The Redskins Chronicle

A Journey Through the History of the Redskins 1937-2008

by Rich Tandler

To Mom

Acknowledgement

The research for this book was done using the game accounts that are the work of dozens of talented and dedicated writers. These reporters were employed by the Richmond Times-Dispatch, the Washington Post, the Associated Press, and other fine news organizations. Their work in capturing the action and emotion of each of the 1,040 games described here and their outstanding work in reporting the day to day happenings surround the team is the reason that the tradition of Redskins football can be recaptured and relived in these pages. I hesitate to mention any names for fear of omitting the names of some excellent sources. I appreciate their talent and I thank them for their effort.

Thanks also to my daughter Katie for her artistic eye and help in making the cover.

Also by Rich Tandler
The Redskins From A to Z
The Washington Redskins Game by Game 1937-2004

Gut Check
The Complete History of Coach Joe Gibbs' Washington Redskins

Hokie Games
Virginia Tech Football Game by Game 1945-2006

For information on obtaining any of these titles contace the author at:
rich.tandler@gmail.com

ISBN: 978-0-9723845-3-7

This book is available in quantity at special discounts for groups and wholesalers. Contact the publisher at the address or email below

All brand names and product names used in this work are trademarks, registered trademarks, brand names, or trade names of their respective holders. His book is not an official publication of the Washington Redskins or the National Football League.

Game by Game Sports Media
5705 Laurel Trail Road
Midlothian, Virginia 23112
www.RedskinsChronicle.com
Your comments and questions are welcome
Rich.tandler@gmail.com

Foreword

When I wrote **The Redskins From A to Z in 2002** I subtitled it "The Complete History of the Redskins". The book did great and drew acclaim as an indespensible reference for both fans the media. As I got around to updating it, though, I realized that the book wasn't quite complete. Sure, it retold the entire on-field history of the team but the story of what went on between those games was left untold.

It was like I'd built a great, big house but it wasn't furnished. There was nothing on the walls, no carpets. A to Z was a good book, it was functional, but it wasn't a finished product.

The Redskins Chronicle is that finished product.

Enjoy the journey.

Rich Tandler
rich.tandler@gmail.com

Key Redskins Games 1937-2008

1	9/15/1937	REDSKINS 13, Giants 3	First game for Washington Redskins
4	12/5/1937	Redskins 49, GIANTS 14	Skins take division, Battles leads the way
4	12/12/1937	Redskins 28, BEARS 21	Sammy slings Skins to NFL Championship
9	10/1/1939	REDSKINS 0, Giants 0	Only scoreless game
10	10/15/1939	REDSKINS 44, Pirates 14	NFL's first 99-yard TD pass, Filchock to Farkas
12	11/19/1939	REDSKINS 20, Cardinals 7	Farkas scores NFL-record 11th TD of season
16	12/1/40	REDSKINS 13, Eagles 6	Skins clinch division but Philly's O'Brien the star
17	12/8/1940	Bears 73, REDSKINS 0	73-0!
22	9/27/1942	Giants 14, REDSKINS 7	Only loss of championship season
24	11/8/1942	REDSKINS 28, Cardinals 0	Baugh runs, passes, picks Skins to win.
26	12/13/1942	REDSKINS 14, Bears 6	Skins stun "unbeatable" Bears for NFL title
28	10/31/1943	Redskins 48, DODGERS 10	Baugh slings six TD passes in rout
28	11/14/1943	REDSKINS 42, Lions 30	Sammy throws four TD's, gets four INT's
30	12/19/1943	Redskins 28, GIANTS 0	Skins rout Giants in Division Playoff
30	12/26/1943	BEARS 41, Redskins 21	Bears gain revenge, take NFL title from Skins
38	12/16/1945	RAMS 15, Redskins 14	Bad bounces doom Skins in title quest
46	11/23/1947	REDSKINS 45, Cardinals 21	Baugh thanks fans on his day with six TD tosses
49	10/31/1948	REDSKINS 59, Yanks 21	Baugh throws for 446 yards, 4 TD's
66	12/14/1952	REDSKINS 27, Eagles 21	LeBaron's sneak shocks Eagles
74	10/1/1955	Redskins 31, EAGLES 30	21 points in 137 seconds beats Philly
86	11/9/1958	REDSKINS 45, Cardinals 31	LeBaron tosses five TD's
97	10/1/1961	Giants 24, REDSKINS 21	DC Stadium opens
100	12/17/1961	REDSKINS 34, Cowboys 24	23-game winless streak over as James scores 4
101	9/23/1962	Redskins 17, BROWNS 16	Mitchell returns to haunt former team
111	9/13/1964	Browns 27, REDSKINS 10	Four Hall of Famers debut for Skins
119	11/28/1965	REDSKINS 34, Cowboys 31	Skins climb out of 21-point hole, beat Dallas
125	11/27/1966	REDSKINS 72, Giants 41	Still the highest-scoring game ever
140	12/14/1969	REDSKINS 17, Saints 14	St. Vincent's Skins clinch winning season
147	10/3/1971	Redskins 20, COWBOYS 16	Skins win in rain in Big D
150	12/13/1971	Redskins 38, RAMS 24	Skins clinch playoffs in Allen's return to LA
151	12/26/1971	49ERS 24, Redskins 20	Niners rally, beat Skins in first playoff since '45
154	10/22/1972	REDSKINS 24, Cowboys 20	Jurgensen, Brown lead rally past Dallas
154	10/29/1972	Redskins 23, Giants 16	Sonny limps off, Brown spurs win
157	12/31/1972	REDSKINS 26, Cowboys 3	Skins stomp Cowboys for NFC title
158	1/14/1973	Dolphins 14, Redskins 7	Dolphins' perfection comes at Redskins' expense
160	10/8/1973	REDSKINS 14, Cowboys 7	Houston stops Garrison at the goal line
165	10/13/1974	REDSKINS 20, Dolphins 17	Sonny's last minute drive beats Miami
167	11/28/1974	COWBOYS 26, Redskins 23	Clint Longley
172	11/16/1975	CARDINALS 20, Redskins 17 OT	Mel Gray
178	12/12/1976	Redskins 27, COWBOYS 14	Riggins' TD pushes Skins into playoffs
185	10/2/1978	REDSKINS 9, Cowboys 5	Skins move to 5-0 with win over Dallas
193	12/16/1979	COWBOYS 35, Redskins 34	Captain Comeback kills Skins' chances
200	10/11/1981	Redskins 24, BEARS 7	Gibbs gets first "W"
207	12/19/1982	REDSKINS 15, Giants 14	Moseley's record-setter lifts Skins into playoffs
210	1/22/1983	REDSKINS 31, Cowboys 17	We want Dallas! We want Dallas!
210	1/30/1983	Redskins 27, Dolphins 17	Hog Day Afternoon in the Rose Bowl
214	10/2/1983	REDSKINS 37, Raiders 35	Theismann, Washington lead late comeback
218	12/11/1983	Redskins 31, COWBOYS 10	The Game: "No, Danny, no!"
219	1/1/1984	REDSKINS 51, Rams 7	Green stars in record playoff rout
219	1/8/1984	REDSKINS 24, 49ers 20	Moseley's FG trumps Montana comeback
220	1/22/1984	Raiders 38, Redskins 9	Black Sunday
225	12/16/1984	REDSKINS 29, Cardinals 27	Monk breaks record, Skins snare division
230	11/18/1985	REDSKINS 23, Giants 21	Theismann breaks leg, Schroeder rallies Redskins
239	1/3/1987	Redskins 27, BEARS 13	Redskins show up, shuffle Bears out of playoffs

243	10/19/1987	Redskins 13, COWBOYS 7	The Replacements hang on for miracle win
247	1/10/1988	Redskins 21, BEARS 17	Green hurdles Skins past Bears
248	1/17/1988	REDSKINS 17, Vikings 10	Redskins, Green hold off Vikes, win NFC
248	1/31/1988	Redskins 42, Broncos 10	The Quarter
266	11/4/1990	Redskins 41, LIONS 38 OT	Rutledge leads comeback from 21 behind
266	11/12/1990	EAGLES 28, Redskins 14	The Body Bag Game
269	1/4/1991	Redskins 20, EAGLES 6	Revenge of the Body Bags
273	10/27/1991	Redskins 17, GIANTS 13	Redskins break Giants Jinx in Meadowlands
276	1/4/1992	REDSKINS 24, Falcons 7	Seat cushions fly to celebrate playoff win
278	1/26/1992	Redskins 37, Bills 24	Rypien, Skins are Super in Minnesota
285	9/6/1993	REDSKINS 35, Cowboys 16	Petitbon's debut a smashing success
292	10/23/1994	Redskins 41, COLTS 27	Gus Bus drives to win over Indy
299	12/3/1995	Redskins 24, COWBOYS 17	Lighting strikes twice; Skins stun Cowboys
305	12/22/1996	REDSKINS 37, Cowboys 10	Farewell to RFK
307	9/14/1997	REDSKINS 19, Cardinals 13 OT	Westbrook's OT catch wins JKC Stadium opener
309	11/23/1997	REDSKINS 7, Giants 7 OT	Gus hits the wall
319	10/3/1999	REDSKINS 38, Panthers 36	Johnson rallies Skins from 21 behind
322	12/26/1999	Redskins 26, 49ERS 20, OT	Johnson to Centers clinches division
323	1/15/2000	BUCS 14, Redskins 13	Bad snap costs Skins chance at playoff win
333	10/21/2001	REDSKINS 17, Panthers 14 OT	Arrington INT return saves season
353	9/12/2004	REDSKINS 16, Buccaneers 10	Gibbs is triumphant in second coming
360	9/19/2005	Redskins 14, COWBOYS 13	Moss to Brunell strikes twice to stun Cowboys
365	12/18/2005	REDSKINS 35, Cowboys 7	Skins flatten Dallas to highlight late season rally
365	1/7/2006	Redskins 17, BUCCANEERS 10	Defense gets Gibbs first playoff win since 1992
379	12/30/2007	REDSKINS 27, Cowboys 6	Skins honor #21 with a playoff-clinching win

1937
Head Coach: Ray Flaherty
Record: 8-3, First in NFL East
Playoffs: 1-0, Won NFL Championship

Honors: Sammy Baugh All NFL; Cliff Battles All NFLDec 12, 1936

Skins Tab Baugh in Draft
TCU All-American passer drafted with sixth pick

Redskins On the Move to D.C.

Dec 16, 1936—The Boston Redskins will be moving to Washington, D.C. for the 1937 season, team owner George Preston Marshall announced. The team will play its home games in Griffith Stadium.

Marshall cited poor attendance and resulting mounting financial losses as the reasons for moving south. The apathy was so great in Beantown that Marshall decided to forego having home-field advantage in the 1936 season NFL Championship Game and moved the contest to New York.

Baugh Makes Early Impression

Sep 7—Redskins coach Ray Flaherty was introducing rookie Sammy Baugh, who will be playing tailback in the team's Single Wing offense, on the intricacies of NFL football during the opening of training camp.

"On forward passes the receivers don't want to bend for the ball and they don't want it too high," Flaherty said. "They like 'em right around the eye."

Baugh quickly asked, "Which eye, coach?"

The Washington offense should be a powerful force this season if Baugh lives up to even a fraction of his reputation and confidence. Riley Smith will be the quarterback, calling the plays in the huddle and the audibles from his spot behind tackle. The wingback is Cliff Battles, an established star who has been the team's lynchpin for several years.

9/16/37	REDSKINS (1-0) 13, Giants (0-1) 3			24,492	
NYG	0	0	3	0	3
Was	3	0	0	10	13
NYG	FG Manton				
Was	TD R. Smith; PAT R. Smith; FG R. Smith 2				

Griffith Stadium—Riley Smith scored all of Washington's points, including the game's only touchdown on a 60-yard interception return as the Redskins successfully debuted under the lights in D.C.

Making his first pro appearance, Sammy Baugh led his team to a score the first time it had the ball. And two pass completions—one to Ernie Pinckert, the other the Charley Malone—sandwiched around a couple of Baugh runs set up Smith's 18-yard field goal. That proved to be the only score of the first half, thanks to a goal line stand by the Redskins that kept New York out of the end zone after the Giants had attained a first and goal at the three.

New York battled back, tying the game in the third quarter on Tily Manton's field goal. Smith booted a field goal through the uprights in the fourth quarter to push the home team back into the lead. Taking to the air, the Giants responded and seemed to be moving towards either a tying or go-ahead score. That was until Smith swooped in, stole an errant aerial at the Washington 40 and ensured that the 24,492 new Redskins fans would go home happy

as he zipped 60 yards down the sideline for the clinching touchdown.

9/24/37	Cardinals (2-1) 21, REDSKINS (1-1) 14			22,367	
Chi	14	0	0	7	21
Was	7	0	7	0	14
Chi	TD Tinsley 3; PAT Baker 3				
Was	TD Malone, Battles; PAT Smith 2				

Griffith Stadium—Chicago's George Grovsner threw three touchdown passes to Gaynell Tinsley, the final one breaking a fourth quarter tie as the Cardinals defeated the Redskins 21-14.

The first scoring connection between the Chicago tandem came five minutes into the game to give the visitors a 7-0 lead. Sammy Baugh led the Redskins right back, tying the game with a scoring toss to Charley Malone. Before the opening period was over, however, the Cards had reclaimed the lead. From the Washington 44, Grovsner zipped a pass to Tinsley, who was conspicuously all alone in the flat about four yards past the line. The receiver easily completed the touchdown play with about a half dozen Redskins in futile pursuit.

The score remained 14-7 until the third quarter when Cliff Battles came to life and started displaying his running skills to help move the Redskins to the Chicago 12. Then Battles shifted to pass catcher and gathered in Baugh's pass to tie the game at 14.

Apparently that served to wake up the Chicago offense as they soon moved to the third Grovsner-to-Tinsley touchdown hookup in the fourth quarter. Baugh and the Redskins battled back as Sammy slung a 40-yard pass to Wayne Millner to spur a drive to the Cardinal 13. That was as far as they would get, however, as a third-down pass grazed off of Millner's fingertips and Baugh's final toss went awry. The relieved Cards ran off the remaining five minutes.

Flaherty: Baugh, Battles to Team Up

Sep 29—Redskins coach Ray Flaherty has decided to take a double-barreled approach in his offensive backfield.

Citing a need to have a versatile attack that keeps opponents honest, Flaherty has scrapped plans to have star backs Sammy Baugh and Cliff Battles alternate in the lineup. Both Baugh, quickly developing into a premiere passing threat in his rookie year, and Battles, an outstanding power rusher, will be in the backfield for most offensive plays.

The Redskins had major problems protecting Baugh during their 21-14 loss to the Cardinals last Sunday. In addition to trying to keep the opposing defense guessing by teaming Baugh and Battles in the same backfield, Flaherty also took a more fundamental approach to pass blocking. He put the linemen through a rigorous workout today. The front line was warned that the likes of Dick Frayne and "Father" Lumpkin of the Brooklyn Dodgers, their opponents this Sunday, could make life miserable for Baugh if they don't do their jobs.

10/3/37	REDSKINS (2-1) 11, Dodgers (2-2) 7			16,253	
Bkn	0	0	0	7	7
Was	0	6	3	2	11
Bkn	TD Barrett; PAT Kerchival				
Was	TD Milner; FG Smith; Safety McChesney				

Griffith Stadium—Wayne Millner took matters into his own hands to break a scoreless tie late in the first half and the Redskins held off the Dodgers by a score of 11-7.

With 19 seconds remaining before intermission, Brooklyn lined up to punt. Millner broke though and blocked the kick, with the ball bouncing out of bounds at the Dodger 26. Then Millner lined up at the left end position, cut across the field and caught Sammy Baugh's accurate missile at the five. A desperation tackle attempt served to propel Millner into the end zone and the Redskins led 6-0.

The Redskins preyed on the Dodger punting team to set up all of their second-half points as well. In the third quarter, Cliff Battles took a booming punt from Ed Kerchival at his own 30, dodged a pair of Brooklynites and took off on a 55-yard jaunt to the Dodger 25. The drive stalled there and Riley Smith was called in to kick a field goal, pushing the home team's lead up to 9-0. Turk Edwards blocked a fourth-quarter punt through the end zone for a safety to extend the margin to 11-0.

Brooklyn gamely fought back, scoring a touchdown with six minutes left and then regaining possession. Ed Kawal saved the day for the Skins as he intercepted a pass to seal the victory.

10/10/37	Eagles (1-4-1) 14, REDSKINS (2-2) 0				9,000
Phi	7	0	0	7	14
Was	0	0	0	0	0
Phi	TD Hewitt, Harper; PAT Reese 2				

Griffith Stadium—The Eagles got ahead early and then held off Washington marches deep into their territory twice to claim a 14-0 win.

End Bill Hewitt was the star on the Eagles' first-quarter touchdown drive, catching passes from two different pitchers to move into the end zone. The first was a fingertip grab of an Emmett Mortell toss that advanced the Eagles 29 yards to the Washington 15. From there, it was Dave Smuckler's turn to pull the trigger and Hewitt gathered in his pass in the end zone for the touchdown.

Late in the second quarter, Sammy Baugh came into the game and moved the Redskins to the Eagle 18 with passes to Ed Justice and Max Krause. A couple of Krause runs and an offside penalty helped push the ball to the one, but time was running short. It ran out, in fact, when Hewitt stopped Don Erwin short of the goal line and the gun sounded.

On a trick play, big lineman Turk Edwards wound up with the ball when the Eagles kicked off to start the second half and Edwards knew which direction to go in. By the time Philadelphia had figured out what was going on and had chased Edwards down, he had lumbered all the way to the Eagle 38. A pass from Cliff Battles to Erwin garnered a first down at the 12 and a reverse on the next play got the ball down to the seven. That was as far as they got, however, and they gave the ball up on downs.

That would be Washington's last threat as Mortell put on a spectacular punting display that kept the Redskins pinned deep in their own territory for most of the rest of the game. Philly held on to win despite being outgained 275 yards to 74.

10/17/37	REDSKINS (3-2) 34, Pirates (2-4) 20				12,385
Pit	0	13	0	7	20
Was	7	0	13	14	34
Pit	TD McNally 2, Thompson; PAT Weinstock, Niccolai				
Was	TD Battles 3, Malone, Justice; PAT R. Smith 4				

Griffith Stadium—Cliff Battles scored three touchdowns from distances averaging 65 yards as the Redskins rallied in the second half to move past Pittsburgh 34-20.

Battles' first touchdown came on defense. On the third play of the game he picked off a short pass at his own 35, headed

towards the sideline, found some excellent blocking and scored standing up after a 65-yard return.

When they had the ball in the first half, the Redskins could not do much with it and Pittsburgh jumped to a 13-7 lead with two second-quarter touchdowns. Player-coach Johnny "Blood" McNally had a hand in both, catching a pass for the first score and then throwing a 65-yard scoring strike to Tuffy Thompson.

The Redskins were just toying with their guests. Before 20 minutes had elapsed in the second half, the Redskins had scored four touchdowns to take a 34-13 lead. Battles swept around end for 60 yards for one TD and then found gobs of daylight off tackle, dashing 71 yards for another. Sammy Baugh found his range on scoring tosses to Charley Malone and Ed Justice.

With a 21-point lead, coach Ray Flaherty emptied the bench and sent Battles into the locker room for a well-deserved early shower. As Shirley Povich of the Post said of Battles, "He had a fair day."

10/24/37	Redskins (4-2) 10, EAGLES (1-6-1) 7				13,167
Was	0	0	7	3	10
Phi	0	7	0	0	7
Was	TD Malone; PAT R. Smith; FG R. Smith				
Phi	TD Carter; PAT Smuckler				

Municipal Stadium—Riley Smith kicked a 27-yard field goal with less than a half minute left to play to lift the Redskins past the Eagles 10-7. Cliff Battles set up the score with a clutch interception and return.

The win was of the ugly genre. The Redskins, particularly Battles, had a difficult time holding on to the ball all day allowing the lowly Eagles to stay with them all the way. In fact, Philly held a 7-0 halftime lead, thanks to a touchdown set up by a Sammy Baugh fumble at the Washington 38. From there, Emmett Mortell whipped a throw to Joe Carter, who was alone at the seven. Carter easily stepped into the end zone for the score.

The score stayed there until five minutes remained in the third quarter when the Redskins suddenly struck back. From his own 41, Baugh dropped back and went deep to Charley Malone. The lanky end caught the ball around the Eagle thirty, dismissed an Eagle safety with a nifty cut, and made it into the end zone standing up.

The score remained tied late into the fourth quarter. The Eagles were forced to punt but Battles fumbled the kick and Philadelphia retained possession at the Washington 45.

The star back more than atoned for his error soon after that, picking off a pass and returning it 42 yards. He then hammered the ball into the line for 21 more yards from scrimmage and the Redskins were at the Eagle 21. With 25 seconds left, Smith's place kick sailed through the uprights with plenty to spare.

10/31/37	Redskins (5-2) 21, DODGERS (2-5) 0				22,300
Was	7	0	14	0	21
Bkn	0	0	0	0	0
Was	TD Baugh, Irwin, Kahn; PAT R. Smith 3				

Ebbets Field—Turk Edwards blocked a punt to set up a Sammy Baugh touchdown run, giving the Redskins all the points they would need to beat Brooklyn. For good measure, the visitors locked it up with two more touchdowns early in the third quarter to make the final 21-0

In the first quarter, the Washington offense drove effectively enough to maintain a solid field position edge, an advantage that paid off when Edwards blocked the punt of Brooklyn's Dick Crayne. Wayne Miller picked the ball up at the 12 and stumbled forward to the four before being brought down. From there, Baugh faked a handoff into the line and took it in himself.

With the Dodgers having difficulty getting past midfield against a stout Washington defense, the Redskins played it conservatively for the rest of the first half before putting it away just after intermission.

Baugh got things started when he returned a punt 20 yards to the Washington 40. He showed more fancy footwork as he faded back deep, started to run to his left, stopped, whirled around and lofted a deep pass to Riley Smith, who was among friendly jerseys at the Brooklyn 30. Smith gathered the pass in, broke one tackle and made it down to the two. From there, Don Irwin smashed over the goal line and it was 14-0. Later in the period, another Baugh pass set up a short TD run by Ed Kahn to account for the final score.

Redskins Rough Up Baltimore Blue Birds

Nov 3—The Redskins did what was expected as they pounded the Baltimore Blue Birds 41-7 in an exhibition game at Oriole Park. The Charm City crowd still had something to cheer about as Leroy "Sunshine" Campbell displayed passing skills that matched those of the more-heralded Sammy Baugh.

Time after time, Campbell's passes found their marks. Had his team possessed pass-catchers of the skill level that Baugh had, the score may well have been much closer.

As it was, the Redskins jumped to a 7-0 lead on Cliff Battles' touchdown run less than three minutes into the game. Baugh ran it in from the five a couple of minutes later.

It remained 14-0 at halftime, but Riley Smith bolted 64 yards for a touchdown on the second play of the third quarter.

11/13/37	PIRATES (4-6) 21, Redskins (5-3) 13			12,240
Was	6	0	0	7	13
Pit	7	2	3	9	21
Was	TD Pinckert, Justice; PAT R. Smith			
Pit	TD Davidson, Karcis; PAT Weinstock; FG Niccolai 2; Safety Mayhew			

Forbes Field—The Pirates scored twice in the game's last three minutes to erase a one-point Washington lead and walk off with a 21-13 victory.

The Redskins gained a 7-0 lead midway through the first quarter. Don Irwin and Cliff Battles pounded though the Pittsburgh line to pace the 10-play march that covered 55 yards. The payoff came in dramatic fashion as they faced fourth down at the Pirate three. Riley Smith took a handoff from Battles, stopped, and fired a strike into the waiting arms of Ed Pinckert in the end zone. Smith's point after attempt was blocked and it was 6-0.

Pittsburgh seized the lead in short order. On the first play following the kickoff Bill Davidson found daylight through the right side of the line and was gone 69 yards down the sideline for the touchdown. Pittsburgh led 7-6 following the extra point. A Sammy Baugh fumble led to a safety that upped the Pirate lead to three points at the half. Another fumble—this one by Battles—set up a field goal that had the home team up 12-6 going into the last quarter.

Early in the fourth quarter, the Redskins let a golden opportunity to score slip away. They blocked a punt and gained possession at the Pirate 24 but the offense stalled at the five. However, they did gain the advantage in field position and capitalized on their next possession. Baugh faded back past midfield and threw to Ed Justice, who caught the ball around the Pirate 25. The safety had Justice by the foot, but the back wriggled out of the defender's grasp and dashed in for the score. This time Smith converted and Washington had a 13-12 lead with five minutes to play.

But Pittsburgh was up to the challenge. They drove smartly down the field from their own 28 to the Washington 25 and Armand Niccolai booted a 41-yard field goal to give his team the lead with three minutes left. Then, after a Steeler interception doomed the Redskins' chances of winning, John "Bull" Karcis trampled the Washington secondary en route to a 21-yard touchdown run to seal it for Pittsburgh.

11/21/37	Redskins (6-3) 16, RAMS (1-9) 7			3,500
Was	6	0	10	0	16
Cle	0	7	0	0	7
Was	TD Irwin, R. Smith' PAT R. Smith; FG R. Smith			
Cle	TD Goddard; PAT Snyder			

Municipal Stadium—Riley Smith scored 10 third-period points to push the Redskins past Cleveland 16-7 in a game played in the midst of a howling blizzard.

Washington scored first, a marked advantage in a game that would see playing conditions deteriorate as it wore on. Cliff Battles led the way on the 58-yard advance with a 15-yard run then a 10-yard pass completion to Wayne Millner, followed by another run—this one good for a first down at the eight. On fourth down from the four, Don Irwin found a seam through the line and bore through for the score. A bad snap aborted the point after attempt and it was 6-0 Redskins.

That lead held until the final play of the first half. The Rams' Ed Goddard intercepted Sammy Baugh's pass somewhere near midfield—with the six inches of snow on the field at the outset of the contest growing by the minute, it was hard to tell exactly where—and returned it to the 23. On the last play of the half, Goddard took it over the goal line on fourth down. The point after gave Cleveland a one-point lead as the teams made their way to the welcome shelter of the locker room.

In the third quarter, it was Battles leading the charge and Smith finishing things off. Going mostly up the middle, it was Battles slogging through the white stuff for good gains to set up Smith's 20-yard field goal to give the Redskins a 9-7 lead they would not relinquish. Battles continued to plough through the Cleveland line for yardage down to the four. From there, Battles faked a pass and handed to Smith, who scampered around end into the end zone. This time, Smith's conversion was good and the Redskins had a nine-point lead. It might as well have been ninety points as the weather shut down both teams' offenses the rest of the day.

Nov 22

Battles Gets Hitched on Off Day
Back stays in Cleveland, marries former Miss Dorothy Kaufman

Skins 2-1 Underdogs to Packers

Nov 26—Although the Redskins have a record that is virtually identical to that of the Green Bay Packers, the home team will be a decided underdog as it vies to stay in the hunt for the Eastern Conference title.

In local betting circles the odds are 2-1 in favor of the Packers. Although the Skins come in at 6-3 while the Green Bay is 7-3, it is generally thought that the Packers have built their record against the tougher competition in the Western Conference.

If a local would like to wager even money, he can get the Redskins plus anywhere from 7 to 13 points.

Should the Redskins win, their game the following Sunday in New York against the Giants could be for the Conference championship and a spot in the NFL title game against the winner of the West.

11/28/37	**REDSKINS (7-3) 14, Packers (7-4) 6**				30,000	
GB	6	0	0	0		6
Was	0	0	7	7		14
GB	TD Hutson					
Was	TD Battles, Malone PAT R. Smith 2					

Griffith Stadium—Needing a win to have a shot at the Eastern title the following week in New York, the Redskins didn't disappoint the 30,000 who turned out to cheer them on. Charley Malone set up one touchdown with a key reception and scored the other on a pass from Sammy Baugh as Washington beat the Packers 14-6.

Green Bay struck first, driving 61 yards for a TD before Washington had gained even a yard on offense. After Don Hutson's nine-yard, fourth down scoring catch, though, Baugh blocked the conversion attempt and the game turned Washington's way.

Although Sammy Baugh and Cliff Battles were ripping through the Packers' line, the Skins still trailed 6-0 at halftime. The Redskins broke through in the third quarter after Malone made a fingertip catch for a 59-yard gain that led to Battles' two-yard scoring burst.

Malone scored the second touchdown himself, juggling the Baugh pass before snaring it, breaking a tackle and running the final five yards into the end zone to complete the 18-yard play. Green Bay didn't cross the Washington 29 after that, and the crowd, which Shirley Povich of the Post repeatedly described as a "mob," went home deliriously happy.

Dec 3

Redskins Sell out Ticket Supply for Game in New York
5,000 tix snapped up, more ordered

12/5/37	**Redskins (8-3) 49, GIANTS (6-3-2) 14**				58,285	
Was	14	7	7	21		49
NYG	0	0	14	0		14
Was	TD Battles 2, M. Krause, Justice, Milner 2, R. Smith; PAT R. Smith 7					
NYG	TD Cuff, Leemans; PAT Manon 2					

Polo Grounds—You often hear of a team invading a city for a road game, and it's usually hyperbole, but that's exactly what the Redskins did to New York in the first trip the Washington Redskins made to the Big Apple. Between ten and twelve thousand fans boarded trains at Union Station to make the trek to the Polo Grounds to watch the two teams battle for the Eastern Conference title on the last day of the regular season. A 150-piece marching band made the trek as well. On arrival, owner George Preston Marshall led an impromptu parade down Seventh Avenue to Columbus Circle and the fans were marching along in step.

Cliff Battles set the tone, leading the way on a grinding, 83-yard drive that he ended with a two-yard touchdown run. Later in the first, he galloped around left end for 75 yards to the Giants' five. Two plays later, Battles scored again and it was 14-0. A second-quarter drive started at midfield and ended when Max Krause scored on an up-the-middle run from five yards out.

A break got the Giants on the scoreboard as one of their passes bounced off of Erny Pinckert's hand and into the arms of the Giants' Ward Cuff, who scampered 45 yards for the Giants' first score. A second Giants touchdown a few minutes later tied it

up and had the Redskins' and their traveling faithful worried. The Giants, after all, had allowed just 60 points all season.

But that didn't stop Sammy Baugh, Battles, and company. Ed Justice was wide open on a 48-yard touchdown pass and, early in the fourth quarter, got more breathing room when Wayne Milner blocked a Giants' punt and fell on the ball in the end zone to make it 35-14. The Skins weren't done yet. Battles intercepted a long pass at the Washington 20, broke a couple of tackles, reversed his field twice, cut back and didn't stop until he ran out of gas and was caught from behind at the New York one. Riley Smith got the score on the next play and, after Ray Flaherty emptied the bench, the Redskins scored once more on a Max Krause TD run of five yards. They were headed to Chicago to play the Bears for the NFL title.

The Redskins fans in the Polo Grounds stormed the field, tearing down the goal posts and reveling long after the final gun. Another gathering of 5,000 greeted the Redskins at Union Station when the trains arrived back in Washington.

Halas Hails the Redskins

Dec 9—Asked to name his All-NFL team as his Chicago Bears prepared to host the Washington Redskins for the NFL championship, Coach George Halas didn't hesitate. He rattled off the names of Battles, Baugh, Millner, and the other eight Redskins starters.

"That's the greatest football team ever put together," said Halas, perhaps going overboard in an effort to keep from saying anything inflammatory to rile up the Skins.

Indeed, Halas wanted to make sure that his praise reached its intended targets. "Please see that these selections get in the paper before Sunday," he told reporters.

Skins' QB Smith Predicts Victory

Dec 11—Washington quarterback Riley Smith had some rather bold statements today on the eve of the Redskins' NFL title tilt with the Bears.

"We are going out tomorrow to pass the Bears into the ground," Smith said. "Washington will beat the Bears and Sammy Baugh will be the man responsible."

NFL Championship Game
Sunday, December 12, 1937
Wrigley Field
Chicago, Illinois

12/12/37	**Redskins 28, BEARS 21**				15,878	
Was	7	0	21	0		**28**
Chi	14	0	7	0		**21**
Was	Battles 7 run (R. Smith kick)					
Chi	Manders 10 run (Manders kick)					
Chi	Manders 39 pass from Masterson (Manders kick)					
Was	Millner 55 pass from Baugh (R. Smith kick)					
Chi	Manske 4 pass from Masterson (Manders kick)					
Was	Millner 78 pass from Baugh (R. Smith kick)					
Was	Justice 35 pass from Baugh (R. Smith kick)					

It was, according to the Post, "Baugh over brawn" as Slingin' Sammy led the Redskins to their first title at a frozen Wrigley Field in Chicago. With his team trailing 14-7 going into the third quarter, Baugh threw three touchdown passes, the first two tying the game and the third putting the Redskins ahead to stay.

With both teams sporting basketball shoes on the frosty turf, the visitors struck first, moving 53 yards to a score, the payoff coming as Cliff Battles dove over the goal line to complete an eight-yard run. The Bears tied the score three minutes later and took the lead shortly after that on a 50-yard pass play to Jack Manders.

After a scoreless second quarter, Baugh went to work. From the Bears 45, he hit Wayne Milner in stride with a bullet at the Chicago 35 and Milner raced across the goal line to tie the game. The Bears answered immediately, going 77 yards for a TD to take a 21-14 lead. Baugh again went to Milner, this time for a 78-yard TD and Riley Smith's conversion tied the game once more. After the Bears punted, Baugh faked a short pass and went long to Ed Justice, who scored easily.

The fourth quarter featured numerous fights and turnovers and no scoring threats. The Redskins got a scare late as Battles fumbled and the Bears recovered at their own 42. The desperation drive was quickly terminated; however, when Smith picked off a Bears pass at the Washington 30 and one dive into the line later, the Washington Redskins were champs.

Champion Redskins to Head West

Dec 13—The Redskins will not be returning to Washington for a victory parade.

After beating the Chicago Bears 28-21 to claim the NFL title, the players will head to their offseason homes straight from the Windy City. Then, following a few weeks of well-earned rest and relaxation, they will reassemble on the West Coast for a series of lucrative exhibition games.

Among the tilts scheduled are some rematches with the Bears squad that they just defeated, as well as some exhibitions against some pro and college all-star teams.

1938
Head Coach: Ray Flaherty
Record: 6-3-2, Second in NFL East

Honors: Sammy Baugh All-NFL; Riley Smith All-NFL; Turk Edwards All-NFL; Les Olsson All NFL

Battles Headed to Columbia?

Feb 15—Cliff Battles, one of the key components to the Redskins drive to the NFL title in their first season in Washington, may be leaving the District of Columbia for Columbia.

The league's best ground gainer in 1937 visited with team owner George Preston Marshall for contract talks. In his pocket, Battles had the ultimate weapon in such negotiations—an unsigned contract from another organization. He has received an offer to be an assistant coach at Columbia University and many believe that he seems to be inclined to accept it.

Marshall himself thinks so. "Battles is a great ball player and a fine boy," he said. "I offered him a healthy raise over what he what he received last year. . . However, his mind seems to be made up on the college coaching proposition."

According to reports, Battles will receive about $1,000 more a year to coach football for the Lions than he would to play ball for the Redskins. In addition, the offseason income opportunities in New York are expected to be greater than they are in D.C.

Baugh Signs Three-Year Deal

Aug 2—Sammy Baugh has decided to pursue his sports career on the gridiron rather than on the diamond.

Baugh ended his flirtation with baseball by signing a three-year deal to become the highest-paid player in the NFL. He had signed a three-year contract with the St. Louis Cardinals in February.

Something besides the dollars may have persuaded Baugh to stay with the Redskins rather than the Redbirds. After spring training the Cards sent Baugh to the minors for some more seasoning. After signing with the NFL's Skins in 1937, Baugh dominated that league, leading his team to the league title in his rookie year.

9/11/38	**Redskins (1-0) 26, EAGLES (0-1) 23**				20,000
Was	7	7	12	0	26
Phi	3	13	7	0	23
Was	TD Krause 3, Young; PAT Masterson 2				
Phi	TD Carter 2, Smuckler; PAT Reese 2; FG Reese				

Municipal Stadium—After Sammy Baugh went out with a separated shoulder just before halftime, it appeared the Redskins would need a miracle to win. If a 62-yard touchdown pass from Baugh's seldom-used backup to makeshift receiver Bill Young, an interior grunt by trade, doesn't qualify as miraculous, then nothing on a football field does.

Although he wasn't involved in the game-winning score, Max Krause scored Washington's other three touchdowns. The first came in the opening period when he took the ball on a fake reverse and galloped 48 yards for a touchdown and a 7-0 lead.

The lead evaporated amidst a barrage of Washington fumbles. Three times the Redskins put the ball on the ground and three times the Eagles scored to take a 16-7 lead.

Late in the half, the Redskins rallied to climb back into it. Baugh's last play of the game came when he was pounded to the turf in the process of launching a 57-yard pass to Krause, who caught the ball at the Eagle 20 and scored easily.

The challenge in the second half for the Redskins was to produce offense without Baugh, who had completed 12 of 13 passes before exiting the game. Initially, it was Krause who responded. He took the ball on a reverse, threaded his way through the initial wave of defenders and outran the rest of them, going 71 yards to put his team into the lead at 20-16.

Again, a fumble cost the Redskins as Philly turned a takeaway into Joe Carter's second touchdown of the game to reclaim the lead at 23-20. But Washington pulled one from deep inside its bag of tricks.

At the Redskin 38 from a spread formation on an unbalanced line, Bill Hartman, in because of Baugh's injury, went back to pass. The formation had left Young as an eligible receiver. The Eagles could scarcely be blamed for ignoring the 245-pound guard as he lumbered down the middle of the field. They surely regretted their decision, though, as Hartman tossed to Young at the Eagle 35. The defense could only watch as Young found another gear and swiftly covered the remaining ground to the end zone. Washington led 26-23 and held on for the win.

Baugh to Miss Three Weeks
Injured passer will be out as separated shoulder heals

9/18/38	REDSKINS (1-0-1) 16, Dodgers (0-0-1) 16				23,000
Bkn	10	0	0	6	16
Was	0	13	0	3	16
Bkn	TD Parker; PAT Kercheval; FG Kercheval 3				
Was	TD Justice 2; PAT Masterson, FG Masterson				

Griffith Stadium—Bob Masterson's field goal with 10 seconds left pulled the Redskins into a 16-16 tie with Brooklyn.

The Dodgers jumped to a 10-0 lead in the first quarter. After Ralph Kercheval kicked a field goal, Ace Parker zipped through the middle on a reverse for 27 yards to the Washington 12. A holding penalty pushed Brooklyn back, but that didn't faze Parker and his mates. Three plays later, Joe Maniaci tossed a touchdown pass to Parker.

In the second quarter, it was the Redskins' turn. Bill Hartman completed passes to Bill Masterson and Ed Justice to get a drive started. Then, from the Brooklyn 22, Hartman faked an end run, drifted back and lofted a pass to Justice in the end zone. Justice settled under it and hauled it in for the touchdown.

Later in the second, Hartman again connected with Justice for a score, but this drive belonged to Andy Farkas. The fullback got the drive started with a 21-yard punt return before bolting for eight more from scrimmage. Hartman took advantage of the defense's wariness of Farkas by faking to him and then launching a pass to Justice to the Dodger 18. Soon after that, it was Hartman to Justice again for the score and a 13-10 lead.

The lead held into the fourth quarter, but the Dodgers clawed back, retaking the lead on a pair of Kercheval field goals. It appeared that the Redskins were destined to lose, but they got new life when Dick Tuckey launched a 40-yard pass to Justice. The play carried to the Dodger 10 and, with time running out, Masterson drilled the three-pointer to give the Redskins a thrilling, if unsatisfying, deadlock.

9/25/38	REDSKINS (2-0-1) 37, Rams (0-3) 13				24,389
Cle	0	0	0	13	13
Was	3	7	21	6	37
Cle	TD Pincura, Peterson; PAT Peterson				
Was	TD Farkas 3, Edwards, Irwin; PAT Masterson, Farkas 2, Karamatic; FG Karamatic				

Griffith Stadium—Rookie back Andy Farkas had a breakout day, scoring three touchdowns to lead the Redskins to an easy 37-13 win over Cleveland.

Washington led 3-0 over the lowly Rams when Farkas entered the game to a thunderous ovation in the second period. He got things going by returning a punt 10 yards and then, along with Bill Hartman, carried the load as the Redskins drove for a touchdown. From less than a yard out, Farkas followed a devastating block by Turk Edwards over the goal line. He then lined up and booted the extra point for a 10-0 lead.

Farkas and the Skins were just getting warmed up. Three minutes into the second half, they were on the board again. Wayne Millner made a spectacular fingertip grab of a Hartman pass to set them up at the Ram 16. Soon after that, Farkas carried from the seven and was tackled to the ground, but not until he had nosed across the goal line. His point after made it 17-0 and the rout was on. He wasn't finished yet, though.

Cleveland punted and Farkas fielded it at his own 35. He was a determined picture of churning arms and swiveling hips as he

skillfully picked his way through the coverage and wasn't stopped until he'd gone 45 yards to the Ram 20. Three plays later, from the 12, he hopped, skipped and jumped his way through the remaining territory to the goal line.

Farkas then went to the sideline for the day to a roar that made the ovation that ushered him into the game look weak. The Redskins extended their lead to 31-0 when Millner blocked a punt and Turk Edwards plopped on the ball in the end zone. The Rams saved some face with two fourth-quarter touchdowns.

10/9/38	Giants (2-2) 10, REDSKINS (2-1-1) 7					35,000
NYG	3	0	0	7	-	10
Was	0	7	0	0	-	7
NYG	TD Howell; PAT Cuff; FG Cuff					
Was	TD Masterson; PAT Masterson					

Griffith Stadium—Ed Danowski threw an 18-yard touchdown pass to Jim Howell in the fourth quarter to push the Giants past the Redskins 10-7.

Washington handed New York an early lead. Max Krause fumbled on the first play from scrimmage and New York recovered at the Redskin 25. The Giants got as far as the 10, but the defense stiffened and they had to settle for Bill Cuff's 17-yard field goal.

Washington responded after an exchange of punts gave them a short field to work with. The Skins had to go just 54 yards to cross the goal line and did so in short order. It took just three plays, the last a pass from Sammy Baugh to Bob Masterson. The wiry end caught the ball in stride at the 20, eluded Tuffy Leemans, and stepped into the end zone for a 7-3 Washington lead.

Both defenses dug in and the Redskins maintained their four-point margin into the fourth quarter. At that point Danowski found his stride and began passing over and through the Washington defense. Starting from the New York 29, Danowski moved his team towards pay dirt. He shot a bullet to Jim Poole for 33 yards to the Washington 34 and then twice went to Hank Soar for six and seven yards. Two plays later, Danowski drew a bead on Howell and fired a pass to him at the goal line. Howell gathered it in and stepped across the stripe for the go-ahead touchdown with six minutes left.

The Redskins did respond, driving into Giant territory behind Bill Hartman's passing. At the Giant 37, however, Baugh replaced Hartman and his pass went through the hands of Don Irwin and into those of New York's Dale Burnett. The Giants burned off the remaining three minutes of the clock.

Redskins Bolster Backfield, Acquiring Filchock, Manton

Oct 10—The Redskins are not a team that takes defeat lying down.

After their first loss of the season, the team moved to strengthen its backfield by obtaining the services of Frank Filchock and ex-Giant Tillie Manton. Filchock's contract was purchased from Pittsburgh for $1,000 while Manton was claimed on waivers from the Giants.

Ex-Pirate Filchock is the league's leading touchdown passer. His presence will enable the team to rest star Sammy Baugh and provide a viable option when Baugh is injured, as he has been since the season opener.

Manton, who played with Baugh at TCU, has been among the NFL's best placekickers since coming into the league in 1936.

Both of the new Redskins are expected to play when the team travels to Detroit to battle the Lions next Sunday.

10/16/38	Redskins (3-1-1) 7, LIONS (2-2) 5			42,855	
Was	0	0	7	0	7
Det	5	0	0	0	5
Was	TD Farkas; PAT Smith				
Det	FG Monahan; Safety team				

Tiger Stadium—Andy Farkas scored the go-ahead touchdown in the third quarter to push the Redskins past Detroit by a score of 7-5. The score came with a major assist from "Wee Willie" Wilkin.

Detroit took a 5-0 lead in the first quarter with a field goal and a safety. The two points were a gift from Farkas, who ran back into the end zone on his own in an attempt to elude tacklers. He was nailed back there for the safety.

The game turned in the third period. The Lions lined up to punt. Ace Gutowsky had the unenviable task of attempting to block the 240-pound Wilkin. At the snap, Wilkin slammed into Gutowsky and drove him back, so far back that the punt went off the back of the blocker's helmet and out of bounds at the Lion 17. Soon after, the Redskins were at the one-foot line. Farkas gained six inches on each of his two carries from there and the Redskins were up 7-5.

The Lions' best chance to respond came in the game's dying minutes. They drove to the Washington 30 and Regis Monahan lined up to attempt a 37-yard field goal with half a minute to play. Bob McChesney, however, led a tidal wave of rushers and the attempt was blocked to give the Redskins the win.

10/23/38	REDSKINS (4-1-1) 20, Eagles (2-4) 14				26,150	
Phi	0	0	7	7	-	14
Was	7	0	7	6	-	20
Phi	TD Ramsey, Carter PAT Reese 2					
Was	TD Smith, Farkas 2 PAT Smith 2					

Griffith Stadium—Andy Farkas scored two touchdowns and the Redskins held off the Eagles.

Philadelphia came out gambling, recovering an onside kick on the game's first play. But Washington soon gained the advantage after Les Olsson stopped Dave Smuckler for no gain on fourth down at the Redskins 38. Bill Hartman faded back and floated the ball to Riley Smith at the Eagle 32. Safety Jay Arnold was in the vicinity, but only close enough to make a futile dive at Smith's ankles as the receiver crossed the five-yard line on his way to the end zone. Smith booted the extra point to make it 7-0.

It remained that way until the third quarter. Farkas capped an 11-play, 58-yard drive with a touchdown run to push the Washington lead to 14-0. It appeared the margin would be sufficient as the Eagles were completely inept in their ground game, thanks largely to the fierce headhunting of the likes of Olsson and tackle Jim Barber. On the day, Philly mustered just 18 yards rushing.

But the Eagles weren't done as they took the alternate route downfield. Emmett Mortell threw two touchdown passes to put a scare into the Redskins, but the Skins drove to Farkas' second score of the game in the fourth quarter to secure the win.

10/30/38	Redskins (4-1-2) 6, DODGERS (2-3-2) 6				29,913	
Was	3	0	0	3		6
Bkn	6	0	0	0		6
Was	FG Smith 2					
Bkn	TD Kercheval					

Ebbets Field—Riley Smith kicked two field goals to account for all of the Redskins' points in the 6-6 deadlock, but he also wore goat horns as he missed a 24-yard attempt in the last minute that would have won it.

The way things started out, it didn't look as though anything late in the game would matter. The Redskins took the opening kickoff and embarked on an efficient seven-play drive spurred by the passing and running of Bill Hartman. Smith put a 31-yard field goal through the uprights and the Redskins held a 3-0 lead.

Washington regained possession and appeared to be moving in for more when disaster struck. Beattie Feathers intercepted Hartman's pass at the Dodger 30 and picked through the Redskins for a 49-yard return to the 21. Soon after that, Ralph Kercheval found some blocking and skirted around the left side for a touchdown. Kercheval missed the point after and it was 6-3.

The score remained there throughout the second and third periods as the Redskins showed considerably more prowess at moving the ball than their opponents—Washington gained 202 yards to 97 for Brooklyn—but no more ability to turn the yardage into points.

Finally, in the fourth quarter, the Skins found an offensive combination that would work. Sammy Baugh and Frank Filchock took turns playing pitch and catch and the Redskins moved into position for Smith's tying field goal midway through the period. Then Filchock intercepted a pass at the Washington 39 with five minutes to play. Baugh completed passes to Charley Malone, Filchock and Wayne Millner to down to the Brooklyn 20. The drive stalled there, however, and Smith came in to try to win it with 50 seconds left. The place kick started off looking good, but it tailed outside of the upright and was no good.

Player accuses Marshall of 'Chiseling'

Oct 31—All is not well with the first-place Washington Redskins.

According to a player who wishes to remain anonymous, many members of the team are disgruntled over the pay that the players have received for playing in exhibition games during the season.

Actually, it's the fact that there hasn't been any extra pay for the extra work that is the sticking point.

They didn't mind playing the exhibitions for free when the team was operating at a loss. "But now the club is making money—a lot of it—and we want to be paid," said the player.

Around the NFL all of the other teams pay their players for exhibitions. Many Redskins player contracts contain clauses calling for pay for the exhibition games, but amounts are not specified.

"Marshall isn't doing himself any good by chiseling on us," said the anonymous team member.

11/6/38	Redskins (5-1-2) 7, PIRATES (2-6) 0				12,910	
Was	0	0	0	7		7
Pit	0	0	0	0		0
Was	TD Karamatic PAT Manton					

Forbes Field—Sammy Baugh shook off the frustration of one of the worst days of his career and fired the game-winning touchdown pass to rookie fullback George Karamatic in the fourth quarter.

Baugh wasn't the only one having a bad day. Through the first three quarters of the game, the Redskins drove inside the Pittsburgh 20 seven times, inside the 15 four of those times. However, Riley Smith and Tillie Manton each missed two field goals and the game remained scoreless after three quarters.

Early in the fourth, it looked like the Pirates were going to be the ones who would scratch the scoreboard first. Whizzer White completed a pass to Jess Tatum for 12 yards to the Washington 27. Tatum, however, fumbled the ball and Baugh initiated his chance at redemption by falling on it.

Baugh got things started with a nine-yard pass to Bob Masterson, just his second completion in twelve attempts on the day. Karamatic got the first down at the 37 and then carried twice more to key the move to the Pittsburgh 39.

Baugh fumbled the snap from center but recovered quickly and spotted Karamatic in the flat about 10 yards downfield. The passer's tight spiral was on target and Karamatic broke the attempted tackle of his closest pursuer. He then headed toward the goal, paused for a moment to allow Charley Malone and Bill Young to clear out the remaining obstacles, and burst through the goal posts for the touchdown. Manton converted and it was 7-0.

The score hardly clinched the win. Picking up where they had left off prior to Tatum's fumble, the Pirates moved deep into Washington territory. The big play was a 33-yard completion from White to Bill Davidson. That earned a first down at the 15, but the drive would die there. Jim Karcher nailed Stu Smith for a seven-yard loss on a reverse on third down and White's desperation fourth down pass fell harmlessly to the turf.

11/14/38	BEARS (5-4) 31, Redskins (5-2-2) 7					21,817
Was	0	0	0	7	-	**7**
Chi	0	17	2	12	-	**31**
Was	TD Filchock PAT Manton					
Chi	TD Francis, Maniaci, Manders 2 PAT FG Manders					
	Safety team					

Wrigley Field—Playing a brand of football that continually crossed the line between tough, hard play and felonious assault with intent to maim, the Bears pounded the Redskins 31-7.

An example of the latter, criminal brand of play came on the third play of the game. George Karamatic fielded a punt at his own 30. The Bears' Joe Stydahar employed an unusual tackling technique as he punched Karamatic square in the mouth, causing the Washington fullback to take leave of both his consciousness and the ball. Chicago did not score points off of the turnover, but gained a major advantage—Stydahar's actions did not draw a flag from the officials.

Redskin owner George Preston Marshall became so incensed by the "let 'em fight" philosophy of the officiating crew that he jumped out of the stands during the first quarter, cornered the referee and demanded the Bears be penalized.

While the rough stuff drew most of the attention, the Bears probably didn't need it anyway as they proceeded to assail the Redskins on the scoreboard in the second quarter. They moved 65 yards to a touchdown by Sam Francis in the second quarter. After that an interception and a long pass from Bernie Masterson to Les McDonald set up a TD run by Joe Maniaci and the rout was on. The Redskins would not score until Chicago was ahead 31-0 and resting most of its starting pugilists.

11/27/38	REDSKINS (6-2-2) 15, Pirates (2-8) 0				25,335
Pit	0	0	0	0	0
Was	3	0	0	12	15
Was	TD Millner, McChesney FG Manton				

Griffith Stadium—Sammy Baugh threw for two touchdowns in the final six minutes of the game to break open a tight contest as the Redskins shut out the Pirates 15-0.

Washington got on top early as Tillie Manton kicked a 22-yard field goal just two minutes into the game. After that, though, the offense went into a slumber that lasted more than 50 minutes of play.

Perhaps they were content to watch the spectacular play of Pittsburgh's Byron "Whizzer" White. According to Shirley Povich of the Post, White "was a dazzling fellow, with his shifty gallops and for the 45 minutes he played was a constant menace to the Redskins." Not enough of a menace to get the Pirates on the scoreboard, mind you, but entertaining nonetheless.

Held out with a variety of injuries that had piled up over the course of the season, Baugh came into the game late in the third quarter. A steady rain had made the field muddy and the ball slick—hardly ideal passing conditions. Undeterred, Baugh faded back from his own 43 and zipped a low spiral to Wayne Miller. The ball went just over White's fingertips and the only thing that could stop the receiver after the catch was the sideline. He averted that obstacle, completing the 57-yard scoring play to give his team a 9-0 lead with six minutes remaining.

Three minutes later, Baugh struck again. This time his target was Bob Masterson, who took the pass from the Pittsburgh 44 in perfect stride in the end zone to account for the final score.

12/4/38	GIANTS (8-2-1) 36, Redskins (6-3-2) 0					57,461
Was	0	0	0	0	-	**0**
NYG	14	0	10	12	-	**36**
NYG	TD Gelatka 2, Soar, Karcis, Cuff PAT Cuff 3, FG Cuff					

Polo Grounds—Just like the previous year, it was all there again: a trip to New York to decide the Eastern division title on the season's final day. Another 12,000 Washingtonians made the trek to the Polo Grounds to cheer the Redskins on.

Once again, the game was a rout, but this time the Redskins were on the losing end of it. Washington crossed midfield just three times, fumbled seven times, got behind early and never showed any sign of being able to catch up.

The tone was set early on. On the Redskins' first possession, Ward Cuff intercepted a Sammy Baugh pass and the Giants were in business at the Washington 43. On the very next play, Hank Soar broke through the middle of the line, got past the entire defense ten yards past the line and was gone for the touchdown.

The pattern of Redskin mistake, Giant touchdown recurred later in the first quarter. Baugh and fullback George Karamatic got their signals crossed and neither attempted to field the snap from center Jim Carroll; the ball sailed between the two of them. Jim Howell recovered for the Giants at the Washington 39. Four plays later, Bull Karcis scored on a short run to put New York up 14-0.

It remained that way until the third quarter when Cuff kicked a field goal—the score, of course, having been set up by a Washington fumble. Trailing 17-0, the Redskins made their one bid to make a contest out of it as they drove to the Giant ten behind Frank Filchock. From there, however, Filchock was smashed as he tried to pass and Cuff picked the ball out of the air and raced 90 yards to slam the door on any hopes for a miracle.

Baugh summed it up after the game saying, "Everything went wrong. Nothing clicked.

1939
Head Coach: Ray Flaherty
Record: 6-3-2, Second in NFL East

Honors: Frank Filchock All-NFL; Andy Farkas All-NFL; Turk Edwards All-NFL; Jim Barber All-NFL; Bo Russell All-NFL

Redskins to Train in Spokane

Feb 3—Redskins General Manager Jack Espey announced today that the team will train for the 1939 season in Washington.

That's in the state of Washington, in the city of Spokane, not in the District of Columbia.

Citing a need to escape the heat and humidity that permeate D.C. in the summer, coach Red Flaherty negotiated a deal with Spokane's Athletic Round Table to hold the team's training camp in the Northwest. The Redskins will travel nearly 2,500 miles to get from Washington to Spokane, the longest trip any sports team has ever made from its home base to its training site.

Not only is the weather better in Spokane, the financial climate there for the Skins isn't too bad, either. The team will receive an undisclosed guaranteed payment for holding their practices there.

While the practice site was not announced, it is thought that Gonzaga University would welcome the team as Flaherty is a proud alum of the school.

Feb 9

Turk Edwards Will Play in '39
Retirement rumors surrounding team captain dispelled

9/17/39	Redskins (1-0) 7, EAGLES (0-1) 0			33,258	
Was	0	0	0	7	7
Phi	0	0	0	0	0
Was	TD Malone; PAT Russell				

Shibe Park—Sammy Baugh threw a 30-yard touchdown pass to Charley Malone on the first play of the fourth quarter for the game's only touchdown. The Redskin defense made it stand up despite a dazzling performance by Philadelphia's Dave O'Brien.

Three times during the game's first three quarters, O'Brien brought his team near the Washington goal line, but came up empty on each trip. Their best chance came early in the proceedings. The Eagles took the opening kickoff and O'Brien led a march sixty yards to a first down at the Redskin 15. The foray ended when O'Brien fumbled and Clem Stralka recovered for the Skins.

Washington blew a golden opportunity early in the second. Turk Edwards blasted through the line and blocked a punt, setting the offense up at the Eagle 13. Wayne Millner managed to get his hand on one of Baugh's passes in the end zone despite the fact that Woody Dow was climbing all over his back, but the end dropped the ball. Andy Farkas fought for five yards to the eight but the drive died there.

Baugh and Malone got credit for the touchdown but an assist must go to Frank Filchock. On the last play of the third period, he fielded a punt at his own 44 and faced a sea of Philly jerseys. He dodged, broke tackles, fought, and bulled his way for 26 yards to the Eagle 30.

After they changed ends of the field, Baugh drifted while looking for a receiver. The search was conducted at a leisurely pace as he enjoyed excellent protection. Baugh found Malone open at the goal line, the pass was perfect and the receiver stepped into the end zone for the touchdown. The Eagles never seriously threatened after that.

Over 31,000 Expected for Giants

Sep 25—While some good seats remain for The Redskins' Sunday home opener against the New York Giants, you'd better hurry if you want to attend the clash of the last two NFL champions.

The Redskins, who won the league title in 1937, announced today that advance sales for the game against the Giants, the defending NFL champions, have broken all previous records. They expect 31,000 tickets will be sold by game time.

Coach Ray Flaherty took advantage of his team's week off to go and scout the Giants in person as they played the Philadelphia Eagles. He came back from the trip thinking the same as he did when he left—those guys are good.

"I saw a lot of things about the Giants that I already knew," said Flaherty. "They're big and fast and tough and they play the same kind of game they always played."

10/1/39	REDSKINS (1-0-1) 0, Giants (1-0-1) 0			26,341	
NYG	0	0	0	0	0
Was	0	0	0	0	0

Griffith Stadium—In a game-long driving rainstorm the Redskins outplayed the Giants by nearly every measure, but were only able to slog off with a scoreless deadlock.

The Redskins' best chance to score came early in the second quarter. Sammy Baugh entered the game and flipped an eight-yard pass to Charley Malone to get things started. Andy Farkas fought for a first down at the 28 and then took another short pass from Baugh and gingerly splashed his way down the sideline for 12 yards. Then it was Farkas again with the carry for a first down at the four. The Giant defense dug in there, however, and Baugh mishandled the snap on the attempted field goal. The Redskins came up empty.

Another great opportunity went by the wayside later in the second after Frank Filchock found good enough footing to return a punt 40 yards to the Giants 22. Ward Cuff picked off Baugh in the end zone to quickly snuff that threat.

The Giants had their chances to scratch the scoreboard as well, but they missed three field goals. Washington rushed for 158 yards to 77 for New York and the Redskins held New York to –3 yards passing.

10/8/39	REDSKINS (2-0-1) 41, Dodgers (2-2-1) 13			27,092	
Bkn	0	6	7	0	13
Was	7	7	7	20	41
Bkn	TD Kosel, Parker; PAT Kercheval				
Was	TD Filchock, Justice, Farkas 2, Russell, Todd; PAT Masterson 2, Russell 3				

Griffith Stadium—Andy Farkas scored two touchdowns to lead an offensive explosion to beat Brooklyn. The Redskins broke open a competitive game in the fourth quarter to take a 41-13 win.

The Redskins led 14-6 at halftime. Taking possession after the opening kickoff they drove 43 yards to Frank Filchock's five-yard touchdown run. Then, in the second period rookie Jim German fielded a punt and dashed 50 yards to put the Redskins in business at the Brooklyn 25. A few plays later German finished the job with a touchdown pass to Ed justice.

The Dodgers pulled closer on a Stan Kosel touchdown and it was 14-6 at intermission. The teams exchanged touchdowns in the third period and it still was very much a contest going into the fourth quarter with the Redskins up 21-13.

Finally, the Redskins pulled away. Farkas scored his second touchdown to cap a 60-yard drive. The back blasted through the line from two yards out. Later in the fourth Bo Russell blocked a Brooklyn punt, falling on the ball for the score.

The Redskins piled up 430 yards of offense to 300 for Brooklyn. Washington's edge was particularly pronounced in the rushing department, where the Redskins held an advantage of 229 yards to just 41 for the Dodgers.

10/15/39	REDSKINS (3-0-1) 44, Pirates (0-5) 14				25,982
Pit	7	7	0	0	14
Was	13	6	19	6	44
Pit	TD Francis, McDonough; PAT Niccolai 2				
Was	TD German 2, Farkas 2, Todd 2, Justice; PAT Russell, Todd				

Griffith Stadium—The Redskins broke open a tight game with 19 unanswered points in the third quarter and went on to rout Pittsburgh. The first score of that outburst came on a record-setting 99-yard pass from Frank Filchock to Andy Farkas.

The Pirates helped the Redskins get off to a quick start by fumbling away the opening kickoff at their own 14. On the next play Jim German broke a tackle in the backfield and scooted down the sidelines across the goal line for a 6-0 lead.

After Pittsburgh scored to take a 7-6 lead, German struck again. He took the ensuing kickoff at the three, waited for his blocking wall to form and turned on his speed for an 84-yard return to the Pittsburgh 13. Evidently not winded by his long jaunt, German took it the rest of the way with one carry inside the one and the next into the end zone. The conversion was good this time and Washington led 13-7.

Not for long, though. Coley McDonough returned the kickoff 56 yards to get things going for the Pirates. A few plays later Carl Littlefield scampered down to the one, but the Redskins repelled three straight plunges from there. On fourth down, however, Pittsburgh recognized the futility of trying to score on the ground and McDonough caught a flip from Lou Thomasetti for a 14-13 lead.

A 31-yard completion from Filchock to Charley Malone and a pass interference call in the end zone led to a one-yard scoring run by Andy Farkas to propel the Redskins into the lead before halftime. Then, early in the second half, Filchock and Farkas got their names indelibly into the record books.

The Redskins were backed up to their own one by a holding call. Filchock drifted back halfway to the end line and tossed an innocent-looking little pass to Farkas at the four. The back took off downfield and dismissed the Pirate safetyman at around the 30. Redskin blockers appeared and Farkas had an escort. He kept running and was free of any hostile players by the time he got to midfield. But Farkas did have company in the form of end Charley Malone, with him stride for stride to enjoy the end of the record romp.

Trailing 25-14, the Pirates were forced to abandon the ground game that had kept them in the contest and their offense went into the tank. Dick Todd extended the lead with a 24-yard TD reception from Filchock and Todd turned it into a rout later in the third with a spectacular 60-yard touchdown run.

Farkas Wins 'Outstanding Redskin' Award, Team Sets Scoring Mark

Oct 16—Back Andy Farkas was honored for his performance against the Pirates on Sunday by being given the "Outstand Redskin" award.

Farkas scored two touchdowns to pace a 44-14 romp over Pittsburgh.

One of the touchdowns put him indelibly in the NFL record book along with teammate Frank Filchock. The two combined for a 99-yard touchdown pass, although Farkas did most of the work. He took Filchock's short toss from the end zone at the four and masterfully followed his blockers into the clear for the score.

Farkas also posted two touchdowns the previous week in Washington's 41-13 pasting of Brooklyn and in doing so he helped the Redskins set another NFL record. Never before has one team scored 40 points or more in back-to-back games.

10/22/39	Redskins (4-0-1) 21, PIRATES (0-6) 14				8,602
Was	14	0	7	0	21
Pit	0	7	0	7	14
Was	TD Millner, Farkas, Irwin; PAT Farkas, Russell 2				
Pit	TD Boyd, Brumbaugh; PAT Niccolai 2				

Forbes Field—The Redskins jumped to a 14-0 lead in the first quarter, but had to hold off a late Pirate bid to tie the game in the late going to escape with the win.

Washington scored its first touchdown with less than two minutes elapsed in the game. A short punt against the wind set them up at their own 46. Three plays later Frank Filchock faded back to his right and launched one deep. Wayne Millner made a leaping catch at the 20 and ran in untouched.

On their next possession, the Redskins came up empty after a foray to the Pittsburgh five, but they cashed in on their next opportunity. The wind advantage helped again as they started from the Pirate 40 after another short punt. Filchock threw a short pass to Andy Farkas. The back got some momentum going, bounced off of a couple of tacklers at around the 30, and raced in for the touchdown to make it 14-0.

Pittsburgh recovered in the second quarter with a touchdown pass from Coley McDonough to Sam Boyd to cut the lead to 14-7 at halftime, but Redskins regained their two-TD lead on their first possession of the second half. Starting from their own 19, they moved to the Pirate 25 with a combination of Filchock's passing and some good running by Jim Johnston. From there Farkas tried to gain a few yards up the middle, but the blockers had done their jobs so well that Andy found open ground all the way to the end zone.

The previous week a Farkas touchdown early in the second half had broken up a close game against Pittsburgh and started the Redskins to an easy win, but that would not be the case this week. Early in the fourth quarter, McDonough let fly with a long pass to Boyd Brumbaugh, who followed a block that eliminated safetyman Farkas and raced over the goal line to complete the 72-yard touchdown play to pull Pittsburgh back within a touchdown.

Washington tried to respond but Filchock threw an interception and the Pirates were knocking at the door at the Washington 22. The immediate threat was nullified when Farkas returned the favor by intercepting McDonough.

Pittsburgh launched its final assault from its own 25 with five minutes left. McDonough got a nine-yard completion and then found Boyd in the clear. The receiver caught the ball in Redskin territory at the 45 at full speed and for a fleeting moment it appeared that the game would be tied. Ed Justice, however, flashed into the picture and hauled Boyd down from behind at the 20. Perhaps inspired by Justice's heroics, the defense stiffened and Pittsburgh advanced no further. McDonough's desperate fourth-down pass bounced harmlessly off the crossbar ensuring that the Redskins would hang on for the win.

10/29/39	**PACKERS (5-1) 24, Redskins (4-1-1) 14**				24,308
Was	0	7	0	7	14
GB	7	10	0	7	24
Was	TD Farkas, Todd; PAT Russell 2				
GB	TD Hinkle, Bruder, Laws; FG Engebreteen				

State Fair Park, Milwaukee—Perhaps the Redskins could have made a classic contest out of this midseason battle of league powerhouses, but we'll never know. Washington passers threw six interceptions, Washington rushers fumbled four times, and Washington receivers dropped several catchable passes, allowing the Packers to claim an easy victory.

Green Bay earned its first score by driving 71 yards in eight plays. The Redskins responded by driving to the Packer 17 at the start of the second quarter. At that point, however, the game turned as Charley Brock intercepted Sammy Baugh's pass and returned it 58 yards. Jim Johnston pulled Brock down from behind at the Washington 33, but that only delayed the touchdown. A few plays later Cecil Isbell threw a touchdown pass to Hank Bruder and the Packers were up 14-0.

Andy Farkas manufactured an answer pretty much on his own, gaining all of the yardage in a two-play, 49-yard touchdown burst. On the first play he was nearly trapped for a loss, but worked his way free for 41 yards to the eight. He took the most direct route the rest of the way, rocketing straight up the middle to cut the Packer lead in half.

After regaining possession, the Redskins reverted to their form for this game. Frank Filchock's pass had just left his hand when it fell into the hands of Moose Mulleneaux. The Packer end rambled down to the Redskin 26 to set up a field goal. The score was 17-7 at the half.

The die was cast. A Baugh interception and return to the Packer 11 was followed by a Don Irwin fumble. Farkas returned a punt 38 yards to the Green Bay 30, but Irwin dropped a sure touchdown before Wayne Millner fumbled it back to the Packers. Farkas returns a punt 30 yards; Irwin fumbles again.

On the last play of the third quarter, Baugh threw an interception at midfield and Green Bay moved in for the kill. Isbell helped get it done on the ground and through the air, with a pass to Don Hutson that gained 14 yards. After that Isbell turned his attention to Don Laws, who caught a pass for ten and then took the handoff to score the clincher.

Redskins 'Too Tight,' Flaherty Says

Oct 30—The Redskins did not lose to the Packers on Sunday because they were not up for the game. In fact, according to coach Ray Flaherty, they were too excited for the battle of top teams.

"My fellows were too tight, too tense in there," said Flaherty. "They were overanxious and that's why they fumbled. They dropped passes a 10-year-old could have caught."

While paying tribute to the Packers, Flaherty clearly thinks the Redskins should have won. "Make no mistake, that's the best Packer team in years, but the Redskins are good enough to lick 'em."

Doing the math, counting points lost due to giveaways and Packer touchdowns set up by interceptions, it's easy to see the Redskins winning the game by 35-7.

11/5/39	**REDSKINS (5-1-1) 7, Eagles (0-5-1) 6**				20,440
Phi	0	6	0	0	6
Was	7	0	0	0	7
Phi	TD Carter				
Was	TD Malone; PAT Russell				

Griffith Stadium—Sammy Baugh threw a touchdown pass to Charley Malone four minutes into the game. The elements, the Washington defense, and some good fortune all helped allow that to hold up over the remaining 56 minutes as the Redskins eked out a 7-6 win.

In a driving rainstorm that made a quagmire of the field— Shirley Povich of the Post wrote of the spectators sitting on the "concrete banks of Lake Griffith"—Baugh got his team a critical field position advantage with a 70-yard quick kick to the Washington 10. The next time the Redskins got the ball they were at the Eagle 48.

It didn't take long for Baugh and the Skins to get into the end zone. A pair of passes to Jim Johnston advanced the ball to the 20. From there, Baugh's pass knifed through the raindrops and into Malone's hands in the end zone. Rookie Bo Russell booted the extra point.

A roughing-the-kicker call kept alive a second-quarter drive that resulted in a TD pass from Emmett Mortell to Joe Carter. However, the Eagles' good fortune did not continue as Franny Murray missed the extra point and the Washington lead held at 7-6.

For the rest of the second and the entire third quarter, the Skins were on the attack offensively but continually bogged down and unable to score. Meanwhile, the Eagles didn't mount a serious threat until the fourth quarter.

In reality, the Eagles' best chance to take a fourth-quarter lead came not as a result of an efficient Philly offense but of a poor punt by Baugh. That set the Eagles up at the Washington 14, but Philly came up empty when a fourth-down pass was incomplete. The Eagles never came close to scoring again.

Nov 9

Baugh Will Not Start vs. Dodgers
Flaherty will go with Filchock-Todd combo in effort to spur offense

11/12/39	**Redskins (6-1-1) 42, DODGERS (4-4-1) 0**				28,000
Was	7	14	7	14	42
Bkn	0	0	0	0	0
Was	TD Farkas 3, Millner, McChesney, Todd; PAT Masterson 3, Russell 3				

Ebbets Field—Andy Farkas scored three touchdowns to pace the Redskins' 42-0 rout of Brooklyn.

It took just 15 seconds for Farkas to tally his first six points. He took the opening kickoff at his nine, followed a wedge of blockers for about 25 yards and then broke sharply towards the left sideline and into the clear. Safetyman Ace Parker awaited Farkas past midfield, but the runner got past him and completed the 91-yard jaunt.

The Washington offense didn't get cranked up until the second quarter and Farkas was the main driver in a four-play, 60-yard touchdown drive. He carried twice for a first down at midfield, and then Sammy Baugh passed to Wayne Miller for 16 yards to the Dodger 34. On the next play Farkas took a handoff, headed around right end, shook free from a pair of tacklers in the backfield and was off to the right corner of the end zone to make it 14-0. Before halftime Baugh had connected with Millner again, this time for a 34-yard touchdown.

If the game wasn't already a rout at 21-0, Farkas went to work to make it one in the third quarter. Starting from the Redskin 39, Farkas carried on ten plays as Washington move relentlessly downfield. Charley Malone offered an occasional break for Farkas by gathering in two Frank Filchock passes for a total of 27 yards. It was Farkas, though, who finished the drive by making his way over right tackle for the final two yards into the end zone. Dick Todd's 80-yard punt return provided yet another highlight and wrapped up the scoring in the fourth quarter.

Almost overlooked in the scoring explosion was the shutout the Washington defense posted. The Washington line was a brick wall containing Parker, the Dodgers' offensive haymaker, all day long. Only three times did Brooklyn move into Redskin territory.

11/19/39	**REDSKINS (7-1-1) 28, Cardinals (1-9) 7**				26,667
Chi	0	0	7	0	7
Was	7	6	6	9	28
Chi	TD Barbatsky; PAT Smith				
Was	TD Farkas 2, Johnston, Todd; PAT Farkas; FG Russell				

Griffith Stadium—For the second straight week the story was Andy Farkas. The back scored two touchdowns to run his total for the season to 11, an NFL record, leading the Redskins to an easy 28-7 win.

As he had the previous week, Farkas scored on a long play in the early going. Washington received the kickoff, but Red Morgan fumbled and Ki Aldrich recovered for the Cardinals at the Washington 30. All the Cards could muster out of the opportunity was an unsuccessful field goal attempt. On the Redskins' first play after the touchback, Farkas took a screen pass from Frank Filchock. He had a phalanx of blockers in front of him and he burst into the secondary. A cut to the sideline allowed him to elude all but one pursuer and the Cardinal safetyman was chasing Farkas from midfield down to about the Chicago 25. At that point Charlie Malone dispatched the defender with a nice block and Farkas cruised the rest of the way across the goal line.

In the second quarter Dick Todd intercepted a Cardinal pass to set up another touchdown. This time Sammy Baugh was at the helm as the Redskins took over in Chicago territory at the 33. It took two plays for Baugh to find the speedy Jim Johnston behind the defense and Baugh's pass was well timed, hitting the back in stride at the six. Johnston scored unchallenged to make it 13-0 at the half.

After intermission, Chicago managed a touchdown when tackle Al Barbatsky scooped up a Redskin fumble and scooted 61 yards into the end zone. That was it for the Cards, though, as it took the Redskins just four plays to score after the kickoff. Farkas caught a touchdown pass from Todd, this one from a more pedestrian distance of 19 yards, to cap the drive.

Record Crowd Expected for Lions

Nov 23—Washington Redskins officials announced that 6,000 additional seats for Sunday's game between the Redskins and the Detroit Lions have been opened up for sale.

The seats are in what is the center field stands in the baseball configuration of Griffith Stadium. They do not offer an ideal view for football but, given the demand for tickets, the team decided to release them for sale.

The team estimated that 35,000 will be in attendance and that would be a record crowd for a Redskins game.

11/26/39	**REDSKINS (8-1-1) 31, Lions (6-4) 7**				36,183
Det	0	7	0	0	7
Was	7	0	14	10	31
Det	TD Ryan; PAT Hanneman				
Was	TD Malone, Millner 2 Justice,; PAT Russell 2, Todd, Johnston; FG Masterson				

Griffith Stadium—The Redskins scored 24 unanswered points in the second half to break a halftime tie and beat the Lions.

Washington took a 7-0 lead on a circus touchdown catch by Charley Malone. From the Lion 48, Frank Filchock launched a pass to him, but Detroit's Lloyd Cardwell tightly covered him. Malone played defensive back, knocking the ball away from Cardwell. The two wrestled for the ball as it dropped towards the ground. The receiver won the battle and outran the rest of the defense into the end zone.

Detroit tied it before halftime and made a bid to take the lead early in the third quarter, but Chuck Hanneman's field goal attempt was short. Andy Farkas fielded the ball on the bounce and returned it to his own 35. From there, the Redskins moved down the field largely on the strength of Filchock passes to Malone. The payoff, though, came as Filchock found a different target. From the Lion 26, Wayne Millner bolted into the end zone and appeared to be under close watch by a pair of Lion backs. With perfect timing, Filchock whipped the ball to Millner and the end turned around the moment the ball arrived, confounding the would-be defenders and notching six points as he caught the pass. Bo Russell converted to make it 14-7.

The Redskins extended their lead on a wild play before the third quarter ended. From the Washington 34, Filchock headed up the middle. After gaining 12 yards he stopped and lateraled to Vic Carroll. He moved in to Lion territory but, perhaps too anxious to score, Carroll fumbled. The man on the spot for the Redskins was Ed Justice, who scooped up the ball from the ground and finished the three-headed touchdown play. In the fourth quarter Sammy Baugh's touchdown pass to Millner and Bob Masterson's field goal finished out the scoring.

Flaherty: Redskins Sharp Mentally

Nov 29—The Redskins are ready, according to their coach.

The team was sharp mentally as they waxed the Detroit Lions 31-7 and Ray Flaherty expects them to remain in that state as they travel to New York to face the Giants with the Eastern Conference title on the line.

"If there is no letdown, if the Redskins take the field in the same proper spirit, I think we should win," said Flaherty.

There is no question that fans of the Redskins are in the proper spirit for the game. The team's allocation of 15,000 seats in the Polo Grounds was snapped up quickly and the trains running from Washington, D.C. to New York will be packed with Burgundy and Gold clad revelers.

Flaherty is dismissing reports that as many as seven Giants, including star back Tuffy Leemans, are suffering from injuries that may keep them out of the game.

"They may not be in the best shape," said Flaherty. "But they are likely to be the liveliest set of cripples that ever went on the field."

12/3/39	GIANTS (9-1-1) 9, Redskins (8-2-1) 7				62,404
Was	0	0	0	7	7
NYG	3	3	3	0	9
Was	TD Masterson; PAT Masterson				
NYG	FG Cuff 2, Strong				

Polo Grounds—For the second straight year, the Redskins lost in New York in a division-deciding game. But, unlike last year's rout, this one was as close as it gets.

In as bizarre an ending as the team has ever seen, an apparent game-winning field goal by Bo Russell that was called wide right by Referee Bill Halloran sparked a wave of fights in the stands and many of the 12,000 Redskins fans present stormed the field.

Another 8,000 fans greeted the team at Union Station on its return, chanting "we wuz robbed" well into the night. George Preston Marshall vowed that Halloran would never work another game. While Marshall's influence is disputed, Halloran never did. But that's the end of the story; let's go back to the beginning.

The Giants had built up a 9-0 lead through three quarters on three field goals, two by Ward Cuff and the other by Ken Strong. Washington's only real threat in the first half came when they drove to a first down at the Giant one, but Tuffy Leemans intercepted a pass in the end zone to kill that opportunity.

It appeared that the Giants' defense, led by Steve Owens, would be sufficient to get the job done as the game wore on late into the fourth quarter. The equation changed dramatically when Wee Willie Wilkin broke up the middle and blocked Len Barnum's punt and Clyde Shugart recovered the ball at the Giant 19. After being thrown for a one-yard loss, Frank Filchock lofted a pass into the end zone. It appeared that Barnum was there to make the play on the ball, but he flailed at it and missed, enabling Bob Masterson to haul it in for the score. Masterson then booted the point after to cut the New York lead to 9-7 with 5:47 left to play.

The Redskin defense then held New York and, although Barnum got his punt off this time, Dick Todd popped through to get 30 yards on the return to near midfield. Runs by Filchock and Todd moved it down to the Giant 28 before Filchock took to the air and threw to John Spirida for a first down at the seven. One play later, Russell came in and Filchock set up to hold at the 15. It seemed that everyone in the stadium except for referee Halloran thought the field goal was good. Unfortunately, his was the only opinion that mattered.

1940
Head Coach: Ray Flaherty
Record: 9-2, First in NFL Eastern Division
Playoffs: 0-1, lost NFL Championship Game

Honors: Jim Barber All NFL; Sammy Baugh All NFL; Steve Slivinski All NFL; Dick Todd All NFL

Redskins Boost Single Ticket Prices

Mar 23—The Redskins announced today that prices will increase for those who buy tickets to individual games.

Tickets that previously cost $1.65 will go up to $2.50 while the more desirable seats have been bumped up from $2.20 to $3.00.

Cost for season tickets, which range from $6.60 to $13.20, will remain the same. That means that fans who plunk down for the entire six-game slate in advance will save from $4.20 to $6.60 compared to the single-ticket prices.

9/15/40	REDSKINS (1-0) 24, Dodgers (0-1) 17				32,763
Bkn	0	0	10	7	17
Was	7	10	0	7	24
Bkn	TD Gussie, McFadden PAT Parker 2 FG Kercherst				
Was	TD Justice, Filchock, Todd; PAT Russell 3; FG Russell				

Griffith Stadium—The Redskins held a 17-0 halftime lead but had to endure some anxious moments in the final 30 minutes before coming out with a 24-17 win over the Dodgers.

After the kickoff, Washington had possession at its own 27 and moved in smartly for a score. Passes from Sammy Baugh to Jim Johnston and Ed Justice got them into Brooklyn territory. Soon after that, Baugh went back to Justice again, this time for 42 yards and the touchdown for a 7-0 lead.

After Haywood Sanford kicked a field goal, Frank Filchock engineered the next TD drive, with a considerable assist from end Bob McChesney. From midfield, Filchock launched a missile towards McChesney, who was running down the left sideline with two defenders on his heels. The receiver somehow managed to haul in the pass at the six. Filchock stumbled over the goal line on the next play for a 17-0 lead.

In the second half, the Dodgers scratched the scoreboard by driving to a touchdown, but it took a bit of good fortune to get it done. Ace Parker's pass from deep in Washington territory bounced off of Justice and into the waiting arms of rookie guard Mike Gussie, who stepped in from the three for a touchdown. A Baugh fumble that led to a Brooklyn field goal made things quite uncomfortable for the Redskins.

The Dodgers returned the favor, though, as they fumbled and Ernie Pinckert recovered for Washington at the Redskin 38. Dick Todd then galloped to the Brooklyn 16 and scored two plays later when Filchock flipped a short pass to him at the eight. He was able to get in from there.

Brooklyn scored a fourth-quarter touchdown to make it a seven-point game, but the Washington defense held them out of the end zone after that.

Skins Prepare for Giants Without Baugh

Sep 16—The wounded shoulder of star passer Sammy Baugh is a great concern for the Redskins as they prepare to host the rival New York Giants on Sunday.

Baugh injured the joint while making a block during Washington's 24-17 win over Brooklyn last Sunday. Trainer Doc Mauro said there was no bone damage in the area and that it's likely a bruised muscle causes the pain.

While the injury is thought to be minor, it could hinder preparation for the game against the Giants.

Also getting in the way of getting ready for the game could be a lack of equipment. Thieves broke into the team's field house at Anacostia Park and made off with some $200 worth of equipment. The team will have to replace the helmets, shoes, and jerseys that were stolen.

9/22/40	**REDSKINS (2-0) 21, Giants (0-1-1) 7**				34,712
NYG	0	0	7	0	**7**
Was	7	7	0	7	**21**
NYG	TD Poole PAT Cuff				
Was	TD Johnston, Moore, Todd PAT Masterson, Russell 2				

Griffith Stadium—A key goal line stand in the third quarter and a 76-yard, fourth quarter punt return by Dick Todd helped the Redskins hold off the Giants.

The Redskins held a 14-0 halftime lead on the strength of touchdowns by Jim Johnston and Wilbur Moore, but the Giants got back into it. In the third quarter, Jim Poole scored one TD for the Giants and soon had his team knocking on the door again when he caught Tuffy Leemans' pass for a 15-yard gain to the Washington three. Sammy Baugh and Johnston nailed him there, but it appeared the game was on the verge of being tied.

New York mustered two yards on three plays and faced fourth and goal at the one. Leemans had a hole for a moment, but the gap was quickly filled by guard Dick Farman, who nailed Leemans for a three-yard loss and gave possession back to the Redskins.

The home team was far from out of the woods at that point, but Todd took care of that midway through the fourth quarter. He fielded Kay Eakin's punt at his own 24, picked his way through the coverage, watched Vic Carroll dispatch the last possible tackler, and sped into the end zone for the clinching score.

Edwards Injured in Freak Accident

Sep 22—Prior to the Redskins' 21-7 win over the New York Giants, lineman Turk Edwards suffered a freak knee injury as he went returned to the sidelines following the opening coin toss. The injury kept him out of the game and is expected to keep him sidelined for another week.

Editor's note: The injury would keep Edwards out much longer. He would appear in just one more game for the Redskins before being forced to retire.

10/6/40	**Redskins (3-0) 40, STEELERS (1-2-2) 10**				8,602
Was	14	7	13	6	**40**
Pit	3	0	7	0	**10**
Was	TD J. Johnston 3, Seymour 2, Millner PAT Masterson 2, Russell, Sanford				
Pit	TD Condit PAT Niccolai FG Niccolai				

Forbes Field—Jim Johnston scored three touchdowns to lead the 40-10 rout of the Steelers.

Pittsburgh took the opening kickoff and drove for a field goal, but the Redskins moved immediately after that to establish dominance, marching 82 yards for a touchdown. Sammy Baugh got things started with a 20-yard run and then a completion to Johnston got them near midfield. After a pass interference call moved the Redskins into Steeler territory at the 31, Johnston caught a pass for five yards and then carried five straight times to score the touchdown.

On the next possession, Johnston took a short pass from Baugh, built up some steam, found a phalanx of blockers, and rolled 64 yards to the Steeler 11. Four plays later, Bob Seymour carried it into the end zone to make it 14-3. They extended the lead to 21-3 at halftime when Wayne Millner snatched Frank Filchock's pass right out of the hands of would-be defender George Klick at the goal line.

In the third quarter, Johnston made another big play as he snuck in at full speed and picked off Bill Patterson's pass at the Washington 39. There was no catching him—he never broke stride in going 61 yards for the TD. There was no catching the Redskins either as Johnston scored again on a one-yard plunge later in the period or Seymour ran in for another six in the fourth quarter.

Flaherty Ramps Up Preparation for Cards

Oct 10—The longer a team goes undefeated in a season, the more coaches tend to worry.

Ray Flaherty is no exception.

Today he ran his players through a two-hour practice in preparation for Sunday's game against the Chicago Cardinals. After that, the mental preparation was extended as well as the skull sessions went on well into the night.

Flaherty is concerned that his 4-0 team is taking the home game against the 1-1-3 Cardinals too lightly.

10/13/40	**REDSKINS (4-0) 28, Cardinals (1-2-3) 21**				33,694
Chi	14	7	0	0	**21**
Was	14	0	7	7	**28**
Chi	TD McCullough, Madden, Goldburg PAT Zontina 2, Clark				
Was	TD Todd, Millner, Masterson, Moore PAT Masterson 2, Sanford 2				

Griffith Stadium—Faced with a second-half deficit for the first time all year, the Redskins showed they had what it takes to come from behind and win. Frank Filchock's fourth-quarter touchdown pass to Bob Masterson put Washington ahead of the Cardinals to stay.

The first quarter involved a furious exchange of touchdowns with Dick Todd and Wayne Miller scoring six points each for Washington. Hugh McCullough and Lloyd Madden got TD's for the Cards, and it was tied at 14 going into the second quarter.

A fumble by Todd backed the Redskins up deep in their own territory and Chicago had excellent field position at the Washington 35 after the punt. Three plays later, Marshall Goldberg raced around end and, encountering little resistance from the defense, scooted 24 yards for a touchdown and a 21-14 lead. Frank Filchock threw a pair of interceptions that prevented the Redskins from threatening before halftime and the Cardinals took their seven-point lead into the locker room.

The Redskins tied it up soon after intermission. They took the second-half kickoff and marched 74 yards to a 20-yard touchdown pass from Sammy Baugh to Wayne Millner. The drive was a deft mixture of running plays and Baugh passes. Besides the touchdown, the prettiest play on the drive was a run fake where Baugh crouched down, headed up the middle, stopped and, still hunched over, popped a nice pass to Charley Malone for 12 yards to the 20.

The game winner came in the fourth quarter. On the last play of the third, Chicago punted and Todd returned it 24 yards to the Washington 39. Soon after that, a pass from Filchock to Jim Meade got them into Cardinal territory at the 44. Todd and Filchock alternated running plays to move down to the 20. Two plays later, they faced third and 11 from the 21.

Filchock went back to pass and found himself under a heavy rush. He heaved a wobbler to Masterson who, unlike the passer, didn't have a defender anywhere near him. The end fielded the ball at around the eight while running backwards and stepped into the end zone. Bo Russell's extra point put Washington up by the final margin of 28-21. A Todd interception ended Chicago's best chance to tie it up after that.

10/20/40	**REDSKINS (5-0) 34, Eagles (0-6) 17**				28,500
Was	7	14	6	7	**34**
Phi	3	14	0	0	**17**
Was	TD Todd 2, Masterson, Seymour, Millner; PAT Masterson 4				
Phi	TD Riffle, Looney PAT Murray, FG Somers				

Shibe Park—Sammy Baugh pitched two touchdown passes in the last three minutes of the first half to put the Redskins ahead to stay as they easily beat the Eagles.

Philadelphia jumped to an early lead, with some help from the Redskins. A pair of fumbles led to a touchdown and field goal for the Eagles. In between, Washington got a touchdown of its own and the Eagles led 10-7 when they intercepted a Frank Filchock pass at their own 24. They drove 76 yards to a touchdown by Don Looney to take a 17-7 lead.

The Redskins, with Baugh leading the charge, quickly moved to take control before halftime. From his own 28, Baugh took the snap, juggled it for a moment and delivered a mortar shot that landed in the hands of Bob Masterson, who caught it in stride at the 11 and then put on a burst of speed to get into the end zone. For good measure, the touchdown catcher booted the extra point as well, cutting the Eagle lead to 17-14.

Baugh then helped the offense get the ball back when he batted down Davy O'Brien's third-down pass, forcing a punt that Dick Todd returned to the Washington 40 with a minute and a half left before intermission. One Baugh pass to Todd got Washington into Eagle territory and then Baugh went back to Todd, this time for the kill. Todd approached the ball as he was crossing the field and somehow managed to catch the ball with one hand as he bumped into the defender in the end zone.

That gave Washington a 21-17 halftime lead and the visitors held Philly at bay in the second half while scoring two more touchdowns.

10/27/40	**Redskins (6-0) 20, Lions (3-3-1) 14**				28,909
Was	7	6	0	7	20
Det	0	7	7	0	14
Was	TD Johnston, McChesney, Todd; PAT Masterson, Russell				
Det	TD J. Moore, Weiss; PAT Hanneman 2				

Detroit University Stadium—Dick Todd was a terror on both offense and defense and his 61-yard touchdown run in the fourth quarter was the game-winning score.

The way the Redskins started out, it didn't appear that any late-game heroics would be needed. Two and a half minutes into it, they had a 7-0 lead thanks to Jimmy Johnston's 65-yard tear on a reverse.

Then Todd got into the act, intercepting Whizzer White's pass near midfield. First, he ran for 15 and then, after a holding call against the Skins, made an impossible catch of a Frank Filchock pass with a Lion defender draped on his shoulders for a gain of 35. Soon after that, from the ten, Filchock lobbed a pass to Bob McChesney in the corner of the end zone for a touchdown and a 13-0 lead in the second quarter.

The home team, however, began to climb back into it. Later in the second, Washington had a chance to break it wide open with possession in Detroit territory, but the Lions intercepted Filchock in the end zone and returned it to their own 15. From there, they marched 85 yards and got on the scoreboard with a touchdown on a pass from Cotton Price to June Moore.

It really got interesting in the third quarter when, again, a Redskin turnover in Lion territory proved very costly. Sammy Baugh shot a shovel pass to Wayne Millner, who was swarmed under as he tried to lateral back to Baugh. The ball came free and bounced into the arms of Harry Weiss, who scooped it up and raced 76 yards for the go-ahead score.

The 14-13 score held into the fourth quarter. From the Washington 39, Todd started out around right end, but then spied a hole in the middle and darted into it. He went streaking across the field, heading for the left corner. At one point, he came to a near-complete stop to let his blocking reform and then cut back again to outrun his pursuers to the end zone. Bo Russell kicked the extra point to make it 20-14.

Two possessions later, the Lions made their last bid. Starting with about three minutes left, they moved from their own three to the Washington 16. The last gasp expired, though, when Willie Wilkin and Bob Masterson broke through and nailed Price for a 20-yard loss as time ran out.

11/3/40	**REDSKINS (7-0) 37, Steelers (1-2-6) 10**				31,204
Pit	3	7	0	0	10
Was	6	7	7	17	37
Pit	TD Platukis; PAT Niccolai; FG Niccolai				
Was	TD Johnston 2, Todd, Filchock, Masterson; PAT Masterson, Russell 3; FG Masterson				

Griffith Stadium—Sammy Baugh and Frank Filchock combined to complete 14 of 15 passes for 204 yards as the Redskins roared past the Steelers.

Pittsburgh got off to a 3-0 lead by driving to a field goal, but the Redskins responded quickly with a 39-yard touchdown pass from Baugh to Jimmy Johnston.

Then it was Filchock's turn as he led a masterful drive from his own 34. Passes to end Bob McChesney and fullback Dick Todd moved the Redskins deep into Steeler territory. From the 12, Filchock took to the ground, faking a reverse and then scooting untouched up the middle into the end zone for a 13-3 lead.

The Steelers responded by scoring a touchdown on a pass from Billy Patterson to George Platukis, who beat rookie back Bob Seymour in the left corner of the end zone. The point after made it 13-10, and that's where it stood at intermission.

The second half was all Washington. Midway through the third quarter, Baugh threw a screaming pass into the arms of Wayne Millner to get into Steeler territory at the 40. From there, Baugh arched a perfect lob right into the arms of a streaking Johnston, who snared it right in stride and rolled into the end zone for a 20-10 lead.

Pittsburgh's spirit flagged after that and the Redskins poured on 17 more points in the fourth quarter

11/10/40	**DODGERS (5-3) 16, Redskins (7-1) 14**				33,864
Was	0	0	0	14	14
Bkn	7	2	7	0	16
Was	TD Masterson, Seymour; PAT Masterson, Millner				
Bkn	TD Shetley, Parker; PAT Parker 2; Safety Todd tackled in end zone by Cassiano				

Ebbets Field—The Dodgers piled up a 16-0 lead through three quarters and then held off a furious aerial barrage by Sammy Baugh and the Redskins to hand Washington its first defeat of the season.

Brooklyn used a bit of razzle-dazzle to get on the board in the first quarter. End Waddie Young took a pass from Ace Parker at the Redskin six and, with Baugh clinging to him, flipped a lateral to rookie Rhoten Sheteley, who easily stepped across the goal line. Parker converted and it was 7-0.

In the second period, a quick kick caught the Redskins by surprise and they were backed up to their own eight. Dick Todd watched the snap go past him. He chased the ball down in the end zone, but was snowed under by a mob of Brooklynites, led by Dick Cassiano. The safety gave the Dodgers the 9-0 lead they carried into intermission.

Brooklyn put the visitors in a real hole in the third quarter. George Cafego lofted a pass over the head of defender Jimmy Johnston and into the hands of Parker for a 38-yard touchdown and, after Parker's conversion, a 16-0 lead.

Even if the score hadn't dictated that Washington abandon the running game at that point, the results of their feeble attempts to rush the ball certainly would have. For the game, the Redskins mustered a meager 19 yards on the ground.

But needing to pass isn't such a bad thing when you have Baugh doing the throwing, and four Slingin' Sammy specials equaled 85 yards and a touchdown early in the fourth quarter. The payoff was a pitch to the left corner of the end zone to Bob Masterson.

The defense forced Brooklyn to punt and Dick Todd's 16-yard return set the Skins up at their own 46. Passes to Todd and Johnston got the ball to the 11 and the Baugh went to Masterson for eight yards to the three. From there, they elected to try to smash it, which Bob Seymour did five plays later. Masterson kicked the point after and it was 16-14 with two minutes left.

An onside kick attempt failed, but Washington did get one more chance from its own 12 when the Dodgers punted again. A lateral attempt went astray, however, and Brooklyn recovered the loose ball and killed the clock.

Farkas Out vs. Bears

November 15—Star back Andy Farkas has been ruled out of the Redskins' upcoming game against the Chicago Bears. A lingering knee injury will keep the star back on the sideline.

The contest is being billed as a preview of the NFL championship game. The 8-1 Redskins suffered their first loss last week but they still hold the lead in the Eastern Conference. Chicago is 6-2 and sits atop the Western Conference.

11/17/40	**REDSKINS (8-1) 7, Bears (6-3) 3**				35,231
Chi	3	0	0	0	3
Was	0	7	0	0	7
Chi	FG Manders				
Was	TD Todd; PAT Russell				

Griffith Stadium—With a last-second goal line stand, the Redskins held off the Chicago Bears and claimed a 7-3 win in what was billed as a preview of the NFL championship game.

The game's only two scores came on back-to-back possessions. Chicago set up its lone field goal by recovering a fumble at its own 36. Quarterback Sid Luckman ran for seven yards before flipping a lateral to George McAfee, who headed left, reversed his field and then picked his way through the defense for 19 yards to the Washington 30. The incursion stalled there and Jack Manders booted a 38-yard field goal.

The ensuing kickoff went out of bounds and the Redskins took over at midfield. Sammy Baugh threw to Wayne Millner for eight yards. When the second quarter started, Frank Filchock rotated in at quarterback and nearly killed the drive when he threw the ball right to McAfee. Fortunately, a penalty nullified the interception and the Skins were back in business. Soon after that, Filchock floated a perfect pass to Dick Todd at the 16. The fullback faked Eggs Manske into a stagger and then broke a couple of tackles, including one attempt by big Lee Artoe, and stepped into the end zone.

Before the half ended, the Bears entered into Washington territory only to come up empty after an interception. That set the pattern for the second half. Six times in the final 30 minutes the Bears had the ball inside the Washington 40—including three trips inside the 15—and came up empty each time. A combination of turnovers, penalties and tough defense kept the Bears out of the end zone. Washington was even less productive offensively, with its only good chance to score ending when, from the Bear 13, Saul Sherman picked off Baugh's pass in the end zone.

The Bears got a jumpstart on their final attempt to take the lead when a roughing penalty set them up at the midfield stripe. On the first play, Sid Luckman arched a beautiful pass to Bob Swisher, who appeared to be alone at the 25. In desperation, Bob Titchenal found an extra burst of speed and got a hand on the ball at the last instant.

The sense of relief didn't last for long. With the clock ticking down below 90 seconds, Luckman launched another nice pass,

and this one found its target. McAfee caught it at the three and Todd just managed to trip him up inches short of the goal line.

Then the Bears committed their last and most costly penalty when they took too much time to get off a play and the official marked them back to the five. Five seconds left, five yards and a few inches to go.

Willie Wilkin and Mickey Parks got a fierce rush on the first play and slapped down Bob Snyder's first pass attempt. Then, on the final play, Luckman passed into a mass in the end zone that included Bill Osmanski and a slew of defenders. The receiver got his hands on the ball but couldn't tuck it away as the defensive horde descended. The ball fell harmlessly to the ground as the final gun sounded.

11/24/40	**GIANTS (6-3-1) 21, Redskins (8-2) 7**				46,439
Was	0	0	7	0	**7**
NYG	14	0	0	7	**21**
Was	TD Justice; PAT Masterson				
NYG	TD Mellus, Soar, Leemans; PAT Barnum 3				

Polo Grounds—The Giants scored two touchdowns in the first 12 minutes of play and made the lead stand up over the remaining 48 minutes to upset the Redskins.

A solid tackle on the part of the Washington defense wound up costing the Redskins six. Len Barnum threw a pass to Jim Lee Howell, who eluded Sammy Baugh's grasp and headed downfield. Two Redskins smashed into Howell around the 20, separating the receiver from the ball. However, John Mellus scooped the ball up and covered the remaining 21 yards for the touchdown.

One of five New York interceptions on the day set up their second touchdown. Baugh's pass intended for Wayne Millner was batted in the air and Howell picked it off at the Washington 23. Two plays later, a connection between Barmun and Howell got the Giants inside the one and Hank Soar pounded it in from there on the next play.

With the Redskins suffering through an off day by Baugh, who was four of 13 passing, Washington just couldn't catch up. Late in the third quarter, Baugh did manage a touchdown pass, a five-yarder to Ed Justice to make it 14-7. A fumble by Bob Seymour at the New York five ended Washington's last chance to tie the score.

12/1/40	**REDSKINS (9-2) 13, Eagles (1-10) 6**				25,838
Phi	0	0	0	6	**6**
Was	0	6	7	0	**13**
Phi	TD Emmons				
Was	TD Moore, Todd; PAT Masterson				

Griffith Stadium—The Redskins clinched the NFL Eastern Division crown and the right to host the Chicago Bears in next week's NFL Championship game as they got by a game Eagles team.

Clearly overshadowing the winning effort of the Redskins was the play of Philadelphia's Davy O'Brien. The 5-7, 151-pound back shattered single-game records for completions and passing yardage as he tried mightily to lead his team to the upset. O'Brien threw 60 passes and his 31 completions broke Sammy Baugh's mark of 21, set earlier this season. His 314 yards through the air also set a new league mark by a considerable margin.

Making O'Brien's performance even more special was the fact that it was his last professional game. The next day, he was reporting to work at the Federal Bureau of Investigation. After the game, Washington coach Ray Flaherty gave O'Brien the game ball.

"Take it," said Flaherty. "You deserve it, kid."

The Redskins got their offense going in the second quarter after Dick Todd returned a punt to his own 45. Roy Zimmerman pounded out 14 yards to the 26. Wilbur Moore scored the touchdown on a reverse after breaking a tackle and picking up an escort of blockers into the end zone. The point after was missed and it was 6-0.

Todd was the workhorse on Washington's next scoring drive, which started four minutes into the second half. Five carries by Todd got the ball near midfield, and then Baugh took to the air, hitting Charley Malone for nine yards. Then it was Ed Justice, ploughing for 18 yards on a reverse to get to the Eagle eight. Todd toted it three times from there, the last a six-yard touchdown run. This time the point after was good and it was 13-0.

The Eagles cause seemed doomed after Baugh got off an 85-yard punt that pinned them back at their two. However, a dozen O'Brien passes later, they were in the end zone on the tenth completion of the drive, this to Frank Emmons who broke a tackle near the three and crossed the goal line. The conversion failed so the score remained 13-6.

O'Brien and the Eagles mounted one more threat. With 48 seconds left, they had moved to the Washington 24. For a moment, Joe Wendlick was in the open and O'Brien threw to him in the end zone. Todd, however, came out of nowhere to bat it away at the last instant and, two plays later, the Redskins walked off winners.

So did Davy O'Brien.

Baugh Will Play For Skins in '41 For 'Good Contract'

Dec 6—Washington Redskins star passer Sammy Baugh took time from preparing for the NFL title game against the Chicago Bears to talk about his future.

Nixing rumors that he was going to accept an offer to coach, the record-setting back said that he wants to return to the Redskins—if the gets what he calls a "good contract."

The coaching offer was believed to carry an annual salary in the vicinity of $10,000. It is presumed that Baugh would want considerably more than that to continue to expose his body to the rigors of playing on the field.

The Bears are 7-5 favorites in Sunday's title tilt in Griffith Stadium. City officials are asking fans to leave their homes early.

NFL Championship Game Sunday, December 8, 1940 Griffith Stadium Washington, D. C.

12/8/40	Bears 73, REDSKINS 0				36,034
Chi	21	7	26	19	73
Was	0	0	0	0	0
Chi	Osmanski 66 run (Manders kick)				
Chi	Luckman 1 run (Snyder kick)				
Chi	Maniaci 42 run (Martinovich kick)				
Chi	Kavanaugh 30 pass from Luckman (Snyder kick)				
Chi	Pool 15 interception return (Plassman kick)				
Chi	Nolting 23 run (kick failed)				
Chi	McAfee 34 interception return (Stydahar kick)				
Chi	Turner 24 interception return (kick failed)				

Chi	Clark 44 run (kick failed)
Chi	Famigletti 2 run (Mancini pass from Sherman)
Chi	Clark 1 run (pass failed)

There is no doubt.

The Chicago Bears are the best pro football has to offer, and the second best, the Redskins, aren't even close.

On their first two possessions, the Bears showed that they could not only score at will, but any way they chose to. On their second play, Bill Osmanski swept around left end for 66 yards and a touchdown. On their next possession, Chicago went from big plays to little plays, taking 17 snaps to move 80 yards to their second score, this one coming on a one-yard blast by Sid Luckman.

By halftime, the Bears had slowed down somewhat—albeit with a 28-0 lead. While a Washington rally to win seemed out of the question, the game appeared to be shaping up as your garden-variety rout. It ended up being far from that, however.

The Redskins were forced to take to the air on almost every play and, of course, the Bears knew this. On the day, Chicago intercepted eight Redskin passes. Three times in the third period, Chicago picked off a pass and returned it for a touchdown. When the Bears got the ball on offense, Ray Nolting got a touchdown on a 23-yard run. At the end of the third, it was 54-0.

The Bears did not let up. Harry Clark scored two touchdowns on runs of 44 and two yards. In between, the Bears recovered Frank Filchock's fumble at the Washington two and pushed it in from there. Just for fun, they faked the kick for the conversion and Sollie Sherman passed to Joe Maniaci for the single extra point. That was about the only thing that the Bears did that could be considered rubbing it in.

The Redskins were left to wonder what might have happened if they had converted an early chance to score. After Osmanski's early romp, Max Krause returned the kickoff 54 yards into Bear territory at the 40. Two plays later, Charley Malone was wide open at the four, but he dropped Sammy Baugh's well-thrown pass. The subsequent field goal attempt was missed and the Redskins came away empty.

When asked about what might have happened if Malone had held on to that pass, almost every Redskin replied that the final score would have been different—probably 73-7.

Team Quit, Marshall Says

Dec 8—Redskins owner George Preston Marshall expects to get what he pays for and, in his eyes, he did not as his team went down to an historic 73-0 title game defeat against the Chicago Bears.

"Those guys out there today quit," said Marshall to reporters in the dressing room after the game.

He then named names.

"[Frank] Filchock's quarterback was awful," he ranted. "Two of the highest salaried backs in the league, Dick Todd and Andy Farkas, stood in the backfield and not once carried the ball."

"It'll show up in next year's salaries. We have some good rookies and we'll get some more," the owner said.

Ray Flaherty also was disappointed but more measured in his comments. "The Bears couldn't miss today, they did everything right," the coach said. "We were just completely demoralized."

1941

Head Coach: Ray Flaherty
Record: 6-5, Third in NFL East

Honors: Willie Wilkin All NFL

Griffith Stadium to Get Grid Expansion

Jan 10—The Redskins signed a new lease and are secure in their home for at least five more years. The landlords showed their appreciation by agreeing to expand their house.

Stadium owner and namesake Clark Griffith agreed to keep allowing the Redskins to share his facility with his baseball team and also agreed to expand the seating for football by 2,500 seats.

The expansion will increase the capacity to about 38,500.

Redskins Camp Moves to San Diego

Mar 27—The Redskins announced that they have accepted an invitation from the mayor of San Diego to hold their training camp in the Southern California city.

The nexus of the move south from Spokane, Washington, where the team has trained the last two years, was a suggestion by former Redskin regular Erny Pinckert. The nine-year starter for the Skins said that owner George Preston Marshall should check out his new home as a possible training site. The legendary great weather in the area, with minimal rainfall and moderate temperatures, was a major selling point along with a large presence of U.S. military personnel.

Team General Manager Jack Espey will fly to San Diego sometime in the next few weeks to work out final details of the agreement. Among the details to be finalized is an intrasquad scrimmage that would benefit the San Diego Police Relief Association.

The Redskins will be the first NFL team to train in California.

Flaherty: Farkas Fit to Play

Sep 11—Redskins coach Ray Flaherty thinks that Andy Farkas' knee is sufficiently healed and that the star fullback needs to get onto the field.

Farkas disagrees, but isn't going to argue with his coach.

After missing most of the 1940 season with the knee problem, he has yet to participate fully in training camp. It has been reported that the injury may threaten his career. However, Flaherty today insisted that Farkas was in condition to play and that he was growing weary of "babying" him.

"That's up to the coach," said Farkas, "but I don't believe that my knees are strong enough to play."

The Farkas matter wasn't the only thing drawing the coach's ire. Unhappy with the performance of the team, Flaherty put the Redskins through a special practice session. The timing was unusual as it took place just eight hours before the team was to face the Pacific all-star team in an exhibition game.

9/28/41	Giants (2-0) 17, REDSKINS (0-1) 10			35,677	
NYG	7	0	7	3	17
Was	0	7	0	3	10
NYG	TD Poole, Dennery; PAT Cuff, Marefos; FG Cuff				
Was	TD Filchock; PAT Masterson; FG Masterson				

Griffith Stadium—The Redskins were their own worst enemies, fumbling five times and throwing five interceptions in a lackluster 17-10 loss to the Giants.

After a furious exchange of turnovers early on, New York took a 7-0 lead after Tuffy Leemans intercepted a Sammy Baugh pass in Washington territory. Five plays later, Washington's Ki Aldrich tipped Leemans' pass in the end zone, but it found the arms of Jim Poole for a 7-0 Giant lead.

The Redskins got on the board in the second quarter. Willie Wilkin partially blocked a New York punt and the ball fluttered into the arms of Frank Filchock. After partially blocking the kick, Wilkin fully blocked the last remaining obstacle in the way of Filchock, who completed a 68-yard dash to knot the score at seven. Another New York interception killed an opportunity for the Redskins to take a halftime lead.

In the third quarter, the Giants took the lead with a bit of trickery. Marion Pugh took the snap and lateraled to Andy Marefos. He waited for a moment and then threw a 30-yard pass to Vince Dennery, who caught it in full stride at midfield and didn't stop until he'd crossed to goal line. Early in the fourth quarter, the Redskins tried and failed to convert a fourth down from their own 29, leading to a New York field goal and a 17-7 lead

Another nice run by Filchock, this one 51 yards from scrimmage, got the Redskins down to the New York 10. They moved to the three where they faced fourth down. Curiously, with four minutes left, the call was to try a field goal. Bob Masterson made it, but the Redskins didn't get the ball back until 90 seconds remained and the final New York interception ended it.

Flaherty Benches 10 of 11

Oct 1—It's not unusual for a coach to make a couple of changes to his starting lineup after a team performs poorly. It is unusual to sit virtually the entire starting team.

When the Redskins take the field on Sunday against the Brooklyn Dodgers, back Bob Hoffman will be the only player in the lineup who started last week against the Giants. The other ten starters will change.

Hoffman will line up alongside Frank Filchock, Wilbur Moore and Dick Todd. That trio replaces Sammy Baugh, Ed Justice, and Andy Farkas.

The line will consist of ends Bob Masterson and Frank Clair (replacing Wayne Millner and Bob McChesney), tackles Wee Willie Wilkin and Jim Barber (Bill Young and Fred Davis), Guards Clem Stralka and Clyde Shugart (Dick Farman and Steve Slivinski) and center George Smith (Ky Aldrich).

10/5/41	REDSKINS (1-1) 3, Dodgers (2-1) 0			32,642	
Was	0	0	3	0	3
Bkn	0	0	0	0	0
Was	FG Aguirre				

Griffith Stadium—Joe Aguirre kicked a 34-yard field goal in the third quarter and the Washington defense made it stand up as the Redskins beat Brooklyn.

In the second quarter, it twice looked like Washington had taken a lead. First, Wilbur Moore caught Frank Filchock's pass in the end zone—almost. It was ruled that Moore was out of bounds. Then Sammy Baugh's pass found Ed Justice for an apparent TD.

The Redskins, however, were penalized for not having enough men on the line and the score was nullified.

After Aguirre's kick—the only one of six field goal attempts on the day that was successful—the Redskins got one of a few scares they had to endure before claiming the win. Bill Leckonby took the ensuing kickoff and weaved his way through traffic before he was finally brought down at the Washington 19. Most of the runback, though, was wiped out as the Dodgers were penalized for an illegal block near midfield. A final drive for Brooklyn died on the Washington 25 as Fred Davis recovered a Dodger fumble.

10/12/41	Redskins (2-1) 24, STEELERS (0-4) 20				18,733
Was	7	3	14	0	24
Pit	0	7	0	13	20
Was	TD Todd 2, R. Hare; PAT Masterson 3; FG Aguirre				
Pit	TD Riffle, Jones, Brumbaugh; PAT Niccolai 2				

Forbes Field—Dick Todd scored two touchdowns as the Redskins led 24-7 entering the final period, but Washington had to withstand a fourth quarter rally to hang on and defeat the winless Steelers.

The visitors held a 10-7 halftime lead thanks to a 10-yard touchdown run by Todd and Joe Aguirre's 39-yard field goal. In the third period, they expanded the lead on Todd's second touchdown, this one on an eight-yard scamper. Then a poor punt gave Washington good field position which they cashed in with Ray Hare's short TD burst, making it 24-7 going into the fourth quarter.

Pittsburgh coach Buff Donelli had said he would find a new group of players if his current crop didn't become more competitive and through 45 minutes it looked as though the coach would have to make good on his threat. But in the fourth the Steelers came alive and nearly killed the Skins.

Pittsburgh drew within 10 early in the fourth when Coley McDonough launched a 41-yard touchdown pass to rookie back Art Jones. Then Bob Seymour fumbled and John Woudenberg recovered for the Steelers. Soon after that Boyd Brumbaugh bulled over from a short distance. The point after was blocked, so it remained 24-20. An onside with a little less than three minutes remaining failed and a final desperate possession by Pittsburgh went nowhere.

Skins 'Celebrate' Win With Tough Practice

Oct 14—What would have happened if they had lost?

Redskins coach Ray Flaherty, unhappy with his team's execution and effort in a 24-20 win over the winless Pittsburgh Steelers, put the Redskins through a long, tough practice today.

According to some, it was the most challenging session since training camp.

10/19/41	Redskins (3-1) 21, EAGLES (0-6) 17				19,071
Was	0	14	0	7	21
Phi	14	0	3	0	17
Was	TD Justice, Farkas, Masterson; PAT Aguirre 2, Masterson				
Phi	TD Humbert, Kreiger; PAT Basca 2; FG Basca				

Shibe Park—Two Sammy Baugh touchdown passes helped the Redskins overcome deficits of 14-0 after one quarter and 17-14 entering the fourth period to beat Philadelphia 21-17.

The Eagles took the lead on their second possession of the game. Tommy Thompson worked them down the field with accurate passing and then capped the drive with a four-yard scoring toss to rookie end Dick Humbert. Thompson never saw his second TD pass—a 40-yarder to another rookie, Bob Kreiger—as Jim Barber nailed the quarterback an instant after the release of

the ball. Thompson bounced right up, though, buoyed by his team's 14-0 margin.

Washington tied it up by halftime with an assist from the Eagles. Baugh and Ki Aldrich forced an Eagle fumble that later resulted in a four-yard touchdown run by Andy Farkas. Philly's Jim Castiglia returned the ensuing kickoff 74 yards, but negated his effort by fumbling back to the Redskins on the very next play. After that, with less than a minute to go in the half, Baugh effortlessly threw a long pass right on the money that Ed Justice caught and then stepped in for the tying score.

The Eagles stopped turning the ball over after halftime and put together a drive that culminated in a 15-yard field goal by Mike Basca. That lead held until less than three minutes remained in the game. Then, from the Eagle 30, Baugh threw to Bob Masterson, who caught the pass at the two and stepped in for the winning touchdown.

10/26/41	REDSKINS (4-1) 17, Rams (2-5) 13				32,280
Cle	0	6	0	7	13
Was	10	7	0	0	17
Was	TD Todd, McChesney; PAT Masterson, Aldrich; FG Masterson				
Cle	TD Hickey, Hall; PAT Adams				

Griffith Stadium—Dick Todd's 71-yard punt return for a touchdown sparked the Redskins' win over Cleveland.

Todd's play came early in the first period with Washington leading 3-0. He took Parker Hall's punt at his own 29 and immediately shot through the first wave of opposition. In the blink of an eye he was in the clear with only Hall, back as the safety, to beat. Hall maneuvered for the best angle and then moved in. The returner dispatched him with a stiff arm, nearly losing his balance in the process. Todd regained his footing and cruised the rest of the way for a 10-0 Washington lead.

In a drive that bridged the first and second periods, Sammy Baugh marched the Redskins downfield using passes to Ed Justice and Bob McChesney. From the Cleveland 14, two passes were incomplete but the third was a low bullet to McChesney in the end zone. The home team led 17-0.

Cleveland got on the board late in the first half after Andy Farkas fumbled the ball away at the Washington 24. After two passes to Johnny Drake, Hall threw to rookie Howard Hickey in the end zone. The point after attempt was blocked and the Rams trailed 17-6 at the half.

The Washington offense went to sleep after intermission, getting its initial first down of the second half in the final seconds of the game. Cleveland had two opportunities to take advantage but could only convert one of them. Riley Matheson intercepted Frank Filchock's pass and the Rams were in business at the Washington 11. Drake charged into the line three times and Cleveland was still left with more than two yards to go for a first down, and more than three for a touchdown. Drake charged as if he was going to try to bull rush for the necessary yardage, but he pulled up and fired a pass into the end zone that whistled just past the intended receiver.

Cleveland cashed in on its second chance, driving downfield on Hall's passing. Hickey made a shoestring catch at the Washington one and Hall took it over himself three plays later. The Rams had two more possessions but interceptions by Ki Aldrich and Bob Titchenal wrapped things up for the Redskins.

11/2/41	REDSKINS (5-1) 23, Steelers (0-7) 3				30,755
Pit	0	3	0	0	3
Was	7	10	0	6	23
Pit	FG Niccolai				
Was	TD Moore, Farkas, Carroll; PAT Masterson, Aguirre; FG Aldrich				

Griffith Stadium—The Redskins dominated play on both sides of the ball and cruised to an easy 23-3 triumph over the Steelers.

Wilbur Moore got the scoring started in the first period when he took a handoff on a reverse, followed the blocking of Jim Barber and Bob Titchenal, and scooted down the left side to score easily. It would be Moore's last contribution of the season as, soon after that, he sustained a broken collarbone that will sideline him for the balance of the year.

On this day, at least, it didn't matter. Washington outgained its hapless opponents by a margin of better than seven to one (340 yards to 48) and held the Steelers to just four first downs. After the teams exchanged field goals in the second quarter, Sammy Baugh led a scoring drive just prior to halftime. From the Pittsburgh 17, all of Baugh's receivers were covered but the defense was paying scant attention to Sammy himself. He took off for the goal line and wasn't dragged down until he reached the two-yard line. Andy Farkas took it over from there and Washington held a 17-3 lead.

They sat on that margin during the second half, having no inclination to do anything other than burn time off the clock. Vic Carroll capped off the scoring with a 30-yard interception return for a touchdown.

11/9/41	DODGERS (5-3) 13, Redskins (5-2) 7			31,713
Was	0	7	0	0	7
Bkn	0	7	0	6	13
Was	TD Seymour; PAT Aldrich			
Bkn	Manders, Wemple; PAT Condit			

Ebbets Field—Sammy Baugh's desperate fourth-down pass was intercepted deep in Brooklyn territory in the closing minute and the Dodgers hung on the defeat the Redskins.

The home team scored first and last. Bruiser Kinard blocked Baugh's punt late in the first period and the Dodgers took over at the Washington 14. Early in the second, Pug Manders wormed his way for the final yard and it was 7-0 Dodgers.

Andy Farkas returned the ensuing kickoff to his own 32 and the Redskins embarked on a scoring drive from there. A strong rain was falling, but Baugh decided that it would be no impediment to taking to the air. He launched a pass toward Wayne Millner that appeared to be too long but the receiver found an extra burst of speed, lunged to catch the slick pigskin, and staggered out of bounds at the 12-yard line after a 53-yard pickup. On the next play, the Dodgers paid scant attention to Bob Seymour and Baugh found him all alone in the end zone for the tying touchdown.

That would turn out to be one of just two incursions into Brooklyn territory on the day with the other being the final, futile drive. Throughout the third quarter and into the fourth, the Dodgers were able to gain favorable field position and finally took advantage, moving in for the kill from their own 48. It took them just four plays to score on a 24-yard pass from Dean McAdams to rookie end Don Wemple. The point after was missed, opening the door for the Redskins. They couldn't quite get through it.

The Redskins took possession at their own 20 with 2:45 to play. Baugh just overthrew Seymour on what would have been a sure touchdown. Then, on fourth down, Baugh whipped one on the money to Vic Carroll, who made it into Brooklyn territory at the 45 with 1:45 left. Baugh's next aerial went to Al Kruger down at the 12. That was as far as they got as a delay penalty and a sack led to fourth down at the 29. Bill Leckeonby stepped in front of Baugh's last pass for an interception to clinch the win for Brooklyn.

Todd May Miss Rest of Season

November 9—The Redskins' hopes of repeating as Eastern Conference champions took a jolt today.

It was revealed that halfback Dick Todd suffered a badly torn ligament in his right leg in the team's loss to the Dodgers on Sunday. Team doctor Pete Moran said that the shifty runner will miss three or four weeks of action.

Since the Redskins have only four games remaining in the regular season, it's possible that Todd won't return until a potential playoff or NFL championship game should the team qualify.

11/16/41	BEARS (7-1) 35, Redskins (5-3) 21			30,095
Was	0	7	7	7	21
Chi	7	14	7	7	35
Was	TD Farkas, Cifers, Seymour; PAT Aldrich 2, Aguirre			
Chi	TD Gallarneau, Standlee, McAfee 2, Nowaskey; PAT Snyder 4, Stydahar			

Wrigley Field—The Redskins improved their performance versus their last meeting with the Bears by 59 points—and still were defeated soundly by Chicago.

Looking for a measure of revenge for the previous season's 73-0 destruction at the hands of the Bears in the championship game, the Redskins had difficulty staying within striking distance for most of the game. After the home team took a 7-0 lead in the first quarter, Andy Farkas tied it up with a scintillating 51-yard punt return for a touchdown in the second.

That would prove to be the high-water mark for the Redskins. The Bears quickly moved to take command. After the ensuing kickoff was returned to the Chicago 35, Sid Luckman threw to Ken Kavanaugh for 18 yards into Washington territory. Two plays later, Ray McLean glided through traffic for 24 yards to the nine and Norm Standlee ran it over soon after that. The next Bears score was a George McAfee production as he returned a punt 54 yards and then caught Bob Snyder's pass in the end zone to give the Bears a 21-7 halftime lead.

A seven-minute drive in the third quarter pulled the Redskins within seven. From the Chicago 14, Sammy Baugh slung a cross-field pass to Ed Cifers for the touchdown.

But Chicago soon expanded its 21-14 lead. Under heavy pressure from his own 32, Baugh threw an ill-advised pass that Standlee intercepted and returned down to the four. McAfee fumbled on the next play but Bob Nowaskey scooped up the ball and got the touchdown for the Bears. On their next possession, the Bears put it away with a 96-yard touchdown drive that ended with Snyder's touchdown pass to McAfee.

> **Nov. 18**
> ## 55,000 Expected to See Skins-Giants Clash
> *At least 5,000 at Polo Grounds will be from DC*

11/23/41	GIANTS (8-2) 20, Redskins (5-4) 13			49,317
Was	0	0	0	13	13
NYG	0	0	10	10	20
Was	TD McChesney, Seymour; PAT Aguirre			
NYG	TD Franck 2; PAT Cuff 2; FG Cuff, Marefos			

Polo Grounds—The Giants scored 10 points in 55 seconds late in the game to trump a fourth-quarter Washington rally and defeat the Redskins. In the process, New York clinched the Eastern Division title, eliminating the Redskins.

Neither team seemed anxious to try much offensively on the muddy field in the first half, which ended as it had started with both teams having no points. It was a different story in the third quarter as the Giants held the ball for 13 minutes and took a 10-0 lead. Early in the period, George Franck returned a punt into Washington territory at the 49 and then, eleven plays later on third down at the three, Franck eluded the desperate grasp of Frank Filchock and slipped into the end zone. Later in the third, another Franck punt return, this one to the Washington 30, led to a field goal by Andy Marefos and a 10-0 New York lead.

It was then that the Redskins moved to get back into the game. Bob Seymour returned the ensuing kickoff to the Washington 41. From there, Sammy Baugh completed two passes and ran for 10 yards to the Giant 45. On third down from there, Baugh threw a dart that stuck in the hands of Bob McChesney—make that the *hand* of McChesney, as the end was playing with a cast on one of his paws. He made the reception at the eight, hurdled a Giant defender, and scored untouched. The point after was blocked, but the Redskins had life.

A fumble caused by Bill Young and recovered by Seymour on the first play after the kickoff put Washington back in business at the New York 27. Starting with about 12 minutes left to play, it took six plays before Seymour battled for the last foot over the goal line. This time the point after was good and, suddenly, the Redskins had the lead at 13-10.

About five minutes later, the Giants struck back just as quickly and it was sudden death for Washington. Ward Cuff booted a 38-yard field goal to tie the game at 13 with less than five minutes showing on the clock. Then, on the Redskins' first play from scrimmage, Jim Poole intercepted Baugh's pass and returned it to the eight. On the next play, Franck scored on a reverse to push the Giants back in front. A final drive by the Redskins fizzled at the New York 35, as did their hopes of returning to the NFL championship game.

11/30/41	Packers (10-1) 22, REDSKINS (5-5) 17			35,594	
GB	0	0	13	9	22
Was	10	7	0	0	17
GB	TD Hutson 3; PAT Hutson 2; Safety R. Hare downed in end zone				
Was	TD Filchock, Seymour; PAT Aguirre, Aldrich; FG Masterson				

Griffith Stadium—Don Hutson caught nine passes, three of them for touchdowns, as the Packers rallied from 17 points down to defeat the Redskins.

Frank Filchock was the main force as Washington jumped to a 10-0 lead in the first quarter. He led a 67-yard, 14-play drive that he capped with an 11-yard run into the end zone on a reverse. Later in the period, Filchock completed a 15-yard pass to Bob Seymour to set up a 28-yard field goal by Bob Masterson.

In the second period, Sammy Baugh was the driver. He intercepted a pass intended for Hutson and returned it to midfield. A couple of plays later from the Packer 40, he launched a pass to Seymour, who caught it inside the ten. The receiver fought off a couple of tackles and eased over the goal line for a 17-0 lead.

Green Bay, meanwhile, could do nothing on offense. Their deepest penetration during the first 30 minutes of play was to the Washington 25. That would all change in the second half, with some help from the Redskins.

Filchock fumbled early in the third quarter and beefy lineman George Svendsen fell on it at the Washington 29, a move which led to Hutson's first TD catch. Next, Svendsen reached up and plucked a Filchock pass out of the air at the line of scrimmage and hoofed it 45 yards down to the three before being caught. Hutson made a fingertip grab of Cecil Isbell's pass for a touchdown. The point after following the first Packer touchdown was missed, so it was 17-13 Redskins entering the final quarter.

Early in the fourth, Isbell drove the Pack steadily downfield to the Washington 40. Hutson got single coverage from Seymour and beat him to haul in Isbell's pass at the 10. He shrugged off Seymour's tackle attempt and, with no other Redskin in sight, easily strode into the end zone for a 20-17 lead.

On the ensuing kickoff, Ray Hare started to return it out of the end zone, thought better of it and then retreated back across the goal line, thinking it would be a touchback. However, since Hare had provided the impetus for the ball to reenter the end zone, it was a safety and Green Bay led by five.

Baugh got his team as close as the Packer four, but Washington couldn't punch it in.

12/7/41	REDSKINS (6-5) 20, Eagles (2-8-1) 14			27,102	
Phi	7	0	7	0	14
Was	0	7	0	13	20
Phi	TD Banta, Piro; PAT Basca 2				
Was	TD Krueger, Aguirre 2; PAT Aguirre 2				

Griffith Stadium—Sammy Baugh led a fourth-quarter comeback win for the Redskins, but the events on the field were far overshadowed by the commotion in the stands and press box due to events half a world away.

Just as the game got underway, word of the Japanese sneak attack on Pearl Harbor was beginning to filter through Washington. While the news was not announced over the public address system, the stadium announcer was quite busy, raising suspicions that something was up. Page after page came over the PA system, asking all manner of VIP's, many with military titles, to call their offices. As the Eagles scored in the first quarter, marching 89 yards in 11 plays to a short touchdown run by Jack Banta, word came to the press box: "The Japanese have kicked off war now!" was the Washington Post's message to its reporters covering the game. "Keep it short," the message continued, meaning that little space would be devoted to game recaps in the next day's edition.

The Eagles held their lead until just 14 seconds remained in the first half. From the Philly 19, Baugh zipped a pass to Al Krueger at the two and the end stepped over the goal line. Joe Aguirre's extra point tied the game at seven.

By this time, the buzz around the press box was beginning to spread through the stands. Philadelphia scored another touchdown to take a 14-7 lead into the fourth quarter, but the specter of a Redskins defeat did not seem to be nearly the calamity it would have been just a few hours earlier.

Washington started on its own eight-yard line and Baugh led the 92-yard drive into the end zone. That march culminated in Baugh's 19-yard pass to Joe Aguirre. The rookie end leapt high to gather in Baugh's bullet in the end zone. A chance to tie, though, was missed when Aguirre misfired on the conversion attempt.

It didn't make any difference as Baugh's passing and Andy Farkas' running had the Redskins right back on the Eagles doorstep at the four. Baugh again went to Aguirre, who caught Baugh's pass over his shoulder in the end zone for the deciding score.

Both teams left the field facing uncertain futures, knowing that, as able-bodied gridiron warriors, a place on the real battlefields in the Pacific and in Europe might well be their next calling.

Skins' Draft Focused on Availability As Much As Football Ability

Dec 22—As the Redskins prepared their list of players they would like to take in the NFL's annual player selection meeting, another draft weighed heavily in their evaluation process. That, of course, is the one being conducted by Uncle Sam.

In addition to examining what a particular player did on the collegiate gridiron, the team looked at a number of off-field aspects of the man as well. In particular, the Redskins and other teams looked for situations that would keep a player out of the Army for at least a year, preferably longer, so that he could play football.

For example, the Redskins' first pick was unheralded back Orban Sanders. While coach Ray Flaherty and his staff did receive good scouting reports on the Texas University reserve's play, one personal situation stood out. Sanders is married, making it unlikely he will be required to serve in the armed forces—at least during the upcoming season.

George Peters was an outstanding blocker and linebacker at Oregon State, but his best asset in this draft was his birth certificate. At just 20 years old, it's likely that he'll get in at least a season in the NFL before being called to serve on fields of real battle in distant lands.

In an ordinary draft a player like Milton "Tiny" Croft of Little Ripon College may well have been passed over. However, at 275 pounds he exceeds the Army's weight limit by a considerable margin, so the Skins tabbed him with their 18th-round selection.

1942
Head Coach: Ray Flaherty
Record: 10-1, First in NFL East
Playoffs: 1-0 Won NFL Championship

Honors: Sammy Baugh All-NFL; Andy Farkas All-NFL, Bob Masterson All-NFL; Willie Wilkin All-NFL; Steve Slivinski All-NFL; Ed Cifers All-NFL

Redskins Defeat Army Stars 26-7

Aug 30—Sammy Baugh's passes set up three touchdowns as the Redskins overwhelmed a team of Army all stars 26-7.

The game, a war benefit was played in front of over 60,000 fans in the Los Angeles Coliseum.

Major Wallace Wade, the Duke University coach who is directing the Army team, saw his charges get off to a good start as former Texas A&M back Johnny Kimbrough bolted 58 yards for a touchdown on the game's third play.

After one Redskin drive ended when Kimbrough intercepted a Baugh pass, the Redskins regained possession and took control of the game. Baugh was in midseason form as he distributed passes to Andy Farkas, Bob Titchenal and Ed Justice in the course of a 76-yard touchdown drive. The payoff came early in the second quarter on an eight-yard Baugh-to-Titchenal pass in the corner of the end zone.

A 12-play, 69-yard drive put the Redskins ahead to stay later in the second period. Baugh again moved the Skins downfield with accurate passes and Dick Todd scooted 18 yards for the go-ahead touchdown.

The game was part of a series of exhibitions played by Wade's team composed of gridiron stars drafted into the Army against NFL squads. Proceeds from the games will go to the Army Emergency Relief fund.

9/20/42	REDSKINS (1-0) 28, Steelers (0-2) 14			30,759
Pit	0	0	14	0	14
Was	0	7	7	14	28
Pit	TD Dudley, Riffle; PAT Sandig 2			
Was	TD Juzwik 2, Aldrich, Justice; PAT Juzwik, Masterson 3			

Griffith Stadium—The upset-minded Steelers took a 14-7 lead in the third quarter, but the Redskins tied it up with a return of a blocked field goal and went on to clinch the win in the fourth quarter.

The Redskins held a 7-0 lead at halftime, with their lone touchdown coming as a result of a blocked punt. With the Skins trailing by seven in the third quarter the Redskins scored again via the blocked kick, a field goal attempt this time. The ball hit right between the "3" and the "8" on center Ki Aldrich's jersey. Aldrich scooped the loose ball up with one hand at the 32 and was unchallenged as he raced 68 yards for the tying score.

On the last play of the third quarter, Dudley got off a poor punt and Washington took over at the Steeler 39. Twelve seconds into the final period, the Redskins took the lead on a touchdown jaunt by the rookie Juzwik, who followed some interference by Joe Zeno. Juzwik then kicked the extra point to give his team a 21-14 lead. Ed

Justice added the clinching score when he took a short pass from Sammy Baugh and zipped in for the TD.

Flaherty Unhappy With Play, Plans Tough Week

Sep 21—Unhappy with the fact that his team had to rally in the second half to beat a weak Steelers team, Redskins coach Ray Flaherty will go about trying to make things better.

The team will practice in pads most of the coming week with plenty of full-contact tackling and scrimmaging. Normally the end of training camp and the start of the regular season signal an end to such rough practice sessions.

But Flaherty believes his team is much better than it showed against Pittsburgh, and he also believes the hard practices will help their talent show up on the field.

Sep 26

Filchock Leads Preflights Over Penn
Redskins star leads Georgia Preflight Naval Cadet squad past mighty Quakers

9/27/42	Giants (1-0) 14, REDSKINS (1-1) 7			34,700
NYG	7	0	7	0	14
Was	0	7	0	0	7
NYG	TD Walls, Adams; PAT Cuff 2			
Was	TD Seymour; PAT Masterson			

Griffith Stadium—On a muddy field in a driving rainstorm, the Giants sent the Redskins to one of the most improbable defeats in their history. New York had no first downs, gained a net of one yard of rushing, completed one pass but scored two touchdowns and beat the Redskins.

The one completion was huge for New York. Figuring that the field would do nothing but get worse, the Giants went for the early lead and got it when Tuffy Leemans launched a 50-yard touchdown pass to Will Walls. Ward Cuff made the conversion and New York had a 7-0 lead.

In the second period, the Redskins got the tying score, needing considerably more effort than the Giants did for their quick strike. During their 44-yard march Washington had to convert no fewer than three fourth downs. Bob Seymour capped it with a dive into the end zone and Bob Masterson's extra point tied it up.

Much of the third quarter was a punting duel with the Redskins' Dick Poillon constantly booting the Giants into trouble—his punts were downed at the New York six, four and three yard lines—and John Chicherneo kicking the Giants out of the hole. Washington's best scoring chance came after a bad snap forced a field goal attempt to be aborted. Kicker Masterson alertly threw towards Steve Juzwik in the end zone, but Cuff knocked it away.

The game-breaking play came when Poillon's pass found its way into the hands of New York's O'Neale Adams. Andy Farkas appeared to be in position to make a quick tackle, but he didn't turn around in time. The rookie back slogged through the mud 66 yards with the interception for the touchdown. Cuff again converted and the Giants had a seven-point lead.

It may as well have been a 70-point lead. The Redskins were unable to mount anything resembling a drive. When the final gun sounded, the teams headed for shelter, something that many in the crowd had done much earlier.

10/4/42	Redskins (2-1) 14, EAGLES (1-3) 10				16,000
Was	7	0	0	7	14
Phi	3	7	0	0	10
Was	TD Todd, Farkas; PAT Todd, Masterson				
Phi	TD Williams; PAT Barnum; FG Barnum				

Shibe Park—Andy Farkas scored the go-ahead touchdown in the fourth quarter to push the Redskins past a game Eagle squad.

Philly twice went into the lead in the opening 30 minutes. First, Tommy Thompson's 31-yard run set up a 30-yard field goal by Len Barnum. Later in the first period, Dick Todd took a short pass from Sammy Baugh, found a squadron of blockers and sped 54 yards for the touchdown. For good measure, Todd booted the extra point for a 7-3 Washington lead.

In the second quarter Philadelphia's Ted Williams embarked on a scoring run that netted 34 yards from scrimmage but covered at least twice that many yards in terms of ground that Williams covered. He zigged and zagged through at least a half dozen tackle attempts, picked up a final block and stepped into the end zone. Barnum's point after gave the Eagles a 10-7 lead.

The home team's margin held into the fourth quarter and the Redskins were nervously staring at the possibility of a second straight loss until Baugh and Farkas teamed up to push the Redskins into the lead.

First Baugh got things going with passes to Al Kreuger and Todd, both good for first downs. Then Farkas snuck into the secondary uncovered and was heading towards the left corner when Baugh cut loose with a perfect pass. Farkas and the ball met at around the 15-yard line and Farkas nearly scored before being hauled down from behind at the two. It didn't matter as Farkas barged into the end zone on the next play to give the Redskins the win.

Oct. 2

Juzwik Called to Service
Rookie back, averaging five yards a carry, called to duty in Navy

---

10/11/42	REDSKINS (3-1) 33, Rams (2-3) 14				33,250
Cle	0	0	0	14	14
Was	7	7	19	0	33
Cle	TD Manani, Lazetich; PAT Clay 2				
Was	TD Wilkin, Todd, Moore, McChesney; PAT Masterson 2, Farkas 2; FG Zimmerman; Safety Pritchard tackled by Wilkin				

Griffith Stadium—In their most dominating performance in nearly two years, the Redskins piled up a 33-0 lead and coasted to the win over Cleveland.

Late in the first quarter, the Rams stopped a Washington drive and took over on the Redskin eight. They didn't stop the Redskins for long. They went three and out and Cecil Hare blocked the punt.

Willie Wilkin flopped on the ball in the end zone for a 7-0 Washington lead. Later, in the second period, Dick Todd dodged his way through traffic into the end zone to complete a 15-yard touchdown run, making it 14-0 at halftime.

And the home team was just getting warmed up. Bob Titchenal got things in motion when he recovered a fumble. From the Ram 21, Baugh threw a floating pass towards Wilbur Moore, who easily gathered it in over his shoulder to push the lead up to three touchdowns.

It started to get ugly for the visitors after Andy Farkas returned a punt 20 yards into Cleveland territory and Baugh whipped a scoring pass that Bob McChesney picked off of his shoetops. Pressing to get back into it, a center snap sailed well over the head of Cleveland's Bosh Pritchard. All he could do is fall on it in the end zone and Wilkin got two more points when he tagged him down. After Roy Zimmerman's field goal, coach Ray Flaherty emptied the bench and the Rams salvaged some degree of respectability with two fourth-quarter touchdowns. The clock ran out with the Redskins on the Cleveland three-yard line.

10/18/42	Redskins (4-1) 21, DODGERS (2-2) 10				25,635
Was	0	14	7	0	21
Bkn	0	10	0	0	10
Was	TD Todd 2, Kovatch; PAT Masterson 2, Zimmerman				
Bkn	TD Manders; PAT Condit; FG Condit				

Ebbets Field—Sammy Baugh threw three touchdown passes, two of them to Dick Todd, as the Redskins beat the Dodgers.

Brooklyn broke out on top in the second period after Merlyn Condit broke free for a 60-yard run to the Washington four. Three plays later, Pug Manders fought his way into the end zone and Condit's conversion gave the home team a 7-0 lead.

That started a back-and-forth pattern that persisted until halftime. With about six minutes left, Baugh's first pass completion of the game got a touchdown drive rolling. From the Dodger 28, Baugh flipped a short pass to Todd, who raced in for the tying touchdown. Then Condit caught a long bomb from Dean McAdams at the Washington 15. That led to a field goal by Condit and the Dodgers grabbed a 10-7 lead with about three and a half minutes left in the half.

The Redskins went into the lead to stay before intermission. Todd returned the kickoff 40 yards to his own 46 and then caught a Baugh pass at the Brooklyn 26 to convert a fourth down. The pitch-and-catch combination kept rolling, connecting three more times, the last a four-yard touchdown that put Washington into the lead.

The Redskins missed one chance to put the game away when they couldn't push it over after moving to a first and goal at the four. They did manage to ice it when Baugh's third touchdown toss of the day went to Johnny Kovach.

End Malone Comes Back

Oct 23—Charley Malone, who was a stalwart on the Redskins' first NFL champion team, ended his retirement today to rejoin the team.

The 6-4 end out of Texas A&M was among the Redskins' leading receivers from 1934 through the 1940 season. He was a favorite target of Sammy Baugh from the moment the quarterback joined the team as a rookie in 1937. Malone averaged 15 yards a catch that year as the Redskins won the NFL title in their first season in Washington.

Malone joins a squad that has suffered depletion both from injuries and players getting called into the armed services.

10/25/42	**Redskins (5-1) 14, STEELERS (3-3) 0**			35,176	
Was	0	7	7	0	14
Pit	0	0	0	0	0
Was	TD Todd, Cifers; PAT Masterson 2				

Forbes Field—An overflow crowd in Pittsburgh watched the Redskins shut out the Steelers to take a stranglehold on the Eastern Division lead.

The two teams came just seconds away from having a scoreless first half before Sammy Baugh intervened. His passes accounted for 65 of the 80 yards the Redskins drove to take the lead. Baugh finished it off with 14 ticks of the clock left in the half when he fired to Dick Todd in the corner of the end zone from four yards away.

Pittsburgh managed to put a scare into the Redskins a few times, but Wilbur Moore, Todd and Ed Justice made touchdown-saving tackles. Armand Niccolai missed two field goals to blow a couple of other good scoring chances.

The Redskins didn't display much offensively after the half-ending drive, with their deepest offensive penetration in the second half reaching just the Steeler 35. They didn't need offense, though, as they scored again late in the third when Willie Wilkin blocked Bill Dudley's punt and Ed Cifers collected the bouncing ball in the end zone for the clinching score.

11/1/42	**REDSKINS (6-1) 30, Eagles (1-7) 27**			32,658	
Phi	0	6	14	7	27
Was	7	0	20	3	30
Phi	Cabrelli, Pritchard, Pate, Davis; PAT Erdlitz 3				
Was	TD Farkas 2, Cifers, R. Hare; PAT Masterson 3; FG Masterson				

Griffith Stadium—At the crack of the final gun, Bob Masterson's 10-yard field goal went through the uprights to give the Redskins a wild, hard-fought win over the lowly Eagles.

After a fairly pedestrian first half, the teams scored in bunches in the third quarter. The Redskins led at intermission 7-6 and it took just 12 seconds for them to expand their margin after the second half got underway. Ted Williams fumbled the second-half kickoff and Ed Cifers picked up the loose ball, zooming 25 yards into the end zone. A few minutes later, Andy Farkas twisted through the line for 20 yards and a touchdown and it seemed that Washington had things well in hand with a 20-6 lead.

Not so fast, said the Eagles. Rookie Bosh Pritchard took Bob Masterson's kickoff at the three and cut across the field in search of an opening. When the Redskins closed in on him, he faked a lateral and used the split second of doubt to break into the clear. Willie Wilkin seemed to have a shot at him but grabbed nothing but air. A convoy of blockers eliminated any remaining potential tacklers and Pritchard strode down the sideline to complete the 97-yard touchdown jaunt, cutting the Washington lead to 20-13.

The Redskins had little time to contemplate their narrowed lead since soon the game was tied. On the first play after the kickoff, Ed Justice fumbled. Guard Rupert Pate fell on the ball, bounced up, and chugged 53 yards for a touchdown.

Just like Washington, Philly had no time to plot a strategy for the new game situation. Ray Hare fielded the ensuing kickoff at the five and burst up the middle, putting distance between himself and his pursuers with every step. By the time he approached midfield, he was 15 yards ahead of the pack and he crossed the goal line a good 25 yards ahead of the nearest Eagle.

The young team from Philly refused to quit and tied the game with less than five minutes to go when Bob Davis scored from 15 yards out on a reverse. That left the crowd pleading "let's go Sammy," imploring the team's star to pull this one out.

He and Masterson did not disappoint. Runs by Farkas and passes to Hare and Cifers moved the home team inside the 10.

They lined up for a field goal from the 12, but it was a fake and Baugh whipped a pass to Masterson, who got down to the five. After one more incompletion with just a couple of seconds left, Masterson lined up at the 10 on a nasty angle. Baugh's took a perfect snap and placed it down for Masterson, who was the only calm person in the stadium. His kick was true and the Redskins got the win.

11/8/42	**REDSKINS (7-1) 28, Cardinals (3-5) 0**			35,425	
Chi	0	0	0	0	0
Was	14	7	7	0	28
Was	TD Masterson 2, R. Hare, Moore; PAT Masterson 3, Todd				

Griffith Stadium—The arm, hands and toe of Sammy Baugh were the key elements in the Redskins' rout of the Cardinals.

It was the toe that was on display first as Baugh's 74-yard quick kick bottled Chicago up and eventually resulted in the Redskins getting possession at the Cardinal 30. Soon after that, Baugh went to Bob Masterson over the middle. The end was past the defense when he caught the ball and easily scored.

Chicago threatened to tie it up on their next possession, but Baugh intercepted a pass and that was that as far as the scoring chance went.

Later in the first quarter, Baugh again went to Masterson, this time for 15 yards and a first down at the Chicago 42. On the next play, Baugh handed off to Ray Hare on a quick opener up the middle. The play worked exactly as designed as the center of the line opened up quickly, and Hare made a beeline for the end zone. He made it virtually unchallenged and Masterson's extra point made it 14-0.

If that didn't wrap it up against the punchless Cards, a hotly disputed touchdown in the second quarter did. From the Chicago 18, Baugh flipped a short pass to Wilbur Moore, who found a wedge of blocking and made his way towards pay dirt. At around the three the pursuit caught up with him and he lunged for the goal line, falling across. At some point—just where was the matter of contention—the ball came loose and rolled out of the end zone. One official called it a touchdown; another called it a touchback with possession going to Chicago. It appeared that the latter opinion had prevailed as the ball was placed on the 20, but after more discussion they put six points on the board for the home team. This sent Cardinal coach Jimmy Conzelman onto the field in a rage in an understandable but futile attempt to get the call reversed again.

Bill Young recovered a fumble in the third quarter to set up the second Baugh-to-Masterson touchdown. One Cardinal incursion deep into Washington territory ended with Hare intercepting a pass in the end zone; another faded away because of a holding penalty.

11/15/42	**Redskins (8-1) 14, GIANTS (3-5) 7**			30,879	
Was	0	0	14	0	14
NYG	0	0	0	7	7
Was	TD Farkas 2; PAT Masterson 2				
NYG	TD Adams; PAT Cuff				

Polo Grounds—Just like their last meeting, the Redskins dominated the Giants statistically. Just like on September 27, the Redskins squandered numerous scoring opportunities. Just like that previous game, the score was 14-7 in favor of the visiting team. Unlike last time, however, it was the Redskins who came out on top.

Six times during the first half, the Redskins got inside the New York 20 and six times they came up with nary a point. They would march down the field using a clever mixture of plays and weapons and then blow it about every way you can—fumbles, interceptions, losing it on downs, take your pick. It was a scoreless game at the half and the Redskins left the field frustrated, as the Giants were relieved.

Games often turn on the smallest of things. This one swung in Washington's favor when a Giant player was a foot or two offside as his team was executing the second-half kickoff. Andy Farkas had returned the kick to his own 30, a decent field position but the Skins had a hunch that they could do better. They had the Giants do it over.

Farkas took the kickoff at the six, turned on the speed and then waited a moment for his blocking to form. He spied open field to the right and took off that way. Kicker Ward Cuff was the last man with a shot but Ed Justice dispatched him with a brush block and that was that. Farkas easily completed the 94-yard touchdown return and Bob Masterson's extra point made it 7-0.

The Redskins doubled their lead the next time they got the ball. For obvious reasons the Giants were wary of Farkas' return prowess, and they didn't even wait until he fielded the ball before ploughing into him after they punted. The resulting penalty got the Redskins started on their own 30.

Passes to Ed Cifers and Masterson moved the ball to the Giant 25. Baugh continued firing away, throwing to Cifers and Justice to get a first down at the one-yard line. Ray Hare got the first foot towards the goal; Farkas got the second. Then Farkas got the third and final 12 inches, Masterson converted and the Redskins were up 14-0.

In the fourth quarter, Washington got the worst of an exchange of punts and New York had to drive just 33 yards to pull within seven on Tuffy Leemans' TD pass to O'Neal Adams. That was it for the Giants, however, as they didn't threaten again.

11/22/42	**REDSKINS (9-1) 23, Dodgers (2-6) 3**			34,450
Bkn	3	0	0 0	3
Was	0	6	7 10	23
Was	TD C. Hare 2, Baugh; PAT Farkas, Poillon; FG Poillon			
Bkn	FG Condit			

Griffith Stadium—After a slow start the Redskins, behind two touchdowns by Cecil Hare, pulled away from the Dodgers and clinched the NFL Eastern Division title.

It wasn't as though the Redskins didn't have any chances to take control of the game earlier. After Brooklyn scored first on a Merlyn Condit's 37-yard field goal, their score came after Andy Farkas fumbled, giving the Dodgers prime field position.

Nobody could accuse Farkas of moping over his mistake. He took the ensuing kickoff a yard deep and galloped 71 yards to the Brooklyn 30. A pair of Sammy Baugh completions to Ed Cifers had them knocking on the door at the six. Farkas carried four times and after the last run, from about six inches away, the referee started to raise his arms to signal a touchdown, but pulled them back to his side and placed the ball back on the six inch line again and it was the Dodgers' ball.

It nearly took until halftime for the Redskins to get on the scoreboard. A pass interference call greatly aided a 72-yard drive to the go-ahead TD.

From the Dodger 33, Baugh flipped a short pass to Hare, who darted and bulled his way into the end zone. The conversion attempt failed and the Redskins took a 6-3 lead into the locker room.

Another foray deep into Dodger territory after the second-half kickoff also led to no points, so Baugh decided to take matters into his own hands.

The next time they got close to pay dirt, Baugh took off from the 16, racing into the end zone as the defensive backfield diligently covered Baugh's potential receivers. This time the

conversion was good and the home team had some breathing room at 13-3.

Hare's second touchdown came when he scooped up a Dodger fumble and raced 43 yards. Dick Poillon's 33-yard field goal finished off the scoring.

Where's the Coach?

November 28—With their berth in the NFL Championship game secure, the Redskins enjoyed a rare Saturday off prior to their Sunday clash with the Detroit Lions.

As players puttered around the Motor City, the whereabouts of their head coach, Ray Flaherty, was a mystery. Assistant coach Turk Edwards was placed in charge of handling any team situations that may have come up but the team did not say where Flaherty was.

It is believed that Flaherty was in Washington receiving his commission as a Lieutenant Commander in the Naval Reserves. If that is the case, he will be able to lead the team in the title game, scheduled for December 13 at Griffith Stadium. Soon after that, however, Flaherty will be reporting for active duty.

11/29/42	**Redskins (10-1) 15, LIONS (0-11) 3**			6,044
Was	0	0	8 7	15
Det	3	0	0 0	3
Was	TD Farkas, Cifers; PAT Poillon; Safety Wilkin blocked punt out of end zone			
Det	FG Pavelec			

Briggs Stadium—Sammy Baugh's scheduled day off was cancelled after the winless Lions led 3-0 at halftime and Baugh came through, throwing two second-half touchdown passes to lead the win.

Ted Pavelec's 25-yard field goal in the first quarter was the only scoring until three minutes into the second half. Willie Wilkin and Dick Farman separated Detroit's Tommy Coleila from the ball and Wilkin recovered. Three plays later, Baugh danced in the backfield as Andy Farkas tangled with defender Ned Matthews. At the release of the ball, Farkas pushed free and caught Baugh's pass in the end zone for a 6-3 lead.

Wilkin, who also was supposed to get considerable rest on this day, provided the Redskins with their next score. After Ray Hare fumbled away a touchdown opportunity at the Detroit one, the defense forced the Lions to punt. Charging up the middle, Wilkin blocked the punt and it bounced out of the end zone for a safety.

The Redskins took the ensuing kickoff back to the Lion 42 and Baugh's passes to Ray Hare and Ed Justice moved them down to the 16. From there, early in the fourth quarter, Baugh slung a TD pass to Ed Cifers to wrap it up.

Dec. 11

Flaherty: Redskins Ready 'With No Excuses'
Team has light practice and short meeting before being dismissed

---

Fifteen Redskins Slated to Join Service

Dec 12—Whether the Redskins win or lose the NFL Championship game tomorrow, life is about to change drastically for at least half of the players, their coach, and some others associated with the team.

Some 15 Redskin players are slated to join various branches of the Armed Forces within weeks of the close of the football season. Star tackle Bill Young will soon be Chief Petty Officer Young of the

U.S. Navy. Guard Clem Stralka and center Ki Aldrich will undergo similar changes in titles.

Johnny Kovatch and Ed Beinor are going to be Second Lieutenants in the Marines. A number of other players such as Ed Justice and Bob Seymour are going to be a part of boxer Gene Tunney's physical fitness program.

One player who won't be reporting for military duty is star passer Sammy Baugh. He will serve by returning to his ranch in Texas to raise beef cattle, a commodity considered to be a wartime necessity.

NFL Championship Game
Sunday, July 13, 1942
Griffith Stadium
Washington, D.C.

12/13/42	**REDSKINS 14, Bears 6**				36,006
Chi	0	6	0	0	6
Was	0	7	7	0	14
Chi	Artoe 52 fumble return (kick failed)				
Was	Moore 39 pass from Baugh (Masterson kick)				
Was	Farkas 1 run (Masterson kick)				

In a game that nobody, maybe not even the Redskins, thought they could win, Washington took the NFL Championship away from the unbeaten and supposedly unbeatable Chicago Bears.

The Bears had ransacked their way through their 11-game schedule, going 11-0. They won their games by an average of more than four touchdowns, and that counts the first five games of the season when they were just rounding into form. In the final six contests, the Bears had dispatched their opposition by a combined score of 199-14. Over two seasons, the Bears had won 18 in a row and were the two-time defending champions. The first of those two titles had come at Griffith Stadium by a score of 73-0. This contest pitted virtually the same two teams against each other.

In the face of that set of facts, the Bears were overwhelming favorites to walk all over the Redskins. Those who wanted to lay down money on the game could have their pick of eight to one odds in favor of Chicago or Washington plus 20 points. Even the members of the local press, normally big Redskins boosters, were not very optimistic about the home team's chances. The day of the game, Merrill Whittlesey of the Post wrote, "Tossing sentiment aside for what we think is better judgment and respect for perhaps the greatest team of all time, we'll string along with the Bears," picking Chicago to prevail by three touchdowns.

Whittlesey was singing a different tune afterwards. "If ever a team reached the peak of football perfection the Redskins did yesterday. As a farewell gift to their coach, Ray Flaherty, who leaves tonight to receive a lieutenant's commission in the United States Navy, the Redskins brought out their best and today stand as the champions of the pro football world."

Flaherty wasn't the only one trading in battle on the gridiron for real war. Chicago coach George Halas was in a U.S. Navy uniform at the game, having handed the reigns over to his assistants to receive his commission earlier that year. At least half of the players on each team would almost certainly be entering the service before the next football season began.

The weather was what the Bears were used to—cold and windy—when the game started. It got a lot colder for the 36,006 in attendance two minutes into the second quarter when, on the first snap the Redskins took in Bear territory, Dick Todd fumbled. As the ball danced on the ground at Todd's ankles, Lee Artoe picked it up

and rambled unchallenged 52 yards for a touchdown. Artoe missed the extra point wide left and the Bears held a 6-0 lead.

Not panicking, the Redskins played it close to the vest. After the ensuing kickoff left them in poor field position, Sammy Baugh quick kicked 61 yards. Chicago converted a fourth and inches when Bill Osmanski took the snap and got the needed distance. It appeared they were about to display their expected dominance as they moved toward Redskin territory.

That is, until Wilbur Moore snatched a pass away from Chicago's John Siegel and returned it 14 yards to the Bear 42. Two Cecil Hare runs got to the 39. Then Baugh faded back, pumped once and quickly launched to Moore, who was behind Sid Luckman down the middle by a couple of steps. Moore leapt into the air, snared the pass, and tucked it away as he took a step over the goal line. Bob Masterson's extra point gave the Redskins a 7-6 lead.

The Redskins' second TD, scored with five minutes left in the third period, belonged to Andy Farkas. He returned a punt to the Chicago 44. Four plays later, from the 25, Farkas carried four straight times, getting clobbered on the last one as the ball popped loose—but only after he had crossed the goal line with it securely in his grasp. Again Masterson's conversion was true and the Redskins were beginning to make believers out of the doubters.

Baugh's punting—he averaged 52 yards per boot on the day—helped keep the Bears pinned back in their own territory for much of the remaining 20 minutes. Still, the mighty Bears threatened twice more. The first time they got down to the Washington 15, but Baugh snuck in and intercepted Frank Maznicki's pass to kill that drive and the last realistic chance for the Bears to get back into the game.

Still, Chicago clung to hope with three minutes left after a pass from Charley O'Rourke to Maznicki got them down to the Washington 2, with Baugh popping into the picture to save what seemed to be a sure touchdown. The Redskins would not yield, however. Willie Wilkin bottled up Osmanski for no gain and then an offside penalty negated an apparent touchdown, pushing the Bears back five yards to the six. Osmanski tried twice more and had to battle for every inch as Bill Young and Dick Farman brought him down at the three. On fourth down, O'Rourke's pass bounced out of Bob Nowasky's hands and harmlessly onto the turf with about a minute left.

The goalposts went down and the party continued late into the night.

Redskins to Face Stars in 'Pro Bowl'
Dec 14—The World Champion Redskins' reward for beating the powerful Chicago Bears is to take on what may be an even more talented group of players. This time, however, the stakes will not be nearly as high.

The Redskins will play a group of 32 NFL all-stars from the league's other teams in Philadelphia on December 27. The exhibition will benefit the United Seaman's Service fund.

Washington Coach Ray Flaherty was granted a delay in his pending entry into the Navy to coach the Redskins in the game. All of the players and coaches involved will be contributing their services.

Dec 14

Redskins Vote 34 Full Title Shares
Players, coaches, trainer each will get $976.48;
payout amount is NFL record high

1943
Head Coach: Dutch Bergman
Record: 6-3-1, Tied for first in Eastern Conference
Playoffs: 1-1, Lost NFL Championship Game

Honors: Joe Aguirre All NFL; Sammy Baugh All NFL; Dick Farman All NFL

Redskins Name Bergman as New Coach

February 17—The Redskins have named Arthur J. "Dutch" Bergman their new head coach. He replaces the highly successful Ray Flaherty, who left to join the Navy.

At Notre Dame, Bergman lined up in the backfield with the legendary George Gipp. He ran up a record of 59-31-4 as the head coach at Catholic University and, most recently, was the Redskins' top scout.

Said team owner George Preston Marshall, "We look forward with high confidence to successful years with him in command of the Redskins."

Much Still Up In the Air For Redskins

Aug 27—After five weeks on the road, the Washington Redskins settled into their training camp location close to home in College Park, Maryland.

Maybe "settled" isn't quite the right word. The team still is in search of players to stock a roster that, like most around the league, has been depleted by the war.

The situation has given rise to some unconventional tryouts. George Mulligan played for Dutch Bergman at Catholic University and the new coach will give his former end a tryout.

That's not unusual on its face. What makes it odd is the fact that that Mulligan has been out of football for five years. But he works for the federal government and he's in town and available, so he'll get a look.

For the players already on the team, such matters as where they are going to live during the season are as yet undecided. During camp, they will take up residence in a University of Maryland fraternity house. It's not yet known if such an arrangement will be made for the regular season or if the individual players will be on their own when it comes to housing.

10/10/43	**REDSKINS (1-0) 37, Dodgers (0-3) 0**				35,540
Bkn	0	0	0	0	0
Was	14	0	6	7	27
Was	TD Moore 3, Farkas; PAT Masterson 2, Jenkins				

Griffith Stadium—The Redskins opened their defense of the NFL championship in grand style, rolling up 431 yards of offense in routing the Dodgers.

It took just a shade over a minute for the Redskins to jump out on top. In fact, the 7-0 lead was almost achieved on the opening kickoff, but Andy Farkas was hauled down near midfield. Wilbur Moore got the team the rest of the way when Sammy Baugh whipped a short pass to him. The back cut to the sidelines and put on a burst of speed that left the defense in a futile chase to the end zone. That alone would prove to be enough to beat the woeful Dodgers, who hadn't scored in their first two games and wouldn't scratch the scoreboard in this one, either.

Later in the first, the Redskins ground out an 80-yard drive for their second touchdown. Farkas capped the march by making a

leaping catch of Baugh's pass down at the three and fighting his way into the end zone.

Moore tallied two more TD's in the second half. An assist on the first one goes to Farkas, who carried for 26 yards to get the Redskins down close. Credit Steve Slivinski for helping as well as he wiped out three Brooklynites with one block, allowing Moore to scamper around end for six points. His other touchdown came on a six-yard pass from Baugh to cap a drive started by Clyde Shugart's fumble recovery.

10/17/43	**Redskins (2-0) 33, PACKERS (2-1-1) 7**				23,058
Was	13	7	6	7	**33**
GB	0	0	0	7	**7**
Was	TD Farkas 2, Moore 2, Aguirre; PAT Aguirre 3				
GB	TD Hutson; PAT Hutson				

State Fair Park, Milwaukee—It was one thing beating the lowly Dodgers at home the previous week; this was quite another. The Redskins went on the road and smacked the powerful Packers around in the course of winning handily.

The Washington line dominated the Packer front during the course of an 80-yard touchdown drive that opened the scoring in the first quarter. Even the Packers who remained standing were unable to tackle Wilbur Moore as he slipped and dodged tackles on his way to a 47-yard gain to the Packer 33. From there, Andy Farkas pounded behind the bulldozing forward line for several plays before scoring from about six inches away.

After the kickoff, the Redskins exhibited the same dominance on defense as they had on offense and the Packers went three and out. A pass from Sammy Baugh to Moore started the 46-yard march. From the Packer 12, Baugh sloughed off a couple of tackles, buying enough time for Moore to find a slender seam in the defense. Baugh threaded the needle with this pass and Moore caught it for a 13-0 lead.

It was more of the same in the second quarter as the Washington line continued to dominate. Again getting good field position thanks to stout defense, the Redskins started from the Green Bay 47. Bob Seymour powered through the line twice for a total of 26 yards. Following a Baugh pass to Moore, it was Seymour up the middle again, to the eight. Moore took another pass from Baugh just in front of the goal line and navigated the remaining one step necessary for six more points. Joe Aguirre added the point after and it was 20-0.

In the second half, Baugh flipped a short TD pass to Farkas and then Sammy intercepted a pass to set in motion another touchdown drive that made it 33-0. That score came on a toss from Baugh to a wide-open Aguirre. Green Bay didn't score its meaningless touchdown until after that.

10/24/43	**REDSKINS (3-0) 13, Cardinals (0-5) 7**				35,540
Chi	0	0	0	7	7
Was	0	0	13	0	13
Chi	TD Rucinski; PAT Stokes				
Was	TD Aguirre, Farkas; PAT Masterson				

Griffith Stadium—Andy Farkas' long return of second half kickoff brought the listless Redskins to life and helped lift them to a tight 13-7 win over the Cardinals, who were 24-point underdogs.

Whether it was good defense or poor offense—probably a bit of both—the two teams failed to score in the first half. After intermission, Farkas fielded the kickoff a yard deep in the end zone and patiently waited for his blocking wedge to form. He followed it for a while before darting towards the sideline. Looking for another blocker around midfield, Farkas found Sammy Baugh. The star passer turned into Slammin' Sammy as he removed obstacles from Farkas' path. But Chicago's Johnny Martin snuck up from behind and knocked the ball out of the returner's grasp.

Farkas' effort was not in vain, though, as the Redskins retained possession while the ball went out of bounds at the six. Two plays later Baugh fired a pass into the chest of Joe Aguirre, who was in the end zone. Aguirre latched on to the pass for the touchdown.

Nine minutes later Farkas scored a touchdown from less than a foot out to extend the lead to 13-0 and the Griffith Stadium crowd began to breathe a bit more easily. Perhaps the Skins did, too, but the Cardinals were not done. A Baugh quick kick had backed them up to their own six, but Chicago drove relentlessly downfield behind the passing of Walt Masters. A 50-yard completion to Johnny Grigas was the big play. On the play, Wilbur Moore tipped the ball but it dropped into the receiver's hands anyway. Two plays later, Masters threw to Eddie Rucinski for a touchdown. Lee Stokes made it 13-7 with the conversion.

Moore was tossed for a loss on fourth down and the Cardinals took over at their own 40 with five minutes left. They drove to the Washington 19 before Moore saved the day with an interception and 44-yard return. The Redskins were able to run the clock out after that.

10/31/43	**Redskins (4-0) 48, Dodgers (0-6) 10**				11,471
Was	7	14	13	14	48
Bkn	10	0	0	0	10
Was	TD Moore 2, Seymour, Aguirre 2, Farkas 2; PAT Masterson 6, Pasqua				
Bkn	TD Manders; PAT Kinard; FG Kinard				

Ebbets Field—Sammy Baugh threw an NFL-record six touchdown passes as the Redskins routed the Dodgers 48-10.

Truth be told, the receivers deserve the lion's share of the credit for Baugh's first two scoring tosses. With two minutes gone in the game, Joe Aguirre took a short, crossfield throw from Baugh and scooted 44 yards into the end zone. Then, with about three minutes left in the first half, Wilbur Moore took another flip from Baugh and negotiated slippery footing down the sideline 52 yards for the score.

The Redskins trailed 10-7 before Moore's TD started a 41-0 scoring run. Before the half was out, the Redskins recovered a fumble and Baugh tallied touchdown pass number three from the Dodger 25 with a precision rocket to Bob Seymour.

After intermission, Baugh went back to work. He teamed up with Aguirre twice, once for 39 yards to the nine, and then Baugh threw a quick jump pass to the end for six points. The next scoring aerial was from longer distance—71 yards. Baugh's pass to Moore covered about half of the distance and Moore sprinted down the sideline for the rest.

Under normal circumstances, with a 34-10 lead in the fourth quarter, Baugh and his first-string mates would have been given the rest of the day off. But with Sammy having tied the record, they went back into the game to get him another touchdown pass. Andy Farkas caught it from 25 yards.

11/7/43	**Redskins (4-0-1) 14, EAGLES (3-2-1) 14**				32,541
Was	0	7	0	7	14
Phi-Pit	0	7	0	7	14
Was	TD Moore, Rymkus; PAT Masterson 2				
Phi-Pit	TD Cabrelli, Steele; Zimmerman 2				

Shibe Park—Bob Masterson blocked a fourth-quarter punt that Lou Rymkus returned for a touchdown to give the Redskins a fourth-quarter lead, but former Redskin Roy Zimmerman led the combined Philadelphia-Pittsburgh team to a responding score and the game ended in a 14-14 deadlock.

The Eagles broke out on top in the second quarter. After Zimmerman pinned the Redskins back at their six with a nice punt, Larry Cabrelli timed out a Sammy Baugh flank pass perfectly, picked it off and easily scooted 30 yards down the sidelines for a touchdown.

Baugh got off a 74-yard quick kick to turn the field position back into the Redskins' favor and led to the tying score. A pass interference call after Washington regained possession moved them down to the Eagle 20. From there, Wilbur Moore shook the coverage and caught Baugh's pass between the goal posts to knot the score at seven.

A barrage of turnovers marked the third quarter with neither team able to take advantage. With the game still tied at seven, Zimmerman lined up to punt from his own 23. Masterson jumped up and swatted the ball down. Rymkus had trouble getting a handle on the ball but managed to fumble it into the end zone, where he fell on it for the score. The conversion by Masterson was good and Washington led 14-7.

It took less than two minutes for the Eagles to respond. From the Redskin 35, Ernie Steele took a handoff and broke into the clear. Bob Seymour finally caught up to him but managed only to knock him into the end zone at the flag.

The Redskins had a shot at reclaiming the lead with a drive to the Eagle 30, but it fell apart there. Baugh, who had been under a withering pass rush all day, was sacked for a five-yard loss. A penalty on top of that set up third and 23 from the 43. Masterson's field goal attempt was not good. Washington had one more possession, but Baugh's desperation pass was intercepted at the final gun.

11/14/43	**REDSKINS (5-0-1) 42, Lions (3-5-1) 20**				35,540
Det	0	0	13	7	20
Was	7	14	7	14	42
Det	TD Matheson, Sinkwich, Calihan; PAT Lio				
Was	TD Masterson 2, Seymour, Rymkus, Farkas, Aguirre; PAT Masterson 4, Aguirre 2				

Griffith Stadium—Sammy Baugh put on quite a show, throwing four touchdown passes, intercepting four Detroit passes, getting off an 81-yard punt and recovering a fumble just for good measure, as the Redskins thumped the Lions 42-20.

Washington built a 21-0 halftime lead. Two of the touchdowns came on Baugh passes. The first was a 10-yard dart to Bob Masterson; the other traveled 28 yards to Bob Seymour. In between, Lou Rymkus tipped a screen pass, gathered it in and stepped 12 yards unchallenged into the end zone to account for the half's other TD.

The Redskins moved quickly to take what appeared to be complete command in the second half as they drove 73 yards in six plays at the outset of the third quarter. From the Lion 10, Baugh scrambled around long enough to find Masterson in the end zone for a 28-0 lead.

Detroit made a bid to get back into the contest when Frankie Sinkwich returned a punt 77 yards to the Redskin 22. On the next play, however, George Smith smashed into ball carrier Harry Hopp, forcing a fumble that Baugh recovered.

Sinkwich then rallied his team almost single-handedly. He threw touchdown passes of 22 yards to Jack Matheson and 40 yards to Bill Callihan. That wasn't quite enough to make the Redskins sweat, though, so he added a 39-yard interception return for another touchdown and, suddenly, it was 28-20.

The performance by Sinkwich sufficiently aroused the Redskins and they tallied two more touchdowns in the remainder of the fourth quarter to put it away. The first came on a short run by Andy Farkas and the second on Baugh's final touchdown pass, this one to Joe Aguirre from four yards.

Four Players, Including Baugh, Miss Practice

November 18—Sammy Baugh emerged from his four-TD pass, four-interception performance against the Lions unscathed. However, after engaging in a game of touch football, the Redskins star has an injured leg that forced him to miss Thursday's practice.

He wasn't the only one to miss the preparations for the upcoming game against the Bears, a battle of unbeaten teams. Willie Wilkin, Bob Masterson and Dick Farman also sat out the workout with various leg injuries. Farman's injury appears to be the most serious as he did not even go to the stadium.

Chicago coaches Hunk Anderson and Luke Johnsos expressed skepticism over the severity of the injuries. They indicated that they expect the Redskins to be at full strength for the game, a rematch of last year's NFL title game and a possible preview of this year's championship tilt.

11/21/43	**REDSKINS (6-0-1) 21, Bears (7-1-1) 7**			35,672
Chi	0	0	0	7	7
Was	7	7	7	0	21
Chi	TD McLean; PAT Snyder			
Was	TD Moore, Farkas, Piasecky; PAT Masterson 3			

Griffith Stadium—The Redskins dominated the Bears on both sides of the ball, running up a 21-0 third quarter lead and coasting to a 21-7 win.

The Redskins resorted to a trick play, the Statue of Liberty, to get their first touchdown. Sammy Baugh, hobbled by a bum knee, came into the game on third and six from the Bear 20. With Baugh in the passing pocket, most of the offensive team moved to the right, with the defense following along. Wilbur Moore reversed direction, and slipped behind Baugh, who had the ball held in passing position. Moore snatched the ball and took off into an open left side of the field. Clyde Shugart and Steve Slivinski were there to handle any obstacles and Moore scored untouched.

The Redskin defense kept Chicago bottled up. The Bears' Sid Luckman had set an NFL record the previous week by throwing seven touchdown passes in a game against the Giants, but it was apparent that this day would not be nearly as productive. Chicago had run just one play before Moore scored and had visited Redskin territory only once before the Redskins scored again in the second quarter.

This time there was no trickery involved, just domination of the Bear defense as Washington moved 70 yards. Runs by Moore and Ray Hare helped get the ball down to the Chicago 17. From there, Baugh limped back and spotted Andy Farkas cutting towards the corner of the end zone. Sammy showed that there was nothing wrong with his slingshot as he lofted a perfect pass to Farkas for a 14-0 lead.

The score remained there until late in the third period. The Bears had mustered a drive into Redskin territory, but Wilbur Moore tipped a pass and Al Piasecky intercepted at the 33. Soon after that, Frank Seno found an opening up the middle and burst through it. Only a desperate, leaping tackle by Harry Clark kept Seno from going all the way. Clark's play prevented a touchdown only for two plays as George Cafego tossed a seven-yard pass to Piasecky for the score.

The Bears averted a shutout when Ray McLean took a short pass from Luckman and flashed 58 yards for a touchdown, but

Washington had things well in hand by then. At the final gun the Redskins were knocking on the door at the Bear four.

11/28/43	**Eagles (5-3-1) 27, REDSKINS (6-1-1) 14**			35.826
Phi-Pit	7	0	7	13	27
Was	0	0	7	7	14
Phi-Pit	Thurbon 2, Steele, Hinkle; PAT Zimmerman 3			
Was	TD Masterson, Aguirre; PAT Masterson, Aguirre			

Griffith Stadium—The Redskins' hopes for an undefeated season were dashed as their former teammate Roy Zimmerman led Philadelphia-Pittsburgh past Washington 27-14.

Zimmerman ran the Eagles' T-formation offense flawlessly all day, especially during his team's scoring drive in the first quarter. The march went 82 yards with Zimmerman gaining chunks of yardage on the ground, among others. Bob Thurbon got the touchdown on a six-yard run and Phil-Pitt led 7-0.

The Redskins didn't threaten the lead during the first half. In fact, they mustered just 23 yards of offense in the opening 30 minutes.

George Cafego shanked a punt, giving the visitors a chance to extend their lead early in the third quarter. The 17-yard kick traveled just to the Eagle 38 and Zimmerman promptly led his team 62 yards for the score with Thurbon again tallying the six points on a run, this one from the eight.

The Redskins blocked a Zimmerman punt to gain possession at the Eagle 22, leading to a touchdown pass from Sammy Baugh to Bob Masterson. Washington then regained possession with a chance to tie, but 60-minute man Zimmerman punctured the comeback balloon with an interception. Ernie Steele's 47-yard touchdown run off tackle soon followed. In the fourth quarter, a short return of a blocked punt gave the Eagles a 27-7 lead, rendering Baugh's 12-yard touchdown pass to Joe Aguirre late in the contest meaningless.

Dec 4
Redskins Can Wrap Up Division
Win in New York would give Washington second straight Eastern Crown

12/5/43	**GIANTS (5-3-1) 14, Redskins (6-2-1) 10**			51,308
Was	3	0	7	0	10
NYG	0	0	7	7	14
Was	TD Farkas; PAT Masterson; FG Masterson			
NYG	TD Paschal 2; PAT Cuff 2			

Polo Grounds—Needing just a tie to wrap up the Eastern Division title, the Redskins blew a 10-0 third-quarter lead and lost to the Giants 14-10.

The first half generated a lot of offense, mostly on Sammy Baugh passes and the running of New York's Bill Paschal and Ward Cuff. The only scoring, however, came on a wobbly 26-yard Bob Masterson field goal in the first quarter and the Redskins led 3-0 at halftime.

After taking the second-half kickoff, Washington made its bid to wrap up the division. From his own 38, Baugh mixed timely passes with the hard running of Andy Farkas to move to a first down at the Giant five. From there, Farkas slammed into the line three times, getting closer to the goal line with each carry until he made it into the end zone on the third. Masterson booted the extra point and the Redskins were less than 25 minutes away from a trip to the title game.

It was then, however, that the running of Paschal and Cuff began to show results for the home team. First Paschal broke off a 31-yard run; Cuff then gained 22 yards to the Redskin 20. Paschal took it in from there, gaining 18 yards before the final two into the end zone. Cuff converted and it was 10-7.

Early in the fourth quarter the Redskins pushed into Giant territory, but a holding call helped abort that promising drive. After an exchange of punts, New York took possession at its own 45 with less than five minutes left.

Their game-winning assault took just two Paschal runs. He gained two yards on first down. On the next play, the back took the ball, hesitated for a moment, and then zipped past the line and into the clear. With every step, Paschal lengthened the distance between himself and the Redskin defense, and he went all the way—53 yards for the touchdown. Cuff again kicked the point after to give New York a 14-10 lead.

Baugh completed a pass to Joe Aguirre for a first down at the Washington 45, but that was as far as the Redskins would get. Four incompletions later, the Giants regained possession and ran out the clock.

12/12/43	Giants (6-3-1) 31, REDSKINS (6-3-1) 7			35,540
NYG	0	14	10	7	31
Was	0	7	0	0	7
NYG	TD Pritko, Liebel, Cuff, Walls; PAT Cuff 4; FG Cuff			
Was	TD Aguirre; PAT Masterson			

Griffith Stadium—The Redskins' second chance to wrap up the division title was buried under an avalanche of Giant points in the second and third quarters. The two teams finished the regular season tied atop the Eastern Division and will meet in a playoff next week in New York.

The Redskins scored first as they had the previous week. They moved downfield to the New York 28 where Sammy Baugh zipped a precise pass to Joe Aguirre in the end zone. Bob Masterson converted and the Redskins led 7-0.

New York tied the score when Ray Hare blocked a Baugh punt. Yes, Hare does play for the Redskins, but he was bulled and spun into the backfield by Frank Cope on the play. The kick ricocheted off of Hare's helmet and into the end zone where New York's Steve Pritko fell on it for the tying score.

On their next possession the Giants took the lead for good. From his own 44, Emery Nix launched a beautiful pass that Frank Liebel caught in stride at around the Redskin 20. Frank Seno's futile, desperate diving tackle attempt at around the 10 was the only opposition Liebel faced as he ran into the end zone. Ward Cuff kicked the conversion to give New York a 14-7 halftime lead.

Washington never threatened to rally in the second half. While the Giants tallied 10 points in the third quarter by grinding out drives to a touchdown run by Cuff and Cuff's 18-yard field goal, the Redskins mustered just eight yards of offense in two possessions. New York capped the rout with a 33-yard touchdown pass from Nix to Will Walls in the fourth quarter.

Have the Skins Run Out of Gas?

Dec 12—A funny thing happened while the Redskins were cruising to their second straight NFL Championship game appearance.

They ran out of gas.

Since beating the Bears to up their record to 6-0-1, the Redskins have lost three straight. They needed just a tie in one of their final two games, a home and home set against the Giants, to wrap up the Eastern Division. But the Giants swept the two games, forcing a playoff for the division.

The reason that many on the team are giving for their late season slump is simple—too much football. Their season started on July 20 with drills in San Diego. Breaks from the game have been few and far between. The physical strain on the players has been heightened by the fact that their ranks have been thinned due to the war.

Unless they find a way to pull it together next Sunday in the Polo Grounds, they will have a long offseason to rest and reflect in their lost opportunity.

Eastern Division Playoff
Sunday, December 19, 1943
Polo Grounds
New York, New York

12/19/43	Redskins 28, GIANTS 0			42,800
Was	0	14	0	14	28
NYG	0	0	0	0	0
Was	TD Farkas 3, Lapka; PAT Masterson 4			

The third time was indeed a charm.

After losing twice to the Giants in the final two regular season games to make this game necessary, the Redskins finally solved the New York offense and pitched a shutout to earn a trip to Chicago to play for the NFL title.

The Redskins missed on their first big scoring chance after blocking a New York punt as Andy Farkas was stopped short of the goal line on fourth down. Farkas wasn't stopped shy of the goal line on his subsequent opportunities. Anvil Andy, as the press called him, pounded in three touchdowns, all from short range.

Sammy Baugh set up each of Farkas' scores with aerial strikes that earned first and goal situations inside the Giant 10. The first of the three went to Wilbur Moore, who was knocked out of bounds at the Giant four. Farkas carried three times, pushing across the goal line on the last effort. Bob Masterson kicked the extra point for a 7-0 Washington lead.

Later in the second period, the Redskins put together a 56-yard drive to the end zone. Baugh masterfully mixed Farkas runs with passes to Joe Aguirre and to Masterson. One of Aguirre's catches gained a first down at the seven. Again, Farkas bucked into the line three times, getting over on the last one.

As the game wore on, it became more and more apparent that the Redskins' 14 points would be plenty to win with. The backfield rushing duo of Ward Cuff and Bill Paschal, which had been so potent in the Giants' two wins over Washington, mustered just 41 yards. And Emery Nix, who had thrown for two touchdowns in the regular season finale, managed just 57 through the air for his team, none of those yards carrying much significance. New York did not set foot in Washington territory on offense the entire first half.

George Cafego kept the Giants bottled up with some precision quick kicks in the third quarter and the Redskins scored twice in the fourth to complete the rout. Farkas got his third TD of the day after Baugh intercepted a pass. Then Baugh capped a 51-yard drive with an 11-yard touchdown pass to Ted Lapka.

NFL Championship Game
Sunday, December 26, 1943
Wrigley Field
Chicago, Illinois

12/26/43	BEARS 41, Redskins 21			34,320
Was	0	7	7	7	21
Chi	0	14	13	14	41
Was	Farkas 1 run (Masterson kick)			
Chi	Clark 31 pass from Luckman (Snyder kick)			
Chi	Nagurski 3 run (Snyder kick)			

Chi	Magnani 36 pass from Luckman (Snyder kick)
Chi	Magnani 66 pass from Luckman (kick failed)
Was	Farkas 17 pass from Baugh (Masterson kick)
Chi	Benton 29 pass from Luckman (Snyder kick)
Chi	Clark 16 pass from Luckman (Snyder kick)
Was	Aguirre 26 pass from Baugh (Aguirre kick)

Sid Luckman threw five touchdown passes to lead the Bears to a rout of the Redskins and to the NFL title that Washington had taken from them a year earlier.

Redskin star Sammy Baugh did not get much of a chance to match Luckman as he missed most of the game's first 35 minutes after sustaining a concussion in the early going. It's doubtful, though, that the Redskins would have beaten the Bears even with Baugh going to distance; it simply was Chicago's day.

The Redskins did score first, with Wilbur Moore making two spectacular catches of George Cafego passes to set up a short touchdown run by Andy Farkas. The Bears, however, were ahead 20 points by the time the Redskins scored again.

They tied the game on a screen pass from Luckman to Harry Clark. Luckman then produced a couple of key runs for first downs to set up a three-yard touchdown blast by Bronco Nagurski to give the Bears a 14-7 lead at halftime.

In the third quarter, the Bears wrapped it up with a pair of Luckman TD passes to Dante Magnani. They were both things of beauty (if you were not a Redskins supporter, anyway). On the first, Luckman hit Magnani in the flat at the Redskin 36 and the receiver danced, dodged and wove his way through the defense to score standing up. On the next, the Redskins again were fooled by the screen pass. It seemed like the entire defense poured through to try to get to Luckman, who calmly flipped the ball to Magnani. The part of the defense that wasn't red-faced in the Bear backfield was wiped out by the phalanx of blockers formed in front of the receiver as he sprinted 66 yards for a 27-7 Bear lead.

Farkas caught a touchdown pass from Baugh late in the third period to give Washington a glimmer of hope at 27-14, but the Bears owned the fourth quarter. They held the ball for the first 11:50 of the period. They first patiently moved downfield and scored on Luckman's fourth scoring pass of the day, to Harry Clark. Evidently not believing that their 34-14 lead was secure enough, the Bears executed an onside kick and retained possession. Luckman's final TD pass of the day, to Jim Benton, ensued.

The Redskins did muster another score, this one on a Baugh pass to Joe Aguirre, but it was far too little and way too late.

1944
Head Coach: Dud DeGroot
Record: 6-3-1, Third in NFL East

Honors: Joe Aguirre All-NFL; Frank Filchock All-NFL;

Jan 29

Bergman Resigns as Redskins Coach
After one year, 'Dutch' quits,
cites 'other interests'

Mar 19

Dudley DeGroot Named Redskins Coach
Former coach at Rochester signed
to five-year deal

Skins To Try Out T-Formation in Scrimmage

Aug 19—A lot will be different when the Redskins take the field for the first time in 1944 in an intra-squad scrimmage at Balboa Stadium in San Diego.

New head coach Dudley DeGroot will coach one half of the split squad while the other half will be in the hands of special advisor Clark Shaughnessy.

Shaughnessy is responsible for another major change in the look of the team—he was brought in to install the T-formation on offense. The Redskins are among a number of teams moving to the new offense in which the quarterback will take the snaps directly from the center.

The scrimmage is expected to be a wide-open affair with Sammy Baugh taking the snaps for DeGroot's team. The adjustment of Baugh, of course, will be critical to the success of the T-formation for the Redskins.

Rookies Bunk Morris and Mike Mica will start in the backfield for Shaughnessy's squad along with Andy Farkas and Wilbur Moore.

Baugh Decides to Go to Texas

Sep 21—The choice that the Texas draft board presented to Sammy Baugh was simple. He either had to return to his cattle ranch and actively engage in that essential occupation or he could play football and risk being drafted into the Army.

After taking a day to consider the two options, Baugh decided to pack his bags and go to Texas.

Since the start of the war Baugh has been receiving a draft deferral because of his cattle ranch. However, the draft board decided that if his ranch could operate while Baugh was playing games on the gridiron, it could operate while he served in the military.

Baugh will depart for the ranch immediately. Frank Filchock will take over as the Redskins' starting quarterback. It's possible that Baugh could return to football later in the season without being exposed to the possibility of being drafted.

10/8/44	Redskins (0-0-1) 31, EAGLES (1-0-1) 31				32,549
Was	6	6	12	7	31
Phi	7	14	3	7	31
Was	TD Moore 2, Dye, Fuller, Seymour; PAT Aguirre				
Phi	TD Bleeker, Hinkle, Ferrante, Banta; PAT Zimmerman;				
	FG Zimmerman				

Shibe Park—This was a game of "couldn't quite" for the Redskins. They couldn't quite master the point after touchdown play, making just one of five attempts due to a variety of errors. And they couldn't quite keep ex-Redskin Jack Banta out of the end zone with six seconds left to preserve a lead, settling instead for a 31-31 tie with the Eagles.

One aspect that worked quite well for the Redskins was the passing of Frank Filchock. After Philly took a 7-0 lead, he led his team right back, driving 48 yards to an 18-yard scoring pass to Wilbur Moore. Filchock had to buy time by scrambling around in the backfield before stopping and firing to Moore in the end zone.

The shape of things to come was set when the center snap was bad on the conversion attempt and the holder Filchock was unable to handle it. On the day, Filchock completed 25 of 33 passes for 291 yards and four touchdowns.

The Eagles responded by driving to one touchdown and taking advantage of an interception to score another, extending their lead to 21-6 as halftime approached. Before intermission, however, Washington was able to get another touchdown on the board on Filchock's pass to Les Dye. This time, things were different on the conversion attempt—it was blocked.

Philly responded with a Roy Zimmerman field goal to go up 24-12, but the Redskins scored 19 unanswered points to assume the lead. The final points came in the fourth quarter on another touchdown pass from Filchock to Moore. The receiver had to fight and carry Eagles along for the final five yards of the play. Finally, Joe Aguirre was able to get an extra point away cleanly and Washington led 31-24.

With time ticking down, however, Banta took a short pass from Allie Sherman and fought his way into the end zone. Former Redskin Zimmerman added his fourth conversion to knot the final score.

10/15/44	Redskins (1-0-1) 21, Yanks (0-3) 14				17,758
Was	7	7	0	7	21
Bos	0	7	7	0	14
Was	TD Seymour 2, Lapka; PAT Aguirre 3				
Bos	TD Cafego, Crowley; PAT Lio				

Fenway Park—Frank Filchock's 45-yard touchdown pass to Ted Lapka early in the fourth quarter lifted the Redskins past Boston.

A poor punt by the Yankees' Ken Steinmetz gave the Redskins good field position to start their first touchdown drive. From his own 43, Filchock got things started by passing to Wilbur Moore for 20 yards. A few plays later, Filchock threaded the needle to Lapka for a first down at the Boston 15. Bob Seymour soon scored the first of his two touchdowns on the day and Joe Aguirre's conversion gave the visitors a 7-0 lead.

The Yanks were not flustered by the relative ease at which the defending division champions moved downfield to score. They came right back, taking less than two minutes to score on a two-yard run by George Cafego.

Before halftime, Washington had regained the lead. On a drive starting from his 21, Filchock masterfully mixed runs and passes to march down to the Boston 20. From there Seymour took a handoff and headed around left end. Frank Seno cleared a path by taking out two Yankee defenders with one block, enabling Seymour to get outside and slant into the end zone for a 14-7 lead.

Determined to stick around in this one, Boston got an opportunity to tie it up early in the third quarter after Seno fumbled and Ed Franco recovered at the Washington 29. On fourth down, the Redskins correctly anticipated a pass and Seymour got his hands on the ball intended for Joe Crowley. The ball, however, wound up in Crowley's hands anyway and he scored easily from the five.

The score remained knotted until the fourth quarter. From the Boston 45, Filchock faded back, pump-faked the secondary out of position and then let fly to Lapka down the sideline. The receiver stretched out to catch the ball at around the 20 and sprinted the rest of the way into the end zone. Aguirre's third conversion gave the Redskins a 21-14 lead.

The only threat that Boston mounted after that was a big one, but the Redskins survived. A 12-yard punt gave the Yanks possession near midfield. They made their way down to the seven with a minute and a half to play but Cafego fumbled and Lapka recovered to end the peril.

Baugh Back, Will Play Part Time

Oct 20—Sammy Baugh flew into Washington Airport and grabbed a cab down to Griffith Stadium, arriving in time to take part in today's practice.

The Redskins will play their home opener on Sunday against the Brooklyn Tigers. Coach Dudley DeGroot said that Baugh, who has not been with the team for three weeks after returning to his cattle ranch on orders from the Texas draft board, would play in a part-time role.

During the workout, Baugh showed that his skills had not deteriorated much during his layoff, if at all. In particular, his punting was very strong as he boomed kick after kick. While Frank Filchock has done a nice job replacing Baugh at quarterback, Sammy's top-notch punting has been sorely missed.

Baugh's availability for games will be determined on a week-to-week basis.

10/22/44	REDSKINS (2-0-1) 17, Tigers (0-4) 14				35,000
Bkn	0	7	0	7	14
Was	0	14	0	3	17
Bkn	TD Manders, Masterson; PAT Kinard 2				
Was	TD Moore, Aguirre; PAT Aguirre 2; FG Aguirre				

Griffith Stadium—The Redskins blew a 14-0 second-quarter lead but managed to pull out a 17-14 win on Joe Aguirre's 39-yard field goal with 10 minutes left to play.

After a first quarter that was free of both scoring and action, things heated up considerably in the second. The Redskins embarked on a seven-play, 68-yard foray to the end zone. Frank Filchock, doing most of the passing despite the return of Sammy Baugh, got it going with a 29-yard pass to Aguirre, who made a leaping grab. A bit later, Filchock went to Frank Seno for 23 yards to the Brooklyn one. Wilbur Moore smashed over three plays later.

On its next possession, the home team rolled downfield once again. This drive started at the Redskin 16. Filchock went to Bob Seymour for 12 yards and then Al Piasecky made a nice one-handed catch for another first down. A pass from Filchock intended for Moore fell incomplete, but the play gained 38 yards to the Tiger eight nonetheless due to a pass interference flag. On third and goal from the nine, Filchock zipped a spiral to Aguirre in the end zone. The receiver also kicked the conversion to make the score 14-0 with just under three minutes remaining in the half.

That proved to be enough time for the Tigers to respond. Aguirre booted his kickoff into the end zone, so Brooklyn had it at its 20 after the touchback. Cece Johnson got warmed up by throwing to Bob Masterson for 12 yards. He then pitched long to Joe Carter, who hauled it in and wasn't hauled down until he reached the Redskin 12. Soon after that, Pug Manders burrowed his way two yards into the end zone and it was 14-7 at the half.

The third quarter contained just as much scoring and excitement as the first—none—but things got interesting again in the fourth. Brooklyn drove 70 yards to tie the score with the payoff coming on a pass from Johnson to ex-Redskin Masterson. Later, it appeared that the Tigers had taken the lead on Manders' 38-yard run over the goal line, but an offside penalty negated the play. Brooklyn ended up with fourth down and decided to punt.

Frank Seno fielded the kick at his four. He twisted, dodged, and broke tackles, leaving a 60-yard trail strewn with would-be tacklers before he was finally hauled down at the Tiger 36. The Redskins could only advance it four more yards from there, so Aguirre came in to try a 39-yard field goal. As the attempt sailed through the air, there was no question that it had the necessary accuracy, but it appeared that it might be short on distance. It had enough by a few inches as the ball hit the crossbar and snuck over it.

Interceptions by Andy Farkas and Mike Micka killed Brooklyn attempts to score after that.

10/24/44	REDSKINS (3-0-1) 42, Chi-Pit (0-5) 20				35,540
Chi-Pit	0	0	7	13	20
Was	7	7	7	21	42
Chi-Pit	TD Grigas 2, Currivan; PAT Baker 2				
Was	TD Aguirre 2, Moore, Seymour 2, Turley; PAT Aguirre 2, Weldon 2				

Griffith Stadium—The Redskins allowed the combined Chicago-Pittsburgh team to stay in the game for most of the day, but finally some brilliant individual efforts allowed Washington to come away with a 42-20 victory.

It did not appear that the Redskins would be sweating it out in the fourth quarter after they took a 14-0 halftime lead. Twice Joe Aguirre managed to completely elude any coverage by the defensive secondary and twice, from 58 and 47 yards, Frank Filchock found him and launched passes accurate enough to have been completed with a defender in close proximity. Aguirre caught his breath and booted the extra point after each catch and the Redskins were in cruise control.

In the third quarter, Wilbur Moore fumbled, setting up a touchdown by John Grigas that cut the lead in half. Moore made up for his miscue in style. On third and 17 from the Washington 25, Filchock crossed up the defense, expecting a pass, by handing to Moore off left tackle. The runner got good blocking at the line and then followed Bob Seymour's interference to some daylight down the sideline. At the 35, still well short of the first down, he appeared to be bottled up, but he cut into the clear. Moore faced his last obstacle two yards from the end zone when Bob Thurban made a desperate, diving tackle attempt, but Moore's momentum was too great and he crash landed into the end zone.

But Chi-Pitt wouldn't go away. A 53-yard drive that bridged the third and fourth quarters culminated in a fourth-down touchdown pass from Grigas to Don Currivan that covered five yards. The Redskins finally pulled away when two interceptions, one by Moore the other by Sammy Baugh, set up a pair of touchdowns for a 35-13 lead. Apparently, Washington didn't feel comfortable with any lead as Filchock threw a 34-yard touchdown pass to rookie Doug Turley with two seconds left to make the final 42-13.

11/5/44	REDSKINS (4-0-1) 14, Rams (3-3) 10				35,540
Was	0	14	0	0	14
Cle	3	0	0	7	10
Cle	TD Jones; PAT Zontini; FG Zontini				
Was	TD Dye, Aguirre; PAT Aguirre 2				

Griffith Stadium—The Redskins scored two touchdowns in a four-play span in the second quarter—and that was all they needed to beat the Rams 14-10.

Cleveland had opportunities to build a lead in the first quarter, but they netted just a Lou Zontini field goal out of trips to the Washington 19 and four yard lines. In fact, the Rams spent much of the day moving up and down the field with little or nothing to show for it. They gained 407 yards on the day, compared to the Redskins' 197.

Looking at those numbers, one would expect that the Redskins needed some good fortune to come out on top in this one and that indeed was the case. On second and one at his own 48, Frank Filchock crossed up the Ram defense by throwing deep to Les Dye. Although back Tom Coiella was playing the run, he recovered in time to tip the ball away from Dye. The rookie end kept his concentration on the ball and gathered it in at around the Cleveland 30. Coiella again recovered and had a shot at Dye at

around the 15, but Dye skipped out of his diving attempt and dashed into the end zone.

Cleveland's Johnny Karrs fumbled and Frank Walton recovered for the Redskins at the Ram 19. Two plays later, Filchock went to Joe Aguirre in the end zone. Although the intended receiver had a defender on either side of him, Filchock somehow got him the ball —and Aguirre somehow caught it. Aguirre lined up and kicked his second point after of the day and the Redskins led 14-3.

Throughout the rest of the second and the entire third quarter, the Rams continued their pattern of putting together a promising drive and then failing to convert it into points. They finally got on the scoreboard again midway through the final period when they drove 76 yards to a 38-yard Harvey Jones touchdown run to pull within four.

With less than two minutes remaining, Cleveland took possession at its own 25 for a last, desperate drive. The clock kept ticking as the Rams converted a fourth down and then quarterback Albie Reisz scrambled 24 yards to the Washington 37. Two heaves to the goal line, though, did not connect and the Redskins survived.

11/12/44	Redskins (5-0-1) 10, Tigers (0-7) 0				20,404
Was	0	0	0	10	10
Bkn	0	0	0	0	0
Was	TD Seymour; PAT Aguirre; FG Aguirre				

Ebbets Field—Sammy Baugh's 71-yard touchdown pass to Bob Seymour broke up a scoreless tie in the fourth quarter as the Redskins finally shook loose of the Tigers.

The Redskins had their chance to go up early, but three trips into Tiger territory resulted in two missed field goals and an interception. In the third, Brooklyn missed a good scoring chance when Bob Masterson's 36-yard field goal attempt was partially blocked and the Redskins took possession at their own eight.

The Skins were unable to move and Sammy Baugh kicked out to the Tiger 48. From there, Brooklyn moved to a first and goal at the five. On first down, Ray Hare gained one and then Pug Manders navigated down to the one. Twice more Manders hurled himself into the Redskins front wall, which turned to stone. Both thrusts were repelled, the second mere inches from pay dirt.

Baugh shanked a punt after that and the Dodgers were back in business at the Washington 17. This time, they marched backwards and wound up giving the ball up on downs at the 34. On the next play, lightning struck.

Baugh sent all but one of his receivers out to the right. The exception was Seymour, who bolted into the flat on the left. The quarterback got the ball to his end in the blink of an eye and Seymour was off after catching the pass in stride at around the Washington 40. Nobody challenged Seymour until he reached the Tiger 25, where Vaughn Stewart had a shot. Into the picture came Andy Farkas who threw a block that was far from devastating but effective as it pushed Stewart off balance and allowed Seymour to make his way the rest of the distance.

Aguirre added a 35-yard field goal from a difficult angle to account for the final score.

11/19/44	Eagles (5-0-2) 37, REDSKINS (5-1-1) 7				35,540
Phi	7	13	3	14	37
Was	7	0	0	0	7
Phi	TD Van Buren, Bleeker, Hinkle, McDonald, Steele; PAT Zimmerman 4; FG Zimmerman				
Was	TD Moore; PAT Aguirre				

Griffith Stadium—For much of the first six games of the seasons, the Redskins had gone undefeated by becoming adroit at pulling out games when they had been outgained and outplayed. It all came crashing down around them on this day when the Eagles outplayed, outgained, *and* outscored the Redskins.

The home team did all of its scoring in the game's first minute and 15 seconds. That's how long it took for them to return the opening kickoff and run two plays. On the second snap, Frank Filchock started to run, pulled up shy of the line of scrimmage and fired a pass to Wilbur Moore. The back caught at the Eagle 35 and took advantage of a nice block by Joe Aguirre to negotiate a course to the end zone.

Philly tied the game late in the first period after Steve Van Buren returned a punt 19 yards to the Redskin 32. Two plays later, Van Buren finished the job by taking a handoff and bolting 20 yards for a touchdown.

By the time halftime came around, the Eagles had begun to establish their dominance. They drove 67 yards to one touchdown to take the lead and then Jack Hinkle intercepted a Baugh pass and streaked 50 yards for a touchdown, making it 20-7 at intermission.

A Roy Zimmerman field goal made it 23-7 midway through the third. After that, the more desperate the Redskins grew, the more opportunistic the Eagles became as they turned an interception and a fumble recovery into 14 more points.

11/26/44	REDSKINS (6-1-1) 14, Yanks (2-4) 7				35,540
Bos	0	0	7	0	7
Was	7	0	7	0	14
Bos	TD Ranspot; PAT Lio				
Was	TD Akins, Moore; PAT Aguirre 2				

Griffith Stadium—Sammy Baugh's touchdown pass to Wilbur Moore gave the Redskins a third-quarter lead and they were able to hang on to beat Boston.

The home team drove 71 yards to break out on top in the first quarter. Frank Atkins was the major force in the drive, carrying nine times for 36 yards. A connection between Sammy Baugh and Wilbur Moore for 20 yards was of considerable aid as well, and Atkins capped the drive with a one-yard TD plunge for a 7-0 lead.

That lead held until early in the third quarter. Atkins fumbled the ball away to the Yanks at his own 29. A touchdown pass from Leo Stasica to end Keith Ranspot soon ensued and the game was tied at seven.

The Yanks got some more help when Bob Seymour fumbled a few plays after the kickoff and they were in business at the Washington 29. They gained a first down at the 19, but then lineman Al Piasecky put an end to things. First he nailed the runner for a 10-yard loss on a reverse. After that, when Boston attempted a 27-yard field goal, he busted through the line and blocked it.

Later in the third, a couple of passes from Baugh to Les Dye and a nice run by Andy Farkas got the Redskins into Boston territory. Then Baugh discovered Moore near the goal line and hit him with a perfect strike. Moore trotted over and Aguirre nailed the point after. Boston didn't seriously threaten after that.

12/3/44	GIANTS (7-1-1) 16, Redskins (6-2-1) 13				47,457
NYG	10	0	0	6	16
Was	0	10	3	0	13
Was	TD Moore; PAT Aguirre; FG Aguirre 2				
NYG	TD Petrilas, Paschal; PAT Strong; FG Strong				

Polo Grounds—The Redskins proved today that they were capable of playing all possible types of football games. Prior to this contest, they had played poorly and lost, played poorly and won and had played well and won. In this game, they played well and lost, completing the matrix. In the end, a holding call on a successful field goal ruined their bid to come out with at least a deadlock against New York.

To get into contention, Washington had to fight back from a first-quarter deficit. Bill Petrilas intercepted Frank Filchock's second pass of the game and rolled 28 yards for a touchdown with

just over a minute gone by in the game. The Giants then drove to a short Ken Strong field goal to make it 10-0.

The Redskins had the score knotted up by halftime. Sammy Baugh came into the game and promptly got his slingshot arm loosened up. He completed passes to Joe Aguirre and Bob Seymour to advance into Giant territory. Then Seymour turned runner, carrying some Giants on his back as he advanced to a first down at the New York 18. Soon after that, from the eight, Wilbur Moore sidestepped the coverage of Ward Cuff and Baugh's pass was right on the money. A minute and a half before halftime, Aguirre connected on a 43-yard field goal to tie the score at 10.

The Redskins' third-quarter drive to take the lead was anything but routine. To start things off, Andy Farkas lost his balance while fielding the second-half kickoff and stepped out of bounds at his own four. The Redskins couldn't move and Baugh lined up behind the goal line to punt. However, Baugh used his arm instead of his toe, passing to Aguirre for 14 yards and a first down.

The march downfield continued, stalling at the New York 29. From the 35, the Redskins lined up to attempt a field goal but the holder Baugh sprang up and again threw to Seymour for a first down. From a conventional T formation, Baugh passed again, this time to Andy Farkas, who fumbled. Apparently determined to retain possession, Baugh successfully fought to recover the ball for a first down at the 17. Four plays later, the Redskins played it straight, lining up for a field goal and kicking it. Aguirre's boot was through the uprights for a 13-10 lead.

The margin held until deep in the fourth quarter. Howie Livingston gave New York a lift with an interception at midfield. Cuff then showed that the Redskins aren't the only team on the field that can catch a break when he fumbled the ball, recovered and then navigated around the defense for 23 yards to the Redskin 25. With about three and a half minutes to play, Bill Paschal powered across the goal line for the go-ahead score.

Washington responded, efficiently moving into position for a 37-yard field goal attempt. With 1:28 to play, Aguirre's attempt was right down Broadway. The visitors' celebration was ended quickly, however, when it was discovered they had been penalized for holding and Aguirre would have to try again, this time from 52 yards out. Aguirre's kick passed just under the crossbar and New York ran out the rest of the clock.

12/10/44	Giants (8-1-1) 31, REDSKINS (6-3-1) 0				35,540
NYG	14	7	0	10	31
Was	0	0	0	0	0
NYG	Cuff, Leibel 2, Avedesian; PAT Strong 4; FG Cuff				

Griffith Stadium—Needing to win to have a shot at a playoff for the division title, the Redskins came up completely empty, playing poorly in all phases of the game in the course of getting shut out by New York.

It didn't take long for the sellout home crowd to figure out their team's season would be ending sooner rather than later. It took less than six minutes for the Giants to establish a 14-0 lead. The first drive to a touchdown, scoring on Arnie Hebner's 25-yard touchdown pass to Ward Cuff. Soon after that, Sammy Baugh fumbled, the Giants recovered at the Washington 21 and Hebner threw another touchdown pass, this one to Frank Leibel.

An interception killed a Redskin drive into New York territory and Wilbur Moore's 26-yard run to the Giant 26 was wasted as well. Hebner and Leibel connected for another score, this one from 44 yards, and the rout was on.

In the fourth quarter, Cuff kicked a field goal and guard Charley Avedesian intercepted a Baugh pass and motored 48 yards to account for the final, embarrassing margin.

1945
Head Coach: Dud DeGroot
Record: 8-2, First in NFL East
Postseason: 0-1, lost in NFL Championship Game

Honors: Joe Aguirre All-NFL; Steve Bagarus All-NFL; Sammy Baugh All-NFL; Frank Akins All-NFL

Feb 11
Redskins' Annual West Coast Trip in Jeopardy
War time travel deemed non-essential being cut back

Bagarus Set to Join Redskins

Sep 25—It looks like the Redskins will be getting the services of a 26-year-old rookie soon.

Former Notre Dame star Steve Bagarus apparently is getting his discharge from the Army after serving for nearly four and a half years. The halfback is set to fly from the West Coast as soon as the paperwork for his discharge has been completed.

The Redskins have received a taste of Bagarus' talents. He played in two exhibition games last year and his performance both running and passing was outstanding. On several occasions last season it appeared that Bagarus might be able to play, but he remained on active duty.

Bagarus has kept his football skills sharpened by playing for some Army teams.

10/7/45	**YANKS (2-0) 28, Redskins (0-1) 20**				25,000
Was	0	6	7	7	20
Bos	0	14	7	7	28
Was	TD Bagarus, Akins; PAT Aguirre 2				
Bos	TD Manders, Currivan, Matthews, Grigas; PAT Lio 4				

Fenway Park—The balanced Yanks scored twice on the ground and twice through the air, controlling the line of scrimmage to upset the Redskins 28-20.

Midway through the second quarter on a muddy field, Steve Bagarus, making his NFL debut with Washington, scored the game's first touchdown. The drive got started when Bob Seymour intercepted a pass at the Boston 37. Sammy Baugh masterfully mixed runs and passes to move to the six. On second down from there, Baugh fired over the middle to Bagarus at the goal line. The rookie out of Notre Dame made a spectacular catch, latching onto the ball while doing a back summersault into a puddle in the end zone. The point after was missed so the Redskins led just 6-0.

Boston was in the lead for good by halftime. They took the kickoff and immediately embarked on a 60-yard incursion into the Washington end zone. George Cafego's 30-yard completion to Bob Davis moved the Yanks into scoring position at the Washington 20. Pug Manders got the touchdowns with a smash from the one. Scotty Gudmundson threw a 43-yard scoring pass to Don Currivan to extend the lead to 14-6 at intermission.

The Redskins pulled within a point in the third on Frank Akins' short TD run, a score set up when Doug Turley recovered a fumble at the Boston 38. The home team, however, responded immediately, reestablishing their eight-point lead on a touchdown pass from Davis to Ned Matthews. The receiver, in fact, wound up in the same puddle—by this point more of a pond—which Bagarus had splashed down in earlier.

Any hopes for a comeback were dashed after Augie Lio intercepted a Baugh pass near midfield and returned it to the Redskin 20 on the last play of the third period. On the second play

of the fourth, Grigas swept to the right to score from the four to make it 28-13.

10/14/45	**Redskins (1-1) 14, STEELERS (0-3) 0**				14,050
Was	0	7	0	7	14
Pit	0	0	0	0	0
Was	TD Dye, Rosato; PAT Aguirre 2				

Forbes Field—The Redskins were dominant defensively and just productive enough on offense to earn a 14-0 victory in Pittsburgh.

Washington had a couple of false starts offensively before scoring. First Sammy Baugh threw an apparent touchdown pass to Frank Filchock, but a clipping call negated that one. Then Baugh threw Wilbur Moore at the ten, but the perfect pitch slid between the receiver's palms. Finally, Baugh threw to Les Dye for seven yards and a touchdown.

That would have been plenty, as it turned out. The Steelers barely topped 100 yards of offense. They seemed to have a chance to get back into it in the third quarter when they moved inside the Washington 35. However, they were forced to attempt a field goal from 40 yards out. The kick of Joe Coomer, a 285-pound lineman, was straight down the middle, but considerably short—by about 20 yards.

Frank Akins set up the Redskins' insurance touchdown with a 31-yard run on a reverse in the fourth quarter. A few plays later, Sal Rosato fought into the end zone from two yards away for the score.

10/21/45	**REDSKINS (2-1) 24, Eagles (1-2) 14**				34,788
Phi	0	7	0	7	14
Was	3	7	7	7	24
Phi	TD Van Buren 2; PAT Zimmerman 2				
Was	TD Rosato, Akins 2; PAT Aguirre; FG Aguirre				

Griffith Stadium—Frank Filchock kept his team in the lead with a fourth-quarter interception deep in his own territory and the Redskins then drove 92 yards for the clinching touchdown and beat the Eagles 24-14.

After a Joe Aguirre field goal, the Eagles put together their only sustained drive of the first half to take a 7-3 lead. Running back Steve Van Buren got things started with a 24-yard punt return and then finished things off with a 15-yard touchdown run.

For most of the day the Washington defense, led by Wilbur Moore, Cecil Hare and Aguirre, kept Van Buren bottled up, holding him to 91 yards on 14 carries, far under his average.

Sammy Baugh came out firing to put the Redskins back into the lead before intermission. He completed one pass to Steve Bagarus for 21 yards and then slung two to Aguirre, the second good for 24 yards to the Eagle 17. Four plays later Sal Rosato scored from close in and Aguirre's conversion made it 10-7.

To open the second half, the Redskins drove from their own 20 to within inches of the goal line. Although they gave it up on downs there, they took advantage of the resulting field position after Roy Zimmerman punted from the end zone. Steve Bagarus returned the punt 23 yards to the Philly 32. Baugh threw a sizzling pass to Aguirre for 21 yards to the nine and it took Frank Akins two carries to reach pay dirt from there. Akins was the workhorse all day long, carrying 24 times for 168 yards.

The Redskins did not have much time to get comfortable with their 17-7 lead. Working from their own 13 after the kickoff, the Eagles steadily marched towards the goal line in a drive that spanned the third and fourth quarters. Van Buren got the TD on a four-yard run and it was 17-14.

Unable to move the team, Baugh punted back to Philadelphia, who took possession at their own 33. They moved downfield until Filchock made his saving interception at the eight. There was still plenty of work to do, though, and Akins helped get it done. His 30-yard burst off left tackle got his team out of the hole and six plays later he slammed up the middle into the end zone from four yards out to clinch the game.

10/28/45	**Redskins (3-1) 24, GIANTS (1-2-1) 14**				55,461
Was	0	10	7	7	24
NYG	7	0	0	7	14
Was	TD Moore, Akins, Millner; PAT Aguirre 3; FG Aguirre				
NYG	TD Weiss, Livingston; PAT Strong 2				

Polo Grounds—Sammy Baugh showed why he's, well, Sammy Baugh as he passed the Giants silly and intercepted two passes, returning one 80 yards to set up a touchdown, to lead the Redskins past New York 24-14.

Baugh did not get off to an auspicious beginning. His fumble at his own 33 gave the Giants a short field to drive to the game's first touchdown. After two incompletions, Marion Pugh threw to John Weiss in the flat. The end took off down the sideline, broke a Baugh tackle attempt, and scooted into the end zone for a 7-0 New York lead.

Steve Bagarus got the Redskins' tying drive in motion with a 22-yard punt return to the Washington 45. Baugh then threw to Bagarus for 21 and then, a few plays later, to Doug Turley for 15 yards to the Giant 17. Then Baugh went to yet another target, Wilbur Moore, who had escaped detection by the New York secondary as he made his way to the end zone. The pass was on target and Joe Aguirre's conversion tied the game at seven. Aguirre booted a 37-yard field goal before halftime and the Redskins led 10-7 at the break.

The Redskins extended their lead when they took the second-half kickoff and advanced 72 yards into the end zone. First Moore got clear of the Giant defense again, this time on a run on a reverse, and he rambled 27 yards to the Washington 45. Then a pass to Bagarus gained 26 yards. (If you haven't figured it out by now, Bagarus was Baugh's favorite target on the day, catching seven balls for 128 yards.) That made it first and goal at the five. On fourth down from the three, Akins rammed it over to make it 17-7.

The Giants were threatening to get back into it early in the fourth quarter when Baugh the defender struck. He grabbed a pass intended for Frank Liebel on the 15 and ran helter-skelter past, around, and through the Giants until he was finally hauled down at the New York five. On the next play, Baugh finished the job with a snappy touchdown pass to Wayne Millner.

Todd Returns to Redskins

Oct 30—The Redskins regained a link to their glorious past and some possible backfield help for the present when Dick Todd rejoined the team.

The speedy, shifty back out of Texas A&M received his discharge from the Army after missing two full seasons and part of the current one. He scored 19 touchdowns from 1939 through 1942 seasons and was a prime threat out of the backfield both running and receiving.

Center Ki Aldrich, who also was a standout from '39 through '42, also is expected to be released from the service soon. He could be with the team in time for their next game.

11/4/45	**REDSKINS (4-1) 21, Cardinals (1-6) 21**				35,000
Chi	0	7	7	7	21
Was	14	7	0	3	24
Chi	TD Poole, Seno, Cantor; PAT Kuharich 3				
Was	TD Moore, Akins, Seymour; PAT Aguirre 3; FG Aguirre				

Griffith Stadium—The Redskins blew all of a 21-0 lead but got a last-minute field goal from Joe Aguirre to edge the Cardinals 24-21.

Washington built its lead in the game's first 20 minutes. Wilbur Moore got things started in spectacular fashion. From his own 43 he swept around left end and broke into the clear. With every step he put more distance between himself and the pursuing defenders. Only when Moore let up a bit as he approached the goal line did a potential tackler get anywhere near him and even Jim Poole's attempted diving stop caught only air.

Bob Seymour didn't score the next touchdown, but did great work to set it up. First he intercepted Paul Christman and returned the ball eight yards to the Cardinal 14. He then carried twice to within a yard of the end zone. Frank Akins got credit for the six points when he carried it the rest of the way from there.

It worked out for Seymour, though as he scored a TD that someone else did most of the work for. In the second quarter the Redskins faced fourth and eight at their own 35. Sammy Baugh faked a punt and flipped a short pass to Mike Micka. The fake left the Cards utterly fooled and Micka was off to the races. He made it within a yard of the goal line. Seymour came in and smashed over from there to make it 21-0.

Any thoughts that this would be a Sunday walk in the park were quickly dissipated as the Cardinals scored touchdowns late in the second and early in the third quarters. The first one came on a pass from Christman to Poole, the second on a nice 48-yard run by Frank Seno.

After that, though, the Washington defense stiffened and it appeared their 21-14 lead would hold up as the game wore on to midway through the fourth quarter. Chicago faced fourth and 27 at its own 14. Christman gambled it all from there, launching a pass to end Bill Dewell, who hauled it in for 29 yards and a first down. Then Christman, taking advantage of the stunned defense, went to Eddie Rucinski for 22 yards to the Redskin 35. A few plays later Christman went back to Rucinski, down to the four and two plays later Leo Cantor negotiated the final three yards to the end zone. Joe Kuharich booted his third extra point to knot the score at 21 with 3:38 left to play.

Just as it was slipping from their grasp, the Redskins managed to snag control again. Kuharich's kickoff was short and Ray Hare fielded it at the Washington 42. Three Baugh passes to Aguirre resulted in two completions and an interference call and the Skins had a first down at the Cardinal 23. Micka carried for a first down at the 12 and Aguirre lined up to kick with 24 seconds on the clock. From the 18, the placement was picture perfect, end over end and right down the middle.

Nov 7

Stralka to Return for Yanks Game
Georgetown product 'Little Bull' comes back after three years in Navy

11/11/45	**REDSKINS (5-1) 34, Yanks (3-3-1) 7**		34,788		
Bos	0	0	7	0	7
Was	3	3	14	14	34
Bos	TD Currivan; PAT Lio				
Was	TD Bagarus, Seymour, Condit, Millner; PAT Aguirre 2, Condit, Weldon; FG Aguirre 2				

Griffith Stadium—Four different players scored second-half touchdowns for the Redskins as they ran roughshod over the Yanks, avenging their only defeat of the season.

Things started off rather slowly for the home team, as the Skins were able to tally just two Joe Aguirre field goals in the game's first 30 minutes. The low score was largely a result of the number of penalties called, with most of the infractions going against the Redskins. On the day, the penalty horn blew 21 times, with 16 penalties for 120 yards being marched off against the locals.

In the second half, the Skins managed to steer clear of the penalties and things started to click. It took just 55 seconds for them to expand their lead in the third period. Steve Bagarus returned the kickoff to his own 40 and a roughness penalty against Boston moved it into Yank territory at the 45. Two plays later Sammy Baugh flipped a pass to Bagarus in the flat. All it took was one block and a burst of speed for the back to negotiate the 41 yards into the end zone. Aguirre added the point to make it 13-0.

After Bob Seymour wove his way for 23 yards and another touchdown about nine minutes later, the rout was on. After Boston drove to its only touchdown late in the third, the Redskins' offense kept going. Merle Condit broke a couple of tackles and scored from 20 yards out to make it 27-7. Apparently not thinking that the lead was safe, with 10 seconds left Frank Filchock threw a seven-yard TD pass to Wayne Miller to account for the final score.

11/18/45	**REDSKINS (6-1) 28, Bears (1-7) 21**		34,788		
Chi	7	14	0	0	21
Was	7	7	0	14	28
Chi	TD Kavanaugh 2, Wilson; PAT Gudauskas 3				
Was	TD Bagarus 2, Condit 2; PAT Aguirre 4				

Griffith Stadium—The Redskins scored two touchdowns in the fourth quarter to rally past the Bears and claim a 28-21 victory.

This edition of the Bears is far from the NFL powerhouse it was just a few years ago; Chicago came in at 1-6, barely out of the Western Division cellar. Nevertheless, they had the Redskins playing catch-up all day long. Sid Luckman opened the scoring with a 33-yard touchdown pitch to Ken Kavanaugh. Washington responded with a nine-play, 72-yard drive to pay dirt. Steve Bagarus hauled it over, eluding at least four good tackle attempts by the Bears in the course of his 17-yard run.

The pattern was set: Kavanaugh unties it, Bagarus ties it. Chicago retook the lead on another Luckman-to-Kavanaugh connection, this one covering 48 yards. In response, Sammy Baugh flipped to Bagarus in the flat from his own 32. The rookie back slipped one tackle, cut back, and was in the clear until he approached the Bear 20. There two defenders converged on him, but he wriggled through and completed the 68-yard scoring play.

Again the Bears took the lead on a Luckman TD pass, this one to George Wilson. Chicago's 21-14 halftime lead stood until the fourth quarter. The Redskins did have a good chance to score in the third, but lost the ball on downs after achieving a first down at the Chicago 20.

The Redskins tied it up for the third time early in the fourth quarter. Bagarus didn't score the touchdown, but he got things started when he fielded Luckman's punt at midfield and tightroped the sideline for 28 yards to the 22. Frank Akins carried the ball in his arms and a few Bears on his back for 18 yards and, from the four, Merle Condit ploughed over. Aguirre's tying conversion sent the Griffith Stadium crowd into a further state of frenzy with 12:30 left.

The Washington defense stuffed the Bears and Luckman punted back. Again Bagarus ripped off a nice return, 18 yards to the Bear 39. Three plays later, Washington responded to a fourth and nine with Dick Todd. On his first offensive play of the year, he swept around right end for 30 yards down to the eight. After Akins carried for five, Condit again lugged it the rest of the way and Aguirre's point after made it 28-21 with about eight and a half minutes to play.

The Bears did not give up, driving into Redskins territory only to be stopped on downs. Then, after Washington burned all but 24 seconds off the clock and punted, Luckman completed a desperation pass to Kavanaugh. Moore hauled the receiver down at the Redskin 25 as time expired.

11/25/45	**EAGLES (6-2) 16, Redskins (6-2) 0**		37,306		
Was	0	0	0	0	0
Phi	0	7	6	3	16
Phi	TD Steele, Van Buren; PAT Zimmerman; FG Zimmerman				

Shibe Park—The Eagles bottled up the Washington rushing game, played a pass defense that baffled Sammy Baugh, and got just enough offense to whip the Redskins 16-0 to tie for the Eastern Division lead.

Neither team could move the ball much during the first half—good defense, poor offense, take your pick. It would have been a scoreless deadlock had Baugh not thrown an interception that Baptiste Manzini returned to the Washington 16 with two and a half minutes to go in the half. Three plays later, on fourth and nine, three Eagles teamed up to score. Roy Zimmerman threw a pass to Ben Kish at about the ten. Kish tossed a lateral to a streaking Ernie Steele, who scored untouched. Zimmerman kicked the extra point to make it 7-0 just 59 seconds before intermission.

The Eagles widened their lead in the third quarter after an exchange of punts, again scoring on a fourth-down play. From the Washington 45, Zimmerman flipped a pass to Steve Van Buren in the flat. It appeared that the Skins had him hemmed in before he got first-down yardage, but he fought his way through and was gone. Zimmerman missed the conversion so the score stayed 13-0.

With their ground game rendered utterly impotent by the Eagle defense—they totaled just 23 yards rushing on the day—the Redskins were unable to mount a threat. Zimmerman kicked a short field goal midway through the fourth quarter to account for the final score.

12/2/45	**REDSKINS (7-2) 24, Steelers (2-8) 0**		34,788		
Pit	0	0	0	0	0
Was	7	7	0	10	24
Was	TD Bagarus 2, Turley; PAT Aguirre 3; FG Aguirre				

Griffith Stadium—After taking a week off in Philadelphia, the Washington offense showed up in grand form in this one, with Sammy Baugh throwing three touchdown passes, two of them to Steve Bagarus, as the Redskins thumped the Steelers 24-0.

The first B-to-B connection came on the fourth play of the game. From his own 30, Baugh faded back and threw to Bagarus in the flat. The running back had some room to his right initially, but appeared to be hemmed in around the Steeler 45. He kicked his speed into another gear, however, and broke back into the clear. Bagarus' teammates had hustled downfield and a half dozen of them were there to provide him with an escort for the final 15 yards.

In the second quarter, Baugh struck again, this time to end Doug Turley. That play capped a 61-yard drive that saw Frank Akins run for good yardage and Joe Aguirre catch two Baugh passes for nice gains. Aguirre fumbled at the 15 after the second catch, but Turley alertly covered the ball. From the Steeler nine,

Sammy found Turley wide open at the four and the end trotted in for the score.

Pittsburgh threatened often but couldn't dent the scoreboard. Steeler drives into Washington territory reached the 4, the 13, the 15, the 17 and the one-foot lines, but each time the defense stiffened and Pittsburgh went away empty.

The 14-0 lead held into the fourth quarter. The home team was in a bit of a jam, backed up to its own three-yard line. Baugh threw a risky pass to Cecil Hare that the back caught two yards deep in the end zone. The gamble paid off as Hare found daylight and raced 66 yards to the Steeler 31.

Bagarus pounded into the line for two and then snared Baugh's pass at the 10. He took off in the only direction where there were no Steelers: parallel to the goal line. In his journey he bowed back as far as the 12, but eventually took an angle towards the goal line. Eluding some tacklers on his own and getting a nice block from Bob DeFruiter, Bagarus finally made his cut for the end zone and scored standing up. Aguirre's third extra point of the day made it 21-0, and he added a field goal later in the fourth to close out the scoring.

The 24-0 final score was not the only good news the day brought for Washington. Word came that the Giants had beaten the Eagles 28-21, meaning that the Redskins held a one-game division lead with only a game against New York remaining. A win or tie would give Washington the division title.

12/9/45	REDSKINS (8-2) 17, Giants (3-6-1) 0			34,788
NYG	0	0	0	0	0
Was	3	0	7	7	17
Was	TD Dye, Akins; PAT Aguirre, Baugh; FG Aguirre			

Griffith Stadium—Sammy Baugh controlled the Giant defense, the entire Redskin defense dominated New York's offense and after a 17-0 victory, the Redskins owned the NFL Eastern Division championship.

Baugh's numbers were not among his best ever, but his performance was. He completed 11 of 19 passes for 150 yards and one touchdown, but it seemed as though every completion was in a clutch situation and the threat of his aerials opened up the Washington ground game to the tune of 296 yards rushing on the day.

Perhaps before or after the game, the Giant offense visited the end of the field that the Redskins defended but they didn't during the competition; New York did not take a snap there all day, so thorough was Washington's command of this matchup.

Even give their superiority on both sides of the ball, the Redskins led just 3-0 at the half, having driven 54 yards to Joe Aguirre's first-quarter field goal. It was different in the third quarter as Washington marched 54 yards for a touchdown. Frank Akins carried much of the way as the Redskins made it to the Giant 24. On second down, Baugh faded back and fired to the five to Les Dye, who made two defenders look foolish in short order. First, he took the ball away from Bill Petrillas, who had his hands on it and then eluded Ward Cuff's attempted tackle on his way into the end zone.

Both sides sensed that the 10-0 lead was probably insurmountable. The Redskins seemed content to grind out huge chunks of time off the clock and the Giants seemed anxious to start their offseason. Following a New York fumble that Alex Piasecky recovered at the Giant 17, the Redskins took three plays to tally one more touchdown on Frank Akins' one-yard run.

If there was any doubt this was the Redskins' day, it was erased on the conversion attempt. The Giants blocked Joe Aguirre's kick, but Washington got the point anyway after holder Baugh scooped up the bouncing ball and dashed into the end zone. It was Baugh's seventh career point scored, his first since getting a touchdown during his rookie 1937 season.

Dec 14

Bagarus Named All Pro
Rookie back is lone Redskin to garner honors

NFL Championship Game
Cleveland Municipal Stadium
Cleveland, Ohio

12/16/45	RAMS 15, Redskins 14			32,178
Was	0	7	7	0	14
Cle	2	7	6	0	15
Cle	Safety Baugh pass from own end zone hit goal post			
Was	Bagarus 38 pass from Filchock (Aguirre kick)			
Cle	Benton 37 pass from Waterfield (Waterfield kick)			
Cle	Gillette 53 pass from Waterfield (Waterfield kick)			
Was	Seymour 8 pass from Filchock (Aguirre kick)			

The purpose of the goalposts is to define the area through which a field goal or extra point attempt must travel to score points; the crossbar and the posts themselves aren't supposed to be a factor in the game. But twice during this game the ball struck the goal post structure and, combined with a few other unusual and unfortunate happenings, those bounces—along with a stiff Cleveland Ram defense—cost the Redskins the NFL championship.

The first oddity occurred prior to the opening kickoff. Winter had struck Cleveland early and despite the best efforts of the grounds crew, the field was frozen solid at game time, rendering regular football cleats an impediment to gaining traction rather than an aid. Anticipating this, the Redskins had brought along basketball sneakers from Washington and the players were putting them on prior to the game. As game time approached, the Rams coach Adam Walsh got wind of this and, not having access to sneakers, approached Washington coach Dudley DeGroot and pleaded with him not to use theirs. Incredibly, DeGroot agreed.

(Note: DeGroot's sportsmanship cost him his job. As both teams slipped and slided around the field on their cleats in the first half, owner George Preston Marshall wondered what had happened to the sneakers and went into the clubhouse at halftime. He confronted the coach and DeGroot refused, saying that he had a "gentlemen's agreement" to not use the sneakers. Marshall hit the ceiling and, for all intents and purposes, DeGroot's career as Redskins coach ended right then and there.)

The first goal post incident came after the Redskins stopped a Cleveland sortie that ended on downs at the Washington six. A few plays later, Sammy Baugh dropped into the end zone to pass. He spotted Wayne Millner open at the 10, but his pass smacked off of the upright. Under the rules, that scored a safety for the Rams and it was 2-0 at the end of the first quarter.

(Note: Prior to the 1946 season the rule was changed so that such a play would simply result in an incompletion.)

Unfortunately, that slightly errant toss would prove to be Baugh's only significant contribution to the outcome. He aggravated a rib injury and played only a few minutes after the opening period.

Frank Filchock stepped in for Baugh and certainly was up to the task. Soon after Ki Aldrich intercepted a Bob Waterfield pass at the Ram 48, Filchock went deep to Steve Bagarus, who wrestled the ball away from Waterfield near the sideline. Waterfield recovered and tried to tackle Bagarus but the back eluded the attempt and completed the 38-yard touchdown play. Joe Aguirre's point after gave Washington a 7-2 lead.

Cleveland stormed back, driving 70 yards to recapture the lead with three and a half minutes left in the half. The payoff came on a 37-yard touchdown pass from Waterfield to Jim Benton. Waterfield's point after attempt was partially blocked by the Washington line. It wobbled to the crossbar, struck it, bounced into the air and fell to the ground on the far side of the bar. The point proved crucial for the Rams as the game unfolded.

Cleveland led 9-7 at the half and struck for more shortly after intermission. They drove 81 yards (96 counting the 15-yard holding penalty they had to overcome) and scored on another long Waterfield TD pass. This one went to Jim Gillette and covered 44 yards. Gillette got behind the secondary, caught Waterfield's pass in stride at the ten and covered the rest of the distance unchallenged. It remained 15-7 as the conversion failed.

The Redskins responded late in the third with a 70-yard sortie. Bob DeFruiter got things started with a 15-yard run before Filchock went down the middle to Bagarus. The back broke into the clear and wasn't hauled down until he reached the Ram six. Three plays later, on the next-to-last play of the quarter, Filchock's fourth-down pass found Bob Seymour all alone in the end zone.

Aguirre's second conversion pulled the Redskins within a point at 15-14.

They couldn't quite overcome the deficit provided by the fluke safety and the lucky extra point. It's very important to note that the Rams' defense also had a great deal to do with the Redskins' defeat. They held the Redskins to just 33 yards rushing on the day. While Filchock filled in admirably for Baugh, he just couldn't get it done without a ground game. Certainly this was no fluke win for Cleveland.

Washington did manage to manufacture a couple of chances in the fourth quarter, but Aguirre failed to connect on two field goal attempts.

His first chance was the best one. With 6:26 remaining Aguirre sent a 31-yarder high and long. The official hesitated for a moment before signaling no good. It was a couple of feet wide to the right. With just over two minutes to go, his 46-yard try was well short. The Redskins got their hands on the ball once more, but for just one play as Albie Reisz intercepted Filchock's pass and the Rams ran out the clock.

1946
Head Coach: Turk Edwards
Record: 5-5-1, Tied for Third in Eastern Division

Honors: John Adams All-NFL; Steve Bagarus All-NFL

Filchock Traded to Giants

Jan 8—The passer who has stood in the shadow of Sammy Baugh for eight years will do so no more.

The Redskins announced today that they have traded Frank Filchock to the New York Giants. Washington will receive star tackle Paul Stenn and, possibly, quarterback Tommy Mont.

Mont, a former star at Maryland, currently is in the Army and stationed in Germany. Should he want to play football when he returns, it will be with the Redskins. If he decides not to play, the Redskins will select another player from the Giants or they will receive cash.

Filchock has proven to be a highly capable backup to Baugh since joining the team in 1938. Most recently, he nearly led the team to a win in the NFL Championship game, throwing two touchdown passes to account for all of the scoring in the Redskins' 15-14 loss to the Rams.

Jan 18
Turk Edwards Named Redskins Coach
DeGroot resigns, to coach AAFC LA Dons

Sep 9
Flaherty Back But Not With Skins
Former Redskins' coach will lead NY Yanks

9/28/46	REDSKINS (0-0-1) 14, Steelers (1-0-1) 14				33,621
Pit	0	0	0	14	14
Was	7	7	0	0	14
Pit	TD Jansante, Dudley; PAT Dudley 2				
Was	TD Saenz, Todd; PAT Poillon 2				

Griffith Stadium—The Redskins cruised into the fourth quarter with a 14-0 lead but had to hold their breaths as a last-second field goal attempt went wide, allowing them to escape with a 14-14 tie with Pittsburgh.

Washington built its lead by scoring touchdowns in each of the first two quarters. On their initial possession, they marched 61 yards into the end zone, scoring on a run by Eddie Saenz.

Sammy Baugh passed for just nine yards on that drive. The next one featured his talents a bit more as his aerials accounted for 47 of the 84 yards. Still, the end zone was broached on the ground, with Dick Todd doing the honors.

A bonehead penalty cost the Redskins three points in the third quarter. Jack Jenkins started to come off of the field as Dick Poillon lined up for a 32-yard field goal attempt. The Washington bench, for some reason, waved him back onto the field. By the time Jenkins realized the mistake and reversed his direction to get off of the field, the ball was snapped. Poillon's attempt split the uprights, but it didn't count due to the infraction. His second try was low and wide. It didn't appear to be significant at the time, but those things have a way of coming back to haunt you.

Pittsburgh started to rally late in the third quarter, embarking on a drive from its own 20. John Clement capped the march early in the fourth quarter by throwing an 18-yard touchdown pass to rookie end Yal Jansante. Bill Dudley kicked the extra point and the Steelers trailed 14-7.

If that scared the Redskins, they were terrified by what happened on the play following the kickoff. Sal Rosato fumbled after a 14-yard run and the Steelers recovered at the Washington 33. They moved to a first down at the two. Dudley cracked the goal line in two tries, got up and kicked the tying conversion with 3:34 remaining.

The Redskins got a drive going, but gave it up on downs at midfield. Two passes by Clement got them to the Washington 11 and, after a five-yard penalty against Pittsburgh for excess time-outs, Dudley trotted out to try and win it from the 25 with 10 seconds left. The roar from the crowd when the referee signaled no good was one of joy mixed with relief.

10/6/46	REDSKINS (1-0-1) 17, Lions (0-2) 16				33,569
Det	0	7	0	9	16
Was	0	7	10	0	17
Det	TD Cifers, Frutig; PAT Tassos 2; Safety punt blocked				
	out of end zone				
Was	TD Saenz, Gaffney; PAT Poillon 2; FG Poillon				

Griffith Stadium—For the second week in a row the Redskins and their home crowd had to watch and hope that an opponent missed a potential game-winning field goal. Like Bill Dudley's late boot last week, Damon Tassos' kicked missed but, unlike the previous week, the Redskins held the lead at the time and thus were able to chalk up their initial win of the season.

The game was scoreless through the first 26 and a half minutes of play. Washington got on the board first with a 57-yard drive into the end zone. The payoff came on Sammy Baugh's perfect pass that Eddie Saenz caught at the Lion eight. The speedster easily strode into the end zone to complete the 30-yard scoring play. It took just a shade over a minute for Detroit to respond with a quick-strike invasion that resulted in a 20-yard touchdown pass from Dave Ryan to Bobby Cifers.

As the Steelers had the week before, the Lions had to rally in the fourth quarter to get a shot at their potential winning kick. Washington had made its move in the third quarter, scoring 10 points to take a 17-7 lead into the final stanza. First the Skins drove from their own 30 to the Lion 19, where things bogged down. Dick Poillon came in to boot a 25-yard field goal. Then, Steve Bagarus intercepted a pass at his own 17, dodged and slipped tackles and was caught by the last Lion with a shot after a 41-yard return to the Detroit 42.

Baugh took advantage immediately. Jim Gaffney got himself open at the 20 and Baugh's precise pass hit the receiver in stride, allowing Gaffney to flash into the end zone unchallenged. Poillon converted and the home team led by 10 going into the fourth.

The Lions were game. They turned a key defensive stand that bottled the Redskins up deep in their own territory into nine points. First, they blocked Baugh's punt and the ball rolled out of the end zone for a safety. Then Ryan returned the ensuing free kick 27 yards to the Washington 38. One apparent Lion touchdown was nullified by a motion penalty, but they eventually got the TD on a seven-yard pass from Ryan to Ed Frutig.

With less than five minutes left, Detroit kicked onside and recovered. Two Ryan passes had them down to the Washington 26. Two more plays lost four yards and Tassos was called on to put his team ahead with just under two minutes left. The drama dissipated soon after the foot met the pigskin. It had no chance, well short and wide.

10/13/46	**REDSKINS (2-0-1) 24, Giants (2-1) 14**			33,651
NYG	0	7	7	0	14
Was	7	0	7	10	24
NYG	TD Paschal, Filipowicz; PAT Strong 2			
Was	TD Jenkins, Bagarus 2; PAT Poillon 2; FG Poillon			

Griffith Stadium—The Redskins scored 10 fourth-quarter points to break open what had been a nip-and-tuck battle and defeated the Giants.

Washington scored the first time they had the ball, but it took a while—more than 10 minutes. That's how much clock they used while driving 87 yards to the goal line. The first 61 yards were attained strictly on the ground, with Frank Akins, Steve Bagarus and Dick Todd advancing the ball steadily downfield. A holding call on a play from the New York 26 forced Sammy Baugh to do what he does best: take to the air. A pass to Todd quickly earned a first down at the 14. Ed Cifers then caught another Baugh bullet for 12 yards to the two. It took Jack Jenkins two plays to power it over from there. Dick Poillon converted and Washington was up 7-0.

Moving in part due to the arm of former Redskins passer Frank Filchock, New York tied the score in the second quarter. Filchock's 33-yard completion to Frank Liebel helped move the Giants to the Washington 30. From there, Bill Paschal found a crack up the middle and slipped through it, breaking it all the way for the touchdown to tie it at seven.

In the third quarter, the Redskins again pulled ahead only to see the Giants even the score by the end of the period. On Washington's fifth play from scrimmage after intermission, Baugh dropped back from his own 49 and hit a streaking Bagarus in stride around the Giant 40. While more than half a dozen New

Yorkers seemed to have a shot, Bagarus eluded them all and scored standing up. Later in the third, Hank Soar's interception and return set up a 46-yard Giants drive that culminated in Filchock's nine-yard dart to Steve Filipowicz, who was standing on the goal line. Strong's conversion made it 14-14 going into the final quarter.

Eddie Saenz jump-started the Redskins' subsequent possession with a 37-yard kickoff return to the Washington 45. Then Baugh went to Bagarus into Giant territory at the 37. A few plays later the Redskins had second and inches at the 14. With the defense crowding the line to stop the anticipated running play, Baugh crossed them up by passing, launching a strike to Bagarus, who gained control just before stepping out of bounds in the corner of the end zone. There was still 13:05 to be played, but the Redskins intercepted Filchock twice and Poillon booted a field goal to preserve the win.

10/20/46	**Redskins (3-0-1) 14, YANKS (0-4) 6**			24,357
Was	7	0	7	0	14
Bos	6	0	0	0	6
Was	TD Todd, Saenz; PAT Poillon 2			
Bos	TD Micka			

Fenway Park—A stout defense and just enough offense carried the Redskins to a 14-6 win over Boston.

The defense, led by the front wall of Ki Aldrich, Paul Stenn, Ed Cifers and Doug Turley, held the Yanks to just 52 yards of offense on the day. They kept Boston out of the end zone, the Yanks' lone score coming on an interception return with the game less than two minutes old. Mike Micka latched on to the errant Sammy Baugh toss and raced 42 yards for a 6-0 lead. Doug Eliason missed the point after and it was 6-0.

Washington responded promptly. Dick Todd got his team good field position by returning the ensuing kickoff to his own 42. The Redskin offense progressed steadily downfield, with Steve Bagarus and Jack Jenkins picked up good chunks of yardage between the occasional Baugh passes. Todd finished what he had started, pushing it across the goal line from short range. Dick Poillon and his mates properly executed the extra point and Washington took a 7-6 lead.

The Redskins' lead was seriously threatened just once, with that scare coming in the third quarter. Boston pieced together its only sustained drive of the day and moved from its 23 to the Washington eight, but it came undone as the Yanks again were unable to make a short kick. This was a 16-yard field goal attempt that Gary Famigletti just flat missed.

After that, the Redskins were stopped on downs at the Boston two. The drive wasn't for naught, however, as the Skins took advantage of the resulting favorable field position. As it had been doing all day, the defense stopped the Yanks cold and Boston punted from its own end zone. Jim Youel returned the boot 20 yards to the Yank 31. Three plays later Baugh zipped a pass to Eddie Saenz at the two. The back fought through a tackle and dove over for the clinching TD.

10/27/46	**Eagles (3-2) 28, REDSKINS (3-1-1) 24**			33,691
Phi	0	0	14	14	28
Was	10	14	0	0	24
Phi	TD Pritchard, Steele, Steinke, Ferrante; PAT Lio 4			
Was	TD Rosato 2, Lapka; PAT Poillon 3; FG Poillon			

Griffith Stadium—It's amazing how much a team can lose in just 30 minutes. In that one half of football on this day, the Redskins lost a 24-0 lead, the football game, and their status as Eastern Division leaders.

The 24-point margin was built methodically in the first half. Washington drove to a pair of Sal Rosato touchdown runs and a Dick Poillon field goal. Rosato's second score came late in the half and the Eagles fumbled the ensuing kickoff. The ball rolled back into the end zone, where Ted Lapka pounced on it for the easy TD.

Often in games like this a play that seems insignificant at the time is, in retrospect, the turning point. Such a moment occurred early in the third quarter. Jim Youel had just returned a punt to the Eagle 25 and the home team was on the verge of turning the game into a certified rout. It never happened as Poillon fumbled and Rudy Smeja recovered for Philly at the 30. Four plays later, the Eagles were in the end zone and it was 24-7.

Suddenly, the Eagles had confidence and the Redskins started playing scared. Philadelphia drove to another touchdown; this one coming on a one-yard sweep by Ernie Steele and it was 24-14 going into the fourth quarter.

The Eagles' momentum was blunted momentarily when they missed a field goal, but they picked it right back up on their next drive. They moved 66 yards behind the passing of Tommy Thompson. He completed four passes on the drive, the last one going to Gil Steinke for eight yards and the score. It was 24-21 with 5:11 to play.

While Poillon's earlier fumble was an unnoticed pivotal moment, the one that occurred with just under three minutes left was quite obvious at the time. On fourth and was at their own 40, the Redskins decided to go for the first to retain possession rather than punt away to the red-hot Eagle offense. The Skins got the worst of both worlds after Rosato was stuffed for no gain; the Eagles had both the ball and great field position.

Thompson handed the ball off twice and got a first down at the 30. From there he completed the comeback by throwing to Jack Ferrante, who gathered in the pass at the goal line. Augie Lio's fourth conversion made it 28-24 with 1:34 to play.

After the kickoff the Redskins did manage to move from their own 20 to near midfield, but Steele intercepted Baugh's desperation heave to put a bow on it for the Eagles.

Edwards: 'We Gambled and Lost'

Oct 27—Redskins coach Turk Edwards apparently didn't make the call to go for it on fourth and one with 2:55 left and his team clinging to a three-point lead over the Eagles. But he did nothing to stop it, either.

"I guess I could have stopped that play," said Edwards. "I probably should have.

"We gambled and lost," he said.

On the play in question, which started at the Washington 40, the Eagles sniffed out the handoff to Sal Rosato and stuffed him for no gain.

The play was the most noticeable element of the team's collapse but you don't lose a 24-point halftime lead on one play.

"That (the fourth-down play) isn't all that worries me," said Edwards. "How could we blow a 24-point lead?"

The question hung in the air, unanswered.

11/3/46	**STEELERS (4-2-1) 14, Redskins (3-2-1) 7**				39,060
Was	0	0	0	7	7
Pit	7	0	0	7	14
Was	TD Baugh; PAT Poillon				
Pit	TD Dudley, Lach; PAT Condit 2				

Forbes Field—Bill Dudley returned an interception 81 yards for a first-quarter touchdown and the Redskins could never quite recover as they fell to the Steelers.

The early momentum belonged to the visitors. A 34-yard pass from Sammy Baugh to Steve Bagarus had the Redskins in Steeler territory, but Chuck Cherundola ended that threat with an interception at the 17. The Redskins didn't lose much as they forced the Steelers to punt and Dudley shanked it out of bounds at his 33. Baugh came out firing, but Bullet Bill leapt up and snared

the pass at the 19. Dudley shot down the sideline with his teammates dispatching the few Redskins that he couldn't outrun. His last potential obstacle was Baugh at around the 10, but Sammy's diving attempt failed and Dudley scampered into the end zone.

Again the Redskins threatened as Bagarus returned the ensuing kickoff 51 yards to the Steeler 32. The offense couldn't move and Dick Poillon missed a 36-yard field goal attempt. Forays into Pittsburgh territory in the second and third quarters also came up empty for Washington.

Pittsburgh wrapped it up in the fourth quarter. Dudley returned a punt 53 yards to the Redskin 14 and, although the subsequent field goal try was blocked, the return gave the Steelers the field position advantage. It paid off after Charley Seabright intercepted Baugh at the Washington 29. Shortly after that, Steve Lach went off tackle for five yards and a touchdown. Merle Condit's extra point made it 14-0.

Baugh snuck in from the one to avert the shutout for the Redskins. They had a shot to tie it up in the dying moments after two passes from Baugh to Eddie Saenz moved the Skins to the Steeler 37. On the next play, though, Baugh was trapped for a 22-yard loss, ending any thoughts of a miracle comeback.

11/10/46	**REDSKINS (4-2-1) 17, Yanks (0-7) 14**				33,691
Bos	0	7	7	0	14
Was	0	3	7	7	17
Bos	TD Famigletti, Davis; PAT Scollard 2				
Was	TD Todd 2; PAT Poillon 2; FG Poillon				

Griffith Stadium—A limping Sammy Baugh came off the bench in the fourth quarter to lead a fourth-quarter touchdown drive that pushed the Redskins past Boston 17-14.

After a scoreless first period, the winless Yanks took possession at their own eight and embarked on an impressive 92-yard TD drive. The main movers were Paul Governali, who completed three passes, and Johnny Grigas, who tore off a 34-yard run. Gary Famigletti chalked up the six points when he smashed it over from the one and Nick Scollard added the conversion.

With Jack Jenkins in the quarterback slot in place of Baugh, the Redskins moved from their own 20 to the Boston 24, with a 35-yard connection between Jenkins and Jim Peebles gaining the lion's share of the yardage. The foray faltered, however, and they had to settle for Dick Poillon's 34-yard field goal and a 7-3 halftime deficit.

The teams exchanged touchdowns in the third quarter, so Boston still held its four-point lead going into the fourth. Baugh, who was nursing both a charley horse and a torn rib cartilage, entered the fray with the ball resting at the Washington 49. We don't know if his injuries hampered his ability to sling the ball because he didn't drop back to pass. The Yank defense was unsure, too, so they played loose just in case. That allowed the Redskins to cover the entire 51 yards to pay dirt on the ground, with Dick Todd covering the final 29 yards. Poillon's point after put the Redskins up 17-14.

The Yanks weren't finished. They drove to the Redskin nine before being undone by a 15-yard penalty that forced a desperation pass attempt on fourth that the home team smothered to preserve the win.

11/17/46	**BEARS (6-1-1) 24, Redskins (4-3-1) 20**				43,315
Was	7	3	7	3	20
Chi	0	17	0	7	24
Was	TD Todd, Peebles; PAT Poillon 2; FG Poillon 2				
Chi	TD J. Osmanski, Clarkson, Keene; PAT Maznicki 3; FG Maznicki				

Wrigley Field—Sid Luckman's 42-yard touchdown pass to Jim Keene with 2:50 to play lifted the Bears past the Redskins 24-20.

The Redskins scored first, taking advantage of a weak punt to take possession at the Chicago 37. After Wilbur Moore and Dick Todd carried down to the 28, Sammy Baugh took to the air. He twice threw to Todd; the first one moved the ball to the 16, and the second moved it into the end zone. Todd made a spectacular catch, tumbling hard against a Wrigley Field barrier just outside of the end line.

After Chicago's Frank Maznicki and Washington's Dick Poillon exchanged field goals early in the second period, the rest of the first half belonged to the Bears. Joe Osmanski capped an 80-yard drive with a four-yard run before center Stuart Clarkson snagged a Baugh pass out of the air and raced 60 yards into the end zone for a 17-10 lead at the break.

Steve Bagarus got things going for the Redskins' tying drive with a 26-yard punt return to the Bear 48. Two plays later, Baugh flipped a pass to Jim Peebles in the flat. The Chicago defender gambled for the interception and lost. Peebles turned and ran in for the TD untouched.

Early in the fourth quarter on a play from the Chicago 46, Bagarus caught a dart from Baugh and weaved his way down to the eight. Alas, a clipping call pushed the line of scrimmage back to the 21. Three plays later, Poillon kicked a 22-yard field goal to put the Redskins ahead by three with about 10 minutes to play.

For a while it appeared the lead would be safe as the Washington defense had the answer for each Chicago attempt to move into scoring position. With around five minutes left, the Skins' offense had a nice drive going in Bear territory. Rather than pushing in for the clinching score, though, disaster struck as Jim Gaffney fumbled and Chicago recovered at its own 38. A penalty pushed Chicago back to the 24, but that didn't bother Luckman as he threw to Keene for 34 yards to the Washington 42. Although one would think that the defense would pay particular attention to Keene after such a play, the Bear end was virtually unguarded as he ran his pattern to the 22. Luckman's pass was on the money and Keene scored easily.

11/24/46	Redskins (5-3-1) 27, EAGLES (4-5) 10				36,683
Was	7	7	0	13	27
Phi	3	0	0	7	10
Was	TD Youel, Saenz, Aldrich, Poillon; PAT Poillon 3				
Phi	TD Prichard; PAT Lio; FG Lio				

Shibe Park—Jim Youel ran for one touchdown and threw for another to lead the Redskins past the Eagles.

Philadelphia held a 3-0 lead when Youel came in to give Sammy Baugh a rest in the first quarter. Youel moved the team to the Eagle 37, and then took matters into his own hands. He faked to a couple of backs, but unbeknownst to the Eagle defense he kept the ball tucked in his own belly. The right side was devoid of blockers, all of whom were putting up interference for the backs who didn't get the ball, but that was OK because there wasn't a defender in that direction, either. Youel took off through the open field and scored easily.

In the second quarter, the Eagles were threatening when Wilbur Moore saved the Redskins with an interception at his own 10. He returned it 21 yards to the 31 and Youel and the Skins were back in business.

They struck quickly. Steve Bagarus made a great catch of a Youel pass for 26 yards and then Jim Gaffney caught one for seven. From the Eagle 37, Eddie Saenz snuck through the middle of the line, turned on the speed, and was wide open when Youel hit him in stride at the 14. Saenz covered the remaining distance to pay dirt in a flash, and it was 14-3 at the half.

After intermission, the Eagles abandoned the running game and tried to catch up with the passing of Tommy Thompson and Roy Zimmerman. In the third quarter, the strategy was unproductive as they failed to score. In the fourth, it was

disastrous as Ki Aldrich latched onto one of Thompson's passes and scooted 27 yards for a touchdown. On their next possession the Redskins ground out a time-consuming 53-yard drive that culminated in a one-yard scoring smash by Dick Poillon.

12/1/46	Packers (6-4) 20, REDSKINS (5-4-1) 7				33,691
GB	0	7	6	7	20
Was	0	0	7	0	7
GB	TD Fritsch 3; PAT Fritsch 2				
Was	TD Bagarus; PAT Poillon				

Griffith Stadium—The Redskins gave up 300 yards rushing, threw four interceptions and fumbled seven times during a 20-7 loss to Green Bay.

The Packers had some trouble getting untracked, with three promising drives into Redskin territory resulting in a missed field goal, a lost fumble and an interception. They got another opportunity when Bruce Smith intercepted Sammy Baugh's pass at the Washington 31 and returned it to the 14. Ted Fritsch capitalized a few plays later when he scored the first of his three touchdowns on the day from one yard out and then kicked the extra point to give his team a 7-0 halftime lead.

It was déjà vu all over again in the third quarter with an interception deep in Redskins territory setting up a short Fritsch TD run. This time, though, he missed the extra point so the Packer lead was 13-0.

The Redskins finally managed to hold on to the ball long enough to piece together an 82-yard touchdown drive. Jim Youel nicely mixed running plays with Steve Bagarus and Eddie Saenz getting good yardage with passes to a variety of targets. The last target was Bagarus. On third down from the Packer six, they ran a version of a sleeper play with Bagarus going in motion before just standing there and looking at the snap of the ball, as though the play would be going away from him. This induced Smith, his defender, to turn his attention elsewhere. Bagarus zipped into the end zone and Youel had the ball there for him.

Even after Dick Poillon's conversion cut the Green Bay lead to 13-7, there still wasn't much of a feeling that the Redskins were really back in the game. This feeling was affirmed in the fourth quarter when Youel fumbled at the Washington 37. Fritsch got 23 yards on the next play and, right after that, got the remaining 14 for the touchdown. Washington worked its way down to the Packer 10 late in the game, but that threat was ended with—you guessed it—an interception.

The only bit of good news on the day was that the New York Giants lost to the LA Rams. That meant that if the Redskins were able to beat the Giants in New York the next week, the two teams would finish the regular season tied for the Eastern Division title, forcing a playoff.

Playoff in D.C. if Skins Beat Giants

Dec 2—Should the Redskins beat the Giants on Sunday to force a playoff for the NFL Eastern Division title, that tilt will take place at Griffith Stadium.

Despite their loss to the Packers on Sunday, the Redskins still have a shot at returning to the league championship game thanks to the Los Angeles Rams. They defeated the Giants 31-21, leaving the Redskins within one game of New York for the division lead.

The scenario is simple: if the Redskins beat the Giants at the Polo Grounds, they will be tied for first place. The teams will then meet again one week later in Washington with the winner advancing and the loser going home. If the Giants win, they take the division and the Redskins are done.

12/8/46	GIANTS (7-3-1) 31, Redskins (5-5-1) 0				50,337
Was	0	0	0	0	0
NYG	3	14	14	0	31
NYG	TD Paschal, Liebel, Franck, Filipowicz; PAT Strong 4; FG Strong				

Polo Grounds—The Redskins' season came to a crashing halt as they were trounced by the Giants. A Redskin win would have forced a playoff for the division title.

A large helping of salt was added to the wound by the fact that the main mover in the Giants' win was quarterback Roy Zimmerman, a player that the Redskins had traded to the Giants during the previous offseason. He had a hand in three of the Giants' four touchdowns.

Trailing 3-0 in the second quarter, the Redskins mounted one of their few offensive threats of the day. Jim Youel connected with Eddie Saenz for 66 yards to the Giant 23. On the next play, though, Zimmerman stepped in front of Youel's pass at the four and picked it off, returning it to the 19 yards to the 23.

From there, the Giants embarked on their first touchdown drive. It appeared that the Redskins had stopped it when they forced the Giants to punt from their own 40, but a roughing-the-kicker penalty kept the drive alive for New York. From the

Washington 42, Zimmerman found Jim Howell open and the end made it down to the one before he was stopped. Bill Paschal ploughed to pay dirt on the next play. Before halftime, New York drove 61 yards to a touchdown pass from Zimmerman to Frank Liebel, giving them a 17-0 lead.

Late in the second quarter, the Redskins had a chance to make some noise as Sammy Baugh's pass headed towards Eddie Saenz, who was wide open at the Giant two. As one would expect the way things were unfolding on this day, Saenz dropped the pass.

New York wrapped up the game and the division title in the third quarter, scoring two touchdowns. One came on a 33-yard pass from Zimmerman to George Franck, who made a nice, juggling catch as he fell into the end zone. Then Steve Filipowicz picked off Baugh's pass and raced 31 yards to close out the scoring

---

Dec 30

Edwards to Remain as Head Coach
Rumors of Shaughnessy promotion unfounded

1947
Head Coach: Turk Edwards
Record: 4-8, Fourth in Eastern Division

Honors: Sammy Baugh All-NFL

Jan 10

Shaughnessy Joins Redskins Full Time
T-formation master quits head coaching post at Maryland

Bagarus Traded to Rams

Jan 18—Talented problem child Steve Bagarus officially became more trouble than he was worth today as the Redskins traded him to the Los Angeles Rams.

In exchange for the Notre Dame product, the Redskins receive 220-pound fullback Ralph Ruthstrom and halfback Tom Farmer. Although neither individual has Bagarus' talent, they hopefully won't be the headache that he brought.

It started midway through his first season in 1945. The 26-year-old rookie, his start to pro football delay by service to the Army, became an instant star and demanded more money during the season. This just isn't done and the demand drew the ire of team owner George Preston Marshall.

After the season, Marshall told his accountant to prepare an $1,800 bonus check for Bagarus. While the payment was being processed, the player complained to a sportswriter that Marshall was cheap and ungrateful. Marshall instructed his account to tear up the bonus check.

Incidents such as that and other various violations of team rules and policies led to the departure of the player who wore uniform number 00.

9/28/47	EAGLES (1-0) 45, Redskins (0-1) 42				35,406
Was	0	14	14	14	42
Phi	10	14	14	7	45
Was	TD Nussbaumer; Taylor 3, Saenz, Poillon; PAT Poillon 6				
Phi	TD Pihos 2, Van Buren 2, Sherman, Armstrong; PAT Patton 6; FG Muha				

Shibe Park—Sammy Baugh threw five touchdown passes to make a big contribution the point total in the highest-scoring game

in NFL history. Despite Baugh's heroics, the Eagles had a greater share of those 87 points than did the Redskins when the game ended.

In fact, the Eagles had more points than the Skins during the most of the game. The only time Washington held the lead was a brief span in the second quarter after scoring two touchdowns to erase a 10-0 deficit. Baugh served up both of them—one a 25-yarder to Bob Nussbaumer, and the other covering 62 yards to Hugh Taylor.

As was stated, the Redskins did not have much time to enjoy their lead. They owned it for 17 seconds, which is the amount of time it took Steve Van Buren to field the kickoff following Taylor's TD on the five and return it 95 yards for a touchdown. It wasn't very long at all considering that Van Buren's path to the goal line was fairly unimpeded by any Redskins attempting to tackle him. The Philly lead grew to 24-14 by halftime as the Eagles drove 58 yards to a one-yard touchdown run by Allie Sherman.

The Redskins answered in the second half as Eddie Saenz took the kickoff at his own six and dashed 94 yards for a touchdown to pull the Redskins back within three.

But the Eagles were up to the challenge. Van Buren capped a 63-yard drive with a one-yard TD plunge and Tommy Thompson threw a 21-yard scoring pass to Pete Pihos. It looked as though the Redskins were done at 38-21, but they made the Eagles fight for it. Washington marched 65 yards for a touchdown with Baugh throwing to a wide-open Dick Poillon in the end zone on fourth and goal at the five. The Eagles, however, pushed their lead back up to 17 early in the fourth quarter as Thompson threw to Neill Armstrong, who landed in the end zone after catching the pass.

Undaunted, Baugh kept firing. He threw two fourth-quarter touchdown passes to Taylor, the second coming with 4:26 to play. Sammy didn't get another chance to sling, however, as the Eagles ran out the clock after that.

Three Redskins Cut, Lack of Hustle Cited
DeFruiter, Gaffney, Avery
waived after loss to Eagles

10/5/47	REDSKINS (1-1) 27, Steelers (1-2) 26			36,585
Pit	3	7	14	2	26
Was	0	7	13	7	27
Pit	TD Lach, Sullivan, Compagno; PAT Glamp; FG Glamp; Safety Baugh stepped out of end zone
Was	TD Taylor, Nussbaumer, Farmer, Poillon; PAT Poillon 3

Griffith Stadium—The Redskins held on at the end to take a wild game from the Steelers. There were seven lead changes during the first 59 minutes and 35 seconds and the Redskins were fortunate that there wasn't an eights change as Joe Glamp's field goal attempt with 25 seconds to play bounced off the left upright.

Glamp gave his team a 3-0 lead in the first quarter when he booted a three-pointer. Washington responded with a quick strike. On the first play of the second period, Sammy Baugh threw to Bob Nussbaumer, who was open going down the sideline and dashed over the goal line to complete the 54-yard scoring play. Dick Poillon kicked the extra point to give Washington a 7-3 lead.

The score stayed the same until less than a minute remained before intermission. That's when Johnny Clement faded back from the Washington 15 and fired to Steve Lach, who caught the ball shy of the end zone and carried about a half dozen Redskins over the goal line for a 10-7 lead.

The two teams each scored two touchdowns in the third period with the lead changing hands after each one. At the end of the period, it was 24-20 Pittsburgh. The Steelers threatened to expand their lead in the fourth quarter as they marched to the doorstep of the end zone only to have the Washington defense slam it shut at the two. The ensuing field position, however, aided the Steelers as Baugh went back into his own end zone to pass and accidentally stepped on the end line to award two points to Pittsburgh.

After the free kick, the Steelers drove into field goal position, but Glamp missed, keeping the Redskins alive. They took full advantage, embarking on an 80-yard touchdown march. A 35-yard pass from Baugh to Eddie Saenz was the big gainer and a nine-yard dart from Baugh to Sal Rosato pushed it to the one. Tom Farmer blasted it over from there and Dick Poillon converted to make it 27-26.

The Steelers' offense then did what it needed to do, moving into field goal position. Glamp was just a few inches wide of doing what he needed to do.

10/12/47	REDSKINS (2-1) 28, Giants (0-2-1) 20			36,533
NYG	7	0	0	13	20
Was	7	7	7	7	28
NYG	TD Paschal, White, Franck; PAT Strong 2
Was	TD Baugh 2, Saenz 2; PAT Poillon 4

Griffith Stadium—Sammy Baugh matched his career total by scoring two touchdowns, Eddie Saenz scored two more, and the Redskins went on to an easy win over the Giants.

New York practically had its only lead of the game handed to it. Dick Poillon fumbled at the Giants 13 and Ray Poole recovered. Three plays later Bill Paschal scooted around right end and scored from the four to make it 7-0.

Their lead was short lived. The Redskins took the ensuing kickoff and showed why they were 14-point favorites. Baugh passes to Joe Tereshinski, who made a nice shoestring catch, and Poillon moved the Skins to the Giant 23. Then Poillon showed that he was determined to make up for his earlier miscue by going off left tackle and fighting his way to the one. It took two quarterback

sneak tries for Baugh to get it over the goal line. Poillon converted to tie it at seven. In the second period, Saenz got off a nice punt return to set up another Baugh scoring sneak to put the Redskins in front to stay.

In the third quarter, the Redskins capitalized on two of their unfair advantages. From his own 30, Baugh unleashed a pass that carried from behind the 26 to the Giant 33. Nobody else can throw it that far with accuracy. Saenz outran the defense to catch the ball and sped past the remaining Giant defender for the touchdown. Few have that kind of speed.

The Redskins seemed content with their 21-7 lead. A touchdown run by Jim White cut into that lead in the fourth quarter and got the attention of the Skins immediately, especially Saenz. He took the ensuing kickoff at the six and was gone in a flash. One Giant had a shot at midfield, but a convoy of blockers took care of that and Saenz dashed in for the score. That rendered a late score by the Giants meaningless.

10/19/47	PACKERS (3-1) 27, Redskins (2-2) 10			23,570
Was	0	7	3	0	10
GB	10	0	0	17	27
Was	TD Lookabaugh; PAT Poillon; FG Poillon
GB	TD Fritsch, Luhn, Forte; PAT Cuff; FG Cuff, Fritsch

State Fair Grounds, Milwaukee—The Packers scored 17 unanswered points in the fourth quarter to break up a tie game and beat the Redskins 27-10.

Green Bay also opened the game with a scoring run, this one of 10-0. After driving 80 yards to a two-yard touchdown run by Ted Fritsch, the Packers got the ball back quickly when end Paul McKee fumbled and Bob Forte recovered at the Packer 45. From there, they drove to a 14-yard field goal by Ward Cuff.

There were no scoring explosions for the Redskins. Their only touchdown came after Dick Todd intercepted a pass at his 40, broke free of a shirt tackle attempt, and ran down to the Packer 10. Three plays later, Sammy Baugh threw a pass to John Lookabaugh at the goal line and the end fell into pay dirt for the score. Perhaps "threw" is not the most apt term to use for Baugh's action. Put it this way—the ball was delivered with such velocity that Lookabaugh had no choice but to catch it, as it would have gone right through him otherwise.

Dick Poillon's third-quarter field goal tied it up going into the fourth, but from then on it was all Packers. On the second play of the final period, Tony Candeo threw his first pass of the game and Nolan Luhn caught it for 26 yards and a touchdown. Later, Fritsch boomed a 49-yard field goal and Forte intercepted Baugh, rambling 88 yards to account for the final score.

10/26/47	Bears (3-2) 56, REDSKINS (2-3) 20			36,591
Chi	14	0	21	21	56
Was	0	7	6	7	20
Chi	TD Gallarneau, Holovak, Keane, Turner, Cifers, McAfee, Minini, Fenimore; PAT McLean 7, Luckman
Was	TD Saenz, Duckworth 2; PAT Poillon 2

Griffith Stadium—Before the biggest crowd in Washington sports history, the Bears laid waste to the host Redskins. They racked up eight touchdowns, six of them in the second half. Eight different Chicago players scored the TD's in the course of the 56-20 pasting.

This was a reasonably competitive affair for about two and a half quarters of play. The Bears jumped to a 14-0 lead in the first quarter, but the Redskins battled back with a 60-yard scoring drive. The payoff came when Eddie Saenz fought over the goal line from a yard out and it was 14-7 at intermission.

Chicago got right down to business in the third, tearing off a five-play, 80-yard drive that culminated in Sid Luckman's 18-yard touchdown pass to Jim Keane. The home team kept the crowd in it by responding with an impressive march of its own, moving 70 yards to the Bear eight. Then disaster struck.

Sammy Baugh threw to where he thought his receiver would be, but there at the four stood Chicago's Bulldog Turner instead. The 235-pound center roared down the right sideline with several Redskins in hot pursuit. Don Avery had a shot before being dispatched with a nice block and Baugh wound up being dragged into the end zone after getting a hold of Turner's jersey inside the 10. Suddenly it was 28-7 and the rout was on.

Redskins Scrimmage Day After Rout

Oct 27—The Bears pounded on them Sunday, and the Redskins pounded on each other the next day.

In a rare Monday scrimmage the Skins went back to basics, working on some skills that eluded them during their 56-20 loss to Chicago.

Coach Turk Edwards promised that this would not be the last full-contact session. "We will scrimmage constantly until we learn to knock somebody down," Edwards said. "The Redskins seem to have forgotten whatever they knew about tackling and blocking."

The only Redskins who were excused from the drills were those who were injured. The most severely banged-up player was rookie end Joe Tereshinski, who will miss a couple of weeks with a dislocated elbow.

11/2/47	Eagles (4-2) 38, REDSKINS (2-4) 14			36,591
Phi	14	3	14	7	38
Was	7	0	0	7	14
Phi	TD Pihos 2, Ferrante, Van Buren 2; PAT Patton 5; FG Patton			
Was	TD Saenz, Youel; PAT Poillon 2;			

Griffith Stadium—It was a case of too much Pete Pihos and Steve Van Buren for the Redskins as the Eagle stars scored two touchdowns each in the Philly romp.

Pihos did his damage in the first quarter using two quite different methods. After the Redskins went three and out following the opening kickoff, Sammy Baugh lined up to punt. The ball traveled about six inches into the belly of Pihos. Somehow, he managed to maintain control of the ball and run 26 yards for a touchdown. Five minutes later, Pihos caught a 10-yard touchdown pass from Tommy Thompson.

Baugh and the Redskins drove to the threshold of the goal line, coming within two inches of the stripe, but they failed to dent Philadelphia's 14-0 lead when they lost it on downs at that point. The drive was not a totally fruitless, however, as Washington had good field position at their own 47 after the Eagles punted. They again moved down into scoring territory and this time cashed in on Baugh's three-yard touchdown pass to Eddie Saenz on the final play of the first quarter.

The lone highlight of the second period was a goal line stand that denied the Eagles after they reached the one-yard line. Later, Cliff Patton kicked a field goal and Philly led 17-7 at the half.

It took just three plays for Philadelphia to establish its dominance in the second half. Van Buren returned the second-half kickoff 54 yards and shortly after that he took the ball on a reverse and rolled 23 yards to make it 24-7. On the Redskins' next possession, Ernie Steele intercepted a Baugh pass, setting up Van Buren's 37-yard touchdown run. The Eagles stretched their advantage to 38-7 in the fourth quarter as both teams emptied their benches. Jim Youel snuck into the end zone on the game's final play to post the other Redskin TD.

11/9/47	STEELERS (6-2) 21, Redskins (2-5) 14			36,257
Was	0	7	0	7	14
Pit	7	7	7	0	21
Was	TD Taylor, Castiglia; PAT Poillon 2			
Pit	TD Lack, Compagno, Clement; PAT Glamp 3			

Forbes Field—A fourth-quarter rally by the Redskins was stopped six feet—and one arm—short of success as they fell in Pittsburgh 21-14.

The arm belonged to an unidentified Steeler and got in the way of what looked to be the game-tying touchdown pass with a minute to play.

Pittsburgh built a 14-0 lead in the first half. Working exclusively on the ground, the Steelers drove 69 yards to their first score, which came on a one-yard burst by Steve Lach. Then, after Sammy Baugh's punt from deep in his own territory carried to just the Washington 40, the Steelers were back in business. They then took to the air with success as Johnny Clement went to Val Jansante for 28 yards to the 12. Back to the ground attack as Tony Compago carried twice, once for ten and then for the final two yards for the score, making it 14-0.

The Redskins got on the board before halftime on a drive that started at their own 26. After handing off a few times, Baugh decided to speed up the pace of the advance and threw to Joe Duckworth for 27 yards to the Steeler 26. On the next play, Hugh Taylor was the target, just over the goal line on the right sideline. Dick Poillon's point after made it 14-7 at the half.

In the third quarter, Clement ran 17 yards for what would prove to be the winning points, hurdling over two Redskin defenders near the goal line in the process. That put his team up 21-7.

Washington would lose, but would go down swinging. Baugh completed three passes to Bob Nussbaumer to help move the Skins from their own 39 to the Steeler three. From there, Jim Castiglia smashed into the line four times, the last try getting him into the end zone at the two early in the fourth quarter.

Late in the game, Baugh came out slinging from his own 21 in a bid to tie. Passes to Taylor and Poillon pushed into Steeler territory. Then Baugh found Poillon alone at the 30 and the end rolled all the way down to the seven. Two runs by Castiglia and a quarterback sneak by Baugh inched the line of scrimmage down to the two. One more play with a minute to go.

Baugh went to Doug Turley, who was in a crowd but appeared to have some separation from his defenders. The pass was on target, but someone's arm got in the way and the ball fell to the turf.

Just Five Players Away, Marshall Says

Nov 14—Despite what their 1-5 record may say about the current state of the team, the Redskins are not that far away from a return to glory, at least in the eyes of owner George Preston Marshall.

"We thought we were going to have our greatest team of all time this year," said Marshall. The team is falling short of that expectation primarily because of inexperience, according to Marshall. There are 13 rookies on the roster.

But the team can turn the corner soon, says Marshall. "With the cream of what we have and five good additions, we'll be right back up there in 1948."

He said that three of the five need to be backs. Presumably, the other two should man the interior line, which has had difficulty preventing penetration all year long.

It will be difficult to count on the draft to restock the talent as the bidding for players is fierce due to competition from the All-America Football Conference. They hope to get some talent from their Wilmington, Delaware farm team.

The star in Wilmington is Tommy Mont, who started the season as Sammy Baugh's understudy. He has moved to running back and his NFL future may lie there.

11/16/47	LIONS (3-6) 38, Redskins (2-6) 21			17,003	
Was	7	0	0	14	21
Det	14	10	7	7	38
Was	TD Nussbaumer, Poillon, Duckworth; PAT Poillon 3				
Det	TD Mote, Madarik, Dudley, Watt 2; PAT Zimmerman 5; FG Zimmerman				

Briggs Stadium—The Redskins went into Detroit and had one of their worst outings of the year against the worst team the NFL West had to offer. Rookie quarterback Clyde LeForce threw three touchdown passes to lead the Lions to a 38-21 rout of Washington.

It started going downhill early. Bob DeFruiter intercepted the pass of Sammy Baugh and the former Redskin returned the ball seven yards to the Washington 43. A holding penalty pushed Detroit back, but it didn't matter. From the Redskin 47, LeForce flipped a screen to Kelly Mote. His blockers got Mote down to the ten and he did the rest from there, breaking two tackles on his way in for the touchdown.

The Redskins looked like they might make a game of it as they took the ensuing kickoff and drove to tie the game. Baugh passes to Hugh Taylor and Eddie Saenz helped them move to the Detroit 23. From there, Baugh found Bob Nussbaumer open in the end zone and delivered to the end for the score.

But that would prove to be the high point for the Redskins. They were active contributors to their own demise. Detroit recaptured the lead for good after Eddie Saenz fumbled the ball away to them at the Washington 25. Bill Dudley made a spectacular catch of a LeForce pass at the four and Tippy Madarik carried for the TD from there. In the second period, after a Lion field goal, Bill Ward blocked Baugh's punt, setting up a short scoring run by Dudley and it was 24-7 at the half.

The Lions removed any potential for suspense in the third quarter when LeForce threw a 75-yard touchdown bomb to Joe Watt.

11/23/47	REDSKINS (3-6) 45, Cardinals (7-2) 21			35,362	
Chi	0	7	7	7	21
Was	7	10	14	14	45
Chi	TD Kutner, Harder, Angsman; PAT Harder 3				
Was	TD Poillon, McKee 2, Taylor, Rosato, Wilde; PAT Poillon 6; FG Poillon				

Griffith Stadium—Note to George Preston Marshall: Have a Sammy Baugh Day more often.

Before the game, Baugh was given a station wagon with "Slingin' Sam—The Redskin Man" emblazoned on the side. As the game unfolded, it was very apparent that Baugh was quite thankful for the gift. All he did was throw for 355 yards and six touchdowns to drive the Redskins past the Cardinals.

The Redskins started their second possession at midfield and embarked on a quick TD drive from there. The most spectacular play came when Dick Poillon made a one-handed stab of a Baugh pass for a 15-yard gain to the four. Two plays later Baugh made it a bit easier for Poillon, drilling the pass right into his receiver's breadbasket just across the goal line for a 7-0 lead.

Despite a clipping penalty, Baugh still started the next drive in fairly good field position at his own 42. After working down to the Cardinal 37, Baugh went to Paul McKee on a deep slant and his pass hit the receiver right in the hands. McKee was hauled down at the four. Three plays later he ran another slant, this one into the end zone, and Baugh was on target again for a 14-0 Washington lead 33 seconds into the second period.

Baugh proved that he was human when he threw an interception that set up Chicago's first touchdown. Poillon booted a field goal with a minute left in the second to make it 17-7 at the break.

It took just nine offensive plays after intermission for the Redskins to take command of the game. Five of them came after

they took the kickoff starting from their own 26. Sal Rosato carried three times and Baugh threw to Doug Turley, advancing the ball to the Cardinal 34. From there, Baugh lofted a scoring pass to Hugh Taylor.

Al DeMao intercepted Paul Christman's pass and returned it to the Chicago 19. On fourth down Baugh dropped a screen pass to Rosato. There were four blockers and just two defenders between the back and the goal line and Rosato took advantage of these odds to score easily. The Redskins were up 31-7.

The Skins coasted after that as Baugh racked up TD passes number five and six to McKee and George Wilde, respectively, in the fourth quarter.

Nov 27

Baugh Wrecks Car He Got On His "Day"
Star QB suffers minor injuries, station wagon worse off

11/30/47	YANKS (4-5-1) 27, Redskins (3-7) 24			24,800	
Was	0	3	14	7	24
Bos	3	10	7	7	27
Was	TD Castiglia 2, Nussbaumer; PAT Poillon 3; FG Poillon				
Bos	TD Crisler, Currivan, Golding; PAT Maznicki 3; PAT Maznicki 2				

Fenway Park—Sammy Baugh had the prettier numbers but opposing passer Boley Dancewicz produced the most points as the Yanks defeated Washington 27-24.

In the first quarter it appeared that a 61-yard completion from Dancewicz to Don Currivan would go for naught when Fred Boensch intercepted a Dancewicz pass. But Boensch fumbled the ball at the Washington 15 on his return and four plays later, Frank Maznicki booted a 27-yard field goal.

The three points turned out to be pivotal as the game wore on. Boston stretched its lead to 10-0 after a weak punt by Dick Poillon led to a 29-yard touchdown pass from Dancewicz to Harold Crisler. Washington fought back with a Poillon field goal that followed Eddie Saenz's punt return to the Boston 36, but the Yanks regained their 10-point lead with another Maznicki three-pointer just before intermission.

Things heated up in the third quarter. The first time the Skins had the ball they marched 64 yards in 13 plays for a touchdown. Baugh's aerials accounted for 54 of those yards. Jim Castiglia bulled over from the one for the TD.

On its next possession it took just four plays for Washington to take the lead. The big play in the 63-yard sortie was Baugh's 54-yard bomb to Saenz and a pass interference penalty positioned the Redskins at the one. Castiglia again fought the ball into the end zone for a 17-13 Redskin lead.

The lead disappeared faster than you could say "Dancewicz." Three plays after the kickoff, the Boston passer found Don Currivan wide open at midfield and the receiver easily completed the 67-yard scoring play untouched.

Baugh was on fire, in the midst of completing 14 straight passes as he led a 55-yard advance to wrest the lead back from the home team. Castiglia also played a key role with a few carries to keep the defense honest. With 10 minutes to play, Baugh threw to Bob Nussbaumer from the Boston six. The end made a spectacular diving catch to put Washington up 24-20.

But Dancewicz responded with a mini-streak of his own, completing four straight passes to account for all of the yardage in their 72-yard scoring foray. The payoff came on his 24-yard pass to Joe Golding, who scooted into the end zone just out of Jack Jenkins' grasp.

Getting the ball back at his own 18 with four minutes left, Baugh completed consecutive passes numbers 12, 13 and 14, but his next three fell incomplete and he was sacked on fourth down.

On the day, Baugh was 20 of 29 and had one touchdown pass while Dancewicz was just nine of 20, but had the three TD tosses.

12/7/47	GIANTS (2-2-7) 35, Redskins (3-8) 10				25,594
Was	0	3	0	7	10
NYG	14	0	7	14	35
Was	TD Saenz; PAT Poillon; FG Poillon				
NYG	TD Livingston 2, Poole 2, Chevarko; PAT Strong 5				

Polo Grounds—Two weeks after whipping one of the league's best teams in the Chicago Cardinals, the Redskins found themselves at the wrong end of a trouncing—this one administered by one of the league's worst teams, the New York Giants. Paul Governali threw four touchdown passes to lead the G-Men past the Redskins.

It took just 11 minutes for the Giants to establish their dominance. On the Redskins' first possession Howie Livingston wrestled the ball away from Bob Nussbaumer to get credit for an interception of Sammy Baugh. Five plays later, Livingston had the ball in the end zone, a recipient of Governali's first touchdown pass. The quarterback's next TD toss came on the first play of the Giants' next possession. This one was also to Livingston and it traveled 53 yards.

After throwing six touchdown passes against the Cardinals, Baugh was frightfully ineffective in this game and all the Skins could muster before the half was an 18-yard Dick Poillon field goal.

That would be the last score the Redskins would get before the game was well out of reach. After Washington drives died at the New York 13 and at midfield, Governali wrapped it up with a 42-yard scoring pass to Jim Poole to make it 21-3. Jim Youel replaced Baugh when it got to be 35-3 and Eddie Saenz tallied the visitors' lone touchdown with a 17-yard touchdown catch from Youel.

12/14/47	REDSKINS (4-8) 40, Yanks (4-7-1) 13				33,226
Bos	6	0	0	7	13
Was	6	14	6	14	40
Bos	TD Maznicki, Currivan; PAT Maznicki				
Was	TD Castiglia 2, Poillon 2, Turley, Tereshinski; PAT Poillon 4				

Griffith Stadium—The Redskins closed out their worst season ever with one of their best games of the year as they pounded the Yanks.

Boston was handed a 6-0 lead in the early going when Sal Rosato fumbled on a line plunge and Frank Maznicki picked the ball up and rolled 50 yards for a touchdown. Perhaps tired from his just-completed jaunt, Maznicki missed the ensuing conversion attempt.

It was all Redskins after that. Jim Castiglia was the main force on his team's game-tying drive, getting some good yardage on laterals from Sammy Baugh before eventually pounding over from the one. In the second quarter, working from the Boston 16, Baugh hit Poillon with a pass at the five. The receiver fought through an attempted tackle by Maznicki and scored to give his team the lead for good. Before halftime, Castiglia started to turn it into a blowout with a 30-yard jaunt to pay dirt.

At halftime, Santa Claus was supposed to parachute onto the field for the climax of the halftime show, but he overshot his target and wound up on the roof of a building near the stadium. Fortunately, Baugh was much more accurate than Kringle as his pass to Doug Turley gained 17 yards to the Yankee one-foot line. Poillon carried it in from there and the rout was certified.

Boston did score a fourth-quarter TD, but Baugh responded with a pair of scoring tosses about two minutes apart. The first one went to Turley and covered six yards; the other was a nice 20-yarder that Sammy placed right in Joe Tereshinski's hands in the end zone.

1948
Head Coach: Turk Edwards
Record: 5-7, Second in NFL East

Honors: Sammy Baugh All-NFL

Skins Trade Rights to Conerly to Giants
Jan 20—The Redskins traded the draft rights to Mississippi All-America back Charley Conerly to the New York Giants in exchange for halfback Howie Livingston and a player to be named later.

The move means that the team is casting its lot with Harry Gilmer, their top pick in the recent draft, to be Sammy Baugh's backup and possible successor at quarterback. The Alabama star has signed a contract with Washington.

10/26/48	REDSKINS (1-0) 17, Steelers (0-1) 14				32,593
Pit	7	7	0	0	14
Was	7	0	0	10	17
Pit	TD Clement, Glamp; PAT Glamp 2				
Was	TD Castiglia, Turley; PAT Poillon 2; FG Poillon				

Griffith Stadium—Dick Poillon kicked a 28-yard field goal with 20 seconds left to push the Redskins past the Steelers 17-14.

Poillon's kick capped a 10-point fourth-quarter rally to overcome a 14-7 deficit going into the final stanza. Doug Turley had tied the game earlier in the period with a fumble return for a touchdown.

The Redskins jumped on top in the first quarter, but Pittsburgh answered with two TD's before halftime. Washington took the opening kickoff and drove 73 yards to pay dirt, the touchdown coming when Sammy Baugh flipped a short pass to Jim Castiglia, who raced into the end zone to complete the 23-yard play. Pittsburgh answered as quarterback Johnny Clement scrambled 28 yards for a touchdown and then threw a 39-yard touchdown pass to Joe Glamp. The Steelers' second score came just before halftime and gave them a 14-7 lead.

The Washington defense put the clamps on Glamp, Clement and company for much of the second half, but the Redskin offense was equally stymied. The break the Skins needed came with 6:45 left in the game. Clement dropped back to pass at his own 44 and Mike Roussos ploughed into him. The ball bounced back to the 33 where Turley scooped it up and dashed in for the TD unchallenged. Poillon's extra point tied the game at 14.

Pittsburgh responded with a kickoff return into Washington territory at the 40. A few plays later it was looking even bleaker as Elibie Nickel took a pass and found some running room. Dan Sandifer, though, saved the game with a crunching tackle that popped the ball loose. The rookie then recovered the loose ball to give Baugh and the offense one last chance with 1:05 to play.

Two passes was all it took to get the Redskins down to the Steeler 17. A long, floating pass from Baugh to Hal Crisler covered the lion's share of the yardage. With 20 seconds left, Poillon lined up at the 28 with a slight angle to the right and drilled his kick through.

10/3/48	REDSKINS (2-0) 41, Giants (1-1) 10				32,593
NYG	3	0	7	0	10
Was	0	14	7	20	41
NYG	TD Scott; PAT Younce; FG Younce				
Was	TD Quirk, Crisler 2, Baugh, Sandifer, Castiglia; PAT Poillon 5				

Griffith Stadium—The Redskins outgained New York by a margin of better than four to one and pulled away from the Giants in the second half for the win.

The Giants got on the board first and were nominally in contention down just 14-10 in the third quarter. Len Younce booted a 28-yard field goal to account for the game's first score, but the Redskins responded early in the second period. Two Sammy Baugh passes to Dick Todd sparked a 73-yard drive that culminated in Ed Quirk's one-yard touchdown smash. Then Tommy Mont took the spotlight. He intercepted a pass to give Washington possession at its own 40 and finished up the drive when, filling in for an injured Baugh, he tossed a 35-yard touchdown pass to Hal Crisler. The Redskins led 14-3 at intermission.

Dick Poillon's weak punt and a pass interference penalty helped set up New York's only touchdown of the day, a four-yard run by Joe Scott, and it was 14-10. It was then that the Redskins established their dominance and tore off four unanswered touchdowns the rest of the way.

Dan Sandifer had a major hand in the first two TD's. First he returned a punt to midfield, and Baugh, still ailing but playing anyway, passed twice to Crisler and once to Bob Nussbaumer to get to the three. Two plays later, Baugh snuck it into the end zone for a 21-10 lead. Then, in the fourth quarter, the Redskins were back at their own 14. Baugh faded back to near the goal line before launching a rocket to Sandifer at midfield. The rookie was behind the defense, making a textbook over-the-shoulder catch and easily outdistancing the defense to pay dirt.

The Redskins continued to pour it on. Crisler caught his second touchdown pass of the day, this one from Baugh, and Jim Castiglia dragged a tackler over the goal line to score from four yards out to cap the scoring.

When it was over, the Redskins had outgained New York by an astounding 485 yards to 110. Confirming Washington's dominance was their edge in first downs, 24 to four.

10/10/48	STEELERS (2-1) 10, Redskins (2-1) 7				28,969
Was	0	0	0	7	7
Pit	0	0	7	3	10
Was	TD Crisler; PAT Poillon				
Pit	TD Clement; PAT Glamp; FG Glamp				

Forbes Field—Two weeks after losing to the Redskins on a late field goal, the Steelers turned the tables on Washington, getting a 12-yard field goal from Joe Glamp with 33 seconds left to take the win.

The game was scoreless until midway through the third quarter. This a due in part to solid defense played by both teams. The larger factors in the lack of scoring, however, were the numerous fumbles committed by both teams and the league-record 23 penalties called by the officials. One might suspect some home cooking as 17 of those infractions were against the visiting Redskins.

The Steelers got the break they needed when Bob Nussbaumer fumbled a punt and they took over at the Washington 20. Soon after that, quarterback Johnny Clement snuck up the middle two yards over the goal line and Glamp's conversion made it 7-0.

After the ensuing kickoff, the Redskins embarked on a 65-yard touchdown march. Well, perhaps it's not accurate to call it a march as it was a meandering, back-and-forth path they took to pay dirt due to six penalties called during the possession. Dick Todd returned the kickoff to the 35, but an unsportsmanlike conduct penalty immediately backed them up. Ed Quirk ran for 14 yards, Bob Nussbaumer caught two Sammy Baugh passes for 14 yards each but after all three of those plays major fouls were called against the Redskins.

They finally staggered to the Steeler 19. From there, Baugh fired a bullet to Hal Crisler, who had run away from the defense in the right corner of the end zone. After scanning the field for penalty flags and finding none, they lined up for the extra point and Dick Poillon's kick was good to tie the game with about four minutes gone in the fourth quarter.

Neither team mounted a serious threat until the Steelers' game-winning drive, which received some assistance from the men in stripes. Pittsburgh took possession on downs at the Washington 41 with about a minute and a half to go. It appeared that Nussbaumer had squashed the threat when he intercepted Clement's pass, but a penalty against the Redskins nullified the turnover. Then Glamp missed a 21-yard field goal, but the Redskins were offside. Another offside pushed the line of scrimmage down to the three and Glamp's game-winner came on the next play.

Judge Upset with Marshall Actions, Remarks

October 15—George Preston Marshall should be more careful about the people with whom he picks fights. It's not good to make an enemy of a judge.

But Marshall did just that at the conclusion of the Redskins' 10-7 loss to the Steelers. After one penalty kept alive a late Pittsburgh drive, an offside call negated a blocked field goal. Joe Glamp then booted the game winner for the Steelers on the second chance with 33 seconds left.

At the end of the game, Marshall rushed the field and protested the penalty. Exactly what he said is unclear, but his comments drew the ire of one of the targets of his remarks, Judge Samuel Weiss of the Pennsylvania Court of Common pleas.

Weiss, a former U. S. Congressman, was one of the officials during the game and apparently Marshall thought that he was less than honorable.

"George Marshall has questioned my integrity," Weiss said. "I won't allow him or anyone else to do that.

Weiss denied a report that he would resign as an official if Marshall was not disciplined for his actions and words.

Even though films examined by Washington-area reporters clearly indicated that the Redskins were not offside on the play in question, Marshall had calmed down a few days later. He did point out, however, that of the five officials working the game, four were residents of Pennsylvania.

10/17/48	Eagles (2-1-1) 45, REDSKINS (2-2) 0				35,584
Phi	14	10	14	7	45
Was	0	0	0	0	0
Phi	TD Pihos, Van Buren 3, Pritchard, Steele; PAT Patton 6; FG Patton				

Griffith Stadium—"I don't care to discuss anything tonight."

That was George Preston Marshall's lone utterance after the game and it was quite appropriate since there really wasn't much to talk about concerning the Eagle's trouncing of Marshall's squad.

This one was a blowout from the get-go. The Eagles scored on their first four possessions and failed on the fifth only because time expired in the first half. In the first quarter, they reeled off long drives that resulted in touchdowns by Pete Pihos and Steve Van Buren. In the second, Jack Myers intercepted a Sammy Baugh pass to set up a field goal before Philly put together another sustained drive: this one 67 yards to Van Buren's second TD of the day, and a four-yard run to make it 24-0 at intermission.

Meanwhile, the Redskins were going nowhere—not that they had many opportunities to advance the ball. The Eagles were in the process of racking up a league record-tying 28 first downs for the game, eating up both yards and clock.

In the second half, Washington did manage to advance to the Eagle 13, but gave the ball up on downs at that point, losing their only genuine scoring opportunity. Their deepest penetration other than that was the Philadelphia 47.

10/24/48	Redskins (3-2) 23, PACKERS (3-3) 7			28,572	
Was	6	7	0	10	23
GB	7	0	0	0	7
Was	TD Sandifer, Farmer, Todd; PAT Poillon; FG Poillon				
GB	TD Goodnight; PAT Cody				

State Fair Park, Milwaukee—Dan Sandifer returned the opening kickoff 96 yards for a touchdown to spark the Redskins' win over the Packers.

From the four, Sandifer found his wall and broke into open ground at his own 20. As he approached the goal, a trio of Packers was gaining ground and one caught up to him at around the five. All the hit did, though, was propel him into the end zone. Dick Poillon missed the conversion and it was 6-0 twelve seconds into the game.

Green Bay responded, taking the ensuing kickoff and acting like the 14-point favorites that they were. The drove 80 yards to a touchdown with the payoff coming on a 14-yard touchdown pass from Jack Jacobs to Clyde Goodnight.

That was the first of five excursions the Pack made inside the Washington 15, but the only one that produced any points. On some occasions the Redskin defense rose to the occasion and drew the line right there; on others, the Packers shot themselves in their collective foot.

The Redskins didn't penetrate Green Bay territory nearly that frequently, but they were much more efficient when they did. They failed to score just twice after crossing the midfield stripe, with the clock running out on them at halftime and at the end of the game.

Washington took the lead for good early in the second quarter with one of their successful invasions of Green Bay's end of the field. After taking a punt on their own 38, Sammy Baugh put together a nice mix of runs and passes to steadily move his team towards the goal line. They converted a fourth and two at the three as Poillon squeezed out the necessary distance with little to spare. On the next play Tom Farmer got the last yard and Poillon booted the point after for a 13-7 lead.

It stayed that way through the third quarter, with the Redskins living on the edge with all of the Packer threats. Following one of those threats that died at the Washington three the Skins launched their game-clinching drive. They advanced the first 64 yards relying exclusively on the ground game, with a pair of penalties on Green Bay helping things along. From the 33, Baugh took to the air, going to Dick Todd for 15 yards to the 18. Two plays later Todd took a shovel pass from Baugh, weaved his way through the defense taking advantage of blocks by Doug Turley and Fred Boensch, and crossed the goal line standing up.

Sandifer intercepted a pass soon after that and Poillon closed out the scoring with a 20-yard field goal with 10 minutes left to play.

10/31/48	REDSKINS (4-2) 59, Yanks (2-5) 21			29,758	
Bos	14	0	7	0	21
Was	14	14	10	21	59
Bos	TD Paschal 2, Golding; PAT Zimmerman 3				
Was	TD Sandifer 2, Todd 2, Poillon, Hartley, Tereshinski, Crisler; PAT Poillon 8; FG Poillon				

Griffith Stadium—The Redskins scored early and often, racking up eight touchdowns to rout the Yanks. Sammy Baugh provided a good chunk of the offense as he passed for a league-record 446 yards. Four of his throws were good for touchdowns from distances ranging from 38 to 78 yards.

Boston got on the board first after recovering a fumble at the Washington 18. Bill Paschal went up the gut four times, scoring on the last try from two yards out.

The Redskins responded with two quick touchdowns, both scored by Dan Sandifer. From his own 28, Baugh hit the rookie back in full stride at midfield. With each step Sandifer opened more daylight between himself and his lone pursuer and he scored easily. A few plays after the ensuing kickoff Sandifer stepped in front of Roy Zimmerman's pass, picked it off, faked three potential tacklers onto the ground, and completed a 35-yard return for the TD.

Before the first quarter was out the Yanks had tied it by driving 80 yards to a touchdown connection between Zimmerman and Paschal that covered 22 yards. That would prove to be the high water mark for the visitors.

One second-quarter touchdown drive started with Sandifer's second interception, and another after Howard Hartley recovered a fumble at the Redskin 38. Both scores came on Baugh passes. Dick Todd got the first, a 76-yard catch and run, and Hal Crisler received the other from 49 yards out. Those scores and Dick Poillon's conversions made it 28-14 at halftime.

Baugh got his final scoring pass of the day to cap a 72-yard foray that started after the second-half kickoff. This one went to Todd again and covered 38 yards.

Poillon added a field goal to make it 38-14 going into the final period. The highlight of the Skins' three fourth-quarter scores was Sandifer's second scoring interception return of the day. This one of 48 yards was made of equal parts speed and elusiveness.

Bagarus is Back

Nov 5—Steve Bagarus is back.

The 1945 All-Pro back returned to the Redskins after spending a season with the Los Angeles Rams. In need of depth in the backfield, the team evidently is willing to forget the troubles that led to the departure of Bagarus after the 1946 season.

11/7/48	Redskins (5-2) 23, YANKS (2-6) 7			9,867	
Was	6	3	7	7	23
Bos	0	7	0	0	7
Was	TD Mont, Poillon, Farmer; PAT Poillon 2; FG Poillon				
Bos	TD Heywood; PAT Zimmerman				

Fenway Park—Tommy Mont, who came in for an injured Sammy Baugh, made a dazzling run for the Redskins' first score in the win over the Yanks.

As for Baugh, he recovered quite nicely, coming back to throw two second-half touchdown passes to wrap it up for the Skins.

Dick Poillon helped give Washington a field position advantage with a punt that bounced out-of-bounds at the Boston six. The Yanks quick kicked, and Dan Sandifer returned the boot to the Boston 46. From there, Baugh passed for a first down and was trying to pass again when the pocket collapsed. He tried to make what he could up the middle, but he was trapped and injured an ankle.

After Baugh was carried from the field, Mont stepped behind center with the line of scrimmage at the 34. He dropped back to pass, but saw an opening and took off towards the right sideline. After waiting for and receiving a couple of blocks around the 20, he reversed his field and cut a diagonal swath to the end zone and it was 6-0.

Mont then led a drive to a 16-yard Poillon field goal early in the second quarter. Later in the second, Jim Castiglia fumbled while running off tackle and the Yanks recovered at the Redskin 42. One play later, it was 9-7 as Roy Zimmerman threw to Ralph Heywood at the 30. One block took care of the only obstacle between Heywood and the goal line and Zimmerman booted the point after.

That would prove to be as close as it would get. The Redskins opened the third quarter with Baugh back at the helm and his 37-yard pass to Bob Nussbaumer was the big gainer in a 68-yard TD drive. The payoff came when Poillon went to his knees to gather in Baugh's pass from four yards out. A Boston fumble led to a 10-yard, fourth-quarter touchdown bullet from Baugh to Tom Farmer.

11/14/48	REDSKINS (6-2) 46, Lions (1-7) 21				32,528
Det	7	7	0	7	21
Was	3	0	16	27	46
Det	TD Wilson, Margucci, Dudley; PAT Pregulman 3				
Was	TD Todd 2, Quirk 2, Farmer, Nussbaumer; PAT Poillon 4, Peebles; Safety Koniszewski				

Griffith Stadium—The Redskins blew by the Lions with 27 unanswered points in the fourth quarter to take the win.

The victory was not nearly as easy as the final score would indicate. Detroit held a 14-3 lead at halftime after turning an interception into one touchdown and putting together a 50-yard drive for another. Washington had a good first-half drive itself, moving 84 yards in 16 plays. It was all for naught, though, as Sammy Baugh's fourth-down pass from the Lion six fell incomplete.

The home team climbed into the lead in the third quarter. Baugh capped a nice drive when he threw a five-yard TD pass to Dick Todd. Then Clyde Erhardt picked off a pass to set up a two-yard touchdown smash by Ed Quirk. Finally, late in the period, tackle John Koniszewski took aim at Bill Dudley in the end zone and nailed the star back for a safety to make the score 19-14.

Detroit was not done, however. Jim Gillette pilfered Baugh's pass and returned it to the Washington 41 early in the fourth quarter. Fred Enke quickly took advantage, firing to Bob Mann for 22 yards and for 13 to Dudley in the end zone for a 21-19 lead. The stage seemed to be set for a taut, seesaw finish.

It was not to be; Hal Crisler helped see to that. First Crisler caught a slant from Baugh in stride and wasn't dragged down until he'd gained 55 yards. Shortly after that Quirk bucked across from two yards out to push Washington into the lead 26-21. Then Crisler drew a bead on an Enke pass and picked it off to set the Skins up in Lion territory. That led to Baugh's 13-yard touchdown pass to Todd and the rout was on.

Dan Sandifer intercepted his eleventh pass of the year, tying an NFL record. After that pick, Baugh threw his third touchdown of the day, this one going to Ed Farmer. Sammy slung TD pass number four on the day to Bob Nussbaumer with just a few ticks left on the clock.

11/21/48	EAGLES (7-1-1) 42, Redskins (6-3) 21				36,254
Was	0	14	0	7	21
Phi	14	7	14	7	42
Was	TD Crisler 2, Poillon; PAT Poillon 3				
Phi	TD Van Buren, Armstrong, Myers, Craft, Pihos, Ferrante; PAT Patton 6				

Shibe Park—The Redskins came into the game with a chance to pull within a half game of the division-leading Eagles, but they laid an egg, leaving with only the faintest title hopes.

Philly took care of matters early, dashing to a 21-0 lead in the second quarter. Their three touchdowns came at the end of three

businesslike, sustained drives. After the third score, a 29-yard Jack Myers dash off tackle that was embarrassingly easy, the Redskins made their bid to make it a competitive game.

With possession at their own 28, the Redskins embarked on a drive. Sammy Baugh completed passes to Dan Sandifer and Dick Todd for 10 and 11 yards, respectively. In between, Dick Poillon dashed for 14 yards and the Skins were at the Eagle 30. From there, Hal Crisler completely eluded the Eagle defense and was alone when Baugh spied him in the end zone and pitched it to him for the score.

Late in the half Baugh struck again. Passing from his own 21, he was trapped and knocked down but was able to bounce up and fling another one to Crisler, who was waiting at midfield, again with no Eagle within shouting distance. Hal covered the remaining half of the field in short order and Poillon's extra point made it 21-14 at the half.

Just after intermission they had an excellent opportunity to tie it up after George Cheverko intercepted Tommy Thompson's pass at the Eagle 36. The threat didn't last long as Steve Van Buren zeroed in on Baugh's pass on the very next play and picked it off at the 25. If that didn't break the Redskins' collective back, the ensuing drive did. After the Eagles pounded out 50 yards exclusively on the ground, Thompson lofted a pass over the head of Cheverko and into the hands of Russ Craft for a 25-yard TD pass to make it 28-14.

It was 35-14 before the Redskins scored again, on a 93-yard fumble return for a touchdown by Poillon.

11/28/48	BEARS (9-1) 48, Redskins (6-4) 13				42,299
Was	0	7	0	6	13
Chi	20	21	0	7	48
Was	TD Bagarus, Youel; PAT Poillon				
Chi	TD McAfee, Evans 2, Kavanaugh, Keane, Kindt, Gulyanics; PAT Lujack 6				

Wrigley Field—Handing a superior opponent the ball three times on fumbles in the first four minutes of play is a recipe for disaster, and that's what the Redskins cooked up in Chicago. The Bears capitalized on all three of those early turnovers for a 20-0 lead and never looked back in the course of thrashing the Skins.

The Redskins' generosity started up early as Howard Hartley fumbled on their first play from scrimmage and the Bears took over at the Washington 14. Two plays later George McAfee barreled over from the one for a 7-0 Bear lead.

The next time the Bear offense took the field it was 20-0. That unit wasn't needed to cash in on the next two Washington fumbles as defensive back Fred Evans scooped each of them up before breezing into the end zone. First it was Bob Nussbaumer on the giving end with Evans scoring from 10 yards out, then Hartley coughing it up for a second time and Evans going 16 yards. Johnny Lujack's conversion after the third score failed—about the only thing to go right for the Redskins.

Washington then made some noise, twice driving deep into Bear territory, but came up empty each time. The Bears decided to show that they could get it done of offense after the second failed Redskin thrust. They moved 96 yards behind the passing of Sid Luckman, with Luckman's final pass of the drive covering 10 yards to Ken Kavanaugh to make it 27-0.

It was 34-0 before the Redskins managed a score. It took them 12 plays to cover the 68 yards to the end zone. The drive was largely a Sammy Baugh production with his passes going to Doug Turley and Steve Bagarus covering large chunks of ground down to the Chicago 14. From there, Bagarus found a hole in the coverage and was wide open down the middle a few steps from the goal line when Baugh zipped the ball to him and the receiver scored easily.

They probably didn't need to, but the Bears responded quickly, embarking on a penalty-aided drive to make it 41-7 just before halftime. It remained that way until the fourth quarter when the Redskins finally got their chance to capitalize on a Bear mistake. Jim Peebles recovered a fumble at the Bear 25 and Jim Youel scored from the one on a quarterback sneak.

12/5/48	Rams (5-5-1) 41, REDSKINS (6-5) 13				32,970
LA	7	20	14	0	**41**
Was	0	7	6	0	**13**
LA	TD Gehrke 2, Hoerner, Washington, Bouley,				
	Hoffman; PAT Waterfield 5				
Was	TD Todd, Taylor; PAT Poillon				

Griffith Stadium—For the third straight week the Redskins gave up more than 40 points to an opponent as the Rams took their turn at spanking the hapless Redskins.

Just like the week before against the Bears, the Redskins made mistakes that helped their opponent to an early lead. Sammy Baugh's arm was hit as he attempted to pass and the ball fluttered into the arms of Dick Hoerner, who returned the pick to the Washington 47. Soon after that, Hoerner was on the receiving end of 17-yard touchdown pass from Bob Waterfield, catching the ball at around the 10 and easily gliding into the end zone. The Rams had less ground to cover after the next Washington turnover, just 16 yards after Baugh and Eddie Saenz botched a handoff. It took them two plays, the second a TD pass from Waterfield to Gil Bouley. Howard Hartley blocked Waterfield's conversion attempt so it was 13-0 with five minutes elapsed in the second quarter.

It got to 20-0 before the Redskins could muster a score. Jim Castiglia ran a kickoff back to the Washington 48 and Baugh and Dick Todd took over from there. Todd made a spectacular stab of one pass for a 24-yard gain and later was wide open for a more routine grab of Baugh's seven-yard pitch for a touchdown to make it 20-7.

Fred Gehrke quickly dumped cold water on any comeback hopes that may have started simmering, however, when he took the ensuing kickoff and burst up the middle. He broke through the wall at around the 30 and after that the only man who could catch him was safety Dan Sandifer. It looked as though the defender had an angle on Gehrke but all Sandifer could get a hold of was turf on a diving attempt at the returner's ankles at the five.

With the score 27-7 at intermission, Waterfield tossed two third-quarter TD passes to turn the rest of the proceedings into extended garbage time.

12/12/48	Redskins (7-5) 28, Giants (4-8) 21				23,158
Was	0	7	14	7	**28**
NYG	7	7	0	7	**21**
Was	TD Todd, Quirk, Taylor 2; PAT Poillon 4				
NYG	TD Minisi, Swiacki, Costes; PAT Younce 3				

Polo Grounds—Sammy Baugh threw his third touchdown pass of the day, a 66-yarder to Hugh Taylor with just over a minute remaining in the game, to pull the Redskins past the Giants.

The hosts drew first blood in this seesaw contest. They jumped to a 14-0 lead through the first quarter and a half of play. Francis Regan got things going for New York when he cut short a promising Washington drive with an interception of Baugh at the Giant 32. Charley Conerly led an efficient scoring drive of seven plays from there, completing passes to Ray Poole and Jim Swiacki to move into position for the payoff pitch. That went to Skippy Minisi, who put a move on Tommy Mont to get clear to gather in Conerly's 14-yard pass.

In the second quarter it was again Conerly torching the Redskins with his arm. The Giant quarterback's precision tosses moved his team 76 yards for a touchdown, the score coming on a five-yard pass to Swiacki. Len Younce converted to make it 14-0.

The Redskins started to climb back into it shortly before halftime. For a change, it was another team giving the Skins an assist as New York coughed the ball up at its own 27. It took just one play of classic Baugh to get into the end zone. He waited patiently as Dick Todd got position on his defender Tex Coulter and then fired the ball into the only spot where it could be complete. Todd and Coulter slid into the end zone together as the defender was clutching the receiver, who had a firm grip on the ball. The teams went into the locker room with New York up 14-7.

It took less than six minutes for Washington to even things up. Ed Quirk punched it over from a yard out to cap a 60-yard thrust and Dick Poillon's point after knotted it at 14. Clearly having the momentum now, the Skins quickly moved into the lead on their next possession with Taylor spinning to avoid defender Ken Keuper as he caught Baugh's 24-yard offering for the score.

The Giants were not done. They embarked on an 82-yard march to tie it up, with 35 of those yards coming on Redskin penalties. Ray Costes tallied the tying points as he pushed his way through the middle for the final yard to pay dirt early in the fourth quarter.

Three subsequent Washington possessions came up empty and a tie appeared to be likely as the Redskins worked from their own 34 with less than 90 seconds left to play. Then Baugh and Taylor teamed up again, with Sammy airing it out to the Giant 25. Taylor was guarded by Carl Fenneme, but he worked his way free to catch the pass. The defender wound up on the ground due to a clever fake by Taylor and the end easily trotted in for the winning touchdown.

1949
Head Coach: John Whelchel (3-3-1), Herman Ball (1-4)
Record: 4-7-1, Fourth in NFL East

Dec 28	
Edwards out as Redskins Coach	
Turk is moved to executive post, search is on for successor	

Bryant Turns Down Redskins Job

Dec 31—Former Maryland head coach Paul "Bear" Bryant has turned down an offer to become head coach of the Redskins.

Bryan, currently the coach at Kentucky, said that he felt an obligation to finish what he started with the Wildcats. He was the first choice of the Redskins to replace Turk Edwards. Now the search for Edwards' successor will start anew.

Feb 5	
Adm. John Whelchel is Redskins' New Coach	
Former Navy coach has been out of football five years	

May 26	
Baugh's Last Year?	
Reports indicate Slingin' Sammy may retire after '49 campaign	

9/26/49	**CARDINALS 38 (1-0) 38, Redskins (0-1) 7**			24,136
Was	0	7	0	0	7
Chi	7	7	7	17	38
Was	TD Sandifer; PAT Poillon			
Chi	TD Trippi 2, Harder 2, Dimancheff; PAT Harder 5; FG Harder			

Comiskey Park—The Cardinals toyed with the Redskins for a half and then broke the game open with 24 unanswered points in the final 30 minutes.

It took just a few minutes for Chicago to get on the board as Paul Christman tossed a 34-yard scoring pass to Charley Trippi. Early in the second quarter, the Redskins responded, driving 86 yards into the end zone. Sammy Baugh targeted Hal Crisler and Eddie Saenz for completions for first downs and capped the march with a five-yard bullet to Dan Sandifer. Dick Poillon's conversion tied it at seven.

That would be as close as the Redskins would get. Chicago star Trippi personally manufactured the next Cardinal score with a nice punt return, a 28-yard jaunt off left tackle to get his team close to the last stripe and then a three-yard slant into the end zone.

The scoreboard saying that the Redskins were in the game at the half at 14-7 was an illusion. Reality came early in the third quarter as the Trippi and Pat Harder swept through the Redskins run defense, such as it was, for large chunks of yardage in a ground-based touchdown drive. Harder took the scoring honors this time, ploughing a 14-yard path to the goal line to make it 21-7.

If that wasn't the clincher, it came on the second play of the fourth quarter when Harter scored again, this time from a yard out. Trippi was the main mover in that drive, breaking into the open in a quick-hitter for 55 yards to the Washington 19.

10/3/49	**Redskins (1-1) 27, STEELERS (1-1) 14**			30,000
Was	6	0	14	7	27
Pit	0	14	0	0	14
Was	TD Taylor 2, Sandifer; PAT Goode 3			
Pit	TD Papach, Nuzum; PAT Glamp 2			

Forbes Field—Sammy Baugh threw three touchdown passes as the Redskins rallied in the second half to beat the Steelers.

The visitors took a 6-0 first-quarter lead on Baugh's first TD pass of the day, a perfectly placed, 25-yard lob to Hugh Taylor. They had moved into Steeler territory via the ground route with Rob Goode carrying much of the load. After getting to the 37 that way, Baugh took to the air with completions to Taylor and Harry Dowda preceding the payoff pitch.

Pittsburgh owned the second quarter. They got off to a good start late in the first when an exchange of punts gave them good field position at their own 44. Bobby Gage went back to pass and seemed to be trapped, but he broke free and scooted 26 yards to the Redskin six. After two line smashes gained four yards, George Papach found a big hole and blew through it for the touchdown. Joe Glamp booted the point after for a 7-6 Steeler lead.

Five minutes later, the Steelers expanded their lead. Starting from their own 35, they ran the ball seven straight times to get it into the end zone. The score came on a 27-yard reverse with Jerry Nuzum carrying around left end. Glamp again converted and Pittsburgh took a 14-6 lead into the locker room.

Baugh found his stride again in the third quarter. He first went to Dan Sandifer for 35 yards and a touchdown to pull his team within 14-13. Then, later in the third, Baugh zeroed in on Taylor again, this time with a 58-yard bomb that put the Redskins ahead to stay.

10/9/49	**Giants (2-1) 45, REDSKINS (1-2) 35**			30,073
NYG	14	10	21	0	45
Was	14	7	0	14	35
NYG	TD Roberts 3, Scott, Mullins, Fischer; PAT Agajanian; FG Agajanian			
Was	TD Taylor 2, Stout, Crisler, Livingston; PAT Poillon			

Griffith Stadium—The Giants scored 21 points in a span of less than three minutes in the third quarter to pull away from the Redskins.

During the first half, this was a competitive, entertaining affair with signal callers Sammy Baugh and Charley Conerly engaged in a passing duel. The Redskins started the game with Harry Gilmer at the quarterback slot but Baugh replaced him after the starter threw two interceptions. The Giants missed a field goal attempt after the second pick that Gilmer threw, but the first led to a 12-yard touchdown run by Choo-Choo Roberts.

Sammy came out firing, making Bones Taylor his favorite target. The pair connected for six and 31 yards before, from the Giant 28, Baugh flipped to Taylor at the 17. The end had only to elude an attempted ankle tackle near the goal line to score, and he did so with ease.

The furious pace continued as a pass interference call moved the Giants to the Washington 10, leading to Joe Scott's one-yard scoring blast. It took the home team just two plays after the kickoff to even it back up. Again it was Sammy to Bones, this time covering 78 yards as Taylor caught the pass near midfield and outsprinted the Giants to the end zone.

Washington moved into the lead in the second period after Howie Livingston intercepted Conerly to give the Skins possession at the Giant 46. Baugh moved his team with his arm and his legs, scrambling for 16 yards before zipping an 11-yarder to Dan Sandifer. Fullback Pete Stout pounded out the last yard and Dick Poillon's conversion made it 21-14.

The Giants garnered a touchdown and a field goal before intermission to take a 24-21 lead. There was little indication that that was the beginning of the end for the Redskins. Gilmer returned at quarterback in the third and dropped a nice pass into the arms of Taylor, who was still in full stride as he crossed the goal line. A penalty, however, nullified the TD and the Redskins wound up punting. The Giants' scoring outburst ensued.

It started with a lightning-quick drive. Conerly passed to Ray Poole for 29 yards and then went to Cletus Fischer for 26 and a touchdown. On the play after the kickoff, Harry Dowda fumbled and the Giants were back in business. Two plays later Roberts completely eluded detection by the Washington defense and was all alone to gather in Conerly's 25-yard touchdown pass for a 38-21 lead.

The Skins' situation at that point was desperate but not hopeless, given the seesaw nature of the contest. Sandifer raised hopes by taking the ensuing kickoff at the two and heading first to his right, then to the left for 70 yards before being dragged down. Baugh went back in and moved them to a first and goal at the three. Then disaster struck.

Emlen Tunnell intercepted Baugh's pass in the end zone and ran it out to the Giant 38. A two-yard loss was only a temporary setback as Roberts took a handoff, found a huge hole up the middle, kicked it into high gear and rolled untouched to a touchdown.

Trailing 45-21 going into the fourth quarter, Gilmer directed two touchdown drives to make the final a bit more respectable.

10/16/49	REDSKINS (2-2) 38, Bulldogs (0-4) 14				26,278
NY	0	7	7	0	14
Was	7	14	7	10	38
NY	TD Layne, Heywood; PAT Scollard				
Was	TD Stout, Crisler 3, Dowda; PAT Poillon 5; FG Poillon				

Griffith Stadium—Sammy Baugh threw four touchdown passes, three of them to Hal Crisler, to lead to Redskins to an easy win over the Bulldogs.

New York started out as though it intended to make a game of it. Bobby Layne led them 67 yards down to the Washington two, but halfback Joe Golding fumbled while fighting for the stripe. Frank Seno recovered in the end zone for a touchback.

Midway through the first quarter Baugh got the Redskins moving. He completed three passes to Dan Sandifer to spark a 44-yard touchdown drive. Jeff Stout got the six points when he bulled over from a half yard out.

Shortly after the second quarter commenced the Bulldogs coughed the ball up again, this time at the Redskin 30. The ensuing touchdown drive was capped by a spectacular play by Crisler. As he got his hands on Baugh's 25-yard pass, his body was horizontal to the ground, which was a few feet underneath him. The wingback tucked the ball in as he somersaulted into the end zone. Baugh's second TD pass to Crisler came two and a half minutes later to make it 21-0.

The Bulldogs did dent the scoreboard before halftime as Layne snuck over from less than a foot out, and put a brief scare into the home team by driving 64 yards for a touchdown early in the second half. Layne then led another drive that threatened to tie the score, but it fizzled at the Washington 23

That was enough to wake up the Skins' offense. They quickly moved to the New York 44 with two Baugh passes with a few runs mixed in. From there it was Baugh to—who else? —Crisler. He took the pass at the 25, spun away from his defender and raced over the goal line.

That made it 28-14 and Dick Poillon extended the lead to 17 on the first play of the fourth quarter with a field goal. Baugh's fourth touchdown pass covered 67 yards and went to Harry Dowda. The rookie took the pass at around the Bulldog 31, twisted away from an attempted tackle and scooted into the end zone.

10/23/49	EAGLES (4-1) 49, Redskins (2-3) 14				28,855
Was	7	0	7	0	14
Phi	14	21	7	7	49
Was	TD Goode, Stout; PAT Poillon 2				
Phi	TD Van Buren, Pritchard 2, Thompson, Armstrong, Ziegler; PAT Patton 7				

Shibe Park—The Redskins were pathetic in falling to the Eagles for the fifth straight time.

It took 10 minutes for Philadelphia to establish its dominance. First Tommy Thompson launched a 75-yard touchdown pass to Bosh Pritchard and then Steve Van Buren pushed his way over from three yards out culminating a 31-yard drive after an interception.

The Redskins did respond. Rob Goode took a handoff from this own 46 and found large quantities of daylight up the middle. Frank Reagan gave chase but the running back was as good as gone.

That was the high water mark for the Redskins. In the second quarter the Eagles drove 57 yards to Thompson's one-yard sneak for one touchdown and then the quarterback used his arm, launching a 77-yard TD bomb to Pritchard. The receiver split the defenders and streaked down the middle of the field to pay dirt. Another Eagle touchdown made it 35-7 at the half and both sides emptied their benches after intermission.

Philadelphia had racked up at least 40 points in four of the games in their current streak of dominance over the Redskins, scoring 38 in the other "contest."

10/30/49	Redskins (2-3-1) 14, BULLDOGS (0-5-1) 14				3,678
Was	0	7	7	0	14
NY	7	0	0	7	14
Was	TD Taylor, Cochran; PAT Poillon 2				
NY	TD Golding, Scollard; PAT Scollard 2				

Polo Grounds—After getting pounded by a good team the week before, the Redskins explored another depth of mediocrity: tying the winless Bulldogs. New York's performance could hardly be attributed to home field advantage as an intimate gathering of 3,678 witnessed this one at the Polo Grounds.

The Bulldogs got on the board first, driving 76 yards for a touchdown with the game less than six minutes old. Bobby Layne was the prime mover in the march, first hitting Nick Scollard for 34 yards to get his team close and then firing to Joe Golding for the final six yards.

After a couple of drives fizzled out, the Redskins evened it up in the second period. The scoring march was, as usual, a Sammy Baugh production. Bones Taylor was the favored target as he first caught a pass goof for 28 yards to midfield and then gathered in a 50-yard bomb from Baugh for the TD. On the touchdown play, defender Harold Prescott went to knock the ball down but the pass was perfectly placed and Prescott waved at air before waving goodbye to Taylor as the end rolled across the goal line.

There was precious little action after that until midway through the third quarter when Dan Sandifer jump-started a touchdown drive when he returned a punt to the 'Dog 36. Fullback Leon Cochran was the workhorse, first catching a 17-yard pass to the 11 and then ploughing over from the one to put his team up 14-7.

The lead proved to be short-lived. Baugh threw an interception and the Bulldogs took possession at the Washington 40. Two plays later Scollard beat Sandifer down the sideline and gathered in Layne's pass to knot it up at 14.

Each team threatened in the late going, but both came up empty. Baugh completed a pass to Hal Crisler, who wasn't satisfied with a 37-yard gain to the Bulldog 34. He attempted a lateral to Eddie Saenz but the pitch went awry and New York's Jim Wade wound up with the ball. The Bulldogs then moved into position to attempt a 39-yard field goal, but it was short.

The same could be said of the Redskins' efforts on this day.

11/6/49	REDSKINS (3-3-1) 27, Steelers (4-3) 14			26,038
Pit	0	7	7	0	14
Was	0	7	0	20	27
Pit	TD Finks, Shipkey; PAT Glamp 2			
Was	TD Taylor, Stout 2, Dowda; PAT Poillon 3			

Griffith Stadium—The Redskins exploded for 20 fourth-quarter points to move past the Steelers and take the win.

The teams exchanged second period touchdowns and went into the locker room tied at seven. The home team drew first blood with Harry Gilmer jumping in the air to launch a bomb from just outside midfield. Bones Taylor was in a crowd at the six and somehow came up with the ball. He pushed his way over the goal line back first. Pittsburgh responded immediately, embarking on an 80-yard drive that culminated in Jim Finks' five-yard touchdown run.

A drive consisting of 11 runs and one pass play worked for 66 yards and six points for the Steelers early in the third period. Fullback Jerry Shipkey blasted for the final inches for a 14-7 Steeler lead.

Little transpired between then and the outset of the fourth quarter that would indicate that the Redskins would suddenly break out of their scoring doldrums. After a punt on the first play of the final period, they had possession at their own 26. The play call was conservative, fullback Pete Stout off left tackle.

The Skins got more than they bargained for. Stout found daylight and continued towards the left sideline. The only Steeler to have a shot at him tried to push him out-of-bounds at midfield, but the would-be tackler missed and Stout was gone.

A few minutes later Dick Poillon tried to break the tie with a 40-yard field goal but it was just short. The Steelers had the ball, but not for long as Al DeMao batted Layne's pass into the air and Howie Livingston pulled it in and rumbled to the Pittsburgh 42. Sammy Baugh zipped a pass to Taylor for 11 yards and then went to Rob Goode, who was tackled just inches shy of pay dirt. Stout got the remaining distance on the next play. Poillon missed the extra point so it remained 20-14.

Pittsburgh responded quickly with quarterback Jim Finks throwing to Elbie Nickel for 30 yards and a first down in Washington territory at the 39. Dan Sandifer killed the rally attempt on the next play, stepping in front of Finks' pass and flashing 59 yards to the Steeler 17. Harry Dowda blasted in from a yard out to close the scoring.

Nov 7

Whelchel Out After 7 Games
by 'Mutual Consent'
Line coach Herman Ball takes
over as interim head man

11/13/49	Eagles (7-1) 44, REDSKINS (3-4-1) 21			31,170
Phi	14	16	14	0	44
Was	7	0	7	7	21
Phi	TD Pritchard, Scott, Ferrante 2, Van Buren, Pihos; PAT Patton 5; FG Patton			
Was	TD Stout, Dowda, Taylor; PAT Poillon 3			

Griffith Stadium—New coach, same story.

George Preston Marshall fired coach John Whelchel during the week, but Herman Ball, the new pilot, was equally unable to lift the squad to a state where it could be competitive with the Eagles. Philadelphia jumped to a 30-7 halftime lead and coasted to the win.

The Eagle offense was dominant. Tommy Thompson threw four touchdown passes and Steve Van Buren led a varied rushing attack that racked up 254 yards. As a result of the Philly offense's efficiency, the Eagles did not punt the ball once, a feat achieved just once before in league history.

The Philadelphia attack started to bully the Skins from the get-go. Van Buren powered an 80-yard drive after the opening kickoff. Bosh Pritchard got the payoff, scoring on a five-yard run.

Washington, with Harry Gilmer calling the signals, responded immediately. Gilmer hit Dan Sandifer for 28 yards to midfield and then, a few plays later, launched one to the five. As defender Russ Craft stood there waiting to intercept the ball, Pete Stout swooped in, took it away from Craft and scampered into the end zone to tie the game.

The deadlock lasted three plays after the ensuing kickoff. Thompson threw to Clyde Scott, who was off to the races. Only Tommy Mont stood between Scott and pay dirt and the runner dispatched the defender at around the Washington 30 and was pulling up as he approached the goal line.

Cliff Patton kicked a field goal early in the second period to stretch the Eagle lead to 17-7. Doubts about the outcome were completely erased soon after that when Thompson threw a 14-yard TD pass to Jack Ferrante. Bob Goode had the receiver in his arms shy of the goal line, but Ferrante shook loose and dove over the stripe.

A Van Buren touchdown made it 30-7 at the half and Thompson got TD passes number three and four in the third quarter to certify the rout. In between, Harry Dowda scored on a nifty 21-yard run to provide a small thrill for those remaining at Griffith Stadium.

11/20/49	BEARS (6-3) 31, Redskins (3-5-1) 21			30,148
Was	7	0	0	14	21
Chi	7	17	7	0	31
Was	TD Shoener, Mont 2; PAT Poillon 3			
Chi	TD Keane 2, Boone, Kavanaugh; PAT Lujack 4; FG Blanda			

Wrigley Field—Johnny Lujack threw three touchdown passes and Sid Luckman added one more as the Bears easily handled the Redskins.

Washington broke out on top in the first quarter when Joe Tereshinski slammed into Lujack and the ball popped loose. Herb Shoener scooped it up and had an unchallenged 32-yard romp into the end zone.

An interception by Harry Dowda cut off the first Bear bid to tie it up, but Chicago came storming back on its next possession. From the Washington 40, Lujack was on target to J. R. Boone at the 20. He broke free from one defender, dispatched another with a nice fake and rolled across to goal line to tie the game.

George Blanda booted a 15-yard field goal early in the second period to put the Bears in the lead for good. The home team wrapped it up with two more touchdowns before halftime, both on passes from Lujack. The second one was the most dazzling play of the day. From his own 19, Lujack faded back and launched to Ken Kavanaugh, who was uncovered at the Washington 30. The end gathered in the pass and had to press only slightly to beat Dowda and Clyde Goodnight into the end zone to make it 24-7 at the half.

Luckman passed for the Bears' final touchdown of the day five minutes into the second quarter, with Jim Keane on the receiving end. In the fourth, the Redskins made the final more respectable with two Sammy Baugh touchdown passes to Tommy Mont.

Nov 22

Baugh Will Be Back Next Year
QB signs '50 contract, says he "gets tired" working on his ranch

11/27/49	GIANTS (6-4) 23, Redskins (3-6-1) 7			12,985
Was	7	0	0	0	7
NYG	0	10	0	13	23
Was	TD Taylor; PAT Poillon			
NYG	TD Roberts 2, Swiacki; PAT Agajanian; FG Agajanian			

Polo Grounds—Charlie Conerly, who was briefly the property of the Redskins a few years earlier, threw two four-quarter touchdown passes to wrap up the Giants' 23-7 win.

The Redskins got off to a 7-0 lead in the first quarter. Behind the passing of Sammy Baugh, the Redskins moved smartly from their own 35 to the Giant 40. It appeared that they had come up empty after the march bogged down there and Dick Poillon missed a field goal. The Giants, however, were offside and Baugh made them pay for their mistake a few plays later.

From the 38, Hugh Taylor ran a deep slant and Baugh hit him in the numbers at the four. The speedy wingman was unchallenged as he strode into the end zone.

That proved to be the high point for the visitors. A Conerly-led drive after the kickoff netted a second-quarter field goal to cut the lead to 7-3. Before halftime, Em Tunnell returned a punt to the Washington 31 and Choo-Choo Roberts carried the first 30 yards and then the final three feet over the goal line to give New York a 10-7 lead.

The margin looked more and more safe as snow fell on the field, making things increasingly problematic for the offenses. That was certainly true for the Redskins, who didn't threaten to score until it was well out of reach in the fourth quarter.

Conerly and the Giants, though, took the third quarter to adjust to the white stuff and then clinched it in the fourth. After a holding penalty backed them up to their own 24, two passes was all it took to reach pay dirt. The first was a 34-yard screen to Ray Coates, the second a 42-yard strike to Roberts. Dan Sandifer and Harry Dowda were nearby, but Roberts made the catch at the three and scored easily. Later, Tunnell intercepted Harry Gilmer's pass at the Washington 38, setting up Conerly's final TD toss—a 19-yarder to Bill Swiacki.

12/4/49	REDSKINS (4-6-1) 30, Packers (2-9) 0			23,200
GB	0	0	0	0	0
Was	0	13	17	0	30
Was	TD Quirk, Hollar, Baugh; PAT Poillon 3; FG Poillon 3			

Griffith Stadium—The Redskins intercepted four Green Bay passes and allowed just 105 yards rushing as they shut the Packers down and out.

Washington took command with 13 second-period points. Early in the period Ed Quirk finished off a drive with four straight carries covering the final 29 yards over the goal line. Dick Poillon booted a pair of field goals, the second coming from 21 yards on the final play of the half.

The Redskins picked up right where they left off after intermission. Sammy Baugh went back to pass from the Packer eight and, finding nobody open, the 13-year veteran scampered in for the touchdown.

A pair of interceptions, one by Al DeMao and the other by Rob Goode, set up Washington's final two scores. DeMao's pick led to a short TD smash by John Henry Hollar and Goode's led to Poillon's third field goal of the day.

12/11/49	RAMS (8-2-2) 53, Redskins (4-7-1) 27			44,899
Was	7	0	7	13	27
LA	20	14	6	13	53
Was	TD Sandifer, Taylor, Hollar, Baugh; PAT Poillon 3			
LA	TD Shaw 4, Fears 2, Hoerner, Smith; PAT Waterfield 4, Gehrke			

Los Angeles Coliseum—(Where do you start? Which Ram passing exploit warrants lead consideration? How about the six touchdown passes that Ram quarterbacks Bob Waterfield and Norm Van Brocklin combined for—or how about the 10 passes that end Tom Fears caught to establish an NFL record for catches in a season? Perhaps, but Billy Shaw's four touchdown catches takes the cake, so here goes:)

Billy Shaw caught four touchdown passes to lead the Rams to a rout of the Redskins. The win enabled Los Angeles to clinch the NFL Western Conference title, an honor they held last year when they were in Cleveland.

There really isn't much of a point of rehashing this one. The Rams jumped to a 14-0 lead in the game's first six minutes and were on cruise control the entire game.

Defensive linemen Dick Huffman and Freddie Naumetz were in the faces of quarterbacks Sammy Baugh and Harry Gilmer all day, killing most Redskin drives before they got started. LA led 34-7 at the half and increased its margin to 53-14 in the fourth quarter before the Redskins scored two TD's in the last four minutes.

1950
Head Coach: Herman Ball
Record: 3-9, Sixth in NFL American Conference

Honors: Bill Dudley Pro Bowl; Harry Gilmer Pro Bowl; Paul Lipscomb Pro Bowl

Jan 9
After 18 Seasons, Edwards Leaves Redskins
Former star lineman, head coach departs for sporting goods business

Redskins Trade for Dudley, Draft Justice, LeBaron

Jan 22—The Redskins made a flurry of moves to try to add more firepower to their offense, trading for one star and drafting two players who may become stars.

The established player was Bill Dudley, the former University of Virginia All-American who twice led the NFL in rushing for the Steelers. The two-time Pro Bowl participant has been with Detroit for the past three years and the Redskins dealt end Dan Sandifer to the Lions in a straight player transaction.

The Redskins tabbed two highly productive backs in the draft. Charley "Choo-Choo" Justice, the two-time All-American out of North Carolina, may or may not end up donning a Redskins uniform. He has accepted a position with a North Carolina medical foundation and has said that he will not play pro football, which is why he lasted until the 16th round of the draft. The Redskins will attempt to persuade him otherwise.

In the 10th round, Washington took quarterback Eddie LeBaron, an All-America performer at Pacific. He will compete to back up and eventually succeed Sammy Baugh at quarterback for the Redskins.

July 27
LeBaron Called to Marine Service
Will play in College All-Star Game then head for active duty; Korean deployment possible

9/17/50	Redskins (1-0) 38, COLTS (0-1) 14			26,000	
Was	7	7	10	14	38
Bal	0	0	14	0	14
Was	TD Taylor 3, Goode, Dowda; PAT Dudley 5; FG Dudley				
Bal	TD Mutryn, Mazzahti; PAT Grossman 2				

Memorial Stadium—Bones Taylor caught three touchdown passes to pace the Redskins in their rout of Baltimore.

Sammy Baugh threw for three scores, including two of Taylor's TD catches. Their first scoring hookup, a 27-yarder, came after Laurie Niemi recovered a Colts fumble at the Baltimore 33 and gave the Redskins a 7-0 first-quarter lead that they would not relinquish.

The Redskins scored again on Taylor's 54-yard scoring pass thrown by Baugh's relief pitcher, Harry Gilmer, who made a terrific play fake and had Taylor wide open. That gave the visitors a 14-0 lead at halftime, but the Colts were not done. Chet Mutryn scored on a 34-yard run in the third quarter to cut the lead in half.

Baugh had the answer, though—a 56-yard screen pass to Bob Goode for a touchdown and a 30-yard pass to Taylor that set up Bill Dudley's 11-yard field goal and it was 24-7.

The Washington defense did its part, getting pressure on Baltimore quarterback Y. A. Tittle all day long. They sacked him for 23 yards in losses and kept him out of rhythm.

9/24/50	PACKERS (1-1) 35, Redskins (1-1) 21			14,109	
Was	7	0	7	7	21
GB	0	14	14	7	35
Was	TD Livingston 2, Goode; PAT Dudley 3				
GB	TD Cook, Grimes 2, Canadeo, Coutre; PAT Fritsch 5				

Wisconsin State Fair Park—The Packers, 20-point underdogs, scored twice in a two-minute span in the second quarter to take the lead and then pulled away for the upset win.

The Redskins drove 82 yards in the first quarter, the march capped by Sammy Baugh's 44-yard touchdown pass to Howie Livingston. Washington had possession in the second quarter, but gave it up when Bob Goode received a jarring hit by Carl Schuette and fumbled. The Packers recovered at the Washington 21 and scored when Paul Christman threw a touchdown pass to Ted Cook.

The Redskins were forced to punt on their ensuing possession and Billy Grimes fielded the kick at his own 15. Washington missed a tackle at the point where he caught the ball and Grimes was gone—85 yards for a touchdown. Green Bay was up 14-7.

The home team upped its lead to 21-7 in the third quarter before Bob Goode tried to make a game of it. Goode raced untouched 80 yards for a touchdown, setting a team record for the longest run from scrimmage.

They couldn't take advantage. A blocked punt led to another Green Bay touchdown and it was 28-14. The Packers coasted to win.

10/1/50	Steelers (1-2) 26, REDSKINS (1-2) 7			25,008	
Pit	3	7	7	9	26
Was	7	0	0	0	7
Pit	TD Gage, Nickel, Rogel; PAT Geri 3; FG Geri; Safety Stautner				
Was	TD Taylor; PAT Dudley				

Griffith Stadium—The Redskins, as the Washington Post put it, played "like cigar store Indians, just standing there." The previously winless Steelers recovered from an early Washington lead to methodically grind down the home team in an easy win.

The early Washington lead came courtesy of a 70-yard touchdown bomb from Harry Gilmer to Bones Taylor. That was the end of the Redskins' highlights for this one. Bobby Gage returned the ensuing kickoff 51 yards before setting up a 41-yard field goal by Joe Geri to cut the Redskins' lead to 7-3. The Steelers had the lead by halftime thanks to a 12-yard touchdown run by Gage.

It didn't get any better in the second half; the Washington offense was ineffective and the defense couldn't stop the Steelers. The final insult came with Pittsburgh leading 24-7: tackle Ernie Stautner nailed Gilmer in the end zone for a safety.

When all was said and done the Redskins had outgained the Steelers 289 yards to 238. But a big chunk of that yardage came on that one early 80-yard Gilmer-to-Taylor connection and Pittsburgh largely controlled the action the rest of the way. Washington also was hurt by 67 yards in penalties.

10/8/50	Giants (3-0) 21, REDSKINS (1-3) 17			19,288	
NYG	7	0	7	7	21
Was	7	7	0	3	17
NYG	TD Griffith, Roberts 2; PAT Poole 3				
Was	Gilmer, Dudley; PAT Dudley 2; FG Dudley				

Griffith Stadium—The Redskins had a 17-14 lead with five minutes to play, but let it slip away. Charlie Conerly of the Giants threw a 38-yard touchdown pass to Gene Roberts to cap an 84-yard drive to take the game.

Washington took a 14-7 lead into the locker room at halftime. They drove to a touchdown the first time they had the ball, moving eight plays to a one-yard sneak by Harry Gilmer. In the second quarter, they turned the recovery of a fumbled punt at the New York nine into seven points on Bill Dudley's four-yard touchdown catch and his subsequent conversion.

It took the visitors six minutes into the second half to tie the game. Roberts ran it over from three yards out. Washington drove right back and kicked a field goal but, in a decision that was highly questionable in hindsight, coach Herman Ball decided to take the points off the board and accept an offside penalty against the Giants. With a first down at the nine, the Redskins still couldn't punch it in; the next field goal attempt by Dudley missed. The score remained tied.

A Gilmer pass to Bones Taylor netted 60 yards and led to a Dudley field goal on the first play of the fourth quarter to put the Redskins up 17-14. They were able to survive the visitors' onslaught until the Giants took possession at their own 16 midway through the final period. Their game-winning drive was almost short-circuited at the start when defensive ends Ed Berrang and Roland Dale had a bead on Conerly two yards deep in his own end zone. The quarterback averted disaster by hitting halfback Forrest Griffith with a 28-yard pass and the Giants continued the march towards Conerly's game-winner to Roberts. A fumble killed the home team's chances of pulling it out at the end.

Justice to Play for Redskins

Oct 15—Charley Justice, who zig-zagged his way across football fields on his way to All-America status at North Carolina, has taken one final change of direction as an amateur athlete.

After months of on-again, off-again negotiations with the Redskins, who took Justice in the 16th round of this year's draft, he has decided to join the play-for-pay group in Washington.

Justice will start practicing immediately and should be ready to play by the Redskins' next game against the Chicago Cardinals in Washington. He will wear jersey number 22—the same one he made famous in Chapel Hill.

10/22/50	Cardinals (2-3) 38, REDSKINS (1-4) 28			27,856	
Chi	10	28	0	0	38
Was	7	7	7	7	28
Chi	TD Angsman, Wham, Shaw, Trippi, Polsfoot; PAT Harder 5; FG Harder				
Was	TD Taylor 3, Goode; PAT Dudley 4				

Griffith Stadium—The Cardinals scored 28 points in the second quarter and coasted to a 38-28 win over Washington.

The teams traded quick touchdown drives in the first quarter. It took Chicago three plays to go 49 yards and score on Elmer Angsman's two-yard plunge. The Redskins answered 33 seconds later as Hall Haynes returned the ensuing kickoff 61 yards to set up Harry Gilmer's 20-yard touchdown pass to a wide-open Bones Taylor. A Chicago field goal had the visitors up 10-7 entering the decisive second quarter.

It got off poorly for the Redskins when, driving at their own 45, Sammy Baugh called a pitchout to Bill Dudley. As Morris Siegel of the Post said, "It worked perfectly—for the Cards." Defensive end

Tom Wham sniffed the play out, grabbed the pitch and rolled unchallenged into the end zone.

It got a bit brighter for the Redskins after Ed Quirk intercepted a pass for the Redskins at the Chicago 33. On the very next play, Gilmer executed a beautiful play fake to the newly-acquired Charlie Justice. Gilmer again threw a touchdown pass to Taylor, cutting the Cardinal lead to 17-14. That would prove to be the high-water mark for the Redskins.

Things started going downhill when quarterback Frank Tripuka threw a medium-range pass to end Bob Shaw, who stiff-armed a would-be tackler out of the way to complete a 64-yard scoring play. It got worse when Dudley fumbled a punt deep in Washington territory, setting up Charlie Trippi's eight-yard touchdown run. With less than a minute to go in the period, Tripuka unleashed a bomb to end Frank Polsfoot, who caught the ball at the Washington 30 and eluded one tackler on the way to completing the 81-yard play.

The Redskins did outscore Chicago 14-0 in the second half, but that served only to make the final score more respectable.

10/29/50	EAGLES (5-1) 35, Redskins (1-5) 3			33,707	
Was	3	0	0	0	3
Phil	0	14	0	21	35
Was	FG Dudley				
Phil	TD Van Buren, Pihos, Muha, Ledbetter, Green; PAT Patton 5				

Shibe Park—Sammy Baugh had one of his worst games in his pro career, completing more passes to the other team than to his own, as the Eagles pounded the visiting Redskins.

Early on, it appeared the Redskins were getting in position to hang with the Eagles, who were 17-point favorites. They drove to a Bill Dudley field goal before Choo Choo Justice broke off a 71-yard run that brought his team to a first and goal at the nine. An attempted lateral was botched on the next play and the Eagles recovered. Justice's effort was for naught.

The Eagles then took charge. After a 39-yard completion from Tommy Thompson to Jack Myers, Steve Van Buren powered over to give the Eagles the lead. After Washington came up short on fourth and two, Philly got a 39-yard TD toss from Thompson to end Pete Pihos to take a 14-3 lead into the locker room.

The Redskins stiffened defensively and the 11-point margin held until there were eight minutes left to play. Then, however, the Eagles scored two quick TD's to wrap it up. The Eagles' Joe Muha stepped in front of a short Baugh pass attempt and intercepted it, returning it 16 yards for six points. Just 38 seconds later, Baugh had the ball knocked out of his hands. End John Green gathered it in at the two and stepped in, making it 28-3. Yet another interception of Baugh set up the Eagles' final TD.

On the day, Baugh completed three of nine passes, with four interceptions.

11/5/50	GIANTS (5-2) 24, Redskins (1-6) 21			23,909	
Was	0	7	14	0	21
NYG	7	0	7	10	24
Was	TD Justice, Goode, Drazenovich; PAT Dudley 3				
NYG	TD McChesney, Tidwell, Swiacki; PAT Poole 3; FG Poole				

Polo Grounds—The Redskins led 21-14 late in the fourth quarter, but they were unable to hold on as the Giants won 24-21 on a 40-yard field goal by Ray Poole with four seconds left. An errant lateral by rookie halfback Choo Choo Justice set up New York's winning points.

A 60-yard drive that ended with Sammy Baugh throwing an eight-yard touchdown pass to Justice just 16 seconds before halftime tied the game at seven at intermission. In the third quarter, a Washington fumble led to a Giants touchdown to give New York the lead at 14-7.

Washington turned the tide when Ed Berrang blocked Tom Landry's punt and recovered on the Giants' six yard line. Two plays later, Bob Goode bulled over the goal line and Bill Dudley's extra point tied it at 14.

It took just two minutes for the Redskins to untie it on a 44-yard drive. Dudley had the big run, a 23-yard jaunt to the New York 7. On second and goal, Chuck Drazenovich carried it in and it was 21-14.

The Redskins blew a golden opportunity to expand their lead when they didn't convert after recovering a fumble at the Giants' 12, but it seemed that they were in little jeopardy—especially when the Giants got the ball on their own 11 with four minutes left to go. But Chuck Conerly got them out of the hole and, two minutes later, faced a fourth and 12 at the Washington 26. Conerly's pass to Bill Swiacki was a couple of yards short of a first down and both Drazenovich and Harry Dowda hit the receiver almost immediately. Swiacki recovered, though, and rolled in for the tying touchdown.

Still, it seemed the Redskins would do no worse than tie and were moving downfield when, on a play that started at the Washington 35, Bones Taylor caught a short pass and lateraled to Justice. The rookie then attempted to lateral to guard Cas Witucki but, instead, tossed it into the arms of Landry, who was tackled at the Washington 41 with 37 seconds left. Four plays later, Poole's wind-aided 40-yarder won the game for the Giants.

11/12/50	Eagles (6-2) 33, REDSKINS (1-7) 0			29,407
Phil	3	7	13	10	33
Was	0	0	0	0	0
Phil	TD Ziegler, Van Buren, Parmer, Ledbetter; PAT Patton 3; FG Patton 2			

Griffith Stadium—Sometimes, the statistics don't tell the story of a game. In this one, they did.

All you really have to know about this game is that the Eagles outgained the Redskins 474 yards to 127, but here's some more anyway. Halfback Steve Van Buren nearly outgained the Redskins with his rushing yards alone, piling up 108 on the ground on 23 carries. Philly intercepted five passes and recovered four fumbles. They snapped the ball on offense 77 times; the Redskins could claim only 47. The home team ventured into Eagles territory just twice, with one of those on a nifty 50-yard kickoff return by Charlie Justice. Unfortunately, it was 23-0 at the time.

The Eagles led just 10-0 at halftime, but quickly broke it open. After taking the second-half kickoff, they faked a punt on fourth and seven at their own 30 and Frank Reagan bolted 40 yards to the Washington 30. Three plays later, Van Buren powered over from 11 yards out, and the Eagles rolled on from that point.

11/19/50	BROWNS (8-2) 20, Redskins (1-8) 14			21,908
Was	0	7	7	0	14
Cle	0	13	0	7	20
Was	TD Haynes, Goode; PAT Dudley 2			
Cle	TD Lavelle, Phelps; PAT Groza 2; FG Groza 2			

Cleveland Municipal Stadium—The Browns drove 80 yards to the go-ahead touchdown late in the game and survived a 71-yard kickoff return by Washington's Eddie Saenz to hang on to beat the Redskins 20-14.

Washington trailed by 13-7 at the half, but it could have been worse if not for a couple of defensive stands that turned Cleveland touchdown opportunities into Lou Groza field goals. Washington had scored when Hall Haynes picked off Otto Graham's pass and romped 40 yards down the sideline for a touchdown.

The game turned in the Redskins' favor in the third quarter when, after they had moved smartly to the Browns' 20, halfback Charlie Justice pulled up and hit Saenz with a 17-yard pass to the three. Bob Goode took it over a couple of plays after that and Bill Dudley's extra point put the underdog visitors up 14-13.

The lead was still one when Cleveland took possession at its own 20 with nine minutes to play. Graham engineered a masterful drive. After Marion Motley carried twice for a total of 21 yards, Graham faked the handoff to Motley and handed instead to halfback Dopey Phelps, who scooted for 12 yards. Soon after that, with less than four minutes showing on the game clock, Graham called the same play and Phelps scooted around end eight yards for the go-ahead touchdown.

The home team had to endure a major scare before chalking this one up in the win column. Saenz took the ensuing kickoff two yards deep in the end zone and didn't stop running until Ken Gorgal brought him down at the Cleveland 31. The Redskins got to the 16 before a fourth-down pass came up short.

11/26/50	REDSKINS (2-8) 38, Colts (1-9) 28			21,275
Bal	7	0	7	14	28
Was	0	17	7	14	38
Bal	TD Stone, Salata, Zalejska, Crisler; PAT Kissell			
Was	TD Baugh, Goodnight 2, Taylor, Saenz; PAT Dudley 5; FG Dudley			

Griffith Stadium—The Redskins broke an eight-game losing streak by beating the Colts for the second time this year. Sammy Baugh completed 22 of 35 passes for 291 yards and three touchdowns to pace the winners.

Washington had to survive a couple of long-distance scoring plays by the Colts to claim this one. Less than three minutes into the game, Baltimore halfback Billy Stone outran the entire Redskins defense en route to a 72-yard touchdown run to give the Colts a 7-0 lead. Late in the game, George Buksar intercepted a pass at his own one, returned it 17 yards and then lateraled to Ernie Zalejski, who took it the rest of the way for a 99-yard touchdown play.

In between, the Redskins largely controlled the game, but it was still a contest late in the third quarter with the home team up just 17-14. Then Baugh moved the Redskins 86 yards in just five plays. The big thrusts were a 42-yard run by Choo Choo Justice and the capper: Baugh's 21-yard TD pass to Clyde Goodnight. That put Washington up 24-14 with two minutes left in the third.

Four minutes later, Washington scored again, allowing them to survive the stunning 99-yard interception and lateral play that followed.

12/3/50	Redskins (3-8) 27, STEELERS (5-6) 7			19,741
Was	7	10	0	7	24
Pit	0	0	0	7	7
Was	TD Dudley, Saenz, Goode; PAT Dudley 3; FG Dudley			
Pit	TD Nickel; PAT Geri			

Forbes Field—Bill Dudley's 96-yard punt return for a touchdown sparked the Redskins to the upset over the Steelers. Seven interceptions of Pittsburgh passes also lent considerable aid to Washington's victory in snowy, muddy conditions at Forbes Field.

There's little doubt that coach Herman Ball and most others with an interest in the Redskins were displeased when Dudley made an over-the-shoulder grab of Joe Geri's punt at the Washington four, just inches from the sideline, a high-risk maneuver with little chance of a reward. The longshot came through, as the Steelers apparently were taken aback that Dudley fielded the ball and didn't react until "Bullet" had sped for 20 yards. When they did go after Dudley, Redskins blockers were in position to wipe them out and Dudley went all the way. For good measure, he kicked the point after for a 7-0 lead.

The Redskins capped an 87-yard march with a pass from Sammie Baugh to Eddie Saenz and then turned an interception into a Dudley field goal to make it 17-0 at halftime.

Probably figuring that he hadn't contributed enough to his team's cause, Dudley picked off a pass to set up Washington's final score, a two-yard run by Bob Goode.

12/10/50	Browns (10-2) 45, REDSKINS (3-9) 21			30,143	
Cle	0	14	14	17	45
Was	7	7	7	0	21
Cle	TD Jones 2, Baumgardner, Lahr, Groza, Phelps; PAT Groza 6; FG Groza				
Was	TD Justice, Taylor, Dudley; PAT Dudley 3				

Griffith Stadium—The Redskins stayed with the Browns for the first half of the game and took a seven-point lead in the third quarter but were outscored 31-0 the rest of the way. Most of the damage was done by Cleveland quarterback Otto Graham, who passed for 321 yards and four touchdowns.

Things looked pretty good for the Redskins at halftime. Sammy Baugh and Harry Gilmer had each thrown a touchdown pass and the score was deadlocked at 14. In addition, Marion

Motley, Cleveland's powerful, star fullback, had been ejected for throwing an elbow on the final play of the first half.

It looked even better in the third quarter when Joe Bartos intercepted one of Graham's passes at Cleveland's 37. Soon after that, Bill Dudley went 23 yards for a touchdown and it was 21-14 Washington.

That was it for the Redskins, however. Graham threw nine straight passes, the last one to Dub Jones for the tying touchdown. Soon after that, a Baugh pass was deflected, Warren Lahr picked it off for Cleveland and ran 18 yards for the go-ahead score. The visitors completed the rout in the fourth quarter when Lou Groza caught a touchdown pass on a tackle-eligible play and Dopey Phelps returned a punt 54 yards for a touchdown.

1951
Head Coach: Herman Ball, Dick Todd
Record: 5-7 (Ball 0-3, Todd 5-4), Third in NFL American Conference

Honors: Sammy Baugh Pro Bowl; Bill Dudley Pro Bowl; Rob Goode Pro Bowl; Paul Lipscomb Pro Bowl; Laurie Niemi Pro Bowl

---

Jan 6

Justice to Leave Redskins
Will go to coach Tar Heel backfield after one season

Jan 25

Ball Will Remain as Redskins Coach
After search, Marshall decides to stand pat

9/30/51	LIONS (1-0) 35, Redskins (0-1) 17			27,831	
Was	3	7	7	0	17
Det	7	7	7	14	35
Was	TD Drazenovich 2; PAT Dudley 2; FG Dudley				
Det	TD Doran, Layne, Hoerneschemeyer, Walker, Harder; PAT Walker 5				

Tiger Stadium—Bobby Layne threw for two touchdowns, scored another, and paced the Lions to 515 yards of total offense in the win over Washington.

Despite the lopsided final score and the Lions' decided statistical edge (Washington gained 388 yards), the Redskins found themselves in a position to take the lead in the fourth quarter. In fact, they had a couple of good chances.

The best came early in the quarter with Detroit leading 21-17. Behind the running of Bill Dudley, Chuck Drazenovich, who scored the Redskins' two touchdowns, and Rob Goode, they moved down to the Lions' five yard line. But then the wheels came off then. Two runs lost three yards, Harry Gilmer overthrew an open Eddie Saenz in the end zone, and Gilmer's fourth-down pass intended for Dudley was broken up. The ball went over on downs.

The Lions were forced to punt from their own territory five minutes later, but this opportunity was squandered when the Redskins were flagged for holding on the play, giving the Lions a first down and new life. That was all that the Lions needed as, seven plays later, Doak Walker took a pitchout from Layne and sped 21 yards for the clinching score.

10/7/51	Giants (1-0-1) 35, REDSKINS (0-2) 14			23,600	
NYG	14	7	7	7	35
Was	0	7	0	7	14
NYG	TD Price, Stribling, Conerly, McChesney, Rote; PAT Poole 5				
Was	TD Drazenovich, Taylor; PAT Dudley 2				

Griffith Stadium—The Giants converted four interceptions into four touchdowns, which was all they had to do to rout the Redskins.

What was particularly painful about the performance was the fact that the player who helped make Washington pay for its errant quarterbacking was New York QB Charlie Conerly. He was property of the Redskins until they traded him away to their division rivals a few years prior. All he did was throw for three TD's and score a fourth himself.

The Redskins won the opening coin toss and elected to receive—a strategic error, as things turned out. Harry Gilmer threw the first of his three interceptions, this one to Otto Schnellenbacher, who legged it back 17 yards to the Washington 28. The Giants scored in four plays on a one-yard run by Eddie Price.

Later in the quarter it was the same story, this time with Tom Landry picking off Gilmer's throw and returning it to the Washington 10. On third down, Conerly found Bill Stribling near the goal line and the end went over for the score to make it 14-0.

The home team responded in the second quarter by driving 74 yards to a short touchdown run by Chuck Drazenovich to cut the lead to 14-7. Any good feelings about the outcome for Redskins fans were fading before halftime, though, as the Giants scored again on Conerly's one-yard sneak. An Em Tunnell interception led to a third quarter Conerly touchdown pass to end Bob McChesney, and the Redskins were done.

10/14/51	BROWNS (2-1) 45, Redskins (0-3) 0			33,968	
Was	0	0	0	0	0
Cle	7	7	17	14	45
Cle	TD Young, Carpenter, Graham, Cole, Phelps, Orstaglio; PAT Groza 6; FG Groza				

Cleveland Municipal Stadium—Although the defending champion Browns didn't need any help, the Redskins provided them with plenty, throwing three interceptions and losing three fumbles. Cleveland graciously accepted the Redskins' gifts and rolled to the big shutout win.

Things got off to a bad start when Harry Gilmer was sacked and coughed the ball up. Defensive end George Young found the ball and 47 yards of open field in front of him. It was 7-0 Cleveland with the game less than two minutes old.

The score stayed there until Otto Graham led the Browns on a 60-yard scoring drive, with Ken Carpenter taking it over to cap the drive and push the halftime lead to 14-0.

Sammy Baugh replaced Gilmer as the signal caller in the second half and the switch wasn't exactly a smashing success. Twice Baugh and his fellow backs botched handoff attempts. Twice the Browns recovered the ball after the miscues. Twice the Browns converted the turnovers into scores. The first came on Lou Groza's 27-yard field goal, the second on Dopey Phelps' 14-yard touchdown run.

Todd Named Coach After Halas Nixes Anderson Deal

Oct 19—When the dust settled after a wild day, Dick Todd stood as the head coach of the Washington Redskins.

He succeeded Hunk Anderson, who lasted about five hours in the job. After a press conference introducing Anderson to succeed Herman Ball, the Bears' George Halas threw a monkey wrench into the works.

Even though Anderson was not working for the Bears—he was a salesman for a Detroit steel firm—he still had a contact with the Bears, for whom he coached in the 1940's. And Halas wouldn't let him out of it unless the Redskins relinquished tackle Paul Lipscomb as compensation.

Washington owner George Preston Marshall refused and then turned to Todd, a former star runner for the Redskins and their backfield coach.

Ball will remain with the organization as its chief scout.

10/21/51	REDSKINS (1-3) 7, Cardinals (1-3) 3				22,690	
Chi	0	0	3	0		3
Was	0	7	0	0		7
Chi	FG Yablonski					
Was	TD Thomas; PAT Dudley					

Griffith Stadium—Sammy Baugh attempted just seven passes on the day, but one of them was a 46-yard scoring pass to George Thomas in the second quarter. That was all the Redskins needed to get past the Cards. George Buksar also played a big hand in the win, getting an interception before tipping away a crucial fourth-down pass in the waning minutes. Both plays happened in the fourth quarter and killed Chicago bids to take the lead.

The touchdown pass came in the second quarter. The Cardinals missed a 34-yard field goal attempt, giving Washington the ball at its own 20. From there, Bob Goode and Bill Dudley ran the ball down to Chicago's 32-yard line. A roughing penalty and seven-yard loss on a sweep, though, pushed them back near midfield. On third and long, Baugh found Thomas, who had had gotten slightly behind his defender, Ray Ramsey. A combination of a good throw and a terrible misplaying of the ball by Ramsey led to six points for Washington. Dudley's extra point made it 7-0. The lead held at the half.

A Chicago field goal made it 7-3 early in the third period. In the rest of the quarter, each team—first the Cardinals, then the Redskins—drove deep into the other's territory only to give the ball up on downs.

In the fourth quarter, Buksar killed a promising Cardinal drive with an end-zone interception on a play from the five. In the final two minutes, it was Buksar to the rescue again as he got his hand on a fourth-down pass attempt from the Washington four to preserve the win.

10/28/51	Redskins (2-3) 27, EAGLES (2-3) 23				20,437	
Was	0	14	3	10		27
Phil	3	7	7	6		23
Was	TD Goode, Thomas, Dudley; PAT Dudley 3; FG Dudley 2					
Phil	TD Walston, Van Buren, Scott; PAT Walston 2; FG Walston					

Shibe Park—Bill Dudley scored 10 points in the fourth quarter to give the Redskins the lead over the Eagles and Washington held on for the win.

The Redskins were trailing 10-0 in the second period when they got things going offensively. A couple of completions from Sammy Baugh to Bones Taylor set up a short touchdown run by Rob Goode and Dudley's extra point made it 10-7. A few minutes later, Baugh got his team from its own nine to pay dirt with a 38-yard strike to Gene Brito and a 53-yard touchdown toss to George Thomas. The visitors held that 14-10 lead at the half.

The Eagles came out and untied it in short order with a 58-yard TD march capped by Steve Van Buren's one-yard plunge. Washington answered, though, moving from their own 24 to the Philly six before settling for Dudley's game-tying 14-yard field goal.

Five and a half minutes into the final period, Dudley booted another three-pointer to put Washington up 17-14. That set the stage for Ed Salem.

The rookie back picked off an Eagle pass and ran it back 16 yards to the Philadelphia 28. Soon after that, Dudley sailed wide and into the end zone from nine yards out for the clincher.

11/4/51	Bears (5-1) 27, REDSKINS (2-4) 0				31,737	
Chi	3	14	7	3		27
Was	0	0	0	0		0
Chi	TD Hunsinger, Kindt, Kyovich; PAT Blanda 3; FG Blanda 3					

Griffith Stadium—The Bears brought a resounding end to the Redskins' modest two-game winning streak with a crunching 27-0 win.

The Bears dominated all phases of the game and two in particular, which turned out to be decisive. They ran the ball 51 times and averaged six yards a pop. That works out to 303 yards on the ground, allowing them to control the clock. In addition to that, Chicago harassed Washington quarterbacks Harry Gilmer and Sammy Baugh all day long with a strong pass rush. The two Washington signal callers combined for just 80 yards passing and threw three interceptions.

As if the visitors needed any more help, the Redskins lost three fumbles, the first of which set up the Bears' first touchdown. With Chicago leading 3-0, receiver George Thomas had the ball knocked out of his hands and the Bears' Brad Rowland recovered at the Washington 41. Three plays later, Chuck Hunsinger crashed over from five yards out for a 10-0 Chicago lead. A 70-yard scoring drive that culminated in Mike Romanik throwing an eight-yard touchdown pass to Don Kindt just seconds before halftime put the Bears up 17-0. The way things were going, it might as well have been 170-0; Washington never threatened in the second half.

11/11/51	GIANTS (5-1-1) 28, Redskins (2-5) 14				21,242	
Was	0	7	0	7		14
NYG	14	0	7	7		28
Was	TD Goode, Taylor; PAT Dudley 2					
NYG	TD Mote, Scott, Price, Schnellbacher; PAT Poole 4					

Polo Grounds—Sammy Baugh threw his sixth interception with less than three minutes left in the game and Otto Schnellbacher took it back all the way—40 yards for the clinching touchdown.

Early on, it looked like there would be no need for late-game heroics for New York to wrap this one up. The Giants drove 70 yards for one touchdown and were given a gift to set up another. After Kelly Mote caught a touchdown pass from Charley Conerly, Baugh and Rob Goode botched a handoff and New York had possession at the Washington 21. A five-yard penalty meant that Joe Scott's touchdown dash around end covered 26 yards.

After that, the Redskins settled down and went about the business of making a ball game out of this one. A Baugh pass to Harry Dowda covered 48 yards to the Giants two and Goode crashed over three plays later to cut the Giants' lead in half.

Another fumble, this one by Bill Dudley after a pass reception at his own 16, gave New York a short field again. From a half yard away, Eddie Price scooted over to stretch his team's lead to 21-7.

Midway through the fourth quarter, the Redskins struck back. Baugh heaved a 40-yard completion to Dudley that got his team to the New York 28. Then Baugh faked a pass towards Harry Gilmer on the left side, a maneuver that sucked in Giants' defensive back Tom Landry, who was supposed to be guarding Bones Taylor on the right side. Taylor gathered in Baugh's toss and zipped into the end zone to make it 21-14.

Washington got the ball back and was looking for the tying score when Schnellbacher stepped in front of Baugh's pass and rolled 40 yards down the sideline to put the game out of reach.

11/18/51	**Redskins (3-5) 22, STEELERS (2-5-1) 7**			15,060	
Was	0	6	3	13	**22**
Pit	0	7	0	0	**7**
Was	TD Goode 2; PAT Dudley; FG Dudley 3				
Pit	TD Mathews; PAT Geri				

Forbes Field—In freezing temperatures and intermittent snow, Rob Goode scored two touchdowns and Bill Dudley more than made up for a botched extra point attempt with three second-half field goals as the Redskins won in Pittsburgh 22-7.

Washington scored first after Sammy Baugh threw a pass that Gene Brito made a leaping grab of at the Steelers two. The 26-yard gainer was the last play of the first quarter. On the initial play of the second, Goode took it over for six. Dudley's point after attempt was missed about every way you can blow it—low, wide, and blocked. It broke a string of 39 consecutive successful conversions for Dudley.

Pittsburgh tied the score about three minutes later on a dazzling 68-yard punt return by Ray Matthews. Joe Geri's point after pushed the home team into a 7-6 lead.

That lead held until about three minutes were left in the third period. A Redskins drive stalled at the Pittsburgh 23 and Dudley kicked a 30-yard field goal for a 9-7 lead. In the fourth, Dudley salvaged two more drives that fizzled at the Pittsburgh 30 with a pair of 37-yard field goals.

With the Redskins up 15-7, Harry Gilmer set up the clincher with a 29-yard punt return to the Steeler 20. Three plays later, Goode went over from the nine. Dudley started a new streak by kicking the point after.

11/25/51	**REDSKINS (4-5) 31, Rams (6-3) 21**			26,307	
LA	7	0	0	14	**21**
Was	7	14	10	0	**31**
LA	TD Williams, Hirsch, Boyd; PAT Waterfield 3				
Was	TD Goode 2, Taylor, Dudley; PAT Dudley 4; FG Dudley				

Griffith Stadium—The Redskins racked up 371 yards rushing in the course of thumping the Rams in a game that was not nearly the contest the 31-21 final score might indicate.

It didn't start off well for the Redskins. Jerry Williams intercepted Sammy Baugh's first pass of the game and sped 17 yards over the goal line for a 7-0 lead for LA. The Redskins responded, though, as Rob Goode capped a 68-yard drive with a short plunge to tie the game at seven. Another solid drive, this one of 64 yards, led to Goode's second touchdown run of the day—this one from three yards out. In addition to his two scores, Goode racked up 148 yards rushing on the day.

The Rams drove into Washington territory behind the passing of Norm Van Brocklin, but Bob Waterfield was wide left on a 26-

yard field goal attempt and it remained 14-7. That is, until the Redskins drove 80 yards, with passes from Baugh to Bones Taylor and George Thomas picking up key gains. The payoff came with 1:45 left in the half on another Baugh-to-Taylor connection, this one from 24 yards away.

On their initial possession of the second half, the Rams mounted a drive behind Waterfield, who had replaced an injured Van Brocklin. But the Rams fumbled and Walt Yowarsky recovered at the Washington 23. Immediately Goode broke off a 38-yard run into Ram territory that set up a Bill Dudley field goal. If that didn't clinch it, the next sequence did. Al DeMao intercepted, Goode ripped off a 33-yard run and Dudley scored. This time Dudley scored six on a pass from Baugh. Make it seven—he kicked his third conversion of the game to give the Redskins a 31-7 lead. Two fourth-quarter TD's served only to save some face for the Rams.

12/2/51	**Eagles (4-6) 35, REDSKINS (4-6) 21**			23,738	
Phil	14	7	7	7	**35**
Was	0	7	7	7	**21**
Phil	TD S. Van Buren 2, Scott, Walston 2; PAT Walston 5				
Was	TD Dudley, Goode 2; PAT Dudley 3				

Griffith Stadium—The Eagles pounded the Redskins into submission, rushing for 297 yards and racking up 32 first downs in the course of an easy win.

The Eagles jumped out to a 14-0 lead in the first quarter. Rob Goode fumbled, setting up a short drive to a two-yard scoring run by Steve Van Buren. Later in the period, Clyde Scott zipped untouched into the end zone, and the rout was on.

Washington did have a response—a short Bill Dudley touchdown run set up by Harry Gilmer's 38-yard punt return into Philly territory made it 14-7. But that would be as close as the Redskins would get as the Eagles scored another touchdown before halftime and went into the locker room with a 21-7 lead.

They expanded that margin in the third quarter when Bobby Walston caught a 14-yard touchdown pass from Adrian Burk. The Redskins came back and scored on Rob Goode's six-yard touchdown run to give them a shot going into the fourth quarter trailing 28-14.

Goode ran for 100 yards on the day on 16 carries.

Philadelphia put it away in the fourth quarter with another Burk-to-Walston scoring pass, this one from 10 yards out. Goode did tally a cosmetic touchdown on a two-yard burst later in the fourth quarter.

12/9/51	**Redskins (5-6) 20, CARDINALS (2-9) 17**			9,459	
Was	10	0	0	10	**20**
Chi	7	7	0	3	**17**
Was	TD Tereshinski, Goode; PAT Dudley 2; FG Dudley 2				
Chi	TD Paul, Polsfoot; PAT Patton 2; FG Patton				

Comiskey Park—Bill Dudley kicked an 18-yard field goal with 15 seconds left to give the Redskins the win over the Cardinals. Gene Brito's jaw-dropping catch of a Sammy Baugh pass set up the game-winning boot.

Washington took a 10-7 lead in the second quarter when Baugh found a wide-open Joe Tereshinski in the end zone on fourth down for an eight-yard touchdown. That lead evaporated before halftime in striking fashion when Chicago converted a second down and 42 to go. Jim Hardy found Fran Polsfoot for 72 yards and a touchdown.

After a scoreless third quarter, Rob Goode put the Redskins up 17-14 with a three-yard touchdown run just six seconds into the final period. The Cards tied it soon after that on Cliff Patton's 17-yard field goal.

It was still tied when the Redskins took over at their own 12 with three minutes to play. Dudley caught a pass for 14 yards that got the Skins out of the hole. Subsequent runs by Johnny Papit and Goode got Washington near midfield. Soon after that, from the Chicago 39, Baugh threw to the well-covered Brito, who stole the ball away from a pair of would-be defenders and came down at the 11-yard line. Dudley came in immediately and booted the game winner.

12/16/51	Steelers (4-7-1) 20, REDSKINS (5-7) 10				18,096
Pit	0	0	0	20	20
Was	3	7	0	0	10
Pit	TD Chandnois, Roger, Geri; PAT Geri 2				
Was	TD Tereshinski; PAT Dudley; FG Dudley				

Griffith Stadium—Pittsburgh quarterback Jim Finks, an emergency replacement, led a 20-point fourth quarter rally on a snow-covered field to pull his team past the Redskins.

Going into the final period, Washington's 10-0 lead looked quite safe. The margin had been built on Bill Dudley's 15-yard, first-quarter field goal and a 17-yard TD connection between Sammy Baugh and Joe Tereshinski. The touchdown was set up when Harry Gilmer intercepted a Pittsburgh pass and returned it to the Steelers 20.

Pittsburgh wasn't able to accomplish much even with Chuck Ortman, their starting quarterback, in the lineup. When Finks entered the game after Ortman was hurt in the third period, there was little reason to think that a Steeler rally was imminent.

But it was. Early in the fourth quarter, Finks threw a 40-yard touchdown pass to Lynn Chandois to make it 10-7. Then he completed four passes to get the Steelers from their own 18 to the Washington three. Joe Geri punched it in from there and, suddenly, the Redskins' outlook was as bleak as the weather. Finks ensured the forecast would remain unchanged as he scooted 24 yards to the Washington four to set up the clincher, another Geri run.

Goode Just Misses on Rushing Title

December 17—Rob Goode led the NFL in rushing for most of November and December, but he couldn't quite win the crown for the entire season.

Eddie Price of the New York Giants finished the season with 971 yards on the ground, nosing out Goode, who had 951.

Price had to work considerably harder to gain his yardage. He had 271 carries while Goode toted the rock 208 times.

Goode will have to settle for the consolation prize of leading the league in rushing touchdowns with nine.

1952
Head Coach: Curly Lambeau
Record: 4-8, Sixth in NFL American Conference

Honors: John Williams All-NFL, Pro Bowl; Harry Gilmer Pro Bowl; Paul Lipscomb Pro Bowl; Hugh Taylor Pro Bowl

Jan 25
Todd to Return as Coach
Team makes official what has been long rumored

Jan 25
Goode Heads to Boot Camp
Marine commitment will interrupt promising career

Mar 1
Justice to Return
Star back will give up UNC coaching job, return to Redskins' backfield

May 16
Redskins Lose Top Draft Pick to Baseball
$30,000 bonus lures Larry Isbell to Bosox

Todd Quits After Spat With Marshall, Lambeau Hired as Redskins Coach

Aug 23—The Redskins today named Early (Curly) Lambeau, who won six NFL titles as coach of the Green Bay Packers, as their head coach.

He takes over for Dick Todd, who resigned suddenly two days ago after the team lost its second straight exhibition game. After the game Todd exchanged angry words with team owner George Preston Marshall. Presumably, that exchange led to Todd's departure.

The hiring of Lambeau wasn't the only preseason shakeup in the coaching staff. Backfield coach Jerry Neri, who may have been in line to succeed Todd had Lambeau not been available, resigned this morning. Sammy Baugh will become a player-coach and assume Neri's duties.

August 28
Quarterback LeBaron Gets Discharge
Korean War hero will join Redskins soon

9/29/52	Redskins (1-0) 23, CARDINALS (0-1) 7				17,837
Was	3	14	0	6	23
Chi	0	0	7	0	7
Was	TD Dowda, Taylor, Ventuno; PAT Bagdon 2 FG Bagdon				
Chi	TD Sitko; PAT Geri				

Comiskey Park—The Redskins jumped to a 17-0 halftime lead and easily beat the Cardinals. Sammy Baugh paced the attack, completing 11 of 15 passes.

Ed Bagdon kicked a 29-yard field goal to account for all of the first-quarter scoring. Early in the second period, a 14-yard Cardinal punt led to Baugh's touchdown pass to Harry Dowda.

Later in the first, Jim Ricca recovered a fumble near midfield that Baugh converted with a five-yard touchdown pass to Bones Taylor and it was 17-0. The Redskins had a chance to extend their lead but the clock expired with the ball at the Cardinal four.

Chicago got on the board in the third quarter after Tony Kilmek intercepted a Baugh pass, giving the Cardinals possession at the Redskin 35. Four plays later, Emil Sitko ran it in from the seven to cut the Washington lead to 17-7.

That would be as close at Chicago would get. John Yonaker blocked a punt to set the Redskins up at the Cardinal three. On the next play, Sam Venuto's run closed out the scoring.

Washington didn't pile up huge offensive numbers but they comfortably outgained the Cards. The Redskins got 283 yards of offense compared to a paltry 104 for Chicago. The Cardinals netted just 38 passing yards.

10/5/52	PACKERS (1-1) 35, Redskins (1-1) 20			9,657	
Was	7	0	7	6	20
GB	7	14	7	7	35
Was	TD Rykovich, Taylor, Ferris; PAT Bagdon 2				
GB	TD Howton, Reid, Canadeo, Cone, Rote; PAT Cone 5				

Marquette Stadium—Rookie Vito Parilli got the scoring started with a 90-yard scoring bomb to end Bill Howton, getting the Packers started towards an easy win over the visiting Redskins.

After the Parilli-to-Howton bomb, Washington did manage to tie the score later in the first period with a 71-yard touchdown march. Julie Rykovich caught a 42-yard pass to the Green Bay 36 to get things started and a few plays later he ran for nine to the 13. The touchdown came from a 13-yard pass from Harry Gilmer to Rykovich.

But the Packers pulled away by running off 21 unanswered points in the second and third quarters. Parilli threw another touchdown pass—this one from a more pedestrian distance of 28 yards—to Tobin Rote and the Packer defense kept the pressure on Washington quarterbacks. Particularly under the gun was rookie signal caller Eddie LeBaron, who was sacked time after time and buried after seemingly every pass attempt.

LeBaron had a decent day passing personally, especially considering all of the pressure, posting 191 yards. But the seven sacks knocked 54 yards off of the team total.

Still, given the Redskins' defensive problems it's doubtful that LeBaron could have done much good even if he had enjoyed ample time to throw. Green Bay racked up 420 yards of total offense.

10/12/52	Cardinals (2-1) 17, REDSKINS (1-2) 6			24,600	
Chi	7	0	0	10	17
Was	0	0	6	0	6
Chi	TD Trippi (1 run), Cross (14 run); PAT Geri 2; FG Geri				
Was	TD Rykovich (2 run)				

Griffith Stadium—The Redskins had their chances but didn't manage to take advantage of them in dropping their home opener to a team they'd beaten by 16 on the road just three weeks earlier.

Chicago took a 7-0 lead in the first quarter on Charley Trippi's one-yard quarterback sneak. The home team tried to respond but Charlie Justice just missed a connection on a pass from Eddie LeBaron before Ed Bagdon badly missed a field goal attempt.

The 7-0 score held until the third quarter when Julie Rykovich scored on a two-yard run. The score came after a Cardinal fumble on a punt attempt gave the Redskins possession on the Chicago 23. In taking advantage of an opportunity for the only time all day, Washington still needed to convert two fourth downs to move the 23 yards. Bagdon's point after attempt was low and the Cards held the lead at 7-6.

Washington tried to build on its newly-seized momentum by again taking advantage of favorable field position, this time starting at the Chicago 41 after a punt. They moved to the nine, but the drive stalled and the Cardinals eventually regained possession at their own 24.

Chicago then turned the flow of the contest its way, moving to the Washington 21 early in the fourth quarter, getting a Joe Geri field goal from 40 yards out to force the Redskins into a position where they would need a touchdown to win at 10-6.

It appeared that Washington was on its way to a score, driving to midfield. It was there, however, that Sammy Baugh fumbled and the Cards recovered at the Redskins' 47 to kill that potential threat. Washington got the ball back, but Rykovich dropped a pass that was a potential long gainer and that was it for the home team. Billy Cross raced 14 yards for the final score with 28 seconds left.

10/19/52	Redskins (2-2) 28, STEELERS (0-4) 24			22,605	
Was	14	0	7	7	28
Pitt	7	10	0	7	24
Was	TD Williams, Heath, Taylor 2; PAT LeBaron 4				
Pitt	Nickel 2, Hays; PAT Kerkorian; FG Kerkorian				

Forbes Field—Eddie LeBaron was a giant in the fourth quarter, leading the Redskins on two critical drives to key his team's win.

By halftime it certainly did not appear that LeBaron would wind up in any sort of hero's role. With Washington leading 14-7 in the first quarter, a 17-yard LeBaron punt led to a Pittsburgh field goal. That was a slip up; what he did next was a genuine—well, *you* fill in the verb.

He forced a pass after scrambling far behind the line and Pittsburgh's George Hays batted the ball in the air, snagged it at the Washington one and stepped in for the go-ahead touchdown.

Washington retook the lead in the third quarter after driving 58 yards to Harry Gilmer's 17-yard scoring pass to make it 21-17. An interception by Pittsburgh's Ed Kissell at the outset of the fourth quarter led to a 37-yard touchdown pass from Jim Finks to end Elbie Nickel, who split two defenders to get to the pass. That put the Steelers up 24-21 and set up the LeBaron-led rally.

It wasn't all Eddie, to be sure. After LeBaron threw a picture-perfect strike to Bones Taylor for a 38-yard touchdown to give the Redskins the lead, Pittsburgh mounted a drive. Paul Lipscomb ended that with a shoestring tackle of back Ed Modzelewski at the Washington 45 and the Redskins soon had the ball back.

An eight-yard pass from LeBaron to Gene Brito kept the drive alive by converting a third and six. As the clock ran down to two minutes, Washington faced a fourth and three at the Pittsburgh 34. LeBaron appeared to be trapped as he faded back to pass, but he eluded several would-be tacklers and zipped a pass across the field that Julie Rykovich caught and then the receiver successfully fought for the first down.

After that, the Washington drive was a success—even though it didn't result in any points—as the Redskins drove to the two before allowing time to run out.

10/26/52	BROWNS (4-1) 19, Redskins (2-3) 15			32,496	
Was	0	13	0	2	15
Cle	3	3	3	10	19
Was	TD Drazenovich 2; PAT LeBaron; Safety Graham tackled in end zone by Berrang				
Cle	TD Graham; FG Groza 4; PAT Groza				

Cleveland Municipal Stadium—The Redskins held the lead entering the fourth quarter and had a couple of chances to steal it back after they lost it, but they still fell short of upsetting Cleveland.

The visitors erased a 3-0 deficit entering the second quarter with two touchdowns by Chuck Drazenovich. The first was the ending of a drive that Eddie LeBaron kept alive with a fake punt to convert a fourth and one at the Cleveland 43. A Charlie Justice run and subsequent roughing call against the Browns pushed the ball to the 14. From there, Leon Heath got it down to the two and Drazenovich crashed over from there. LeBaron missed the conversion attempt.

After Lou Groza's field goal—the second of four on the day for "The Toe" tied the game—Washington embarked on an 80-yard drive to retake the lead. The march got off to a good start when Harry Gilmer threw to Julie Rykovich for 25 yards. After that runs by Gilmer and Johnny Papit moved the ball downfield, LeBaron fired a pass to Gene Brito at the one and Drazenovich got his second short TD run from there. This time LeBaron's point after was good and it was 13-6.

Groza booted field goals in the third and fourth quarters to cut the margin to 13-12. Then quarterback Otto Graham, who had been having an ordinary game, made the big play for the Browns. He tossed a nice, 56-yard pass to Sherman Howard that landed his team on the Washington one. Graham snuck it over from there to give Cleveland a 19-13 lead.

Washington roared back and seemed to have made a big play of its own. Rykovich caught a fourth-down pass from LeBaron and broke free for a 31-yard gain to the Cleveland 18. There, however, Rykovich was sandwiched between two defenders and fumbled, with the Browns recovering.

The defense pushed Graham and the Browns back, though, forcing a fourth and long with 1:15 to go. Rather than punt from deep in his own territory, Graham took an intentional safety to make the score 19-15 and allow a free kick from the 20. LeBaron desperately tried to get into scoring range, but the clock ran out with the ball near midfield.

11/2/52	Steelers (2-4) 24, REDSKINS (2-4) 23			25,866	
Pitt	7	10	7	0	24
Was	7	0	0	16	23
Pitt	TD Dodril, Mathews, Rogel; PAT Kerkorian 3; FG Kerkorian				
Was	TD LeBaron, Taylor, Justice; PAT Rykovich 3; Safety Finks tackled in end zone by Hennessey				

Griffith Stadium—A furious fourth quarter rally came up short as the Redskins fell to the Steelers.

Washington trailed 24-7 entering the final period, but soon the Skins were knocking on the door. They had driven from their own two to a first and goal at the Pittsburgh three. The big play on the drive was a 57-yard completion from Eddie LeBaron to Bones Taylor. In an unusual occurrence, Taylor was caught from behind at the six, but it didn't seem to matter much at the time as a penalty pushed the ball to the three. In four tries, however, the Redskins couldn't push it over and the Steelers took over on downs. The drive did result in some points as end Jerry Hennessey tackled Pittsburgh quarterback Jim Finks in the end zone for a safety that made the score 24-9.

But LeBaron and Taylor weren't done. The two connected on a 40-yard touchdown pass with about six minutes left to pull the Redskins within eight. On the next possession, Taylor came back to grab a short, wobbly LeBaron pass at the Pittsburgh 25 and carried it down to the 13. Right after that, LeBaron threw to Charlie Justice for a touchdown and it was 24-23.

The home team got the ball back with time for one final prayer of a rally, but it came up short as LeBaron's pass was intercepted in Steeler territory.

11/9/52	EAGLES (4-3) 38, Redskins (2-5) 20			16,392	
Was	0	7	6	7	20
Phil	14	14	7	3	38
Was	TD Williams, Drazenovich, Taylor; PAT Buksar 2				
Phil	TD Stevens, Grand 2, Husvar, Jarmoluk; PAT Walston 5; FG Walston 2				

Shibe Park—The Redskins' play matched the climate on this dull and dreary day. The Washington offense, defense and kicking teams were equally inept in this defeat.

The Eagles got their first score when Don Stephens returned a punt 44 yards for a touchdown to make it 7-0. Soon after Eddie LeBaron botched a pitchout and the Eagles recovered at the Washington eight, bringing it to 14-0.

The visitors did manage to cut that lead in half with a touchdown punt return of their own, this one of 74 yards by Johnny Williams. That play, however, only seemed to wake up the Eagles. They scored two more touchdowns before halftime. One

was the result of a 68-yard drive; the other came after 240-pound tackle Mike Jarmoluk picked up a Washington fumble and rumbled 16 yards for a touchdown.

Any thoughts of a miracle rally were quickly dissipated when Philly took the second half kickoff and drove 73 yards for a touchdown to make it 35-7.

The Redskins had a good enough rushing game, posting 120 yards on the ground. But their defense couldn't stop the Eagles, who pounded for 231 yards.

11/16/52	49ers (6-2) 23, REDSKINS (2-6) 17			28,997	
SF	3	0	6	14	23
Was	7	7	3	0	17
SF	TD Perry, McElhenny, Wilson; PAT Soltau 2; FG Soltau				
Was	TD Taylor, Brito; PAT Buksar 2; FG Buksar				

Griffith Stadium—The Redskins appeared to be on their way to a big upset over San Francisco, but they couldn't hold on to a fourth-quarter lead and lost to the 49ers. Y. A. Tittle's 31-yard touchdown pass to Bobby Wilson with 3:31 to play was the game-winner, but a highly questionable play call by Eddie LeBaron gave the visitors considerable aid in pulling this one out of the fire.

Trailing 3-0 in the first quarter, the Redskins got rolling on offense. LeBaron and Bones Taylor connected for eight yards to the Washington 47. Then the two tried for bigger things and Taylor fought off two defenders to make a spectacular catch of LeBaron's long pass, gaining 38 yards to the nine. Two plays later LeBaron danced with who brung him as he faked a sweep, stopped and tossed a six-yard touchdown pass to a wide-open Taylor. George Buksar's extra point made the score 7-3.

It stayed that way until just before halftime. With 20 seconds left, Chuck Drazenovich picked off a Tittle pass and returned it 39 yards to the 49ers 36. Soon after that, Harry Gilmer connected with Gene Brito at around the 20 and the end dove the last few yards into the end zone with three defenders converging on him, completing the 26-yard touchdown play as time ran out in the half.

San Francisco rolled 70 yards after taking the second half kickoff to narrow the score to 14-9. The Redskins responded with a 35-yard field goal by Buksar and the lead was a more comfortable eight entering the final period.

Washington failed to get any points from a first and goal at the San Francisco nine and 49ers rookie Hugh McElhenny raced 46 yards for a touchdown to cut the lead to a single point, but the Redskins still seemed in control. With three and a half minutes to play, Washington had the ball with a third and two at its own 32. LeBaron's call was a pass, a decision that Curly Lambeau later said was "a bad call, what's the use of kidding yourself?" It turned from questionable into disaster as the receiver of the pass turned out to be the 49ers Sam Cathcart. He returned it from the Washington 46 to the 32. Two plays later, Tittle threw to Wilson, who took the ball at the 21 and benefited from a couple of missed tackles as he rolled into the end zone.

11/23/52	Giants (6-3) 14, REDSKINS (2-7) 10			21,125	
NYG	0	0	7	7	14
Was	3	0	7	0	10
NYG	TD Rote, Price; PAT Conerly, Poole				
Was	TD Heath; PAT Buksar; FG Buksar				

Griffith Stadium—The Redskins led the Giants 10-0 in the late stages of the third quarter but a Tom Landry interception set up the go-ahead score for the Giants as they rallied for the win.

The truth is that the game should not have been that close entering the late going. In the first half, the Redskins had three marvelous scoring opportunities and just three points to show for them. They drove 50 yards with the opening kickoff, but that drive resulted in George Buksar missing a 31-yard field goal attempt. A second march, this one of 75 yards, resulted in another field goal attempt by Buksar. This one was good and it was 3-0. The third foray into New York territory saw a touchdown get called back by a penalty and again resulted in zero points. Fortunately, the Giants were only able to mount one threat, but Ray Poole missed a 37-yard field goal attempt.

Leading 3-0 in the third quarter, the Redskins finally broke through for a touchdown, even though it seemed for a moment that the drive had again ended in futility. A nice return of a Landry punt by Charlie Justice set the home team up at its own 43. Julie Rykovich then ran for 15 yards and Eddie LeBaron passed to Leon Heath for another 15. The Giants soon intercepted LeBaron, but were flagged for pushing off the receiver and Washington had a first down at the 14. Four plays later, Heath scored standing up from the three to make it 10-0.

That score served to wake up the slumbering New York offense. After the ensuing kickoff, the Giants moved 59 yards to a touchdown. A 35-yard pass from Fred Benners to Joe Scott was the big gainer and Kyle Rote got over the goal line on a two-yard run. Charlie Conerly ran the conversion attempt over the goal line after a Redskin appeared in position to block the kick. The Giants would have had another attempt had Conerly been unsuccessful as the onrushing Redskins had been flagged for being offside.

Soon after that, Landry intercepted LeBaron's pass at the New York 42 and returned into Redskins territory at the 48. It didn't take long for the Giants to convert, as they moved smartly downfield and scored on Eddie Price's 14-yard run to make it 14-10. Washington didn't threaten after that and the Giants killed much of the remaining time with a drive to the Redskins 10.

Nov 27

Where's Sammy?
Baugh rides the bench despite Skins' 2-7 mark

11/30/52	Browns (7-3) 48, REDSKINS (2-8) 24				22,679
Cle	7	14	13	14	48
Was	14	3	0	7	24
Cle	TD Jagade, Speedie, Graham 2, Jones, Carpenter, Lavelli; PAT Groza 6				
Was	TD Taylor, Gilmer, Heath; PAT Buksar 3; FG Buksar				

Griffith Stadium—The Browns broke open a close game in the third quarter by scoring 13 unanswered points and continued on to rout the Redskins.

Washington held leads of 14-0 and 17-7 in the early going. An interception by Chuck Drazenovich and a fumble recovery by Johnny Williams set up two touchdowns in the first five minutes of play. After the Browns righted the ship and scored a touchdown, Otto Graham threw another interception and George Buksar kicked a field goal for a 17-7 lead in the second quarter.

It soon became apparent that the Browns were just warming up. By halftime they had claimed the lead on Graham's 24-yard touchdown pass to receiver Mac Speedie and a short touchdown run by Graham to make it 21-17.

It got no better in the third quarter. Hard-charging fullback Harry Jagade kept eating up yardage (147 yards on 16 carries) and the Browns kept scoring. The back breaker came with the Redskins still clinging to faint hope at 27-17. Ken Carpenter fielded a punt at this own 46 and went all the way to put it out of reach, if it wasn't already.

12/7/52	Redskins (3-8) 27, GIANTS (6-5) 17				21,237
Was	0	13	7	7	27
NYG	3	7	7	0	17
Was	TD Taylor 3, Papit; PAT Buksar 3				
NYG	TD Landry, McChesney; PAT Poole 2; FG Poole				

Polo Grounds—Washington spotted the Giants a 10-0 lead before roaring back on the strength of three touchdown catches by

Bones Taylor to take the upset in Gotham. The three Taylor scores came off of the arm of Eddie LeBaron, who had a fourth TD pass to Johnny Papit.

New York's Emlen Tunnell returned a punt 61 yards to set up his team's first score, a 15-yard field goal by Ray Poole. In the second quarter, a fumble recovery and subsequent 67-yard return to the Washington seven led to a touchdown run by Tom Landry. At least five Redskins appeared to have a shot at New York's defensive ace who was filling in at quarterback due to injuries, but Landry eluded them all and completed the scoring run for a 10-0 lead.

But the Redskins took the lead before halftime. From his own 34, LeBaron found Taylor wide open at the Giants 25. Even though Taylor had to wait momentarily for the ball to fall into his arms, he was still unchallenged as he strode into the end zone to complete the 66-yard play. Less than two minutes before the break, the combo hooked up from long distance again, with Taylor shaking his would-be defender and LeBaron hitting his receiver in perfect stride for a 50-yard touchdown. Although the point after was blocked, the game had clearly swung the Redskins' way at 13-10.

Washington expanded the lead in the third quarter after Joe Scott of the Giants made an ill-advised lateral attempt as he was being tackled and Laurie Niemi recovered the errant toss at the New York 43. The visitors advanced rapidly and scored on LeBaron's 13-yard pass to Papit, who made a leaping grab to put his team up 20-10.

As has been the pattern this season, the Redskins could not do it the easy way. The Giants scored to cut the lead to 20-17. After that, the Redskins had three possessions that ended inside the New York 15—and all without points. Finally in the fourth quarter Taylor again shook a hapless defender, LeBaron got him the pass once more and the Redskins had their first win over the Giants since 1948.

So Long, Sammy

Dec. 8—When Sammy Baugh signed his first contract with the Redskins, a Washington Post scribe opined that "he should go places in the pro game."

Rarely has a writer's prognostication proven to be more accurate.

Not only has Baugh gone places, he's taken the team with him. Washington claimed two NFL titles in Baugh's first six years in the league and played for the championship a total of five times thanks largely to Baugh's powerful, accurate right arm.

The team announced today that Baugh, who has passed for more than 12 miles worth of yardage in his 16-year career, will retire at the end of the season.

Speculation about Baugh's retirement has become an annual event around Washington, D.C. In fact, in 1938, his second year in the league, he said, "I'm going to play only one more year of pro football anyhow."

He stayed around a lot longer, of course, and for that the Redskins and their fans will be eternally grateful.

12/14/52	REDSKINS (4-8) 27, Eagles (7-5) 21				22,468
Phil	7	7	0	7	21
Was	7	7	0	13	27
Phil	TD Ziegler, Pollard, Jarmoluk; PAT Walston 3				
Was	TD Brito, Williams, Taylor, LeBaron; PAT Buksar 3				

Griffith Stadium—It was, as the Washington Post said, "well-nigh unbelievable." Eddie LeBaron's one-yard touchdown plunge with 18 seconds left gave the Redskins a stunning upset of Philadelphia. The Eagles were doubly stunned as the loss knocked them out of a chance to host a playoff game against the

Cleveland Browns to determine the NFL American Conference title.

At the outset, it didn't appear there were any surprises in store. Before the game was a minute old, the Eagles had a 7-0 lead. Al Pollard returned the opening kickoff 66 yards to the Washington 30 and two plays later the Eagles scored on Bobby Thomason's 19-yard touchdown pass to Frank Ziegler. The Redskins battled back to tie the game on Eddie LeBaron's 23-yard touchdown pass to Gene Brito.

In the second quarter, the teams exchanged touchdowns set up by interceptions. The Eagles went first, scoring on Al Pollard's two-yard run after Joe Sutton picked off LeBaron's pass and returned it 23 yards to the Washington 25. Then Johnny Williams grabbed one of Thomason's throws, found a block by Joe Tereshinski and scooted all the way, 38 yards to again knot the score, this time at 14.

It stayed that way until the fourth quarter when another interception was returned for a touchdown. This time, it was Eagles defensive tackle Mike Jarmoluk who sniffed out a short LeBaron pass intended for Harry Gilmer, grabbed the ball and got his 6-5, 240-pound frame moving rapidly enough to outrun the Redskins and score from 45 yards out.

Trailing 21-14, the Redskins went to work. Bones Taylor, who had drawn double and triple coverage most of the day, found some operating room and caught a Harry Gilmer pass for 51 yards to the Philly 16. Two plays later, Taylor was open again and LeBaron hit him for 11 yards and the tying score with 4:45 to go.

Desperation set in for the Eagles. A tie was as fatal to their playoff hopes as a loss. They faked a punt in an attempt to convert a fourth and six. Adrian Burk threw to Bob Walston. The receiver was going to be stopped short of the first down, so he lateraled to nobody in particular. The recipient wound up being Washington's Harry Dowda, who recovered the ball at the Eagles 42. Several plays later, Charlie Justice scooted 16 yards to the one and LeBaron snuck it over on the next play to give the Skins the win. The Eagles sent packing.

This was Sammy Baugh's last game. He quarterbacked the team in just one series and did not attempt a pass. As Baugh left the locker room, a reporter stated the obvious to team owner George Preston Marshall, "Guess you hate to see him go." Marshall answered on behalf of all football fans with a simple, "Yep.

1953
Head Coach: Curly Lambeau
Record: 6-5-1, Third in NFL Eastern Conference

Honors: Gene Brito Pro Bowl; Don Boll Pro Bowl; Gene Lipscomb Pro Bowl

Canadian Teams Make Serious Bids

Feb 25—Redskins draft picks Dick Modzelewski and Jack Scarbath are among some Washington players weighing offers to play football north of the border in 1953.

The Canadian Football League has started to offer big-money contracts to both established and potential NFL stars and it may force Redskins owner George Preston Marshall to reconsider his notoriously tight-fisted ways when it comes to paying players.

Defensive tackle Paul Lipscomb, who has been selected to play in the last two Pro Bowls, also has received an attractive offer from the CFL.

9/27/53	Redskins (1-0) 24, CARDINALS (0-1) 13				16,055
Was	7	0	0	17	24
Chi	7	3	3	0	13
Was	TD Justice, Drazenovich, Heath; PAT Dudley 3; FG Dudley				
Chi	TD Olszewski; PAT Summerall; FG Summerall 2				

Comiskey Park—The Redskins took advantage of a pair of Cardinal fumbles to jump into the lead in the fourth quarter, taking the win from Chicago.

The Cardinals led 13-7 and had possession in their own territory when Leon Heath nailed Billy Cross, separating the runner from the ball. Gene Brito scooped it up for the Redskins and made it down to the one yard line on the last play of the third quarter. On the final period's initial play, Chuck Drazenovich finished the job, smashing over from there. Bill Dudley's extra point pushed the Redskins into a 14-13 lead.

It was then Wally Triplett's turn to contribute to the Redskins' cause. He bobbled Dudley's kickoff at the seven, recovered, headed upfield and coughed it up for good at the 20, where Dudley recovered. Soon after that, Dudley's field goal gave Washington a 17-13 lead. The Cardinals gave the ball up on downs in a controversial measurement and Washington drove 46 yards to the clinching score, Leon Heath's 14-yard scamper.

10/2/53	Redskins (1-0-1) 21, EAGLES (0-1-1) 21				19,099
Was	7	7	7	0	21
Phil	7	7	0	7	21
Was	TD Niemi, Taylor 2; PAT Dudley 3				
Phil	TD Pihos 2, Burk; PAT Walston 3				

Shibe Park—The Eagles' Bobby Walston missed a 27-yard field goal with 40 seconds left, enabling the Redskins to hang on for a 21-21 tie with Philly.

Play was rather sloppy through much of the game. A Redskin fumble set up Philadelphia's first touchdown, which came on a pass from Adrian Burk to Pete Pihos. Then the Eagles came up with some brotherly love of their own as Burk fumbled deep in his own territory. Laurie Niemi pounced on it at the two and skidded untouched into the end zone to tie the score at seven.

After trading touchdowns again in the second quarter, the Redskins grabbed the lead in the third. Jack Scarbath pitched a TD pass to Bones Taylor, their second scoring hookup of the game. Then Scarbath scrambled for 40 yards into Eagle territory, setting up a Bill Dudley field goal attempt. Chuck Bednarik blocked it, though, and Tom Brookshier recovered it at the nine.

From there, the Eagles embarked on a game-tying drive, with Burk ramming it over for the last yard. After regaining possession, they again were on the march and moved to a first down at the Washington 17 with just under two minutes to play. But the defense stiffened and Walston's attempt was wide left.

10/11/53	REDSKINS (2-0-1) 13, Giants (0-3) 9				26,241
NYG	2	7	0	0	9
Was	10	0	3	0	13
NYG	TD Gifford; PAT Clay; Safety Long tackled Doll in end zone				
Was	TD Taylor; PAT Dudley; FG Dudley 2				

Griffith Stadium—Jack Scarbath threw a 38-yard touchdown pass to Bones Taylor in the first quarter to give the Redskins a 10-0 lead, and the Washington defense held the Giants at bay the rest of the way to help claim the 13-9 win for Washington.

Scarbath's touchdown to Taylor was the less spectacular of the two passes he completed in succession to quickly move the team 88 yards. The first was a 50-yarder to Charlie Justice.

Up 10-0, Washington gave nine points back to its guests. First, Don Doll tried to make something out of an interception return and backed up from his own five into the end zone, where Buford Long, the intended receiver, tackled him for a safety. In the second period, the Giants scored on an interception again. This time, it was their own pick. Tom Landry grabbed Eddie LeBaron's pass at the Washington 35 and returned it to the 16, where LeBaron tackled him. Before he was down, though, Landry lateraled to Frank Gifford, who completed the scoring run.

At 10-9, the Redskins went into a shell offensively, determined not to give the Giants any more opportunities. Washington attempted just two passes after intermission, and was content to pound the ball on the ground. Washington rushed for 215 yards and the defense did its part by holding the Giants to 104 on the ground. New York was even more inept through the air, netting just 37 yards on 30 pass attempts. Bill Dudley's third-quarter field goal provided the final margin.

10/18/53	Browns (4-0) 30, REDSKINS (2-1-1) 14				33,963
Cle	3	10	0	17	30
Was	0	7	0	7	14
Cle	TD Graham, Lavelli, Reynolds; PAT Groza 3; FG Groza 3				
Was	TD Taylor, Cloud; PAT Dudley 2				

Griffith Stadium—The Redskins surprised the Browns by taking a 14-13 lead in the fourth quarter on a 28-yard touchdown interception return by Jack Cloud. Cleveland regrouped quickly, however, scoring the last 17 points of the game to claim the win.

Washington entered the fourth quarter trailing 13-7, having scored on the first play of the second period on a beautiful 61-yard touchdown pass from Jack Scarbath to Bones Taylor. On the play, Taylor smoked his defender and Scarbath hit him in stride around the Cleveland 20. That gave the home team a 7-3 lead.

Cleveland responded before halftime by driving to Lou Groza's second field goal and quarterback Otto Graham's short touchdown run to take a 13-7 lead at intermission.

It stayed that way through the third quarter. Then early in the final period, Cloud latched on to a Graham pass and took advantage of a block by Jim Ricca to scamper 28 yards for the touchdown. The Redskins went into the lead, the Griffith Stadium crowd of nearly 34,000 went into a frenzy, and the Browns went to work.

Cleveland retook the lead at 20-14 on a 25-yard pass from Graham to Dante Lavelli. Washington was trying to respond when Harry Dowda fumbled and the Browns recovered at the Washington 38. Graham crossed the Redskins defense up by running for 20 yards on third and 15. Soon after that, rookie Billy Reynolds wrapped it up with a nine-yard touchdown run.

10/25/53	COLTS (3-2) 27, Redskins (2-2-1) 17				34,031
Was	7	3	0	7	17
Bal	3	7	10	7	27
Was	TD Baker, Justice; PAT Dudley 2; FG Dudley				
Bal	Taliaferro 2, Huzvar; PAT McPhail 3; FG Rechichar				

Memorial Stadium—The Colts scored 10 points in the third quarter to break a halftime tie and then ground out a killing fourth-quarter drive to preserve a 27-17 win over the Redskins.

Sam Baker gave the Redskins a 7-0 lead just over two minutes into the game with a nifty 32-yard touchdown run on a reverse. After the Colts took a 10-7 lead in the second quarter, the Redskins tied it up just before halftime after Bones Taylor caught two passes for 33 yards and Bill Dudley booted a 36-yard field goal.

Redskin mistakes cost the team dearly in the third quarter. First, Charlie Justice fumbled at the Colts 27 and Don Shula

recovered for Baltimore. Then Tom Keane picked off an Eddie LeBaron pass and took it back 36 yards to the Washington 17. Soon after that, fullback John Huzvar was stuffed at the line of scrimmage but had the presence of mind to lateral back to tailback George Taliaferro, who rolled in for a touchdown to put the Colts up 17-10. On the next Redskins series, Jack Scarbath messed up a handoff and Artie Donovan recovered for the Colts. That set up a field goal to give Baltimore a 20-10 lead.

The visitors tried to make a game of it in the fourth quarter when Justice sped 10 yards to score, standing up to make it 20-17 with about eight minutes remaining. However, the Colts ground out any hopes of a comeback by eating up all but 17 seconds of the remaining time with a 63-yard, 14-play touchdown drive. Huzvar scored the clinching touchdown from two yards out.

11/1/53	BROWNS (6-0) 27, Redskins (2-3-1) 3				47,485
Was	0	3	0	0	3
Cle	3	3	7	14	27
Was	FG Dudley				
Cle	TD Graham 2, Reynolds; PAT Groza 3; FG Groza 2				

Cleveland Municipal Stadium—The Browns toyed with the Redskins for a half and then took advantage of second half mistakes by Washington to roll to the easy win.

Washington came out gambling, with Eddie LeBaron taking off to run 24 yards out of punt formation on fourth and three on the Redskins' first offensive series. The visitor trailed by just three at the half—and that was after having blown a golden scoring opportunity. Leon Heath fumbled on a first and goal carry at the Cleveland four and the Browns recovered.

The errors continued in the second half. Charlie Justice fumbled a punt and Cleveland recovered at the Washington 44. Otto Graham set up his own short scoring run by passing to Dante Lavelli for 24 and then to Dub Jones for 15.

The Redskins were game, driving to the Browns 27. It ended there, however, when Tommy James picked off a LeBaron pass. A blocked punt led to another Graham touchdown and that sealed it for the Browns.

Washington was done in by its own errors. On the day the Redskins threw four interceptions and fumbled twice, losing both of them. The Browns suffered one interception but other than that they were clean in the giveaway category.

11/8/53	REDSKINS (3-3-1) 28, Cardinals (0-7) 17				19,654
Chi	7	10	0	0	17
Was	7	7	0	14	28
Chi	TD Stonesifer, Tagler; PAT Summerall 2; FG Summerall				
Was	TD Taylor, LeBaron, Heath 2; PAT Dudley 4				

Griffith Stadium—It appeared as though the Cardinals were about to break their season-long winless streak as they held both a 17-14 lead at the outset of the fourth quarter and a first and goal at the Washington nine. What seemed to be inevitable did not occur, however, as the Washington defense—Eddie LeBaron, Fran Polsfoot, and Leon Heath, with help from others—turned the dire situation around and led the Redskins to the win.

A Charlie Justice fumble late in the third period had put the Cardinals in position to wrap this one up, giving the visitors possession at the Washington 23. On the next play, Charlie Trippi ran to the nine for a first and goal as the third quarter expired. Three plays later, Chicago faced fourth down at the two. Quarterback Jim Root tried to sneak it over from there, but he couldn't sneak past Jim Ricca, Paul Lipscomb, and Knox Ramsey; they planted Root a foot short of the end zone.

The Redskins couldn't move the ball and the Cards soon had possession again at the Washington 41. The defense held again, this time taking over on downs at the 25 midway through the final quarter. From there, LeBaron and the offense got things going.

LeBaron went back to pass, and it was evident that the Cards knew what the play call would be. They had about a half dozen rushers zeroing in on LeBaron, but they ended up getting, well, zero. LeBaron eluded all of them and found ex-Card Polsfoot open down the sidelines. Polsfoot sped to the Cardinal nine before being knocked out of bounds. Two plays later, Heath scored from inches out and Washington led 21-17. A 36-yard Justice run spurred a 62-yard drive to the clinching score in the final minutes, another short touchdown run by Heath.

11/15/53	Bears (2-6) 27, REDSKINS (3-4-1) 24			21,392
Chi	7	6	7	7	27
Was	0	14	10	0	24
Chi	TD Hoffman 2, Macon; FG Blanda 2; PAT Blanda 3			
Was	TD Justice, Taylor, Heath; FG Dudley; PAT Dudley 3			

Griffith Stadium—The Redskins took a 24-20 lead into the fourth quarter but saw it disappear when Eddie Macon caught a nine-yard touchdown pass from George Blanda and Chicago held on for the win.

The Bears jumped to an early 10-0 lead and it seemed that the rout might have been on—until Washington rallied behind quarterback Jack Scarbath. The ex-Maryland star did a credible job of imitating the man he usually backed up, Eddie LeBaron, to create his team's first touchdown.

From the Chicago 32, Scarbath went back to pass and he appeared to be dead meat as Bear defenders converged on him from all directions. Somehow, he managed to elude the onrushers and continued searching for a receiver. He pulled up when he saw Charlie Justice open in the end zone. Justice was pretty creative on the play himself. He was supposed to be one of Scarbath's blockers but, having failed in that role along with a few teammates, he took off downfield to be the quarterback's safety valve receiver. "Choo Choo" almost lost the score as the ball came loose, but he held on just long enough for the official to signal a touchdown.

That score was rather ugly, but Scarbath's next TD pass was a thing of beauty. He found Bones Taylor in the receiver's familiar long stride and hit him for a 71-yard touchdown that gave the home team a 14-13 halftime lead.

Early in the third quarter, the Redskins expanded their lead. Gene Brito stole the ball from Chicago fullback Fred Morrison, giving Washington possession at the Bears' 27. Justice ripped off runs of 5, 11, and 8 yards to get his team to the two. Leon Heath carried it over from there and the Redskins enjoyed an eight-point lead at 21-13.

The Bears immediately took back the momentum, moving 77 yards to cut the lead to one. A Bill Dudley field goal stretched the margin to 24-20 entering the fourth.

Macon scored his game winner on a pass from George Blanda with five minutes gone in the fourth quarter. Washington had a chance to tie or take the lead midway through the period but a drive stalled in Chicago territory and Dudley missed a 27-yard field goal attempt.

11/22/53	Redskins (4-4-1) 24, GIANTS (2-7) 21			16,887
Was	0	0	7	17	24
NYG	0	14	0	7	21
Was	TD Taylor, LeBaron, Justice; PAT Dudley 3; FG Dudley			
NYG	TD Gifford, Rote, Price; PAT Clay 3			

Polo Grounds—Looking dead in the water in the first half, the Redskins came to life and rallied for the win in New York. The resurrection was a team effort, with quarterback Eddie LeBaron, offensive backs Bill Dudley and Charlie Justice and defender Johnny Williams leading the way.

It was 14-7 New York late in the third quarter and the Giants were trying to extend their lead as Frank Gifford attempted a 35-yard field goal. He missed it badly and Washington took over at its own 20. LeBaron passed the team into enemy territory and Dudley booted a 37-yard field goal to make it 14-10.

Then Williams got into the act, intercepting a Charlie Conerly pass to set Washington up at its own 33. Two plays later, LeBaron threw to Justice, who had gotten behind Tom Landry, and Charley chugged to the New York 18 for a 53-yard gain. Dudley then sped to the three. From there, LeBaron found his intended receiver stuffed at the line, so he took off around the left end and scored to put his team up 20-14.

Again, Williams got the ball back for his team, this time grabbing a tipped ball out of the air at the New York 28. Soon after that, Justice followed a block by guard Steve Witucki and rolled in for a 15-yard touchdown and a 24-14 lead. That rendered a late New York TD meaningless and Washington walked off with the win.

Nov 23

Drazenovich Suspended Without Pay
Lambeau cites 'improper attitude' on part of star linebacker, fullback

---

Nov 26

Drazenovich Reinstated
Player, Lambeau meet and resolve differences

11/29/53	Redskins (5-4-1) 17, STEELERS (4-6) 9			17,026
Was	0	7	0	10	17
Pitt	2	0	0	7	9
Was	TD Taylor, Rykovich; PAT Dudley 2; FG Dudley			
Pit	TD Chandois; PAT Bolovac; Safety Ferry tackled Heath in end zone			

Forbes Field—Bill Dudley's 41-yard field goal in the fourth quarter put the Redskins ahead of the Steelers and then Eddie LeBaron's short TD toss to Julie Rykovich wrapped up the win in Pittsburgh.

Johnny Williams' stirring 70-yard punt return set up a touchdown pass from LeBaron to Bones Taylor in the second quarter and Washington held a 7-2 halftime lead. Pittsburgh turned things its way in the second half, scoring one touchdown and threatening to score another by recovering a fumble on the ensuing kickoff to regain possession at the Washington nine. The defense stiffened and it appeared the Steelers had settled for a 16-yard field goal to take a 12-7 lead. Pittsburgh was denied the points, however, on an illegal procedure penalty and lined up to try the kick again. This time it was a fake as holder Lynn Chandois threw to Jim Brandt, who made it as far as the four yard line. Brandt was denied by Jim Ricca and Don Doll, who combined to make a sure stop to kill the threat.

It was from that point that the Redskins moved into Steeler territory to give Dudley the opportunity to put Washington in the lead. His 41-yarder was good and the visitors reclaimed the lead.

Washington wrapped it up in the late going when Laurie Niemi and Dick Modzelewski crushed the Steelers' Bill Mackrides, relieving the carrier of the ball. Gene Brito pounced on it at the Steeler 10 and LeBaron's four-yard scoring toss to Rykovich ensued shortly thereafter.

12/6/53	REDSKINS (6-4-1) 10, Eagles (6-4-1) 0			21,579
Phil	0	0	0	0	0
Was	0	0	0	10	10
Was	TD Dowda; PAT Dudley; FG Dudley			

Griffith Stadium—In a downpour that turned the stadium turf into a venue more suitable to mud wrestling than football, the Redskins scored twice in the game's final five minutes to beat the Eagles.

Philadelphia, which had averaged more than 400 yards per game in total offense, found itself spinning its wheels. The Eagles gained just 66 yards rushing and 81 through the air. The only time it appeared they were threatening the Washington goal line, it turned out to be but a momentary illusion. In the third period, Chuck Bednarik intercepted Eddie LeBaron's pass at the Washington 37 and ran it back to the 18. An official's flag, however, nullified the runback and the Eagles were pushed back to the 50. As it turned out the Eagles never took a snap from closer than the Washington 38.

The home team managed triple digit yardage totals in both rushing (159) and passing (119), but as the game slogged on it seemed as though both teams would be scoreless as they couldn't turn their yardage into points.

Until the fourth quarter, that is. LeBaron completed a pass to Al Dekker to convert a third down to get the drive started. Then it was turned over to Paul Barry, a powerful backup runner who was able to find his feet in the muck and break off runs of 22, 5, 11, and 6 yards. After LeBaron sneaked for a first down inside the 10, he called for three line plunges that ran the clock down to about four minutes. Bill Dudley came in and booted a 16-yard field goal to give Washington a 3-0 lead.

After the ensuing kickoff, Don Doll picked off a pass by the Eagles' Bobby Thompson. Then, after the Redskins had punted, Harry Dowda removed all doubt when he intercepted Adrian Burk's pass and slogged 23 yards down the sideline for a touchdown with 44 seconds to play.

12/13/53	Steelers (6-6) 14, REDSKINS (6-5-1) 13				22,057	
Pitt	0	0	0	14		14
Was	7	3	3	0		13
Pitt	TD Chandnois, Butler; PAT Bolkovac 2					
Was	TD Dekker; PAT Dudley; FG Dudley 2					

Griffith Stadium—The Redskins held a 13-0 lead going into the fourth quarter and, certainly, many on the team were figuring out how to spend the $400 per man they would receive for finishing in second place. Pittsburgh had other plans, however, and Jack Butler took the cash out of the Redskins' pockets when he picked off Eddie LeBaron's ill-advised pass from the Washington one and sauntered five yards to the winning touchdown.

The game started exactly as the Redskins wanted it to. They took the opening kickoff and marched 72 yards in seven plays to a touchdown with Julie Rykovich doing some excellent running along the way. The payoff came on LeBaron's 34-yard touchdown pass to Al Dekker.

Washington's defense did its part to preserve the 7-0 lead, stopping the Steelers three times in the first half on fourth down plays. Bill Dudley booted a 39-yard field goal on the last play of the first half and kicked another three-pointer in the third quarter to extend the lead to 13-0.

Pittsburgh scratched the scoreboard after driving from its 37 to the Washington 23. On the first play of the fourth quarter, Lynn Chandnois took a pitch from Ray Matthews, who had been stuffed at the line. Chandnois scooted into the end zone and it was 13-7.

Later in the fourth, it was the classic good news, bad news scenario for the Redskins. The good news was that the defense put on a magnificent goal line stand to deny the Steelers the go-ahead score. The bad news was that they were backed up at their own one.

The worst news was that, on third down, LeBaron made a play call that was highly questionable at best, throwing short to Charlie Justice. Butler made his fourth interception of the day and had an easy five-yard run into the end zone to give Pittsburgh the lead. Another interception of LeBaron, this one by Dick Flanagan, clinched it for the Steelers in the final minutes of play.

1954
Head Coach: Joe Kuharich
Record: 3-9-0, Fourth in Eastern Conference

Honors: Dick Alban Pro Bowl; Rob Goode Pro Bowl; Hugh Taylor Pro Bowl; Billy Wells Pro Bowl

---

Mar 23
LeBaron Jumps North
QB notifies team that he's going to play in Canada in 1954

Lambeau Fired After Scuffle With Marshall, Kuharich named coach
Aug 22—The dean of NFL head coaches is out of a job.

Redskins owner George Preston Marshall today fired Curly Lambeau as his team's head coach. The dismissal followed an early-morning shoving match between Marshall and Lambeau, a dustup which took place in the lobby of the team hotel in Los Angeles following the Redskins' 30-7 exhibition loss to San Francisco.

Line coach Joe Kuharich was named Washington's new head coach.

The seeds of the dispute and subsequent firing apparently came when Marshall saw three players going to their rooms carrying beer. Marshall is against his players drinking.

Neither had much to say regarding the shoving match. "I have no statement, no comment of any kind to make on the incident," Marshall said. "I won't discuss it."

Lambeau, who was about to embark on his 36th consecutive season as a head coach, was formally fired during a 10-minute meeting with Marshall about seven hours after the initial dispute. "I hold no animosity," Lambeau said after that. "It was just an unfortunate thing, part of the game."

There was a minor aftershock to all of this as defensive back Don Paul left the team. "If Curly goes, I go too," he said.

Sep 10
Janowicz Released From Baseball Contract to Sign with Redskins
Former Ohio State star, '54 draft pick of Skins, leaves Pirates for Washington

9/26/54	49ERS (1-0) 41, Redskins (0-1) 7				34,548	
Was	0	0	7	0		7
SF	13	14	0	14		41
Was	TD Scudero; PAT Kincaid					
SF	TD Wilson, Tittle, R. Berry, Perry 2, J. H. Johnson; PAT Perry 5					

Kezar Stadium—The Redskins were down 13-0 before the game was five minutes old and offered little resistance in being downed by the 49ers.

San Francisco's Joe Perry is nicknamed "Jet" and he lived up to the moniker by kicking in the afterburners and cruising 52 yards to the Washington six early in the first quarter. Soon after that, he scored on a much shorter flight of one yard.

On the first play after the ensuing kickoff, Billy Wells fumbled and the 49ers were back in business at the Washington 37. The result was a five-yard touchdown pass from Y. A. Tittle to end Billy Wilson and a 13-0 San Francisco lead.

Things didn't get any better in the second quarter as the 49ers scored twice to make it 27-0. The lone Redskins score came in the third quarter following a poor punt that put the Redskins in position at the San Francisco 24. Jack Scarbath threw a 12-yard touchdown pass to Joe Scudero to cut it to 27-7, but the Niners scored twice more in the fourth.

10/2/54	STEELERS (2-0) 37, Redskins (0-2) 7			22,402
Was	0	0	0	7	7
Pitt	13	14	7	3	37
Was	TD Dorow; PAT Felton			
Pitt	TD Nickel, Lattner, Rogel, Sulima, Brandt; PAT Held 4; FG Held			

Forbes Field—For the second straight week, the halftime score was 27-0 and, just like they were in San Francisco the week before, the Redskins were on the short end of that tally. They did manage a score to avert a shutout once again, but that was the extent of their success.

Pittsburgh quarterback Jim Finks was forced to leave the game to get a couple of stitches over his eye due to a fierce hit by Washington's Walt Yowarsky. That didn't faze the driving Steelers at all. Backup quarterback Paul Held got his first NFL action behind center and promptly threw a 25-yard touchdown pass to end Elbie Nickel.

Finks reentered the game and paid back the Washington defense by winging a pass 43 yards to Ray Matthews to move his team to the Washington one. From there, Johnny Lattner bulled over and it was 13-0. The Steelers continued to roll.

The score that averted the shutout came in the fourth quarter. Al Dorow was in the game replacing the ineffective Jack Scarbath. The backup found throwing room against a Steeler defense that was playing loosely and, with a 37-0 lead, had little interest in the proceedings at that point. In any case, Dorow completed passes to Bones Taylor, John Carson and Ed Barker, the last one moving the Skins 29 yards to the Pittsburgh one. Dorow sneaked it over from there.

10/10/54	Giants (2-1) 51, REDSKINS (0-3) 21			21,217
NYG	17	14	3	17	51
Was	0	14	7	0	21
NYG	TD Schnelker 3, Johnson, MacAfee, Wilkins; PAT Agajanian 5; FG Agajanian 3			
Was	TD Wells, Barker 2; PAT Felton 3			

Griffith Stadium—The Giants jumped to a 17-0 lead in the first quarter and never looked back, routing Washington in its home opener.

The Redskins did manage to push New York a bit in the second quarter by scoring two touchdowns, but the Giants had an answer for each of them. Billy Wells got the home crowd on its feet for one of the few times on the day with a 68-yard touchdown run. He was tripped up a bit as he got through the line, but got his feet back under him quickly. Wells rolled in for the score with a couple of Giant defenders in fruitless pursuit.

That made it 17-7, but New York quarterback Charley Conerly soon threw a 23-yard touchdown pass to Ken MacAfee to push New York's margin back to 17. Then Jack Scarbath got credit for throwing a 32-yard touchdown pass to Ed Barker, but in reality, the score was all Barker's. The end took Scarbath's short toss, sidestepped two defenders and then had to fight his way into the end zone after he was hit at the four.

That pulled Washington back within 10, but that was as close as it got. Conerly threw 20 yards to Bob Schnelker to give the Giants a 31-14 halftime lead. Washington did manage another touchdown in the third quarter on Scarbath's seven-yard touchdown pass to Barker, but the Giants' dominance was never threatened.

10/17/54	Eagles (4-0) 49, REDSKINS (0-4) 21			22,051
Phil	7	14	14	14	49
Was	7	0	14	0	21
Phil	TD Walston 3, Pihos 3, Ledbetter; PAT Walston 7			
Was	TD Barker, Atkeson, Taylor; PAT Felton 3			

Griffith Stadium—Philly quarterback Adrian Burk tied an NFL record by throwing for seven touchdowns, accounting for all of his team's TD's as the Eagles smashed the Redskins.

Actually, the Redskins were in this one as halftime approached. They trailed just 14-7 thanks to Al Dorow's 14-yard touchdown pass to Ed Barker in the first quarter. It appeared that Dick Alban had given the home team a big boost when he picked off Burk's pass at the Washington two and took it back to his 21. Alban fumbled, though, giving the ball right back to the Eagles. Soon Burk had TD pass number three, a 19-yard toss to end Pete Pihos and it was 21-7 at halftime. On the day, Pihos caught three of Burk's scoring passes, as did teammate Bobby Walston. In addition, Walston booted all seven extra points, giving him 25 points on the day.

Any thoughts the Redskins might have had of getting back into it were quickly squashed early in the second half when two defenders sandwiched Jack Scarbath deep his own territory. The quarterback fumbled and Chuck Bednarik recovered at the nine. Touchdown pass number four for Burk ensued, a five-yarder to Walston.

There was some momentary excitement for the home fans. Following the score, fullback Dale Atkeson took the kickoff back 99 yards for the longest scoring play in team history. He followed the wedge up the middle, was nearly tripped up at the 30 by ex-Redskin Harry Dowda, broke into the clear, and accepted teammate Bob Goode's escort to the end zone.

The return did little to add any doubt to the outcome of the game; the only suspense remaining was if Burk would get his seventh touchdown pass. Burk had been pulled from the game in the fourth quarter after his sixth, but when assistant coach Charley Gauer pointed out to head coach Jim Trimble that Burk had a chance to tie the record, Burk was put back in with 33 seconds left. He got number seven on a low pass that Pihos scooped up in the end zone with 20 seconds on the clock.

10/24/54	GIANTS (4-1) 24, Redskins (0-5) 7			22,507
Was	0	0	7	0	7
NYG	3	14	0	7	24
Was	TD Dorow; PAT Felton			
NYG	TD Schnelker, Long, Price; PAT Agajanian 3; FG Agajanian			

Polo Grounds—The Redskins were game but still didn't have nearly enough to beat the Giants.

Just as they did in the teams' previous meeting two weeks earlier, the Giants jumped out to a 17-0 lead. This time, though, instead of doing it in the first quarter, it took them the entire first half. When Frank Gifford fumbled the second-half kickoff and Bob Morgan recovered for Washington at the New York 33, the Redskins had an opportunity that they took full advantage of. Billy Wells took a pass from Al Dorow and twisted and turned for six yards before he got another 15 tacked on when the Giants roughed him after the whistle. From the 14, Dorow threw to Joe Scudero at the two and then the quarterback took it over himself from there.

With the score still 17-7 late in the third, Washington was driving, having clicked off a couple of first downs to get near midfield. Then, on a third and one, from his own 47, Dorow called a reverse with Scudero. The play lost eight yards and hopes of a comeback were just about done. New York quarterback Charley Conerly clinched it when, after being chased out of the pocket by Ralph Felton, he flipped an underhand pass to Eddie Price. The fullback rolled into the end zone to complete a 26-yard scoring play.

10/31/54	REDSKINS (1-5) 24, Colts (1-5) 21				23,567
Bal	0	7	7	7	21
Was	7	14	0	3	24
Bal	TD Young, Edwards, Toth; PAT Kerkorian 3				
Was	TD Atkeson 2, Wells; FG Janowicz; PAT Janowicz 3				

Griffith Stadium—The Redskins built a 21-7 first half lead and were able to keep the Colts at bay in the final half to claim their first win of the year.

Not only had Washington failed to win a game in its previous five starts, but the Redskins had not been in the lead at any time during those games. That ended when Al Dorow led Washington 60 yards down the field to a touchdown in the first quarter. A 19-yard run by Billy Wells and a nice catch by John Carson got the home team down to the five. Fullback Dale Atkeson soon scored to put Washington up 7-0.

An alert play by Bob Goode, who had lost his starting job to Atkeson, helped the Redskins up their lead in the second quarter. Vic Janowicz attempted a 40-yard field goal but the kick was low and it went into the Colts' line. Goode picked the ball up and battled his way to the Baltimore 17 to pick up a first down. Soon after that, Atkeson had his second touchdown and Washington led 14-0.

After Buddy Young scored for Baltimore to cut the lead in half, Dick Alban intercepted a pass from Cotton Davidson and the Redskins were in business. The subsequent scoring play went in the books as belonging to Dorow and Wells, but Goode and Joe Scudero should be credited as well. Goode's block enabled Dorow to get off the pass to Wells. Scudero made a fine sideline block to help spring Wells to complete the 48-yard touchdown play, pushing the Redskins to a 21-7 lead at the half.

It appeared as though the Redskins couldn't stand their good fortune. On the first play following the second half kickoff Dorow and Wells got their signals crossed on a handoff and the Colts recovered the fumble to set up a touchdown and slice the lead back to seven at 21-14. Baltimore threatened again after intercepting a Dorow pass, but a goal line stand stuffed the drive at the Washington five.

Janowicz was good on a 14-yard field goal attempt with 10 minutes left. His team would need those three points as Baltimore scored again as quarterback Gary Kerkorian drove the Colts to Zollie Toth's short touchdown run. With about four minutes left, Baltimore was threatening again after Kerkorian completed a pass to Jack Bighead that was good for 25 yards to the Washington 39. On the next play, though, Chuck Drazenovich slammed into Baltimore's Royce Womble, who had just received a short pass from Kerkorian. The hit forced a fumble that Scudero recovered at the Washington 27 to preserve the win.

11/7/54	BROWNS (4-2) 62, Redskins (1-6) 3				52,158
Was	0	3	0	0	3
Cle	13	14	21	14	62
Was	FG Janowicz				
Cle	TD Graham, Bassett, Jones, Brewster 2, Lavelli, Morrison, Gorgal; PAT Groza 5, Konz 3; FG Groza 2				

Cleveland Municipal Stadium—The scoreboard didn't lie.

It's tough to imagine that one team on a given day is really 59 points better than another, but it would be difficult to argue otherwise in this case. The Browns earned this rout. Cleveland racked up 33 first downs to four for Washington. The Browns recorded more than 250 yards both rushing and passing; the Redskins could not reach 40 yards in either category. It got ugly early, worse in the middle, and no better in the late going.

The only moment of hope for the Redskins came in the second quarter when Otto Graham, the Browns' All-Everything quarterback, had to leave the game with an injured arm with Cleveland leading 13-3. Washington had managed to hold the Browns to field goals twice and perhaps this was their chance to get back into it.

Nope. George Hatterman came in and threw three touchdown passes and the Browns never missed a beat. When Graham returned, he had a 41-3 lead.

Nov 12

Despite 59-Point Loss, 1-6 Record, Marshall Sees Better Days Ahead
Young squad will win championship within two years, says team owner

---

11/14/54	REDSKINS (2-6) 17, Steelers (4-4) 14				19,388
Pitt	0	7	0	7	14
Was	0	7	3	7	17
Pitt	TD Lattner, Nickel; PAT Kissel 2				
Was	TD Wells, Taylor; PAT Janowicz 2; FG Janowicz				

Griffith Stadium—Jack Scarbath threw a 42-yard touchdown pass to Bones Taylor on the first play of the fourth quarter to give the Redskins the win over Pittsburgh.

The Steelers were threatening to score first when Chuck Drazenovich picked off a Jim Finks pass at the Washington 11. A good chunk of the ensuing 89-yard touchdown drive came when Scarbath flipped a short pass to fullback Dale Atkeson, who ran around and through the defense for a 45-yard gain to the Steelers 28. Three plays later, Billy Wells made a neat cutback on a sweep and zipped nine yards into the end zone to make it 7-0.

Pittsburgh tied it up before halftime on Finks' touchdown pass to Johnny Lattner. It was third and one from the Washington 32 when Finks found his back all alone at the 10, and Lattner strolled in for the score.

Vic Janowicz booted a 32-yard field goal in the third quarter to push the Redskins back into the lead at 10-7. Then Scarbath connected with Taylor to open the final period and extend the lead to 10. The Steelers answered with a touchdown of their own, but the Redskins managed to burn off most of the game's last seven minutes by continuing their domination on the ground. On the day, Washington rushed for 258 yards, Pittsburgh 66.

11/21/54	CARDINALS (2-7) 38, Redskins (2-7) 16				15,619
Was	7	7	2	0	16
Chi	7	10	14	7	38
Was	TD Taylor, Wells; PAT Janowicz 2; Safety Ricca tackled McHan in end zone				
Chi	TD Matson 4, King; PAT Summerall 5; FG Summerall				

Comiskey Park—Ollie Matson scored four touchdowns, two of them from a long distance, as Chicago broke open a tight game in the second half and defeated the Redskins.

Matson wasn't the only one of the field ripping off long scoring runs. In the second quarter, Billy Wells busted an 88-yard touchdown run. That was the longest scoring run from scrimmage in team history and, more importantly at the time, it tied the game at 14 with halftime approaching. The Cardinals snatched the lead back on the last play of the half on a 37-yard field goal by Pat Summerall.

Matson saw to it that Chicago would stay ahead. With about two and a half minutes gone in the second half, he displayed his speed when he popped through the line and raced 62 yards for his second touchdown of the day. Later in the third quarter, he showed his power when he cut back and ran through a bevy of would-be tacklers to complete a 15-yard touchdown run. Then, with just over a minute to play, Matson left Dick Alban and Rob Goode in his dust as he jetted 79 yards for the final score of the game.

11/28/54	EAGLES (6-4) 41, Redskins (2-8) 33			18,517
Was	10	7	7	9	33
Phil	6	7	21	7	41
Was	TD Goode, Justice, Taylor, Dorow; PAT Janowicz 2, Felton 2; FG Janowicz			
Phil	TD Giancanelli 3, Pihos, Williams; PAT Walston 5; FG Walston 2			

Shibe Park—Adrian Burk wasn't going to sneak up on the Redskins this time. No sir, the Redskins were ready for the Eagles' part-time quarterback who threw for a record seven touchdowns against them at Griffith Stadium six weeks earlier in a game Washington lost by 28 points. This time, Burk, who had been spending a lot of time on the bench since his remarkable performance on October 17, passed for just five touchdowns. The Skins managed to slash their margin of defeat to a mere eight points.

The Redskins were in this one until their own mistakes became their undoing. Each team handed the other numerous opportunities as the game unfolded; the teams combined to lose the ball 12 times on fumbles.

Washington had a 17-6 lead in the second quarter, but the Eagles roared back to take the lead at 20-17 in the third quarter. Facing a fourth and two near midfield, Charlie Justice faked a punt and a combination of outstanding blocking and great running got Choo Choo into the end zone to complete a stunning 51-yard scoring jaunt. The 17-point underdogs had a 24-20 lead.

From deep in their own territory, though, the Redskins soon justified their underdog status. An errant pitch by Jack Scarbath handed the Eagles possession at the Washington seven and Burk soon had his team back on top with a touchdown pass to Pete Pihos. Then Rob Goode missed a tackle that allowed Jerry Williams to take a short Burk toss and ramble 84 yards for a touchdown to put it out of reach for Washington.

12/5/54	Browns (8-2) 34, REDSKINS (2-9) 14			21,761
Cle	7	10	10	7	34
Was	7	0	0	7	14
Cle	TD Bassett 2, Konz, Ratterman; PAT Groza 4; FG Groza 2			
Was	TD Taylor, Justice; PAT Felton 2			

Griffith Stadium—This one was not nearly as dreadful as the 62-3 whipping the Browns had laid on the Redskins some weeks back, but Cleveland's win was decisive nonetheless.

The Redskins took the opening kickoff and drove 73 yards in nine plays. The capper was Al Dorow's 13-yard touchdown pass to Bones Taylor. The end caught the ball at around the five and dragged defender Ken Konz into the end zone.

That was the high water mark for Washington. The Browns took the ensuing kickoff and drove to tie the score on Maurice Bassett's five yard touchdown run. Then Konz got a measure of revenge for his humiliating moment on Taylor's TD when he picked off a pass and encountered little opposition in rolling 25

yards to a touchdown. A Billy Wells fumble set up a Lou Groza field goal and the Browns were up 17-7 at the half.

Cleveland wrapped it up in the third quarter. Dante Lavelli made a spectacular, fingertip grab of Otto Graham's pass, a play that gained 64 yards to the Washington 15. From there, Graham ran it down to the one and Bassett got his second touchdown.

There was one more moment of excitement for the home team, but it came after the outcome had been decided. At the Washington 20 with four minutes left and the score 34-7, Dorow threw to Charlie Justice around the Redskins 40. When his defender gambled for the interception and missed, Justice was off to the races. He outmaneuvered and outran the remaining defenders to complete the 80-yard touchdown play.

Tackle Dave Sparks Dies After Game

December 5—Redskins tackle Dave Sparks collapsed and died of an apparent heart attack about three hours after Washington's game against Cleveland ended.

Sparks, 26, had played almost the entire game and appeared to be suffering from nothing more than the normal bumps and bruises associated with the game. He went to have dinner at the home of a friend and complained of chest pains. Soon after that he collapsed and was pronounced dead at Arlington Hospital about 30 minutes later.

> **Dec 9**
>
> ## Eddie's Back
> *LeBaron signs with Skins for '55 season after a year in Canadian league*

12/12/54	REDSKINS (3-9) 37, Cardinals (2-10) 20			18,107
Chi	0	13	0	7	20
Was	13	17	7	0	37
Chi	TD Sugar, Olszewski, Romanik; PAT Summerall 2			
Was	TD Ricca, Taylor 3, Justice; PAT Felton 4; FG Felton			

Griffith Stadium—Finally, in their 12th and final game of the year, the Redskins were on the good end of a blowout. Al Dorow passed for four touchdowns, three of them to Bones Taylor, and the Redskins dominated the visitors from Chicago.

Things got off to an auspicious start for the Redskins when Cardinal quarterback Lamar McHan dropped the ball and lineman Jim Ricca scooped it up and rumbled 25 yards for a touchdown. Then Dorow found Taylor a pair of scoring passes and it was 20-0.

The Redskins handed six points back to Chicago when Dorow's wild pitchout wound up on the ground at the Washington five where end Leo Sugar gratefully accepted the gift and walked in for the touchdown.

But Washington quickly dampened any spark the Cardinals may have had when Dorow again connected with Taylor, who was wide open in the end zone. It was 30-13 by halftime, making Santa's annual visit to the stadium a very merry one.

On the day, Taylor caught five passes for 106 yards. The Redskins piled up 464 yards of offense. The attack was well balanced as they picked up 221 on the ground and 243 in the air.

The Redskins were fortunate that they Cards turned the ball over seven times as they were guilty of five giveaways themselves.

1955
Head Coach: Joe Kuharich
Record: 8-4, Second in Eastern Conference

Honors: Gene Brito Pro Bowl, All-NFL; Chuck Drazenovich Pro Bowl; Eddie LeBaron Pro Bowl; Volney Peters Pro Bowl; Joe Scudero Pro Bowl; Torgy Torgeson Pro Bowl; Harry Ulinski Pro Bowl

9/24/55	Redskins (1-0) 27, BROWNS (0-1) 17				30,041
Was	6	7	7	7	27
Cle	0	3	14	0	17
Was	TD Carson 2 (24 pass from LeBaron, 17 pass from LeBaron), Janowicz (13 run), LeBaron (13 run) PAT Janowicz 3				
Cle	Brewster (21 pass from Ratterman), Renfro (8 pass from Ratterman); PAT Groza 2; FG Groza (44)				

Cleveland Municipal Stadium—Eddie LeBaron, in his first game back after a one-year defection to the Canadian Football League, ran for one touchdown and threw for two others as the Redskins stunned the Browns. It was the first time the Redskins had beaten the Browns in ten tries.

LeBaron had a big hand in Washington's other touchdown as well. In the first quarter, he completed a long pass to Leo Elter, who was dragged down at the Cleveland three after a 70-yard gain. On the next play, Vic Janowicz carried it into the end zone to put Washington up 6-0.

Not only had Cleveland always beaten Washington, the Redskins had rarely even enjoyed a lead in any of the previous nine games. In the second quarter, though, they found themselves up 13-0, thanks to LeBaron's first touchdown pass, a 24-yarder to John Carson.

The Browns being the Browns, they weren't about to just go away. Lou Groza kicked a 44-yard field goal to make it 13-3 at the half and then, in the third quarter, drove 80 yards and made it 13-10 on George Ratterman's 21-yard touchdown pass to end Darrell Brewster.

Rather than fold up, though, the Redskins fought back. Another LeBaron-to-Carson touchdown connection, this one from 14 yards, put the Redskins up 20-10. Cleveland scored another touchdown on Ratterman's eight-yard pass to Ray Renfro and it was 20-17 going into the fourth quarter.

Then it was Eddie's turn. From the Cleveland 13 with about six minutes left, LeBaron ran to his right, then faded backwards, found an opening off to the left and scampered into the end zone for the clinching score. All 11 Cleveland defenders had a shot at LeBaron, but he managed to elude each of them.

10/1/55	Redskins (2-0) 31, EAGLES (1-1) 30				31,891
Was	0	0	28	3	31
Phil	3	6	14	7	30
Was	TD Janowicz 2 (19 pass from LeBaron, 1 run), Thomas (2 free kick recovery), LeBaron 1 run; PAT Janowicz 4; FG Janowicz 20				
Phil	TD Giancanelli (13 pass from Thomason), Pihos (16 pass from Thomason), Norton (36 pass from Thomason) Stribling (from Tomason); PAT Walston 2, Bielski; FG Walston (25)				

Connie Mack Stadium—Washington racked up 28 points in the third quarter, 21 of them in a span of just over two minutes, to stun the Eagles.

Philly was rolling along with a 16-0 lead when Gene Brito recovered a fumble at the Eagles 32. Eddie LeBaron then passed

to John Carson to the 21 and to Vic Janowicz for 19 and the touchdown.

Norb Hecker's ensuing kickoff took an odd bounce to stay inbounds and rolled towards the Philadelphia goal line. Possibly forgetting that it was a free ball or perhaps hoping that it would roll into the end zone where they could fall on it for a touchback, the Eagles watched as the ball rolled. Washington's Ralph Thomas, however, got a bead on the ball, dove on it at the two and slid in for a touchdown.

Yet another Philly miscue led to yet another Washington touchdown. Jerry Norton, whose fumble had set up the first score, dropped the ball after catching a pass on the Eagles' first play from scrimmage and Torgy Torgeson recovered at the Eagles 13. Two plays later, Janowicz put his team into the lead at 21-16 with a one-yard touchdown run.

Philadelphia reclaimed the lead when Norton did some atoning for his errors by catching a 36-yard scoring pass from Bobby Thomason. It was one of four touchdown passes on the day for Thomason.

Washington's offense finally made a move without the aid of its defense late in the third. LeBaron threw a pass to Bert Zagers, who was dragged down at the one after a 57-yard gain. On the quarter's final play, LeBaron scored on a sneak and Washington was in the lead to stay at 28-23.

Janowicz booted a 20-yard field goal in the fourth quarter that proved decisive. Thomason's fourth TD toss of the day, this one to Bill Stribling, pulled Philadelphia within one at 31-30, but the Redskins ran the final three minutes off the clock and walked off victorious.

10/9/55	Cardinals (2-1) 24, REDSKINS (2-1) 10				26,337
Chi	7	3	7	7	24
Was	3	0	0	7	10
Chi	TD Nagler (8 pass from McHan), McHan (1 run), Hammack (2 run); PAT Summerall 3; FG Summerall (43)				
Was	TD Janowicz (1 run); PAT Janowicz; FG Janowicz (18)				

Griffith Stadium—After twice winning on the road as 10-point underdogs, the favored Redskins laid an egg in their home opener, losing to the Cardinals.

Vic Janowicz booted an 18-yard field goal six minutes into the game to give the Redskins their only lead at 3-0. Soon after that, however, John Carson was hit and fumbled after gaining 21 yards on a pass and Chicago recovered at its own 48. The Cardinals drove to a touchdown, which came when Gern Nagler made a nice, one-handed catch of Lamar McHan's pass in the end zone. That gave them a 7-3 lead they never relinquished.

After a gutty goal line stand denied the Cardinals a chance to extend the lead, Eddie LeBaron promptly opened the door for Chicago again by throwing a short pass that lineman Fred Wallner intercepted and returned to the Washington eight. Four plays later McHan snuck over from the one to make it 14-3.

In the fourth quarter after Chicago had extended its lead to 24-3, Ralph Guglielmi, the team's first-round draft pick, came into the game at quarterback. It's safe to say that the Cards were playing soft defensively and were somewhat disinterested in the proceedings but, nevertheless, the rookie led his first touchdown drive. His passes got his team close enough for Janowicz to dive over from the one to make the final 24-10.

10/16/55	Browns (3-1) 24, REDSKINS (2-2) 14				29,168
Cle	7	3	14	0	24
Was	7	0	0	7	14
Cle	TD Modzelewski 2 (6 run, 5 pass from Graham), Michaels (25 interception return); PAT Groza 3; FG Groza (41)				
Was	TD Atkeson (15 run), Hecker (9 pass from LeBaron); PAT Janowicz 2				

Griffith Stadium—The Browns broke open a tight game with two touchdowns in the third quarter and held off the Redskins to claim the win.

A nice 15-yard touchdown run by fullback Dale Atkeson tied the game at seven in the first quarter and Washington went into the locker room at halftime down 10-7.

Cleveland established control of the contest by taking the second half kickoff and embarking on a 77-yard touchdown drive. Otto Graham completed four of five on the march, the last completion a touchdown pass covering five yards to Ed Modzelewski. It was the second touchdown of the game for the former Maryland All-American known as "Mighty Mo."

Rookie Ralph Guglielmi then came into the game at quarterback and promptly threw a pass right into the hands of Walt Michaels. The linebacker accepted the gift and rumbled 25 yards for a touchdown to make it 24-7.

In the fourth quarter, Washington attempted to rally when Eddie LeBaron found Norb Hecker for nine yards and a touchdown to narrow the Cleveland lead to ten at 24-14. Hecker then executed a textbook onside kick and it appeared that any of five Redskins would pounce on the ball, but Michaels wound up with it. Cleveland killed the clock.

10/23/55	Redskins (3-2) 14, COLTS (3-2) 13				51,387
Was	0	0	7	7	14
Bal	0	3	10	0	13
Was	TD LeBaron 2 (1 run, 1 run); PAT Janowicz 2				
Bal	TD Ameche (3 run), PAT Rechiehar; FG Rechiehar 2 (50, 27)				

Memorial Stadium—The Redskins twice came from behind and held off the Colts to send most of a record Memorial Stadium crowd of more than 51,000 home unhappy. The folks in the crowd, though, couldn't complain they didn't get their money's worth in paying for admission to this taut, exciting game.

Baltimore's Bert Rechiehar booted a 50-yard field goal to account for the only score in a first half marked by spirited hitting. The Colts kicker and—remember this—defense back then doubled the lead with a 27-yarder in the third quarter.

Joe Scudero returned the ensuing kickoff 24 yards to the Washington 30. On second and four from his own 48, Eddie LeBaron uncorked a long pass intended for John Carson. Rechiehar was covering Carson and deflected the pass. Somehow, Carson recovered and caught the pass for a 50-yard gain to the two. LeBaron called his own number, sneaking it over from there to put Washington up 7-6.

That lead didn't last long. Buddy Young took the kickoff back from the goal line to the Colts 43, with Jim Norman making a touchdown-saving tackle. Well, it saved a touchdown temporarily anyway. The Colts drove to the three and Alan Ameche ran it over from there to give the home team the lead again at 13-7.

Washington went back up on top on its next possession. A roughing the passer call got the drive jump started before Carson

made an excellent leaping catch of a LeBaron pass to the Baltimore 29. Bert Zagers ran up the middle for 17 more yards to the nine. Three plays later, LeBaron again snuck it over the goal line to give his team a 14-13 lead with 12 minutes to play.

The Colts had a couple of opportunities to retake the lead, but came up short. Rechiehar missed a 52-yard field goal attempt and Joe Scudero picked off a pass in Washington territory to seal it with less than three minutes left.

10/30/55	GIANTS (2-4) 35, Redskins (3-3) 7				17,402
Was	0	0	7	0	7
NYG	7	0	21	7	35
Was	TD Janowicz (48 pass from LeBaron; PAT Janowicz				
NYG	TD Patton 2 (98 kickoff return, 69 punt return), Webster 2 (32 run, 41 pass from Conerly) Rote (36 pass from Conerly); PAT Agajanian 4; Conerly				

Polo Grounds—The Giants scored three third-quarter touchdowns to break open a tight game and went on to trounce the Redskins.

Jim Patton got things off on the right foot for New York when he took the game's opening kickoff back 98 yards for a touchdown and a 7-0 New York lead. Washington had only one real threat in the first half and it ended when the officials ruled that Norb Hecker had trapped an Eddie LeBaron pass in the end zone and it remained 7-0 at halftime.

Alex Webster did the Redskins in during the third quarter. He scored on a 52-yard run and then caught a 41-yard TD pass from Charley Conerly. On the latter play, he slipped an attempted tackle by Hecker at the 23 and fought through Joe Scudero to get into the end zone.

In between Webster's scores, Washington got its only touchdown on a 48-yard pass play from LeBaron to Vic Janowicz. The score served only to elude a shutout. With the score 28-7 in the fourth quarter, Patton struck again, going 69 yards with a punt return to provide the final margin.

11/6/55	REDSKINS (4-3) 34, Eagles (2-4-1) 21				25,741
Phil	0	7	0	14	21
Was	0	17	10	7	34
Phil	TD Pihos (19 pass from Thomason), Walston (23 pass from Thomason), Stribling (5 pass from Thomason); PAT Bielski 3				
Was	TD Barni (17 fumble recovery), Guglielmi (2 run), Monachino (2 run), Zagers (3 run); PAT Janowicz 4; FG Janowicz 2 (45, 33)				

Griffith Stadium—The Redskins held Philadelphia to 43 yards on the ground and recovered six Eagle fumbles, and breezed to a 34-21 victory.

The game was scoreless going into the second quarter, but the Redskins took command thanks to the Eagles' mistakes. Gene Brito slammed into Philly's Ted Wegert, separating the runner from the ball. Defensive back Roy Barni scooped the ball up at the Eagles' 17 and scooted into the end zone for a 7-0 Washington lead.

Next, it was former Redskin Rob Goode's turn to cough it up and Chet Ostrowski recovered at the Philly 43. That led to Vic Janowicz's 43-yard field goal. Then, on the ensuing kickoff, Wegert fumbled again and Ralph Felton got possession for the Skins at the Philadelphia 29. After Ralph Guglielmi tossed a short pass that Leo Elter turned into a 28-yard gain, the quarterback bootlegged it over for a 17-0 Washington lead.

Eddie LeBaron took over at quarterback in the second half and completed the rout. A 47-yard pass to John Carson led to a short TD run by Jim Monachino. In the fourth quarter, LeBaron teamed up with Bert Zagers to put it away. The quarterback threw a pass to Zagers, who fought his way for 35 yards to the Eagles 19. LeBaron then scrambled to the three and subsequently handed to Zagers, who ran in for the touchdown.

11/13/55	REDSKINS (5-3) 7, 49ers (3-5) 0				25,112
Was	0	0	7	0	7
SF	0	0	0	0	0
Was	TD Zagers (13 run); PAT Janowicz				

Griffith Stadium—Defensive end Gene Brito and halfback Bert Zagers produced the game's only touchdown as the Redskins got a shutout win over San Francisco.

The first half consisted mostly of the Redskins gearing up to repel San Francisco scoring threats. Four times the visitors had first downs inside the Washington 27. Washington stuffed quarterback sneaks, nailed runners and passers for huge losses and watched as their opponents missed three field goals. They felt fortunate to still be in a scoreless game late in the third quarter when Brito and Zagers struck.

It was Brito's turn first. He chased quarterback Y. A. Tittle backwards and nailed the would-be passer, sending the ball rolling towards the sideline. The defender had a bead on it and recovered the fumble at the San Francisco 33.

Zagers then took it most of the rest of the way. Eddie LeBaron passed to the back for 17 yards to the 16. After Jim Monachino ran three yards, Zagers ran 13 yards for the score. Assists on the nice cutback effort went to fullback Leo Elter and guards Red Stephens and Walt Houston, all of whom bulldozed the path for Zagers.

San Francisco didn't mount a serious threat in the fourth quarter, although they did gain possession at their own 48 with 52 seconds left. The clock ran out on their effort to tie it up.

11/20/55	Redskins (6-3) 31, CARDINALS (3-5-1) 0				16,901
Was	14	0	0	17	31
Chi	0	0	0	0	0
Was	TD Zagers (55 punt return), Janowicz (8 pass from Guglielmi), Carson (31 pass from LeBaron), Monachino (10 run); PAT Janowicz 4; FG Janowicz (20)				

Comiskey Park—The Redskins scored early and late and controlled the ball on the ground in between to post the rout of the Cardinals.

Bert Zagers got things jump started when he took the game's first punt, twisted away from the coverage and was off, scoring on a 55-yard run just over a minute into the game. Later in the first quarter, the Redskins drove 57 yards to another score. The first ten plays of the drive were runs, the eleventh an eight-yard touchdown pass from Ralph Guglielmi to Vic Janowicz.

Throughout the second and third quarters, the Redskins maintained their grip on their opponents, although they blew a couple of opportunities to expand their lead when Janowicz misfired on a pair of field goal tries.

In the fourth, the Redskins wrapped it up as they drove to a touchdown pass from Eddie LeBaron to John Carson. Interceptions set up a Janowicz field goal and a Jim Monachino touchdown run to complete the blowout.

11/27/55	Redskins (7-3) 23, STEELERS (4-6) 14				21,760
Was	7	7	9	0	23
Pit	0	7	7	0	14
Was	TD Elter 2 (20 run, 33 run), Scudero (49 punt return); PAT Janowicz, Hecker; FG Janowicz (13)				
Pit	TD Mathews (61 pass from Finks), Watson (62 pass from Finks); PAT Weed 2				

Forbes Field—Leo Elter scored two touchdowns rushing to lead the Redskins over the host Steelers. The remarkable thing about this contest was that Washington won despite failing to complete a single forward pass.

Ralph Guglielmi was 0-2 passing and Eddie LeBaron missed all six of his attempts, but they knew they had a good thing going in the ground game. While the passing game netted minus 29

yards, Guglielmi and LeBaron handed off to backs who rushed for 329 on the day.

Both of Elter's TD's came in the first half. The first was a 20-yard jaunt that gave his team a 7-0 lead. Then, after the Steelers had tied the game on Jim Finks' 61-yard scoring bomb to Ray Mathews, Elter weaved his way behind his blockers and through the defense 33 yards for the touchdown that put the Redskins ahead 14-7 at halftime. Chuck Drazenovich set up that TD by intercepting Finks' pass at the Washington 39.

In the third quarter, Joe Scudero caught a punt at midfield then ran backwards about ten yards, trying to find some room to operate. He found it, blowing by at least half of the Steelers' coverage team en route to a 49-yard touchdown run. That run and Vic Janowicz's field goal enabled the Redskins to withstand another long TD pass by Finks, this one to Sid Watson.

12/4/55	Giants (5-5-1) 27, REDSKINS (7-4) 20				28,556
NYG	7	10	3	7	27
Was	0	20	0	0	20
NYG	TD Heinrich (5 run), Gifford (1 run), Rote (26 pass from Conerly); PAT Agajanian 3; FG Agajanian 2 (38, 35)				
Was	TD Scudero (94 kickoff return), Elter (28 pass from LeBaron), Thomas (9 pass from Guglielmi); PAT Baker 2				

Griffith Stadium—The Redskins' unlikely pursuit of the Eastern Conference title came to a gut-wrenching halt today as a desperate drive to tie the game in the closing minute ended with a New York interception.

Early on, it seemed as though the Giants would need no late heroics to win this one. They jumped to a 14-0 lead in the second quarter, arriving at that score when Frank Gifford bulled over for a one-yard touchdown run. The home team came to life immediately after that. Joe Scudero fielded the ensuing kickoff at the six and blazed untouched through the coverage team for 94 yards and a touchdown to cut the lead in half.

It appeared that the comeback attempt would be short lived when New York's Jim Patton nearly duplicated Scooter's feat, breaking the next kickoff for big yardage. Ralph Thomas saved the touchdown by knocking Patton out of bounds after a 65-yard gain. The Giants had to settle for a field goal and a 17-7 lead.

The Redskins came right back behind Eddie LeBaron. Operating from his own 30, the quarterback completed passes to John Carson, Dale Atkeson, and Thomas to carry the team to the New York 28. From there, LeBaron tossed one into the end zone. The pass appeared to be headed for the wrong hands as two defenders converged on it. Fortunately, it bounced out of the hands of Herb Rich and into the waiting arms of Leo Elter. The conversion was blocked and the Giants' lead was four at 17-13 with about three minutes left before halftime. Rich would have better fortune in the end zone later in the game.

The Redskins crossed the Giants up with an onside kick attempt. The element of surprise worked to perfection and Roy Barni recovered for Washington at the New York 43. LeBaron ran for seven yards, but was shaken up on the play and Ralph Guglielmi came in at quarterback. He immediately made a key play, throwing a perfect pass to Bert Zagers while on the run. Two plays later Guglielmi found Thomas for an eight-yard touchdown pass. The Giants again got a hand on the conversion attempt, but Norb Hecker's effort slithered over the crossbar anyway and Washington had the lead. Starting with Gifford's touchdown, the teams had combined for 30 points in about eight minutes of play.

But that would be all the scoring the Redskins could muster. The visitors tied the game on a 35-yard field goal by Ben Agajanian, a score that was set up by Atkeson's fumble at the his own 39.

After an exchange of punts left New York with favorable field position at the Washington 49, the Giants moved in for the kill. Charley Conerly threw to ex-Redskin Alex Webster for 17 yards and then caught the Redskins in a coverage foul-up. Kyle Rote was wide open to catch Conerly's 26-yard touchdown pass to give New York the lead for good.

The Redskins threatened in the fourth quarter, but missed a field goal with about six minutes left. They got the ball back at their own 39 with time for one more go at gaining the tie, which would have kept them in the running for the conference crown. LeBaron threw for 11 to Carson, to Charley Jones for 21 and Atkeson for 13, and then went back to Carson for another 17 to the New York six. Two plays later, it appeared that LeBaron's pass was headed for Jones' hands in the end zone, but Rich cut in at the last second and intercepted with 1:03 left to play.

12/11/55	**REDSKINS (8-4) 28, Steelers (4-8) 17**			20,547	
Pitt	0	14	3	0	**17**
Was	7	0	7	14	**28**
Pitt	TD Rogel (1 run), Mathews (29 pass from Finks); PAT Weed 2; FG Weed (9)				
Was	TD Elter (22 run), Thomas (11 pass from LeBaron), Atkeson (5 pass from LeBaron), Janowicz (1 run); PAT Janowicz 4				

Griffith Stadium—Two goal line stands kept the Redskins in the game and Eddie LeBaron spurred the rally that pulled them past the Steelers.

Pittsburgh led 14-7 as halftime neared and were threatening to make it worse after Jim Monachino fumbled a Steeler punt to set the visitors up at the Redskin 33. They drove to the three, but Gene Brito saved the day with a tremendous effort. He chased down Fran Rogel on an end around, stripped the ball from the back, and recovered the fumble with 30 seconds left until halftime.

After halftime, the Steelers got close again, but had to settle for Tad Weed's nine-yard field goal for a 17-7 lead. It was then that the Redskins woke up. Greatly aiding in the process was the play of quarterback LeBaron, who was inserted into the lineup in place of starter Al Dorow after intermission. Working from his own 29, LeBaron quickly went to work, connecting with Monachino for 15 yards and then with end Ralph Thomas for 25 more. John Reger caught Thomas from behind at the 16, but Thomas couldn't be denied three plays later when he gathered in LeBaron's pass in the deep corner of the end zone to cut the deficit to 17-14.

On the last play of the third quarter Monachino broke loose from down the sideline for 35 yards to the Pittsburgh 16. After gaining a first down at the five, Vic Janowicz lost a yard. The Steeler defense dug in, expecting another run. For some reason they didn't pay any attention to Atkeson, who was able to slip over the goal line uncovered and take in LeBaron's pass to give the Redskins the lead. Vic Janowicz closed out the scoring later in the fourth, setting a team scoring record with 88 points.

Dec 19

Kuharich Gets Three-Year Deal
8-4 record earns coach extension

1956
Head Coach: Joe Kuharich
Record: 6-6, Third in Eastern Conference

Honors: Sam Baker Pro Bowl; Gene Brito Pro Bowl, All-NFL; Al Dorow Pro Bowl; Chuck Drazenovich Pro Bowl; Leo Elter Pro Bowl; Dick Stanfel Pro Bowl, All-NFL; Torgy Torgeson Pro Bowl

---

Kuharich Turns Down Huskies, Will Stay In D.C.

Feb 10—Joe Kuharich will be doing his coaching in the District of Columbia in 1955 and not in Washington state.

A report appearing in the Seattle Times earlier this week stated that Kuharich "will be the new coach of the University of Washington football team."

The report was inaccurate, but there was some fire along with the smoke. Kuharich today admitted that he had discussed the possibility of making the jump to the college game through some friends. After considering his options, however, he decided to remain with the Redskins.

Apr 23

Alban Traded to Lions
DB swapped for guard Dick Stanfel

Janowicz Injured in Auto Accident

Aug 18—The promising career of Redskins halfback Vic Janowicz is in jeopardy after he was seriously injured in an automobile accident.

Janowicz was a passenger in a car that ran into a telephone pole. He was thrown from the vehicle and remains unconscious.

The accident came as he was returning from a party at the house of teammate Gene Brito, who lives about an hour from the team's training camp site at Occidental College. Just a few blocks from Occidental, the driver lost control of the car and ran into the pole.

Janowicz set a team record by scoring 88 points in 1955, working double duty as a halfback and a place kicker. His 397 rushing yards led the team.

Dorow Hospitalized After Crash

August 20—Quarterback Al Dorow has been hospitalized with injuries sustained in an automobile accident. The crash, caused by a drunk driver, claimed the life of his mother-in-law, Bernadine Alison.

Dorow was released from a hospital near the scene of the accident, which is about 65 miles from the Redskins training camp in Los Angeles. When he returned to Occidental College, Dorow complained of back pain and checked in to Hollywood Presbyterian Hospital.

At the same facility, teammate Vic Janowicz is recovering from injuries sustained in a separate car wreck.

Dorow has two broken ribs, a contusion of the kidney and strained back ligaments.

Mrs. Alison was killed instantly when she was thrown from the car after it collided with a Jeep that suddenly pulled onto the road.

9/30/56	**STEELERS (1-0) 30, Redskins (0-1) 13**			27,718	
Was	0	6	0	7	13
Pit	7	7	9	7	30
Was	TD Meilinger (15 pass from LeBaron); PAT Baker; FG Baker 2 (42, 41)				
Pit	TD Chandois 3 (2 run, 4 run, 17 pass from Marchibroda, Marchibroda (1 run); PAT Glick 3; FG Glick (27)				

Forbes Field—Veteran halfback Lynn Chandois scored three touchdowns and set up another for the Steelers as they easily beat the visiting Redskins.

The Redskins had their best chances to get into the game in the second quarter when they twice drove into Steeler territory. Twice, however, they had to settle for Sam Baker field goals. After the second successful kick, which pulled the Redskins to within 7-6, Chandois killed any momentum when he returned the ensuing kickoff 91 yards to the Washington 14. That led to a one-yard sneak for a touchdown by quarterback Ted Marchibroda and a 14-6 halftime lead for the Steelers.

Pittsburgh quickly put it away in the third period. Dale Atkeson fumbled and Jack Butler recovered for the Steelers at the Washington 17. On the next play, Marchibroda threw a nice pass that found Chandois just as the receiver crossed to goal line and it was 21-6.

Washington's deficit grew to 30-6 before they scored their only touchdown—largely a gift from Jack Scarbath, their former quarterback who had replaced Marchibroda during garbage time. Scarbath threw a pass directly into the arms of defensive back Roy Barni at the Pittsburgh 40. Barni returned the interception to the 26. Soon after that, Eddie LeBaron threw a 15-yard touchdown pass to rookie Steve Meilinger.

10/6/56	**EAGLES (1-1) 13, Redskins (0-2) 9**			26,607	
Was	0	6	3	0	9
Phil	0	7	0	6	13
Was	Atkeson (3 run); FG Baker (38)				
Phil	Schaefer (2 run), Thomason (1 run); PAT Walston				

Shibe Park—The Eagles scored a touchdown on a one-yard sneak by Bobby Thomason with just under four minutes left to come away with a win over the Redskins.

Sam Baker went 32 yards with a fake punt to set up Washington's first touchdown. The play set them up at the Philly 27 and they soon scored on Dale Atkeson's three-yard burst. Baker's point after attempt was wide and it was 6-0 Redskins.

The Eagles converted a fourth and one at the Washington five, leading to their first score, a two-yard touchdown run by Don Schaefer. Their conversion was good and they took a 7-6 lead into halftime.

With 6:45 remaining the in the third period, Washington went back into the lead on Baker's 38-yard field goal. A 26-yard gain on Al Dorow's pass to Atkeson was the key play in the drive to Washington's 9-7 lead.

It appeared the lead might hold as the game moved into the fourth quarter, but the Eagles embarked on the game-winning drive from their own 37. Thomason completed a pair of key passes to Skippy Giancanelli and Schaefer to move the Eagles downfield. Thomason snuck over from the one to push the Eagles back into the lead at 13-9 with 3:40 left. Jerry Norton intercepted Dorow's pass at the Philadelphia 20 with 2:05 to go to kill the Skins' last bid.

10/14/56	**Cardinals (2-1) 31, REDSKINS (0-3) 3**			25,794	
Chi	7	7	7	10	31
Was	0	0	3	0	3
Chi	TD Bernardt (95 punt return), Root (1 run), Matson (105 kickoff return), Burl (19 pass from McHan); PAT Summerall 4; FG Summerall (23)				
Was	FG Baker (19)				

Griffith Stadium—The Cardinals got two long kickoff returns for touchdowns from Frank Bernhardt and Ollie Matson as they trounced the Redskins.

Bernhardt's big play came just three minutes into the game on a 95-yard punt return. He went untouched through the Redskins to give his team a 7-0 lead.

Chicago drove 94 yards to extend its lead in the second quarter, scoring a touchdown on quarterback Jim Root's one-yard plunge to go up 14-0 at halftime.

Just as the home team got a small buzz going in the crowd by driving deep into Chicago territory to score on Sam Baker's 19-yard field goal, Matson silenced the stadium and wrapped it up for his team.

He took Norb Hecker's kickoff five yards deep in the end zone and the former Olympian showed off his speed, dashing all the way for a touchdown. Hecker seemed to have a shot at him at the Washington 35, but Matson kicked in a higher gear and Hecker's arms found nothing but the air stirred up by the sprinter's afterburners. That made it 21-3 and the rout was assured.

Considering the score, the Cardinals enjoyed a rather slim statistical margin. They outgained the Redskins 286 yards to 230. That statistic, of course, punctuates the importance of the kickoff returns as the difference between a competitive game and a rout.

10/21/56	**REDSKINS (1-3) 20, Browns (1-3) 9**			23,332	
Cle	3	6	0	0	9
Was	0	7	7	6	20
Cle	FG Groza 3 (47, 30, 12)				
Was	TD Elter (5 run), James (9 pass from LeBaron); PAT Baker 2; FG Baker 2 (32, 16)				

Griffith Stadium—Halfback Leo Elter rushed for 91 yards on 16 carries and Eddie LeBaron led touchdown drives in the second and third quarter to lead the Redskins past the Browns.

Elter's day got off to an inauspicious beginning when he killed a promising opening drive by fumbling the ball at the Cleveland 12. Cleveland drove to the first of three Lou Groza field goals, although they lost their starting quarterback in gaining the lead. George Ratterman suffered a serious knee injury on a quarterback sneak during that drive and, although Babe Parilli finished off the march to Groza's three-pointer, the Browns struggled on offense the entire game.

Two pass interference calls helped the Redskins move in for their first touchdown. The second one was in the end zone, giving Washington a first down at the Cleveland one. Elter fought to pay dirt from there and the Redskins had the lead at 7-3. Cleveland claimed the lead back on Groza's second and third field goals, the latter with just 20 seconds left in the first half.

Midway through the third quarter, the Redskins took possession at their own 20 and embarked on the game-winning march. LeBaron kept it mostly on the ground, handing off to Elter, Dale Atkeson and Tom Runnels for good chunks of yardage. From the Cleveland nine, the signal caller decided to mix it up, throwing to a wide-open Dick James in the end zone. The catch was anything but routine with James juggling the ball and then getting a grasp on it as he rolled near the end line. Sam Baker's point after put Washington up 14-9.

The home team wrapped it up with two Baker field goals in the fourth quarter. One followed a fumble recovery by J. D. Kimmel at the Browns 13 and the other capped a late, time-killing drive in the last five minutes.

10/28/56	Redskins (2-3) 17, CARDINALS (4-1) 14				50,553
Was	0	3	14	0	17
Chi	14	0	0	0	14
Was	TD James (34 pass from Dorow), Meilinger (40 pass from Dorow); PAT Baker 2; FG Baker (22)				
Chi	TD Boydston (39 pass from McHan), Olszewski (6 run); PAT Summerall 2				

Comiskey Park—Al Dorow passed for two third-quarter touchdowns to rally the Redskins past Chicago, dealing the Cards their first loss of the year.

Dorow came into the game in the third quarter with the Cardinals up 14-3. Starting quarterback Eddie LeBaron was shaken up when he was roughed by an overzealous defender, who was flagged for a personal foul on the play, moving the ball to the Chicago 46. Three plays later, he threw a 34-yard touchdown pass to rookie back Dick James, who took advantage of a neat block by end Steve Meilinger and the Redskins pulled within four at 14-10.

Chicago was poised to respond as Dave Mann made a nice one-handed catch and picked up 23 yards into Washington territory at the 28. It was there that he fumbled, however, and Art DeCarlo made the recovery for the Redskins.

It took just two plays for Washington to take the lead. Meilinger got behind his defender and Dorow hit him with a 40-yard strike for the touchdown.

After that, the Cardinals fumbled or threw away some late scoring chances and the Redskins walked off winners.

Janowicz Gets Game Ball

Oct 29—He didn't play, but the presence of Vic Janowicz was felt on the field as the Redskins overcame a bad start to beat the Cardinals.

The young back, who suffered a severe concussion in a car crash during training camp, was at a game for the first time since the accident. He sat on the bench and seemed to serve as inspiration as the team battled back from a 14-0 first-quarter deficit.

"Who knows?" said coach Joe Kuharich. "Maybe Vic being there was a factor in all of the extra drive all the boys kept displaying."

The players awarded Janowicz a game ball as a token of their support. They also gave him something a bit more substantial, a check for $1,300 from the fund to which the players and coaches have been contributing $10 a week to help defray his medical expenses.

Oct 30

Billy Wells Rejoins Redskins
Halfback is on leave from the Army

11/11/56	REDSKINS (3-3) 18, Lions (6-1) 17				28,003
Det	0	3	7	7	17
Was	3	10	0	5	18
Det	TD Gedman (1 run), Middleton (10 pass from Layne); PAT Layne 2; FG Layne (22)				
Was	TD James (41 run); PAT Baker; FG Baker 3 (16, 20, 27); Safety Lary of Detroit stepped out of end zone.				

Griffith Stadium—Again the Redskins played the role of giant killers, knocking off a previously unbeaten team for the second straight week. Sam Baker kicked three field goals to help hand the Lions their first loss after six straight wins to open the season.

Following Baker's first field goal, Dick James scored Washington's only touchdown on a spectacular 41-yard run. He took a pitchout from Al Dorow and found a solid block from guard

Red Stephens as he cut back into the secondary. The last obstacle between James and the end zone was Bob Long, who waited at the 10. The would-be tackler wound up with James' helmet—but it no longer contained the rookie runner's head. James was standing in the end zone hatless but happy with the 10-0 Washington lead.

The two teams exchanged field goals before halftime and the Skins maintained their 10-point margin. The crowd at Griffith Stadium was beginning to sense an upset in the making. The enthusiasm was dampened, temporarily, in the third quarter, when Leo Elter fumbled and linebacker Joe Schmidt recovered for the Lions at the Washington 13. Six plays later, Detroit scored on Gene Gedman's one-yard plunge to make it 13-10.

With the same score in the fourth quarter, Detroit coach Buddy Parker made a decision that was bold but maybe not very bright. Facing fourth down at his team's own five, Parker ordered punter Yale Lary to step out of the end zone and take a safety rather than punt from deep in his own territory. That is often a sound strategy when your team is in the lead, but a questionable idea when it puts your team in a position where it has to score a touchdown and hold its opponent scoreless to win the game.

The Lions accomplished the former, but not the latter. Baker booted a 27-yard field goal with under two minutes left to give his team an eight-point lead. Detroit did manage to score its touchdown, a 10-yard pass from Bobby Layne to David Middleton. The Redskins, though, wrapped it up when they recovered an onside kick attempt with 1:18 to go. Dorow killed the clock with a couple of sneaks.

11/18/56	REDSKINS (4-3) 33, Giants (6-2) 7				26,261
NYG	0	0	7	0	7
Was	7	17	3	6	33
NYG	TD Schnelker (12 pass from Gifford); PAT Agajanian				
Was	TD Wells 2 (15 run, fumble recovery in end zone), Carson (7 pass from Dorow), Meilinger (51 pass from Dorow); PAT Baker 3; FG Baker 2 (49, 28)				

Griffith Stadium—Unlike the Redskins' two previous opponents, the Giants were not unbeaten; they were merely 6-1 and in first place in the Eastern Conference. But the Giants—like the last two opponents—were jolted by the Skins as Washington ran up a 24-0 halftime lead en route to a 33-7 trouncing of New York.

The Redskins were stuffed three and out on their initial possession but, in a foreshadowing of how the game would go on this day, the Giants were called for roughing punter Sam Baker. The Redskins had a first down at their own 25. They took advantage of their good fortune by driving to Billy Wells' 15-yard touchdown run.

Before the end of the first quarter, Washington recovered a Giants fumble at the New York 37 and moved to a 14-0 lead on Al Dorow's seven-yard touchdown pass to John Carson early in the second period.

After Baker kicked a field goal to make it 17-0, the Redskins had the ball at the New York 40 shortly before halftime and pulled out a trick play. The play, a pass by halfback Tom Runnels to Wells, fooled the heck out of the Giants as nobody was near the receiver. But Wells had to come back for Runnels' throw and was pushed out of bounds at the six. For a moment, it seemed that the Redskins had blown a golden scoring opportunity when, a few plays later, Dorow fumbled as he struggled to get the ball over the plane of the goal line. The alert Wells turned potential disaster into triumph as he fell on the ball in the end zone for a touchdown and a 24-0 lead.

The second half was marked by a couple of superb plays that helped the Griffith Stadium crowd celebrate the big win. Baker kicked a 49-yard field goal, the longest ever at Griffith Stadium and the longest anywhere by a Redskin. Then, in the fourth quarter, end Steve Meilinger grabbed a Dorow pass that three Giants defenders appeared to have a shot at intercepting, spun away and rolled his 220-pound frame over the goal line to complete a 51-yard scoring play.

11/25/56	Redskins (5-3) 20, BROWNS (3-6) 17				22,878
Was	7	0	6	7	20
Cle	7	7	0	3	17
Was	TD Hecker (18 fumble recovery), Carson (26 pass from LeBaron); PAT Baker 2; FG Baker 2 (41, 19)				
Cle	TD Konz (65 punt return), Basset (4 run); PAT Groza 2; FG Groza (42)				

Cleveland Municipal Stadium—Eddie LeBaron threw a 26-yard touchdown pass to John Carson with a minute and a half left in the game to pull the Redskins past the Browns.

Washington took a 7-0 lead when defensive back Norb Hecker got a good bounce on a Cleveland fumble, snagged the ball and zoomed 18 yards for a touchdown. Cleveland dominated the rest of the half but, thanks to that fortunate bounce, the Browns held just a 14-7 lead at halftime.

Sam Baker kicked a pair of field goals in the third quarter to pull Washington within one point. Starting at the outset of the final quarter, Cleveland responded, taking 13 plays—all runs—to move from their own nine to the Washington 36. From there, Lou Groza booted a 42-yard field goal that put his team up 17-13 with four minutes left in the game.

It appeared the Redskins' comeback effort was dead when Sam Baker had to punt with three minutes left. Incredibly, tackle Don Colo was called for roughing the punter, resurrecting the Redskins' hopes. Working from his own 34, LeBaron completed five straight passes, including the game winner to Carson. The receiver was double covered by Don Paul and Junior Wren, but LeBaron's pass was perfect and the Redskins had their fifth straight win.

12/2/56	GIANTS (7-2-1) 28, Redskins (5-4) 14				46,351
Was	7	0	0	7	14
NYG	14	0	7	7	28
Was	TD Meilinger (6 pass from Dorow), Paluck (76 fumble return); PAT Baker 2				
NYG	TD Gifford 3 (6 run, 14 pass from Conerly, 11 run), MacAfee (29 pass from Gifford; PAT Agajanian				

Yankee Stadium—Frank Gifford proved to be a classic triple threat, throwing for one touchdown, scoring one on a pass reception and getting two on the ground. That gave him a hand in all of the Giants' scores as they knocked off the Redskins. The loss dealt a serious blow to Washington's division title aspirations as it wound up two games behind in the loss column with three to play for the Redskins, and two to go for New York.

Gifford got the Giants off to a 7-0 lead in the first quarter when he capped an 81-yard drive by throwing a 29-yard touchdown pass to Ken MacAfee. Joe Scudero fumbled the ensuing kickoff and New York recovered at the Washington eight. Shortly after that, Gifford ran off tackle for six yards and a touchdown to give New York a 14-0 lead.

The Redskins pulled back within seven after Leo Elter's 48-yard run set up a six-yard touchdown pass from Al Dorow to Steve Meilinger. Washington had a golden opportunity to tie it up just before halftime when Art DeCarlo recovered a fumbled punt at the New York 24, but Emlin Tunnell intercepted Dorow in the end zone to kill the threat.

The Giants methodically moved 80 yards in the third quarter to tighten the noose around the necks of the Redskins. Gifford got the score in a 14-yard pass from Charley Conerly. Another sustained drive, this one of 69 yards, choked off the Redskins' chances in the fourth quarter as Gifford rolled 11 yards for a 28-7

lead. Joe Scudero scooted 76 yards with a fumble recovery to make it 28-14, but Washington didn't threaten after that.

12/9/56	REDSKINS (6-4) 19, Eagles (3-7-1) 17				22,333
Phil	10	0	7	0	17
Was	0	3	7	9	19
Phil	TD Keller (45 run), Burnine (11 pass from Schaefer); PAT Walston 2; FG Walston (17)				
Was	TD Elter (4 run), Carson (5 pass from Dorow); PAT Baker; FG Baker 2 (17,21)				

Griffith Stadium—Sam Baker's 21-yard field goal with 25 seconds left to play pushed the Redskins past the Eagles in rainy, muddy conditions on the stadium field. Baker's heroics made up for a pair of misses earlier in the fourth quarter that left his team in a position where they had to come back.

Actually, the Eagles' play contributed to Washington's need to come from behind as well. Leading 10-3 at the half, the Eagles stretched their lead with their first possession of the third quarter. From the Washington 11, quarterback Bobby Thomason crossed up the Redskins with his play call. He lateraled to fullback Don Schaefer, who threw to a wide-open Hank Burnine for a touchdown and a 17-3 lead.

The home team then came to life. Al Dorow replaced an ineffective Eddie LeBaron at quarterback and promptly led the team 74 yards to its first touchdown. Passes to Steve Meilinger and Billy Wells gained much of the yardage in the drive, along with some nice runs by Tom Runnels. Leo Elter got the scoring honors, bulling his way over the goal line from the four. Baker's point after pulled the Redskins within 17-10.

Washington started in next touchdown drive in the fourth quarter at its own 30. As it turned out, they wound up needing to cover 88 yards to get to the end zone as a clipping penalty backed them up to the 12. A pass to John Carson got them to midfield and then Runnels made the play of the game, reeling in a tipped ball while surrounded by three defenders. The result was a 44-yard gain to the Philly six. Dorow threw a five-yard touchdown pass to Carson soon after that. The drenched crowd exploded with delight, but had its enthusiasm dampened when Baker's tying conversion attempt bounced off the left upright and was no good.

Later in the final period, Baker was short on a 42-yard attempt and was left to hope the offense could again get him into a position to redeem himself. It came after his team had taken possession at its own 32 and deftly moved to the Eagles 15. Baker's 21-yard boot was true with 25 seconds left and the Redskins had their first lead at 19-17.

12/16/56	Steelers (5-7) 23, REDSKINS (6-5) 0				21,097
Pit	0	7	0	16	23
Was	0	0	0	0	0
Pit	TD Watson (1 run), Matthews (48 pass from Marchibroda), Butler (10 pass from Marchibroda); PAT Watson 3; Safety Dorow tackled in end zone by Dodrill				

Griffith Stadium—Pittsburgh broke open what was a tight game on the scoreboard with 16 fourth-quarter points to earn the shutout win over the Redskins.

It's important to note that the game was tight on the scoreboard, but not in reality. Washington's deepest "penetration" into Steeler territory was to the 30 and that happened twice: once after a 59-yard punt return by Tom Runnels, and again after a shanked Steeler punt. They could advance no further either time.

To say the offense was ineffective would be to praise it with faint damnation. Washington mustered 70 yards on the ground, bad enough against a mediocre defense. It was the passing numbers that were truly pathetic, with Eddie LeBaron and Al Dorow teaming up to complete three of 13 for a net of 15 yards. They had as many interceptions as completions.

One might want to note that the game was played in sloppy, muddy conditions and explain Washington's lack of offense that way, but it wouldn't fly. Steeler quarterback Ted Marchibroda threw for two touchdowns and passed his team into position for its other touchdown. On the same field, Marchibroda passed for 180 yards. That was the difference in this one.

12/23/56	COLTS (5-7) 19, Redskins (6-6) 17				32,994
Was	3	7	7	0	17
Bal	0	6	0	13	19
Was	TD Meilinger (35 pass from Dorow), Runnels (14 pass from Dorow); PAT Baker 2; FG Baker (8)				
Bal	TD Ameche (1 run), Moore (7 run), Mutscheller (53 pass from Unitas); PAT Kerkorian 1				

Memorial Stadium—Johnny Unitas threw a long touchdown pass to Jim Mutscheller with 15 seconds left to pull the Colts past the Redskins.

Norb Hecker seemed to have Mutscheller well defended on the play and even got a hand on the ball, tipping it into the air at about the five, but the deflection went right to the offensive player and Mutscheller secured the ball and completed the 53-yard play.

The Redskins were outgained by better than a two to one margin—453 yards to 220—but they led 17-6 going into the fourth quarter. They scored in the first quarter when coach Joe Kuharich decided to kick a field goal with the line of scrimmage at the Baltimore one-foot line. Baker's eight-yarder made it 3-0. After the Colts responded by driving to Alan Ameche's one-yard touchdown plunge, Al Dorow threw touchdown passes in the second and third periods to give his team its 11-point led. In a foreshadowing of things to come, Dorow's second TD pass was tipped by a Colt defender before Tom Runnels latched onto it for a 14-yard scoring play.

The Colts stormed back. They pulled within five at 17-12 on Lenny Moore's seven-yard touchdown run early in the fourth. With the score the same and the clock winding down, the Redskins dodged a bullet. Runnels fumbled and Gino Marchetti recovered for the Colts at the Washington 34 at the two-minute warning. Unitas completed a pass to Mutscheller, but Hecker knocked the ball out of the receiver's hands and Joe Scudero scooped it up at the 11 with 1:14 left.

One first down would have allowed them to kill the clock, but they didn't get it. With 44 seconds left, Baker punted and the stage was set for the heroics of Unitas and Mutscheller. An attempt to match the Colts' miracle didn't come close; Baker's 65-yard field goal attempt on the final play was well short.

Marshall: New Stadium a 'Must'

Dec 28—George Preston Marshall wants to keep the Redskins in Washington. He also says that goal will be impossible to achieve without a new stadium.

He put it quite simply. Griffith Stadium is outdated and he couldn't turn a profit with his team playing in it. And the clock is ticking, given that the team's lease at that stadium is set to expire in 1960. Fast action, Marshall said, is "vital".

Unless new facilities are built, "I'd have to leave town," Marshall said.

The most promising plan on the board has the new stadium being built near the D. C. Armory. It would be a multipurpose facility that would feature stands that would roll underneath the stadium structure for a baseball configuration and roll out for football.

1957
Head Coach: Joe Kuharich
Record: 5-6-1, Fourth in Eastern Conference

Honors: Gene Brito All-NFL, Pro Bowl; John Carson All-NFL, Pro Bowl; Chuck Drazenovich All-NFL, Pro Bowl; Eddie LeBaron Pro Bowl; Jim Podoley Pro Bowl; Dick Stanfel All-NFL, Pro Bowl

---

Jan 5
Bill Would Build New Stadium Near Armory
Arkansas Rep. Harris introduces legislation

Roy Barni Shot to Death

July 22—Roy Barni went outside of his tavern in an effort to be a peacemaker in a dispute. That ended up costing him his life.

The Redskins' starting defensive back, 29, was shot three times by James D. Invirnizzi, 62, who had known Barni since the player was a boy. Invirnizzi and another man left The Huddle, a San Francisco tavern owned by Barni, in a heated dispute and Barni followed them outside. A witness saw Invirnizzi draw a gun and fired three shots at Barni, who staggered back into the tavern and collapsed.

He died a short time later at a local hospital.

All-Rookie Backfield Behind LeBaron Tonight

September 7—Youth will be served when the Redskins face the Colts in an exhibition game tonight.

In the backfield behind quarterback Eddie LeBaron will be a trio of promising rookie backs. Ed Podoley, the Skins' fourth-round pick out of Central Michigan, and Eddie Sutton, selected out of

North Carolina in the third, will be the halfbacks. Don Bosseler, the team's first-round draft pick out of Miami, will line up at fullback.

The Redskins are hoping the youth movement will bolster their running game, which ranked dead last in the 12-team NFL. They averaged 3.5 yards per carry and scored just five touchdowns all year.

Sep 9
Skins Deal for Rudy Bukich
Team gets strong-armed QB from Rams

Sep 15
QB Dorow Dealt to Eagles
Impressed with Bukich, team trades backup

9/29/57	STEELERS (1-0) 28, Redskins (0-1) 7				27,452
Was	0	0	7	0	7
Pit	0	7	7	14	28
Was	TD Podoley (38 pass from LeBaron); PAT Baker				
Pit	TD Mathews (25 pass from Morrall), Young (2 run), Girard 2 (42 pass from Morrall, 32 pass from Morrall); PAT Glick 4				

Forbes Field—Earl Morrall, acquired just days earlier in a trade, passed for 248 yards and three touchdowns as the Steelers easily beat the Redskins in the season opener.

Former Redskin Dick Alban got things going for his new team in the second quarter when he picked off Eddie LeBaron's sideline pass at the Pittsburgh 35 and returned it all the way to the Washington 25. On the next play, Morrall threw a perfect pass to Ray Mathews in the end zone and it was 7-0.

The visitors tied it up in the third quarter. Pittsburgh punted from deep in its own territory and Joe Scudero returned the boot to the Pittsburgh 38.

Taking a page from Morrall's book, LeBaron decided to go for it all on the first play. He threw to Jim Podoley in the end zone. The receiver had to battle two Steeler defenders for the ball, but Podoley came down with it and Sam Baker's extra point tied the game at seven.

It didn't remain tied for long. The Steelers took the ensuing kickoff and drove 72 yards for a touchdown. Morrall drove his team downfield steadily, mostly through the air, and Dick Young scored the six from three yards out.

Another interception of LeBaron, this one by Jack Butler, set up another Morrall touchdown pass. His final TD toss—his second to Mathews—came late in the final period.

Skins Add Veteran DB Don Shula

September 30—The Redskins made a move today to patch up a defensive backfield that was torched on Sunday by signing defensive back Don Shula.

The six-year veteran recently was let go by the Colts, who are rebuilding with younger players. Shula has a nose for the ball, boasting 18 career interceptions.

He will step into a right wingback position. That became an area of concern during Sunday's 28-7 loss to the Steelers. Earl Morrall lit up the Redskins for 248 yards passing and three touchdowns.

10/6/57	Redskins (1-1) 37, CARDINALS (1-1) 14			18,278	
Was	6	7	14	10	37
Chi	7	7	0	0	14
Was	TD Carson (19 pass from LeBaron); Sutton 2 (18 run, 5 run); Bosseler (1 run); PAT Baker 4; FG Baker 3 (12, 32, 16)				
Chi	TD Nagler 2 (83 pass from McHan, 36 pass from McHan); PAT Summerall 2				

Comiskey Park—The Redskins outscored the Cardinals 24-0 in the second half to break open a tight game in Chicago.

Washington took a 6-0 first-quarter lead by driving to two Sam Baker field goals, but Chicago wiped that out in a hurry. Gern Nagler got behind defender Norb Hecker and caught Lamar McHan's bomb for 83 yards and a touchdown.

The Redskins retook the lead when John Carson leapt into the air and grabbed Eddie LeBaron's pass just outside the end zone, stepping in to complete a 19-yard touchdown play with about two minutes to go in the half.

Hoping to capitalize on the momentum, coach Joe Kuharich called for an onside kick, but Pat Summerall recovered for the Cards at the Washington 38. On the next play, McHan and Nagler made the Redskins pay for Kuharich's gamble, hooking up for a 38-yard touchdown pass and a 14-13 lead at the half.

In the third quarter, Washington took the lead for good. Dick James' 21-yard punt return to the Chicago 26 led to Ed Sutton's 18-yard touchdown run, and later in the period Sutton scored again, this time from three yards to cap a 66-yard scoring thrust. That put the Redskins up 27-14 going into the final quarter.

A 51-yard halfback pass from Sutton to Ed Podoley set up a one-yard touchdown run by Don Bosseler in the fourth period. Baker's third field goal closed out the scoring.

10/13/57	Giants (2-1) 24, REDSKINS (1-2) 20			30,086	
NYG	7	7	7	3	24
Was	6	0	7	7	20
NYG	TD Schnelker 2 (66 pass from Gifford, 2 pass from Conerly) Gifford (1 run); PAT Agajanian 3; FG Agajanian 3				
Was	TD Podoley (82 pass from LeBaron), Carson (12 pass from LeBaron); PAT Baker 2; FG Baker 2 (15, 41)				

Griffith Stadium—The Giants stunned the Redskins with a 66-yard halfback option pass for a touchdown on the game's first play from scrimmage. Washington never quite seemed to recover from the bomb, which Frank Gifford threw to Bob Schnelker, and lost to the Giants.

The Redskins offense twice drove into Giants territory in the first quarter, only to be forced to settle for field goals. There was just a yard to go for a first down prior to both of Sam Baker's three-pointers—one from 18 yards, the other from 41—but coach Joe Kuharich played it close to the vest.

The Giants went up 14-6 in the second quarter when Gifford powered over from a yard out. That was the score at halftime, but the Redskins responded in the third period with a big play. From the Washington 18, Eddie LeBaron scrambled to his right and saw Jim Podoley near midfield. The quarterback launched a high, long one in Pododley's direction. The receiver reached over the head of New York defender Jim Patton, caught the ball a whisker away from the sideline, and headed towards the goal line. Podoley had to take an angle to elude the last New York defender and crossed into the end zone right under the goal posts. Baker's point after made it 14-13.

That was as close as the Redskins would get. Charley Conerly flipped a two-yard touchdown pass to Schnelker and Ben Agananian booted the longest field goal in Griffith Stadium history, a 50-yarder, to put New York up by 11. That enabled them to survive LeBaron's 12-yard touchdown toss to John Carson in the fourth quarter.

10/20/57	Cardinals (2-2) 44, REDSKINS (1-3) 14			23,159	
Chi	21	10	6	7	44
Was	0	7	7	0	14
Chi	TD Matson 2 (56 run, 49 pass from McHan), Lewis 2 (39 pass from McHan, 8 pass from McHan), McHan (18 run), Sugar (fumble recovery in end zone); PAT Summerall 5; FG Summerall (17)				
Was	Podoley (11 pass from LeBaron), Meilinger (7 pass from LeBaron); PAT Baker 2				

Griffith Stadium—Ollie Matson ran for 155 yards and scored two touchdowns to pace the Cardinals to the romp over the Redskins.

Matson gave his team a 7-0 lead with a run that had him flat on his face and left the Redskins with egg on their faces. From the Washington 44, he broke a tackle at the line and broke into the clear for about 10 yards and then fell down, untouched. Although there were some defenders in the vicinity, none of them jumped on Matson to keep him down so the runner got back on his feet and completed the 56-yard touchdown jaunt.

It quickly got uglier for the Redskins. Before the first quarter was finished, Lamar McHan threw a 39-yard touchdown pass to Woodley Lewis and then scrambled 18 yards to make it 21-0 in the first quarter.

It didn't get much better for the home team. Eddie LeBaron found Jim Podoley all alone in the end zone for an 11-yard touchdown pass, but the Redskins would get no closer to the Cards. By halftime, Pat Summerall's 17-yard field goal and McHan's second touchdown pass to Lewis had Chicago up 31-7 and the Cardinals coasted in the final 30 minutes.

10/27/57	Redskins (2-3) 31, GIANTS (3-2) 14				40,416
Was	14	7	7	3	31
NYG	7	7	0	0	14

Was	TD Sutton (23 run), Zagers (76 punt return), Carson (25 pass from LeBaron), Bosseler (1 run); PAT Baker 4; FG Baker (22)
NYG	TD Webster (10 pass from Conerly), Conerly (3 run); PAT Agajanian 2

Yankee Stadium—The Redskins scored two touchdowns on consecutive touches in the first quarter and handled the Giants the rest of the way.

New York started off as if it might dominate. The home team moved smartly downfield after the opening kickoff, taking 10 plays to move 80 yards to Charley Conerly's 10-yard touchdown pass to Alex Webster. The Redskins, though, responded swiftly and surely.

First, Ed Sutton popped free for a 23-yard touchdown run later in the first quarter. Then, after the defense held the Giants, Bert Zagers took a punt at his own 24. He headed up the middle and then found some running room to the outside. Don Boll and Steve Meilinger provided interference as Zagers tightroped down the sidelines all the way for the touchdown.

New York immediately battled back, moving to the Washington 31. The Redskins' front line came up big, stuffing Bobby Epps on consecutive carries with just a yard to go for the first down. Having grabbed momentum back, the Skins immediately embarked on a 69-yard touchdown drive. Eddie LeBaron completed a pass to Joe Walton for 21 yards to the New York 33 and then whipped another 21-yarder—this one to John Carson—for a touchdown. Sam Baker's conversion made it 21-7 with about four minutes gone in the second quarter and the Redskins were on their way.

The Giants drove 63 yards to Conerly's one-yard touchdown run to make it 21-14 at halftime, but the Redskins owned the second half. Dick James picked off one of Conerly's passes, setting Washington up at its own 41. From there, LeBaron threw to Jim Podoley for 15 yards, to Carson for 17 and then to Don Bosseler for 15 down to the one. From there, Bosseler finished it off with a scoring plunge to make it 28-14. Sam Baker's 22-yard field goal finished off the scoring in the fourth quarter.

Meanwhile, James, Zagers, Norb Hecker and Don Shula were blanketing the New York receivers and Conerly was unable to mount any serious scoring threats.

11/3/57	BROWNS (5-1) 21, Redskins (2-4) 17				52,936
Was	0	3	7	7	17
Cle	7	0	7	7	21

Was	TD Sutton (8 run), Zagers (56 punt return); PAT Baker 2; FG Baker (11)
Cle	TD Brown 2 (3 run, 9 run), O'Connell (1 run); PAT Groza 3

Cleveland Municipal Stadium—Jim Brown rushed for 109 yards and two touchdowns to lead Cleveland over the Redskins.

After Brown scored standing up to cap an 80-yard drive on his team's first possession, the Redskins scored 10 straight points to take a 10-7 lead in the third quarter. The first three came on Sam Baker's 11-yard field goal with just seconds left in the first half. The big play on that 63-yard drive was a 39-yard pass from backup quarterback Rudy Bukich to Ed Podoley. Chuck Drazenovich intercepted a Cleveland pass to set up Ed Sutton's eight-yard touchdown run to put the Redskins in the lead.

The Browns reclaimed the lead soon after that. Quarterback Tommy O'Connell got hot, moving Cleveland downfield with throws to Darrell Brewster.

Brown finished up the job with a nine-yard run.

The home team extended its lead in the fourth quarter soon after Preston Carpenter gained 39 yards on an end around. That

took the Browns to the Washington 26 and they moved in, scoring on O'Connell's one-yard sneak to make it 21-10.

Bert Zagers made it close with a dazzling 56-yard punt return with less than six minutes left, but the Browns preserved their four-point lead the best way you can. They took the ensuing kickoff and ground out a clock-killing drive, with Brown and Lew Carpenter making key gains to move the chains.

The Redskins did not get the ball back.

11/10/57	Colts (4-3) 21, REDSKINS (2-5) 17				33,149
Bal	7	7	0	7	21
Was	0	7	7	3	17

Bal	TD Berry 2 (67 pass from Unitas, 11 pass from Unitas), Unitas (3 run); PAT Rechichar 3
Was	TD Podoley (3 run), Bosseler (1 run); PAT Baker 2; FG Baker 37

Griffith Stadium—Johnny Unitas ran for one touchdown and threw for two more, including one with 40 seconds left, to push the Colts past the Redskins. Eddie LeBaron twice lost his handle on the ball in the late going, miscues that proved fatal to the Redskins.

The Colts jumped to a 14-0 lead in the first half on Unitas' two TD passes, both of which went to end Raymond Berry. The first was a 67-yard play where Unitas hit his target in stride and Berry zoomed into the end zone. The second was not quite as spectacular but just as pretty as Berry jumped over three defenders to haul in Unitas' pass near the goal line and fell over the stripe to complete an 11-yard play.

You weren't supposed to be able to run against the Colts' vaunted defensive line that boasted such stalwarts as Artie Donovan, "Big Daddy" Lipscomb and Gino Marchetti, but that's just was the Redskins did to get back into the game. Leo Elter, Jim Podoley and Don Bosseler all pounded that line with great success as the Redskins moved 89 yards for a touchdown to get back into the game. Podoley scored it on a three-yard run and it was 14-7 at halftime. Less than five minutes into the second half, the Redskins tied the game. Baltimore's Alan Ameche fumbled and Dick James recovered at the Colts' 31. Bosseler powered for 19 yards to the one and then took it over from there.

Early in the fourth quarter, Sam Baker made up for two earlier misses by booting a 37-yard field goal to put his team into the lead. Baker's earlier misses were from 39 and 41 yards.

It appeared the home team was moving in for the kill when LeBaron fumbled as he was scrambling for yardage at the Baltimore 20. The Colts recovered and Unitas launched the game-winning drive. Twice Unitas went to his favorite target, Berry—once for 42 yards, the second time for 13 yards to the six. Unitas took it into his own hands, running twice to get the six yards for the go-ahead touchdown with 40 ticks left on the clock.

LeBaron threw to Steve Meilinger, John Carson and Podoley to get down to the Baltimore 20 with enough time remaining for one play. The quarterback couldn't find anyone open, but he had good protection and stood in the pocket waiting for a receiver to break free. Just as he was going into his throwing motion, Baltimore's Don Joyce broke through the blocking wall and slapped the ball out of LeBaron's hand. The Colts fell on the ball with three seconds left.

11/17/57	REDSKINS (2-5-1) 30, Browns (6-1-1) 30				27,722
Cle	3	7	3	17	30
Was	6	3	14	7	30

Cle	TD Hanulak (3 run), Brewster 2 (10 pass from O'Connell, 23 fumble recovery); PAT Groza 3; FG Groza 3 (10, 35, 23)
Was	TD Elter 2 (4 run, 16 run) Bosseler (7 run), Meilinger (34 pass from LeBaron); PAT Baker 3; FG Baker (25)

Griffith Stadium—Those missed extra points—they'll always come back to haunt you.

It's a cliché, to be sure, but it became one because it happens so often, as it did in this game. Cleveland's Bill Quinton blocked Sam Baker's first-period conversion attempt. That lost point enabled Lou Groza's 23-yard field goal to tie the game at 30-30 with 13 seconds left on the clock.

Earlier in the fourth quarter, the Browns got one very fortunate bounce that enabled them to stay in the game. The Redskins had taken a 30-20 lead when Steve Meilinger caught a 33-yard touchdown pass from Eddie LeBaron.

The powerful end took LeBaron's short toss near the sideline, broke a tackle and rolled into the end zone.

Cleveland had the ball with less than four minutes left and coach Paul Brown, signaling the plays in to quarterback Tom O'Connell, kept the ball in the air. A pass to Pres Carpenter carried them down to the Washington 25, but Carpenter seemed to attempt a lateral while being tackled; the ball popped loose and was bouncing along on the ground for the taking. Unfortunately, it was taken by Browns receiver Darrel Brewster, who scooped the ball up in stride and sped 23 yards into the end zone. Lou Groza's extra point pulled Cleveland within 30-27. The Redskins were unable to kill the clock and Cleveland moved smartly downfield to get in position for Groza's tying boot.

11/24/57	EAGLES (3-6) 21, Redskins (2-6-1) 12			20,730	
Was	3	6	3	0	12
Phil	0	7	7	7	21
Was	FG Baker 4 (18,19,10,26)				
Phil	TD McDonald (61 pass from Jurgensen, 36 pass from Jurgensen), Bielski (9 pass from Jurgensen); PAT Walston 3				

Connie Mack Stadium—Rookie quarterback Sonny Jurgensen passed for three touchdowns to lead his Eagles over the Redskins 21-12. Jurgensen's efforts trumped Sam Baker's team-record four field goals.

Washington held a 6-0 lead in the second quarter thanks to Baker's first two field goals, which came from 18 and 19 yards out. The close-range field goals were not a good sign for the visitors as Jurgensen was about to get cranked up. He teamed up with Tommy McDonald for Philly's first score. McDonald made a leaping catch over defender Joe Walton and cut back to the middle of the field, racing untouched to complete the 61-yard touchdown play.

The Redskins pushed back into the lead before halftime, again getting close to the end zone but not into it. Baker's 10-yard field goal made it 9-7.

Philadelphia took control early in the third quarter. A lightning quick 76-yard drive put them in front to stay. Jurgensen completed passes of 47 yards to Bobby Walston and 19 to Dick Bielski to move his team to the Washington nine. From there, Jurgensen went back to Bielski, looping a nine-yard pass to the receiver for the touchdown.

After Baker kicked another field goal and Jurgensen and McDonald hooked up for another touchdown, the Eagles held a 21-12 lead midway through the fourth quarter. Washington was threatening to make a game of it when Don Bosseler fumbled at the Philadelphia 11 to end the Skins' hopes.

12/1/57	Redskins (3-6-1) 14, BEARS (4-6) 3			39,148	
Was	14	0	0	0	14
Chi	0	3	0	0	3
Was	TD Sutton (4 run), Podoley (10 pass from LeBaron); PAT Baker 2				
Chi	FG Blanda (49)				

Wrigley Field—For the first time since their first season in Washington, the Redskins won at Wrigley field. That 1937 game gave the Skins the NFL title. While the stakes were much lower this time, the performance was still impressive.

All of the Redskins' points came in the first quarter. After they took possession after taking a punt at its own 28, Eddie LeBaron got things going with a 15-yard pass to Tom Braatz. Then, after a series of runs moved the ball into Bear territory at the 46, LeBaron took to the air again, going to Jim Podoley. After an 18-yard gain, the ball was wrestled out of Podoley's grasp, but he managed to regain control and lateral to fellow rookie back Don Bosseler, who scooted down to the nine. From there, Ed Sutton carried twice; the second one covered four yards into the end zone with 8:29 left in the first period.

Washington had a great opportunity to expand its lead after blocking a punt to set up first and goal at the four, but the Bears put on a goal line stand and the Redskins gave the ball up on downs.

Chicago could only drive out to its 19 and punted back to the Redskins. LeBaron passes to Podoley and John Carson each covered 23 yards and they were knocking on the door at the Chicago 10. On the next play, LeBaron scrambled to his right and then reversed his field. While the Bears were fiercely rushing the quarterback, they neglected to cover Podoley, who was all alone in the end zone. LeBaron flipped the ball to him and Sam Baker's second conversion made it 14-0.

Although the Redskins didn't score any more, they still controlled the contest on both sides of the ball. Bears coach Paddy Driscoll delivered a backhand compliment, saying of his team, "We couldn't run, we couldn't pass and our defense was lousy."

The Bears' deepest offensive penetration of the day was the Washington 43. They did convert on that opportunity as George Blanda booted a 49-yard field goal.

12/8/57	REDSKINS (4-6-1) 42, Eagles (4-7) 7			21,304	
Phil	0	0	0	7	7
Was	7	14	7	14	42
Phil	TD Dorow (1 run); PAT Walston				
Was	TD Bosseler (1 run, 1 run, 5 run), Sutton (17 pass from LeBaron), Podoley (9 run), Elter (50 pass from LeBaron); PAT Baker 6				

Griffith Stadium—Don Bosseler ran for three touchdowns and Eddie LeBaron threw for two more as the Redskins routed the Eagles.

The game was played in a steady drizzle, weather conditions that generally do not favor the offense. And, certainly, it didn't help Philly's attack any as Eagle quarterbacks threw five interceptions and were unable to push their team past the Washington 42 until the Redskins had racked up 42 points. The Skins' offense, in contrast, was in high gear.

The Redskins scored on their first possession, moving 68 yards in 11 plays behind LeBaron's passing. Bosseler capped the march with a one yard touchdown run.

In the second quarter, the Redskins took advantage of two turnovers to expand their lead to 21-0. First, Dick James intercepted a pass at the Eagle 35 and Jim Podoley converted soon after with a nine-yard run. Then the Eagles fumbled a punt with Steve Meilinger recovering at the Philly 17. From there, LeBaron fired a touchdown pass to Ed Sutton.

Any thoughts the Eagles may have had of mounting a comeback were dashed in the third period. On a play from midfield, fullback Leo Elter managed to elude the Eagles' coverage entirely and was 20 yards in the clear when LeBaron threw to him for a touchdown to make it 28-0. Two fourth quarter interceptions—one by Ralph Felton, the other by Joe Walton—preceded Bosseler's final two TD runs.

12/15/57	**REDSKINS (5-6-1) 10, Steelers (4-7) 3**			22,577	
Pit	3	0	0	0	**3**
Was	0	3	0	7	**10**
Pit	FG Glick (35)				
Was	TD Baker (10 run); PAT Baker; FG Baker 45				

Griffith Stadium—Sam Baker scored all 10 of the Redskins' points as Washington ended its season with its third straight win, this one over the Steelers.

Gary Glick's 35-yard first-quarter field goal—according to Shirley Povich in the Post, "a ridiculous kick, cock-eyed and with no spin after leaving his toe and the only time Glick is proud of it is when the thing goes over the bar and between the posts"—gave Pittsburgh a 3-0 lead in the first quarter. Baker matched it with a 45-yard three-pointer in the second period.

With the score still tied late in the third quarter, Don Bosseler got the Skins near scoring position with a 46-yard run to the Pittsburgh 15. Penalties pushed them back outside the 20 on two occasions, but eventually they fought to a fourth down at the 11. On the first play of the fourth quarter, Baker trotted into the game to attempt the go-ahead field goal.

At least that's what everyone, in particular and most importantly the Steeler defense, thought was going to happen. Holder Tom Runnels took the snap, waited for the rushers to get moving and then flipped the ball to Baker, who was on about the 20. The kicker-turned-runner built up a head of steam while heading around right end, broke a couple of tackles and ran through the end zone for the winning touchdown.

1958
Head Coach: Joe Kuharich
Record: 4-7-1, Fourth in NFL East

Honors: Gene Brito Pro Bowl, All-NFL; Chuck Drazenovich Pro Bowl; Eddie LeBaron Pro Bowl; Jim Schrader Pro Bowl; Dick Stanfel Pro Bowl, All-NFL

Jan 26
Marshall: Armory Site OK
Engineering firm will recommend East Capitol St. location to Congress

Feb 10
Brito Will Play in '58
All-Pro DE persuaded by fans to put off retirement

Kuharich Gets New Deal, More Juice

Mar 3—The Redskins announced that they have signed Head Coach Joe Kuharich to a five-year contract and that his responsibilities in the organization have been increased.

"We burned up Kuharich's old contract, which still had a year to run, and gave him a new one," said team owner George Preston Marshall.

"I personally felt that Joe deserved it."

Kuharich's new role is being compared to Paul Brown's of the Cleveland Browns. In addition to coaching duties, Kuharich will take on some of the responsibilities normally held by a vice president and general manager.

His annual salary was not revealed, but it is estimated that he will make about $17,500 per year with bonuses and incentives that could push the annual take over $20,000.

June 20
Guglielmi To Get Air Force Discharge
QB will rejoin team after two-year absence

July 7
Despite Stadium Delays, Marshall Says Skins Will Stay
'As long as I am head of the Redskins, the team will remain in Washington'

Redskins, Board Come to Agreement on Stadium Lease, Work to Start Soon

Sep 3—The Washington Redskins will have a new home within a few years.

The team and the District Armory Board have come to an agreement on a lease for a new stadium to be built on the Armory grounds on East Capitol Street in Southeast Washington, D.C. With a tenant in place, construction is expected to start almost immediately. The building will be ready in 1960 or by early 1961 and will seat 50,000 for football.

Redskins owner George Preston Marshall agreed to pay 10 percent of the team's gross revenue from the stadium and will get a share of program and other souvenir sales.

Costs for the as-yet unnamed stadium are estimated to be between $7.5 million and $8.6 million.

9/28/58	**Redskins (1-0) 24, EAGLES (0-1) 14**			36,853	
Was	0	10	0	14	**24**
Phil	7	0	7	0	**14**
Was	TD Carson (28 pass from LeBaron), James (3 run), Bosseler (1 run); PAT Baker 3; FG Baker (33)				
Phil	TD Barnes (1 run), Van Brocklin (1 run); PAT Walston 2				

Franklin Field—Dick James made key plays on both offense and defense to help push the Redskins past Philadelphia.

James' big heroics as a defender came near the end of the first half. With Washington clinging to a 10-7 lead, quarterback Norm Van Brocklin had his Eagles threatening with a second and two at the Washington 20. On the run, he threw to end Bobby Walston, who appeared to have position on the shorter James in the end zone. Not to be denied, James timed his jump perfectly and knocked the pass harmlessly to the ground. Philly eventually lost the ball on downs and Washington held its three-point lead at the half.

In the third quarter, for the second time on the day, the Eagles took advantage of a Redskins fumble and drove a very short way to a touchdown. This time, Van Brocklin cashed in on Jim Podoley's fumble that Philadelphia had recovered on the Washington 15 by sneaking it over from a yard out. In the first quarter, the Eagles had to drive all of 14 yards for their initial score after a fumble recovery.

Trailing 14-10 late in the third quarter, James and the Redskins went to work. The 5-9 speedster gained 42 of the 62 yards needed for his team to take the lead for good. Included were a 14-yard run, an 18-yard pass reception and a carry for the final three yards and the touchdown. Sam Baker's extra point put Washington up 17-14.

The Redskins clinched it after coach Joe Kuharich had sent Baker onto the field for a field goal attempt on fourth and one at the Eagles' 13. Quarterback Eddie LeBaron, though, showed some swagger when he waved Baker off the field and made his fourth-down play call. James made LeBaron look good by popping a five-yard run for the first down. Soon after that, Don Bosseler bulled over from the one.

10/4/58	**CARDINALS (1-1) 37, Redskins (1-1) 10**			21,824	
Was	0	0	3	7	**10**
Chi	7	10	7	13	**37**
Was	TD Carson (20 pass from Bukich); PAT Baker; FG Baker (34)				
Chi	TD Crow 2 (83 run, 2 run), Boydston (16 pass from Reynolds), Sears (18 pass from Reynolds), Matson (51 pass from McHan); PAT Conrad 4; FG Conrad (18)				

Comiskey Park—Rookie running back John David Crow bolted 83 yards for a touchdown on the game's first play from scrimmage and the Cardinals never looked back as they routed the Redskins.

Crow scored again in the second quarter, this time on a more pedestrian two-yard run to push his team in front 14-0. Another Cardinal rookie, Bobby Conrad, kicked the conversions after each of Crow's TD's and then booted an 18-yard field goal to make it 17-0 at the half.

After Sam Baker got the Skins on the board with a 34-yard field goal about six minutes into the second half, yet another Chicago first-year player got into the act in a big way. M. C. Reynolds stepped in for veteran Lamar McHan, who had aggravated an elbow injury, and threw two second-half touchdown passes to help put the Redskins away.

The visitors got their one touchdown on a 20-yard pass from Rudy Bukich to John Carson. Dickey Lynn set that one up for Washington with his second interception of the game.

The Cardinals piled up a huge margin statistically, outgaining the Redskins by a margin of better than 2-1 (531 yard to 247). The domination was complete as that margin held in both rushing yards (261-133) and passing (270-114).

10/12/58	**Giants (2-1) 21, REDSKINS (1-2) 14**			30,348	
NYG	14	0	0	7	**21**
Was	0	14	0	0	**14**
NYG	TD Gifford 6 run (Summerall kick)				
NYG	Schnelker 41 pass from Heinrich (Summerall kick)				
Was	Podoley 39 pass from LeBaron (Baker kick)				
Was	Sutton 1 run (Baker kick)				
NYG	McAfee 10 pass from Conerly (Summerall kick)				

Griffith Stadium—The Redskins held New York to a standoff for more than three quarters, but the Giants came up with the clutch plays in the final period and won the game.

Initially, it seemed the Giants were in for an easy time. They jumped to a 7-0 lead the first time they had the ball, driving 72 yards to a six-yard touchdown run by Frank Gifford. While Gifford got credit for the score, the force behind the march was fullback Mel Triplett, who gained 68 yards in the drive.

After Don Heinrich threw a 41-yard touchdown pass to Bob Schnelker, New York held a 14-0 lead at the end of the first quarter. The second period belonged to Washington.

Eddie LeBaron and Jim Podoley teamed up for the Redskins' first score, the quarterback throwing over the defense to the running back for a 39-yard touchdown play. Then Joe Scudero picked Alex Webster's fumble out of the air and returned it to the New York 34. Soon after that, LeBaron passed for 28 to Don Bosseler, a play that carried to the one yard line. Ed Sutton took it over from there to tie the game at 14.

The score was still deadlocked in the fourth quarter when Charley Conerly came into the game at quarterback. Washington traded Conerly to the Giants in 1945, and Conerly has spent much of the time since making the Redskins regret the move. This day was one of those times. Conerly threw to Gifford, who made a fingertip snag for a 41-yard gain to the Washington 17. A few plays later, Conerly pumped, scrambled, pumped again and finally unleashed a 10-yard touchdown pass to Ken McAfee. New York preserved its lead with an interception, holding the ball until the clock expired.

10/19/58	**REDSKINS (2-2) 37, Packers (0-3-1) 21**			25,228	
GB	0	0	0	21	**21**
Was	10	10	14	3	**37**
Was	Olszewski 45 run (Baker kick)				
Was	FG Baker 44				
Was	Walton 19 pass from LeBaron (Baker kick)				
Was	FG Baker 38				
Was	Anderson 33 pass from LeBaron (Baker kick)				
Was	Sutton 7 run (Baker kick)				
GB	McGee 80 pass from Parilli (Hornung kick)				
GB	Hornung 3 run (Hornung kick)				
Was	FG Baker 22				
GB	Taylor 31 pass from Parilli (Hornung kick)				

Griffith Stadium—Johnny Olszewski ran for 165 yards on 21 carries to lead the Redskins over Green Bay. Included in Johnny O's efforts was an inspiring 45-yard touchdown blast that sparked a 34-0 scoring run that buried the Packers.

In the first quarter, on a play from the Green Bay 45, Olszewski took a handoff from Eddie LeBaron and broke into the clear. He slowed down briefly at the 20 to allow Ed Podoley to remove one of the two remaining obstacles between himself and the goal line. The other was an unfortunate defensive back named Billy Kinard who was positioned at around the 10. Olszewski didn't try to juke the defender and didn't sidestep him—he blasted right *through* him, scoring standing up.

Before the quarter was finished, the Redskins drove to a Sam Baker field goal that extended the lead to 10-0. The big mover in that march was, not surprisingly, Johnny O, who gained 32 of the 41 yards.

Having softened up the Green Bay defense with the run, LeBaron decided it was time to take to the air. He threw touchdown passes of 19 yards to Joe Walton in the second quarter and 33 yards to Bill Anderson. On the second one, LeBaron used his short stature to his advantage as defensive back Alton Romine lost sight of the quarterback and, for a brief moment, thought the play was a run. That was enough of an opening for LeBaron as the quarterback hit the receiver in stride. Anderson dragged the beaten Romine into the end zone for a 27-0 lead.

The Redskins stretched their margin to 34-0 on Ed Sutton's nine-yard run later in the third quarter. An 80-yard touchdown pass from Babe Parilli to Max McGee started off a face-saving 21-point fourth quarter for the Packers.

10/26/58	**COLTS (5-0) 35, Redskins (2-3) 10**			54,403	
Was	7	0	3	0	**10**
Bal	7	14	14	0	**35**
Was	Zagers 4 run (Baker kick)				
Bal	Moore 12 run (Myhra kick)				
Bal	Berry 17 pass from Unitas (Myhra kick)				
Bal	Ameche 4 run (Myhra kick)				
Was	FG Baker 31				
Bal	Lyles 101 kickoff return (Myhra kick)				
Bal	Berry 48 pass from Unitas (Myhra kick)				

Memorial Stadium—Johnny Unitas threw two touchdown passes to Ray Berry and Len Lyles returned a kickoff 101 yards for a touchdown as the Colts manhandled the visiting Redskins.

Washington did manage to take a 7-0 lead in the first quarter on Bert Zagers' four-yard touchdown run, but the Colts soon established their dominance.

It seemed the Colts had their opponents intimidated. After Baltimore tied the game on Lenny Moore's 12-yard touchdown run, Washington faced a third and 12 at its own 27. Rather than attempt a pass and face the fierce rush of the likes of Art Donovan and Gino Marchetti, the Redskins punted. Sam Baker got off a nice 57-yard boot, but the Colts marched right back down the field and scored on the first Unitas to Berry connection, this one from 17 yards out.

It was 21-7 before the Redskins got on the board again with a 31-yard Baker field goal. Any hope for a comeback that score may have created was quickly dashed as Lyles took Baker's kickoff a yard deep in the end zone, hesitated as his blocking wall formed and took off for the goal line. Lyles easily got by Baker at the Colts 45 and completed the 101-yard return for a touchdown.

11/2/58	STEELERS (2-4) 24, Redskins (2-4) 16			19,525	
Was	3	3	0	10	16
Pit	0	14	0	10	24
Was	FG Baker 13				
Pitt	Orr 19 pass from Layne (Miner kick)				
Was	FG Baker 27				
Pitt	Younger 1 run (Miner kick)				
Was	FG Baker 12				
Pitt	Mathews 62 pass from Layne (Miner kick)				
Pitt	FG Miner 42				
Was	Walton 26 pass from Guglielmi (Baker kick)				

Pitt Stadium—It was one thing to be routed by the undefeated Colts the week before, but to have the Steelers gain their second win of the year at the Skins' expense was quite another.

As was the case the week before, the Redskins got off to a good start. Eddie LeBaron hit Jim Podoley on a 15-yard pattern that Podoley turned into a 45-yard gain by eluding his defender and racing to the Pittsburgh 25. After getting a first down at the 13, though, former Redskin Dick Alban got the first of his three interceptions of LeBaron on the day. Washington recovered quickly as Joe Scudero recovered Bobby Layne's errant lateral at the Pittsburgh 15. Three plays later, Sam Baker's 13-yard field goal had Washington ahead 3-0.

Alban again intercepted LeBaron deep in Steeler territory and this time Layne and the Pittsburgh offense took advantage. After Alban's pick at the one, Layne took his team 99 yards for a touchdown. The big play was a 49-yard connection between Layne and end Jimmy Orr that got them to the Washington 27 and, soon after that, Layne and Orr hooked up again for 19 yards and the touchdown.

Pittsburgh answered another Baker field goal with another long touchdown drive. They moved 80 yards swiftly and smoothly, scoring on the aptly-named Tank Younger's one-yard charge into the end zone to take a 14-6 lead at halftime.

Washington's defense was a bit more stout in the third quarter, twice forcing the Steelers to attempt field goals after drives and blocking both of them. On the first play of the fourth quarter, Baker's third field goal of the day pulled the Skins within five at 14-9.

It didn't take long for Layne to put it out of reach. From the Pittsburgh 38, a play action fake by Layne sucked in the defense, leaving Ray Mathews all alone. Layne hit his receiver in stride at around the Washington 30 and Mathews easily rolled the rest of the way for the score and a 21-9 lead. Following an insurance field goal by the Steelers, Washington scored a touchdown in the waning seconds on Ralph Guglielmi's 26-yard pass to Joe Walton.

11/9/58	REDSKINS (3-4) 45, Cardinals (2-4-1) 31			26,196	
Chi	3	7	14	7	31
Was	14	24	7	0	45
Was	Olszewski 2 run (Baker kick)				
Chi	FG Conrad 45				
Was	Walton 5 pass from LeBaron (Baker kick)				
Was	Podoley 20 pass from LeBaron (Baker kick)				
Was	Podoley 10 pass from LeBaron (Baker kick)				
Was	Walton 18 pass from LeBaron (Baker kick)				
Chi	Nagler 14 pass from McHan (Conrad kick)				
Was	FG Baker 18				
Was	Walton 38 pass from LeBaron (Baker kick)				
Chi	Lewis 58 pass from McHan (Conrad kick)				
Chi	Lewis 34 pass from McHan (Conrad kick)				
Chi	Matson 8 pass from McHan (Conrad kick)				

Griffith Stadium—Eddie LeBaron threw five touchdown passes, including three in a decisive 24-point second quarter, to pull the Redskins over the Cardinals.

Washington's first score didn't come on a LeBaron pass but on a two-yard run by Johnny Olszewski—though it was largely the result of LeBaron's 67-yard pass to Ed Podoley. The back snuck down the right sideline, took LeBaron's pass over a linebacker's head and took off towards the goal line. Defensive back Dick Nolan got an angle on Podoley and stopped him at the four. Two plays later the ex-Cardinal Johnny O scored to make it 7-0.

LeBaron got warmed up for the big second quarter by throwing to Joe Walton for a touchdown, the first of three scoring connections between the two. Leading 14-3 entering the second stanza, LeBaron and the Skins poured it on. The quarterback partnered with Podoley for 20 yards and six points, went to Podoley once more for 10 and a score, and then hooked up with Walton again for 18 and another touchdown. By the time the quarter was over, Sam Baker had added an eight-yard field goal and the Redskins led 38-10.

LeBaron and Walton kept it going after halftime. From the Chicago 38, the quarterback faked a handoff and zipped a pass to his end. Walton had to deal with the annoyance of a Chicago defender who was draped all over him, but he ignored the obstacle and caught the touchdown pass to wrap up the scoring for the home team. The Cards kept the celebrating crowd entertained by scoring three touchdowns on some nice passes from Lamar McHan, but the contest had long since been decided.

11/16/58	Browns (6-2) 20, REDSKINS (3-5) 10			32,372	
Cle	7	3	0	10	20
Was	7	3	0	0	10
Cle	Brown 1 run (Groza kick)				
Was	Podoley 64 pass from Guglielmi (Baker kick)				
Was	FG Baker 35				
Cle	FG Groza 10				
Cle	FG Groza 26				
Cle	Brown 4 run (Groza kick)				

Griffith Stadium—Jim Brown rushed for 152 yards and two touchdowns as his Cleveland team pulled away from a game Redskins squad in the final minutes.

The Browns got a big play early: a 74-yard pass from Milt Plum to end Preston Carpenter. That play wound up at the Washington six, and Brown scored the touchdown from there for a 7-0 lead.

Washington responded in kind. From the Washington 36, Ralph Guglielmi launched a bomb to a wide-open Ed Podoley. The back, who was split wide on the play, juggled the ball for a moment, but managed to gather it in and complete the 64-yard touchdown play to tie the game at seven.

The teams exchanged field goals in the second period and the 10-10 tie lasted until late in the fourth quarter. Cleveland finally broke through by driving 58 yards to a 26-yard field goal by Lou Groza with slightly more than two minutes remaining. After that, defensive back Don Paul broke the Redskins' backs with an interception that he returned to the Washington 11. After two carries by Brown, Cleveland had the clinching touchdown with just a minute left on the clock.

Brown's rushing yardage for the game pushed him past the regular season rushing mark of 1,146 yards that Steven Van Buren had set. Brown, with 1,163 yards so far, took just eight games to surpass Van Buren's record, set in a 12-game season.

11/23/58	**GIANTS (6-3) 30, Redskins (3-6) 0**				46,732
Was	0	0	0	0	**0**
NYG	6	10	7	7	**30**
NYG	FG Summerall 41				
NYG	FG Summerall 37				
NYG	FG Summerall 20				
NYG	MacAfee 10 pass from Conerly (Summerall kick)				
NYG	Gifford 13 pass from Conerly (Summerall kick)				
NYG	Schnelker 4 pass from Heinrich (Summerall kick)				

Yankee Stadium—Veteran quarterback Charley Conerly was a very efficient nine of 14 passing and led the Giants to a 30-0 skunking of the Redskins. Conerly passed for 154 yards and two touchdowns.

Conerly and the Giants didn't need much help, but the Redskins gave it them anyway. On the fourth play from scrimmage, Johnny Olszewski fumbled the ball away to New York at the Washington 47. That led to a 41-yard Pat Summerall field goal. Two more three-pointers by Summerall had New York up 9-0 in the second quarter.

By then, Conerly was warmed up and led a 95-yard touchdown drive. The big play on the march was a 32-yard pass from Conerly to Mel Triplett, culminated when Ken MacAfee caught a 10-yard pass from Conerly. Summerall's extra point made it 16-0.

Washington kept giving opportunities in the second half—and the Giants kept taking advantage of them. A fourth-down gamble near midfield failed when Ed Podoley gained just two of the needed three yards and New York took over. Soon after Conerly passed to Triplett again for 19 and Frank Gifford got the final 25 yards—12 on a run and 13 and the touchdown on a Conerly pass.

Conerly was rested in the fourth quarter and sub Don Heinrich finished off the rout with a four-yard touchdown pass to Bob Schnelker.

11/30/58	**BROWNS (8-2) 21, Redskins (3-7) 14**				33,240
Was	7	0	7	0	**14**
Cle	7	0	0	14	**21**
Was	Bosseler 4 run (Baker kick)				
Cle	Renfro 30 pass from Plum (Groza kick)				
Was	Watson 7 pass from LeBaron (Baker kick)				
Cle	Carpenter 3 run (Groza kick)				
Cle	Plum 1 run (Groza kick)				

Cleveland Municipal Stadium—With Jim Brown bottled up by a fired-up Washington defense, quarterback Milt Plum was the hero for Cleveland, scoring one touchdown and passing for another to rally his team past the Redskins.

Washington literally ground out a drive on its first possession to take a 7-0 lead. All of the 76 yards came via the running game with Don Bosseler and Ed Sutton tearing off big chunks of yardage. Bosseler got the touchdown by bullying his way through the defense for the final four yards.

Cleveland gambled and won big after the ensuing kickoff. They drove from their 23 to the Washington 30, where they faced fourth and 11. Despite the presence of their reliable kicker Lou "The Toe" Groza, Cleveland went for it. And they got it all, with Plum rolling away from pressure to get a pass to Ray Renfro, who had broken free inside the 10. He scored unchallenged and the game was tied.

Sam Baker missed a 45-yard field goal near the end of the first half and the score was still deadlocked at intermission. In the third quarter Baker made up for his miss by pinning the Browns back at their nine with a textbook coffin corner punt. Cleveland was unable to move and Washington had great field position at its own 46 after the punt.

A pass from Eddie LeBaron to Joe Walton and a personal foul flag against the Browns moved the Skins to the 10. Shortly after that, from the seven, LeBaron juked the Browns out of their shoes with what the Post called "the slickest fakery of the contest." He started going with the flow of the play to the right but suddenly reversed his field. Halfback Sid Watson had delayed for a moment and snuck free in the left flat. He was so wide open—nobody was within 20 yards—that the only worry was an overthrow or a drop. Neither happened and Watson strolled in for a 14-7 Washington lead.

Cleveland drove 91 yards to tie the game, but it took a big play combined with a big break to do it. Plum threw a long pass to Renfro, and Doyle Nix made a shoestring tackle after a 45-yard gain. Renfro lost the ball when he was tackled and the Redskins recovered, but officials ruled that the whistle had blown prior to the fumble.

After that, the Browns went to a trick play. From the Washington 41, Brown, who rushed for just 12 yards on the day, took a handoff and headed up the middle. He stopped and pitched the ball back to Plum. The quarterback passed to end Pete Brewster for a 38-yard gain down to the three. Lew Carpenter scored from there after several Redskins had a shot at him—including Dick James, who rode into the end zone on Carpenter's back.

After Baker missed a 44-yard field goal attempt, the Browns moved in for the winning score. Carpenter was the main mover of the drive, running for 15 yards before catching a pass for 13. After Plum scrambled for 22 to the Washington 37, Carpenter broke through the line and appeared headed for the end zone, but he stumbled and was brought down at the 10. It was Carpenter one more time to the three, but Plum got the six points on a sneak two plays later. Groza's extra point made it 21-14 and Washington was unable to answer.

12/7/58	**REDSKINS (3-7-1) 14, Steelers (6-4-1) 14**				23,370
Pit	0	0	7	7	**14**
Was	0	14	0	0	**14**
Was	Bosseler 7 run (Baker kick)				
Was	Bosseler 2 run (Baker kick)				
Pit	Orr 55 pass from Layne (Miner kick)				
Pit	McClairen 28 pass from Layne (Miner kick)				

Griffith Stadium—Bobby Layne gave, and then he took away.

The Pittsburgh quarterback twice threw passes that Bert Zagers intercepted for the Redskins, setting up two touchdowns and a 14-0 Redskins lead. In the second half, however, Layne made up for his early poor play by throwing two touchdown passes as the Steelers tied Washington.

The first theft came just before the end of the first quarter as Bert Zagers latched on to Layne's wobbly aerial at the Washington 39 and zipped to the Steelers 24. Three plays later, early in the second period, Don Bosseler took a pitchout, followed a block by Dick Stanfel and fought his way over the goal line for a seven-yard touchdown run and a seven-point lead for Washington.

Again, Zagers picked off Layne and got a good runback, 26 yards to the Steelers 33. And again, Bosseler was the one to finish things off for the Redskins, dragging defender Dean Derby into the end zone for a 14-0 lead. In addition to the two touchdowns, Bosseler rushed for 145 yards on the day.

The game then entered a stretch that was a combination of good defense and horrid offense. At one point, the two teams combined for nine consecutive plays without a positive yard made on any of them. Pittsburgh once faced a fourth and 55.

In the third quarter, the Redskins had a shot at extending their lead to three touchdowns, but Derby intercepted Ralph Guglielmi's pass in the end zone and the tide was turned. From his own 45, Layne found end Jim Orr, who had gotten behind defender Doyle Nix. Orr caught the pass over the desperation flailing for Nix and cruised the remaining 20 yards for the score.

From their own 39, the Steelers launched their game-winning drive. After Layne successfully converted a fourth down on a sneak to the Washington 24, he took to the air again. This time his target was Jack McClairen, who made a superb catch in the end zone to tie the game. Eddie LeBaron came into the game in place of Guglielmi, but was unable to move the team.

12/14/58	**REDSKINS (4-7-1) 20, Eagles (2-9-1) 0**				22,621
Phil	0	0	0	0	0
Was	3	10	0	7	20
Was	FG Baker 30				
Was	FG Baker 18				
Was	Sutton 2 run (Baker kick)				
Was	Anderson 71 pass from LeBaron (Baker kick)				

Griffith Stadium—Seven Redskins gained at least 10 yards rushing and the Washington defense held the Eagles to a net of seven yards on the ground, closing out the season with a shutout win.

Soon after Vice President Richard Nixon presented the retiring Gene Brito with the keys to a new car, a blocked punt set up the game's first score—a 30-yard field goal by Sam Baker. Soon after that, Dick Lynch made a spectacular, leaping interception and the Redskins were back in business at their own 40. The subsequent drive was aided by a roughing penalty against the Eagles, but the man they roughed, Eddie LeBaron, was sent to the bench and Ralph Guglielmi came in at quarterback. Googs led the Skins to the 11, but the march stalled there and Baker booted another field goal to make it 6-0.

Towards the end of the second quarter, Guglielmi threw an interception, but Philly returned the favor when Gene Cichowski fell on an Eagles fumble at the Washington 30. Then Guglielmi led a 70-yard touchdown drive that culminated with Ed Sutton's two-yard run. Washington led 13-0 at halftime.

LeBaron came back into the game in the second half and teamed up with Bill Anderson to provide the second-half's lone highlight. From the Washington 29, the quarterback threw a pass that Anderson stretched out for just past midfield. The effort to catch the ball caused the receiver to stumble a bit, but Anderson kept his footing and was gone, completing the 71-yard touchdown pass untouched with his familiar, long strides.

1959
Head Coach: Mike Nixon
Record: 3-9, Fifth in NFL East

Honors: Bill Anderson Pro Bowl; Don Bosseler Pro Bowl; Jim Schrader Pro Bowl; Bob Toneff All-NFL, Pro Bowl

---

Kuharich to Notre Dame, Nixon to Coach Skins

Dec 22—Just a year after signing a five-year contract extension, Joe Kuharich is flying the Redskins coop. He is soon to be introduced as the next head coach of his alma mater, Notre Dame.

Mike Nixon, Kuharich's top assistant, will take over the top job in Washington, D.C.

Nixon is not out of the typical football coach mold. His resume includes time spent as a coal miner, as an official in the United Mine Workers union, and as a third baseman in the Southern Association. He also was elected to the Pennsylvania state legislature.

Sep 23

Eisenhower Signs Stadium Bill
Final hurdle cleared, construction to begin

9/27/59	**CARDINALS (1-0) 49, Redskins (0-1) 21**				21,892
Chi	7	14	14	14	49
Was	0	0	14	7	21
Chi	TD Conrad 3 (58 run, 35 run, 5 pass from Reynolds), Crow (9 pass from Hill), Randle (22 pass from Hill), Hill (27 run), Lewis (83 pass from Reynolds); PAT Conrad 7				
Was	TD James 3 (41 pass from LeBaron, 4 run, 3 run); PAT Baker 3				

Soldier Field—Bobby Joe Conrad scored 25 points on three touchdowns and seven extra points to lead the Cardinals' rout over the Redskins.

This one was over quickly. Late in the first quarter, Chicago quarterback King Hill found John Crow wide open in the end zone for a nine-yard touchdown pass, Conrad scored his first touchdown less than four minutes later on a well-executed 35-yard reverse and, just before halftime, Hill threw a 22-yard touchdown pass to Sonny Randle. The score was 21-0 at halftime.

Dick James matched Conrad's touchdown output by scoring three but, unlike Conrad, he had no help from his teammates. That includes the Washington defense; each time that James scored, the Cardinals drove the ensuing kickoff back for a touchdown.

The final TD for the Cardinals was the ultimate garbage time score. With just seconds left on the clock, reserve quarterback M. C. Reynolds let fly with a long pass to receiver Woodley Lewis, who gathered the ball in and strolled into the end zone to complete an 83-yard final embarrassment for the soundly defeated Redskins.

Nixon: No More Mr. Nice Guy

September 28—When he was the top assistant coach of the Redskins, Mike Nixon was the players' buddy, taking them to the movies some nights and serving as a sounding board for their personal problems.

After a blowout loss to the Cardinals in his debut as the team's head coach, that's all changed.

"I've ceased being a nice guy," said Nixon.

"I'm amazed and disappointed at the lack of effort of many on this team," he continued. "They're making me harsh."

Nixon demonstrated that his new tone was more than just talk as he announced six changes to the defensive lineup after the Redskins gave up 569 yards in total offense to the Cardinals.

10/4/59	Redskins (1-1) 23, STEELERS (1-1) 17			26,570	
Was	3	6	14	0	**23**
Pitt	0	0	10	7	**17**
Was	TD Anderson (70 pass from Guglielmi), Watson (26 pass from Guglielmi); PAT Baker 2; FG Baker 3 (43, 47, 25)				
Pitt	TD Brewster (33 Pass from Layne), Krutko (2 run); PAT Layne 2; FG Layne 32				

Pitt Stadium—Ralph Guglielmi passed for 235 yards and two touchdowns and Dick James picked off a pass to kill a late rally bid as the Redskins upset the Steelers.

Guglielmi pushed the Redskins to a 23-3 lead before James' late heroics became necessary. Sam Baker provided all of the scoring in the first half with three field goals, two of them from long range.

Then, in the third quarter, Guglielmi teamed up with Bill Anderson to get the Skins into the end zone in spectacular style. On a play from the Washington 30, Anderson got so wide open from would-be defenders Dick Alban and Dean Derby that only a drop or a bad pass would prevent a touchdown. Both the QB and receiver did their jobs, and Anderson rolled in to complete the 70-yard scoring play. Before the quarter was out, Guglielmi connected with Sid Watson from 26 yards for another touchdown that extended Washington's lead to 23-3.

Bobby Layne brought his team back, throwing a 33-yard touchdown pass to Darrell Brewster and setting up a second touchdown with a completion to Jimmy Orr that carried to the Washington 27. Leading by just six, the Redskins had to punt the ball back to Pittsburgh with 1:40 left to play. Layne unleashed a long pass intended for Buddy Dial, but James came in and stole the ball away at the Washington 20 to clinch the win for the visitors.

10/11/59	REDSKINS (2-1) 23, Cardinals (2-1) 14			25,937	
Chi	7	0	0	7	**14**
Was	7	0	7	9	**23**
Chi	TD Hill 2 (1 run, 1 run); PAT Conrad 2				
Was	TD Bosseler (1 run), Anderson (58 pass from Guglielmi), Sutton (1 run); PAT Baker 3; Safety Hill tackled in end zone				

Griffith Stadium—Ralph Guglielmi's 58-yard touchdown pass to Bill Anderson broke a 7-7 tie in the third quarter and the Redskins went on to beat the Cardinals.

Cardinal fumbles greatly contributed to the Washington cause. In the first quarter, Ed Meadows recovered a botched handoff at the Chicago 40. It took seven plays for the Redskins to hammer across the goal line, with Don Bosseler doing the honors on a one-yard plunge. Chicago earned its tying score by marching 93 yards to a touchdown on a quarterback sneak by King Hill.

The score remained there until the third quarter. The Cards were driving in Washington territory, but they coughed the ball up again and the Skins were in business at their own 42. From there, Guglielmi dropped back and enjoyed excellent protection as Anderson worked his way through the coverage. The end was wide open as he hauled in the pass at around the 13 and sauntered in for the score.

In the fourth quarter, the Redskins scored without the benefit of a takeaway, driving 61 yards to Ed Sutton's one-yard TD dive. Trailing 21-7, Hill rallied his team to one more touchdown, again sneaking it into the end zone from the one. The Redskins burned off much of the remaining time before giving Chicago possession again with 35 seconds left. Thoughts of a miracle comeback vanished when Hill was trapped in the end zone for a safety.

10/18/59	Steelers (3-1) 27, REDSKINS (2-2) 6			29,260	
Pitt	14	7	0	6	**27**
Was	6	0	0	0	**6**
Pitt	TD Krutko 2 (1 run, 4 run), Tarasovic (38 fumble recovery); PAT Layne 3; FG Layne 2 (23,22)				
Was	FG Baker 2 (39, 30)				

Griffith Stadium—Normally, Santa Claus doesn't visit Griffith Stadium until December, but you would have thought the jolly old soul had dressed in a Redskins uniform on this day. Washington giveaways set up every one of the Steelers' points as Pittsburgh got an easy win.

The Skins' giving spirit started early. On the first play from scrimmage, quarterback Ralph Guglielmi dropped the ball without being hit. It seemed as though he could have fallen on the ball, but the Steelers' George Tarasovic scooped it up instead, rolling to the Washington seven. Three plays later, Larry Krutko scored to put the visitors up 7-0.

It quickly got worse. On the Redskins' next possession, Guglielmi fumbled again, this time being separated from the ball by a hit from Ernie Stautner. Again Tarasovic recovered and now took it in himself, scooting unchallenged 38 yards for a 14-0 lead with less than five minutes elapsed in the game.

Later in the first quarter, the Steelers tried to return their hosts' generosity, but the Redskins couldn't quite take full advantage. A Pittsburgh fumble that Bob Toneff recovered and a Gary Glick interception started two possessions in Steeler territory, but the Redskins came away with just a pair of Sam Baker field goals. It was 14-6 at the end of the first period.

It stayed that way until late in the second. The play called for Bill Anderson to lateral to a trailing back. The trailer wasn't there, but Anderson lateraled anyway; the Steelers fell on the loose ball and were in business at the Washington 33. Soon after that, Krutko smashed over again and the Steelers led 21-6 at the half.

The Redskins held on to the ball in the third quarter, but could only get close enough for two long-distance field goal attempts by Sam Baker. Both boots, from 56 and 54 yards, had no chance. Pittsburgh put it away in the fourth quarter with a pair of field goals—both set up by Washington turnovers, naturally.

10/25/59	BROWNS (3-2) 34, Redskins (2-3) 7			42,732	
Was	0	0	7	0	**7**
Cle	6	7	7	14	**34**
Was	TD Anderson (28 pass from Guglielmi); PAT Baker				
Cle	TD Mitchell 2 (76 pass from Plum, 15 pass from Plum), Brown (30 run), Carpenter (12 pass from Plum), Modzelewski (10 pass from Plum); PAT Groza 4				

Cleveland Municipal Stadium—The headline in the Post read, "Redskins Just Plum(b) Beaten." Cleveland quarterback Milt Plum threw for 253 yards and four touchdowns to pace his team over the Redskins.

Actually, Bobby Mitchell should get most of the credit on Plum's first TD pass. Plum threw him a short pass in the flat and Mitchell high-stepped down the sideline to complete a 76-yard touchdown play. Lou Groza missed the extra point and it was 6-0 at the end of the first quarter.

In the second, Jim Brown did what he has done so often. From the Washington 30, he took a handoff and it appeared that he had been stopped at the line for a minimal gain. However, Brown bounced off the line and found daylight, rolling 30 yards into the end zone for a 13-0 lead.

Plum and Cleveland put it away early in the second half with an assist from the Redskins. Guglielmi threw an interception and the Browns took advantage when, from the Washington 15, Plum rolled right and threw back to Mitchell on the left. The receiver didn't need his outstanding speed this time as he strolled into the end zone.

The Redskins scratched the scoreboard on Guglielmi's 28-yard touchdown pass to Bill Anderson, but Plum threw two more touchdown passes in the fourth quarter to top off the rout.

11/1/59	EAGLES (4-2) 30, Redskins (2-4) 23				39,854
Was	0	9	0	14	23
Phil	10	20	0	0	30
Was	TD Bosseler 2 (41 run, 1 run), Podoley (8 pass from LeBaron); PAT Baker 2; FG Baker (24)				
Phil	TD Barnes (61 run), Peaks (2 run), Walston (22 pass from Van Brocklin), McDonald (3 pass from Van Brocklin); PAT Walston 3; FG Cothren (46)				

Franklin Field—The Redskins were a foot short of coming all the way back from a 30-9 deficit going into the fourth quarter as a goal line stand saved the game for the Eagles.

For the first 45 minutes, it looked as though it would be an easy win for the home team. Five minutes into it, Billy Barnes took a handoff, followed some nice blocks and busted loose on a 61-yard scoring run. By the time four seconds had elapsed in the second quarter, a wind-aided 46-yard field goal by Paige Cothren and a short touchdown plunge by Clarence Peaks had given the Eagles a 16-0 lead.

Then the Redskins' running attack, led by Don Bosseler, got into gear. Bosseler scored one touchdown on a 41-yard pop through the middle of the line and he and Dick James carried the ball to get the Skins in position for Sam Baker's 24-yard field goal attempt which made it 16-9.

The Eagles responded in a big way in the last two minutes of the half. Quarterback Norm Van Brocklin led a rapid advance downfield that culminated in his 22-yard touchdown pass to Bobby Walston with 45 seconds to go in the half. Disaster struck as Chuck Weber intercepted Eddie LeBaron's pass and, as he was going down, flipped a lateral to Jim Carr, who took it to the Washington three. On the next play, Van Brocklin faked to Peaks and threw to Tommy McDonald, who made a nice diving catch in the end zone. Walston's extra point made it 30-9 at the half.

Another ground-based march got the Redskins deep into Philly territory early in the second half, but a botched handoff between LeBaron and James gave the ball back to the Eagles on their 14. It seemed the door was closing on the Redskins' chances as the third quarter wound down with them facing a 21-point deficit.

They got a foot in the door late in the period when Ralph Felton picked off a Van Brocklin pass at the Eagles' 42. Passes to Jim Podoley and James moved the Redskins close and Bosseler bulled over from the one to make it 30-16. Then a Peaks fumble and Bob Toneff's recovery at the Eagle 27 led to LeBaron's eight-yard TD pass to Podoley. The once-formidable Philadelphia lead was cut to a touchdown.

But the Redskins couldn't quite get it. After the Eagles missed a field goal, Washington started its final, desperate drive. LeBaron made a nice pass and Bill Anderson made a nicer catch to convert a fourth and ten at the Washington 48. Anderson made it to the three where Tom Brookshier made the tackle. On first and goal, Dick Haley went around end and was tripped up a foot short of the goal line by Jess Richardson. On the next three plays, LeBaron handed to Bosseler, who had tied a team record in gaining 168 yards on the day. Three times, the suddenly-stout Eagle line repelled Bosseler. On the last play, Marion Campbell torpedoed in to nail Bosseler for a loss, slamming the door shut on the Redskins' rally.

11/8/59	REDSKINS (3-4) 27, Colts (4-3) 24				32,773
Bal	0	7	3	14	24
Was	3	7	0	17	27
Bal	TD Mutscheller 2 (19 pass from Unitas, 3 pass from Unitas), Richardson (12 pass from Moore); PAT Myrha 3; FG Myrha (21)				
Was	TD Walton 2 (19 pass from LeBaron, 22 pass from Sutton), Anderson (17 pass from LeBaron; PAT Baker 3; FG Baker 2 (46, 43)				

Griffith Stadium—Sam Baker calmly knocked through a 46-yard field goal with eight seconds to play to boost the Redskins to a 27-24 upset over the defending champion Colts. Linebacker Tom Braatz set up Baker's heroics when the picked off Johnny Unitas' pass and returned it to the Colt 39.

Baker's kick boosted the fourth-quarter scoring total to a combined 31 points in a game that had been a taught defensive struggle for most of the first three quarters. The Redskins scored the first half's only touchdown on Eddie LeBaron's 19-yard pass to Joe Walton in the second quarter to take a 7-3 halftime lead. A Baker field goal boosted the lead to 10-3 before Unitas tied it up with a 19-yard scoring pass to Jim Mutscheller and it was 10-10 going into the fourth quarter.

After an exchange of touchdowns, Washington took a 24-17 lead with 3:40 left to play when LeBaron threw a 17-yard touchdown pass to Bill Anderson. The next play from scrimmage was nearly disastrous for the Colts as Unitas dropped the ball and it appeared that Washington's Art Gob had a clear shot to the ball and goal line. However, center Buzz Nutter somehow came up with the ball at the Colt 11. From there, Unitas righted the ship, throwing to Raymond Berry for 18 yards on a third and 19 and then going to Lenny Moore for 22 on fourth and one. From the Redskin 12, Unitas crossed up the Redskins by handing off to Moore, who threw to rookie end Jerry Richardson in the end zone to tie the game.

The Redskins couldn't move and had to punt to the Colts. Johnny U's magic ran out as Braatz intercepted his pass and Baker sent the crowd into frenzy with his game-winning kick.

11/15/59	Browns (6-2) 31, REDSKINS (3-5) 17				32,206
Cle	14	0	10	7	31
Was	7	7	3	0	17
Cle	TD Mitchell 3 (90 run, 23 run, 6 run), Renfro (39 pass from Plum); PAT Groza 4; FG Groza (35)				
Was	TD Olszewski (19 run), James (4 run); PAT Baker 2; FG Baker (14)				

Griffith Stadium—You might have known it was going to be Bobby Mitchell's day when he ran 90 yards for a touchdown less than three minutes into the game. That was only the beginning for the Cleveland star as he rushed for 232 yards and three touchdowns on just 14 carries. Mitchell's fireworks upstaged a great game by his Washington counterpart, Johnny Olszewski. The Redskins back gained a team-record 190 yards on the ground in a losing cause.

Mitchell's long-distance jaunt and a 39-yard touchdown pass from Milt Plum to Ray Renfro had Cleveland ahead 14-0 with less than half of the first quarter gone. It looked like a long day was in store for the home team and its fans, but the Redskins battled back. A 65-yard run by Olszewski was the key to a drive that ended with Dick James' four-yard scoring run. After James fumbled at the Cleveland three to end a scoring threat, a short Browns punt gave Washington good field position at the Cleveland 38. Johnny O zipped 19 yards to tie the game at 14 at the half.

Cleveland, battling for a share of the Eastern Conference lead, turned it on in the second half. Lou Groza kicked a 35-yard field goal that put the Browns ahead to stay. Then LeBaron threw a horrible pass right to linebacker Galen Fiss at the Washington 25 to set up Mitchell's second touchdown of the day, an eight-yard run, and Cleveland had a 10-point lead.

After Sam Baker's 14-yard field goal cut the lead back to 24-17, Mitchell and the Browns moved in for the kill. Mitchell broke free for 39 yards to the Washington 39 and, two plays later, scooted 23 yards for a 31-17 lead for his team.

Mitchell's 232 yards rushing was the second-best total for a game in NFL history, but it didn't even give him the team record as teammate Jim Brown held the league mark with 237 yards.

Olszewski bested the team record of 168 yards set by Frank Atkins in 1945 and tied by Don Bosseler just two weeks prior to this game. Olszewski had the record by intermission with 177 yards at halftime, but the Browns clamped down on him in the second half.

11/22/59	Packers (4-5) 21, REDSKINS (3-6) 0				31,853
GB	0	14	7	0	21
Was	0	0	0	0	0
GB	TD Knafeic (11 pass from Starr), McGee (10 pass from Starr), Hornung (5 run); PAT Hornung 3				

Griffith Stadium—For the first time in his four-year career, Green Bay quarterback Bart Starr walked off the field a winner as the Packers shut out the Redskins 21-0.

Starr threw for two touchdowns, both in the decisive second quarter. His first went to Gary Knafeic for 11 yards to give his team a 7-0 lead.

The Redskins were looking to cut into that lead as halftime neared. Sam Baker attempted at 34-yard field goal, but Henry Jordan broke through and blocked the kick. Hank Gremmlinger picked up the loose ball, reversed his field and wound up at midfield. Starr's second TD pass of the quarter went 10 yards to Max McGee with 47 seconds left in the half.

Starr directed a 79-yard touchdown drive early in the second half to put this one away. Paul Hornung capped the drive with a five-yard touchdown run. The Redskins had their chances throughout the game, but forays deep into Packer territory wound up either with turnovers or the ball given over on downs.

11/29/59	GIANTS (8-2) 45, Redskins (3-7) 14				60,982
Was	0	0	7	7	14
NYG	14	24	0	7	45
Was	TD Podoley (9 pass from LeBaron), Anderson (15 pass from LeBaron); PAT Baker 2				
NYG	TD Webster 2 (10 run, 1 run), Schnelker 2 (34 pass from Conerly, 7 pass from Conerly), Rote (2 pass from Conerly), King (24 pass from Gifford); PAT Summerall 6; FG Summerall (31)				

Yankee Stadium—On Charley Conerly Day at Yankee Stadium, it was the New York quarterback's world and he wasn't about the let the Redskins live in it—at least, not for long. He and his teammates built a 38-0 halftime lead and never looked back in smothering the Skins.

Conerly was a bit tight when the game started, or perhaps a bit distracted by the Cadillac and Corvette he received before the game. He missed badly on his first two passes and Don Chandler lined up in punt formation. It was a fake and 24 yards later, the Giants had a first down at the Washington 32. It didn't take any more than that for the Redskins to come unglued. Alex Webster scored from 10 yards out and the rout was on.

Before the quarter was out, Conerly had thrown a two-yard touchdown pass to Kyle Rote and moved his team deep into Washington territory again when the first quarter ended. Pat Summerall's 31-yard field goal opened the flood of New York scoring in the second period. Don Bosseler fumbled and Cliff Livingston recovered for the Giants at the Redskin 29. Soon after that, Conerly hit Bob Schnelker for seven yards and a 24-0 lead. Conerly and Schnelker hooked up again later in the period. The receiver made a spectacular, juggling catch for a 34-yard TD, a grab that left would-be defender Gary Glick an awed spectator. Frank Gifford's 24-yard touchdown toss to Phil King on a halfback option capped the first half scoring.

The Redskins did not give up, driving for two touchdowns in the second half. Eddie LeBaron threw for both of them, one for nine yards to Jim Podoley and the other 15 to Bill Anderson. By then Conerly was on the bench, possibly thinking of the sights he'd see on the European vacation he'd been given.

12/6/59	Eagles (7-4) 34, REDSKINS (3-8) 14				24,325
Phil	3	17	0	14	34
Was	0	0	7	7	14
Phil	TD McDonald 3 (50 pass from Van Brocklin, 35 pass from Van Brocklin, 6 pass from Van Brocklin), Barnes (1 run); PAT Walston 4; FG Cothren 2 (21, 16)				
Was	TD MacAfee (4 pass from LeBaron), Anderson (75 pass from LeBaron); PAT Baker 2				

Griffith Stadium—It's hard to know exactly what drove all but a handful of the 24,325 paying fans out of Griffith Stadium and on their way home well before this game ended. Perhaps it was the steady rain that grew heavy in the second half. Perhaps it was the officials, who dragged the game out by throwing 20 penalty flags. The vote here is that it was the play of the Redskins, who were uncompetitive for the fourth straight week.

Tommy McDonald and Norm Van Brocklin teamed up to make the Redskins' life as miserable as the weather. After two Paige Cothren field goals gave Philly a 6-0 lead, McDonald faked his man Ben Scotti onto the turf and caught a 35-yard pass from Van Brocklin for the touchdown. Before the half was out, McDonald caught another scoring pass from his quarterback, this one from six yards, and it was 20-0 at halftime.

The Redskins started making some noise, scoring on a four-yard touchdown pass from Eddie LeBaron to Ken MacAfee to pull within 20-7 and then recovering a fumble in Eagle territory. But an apparent first-down run by Dick James was nullified by a motion penalty and the threat, mild as it was, ended. That started the crowd's trek to the exits. The exodus began in earnest after McDonald again smoked the hapless Scotti and caught a 50-yard TD pass from Van Brocklin.

Dec 9

Drazenovich to Retire
Star linebacker will play last game on Sunday

12/13/59	Giants (10-2) 24, REDSKINS (3-9) 10				26,195
NYG	7	0	10	7	24
Was	7	3	0	0	10
NYG	TD Morrison 2 (9 pass from Conerly, 1 run), Rote (26 pass from Conerly); PAT Summerall 3; FG Summerall (14)				
Was	TD Haley (3 run); PAT Baker; FG Baker (39)				

Griffith Stadium—Although the Redskins accomplished a 41-point turnaround from their disastrous first half two weeks before at Yankee Stadium, they still didn't have enough to beat the Giants.

The Redskins led 10-7 at halftime on the strength of Sam Baker's 39-yard field goal and a three-yard touchdown run by Dick Haley. They had trailed 38-0 at the half in their previous meeting with New York.

While the Giants had already clinched the Eastern Conference title, it was apparent they didn't want to go into the championship game on a losing note. In the third quarter, they made a lightning-quick advance into the end zone, moving 80 yards in four plays. Frank Gifford picked up 19 yards on a run, then another 19 on a pass from Charley Conerly. Conerly then turned to Kyle Rote, who caught passes for 25 and 26 yards, the second of which scoring a touchdown that put the Giants ahead to stay.

After Pat Summerall's field goal put the Giants up 17-10, New York did get a couple of scares. The first happened when Ed Sutton caught Eddie LeBaron's pass at the Washington 40 and sped into the end zone to score an apparent 80-yard touchdown. An official's flag, however, brought this one back with a backfield in motion penalty. Later the Redskins drove down to the New York two. This time the Giants stopped Sutton, dragging him down a yard shy of the goal line on fourth down. Soon after that, Don Henrich, subbing for Conerly behind center, led a 77-yard drive to the clinching touchdown.

1960
Head Coach: Mike Nixon
Record: 1-9-2, Sixth in NFL Eastern Conference

Honors: Bill Anderson Pro Bowl; Bob Khayat Pro Bowl;
Jim Schraeder All NFL; Bob Toneff Pro Bowl, All NFL

Jan 1
Top Draft Pick Richie Lucas Signs with AFL
*Former Penn State star QB inks deal
with Buffalo Bills*

Feb 16
Eddie LeBaron to Retire
Diminutive star QB will work in Texas law firm

June 24
LeBaron Dealt to Cowboys for G Ray Krouse Plus No. 1, No. 6 picks
*After change of heart about playing,
QB dealt to expansion Dallas team*

Guglielmi Finally Gets His Shot

July 30—Usually a top-five pick in the draft has a clear path to becoming a starter. Such has not been the case for Ralph Guglielmi, the No. 4 overall selection in the 1955 draft.

The former Alabama star has started nine games at quarterback in the five years since coming to Washington. He missed two complete seasons due to military service. And when Guglielmi has been with the team, he has been stuck behind Eddie LeBaron on the depth chart.

With LeBaron gone—traded to the expansion Dallas Cowboys—the starting job is now Ralph's to win or lose. And, at least in the short term, it appears unlikely that he will lose the job to either of his designated backups, former Cardinal Mack Reynolds or second-year player Eagle Day.

September 17
Skins Rebuffed in Bid for Jurgensen
Eagles won't give up promising backup QB

9/25/60	COLTS (1-0) 20, Redskins (0-1) 0			53,818	
Was	0	0	0	0	0
Bal	0	7	10	3	20
Bal	Moore 4 run (Myhra kick)				
Bal	FG Myhra 28				
Bal	Berry 13 pass from Unitas (Myhra kick)				
Bal	FG Myhra 18				

Memorial Stadium—The Redskins defense was game but the offense was punchless as the Colts pulled away in the second half for a 20-0 win.

About the only significant action in the first 20 minutes of play was a round of fisticuffs between Baltimore's Ordell Braase and Washington rookie Fran O'Brien. Baltimore quarterback Johnny Unitas didn't complete a pass until the second quarter and his Washington counterpart (well, in position, anyway) Eagle Day was spending his time evading the pass rush coming from the likes of Art Donovan and Gino Marchetti.

Unitas got untracked in the second quarter. He led an 85-yard drive to a touchdown, moving the team downfield on passes to Alan Ameche, Art DeCarlo and Alex Hawkins. The payoff came on Lenny Moore's four-yard run inside tackle.

A 23-yard pass from Day to Bill Anderson came on the Redskins' ensuing drive. After Don Bosseler ran down to the Baltimore 34, Ed Khayat tried a 42-yard field goal, but it missed.

The Redskins committed the killer mistake late in the third quarter. Trailing 10-0, they fumbled the ball away to the Colts, who recovered at the Washington nine. Shortly after that, Unitas passed 13 yards to Raymond Berry to wrap it up for the home team.

On the day, the Redskins mustered just 113 yards of offense.

10/9/60	REDSKINS (1-1) 26, Cowboys (0-2) 14			21,142	
Dal	0	7	0	7	14
Was	3	10	3	10	26
Was	FG Khayat 15				
Dal	Clarke 32 pass from LeBaron (Cole kick)				
Was	James 7 pass from Guglielmi (Khayat kick)				
Was	FG Khayat 29				
Was	FG Khayat 38				
Was	FG Khayat 10				
Dal	Bielski 1 pass from LeBaron				
Was	Olszewski 1 run (Khayat kick)				

Griffith Stadium—Ralph Guglielmi was a very efficient 10 of 16 passing for 237 yards and a touchdown as he bested the quarterback he had been in the shadow of for two seasons, Eddie LeBaron. The Redskins beat the Cowboys 26-14 in the first meeting ever between the two teams.

The Redskins led 3-0 on the first of four Bobby Khayat field goals until Frank Clark did an outstanding balancing act to get the Cowboys on the board. The Dallas receiver gathered in LeBaron's pass at around the Washington 20, bounced off of two defenders, absorbed another hit by Jim Crotty inside the 10 and completed a 32-yard touchdown play.

The Redskins responded to reclaim the lead before halftime. A screen pass that looked rather confused and disorganized suddenly took shape as Don Bosseler found some nice blocking and ripped off a 50-yard gain to the Dallas seven. From there, Guglielmi found Dick James all alone in the end zone.

An interception by Gary Glick and two nice offensive thrusts set up Khayat's other three field goals and Washington led 19-7 in the fourth quarter. It was then that LeBaron made things interesting. He drove Dallas to the Washington two-inch line where he threw the shortest touchdown pass in NFL history to Dick Bielski, shortening the lead to 19-14. The Griffith Stadium crowd, with its chances of seeing the home team break a 12-game losing streak in jeopardy, got restless.

But Guglielmi kept the Cowboys at bay. He completed passes to Bill Anderson and rookie Sam Horner to move his team to the Dallas two and Johnny Olszewski ran it over from the one, securing the win.

10/16/60	**Redskins (1-1-1) 24, GIANTS (3-0-1) 24**				60,625
Was	0	3	7	14	24
NYG	3	14	7	0	24
NYG	FG Summerall 48				
NYG	Gifford 2 run (Summerall kick)				
Was	FG Khayat 50				
NYG	Rote 6 pass from Shaw (Summerall kick)				
Was	Bosseler 2 run (Khayat kick)				
NYG	Gifford 2 run (Summerall kick)				
Was	Olszewski 1 run (Khayat kick)				
Was	Podoley 20 pass from Guglielmi (Khayat kick)				

Yankee Stadium—Ralph Guglielmi threw a 20-yard touchdown pass to Jim Podoley to cap a furious comeback to tie the Giants 24-24.

The Redskins scored two touchdowns in a two-minute span to gain the deadlock, with the Googs-to-Podoley connection coming with less than 25 seconds left.

The Redskins trailed 17-3 at halftime, their lone highlight coming on a team-record 50-yard field goal by Bobby Khayat. In the third quarter, Don Bosseler scored on a two-yard run to cap an 80-yard drive and narrow the margin to seven, but Johnny Olszewski muffed a pitchout and the Giants recovered at the Washington 23. The home team converted the turnover into seven points, with Frank Gifford scoring on a two-yard run. The two-touchdown lead held well into the fourth quarter. Washington raised some hopes by driving to a one-yard TD plunge by Olszewski, but just 2:07 remained.

What the Skins needed was a perfectly executed onside kick—and that's exactly what they got. Khayat popped the ball into the air in the direction of Jim Patton. Ben Scotti pounded Patton as soon as the Giant touched the ball and Vince Promuto fell on it at the New York 49. Three plays gained netted just one yard, but Guglielmi converted the fourth down with a pass to Joe Walton that gained 12. A pair of pass interference calls on New York got the Redskins to the Giant 24. Rookie Tom Osborne caught a pass good for a first down at the 13, but a vicious sack knocked them back to the 20. Guglielmi's response to his tormentors was the clutch game-tying pass to Podoley, who beat Lindon Crow and fell into the end zone.

10/23/60	**REDSKINS (1-1-2) 27, Steelers (2-2-1) 27**				25,292
Pit	7	3	7	10	27
Was	7	3	7	10	27
Was	Olszewski 1 run (Khayat kick)				
Pit	Tracy 7 pass from Bukich (Layne kick)				
Was	FG Khayat 17				
Was	FG Layne 17				
Pit	Lewis fumble recovery in end zone (Layne kick)				
Was	Walton 25 pass from Guglielmi (Khayat kick)				
Was	Anderson 12 pass from Guglielmi (Khayat kick)				
Pit	FG Layne 15				
Pit	Dial 27 pass from Bukich (Layne kick)				
Was	FG Khayat 43				

Griffith Stadium—The Redskins earned their second consecutive come-from-behind tie when Bob Khayat booted a 43-yard field goal with 45 seconds left to create a 27-27 deadlock with the Steelers. Pittsburgh missed a chance to win with 15 seconds remaining as Bert Rechichar's 44-yard try bounced off the crossbar.

If there were ever two teams fit to be tied, these two filled the bill. They matched each other's scoring quarter by quarter. Each team gained 119 yards rushing and the difference in the passing yardage was just 14 in favor of the Steelers (264 yards to 250).

With the game tied at 17 going into the final quarter, the Redskins moved to take the lead behind Ralph Guglielmi. Facing a third and 22, the quarterback escaped a fierce pass rush, scrambled and threw a beauty of a pass on the dead run. Ed Podoley gathered it in for a first down at the Pittsburgh 16. Again

facing third down, Guglielmi zipped a 12-yard touchdown pass to Bill Anderson to put the Redskins ahead.

The Steelers battled back. A 51-yard connection between quarterback Rudy Bukich and receiver Buddy Dial set up a field goal, another was good for 27 yards and a touchdown to put Pittsburgh back into the lead.

Guglielmi responded with passes to Joe Walton and Anderson to get things going and then he passed to Don Bosseler for a first down at the Steeler 32 at the two-minute warning. A fumble and penalty stalled the drive from there, but Khayat saved the day with his long boot.

10/30/60	**Browns (4-1) 31, REDSKINS (1-2-2) 10**				32,086
Cle	0	14	17	0	31
Was	0	3	0	7	10
Cle	Brown 25 run (Baker kick)				
Was	FG Khayat 12				
Cle	Renfro 23 pass from Mitchell (Baker kick)				
Cle	Nagler 53 pass from Plum (Baker kick)				
Cle	FG Baker 21				
Cle	Mitchell 3 run (Baker kick)				
Was	Bosseler 1 run (Khayat kick)				

Griffith Stadium—Bobby Mitchell scored one touchdown and connected on his first NFL pass for another score as the Browns pulled away from the Redskins for a 31-10 victory.

Washington was trailing just 7-3 in the first quarter when Mitchell got things going. He fielded what appeared to be a good punt by Eagle Day and scampered for a 28-yard return as the last man, Don Lawrence, prevented the touchdown with a good open-field tackle.

Make that Lawrence *delayed* the touchdown. From the Washington 23, Mitchell swept right, pulled up and threw a pass to Ray Renfro in the end zone. It was a perfect strike, but just about any old toss would have done as there was nobody anywhere near Renfro.

That made it 14-3 and the Browns put it out of reach with an odd play that left the Griffith Stadium crowd in a stunned silence. Milt Plum threw a routine short pass to Gern Nagler. Defensive back Billy Brewer appeared to be in position to stop Nagler for a short gain, but didn't make a move towards the receiver—allowing Nagler to gallop 53 yards untouched for the touchdown. After the game, Brewer explained he had lost the ball in the sun and had no idea what was happening.

11/6/60	**CARDINALS (4-3) 44, Redskins (1-3-2) 7**				22,458
Was	0	0	7	0	7
StL	7	16	7	14	44
StL	Randle 14 pass from Roach (Conrad kick)				
StL	FG Perry 18				
StL	FG Perry 21				
StL	Randle 7 pass from Roach (Conrad kick)				
StL	FG Perry 23				
Was	James 3 run (Khayat kick)				
StL	Crow 4 run (Conrad kick)				
StL	Randle 3 pass from Roach (Conrad kick)				
StL	Crow 3 run (Conrad kick)				

Busch Stadium—Sonny Randle caught three touchdown passes from quarterback John Roach to pace the 44-7 trouncing of the Redskins.

Roach, completing just 34 percent of his passes coming in, went 13 for 16. Running back John David Crow was an offensive force as well, running for 75 yards and scoring two touchdowns.

This is the Cardinals' first season in St. Louis, giving that city a pro football team for the first time since 1934. This game left Redskins fans wondering if Washington had a pro team playing there. St. Louis led 23-0 at halftime and the Redskins were never competitive.

Even when handed opportunities, the hapless visitors couldn't convert. Joe Driskill of the Cardinals fumbled the second-half kickoff and Sam Horner recovered for the Redskins at the St. Louis 21. On fourth and four at the 15, Washington tried to trick the home team by sending Jim Podoley up the middle. The Cardinals were not fooled as Podoley was stuffed a good two yards short of a first down.

Among other lowlights, the Redskins managed just nine first downs and allowed a fourth and 17 conversion on a fake punt by St. Louis.

Redskins Hold Rare Monday Workout

Nov 7—Following back-to-back losses during which they were outscored 71-17, the Redskins held a strenuous workout on what normally is a day of leisure for NFL players.

The practice, which lasted about an hour and 10 minutes, was closed to the press but all indications were that it was a full-bore session. According to coach Mike Nixon, who said that the Redskins did "nothing right" in their 44-7 loss to St. Louis, some of his players needed to be taught a lesson.

"I am of the opinion that some of our kids feel pro football is a lark," Nixon said. "They think they can put on a suit Sunday and go out and play well. They can't, you've got to prepare all week."

Nixon is mulling a possible switch at quarterback. Starter Ralph Guglielmi has been far from the only problem with the team's performance, but he hasn't helped matters much either. Backup M. C. Reynolds is the likely starter should Guglielmi be benched.

11/13/60	**EAGLES (6-1) 19, Redskins (1-4-2) 13**			39,361	
Was	3	0	7	3	13
Phi	0	3	6	10	19
Was	FG Khayat 18				
Phi	FG Walston 22				
Phi	McDonald 10 pass from Van Brocklin (kick failed)				
Was	Anderson 11 pass from Guglielmi (Khayat kick)				
Was	FG Khayat 17				
Phi	Walston 28 pass from Van Brocklin (Walston kick)				
Phi	FG Walston 10				

Franklin Field—The Redskins battled and led the Eagles most of the way before falling in the fourth quarter. Norm Van Brocklin threw a 28-yard touchdown pass on fourth down to put Philadelphia ahead to stay.

Philadelphia gave the Redskins an early opportunity when Tom Brown fumbled the opening kickoff and Pat Heenan recovered for the Redskins. They had to settle for a field goal but for the first time in three weeks, they held the lead in a game.

After tying it up before halftime, the Eagles moved in front after Ralph Guglielmi tossed up a wounded duck of a pass that Don Burroughs of the Eagles intercepted at the Philly 48. After Ted Dean scampered 32 yards to the Washington nine, Van Brocklin hit Tommy McDonald with a 10-yard touchdown pass that was successful despite excellent coverage by Ben Scotti.

The Eagles missed the point after, though, opening the door for the Redskins to retake the lead before the end of the quarter. Guglielmi completed passes to Jim Podoley and Bill Anderson before Don Bosseler ground out 17 yards for a first down at the Eagle 25. They moved to the eleven and Anderson beat Tom Brookshier's coverage. Guglielmi's pass was on target, and Bobby Khayat's point after gave the Redskins a 10-9 lead as the fourth quarter started.

Washington drove to a 17-yard Khayat field goal early in the fourth to extend the lead to four, but the Redskins couldn't stand their good fortune. A poor punt by Eagle Day put the Eagles in scoring position at the Washington 30. The defense stiffened and Van Brocklin faced fourth and eight at the 28. The quarterback threw a strike to Bobby Walston, who caught the pass inside the

10, knifed between two defenders and got into the end zone, giving the Eagles a 16-13 lead midway through the quarter.

It appeared that Washington had life on the next series when Anderson gathered in a pass as ran it to the Eagle 30, but a penalty nullified the gain and a Walston field goal put it away for Philly.

11/20/60	**Cardinals (5-4) 26, REDSKINS (1-5-2) 14**			23,846	
StL	2	17	7	0	26
Was	7	0	0	7	14
Was	Walton 10 pass from Guglielmi (Khayat kick)				
StL	Safety Olszewski tackled in end zone				
StL	Randle 27 pass from Roach (Conrad kick)				
StL	Randle 7 pass from Roach (Conrad kick)				
StL	FG Perry 26				
StL	Randle 37 pass from Roach (Conrad kick)				
Was	Glick fumble recovery in end zone (Khayat kick)				

Griffith Stadium—For the second time in three weeks, Sonny Randle caught three touchdown passes in a game against the Redskins, paving the way for another easy Cardinal win.

Quarterback Ralph Guglielmi only had to move Washington 10 yards to its first touchdown, the length of his touchdown pass to Joe Walton. St. Louis fumbled a punt and Bob Whitlow recovered at the Cardinal 10. That represented the day's high point for Guglielmi. In the first half, the Skins quarterback completed four passes to Redskins and three to the Cardinals.

Things started to go downhill for the rest of the team later in the first quarter. On a play from the Redskins 10, Johnny Olszewski took a deep handoff from Guglielmi and was tackled in the end zone for a safety. The home team did manage to hold the Cards after they got a first down at the Washington 11, but Cardinal quarterback John Roach and Randle connected twice for touchdowns in the second period and the rout was on.

Looking at some of the statistics it's surprising that the Cardinals didn't win by much more. They posted 515 yards of total offense to just 154 for the Redskins. That included a whopping advantage in rushing yards of 267 to 37.

11/27/60	**STEELERS (4-5-1) 22, Redskins (1-6-2) 10**			22,334	
Was	0	0	7	3	10
Pit	6	7	3	6	22
Pit	FG Tracy 37				
Pit	FG Tracy 31				
Pit	Tracy 28 run (Layne kick)				
Was	James 49 pass from Guglielmi (Khayat kick)				
Pit	FG Layne 21				
Was	FG Khayat 9				
Pit	FG Tracy 26				
Pit	FG Layne 11				

Forbes Field—Tom "The Bomb" Tracy kicked three field goals and ran for a touchdown to pace the Steelers' to a 22-10 win over Washington.

The Redskins offense bombed as well, with an output of 43 yards for the first half, on the way to being outgained 394-181.

Tracy scored all but one of his team's points as the Steelers built a 13-0 halftime lead. Washington made a bid to get back into it in the third quarter when Rod Breedlove made his second interception of the day and returned it 16 yards to the Steeler 49. From there, Dick James went deep, caught Ralph Guglielmi's pass around the 20 and scored easily, cutting the Steeler lead to 13-7.

Quarterback Bobby Layne had an off day, completing just nine of 24 passes for 159 yards. But he worked around his issues by giving the ball to Tracy, who was throwing the ball well.

Tracy had never been successful on a field goal attempt before this game.

The teams exchanged field goals to make it 16-10, but the Redskins couldn't take advantage of a fine kickoff return by James after Tracy's 26-yard field goal made it 19-10. Pittsburgh's fifth field goal of the game, this one by Layne, clinched it for the home team.

12/4/60	**BROWNS (6-3-1) 27, Redskins (1-7-2) 16**				35,211
Was	10	3	3	0	16
Cle	7	17	0	3	27

Was	James 27 run (Khayat kick)
Cle	Brown 30 pass from Plum (Baker kick)
Was	FG Khayat 37
Was	FG Khayat 31
Cle	FG Baker 16
Cle	Kreitling 12 pass from Plum (Baker kick)
Cle	Mitchell 29 pass from Plum (Baker kick)
Was	FG Khayat 35
Cle	FG Baker 15

Cleveland Municipal Stadium—Milt Plum completed just 10 passes and Jim Brown carried only 15 times. But Plum's throws were good for 212 yards and three TD's and Brown gained 135 yards rushing and caught one of Plum's touchdown tosses as the Browns held off the Redskins 27-16.

The Redskins took advantage of a fumble recovery at the Cleveland 34 as Dick James weaved his way for 27 yards and a touchdown to take a 7-0 lead. Brown's touchdown reception tied the game, but Washington fought back, twice driving to Bobby Khayat field goals. The second one came on the first play of the second quarter and the Redskins held an improbable 13-7 lead over the heavily favored Browns.

It took the Browns until five minutes were left in the half to show why they were such prohibitive favorites. With the score 13-10, Brown made a 17-yard run to the Washington 36, and Plum made a couple of nice passes: one to Gern Nagler that carried to the 14, and then 12 yards to Rich Kreitling for the touchdown. Following a Cleveland interception, with just 27 seconds left before halftime, Washington linebacker Dick Lasse was left covering Bobby Mitchell one on one. Plum immediately spotted the extreme mismatch and Mitchell easily shook Lasse, catching Plum's pass for a 29-yard touchdown and a 24-13 lead.

The teams exchanged field goals in the second half and the Browns walked off with the win.

12/11/60	**GIANTS (6-3-2) 17, Redskins (1-8-2) 3**				14,077
NYG	0	0	7	10	17
Was	3	0	0	0	3

Was	FG Khayat 12
NYG	Morrison 9 pass from Conerly (Summerall kick)
NYG	FG Summerall 17
NYG	Scott 15 interception return (Summerall kick)

Griffith Stadium—It had already snowed six inches by game time and it didn't stop then. The Redskins didn't complete a pass and the Giants rushed for a net of minus one yard. The game came down to crucial mistakes and, as has been the case all year long, it was Washington making the key miscues.

New York won the toss and elected to kick off, confident their opponents would be unable to move, but the Redskins moved smartly downfield, mostly on the running of Don Bosseler. The fullback nearly scored a touchdown, but Lee Riley hauled him

down just short of the goal line after a 29-yard run. The New York defense held and Bobby Khayat kicked a field goal from 12 yards out.

For a long time, it appeared the three points would hold up. Late in the third quarter, the Giants lined up to punt somewhere near midfield—by that time, the snow had made it impossible to tell exactly where. Inexplicably, Gary Glick tried to field the ball inside the five and never got the handle. The Giants recovered and two plays later, Charley Conerly passed nine yards to Joe Morrison for the go-ahead touchdown. That would be all the points the Giants would need; the Redskins never threatened after that.

12/18/60	**Eagles (10-2) 38, REDSKINS (1-9-2) 28**				20,558
Phi	7	10	7	14	38
Was	7	7	7	7	28

Phi	McDonald 52 pass from Van Brocklin (Walston kick)
Was	Walton 30 pass from Guglielmi (Khayat kick)
Phi	McDonald 64 pass from Van Brocklin (Walston kick)
Was	James 3 run (Khayat kick)
Phi	FG Walston 23
Phi	Brown 34 pass from Jurgensen (Walston kick)
Was	Anderson 15 pass from Guglielmi (Khayat kick)
Phi	Brown 5 run (Walston kick)
Phi	Retzlaff 57 pass from Jurgensen (Walston kick)
Was	James 1 run (Khayat kick)

Griffith Stadium—The Eagles had already clinched the Eastern Conference title, so they rested Norv Van Brocklin and inserted young quarterback Sonny Jurgensen into the game in the second half to see what he could do. He did plenty, throwing for two touchdowns to pace the Eagles' 38-28 win over the Redskins.

Van Brocklin set the table for Jurgensen by throwing two long touchdown passes to Tommy McDonald in the first half. The Redskins were able to keep pace, though, scoring on Ralph Guglielmi's 30-yard pass to Joe Walton and Dick James' three-yard run. James set up his score himself with a nice reception of Guglielmi's pass for a 37-yard gain to the eight.

The game was tied at 14 nearing halftime, but Van Brocklin engineered a textbook two-minute drill to set up a 23-yard field goal by Bobby Walston to give the Eagles a three-point halftime lead.

A Washington fumble led to Jurgensen's first scoring pass—a 34-yard strike to Tim Brown. The home team climbed back into it with a 15-yard pass from Guglielmi to Bill Anderson to cut the lead back to three, but Jurgensen and the Eagles were just too much. Jurgensen converted a third and 14 with a 71-yard bomb to Brown, who was tackled at the Redskin five. Brown completed the drive by running it over on the next play. Pete Retzlaff caught Jurgy's other scoring pass in the fourth quarter

This was the last NFL game at Griffith Stadium.

Dec 18

Marshall: Nixon Fired
Owner's postgame statement:
'He will not be rehired'

1961
Head Coach: Bill McPeak
Record: 1-12-1, Seventh in NFL Eastern Conference

Honors: Dick James Pro Bowl; Ray Lemek Pro Bowl;
Jim Schrader Pro Bowl; Bob Toneff Pro Bowl, All-NFL

McPeak Hired as Redskins Coach

Dec 19—The Redskins made assistant coach Bill McPeak the youngest head coach in the NFL today.

McPeak, 34, replaces Mike Nixon, who led the Redskins to a 1-9-2 record in 1960, the worst record in the history of the franchise.

At his own request, McPeak was given a one-year contract. "I feel that I can prove myself in a year," he said.

McPeak is just four years removed from his nine-year career as a player for the Pittsburgh Steelers. He was a player-coach his last two years there.

The team would like to retain assistant coaches Abe Gibron and Torgy Torgeson. Both have indicated they will stay on.

Dec 23

Race Ban Hurting Redskins?
Coaches will fail as long as team refuses to allow black players, says writer

---

Dec 27

Redskins Tab Snead, Rutgens in NFL Draft
Team faces competition from AFL in signing QB and DE

Marshall to JFK: Let's Talk Race

Mar 24—Redskins owner George Preston Marshall remained defiant today over his refusal to hire black players to play for his team, but he would be willing to debate the issue with President John F. Kennedy.

"I would consider it a great honor to meet with and discuss this with the president of the United States," said Marshall.

"I'd like to debate the president. I could handle him with words," he continued.

The issue of the Redskins remaining an all-white team has come to the forefront as they prepare to move into a new stadium built on land owned by the federal government. According to Secretary of the Interior Stewart Udall, the head of the department that controls the land, the team's policy runs afoul of a general anti-discrimination policy that Kennedy announced a few days ago.

Marshall claims that the race issue is a moot point. "Our roster is closed," he said. "The draft is over."

"We have been drafting our players primarily from colleges in the South and they don't have [blacks]," Marshall said in justifying his team's stance.

Udall is going after Marshall with more than just words. The team must comply with federal rules, such as the anti-discrimination order, in order to play in the stadium. Should the team not play in the stadium it would be in violation of the 30-year lease that Marshall signed, making the organization subject to heavy financial penalties.

Apr 11

J. Robinson Lauds Udall's Stance vs. Skins
Player who broke baseball color barrier says Secretary's stand is 'inspirational and encouraging'

Aug 15

Redskins Will Employ Blacks in '62
Rozelle will monitor compromise deal

September 12

Guglielmi Traded to Cardinals
QB miffed but will report; Rookie Snead to take over as Redskins starter

---

9/17/61	49ERS (1-0) 35, Redskins (0-1) 3				43,142
Was	3	0	0	0	3
SF	7	14	14	0	35
SF	Stickles 25 pass from Brodie (Davis kick)				
Was	FG Aveni 29				
SF	Stickles 4 pass from Brodie (Davis kick)				
SF	Smith 34 pass from Brodie (Davis kick)				
SF	Connor 10 pass from Brodie (Davis kick)				
SF	Smith 3 run (Davis kick)				

Kezar Stadium—San Francisco gave Norm Snead a rude welcoming into the NFL, intercepting three of the rookie quarterback's passes en route to a 35-3 trouncing of Snead's Redskins.

Snead's issues weren't entirely his fault. His receivers struggled to get open against a tough 49er secondary, and he didn't get much help from a ground game, either. Washington rushed for just 37 yards on the day. In addition, the 49ers rushed the rookie hard all day and he had little time to throw. He was sacked five times for 42 yards in losses.

San Francisco quarterback John Brodie had a hot hand, shredding the Washington secondary for four touchdowns.

A pair of touchdown passes from the 49ers' Brodie to Monte Stickles gave the home team a 14-3 lead. In between, a John Aveni field goal gave the Redskins their only points.

Brodie passed for two more scores in the process of shredding the Redskins' secondary. For the day, he was 16 of 23 for 238 yards and the four TD's.

Another rookie quarterback made his NFL debut in the game as Brodie took a seat in the fourth quarter—Billy Kilmer, out of UCLA, went six for nine with two interceptions.

9/24/61	EAGLES (2-0) 14, Redskins (0-2) 7				50,108
Was	0	0	7	0	7
Phi	0	0	14	0	14
Phi	Retzlaff 52 pass from Jurgensen (Walston kick)				
Was	Dugan 80 pass from Snead (Aveni kick)				
Phi	McDonald 23 pass from Jurgensen (Walston kick)				

Franklin Field—The Redskins gave the defending champion Eagles all they could handle in Philadelphia, but the Skins fumbled a punt to set up the go-ahead score in a 14-7 loss.

Following a slow start last week in San Francisco, the Washington offense did have a respectable showing. Washington posted 325 yards of offense including 106 on the ground. They did hurt their own cause, however, by losing two fumbles.

After a scoreless first half, Eagle quarterback Sonny Jurgensen threw a short pass to Pete Retzlaff, who caught the ball at the Redskins 40, put a move on two Redskins defenders and raced the rest of the way into the end zone.

The lead lasted for 18 seconds. After the ensuing kickoff, Washington quarterback Norm Snead found receiver Fred Dugan behind the Eagles' secondary and hit him in stride for an 80-yard touchdown. John Aveni's extra point tied the score at seven.

Later in the third, Washington's Lew Luce mishandled a punt and the Eagles recovered at the Redskins' 23. On the next play, Jurgensen fired a pass just over the outstretched hands of the Redskins' Ben Scotti and into the hands of flanker Tommy McDonald for the winning touchdown.

10/1/61	Giants (2-1) 24, REDSKINS (0-3) 21				36,757
NYG	7	7	3	7	24
Was	21	0	0	0	21
NYG	Rote 17 pass from Connerly (Summerall kick)				
Was	Bosseler 4 pass from Snead (Aveni kick)				
Was	Hackbart 48 interception return (Aveni kick)				
Was	James 29 pass from Snead (Aveni kick)				
NYG	Shofner 1 pass from Tittle (Summerall kick)				
NYG	FG Summerall 28				
NYG	Tittle 1 run (Summerall kick)				

D.C. Stadium—The Redskins got the crowd going at the christening of D.C. Stadium by scoring three touchdowns in a six-minute span in the first quarter to take a 21-7 lead. The veteran Giants, led by quarterback Y. A. Tittle, spoiled the party by coming back over the game's final 45 minutes to secure the 24-21 win.

The game started ominously for the Redskins. Rookie Jim Kerr fumbled the opening kickoff and Pat Summerall recovered for the Giants at the Washington 24. Kyle Rote gathered in a touchdown pass from Charlie Connerly soon after, and it was 7-0.

Washington immediately answered, driving 69 yards to a touchdown. The payoff came when Norm Snead, under heavy pressure, flipped a four-yard touchdown pass to Don Bosseler.

The next Redskins score had a down side to it. Dale Hackbart intercepted Connerly's pass and sidestepped the Giants' quarterback on the way to a 48-yard touchdown run. The problem was this prompted Giants coach Allie Sherman to bench Connerly in favor of Tittle, who proceeded to go 24 of 41 for 315 yards and rally his team.

The Redskins went up 21-7 after Snead went to Dick James for a 29-yard touchdown, a score set up by John Paluck's interception of Tittle. After that, the Giants' quarterback went to work. In the second quarter, Tittle led a drive that ended when he found a wide-open Del Shofner for a one-yard touchdown pass. Summerall hit a 28-yard field goal to cut the home team's lead to 21-17.

In the fourth quarter, Tittle snuck it over from the one to give the Giants a three-point lead. Kerr gave Washington a chance to answer by making a diving interception with about five minutes left, but the Giants intercepted Snead to end the threat and seal the win.

New York dominated the game statistically. The Giants got 30 first downs to Washington's eight and outgained the Redskins 416-125.

10/8/61	BROWNS (3-1) 31, Redskins (0-4) 7				46,186
Was	0	7	0	0	7
Cle	3	14	0	14	31
Cle	FG Groza 34				
Cle	Mitchell 52 pass from Plum (Groza kick)				
Cle	Mitchell 64 punt return (Groza kick)				
Was	Osborne 6 pass from Snead (Aveni kick)				
Cle	Mitchell 31 run (Groza kick)				
Cle	Renfro 17 pass from Dawson (Groza kick)				

Cleveland Stadium—Bobby Mitchell scored touchdowns three different ways to lead Cleveland's win.

After a Lou Groza field goal, Mitchell caught a 52-yard touchdown pass from Milt Plum. Later in the second period Mitchell returned a punt 64 yards for a pair of second-quarter scores.

The Redskins made a game of it before halftime. They scored on a six-yard Norm Snead pass to Tom Osborne that capped an eight-play, 79-yard drive. Snead's passes accounted for 75 of those yards and Washington was within 17-7 at the half.

The margin stood until the fourth quarter when Mitchell scooted 31 yards around end to his third TD of the game. Ray Renfro finished the scoring by catching a 17-yard pass from Len Dawson.

The numbers in this game are a great argument for those who contend that statistics are for losers: the Redskins (16) had more first downs than did the Browns (13) and passed for 201 yards to 194 for Cleveland.

Fred Dugan was an offensive standout for the Redskins. He caught seven Snead passes for 120 yards.

10/15/61	STEELERS (1-4) 20, Redskins (0-5) 0				15,072
Was	0	0	0	0	0
Pit	17	0	0	3	20
Pit	Carpenter 8 pass from Bukich (Michaels kick)				
Pit	Dial 23 pass from Bukich (Michaels kick)				
Pit	FG Michaels 13				
Pit	FG Michaels 36				

Forbes Field—An intimate gathering of just over 15,000 watched the NFL's last two winless teams play. The Redskins were the ones left unscathed in the win column as Pittsburgh rolled to a 20-0 win.

It was over early as the Steelers scored 17 points in the first quarter. Seven Washington turnovers, six interceptions thrown and a fumble lost during and after that onslaught let Pittsburgh coast to victory.

Lou Michaels set up the first score when he got the first of Pittsburgh's six interceptions on the day and returned it to the Washington 10. That set up a touchdown pass from Rudy Bukich to Preston Carpenter.

Washington quarterback Norm Snead fumbled on the first play after the kickoff and the Steelers recovered. From the Washington 23, Bukich threw to Buddy Dial to make it 14-0. Michaels kicked two field goals—one late in the first quarter, and the other in the final moments of the game—to round out the scoring.

Washington's scoring threats were thwarted by missed field goals and interceptions. John Aveni missed three field goals, including one that was blocked, and Johnny Sample made a fourth-quarter interception in the end zone to kill another drive.

10/22/61	Cardinals (3-3) 24, REDSKINS (0-6) 0				28,037
StL	0	7	3	14	24
Was	0	0	0	0	0
StL	Anderson 42 pass from Guglielmi (Perry kick)				
StL	FG Perry 24				
StL	Gautt 10 pass from Guglielmi (Perry kick)				
StL	Hill 34 interception return (Perry kick)				

D.C. Stadium—It was "Virginia Day" at D.C. Stadium and the Virginia Tech band known as the "Highty-Tighties" performed with flair and precisions.

Too bad the home team couldn't do the same.

The streaks continued to grow—14 consecutive losses, 16 in a row winless, two straight shutouts, 0 for two at their new stadium. Washington was again uncompetitive in dropping this one to the Cards.

Ex-Skins quarterback Ralph Guglielmi threw two touchdown passes to pour some salt in his former teammates' wounds. The first one went to rookie tight end Taz Anderson and covered 42 yards. That was the only scoring in the first half, and the Redskins were still in the game.

Nonetheless, their prospects for winning seemed dim. They were unable to generate an offensive threat, generating just 22 yards of offense in the half. On the day, the Cardinal defense dumped rookie quarterback Norm Snead for losses 11 times.

The Highty-Tighties left the field to cheers; the Redskins returned to the field to booing. The Skins proved they deserved it as they mustered just 67 more yards after intermission. Their deepest penetration on the day was to the St. Louis 33 yard line.

After a third-quarter Gerald Perry field goal made it 10-0, Guglielmi put it out of reach in the third quarter with a 10-yard TD toss to Prentice Gautt. Jimmy Hill put a bow on it for the Cards with a 35-yard touchdown return of an interception.

10/29/61	Eagles (6-1) 27, REDSKINS (0-7) 24			31,066	
Phi	7	7	3	10	27
Was	7	10	0	7	24
Was	Horner 3 pass from Snead (Aveni kick)				
Phi	Retzlafff 46 pass from Jurgensen (Walston kick)				
Was	Bosseler 8 run (Aveni kick)				
Was	FG Aveni 52				
Phi	Retzlaff 11 pass from Jurgensen (Walston kick)				
Phi	FG Walston 14				
Phi	FG Walston 33				
Was	Cunningham 7 pass from Snead (Aveni kick)				
Phi	McDonald 41 pass from Jurgensen (Walston kick)				

D.C. Stadium—The Redskins got the home crowd on their side by holding the Eagles to minus 12 yards rushing, getting a team record 52-yard field goal from John Aveni, intercepting two Sonny Jurgensen passes and scoring a touchdown to take a 24-20 lead with 42 seconds left. But Jurgensen, who passed for 436 yards, produced the final rally by taking his team 80 yards in four plays, the last a 41-yard strike to Tommy McDonald with 12 seconds left to give the Eagles a 27-24 win.

Aveni's field goal, a three-yard touchdown pass from Norm Snead to Sam Horner, and an eight-yard scoring run by Don Bosseler boosted the Redskins to a 17-7 second-quarter lead. Then the world champion Eagles took over, scoring 13 unanswered points from late in the second to early in the fourth quarter to take a 20-17 lead.

With time running out, the Redskins took possession at their own 19. Snead completed passes of 20 yards to Bosseler, nine to Fred Dugan, and 22 to Dick James and the Redskins were down to the Philly 26. Facing a third and four soon after, Snead found Dugan for a first down at the seven. A run for no gain and an incompletion made it third and goal. With Eagles tackle Jess Richardson hanging on, Snead somehow managed to slip a pass to Jim Cunningham in between two defenders in the end zone with 42 seconds left.

But before the home crowd could go home happy, Jurgensen rewrote the ending. From his own 20, he hit Walston twice for 20 and 18 yards and then found McDonald streaking over the middle. The flanker caught the ball in stride and rolled untouched into the end zone.

11/5/61	GIANTS (6-2) 53, Redskins (0-8) 0			56,077	
Was	0	0	0	0	0
NYG	9	16	7	21	53
NYG	Safety Snead tackled in end zone				
NYG	Shofner 38 pass from Tittle (Summerall kick)				
NYG	Gaiters 1 run (Summerall kick)				
NYG	Gaiters 3 pass from Tittle (Summerall kick)				
NYG	Safety Snead tackled in end zone				
NYG	Shofner 13 pass from Tittle (Summerall kick)				
NYG	Shofner 32 pass from Grosscup (Summerall kick)				
NYG	Patton 51 interception return (Summerall kick)				
NYG	Wells 2 run (Summerall kick)				

Yankee Stadium—Things started out ugly for the Redskins—and rapidly rolled downhill from there. Washington suffered its third-worst defeat ever at 53-0.

The reader will be spared the gloomy details here. It took the Giants less than two minutes to take a 9-0 lead by scoring on a safety and the first of three Y. A. Tittle touchdown passes.

Quarterback Norm Snead was sacked in the end zone a second time in the second quarter to give the Giants a 25-0 halftime lead. They poured it on in garbage time in the fourth quarter with backup quarterback Lee Grosscup throwing a scoring pass and Jimmy Patton scoring on an interception return. Another Giants interception set up a final touchdown on a two-yard run by Joel Wells.

Washington mustered just 82 yards of total offense 31 on the ground and 51 in the air.

McPeak: Poor Drafts at Root of Skins' Woes

Nov 6—Everyone in town has a theory about what's wrong with the Redskins. The man most responsible for righting the ship, rookie head coach Bill McPeak, has one that seems to make a lot of sense.

"Look back over the records of the top draft choices. Check who was picked and who's still here."

Players are supposed to make an impact as they enter their third and fourth years in the league. A look at the 1958 draft reveals that just one player from the top five selections—end Bill Anderson—made the team. A year later, the draft class yielded not one player among the top five picks who made the team.

McPeak went on a personal scout tour when he came to Washington, D.C., three years ago, a first for the team. He has Tim Temerario doing that duty this year in hopes of turning around the organization's draft misfortunes.

The Redskins' exclusion of black players from the draft pool was not addressed by McPeak. The team has committed to integrating its roster next season.

11/12/61	Browns (6-3) 17, REDSKINS (0-9) 6			28,975	
Cle	3	7	7	0	17
Was	0	0	6	0	6
Cle	FG Groza 48				
Cle	Renfro 37 pass from Brown (Groza kick)				
Was	Bosseler 1 run (kick failed)				
Cle	Kreitling 9 pass from Plum (Groza kick)				

D.C. Stadium—Cleveland's Jim Brown completed the first pass of his pro career for a touchdown as the Browns handed the Redskins their seventeenth straight loss over two seasons by a score of 17-6.

Following a Lou Groza field goal in the first quarter, Brown took a handoff, pulled up and passed. His toss found a wide-open Ray Renfro for 37 yards and a 10-0 Cleveland lead.

The Redskins had their chances to make a game of it in the first half. Not only did their drives stall short of the end zone but John Aveni missed field goals of 37, 27 and 46 yards to damage Washington's hopes.

Aveni's first miss came right after Groza's field goal. The Redskins answered, putting together a nice drive down to the Cleveland 29, but the drive fizzled and Aveni missed.

The damage caused by the missed field goals was magnified in the third quarter when the Browns fumbled at their own one yard line and Don Bosseler scored from there. Instead of leading, the Redskins were still down 10-6. It stayed that way as Aveni missed the extra point.

Cleveland answered with a touchdown pass from Milt Plum to Rich Kreitling later in the third quarter for the final 17-6 margin.

Nov 13

Ernie Davis Not Interested in Joining Skins
Star Syracuse RB is likely top pick in draft

11/19/61	Redskins (0-9-1) 28, COWBOYS (4-5-1) 28			17,500	
Was	7	14	0	7	28
Dal	7	0	14	7	28
Dal	Clarke 40 pass from Meredith (Bielski kick)				
Was	Snead 1 run (Aveni kick)				
Was	Hackbart 32 interception return (Aveni kick)				
Was	Dugan 9 pass from Snead (Aveni kick)				
Dal	Howton 15 pass from Meredith (Bielski kick)				
Dal	Perkins 2 run (Bielski kick)				
Was	Snead 1 run (Aveni kick)				
Dal	Bielski 3 pass from LeBaron (Bielski kick)				

Cotton Bowl—The Redskins managed to not lose the contest, something that hadn't happened in the last 19 games. Still, the Redskins led 21-7 at halftime, then 28-21 with 7:29 to go in the game, but allowed the Cowboys to rally both times to gain a 28-28 tie.

With the score tied at 21, Dallas was flagged for pass interference in the end zone and Washington got the ball on the Dallas one. Quarterback Norm Snead snuck it over from there to put the Redskins up by seven. The Redskins had gained possession when Dick Lasse and Jim Kerr stopped Dallas on a fourth and one attempt at the Cowboys' 44.

But former Washington quarterback Eddie LeBaron, subbing for an injured Don Meredith, completed three of five passes in the game-tying drive, capped by a three-yard touchdown pass to Dick Bielski with less than two minutes left in the game.

Both Snead and Meredith had hot hands. The Redskins' quarterback passed for 234 yards and a touchdown while Meredith tallied 217 in the air.

Both teams had a chance to untie the game in the final minute. Dallas linebacker Chuck Howley blocked a 41-yard John Aveni field goal attempt with 25 seconds left and, on the game's final play, Bielski was short on a 50-yard attempt.

11/26/61	Colts (6-5) 27, REDSKINS (0-10-1) 6			41,062	
Bal	14	3	7	3	27
Was	0	0	6	0	6
Bal	Mutscheller 10 pass from Unitas (Myrah kick)				
Bal	Hawkins 2 run (Myrah kick)				
Bal	FG Myrah 37				
Was	FG Aveni 30				
Was	FG Aveni 46				
Bal	Moore 54 run (Myrah kick)				
Bal	FG Myrah 37				

D.C. Stadium—For a few fleeting moments, it looked like the Redskins had a shot at ending their 20-game winless streak.

Trailing 17-3 in the third quarter, the Redskins' Andy Stynchula forced Baltimore quarterback Johnny Unitas to fumble and Joe Rutgens recovered at the Colts' 35. A touchdown would have pulled the Redskins within seven and given the portion of the 41,062 in attendance pulling for the Redskins—at least a third had apparently made the trek from Baltimore—something to cheer about.

But it was the same old story. A holding penalty killed the drive and they had to settle for a 46-yard John Aveni field goal. Less than a minute later, Baltimore's Lenny Moore took a handoff from Unitas, went wide left, shook off Stynchula, got a block from receiver Raymond Berry and sprinted down the sideline for a 54-yard touchdown run. Moore, who had run 45 yards on the Colts'

first play from scrimmage, rushed for 122 yards on six carries on the day.

The Baltimore defense took care of the rest of the business, with linemen Gino Marchetti and Ordell Braase taking up residence in the Washington backfield, harassing quarterback Norm Snead and helping hold the Redskins to less than 100 yards of total offense.

12/3/61	CARDINALS (5-7) 38, Redskins (0-11-1) 24			16,204	
Was	7	10	0	7	24
StL	7	0	10	21	38
Was	Aveni 41 pass from Snead (Aveni kick)				
StL	Gautt 2 run (Perry kick)				
Was	Cunningham 8 run (Aveni kick)				
Was	FG Aveni 37				
StL	FG Perry 37				
StL	Conrad 32 pass from Crow (Perry kick)				
StL	Randle 3 pass from Etcheverry (Perry kick)				
StL	Conrad 43 pass from Etcheverry (Perry kick)				
StL	Gautt 1 run (Perry kick)				
Was	Osborne 60 pass from Snead (Aveni kick)				

Busch Stadium—A 10-point Redskins lead late in the third quarter was buried under an avalanche of 31 unanswered points by the Cardinals. Washington recovered to score a late touchdown, but by then it was too late—St. Louis won 38-24.

Rookie Washington quarterback Norm Snead was instrumental in building his team's lead. A 41-yard TD pass to John Aveni accounted for the first score of the game and, after St. Louis tied it at seven, Snead went to Bill Anderson for 29 yards to set up Jim Cunningham's eight-yard touchdown run. Those two touchdowns and a 37-yard John Aveni field goal staked the Redskins to a 17-7 lead that held until five minutes remained in the third quarter.

It started innocently enough when Jerry Perry kicked a 37-yard field goal. Then running back John David Crow threw a 32-yard touchdown pass to Bobby Joe Conrad to tie it at 17 going into the fourth.

Quarterback Sam Etcheverry then broke it open with a pair of touchdown passes: one to Sonny Randle, the other to Conrad. After a Cardinal scoring run, Snead threw a 60-yard touchdown pass to Tom Osborne, but it was too little and too late; the winless streak extended to 22.

Dec 4

Redskins Take Davis With Top Pick
First black player drafted by Washington says he'll take best offer between Skins, AFL

12/10/61	Steelers (6-7) 30, REDSKINS (0-12-1) 14			21,134	
Pit	7	3	14	6	30
Was	0	7	0	7	14
Pit	Mack 10 pass from Layne (Michaels kick)				
Was	Dugan 9 pass from Snead (Aveni kick)				
Pit	FG Michaels 42				
Pit	Carpenter 40 pass from Layne (Michaels kick)				
Pit	Mack 6 pass from Layne (Michaels kick)				
Was	Dugan 11 pass from Izo (Aveni kick)				
Pit	Dial 5 pass from Layne (kick failed)				

D.C. Stadium—Bobby Layne threw four touchdown passes to lead Pittsburgh to a 30-14 win over Washington. The loss extended the Redskins' winless streak to 23 games.

After the Steelers took a first-quarter lead on Layne's first scoring pass, the Redskins looked as though they would go into the locker room at the half tied. Norm Snead threw a nine-yard touchdown pass to Fred Dugan with 38 seconds left in the second quarter. It was one of two scoring catches on the day for Dugan, who finished the game with 50 receptions for the season, a new team record.

But Pittsburgh quickly untied the game, with Layne completing two quick passes for 34 yards to set up Lou Michael's 42-yard field goal with four seconds left until halftime.

That set the tone for the second half as Layne led the Steelers on touchdown drives of 51 and 96 yards.

Despite out gaining Pittsburgh 344 yards to 324, the Redskins again were on the short end of the score. Their primary issue was not an inability to move the ball, but scoring when they got close. Three times they advanced inside the Pittsburgh 15—and three times they came away with no points. John Aveni missed field goal attempts from 33 and 48 yards.

Redskins Sign Hatcher, First Black Player

Dec 9—The Washington Redskins signed fullback Ron Hatcher, their eighth-round pick in the recent NFL draft, to a contract. Although Hatcher faces long odds in trying to make the team, his signing is noteworthy as he is the first black player the team has ever signed.

Redskins Trade Davis Rights to Browns for Mitchell, Jackson

Dec 14—The Redskins have traded a potential star for an established one.

In a deal finalized on draft day 10 days ago but not revealed until today, Washington will send the rights to Syracuse running back Ernie Davis, the first overall selection, to the Browns. In return, the Redskins will get running back Bobby Mitchell and LeRoy Jackson, a first-round selection of Cleveland's in the draft.

Actually, the name of Mitchell has not been formally announced since he still has another game to play this Sunday. Technically the deal is for "a player to be named later," but multiple sources have confirmed the player is indeed named Bobby Mitchell.

Mitchell is black, certainly relieving some of the pressure the Redskins have been under to integrate the team.

However, it's clear that Mitchell was not acquired solely based on race. He's a superstar playing in the shadow of teammate Jim Brown. The Redskins certainly need no introduction to Mitchell as he gained 234 yards from scrimmage against them in just 14 touches in a 1959 game. This season, he scored three touchdowns in a Cleveland rout of the Redskins.

12/17/61	REDSKINS (1-12-1) 34, Cowboys (4-9-1) 24				21,451
Dal	3	0	14	7	24
Was	7	0	21	6	34

Was	James 5 run (Aveni kick)
Dal	FG Bielski 27
Was	James 4 run (Aveni kick)
Dal	Clarke 80 pass from LeBaron (Bielski kick)
Was	James 1 pass from Snead (Aveni kick)
Was	James 38 run (Aveni kick)
Dal	Clarke 65 pass from LeBaron (Bielski kick)
Was	Snead 1 run (kick failed)
Dal	Houston 11 pass from LeBaron (Bielski kick)

D.C. Stadium—It seemed to be a bad omen. During the halftime Christmas festivities, Santa's dog sled got stuck in the mud. The Redskins led 7-3 but had gotten bogged down in the second half many times during the course of their 23-game winless streak. But the guy in the red suit made a nice recovery, jumping out of the sled and dancing the Twist. Things turned out OK for the Redskins, too, as running back Dick James twisted, shifted, turned, and ran through the Cowboys for a team-record four touchdowns. And the Redskins finally won one.

Jim Steffen returned the opening kickoff 43 yards to jump-start the Redskins. James kept the drive alive by catching a 22-yard pass from Norm Snead to convert a third and seven. On second down from the five, James went untouched into the end zone to give Washington a 7-0 lead with just four and a half minutes gone.

Dallas missed a chance to tie the game when Eddie LeBaron's pass intended for a wide-open receiver in the end zone hit the goal post and bounced harmlessly to the ground. They settled for a field goal to pull within 7-3.

In the third quarter, Snead passed to end Bill Anderson for a 41-yard gain. Anderson broke a tackle at the Dallas 37 and rolled another 23 yards to the 14 before being tackled. Shortly after that, James dove over the goal line to tally his second touchdown, this one from four yards out.

The 11-point lead lasted less than a minute. LeBaron threw a bomb to Frank Clarke for an 80-yard touchdown that made it 14-10. Dallas got the ball back and the crowd of 21,451 was starting to squirm. They weren't uncomfortable for long as Rod Breedlove recovered a Dallas fumble at the Cowboys' 33. A roughing the passer call got the Redskins halfway to the goal line before James went the rest of the way, following blocks by Vince Promuto and Ray Lemek to the one and then catching a one-yard flip from Snead to take a 21-10 lead.

Dallas fumbled again and Bob Toneff recovered, giving the Redskins the ball in Dallas territory once more, at the 45. Shortly after that, James had his best run of the day: 39 yards for his fourth touchdown. Lemek wiped out the last Dallas defender at around the 15.

James had a chance to join a select group who had scored more than four touchdowns in a game, but Snead snuck it over from the one in the fourth quarter. For the game, James rushed for 146 yards on 27 carries.

1962
Head Coach: Bill McPeak
Record: 5-7-2, Fourth in NFL Eastern Conference

Honors: Rod Breedlove Pro Bowl; Bobby Mitchell Pro Bowl, All NFL;
John Nisby Pro Bowl; Norm Snead Pro Bowl

Feb 8

Leo DeOrsey Buys 13 Percent of Redskins
D. C. attorney exercises option, Marshall's share of team now down to 55.8 percent

---

Jack Kent Cooke Back In Town

June 19—Canadian millionaire Jack Kent Cooke is in meetings with representatives of the Washington Redskins, vigorously attempting to buy the NFL team.

Cooke already owns the Toronto minor-league baseball team and wants to expand his investments in sports.

Under Cooke's ownership, the Maple Leafs have become as well known for putting on a show as they have for playing baseball games. The team's schedule is loaded with celebrity appearances and other promotions.

9/16/62	Redskins (0-0-1) 35, COWBOYS (0-0-1) 35			15,730
Was	7	7	7	14	35
Dal	7	7	14	7	35

Dal	Marsh 4 run (Baker kick)
Was	Mitchell 6 pass from Snead (B. Khayat kick)
Was	Snead 1 run (B. Khayat kick)
Dal	Clarke 58 pass from Meredith (Baker kick)
Dal	Clarke 11 pass from LeBaron (Baker kick)
Dal	Marsh 6 run (Baker kick)
Was	Mitchell 92 kickoff return (B. Khayat kick)
Dal	Clarke 55 pass from Meredith (Baker kick)
Was	Mitchell 81 pass from Snead (B. Khayat kick)
Was	Snead 1 run (Khayat kick)

Cotton Bowl—Bobby Mitchell made his Redskins debut a smashing success, either scoring or setting up all five of Washington's touchdowns as the Redskins rallied to tie the Cowboys 35-35.

Twice in the second half Dallas took 14-point leads—and twice the Redskins battled back. With the score tied at 14 at the half, the Cowboys scored one touchdown after a 15-play drive and another after Jerry Norton picked off Norm Snead's pass and Dallas drove 40 yards into the end zone.

Then a Cowboy special teamer committed a small mistake that turned out to be huge. He was offside on the kickoff after Dallas' second score, forcing a rekick. Mitchell took the second kick and rolled 92 yards for a touchdown, pulling the Redskins within seven.

But Dallas shook off the stunning return and widened the margin back to 14 early in the fourth quarter. Frank Clark caught a pass from Don Meredith, slipped Bob Pellegrini at the Washington 35, and ran to the goal line to complete a 55-yard touchdown play. It was Clark's third touchdown catch of the game.

Mitchell and Snead matched that touchdown 47 seconds later. From the Washington 19, Snead lofted a long pass downfield. All day long Mitchell had been beating Warren Livingston, his would-be defender. This play was no different as Mitchell was wide open to catch Snead's bomb in stride and he rolled in for an 81-yard touchdown and a 35-28 Dallas lead.

Washington got the ball back with time running out. Facing third and ten at his own 35, Mitchell fooled the Cowboys by taking a few lazy steps down the sideline when the ball was snapped. Suddenly, he burst towards the middle, made a remarkable stab of Snead's pass and wasn't take down until he'd gained 26 yards to the Dallas 39. Four plays later, Snead scored on a one-yard sneak and the game was tied at 35.

Ex-Redskin quarterback Eddie LeBaron completed a 34-yard pass to Clark that set up a 34-yard field goal attempt with eight seconds left. Fortunately, another former Redskin, Sam Baker, missed the attempt badly. The game ended in a tie.

9/23/62	Redskins (1-0-1) 17, BROWNS (1-1) 16			57,491
Was	7	0	3	7	17
Cle	3	10	0	3	16

Was	Steffen 39 fumble return (B. Khayat kick)
Cle	FG Groza 32
Cle	Wilson 1 run (Groza kick)
Cle	FG Groza 12
Was	FG Khayat 33
Cle	FG Groza 37
Was	Mitchell 50 pass from Snead (B. Khayat kick)

Cleveland Municipal Stadium—As Jack Walsh said in the Post, "You can't make up things like this. It actually happened. What happened after that gets more unbelievable."

What can't you make up? The fact that Bobby Mitchell returned to Cleveland where he had been a star performer for four years and scored the game-winning touchdown with a minute and a half left in the game. What actually happened? The dazzling, astounding move that Mitchell made to get free to turn Norm Snead's short pass into a 50-yard touchdown play. What was more unbelievable after that? The Redskins blocked two Lou Groza field goal attempts in the waning seconds, preserving the one-point win.

There were more remarkable events. In the early going Cleveland running back Jim Brown made the first of two critical mistakes when he flipped a lateral to nobody in particular. Defensive back Jim Steffen snared the ball and easily bolted 39 yards for a touchdown and a 7-0 lead.

Cleveland responded with a one-yard touchdown run and two Groza field goals and took a 13-10 lead into halftime. The Browns had some chances to put the Redskins away, but they came up empty after getting a first and goal at the three and later had to settle for a 37-yard field goal on another foray into Washington territory.

The home team's 16-10 lead still looked safe as the Redskins offense was unable to get much going. It looked even more secure when, with about four minutes left to play, Brown took a pass from Jim Ninowski and scooted all the way down to the Washington 33. There, however, linebacker Bob Pellegrini smacked into Brown and the ball popped free. Eddie Khayat pounced on it and the Redskins had one last shot.

They moved to midfield and Snead flipped a pass that Mitchell caught over the middle around the Cleveland 40. A head fake and a wicked cut to the outside had Browns defenders running into each other. From the sideline, one more cut back to the middle got Mitchell free for the touchdown. Bob Khayat's extra point put Washington up 17-16 with 1:36 left.

Ninowski moved his team smartly downfield and it appeared that Mitchell's heroics would be for naught as the usually automatic Groza lined up for a 35-yard field goal attempt on second down with seven seconds left. Dale Hackbart cut through the wall and blocked the attempt. Cleveland recovered the ball and the officials determined there was still a second left. It didn't matter; Bobby Freeman rejected Groza's second attempt from 50 yards and the Redskins survived.

9/30/62	**REDSKINS (2-0-1) 24, Cardinals (1-2) 14**				39,250
StL	0	0	7	7	14
Was	7	7	0	10	24
Was	Mitchell 40 pass from Snead (B. Khayat kick)				
Was	Mitchell 23 pass from Snead (B. Khayat kick)				
StL	Crow 6 run (Perry kick)				
Was	FG Khayat 28				
Was	Cunningham 1 run (B. Khayat kick)				
StL	Crow 1 run (Perry kick)				

D.C. Stadium—Norm Snead and Bobby Mitchell paired up for two touchdown passes as the Redskins beat the Cardinals 24-14.

Both of the scoring connections came in the first half. The first was the result of a great play call by Snead, a play-action pass on third and one at the St. Louis 40. The fake sucked the defense in and Mitchell was wide open.

The second touchdown also came on third down. On third and six from the Cardinals 23, Snead dropped back, rolled to his right and found Mitchell, who had beaten Larry Wilson and Pat Fischer in the end zone. The pass was perfect and it was 14-0. Washington was never threatened after that.

The Mitchell-to-Snead combination had a hand in two of the Redskins' scores in the fourth quarter. A 24-yard completion set up a 28-yard field goal by Bobby Khayat. Later in the fourth, Snead went to Mitchell for 28 yards to key a drive that culminated in Jim Cunningham's one-yard touchdown blast.

That last score rendered John David Crow's one-yard touchdown run later in the fourth mere window dressing.

The visitors were quite generous to their hosts. Crow fumbled four times, with the Redskins recovering all of them. In addition, Cardinal quarterback Sam Etcheverry threw four interceptions. In retrospect, the five-point underdog Redskins should have won by a lot more.

10/7/62	**REDSKINS (3-0-1) 20, Rams (0-4) 14**				38,264
LA	0	7	0	7	14
Was	10	10	0	0	20
Was	FG B. Khayat 30				
Was	Dugan 2 pass from Snead (B. Khayat kick)				
LA	Bass 33 pass from Bratkowski (Villanueva kick)				
Was	FG B. Khayat 46				
Was	Dugan 25 pass from Snead (B. Khayat kick)				
LA	Phillips 55 pass from Miller (Villanueva kick)				

D.C. Stadium—Fred Dugan caught two touchdown passes from Norm Snead to help push Washington to a 20-7 lead and the Redskins managed to hang on for the 20-14 win over the Rams.

Los Angeles helped the Redskins out in the early going by fumbling on their first play from scrimmage. That led to a Bobby Khayat field goal. Before the first quarter was out, Snead had flipped a two-yard touchdown pass to Dugan and Washington held a 10-0 lead. Dick James got things going by returning a punt to the Washington 47. Snead called his own number on fourth and one and his sneak got the first down. Then Don Bosseler popped an 11-yard run on third and ten to move the ball to the Rams nine. The final key conversion came on third and goal at the two when Snead hit Dugan in the end zone.

The Rams came back with a 33-yard pass from Zeke Bratkowski to Dick Bass, but Dugan and the Redskins had the answer. After Bill Anderson hauled in a pass to move the Redskins to the LA 25 with 54 seconds left in the first half, Dugan

caught one pass to get inside the five and then made a beautiful grab of Snead's wobbly pass for the touchdown. Dugan had a defender hanging on to him with another coming over to help, but he still made a falling catch for a 20-7 halftime lead.

The Rams managed to make it interesting in the late going by scoring a touchdown and then blocking a late field goal attempt. Their final bid to steal the win died near midfield, aided greatly by Rod Breedlove's sack of Bratkowski.

10/14/62	**Redskins (3-0-2) 17, CARDINALS (1-3-1) 17**				18,104
Was	7	0	7	3	17
StL	0	3	0	14	17
Was	Mitchell 38 pass from Snead (B. Khayat kick)				
StL	FG Perry 27				
Was	Barnes 2 run (B. Khayat kick)				
StL	Childress 27 pass from Johnson (Perry kick)				
StL	Crow 1 run (Perry kick)				
Was	FG B. Khayat 29				

Busch Stadium—The Redskins blew a 14-3 lead in the fourth quarter but managed a tie 17-17 with the Cardinals when Bobby Khayat kicked a 29-yard field goal with 14 seconds left to play.

Washington held a 7-3 halftime lead on the strength of Norm Snead's 38-yard touchdown pass to Bobby Mitchell. In the third period, they went about the business of expanding the margin. It appeared they would have to give up possession when faced with a third and 22, but Snead went to his favorite target and Mitchell made a juggling catch good for 24 yards and the drive stayed alive. The march consumed more than seven minutes and ended when Billy Barnes pushed in for a two-yard touchdown run. Bobby Khayat's extra point made it 14-3 entering the fourth quarter.

The Cardinals were not done. Quarterback Charley Johnson, seeing his first extended NFL action, brought the Cardinals back into the lead. First, he hit Joe Childress with a 27-yard touchdown pass to pull St. Louis within four as six and a half minutes remained to play. The Redskins were unable to garner a first down and punted back to the Cards. It didn't take long before Johnson threw to Childress again, this time for 42 yards to the Washington one. John David Crow went over from there and, stunningly, the Cardinals led 17-14 with time running out.

There was just enough time left for Snead to throw to—you guessed it—Mitchell for 38 yards to the Cardinals 18. Don Bosseler lost four yards, but got the ball lined up between the goal posts for Khayat. Out of timeouts, the Redskins field goal team had to hustle onto the field and Khayat's game-tying boot was true with 14 seconds left to play.

10/21/62	**Redskins (4-0-2) 27, EAGLES (1-5) 21**				60,671
Was	0	1	3	7	27
Phi	0	7	7	7	21
Was	Mitchell 28 pass from Snead (B. Khayat kick)				
Phi	Cassady 8 pass from Jurgensen (Walston kick)				
Was	Barnes 3 run (B. Khayat kick)				
Was	FG B. Khayat 28				
Was	FG B. Khayat 9				
Phi	McDonald 13 pass from Jurgensen (Walston kick)				
Was	Mitchell 28 pass from Snead (B. Khayat kick)				
Phi	Cassady 47 pass from Jurgensen (Walston kick)				

Franklin Field—Dale Hackbart intercepted Sonny Jurgensen's pass in the end zone with less than two minutes to play to preserve the Redskins' 27-21 win over Philadelphia. The win kept Washington's unbeaten record intact.

After a scoreless first quarter, former Eagle Bobby Freeman picked off King Hill's pass and returned it 40 yards to the Philly 28. On the next play, Norm Snead found Bobby Mitchell on the five and the receiver stepped into the end zone, making it 7-0. Jurgensen answered by hitting Hopalong Cassady with an eight-yard touchdown pass to tie it up.

Dick James, victimized on Cassady's TD catch, jump-started the drive by returning the ensuing kickoff to the Redskin 44. Two passes from Snead to Fred Dugan got the Redskins down to the Philadelphia 14 and Billy Barnes capped the drive by bulling over from three yards out. Bobby Khayat's 28-yard field goal at the gun made the halftime score 17-7.

The home team had a great chance to put the Eagles in a huge hole when Bobby Mitchell took the second-half kickoff back 74 yards to the Eagle 25. Irv Cross got the angle on Mitchell and just tripped him up to prevent the touchdown. The Redskins continued down to the two but had to settle for Khayat's nine-yard field goal and a 20-7 lead.

Khayat later missed a 25-yard field goal attempt and Jurgensen brought his team back into the game by throwing a 13-yard touchdown pass to Tommy McDonald. That score was set up by a 48-yard run by Clarence Peaks.

The Redskins answered in the fourth quarter with Snead's second touchdown pass to Mitchell, this one also from 28 yards. The 13-point lead was not insurmountable, however. Jurgensen also returned to a favorite target, tossing a short pass to Cassady that the receiver turned into a 47-yard touchdown pass. That pulled the Eagles within six with 13 minutes left to play.

Philly had two good chances to take the win away from the Redskins. Bob Harrison picked off Snead's pass at the Redskin 28, but Bob Pellegrini ended that threat when he forced a fumble on a fourth down play and Claude Crabb recovered for Washington at the four. Then, with time running out, Jurgensen converted a third and 16 with a 26-yard pass to Theron Sapp, getting the Eagles to the Washington 17. From there, Jurgensen seemed determined to go to McDonald for the game-winning touchdown, but Hackbart was just as determined to make the game-saving interception.

Hackbart won, taking the pass four yards deep in the end zone and returning it 21 yards to the 17. Washington made sure that Jurgy didn't get another chance as they killed the clock from there.

10/28/62	GIANTS (5-2) 49, Redskins (4-1-2) 34				62,884
Was	7	6	7	14	34
NYG	7	14	21	7	49
Was	Mitchell 44 pass from Snead (B. Khayat kick)				
NYG	Morrison 22 pass from Tittle (Chandler kick)				
NYG	Walton 5 pass from Tittle (Chandler kick)				
Was	Dugan 24 pass from Snead (kick failed)				
NYG	Morrison 2 pass from Tittle (Chandler kick)				
Was	Mitchell 80 pass from Snead (B. Khayat kick)				
NYG	Shofner 32 pass from Tittle (Chandler kick)				
NYG	Walton 26 pass from Tittle (Chandler kick)				
NYG	Gifford 63 pass from Tittle (Chandler kick)				
NYG	Walton 5 pass from Tittle (Chandler kick)				
Was	Snead 1 run (B. Khayat kick)				
Was	Junker 35 pass from Snead (B. Khayat kick)				

Yankee Stadium—New York's Y. A. Tittle tied an NFL record by throwing for seven touchdowns as the Giants outlasted the Redskins.

The veteran New York quarterback's performance far overshadowed a good outing for Washington quarterback Norm Snead. The second-year signal caller accounted for all five of his team's touchdowns by throwing for four and scoring another on a sneak. Snead's first TD pass covered 44 yards to Bobby Mitchell and gave Washington a 7-0 lead in the first quarter. Mitchell smoked pass defender Erich Barnes and Snead had a nice touch on the pass to his receiver.

After the Giants tied the score on Tittle's 22-yard touchdown pass to Joe Morrison, Barnes got a measure of revenge when he intercepted a Snead pass to set up the go-ahead score for his team. That came on ex-Redskin Joe Walton's jaw-dropping catch in the back of the end zone. Bobby Freeman just missed breaking up Tittle's pass on the play, which came from five yards out.

New York led 21-13 at halftime, but the Redskins were not quite done. At the start of the second half, Snead and Mitchell again picked on Barnes. "I looked for an end sweep just a moment too long," Barnes said. "When I looked around to see him (Mitchell), he was gone."

Gone, indeed—for 80 yards and a touchdown, pulling his team within one.

This was the Giants' day, though, and they ran off four unanswered touchdowns—all, of course, on Tittle passes. Two of them went to Walton, giving him three on the day. Another went 63 yards to Frank Gifford. Snead's touchdown on a one-yard sneak and his fourth TD throw, this one to Steve Junker, served only to make the score more respectable.

On the day, Tittle was 27 of 39 passing for 505 yards.

11/4/62	Cowboys (4-3-1) 38, REDSKINS (4-2-2) 10				49,888
Dal	3	7	14	14	38
Was	3	0	0	7	10
Dal	FG Baker 16				
Was	FG B. Khayat 14				
Dal	Falkins 11 pass from Meredith ((Baker kick)				
Dal	Marsh 23 pass from LeBaron (Baker kick)				
Dal	Lockett 4 pass from Meredith (Baker kick)				
Dal	Bullocks 4 run (Baker kick)				
Dal	Clarke 14 pass from LeBaron (Baker kick)				
Was	Hall 1 run (B. Khayat kick)				

D.C. Stadium—Dallas broke open a close game with two third-quarter touchdowns and went on to rout the Redskins 38-10.

The result disappointed a standing room only crowd of 49,888, the largest ever to see a sporting event in Washington.

The Redskins assisted in their own demise with various sins of commission and omission. Trailing 10-3 in the second quarter, quarterback Norm Snead made a brilliant play call on third and one at the Dallas 25, a play action pass that had Dick James in the clear by a good five yards. Apparently afraid of overthrowing James, Snead under threw his receiver and the ball was batted away. A fourth down quarterback sneak was stuffed and the opportunity went by the wayside.

Snead's first pass of the third quarter was even worse, intercepted by Mike Gaechter and returned to the Washington 41. Soon after that, Eddie LeBaron threw a 23-yard touchdown pass to Amos Marsh to make it 17-3.

Later in the third, Marsh helped Dallas put the game away with a 70-yard run down to the Washington four. From there, Don Meredith threw a quick touchdown pass to J. W. Lockett to make it 24-3.

It was 38-3 with time running out by the time the Redskins scored their only touchdown. Rookie quarterback Galen Hall led a garbage-time drive to the Dallas one and then snuck it over with 11 seconds left.

11/11/62	REDSKINS (5-2-2) 17, Browns (4-4-1) 9				48,169
Cle	0	0	9	0	9
Was	0	10	7	0	17
Was	Bosseler 2 run (B. Khayat kick)				
Was	FG B. Khayat 29				
Was	Bosseler 1 run (B. Khayat kick)				
Cle	Renfro 65 pass from Ryan (kick failed)				
Cle	FG Groza 35				

D.C. Stadium—A mix of stout defense, just enough offense and some fortuitous calls by officials combined to help the Redskins beat Cleveland 17-9.

Washington built a 10-0 halftime lead on Don Bosseler's two-yard touchdown run and Bobby Khayat's 29-yard field goal. The TD was set up when one of the two defenders covering Bobby Mitchell interfered with the star receiver, giving Washington a first down at the Cleveland two.

In the second half, the home team got help from both the Browns and the referees to lengthen its lead. Quarterback Frank

Ryan fumbled on the first play of the half and Andy Stynchula recovered for the Redskins at the Brown 33. A third and 12 pass fell incomplete, but again a pass interference flag flew and Washington had a first and goal at the one. After Billy Barnes tried and failed three times to get in, Snead handed to Bosseler, who took it over for the score and a 17-0 lead.

Cleveland fought back to within 17-9 and was threatening to make it a one-point game early in the fourth quarter after moving to a first and goal at the seven. One play after Dale Hackbart nailed Jim Brown for an 11-yard loss, it appeared that Cleveland had scored when Ryan passed to Rich Kreitling, who eluded Claude Crabb at the five and stepped into the end zone. However, another official's flag zapped the Browns as Cleveland was penalized for holding. Crabb made a bold tackle on 235-pound Leon Clark to force a field goal attempt. The defensive back was carried off the field, but his efforts were not in vain. Lou Groza missed the attempt from 24 yards with seven and a half minutes to play.

Cleveland got the ball back quickly, but Ryan threw a first down pass that Bobby Freeman deflected into the hands of Rod Breedlove and the linebacker returned the interception to the Washington 49. The Redskins ate up the last six minutes of the game clock with Billy Barnes and Jim Cunningham getting the carries to pace an infantry march to the Cleveland five as time ran out.

Redskins Get an Extra Day of Rest

Nov 12—In a move spurred by both a desire to reward the team and by necessity, the Redskins were given an extra day off by Coach Bill McPeak.

The reward aspect came from the Redskins having beaten the Cleveland Browns on Sunday 17-9, sweeping the season series from a team that has given them fits for the past decade. Combine that with the fact that the win pushed the Redskins' record to 5-2-2, good for second place in the NFL East.

The team probably needed a day off regardless of the outcome of Sunday's game given the beaten-up condition of many of the players. Among the wounded are defensive back Claude Crabb, still hospitalized after sustaining a concussion on a key tackle, and linebacker Bob Pellegrini, who has a foot injury.

Even those players who are not on the injury list are suffering from the wear and tear of the season.

"We're a bit battered," said McPeak.

11/18/62	STEELERS (6-4) 23, Redskins (5-3-2) 21				23,231
Was	0	7	14	0	21
Pit	3	3	0	17	23
Pit	FG Michaels 37				
Was	Cunningham 9 pass from Snead (B. Khayat kick)				
Pit	FG Michaels 19				
Was	Anderson 47 pass from Snead (B. Khayat kick)				
Was	Barnes 32 run (B. Khayat kick)				
Pit	Mack 22 pass from Brown (Michaels kick)				
Pit	Dial 9 pass from Brown (Michaels kick)				
Pit	FG Michaels 23				

Forbes Field—Lou Michaels kicked a field goal with 13 seconds left to play to complete the Steelers' comeback from a 21-6 deficit midway through the fourth quarter. Michaels' 23-yard chip shot gave Pittsburgh a 23-10 win.

The Redskins held a 7-6 lead at the half and moved quickly to expand the margin. First Norm Snead threw a 47-yard touchdown pass to Bill Anderson, who broke a tackle at the ten to score. Then Bobby Freeman intercepted Bobby Layne and galloped to the Pittsburgh 34. A couple of plays later, Billy Barnes zoomed 32 yards for a touchdown and the Redskins were up 21-6.

It stayed that way until Layne left with an injury and Ed Brown came in at quarterback. With a little more than seven minutes left

to play, Brown tossed a 23-yard touchdown pass to another sub—end Red Mack. Less than four minutes later, Brown went to Buddy Dial for nine yards and a touchdown to make it a one-point game.

Washington took over with 3:45 to go, but couldn't kill the clock and punted to the Steelers, who took possession on their own 34 with 1:37 left to play. Brown went to Mack again, this time for a 36-yard gain to the Washington 24. Soon after that, with just seconds left, the Steelers lined up for a 23-yard field goal attempt. The snap was high and wide, but Brown performed his final heroic act by snaring the errant snap and getting it down in time for the left-footed Michaels to deliver the Redskins a major kick in the gut.

11/25/62	Giants (9-2) 42, REDSKINS (5-4-2) 24				49,219
NYG	7	21	7	7	42
Was	3	7	0	14	24
NYG	Counts 90 kickoff return (Chandler kick)				
Was	FG B. Khayat 27				
NYG	Shofner 20 pass from Tittle (Chandler kick)				
NYG	King 7 run (Chandler kick)				
NYG	Shofner 10 pass from Tittle (Chandler kick)				
Was	Mitchell 15 pass from Snead (B. Khayat kick)				
NYG	Shofner 44 pass from Tittle (Chandler kick)				
NYG	Webster 6 run (Chandler kick)				
Was	James 18 pass from Hall (B. Khayat kick)				
Was	James 48 pass from Hall (B. Khayat kick)				

Yankee Stadium—New York's Johnny Counts set the tone for the day by returning the opening kickoff for a touchdown as the Giants easily beat the Redskins 42-24.

It wasn't so much that Counts scored but the seeming ease with which he covered the 90 yards that made it apparent the Redskins would struggle. Before the first half was out, New York built up a 28-3 lead. Y. A. Tittle threw two touchdown passes to Del Shofner and Phil King scored on a seven-yard run. All the Redskins had for a response was a 27-yard field goal by Bobby Khayat.

Washington did manage a touchdown on the last play of the first half. After Billy Barnes and Bobby Mitchell had dropped certain touchdown passes, Norm Snead gave Mitchell another shot and Bobby came through, catching his 14-yard touchdown pass to make it 28-10 at the half.

The Redskins would not score again before New York had pulled away to a 42-10 lead. Galen Hall relieved Snead at quarterback in the fourth quarter and threw two touchdown passes to Dick James, but it was far too little and way too late.

12/2/62	Eagles (3-8-1) 37, REDSKINS (5-5-2) 14				32,229
Phi	0	14	14	9	37
Was	7	7	0	0	14
Was	Junker 5 pass from Snead (B. Khayat kick)				
Was	James 10 pass from Snead (B. Khayat kick)				
Phi	Brown 99 kickoff return (Walston kick)				
Phi	Retzlaff 12 pass from Jurgensen (Walston kick)				
Phi	Brown 3 run (Walston kick)				
Phi	Brown 10 pass from McDonald (Walston kick)				
Phi	Budd 9 pass from Jurgensen (kick failed)				
Phi	FG Wittenborn 27				

D.C. Stadium—A 14-0 Redskins lead was buried under an avalanche of Philadelphia points as the Eagles pounded Washington 37-14.

The home team started off quickly and efficiently. They took the opening kickoff and drove in for a touchdown with Norm Snead capping the drive with a five-yard pass to Steve Junker. Another drive ended with Snead throwing another touchdown pass, this one for 10 yards to Dick James. The big play in that drive was Snead's 38-yard pass to running back Leroy Jackson. The home crowd was enthusiastic, sensing a rout of the Eagles, who had just two wins coming in.

But any such notions were quickly disabused as Tim Brown returned the ensuing kickoff 99 yards for a touchdown. The speedy Brown raced untouched through the Redskins and the game had its first—and last—momentum swing. By halftime, the Eagles had tied the game on Sonny Jurgensen's 12-yard touchdown pass to Pete Retzlaff.

The Eagles quickly moved to take the lead after intermission, with Brown scoring on a three-yard run. James' fumble recovered by the Eagles inside their own five killed the Redskins' bid to tie it up. The turnover became doubly damaging when Philly drove downfield and stretched the lead to 28-14 on Brown's third touchdown of the game. It came on a 10-yard pass from receiver Tommy McDonald. Emblematic of the Redskins' day, linebacker Dale Hackbart tipped McDonald's weak pass right into Brown's arms.

Any hope of a Redskins rally was dashed when Mike McClellan intercepted Snead's pass near midfield. Snead started the day by completing nine of his first 10 passes for two touchdowns, but his eleventh pass was intercepted and it was all downhill from there.

12/8/62	COLTS (6-7) 34, Redskins (5-6-2) 21				56,964
Was	7	7	7	0	21
Bal	0	14	0	20	34

Was	Jackson 85 pass from Snead (B. Khayat kick)
Bal	Orr 11 pass from Unitas (Harris kick)
Bal	Orr 59 pass from Unitas (Harris kick)
Was	Dugan 17 pass from Snead (B. Khayat kick)
Was	Dugan 20 pass from Snead (B. Khayat kick)
Bal	Bielski 11 pass from Unitas (kick failed)
Bal	Orr 22 pass from Unitas (Bielski kick)
Bal	Hawkins 2 run (Bielski kick)

Memorial Stadium—The Redskins played one of their best games of the year for three quarters, but the Colts dominated the last 15 minutes to take a 34-21 win.

Washington took a 7-0 lead in the first quarter in spectacular fashion. Facing a second and 24 at his own 15, Norm Snead faced extreme pressure as he unleashed a bomb to Leroy Jackson. The running back caught the ball just past midfield, kicked his speed up a notch and outran his pursuers to the goal line.

Another spectacular play denied the Redskins a score later in the first. Bobby Khayat's 40-yard field goal attempt was on target, but receiver R. C. Owens played goaltender, leaping high enough to get his hand above the crossbar to deflect the ball back onto the field. Owens had been practicing the maneuver for a couple of years, but this was the first time it had worked.

After the Colts tied it with an 11-yard touchdown pass from Johnny Unitas to Jimmy Orr, the Redskins lost another scoring opportunity. A penalty wiped out a pass from Snead to Bobby Mitchell that would have set up a first and goal at the five, and a fumbled snap aborted a subsequent field goal attempt. After that, Unitas connected with Orr for a second touchdown, this one from 59 yards, and Baltimore led 14-7.

Before halftime, Snead passed 19 yards to Bill Anderson and 25 to Bobby Mitchell to move his team to the Baltimore 25. Two plays later, Snead faked a draw to Don Bosseler and found Fred Dugan wide open for a 17-yard, game-tying touchdown.

Snead and Dugan connected again for a third-quarter touchdown that pushed the Redskins in front 21-14. Late in the third quarter, they had possession again and Jackson had a hole up the middle. Jackson made the worst of it has he fumbled the ball before accidentally kicked it, allowing linebacker Don Shinnick to recover at the Washington 31. On the next two plays, the Redskins defense stepped up and pushed the Colts back, though

on third and 16, Ray Berry jumped up and made one of his patented spectacular catches for 20 yards and a first down at the 17. Unitas' 11-yard TD pass to Dick Bielski followed soon after that. The Redskins managed to hold on to a one-point lead when Wendell Harris missed the extra point.

On the Redskins' subsequent possession, Shinnick struck again, intercepting Snead's poor throw at the Washington 31 and returning it to the 25. Unitas' third touchdown pass to Orr came from 23 yards and put the Colts ahead 27-21.

Washington countered with a nice drive to move to a first and 10 at the Baltimore 30. Snead tried to throw to Dugan, but that Shinnick fellow got in the way again. The 240-pound linebacker sprinted all the way downfield to provide double coverage on Dugan along with back Jim Welch. Dugan, Shinnick and Welch all went up for the ball—and you only get one guess as to who came down with it. The interception gave the ball back to the Colts at their own eight. Baltimore wrapped it up with Alex Hawkins' two-yard touchdown run with less than two minutes left.

12/16/62	Steelers (9-5) 27, REDSKINS (5-7-2) 24				34,508
Pit	7	7	6	7	27
Was	3	0	7	14	24

Was	FG Khayat 33
Pit	Dial 39 pass from Layne (Michaels kick)
Pit	Hoak 1 run (Michaels kick)
Was	James 25 pass from Izo (Khayat kick)
Pit	FG Michaels 38
Pit	FG Michaels 22
Pit	Carpenter 23 pass from Layne (Michaels kick)
Was	James 49 pass from Izo (Khayat kick)
Was	Anderson 27 pass from Izo (Khayat kick)

D.C. Stadium—Third-string quarterback George Izo threw three touchdown passes, but they were not enough as the Redskins lost to the Steelers 27-24 in the season finale.

Izo was pressed into action after Norm Snead's season ended about 56 minutes early when a crunching hit separated his shoulder. As second-team quarterback Galen Hall had broken his thumb a few weeks earlier, Izo came off the bench to finish up the year.

Snead's injury came in the midst of a drive to a 33-yard Bobby Khayat field goal that gave the home team a 3-0 lead. Before the first quarter was out, Pittsburgh had taken the lead on Bobby Layne's 39-yard touchdown pass to Buddy Dial.

In the second quarter, George Tarasovic intercepted an Izo pass and ran to the Washington 37. A couple of plays later, the game turned on a highly controversial play. From the 43, Layne launched a long pass to Red Mack near the goal line. The receiver and defender Claude Crabb both went up for it. Mack had the ball at first, but Crabb took it away from him and had it in his possession as the two hit the ground. Santa Claus wasn't scheduled to appear until halftime, but he arrived early dressed in a striped shirt. Somehow, the field judge ruled that it was a completion and Pittsburgh had a first and goal at the two. Three plays later, Don Hoak scored and it was 14-3 at the half.

Izo directed a touchdown drive at the outset of the third quarter to pull his team within 14-10. After completing a pass to Dugan to get into Steeler territory, Izo converted a fourth and eight at the 25 with a pass to Dick James, who eluded his defender at the 12 and scored standing up.

Pittsburgh responded immediately, scoring on two Lou Michaels field goals and a touchdown pass by Bobby Layne. Izo's final two TD passes made the final more respectable.

1963
Head Coach: Bill McPeak
Record: 3-11, Sixth in NFL Eastern Conference

Honors: Bobby Mitchell Pro Bowl, All-NFL; Vince Promuto Pro Bowl; Joe Rutgens Pro Bowl; Norm Snead Pro Bowl

Hall of Fame (Charter Class): Sammy Baugh, Quarterback 1937-1952; Curly Lambeau Coach 1952-1953; George Preston Marshall, Founder, 1932-1969

May 1

Redskins to Train in Carlisle, PA
Five-year agreement reached to move camp from Los Angeles to Dickinson College

---

9/15/63	**BROWNS (1-0) 37, Redskins (0-1) 14**			57,618	
Was	0	7	7	0	14
Cle	10	14	3	10	37

Cle	Crespino 4 pass from Ryan (Groza kick)
Cle	FG Groza 42
Was	Richter 7 pass from Snead (Khayat kick)
Cle	Brown 83 pass from Ryan (Groza kick)
Cle	Brown 10 run (Groza kick)
Cle	FG Groza 24
Was	Mitchell 99 pass from Izo (Khayat kick)
Cle	Brown 80 run (Groza kick)
Cle	FG Groza 39

Cleveland Municipal Stadium—Jim Brown topped a record-tying 99-yard touchdown pass from George Izo to Bobby Mitchell by scoring twice from long distance himself as the Browns pounded the Redskins 37-14.

Brown's first long score came shortly after the Redskins had scored on a seven-yard touchdown pass from Norm Snead to rookie end Pat Richter, making the score 10-7 in favor of Cleveland. Any notion that the Redskins would be able to get back into this one was quickly disabused when Brown took a short pass from Frank Ryan, shed the attempted tackles of several would-be defenders and wound up in the end zone with an 83-yard touchdown pass.

Cleveland scored twice more before Izo and Mitchell tied a record that can't be broken. Izo replaced an ineffective (five of 15 passing) Snead and the Redskins were backed up on their own one. The best bet seemed to be to put the ball in the hands of the speedy Mitchell and Izo was smart enough to do that and Mitchell outraced the defense to the end zone.

That score made it 27-14 late in the third quarter, but Brown took care of any lingering doubt as to the outcome by going around end and, ho-hum, breaking some more tackles and rolling 80 yards for a touchdown. On the day, Brown nearly outgained the Redskins by himself, getting 162 yards of 15 rushes and an even 100 of three catches. Washington totaled 272 yards of offense.

9/21/63	**Redskins (1-1) 37, RAMS (0-2) 14**			29,295	
Was	7	6	7	17	37
LA	7	7	0	0	14

LA	Arnett 3 run (Villanueva kick)
Was	James 2 run (Khayat kick)
Was	FG Khayat 38
Was	FG Khayat 31
LA	Arness 6 pass from Bratkowski (Villanueva kick)
Was	Barnes 1 run (Khayat kick)
Was	FG Khayat 44

Was	Snead 1 run (Khayat kick)
Was	Dugan 15 pass from Snead (Khayat kick)

Los Angeles Coliseum—The Redskins broke open a close game with 24 unanswered points in the second half as they trounced the Rams 37-14.

Early on, it looked like it might be a repeat of the Skins 37-14 defeat at the hands of Cleveland six days earlier rather than a reversal of that score. Norm Snead's first pass went right to the Rams' Ed Meador and the interception cost the Redskins seven points as Jon Arnett scored on a three-yard run. The visitors quickly rebounded, though, and took a 13-7 lead on Dick James' two-yard touchdown burst and a pair of Bobby Khayat field goals. Before halftime, LA had reclaimed the lead on Arnett's second touchdown pass, this one coming on a seven-yard pass from Zeke Bratkowski.

Early in the third, still trailing 14-13, the Redskins gambled on fourth and one at the Rams 48 and James failed to make the yard. But the Washington defense dug in and forced a punt. Snead flipped a short pass to James, who more than made up for his earlier failure by deftly maneuvering 77 yards to the Ram two yard line. Billy Barnes scored soon after that and the Redskins had the lead for good.

Injuries reduced LA's famed Fearsome Foursome to a shadow of its usual self and the Redskins controlled the game on the ground with Don Bosseler, Barnes and James combing for most of Washington's 177 rushing yards. Also of great aid to the Redskins' cause were some long punt returns. Runbacks of 45 yards by Jim Steffen, 42 by Johnny Sample and 39 by James all set up Redskins scores.

9/29/63	**REDSKINS (2-1) 21, Cowboys (0-3) 17**			40,101	
Dal	0	7	10	0	17
Was	7	0	7	7	21

Was	Steffen 78 interception return (Khayat kick)
Dal	Marsh 1 run (Baker kick)
Dal	FG Baker 41
Was	James 1 run (Khayat kick)
Dal	Howton 43 pass from Meredith (Baker kick)
Was	Cunningham 1 run (Khayat kick)

D.C. Stadium—Playing on a bad leg, Jim Steffen intercepted three passes, returning one 78 yards for a touchdown, to pace the Redskins past Dallas 21-17.

It was Steffen's first pick returned for a score. Dallas had just seen a 23-yard touchdown pass wiped out by an offensive pass interference call. Steffen intercepted Meredith's next attempt and rolled untouched 78 yards to the end zone.

A face mask call greatly aided Dallas' drive to the tying score in the second quarter and Sam Baker's 41-yard field goal put Dallas ahead 10-7 in the third quarter. The Redskins responded as Norm Snead, booed lustily in the pre-game introductions, directed a 70-yard drive to push his team back out in front. The march got started when Snead converted a third and ten from the 30 with a 13-yard completion to Dick James. Then he snuck Don

Bosseler out on a deep pattern and the fullback made a great, diving catch for a 33-yard gain to the Dallas 21. Bosseler picked up 18 more, this time on a trap play, and Dick James got the score from a yard out three plays later. The Redskins led 14-10.

It was then Meredith's turn for heroics, as he pitched a 43-yard touchdown pass to end Bill Howton to pull Dallas back into the lead before the third quarter was out. Then Baker missed a 40-yard field goal attempt and the Redskins embarked on their game winning drive from their own 20. During the scoring thrust, rookie end Pat Richter caught a pass for an 18-yard gain and then Billy Barnes ran for 10 and caught a swing pass to move to a first down at the Dallas 13. It was Barnes again on the next three plays with three carries that just barely gained enough for a first down at the three. On fourth and goal from the one, Coach Bill McPeak spurned a tying field goal attempt and Jim Cunningham made the gamble pay off by smashing over for the touchdown. Steffen's third interception with 1:46 left sealed the win for the home team.

10/6/63	**Giants (3-1) 24, REDSKINS (2-2) 14**	49,219			
NYG	14	3	0	7	24
Was	0	14	0	0	14
NYG	Shofner 41 pass from Tittle (Chandler kick)				
NYG	Walton 17 pass from Tittle (Chandler kick)				
NYG	FG Chandler 9				
Was	Bosseler 1 run (B. Khayat kick)				
Was	Anderson 11 pass from Snead (B. Khayat kick)				
NYG	Walton 27 pass from Tittle (Chandler kick)				

D.C. Stadium—The Redskins woke up in time to turn a pending rout into a contest, but it wasn't enough to beat the Giants. New York held off an attempted rally and won 24-14.

Y. A. Tittle threw the first of his three touchdown passes to Del Shofner, a 41-yarder that gave New York an early 7-0 lead. Former Redskin end Joe Walton caught the first of his two TD receptions when he grabbed a 17-yarder to make it 14-0. Then, the Redskins defense turned the game around, stopping the Giants after they gained a first and goal at the three, forcing them to settle for Don Chandler's nine-yard field goal.

After that, the Redskins developed some offensive rhythm. Erich Barnes was right with Bobby Mitchell, but the Redskins end made a nice catch at the one anyway to set up Don Bosseler's touchdown smash on the next play. Then the home team got the crowd back into it with an 80-yard drive in the last two minutes of the half. Norm Snead threw to Mitchell for 13, Pat Richter for another 13, and then to Bosseler, who eluded a tackle and sped 24 yards to the New York 27. After scrambling to the 11, Snead found Bill Anderson, who had slipped between a pair of defenders, in the end zone for a touchdown. Washington pulled within three at 17-14.

The Redskins had a chance to take the lead after linebacker Carl Kammerer intercepted a Tittle pass at the Washington 35. Anderson made a great catch to move his team into Giant territory at the 39, but a pair of dropped passes killed the drive there.

Tittle then moved his team in for the kill. One key pass went to Frank Gifford and the other to Walton for 27 yards and the clinching score.

10/13/63	**Eagles (2-2-1) 37, REDSKINS (2-3) 24**	27,264			
Phi	0	16	14	7	37
Was	3	14	7	0	24
Was	FG B. Khayat				
Was	Barnes 3 run (Khayat kick)				
Was	Mitchell 66 pass from Snead (Khayat kick)				
Phi	Goodwin 35 pass from Jurgensen (kick failed)				
Phi	FG Clark 42				
Phi	Brown 3 run (Clark kick)				
Phi	Brown 36 pass from Jurgensen (Clark kick)				
Phi	McDonald 34 pass from Jurgensen (Clark kick)				
Was	Mitchell 35 pass from Snead (Khayat kick)				
Phi	McDonald 9 pass from Jurgensen (Clark kick)				

D.C. Stadium—The Redskins watched a 17-0 lead disappear under a barrage of Sonny Jurgensen touchdown passes and lost to the Eagles 37-24.

With Washington up 3-0, linebacker Carl Kammerer intercepted a pass that teammate John Paluck had deflected to give the Redskins possession just inside the Eagle 10. On the first play of the second quarter, Billy Barnes scored from two yards out to make it 10-0.

It really looked like the home team was on a roll when Norm Snead eluded a rush and threw downfield for Bobby Mitchell. Mitchell caught the pass, faked out would-be tackler Don Burroughs and easily glided in for the touchdown to make it 17-0.

The lead was far from secure. Jurgensen and the Eagles nearly tied it up before halftime. Ron Goodman caught a touchdown pass and a Jurgensen completion to Pete Retzlaff set up six more Philly points. In between, Mike Clark, who had missed the conversion after the first touchdown, hit a 42-yard field goal and it was 17-16 at halftime.

Intermission did nothing to cool down Jurgensen. Touchdown passes to Tim Brown and Tommy McDonald pulled the Eagles out to a 30-17 lead.

The Redskins recovered and Mitchell got the Redskins back into it with a juggling end zone catch and it was 30-24. Washington's defense forced a punt at midfield. Unfortunately, King Hill's boot was a beaut, rolling dead at the one.

Snead tried to pass his team out of the hole, but it only got deeper. His pass bounced off of Jim Cunningham and into the arms of Philadelphia's Dave Lloyd. The linebacker lateraled to Irv Cross, who sped to the Washington 12. On third down from the nine, McDonald eluded Lonnie Sanders and caught Jurgensen's fourth touchdown pass of the day for a 37-24 lead with nine minutes left. Burroughs made up for being burned on Mitchell's longer score by picking off two passes to kill off the Redskins.

10/20/63	**STEELERS (3-2-1) 38, Redskins (2-4) 27**	41,987			
Was	3	14	7	3	27
Pit	7	10	7	14	38
Pit	Brown 1 run (Michaels kick)				
Was	FG Khayat 49				
Pit	Hoak 8 run (Michaels kick)				
Pit	FG Michaels 9				
Was	Snead 1 run (Khayat kick)				
Was	James 36 pass from Snead (Khayat kick)				
Was	James 5 run (Khayat kick)				
Pit	Hoak 1 run (Brown kick)				
Was	FG Khayat 15				
Pit	Haley 24 interception return (Michaels kick)				
Pit	Dial 4 pass from Brown (Michaels kick)				

Pit Stadium—The Redskins came all the way back from a 17-3 deficit to take a three-point lead in the fourth quarter, but two quick mistakes led to 14 Steeler points and a 38-27 Pittsburgh win.

Facing that 14-point deficit in the second quarter, it seemed the futility would continue for the Redskins. An apparent 57-yard touchdown pass from Norm Snead to Bobby Mitchell was called back by a holding penalty and the Redskins were pushed back to their 24. Undaunted, Snead went back to Mitchell, who was off to the races. As the receiver hip-faked defenders into missed tackles, he fumbled the ball but managed to recover it at the Pittsburgh 16 after a 59-yard gain. After Dick James ran for 15 yards to the one, Snead snuck it over to make it 17-10.

The Steelers seemed to have an answer when they drove to the Washington four and Lou Michaels put a field goal attempt through the uprights. An offside penalty on Washington, though, gave the Steelers the option of going for it on fourth and goal at the two. Pittsburgh coach Buddy Parker violated a coaching maxim and took points off the board. The gamble backfired when

Rod Breedlove stuffed Dick Hoak and the Skins took over on downs.

Snead quickly went to work, getting his team well out of the shadow of its own goalposts with a 47-yard connection to Mitchell to the Steeler 45. Soon after that, James took a pitchout from Snead and galloped 36 yards for the tying touchdown.

The teams exchanged third-quarter touchdowns before Snead threw for 51 yards to—you guessed it—Mitchell, setting up Bobby Khayat's 15-yard field goal and Washington led 27-24. The Steelers were forced to punt, Washington regained possession and then it came unraveled for the visitors.

Snead threw his first and only interception of the day and former Redskin Dick Haley returned it 24 yards for the go-ahead touchdown. Before the Redskins could recover, Leroy Jackson fumbled the kickoff and Jim Bradshaw fell on it for the Steelers at the Redskin 22. Soon after that, Ed Brown threw a four-yard touchdown pass to Buddy Dial to clinch the win.

10/27/63	Cardinals (5-2) 21, REDSKINS (2-5) 7			46,921
StL	0	7	7	7	21
Was	0	0	0	7	7
StL	Conrad 14 pass from Johnson (Bakken kick)			
StL	Randle 28 pass from Johnson (Bakken kick)			
StL	Randle 54 pass from Johnson (Bakken kick)			
Was	Richter 28 pass from Izo (Khayat kick)			

D.C. Stadium—In a game Bill McPeak called "a tragedy of errors," the Redskins turned the ball over six times in the process of falling to the Cardinals 21-7.

Quarterbacking is often overrated as a factor in NFL games, but the difference in the performances of the two starting quarterbacks was the critical issue here. St. Louis' Charley Johnson completed 18 of 32 passes for 270 yards and three touchdowns while, in three quarters before being pulled in favor of backup George Izo, Norm Snead completed 11 of 20 for 78 yards and threw two interceptions.

While Snead's ineffectiveness was a problem for the Redskins, it wasn't the only one. The Redskins burned off the first nine and a half minutes of the game clock with a 71-yard drive that culminated with Dick James' fumble at the Cardinal two yard line. Dale Meinert recovered for the Cards, and the tone for the game was set.

Johnson's first two touchdown passes converted third and long situations. On third and ten at the Washington 14, he flipped a short pass to Bobby Joe Conrad, who gave the slip to linebacker Gordon Kelly and scored to give St. Louis a 7-0 halftime lead. The next TD came on third and 14 at the Redskin 28 and Johnson threw a picture-perfect pass to Sonny Randle.

Johnson and Randle combined again to make it 21-0, this score coming on a nice 54-yard bomb in the fourth quarter. Izo connected with rookie Pat Richter for the Redskins' lone tally of the game after that.

Redskins Down But Not Out

October 31—While you can't find a player in the Redskins locker room who is not disappointed, you can't find one who has given up, either.

Guard Vince Promuto says he doesn't know what the answer is to improving on the team's 2-5 record, but he thinks that the parts are in place. "This is a lot better team than the record indicates," the offensive captain said.

"Not to alibi," said Promuto's defensive counterpart at tackle Bob Toneff, "but I feel some of the fellows getting injured early hurt us a lot." He pointed to Johnny Sample, Claude Crabb and Jim Steffan as key players whose absences have affected the team.

Star flanker Bobby Mitchell figures things will improve if only because the team has nowhere to go but up. "We can't do much worse than we have, can we?" he asked rhetorically.

11/3/63	COWBOYS (2-6) 35, Redskins (2-6) 20			18,838
Dal	7	7	7	14	35
Was	0	10	3	7	20
Dal	Folkins 1 pass from Meredith (Baker kick)			
Was	Dugan 41 pass from Snead (Khayat kick)			
Was	FG Khayat 12			
Dal	Clarke 13 pass from Meredith (Baker kick)			
Was	FG Khayat 49			
Dal	Folkins 1 pass from Meredith (Baker kick)			
Was	Dugan 41 pass from Snead (Khayat kick)			
Dal	Stiger 7 run (Baker kick)			
Dal	Clarke 12 pass from Meredith (Baker kick)			

Cotton Bowl—If the previous week's game was a tragedy of errors, this one was a disaster of epic proportions. The Redskins committed seven turnovers in falling to the Cowboys 35-20.

All you have to know of the statistics in this one is that the Redskins outgained Dallas by better than a two-to-one margin (468 yards to 221), but still lost by 15 points.

The key swing in the contest came late in the first half. The Redskins held a 10-7 lead and John Paluck had just given the Redskins a golden opportunity when he intercepted a pass at the Dallas 29 and rumbled down to the three. Norm Snead squandered it when he threw a pass that Mike Gaechter intercepted at the one. That was bad enough, but Gaechter found some running room and returned the ball 86 yards to the Redskin 13. Don Meredith threw a 12-yard touchdown pass to Frank Clarke and the 14-point reversal had Dallas ahead to stay at 14-10.

The Redskins kept fighting, however, and managed to pull within a point at 21-20 after Fred Dugan made a strong run after catching Snead's pass, going 41 yards for a touchdown early in the fourth quarter.

But then the dam broke—and the Redskins' sloppy play caught up with them. Amos Bullocks returned the kickoff after Dugan's score 52 yards to the Washington 40. Soon after that, rookie fullback Jim Stiger scored on a seven-yard run and Dallas led 28-20.

One final mistake ended it for the Redskins. Bobby Mitchell fumbled after catching a pass and Dallas recovered at the 50. Soon after that, Meredith threw another touchdown pass to Clarke to provide the final margin.

Mitchell Tells RFK He'll Run the Ball

Nov 5—The Redskins' 2-8 record has caught the attention of those at the highest levels of our government. Today saw Attorney General Robert F. Kennedy asking Bobby Mitchell what's wrong with the team.

Mitchell didn't offer much in the way of analysis of what has happened so far, but he did offer a possible solution.

"I feel tempted to volunteer to run the ball," Mitchell told the president's brother as the two attended addressed assemblies at local schools.

Mitchell figures his offer would fall on deaf ears. "I understand Coach McPeak has refused to consider the idea because he thinks I'm more valuable as a flanker to catch the bomb."

Kennedy suggested the team could benefit from Mitchell's speed and elusiveness more frequently if he was in the backfield. While Mitchell nodded in agreement, it's unlikely that the only man whose opinion matters—Bill McPeak—will be persuaded to agree, even by the Attorney General.

11/10/63	CARDINALS (6-3) 24, Redskins (2-7) 20			19,917	
Was	0	6	0	14	20
StL	7	3	7	7	24
StL	Paramore 31 pass from Johnson (Bakken kick)				
Was	FG Khayat 37				
StL	FG Bakken 36				
Was	FG Khayat 10				
StL	Conrad 20 pass from Johnson (Bakken kick)				
StL	Randle 14 pass from Johnson (Bakken kick)				
Was	Barnes 2 run (Khayat kick)				
Was	Barnes 4 run (Khayat kick)				

Busch Stadium—Charley Johnson threw three touchdown passes and the Cardinals staved off a late Redskins rally to claim a 24-20 win in St. Louis.

A crucial and controversial call late in the third quarter helped St. Louis open up a 24-6 lead. The Cardinals, leading 17-6, punted to Bobby Mitchell. The ball bounced and, according to the officials, struck Mitchell's leg, a claim that Mitchell vehemently denied. Nonetheless, linebacker Larry Stallings fell on the ball at the Washington 14 and the Cardinals were awarded possession. On the next play, Johnson fired a touchdown pass to Sonny Randle and St. Louis opened up an 18-point lead.

As it turned out, the Cardinals needed every point. Fred Dugan made a great catch of a Norm Snead pass at the Cardinal four to set up a two-yard scoring run by Billy Barnes. With about two and a half minutes to play, Barnes scored again following a 50-yard reception by Frank Budd. The onside kick failed, though, and the Cardinals killed the clock.

11/17/63	Steelers (6-3-1) 34, REDSKINS (2-8) 28			49,219	
Pit	7	7	10	10	34
Was	7	7	0	14	28
Was	Crabb 35 interception return (Khayat kick)				
Pit	Johnson 3 run (Michaels kick)				
Was	Mitchell 19 pass from Snead (Khayat kick)				
Pit	Ballman 67 pass from Brown (Michaels kick)				
Pit	Johnson 1 run (Michaels kick)				
Pit	FG Michaels 27				
Was	Mitchell 20 pass from Barnes (Khayat kick)				
Pit	FG Michaels 18				
Was	Richter 21 pass from Snead (Khayat kick)				
Pit	Ballman 92 kickoff return (Michaels kick)				

D.C. Stadium—It was like a punch in the gut. The home crowd launched into a boisterous celebration when Norm Snead's 12-yard touchdown pass to Pat Richter gave the Redskins a 28-27 lead with 2:38 left on the clock. However, the party was short lived as Gary Ballman returned the ensuing kickoff 92 yards for the winning score.

This game went back and forth throughout. The Washington defense started off the scoring as Claude Crabb intercepted Ed Brown's pass and scooted 35 yards down the sidelines, taking advantage of a nice block by John Paluck. Bobby Khayat's extra point made it 7-0.

Crabb soon went from hero to victim, giving up a 43-yard reception to flanker Buddy Dial, a play that set up John Henry Johnson's three-yard touchdown run to tie the game. The Redskins drove 97 yards to retake the lead with 1:38 left in the half. Bobby Mitchell caught Norm Snead passes of 44, 66 and 19 yards, with the last good for a touchdown.

Before halftime, though, Ballman gave a preview of things to come by scoring on a long play. On this occasion, he got a step on Crabb as safety Dale Hackbart misplayed the ball and Ballman easily gathered it in, completing the 67-yard scoring play.

That play gave the momentum to the visitors. Billy Barnes fumbled and Ernie Stautner recovered for the Steelers at the Redskin 45. Ten plays later, Johnson scored his second touchdown of the day from a yard out. A Walt Michaels field goal pushed the Pittsburgh lead to 10 entering the final period.

Barnes then made a couple of plays to atone for his earlier miscue and get his team back into the game. First, he took a short pass from Snead and turned it into a 54-yard gain. Then, he took a pitchout, pulled up and lobbed a 20-yard touchdown pass to Bobby Mitchell to cut the Steelers' lead to 24-21.

Michaels kicked another field goal to stretch the lead back to six before Snead connected with Richter to send the stadium into a frenzy, a mood on which Ballman quickly dumped cold water. The home team managed to drive to the Steeler 25 after that, but four incompletions ended the Redskins' hopes.

11/24/63	Redskins (3-8) 13, EAGLES (2-8-1) 10			60,671	
Was	3	10	0	0	13
Phi	0	0	0	10	10
Was	FG Khayat 37				
Was	FG Khayat 22				
Was	James 31 pass from Snead (Khayat kick)				
Phi	Brown 25 pass from Jurgensen (Clark kick)				
Phi	FG Clark 45				

Franklin Field—It was an atmosphere fitting of the Redskins' dismal season. They won on the road to snap a seven-game losing streak, but there was no celebrating on the field or in the locker room. Back in Washington, preparations were being made for the funeral of President John F. Kennedy, who had been assassinated in Dallas two days earlier.

The Redskins built up a 13-0 first half lead and then had to hang on. Bobby Khayat kicked two field goals before Dick James made a superb, diving catch of a Norm Snead pass for a 31-yard touchdown to give Washington a 13-0 halftime lead.

The lead held into the fourth quarter and then Eagles quarterback Sonny Jurgensen, who had been shelved with a shoulder injury, got warmed up. He threw a 25-yard touchdown pass to Tim Brown and led the Eagles to a 45-yard field goal by Mike Clark. On the Eagles' last possession, Philly got to the Redskin nine, but Clark missed a potential game-tying field goal from 16 yards.

Commissioner Pete Rozelle made the controversial decision to play the scheduled games in the shadow of the tragedy, a call which obviously sat well in the City of Brotherly Love. One fan said, "I've been coming to these games for years. Look, I'm for the man (Kennedy) and couldn't be any sorrier about this tragic happening. President Kennedy's dead, though, and whether I attend the game or not can't change that." He apparently was echoing the sentiments of many. There were no empty seats evident among the sold-out Franklin Field crowd of 60,671.

12/1/63	Colts (6-6) 34, REDSKINS (3-9) 21			44,006	
Bal	3	13	3	17	36
Was	0	7	6	7	20
Bal	FG Martin 9				
Was	Mitchell 28 pass from Snead (Khayat kick)				
Bal	Mackey 30 pass from Unitas (Martin kick)				
Bal	Berry 2 pass from Unitas (kick failed)				
Was	James 3 run (kick failed)				
Bal	FG Martin 37				
Bal	Hill 10 run (Martin kick)				
Bal	Orr 28 pass from Unitas (Martin kick)				
Bal	FG Martin 41				
Was	Bosseler 1 run (Khayat kick)				

D.C. Stadium—The Colts broke open a close game with 17 unanswered points in the fourth quarter to beat the Redskins 34-21.

The Colts moved smartly down the field after a short opening kickoff to take a 3-0 lead on Jim Martin's nine-yard field goal. In the second quarter, the Redskins took their only lead of the game when Bobby Mitchell eluded defender Bob Boyd and then juggled Norm Snead's pass for a moment before securing it for a 7-3 Redskin lead.

Baltimore reestablished control before halftime with Johnny Unitas throwing two touchdown passes in the last three minutes of the second quarter, a 30-yarder to John Mackey and a two-yard flip to Ray Berry. Martin missed the point after following the second score and the Colts led 16-7 at intermission.

In the third quarter, the Redskins climbed back into the game. From the Washington 20, a screen pass to Dick James was good for 13. Liking the result, Snead tossed another short pass, this one to Don Bosseler. The fullback slipped past linebacker Bill Pellington at around the Colt 40 and rumbled 62 yards to the five. Three plays later, Dick James scored from three yards and, although Bobby Khayat's point after attempt was blocked, it was a ballgame at 16-13.

Another Martin field goal extended the Colt lead to six points entering the final period—when Unitas is at his best. Following a 17-yard screen to Tom Matte with a 15-yard roughness penalty tacked on, the Colts were at the Washington 23. Unitas rolled out and charged to the 10, sending Jerry Hill right up the middle into the end zone.

Washington had a chance to respond but Bobby Mitchell dropped a beautiful Snead pass inside the Baltimore five. Unitas' 28-yard touchdown pass to Orr wrapped it up soon after that.

12/8/63	**GIANTS (10-3) 44, Redskins (3-10) 14**			62,992	
Was	7	0	0	7	14
NYG	3	20	14	7	44
Was	Tracy 4 run (Khayat kick)				
NYG	FG Chandler 48				
NYG	Lynch 42 interception return (Chandler kick)				
NYG	Gifford 8 pass from Tittle (Chandler kick)				
NYG	Katcavage 10 fumble return (kick failed)				
NYG	Morrison 57 pass from Tittle (Chandler kick)				
NYG	Huff 36 interception return (Chandler kick)				
NYG	Gifford 28 pass from Griffing (Chandler kick)				
Was	Mitchell 56 pass from Izo (Khayat kick)				

Yankee Stadium—The Giants took advantage of 10 Washington turnovers to deliver a smashing win over the hapless Redskins by a score of 44-14.

The Giants scored 21 points on runbacks of Washington miscues and set up another 10. The first scoring return came as Washington was enjoying a 7-3 lead in the second quarter. Dick Lynch latched on to a Norm Snead pass in the flat and, 42 yards later, the Redskins led no more. End Andy Robustelli then blindsided Snead and recovered the quarterback's fumble at the Washington nine. Shortly after that, Y. A. Tittle threw an eight-yard touchdown pass to Frank Gifford and the Giants led 17-7.

When the Redskins got the ball back, Robustelli again went to work harassing Snead. This time Norm saw him and scrambled to elude his tormentor, but Robustelli knocked the ball out as Snead attempted to pass. The New York defense now saved the offense the trouble as the other end, Jim Katcavage, scooped the ball up and ran it nine yards for another six for the Giant defense.

Head Coach Bill McPeak pulled Snead in the third quarter, more out of pity than of any realistic hope of replacement George Izo igniting a rally for Washington. In fact, the Giants were the immediate beneficiaries of the switch; Sam Huff picked off one of Izo's first attempts. The linebacker scampered 36 yards into the end zone. Izo did get the Redskins on the scoreboard again,

passing 56 yards to Bobby Mitchell for a touchdown in the fourth quarter, but it mattered not.

Top Pick Charley Taylor Signs

Dec 10—The Redskins have their man.

Shortly after drafting dual-threat running back Charley Taylor out of Arizona State with the third overall pick, the Redskins signed him to a contract today.

Taylor was a two-time All-American for the Sun Devils. He played in the defensive backfield but will earn his NFL paycheck carrying and catching the football. He is expected to add a spark to an offense that ranked dead last in rushing in 1963.

Dec 13

Marshall Associates Take Over Affairs
Ailing Redskins majority owner ruled legally incompetent

12/15/63	**Browns (10-4) 27, REDSKINS (3-11) 20**			40,865	
Cle	10	10	0	7	27
Was	0	7	7	6	20
Cle	FG Groza 42				
Cle	Collins 34 pass from Ryan (Groza kick)				
Cle	FG Groza 42				
Was	Mitchell 92 kickoff return (Khayat kick)				
Cle	Green 33 pass from Ryan (Groza kick)				
Was	Barnes 1 run (Khayat kick)				
Cle	Collins 9 pass from Ryan (Groza kick)				
Was	Barnes 24 pass from Snead (kick failed)				

D.C. Stadium—The Redskins had their chances but, as had been the case all season long, they shot themselves in the foot at key times and ended to season with a 27-20 loss to Cleveland.

Trailing 13-0, the Redskins got back into it after Lou Groza kicked a 42-yard field goal. Groza made the mistake of kicking to Bobby Mitchell, who ran the boot back 92 yards for a touchdown, cutting the lead to 13-7. The Washington defense, however, gave it right back as Frank Ryan, not the most mobile quarterback around, scrambled away from trouble and threw a 33-yard touchdown pass to Ernie Green to make it 20-7 at the half.

The home team got the only score of the third quarter when Billy Barnes bulled in from a yard out to pull the Redskins back within six at 20-14. Cleveland responded in the fourth quarter with another Ryan-to-Collins TD hookup, this one from nine yards out.

Then the Redskins got the break they needed when Jim Shofner fumbled a punt and Vince Promuto recovered at the Cleveland 38. Barnes scored on a 24-yard pass from Norm Snead soon after that and it was 27-20 with 4:55 left.

One step forward, two steps back. Bobby Khayat bounced the extra point try off the upright and the best the Redskins could hope for was a tie. That prospect vanished when Andy Stynchula was flagged for roughing the punter with two minutes left and the Browns were able to kill the clock.

Dec 16

Redskins to Retain McPeak
Despite 3-11 disappointment, coach receives 25 percent raise

1964
Head Coach: Bill McPeak
Record: 6-8, Tied Third in NFL East

Honors: Sam Huff Pro Bowl; Sonny Jurgensen Pro Bowl; Paul Krause Pro Bowl, All-NFL;
Bobby Mitchell Pro Bowl, All-NFL; John Paluck Pro Bowl;
Vince Promuto Pro Bowl; Charley Taylor Pro Bowl

Redskins Trade Snead for Jurgensen

Mar 31—In an exchange of youth and potential for experience and accomplishment, the Redskins sent quarterback Norm Snead to Philadelphia in exchange for their signal caller, Sonny Jurgensen.

Defensive back Claude Crabb also went to the Eagles in the deal, while Jimmy Carr will join Jurgensen in Washington.

Snead, 23, appeared in the Pro Bowl after last season and is considered to be one of the game's rising stars. Jurgensen, who will be 30 when the season starts, is an established star. He received Pro Bowl honors in his first season as a starter in 1961. That year he tied an NFL record by throwing for 32 touchdowns.

The acquisition of Jurgensen emphasizes that the Redskins are in a win-now mode. They went 3-11 last year and it seems certain Coach Bill McPeak won't return if they don't turn things around in 1964.

"[Jurgensen] can take the Redskins right to the top of the Eastern Division," said McPeak.

Apr 10
Linebacker Sam Huff Traded to Redskins
Stynchula, James go to Giants

Graham: Taylor 'Lazy'

Aug 5—Diplomacy may be a key skill in Washington, D.C., but apparently it's one Otto Graham never learned.

Graham is coaching the College All Stars as they prepare for an exhibition game against the NFL champion Chicago Bears. Charley Taylor, the Redskins' top draft pick, is a member of that team. When asked about Taylor, Graham said that Taylor is "a great athlete, but he is very lazy."

"He comes late to practice and is the first to leave. He even misses practice. And it has happened too often for him to be a victim of circumstances," Graham continued. "He seems to have no interest."

Taylor "could have a great future in football or fall flat on his face," Graham said.

Although he's one of the best players on the team, Graham—a former standout quarterback for the Browns—indicated that Taylor would not start the game.

Washington's coach Bill McPeak reportedly is considering filing a letter of protest with NFL commissioner Pete Rozelle over Graham's comments.

9/13/64	**Browns (1-0) 27, REDSKINS (0-1) 13**			47,577	
Cle	0	13	7	7	27
Was	0	10	0	3	13
Was	FG Martin 12				
Was	Taylor 17 run (Martin kick)				
Cle	Collins 23 pass from Ryan (kick failed)				
Cle	Brown 1 run (Groza kick)				
Cle	Brown 1 run (Groza kick)				
Was	FG Martin 14				
Cle	Green 1 run (Groza kick)				

D.C. Stadium—The Redskins built a 10-0 lead in the second quarter, but lost it in a barrage of ill-timed turnovers as the Browns wore down their opponents and grabbed a 27-13 victory.

The Redskins' new-look offense, led by quarterback Sonny Jurgensen, acquired via a trade with the Eagles, and running back Charley Taylor, the team's first-round draft pick out of Arizona, began to click late in the first. From the Washington 12, Jurgensen threw to Pat Richter for 11 yards and Taylor carried three times for a total of 25. With the defense looking for the rookie, Jurgensen then turned his attention to the Skins' established star, Bobby Mitchell. The flanker ran a slant and took Jurgensen's pass for 13 yards down to the three. Taylor got thrown for a loss from there and the Redskins had to settle for Jim Martin's 12-yard field goal for a 3-0 lead.

Safety Paul Krause, the Redskins' second-round pick, paid dividends nearly as quickly as Taylor did. He drew a bead on a Frank Ryan pass, leapt in front of the intended receiver, intercepted the pass and returned it 18 yards to the Cleveland 16. Not to be outdone, Taylor converted the turnover, taking a weak side pitch from Jurgensen, found daylight and fended off safety Larry Benz to score a touchdown, making it 10-0.

The Washington defense stuffed Jim Brown on the next series and Cleveland had to punt. The rookie magic ended as first-year returner Ozzie Clay fumbled Gary Collins' boot, giving the Browns the ball at the Washington 24. The miscue swung the momentum to the Browns instantly and, as it turned out, inexorably.

Two plays after the punt, Krause displayed the nature of rookies as he, in his words, "simply got mixed up" and blew his coverage on Collins. Dave Brady of the Post said Collins "was so wide open that the nearest person to him was a spectator sitting directly above in the overhanging second deck of D.C. Stadium." The Browns missed the point after but were undaunted as they drove 70 yards to Jim Brown's one-yard touchdown run to take a 13-10 halftime lead.

In his Redskins debut, middle linebacker Sam Huff got an interception to kill a Cleveland threat inside the Washington 10, but Mitchell quickly gave it back with a fumble that Walter Beach recovered at the Redskin 34. Soon after that, it was Brown scoring from the one again, and the Browns were beginning to pull away. Their cause was greatly aided when Jurgensen fumbled it away at the Cleveland four, short-circuiting a comeback bid.

9/20/64	**COWBOYS (1-1) 24, Redskins (0-2) 18**			25,158	
Was	3	6	0	9	18
Dal	0	14	3	7	24
Was	FG Martin 31				
Was	FG Martin 41				
Dal	Perkins 1 run (Van Raaphorst kick)				
Dal	Perkins 3 run (Van Raaphorst kick)				
Was	FG Martin 32				
Dal	FG Van Raaphorst 15				

Dal	Renfro 39 interception return (Van Raaphorst kick)
Was	Safety Jordan tackled in end zone
Was	Lockett 29 pass from Izo (Martin kick)

Cotton Bowl—The Redskins had plenty of opportunities on this day, but they just couldn't hold on to them. Ten dropped passes, including at least three that would certainly have been touchdowns, contributed greatly to Cowboys' 24-18 victory.

The first key muff of a pass came in the first quarter following a Sam Huff interception that set the Redskins up at the Dallas 37. Bobby Mitchell lost Cornell Green and was wide open, but dropped Sonny Jurgensen's perfectly-thrown pass. All the scoring Redskins could muster in the first half was three Jim Martin field goals. Dallas got two short Don Perkins touchdown runs to take a 14-9 halftime lead.

Texan Charley Taylor, playing in front dozens of friends and family members, had a chance to give the Redskins the lead in the third quarter on a play from the Redskins 12 yard line. As Jurgensen scrambled free from blitzing Cowboys, Taylor was breaking free from Mel Renfro's coverage near midfield. The pass found Taylor's hands, but the rookie running back dropped it.

The Cowboys began to pull away with a field goal and a 39-yard interception return by Renfro to take a 24-9 lead into the fourth quarter. George Izo replaced a limping Jurgensen at quarterback and things began to happen. Taylor connected with Mitchell on a halfback option good for 41 yards to the Dallas 21. Then Izo's pass was picked off by linebacker Dave Edwards, who promptly fumbled. Lee Roy Jordan recovered the fumble for Dallas in the end zone and the Redskins got two points.

After the ensuing free kick, Izo converted a fourth and five by throwing a 29-yard touchdown pass to J. W. Lockett. The fullback dragged two would-be tacklers into the end zone to pull the Redskins within six at 24-18. The Washington defense rose to the occasion, forcing Dallas to punt. The Redskins had the ball back at their own 35 with over three minutes to go.

After Tom Tracy came up inches short on third down at the Washington 44, Izo came up with an inspired play call. With the Cowboys geared to stuff the expected running play, he sent Mitchell deep. The call was perfect as Mitchell was five yards behind Green and the pass was perfect as it nestled into Mitchell's arms, but the result was a bust as the go-ahead touchdown opportunity slid out of Mitchell's grasp.

9/25/64	**GIANTS (1-2) 13, Redskins (0-3) 10**				62,996
Was	3	7	0	0	10
NYG	0	0	3	10	13
Was	FG Martin 43				
Was	Carpenter 15 pass from Jurgensen (Martin kick)				
NYG	FG Chandler 40				
NYG	FG Chandler 19				
NYG	Wood 1 run (Chandler kick)				

Yankee Stadium—The Redskins held a 10-0 lead until late in the third quarter, but they eventually collapsed under the weight of their own mistakes, including a huge one by Charley Taylor, and lost to the Giants 13-10.

Washington built its lead in the first half with a 43-yard field goal by Jim Martin and a 15-yard touchdown pass from Sonny Jurgensen to Pres Carpenter. The TD came after Sam Huff ended a Giant threat by intercepting a pass at the goal line. The ex-Giant star, returning to Yankee Stadium for the first time as an opponent, ran the interception out to the Redskin 14. From there, Jurgensen led the march to the end zone, with the biggest chunk of yardage coming on his 35-yard completion to Bobby Mitchell.

The Redskins would have further opportunities but couldn't dent the scoreboard again. Breakdowns in the kicking game were rampant as Martin had two field goal attempts blocked and pressure forced Pat Richter to abort a punt attempt, resulting in a fumbled ball going to the Giants.

A pair of Don Chandler field goals—one late in the third, the other early in the fourth quarter—pulled the Giants within 10-6. Then things seemed to turn the Redskins' way as Chandler missed from 15 yards. After that, another New York threat was averted when Jim Shorter intercepted a Y. A. Tittle pass at his 22 with 2:05 left in the game. All the Redskins had to do was hang on to the ball.

But they didn't. Charley Taylor fumbled and the Giants recovered at the 22 with 1:53 to go. Tittle threw to Alex Webster to get the ball two yards from the goal line, but three subsequent plays gained just one yard. On fourth down, rookie Gary Wood replaced Tittle, took the snap and rolled around left end. Linebacker Jimmy Carr had Wood in his sights well behind the line of scrimmage, but missed the tackle. Wood crossed into the end zone with 39 seconds left.

September 28
McPeak Safe, Team Officials Say
Coaching change not planned despite 0-3 start

10/4/64	**Cardinals (3-0-1) 23, REDSKINS (0-4) 17**				49,219
StL	14	0	7	2	23
Was	3	7	0	7	17
StL	Fischer 33 interception return (Bakken kick)				
Was	FG Martin 22				
StL	Crow 1 run (Bakken kick)				
Was	Mitchell 19 pass from Jurgensen (Martin kick)				
StL	Childress 22 pass from Johnson (Bakken kick)				
StL	Safety Izo tackled in end zone				
Was	Tracy 16 run (Martin kick)				

D.C. Stadium—The Cardinals jumped to a 14-3 first-quarter lead and then, aided by a fierce pass rush that had Sonny Jurgensen frustrated all afternoon, held on to beat the Redskins 23-17.

St. Louis took a 7-0 lead on the game's second play when cornerback Pat Fischer snagged a tipped pass and raced 33 yards for a touchdown. The home team responded as Ozzie Clay returned the ensuing kickoff 84 yards, leading to a 22-yard Jim Martin field goal. By the end of the quarter, John David Crow had scored on a one-yard run for the Cards to make it 14-3.

Another big play set up Washington's first touchdown. Sonny Jurgensen completed a 43-yard pass to Bobby Mitchell to set up a 19-yard TD by the same combination.

As the game wore on, the Cardinal pass rush, led by ends Tom Redmond and Don Brumm, wore down Jurgensen and the Washington offense. Jurgensen was sacked eight times for 66 yards in losses. The last sack, by Redmond, came early in the fourth quarter with St. Louis holding a 21-10 lead. Jurgensen slammed the ball on the turf in anger after that, his last play of the game. George Izo came in for the next series and Brumm promptly nailed him in the end zone for a safety and a 23-10 lead.

The Redskins fought back in the late going. Charley Taylor broke loose for a 50-yard run to the Cardinal 16 and on the next play Tom Tracy abandoned a halfback option pass, reversed his field and scurried into the end zone. After all the miseries of the preceding 58 minutes, Washington was within six points with 1:50 to go.

With fourth down and a foot to go on the Washington 47, the Cardinals went for it, with quarterback Charley Johnson plunging into the middle on a sneak. It took two measurements to determine that Johnson had gained the needed inches for the first down. Much to the displeasure of the loudly-booing D.C. Stadium crowd, St. Louis killed the clock to preserve the win.

10/11/64	REDSKINS (1-4) 35, Eagles (2-3) 20				49,219	
Phi	0	0	20	0		20
Was	14	7	7	7		35
Was	Mitchell 29 pass from Jurgensen (Martin kick)					
Was	Lockett 22 pass from Jurgensen (Martin kick)					
Was	Mitchell 9 pass from Jurgensen (Martin kick)					
Phi	Brown 22 run (kick failed)					
Phi	Brown 14 pass from Snead (Baker kick)					
Was	Taylor 66 pass from Jurgensen (Martin kick)					
Phi	Brown 5 run (Baker kick)					
Was	Taylor 74 pass from Jurgensen (Martin kick)					

D.C. Stadium—Sonny Jurgensen welcomed his old team to his new home by throwing five touchdown passes as the Redskins whipped the Eagles 35-20.

Jurgensen's favorite target in the first half was Bobby Mitchell. The flanker caught eight passes, one for a 29-yard touchdown that gave his team a 7-0 lead in the first quarter. His victim for most of those first-half catches was Glenn Glass, who was injured as Mitchell caught a 56-yard pass carried to the Philly nine yard line with 15 seconds left in the half. In came Claude Crabb, who had been dealt to the Eagles as part of the Jurgensen trade. Crabb was in futile pursuit as Jurgensen tossed a pass to Mitchell in the right corner of the end zone for another touchdown. In between, Jurgensen had connected with fullback J. W. Lockett for a 22-yard score and it was 21-0 at halftime.

It would be an understatement to say that the Redskins dominated the first half; they outgained the Eagles 302 yards to two.

While they were unable to continue their supremacy to that degree, the Redskins did manage to hold Philly at arm's length during the second 30 minutes of the proceedings. Tim Brown put a bit of a scare into the home fans, scoring on a 22-yard run and a 14-yard pass from Norm Snead, the quarterback who was the other component in the Jurgensen deal.

Then Jurgensen turned his attention to Charley Taylor. After the Eagles had closed to within 21-13, the running back caught a 66-yard touchdown pass to give the Skins some breathing room. Taylor answered Brown's third TD of the game, by scoring on a 74-yard pass from Jurgensen.

10/18/64	CARDINALS (4-1-1) 34, Redskins (1-5) 28				21,794	
Was	14	0	0	10		24
StL	10	14	0	14		38
Was	Jurgensen 1 run (Martin kick)					
Was	Coia 32 pass from Jurgensen (Martin kick)					
StL	FG Bakken 17					
StL	Randle 11 pass from Johnson (Bakken kick)					
StL	Crow 9 run (Bakken kick)					
StL	Smith 1 pass from Johnson (Bakken kick)					
Was	Mitchell 18 pass from Jurgensen (Martin kick)					
Was	FG Martin 22					
StL	Conrad 12 pass from Johnson (Bakken kick)					
StL	Fisher 37 interception return (Bakken kick)					

Busch Stadium—The Redskins battled back with 10 fourth-quarter points to tie the game, but St. Louis scored 14 points in the game's final 27 seconds to take a 34-28 win.

Washington jumped to a 14-0 lead aided by a pair of takeaways by the defense. First, Paul Krause picked off a Charley Johnson pass at the Washington 22. On the next play, Charley Taylor caught a Sonny Jurgensen pass and raced 77 yards to the one. Jurgensen snuck it over on the next play. Less than a minute later, Johnson fumbled, tackle Joe Rutgens recovered and Jurgensen threw a 32-yard TD pass to Angelo Coia.

The turnover bug bit the Redskins back. After Jim Bakken had kicked a field goal to cut the lead to 14-3, halfback Tom Tracy fumbled and Dale Meinert claimed the ball for St. Louis at the Washington 27. That led to Johnson's 11-yard touchdown pass to Sonny Randle and it was 14-10. In the second quarter, after

another Cardinal TD, Taylor tried his hand at passing with disastrous results. Jerry Stovall intercepted his attempted pitch to Mitchell, and St. Louis was back in business at the Washington 47. Eleven plays later, Johnson flipped a one-yard touchdown pass to tight end Jackie Smith and the home team had a 24-14 halftime lead.

After a scoreless third quarter, the Redskins again played takeaway to get back into the game. Johnny Sample intercepted Johnson and returned the ball 16 yards to the Redskin 44. Taylor picked his way through the defenders for a 37-yard run and then Jurgensen threw a low pass to Bobby Mitchell. The flanker took the pass on his knees at the three, popped up and easily ran in to the end zone. Jim Carr's interception set up Jim Martin's field goal to tie the game at 24. Shortly before that, Angelo Coia had bobbled and dropped a pass in the end zone.

Starting with less than two minutes remaining, though, the Cardinals took advantage of some sloppy tackling to move 73 yards to take the lead on Johnson's 12-yard touchdown pass to Bobby Joe Conrad with 27 seconds left on the clock. Washington had a final, desperation chance, but Pat Fisher intercepted Jurgensen's pass and ran it back 37 yards to score as the clock ran out.

10/25/64	REDSKINS (2-5) 27, Bears (2-5) 20				49,219	
Chi	0	6	7	7		20
Was	0	13	0	14		27
Chi	Bivins 21 pass from Wade (kick failed)					
Was	Mitchell 12 pass from Jurgensen (Martin kick)					
Was	Coia 59 pass from Jurgensen (kick failed)					
Chi	Morris 3 pass from Wade (Jencks kick)					
Was	Coia 10 pass from Jurgensen (Martin kick)					
Chi	Marconi 3 pass from Wade (Jencks kick)					
Was	Carpenter 15 pass from Jurgensen (Martin kick)					

D.C. Stadium—Sonny Jurgensen's fourth touchdown pass of the day went to tight end Pres Carpenter with a minute to play, giving Washington a 27-20 win over the Bears.

The Redskins held a slim 7-6 lead with time running out in the first half as they took possession at their own 41. Chicago inserted five defensive backs into the game to prevent any long passes. The strategy didn't work; Angelo Coia, a former Bear, split two of those backs and was churning at full speed when he gathered in Jurgensen's bomb for a 13-6 halftime lead.

The Bears tied it up in the third by driving 73 yards, mostly through the air. The payoff came on a three-yard touchdown pass from Bill Wade to receiver Johnny Morrison.

In the fourth, the Redskins moved in to take the lead. After Chicago punted from its own end zone, Washington took possession at the Bear 29. Jurgensen handed to Taylor, who then gave the ball to Bobby Mitchell on a reverse. Mitchell got a nice block from Fran O'Brien and made it down to the 12 before being brought down. Soon after that, Coia, who had dropped a potential go-head touchdown pass in the fourth quarter of a loss the week before, completed his transformation from goat to hero when he sped past his defender and took Jurgensen's crisp pass at the goal line. The score was 20-13.

But the Bears were not done. They had to rely almost exclusively on the passing game as the Washington defense had shut down their ground attack. Wade's 53rd pass of the game was a three-yard touchdown pass to fullback Joe Marconi and the game was tied once more.

The key plays on the Skins' winning drive were a 24-yard run with a pitchout by Taylor and Jurgensen's screen pass to Don Bosseler that was good for 18. From the Bear 15 with the clock running down, Jurgensen threw to Carpenter on the right sideline. Safety Richie Petitbon was waiting there for him, but Carpenter made a nice pivot move and Petitbon wound up face down on the turf. Perhaps the defender was able to lift his head in time to see Carpenter speed into the end zone.

11/1/64	**REDSKINS (3-5) 21, Eagles (4-4) 10**				60,671
Was	14	0	7	0	21
Phi	0	0	3	7	10
Was	Taylor 1 run (Martin kick)				
Was	Mitchell 29 pass from Jurgensen (Martin kick)				
Phi	FG Baker 26				
Was	Taylor 2 run (Martin kick)				
Phi	Brown 1 run (Baker kick)				

Franklin Field—The Redskins jumped to a 10-point lead in the game's opening five minutes and held the Eagles at bay the rest of the way to beat Philadelphia 21-10.

Pervis Atkins got things off to a good start when he returned a punt 68 yards to the Eagle one. Charley Taylor plunged over on the next play.

On the ensuing possession, Philly fullback Earl Gros was separated from the ball and Paul Krause gathered it in at the Eagle 22. After a holding call, Sonny Jurgensen zipped a 29-yard touchdown pass to Bobby Mitchell and the Redskins had a quick 14-0 lead.

Although the Redskin offense wasn't able to accomplish much on its own, an inspired defense kept the Eagles bottled up. The frustration quickly spilled into the stands, with quarterback Norm Snead being the particular target of the Philly fans' displeasure. Snead threw two interceptions and his offense was unable to generate anything more than a 26-yard field goal by Sam Baker. It was unfair, however, to lay all the blame at Snead's feet—not with the way Washington defenders like ends John Paluck and Joe Rutgens were living in the Eagle backfield.

After that third-quarter field goal, an alert play by defensive back Johnny Sample gave the Redskins yet another short field with which to work. Philadelphia's Ray Poage held on to a pass reception for a split second before dropping the ball and tumbling out of bounds. The officials hesitated to make a call, but Sample didn't wait for them as he scooped up the ball and ran it back 31 yards to the Eagle 15. The play was ruled a completion and fumble and Washington got the ball. After Jurgensen completed a post to Angelo Coia to the three, Taylor took it to pay dirt and the Redskins led 21-3.

King Hill replaced Snead at quarterback and threw another interception, but he did drive the team to its only touchdown in the last two minutes.

11/8/64	**BROWNS (7-1-1) 34, Redskins (3-6) 24**				76,385
Was	0	3	7	14	24
Cle	0	13	14	7	34
Was	FG Martin 30				
Cle	Green 21 run (Groza kick)				
Cle	FG Groza 11				
Cle	FG Groza 38				
Cle	Collins 13 pass from Brown (Groza kick)				
Was	Mitchell 14 pass from Jurgensen (Martin kick)				
Cle	Warfield 62 pass from Ryan (Groza kick)				
Was	Taylor 10 pass from Jurgensen (Martin kick)				
Cle	Brown 2 run (Groza kick)				
Was	Mitchell 14 pass from Jurgensen (Martin kick)				

Cleveland Municipal Stadium—Jim Brown rushed for 121 yards, scored one touchdown and threw for another to lead his team to an easy 34-24 win over the Redskins.

The Redskins scored first, moving 61 yards to a 24-yard field goal by Jim Martin. After that, though, Cleveland took control. The Browns took the ensuing kickoff and moved 71 yards to a 21-yard touchdown run by Ernie Green. On the play, Green brushed aside an attempted tackle by Paul Krause at the two and scored standing up. Two Lou Groza field goals made the halftime score 13-3.

Cleveland wrapped it up shortly after halftime. Sonny Jurgensen was off balance when he threw a pass and defensive back Larry Benz picked it off, returning it 45 yards to the Washington 10. Shortly after that, from the 13, defensive end John Paluck flattened Brown, but not before the back got a pass away that floated over the heads of Krause and Jim Steffen and into the hands of receiver Gary Collins in the end zone for a 20-3 lead.

The Redskins did try to climb back into it as Jurgensen connected with Mitchell on a 14-yard touchdown pass, but Cleveland had the answer. Frank Ryan threw a 62-yard TD pass to Paul Warfield to end any doubt.

11/15/64	**Redskins (4-6) 30, STEELERS (3-7) 0**				31,587
Was	7	13	10	0	30
Pit	0	0	0	0	0
Was	Taylor 3 run (Martin kick)				
Was	Coia 80 pass from Jurgensen (kick failed)				
Was	Taylor 80 pass from Jurgensen (Martin kick)				
Was	Sample 15 interception return (Martin kick)				
Was	FG Martin 31				

Pit Stadium—Sonny Jurgensen threw two 80-yard touchdown passes in the second quarter to lead the Redskins past the Steelers 30-0. The defense did its part by picking off four passes to help shut out Pittsburgh.

Sam Huff blocked a field goal attempt, setting off the Skins' first scoring drive from their 36. J. W. Lockett carried once and then found a nice block by tackle Riley Mattson to help gain 20 yards on a screen pass. A few twisting Charley Taylor runs got them to the Steeler 24. A few plays later, from the three, Taylor zipped into the end zone for a 7-0 lead.

In the second quarter, a missed field goal gave Washington possession at its own 20—and this time they got it done in a hurry. The line gave Jurgensen all day to throw and speedy receiver Angelo Coia beat one-on-one coverage and was wide open at the Steeler 35. He caught Jurgensen's pass on his fingertips in stride and glided in for the touchdown. The point after was blocked, so the Washington lead was 13-0.

About eight minutes later there was, *ho-hum*, another 80-yard TD pass by Jurgensen. This one also followed a missed field goal. The quarterback sent Coia on the same rout and snuck Taylor in behind him. This time Jurgensen went short to Taylor, who wrestled the ball away from Brady Keys, the victim of the bomb to Coia. In fact, Keys fell to the ground after being outfought for the ball and Taylor flew downfield to complete the play. This time, Jim Martin's point after was good and it was 20-0 at the half.

Johnny Sample scored one for the defense on a 15-yard interception return in the third quarter and Martin's 31-yard field goal later in the period closed out the scoring.

11/22/64	**REDSKINS (5-6) 28, Cowboys (4-6-1) 14**				49,219
Dal	6	0	0	10	16
Was	7	7	7	7	28
Was	Reger 6 interception return (Martin kick)				
Dal	FG Van Raaphorst 15				
Dal	FG Van Raaphorst 32				
Was	Jurgensen 1 run (Martin kick)				
Was	Coia 59 pass from Jurgensen (Martin kick)				
Dal	FG Van Raaphorst 38				
Dal	Stiger 2 run after lateral (Van Raaphorst kick)				
Was	Krause 35 interception return (Martin kick)				

D.C. Stadium—The Redskins' defense hung up four interceptions and seven sacks on Dallas quarterbacks. Two of the interceptions were returned for touchdowns as Washington beat the Cowboys 28-16.

Linebacker John Reger got the game's first score when he picked off Don Meredith's pass in the flat and scooted six yards for a touchdown. Dallas responded with two field goals by Dick Van Raaphorst and it was 7-6 going into the second quarter.

The score remained there until the last minute of the first half. Bob Pellegrini blocked a Dallas punt and Jimmy Carr recovered the ball at the Dallas 39 with 26 seconds left. Sonny Jurgensen passes to Pres Carpenter covered 18 and 20 yards to the Dallas one. On the second play, Carpenter used a nifty pivot move that put Dallas safety Mel Renfro on the ground at the 10 and allowed the receiver to get down to the one before going out of bounds. Two plays later, on the last play before intermission, Jurgensen wedged over from a foot away to make it 14-6 at the half.

The Redskins extended their lead in the third quarter following a diving Paul Krause interception of Meredith at the Washington 36. On third down from the 41, Jurgensen zipped a pass to receiver Angelo Coia, who made a fingertip catch at full speed around the Dallas 40. His defender fell in futile pursuit and Coia blazed into the end zone to give his team a 21-6 lead.

The comfort level for the fans at D.C. Stadium began to diminish in the fourth quarter after Van Raaphorst kicked another field goal. It got downright shaky after Pervis Atkins fumbled a punt that Dallas recovered at the Redskins 10. From the six, Meredith took off for the goal line and, as he was being tackled at the two, flipped a lateral to fullback Jim Stiger, who scored easily. Dallas was within five at 21-16.

The Redskins blew one chance to put it away when they came away from a first and goal at the one with no points. After three plunges into the line went nowhere, Jim Martin's field goal attempt was blocked. With two minutes to go, however, Krause ensured the crowd would go home happy when he intercepted Meredith's pass intended for Buddy Dial at the Cowboy 35, picked up a phalanx of blockers and went in for the clinching score.

11/29/64	REDSKINS (6-6) 36, Giants (2-8-2) 21				49,219
NYG	0	14	7	0	21
Was	7	3	13	13	36
Was	Carpenter 14 pass from Jurgensen (Martin kick)				
NYG	Wood 1 run (Chandler kick)				
NYG	Morrison 16 run (Chandler kick)				
Was	FG Martin 31				
Was	Taylor 24 pass from Jurgensen (Martin kick)				
NYG	Thomas 9 pass from Wood (Chandler kick)				
Was	Mitchell 17 pass from Jurgensen (kick failed)				
Was	Mitchell 32 pass from Jurgensen (kick failed)				
Was	Lockett 3 run (Martin kick)				

D.C. Stadium—Sonny Jurgensen threw for four touchdowns and Paul Krause intercepted two New York passes as the Redskins beat New York 36-21. It was Washington's first win over the Giants in seven years.

The game turned late in the third quarter. The Giants had scored on a nine-yard pass from Gary Wood to Aaron Thomas to take a 21-17 lead. They had the ball back in their own territory when Bob Toneff chased Wood out of the pocket and Joe Rutgens hit the quarterback and the ball popped loose. Linebacker Jim Carr recovered for the Redskins at the New York 17. Jurgensen found Bobby Mitchell open in the back of the end zone for the touchdown. The point after was missed, but the Redskins held a 23-21 lead.

Rookie Clarence Childs' 75-yard kickoff return momentarily took some of the sting out of the Giants' loss of the lead. But on the very next play from the Washington 23, fullback Alex Webster fumbled, John Paluck recovered and a lot of the air was out of the Giants' balloon.

New York did regain possession still trailing by just two, but Krause wrestled a pass away from Thomas for an interception at the Washington 33. The Redskins drove to Jurgensen's fourth TD pass of the day—a 32-yarder to Mitchell—to up their lead to eight at 29-21.

On the first play following the kickoff, Y. A. Tittle, who had replaced the rookie Wood at quarterback, was hit and fumbled.

Ron Snidow recovered for Washington and J. W. Lockett's three-yard touchdown run put it out of reach.

12/6/64	Steelers (5-8) 14, REDSKINS (6-7) 7				49,219
Pit	7	0	0	7	14
Was	0	7	0	0	7
Pit	Johnson 4 run (Clark kick)				
Was	Taylor 36 run (Martin kick)				
Pit	Ballman 47 pass from Brown (Clark kick)				

D.C. Stadium—The Redskins garnered just 82 yards rushing and had they been able to gain 83, Washington would have been able to come out of this game with a tie. In two tries from the one, however, they couldn't buck into the end zone. The Steelers escaped with a 14-7 win.

After the Steelers took a 7-0 lead on John Henry Johnson's four-yard touchdown run, John Paluck recovered a Pittsburgh fumble at the Steeler 36. The Redskins took advantage immediately. On the next play, Charley Taylor took a pitch to the weak side, danced through traffic, followed the path created by a crunching block by tackle Riley Mattson and scooted down the sidelines 36 yards to tie the score.

Neither team was able to generate much offense. Forced to pass due to the lack of a running game, Sonny Jurgensen was sacked five times for 34 yards in losses. Steeler quarterback Ed Brown went back to pass 15 times. He got nine of them off and was sacked the other six times.

One of Brown's five completions turned out to be the gamebreaker. With just under nine minutes left, he found Gary Ballman wide open for a 47-yard touchdown pass to give the Steelers a 14-7 lead.

Bobby Mitchell returned the ensuing kickoff to the Washington 27, where Jurgensen and the offense went to work. A 19-yard pass to Angelo Coia got things started, but on the next play Jurgensen was sacked for a seven-yard loss.

A pass to Taylor got that back and then Jurgensen went back to Coia for 15 yards into Pittsburgh territory at the 40. A third and ten pass to Mitchell gained just nine, but J. W. Lockett picked up the first down on fourth and one. Then a pass interference call got the Redskins down to the 18. Mitchell fumbled a third-down pass, but recovered for a first down at the seven. With just over a minute left, time was becoming a big factor.

After an incompletion, Taylor swept for six yards to the one. J. W. Lockett slammed into the line but was immediately slammed back by tackle Chuck Hinton and linebacker Myron Pottios. Then Taylor tried to go off tackle, but Pottios and safety Jim Bradshaw flew into the backfield and stopped the fourth-down play. Brown took one snap and killed the clock.

Dec 11	**McPeak Signs New Contract** *Two-year extension reward for recovery from slow start*

12/13/64	COLTS (12-2) 45, Redskins (6-8) 17				60,213
Was	7	3	7	0	17
Bal	3	7	14	21	45
Was	Atkins 17 run (Martin kick)				
Bal	FG Michaels 25				
Bal	Berry 30 pass from Unitas (Michaels kick)				
Was	FG Martin 25				
Bal	Hill 7 run (Michaels kick)				
Was	Jurgensen 2 run (Martin kick)				
Bal	Mackey 22 pass from Unitas (Michaels kick)				
Bal	Moore 3 run (Michaels kick)				
Bal	Moore 11 run (Michaels kick)				
Bal	Petties 15 pass from Mattee (Michaels kick)				

Memorial Stadium—The Redskins had battled the Western Conference champs to a stalemate for most of three quarters, but the Colts exploded for four touchdowns to come away with a 45-17 win.

Washington got on the board quickly after Baltimore fumbled the opening kickoff and Vince Promuto recovered for the Redskins at the Colt 26. Soon after that, fullback Pervis Atkins took off to the weak side, catching the Colts completely off guard. He covered the 17 yards to the goal line untouched.

After the Colts took a 10-7 lead, the visitors evened it up before halftime. John Paluck recovered a Johnny Unitas fumble at the Colt 18. They moved to a first and goal at the four but had to settle for Jim Martin's 25-yard field goal. At intermission, the score was tied at 10.

Charley Taylor fumbled in the third quarter and Jerry Logan recovered for Baltimore, setting up Jerry Hill's seven-yard run to push the Colts back ahead. One Washington bid to tie it up again was foiled when Logan intercepted Sonny Jurgensen's pass in the end zone. The Redskins took advantage of their second opportunity after safety Tom Walters picked off a Unitas pass at the Baltimore 36 and returned it to the two. Jurgensen and J. W. Lockett missed connections on a handoff on the next play, but Jurgensen took it around end himself to tie the score at 17.

After the ensuing kickoff, the Colts quickly regained the lead, driving to a 22-yard touchdown pass from Unitas to tight end John Mackey with 49 seconds left in the third quarter. In the next 10 minutes, the Colts established their dominance, scoring three times on two Lenny Moore touchdown runs and halfback Tom Matte's 15-yard touchdown pass to reserve end Neal Petties.

Dec 29
Taylor wins NFL Rookie of the Year
Halfback edges teammate Krause for honor

1965
Head Coach: **Bill McPeak**
Record: **6-8, Fourth in NFL Eastern Conference**

Honors: Paul Krause Pro Bowl; Joe Rutgens Pro Bowl; Charley Taylor Pro Bowl

Hall of Fame: Otto Graham, Head Coach 1966-1968

Apr 30
Leo DeOrsey Dead of Heart Attack
Acting Redskins president was 61

May 8
Edward Bennett Williams Now Acting President
Team succession bylaws dictated that attorney take over after DeOrsey death

---

9/19/65	Browns (1-0) 17, REDSKINS (0-1) 7			48,208	
Cle	3	7	7	0	17
Was	0	0	0	7	7
Cle	FG Groza 20				
Cle	Roberts 80 pass from Ryan (Groza kick)				
Cle	Collins 35 pass from Ryan (Groza kick)				
Was	Coia 21 pass from Shiner (Jencks kick)				

D.C. Stadium—In recent years, it hasn't taken much to turn a Washington-Cleveland matchup in favor of the Browns—and this 17-7 Redskins loss was no exception.

Trailing 3-0 in the second quarter, the Redskins had taken a Jim Steffen interception from their own 36 deep into Cleveland territory. It seemed likely that they would take the lead and would, at worst, come out tied. But Sonny Jurgensen misfired on a few passes and Bob Jencks was wide right on a 22-yard field goal. The Redskins came up empty.

It turned out worse than that. On the next play, Cleveland quarterback Frank Ryan threw to receiver Walt Roberts, who had beaten rookie Rickie Harris on a slant. Roberts juggled the ball for a moment before taking off to complete an 80-yard touchdown play for a 10-0 lead.

After that, the Redskins again drove close to the goal line and came up empty once more. Jencks missed a 17-yard field goal this time.

The home team didn't muster much offense in the second half, scoring just a token touchdown with less than two minutes left. For the day, Washington gained just 24 yards rushing.

9/26/65	COWBOYS (2-0) 27, Redskins (0-2) 7			61,577	
Was	0	0	0	7	7
Dal	7	13	0	7	27
Dal	Hayes 45 pass from Meredith (Villanueva kick)				
Dal	Hayes 11 run (Villanueva kick)				
Dal	FG Villanueva 27				
Dal	FG Villanueva 7				
Dal	Smith 7 run (Villanueva kick)				
Was	Mitchell 22 pass from Jurgensen (Jencks kick)				

Cotton Bowl—For the second straight week, the Redskins managed just an empty touchdown late in the game to avert a shutout as they lost to the Cowboys 27-7.

Dallas built a 14-0 second-quarter lead by utilizing its newest offensive weapon: rookie receiver Bob Hayes. An Olympic champion sprinter, Hayes got a chance to show his stuff early on when Don Meredith got the ball to him and the receiver flashed into the end zone to complete a 45-yard scoring play.

In the second period, Bob Briggs fumbled for the Redskins and Cornell Green recovered at the Redskin 23. A few plays later, Meredith called Hayes' number on an end around. A much slower man certainly could have scored following the blocking wall that accompanied Hayes.

Two field goals by Danny Villanueva pushed the halftime lead to 20-0 and the Redskins were unable to climb back into it. A foray to the Dallas four ended with four unimaginative running plays and they lost the ball on downs. The result was the same after a 49-yard reception by Bobby Mitchell and a 16-yard reception by halfback Danny Lewis gained a first down at the Dallas 16. This time it was four passing plays. Jurgensen misfired on three of them and Mitchell dropped the fourth in the end zone.

Washington's touchdown came with less than five minutes on the clock on Jurgensen's 22-yard pass to Mitchell.

10/3/65	**LIONS (3-0) 14, Redskins (0-3) 10**			52,627	
Was	0	0	0	10	10
Det	0	7	7	0	14
Det	Rasmussen 50 interception return (Walker kick)				
Det	Looney 4 run (Walker kick)				
Was	Shorter 54 fumble return (Jencks kick)				
Was	FG Jencks 34				

Tiger Stadium—The Redskins committed eight turnovers, including six interceptions, and lost to the Lions 14-10 in Detroit.

The score could well have been worse but the Lions turned it over six times themselves, giving up four interceptions and losing two fumbles.

As bad as the interceptions were—one was returned 50 yards for a touchdown by Wayne Rasmussen—it was the two fumbles that did in the Redskins.

In the third quarter, with Washington trailing 7-0, fullback Pervis Atkins fumbled and Darris McCord recovered to give Detroit possession at the Washington four. Soon after that, halfback Joe Don Looney slammed four yards for a touchdown and a 14-0 Lions lead.

In the fourth quarter, the Redskins took advantage of Detroit's sloppy play to get back into it. Jim Shorter picked up a fumble and scooted 54 yards to get the Redskins on the scoreboard. Bob Jencks' 34-yard field goal pulled Washington within four at 14-10. The Tiger Stadium crowd groaned as the Lions went three and out and Pat Studstill shanked a punt 27 yards. The ball landed on the back of unsuspecting linebacker Bob Pellegrini and Detroit recovered at its own 42 with just over two minutes left. They killed most of the rest of the clock from there.

10/10/65	**Cardinals (3-1) 37, REDSKINS (0-4) 16**			50,205	
StL	7	3	13	14	37
Was	0	3	7	6	16
StL	Conrad 36 pass from Johnson (Bakken kick)				
Was	FG Jencks 39				
StL	FG Bakken 8				
StL	FG Bakken 42				
Was	Mitchell 80 pass from Shiner (Jencks kick)				
StL	FG Bakken 28				
StL	Brumm 10 fumble return (Bakken kick)				
StL	Triplett 3 run (Bakken kick)				
StL	Gault 7 run (Bakken kick)				
Was	Hunter 29 pass from Shiner (kick failed)				

D.C. Stadium—The Redskins managed to cut their giveaway output in half from the previous week, from eight to four, but it was still a generous-enough total to help hand the Cardinals an easy 37-16 win.

It started early. One of quarterback Dick Shiner's first passes was off target and the Cardinals intercepted it and had possession at the Washington 36. St. Louis immediately converted as Charley Johnson threw a touchdown pass to Bobby Joe Conrad on the next play for a 7-0 lead.

Trailing 13-3 at halftime, the Redskins tried to let the Cards wrap it up in the third quarter. Charley Taylor fumbled and Chuck Walker of St. Louis recovered at the Washington 12. Johnson returned the favor, though, throwing a pass that Johnny Sample intercepted in the end zone.

From the Cardinal 20, Shiner found Bobby Mitchell behind the secondary and completed an 80-yard touchdown bomb to cut the St. Louis lead to 13-10.

The home team couldn't stand their good fortune. After a Jim Bakken field goal made it 16-10, Washington fullback Pervis Atkins fumbled deep his own territory. Don Brumm scooped it up and easily scooted 10 yards for the touchdown to put it out of reach.

10/17/65	**Colts (4-1) 38, REDSKINS (0-5) 7**			50,405	
Bal	10	14	14	0	38
Was	0	7	0	0	7
Bal	FG Michaels 20				
Bal	Mackey 34 pass from Unitas (Michaels kick)				
Bal	Lorick 12 run (Michaels kick)				
Bal	Haymond 30 interception return (Michaels kick)				
Was	Jurgensen 27 run (Jencks kick)				
Bal	Berry 3 pass from Unitas (Michaels kick)				
Bal	Hill 2 run (Michaels kick)				

D.C. Stadium—The Redskins took sloppy play to new lows, adding dropped passes, missed field goals, untimely penalties and other assorted sins of commission and omission to their repertoire in the course of getting routed by the Colts 38-7.

Washington got into a huge hole early on. After Lou Michaels kicked a 20-yard field goal, center Len Hauss flew a shotgun snap over Sonny Jurgensen's head, resulting in a 25-yard loss. A punt from deep in Redskin territory resulted in excellent field position for the Colts. It took them just three plays to move 47 yards for a touchdown, the payoff coming on Johnny Unitas' 34-yard touchdown pass to tight end John Mackey for a 10-0 lead.

The Redskins missed a few chances to climb back into it in the second quarter. First, Bob Jencks missed a 25-yard field goal attempt. Then, an apparent six-yard touchdown pass from Jurgensen to Bobby Mitchell was nullified by a holding penalty. Jencks missed another field goal after that, this one from 30 yards.

Baltimore wrapped it up in short order after that. Unitas again connected with Mackey, this time for 38 yards, to set up a 12-yard touchdown run by fullback Tony Lorick. Then defensive back Alvin Haymond swooped in front of a Jurgensen pass intended for Mitchell and rolled 30 yards into the end zone to make it 24-0.

Before halftime, the Redskins drove 88 yards for a touchdown, converting three fourth downs along the way. Jurgensen got the last of those conversions himself as he scrambled 27 yards for a touchdown on fourth and four with 33 seconds left in the half.

That only served to ward off the shutout as the Colts emptied the bench in the fourth quarter after a 14-point third period.

Williams, Players Mum After Meeting

October 19—Redskins team president Edward Bennett Williams held a two-hour, closed-door meeting with the players today. No coaches were permitted.

Neither Williams, who built a sterling reputation as a trial lawyer, nor the players would discuss what took place. Williams described it as "a give and take session" and "a family affair."

Williams did make assurances that despite the team's 0-5 start and the exclusion of the coaching staff from the meeting, he was not contemplating making any coaching changes. "We are not going to be persuaded by hysteria," Williams said.

The players were somewhat subdued after the meeting and remained so as they reviewed films of their 38-7 pounding by the Colts and attended a two-hour practice session.

Rookie Hanburger Will Start at Linebacker

October 22—An 18th-round draft pick will be starting on Sunday for the Redskins.

Chris Hanburger, a rookie linebacker out of North Carolina, will take over for 32-year-old Jim Carr as the Redskins take on the Cardinals in an attempt to gain their first win.

"He has been excellent every time we have put him in a game," said Coach Bill McPeak. "He rates a start."

While Hanburger is undersized at 218 pounds, he makes up for it with a fierce competitive nature and a nose for the football.

10/24/65	Redskins (1-5) 24, CARDINALS (4-2) 20			32,228	
Was	3	7	7	7	24
StL	0	10	0	10	20
Was	FG Jencks 17				
StL	Gautt 2 run (Bakken kick)				
StL	FG Bakken 27				
Was	Mitchell 53 pass from Jurgensen (Jencks kick)				
Was	Taylor 14 pass from Jurgensen (Jencks kick)				
StL	FG Bakken 23				
Was	Smith 1 pass from Jurgensen (Jencks kick)				
StL	Triplett 2 run (Bakken kick)				

Busch Stadium—Sonny Jurgensen threw three touchdown passes to lead the Redskins over the Cardinals for a 24-20 win, Washington's first victory of the year.

The Redskins had played 314 minutes of football since the season opened without holding a lead for even a fleeting moment. That changed when Bob Jencks kicked a 17-yard field goal in the final minute of the first quarter.

The novelty of holding the lead didn't have much time to sink in. St. Louis quickly drove 70 yards for a touchdown after the ensuing kickoff and later moved to a 27-yard field goal by Jim Bakken. But unlike the previous five games, the Skins did not roll over and play dead.

By halftime, the game was evened up. With the ball on the Washington 47, the Redskins receivers flooded the Cards' very effective zone defense and Bobby Mitchell broke free around the Cardinal 30. Jurgensen got him the ball and all Mitchell had to do was hip-fake safety Larry Wilson onto the ground. The score was tied at 10.

In the third quarter, the Redskins drove 84 yards to take the lead for good. The drive culminated with another Jurgensen touchdown pass, again flooding the zone to get the receiver open. This time, it was Charley Taylor who caught the 14-yard scoring toss to put Washington up 17-10.

St. Louis responded with a 23-yard Jim Bakken field goal to cut the lead to four, but the Redskins had the answer. Receptions by Pres Carpenter and Mitchell got the Redskins down to the Cardinal one. Rookie tight end Jerry Smith made a leaping catch of Jurgensen's third touchdown pass to pad the margin to 11. That rendered a late TD by St. Louis meaningless.

10/31/65	REDSKINS (2-5) 23, Eagles (2-5) 21			50,301	
Phi	0	0	7	14	21
Was	7	3	0	13	23
Was	Taylor 1 run (Jencks kick)				
Was	FG Jencks 28				
Phi	Gros 1 run (Baker kick)				
Was	Taylor 55 pass from Jurgensen (kick failed)				
Phi	Poage 22 pass from Snead (Baker kick)				
Was	Mitchell 11 pass from Jurgensen (Jencks kick)				
Phi	Gros 18 pass from Snead) Baker kick)				

D.C. Stadium—A drive that produced no points was the key for the Washington offense as the Redskins held off the Eagles 23-21.

Leading 10-7 going into the fourth quarter, Washington extended its margin as Charley Taylor used some fancy footwork to finish up a 55-yard touchdown pass from Sonny Jurgensen. He took the pass at around the Eagle 32, faked defensive back Joe Scarpati into tripping himself and sped the rest of the way to the end zone. The extra point was blocked so the lead was only 16-7.

The Eagles came right back, taking just three minutes to drive to Norm Snead's 22-yard touchdown pass to Ray Poage and cut the lead to two. Washington responded with Jurgensen making key completions to Pres Carpenter and Dan Lewis to move to the Eagles 11. From there, Bobby Mitchell shook free of his defender

and Jurgensen was on target for six points. The point after was good, and the Redskins' lead was back up to nine.

A fake punt keyed Philly's answering drive, with the payoff coming on Snead's 18-yard pass to Earl Gross to cut the lead back to two at 23-21. The four touchdowns occurred in less than nine minutes of play, and it appeared to be one of those games where the last team with the ball wins.

It was—but not in the way one would have thought. After the Eagles score, the Redskins took possession at their own 20 with 6:38 left on the clock. From there, Jurgensen led a clock-erasing drive completing all five of his pass attempts as his team crept down the field. He took the final seconds off the clock himself, running for 16 yards to the Eagle 16 on fourth down as the clock expired.

11/7/65	Redskins (3-5) 23, GIANTS (4-4) 7			62,788	
Was	14	3	0	6	23
NYG	0	7	0	0	7
Was	Krause 31 fumble return (Jencks kick)				
Was	Smith 26 pass from Lewis (Jencks kick)				
Was	FG Jencks 37				
NYG	Mercein 1 run (Timberlake kick)				
Was	FG Jencks 14				
Was	FG Jencks 37				

Yankee Stadium—For much of the first half of the season, the Redskins made things easy for their opponents by presenting them with key turnovers and committing untimely penalties and other critical mistakes. Those who believe that such things even out over the long run got some evidence for that as the Giants bumbled and stumbled their way to a 23-7 loss to Washington.

It started to go downhill quickly for the Giants. In the first quarter, ex-Giant Sam Huff smashed into New York's Steve Thurlow, causing a fumble that Paul Krause picked up at the Giant 31. Krause ran into the end zone unchallenged for a 7-0 Washington lead.

The Giants were soon in position to tie it up, but Johnny Sample picked off Earl Morrall's pass from the Washington 10 to kill the threat.

Washington used the turnover as a springboard to another score. The drive covered 83 yards and ended in a 26-yard touchdown pass by fullback Dan Lewis. Lewis started around right end, pulled up and found Jerry Smith all alone behind a thoroughly fooled New York secondary.

Another interception set up another score, but the touchdown was the Giants'. Harry Carr picked off a Jurgensen pass at the Washington 26 and ran it back to the six. Soon after that Chuck Mercein dove over from the one to make it 14-7.

A Bob Jencks field goal extended the Redskins' lead to 17-7 at halftime. Early in the third quarter, the Giants drove for a first down at the Washington five behind quarterback Phil Wood, who replaced an injured Morrall. Mercein was stopped at the three but Giants tackle Frank Lasky was flagged for punching end John Paluck and New York found itself backed up to the 20. Huff and Lonnie Sanders blocked the subsequent field goal attempt.

Two more field goals by Jencks in the fourth quarter kept the Giants at bay.

11/14/65	EAGLES (3-6) 21, Redskins (3-6) 14			60,444	
Was	0	7	7	0	14
Phi	7	0	7	7	21
Phi	Snead 1 run (Baker kick)				
Was	Lewis 5 pass from Jurgensen (Jencks kick)				
Was	Richter 25 pass from Jurgensen (Jencks kick)				
Phi	T. Brown 4 run (Baker kick)				
Phi	Gros 1 run (Baker kick)				

Franklin Field—A 78-yard pass from Norm Snead to 33-year old tight end Pete Retzlaff set up Philadelphia's game-winning touchdown as the Eagles rallied past the Redskins 21-14.

The game was tied at seven at the half and Washington moved to take the lead in the third quarter. From the Philly 26, Sonny Jurgensen rolled to his left, extracted his foot from the grasp of a couple of Eagle defenders and zipped a pass to Pat Richter at the 11. The tight end pivoted and left defensive back Irv Cross grasping for air as he ran into the end zone to put the Redskins up 14-7.

Philadelphia responded before the quarter was done. A 74-yard drive culminated in Timmy Brown's four-yard touchdown run to tie it up.

The Redskins blew a golden opportunity to recapture the lead early in the fourth quarter. Paul Krause intercepted Snead's pass at the Washington 33 and returned it to the Eagles 41. Fullback Danny Lewis gained 17 yards on the next two plays to move the team to a first down at the 24.

The effort fizzled from there. Joe Scarpati knocked down a pass just before Charley Taylor was able to get a grip on it in the end zone. On third down, Jurgensen was sacked by end Ed Khayat. Bob Jenck's field goal attempt into a strong wind was long enough but wide and the score remained tied.

Later in the period, the Eagles were backed up to their own 15 by a holding penalty. Snead threw to Retzlaff at the 35, where Jim Steffen seemed to have him contained. Retzlaff got by him, though, and wasn't stopped until Paul Krause caught up with him at the six. Four plays later, fullback Earl Gros squeezed into the end zone on fourth down at the one to push the Eagles in front 21-14.

The Redskins had a shot to tie it up in the late going, but defensive tackle John Meyers intercepted Jurgensen's pass from the Philadelphia 38 to snuff out Washington's chances.

11/21/65	Redskins (4-6) 31, STEELERS (2-8) 3		25,052
Was	0	10	14	7	31
Pit	3	0	0	0	3
Pit	FG Clark 34
Was	Lewis 1 run (Jencks kick)
Was	FG Jencks 9
Was	Taylor 8 run (Jencks kick)
Was	Coia 45 pass from Jurgensen (Jencks kick)
Was	Harris 57 punt return (Jencks kick)

Pit Stadium—The Redskins broke open a tight contest in the third quarter and cruised to an easy 31-3 win over Pittsburgh.

Washington was clinging to a 10-3 lead when Pittsburgh quarterback Ed Brown completed a short pass to flanker Gary Ballman. Perhaps due to the wet conditions, Ballman lost his handle on the ball without being touched and Paul Krause picked up the loose ball at the Steeler 38. The safety rolled to the eight where fullback Mike Lind brought him down. On the next play, Charley Taylor took a pitchout and outran Willie Daniel into the end zone to give the Skins some breathing room at 17-3.

Given the Steelers' offensive woes—they crossed midfield only once after a first-period field goal—that was probably an adequate lead, but the Redskins moved in for more. Sam Huff took out two Steelers with one block, springing Rickie Harris free for a 21-yard punt return into Pittsburgh territory at the 49. Soon after that, receiver Angelo Coia split two defenders right down the middle of the field, caught Sonny Jurgensen's pass at the ten and glided into the end zone to complete a 45-yard scoring play.

In the fourth quarter, Harris fielded another punt and finished the job himself, shaking loose for a 57-yard TD return to cap the scoring.

11/28/65	REDSKINS (5-6) 34, Cowboys (4-7) 31		50,205
Dal	14	7	3	7	-	31
Was	0	6	7	21	-	34
Dal	Dunn 6 pass from Meredith (Villanueva kick)
Dal	Green 5 fumble return (Villanueva kick)
Dal	Gaechter 60 blocked FG return (Villanueva kick)
Was	Taylor 26 pass from Jurgensen (kick blocked)
Dal	FG Villanueva 30
Was	Jurgensen 1 run (Jencks kick)
Was	Lewis 2 run (Jencks kick)
Dal	Clarke 53 pass from Meredith (Villanueva kick)
Was	Mitchell 10 pass from Jurgensen (Jencks kick)
Was	Coia 5 pass from Jurgensen (Jencks kick)

D.C. Stadium—The Redskins overcame a 21-point second-quarter deficit and held on to beat the Cowboys 34-31.

Dallas took advantage of some very hospitable behavior by their hosts. Fumbles by Sonny Jurgensen and Charley Taylor and a blocked FG attempt led to a 21-0 Dallas lead in the second quarter. Jurgensen went to Taylor for a 26-yard score before halftime, but the extra point was blocked and it was 21-6 at halftime.

Another Taylor fumble set up an additional Dallas field goal—and then the comeback began in earnest. Jurgensen capped off a 13-play, 90-yard drive with a one-yard sneak for the score and running back Danny Lewis scored on a three-yard plunge at the end of another long drive that bridged the third and fourth quarter. It was 24-20 Dallas.

Dallas quickly snatched the momentum back when Dave Edwards intercepted Jurgensen near midfield and quarterback Don Meredith threw a 53-yard TD to wide receiver Frank Clarke with six minutes left. The comeback appeared over, especially when Dallas answered Jurgensen's 10-yard touchdown pass to Bobby Mitchell with three and a half minutes left with a 56-yard kickoff return to the Washington 41. The defense stiffened, however, and Jurgensen and the Redskins had one more chance from their own 20 with 1:41 left.

The Redskins scored quickly to take the lead—almost *too* quickly. Jurgensen recovered his own fumble and gained nine yards in the process. He then went back to the air, hitting tight end Jerry Smith first for 22 yards and Mitchell for 35 yards to the Dallas 5. On first down, receiver Angelo Coia ran towards the middle, faked a block and cut to the corner where Jurgensen hit him for the TD to make it 34-31 Redskins with 1:04 remaining.

That left Dallas with a little too much time. A 35-yard Meredith to Bob Hayes completion gave Dallas a shot at a tying FG from 44 yards out with seven seconds left. The Redskins and the 50,205 in attendance breathed easily for the first time all day, though, when Lonnie Sanders blocked the attempt to end the game.

"Sonny pulled off a miracle," said Taylor.

12/5/65	BROWNS (10-2) 24, Redskins (5-7) 16		77,765
Was	6	10	0	0	16
Cle	0	7	3	14	24
Was	Taylor 2 run (kick failed)
Cle	Collins 7 pass from Ryan (Groza kick)
Was	Richter 6 pass from Jurgensen (Jencks kick)
Was	FG Jencks 20
Cle	FG Groaz 42
Cle	Hutchinson 14 pass from Ryan (Groza kick)
Cle	Brown 5 run (Groza kick)

Cleveland Municipal Stadium—Two fourth-quarter turnovers were critical as the Redskins lost a 16-7 halftime lead and fell to the Browns 24-16.

Even before those miscues, the Redskins blew a golden opportunity to put some severe pressure on their hosts. With Washington still up by nine in the third quarter, Cleveland lined up to punt in its own territory. The snap sailed far over the head of punter Gary Collins. As Collins chased the ball down, rookie linebacker Chris Hanburger appeared to have a bead on him for a huge loss. But Collins, who has burned the Redskins before in his other role as a wide receiver, managed to elude Hanburger and the rest of the coverage team to gain 16 yards and a first down at the Washington 47. The Browns moved in for a Lou Groza field goal, cutting the Washington lead to six.

The Redskins were moving into Cleveland territory and faced a third and six at the beginning of the fourth quarter. Sonny Jurgensen misfired on a pass intended for Charley Taylor and linebacker Vince Costello intercepted at the Brown 38, returning it to the Washington 39. Later, on third and nine from the 14, quarterback Frank Ryan watched as end Tom Hutchinson shook free of cornerback Lonnie Sanders and fired a perfect strike to his receiver in the corner of the end zone. Groza's extra point put Cleveland ahead 17-16.

The Redskins were attempting to respond with 3:40 to play when end Bill Glass crashed into Jurgensen, forcing a fumble that linebacker Jim Houston recovered at the Washington 18. That set up Jim Brown's five-yard touchdown run to clinch it for Cleveland.

12/12/65	Giants (7-6) 27, REDSKINS (5-8) 10		50,373	
NYG	7	13	0	7	27
Was	10	0	0	0	10
Was	FG Jencks 10			
Was	Mitchell 45 pass from Taylor (Jencks kick)			
NYG	Jones 74 pass from Morrall (Timberlake kick)			
NYG	Thurlow 1 run (kick failed)			
NYG	Jones 72 pass from Morrall (Timberlake kick)			
NYG	Frederickson 10 run (Wood run)			

D.C. Stadium—The Redskins jumped into the lead by scoring 10 points in a 35-second span in the first quarter, but the Giants did all of the scoring the rest of the way in beating the Redskins 27-10. Two long bombs from Earl Morrall to end Homer Jones keyed the comeback.

Lonnie Sanders intercepted Morrall to set up Washington's first score: a 10-yard field goal by Bob Jencks. On the ensuing kickoff Coach Bill McPeak gambled and won as Jerry Smith covered an onside kick at the Giant 45.

A combination of clever play calling and plain good luck gave the Redskins a touchdown on their next play. Charley Taylor, lined up in the slot on the left, took a handoff from Sonny Jurgensen, started to run around right end, pulled up and launched a pass downfield to Bobby Mitchell. Cornerback Spider Lockhart got both hands on the ball, but he bobbled it. Mitchell picked it out of the air and raced the rest of the way for a 45-yard touchdown catch to give the Redskins a 10-0 lead.

About a minute and a half later, the Giants responded. Jones blew a good ten yards past Lonnie Sanders and gathered in Morrall's pass for 74 yards and a touchdown to make it 10-7.

The Giants captured the lead early in the second quarter after Johnny Sample was flagged for interference in the end zone, giving them the ball at the Washington one. Steve Thurlow bulled it over from there. Although Sanders blocked the point after, New York had the lead for good at 13-10.

Later in the period, the Redskins drove all the way to the Giant one yard line. They faced fourth and goal from there and McPeak continued his gambling ways, eschewing the tying field goal attempt and going for the lead. This time, he lost as Danny Lewis was stuffed for no gain and the Giants gained possession.

New York drove 99 yards, with by far the biggest chunk coming on the second Morrall-to-Jones scoring connection. That one covered 72 yards and Jones showed great elusiveness to go with his sprinter's speed to get past Sanders, Jim Steffen and Paul Krause and into the end zone.

The Giants had no problem hanging on to their 20-10 halftime lead; they only allowed the Redskins two possessions in the second half.

12/19/65	REDSKINS (6-8) 35, Steelers (2-12) 14		49,806	
Pit	0	14	0	0	14
Was	14	14	7	0	35
Was	Lewis 10 pass from Jurgensen (Jencks kick)			
Was	Harris 34 interception return (Jencks kick)			
Pit	Ballman 2 run (Clark kick)			
Was	Walters 63 interception return (Jencks kick)			
Pit	Ballman 44 pass from Wade (Clark kick)			
Was	Pellegrini 32 fumble return (Jencks kick)			
Was	Hughley 4 pass from Jurgensen (Jencks kick)			

D.C. Stadium—The Washington defense scored three touchdowns to spark a 35-14 rout of the Steelers.

A contribution came from the Redskin offense as well. In the first quarter, they drove 80 yards for a touchdown following a Pittsburgh punt. The big play happened when Sonny Jurgensen dropped a pass over the linebackers and into the hands of tight end Jerry Smith, who found a block from safety turned receiver Paul Krause and gained 54 yards to the Steeler 11. Shortly after that, Jurgensen flipped to Danny Lewis on a swing pass and the halfback fought off a couple of attempts to bring him down to complete a 10-yard touchdown play.

Less than two minutes later, Rickie Harris started the scoring parade for the defense. He drew a bead on a Tommy Wade pass intended for Gary Ballman and picked it off. After stumbling briefly, Harris found a lane and sped down the left sideline for 34 yards and a touchdown for a 14-0 lead.

Ballman scored twice in the second quarter on a two-yard run and a 44-yard pass reception, but each time the Redskins defense responded with a touchdown return. After Ballman's run, Tom Walters intercepted Wade, found blocks from Sam Huff and Chris Hanburger and scooted into the end zone for a 21-7 lead.

Following Baldwin's scoring catch, the Steelers regained possession. With 27 seconds left in the half, both teams appeared to be offside. Wade backed away from the center, but the ball was snapped anyway. As 21 players looked around in confusion, linebacker Bob Pellegrini noted the lack of a whistle, scooped the ball up and raced 32 yards to a touchdown.

A seven-yard touchdown pass from Jurgensen to halfback George Hughley wrapped up the scoring and Coach Bill McPeak emptied the bench in the fourth quarter.

1966
Head Coach: Otto Graham
Record: 7-7, Fifth in NFL Eastern Conference

Honors: Chris Hanburger Pro Bowl; Sonny Jurgensen Pro Bowl;
Charley Taylor Pro Bowl

Jan 7

Redskins Fire McPeak
Coach and GM didn't have winning record in any of four seasons

---

Graham Hired, Promises Excitement

Jan 25—Otto Graham, the Washington Redskins' new head coach, will not play it safe as coach of the Washington Redskins—even if it means another mark in the loss column.

"I'd rather risk losing some games by, say, 35-28 and have the fans up off their seats with excitement. I think the players would have more fun, too," said Graham.

He knows a little about winning. As quarterback of the Cleveland Browns, he took his team to the league championship game his first 10 years as a pro. Most recently he has been the coach at the United States Coast Guard Academy.

"I think hard work wins football games, but I think football can be fun, too. I am not Vince Lombardi," said Graham, 44. "But I am tough. I am firm but fair."

Team President Edward Bennett Williams echoed Graham on that point. "We [have found] a crack-down coach with a winning background."

Graham made his comments as he prepared to play in the Bob Hope Desert Classic golf tournament. His plans for what to do with the Redskins will remain on hold until he returns from vacation March 10.

Graham's five-year contract is worth $60,000 annually.

Aug 17

Paluck Traded For Stan Jones
Longtime Bear star DT will leave Job Corps to play for Redskins

---

9/11/66	Browns (1-0) 38, REDSKINS (0-1) 14			48,643
Cle	7	0	10	21	38
Was	14	0	0	0	14
Was	Taylor 5 run (Gogolak kick)			
Was	Taylor 32 pass from Jurgensen (Gogolak kick)			
Cle	Kelly 29 run (Groza kick)			
Cle	Collins 20 pass from Ryan (Groza kick)			
Cle	FG Groza 35			
Cle	Warfield 16 pass from Ryan (Groza kick)			
Cle	Green 1 run (Groza kick)			
Cle	Collins 5 pass from Ryan (Groza kick)			

D.C. Stadium—A 14-0 Washington lead fell victim to a 31-0 second-half run by the Browns as Cleveland won the season opener 38-14. The victors were greatly aided by five interceptions off of the arm of Sonny Jurgensen.

Charley Taylor scored both of the touchdowns that gave the Skins the early leg up. The first came on a five-yard run after Brig Owens recovered a fumble at the Cleveland 30. Another Taylor run on the Redskins' next possession—this one for 24 yards—started a drive into Cleveland territory. On second down they flooded the right side and Taylor drew double coverage. It didn't matter as he outran both the linebacker and the cornerback to catch Jurgensen's 32-yard touchdown pass for a 14-0 lead.

Play went downhill for the Redskins the next time they had the ball. End Bill Glass deflected Jurgensen's pass intended for Jerry Smith and linebacker Johnny Brewer picked it off at the 29. On the next play, LeRoy Kelly ran it in for a touchdown, dragging Jim Shorter across the goal line with him.

Washington blew a golden opportunity as halftime approached. Jurgensen completed three straight passes to move to the Cleveland 12. On first down from there, Jurgensen put one in the arms of Pres Carpenter, whose defender had fallen. Carpenter dropped the sure six and Jurgensen was intercepted on third down.

The Redskins still led going into the third quarter, but not for long. A. D. Whitfield fumbled after a reception and Walter Beach recovered at the Washington 32. Two plays later Frank Ryan threw a 20-yard touchdown pass to Gary Collins to tie the score. A few minutes later, a Lou Groza field goal put the Browns in the lead to stay.

It started to unravel near the end of the third quarter when Jurgensen's third interception of the day was converted into seven more points on Ryan's pass to Paul Warfield early in the fourth. Less than two minutes later Erich Barnes brought yet another interception back 54 yards to the one and Ernie Green carried it in from there. Cleveland drove to their final score, another Ryan-to-Collins connection, this one from five yards.

9/18/66	CARDINALS (2-0) 23, Redskins (0-2) 7			40,198
Was	0	7	0	0	7
StL	0	3	3	17	23
StL	FG Bakken 26			
Was	Mitchell 7 pass from Jurgensen (Gogolak kick)			
StL	FG Bakken 13			
StL	FG Bakken 11			
StL	Roland 22 run (Bakken kick)			
StL	Smith 11 pass from Johnson (Bakken kick)			

Busch Stadium—The Cardinals turned two fourth-quarter fumble recoveries into touchdowns to beat the Redskins 23-7.

The Redskins took a 7-3 lead in the second quarter by driving 69 yards to a seven-yard touchdown pass from Sonny Jurgensen to Bobby Mitchell. A grand opportunity to expand the lead was wasted as the first half wound down. Jim Shorter intercepted a Charley Johnson pass at the Washington two and returned it 18 yards to the 20 with 1:10 remaining. Passes to Jerry Smith, A. D. Whitfield and Mitchell quickly had the visitors knocking on the door at the Cards' two. A play with offsetting penalties burned time off the clock, forcing a field goal attempt with two seconds left. The attempt went awry when holder Dick Shiner fumbled the snap and the Skins came up empty.

St. Louis dented the lead with a Jim Bakken field goal in the third quarter before driving to take the lead at 9-7 with another three-pointer early in the fourth. That was bad, but what ensued was disastrous.

John McDowell was part of the gang that tackled Rickie Harris on the kickoff and he stripped the ball away. Dave O'Brien recovered for the Cards at the Washington 25. It took just two plays for St. Louis to cash in on the takeaway as Johnny Roland shook loose from some tacklers at the line and then veered away from safety Paul Krause to score on a 22-yard run. Three plays later, Steve Thurlow fumbled away to the Cards again and St. Louis wrapped it up on Johnson's 11-yard pass to Jackie Smith soon after that.

9/25/66	Redskins (1-2) 33, STEELERS (1-1-1) 27			37,505	
Was	9	0	21	3	33
Pit	0	14	10	3	27
Was	FG Gogolak 41				
Was	FG Gogolak 47				
Was	FG Gogolak 29				
Pit	Ballman 49 pass from R. Smith (Clark kick)				
Pit	J. Bradshaw 27 interception return (Clark kick)				
Pit	Ballman 79 pass from R. Smith (Clark kick)				
Was	Taylor 4 pass from Jurgensen (Gogolak kick)				
Pit	FG Clark 47				
Was	Mitchell 35 pass from Jurgensen (Gogolak kick)				
Was	Taylor 2 run (Gogolak kick)				
Was	FG Gogolak 15				
Pit	FG Clark 42				

Pit Stadium—The Redskins rallied from a 21-9 third-quarter deficit to defeat the Steelers 33-27.

The first quarter belonged to Washington. To be more precise, place kicker Charlie Gogolak owned the opening period. The rookie first-round draft pick booted field goals of 41, 47 and 29 yards to propel his team to a 9-0 lead.

Pittsburgh owned period number two. A bit of confusion allowed Jerry Ballman to slip a good five yards into the clear and he hauled in Ron Smith's 49-yard touchdown pass to make it 9-7. Then, with a minute left before halftime, the home team took the lead when Jim Bradshaw intercepted Sonny Jurgensen's pass and scooted 27 yards to put the Steelers up 14-9 at halftime. It looked like they would take ownership of the game on the second play of the third quarter when Smith warded off a tackler with one hand and threw deep to Ballman with the other. The receiver caught the ball at the Washington 30, eluded the last obstacle inside the 10 and scored for a 21-9 Steeler lead.

The Redskins responded immediately and got back into it with an 80-yard drive that culminated in a four-yard touchdown pass from Jurgensen to Charley Taylor. A Pittsburgh field goal blunted the momentum, but it was only a temporary interruption. A nice kickoff return by Fred Mazurek with a 15-yard roughing penalty tacked on had Washington in business at the Steeler 47. It took just two passes to Bobby Mitchell—one of 12 yards, the second a 35-yard scoring strike—to pull the Redskins within one at 24-23.

Jim Shorter intercepted a pass and returned it to the Pittsburgh 18. Taylor got all of the yardage needed to get to pay dirt with receptions good for 12 and two yards, and then a pair of two-yard runs had Washington leading 30-24.

Gogolak's fourth field goal gave the Skins a little breathing room, but Pittsburgh matched it with more than five minutes to play. The Redskins, however, embarked on a time-consuming drive that ate up all but 34 seconds of the remaining time. Ron Snidow erased all doubt when he stripped Smith of the ball and recovered at the Steeler six.

10/2/66	REDSKINS (2-2) 24, Steelers (1-2-1) 10			47,360	
Pit	0	10	0	0	10
Was	10	0	7	7	24
Was	Taylor 60 pass from Jurgensen (Gogolak kick)				
Was	FG Gogolak 12				
Pit	Hoak 2 run (Clark kick)				
Pit	FG Clark 25				
Was	Mitchell 51 pass from Jurgensen (Gogolak kick)				
Was	Mitchell 70 pass from Jurgensen (Gogolak kick)				

D.C. Stadium—Sonny Jurgensen threw three touchdown passes, all of them covering more than half the length of the field, to lead the Redskins to their second win over the Steelers in as many weeks.

A daring play call got the Redskins started in the first quarter. Facing third and one at his own 40, Jurgensen eyed an eight-man stacked to stop the anticipated run. Charley Taylor fired at a linebacker as if to throw a block, but broke into a pass pattern. The ploy worked perfectly as Taylor was all alone as he took Jurgensen's pass and scored easily for a 7-0 lead. Sam Huff's interception and 17-yard return set up Charlie Gogolak's 12-yard field goal.

The Redskins threatened to break the game open in the second period after Chris Hanburger's fumble recovery set them up at the Steeler six. On fourth and goal, coach Otto Graham went for the kill with a fake field goal attempt but the Steelers sniffed it out. The pass intended for Hanburger went incomplete.

After Gogolak was just short on a 50-yard attempt, the Steelers got back into it. They drove 90 yards to a two-yard touchdown run by Dick Hoak and then marched into Washington territory again to Frank Clark's 25-yard field goal to tie it up with 23 seconds left in the half.

The Pittsburgh resurgence was only temporary. After coming up empty on two more field goal tries, Washington took the lead on Jurgensen's shortest TD pass of the day—a mere 51-yarder to Bobby Mitchell.

The Redskins put it away early in the fourth quarter. On a third-down play from the Washington 30, Mitchell was the fourth option on the play called. Jurgensen found the first three choices wanting and flung it long to Mitchell. The receiver's coverage had deserted him and he gathered in the bomb and strode the remaining 40 yards into the end zone.

Redskins Trade For Joe Don Looney

October 2—The Redskins made a deal for the talented but well-traveled Joe Don Looney today.

The running back will join his fourth NFL team in just over two seasons in the league. He was drafted in the first round by the Giants and has spent time with the Colts and Lions. In exchange for Looney, Washington sent Detroit an undisclosed draft pick.

He seems to have ability but his attitude has been questioned. Last year in Detroit, the coach asked him to go into the game and relay a play to the quarterback. Looney refused, saying, "If you want a messenger, call Western Union."

10/9/66	REDSKINS (3-2) 33, Falcons (0-5) 20			50,116	
Atl	7	10	3	0	30
Was	7	13	6	7	33
Atl	Coffey 4 run (Kirouac kick)				
Was	Taylor 12 run (Gogolak kick)				
Atl	FG Kirouac 47				
Was	Smith 14 pass from Jurgensen (kick failed)				
Atl	Coffey 3 run (Kirouac kick)				
Was	Taylor 86 pass from Jurgensen (Gogolak kick)				
Was	FG Gogolak 10				
Was	FG Gogolak 45				
Was	FG Kirouac 28				
Was	Looney 3 run (Gogolak kick)				

D.C. Stadium—Charley Taylor scored two touchdowns—one on an 86-yard pass from Sonny Jurgensen—to pace the Redskins past Atlanta 33-30.

After Atlanta's Junior Coffey hit pay dirt on the first of his two short touchdown runs, Taylor's first score tied the game at seven. It came on a 12-yard run in the first quarter.

The teams spent the second period trading the lead back and forth. The Falcons broke on top first on Lou Kirouac's 47-yard field goal. Jerry Smith then caught a 14-yard TD pass from Jurgensen and, although the conversion was blocked, the Redskins led 13-

10. The second of Coffey's scoring bursts pushed Atlanta back in front.

Enough of this said Jurgensen and Taylor. The quarterback was under heavy pressure and the receiver drew double coverage, but it didn't matter. Taylor was well in the open when he caught the pass and effortlessly eluded the safety's diving attempt to stop him on the way to completing the 86-yard touchdown play. The Redskins pulled ahead to stay 20-17.

Charlie Gogolak booted a pair of third-quarter field goals to extend the margin and newcomer Joe Don Looney pushed over from three yards out to finish the scoring.

10/16/66	GIANTS (1-4-1) 13, Redskins (3-3) 10	62,865
Was	3 7 0 0	10
NYG	0 3 0 10	13
Was	FG Gogolak 37	
Was	Mitchell 7 pass from Jurgensen (Gogolak kick)	
NYG	FG Gogolak 14	
NYG	FG Gogolak 18	
NYG	Thomas 29 pass from Morrall (Gogolak kick	

Yankee Stadium—New York quarterback Earl Morrall, booed and benched earlier in the game for ineffectiveness, returned to the game to throw the winning touchdown pass to Aaron Thomas with just over four minutes to play to defeat the Redskins.

For a long time it looked as though the 10-0 lead the Redskins had built in the first half just might stand up. A short punt set up a Charlie Gogolak field goal for a 3-0 lead. Then, near halftime, Sonny Jurgensen got the offense cranked up. It was during this drive that Bobby Mitchell caught his only two passes of the day—and he made them count. On the first, he dusted off Spider Lockhart's coverage and hauled down Jurgensen's pass for 51 yards to the New York 24. After a pass to Jerry Smith advanced the ball to the seven, Mitchell's out-and-in pattern had Lockhart bamboozled again and Jurgy's pass was on the mark for a 10-0 lead just after the two minute warning.

The Giants got some life just before half time with Pete Gogolak's short field goal. It remained 10-3 going into the fourth quarter. Gary Wood had replaced Morrall at quarterback, but he was shaken up. Morrall came back in to replace him and led New York to another Pete Gogolak field goal to pull within 10-6.

Meanwhile, on the other side of the field, Jurgensen had also been knocked woozy and Dick Shiner replaced him at signal caller for Washington. The running game had been ineffective (72 yards all day) and the absence of the Skins' star quarterback pretty much killed the threat of the pass, so the Giants quickly regained possession.

Morrall converted a fourth and eight at the Washington 41 to keep the drive alive and finished it off with his pass to Thomas, which came with 4:17 left. Just after the two-minute warning, Charley Taylor was a foot short on a fourth and one rushing attempt and the Giants killed the clock.

10/23/66	REDSKINS (4-3) 26, Cardinals (5-1-1) 20	50,154
StL	7 3 3 7	20
Was	3 6 3 14	26
Was	FG Gogolak 39	
StL	Randle 1 pass from Johnson (Bakken kick)	
Was	FG Gogolak 9	
StL	FG Bakken 37	
Was	FG Gogolak 44	
Was	FG Gogolak 19	
St:	FG Bakken 17	
Was	Mitchell 16 pass from Jurgensen (Gogolak kick)	
Was	Mitchell 44 pass from Jurgensen (Gogolak kick)	
StL	Johnson 2 run (Bakken kick)	

D.C. Stadium—During the week leading up to this contest against the 5-0-1 Cardinals, rain had forced the team to practice on three different fields, including the Lanham Boys Club field and indoors

at the D.C. Armory, adding to the chaotic atmosphere. St. Louis had built its record on the strength of its defense. Led by such stars as Larry Wilson, Jerry Stovall, Larry Stallings and Pat Fischer, they had allowed just three touchdown passes in six games. One would think that you would want to enter the game with all of your offensive weapons deployed.

Not Graham. On the bench was league-leading receiver Bobby Mitchell. Graham had complained about Mitchell's lackluster blocking in a loss to the Giants the week before, so Sonny Jurgensen found himself with Fred Mazurek in the lineup in place of his favorite target.

In one more plot twist, the anticipated move of star running back Charley Taylor to split end became a reality as Taylor saw substantial action both in the backfield and as a wide receiver. Graham called all the turmoil "a family affair."

The Redskins trailed 10-9 at halftime, able to muster just three Charley Gogolak field goals. The third was a 44-yarder that cleared the crossbar just as the half ended. Said Gogolak, "That was a momentum factor, everyone was pretty excited in the dressing room."

Mitchell entered the game in the second quarter, but he wasn't the target of a pass until the third. Taylor had returned a punt 58 yards and Washington faced a third and eight at the St. Louis 14. Jurgensen went to Mitchell in the end zone, but the pass was batted away. The Redskins had to settle for yet another field goal and a 12-10 lead. Jim Bakken answered later in the third with a 17-yard boot for a 13-12 Cardinal lead.

On the final play of the third quarter, the Redskins got the break they needed when linebacker John Reger intercepted a pass at the Cards' 16. On the next play, after changing ends of the field, Jurgensen sent Mitchell on a slant pattern. The receiver zipped free of defender Jimmy Burson and Jurgensen laid the ball in right at the goal line. The Redskins had a 19-13 lead.

"Burson was covering me one on one," Mitchell said. "Sonny threw a perfect pass, that always helps."

Less than three minutes later, Jurgy-to-Bobby clicked again. Following a short punt, the quarterback went in for the kill on first down from the Cardinals 44. Mitchell ran what the team called a "shake pattern" and again shook loose of Burson. "I had to go up for the pass," said Mitchell, "but Sonny put it right where I expected it." The result was a 44-yard touchdown pass and a 26-13 lead.

The Cardinals wouldn't go away. They drove 70 yards for a touchdown and then, trailing by six, got the ball back at their own 20 with 6:11 left. Quarterback Charley Johnson showed great patience in his play calling, keeping the ball on the ground with runs by Johnny Roland, who had 109 rushing yards on the day, and moved St. Louis to a third and six at the Washington 47 with 1:45 left.

Johnson flipped a screen pass to fullback Willis Crenshaw. "The screen had been working real well all day," said Huff. He anticipated the play and moved in to tackle Crenshaw.

"I just buried my head," said Huff, "and hit him with all I had." Huff's head found the ball and it popped free at the 38. Jim Shorter recovered for the Redskins, preserving the upset win.

Taylor Prefers To Stay at Halfback

October 26—While Charley Taylor is willing to try new roles with the Redskins, he'd rather stick with his original position.

Taylor played flanker and returned punts during the Redskins' 26-20 win over the previously-undefeated Cardinals last Sunday. His one punt return went for 58 yards and forced St. Louis punter Jim Bakken to kick away from him the rest of the game. While

Taylor said that he was "honored" to be a part of that unit, he'd rather not do it again.

He said that playing flanker was "all right" but he'd rather stay in the backfield. "I missed the crowd," he said, talking about making his way through the masses at the line of scrimmage.

End coach Ray Renfro is unsure how much Taylor will be used at flanker in the future. "The surprise element will, of course, be gone."

10/30/66	**Redskins (5-3) 27, EAGLES (4-4) 13**			60,658	
Was	3	7	3	14	27
Phi	3	3	7	0	13
Phi	FG Baker 15				
Was	FG Gogolak 17				
Was	Looney 1 run (Gogolak kick)				
Phi	FG Baker 37				
Phi	Gros 13 pass from Snead (Baker kick)				
Was	FG Gogolak 28				
Was	Mitchell 4 pass from Jurgensen (Gogolak kick)				
Was	Smith 4 pass from Jurgensen (Gogolak kick)				

Franklin Field—Jim Shorter is called "The Short Man" but he came up big in Washington's 27-13 win over Philadelphia. His interception and 54-yard return in the fourth quarter sparked a burst of 14 points in less than a minute and a half to push the Redskins past the Eagles.

Charlie Gogolak's 28-yard field goal—his second three-pointer of the day—tied the contest midway through the third period. The Redskins had scored to take a 10-3 first-quarter lead on a one-yard run by Joe Don Looney.

The Eagles had answered with two field goals by Sam Baker and a 13-yard touchdown pass from Norm Snead to fullback Earl Gros.

The Eagles were threatening to move into Washington territory when Shorter grabbed Snead's pass at the Redskin 39 and raced down to the seven. Soon after that, Sonny Jurgensen fired a four-yard touchdown pass to Bobby Mitchell and the Redskins took a 20-13 lead.

It didn't take long for Washington to add on an insurance score. Ben Hawkins fumbled the ensuing kickoff and Pat Hodgson recovered at the Eagle two. On third down from the four, Jerry Smith ran a curl pattern and Jurgensen hit him in the breadbasket for the touchdown, making it 27-13 with 3:49 left.

11/6/66	**COLTS (6-2) 37, Redskins (5-4) 10**			60,238	
Was	3	0	7	0	10
Bal	3	20	7	7	37
Was	FG Gogolak 21				
Bal	FG Michaels 22				
Bal	FG Michaels 12				
Bal	Orr 42 pass from Unitas (Michaels kick)				
Bal	Berry 9 pass from Unitas (Michaels kick)				
Bal	FG Michaels 33				
Bal	Berry 1 pass from Unitas (Michaels kick)				
Was	Taylor 20 pass from Jurgensen (Gogolak kick)				
Bal	Wilson 9 pass from Cuozzo (Michaels kick)				

Memorial Stadium—"The Colts are a better team than we are," said Otto Graham after this one, getting no argument from anyone present. Then he added, "But not that much better"—an opinion that ran contrary to the result on the scoreboard showing a 37-10 Baltimore victory.

The Colts ran off 20 points in the second quarter, getting two field goals by Lou Michaels and a pair of Johnny Unitas touchdown passes. Unitas, who passed for 342 yards on the day, took advantage of some substitutions in the Washington secondary to torch that unit throughout the decisive second period.

After Michael's first field goal, receiver Jimmy Orr slammed on the brakes near the goal line and watched his defender speed by

him as he caught Unitas' floater and then stepped across the goal line. Later, he burned rookie cornerback Billy Clay on a 20-yard catch that set up Raymond Berry's nine yard TD reception to make it 20-3. Michael's second three-pointer of the quarter came with three seconds to go in the half.

Berry had another touchdown catch before the visitors posted their only TD of the day on Sonny Jurgensen's 20-yard pass to Charley Taylor. They were threatening to post another that would have made the final a bit more respectable, but Joe Don Looney fumbled while fighting for extra yardage inside the Colt 10 and Baltimore recovered at the eight.

11/13/66	**Cowboys (6-2-1) 31, REDSKINS (5-5) 30**				50,927	
Dal	7	7	7	10	-	31
Was	6	0	17	7	-	30
Was	FG Gogolak 35					
Dal	Meredith 1 run (Villanueva kick)					
Was	FG Gogolak 33					
Dal	Hayes 52 pass from Meredith (Villanueva kick)					
Dal	Hayes 95 pass from Meredith (Villanueva kick)					
Was	Smith 4 pass from Jurgensen (Gogolak kick)					
Was	Taylor 78 pass from Jurgensen (Gogolak kick)					
Was	FG Gogolak 11					
Dal	Reeves 1 run (Villanueva kick)					
Was	Taylor 18 pass from Jurgensen (Gogolak kick)					
Dal	FG Villanueva 20					

D.C. Stadium—Don Meredith trumped Sonny Jurgensen's miracle comeback by leading the Cowboys 85 yards in the final minute and a half to Danny Villanueva's game-winning field goal.

Dallas turned a 7-6 first quarter lead into a 21-6 margin by working what was nearly an unfair advantage, the speed of receiver Bob Hayes. The Olympic sprinter had won the 100-meter dash in the 1964 games thus earning the title "The World's Fastest Human." He got open for a 52-yard touchdown bomb from Meredith in the second quarter—and he was just getting warmed up.

When Dallas got the ball for its initial second half possession at its own five, Hayes ran a complex pattern known as "outrun the cornerback." He did just that, beating Lonnie Sanders, catching Meredith's pass and putting on the afterburners with Sanders in utterly futile pursuit. It looked as though Hayes would need a drag chute to slow down enough to stay in the stadium, but he decelerated in time after blazing across the goal line.

Jurgensen and the Redskins had the answer. They drove to a four-yard touchdown pass from Jurgensen to Jerry Smith and then showed they had a deep threat of their own. Charley Taylor seemed to be headed into triple coverage when Jurgensen unleashed his pass, but the defenders collided into a pile, freeing Taylor to catch the pass and easily complete the 78-yard touchdown play. That pulled the Redskins within a point and, before the third quarter was out, Charlie Gogolak kicked a short field goal to push them in front 23-21.

Dan Reeves regained the lead for Dallas with a one-yard run, but the Redskins responded. With 5:38 remaining, Jurgensen and Taylor connected for six again, this time from 14 yards and Washington went up 30-28. The teams exchanged punts, with Dallas getting the worst of the trade, gaining possession at its own three. The clocked showed 1:30 remaining and no time outs for Dallas.

"I'm thinking: The game is over," Dallas cornerback Mel Renfro said. "We had lost. No question about it. No time. No timeouts."

Meredith didn't share Renfro's sentiments. He quickly got his team out of the hole with a 26-yard pass to Pete Gent and, a few plays later, moved the Cowboys into field goal position with another toss to Gent, this one covering 25 yards to the Washington 33. Villanueva had a good shot at a field goal from there, but it got considerably easier for him on the next play when Meredith scrambled for six yards and linebacker John Reger committed a foolish personal foul, hitting Meredith when the quarterback was well out of bounds. Villanueva kicked the 20-yard game-winner on the next play with 15 seconds left.

11/20/66	**BROWNS (7-3) 14, Redskins (5-6) 3**			78,466	
Was	0	0	3	0	3
Cle	7	0	7	0	14
Cle	Green 5 pass from Ryan (Groza kick)				
Cle	Kelly 56 run (Groza kick)				
Was	FG Gogolak 20				

Cleveland Municipal Stadium—The usual suspects—key fumbles, dropped passes, critical interceptions, and missed field goals—were the main culprits in Washington's sluggish 14-3 loss to the Browns.

An interception at the Brown 23 by Cleveland's Ernie Kellerman killed a Redskin scoring threat and launched a touchdown march for the Browns. They moved to the Washington five, where Frank Ryan's pass intended for a wide-open Gary Collins hit the goal post. On the next play Ryan avoided the goal line obstacle, calling for fullback Ernie Green to run a flag pattern. The quarterback hit him for a 7-0 lead for the home team.

The Redskins' day was summed up in the second quarter. From the Cleveland 27, Bobby Mitchell broke open and Jurgensen's game-tying pass was right on the money. Mitchell dropped it. Trying to salvage something, Charlie Gogolak was sent out to kick a field goal, but his effort from 39 yards smacked off of an upright and it remained 7-0.

In the third quarter, Sam Huff guessed wrong on a blitz and Leroy Kelly scooted through the opening that the linebacker created, going 56 yards for a 14-0 lead. Gogolak connected on a 20-yard field goal later on in the third, but that was all the scoring the Redskins could muster. Their last good chance to get back into the game ended early in the final period when rookie running back Tom Barrington fumbled and the Browns recovered at their own 18.

11/27/66	**REDSKINS (6-6) 72, Giants (1-9-1) 41**			50,439	
NYG	0	14	14	13	41
Was	13	21	14	24	72
Was	Whitfield 5 pass from Jurgensen (kick blocked)				
Was	Whitfield 63 run (Gogolak kick)				
Was	Owens 62 rumble return (Gogolak kick)				
NYG	Jacobs 6 run (Gogolak kick)				
Was	Whitfield 1 run (Gogolak kick)				
Was	Looney 9 run (Gogolak kick)				
NYG	Wood 1 run (Gogolak kick)				
NYG	Morrison 41 pass from Wood (Gogolak kick)				
Was	Taylor 32 pass from Jurgensen (Gogolak kick)				
NYG	Jones 40 pass from Wood (Gogolak kick)				
Was	Taylor 74 pass from Jurgensen (Gogolak kick)				
Was	Harris 52 punt return (Gogolak kick)				
Was	Owens 60 pass interception (Gogolak kick)				
NYG	Thomas 18 pass from Kennedy (Gogolak kick)				
NYG	Lewis 1 run (Gogolak kick)				
Was	Mitchell 45 run (Gogolak kick)				
Was	FG Gogolak 29				

D.C. Stadium—The Redskins scored on offense, on defense, on special teams, on the ground and through the air in racking up the highest single-game scoring total ever in a regular season NFL game. In a losing effort, the Giants scored 41, making the combined total of 113 points another league record.

It started off tamely enough when Brig Owens intercepted a pass by Giants quarterback Tom Kennedy, setting up a five-yard touchdown pass from Jurgensen to AD Whitfield. It was the start of a career day for Whitfield, a backup running back as he scored three touchdowns. His second one made it 13-0 (Charlie Gogolak

had missed the extra point after the first TD) going into the second quarter.

The Redskins racked up three more touchdowns before halftime. Hanburger barreled into Kennedy, forcing a fumble that Owens recovered and returned 62 yards into the end zone. Whitfield and the player he backed up, Joe Don Looney, scored the other two. The Giants added two scores of their own and it was 34-14 at halftime.

The third quarter was Taylor's time to shine. The receiver scored on Jurgensen touchdown passes of 32 and 74 yards. Jurgy's passing line on the day belies the high scoring nature of the contest—ten of 16 for 145 yards. For his part, Taylor was glad to get on the board, having dropped a sure TD pass earlier in the game.

The Giants matched Washington's scoring in the third period with Gary Wood throwing a pair of touchdown passes of his own. That made it 48-28 going into the fourth quarter. The Redskins defense was certainly capable of blowing such a lead.

But there were more points to be scored by the Redskins. Ricky Harris pushed the Redskins over the 50-point mark when he returned a punt 52 yards for a touchdown. Then Owens stepped in front of a pass from Wood and went all the way with a 60-yard interception return. That touchdown broke the team record for most points scored in a game: the 59 they had scored against the Boston Yanks in 1948. The Giants scored two more touchdowns pushing the total for both teams over 100 points. Just for fun, Otto Graham lined wide receiver Mitchell up at his old running back spot and Mitchell scooted 45 yards for the Redskins' tenth and final touchdown of the day. To recap, they scored a touchdown almost every way you can: four running, three passing and one each on a punt, fumble, and interception return. They also got nine extra points and a field goal.

Oh, yes, the field goal—a very interesting sidebar to the game.

Either thinking it was third down or just wanting to get the heck off the field, Kennedy threw the ball out of bounds on fourth down with nine seconds left. Gogolak trotted onto the field and kicked a 29-yard field goal. After the game, Redskins coach Otto Graham said that he just wanted to give Gogolak some practice. Some accounts said the players had pleaded with Graham to go for breaking 70 points. The best story, though, is that Sam Huff, still mad at the Giants for trading him two years earlier, yelled out "Field goal team, field goal team" himself in hopes that the unit would run on the field in the confusion and rub some salt in the Giants' wounds. No matter why, the three points made the final 72-41.

(Editor's Note: About 11,000 NFL games have been played since this one and, despite rule changes designed to favor the offense and increase scoring, both the Redskins' 72 points and the combined 113 still stand as NFL records.)

Nov 28

Graham Apologizes for Late Field Goal
Final tally against Giants set scoring record for Redskins

12/11/66	**Redskins (7-6) 34, COWBOYS (9-3-1) 31**			64,198	
Was	0	10	7	17	34
Dal	0	7	10	14	31
Dal	Perkins 20 run (Villanueva kick)				
Was	FG Gogolak 42				
Was	Reger recovered blocked punt in end zone (Gogolak kick)				
Dal	FG Villanueva 26				
Dal	Hayes 23 pass from Morton (Villanueva kick)				
Was	Mitchell 11 pass from Jurgensen (Gogolak kick)				

Dal	Reeves 67 run (Villanueva kick)
Was	Smith 11 pass from Jurgensen (Gogolak kick)
Dal	Perkins 6 run (Villanueva kick)
Was	Taylor 65 pass from Jurgensen (Gogolak kick)
Was	FG Gogolak 29

Cotton Bowl—Charlie Gogolak kicked a 29-yard field goal with four seconds left to cap a wild fourth quarter and give the Redskins a stirring 34-31 win over Dallas.

The Cowboys put together a second-quarter drive to take a 7-0 lead on Don Perkins' 20-yard touchdown run, but the Redskins came right back thanks largely to Carl Kammerer. Midway through the second, the defensive end recovered a fumble, setting up a Gogolak field goal to make it 7-3. Later in the period Kammerer broke through to block Danny Villanueva's punt in the end zone and John Reger was right there to fall on the ball for the touchdown, giving the visitors the halftime lead.

After Villanueva kicked a field goal to tie the game at 10, the Cowboys drove 86 yards to reclaim the lead on Craig Morton's 23-yard touchdown pass to Bob Hayes. Washington came right back with a drive of its own. A 41-yard run by A. D. Whitfield got the Redskins down to the Dallas 11 and from there Sonny Jurgensen threw a touchdown pass to Bobby Mitchell. The game was tied at 17 going into the fourth quarter.

The Cowboys made Washington play catch-up as Dan Reeves shook a tackle and went 67 yards for a touchdown. That's the kind of game Jurgensen likes and his 53-yard bomb to Charley Taylor led to his 11-yard scoring toss to Jerry Smith to even it up at 24.

It was Dallas' turn and they drove 72 yards, the last six on Perkins' second scoring run and recaptured the lead. No problem for Jurgensen, who promptly went long to Taylor again, this time for 65 yards and a touchdown with 3:11 remaining.

All the Cowboys needed was a tie to clinch the Eastern Division title, but they couldn't get it. Washington got the ball again and ex-Cowboy Whitfield busted loose for 30 yards to get his team in field goal range. Jurgensen stood next to the official, his hands on his hips, and watched the clock tick down to eight seconds before calling timeout. Gogolak trotted in and his game-winner from 29 yards was perfect.

12/18/66	**Eagles (9-5) 37, REDSKINS (7-7) 28**			50,405
Phi	7	3	7	20	37
Was	7	7	7	7	28

Phi	Woodeshick 1 run (Baker kick)
Was	Smith 18 pass from Jurgensen (Gogolak kick)
Phi	FG Baker 47
Was	Smith 28 pass from Jurgensen (Gogolak kick)
Phi	Retzlaff 24 pass from Hill (Baker kick)
Was	Taylor 11 pass from Jurgensen (Gogolak kick)
Phi	Woodeshick 1 run (kick failed)
Phi	Matson 3 run (Baker kick)
Was	Taylor 26 pass from Jurgensen (Gogolak kick)
Phi	Wells 60 fumble return (Baker kick)

D.C. Stadium—The Redskins were dressed in their home burgundy jerseys, but red suits with white trim would have been more appropriate as they played Santa a week early in dropping this one to the Eagles 37-28.

The Redskins led 14-10 at halftime, having scored on two touchdown passes from Sonny Jurgensen to Jerry Smith. Early in the third quarter, Jurgensen tried to go to Smith again, but safety Joe Scarpati swooped in front of the receiver to intercept the pass. Right after Scarpati's return to the Washington 24, backup quarterback King Hill threw to tight end Pete Retzlaff for the touchdown.

Washington came right back with a 74-yard march that culminated in Jurgensen's 11-yard TD pass to Charley Taylor, who had badly beaten cornerback Al Nelson. Charlie Gogolak's extra point put the Redskins back ahead 21-17

The fourth quarter, though, belonged to the Eagles. Jurgensen fumbled at his own 20 and Philly turned that miscue into a one-yard scoring blast by fullback Tom Woodeshick. Then defensive end John Hultz batted a Jurgensen pass and Fred Whittingham intercepted at the Washington 45. Six plays later, Ollie Matson beat Chris Hanburger to the flag for a three-yard touchdown run and the Eagles led 30-21.

The Redskins managed to put a scare in the Eagles when Jurgensen again connected with Taylor for a touchdown and then recovered an onside kick with a minute and a half left. Needing just a field goal, the Redskins started at the Philadelphia 44. The drive never got started as Taylor caught a first down pass but fumbled. Linebacker Harold Wells recovered and, aided by some uninspired tackling attempts, went 60 yards for the final score.

Dec 19

Taylor NFL's Top Receiver
Midseason switch to wide receiver spurred move to top of league in catches

---

1967
Head Coach: Otto Graham
Record: 5-6-3, Third in NFL Capitol Division

Honors: Chris Hanburger Pro Bowl; Len Hauss Pro Bowl; Sonny Jurgensen Pro Bowl; Jerry Smith Pro Bowl, All-NFL; Charley Taylor Pro Bowl, All-NFL

Graham: Better Year From 'Smarter' Team

Aug 29—Otto Graham said today that he was "far more encouraged" about the prospects for his 1968 team than he was about last year.

Graham's expectations are raised due to an improvement in both brains and brawn.

"We're a much smarter team and therefore stronger," said Graham. Having spent a year in his system, the coach reasoned, the team will know how to react.

Another, more tangible reason Graham believes Washington can improve on its 1967 record of 7-7 is an improved running game. The Redskins invested their first-round pick, the 13th overall, on back Ray McDonald. He's already a bruiser at 230 pounds and Graham would like to see him add about 10 more pounds. Joe Don Looney and Steve Thurlow will carry a share of the load as well.

9/17/67	EAGLES (1-0) 35, Redskins (0-1) 24			60,709
Was	10	7	7	0	24
Phi	14	7	7	7	35
Was	Love 96 kickoff return (Gogolak kick)
Phi	Ballman 59 pass from Snead (Baker kick)
Was	FG Gogolak 30
Phi	Ballman 10 pass from Snead (Baker kick)
Was	Looney 5 run (Gogolak kick)
Phi	Snead 1 run (Baker kick)
Was	Smith 4 pass from Jurgensen (Gogolak kick)
Phi	Woodeschick 40 run (Baker kick)
Phi	Woodeschick 1 run (Baker kick)

Franklin Field—The Redskins got off to a promising start when rookie John Love took the season-opening kickoff back 96 yards for a touchdown, but the Eagles eventually outgunned Washington to come away with a 35-24 win.

Love took the kickoff in front of the goal post at the four and found open ground straight ahead. He rolled down the center of the field untouched to give Washington a 7-0 lead 18 seconds into the season.

The Eagles tied it up two minutes later when Norm Snead threw 59 yards to Gary Ballman for a touchdown, capping a quick 80-yard drive. Washington retook the lead when Snead fumbled and the Redskins recovered, setting up a 30-yard field goal by Charlie Gogolak, who had an injured kicking leg. It was Gogolak's only successful attempt of the day as he missed another and had two blocked, both from short range. Love tried an 11-yard field goal in the fourth quarter and missed as well.

Philadelphia got the lead back before the first quarter ended on Snead's second scoring pass to Ballman. For the second and third quarters, the lead seesawed back and forth with the Redskins taking their last lead in the third quarter when Sonny Jurgensen hit tight end Jerry Smith with a four-yard TD pass.

But Philly's Tom Woodeschick scored the game's last two touchdowns to take away the win. The first was a 40-yard burst up the middle on a draw play that totally fooled the Washington defense. In the fourth quarter, he followed up a 68-yard Snead pass to Ben Hawkins by plunging over from the one.

9/24/67	Redskins (1-1) 30, SAINTS (0-2) 10			74,937
Was	6	14	0	10	30
NO	3	7	0	0	10
Was	McDonald 1 run (kick blocked)

NO	FG Durkee 27
NO	Roberts 36 pass from Kilmer (Durkee kick)
Was	McDonald 36 run (Love kick)
Was	Taylor 40 pass from Jurgensen (Love kick)
Was	McDonald 15 run (Love kick)
Was	FG Love 30

Tulane Stadium—Rookie running back Ray McDonald ran for 98 yards and three touchdowns to spur the Redskins to the win.

McDonald's first scoring run came on a one-yard blast. The conversion, however, was blocked and the Redskins led 6-0.

New Orleans took a lead on a field goal and a 36-yard touchdown pass from Billy Kilmer to Walter "Flea" Roberts. But that was it for the Saints' offense, as Kilmer and his second-half replacement Gary Cuozzo were harassed by the Washington defense, led by middle linebacker Sam Huff.

McDonald gave the Redskins the lead for good in the second quarter by brushing off attempted tackles by five would-be defenders in going 36 yards to make the score 14-10. They expanded their lead before halftime with a 40-yard touchdown pass from Sonny Jurgensen to Charley Taylor.

The visitors put the game away in the fourth quarter with McDonald's third TD run—this one from 15 yards out—and a 30-yard field goal by fill-in kicker John Love.

McDonald bashed his way to 98 yards on 15 carries. Washington rushed for 158 yards as a team and Jurgensen picked up 211 yards through the air.

10/1/67	REDSKINS (2-1) 38, Giants (1-2) 34			50,266
NYG	10	3	7	14	34
Was	3	14	7	14	38
NYG	Koy 22 run (Murdock kick)
NYG	FG Murdock 30
Was	FG Love 27
Was	Love 14 pass from Jurgensen (Love kick)
Was	Jurgensen 1 run (Love kick)
NYG	FG Murdock 29
Was	Mitchell 6 run (Love kick)
NYG	Jones 35 pass from Tarkenton (Murdock kick)
Was	Smith 11 pass from Jurgensen (Love kick)
NYG	Jones 68 pass from Koy (Murdock kick)
Was	Love 2 fumble recovery (Love kick)
NYG	Thomas 11 pass from Tarkenton

D.C. Stadium—Redskins rookie flanker and fill-in kicker John Love scored 20 points on a pair of touchdowns, five extra points, and a field goal. His final touchdown on a fumble recovery provided what proved to be the winning points as Washington defeated the Giants 38-34.

Love scored his team's first 10 points on a field goal, a 14-yard touchdown pass from Sonny Jurgensen and the subsequent extra point. That run tied the game at 10 and the Redskins soon claimed the lead when Jurgensen snuck over from the one to make the score 17-10.

Washington's Bobby Mitchell, a receiver, started the game at running back, giving some punch to the Washington ground attack as well as providing Love a spot in the lineup. Considering Love's performance and Mitchell's 115 yards rushing, the lineup shuffling had to be considered a stroke of genius on the part of Washington coach Otto Graham.

The Redskins led 24-20 entering a wild fourth quarter. They stretched their lead when Jurgensen hit Jerry Smith for 11 yards and a touchdown to make it 31-20. That margin lasted eight seconds. Running back Ernie Koy pulled up and threw to receiver Homer Jones for a 68-yard touchdown to pull New York back within four.

It appeared for a moment that the Giants had repelled a Washington bid to expand its lead again when Les Murdock intercepted a Jurgensen pass at the Giants' two, but Murdock fumbled and Love recovered for a touchdown. Fran Tarkenton's 11-yard touchdown pass to Aaron Thomas was rendered meaningless.

10/8/67	**Cowboys (3-1) 17, REDSKINS (2-2) 14**			50,566	
Dal	0	0	10	7	17
Was	0	7	0	7	14
Was	McDonald 1 run (Love kick)				
Dal	Rentzel 25 pass from Meredith (Villanueva kick)				
Dal	FG Villanueva 27				
Was	Taylor 8 pass from Jurgensen (Love kick)				
Dal	Reeves 36 pass from Meredith (Villanueva kick)				

D.C. Stadium—The Redskins wound up on the wrong end of another thriller with the Cowboys. As has happened so often in the brief but intense series between the two teams, having the lead in the final seconds proved to be more of a curse than an advantage.

After an early flurry of turnovers by both teams, the Redskins got on the board first with a 78-yard second-quarter TD drive. Jurgensen threw to running back A.D. Whitfield for 28 yards and to receiver John Love for 33 and a first down at the Dallas two. Fullback Ray McDonald bowled over from the one and it was 7-0 Washington.

It stayed that way into the third quarter until Meredith hit receiver Lance Rentzel with a 29-yard touchdown pass to knot the score at seven. A Dallas field goal later in the period gave the Cowboys a three-point lead held deep into the fourth quarter.

Then Ricky Harris took a Dallas punt and returned it 41 yards to the Dallas 24. When a series of penalties set up a fourth and two at the 26 with 1:57 left, Jurgensen convinced coach Otto Graham to eschew a tying field goal attempt and go for the first down. Sonny made a genius out of Otto—no small feat—by zipping a pass between two defenders to Mitchell for a first down at the 13. Two plays later, Taylor shook his defender and caught a dart from Jurgensen to send the crowd into premature delirium with 1:10 left.

The Redskins had scored too quickly. Moving from the Dallas 29, Meredith hit Rentzel to get into Redskins territory and then for six more to get to the Washington 36. Dallas faced fourth and four from there with 26 seconds left. The crowd roared, exhorting the defense to make one more play. It didn't happen.

Running back Dan Reeves delayed for a moment before slipping past linebacker Chris Hanburger. All Meredith had to do was recover from the astonishment of seeing Reeves so wide open and hit him with the pass at the 10. The back easily strode into the end zone with ten seconds left. The crowd's roar instantly became stunned silence.

Taylor couldn't get out of bounds in Dallas territory in time to allow for a tying field goal attempt and the Cowboys got the win.

10/15/67	**FALCONS (0-4-1) 20, Redskins (2-2-1) 20**			56,538	
Was	0	7	7	6	20
Atl	0	14	0	6	20
Atl	Coffey 20 run (Traynham kick)				
Was	Taylor 9 pass from Jurgensen (Owens kick)				
Atl	Martin 13 pass from Johnson (Traynham kick)				
Was	Smith 3 pass from Jurgensen (Owens kick)				
Atl	FG Traynham 31				
Was	Mitchell 24 pass from Jurgensen (kick blocked)				
Atl	FG Traynham 31				

Atlanta Stadium—A blocked extra point following the Redskins' go-ahead touchdown with 40 seconds left opened the window for

the Falcons to tie it with a field goal. They climbed through that window when Wade Traynham kicked a 31-yard field goal on the last play to knot the score at 20.

Washington trailed 14-7 at halftime. They had tied it at 7-7 in the second quarter when Charley Taylor hauled in a nine-yard touchdown pass from Sonny Jurgensen. But Atlanta took the lead with a touchdown before halftime.

Again the Redskins battled back, getting another Jurgensen touchdown pass— this one to Jerry Smith—to deadlock the game at 14 going into the fourth quarter. A Traynham field goal regained the lead for Atlanta.

The Redskins took over at their own 17 facing a 17-14 deficit late in the fourth quarter. Sonny Jurgensen and Bobby Mitchell teamed up to torch the Atlanta secondary. The quarterback and flanker connected on passes good for 24 and 28 yards to get into Atlanta territory. Then with 40 seconds left, the two connected again, this time on a 24-yard touchdown pass to put the Redskins up by three.

Atlanta linebacker Tommy Nobis then blocked the attempted point after and the Falcons remained within a field goal. They got it from Traynham, whose 31-yarder at the gun split the uprights.

10/22/67	**Redskins (2-2-2) 28, RAMS (3-1-2) 28**			55,381	
Was	7	7	7	7	28
LA	0	14	7	7	28
Was	Taylor 86 pass from Jurgensen (Absher kick)				
LA	Bass 2 run (Gossett kick)				
LA	Snow 61 pass from Gabriel (Gossett kick)				
Was	Smith 14 pass from Jurgensen (Absher kick)				
Was	Smith 21 pass from Jurgensen (Absher kick)				
LA	Josephson 4 run (Gossett kick)				
Was	Smith 39 pass from Jurgensen (Absher kick)				
LA	Casey 6 pass from Gabriel (Gossett kick)				

LA Memorial Coliseum—For the third straight game, the Redskins were unable to hold a late lead as the Rams scored with just over a minute left to tie the game at 28-28.

The teams battled back and forth all day as they combined for nearly 800 yards of total offense. Sonny Jurgensen threw two first-half touchdown passes as the teams were tied 14-14 at halftime. One of Jurgensen's passes was an 86-yard bomb to Charley Taylor while the other went to tight end Jerry Smith and covered a more pedestrian 14 yards.

The teams exchanged touchdowns in the third quarter. Jurgensen and Smith hooked up again for one from 21 yards. Les Josephson evened it up again by powering four yards into the end zone.

With the score tied at 21 in the fourth quarter, Rickie Harris fielded a punt at the Washington 10 and returned it 51 yards to the LA 39. On the very next play, Jurgensen and Smith combined on their third touchdown pass of the day to give Washington a 28-21 lead.

But Rams quarterback Roman Gabriel brought the Rams back, connecting with receiver Bernie Casey on a six-yard touchdown pass with 1:05 left in the game to produce the 28-28 result.

Oct 25

Joe Don Gone
*Redskins waive Looney after
second straight missed practice*

10/29/67	Colts (5-0-2) 17, REDSKINS (2-3-2) 13			50,574	
Bal	0	7	0	10	17
Was	3	7	0	3	13
Was	FG Mingo 42				
Bal	Hawkins 22 pass from Unitas (Michaels kick)				
Was	Mitchell 16 pass from Jurgensen (Mingo kick)				
Was	FG Mingo 35				
Bal	Matte 7 run (Michaels kick)				
Bal	FG Michaels 30				

D.C. Stadium—In a variation on a theme, it was the Redskins with late opportunities to come from behind to steal a win, but an inability to hang on to the ball combined with a controversial call by the officials allowed Baltimore to escape with a 17-13 victory.

The Redskins took a 13-7 lead in the third quarter when Brig Owens stole the ball away from the Colts' Tom Matte, setting up a 35-yard field goal by the newly-acquired Gene Mingo. The home team still held that lead midway through the fourth quarter, but the Colts came back by scoring ten points in a six-minute span. Johnny Unitas led a 65-yard drive that included just one pass completion, a 23-yarder to tight end John Macke. The drive's key play, however, was a called passing play. Finding nobody open on third and five at his own 40, Unitas took off running to his left. He was tackled on the Washington 48, and when the Redskins' Ron Snidow decided to make sure the quarterback was down, Washington was flagged for a 15-yard personal foul. Three plays later, Matte rolled through would-be tacklers for a seven-yard touchdown run to give Baltimore a 14-13 lead.

After a Lou Michaels field goal with 3:48 boosted Baltimore's lead to four points, the Redskins had two opportunities to reclaim the lead. Both ended with the ball on the ground. Sonny Jurgensen apparently had given the Redskins a first down after hitting Bobby Mitchell for a nine-yard gain to the Colts 49, but three Colt defenders crunched Mitchell and the ball popped loose. In the scramble for the ball, it appeared that Mitchell had reclaimed possession, but the officials saw it otherwise; they awarded the ball to the Colts.

The defense held and Baltimore punted, giving Washington a last-gasp chance from its own 10 with 1:15 left to play. The heart started beating a bit stronger when Jurgensen found John Love for a 23-yard gain, but it stopped altogether when Colts safety Rick Volk forced Love to fumble. Lenny Lyles recovered for Baltimore and the Colts escaped with a 17-13 win.

11/3/67	Cardinals (5-3) 27, REDSKINS (2-4-2) 21			50,480	
StL	0	10	3	14	27
Was	7	7	0	7	21
Was	Owens 45 interception return (Mingo kick)				
StL	Conrad 11 pass from Hart (Bakken kick)				
StL	FG Bakken 35				
Was	Jurgensen 1 run (Mingo kick)				
StL	FG Bakken 17				
StL	Hart 1 run (Bakken kick)				
StL	Roland 1 run (Bakken kick)				
Was	Mitchell 65 pass from Jurgensen (Mingo kick)				

D.C. Stadium—Two Redskins turnovers keyed a 17-0 St. Louis run in the second half to rally the Cardinals to a 27-21 victory.

Washington had used a takeaway of its own to grab a 7-0 lead in the first quarter. Brig Owens picked off a Jim Hart pass and went all the way, 45 yards for a 7-0 lead. After the Cardinals had taken the lead with 10 second-quarter points, A. D. Whitfield set up Washington's second TD with a 44-yard run. Sonny Jurgensen scored it by sneaking over from the one and the Skins led 14-10 at halftime.

Jim Bakken's 17-yard field goal accounted for the only third-quarter scoring and Washington still held a 14-13 lead going into the third quarter. The home team was threatening to expand the margin but safety Larry Wilson intercepted Jurgensen's pass at the St. Louis one and returned it 44 yards. On the next play, Jim

Hart went to tight end Jackie Smith for 54 yards to the one. Hart took it over from there to put the Cards on top 20-14.

Then John Love fumbled a Cardinal punt and Clyde Williams recovered for St. Louis at the Washington 24. Eight plays later, John Roland expanded the lead to 27-14 with a one-yard run.

That rendered a 65-yard Jurgensen to Bobby Mitchell touchdown pass—a catch that the wide-open Mitchell juggled for 15 yards before securing—nothing more than a highlight reel spot.

Graham Blasts Lack of Hustle

Nov 6—Otto Graham today took a shot at some unnamed Redskins for, in his view, failing to give a full effort in a 27-21 loss to the St. Louis Cardinals.

"What worries me," Graham said, "is that I don't think our 40 players gave as much as the Cardinals' 40 players did."

He did not name any names, but he hinted that we might have a clue this coming contract season.

"If you see a player laying down on the job you can't condone it," said Graham. "You cannot fire them unless you can get somebody to replace them but you can remember them next season when it comes time to talk salary."

One player Graham isn't blasting for his play Sunday is kicker Charlie Gogolak, but that's only because the team's top draft pick in 1966 didn't play for the seventh straight game due to a lingering leg injury.

When asked when Gogolak might return, the frustrated coach replied, "I have no idea."

He confirmed that Gogolak has a no-cut contract. "Yes, I am afraid they—the Redskins—gave him one before I got here."

There is frustration growing on many levels as the Redskins, expected to improve on their 7-7 mark last year, sit at 2-4-2.

11/12/67	REDSKINS (3-4-2) 31, 49ers (5-4) 28			50,236	
SF	7	7	7	7	28
Was	0	3	14	14	31
SF	Brodie 14 run (Davis kick)				
SF	Randle 10 pass from Brodie (Davis kick)				
Was	FG Mingo 19				
Was	Smith 2 pass from Jurgensen (Mingo kick)				
Was	Allen 7 run (Mingo kick)				
SF	Willard 2 run (Davis kick)				
Was	Allen 16 pass from Jurgensen (Mingo kick)				
SF	Willard 7 run (Davis kick)				
Was	Smith 15 pass from Jurgensen (Mingo kick)				

D.C. Stadium—Sonny Jurgensen threw a 15-yard touchdown pass to Jerry Smith midway through the fourth quarter to pull the Redskins past San Francisco 31-28.

Washington scored two touchdowns in a 38-second span in the third quarter, both the result of San Francisco turnovers. Linebacker Ed Breding recovered a Ken Willard fumble at the Niners' 26 on the first play from scrimmage after halftime. Seven plays later on fourth down from the two, Jurgensen threaded the needle to Smith to pull Washington to within 14-10.

San Francisco's Doug Cunningham fumbled the ensuing kickoff and kicker Gene Mingo recovered at the visitors' 29 yards. On the first snap, Jurgensen threw to Bobby Mitchell and Kermit Alexander was flagged for pass interference, putting the ball at the seven. Gerry Allen took it into the end zone on the next play, putting his team in the lead 17-14.

That margin lasted until Willard scored for San Francisco on a two-yard run later in the third. Then Allen tallied his second touchdown early in the fourth quarter on a 16-yard pass from Jurgensen. The 49ers came right back, getting another scoring run from Willard—this one from seven yards—to go up 28-24.

A Jurgensen-to-Smith connection jump-started the Redskins' game-winning drive: a 72-yard, 10-play march that ended with

Smith's catching Jurgensen's pass to cover the last 15 yards with just over seven minutes left. San Francisco was unable to move the ball on two subsequent possessions and Washington walked off with the 31-28 win.

11/19/67	**Washington (4-4-2) 27, DALLAS (7-3) 20**				75,538
Was	0	14	6	7	27
Dal	0	6	0	14	20
Was	Smith 29 pass from Jurgensen (Mingo kick)				
Dal	Rentzel 6 pass from Meredith (run failed)				
Was	Smith 4 pass from Jurgensen (Mingo kick)				
Was	Whitfield 14 pass from Jurgensen (kick failed)				
Was	Mitchell 5 pass from Jurgensen (Mingo kick)				
Dal	Clarke 15 pass from Morton (Villanueva kick)				
Dal	Norman 7 pass from Morton (Villanueva kick)				

Cotton Bowl—Four touchdown passes by Sonny Jurgensen staked Washington to a 27-6 lead, but it took a Paul Krause interception in the waning moments to preserve the win for the Skins.

The Redskins got on the board first following a 25-yard punt by Dallas. Jurgensen got excellent pass protection on a third and seven play from the Dallas 29 and was able to watch tight end Jerry Smith breaking free from safety Mike Gaechter on a post pattern and deliver a perfect strike for a touchdown. Dallas got the touchdown back on a touchdown pass from Don Meredith to Lance Rentzel, but failed to even up the score as a bad snap aborted the point after attempt.

Dallas got the ball back and Rentzel was open again, having beaten safety Rickie Harris. Meredith's pass was good, but the receiver bobbled the ball. It popped over Rentzel's shoulder, and Harris accepted the gift, intercepting the pass at the Washington eight. That turnover prevented a Dallas score; the next two Cowboy giveaways set up Redskins touchdowns.

Jim Shorter picked off Meredith with two minutes left in the first half and returned the ball to the Washington 49. Jurgensen completed three straight passes to the Dallas four. From there, Smith again broke free of Gaechter's coverage and caught the touchdown pass to widen the Redskins' margin to 14-6 at the half.

In the third quarter, Dallas receiver Bob Hayes caught a pass for a 25-yard gain, but fumbled it away to the Redskins. Washington drove 75 yards for a touchdown, with Jurgensen passing to running back A. D. Whitfield for gains of 29 yards and then 14 for the score. The point after was blocked and the Redskins led 20-6.

Dallas marched right down the field, driving to the Washington four. Hayes had a half step on Washington defender Dick Smith, but Smith made a spectacular, diving interception in the end zone, taking the ball just out of the receiver's grasp. The Cowboys regained possession with an interception of their own, but were stopped on a fourth down play at their own 12. Washington regained possession.

Jurgensen completed passes to Bobby Mitchell for 29 and Jerry Smith for 13 to get to the Dallas 15. From there, Mitchell got free on a curl pattern and snared Jurgensen's pass just inside the left flag to give the Redskins a 27-6 lead.

Craig Morton replaced the ailing and ineffective Meredith and provided a spark to make a game out of it. After Morton threw one TD pass in the fourth quarter, Dallas recovered an onside kick and racked up another touchdown in less than two minutes. But Krause killed Dallas' hopes by intercepting a Morton pass with 1:13 left to play.

11/26/67	**BROWNS (7-4) 42, Redskins (4-5-2) 37**				72,798
Was	0	17	7	13	**37**
Cle	14	14	7	7	**42**
Cle	Kelly 42 run (Groza kick)				
Cle	Brewer 70 interception return (Groza kick)				
Was	Taylor 23 pass from Jurgensen (Mingo kick)				

Was	FG Mingo 27				
Cle	Ward 104 kickoff return (Groza kick)				
Cle	Warfield 40 pass from Ryan (Groza kick)				
Was	Taylor 15 pass from Jurgensen (Mingo kick)				
Cle	Green 1 run (Mingo kick)				
Was	Allen 1 run (Mingo kick)				
Cle	Kelly 21 run (Mingo kick)				
Was	Mitchell 48 pass from Jurgensen (Mingo kick)				
Was	Allen 1 run (kick failed)				

Cleveland Municipal Stadium—The Redskins were in this one for about 20 seconds—about the amount of time it took for Carl Ward to return a kickoff all the way, sealing the 42-37 win for Cleveland.

They were trailing the Browns 14-0 after the first quarter, but had rallied to within four points midway through the second on a 23-yard touchdown pass from Sonny Jurgensen to Charlie Taylor and a 27-yard Gene Mingo field goal.

That was the end of the rally. Ward took Mingo's kickoff four yards deep in the end zone and didn't stop until he had gone a team-record 104 yards for the touchdown. Soon after that, the home team's Frank Ryan passed 40 yards to Paul Warfield for another touchdown. Suddenly, it was 28-10.

The Redskins played catch up the rest of the way. Washington pulled within 11 a couple of times, first on another Jurgensen-to-Taylor touchdown connection in the second quarter and later on a one-yard run by Gerry Allen in the third quarter. But the Browns responded each time and led 42-24 in the fourth quarter. Two late Redskins scores made the final more respectable but did not alter the outcome.

12/3/67	**REDSKINS (4-5-3) 35, Eagles (5-6-1) 35**				50,461
Phi	7	7	21	0	35
Was	0	14	14	7	35
Phi	Ballman 3 pass from Snead (Baker kick)				
Was	Taylor 7 pass from Jurgensen (Mingo kick)				
Was	Smith 18 pass from Jurgensen (Mingo kick)				
Phi	Hawkins 69 pass from Snead (Baker kick)				
Phi	Woodeschick 13 pass from Snead (Baker kick)				
Phi	Woodeschick 10 run (Baker kick)				
Phi	Hawkins 63 pass from Snead (Baker kick)				
Was	Mitchell 10 pass from Jurgensen (Mingo kick)				
Was	Smith 27 pass from Jurgensen (Mingo kick)				
Was	Larson 3 run (Mingo kick)				

D.C. Stadium—The Redskins came all the way back from a 35-14 deficit to tie the Eagles at 35-35. They had a shot to win it, but Gene Mingo's 36-yard field goal attempt went wide right with seven seconds left.

Washington had built a 14-7 lead on the strength of two Sonny Jurgensen touchdown passes—one to Charlie Taylor, the other to Jerry Smith—but Philadelphia scored four unanswered touchdowns in the second and third quarters and the home team held a 35-14 lead. Norm Snead threw for three of those touchdowns, one to running back Tom Woodeschick and two to receiver Ben Hawkins. Woodeschick tallied the other on a 10-yard run.

Then Jurgensen and the Redskins went to work. They got two touchdowns back before the third quarter ended, both on Jurgensen passes. The quarterback, who was 30 of 50 passing for 366 yards, first found Bobby Mitchell from ten yards out and then Jerry Smith from 27 to pull Washington within 35-28 as the fourth quarter started.

The offensive fireworks diminished in the final period, but the Redskins got what they needed when Pete Larson ran three yards for the tying score with 1:55 left in the game. Washington got the ball back and were in position to take the lead, but Mingo's field goal went awry. The Redskins had to settle for their third tie of the season.

12/10/67	**Redskins (5-5-3) 15, STEELERS (3-9-1) 10**				22,251
Was	0	9	0	6	15
Pit	0	3	0	7	10

Was	Whitfield 2 run (Alford kick)
Was	Safety, blocked punt rolled out of end zone
Pit	FG Clark 20
Pit	Hilton 3 pass from Nix (Clark kick)
Was	Taylor 33 pass from Jurgensen (kick failed)

Pitt Stadium—In a driving rainstorm, Sonny Jurgensen had his worst day of the year, but still managed to find Charlie Taylor for the winning score late in the game as the Redskins beat the Steelers 15-10.

While the offense struggled, the Washington defense and special teams kept things going. After a two-yard touchdown run by A. D. Whitfield, Ed Breding blocked a Pittsburgh punt and the Redskins were awarded a safety when the ball rolled out of the end zone. Safety Paul Krause helped hold the home team at bay by intercepting rookie Pittsburgh quarterback Kent Nix three times. Still, the Steelers took a 10-9 lead early in the fourth quarter by completing a 78-yard drive with a three-yard touchdown pass from Nix to John Hilton.

Later in the fourth, Jurgensen and Taylor finally started connecting. Faced with a third and seven at the Washington 30, the league's leading passer found the league's leading receiver for 16 yards into Steeler territory at the 44. Five plays later, Taylor beat defensive back Bob Hohn for the winning touchdown with just under three minutes left to go. Krause's third interception shut the door on Pittsburgh.

For the game, Jurgensen was nine of 32 for 155 yards with three interceptions and the one touchdown. Many of his incompletions were drops of the wet ball by receivers including Taylor, who had just one catch before the game-winning drive.

12/17/67	**Saints (3-11) 30, REDSKINS (5-6-3) 14**				50,486
NO	0	7	9	14	30
Was	0	0	7	7	14

NO	Abramowicz 80 pass from Kilmer (Durkee kick)
Was	Taylor 6 pass from Jurgensen (Alford kick)
NO	Safety, Love tackled in end zone by Anderson
NO	Schultz 1 run (Durkee kick)
NO	Abramowicz 13 pass from Kilmer (Durkee kick)
Was	Whitfield 23 pass from Jurgensen (Alford kick)
NO	McCall 49 run (Durkee kick)

D.C. Stadium—The Redskins had recovered from a dismal first half to tie the Saints at seven in the third quarter on the strength of a six-yard TD pass from Sonny Jurgensen to Charlie Taylor. On the next series, New Orleans was forced to punt from its own 40. Then, in short order, it all came apart.

John Love fumbled the punt and tried to pick it up in the end zone. The Saints' Dick Anderson tackled Love for a safety. Then Walter "Flea" Roberts returned the ensuing free kick 68 yards to the one, and Randy Schultz took it into the end zone on the next play for a 16-7 Saints lead.

The self-destruction continued. After the kickoff, Jurgensen threw an interception and New Orleans took possession at the Washington 26. Four plays later, Billy Kilmer threw a 13-yard touchdown pass to Danny Abramowicz to stretch the lead to 23-7 and put an end to the competitive phase of the game.

Jurgensen passed for 214 yards, bringing his season total to a league-record 3,747 yards, breaking his own mark set with the Eagles in 1961.

Fancy Passing: Jurgensen, Receivers Set Marks

Dec 17—While the Washington Redskins didn't have a stellar NFL season in terms of wins and losses, they put on one of the best aerial shows in league history.

Quarterback Sonny Jurgensen set an NFL record for passing yards in a year with 3,747 yards. And, as a result of the redhead's throwing prowess, receiver Charley Taylor (70 receptions), tight end Jerry Smith (67) and receiver Bobby Mitchell (60) finished first, second and fourth, respectively, in catches. Never before has an NFL team had three of the top four receivers in a season playing on the same team.

1968

Head Coach: Otto Graham
Record: 5-9, Third in NFL Capitol Division

Honors: Chris Hanburger Pro Bowl; Len Hauss Pro Bowl

Hall of Fame: Cliff Battles, Running Back, 1932-1937; Wayne Millner, End, 1936-1941, 1945

QB Beban, CB Fischer Sign Deals

June 14—The Redskins signed one proven performer and one exciting rookie today.

Pat Fischer, a Pro Bowl cornerback who played out his option with the Cardinals, is the veteran, and quarterback Gary Beban is a newcomer to pro football.

Beban won the 1967 Heisman Trophy at UCLA. He was drafted in the second round by the Los Angeles Rams but he was unable to come to contract terms there. The Redskins shipped their 1969 first-round pick to the Rams for the rights to Beban, who will sign a contract reported to be worth $200,000 over three years.

Beban, who is on the small side for an NFL quarterback at 6 feet tall and 198 pounds, joins a crowded quarterback group in Washington. Sonny Jurgensen is the starter and veterans Jim Ninowski and Harry Theofiledes are the backups.

The rookie doesn't plan to jump right in. "I expect to be undergoing a learning process at first," Beban said. "I have to gain the confidence of the veterans so if I come into a game there won't be a let-down."

The Redskins don't know what they will be giving up for Fischer. The Cardinals are due compensation for losing the free agent and the two teams could not agree on just what that will be. Commissioner Pete Rozelle will make the decision.

Fischer, 28, is a seven-year veteran. At 5'9" he relies on technique and toughness to guard larger receivers. He has done that well enough to earn Pro Bowl honors following the 1965 and 1966 seasons.

July 3

Rozelle Rules: Two Picks for Fischer
1969 No. 2 and 1970 No. 3 go to Cardinals as compensation for CB

9/15/68	**Redskins (1-0) 38, BEARS (0-1) 28**			41,321	
Was	14	14	7	3	38
Chi	7	14	0	7	28
Was	Richter 16 pass from Jurgensen (Gogolak kick)				
Was	Allen 12 run (Gogolak kick)				
Chi	Concannon 7 run (Percival kick)				
Was	Allen 99 pass from Jurgensen (Gogolak kick)				
Chi	Piccolo 12 run (Percival kick)				
Was	Richter 6 pass from Jurgensen (Gogolak kick)				
Chi	Bull 5 run (Percival kick)				
Was	Richter 19 pass from Jurgensen (Gogolak kick)				
Chi	Bull 8 run (Percival kick)				
Was	FG Gogolak 37				

Soldier Field—Sonny Jurgensen threw four touchdown passes, including a 99-yarder to running back Gerry Allen, to help the Redskins outscore the Bears 38-28 in Chicago.

Tight end Pat Richter caught Jurgensen's other three scoring passes, the first of which capped an 80-yard drive following the opening kickoff and gave Washington a 7-0 lead. Allen capped another 80-yard march with a 12-yard scoring run and Washington was up 14-0 in the first quarter.

The Bears were game. A 43-yard run by Gayle Sayers set up a seven-yard TD run by quarterback Jack Concannon. They were threatening to tie the game when Brig Owens intercepted Concannon at the Washington one. Undaunted by the poor field position, Jurgensen dropped deep into his own end zone and fired a strike to a wide-open Allen at the Washington 31. The back went untouched the rest of the way for the record-tying 99-yard play.

Every time Chicago would score, Jurgensen and the Redskins responded. Second-quarter Bear touchdown runs by Brian Piccolo and Ron Bull were negated by a pair of Jurgensen to Richter touchdown passes. Another scoring run by Bull in the fourth quarter brought Chicago back within seven, but the Bears' last hope died with seven minutes left when they gambled and lost on a fourth and three.

For the day, Jurgensen was 14 of 21 passing for 296 yards.

9/22/68	**SAINTS (1-1) 37, Redskins (1-1) 17**			65,941	
Was	0	3	7	7	17
NO	14	6	7	10	37
NO	Whitsell 4 blocked punt return (Durkee kick)				
NO	McCall 8 run (Durkee kick)				
Was	FG Gogolak 13				
NO	FG Durkee 17				
NO	FG Durkee 28				
NO	McCall 4 pass from Kilmer (Durkee kick)				
Was	Smith 23 pass from Jurgensen (Gogolak kick)				
NO	Abramowicz 43 pass from Kilmer (Durkee kick)				
Was	Richter 12 pass from Jurgensen (Gogolak kick)				
NO	FG Durkee 40				

Tulane Stadium—Don McCall became the first Saint to rush for more than 100 yards in a game, gaining 127 to pace the second-

year expansion New Orleans team to a 37-17 pounding of the Redskins.

McCall wasn't the only thorn in the side for the visitors. Defensive back Dave Whitsell opened the scoring when he blocked a Washington punt, scooped it up at the four and went in for the touchdown. Whitsell later blocked a field goal attempt and intercepted a Sonny Jurgensen pass.

This one was ugly early, late and in between. Not that the Saints needed any help, but the Redskins sure were willing to provide them with some as they turned the ball over three times on two fumbles and an interception.

Whitsell's touchdown, two touchdowns by McCall and a pair of field goals staked New Orleans to a 27-3 third-quarter lead. Jurgensen did throw for two touchdowns to narrow the gap, but the Saints defense wouldn't let them come back. Doug Atkins, New Orleans' 38-year-old defensive end, got two long sacks of Jurgensen, each of them fatal to a Redskin drive.

The New Orleans offense displayed perfect balance as they gained 183 yards on the ground and 183 through the air.

9/29/68	**GIANTS (3-0) 48, Redskins (1-2) 21**			62,797	
Was	7	7	0	7	21
NYG	3	21	17	7	48
NYG	FG Gogolak 32				
Was	Allen 1 run (Gogolak kick)				
NYG	Duhon 2 run (Gogolak kick)				
NYG	Jones 82 pass from Tarkenton (Gogolak kick)				
NYG	Tarkenton 3 run (Gogolak kick)				
Was	J. Smith 3 pass from Jurgensen (Gogolak kick)				
NYG	FG Gogolak 43				
NYG	Jones 56 pass from Tarkenton (Gogolak kick)				
NYG	Blye 1 run (Gogolak kick)				
NYG	Lockhart 47 interception return (Gogolak kick)				
Was	Richter 3 pass from Jurgensen (Gogolak kick)				

Yankee Stadium—The Redskins led 7-3 at the end of the first quarter, but Giants quarterback Fran Tarkenton sparked a 21-0 Giants run in the second quarter to send the home team on its way to a 48-21 rout.

Gerry Allen answered a Pete Gogolak field goal with a one-yard scoring run in the first quarter to give Washington that 7-3 lead. But things started going downhill when Spider Lockhart intercepted a Sonny Jurgensen pass to set the Giants up at the Washington 33. Soon after that, Bobby Duhon scored on a one-yard run to give New York the lead for good.

After that, it was Tarkenton's turn. He threw an 82-yard bomb to Homer Jones for one touchdown and ran in from three yards out for another. Washington did respond before halftime with a three-yard scoring pass from Jurgensen to tight end Jerry Smith to cut the halftime deficit to 21-10.

Any hope the Redskins had of getting back into it was buried under a 17-0 Giants avalanche in the third quarter, highlighted by another Tarkenton-to-Jones TD bomb, this one from 56 yards.

10/6/68	**REDSKINS (2-2) 17, Eagles (0-4) 14**			50,816	
Was	0	10	7	0	17
Phi	0	0	0	14	14
Was	FG Gogolak 24				
Was	Jurgensen 4 run (Gogolak kick)				
Was	Taylor 34 pass from Jurgensen (Gogolak kick)				
Phi	Hawkins 26 pass from Snead (Baker kick)				
Phi	Haymond 54 punt return (Baker kick)				

D.C. Stadium—The Redskins took advantage of some Eagle turnovers to build a 17-0 lead in the third quarter and withstood a Philadelphia rally in the fourth to hang on for the win.

An interception by linebacker Mike Morgan put the Redskins in prime position at the Philly two, but the offense moved backwards from there and Charlie Gogolak ended up kicking a 24-yard field goal for a 3-0 lead.

The home team fared better after getting another turnover, this one an interception by defensive back Aaron Martin at the Washington 20. Aided considerably by Eagle penalties, the Redskins drove 80 yards, with Sonny Jurgensen eluding the defense around the right end from four yards out, to take a 10-0 lead with 45 seconds left in the first half.

In the third quarter, Washington managed a touchdown drive that was largely unaided by Philadelphia miscues. During the 80-yard march, Jurgensen completed four passes, the last a 34-yard bullet to Charley Taylor for the touchdown and a 17-0 lead.

The cushion allowed the Skins to withstand two fourth-quarter touchdowns by the Eagles, the second a 54-yard punt return by Alvin Haymond with 45 seconds left. Washington recovered the Eagles' onside kick, and the Redskins ran out the clock.

10/13/68	**REDSKINS (3-2) 16, Steelers (0-5) 13**	50,659

Pit	0	10	0	3	13
Was	3	6	7	0	16
Was	Je. Smith 17 pass from Jurgensen (run failed)				
Was	FG Gogolak 24				
Pit	Jefferson 33 pass from Shiner (Lusteg kick)				
Pit	FG Lusteg 24				
Was	Je. Smith 49 pass from Jurgensen (Gogolak kick)				
Pit	FG Lusteg 30				

D.C. Stadium—A pair of Sonny Jurgensen to Jerry Smith touchdown passes paced the Redskins to a 16-13 win over Pittsburgh. The Redskins quarterback was severely hampered by a bad cold, to the point where he had to sleep for a couple of hours in a storage room at the stadium just to be able to suit up.

The Redskins took a 9-0 lead in the second quarter on the strength of the first Jurgensen-to-Smith scoring connection—the point after failed—and a 24-yard Charlie Gogolak field goal. Pittsburgh erased that lead on a 33-yard touchdown pass from Dick Shiner to Roy Jefferson and a 24-yard field goal by Booth Lusteg. Their conversion following their TD was good, so they led 10-9 at the half.

In the third quarter, a punt pinned the home team back at its own four. On first down from there, Jurgensen was nearly trapped for a safety while attempting to pass, but he eluded the charge and scrambled for 11 yards. That play jump-started what proved to be the game-winning drive. Seven plays later, Jurgensen found Smith cutting across the middle for 49 yards and the touchdown.

The Steelers' Lusteg kicked a 30-yard field goal in the fourth quarter to pull his team within three, but he was wide right on a 33-yard try that would have tied the game with two minutes left to play.

10/20/68	**CARDINALS (3-3) 41, Redskins (3-3) 14**	46,456

Was	7	0	7	0	14
StL	3	21	7	10	41
StL	FG Bakken 28				
Was	Richter 29 pass from Jurgensen (Gogolak kick)				
StL	Shivers 42 run (Bakken kick)				
StL	Roland 1 run (Bakken kick)				
StL	Conrad 32 pass from Hart (Bakken kick)				
Was	Allen 4 run (Gogolak kick)				
StL	Williams 2 pass from Hart (Bakken kick)				
StL	Hart 1 run (Bakken kick)				
StL	FG Bakken 40				

Busch Memorial Stadium—Reserve running back Roy Shivers galloped 42 yards for a touchdown that started a 21-0 second-quarter outburst and pushed the Cardinals past the Redskins 41-14.

St. Louis got on the board first with a 28-yard Jim Bakken field goal. The Redskins took a 7-3 lead entering the second thanks to a 29-yard touchdown pass from Sonny Jurgensen to Pat Richter.

But Shivers erased the lead by taking a pitchout and racing down the left sideline 42 yards for the score.

A pass interference call against Washington's Rickie Harris greatly aided the Cardinals' drive to their second touchdown of the period. Then a high snap aborted a Washington punt attempt and St. Louis took possession at the Redskins' 32. On the next play, quarterback Jim Hart threw to receiver Bobby Joe Conrad for another touchdown and it was 24-7 at halftime.

The Redskins did manage a four-yard touchdown run by Gerry Allen in the third quarter, but the Cardinals answered with two more touchdowns and a field goal to make it a certified rout.

Jurgensen came into the game with a body cast to protect his cracked ribs. He left the game midway through the final period when the outcome had long since been settled.

10/27/68	**Giants (5-2) 13, REDSKINS (3-4) 10**	50,839

NYG	0	3	3	7	13
Was	0	3	7	0	10
NYG	FG Gogolak 10				
Was	FG Gogolak 36				
Was	Barefoot 8 blocked punt return (Gogolak kick)				
NYG	FG Gogolak 18				
NYG	Frederickson 1 run (Gogolak kick)				

D.C. Stadium—Sonny Jurgensen had one of his worst games as a pro. The Giants held possession of the ball for almost the entire second half. Still, the Redskins still had a chance to win or tie this one at the end, but came up on the short end of a 13-10 score.

The Redskins broke a 3-3 tie early in the third quarter when Walt Barnes, at the head of a massive wave of rushers, blocked a New York punt at the Giants' 10. Ken Barefoot scooped it up at the eight and ran it in to give Washington a 10-3 lead.

Besides that, the Redskins barely touched the ball in the second half. Washington got possession with 1:53 left. At that point, the Giants had run 41 plays and the Redskins six. Eighteen of those plays came on a touchdown drive that consumed 9:37 of clock and resulted in what proved to be the game-winning score. Tucker Frederickson scored it on a one-yard run with 6:34 left in the game.

When the home team did regain possession with less than two minutes left, Jurgensen, suffering from broken ribs, managed to get the team moving, getting to the Giants' 35. From there, he missed a wide-open Taylor for what would have been a sure TD. Charlie Gogolak missed a 42-yard field goal with one second remaining.

On the day, Jurgensen was seven for 25 passing for 73 yards.

11/10/68	**Redskins (4-5) 16, EAGLES (0-9) 10**	59,113

Was	3	6	7	0	16
Phi	0	3	0	7	10
Was	FG Gogolak 15				
Was	FG Gogolak 25				
Phi	FG Baker 37				
Was	FG Gogolak 9				
Was	Allen 1 run (Gogolak kick)				
Phi	Hawkins 6 pass from Snead (Baker kick)				

Franklin Field—A 53-yard drive led by backup quarterback Jim Ninowski gave the Redskins a 16-3 lead in the third quarter and the Redskins were able to survive a late Eagle bid and claim a 16-10 win.

The Redskins were able to get close to the end zone in the first half but they continually had to settle for three points. Charlie Gogolak kicked field goals of 15, 25, and nine yards

Washington took a 9-3 lead into the third quarter. Ninowski accounted for the lion's share of the yardage in the touchdown drive. He completed four passes for 48 yards and Gerry Allen culminated the march with a 1-yard touchdown run.

The Eagles threatened often in the fourth quarter, but could just manage a six-yard touchdown pass from Norm Snead to Ben Hawkins. One drive ended when Snead was sacked on fourth and one at the Washington 39 with just over four minutes left and another died when the clock expired with the Eagles at the Washington 18.

The Redskins didn't muster much in the way of passing yardage with just 92 yards through the air. However, they controlled the game on the ground, picking up 175 yards rushing.

11/17/68	Cowboys (8-2) 44, REDSKINS (4-6) 24			50,816
Dal	7	6	17	14	44
Was	0	10	7	7	24

Dal	Hayes 35 pass from Meredith (Clark kick)
Dal	FG Clark 45
Was	Taylor 35 pass from Jurgensen (Gogolak kick)
Dal	FG Clark 34
Was	FG Gogolak 37
Was	Taylor 11 pass from Jurgensen (Gogolak kick)
Dal	FG Clark 13
Dal	Rentzel 14 pass from Meredith (Clark kick)
Dal	Rentzel 9 pass from Morton (Clark kick)
Dal	Perkins 28 run (Clark kick)
Dal	Cole 21 fumble return (Clark kick)
Was	Hanburger 30 interception return (Gogolak kick)

D.C. Stadium—The Redskins took a third quarter lead over the heavily-favored Cowboys, but upset hopes were buried under an avalanche of 31 unanswered Dallas points.

Dallas took a 7-0 lead by driving 94 yards in the first quarter. It took eight plays for them to score on Don Meredith's 35-yard touchdown pass to Bob Hayes. A 45-yard Mike Clark field goal put the Cowboys up 10-0 early in the second quarter.

The home team then made its bid to climb back into the game. Rookie Yazoo Smith ran a punt back 25 yards to the Washington 38. Sonny Jurgensen threw to Charley Taylor for ten yards and then got an 11-yard run by Bob Brunet to get into scoring position. From the 35, Jurgensen had plenty of time to find Taylor, who had shed the attempted coverage of cornerback Cornell Green, in the end zone to cut the lead to 10-7. The teams exchanged field goals before the half and Dallas still had its three-point lead.

Washington took the second-half kickoff and embarked on a quick 75-yard touchdown march. Taylor caught a 47-yard pass from Jurgensen and was tripped up by a shoestring tackle at the 14. He got it in shortly after that when the split the safeties a caught an 11-yard strike from Jurgensen. Charlie Gogolak's point after gave them a 17-13 lead just over a minute into the third quarter.

A Clark field goal pulled Dallas within one before things came unglued for Washington. Bobby Mitchell fumbled the kickoff and Dallas recovered at the Redskins' 20. Two plays later, Meredith hit Lance Rentzel with a 14-yard touchdown pass to put Dallas ahead to stay. Rentzel caught another touchdown pass—this one from Craig Morton who had replaced an injured Meredith—and the rout was on.

While the Cowboys were racking up points offensively, their defense was putting the clamps on the Washington offense. After the touchdown to make it 17-13, the Redskins gained just 25 yards of total offense.

11/24/68	Packers (5-5-1) 27, REDSKINS (4-7) 7			50,621
GB	7	7	10	3	27
Was	0	7	0	0	7

GB	Anderson 1 run (Mercer kick)
GB	Pitts 1 run (Mercer kick)
Was	Richter 2 pass from Jurgensen (Gogolak kick)
GB	Anderson 47 pass from Bratkowski (Mercer kick)
GB	FG Mercer 29
GB	FG Mercer 27

D.C. Stadium—Vince Lombardi had retired and Bart Starr was hurt, but Phil Bengston and Zeke Bratkowski did well enough in their places to lead the Packers to an easy 27-7 win over the Redskins.

Lombardi's Packers were known for ball control on offense. Bengston's squad held the ball all but one minute of the first quarter with two drives. The first covered just 55 yards after taking the opening kickoff. They chewed up six minutes of clock in the process of moving to a one-yard touchdown run by Donny Anderson.

After the Redskins went three and out, Bratkowski engineered an 87-yard touchdown drive that took eight minutes. Elijah Pitts capped that drive with a one-yard scoring burst on the first play of the second quarter to give Green Bay a 14-0 lead.

Starr is known for passing with maximum efficiency. On the two drives, Bratkowski was eight for eight passing.

Washington finally got going offensively late in the second quarter after a Packer drive ended with a missed field goal. From their own 20, the Redskins got their initial first down of the game and moved on 80 yards to score just before halftime on a two-yard pass from Sonny Jurgensen to Pat Richter to cut the lead to 14-7.

Any optimism the touchdown may have created soon dissipated. The Skins got the second half kickoff, but quickly punted back to Green Bay. It took six plays to move 76 yards. The last play was a 47-yard touchdown pass from Bratkowski to Anderson, who broke some attempted tackles on his way to making it 21-7. Two sacks of Jurgensen by Willie Davis aborted Washington's next drive and a pair of field goals wrapped it up for the Pack.

11/28/68	COWBOYS (10-2) 29, Redskins (4-8) 20			66,076
Was	0	7	7	6	20
Dal	3	14	2	10	29

Dal	FG Clark 18
Dal	Baynham 1 run (Clark kick)
Dal	Perkins 9 run (Clark kick)
Was	Taylor 29 pass from Ninowski (Gogolak kick)
Dal	Safety Ninowski fumbled out of end zone
Was	Smith 11 pass from Ninowski (kick failed)
Was	Richter 4 pass from Ninowski (Gogolak kick)
Dal	FG Clark 25
Dal	Cole 5 interception return (Clark kick)

Cotton Bowl—Jim Ninowski, filling in for the flu-ridden Sonny Jurgensen, threw for three touchdowns to bring the Redskins back from a 17-0 first half deficit to a 20-19 lead early in the fourth quarter. The Cowboys, however, scored the last 10 points to elude the upset at home and beat the Redskins 29-20.

The Cowboys' early lead was built largely on the generosity of the visiting team as a pair of fumbles and a pass interference call in the end zone led to a touchdown run and field goal for the Cowboys. The other touchdown came when the Cowboys moved 62 yards in seven plays, the big play coming on a 41-yard strike from Craig Morton to Lance Rentzel. That drive ended with a nine-yard Don Perkins touchdown run and a 17-0 Dallas lead.

Then the Redskins began to climb back into the game. A 30-yard kickoff return by Dick Smith set them up at their own 42. A 15-yard roughing the passer call tacked onto a 13-yard completion put the visitors into scoring range. From the 29, Ninowski hit Charley Taylor on the dead run and the receiver easily scored to cut the lead to 17-7 at halftime.

The comeback train was temporarily derailed when Ninowski was tackled in the end zone and fumbled. Fortunately, the ball rolled out of the end zone and Dallas got two points for the safety. Later in the third, Ninowski converted a second and 48 situation by throwing 56 yards to tight end Jerry Smith at the Dallas six. Shortly after that, Ninowski and Smith connected again, this time on an 11-yard touchdown pass to make the score 19-14.

Brig Owens intercepted a Don Meredith pass on the first play of the fourth quarter and returned it 31 yards to the Dallas 32. It took just two plays for the Redskins to take the lead on Ninowski's third scoring pass, this one to Pat Richter from six yards out. The point after was blocked, but Washington still held a 20-19 lead.

But that was the end of the road for the Redskins. A roughing penalty on the ensuing kickoff gave Dallas good field position and they drove for a field goal to take the lead at 22-19. A fumble on the kickoff return bottled the Redskins up deep in their own territory. On third down from the Washington 12, Ninowski was hit by defensive tackle Jethro Pugh just as he was releasing the ball. It popped into the air and end Larry Cole gathered it in, strolling five yards for the clinching TD.

12/8/68	Browns (10-3) 24, REDSKINS (4-9) 21				50,661
Cle	0	7	7	10	24
Was	7	7	0	7	21
Was	Smith 5 pass from Jurgensen (Gogolak kick)				
Cle	Barnes 40 interception return (Cockroft kick)				
Was	Larson 2 pass from Jurgensen (Gogolak kick)				
Cle	Kelly 1 run (Cockroft kick)				
Cle	FG Cockroft 20				
Cle	Warfield 38 pass from Nelsen (Cockroft kick)				
Was	Taylor 31 pass from Ninowski (Gogolak kick)				

D.C. Stadium—The Redskins threw a scare into the Browns in the first half, but Cleveland pulled away as the game went on and clinched the NFL Century division title.

Following Jim Carroll's recovery of a Leroy Kelly fumble, Sonny Jurgensen led the Redskins 76 yards to a touchdown. The big play was a 56-yard connection from Jurgensen to tight end Jerry Smith and the quarterback returned to Smith for a five-yard touchdown pass, capping the drive and giving the home team a 7-0 lead.

The lead was soon erased when Cleveland defensive end Jack Gregory tipped Jurgensen's pass and cornerback Erich Barnes intercepted it, scooting 40 yards for a touchdown to tie the game.

Unfazed, Jurgensen took the Redskins 83 yards in 13 plays to retake the lead. That drive culminated in a two-yard touchdown pass from Jurgensen to back Pete Larson with 24 seconds left in the first half. The score was 14-7 Washington.

However, Cleveland ran off 17 unanswered points in the second half to take command of the game. They drove 77 yards in eight plays with their first possession of the half. Kelly, the

league's leading rusher, took it the final yard to tie the game at 14. Don Cockroft's 20-yard field goal early in the fourth quarter pushed the Browns into the lead and less than three minutes later Cleveland quarterback Bill Nelsen threw 38 yards to receiver Paul Warfield to pad the lead to 10. Washington managed a touchdown by Charley Taylor with just over a minute left, but that served only to make the final a bit more respectable at 24-21.

12/15/68	REDSKINS (5-9) 14, Lions (4-8-2) 3				50,123
Det	0	0	3	0	3
Was	0	0	0	14	14
Det	FG Walker 17				
Was	Brunet 29 pass from Theofiledes (Gogolak kick)				
Was	Larson 2 run (Gogolak kick)				

D.C. Stadium—Third-string quarterback Harry Theofiledes came off the bench to lead the Redskins to a 14-3 victory over the Lions.

The win was marred by a serious injury suffered by rookie Jim (Yazoo) Smith. Smith, a safety and the team's first-round pick in the most recent draft, was accidentally kicked by a teammate and suffered a broken neck.

Detroit had squandered two golden opportunities to take the lead by fumbling deep in Redskins territory. The most frustrating for the visiting team occurred when they drove 96 yards to the Redskins three and failed to score when back Nick Eddy fumbled the ball away there.

The Lions still held a 3-0 lead going into the fourth quarter when coach Otto Graham inserted Theofiledes into the game. Four plays later, the Redskins grabbed the lead when Theofiledes threw a 29-yard scoring pass to back Bob Brunet.

Charley Taylor drew a 43-yard pass interference penalty that helped the Redskins to a clinching TD with a minute left. That score came on a two-yard Pete Larson run.

(Note: Smith's injury turned out to be career ending for the promising first-round draft choice out of Oregon.)

Dec 30
Smith Gets Surgery, Still in Traction
Condition described as 'good' after three-hour operation

1969
Head Coach: Vince Lombardi
Record: 7-5-2, Second in Capitol Division

Honors: Larry Brown Pro Bowl; Pat Fischer Pro Bowl; Chris Hanburger Pro Bowl; Len Hauss Pro Bowl; Sonny Jurgensen Pro Bowl; Jerry Smith Pro Bowl

Hall of Fame: Turk Edwards, Tackle, 1932-1940

Jan 18
Smith Released From Hospital
DB is 'optimistic' about playing in '69

Jan 24
Smith Says He Won't Play Next Year
Has lost 40 pounds since neck injury

Feb 1
Lombardi Clears Way to Join Redskins
Request for release from his contract expected to be honored by Packers

Feb 3
Graham Out, Lombardi In
Former Packer boss will coach, GM and have option on five percent of team stock

Lombardi: 'Commitment to Excellence'

Feb 6—"It's not true that I can walk across the Potomac," said Vince Lombardi in the press conference introducing him as the head of all things football-related for the Redskins.

"Not even when it's frozen."

While walking on water isn't expected from Lombardi, plenty is. The Redskins haven't had a winning season since 1945 and Lombardi, a living legend if ever there was one, is expected to change that—and quickly.

Lombardi has embraced the challenge. When asked why he came to the Redskins when he could have written his own ticket with any number of teams, he said, "Why did I choose Washington among offers from other cities? Because it is the capital of the world. And I have some plans to make it the football capital."

His plans involve some very simple elements.

"I will demand a commitment to excellence and to victory," Lombardi said. "That is what life is all about, too."

Feb 14

Huff to Return as Player Coach
Star linebacker ends retirement after one year

Marshall Dies, Questions Loom

Aug 9—George Preston Marshall, the founder of the Washington Redskins, died in his sleep in his Georgetown home. He was 72.

As plans for services for Marshall are underway, a battle for control of his football team looms. Marshall has not been active in the operation of the franchise for a number of years as his health has declined.

Currently Jack Kent Cooke of Los Angeles, who also owns the NBA's Lakers, owns 25 percent of the team while coach Vince Lombardi, president Edward Bennett Williams, and attorney Milton King each own five percent. The remainder belongs to Marshall.

The main point of contention is Marshall's intentions as to what to do with his share. His son has claimed that the senior Marshall left it to him. There also is documentation that Marshall wanted to have the stock sold with the proceeds donated to a Washington boy's club.

Going by the stock price of the 50 shares sold to Lombardi, the franchise is valued at $10 million. That seems to be significantly under its true value, as the Philadelphia Eagles recently sold for $16 million.

9/21/69	Redskins (1-0) 26, SAINTS (0-1) 20				73,147
Was	0	14	7	5	26
NO	7	3	3	7	20
NO	Poage 5 pass from Kilmer (Dempsey kick)				
NO	FG Dempsey 13				
Was	Taylor 10 pass from Jurgensen (Knight kick)				
Was	Smith 14 pass from Jurgensen (Knight kick)				
NO	FG Dempsey 43				
Was	Taylor 51 pass from Jurgensen (Knight kick)				
NO	Livingston 1 run (Dempsey kick)				
Was	FG Knight 18				
Was	Safety McNeill stepped out of end zone				

Tulane Stadium—Three Sonny Jurgensen touchdown passes in the second and third quarters gave the Redskins the lead, and Washington survived a late bid by the spirited Saints to take a 26-20 win in Vince Lombardi's coaching debut with the Redskins.

Two of Jurgensen's scoring tosses came in a 40-second span in the second quarter. The first went to Charley Taylor for 10 yards and that was followed up with a 14-yarder to Jerry Smith to put the Redskins up 14-10.

Washington answered a third quarter Tom Dempsey field goal with another Jurgensen-to-Taylor touchdown connection, this one coming from 51 yards out, to give the visitors a 21-13 lead.

In the fourth quarter, New Orleans again pulled within a point on a one-yard scoring run by Andy Livingston. Curt Knight gave the Redskins a little breathing room soon after that with an 18-yard field goal.

In a desperate effort to catch up, New Orleans gave Washington an intentional safety with less than two minutes left, gambling that their defense would hold following the free kick. That part of the gamble paid off as the Saints regained possession, but a Billy Kilmer pass from the New Orleans 49 fell short as the game ended.

9/28/69	BROWNS (2-0) 27, Redskins (1-1) 23				82,581
Was	7	3	0	13	23
Cle	0	10	7	10	27
Was	Smith 6 pass from Jurgensen (Knight kick)				
Cle	Johnson 1 run (Cockroft kick)				
Cle	FG Cockroft 41				
Was	FG Knight 32				
Cle	Johnson 17 run (Cockroft kick)				
Cle	FG Cockroft 23				
Was	Harraway 1 run (kick failed)				
Was	Long 13 pass from Jurgensen (Knight kick)				
Cle	Collins 15 pass from Nelsen (Cockroft kick)				

Cleveland Municipal Stadium—A pair of fourth-quarter touchdowns gave the Redskins the lead, but a 15-yard pass from Bill Nelsen to Gary Collins with just over a minute left gave the Browns the win.

Trailing 20-10 halfway through the fourth quarter, the Redskins drove 70 yards in seven plays to score on a one-yard run by Charley Harraway. The point after was missed, but the Cleveland lead was cut to 20-16. Shortly after that, Leo Carroll recovered a Cleveland fumble at the Browns 13. On the next play, Jurgensen found Bob Long for a touchdown and, following the successful conversion, a 23-20 lead.

The Browns responded with a 74-yard drive. Backup running back Reece Morrison gained 40 of those yards on two runs and an 18-yard pass reception. Right after Morrison's catch Nelsen hit Collins for the winning points with 1:19 left.

10/5/69	Redskins (1-1-1) 17, 49ERS (0-2-1) 17				35,642
Was	0	0	3	14	17
SF	0	7	3	7	17
SF	McNeil 16 pass from Brodie (Davis kick)				
Was	FG Knight 9				
SF	FG Davis 17				
Was	Harraway 3 run (Knight kick)				
SF	Cunningham 17 run (Davis kick)				
Was	Smith 4 pass from Jurgensen (Knight kick)				

Kezar Stadium—A four-yard touchdown pass from Sonny Jurgensen to Jerry Smith rallied the Redskins to a tie with 26 seconds remaining in the game. Washington had a shot to win it on the game's last play, but a 56-yard free kick field goal attempt was off target.

Early in the fourth quarter, the Redskins had tied the game at 10 on a controversial three-yard run by Charley Harraway. On the play, Harraway fumbled the ball as he fought for yardage near the goal line. San Francisco recovered, but the officials ruled that Harraway had scored prior to losing possession.

The 49ers regained the lead about six minutes later. Three completions from John Brodie to receiver Gene Washington got them in position for a 17-yard touchdown run by Doug Cunningham.

Washington's tying drive was greatly aided when San Francisco safety Alvin Randolph was flagged for pass interference at the Niners' two. Three plays later, Jurgensen flipped to ball to Smith and the point after tied the score. The Redskins forced a quick punt and a fair catch allowed them to attempt an uncontested field goal from their own 44. Curt Knight's kick was long enough, but wide left.

Lombardi: There's No Place Like Home

October 6—Vince Lombardi was smiling, an indication of a degree of pleasure with the Redskins' 1-1-1 start to the season.

"Do you realize that the difference between our current record and being undefeated is just four points?" Lombardi asked.

The Redskins' lone loss came a week ago at Cleveland by a score of 27-23.

The three road games to start the season mean that Washington will be playing seven of its last 11 games in the friendly confines of RFK Stadium. And Lombardi is looking forward to some home cooking.

The coach said that being at home will "give the Redskins a lift with their fans pulling for them."

Lombardi knows the team still has a long way to go before it can be a consistent winner. "We have got to improve a lot, but I don't know whether some players will," he said.

"It's obvious we do not have the people who can do certain things."

10/12/69	REDSKINS (2-1-1) 33, Cardinals (2-2) 17			50,481	
StL	3	0	7	7	17
Was	10	13	0	10	33
StL	FG Bakken 34				
Was	FG Knight 37				
Was	Brown 12 run (Knight kick)				
Was	Taylor 11 pass from Jurgensen (Knight kick)				
Was	FG Knight 28				
Was	FG Knight 8				
StL	Roland 6 run (Bakken kick)				
Was	FG Knight 28				
StL	Roland 1 run (Bakken kick)				
Was	Smith 6 pass from Jurgensen (Knight kick)				

RFK Stadium—Curt Knight tied a team record with four field goals and rookie running back Larry Brown rushed for 82 yards to pace the Redskins to a 33-17 win over St. Louis.

Things were going well on both sides of the ball. The defense harassed St. Louis quarterback Jim Hart all day, constantly forcing him out of the pocket and intercepting five of his passes. The front four, led by Ends John Hoffman and Leo Carroll, put continuous pressure on Hart.

The Cardinals got on the board first with a 34-yard Jim Bakken field goal but Brown put the Redskins on top to stay with a 12-yard run in the first quarter, making the score 10-3.

Before the half was over, the Redskins would stretch the lead to 23-3 on the strength of an 11-yard touchdown pass from Sonny Jurgensen to Charley Taylor and the second and third of Knight's field goals.

The game grew a bit sloppy in the second half as a myriad of Washington penalties and turnovers helped the Cardinals to two touchdowns. Washington held the visitors at bay, though, with Knight's fourth field goal and a six-yard touchdown pass from Jurgensen to Jerry Smith.

10/19/69	REDSKINS (3-1-1) 20, Giants (3-2) 14			50,332	
NYG	0	7	7	0	14
Was	0	0	7	13	20
NYG	Morrison 11 run (Gogolak kick)				
NYG	Minniear 2 run (Gogolak kick)				
Was	Harraway 1 run (Knight kick)				
Was	Harraway 15 run (Knight kick)				
Was	Harris 86 punt return (kick failed)				

RFK Stadium—The Redskins had rallied from a 14-0 halftime deficit, but it looked like their efforts might end up being for naught.

With just over three minutes left, Frank Tarkenton had a lane up the middle. It was fourth down and the Redskins were leading by six. A typical Tarkenton scramble surely was about to waste Larry Brown's 102-yard rushing effort, Charley Harraway's two second-half touchdowns and Rickie Harris' 86-yard, go-ahead punt return.

After Tarkenton dropped back from the Washington two, he couldn't find a receiver but saw an opening up the middle and took off towards the goal line. But Sam Huff, Pat Fischer and Leo Carroll quickly filled the hole and Tarkenton was forced to intentionally fumble into the end zone. Harris pounced on it there, and the Redskins preserved the win.

The Redskins appeared to be dead in the water as the visitors built up that 14-0 lead in the third quarter. But the offense came to life and Washington embarked on a 69-yard drive to Harraway's first touchdown, scoring on a one-yard run. Early in the fourth quarter, Harraway raced around left end from the Giants' 15 and, taking advantage of a textbook block by receiver Charley Taylor, got into the end zone to tie the score at 14.

Soon after that, the Giants lined up in punt formation. Flags flew as the Giants were clearly offside. Ernie Koy punted to Harris at the Washington 14. "I knew I might as well grab it, take a chance," said Harris, referring to the penalty situation. "I had nothing to lose even if I fumbled it away."

He did much better than fumble it. Harris headed straight up the middle, cut to the left and followed key blocks by Flea Roberts, Brig Owens and Chris Hanburger into the end zone. Curt Knight missed the extra point, opening the door to the Giants' late bid to win, but Huff, Carroll and Fischer closed it.

Lombardi: 'My Coaching Has To Be Blamed'

Oct 20—Most NFL coaches would be happy to escape with a six-point win against a division rival and move on.

Vince Lombardi is not most coaches.

The person who drew the most criticism in the wake of Washington's 20-14 win over the Giants was himself.

Specifically, Lombardi was dissatisfied with the fact that New York gained 179 yards rushing. "There were gaping holes in our line," he said. "My coaching has to be blamed."

He elaborated, saying that he was too concerned with containing the scrambling of New York quarterback Fran Tarkenton. "As a result, our players had a tendency to wait a bit instead of being more aggressive."

Overall, Lombardi indicated that he was pleased with the team's 3-1-1 record.

10/26/69	Redskins (4-1-1) 14, STEELERS (1-5) 7			46,357	
Was	0	0	14	0	14
Pit	7	0	0	0	7
Pit	Gros 7 pass from Hanratty (Mingo kick)				
Was	Jurgensen 10 run (Knight kick)				
Was	Taylor 17 pass from Jurgensen (Knight kick)				

Pit Stadium—Two touchdowns within a nine-minute span in the third quarter would be all the Redskins would need to beat the Steelers.

Trailing 7-0 at halftime, the Redskins commenced a 10-play, 80-yard drive that ended with Sonny Jurgensen taking it in himself from 10 yards out. Curt Knight's extra point tied the game at seven.

Soon after that linebacker Marlin McKeever intercepted a pass and the ball was returned to the Steelers' eight. Joe Green sacked

Jurgensen on first down, but on the next play the quarterback found Charley Taylor open in the end zone for a 14-7 lead.

Pittsburgh had a couple of chances to tie it up in the late going. An apparent fourth-down touchdown pass from Terry Hanratty to Earl Gros was taken away when the officials ruled that Hanratty had stepped out of bounds prior to releasing the pass. That play came with about three minutes left in the game. Hanratty got the Steelers deep into Washington territory on a last-gasp drive, but they turned it over on downs at the Washington four with six seconds left.

11/2/69	COLTS (4-3) 41, Redskins (4-2-1) 17				60,238
Was	3	0	7	7	17
Bal	3	10	14	14	41
Was	FG Knight 34				
Bal	FG Michaels 49				
Bal	FG Michaels 12				
Bal	Matte7 run (Michaels kick)				
Was	Taylor 19 pass from Jurgensen (Knight kick)				
Bal	Hill 1 run (Michaels kick)				
Bal	Matte2 run (Michaels kick)				
Bal	Matte6 run (Michaels kick)				
Was	Dyer 69 pass from Jurgensen (Knight kick)				
Bal	Havrilak 10 run (Michaels kick)				

Memorial Stadium—The defending NFL champion Colts came into the game as a .500 team, but coach Don Shula shuffled their defensive lineup and they looked like the Colts of old. Baltimore held Larry Brown, the NFL's second-leading rusher, to 14 yards in 14 carries, picked off three Sonny Jurgensen passes and recovered a fumble in the process of defeating Washington 41-17.

The Redskins should have known this wasn't going to be their day when Lou Michaels' 49-yard field goal attempt bounced off the crossbar and went through to tie the game at three in the second quarter. Another Michaels field goal and the first of three scoring runs by halfback Tom Matte had Baltimore up 13-3 at halftime.

The Redskins threatened to get back into it early in the second after the Colts' Willie Richardson fumbled and Pat Fischer recovered for the Redskins. Jurgensen threw a 19-yard TD pass to Charley Taylor and suddenly it was 13-10.

The good feeling didn't last long. Baltimore's Tom Mitchell blocked a punt and recovered it at the Washington six. Three plays later, Jerry Hill scored from a yard out and the rout was on.

11/9/69	REDSKINS (4-2-2) 28, Eagles (3-4-1) 28				50,502
Phi	7	0	7	14	28
Was	0	7	7	14	28
Phi	Keyes 2 run (Baker kick)				
Was	Brown 1 run (Knight kick)				
Was	Harraway 15 pass from Jurgensen (Knight kick)				
Phi	Hawkins 4 pass from Snead (Baker kick				
Was	Taylor 3 pass from Jurgensen (Knight kick)				
Was	Huff 18 interception return (Knight kick)				
Phi	Woodeschick 1 run (Baker kick)				
Phi	Snead 1 run (Baker kick)				

RFK Stadium—On fourth and 25 with just over a minute left and his team trailing by seven, the Eagles' Norm Snead threw up a prayer from the Washington 42. It was answered by a slightly lower authority—the back judge—and Philly got in position to tie this one 28-28.

The Redskins had broken a 14-14 tie by scoring two touchdowns in a 32-second span early in the fourth quarter. Sonny Jurgensen directed a 79-yard drive capped by his three-yard scoring toss to Charley Taylor for a seven-point lead with more than 11 minutes left.

Four plays later, the home team got some breathing room. Sam Huff intercepted Snead's pass at the Philadelphia 18 and just made it across the goal line before being tackled.

But the Eagles were not done. Snead led the Eagles on an 84-yard drive and Tom Woodeschick scored on a one-yard run to pull the Eagles within a touchdown with 5:23 left. The Redskins survived one scare when Sam Baker missed a field goal following a Larry Brown fumble.

Philadelphia regained possession for one last chance. An intentional grounding call on Snead set up a fourth and 25 at the Washington 42. Snead launched a high, arching pass to the left corner of the end zone. While the ball was in the air, Ben Hawkins, the intended receiver, and Mike Bass, the defender, collided at the goal line and both fell to the ground. While it appeared that Hawkins had backed into Bass, back judge Gordon McCarter flagged the cornerback for pass interference. On the next play, Snead snuck over from the one with 55 seconds left. Baker's extra point tied the game.

11/16/69	Cowboys (8-1) 41, REDSKINS (4-3-2) 28				50,474
Dal	17	10	7	7	41
Was	7	14	7	0	28
Dal	FG Clark 36				
Was	Smith 27 pass from Jurgensen (Knight kick)				
Dal	Rentzel 65 pass from Morton (Clark kick)				
Dal	Cole 41 interception return (Clark kick)				
Dal	Hill 3 run (Clark kick)				
Was	Taylor 88 pass from Jurgensen (Knight kick)				
Dal	FG Clark 14				
Was	Smith 11 pass from Jurgensen (Knight kick)				
Dal	Hill 7 run (Clark kick)				
Was	Smith 20 pass from Jurgensen (Knight kick)				
Dal	Reeves 4 run (Clark kick)				

RFK Stadium—Sonny Jurgensen had an uneven day that was emblematic of the Redskins' up and down season. The quarterback was 24 of 35 passing for 338 yards and four touchdowns, with one stretch in the second half where 16 straight passes were caught. Unfortunately, the Cowboys caught three of those. In game of big plays, the Cowboys made more of them and Washington couldn't catch up with Dallas. The Redskins lost 41-38.

Dallas made the first three big plays to turn a 7-3 deficit into a 24-7 lead. Craig Morton made a beautiful throw to receiver Lance Rentzel for 65 yards and a touchdown to put Dallas in the lead. Soon after that, defensive end Larry Cole picked a tipped pass out of the air and rumbled 41 yards for a touchdown. Then Bob Hayes returned a punt 50 yards to the Washington three and Calvin Hill ran it over from there to give his team a 17-point lead.

It was Washington's turn to rip off a big chunk of yardage. With the line of scrimmage at the Redskins 12, a double-teamed Charley Taylor made a nice move to catch a floating Jurgensen pass near midfield and spun free, going all the way for the touchdown.

The Redskins pulled within 27-21 by halftime and had apparently taken the lead on another play of more than 80 yards, this one an 83-yard punt return by Rickie Harris. But Chris Hanburger was flagged for a borderline clip and the score was called back.

The Cowboys extended their lead with another touchdown run by Hill, who rushed for 150 yards on 27 carries on the day. Jurgensen's fourth TD pass, to Jerry Smith, got the Redskins back within six one last time, but Dan Reeves scored on a four-yard run in the fourth quarter to lock it up for Dallas.

11/23/69	REDSKINS (5-3-2) 27, Falcons (3-7) 20				50,345
Atl	7	13	0	0	20
Was	7	10	7	3	27
Atl	Johnson 5 run (Etter kick)				
Was	Smith 16 pass from Jurgensen (Knight kick)				
Atl	FG Etter 18				
Atl	Butler 3 run (Etter kick)				
Was	Brown 2 run (Knight kick)				

Atl	FG Etter 13
Was	FG Knight 38
Was	Harraway 68 pass from Jurgensen (Knight kick)
Was	FG Knight 27

RFK Stadium—A 68-yard screen pass from Sonny Jurgensen to Charley Harraway gave the Redskins the winning points in their 27-20 victory over the Falcons.

The Redskins trailed 20-17 at halftime, but had already taken a big step towards winning by knocking Atlanta starting quarterback Randy Johnson out of the game. Johnson had been the NFL's Offensive Player of the Week the previous Sunday and his replacement, Bruce Lemmerman, was inadequate to say the least.

Washington forced Atlanta to punt on the first series of the second half and took possession at its own 38. Jurgensen was sacked for a six-yard loss by defensive end Claude Humphrey on first down. He decided to make the Falcons pay for their aggressive pass rush. With the defensive line bearing down on him, the quarterback calmly flipped a screen pass to Harraway about four yards behind the line of scrimmage. The fullback appeared to be hemmed in, but he escaped the first wave of tacklers and broke into the open. He rolled untouched for the only touchdown of the second half.

A Curt Knight field goal stretched the lead to 27-20 early in the fourth quarter and the Washington defense made a couple of big plays to make it stand up. Following a shanked punt, Atlanta gained possession at the Washington 18, but the Redskins forced a fumble and Chris Hanburger recovered at the 10 for the home team. Following a later interception, Atlanta moved to the Washington 14. Defensive linemen Dennis Crane and Frank Bosch saved the day, though, quashing the drive with a sack. The Redskins killed the clock.

11/30/69	**Rams (11-0) 24, REDSKINS (5-4-2) 13**				50,352
LA	0	10	0	14	**24**
Was	3	3	0	7	**13**

Was	FG Knight 19
LA	FG Gossett 20
LA	Klein 1 pass from Gabriel (Gossett kick)
Was	FG Knight 19
LA	Truax 3 pass from Gabriel (Gossett kick)
Was	Harraway 1 run (Knight kick)
LA	Ellison 1 run (Gossett kick)

RFK Stadium—The Redskins gave the undefeated visitors all they could handle, but the Rams came up with a blocked punt and a key interception to escape with a 24-13 victory.

Punters Mike Bragg of Washington and Pat Studstill of LA were involved in a punting duel for much of the first half, interrupted only by an exchange of field goals. Bragg was getting the better of the exchanges until Willie Ellison led a jailbreak and got to a Bragg punt just off the kicker's toe, scrambling for the recovery at the Washington 22. After two plays and three penalties on Washington—one of those penalties nullified an end zone interception by Pat Fischer—Roman Gabriel threw a one-yard scoring pass to tight end Bob Klein and the Rams were up 10-6.

The score stayed the same until the first play of the fourth quarter when the Rams drove to the Washington three. Gabriel called the same play as when he threw the scoring toss to Klein earlier, but this time to a different tight end. The result was a three-yard scoring pass to Billy Truax. Washington roared back with a 67-yard touchdown drive that culminated in Charley Harraway's one-yard plunge. Curt Knight's point after pulled the home team back within four with 9:17 left.

The defense forced the Rams to punt and the Redskins took possession at their own six. Soon after that, though, cornerback Jim Nettles cut in front of a pass intended for Charley Taylor at the Washington 39 and returned it to the one. Although a clipping

penalty forced the Rams to put the ball in play at the spot of the interception, the Rams moved in for the kill. It came on Ellison's one-yard touchdown run with just 3:31 left.

12/7/69	**Redskins (6-4-2) 34, EAGLES (4-8) 29**				60,658
Was	7	6	14	7	34
Phi	7	9	3	10	29

Phi	Keyes 2 run (Baker kick)
Was	Taylor 12 pass from Jurgensen (Knight kick)
Phi	Jackson 29 pass from Snead (Baker kick)
Phi	Safety Jurgensen tackled in end zone
Was	FG Knight 12
Was	FG Knight 43
Was	Hoffman recovered fumble in end zone (Knight kick)
Phi	FG Baker 19
Was	Smith 25 pass from Jurgensen (Knight kick)
Phi	FG Baker 47
Was	Brown 1 run (Knight kick)
Phi	Jackson 18 pass from Snead (Baker kick)

Franklin Field—On an ice-covered Astroturf field, a third-quarter fumble recovery in the end zone by rookie defensive end John Hoffman put the Redskins in the lead for good in their win over the Eagles. Washington's victory assured they would finish with at least a .500 record in Vince Lombardi's first season with the team.

After tying the game at seven on a 12-yard touchdown pass from Sonny Jurgensen to Charley Taylor, the Redskins saw the Eagles take a nine-point lead on Norm Snead to Harold Jackson touchdown pass and a safety when Jurgensen was sacked in the end zone for a safety. A pair of Curt Knight field goals prior to halftime cut the Philly lead to 16-13 at the break.

Midway through the third quarter, the Redskins punted and the home team took possession at its own 13. After a three-yard gain, Snead was sacked for a loss back to the eight. He tried passing again and was sacked once more, with disastrous consequences for his team. End Carl Kammerer forced Snead to fumble, Hoffman pounced on it and Washington had a 20-16 lead with 7:54 left in the third.

The Eagles pulled within one on Sam Baker's 19-yard field goal, but the Redskins answered with a 25-yard scoring pass from Jurgensen to Jerry Smith. That and a one-yard touchdown run by rookie running back Larry Brown wrapped up the win for the Redskins.

12/14/69	**REDSKINS (7-4-2) 17, Saints (4-11) 14**				50,354
NO	0	0	7	7	14
Was	7	10	0	0	17

Was	Harraway 12 run (Knight kick)
Was	FG Knight 19
Was	Harraway 30 pass from Jurgensen (Knight kick)
NO	Shy 1 run (Dempsey kick)
NO	Wheelright 5 run (Dempsey kick)

RFK Stadium—Two Charley Harraway touchdowns—one rushing, the other on a pass reception—spurred the Redskins to a 17-0 halftime lead. They had to hang on in the second half to secure the 17-14 victory and assure the team of its first winning season since 1955.

A 25-yard punt return set up Harraway's first score. From the Saints' 12, the Redskins lined up in a tight formation. In a role reversal, halfback Larry Brown threw a block that cleared the way for the fullback Harraway and it was 7-0.

A 47-yard return with an interception by Rickie Harris set up a 19-yard Curt Knight field goal. After a New Orleans punt, Sonny Jurgensen took to the air, completing three of four passes that accounted for all of the 47 yards in the touchdown drive. The last 30 came on a short toss to Harraway, who blew by the linebacker attempting to cover him and went into the end zone untouched.

In addition to Harris' interception during the first half, Mike Bass picked off a Saints pass and Chris Hanburger recovered a fumble, but all the Redskins got of those three turnovers were the three points following Harris' play. It nearly cost the Redskins in the second half.

Rookie quarterback Edd Hargett, subbing for an ailing Billy Kilmer, brought the Saints' offense to life. As a taste of things to come in the second half, Hargett moved his team from its own 20 to the Washington five, but the gun ending the half sounded before he could get off a play from there. Hargett led TD drives of 53 and 97 yards in the second half. In the game's last two minutes, he drove the Saints to the Washington 43, but linebacker Harold McLinton tackled Hargett for no gain on fourth down and the Skins were able to kill the clock.

12/21/69	COWBOYS (11-2-1) 20, Redskins (7-5-2) 10			56,924	
Was	0	3	0	7	10
Dal	10	3	0	7	20
Dal	FG Clark 12				
Dal	Norman 26 pass from Morton (Clark kick)				
Was	FG Knight 33				
Dal	FG Clark 24				
Was	Hanburger 19 fumble return (Knight kick)				
Dal	Hill 6 run (Clark kick)				

Cotton Bowl—Dallas survived a fourth-quarter scare to beat the visiting Redskins 20-10.

The Cowboys got out to a 10-0 first-quarter lead. First Mike Clark kicked a 12-yard field goal. After that Craig Morton led a drive that culminated in a 26-yard touchdown pass to tight end Pettis Norman.

The Redskins countered with a 33-yard Curt Knight field goal but Clark booted another one, this one from 24, and Dallas took a 13-3 lead into the locker room.

The third quarter was scoreless and the Cowboys appeared to be coasting with that 10-point lead and less than 10 minutes left in the game.

But that changed in an instant. Defensive end Frank Bosch stripped the ball from rookie running back Calvin Hill and linebacker Chris Hanburger picked it up and ran untouched 19 yards for a touchdown, cutting the Cowboy lead to 13-10.

Dallas responded immediately, returning the ensuing kickoff to their own 40. From there, staying mostly on the ground, the Cowboys moved in for the clincher—and it came on a six-yard run by Hill.

Washington quarterback Sonny Jurgensen passed for 206 yards to give him an NFL-leading total of 3,102. This was Jurgensen's fifth season with 3,000 or more passing yards.

1970
Head Coach: Bill Austin
Record: 6-8, Fourth in NFC East

Honors: Larry Brown, Pro Bowl, All-NFL;
Chris Hanburger, All-NFC; Len Hauss, Pro Bowl

Redskins, Cowboys in Five-Team NFC East
Jan 16—The Redskins and Cowboys will be battling it out twice a year.

Along with the Giants, Eagles and Cardinals, they will now be together in the NFC East division. New York and Philadelphia are two of Washington's oldest rivals.

June 27
Lombardi Condition 'Excellent' after Surgery
Tumor, portion of colon removed during procedure

July 6
Williams: Lombardi Will Be at Camp
Coach will be out of hospital soon, expects to be present in Carlisle

July 13
NFL Locks Veterans Out of Camps
Strike possibility looms

July 16
Bill Austin Named Interim Coach
Ex-Steelers boss will run team while Lombardi recuperates

July 27
Lombardi Reenters Hospital
Additional surgery planned, details guarded

Aug 4
Labor Deal Reached, Veterans Report
Rookies will have to yield

Vince Lombardi Dies at 57

Sep 3—The Redskins lost a coach and the NFL lost a legend as Vince Lombardi died of cancer today.

Serious questions about Lombardi's health have been raised since he entered Georgetown Hospital for a second time on July 27. A month earlier he had undergone surgery for removal of a tumor and part of his large intestine.

Reports that he was gravely ill have emerged just in the past few days. The Redskins were braced for the worst. Today, the members of the team were unrestrained in expressing their love and respect for Lombardi.

"All of the things a man searches for all his life I found in Coach Lombardi," said tight end Jerry Smith.

Many players chose to make written statements rather than talk to the press during such an emotional time.

Quarterback Sonny Jurgensen, who had one of his best seasons ever under Lombardi in 1969, wrote, "In this short period of time, I grew to love the man."

"I thank God for letting such a man as Coach Lombardi come into my life," wrote safety Brig Owens.

"He had a covenant with greatness," said team president Edward Bennett Williams. "The world of sport has lost its first citizen."

With the Green Bay Packers and the Redskins, Lombardi's record was 105-35-6. His .750 winning percentage is the best among NFL coaches who have at least 100 victories.

Sep 7

Former Heisman Winner Beban Cut
Redskins give up on QB; gave up first-round pick for him in '68

9/20/70	49ERS (1-0) 26, Redskins (0-1) 17				34,984
Was	7	3	0	7	17
SF	7	9	7	3	24
SF	Cunningham 1 run (Gossett kick)				
Was	Brown 75 run (Knight kick)				
SF	Safety Brown tackled in end zone				
SF	Willard 7 run (Gossett kick)				
Was	FG Knight 18				
SF	Witcher 21 pass from Brodie				
Was	Smith 10 pass from Jurgensen (Knight kick)				
SF	FG Gossett 20				

Kezar Stadium—John Brodie completed 17 of 20 passes to lead San Francisco over the Redskins 26-17.

The game spoiled the debut of Redskins head coach Bill Austin, taking the place of Vince Lombardi, who died of cancer earlier this month.

The San Francisco defense did its part to secure the win, sacking Sonny Jurgensen seven times and intercepting a pass to kill a promising drive.

The home team broke on top in the first quarter on a one-yard run by Doug Cunningham. Larry Brown broke free for a 75-yard touchdown run to tie the game at seven later in the first.

Soon after that, though, Brown gave two points right back. He fumbled into his own end zone and had to dive on the ball, giving San Francisco a safety and the lead for good.

San Francisco led 16-10 at halftime and expanded the margin to 23-10 on Brodie's 21-yard touchdown pass to Dick Witcher in the third quarter. Jurgensen rallied the Redskins with a 13-yard TD pass to Jerry Smith in the fourth quarter, but Brodie crafted a masterful, time-killing drive to a Bruce Gossett field goal that provided the insurance points with a minute to play.

9/27/70	CARDINALS (1-1) 27, Redskins (0-2) 17				44,246
Was	7	3	0	7	17
StL	0	13	14	0	27
Was	Brown 5 run (Knight kick)				
Was	FG Knight 36				
StL	Lane 9 run (Bakken kick)				
StL	Rowland 16 pass from Beathard (kick failed)				
StL	Farr 19 interception return (Bakken kick)				
StL	Lane 1 run (Bakken kick)				
Was	Harraway 3 run (Knight kick)				

Busch Stadium—The Cardinals spotted Washington a 10-0 lead before running off 27 unanswered points in the second and third quarters to claim a 27-17 win over Washington.

The Redskins built their lead on the strength of a five-yard run by Larry Brown, who carried 17 times for 114 yards on the day, and a 36-yard Curt Knight field goal.

It seemed the Redskins' fortunes were growing even better when quarterback Jim Hart had to leave the game with a concussion after being knocked out by blitzing linebacker Harold McLinton. However, backup Pete Beathard picked up where Hart left off, completing the touchdown drive that the starter had gotten underway. Later in the second period, Beathard gave the Cardinals the lead for good by throwing six yards to Johnny Rowland to complete a 62-yard touchdown drive. The home team led 13-10 at halftime.

The Cardinal defense wrapped it up with a pair of thefts of Sonny Jurgensen passes in the third quarter. Miller Farr stole the ball out of Jerry Smith's hands and easily rolled 19 yards for a touchdown. Soon after that, Jerry Stovall picked Jurgensen off at

the Washington 30 and returned it to the one. McArthur Lane scored his second touchdown of the game from there to put St. Louis up 27-10.

10/4/70	Redskins (1-2) 33, EAGLES (0-3) 21				60,638
Was	0	13	6	14	33
Phi	7	0	0	14	21
Phi	Bouggess 21 pass from Snead (Moseley kick)				
Was	FG Knight 26				
Was	Smith 26 pass from Jurgensen (Knight kick)				
Was	FG Knight 22				
Was	FG Knight 12				
Was	FG Knight 22				
Was	Taylor 5 pass from Jurgensen (Knight kick)				
Phi	Pinder 40 run (Moseley kick)				
Was	Brown 4 run (Knight kick)				
Phi	Arrington 1 run (Moseley kick)				

Franklin Field—Larry Brown rushed for 110 yards on 27 carries and Sonny Jurgensen threw two touchdown passes to lead the Redskins past the Eagles 33-21.

The host team graciously assisted its visitors, losing three fumbles and tossing up two interceptions. The turnovers set up four Washington scores.

Philadelphia led after one period on a touchdown pass from Norm Snead to Les Bouggess. Mark Moseley converted to give the Eagles a 7-0 lead.

The Redskins then tore off 23 unanswered points. Curt Knight booted a 26-yard field goal to make it 7-3 and then Rickie Harris intercepted Norm Snead's pass, setting Washington up at the Philly 23. Three plays later, Jurgensen threw 26 yards to Jerry Smith to put the Redskins ahead to stay.

After three Curt Knight field goals expanded Washington's lead to 19-7, Chris Hanburger set up a touchdown when he picked off a Snead pass at the Philly 21 and returned it to the nine. A few plays later Jurgensen threw a five-yard touchdown pass to Charley Taylor.

Brown tallied an insurance touchdown by capping a drive with a four-yard touchdown run in the four quarter. That enabled the Skins to survive two fourth-quarter Eagle touchdowns.

Jurgensen completed 14 of 28 passes for 139 yards.

10/11/70	REDSKINS (2-2) 31, Lions (3-1) 10				50,414
Det	0	3	7	0	10
Was	7	10	7	7	31
Was	Taylor 15 pass from Jurgensen (Knight kick)				
Det	FG Mann 36				
Was	FG Knight 31				
Was	Smith 7 pass from Jurgensen (Knight kick)				
Was	Taylor 16 pass from Jurgensen (Knight kick)				
Det	Eddy 4 run (Mann kick)				
Was	Brown 4 run (Knight kick)				

RFK Stadium—It was the Sonny and Larry show once more as Jurgensen passed for 225 yards and three touchdowns and Brown racked up 101 on the ground and scored once, leading Washington over the previously unbeaten Lions.

Not only had Detroit gone unbeaten in three games to open the season, but they had allowed just 17 total points in those games. The Redskins equaled that score by halftime as Jurgensen threw two touchdown passes. The first, to Charley Taylor, came after a Detroit fumble set Washington up at the Lions' 39. Following a Curt Knight field goal, Jurgensen struck again, this time on a seven-yard pass to Jerry Smith to put the home team in control at 17-3 at intermission.

In all, the Redskins racked up 341 yards of total offense. Balance was key as Brown's running opened up things for Jurgensen's aerial attack. When they dropped back to defend against the pass, Brown would start to pound away.

As the Washington defense controlled the Lions, all that remained in the second half was for Jurgensen to throw his third touchdown pass—another strike to Taylor—and for Brown to squeeze over the 100-yard mark in rushing by scoring on a four-yard run late in the game.

10/19/70	RAIDERS (2-2-1) 34, Redskins (2-3) 20				54,471
Was	3	10	0	7	20
Oak	14	6	14	0	34
Oak	Dixon 39 run (Blanda kick)				
Oak	Wells 28 pass from Lamonica (Blanda kick)				
Was	FG Knight 14				
Oak	FG Blanda 35				
Was	FG Knight 34				
Was	Taylor 39 pass from Jurgensen (Knight kick)				
Oak	FG Blanda 21				
Oak	Wells 24 pass from Lamonica (Blanda kick)				
Oak	Wells 24 pass from Lamonica (Blanda kick)				
Oak	C. Smith 16 pass from Lamonica (Blanda kick)				
Was	J. Smith 23 pass from Jurgensen (Knight kick)				

Oakland-Alameda County Coliseum—Raiders fullback Hewitt Dixon scrambled 39 yards for a touchdown on his team's first play from scrimmage, an inauspicious beginning to Washington's first appearance on Monday night football. Oakland led all the way in defeating the Redskins 34-20.

It didn't get much better the second time the Redskins were on defense as Daryle Lamonica found Warren Wells for a 28-yard touchdown pass, the first of three scoring tosses for the Raider QB. The Redskins got close to the goal line late in the first quarter, but had to settle for a 14-yard field goal by Curt Knight.

Washington mounted a bit of a comeback in the second quarter. Knight kicked another field goal and Sonny Jurgensen threw a 39-yard touchdown pass to Charley Taylor, cutting the Raiders' lead to 17-13.

That was the high point for the Skins, however, as George Blanda kicked a 21-yard field goal before halftime and the Raiders drove 77 and 69 yards for third-quarter touchdowns that wrapped it up for the home team. Oakland controlled the game by gaining 226 yards on the ground, compared to just 77 for Washington.

10/25/70	REDSKINS (3-3) 20, Bengals (1-5) 0				50,514
Cin	0	0	0	0	0
Was	10	0	7	3	20
Was	Taylor 10 pass from Jurgensen (Knight kick)				
Was	FG Knight 10				
Was	Taylor 31 pass from Jurgensen (Knight kick)				
Was	FG Knight 30				

RFK Stadium—Usually just two teams are involved in playing any given football game. On this day, though, there were at least three, maybe four teams playing in the contest.

One was the Cincinnati Bengals, and the others wore the Washington Redskins uniform. At times in the game—such as when Sonny Jurgensen was throwing a pair of touchdown passes to Charley Taylor—the Redskins resembled a good NFL team. At others, such as when they drove deep into Cincy territory and had to settle for field goals or were letting the hapless Bengals stay in the game or were having touchdowns called back due to penalties, they looked more like one of the league's bottom dwellers.

That works out to Washington being an average team, and that's what this performance indicated. The Redskins drove 80 yards after taking the opening kickoff, scoring on the first Jurgensen-Taylor TD hookup. They had another golden opportunity when end John Hoffman recovered a fumble at the Cincinnati 12, but settled for a 10-yard Curt Knight field goal.

Much of the rest of the game was marked by the Redskins giving the Bengals chances to score, and then watching them

bumble them away. Larry Brown, who carried 22 times for 110 yards, had a third-quarter touchdown run of 42 yards called back due to a penalty. Then the powerhouse Redskins appeared, bouncing back from adversity. On the very next play, Jurgensen threw 31 yards to Taylor to make it 17-0.

11/1/70	Washington (4-3) 19, BRONCOS (4-3) 3				50,705
Was	3	10	0	6	19
Den	0	0	0	3	3
Was	FG Knight 37				
Was	FG Knight 44				
Was	Smith 17 pass from Jurgensen (Knight kick)				
Den	FG Howfield 36				
Was	Smith 11 pass from Jurgensen (kick failed)				

Mile High Stadium—The Redskins allowed Denver to cross midfield just once in the first half while in the process of building a 13-0 lead and taking the easy win.

Curt Knight started the scoring with a 37-yard field goal in the first quarter. He booted another one—this time from 44—in the second, putting Washington up 6-0.

Then, late in the first half, Sonny Jurgensen led a sustained touchdown drive. The 62-yard touchdown march was capped with a 17-yard touchdown toss from Jurgensen to Jerry Smith to give the Redskins their 13-0 edge.

The third quarter was scoreless as the Redskins were content to let their defense continue to hold the Broncos at bay. Bronco quarterback Pete Liske completed just nine of 25 passes for 86 yards. Floyd Little, Denver's All-Pro running back, was held to 65 yards on 15 carries.

Denver did manage to score on a field goal early in the final period. They regained possession and had a chance to make a game of it. Their hopes were short lived, however, as end Bruce Anderson recovered a Denver fumble at the Broncos' 11-yard line and Jurgensen's second scoring strike to Smith came on the next play.

11/8/70	Vikings (7-1) 19, REDSKINS (4-4) 10				50,415
Min	3	7	3	6	19
Was	7	0	3	0	10
Was	Taylor 2 pass from Jurgensen (Knight kick)				
Min	FG Cox 44				
Min	Osborn 1 run (Cox kick)				
Min	FG Cox 17				
Was	FG Knight 15				
Min	FG Cox 25				
Min	FG Cox 42				

RFK Stadium—Somewhere in the Ironclad Laws of Football, there is rule stating if you hope to upset a superior team, you must take advantage of opportunities when you have them. The 6-1 Vikings were ripe for the plucking, but the Redskins couldn't pull off the upset; they failed to cash in on some golden opportunities.

Actually, they did convert their first foray into Minnesota territory to their maximum advantage as they moved 81 yards to take a 7-0 lead on their first possession. Sonny Jurgensen found receiver Walt Roberts wide open for 49 yards and then Larry Brown ripped 20 yards to the four. Two plays after that, Jurgensen went to Charley Taylor to cap the drive.

The Vikings responded. After a Fred Cox field goal, they ground out a drive that ate up the first 9:03 of the second quarter. They crept forward 73 yards in 19 plays to Dave Osborn's one-yard touchdown plunge.

Faced with a 10-7 deficit, the Redskins drove to the Minnesota 16 and suffered their first blown opportunity after Gary Larsen sacked Jurgensen for a 10-yard loss. Curt Knight missed a 33-yard field goal and the Redskins still trailed by three at the break.

Minnesota's special teams and defense were instrumental in expanding the lead in the second half. Karl Kassulke blocked Mike

Bragg's punt to give the Vikings the ball at the Washington 14, leading to another Cox field goal to make it 13-7.

Washington again responded with a drive—and the glass was only half empty at the end of this one, instead of being bone dry. Knight hit a 15-yard field goal after a drive to the eight.

Trailing by just three, the Redskins got the ball back, but Jurgensen was again nailed by Larsen and lost the ball at the Washington 23. Four plays later, Cox hit his fourth field goal of the game from 24 yards and it was 16-10 early in the final period.

Again, the Redskins drove deep into Minnesota territory and the offense left the field frustrated once more. After moving to a first and goal at the nine with 6:20 left, three straight incompletions ended the Redskins' hopes.

11/15/70	GIANTS (6-3) 35, Redskins (4-5) 33			62,915	
Was	0	12	21	0	33
NYG	7	7	.0	21	35
NYG	Frederickson 1 run (Gogolak kick)				
Was	FG Knight 15				
Was	FG Knight 27				
NYG	McNeil recovered fumble in end zone (Gogolak kick)				
Was	FG Knight 27				
Was	FG Knight 40				
Was	Harraway 57 run (Knight kick)				
Was	Taylor 28 pass from Jurgensen (Knight kick)				
Was	Harraway 2 run (Knight kick)				
NYG	Johnson 5 run (Gogolak kick)				
NYG	Frederickson 57 pass from Tarkenton (Gogolak kick)				
NYG	Johnson 9 run (Gogolak kick)				

Yankee Stadium—Pull out all of the metaphors, mix them up and throw them on the table. With the Redskins leading by 19 points in the fourth quarter, the wheels came off the train; there was a bus wreck. Say it any way you'd like—it was a classic disaster, as though the Hindenburg crashed into the *Titanic*.

In the first half, the Redskins had four opportunities to score touchdowns, but had just 12 points to show for them. They also had a chance to prevent a New York score when the Giants fumbled into the end zone, but receiver Clifton McNeil recovered to give the Giants a touchdown. New York entered the locker room at halftime fortunate to be up 14-12.

In the third quarter, it didn't seem that the missed opportunities would matter. On the first play from scrimmage, Charley Harraway raced 57 yards for a touchdown that put the Redskins on top 19-14. Before the quarter was out, Sonny Jurgensen had directed the team to two more touchdowns. One came on a 28-yard pass from Jurgensen to Charley Taylor, and the other on a two-yard Harraway run.

Washington's 33-14 margin held until 5:19 had elapsed in the fourth quarter. Ron Johnson scored on a five-yard touchdown run to make it 33-21. The slippery slope the Redskins were on suddenly got much slicker as less than two minutes after Johnson's run, Fran Tarkenton threw a little swing pass to fullback Tucker Frederickson. He rumbled 57 yards to a touchdown to pull his team within five at 33-28.

When New York got the ball back on a punt with 4:06 remaining, there were only a couple of differences between the Washington defense and the crowd of 62,915 at Yankee Stadium: the Redskins didn't pay to get in, and they weren't wildly cheering on the Giants' rally. Nevertheless, the Redskins were indeed mere spectators as the Giants rolled downfield to the goal line. Tarkenton completed passes of 20, 13, 10 and 10 yards to move the Giants to the Washington nine. Johnson had a wall of blockers to run behind and scored the winning touchdown with a minute left on the clock. The Hindenburg was sunk.

11/23/70	Cowboys (6-4) 45, REDSKINS (4-6) 21			50,415	
Dal	3	21	14	7	45
Was	7	0	14	0	21
Dal	FG Clark 42				
Was	Smith 20 pass from Jurgensen (Knight kick)				
Dal	Thomas 4 run (Clark kick)				
Dal	Rentzel 27 pass from Morton (Clark kick)				
Dal	Garrison 3 pass from Morton (Clark kick)				
Was	Brown 21 pass from Jurgensen (Knight kick)				
Dal	Washington 100 kickoff return (Clark kick)				
Was	Henderson 12 pass from Jurgensen (Knight kick)				
Dal	Thomas 35 run (Clark kick)				
Dal	Thomas 2 run (Clark kick)				

RFK Stadium—The Cowboys erased a 7-3 Redskins lead by scoring 21 unanswered points in the second quarter, propelling them to an easy 45-21 win.

The Redskins moved 98 yards for a touchdown on their second possession of the game, the payoff coming on a 20-yard pass from Sonny Jurgensen to Jerry Smith. The Redskins were up 7-3 and it appeared that the Cowboys, who had been ripped 38-0 the previous Monday night by the Cardinals, were in for a battle.

Until the second quarter began.

Dallas first scored on a four-yard run by Duane Thomas, who was subbing for the injured Calvin Hill. It was the first of three scoring runs for Thomas, who gained 104 yards on 16 carries for the day. Quarterback Craig Morton added two touchdown passes and it was 24-7 at the half.

The home team got back into it for a brief time. Jurgensen threw a 21-yard TD pass to Larry Brown early in the third quarter to pull his team within ten. That lasted for as long as it took Dallas' Mark Washington to field the ensuing kickoff and return it 100 yards for a touchdown. At 31-14, the rout was on.

11/29/70	Giants (7-4) 27, REDSKINS (4-7) 24			50,415	
NYG	0	10	14	3	27
Was	3	0	7	14	24
Was	FG Knight 27				
NYG	Johnson 1 run (Gogolak kick)				
NYG	FG Gogolak 22				
Was	Roberts 66 pass from Jurgensen (Knight kick)				
NYG	Frederickson 5 pass from Tarkenton (Gogolak kick)				
Was	Henderson 5 pass from Jurgensen (Knight kick)				
Was	Brown 15 pass from Jurgensen (Knight kick)				
NYG	FG Gogolak 20				

RFK Stadium—A comeback bid by the Redskins fell short in the final seconds as Sonny Jurgensen was sacked attempting a pass off of a fake field goal play. Coach Bill Austin eschewed a possible 44-yard attempt by Curt Knight that would have tied the game and the Redskins lost 27-24.

The Giants led 10-3 at halftime, but the Redskins showed an offensive pulse when Jurgensen launched a 66-yard scoring pass to Walter Roberts to tie the game. Then the offense went back to sleep and the Giants scored on two Fran Tarkenton touchdown passes, taking a 24-10 lead and, it seemed, control of the game.

But Jurgensen and the Redskins fought back, moving 73 yards to score on Jurgensen's five-yard touchdown pass to John Henderson on the first play of the fourth quarter. Four minutes later, the Redskins struck again, finishing off a 52-yard drive that tied the game on a 15-yard Jurgensen to Larry Brown touchdown pass.

Washington regained possession and was looking to take the lead when a safety blitz hurried a Jurgensen pass and Willie Williams picked it off at the New York 45. A 38-yard run by Bobby Duhon was the big play that got the Giants into field goal position and Pete Gogolak put it through the uprights to give the Giants a 27-24 lead with just under two minutes to play.

Four pass completions got the Redskins into position to fake the field goal with 17 seconds left, but the entire Giants bench seemed to have the play sniffed out. Rookie defensive back Joe Green headed straight for Jurgensen and got the sack to end the threat.

12/6/70	COWBOYS (8-4) 34, Redskins (4-8) 0				57,936
Was	0	0	0	0	0
Dal	0	7	14	13	34
Dal	Reeves 6 run (Clark kick)				
Dal	Garrison 6 pass from Morton (Clark kick)				
Dal	Garrison 8 run (Clark kick)				
Dal	FG Clark 38				
Dal	FG Clark 15				
Dal	Reeves 1 run (Clark kick)				

Cotton Bowl—A battered Redskin team hung close with Dallas for 30 minutes before the Cowboys broke the game open in the third quarter with two touchdowns. The Redskins suffered their first shutout in nine years, losing 34-0.

Playing without offensive stalwarts Charley Taylor, Larry Brown and Charley Harraway, the Redskins trailed just 7-0 at halftime. Then they made the mistake of putting the second half kickoff into the hands of Mark Washington, who had a critical 100-yard kickoff return in the teams' previous meeting two weeks ago. This time, Washington just reached the Redskins' 30 before being tackled by Mike Bass, but the end result was the same. Craig Morton then threw six yards to Walt Garrison to put Dallas up 14-0.

Soon after that, cornerback Herb Adderly picked off a Jurgensen pass and returned it 30 yards. This led to another Garrison TD—an eight-yard run—to give Dallas a 21-0 lead.

To say the second half belonged to Dallas would be a terrible understatement. In the final 30 minutes, the Redskins managed no first downs, minus two yards passing and 17 yards rushing. Not surprisingly, they failed to get out of their own territory.

12/13/70	REDSKINS (5-8) 24, Eagles (2-10-1) 6				50,415
Phi	3	3	0	0	6
Was	0	7	7	10	24
Phi	FG Moseley 24				
Was	Brown 5 run (Knight kick)				
Phi	FG Moseley 16				
Was	Henderson 56 pass from Jurgensen (Knight kick)				
Was	FG Knight 49				
Was	Jurgensen 1 run (Knight kick)				

RFK Stadium—You could hear the sound of things breaking all over the place at RFK Stadium.

Larry Brown broke the 1,000 yard rushing mark for the season, becoming the first Redskin and 13th NFL player to do so.

A 56-yard touchdown pass from Sonny Jurgensen to John Henderson broke open a tight game in the third quarter.

Finally, the Redskins broke a five-game losing streak that had seen them go from division title contenders to this—a battle to stay out of the NFC East basement.

Brown picked up 85 yards on 21 carries for the day. He got the scoring started for his team when he blasted four yards for a touchdown on the initial play of the second quarter. That gave Washington a 7-3 lead, a margin the Eagles cut to 7-6 by halftime on Mark Moseley's second field goal.

Midway through the third period, Jurgensen found Henderson to expand the lead to 14-6. The home team put the game away in the fourth with a 49-yard field goal by Curt Knight and a touchdown on a one-yard quarterback keeper by Jurgensen.

After Brown surpassed the 1,000-yard mark for the season early in the game, he took the ball he was carrying over to the sideline and flashed the "V" sign, much to the crowd's delight.

Brown had plenty of help as Charlie Harraway picked up 60 yards rushing on 16 carries.

The Redskins defense was tough against the Philadelphia running game. The Eagles were limited to just 51 yards on the ground.

12/20/70	REDSKINS (6-8) 28, Cardinals (8-5-1) 27				50,415
StL	7	3	3	14	27
Was	14	7	0	7	28
Was	Smith 19 pass from Jurgensen (Knight kick)				
StL	Smith 16 pass from Hart (Bakken kick)				
Was	Harraway 3 run (Knight kick)				
Was	Smith 14 pass from Jurgensen (Knight kick)				
StL	FG Bakken 45				
StL	FG Bakken 34				
Was	Harraway 1 run (Knight kick)				
StL	Gilliam 57 pass from Hart (Bakken kick)				
StL	Latourette 32 fumble return (Bakken kick)				

RFK Stadium—The Redskins built a 28-13 lead in the fourth quarter and then had to watch as St. Louis' Jim Bakken lined up for a 21-yard field goal attempt that would have given the Cards the lead with just under four minutes remaining. Fortunately, the veteran kicker pulled the attempt right, and the home team escaped with a 28-27 win.

The Redskins took a 21-7 lead in the second quarter on the strength of two Sonny Jurgensen touchdown passes to Jerry Smith and a three-yard scoring run by Charley Harraway. Bakken snuck a 45-yard field goal over the crossbar with just over a minute left in the half to make it 21-10 at the break.

After another Bakken field goal, the Redskins drove for what seemed to be the clincher. Starting from their own 20, they moved the 80 yards to pay dirt in 12 plays, with Harraway scoring his second touchdown of the day on a one-yard plunge. That made it 28-13 early in the fourth quarter.

There was cause for concern but not worry when Jim Hart found John Gilliam open for 57 yards and a touchdown following Harraway's score. It was time to worry but not panic two plays later when Larry Brown fumbled and Cardinal safety Chuck Latourette returned it 32 yards for a touchdown to cut the Redskins' lead to one. Yes, then it was time to panic.

On the Redskins' first play after Latourette's return, Brown fumbled again and Bob Rowe recovered for St. Louis at the Washington 25. Despite this, the Washington defense remained calm and forced Bakken's errant 21-yard field goal attempt with 3:51 left. Two subsequent St. Louis possessions ended in a sack and a Brig Owens interception.

1971

Head Coach: George Allen
Record: 9-4-1, Second in NCF East
Playoffs: 1-1, lost in Wild Card Game

Honors: George Allen, NFL Coach of the Year; Larry Brown, Pro Bowl, All-NFC; Speedy Duncan, All-NFC; Len Hauss, Pro Bowl, All-NFC; Roy Jefferson, Pro Bowl; Curt Knight, Pro Bowl, All-NFC; Jack Pardee, All-NFC

Hall of Fame: Vince Lombardi, Coach 1969

Williams Delays Coaching Decision

Dec 20—Redskins team President Edward Bennett Williams will delay any announcement of the future of interim head coach Bill Austin until January.

For his part, Austin has indicated that he would not be interested in coming back under a one-year deal.

George Allen Gets 'Feeler' From Skins

Dec 31—It appears that the Redskins are interested in hiring recently-fired Rams coach George Allen, and they have what it takes to lure the coveted coach to Washington, D.C.

Allen said yesterday that he and his agent have received inquiries from a number of teams, Washington among them. To consider an opening, he would have to get the title of general manager as well as head coach and have an opportunity to purchase stock in the team, he said. Allen wants to take over a team that has a chance to win soon.

The Redskins would appear to fit the bill in all three areas. The GM position has been vacant since the death of Vince Lombardi; there don't appear to be any obstacles to Allen obtaining a piece of the team; and the Redskins went 6-8 last year, despite the loss of Lombardi a few weeks prior to the start of the season.

The Future is Now: George Allen Hired as Redskins Coach

Jan 6—Promising to win now, George Allen was introduced as the Redskins' new head coach today.

According to team president Edward Bennett Williams, Allen will have "all of the authority" that the late Vince Lombardi had, meaning complete control of the football end of the operation.

Williams proclaimed that Allen is "the best football coach in the world."

"I am saying unequivocally, unqualifiedly, and unambiguously that this is the last coach I will ever hire," Williams gushed.

For his part, Allen had high praise for several players including quarterback Sonny Jurgensen, calling him "one of the great passers in modern football."

"I plan to win in 1971," said Allen, who is not a believer in long-term rebuilding plans.

Allen, a highly-regarded defensive coordinator in Chicago before going to the Rams, said he will focus on the defensive side of the ball. He noted that the Redskins finished dead last in the 13-team NFC in rushing defense and 12th in total defense.

Allen was 49-17-4 in his five seasons in Los Angeles.

Jan 23

Redskins Trade for Billy Kilmer
Allen sends LB Roussel & undisclosed pick for Saints QB

Allen's Contract Richest Ever

Jan 28—A Los Angeles newspaper has revealed some of the details of the contract George Allen signed as coach of the Washington Redskins. Among the provisions in the deal:

- A $25,000 bonus to sign the contract.
- An annual salary of $125,000 per year for seven years.
- Bonuses for reaching various levels in the playoffs, including $15,000 for making it to the Super Bowl.
- A new house for which the team will pay up to $150,000.
- An option to purchase five percent of the team for $500,000 (pending the outcome of litigation by the estate of George Preston Marshall).
- Permission to keep all money earned from endorsements and radio and TV jobs.

Other perks include expense accounts, a car and driver, and six weeks of vacation a year.

While it is difficult to estimate the value of some of the provisions, it is believed that Allen's is the most lucrative ever for an NFL coach.

Big Deal: Redskins, Rams Swap Players, Picks

Jan 28—George Allen dialed up his old team, the Los Angeles Rams, and negotiated the biggest trade in NFL history.

In all, 15 players and draft picks changed hands between the Rams and the Redskins. In the history of the NFL, there has never been a bigger trade involving two teams.

To the Rams went linebacker Marlin McKeever, first and third round picks in 1971 and third-, fourth-, fifth-, sixth- and, seventh-rounders in 1972. In exchange, the Redskins got linebackers Maxie Baughn, Jack Pardee and Myron Pottios, running back and special teams ace Jeff Jordan, guard John Wilbur, defensive tackle Diron Talbert and a fifth-round pick in 1971.

The fifth-round choice that came to the Redskins didn't stay in Washington for long. Allen immediately dispatched it to Green Bay for the rights to tight end Boyd Dowler. The former Packer tight end had already come to the Redskins as an assistant coach, but Allen wanted to be able to activate Dowler should the Skins need him.

"This is great, terrific for the Redskins," Allen said. "We've upgraded our defense at least twenty-five percent. It's worth at least two victories. Our goal is now nine or ten wins."

Some agreed with Allen, while others were skeptical. Talbert, Allen maintained, was his number one pick, but at age 27 with four years and 44 NFL games on his body, he was hardly the spry youngster that one might get with the tenth overall selection. Linebackers Baughn, Pottios and Pardee were all looking at age 30 in the rear view mirror.

May 11

Redskins Trade for Ron McDole
Three undisclosed picks go to Bills for 290-lb. defensive end

---

Allen's Style Offers Contrast

July 11—Vince Lombardi was, to say the least, vocal during practices. In fact, Dickinson College teachers and secretaries would complain about the language the late legendary coach used while exhorting his troops at Biddle Field. Bill Austin, a Lombardi disciple, didn't employ his mentor's salty language, but his voice carried around the Carlisle campus as well.

In his first practice today, George Allen offered a different style. His voice was rarely audible. He maintained a low profile, spending much of his time with the linebacker group. It was a much more businesslike approach to the game than has been seen in the past few years.

To be sure, Allen exerted his authority. When some were lagging in wind sprints, Allen threatened to make the group run again unless the last man across the finish line met a maximum time.

The pace picked up considerably after that.

Bad Break: Jurgensen Faces Shoulder Surgery

Sep 5—X-rays show Sonny Jurgensen suffered a broken left shoulder when making a tackle after throwing an interception in the third quarter of the Redskins' preseason game in Miami.

Jurgensen is on his way to Oklahoma City where surgery to repair the break will be performed.

When asked why he would risk injury making a tackle in a meaningless game, Jurgensen said, "I cannot ever recall trying to get out of the way of anybody in football. You are supposed to tackle them, aren't you?"

While the injury may put the star quarterback out for the year, no decision has been made regarding placing him on season-ending injured reserve. Billy Kilmer will take the reins of the offense in Jurgensen's absence.

Sep 13

Over the Hill? Final Roster All Veterans
No rookies make squad as Skins prepare for Cards

9/18/71	Redskins (1-0) 24, CARDINALS (0-1) 17			46,805
Was	7	0	14	3	24
StL	0	10	7	7	17

Was	Brown 1 run (Knight kick)	
StL	Smith 8 pass from Hart (Bakken kick)	
StL	FG Bakken 25	
Was	Hanburger 16 fumble return (Knight kick)	
Was	Smith 31 pass from Kilmer (Knight kick)	
StL	Smith 9 pass from Beathard (Bakken kick)	
Was	FG Knight 25	

Busch Stadium—Chris Hanburger gave the Redskins the lead by returning a fumble 16 yards for a third-quarter touchdown as the Redskins won in St. Louis.

Coach George Allen, successful in his Redskins debut, preaches getting takeaways to set up scores and his philosophy was on display in this game. In addition to Hanburger's return, one St. Louis turnover led to an easy score by the Washington offense early in the contest and another put Allen's team in position to score the touchdown that put it away.

In the first quarter safety Richie Petitbon intercepted a Jim Hart pass and returned it 24 yards to the Cardinals' one. Larry Brown scored on the next play and it was 7-0. St. Louis responded with a 66-yard touchdown drive and a Jim Bakken field goal to take a 10-7 lead into the locker room at halftime.

Early in the second half, the Cardinals' Sid Edwards fumbled after catching a pass from Hart. Hanburger scooped it up and rolled 16 yards to the go-ahead touchdown.

About six minutes after that, St. Louis paid the ultimate price for yet another turnover—this one a Brig Owens interception at the Cardinals 39. Billy Kilmer, in for the injured Sonny Jurgensen, threw 31 yards to Jerry Smith for a touchdown and a 21-10 lead.

After St. Louis pulled to within 21-17, the Redskins sealed it with a Curt Knight field goal while four minutes remained. That score was set up by—what else?—a Cardinal turnover.

9/26/71	Redskins (2-0) 30, Giants (1-1) 3			62,795
Was	14	3	3	10	30
NYG	3	0	0	0	3

NYG	FG Gogolak 18	
Was	Taylor 71 pass from Kilmer (Knight kick)	
Was	Pardee 20 interception return (Knight kick)	
Was	FG Knight 52	
Was	FG Knight 32	
Was	Taylor 1 pass from Kilmer (Knight kick)	
Was	FG Knight 13	

Yankee Stadium—Charley Taylor caught two touchdown passes and Jack Pardee returned an interception for another TD as the Redskins routed the Giants 30-3.

There is a fine line between aggressive, physical play and dirty play. In the judgment of the officials, the Redskins played on both sides of that line. Two players—Paul Laaveg and Verlon Biggs—were ejected early for fighting and the Redskins were penalized 15 times. Larry Brown drew the first flag on the game's first play from scrimmage when he threw a punch at New York's Bob Lurtsema. Brown certainly received the worst of the skirmish; in addition to the penalty yardage, he got a nasty, 20-stitch cut on his hand when it caught the defender's facemask.

"I do not like penalties," said George Allen, "but I would rather be aggressive and get penalties than not be aggressive and not get penalties."

The Giants took a 3-0 lead with a field goal but before the first quarter was done, the Redskins had opened up a lead. From the Washington 29, Billy Kilmer froze safety Spider Lockhart with a nice run fake to Charley Harraway. Lockhart had single coverage on Taylor and the receiver blew past the defender, hauling in Kilmer's pass and easily making it over the goal line to give Washington a 7-3 lead. After that, Pardee guessed right on Fran Tarkenton's pass into the flat and was in the clear when he picked it off at the Giant 20 and rolled into the end zone.

Just before halftime, Curt Knight booted a 52-yard field goal—tied for the longest in team history—to expand his team's lead to 17-3. With Tarkenton being bottled up by a defense that sacked him three times, New York was powerless to respond. One sack in particular frustrated Tarkenton. Jimmie Jones chased the mobile quarterback down for a 14-yard loss to the Giant 11. As Jones turned to return to the huddle, Tarkenton threw perhaps his most accurate pass of the day, zinging the ball off the back of Jones' helmet.

After another Knight field goal, Taylor capped a 58-yard drive for the final touchdown with a one-yard reception. Bobby Mitchell was the main man in that drive, catching three straight Kilmer passes for 34 yards.

10/3/71	Redskins (3-0) 20, COWBOYS (2-1) 16				72,000
Was	7	7	3	3	20
Dal	0	9	0	7	16
Was	Harraway 57 run (Knight kick)				
Dal	FG Clark 22				
Was	Jefferson 50 pass from Kilmer (Knight kick)				
Dal	FG Clark 9				
Dal	FG Clark 27				
Was	FG Knight 25				
Was	FG Knight 32				
Dal	Hill 1 run (Clark kick)				

Cotton Bowl—Dallas had beaten the Redskins six straight times, a streak spanning three Washington head coaches, but things appeared to be different here right off the bat. On the second play from scrimmage, fullback Charley Harraway took a pitch on a weak side sweep, followed textbook blocks by Larry Brown, Walter Rock and Roy Jefferson and rolled all the way—57 yards for a touchdown. Washington was in the lead to stay.

Dallas tried to respond and mounted a promising drive, taking 15 plays to move up-field to the Washington 41. The promise died, though, when Mike Clark's field goal attempt from 48 yards was partially blocked. The score stayed 7-0.

Clark did have a successful field goal attempt in the second quarter, but the Redskins had the response. Jefferson took advantage of a slip by his defender and caught a 50-yard TD bomb from Billy Kilmer. The Redskins were up 14-3 and, although Dallas did get two more field goals before halftime, the impression was that the visitors were clearly in the driver's seat.

That impression proved to be accurate. Washington kept the ball on the ground—Kilmer attempted only 10 passes all day, getting over half of his 94 passing yards on the one TD to Jefferson—and set up two Curt Knight field goals to extend the lead to 20-9. Harraway rushed for 111 yards on the day and Larry Brown pitched in another 81.

The defensive highlight was Bill Brundige's long sack of Roger Staubach. A stunt allowed Brundige to take advantage of Diron Talbert's pressure that flushed Staubach out of the pocket. "Roger the Dodger" reversed his field for a second time, but Brundige had Staubach in his crosshairs and nailed him 29 yards behind the line of scrimmage.

Calvin Hill scored a touchdown on a one-yard run with 3:08 left in the game to get Dallas within four. After that, though, Brown rushed for one first down and Harraway for another. The Redskins killed the clock.

Skins Mania: 5,000+ Hail Redskins at Dulles

Oct 3—A frenzied crowd of Redskins fans estimated at 5,000 people was chanting "We're number one!" and "Defense, defense, defense" in the main terminal at Dulles Airport in Virginia.

And when the team actually arrived back from Dallas following its triumph over the Cowboys, things *really* got wild.

Coach George Allen got the biggest cheer as he greeted the crowd composed of infants, the elderly and every age group in between. Allen and team president Edward Bennett Williams were able to exit via a rear door, but the players had to go through the crowd to get to their cars. They signed autographs, posed for pictures and generally marveled that so many would sit in a traffic jam on the airport access road just to catch a glimpse of their conquering heroes.

10/10/71	REDSKINS (4-0) 22, Oilers (0-3-1) 13				53,041
Hou	0	10	3	0	13
Was	6	10	0	6	22
Was	FG Knight 15				
Was	FG Knight 36				
Was	FG Knight 13				
Hou	Sledge 5 pass from Johnson (Moseley kick)				
Was	McDole 18 interception return (Knight kick)				

Hou	FG Moseley 42
Hou	FG Moseley 25
Was	FG Knight 17
Was	FG Knight 39

RFK Stadium—Even Curt Knight, who kicked a team-record five field goals, wasn't very impressed by the Redskins' 22-13 win over Houston. "It wasn't pretty," Knight said, quickly adding, "It counts." Yes, it does count, and the Redskins moved to 4-0.

The 22-13 win delighted the 53,041 at RFK Stadium, the largest crowd ever to witness a sporting event in the District of Columbia.

Washington's defense was dominant. They allowed the Oilers just 46 yards rushing on 21 attempts. They also got five turnovers with two fumbles and three interceptions.

The only Washington touchdown came as a result of one of those interceptions. With the Redskins up 9-7, Oilers quarterback Charley Johnson was forced to scramble back from his 28. He attempted an ill-advised pass that McDole intercepted at the 18. He scored easily, and it was 16-7.

Houston's Mark Moseley kicked field goals late in the second and early in the third quarters, the second drawing his team within three at 16-13. The Redskins defense, led by McDole and Jack Pardee, who had an interception and a fumble recovery, shut Houston down from there, and Knight's last two field goals in the fourth quarter put this one away.

10/17/71	REDSKINS (5-0) 20, Cardinals (2-3) 0				53,041
St>	0	0	0	0	0
Was	10	0	3	7	20
Was	FG Knight 16				
Was	Harraway 1 run (Knight kick)				
Was	FG Knight 11				
Was	Kilmer 3 run (knight kick)				

RFK Stadium—Jack Pardee intercepted three passes and the Redskins had a total of seven takeaways on the day to bury the Cardinals before a delirious sellout crowd. Larry Brown pitched in on behalf of the offense, rushing for 150 yards on 25 carries.

St. Louis turned the ball over at its earliest opportunity. Norm Thompson fielded the opening kickoff and a jarring hit by Bill Malinchak separated the returner from the ball. Terry Hermeling recovered the fumble at the Cardinals' 14, setting up a 16-yard field goal by Curt Knight with just under a minute and a half gone.

The Redskins earned their next score, embarking on a 72-yard drive that consumed almost seven minutes. Charley Harraway gained the last yard on the 12th play, crashing over from the one for a 10-0 Washington lead.

On the rare occasions that the Cardinals were able to start something offensively, the Redskins thwarted them by taking the ball away. With the defense playing takeaway, the Washington offense was doing a good job of playing keep away, gaining 229 yards on the ground. Another Knight field goal in the third quarter and a three-yard TD run by Billy Kilmer in the fourth completed the scoring.

10/24/71	CHIEFS (5-1) 27, Redskins (5-1) 20				51,989
Was	10	7	0	3	20
KC	3	3	7	14	27
Was	C. Taylor 4 pass from Kilmer (Knight kick)				
KC	FG Stenerud 39				
Was	FG Knight 33				
KC	FG Stenerud 15				
Was	C. Taylor 36 pass from Kilmer (Knight kick)				
KC	O. Taylor 26 pass from Dawson (Stenerud kick)				
Was	FG Knight 23				
KC	Wright 15 pass from Dawson (Stenerud kick)				
KC	O. Taylor 28 pass from Dawson (Stenerud kick)				

Municipal Stadium—A costly touchdown pass gave the Redskins a 17-6 halftime lead, but the Chiefs stormed back in the second half on the strength of Len Dawson's three touchdown passes to hand the Redskins their first defeat of the year.

The above-referenced scoring play for Washington was a 36-yarder from Billy Kilmer to Charley Taylor with 43 seconds left in the first half. On the play—Taylor's second TD catch of the day—an attempted tackle caught his ankle the wrong way and broke a bone. Up to that point, he had caught seven passes for 125 yards.

The Chiefs struggled to get anything going offensively in the first half due to a relentless Washington pass rush. Early in the second half, though, the Chiefs began to hit their stride. Dawson found Otis Taylor for 23 yards and a touchdown to pull within four at 17-13.

The Redskins had a chance to extend their lead, but tight end Mack Alston, filling in for an injured Jerry Smith, dropped a pass at the Kansas City three. "I had to come back a little for it," said Alston, "but I should have caught it."

Later, Curt Knight kicked a 23-yard field goal to push the lead back up to seven, but the Chiefs were not done. Starting from their own 18, they moved 82 yards to tie the game. The drive was nearly over before it started as end Ron McDole sacked Dawson and the Chiefs faced third and 18. They converted that one when Taylor broke three tackles to fight his way for 19 yards. "We had them third down and long yardage and we let them get away," said Allen.

Perhaps a bit shaken after that play, the defense allowed Elmo Wright to get open for a 51-yard gain to the Redskins 20. The touchdown came on another Dawson-to-Wright completion, this one from 15 yards.

Unable to mount a consistent ground attack and with their passing game hobbled by the absence of Taylor, Washington had to punt back to KC with less than five minutes left. The Chiefs moved in for the kill. Runs by Ed Podolak, Wendell Hayes and Warren McVea moved the ball to the Washington 28. From there, Taylor made a spectacular one-handed grab of Dawson's pass in the end zone to give the Chiefs a 27-20 lead with 3:59 to play.

"How many guys catch the ball with one hand?" asked Pat Fischer, who was covering Taylor on the play. "I don't think I could have been any closer to him than I was."

The loss did little to dampen the enthusiasm of the Redskins faithful. Some 20,000 of them were on hand to greet the team at Dulles Airport after the return trip.

Oct 24
Bad Break: Taylor Out For the Season
Ankle broken while catching TD to sideline star receiver

10/31/71	REDSKINS (6-1) 24, Saints (2-4-1) 14			53,041	
NO	0	0	0	14	14
Was	0	17	0	7	24
Was	Kilmer 1 run (Knight kick)				
Was	Brown 36 pass from Kilmer (Knight kick)				
Was	FG Knight 47				
NO	Ford 3 run (Durkee kick)				
Was	Fischer 53 interception return (Knight kick)				
NO	Gresham 1 run (Durkee kick)				

RFK Stadium—To be sure, it was more like football follies than a football clinic as the Redskins survived six turnovers to beat the Saints.

The Redskins fumbled away New Orleans' first two punts, but the Saints were only able to muster a failed 33-yard field goal attempt from their good fortune. After the miss, the Redskins drove 80 yards in 12 plays to take the lead. Billy Kilmer scored from a yard out on an option play about 30 seconds into the second quarter.

After fumbling away a scoring chance on their next drive, the Skins got the ball back shortly afterwards and embarked on a 71-yard scoring drive. From the New Orleans 36, Kilmer and fullback Tommy Mason executed a classic play action fake, which sucked in, among others, whoever should have been covering Larry Brown. The halfback easily caught the touchdown pass to give Washington a 14-0 lead. After a Curt Knight field goal, the Redskins lost another golden scoring opportunity just before halftime when Kilmer's pass was picked off in the end zone.

After a scoreless third quarter, an interception and a pass interference call helped New Orleans score on a three-yard run by Jim Ford to cut the lead to 17-7. The Redskins defense responded as Pat Fischer picked off a pass by Ed Hargett and raced down the sideline for the clinching TD.

11/7/71	REDSKINS (6-1-1) 7, Eagles (2-5-1) 7				53,041
Phi	0	0	7	0	7
Was	0	0	0	7	7
Phi	Bull 12 pass from Liske (Feller kick)				
Was	McNeil 32 pass from Kilmer (Knight kick)				

RFK Stadium—Once again, the Redskins committed a flood of turnovers: seven of them (four interceptions, three fumbles). Unlike their six-giveaway game the previous week against the Saints, the Redskins were unable to pull out a win, coming dangerously close to winding up on the losing end to the game Eagles.

After a first half in which scoring threats were few and scores were nonexistent, Philly broke through early in the third quarter. Larry Brown fumbled on the first play of the half and Ron Porter recovered for Philadelphia at the Washington 17. Three plays later, Ron Bull made a nice, over-the-shoulder catch of Pete Liske's 12-yard touchdown pass for a Philly 7-0 lead.

A penalty killed an apparent 45-yard touchdown pass from Billy Kilmer to Boyd Dowler and Curt Knight missed a 46-yard field goal attempt. This left the door open for the Eagles to drive towards what would have been the clinching field goal with just over four minutes left.

That door was slammed shut, though, as Ron McDole blocked Happy Feller's 35-yard attempt and Speedy Duncan picked it up. His 38-yard return and a personal foul penalty had the Redskins in business at the Eagles 38. Two plays later, Kilmer threw a 32-yard scoring pass to Clifton McNeil and Knight's point after tied the game at seven.

The Redskins had to survive another scare to come out with the tie. Liske completed a 31-yard pass to Harold Jackson that took the Eagles to the Washington 25. There were 21 seconds left on the clock when the ball was snapped for that pass play, but the Eagles never got another play off. The defense—particularly McDole—dawdled just enough getting to the line of scrimmage to kill the clock before the Eagles could intentionally ground the ball to set up what would have been a 32-yard Feller field goal attempt. Washington escaped with a tie.

11/14/71	BEARS (6-3) 16, Redskins (6-2-1) 15				55,049
Was	6	6	3	0	15
Chi	0	3	3	10	16
Was	FG Knight 30				
Was	FG Knight 12				
Chi	FG Percival 15				
Was	FG Knight 37				
Was	FG Knight 9				
Was	FG Knight 27				
Chi	FG Percival 42				
Chi	FG Percival 9				
Chi	Pinder 40 run (Butkus pass from Douglass)				

Soldier Field—Dick Butkus earned his reputation by preventing scores, not by catching passes for points. In this game, though, it was a Butkus reception that provided the winning margin for the Bears.

The Redskins appeared to be in control for most of the game, although numerous forays into Chicago territory resulted in field goals, not touchdowns. Curt Knight tied his own team record by kicking five field goals, the last of which put the Redskins ahead 15-3 early in the third quarter.

Eventually, the Redskins would pay for their inability to get into the end zone. The Bears chipped away at the lead, getting two field goals from Mac Percival. The second came early in the fourth quarter and cut the margin to 15-9. A touchdown and point after would give them the lead.

They got the touchdown with 3:14 left when Cyril Pinder found open spaces up the middle on a quick hitter and darted 40 yards for the tying score.

On the point after try, Butkus was lined up in the backfield as a blocker. The snap went over the head of holder Bobby Douglass, who, as luck would have it, was also Chicago's scrambling quarterback. Douglass ran down the ball at the 30 and flipped a desperation toss towards Butkus, who snared the ball in the corner of the end zone for the critical point.

The Redskins had a shot to pull it out in the closing seconds. Sonny Jurgensen replaced Billy Kilmer at quarterback and completed two passes to get his team into Bears territory with 15 seconds left. As Knight's attempt for his sixth field goal of the game, a 45 yarder, got airborne, the wind off of Lake Michigan kicked up and pushed the attempt wide left.

Nov 16
Jurgensen to be Active, Kilmer Will Start
Billy not fazed by presence of star on bench

11/21/71	**Cowboys (7-3) 13, REDSKINS (6-3-1) 0**				53,041
Dal	7	0	3	3	13
Was	0	0	0	0	0
Dal	Staubach 29 run (Clark kick)				
Dal	FG Clark 26				
Dal	FG Clark 48				

RFK Stadium—Roger Staubach scrambled 29 yards for a first-quarter touchdown, giving the Cowboys all the points they would need to defeat the Redskins and take over first place in the NFC East.

Staubach seemed to be in a world of trouble when he dropped back to pass from the Washington 29. Intended receiver Lance Alworth was covered, as were his other potential targets. Diron Talbert was drawing a bead on him. However, the quarterback eluded the grasp of the Redskins tackle, dodged a few others and made it into the end zone.

After the game, Coach George Allen admitted that there really was no way to stop such a play. "We tried to take away his scrambling up the middle, and did. We dogged (sent) middle linebacker Mo Pottios up the middle. But Staubach went to the outside. There is no defense for the scramble. If you tried to set a defense just for that, you would throw off the rest of your defense."

The Redskins struggled mightily on offense. They managed just 65 yards rushing on 21 attempts. When they did get into scoring position, they couldn't convert. One field goal try was aborted when the snap was high and Curt Knight missed a 25-yard attempt when a gust of wind caught the boot and pushed it wide.

With the Redskins trailing 10-0 in the fourth quarter, Allen tried to work up a little magic by bringing Sonny Jurgensen into the game to replace Billy Kilmer. The prospect of anything miraculous happening quickly faded, though, when Jurgensen's first pass was intercepted.

Allen: Talk of Redskins Fold 'Asinine'

Nov 22—With the Redskins going 1-3-1 since their 5-0 start to the season, George Allen is getting a bit testy.

When asked about this midseason slump mirroring his Rams' tendency to cool off after hot starts, Allen said, "This is asinine. We were 6-1 to start the season. I will take that."

"Should we have lost early?" he asked rhetorically.

Allen chose not to comment on the booing that took place when starter Billy Kilmer trotted back onto the field on Sunday with Dallas leading 10-0. Sonny Jurgensen had started to warm up and the boo-birds were apparently disappointed that he didn't enter the game at that point.

Jurgensen did come in later with the score the same, but his first pass was intercepted.

11/28/71	**Redskins (7-3-1) 20, Eagles (3-7-1) 13**				65,358
Was	0	13	0	7	20
Phi	0	0	6	7	13
Was	FG Knight 40				
Was	FG Knight 14				
Was	Jefferson 27 pass from Kilmer (Knight kick)				
Phi	Bailey 1 run (Kick failed)				
Was	Bass 38 interception return (Knight kick)				
Phi	Zabel 1 pass from Liske (Dempsey kick)				

Veterans Stadium—A 27-yard touchdown pass from Billy Kilmer to Roy Jefferson in the second quarter broke a nine-quarter touchdown drought for the Redskins and helped boost Washington to a key road win.

The touchdown came after Curt Knight had kicked field goals of 40 and 14 yards. Starting quarterback Sonny Jurgensen reinjured his left shoulder, which has kept him sidelined for much of the season, during the drive to the first field goal. He was hurt while scrambling 10 yards for a first down; Kilmer came into the game to replace him.

The touchdown drive came late in the first half and covered 50 yards on three Kilmer passes. The first went to Boyd Dowler for 19 yards, and the next to Clifton McNeil for four. Kilmer then found Jefferson in the end zone for the final 27 yards and a 13-0 Redskins lead.

The Eagles cut that margin to 13-6 in the third quarter with an 82-yard touchdown drive capped by Tom Bailey's one-yard touchdown run. The extra point was a miss, and in the fourth quarter a Mike Bass interception return for a touchdown put it away for Washington.

12/5/71	**REDSKINS (8-3-1) 23, Giants (4-8) 7**				53,041
NYG	0	0	0	7	7
Was	13	7	3	0	23
Was	FG Knight 28				
Was	FG Knight 25				
Was	Brown 17 run (Knight kick)				
Was	Brown 2 run (Knight kick)				
Was	FG Knight 44				
NYG	Brown recovered blocked punt in end zone (Gogolak kick)				

RFK Stadium—With the Redskins offense struggling, it was up to the defense to pull this one out. The home team literally stole the victory, intercepting five passes and making some key special teams plays to set up all five Washington scores to beat the Giants.

The tone was set early as Chris Hanburger grabbed a tipped Fran Tarkenton pass and returned it to the New York 24. Unable to move the ball, the Skins called on Curt Knight to give them a 3-0 lead just over a minute into the game. Three plays later, a Myron Pottios interception returned to the New York 10 led to another Knight three pointer.

The Giants' third possession ended with Tarkenton throwing his third interception, this one to end Ron McDole. Despite the

Washington offense's ineptitude, they couldn't mess up three gift-wrapped opportunities in a row. From the New York 37, the Redskins moved in and popped Larry Brown free for a 17-yard touchdown run and a 13-0 lead.

After the Giants' punter muffed a snap, the Skins had to drive all of nine yards to another Brown touchdown run, this one of four yards. In the third quarter, Ted Vactor blocked a 12-yard field goal attempt by the Giants and Washington moved in for its final score, a 44-yard field goal that made it 23-0.

Allen Derides Rams' 'Gadgets'

Dec 8—George Allen fired off a few cross-country shots at his old team, the Rams, as he prepared his Redskins for their big prime-time game next Monday night in Los Angeles.

The target of Allen's barbs was Los Angeles rookie head coach Tommy Prothro—and his fondness for trick plays.

"The Rams are a great gadget team," said Allen. "They use every type of gadget that's ever been used."

Prothro calls a variety of such plays, including fake punts, double reverses and passes off of reverses.

Allen has distain for such tactics. "Over the years I've found gadgets can hurt you more than they help you. For every touchdown you make with them, one will backfire and the other team will get a score."

While we don't know what tricks Prothro has up his sleeve for Monday night, it's likely the Redskins will try to control the ball on the ground and use the run to set up the pass. Such tactics have gotten them to the verge of their first postseason appearance since 1945.

12/13/71	Redskins (9-3-1) 38, Rams (7-5-1) 24				80,402
Was	7	17	7	7	38
LA	10	0	7	7	24
LA	Alexander 82 interception return (Ray kick)				
Was	Jefferson 70 pass from Kilmer (Knight kick)				
LA	FG Ray 32				
Was	FG Knight 52				
Was	McNeil 32 pass from Kilmer ((Knight kick)				
Was	Brown 1 run (Knight kick)				
Was	Jefferson 5 pass from Kilmer (Knight kick)				
LA	Klein 3 pass from Gabriel (Ray kick)				
LA	Ellison 1 run (Ray kick)				
Was	Duncan 46 interception return (Knight kick)				

Los Angeles Coliseum—They say that when something sounds too good to be true, it's probably untrue. The Redskins and their fans probably pinched themselves a few times after this one, but it was, indeed, a reality.

Most Hollywood script writers would shy away from this story line, as the main plot elements were too improbable even for fiction:

• Coach returns to beat the team that fired him the previous year.

• The win gives the coach's team its first postseason berth in 25 years and virtually eliminates his old team.

The coach, of course, is George Allen. He had his new team on the verge of its first playoff game since 1945 coming into this Monday night contest against the Rams, who were in the playoff hunt as well.

It did not start off well for Washington. Kermit Alexander picked off a Billy Kilmer pass and dashed down the sideline 82 yards for a 7-0 Ram lead. A 70-yard bomb from Kilmer to Roy Jefferson tied it up before the first quarter ended. The teams exchanged field goals before L.A. let a couple of golden opportunities slip away. The first time, they had moved to the Washington 18, where a decision to go for a first down on fourth and one backfired when Jack Pardee nailed Ram quarterback

Roman Gabriel on a rollout. The second time, from the Redskin 22, Ted Vactor blocked a field goal attempt.

The block sparked the Washington offense back to life. They drove 62 yards for a touchdown, the payoff coming on Kilmer's 32-yard toss to Clifton McNeil. The Rams fumbled the ensuing kickoff and the Redskins offense was back in business. Seven plays later, Larry Brown bulled it over from a yard out and Washington took a 24-10 lead into the locker room.

It appeared to be turning into a laugher in the third quarter after Mike Bass intercepted Gabriel's pass. Three plays after that, Kilmer threw a five-yard touchdown pass to Jefferson and it was 31-10.

The Rams weren't quite done yet. Gabriel led touchdown drives of 59 and 69 yards in the third and fourth quarters, respectively, to pull his team within a touchdown. They had a couple more possessions to try to tie it up, but the first ended in a punt and the second on Speedy Duncan's 44-yard interception return for the clinching touchdown.

Dec 19

Sonny Setting? Jurgy Contemplates Retirement
QB says frustration over injury has led him to consider calling it quits

12/19/71	Browns (9-5) 20, REDSKINS (9-4-1) 13				53,041
Cle	3	7	3	7	20
Was	3	10	0	0	13
Cle	FG Cockroft 30				
Was	FG Knight 18				
Cle	Collins 17 pass from Nelsen (Cockroft kick)				
Was	Brown 29 pass from Kilmer (Knight kick)				
Was	FG Knight 35				
Cle	FG Cockroft 22				
Cle	Glass 4 pass from Nelsen (Cockroft kick)				

RFK Stadium—The Redskins played gracious hosts to the Browns, turning the ball over four times to assist Cleveland in the win.

The visitors recovered a Larry Brown fumble to set up their first score, a 30-yard Don Cockroft field goal. Curt Knight answered by kicking an 18-yard field goal and the game was tied 3-3 at the end of the first quarter.

In the second period, Cleveland drove to a 17-yard touchdown pass from Bill Nelsen to Gary Collins and it was 10-3.

Washington claimed the lead before halftime. First, Billy Kilmer threw a 29-yard touchdown pass to Larry Brown. Then Knight booted a 35-yard field goal to make it 13-10 at intermission.

The second half belonged to Cleveland as Washington blew a pair of scoring opportunities with turnovers before making the killer mistake.

Mike Howell intercepted a Kilmer pass and returned it 68 yards. That led to a short drive that culminated in Nelsen's four-yard scoring pass to Chip Glass, putting the Browns up by the final margin of 20-13.

The fact that Washington outgained the Browns 346 yards to 223 was testament to George Allen's constant preaching that turnovers usually win or lose games.

Baughn, Gossett Swap Verbal Jabs

Dec 23—It wasn't exactly a verbal clash of the titans given that it involved a player on injured reserve and a place kicker, but Washington's Maxie Baugh and the 49ers' Bruce Gossett have added a little spice to the week leading up to their teams' playoff game.

Gossett, the kicker, started things up when he asked a reporter, "You wonder why players like Tommy Mason and Maxie Baugh support George Allen?"

"Because without him they wouldn't be in football," Gossett continued, answering his own question. "They are not good enough to be working for anyone else but George Allen."

Baugh, on injured reserve and ineligible to play this week, minced no words when he heard of Gossett's commentary. "He (Gossett) is not a player; he's not even an athlete. Ask him how many tackled he's made.

"How many times has he been to the Pro Bowl? Check the record," he said.

The record shows nine Pro Bowl selections for Baugh, three for running back Mason, and zero for Gossett.

Fischer Not Fazed by Pro Bowl Snub

Dec 23—It was an issue that concerned the editorial board of one of the newspapers in the capitol of the free world, but Pat Fischer—the supposed victim—really didn't care about it.

The Evening Star editorial headline read, "Where's Pat?" and lamented the Redskins' star cornerback Fischer's exclusion from the NFC Pro Bowl roster. His selection was widely anticipated but Roger Wehrli, who missed several games for a four-win Cardinal team, made it instead.

It didn't seem to matter much to Fischer. "Oh, I used to get excited about those things, but not anymore," he said. "I don't care about the all-star selections because they are made by a lot of people everywhere who don't even see the games."

He was flattered by the attention from the Evening Star. "They had me right up there under the editorial about the new secretary general of the United Nations and above the one about offshore oil leases."

"I'm making money from those leases," said Fischer, a stockbroker in the offseason.

12/26/71	**49ERS 24, Redskins 10**				45,364
Was	7	3	3	7	20
SF	0	3	14	7	24

Was	Smith 5 pass from Kilmer (Knight kick)
SF	FG Gossett 23
Was	FG Knight 40
SF	G. Washington 78 pass from Brodie (Gossett kick)
SF	Windsor 2 pass from Brodie (Gossett kick)
Was	FG Knight 36
SF	Haskins fumble recovery in end zone (Gossett kick)
Was	Brown 16 pass from Kilmer (Knight kick)

The Redskins had their chances to advance to the NFC title game, but a pair of bad snaps on kicking plays and the failure of a fourth-down gamble to pay off doomed them to a loss in rainy, windy San Francisco.

In the early going, the Redskins blocked a Steve Spurrier punt and Billy Kilmer found Jerry Smith for a five-yard touchdown. In the second quarter, Curt Knight and Bruce Gossett exchanged field goals.

As halftime approached, the Skins held a 10-3 lead and were poised to strike for more after Speedy Duncan returned a punt 47 yards to the San Francisco 12. But, on a play reportedly suggested by President Richard Nixon in a phone call to Allen the night before the game, Roy Jefferson lost 13 yards on an end around. The Redskins were forced to settle for a field goal attempt, but center George Burman bounced the snap in front of holder Sonny Jurgensen and the kick was blocked.

Still leading by seven in the third quarter, an uncharacteristic gamble by Allen failed when Larry Brown was tackled for a two-yard loss on a fourth and inches play at the Niners' 11. On third and short a few plays later, John Brodie executed a beautiful play action fake and uncorked a perfect spiral to receiver Gene Washington, who snared it and ran in for a 78-yard TD to tie the game at seven.

After that, it was the Redskins giving the 49ers opportunities. Unlike Washington, San Francisco took full advantage. First, Rosey Taylor intercepted a Kilmer pass, leading to Brodie's two-yard touchdown pass to tight end Bob Windsor. Then, with the score 17-13 with three and a half minutes left to play, another Burman snap went awry as he bounced one a yard in front of punter Mike Bragg. The ball flew between Bragg's feet and into the end zone. Bob Hoskins of the 49ers pounced on it there for an easy touchdown, making it 24-13.

The Redskins drove to one touchdown on a 16-yard pass from Kilmer to Brown and, after their defense held San Francisco, regained possession at their own 37. With 51 seconds and no timeouts left, the odds of the Redskins scoring were slim to none. Slim left town when Cedrick Hardman sacked Kilmer for a 13-yard loss as the final gun sounded.

1972

Head Coach: George Allen
Record: 11-3, NFC East Champions
Playoffs: 2-1, lost in Super Bowl VII

Honors: Larry Brown, Pro Bowl, All-NFL, NFL Most Valuable Player;
Speedy Duncan, Pro Bowl; Chris Hanburger, Pro Bowl, All-NFL;
Len Hauss, Pro Bowl, All-NFL; Billy Kilmer, Pro Bowl, All-NFC;
Charley Taylor, Pro Bowl

Jan 28
Allen Was Fined At Least Twice in '71
Coach/GM cited for technical violations of roster limit

First Draft Pick Will Fit Right In

Feb 2—After what he called a "relaxing" first day of the draft, George Allen got to work today. He used the team's first selection— in the eighth round—on a player who should fit right in with the Over the Hill Gang.

Allen selected running back Moses Denson out of the University of Maryland-Eastern Shore with that pick—No. 203 overall. Well, not directly out of that school; Denson has been playing for the Montreal Alouettes of the Canadian Football League for the past three seasons.

He will be 28 years old before training camp starts.

Apr 12
NFL Gives Allen Refresher in Tracking Picks
Coach dealt same picks to Chargers, Rams

May 13
Skins Trade Picks for Rosey Taylor
Safety played for Allen in Chicago

Allen Settles Up Overdrawn Draft Picks

May 16—George Allen paid off a draft pick debt with interest today as he worked a deal with the NFL and the San Diego Chargers.

The issue goes back to May of 1971 when the Redskins and Chargers made a trade for defensive back and kick returner Speedy Duncan. Allen thought he was to give up the team's 1974 Nos. 3 and 5 picks with the fifth-rounder improving to a fourth if Duncan was a member of the 1972 team.

However, the Chargers have produced documents showing the two sides had agreed that the picks would be for the 1973 season.

Since it appears certain that Duncan will be sticking around this year, the upgrade is scheduled to take place. However, the Redskins no longer own that '73 fourth-round pick. Allen sent that selection to the Buffalo Bills for defensive end Ron McDole.

Oops.

The matter was resolved when the Redskins swung a deal with the San Francisco 49ers a few days ago. The agreement netted the Redskins safety Rosey Taylor and third- and fourth-round picks for 1973. The Redskins will send those picks to San

Diego and, as a penalty for double-dealing, a 1974 fifth-round pick also will go to the Chargers.

Allen was anything but remorseful about the fiasco. "This whole thing has been grossly exaggerated," he said. "It is a happy conclusion."

May 23
Sloppy Bookkeeping Costs Allen
Draws $5,000 fine for 'conduct detrimental to NFL' in double-trading draft picks

---

Allen's Decision: It's Billy

Sep 7—George Allen today announced that Billy Kilmer will start the season at quarterback for the Redskins. That means Sonny Jurgensen, the team's leader since 1964, will start the year on the bench.

Allen explained that the decision was a reward for Kilmer leading the Redskins to their first playoff appearance since 1945.

"That's the only way it can be," Allen said. "We won with Billy and he's our quarterback. He did an excellent job last year."

Sep 12
Mul-Key makes final cut
Rookie running back/kick returner a product of Allen public tryout

---

9/18/72	Redskins(1-0) 24, VIKINGS (0-1) 21			47,900
Was	7	3	0	14	24
Min	0	7	7	7	21
Was	Malinchak 16 return of blocked punt (Knight kick)			
Min	Jones 1 run (Cox kick)			
Was	FG Knight 30			
Min	Gilliam 11 pass from Tarkenton (Cox kick)			
Was	L. Brown 3 run (Knight kick)			
Was	Harraway 9 run (Knight kick)			
Min	B. Brown 4 pass from Tarkenton (Cox kick)			

Metropolitan Stadium—Bill Malinchak set the tone for the Redskins' 24-21 win over the Vikings on the first series of the game. He blocked a punt by Minnesota's Mike Eischeid, picked it up at the Vikings' 16 and ran in for a touchdown with just over two minutes elapsed in the season.

As things settled in, though, the game swung Minnesota's way. They took a 14-10 lead with 7:01 to play in the third quarter when Fran Tarkenton threw an 11-yard touchdown pass to John Gilliam, who made a spectacular diving grab in the end zone. It might have been worse if not for another big play by special teams. This one happened when Ted Vactor blocked a 44-yard field goal attempt by Fred Cox just before halftime.

After Gilliam's score, Minnesota got the ball back and drove to the Redskins 20, but they fumbled the ball away, giving the Redskins new life. The Washington offense finally got untracked, driving 58 yards to a touchdown; the payoff came on a three-yard Larry Brown run. Again, special teams came through when Bob Brunet crashed into Minnesota's Clint Jones on the kickoff return, jarring the ball loose. Malinchak recovered and two plays later, just 85 seconds after Brown had scored, Charley Harraway took it in around left end to give the Redskins a 24-14 lead. Tarkenton completed a desperation fourth-down touchdown pass to Bill Brown with more than a minute left, but it was too late for the Vikings.

Brown finished the game with 104 yards rushing on 21 carries, while Harraway kicked in 42 on nine carries.

9/24/72	**REDSKINS (2-0) 24, Cardinals (1-1) 10**				53,039
StL	0	3	7	0	10
Was	7	10	7	0	24
Was	Smith 6 pass from Kilmer (Knight kick)				
Was	Bass 32 blocked field goal return (Knight kick)				
StL	FG Bakken 41				
Was	FG Knight 31				
Was	Smith 5 pass from Kilmer (Knight kick)				
StL	Burns 1 run (Bakken kick)				

RFK Stadium—Larry Brown ran for 148 yards to become the Redskins' all-time leading rusher and Jerry Smith caught two touchdown passes to lead the Skins to a 24-10 win over the Cardinals..

Smith's first score came in the opening quarter and gave the Redskins a 7-0 lead. The score came on a play where, according to Smith, the Redskins "just caught them in the right defense." Billy Kilmer threw a strike after a play-action fake and the Redskins were ahead to stay.

Special teams got into the act as well, scoring a touchdown for the second straight week. In the second quarter, Verlon Biggs reached up and swatted down a Jim Bakken field goal attempt. Mike Bass picked it up at the Cardinals' 32 and rolled into the end zone. That gave the Redskins a 14-0 second quarter lead.

"Every time there's a field goal attempt, I figure it's fifty-fifty," said Biggs. "They have a fifty percent chance of making it and we have a fifty percent chance of blocking it."

Brown surpassed Don Bosseler's career mark of 3,112 yards halfway through the second quarter. The home crowd roared as he was given the ball.

The teams exchanged field goals before halftime. Kilmer and Smith put it out of reach in the third quarter with a five-yard TD pitch and catch.

9/30/72	**PATRIOTS (2-1) 24, Redskins (2-1) 23**				60,999
Was	0	14	0	9	23
NE	0	7	10	7	24
Was	Taylor 30 pass from Kilmer (Knight kick)				
Was	Taylor 4 pass from Kilmer (Knight kick)				
NE	Ashton 2 run (Gogolak kick)				
NE	Rucker 11 pass from Plunkett (Gogolak kick)				
NE	FG Gogolak 42				
Was	Smith 9 pass from Kilmer (Knight kick)				
NE	Ashton 24 pass from Plunkett (Gogolak kick)				
Was	Safety punt blocked through end zone				

Schaefer Stadium—Don't take points off the board. That's the coaching dictum George Allen violated in the fourth quarter and that, along with a questionable official's call after a blocked punt, cost the Redskins with this stunning 24-23 loss to the Patriots.

Early on, it didn't seem like Washington would be worried about the outcome in the fourth quarter. They had built a 14-0 lead on the strength of two Billy Kilmer to Charley Taylor touchdown passes. However, the youthful Patriots—led by second-year quarterback Jim Plunkett—were game, rallying with 17 points in the second and third quarters to take a 17-14 lead into what turned out to be a frantic fourth quarter.

The Redskins retook the lead with just over nine minutes left on a nine-yard pass from Kilmer to Jerry Smith. But Plunkett picked the Redskins defense apart like an old pro, driving the Patriots 80 yards for a touchdown and a 24-21 lead. After that, the Redskins had four chances to tie or win the game in the last minute and forty seconds but were unable to convert on any of them.

Actually, they did convert the first one when Curt Knight connected on a 33-yard field goal that tied the score with 1:39 to go. New England, though, was called for roughing the kicker on the play and George Allen elected to take the three off the board and give his offense a chance to win it. But the Redskins couldn't move the ball and Knight's second try to tie it from 27 yards out was wide right.

The Redskins weren't done yet. The defense held the Patriots on three plays and Bill Malinchak blocked Pat Studstill's punt. It appeared that Malinchak had gained control of the ball before it rolled out of the end zone, but the officials ruled otherwise, awarding the Redskins a safety rather than a touchdown.

After the free kick, Washington moved into position to attempt a 50-yard field goal on the game's last play. It was no good; the Patriots escaped with the win.

Taking it Easy? Pats are Patsies to Skins

Sep 29—Fretting is one of the things George Allen does best— and he was in top form today.

The Redskins seem to be taking Sunday's opponent, the 1-1 New England Patriots, too lightly for Allen's liking. "I don't know if we're ready for 'em," he said after practice.

"Yes, I'm serious," he continued. "Everyone is taking them too lightly."

Defensive tackle Diron Talbert didn't necessarily disagree. "Of course, it's hard for some guys to get up for them," he explained. "On paper, we have the better team.

"It's only natural, I suppose."

Talbert didn't think it would take a total team effort for the Redskins to win.

"If three quarters of the guys get up for the game, we should win it," he said.

Are Sonny Days Ahead?

Oct 6—At 2-1, the Redskins may be on the verge of a change at quarterback.

Although Billy Kilmer's performance wasn't a big factor in the Redskins' 24-23 loss to New England (a leaky pass defense was the main culprit), it appears he is being shown the bench. Sonny Jurgensen has stepped up his participation in drills and may well get the starting nod when the Redskins host the Eagles on Sunday.

Coach George Allen, of course, wouldn't confirm or deny anything. He got a bit testy under questioning by reporters on the subject of the starting quarterback. It remains one of the most closely-guarded secrets outside of the confines of CIA headquarters, located near Allen's Virginia residence.

If Allen does start Jurgensen, he will be going with the choice of the people, albeit by a narrow margin. In a poll conducted by a local TV station, 45 percent of respondents said that they liked Sonny as the starter while 42 percent favored Billy.

10/8/72	**REDSKINS (3-1) 14, Eagles (0-4) 0**		53,039		
Phi	0	0	0	0	0
Was	0	0	14	0	14
Was	Brown 2 run (Knight kick)				
Was	Jefferson 35 pass from Jurgensen (Knight kick)				

RFK Stadium—Sonny Jurgensen returned to the starting lineup, but it was the Redskins defense that headlined this game. After a scoreless first half, Washington put up 14 third-quarter points—plenty to beat the Eagles 14-0.

In the first half, Jurgensen struggled through a seven for 17, three interception passing effort, with two of those picks killing drives in the Eagles end zone. Safety Bill Bradley was the culprit on those two takeaways.

The Washington defense allowed the Eagles past midfield just once. That drive ended when Chris Hanburger intercepted a John Reaves pass at the Washington 4.

Jurgensen blamed himself for the first-half woes. "I was very uptight. I was rusty and I threw poorly," he said.

In the second half, Jurgy got untracked, hitting Jerry Smith for 25 yards on the team's first possession, sparking an eight-play, 75-yard TD drive that ended when Larry Brown went over from the two.

The next possession, it took just three plays to cover 63 yards. The last 35 came when Jurgensen hit Roy Jefferson between two defenders at the 20 and the receiver burst past them and into the end zone.

Jurgensen was seven for seven for 128 yards in the second half.

10/15/72	**Redskins (4-1) 33, CARDINALS (2-3) 3**			50,454	
Was	3	7	6	17	33
StL	0	0	3	0	3
Was	FG Knight 30				
Was	Harraway 1 run (Knight kick)				
StL	FG Bakken 46				
Was	FG Knight 8				
Was	FG Knight 42				
Was	FG Knight 36				
Was	Harraway 4 run (Knight kick)				
Was	Brunet 2 run (Knight kick)				

Busch Stadium—Curt Knight kicked three of his four field goals in the third and fourth quarters to help the Redskins pull away from the Cardinals to a 33-3 victory.

The Redskins went up 3-0 in the first quarter on a 30-yard Knight field goal. In the second quarter they expanded their lead to 10-0 when Charlie Harraway powered into the end zone from a yard out.

Although St. Louis gained just 151 yards of offense on the day, the Cardinals were very much in it when Jim Bakken kicked a 46-yard field goal with seven minutes left in the third quarter to pull his team within 10-3.

Then Sonny Jurgensen, who was a very efficient 13 for 18 passing for 203 yards, and Larry Brown, who had 23 carries for 110 yards, helped get the Redskins into scoring position. Although they were unable to punch it in the end zone, Knight converted from eight, 42 and 36 yards.

The rout was on in the fourth quarter. Charley Harraway's second TD of the day put Washington up 26-3 and reserve back Bob Brunet's short run topped off the scoring.

The Cardinals had a hand in their own demise. They fumbled four times, losing two of them, and quarterback Gary Cuozzo threw two interceptions.

10/22/72	**REDSKINS (5-1) 24, Cowboys (4-2) 20**			53,039	
Dal	10	3	7	0	20
Was	0	7	10	7	24
Dal	Sellers 39 pass from Morton (Fritsch kick)				
Dal	FG Fritsch 13				
Dal	FG Fritsch 12				
Was	Brown 19 pass from Jurgensen (Knight kick)				
Dal	Garrison 1 run (Fritsch kick)				
Was	Brown 34 run (Knight kick)				
Was	FG Knight 42				
Was	Harraway 13 run				

RFK Stadium—The Redskins outscored the defending champion Cowboys 17-0 over the last 23 minutes of the game, sending the RFK crowd home deliriously happy over Washington's 24-20 win.

Larry Brown accounted for nearly two thirds of the Redskins' 305 yards of total offense, rushing for 95 yards and catching seven passes for 100. One of those catches in the second quarter went for 19 yards and a touchdown that gave the Redskins their first points. They trailed 13-0 before that score and were fortunate it wasn't worse. On the game's second play, Calvin Hill snuck through the Redskins' secondary and was all alone at the Washington 25. Craig Morton got the ball to him, but Hill dropped it and the stadium breathed a sigh of relief.

But it didn't last long—Morton found Ron Sellers for a TD and Tony Fritsch kicked two field goals. Brown's catch provided only a temporary respite. Right after halftime, the Cowboys methodically drove to a one-yard touchdown run by Walt Garrison to get back to a 13-point lead with just over nine minutes left in the third quarter. That would be all for Dallas.

Sonny Jurgensen "had caused Dallas grief so many times, and at 38, was clearly too old to change," said George Solomon of the Washington Post. After Garrison's score, he found Jerry Smith for 28 yards to the Redskins 48. Four plays later from the Dallas 34, Brown took a pitchout, followed blocks by Terry Hermeling, Charley Harraway and Walt Rock and roared into the end zone. Suddenly, it was 20-14. A field goal on the last play of the third quarter got the Redskins within three.

The go-ahead drive started with 10 minutes left in the game. After throwing to Roy Jefferson for 26 yards, Jurgensen found Brown's midsection amidst three Dallas defenders at the Cowboys 17. From there, it was Harraway for four and again for 13 and the touchdown.

There still was 6:42 left in the game, plenty of time for Dallas to score. The Redskins defense's Pat Fischer and Speedy Duncan each intercepted Morton in the final minutes and Dallas never threatened.

10/29/72	**Redskins (6-1) 23, Giants (4-3) 17**			62,878	
Was	3	6	7	7	23
NYG	0	3	6	7	16
Was	FG Knight 41				
NYG	FG Gogolak 43				
Was	Brown 7 pass from Kilmer (Knight kick)				
NYG	FG Gogolak 14				
NYG	FG Gogolak 22				
Was	Brown 38 run (Knight kick)				
Was	Smith 5 pass from Kilmer (Knight kick)				
NYG	Tucker 10 pass from Snead (Gogolak kick)				

Yankee Stadium—Faced with a very hostile crowd and the loss of the team's star quarterback, Larry Brown came up big as the Redskins beat the Giants 23-16.

Sonny Jurgensen started the game at QB for Washington. As he threw his first pass of the game—a completed 13-yard out to Roy Jefferson—the quarterback felt something pop in his ankle. He suffered a torn Achilles' tendon and is lost for the season.

Not only was Jurgensen the team's field general, he was the holder on place kicks as well. The loss in the latter department was felt after Kilmer threw a seven-yard touchdown pass to Larry Brown in the second quarter. Brig Owens muffed the snap on the point-after try, and the Redskins held just a 9-3 lead. The Giants answered with a second quarter field goal to make it 9-6 at halftime. The stage was set for some second-half fireworks.

With time winding down in the third quarter, the Giants were poised to take the lead, having driven to the Redskins 7. In fact, it looked like New York had grabbed the lead after Norm Snead passed to Ron Johnson for an apparent score. However, the Giants were flagged for pass interference, the TD was nullified and Pete Gogolak's 22-yard field goal tied the game at nine with 3:51 left in the third.

That call did not sit well with fans in the stands in the Bronx. The booing had just begun to settle down when Chris Hanburger and Brown gave them something to be really unhappy about.

The Giants had the ball back and were nearing midfield when Snead threw to Johnson again, this time for a short gain. As Johnson struggled for additional yardage, Hanburger came in and stole the ball right out of the running back's hands. Officials ruled that forward progress had not been stopped and, much to the displeasure of the Yankee Stadium mob, it was the Redskins' ball at the New York 38.

As the boos rolled in on the very next play, Brown took the handoff from Kilmer, zoomed off of right tackle and galloped untouched into the end zone. In fact, the only hostile thing to hit him on the play was the shower of beer he got from the hooligans in the stands near the end zone. This time Owens' hold was good, Curt Knight's kick was through the uprights and the Redskins had a 16-9 lead.

Brown's clutch run was only part of his best rushing day as a Redskin. In fact, it was probably his best game in a Redskin uniform; he took control of the game and came up big when the team needed him. On the day, he carried 29 times for a single-game Redskin record of 191 yards.

The Redskins drove for an insurance score midway through the final period, with the payoff coming on a five-yard Kilmer-to-Jerry Smith touchdown pass. That made a scoring pass from Snead to tight end Bob Tucker with 1:35 left meaningless. Apparently, there was still plenty of beer left—Brown and the Redskins were doused with suds as they left the field with a 23-16 victory.

Oct 30

Heel Surgery May Save Jurgy's Career
QB, 38, looks forward to '73 season after operation to repair Achilles' tendon tear

11/5/72	Redskins (7-1) 35, JETS (5-3) 17			63,962	
Was	7	14	7	7	35
NYJ	7	3	0	7	17
Was	Jefferson 45 pass from Kilmer (Knight kick)				
NYJ	Riggins 1 run (Howfield kick)				
NYJ	FG Howfield 13				
Was	Taylor 70 pass from Kilmer (Knight kick)				
Was	Hanburger 41 pass interception (Knight kick)				
Was	Brown 89 pass from Kilmer (Knight kick)				
NYJ	Maynard 15 pass from Namath (Howfield kick)				
Was	Biggs 16 fumble return (Knight kick)				

Shea Stadium—Billy Kilmer threw touchdown passes of 45, 70 and 89 yards and the defense intercepted three Joe Namath passes to lead a 35-17 rout of the Jets.

The Redskins got on the board first with Kilmer's first touchdown pass, the 45-yarder to Roy Jefferson. New York tied it up on John Riggins' one-yard touchdown burst and Ian Howfield's 13-yard field goal.

Then it was bombs away for Kilmer again. This time he dialed up Charley Taylor for 70 yards and a 14-10 lead that the Redskins never relinquished.

They started to pull away before halftime when Chris Hanburger picked off a Namath pass and scooted 41 yards to make it 21-10 at intermission.

The longest gain came on the shortest pass when Kilmer flipped a screen to Larry Brown at the Washington 11. Brown got good blocks from the front line, burst into the secondary, did a tightrope act down the sideline and picked up a downfield block from Taylor to complete the 89-yard play and put Washington up 28-10.

Namath and the Jets netted just 116 passing yards after subtracting the 32 yards lost on three sacks.

Kilmer completed just seven passes in 16 attempts but netted 222 yards through the air.

Nov 5

The Best Game You Never Saw?
Strikers cut TV cable; game not telecast

11/12/72	REDSKINS (8-1) 27, Giants (5-4) 13			53,039	
NYG	0	7	3	3	13
Was	0	6	7	14	27
NYG	Johnson 1 run (Gogolak kick)				
Was	Smith 18 pass from Kilmer (kick failed)				
NYG	FG Gogolak 12				
Was	Harraway 1 run (Knight kick)				
NYG	FG Gogolak 23				
Was	Brown 5 run (Knight kick)				
Was	Brown 4 run (Knight kick)				

RFK Stadium—In a game that was much closer than the final score indicated, Larry Brown scored two touchdowns in the last 1:05 of the game to give the Redskins a 27-13 win over the Giants.

New York defensive coach Jim Garrett had guaranteed that Brown would not rush for 100 yards after the Redskins' star back had slashed up the Giants for 191 yards in Yankee Stadium two weeks earlier. Brown's last two scoring runs put him over the century mark, giving him 106 yards for the game.

New York came out in the second half looking to expand its 7-6 lead, running a reverse on the second half kickoff that netted 86 yards. But the Giants could muster just a field goal out of it and had to be satisfied with a four-point lead. The Redskins got another scare when Billy Kilmer threw a pass that the Giants' linebacker Jim Files had his hands on. The ball slipped through Files' mitts and into those of Roy Jefferson, keeping alive the 78-yard drive that ended up with a one-yard Charley Harraway run and a 12-10 lead. The Giants had blocked the point after attempt following the Redskins' first touchdown and got a hand on this one, but it made it over the crossbar for a 13-10 advantage.

After a Pete Gogolak field goal tied the game in the fourth quarter, Alvin Haymond returned the ensuing kickoff 40 yards. Starting with 3:51 left, Kilmer sparked a 67-yard drive with a 38-yard pass to Jefferson. Brown capped it off with a five-yard run through a huge hole to put the Redskins up by 20-13 with 1:05 to go.

Ted Vactor killed any New York hopes by intercepting Norm Snead's pass and returning it to the Giants' 10 with just seconds left. In a move that sparked several fistfights and other confrontations, the Redskins decided to try to score again—on Brown's four-yard run. Reserve quarterback Sam Wyche gave the best of several reasons for the decision offered by the Redskins: "We wanted Larry to rub salt in the Giants' wounds."

11/20/72	REDSKINS (9-1) 24, Falcons (5-5) 13			53,039	
Atl	7	3	0	3	13
Was	0	7	14	3	24
Atl	Mitchell 36 pass from Berry (Bell kick)				
Atl	FG Bell 33				
Was	Brown 1 run (Knight kick)				
Was	Brown 28 pass from Kilmer (Knight kick)				

Was	Smith 12 pass from Kilmer (Knight kick)
Atl	FG Bell 17
Was	FG Knight 37

RFK Stadium—The Redskins, aided by a few key Atlanta turnovers, overcame a 10-0 second-quarter deficit and beat the Falcons 24-13.

After the game Atlanta coach Norm Van Brocklin mused, "That's what beat us. The breaks; that was it."

True, but it went both ways. Atlanta had built its lead with a touchdown following an interception and field goal after Ted Vactor fumbled a punt.

Then it was Atlanta's turn to play giveaway. Art Malone fumbled and Chris Hanburger recovered at the Atlanta 42, setting up a one-yard touchdown plunge by Larry Brown. Then, with the Skins up 14-10, Malone fumbled again, with Brig Owens pouncing on it at the Atlanta 11. Washington capitalized when Billy Kilmer threw a 12-yard touchdown pass to Jerry Smith.

In between those gifts, however, is the drive that the Redskins wanted to focus on after the game. They took possession at their own 11 early in the third quarter and embarked on an 11-play drive for a touchdown. Kilmer passes to Charley Taylor and Roy Jefferson ate up large chunks of yardage and the quarterback finished it off with a 28-yard scoring pass to Larry Brown.

Smith's touchdown made it 21-10. All the Falcons could muster in response was a field goal.

11/26/72	**REDSKINS (10-1) 21, Packers (7-4) 16**				53,039
GB	3	3	0	10	16
Was	0	14	0	7	21
GB	FG Marcol 51				
Was	Brown 2 run (Knight kick)				
Was	Smith 25 pass from Kilmer (Knight kick)				
GB	FG Marcol 37				
GB	Lane 6 run (Marcol kick)				
Was	Taylor 5 pass from Kilmer (Knight kick)				
GB	FG Marcol 39				

RFK Stadium—The Redskins clinched a playoff spot by beating the Packers 21-16 at home.

The Redskins built a 14-3 second quarter lead after a Pat Fischer interception set up one touchdown and a six-play, 67-yard drive ended in a 25-yard Billy Kilmer to Jerry Smith touchdown pass.

Even though quarterbacks Scott Hunter and Jerry Taggee would finish the day with a combined five for 19 for 66 yards passing, the Packers would not go away and let the Redskins celebrate.

A 37-yard Chester Marcol field goal (he had opened the scoring with a 51-yarder in the first quarter) cut the lead to 14-6 at halftime. After a scoreless third quarter, MacArthur Lane took it in from six yards to make it a one-point game three minutes into the final period.

It was over for the Packers after that. The Redskins did exactly what they needed to do: embark on a time-consuming drive resulting in a touchdown. Kilmer was masterful on the 10-play, 78-yard drive, going five for five passing and mixing in the running game as well. His completions went to wideouts Roy Jefferson and Charley Taylor, with the payoff coming on a five-yard strike to Taylor with 6:24 left. The drive ate up nearly six minutes and Green Bay never threatened after that.

12/3/72	**Redskins (11-1) 23, EAGLES (2-10) 7**				65,720
Was	3	7	3	10	23
Phi	7	0	0	0	7
Was	FG Knight 9				
Phi	Carmichael 10 pass from Reaves (Dempsey kick)				
Was	Harraway 1 run (Knight kick)				
Was	FG Knight 14				

| Was | FG Knight 46 |
| Was | Taylor 2 pass from Kilmer (Knight kick) |

Veterans Stadium—The Redskins wrapped up their first division title in 27 years by wearing down a game Eagles team. Like many Redskins games this year, this 23-7 win wasn't pretty—but counts just the same.

Washington took an early 3-0 lead after recovering a Philadelphia fumble at the Eagles' six. They couldn't punch it into the end zone so Curt Knight came on to kick a nine-yard field goal.

Philadelphia responded with a 66-yard touchdown drive to take a 7-3 lead. The payoff came on a 10-yard pass from rookie quarterback John Reaves to receiver Harold Carmichael.

But the Redskins answered with a drive of their own: a 15-play, 84-yard beauty that ate up 8:48. Charley Harraway finished it off when he went over from the one to give the Skins a 10-7 halftime lead.

The Eagles were unable to threaten in the second half, but played some good defense of their own to keep within six going into the fourth quarter. Washington put it away in the fourth with a Curt Knight field goal less than a minute into the final period and Kilmer's two-yard toss to Taylor with eight minutes remaining.

Kilmer to Nixon: Shut Up!

Dec 3—President Richard Nixon is a huge fan of the Washington Redskins. He's so much of a fan, in fact, that Billy Kilmer thinks he's hurting the team.

"He's something else," said Kilmer. "He even called the coach on election night to talk about the game."

"But he's really hurting us," Kilmer said, explaining that Nixon's remarks prior to some games get the opposition psyched up.

"I think I'm going to ask George Allen to tell the president not to talk about a game until after we've played in it."

12/9/72	**COWBOYS (10-3) 34, Redskins (11-2) 24**				65,136
Was	0	3	7	14	24
Dal	14	14	3	3	34
Dal	Hill 10 run (Fritsch kick)				
Dal	Hill 26 pass from Morton (Fritsch kick)				
Dal	Garrison 25 run (Fritsch kick)				
Was	FG Knight 16				
Dal	Morton 12 run (Fritsch kick)				
Was	Taylor 10 pass from Kilmer (Knight kick)				
Dal	FG Fritsch 36				
Was	Jefferson 10 pass from Kilmer (Knight kick)				
Was	Taylor 6 pass from Kilmer (Knight kick)				
Dal	FG Fritsch 26				

Texas Stadium—In a game that had no meaning for the Redskins, Dallas clinched the wild card playoff spot in the playoffs by building up a big early lead and hanging on for a 34-24 win.

The Cowboys rolled up a big lead and coasted to a win over Washington. The Redskins had already wrapped up the division title the week before and rested Larry Brown, the NFL's leading rusher.

This one got out-of-hand early. Calvin Hill scored two first-quarter touchdowns—the first on a 10-yard run, and the second on a 26-yard pass from Craig Morton. The Cowboys boosted their lead to 21-0 in the second quarter when Walt Garrison rumbled 25 yards for a touchdown.

Washington dented the scoreboard later in the second on Curt Knight's 16-yard field goal but Morton scrambled 12 yards for a touchdown to make it 28-3 at halftime.

The Cowboys rushed for 246 yards on the game, including 111 by Calvin Hill.

The Redskins fought back in the second half and made the score respectable. In fact, a six-yard pass from Billy Kilmer to Charley Taylor cut the Dallas lead to 31-24 and had possession of the ball in the fourth quarter, but Charlie Waters intercepted Billy Kilmer's pass and Tony Fritsch kicked the clinching field goal.

12/17/72	**Bills (4-9-1) 24, REDSKINS (11-3) 17**			53,039	
Buf	10	0	0	14	24
Was	0	7	10	0	17
Buf	Wyatt 49 interception return (Leypoldt kick)				
Buf	FG Leypoldt 23				
Was	Mul-Key 8 run (Knight kick)				
Was	Brunet 2 run (Knight kick)				
Was	FG Knight 35				
Buf	Simpson 21 run (Leypoldt kick)				
Buf	Braxton 4 run (Leypoldt kick)				

RFK Stadium—"Losing is like death," said George Allen after the Bills beat the Redskins 24-17.

That may be true—but as losses go, this one was more like a mild cold. The Redskins let a 17-10 lead slip away in the fourth quarter and lost to the Bills, but the result did nothing to affect their already-determined playoff fate.

For the second straight week Larry Brown was rested and could only watch as Buffalo's O.J. Simpson gained 101 yards to pass the Redskin star for the NFL rushing title.

Billy Kilmer, a Pro Bowl selection, was on the field, but was playing as though he wanted to join Brown on the sidelines. He had just seven passes caught. Even worse, just four of the receptions were by Redskins; the Bills caught the other three. Alvin Wyatt returned the first INT that Kilmer threw 49 yards for a touchdown. Before the first quarter was over, the Bills' John Leypoldt kicked a 23-yard field goal to give his team a 10-0 lead.

The Washington offense then came alive with a big assist from the Buffalo defense. A pass interference call gave Washington a first down at the Bill eight and Brown's backup Herb Mul-Key, who had drawn the flag, scored from there. Washington took the lead in the third quarter with a 76-yard touchdown drive. Much of the ground in that march was gained by the referee, who walked off two 15-yard penalties against the Bills. Bob Brunet culminated the drive with a two-yard run over the goal line. Later in the third, Curt Knight connected on a 35-yard field goal to expand the Washington lead to 17-10.

Early in the fourth quarter, Simpson tied it with a 21-yard run, the capper of a 14-play, 80-yard drive. As the Redskins were trying to get into position for a game-winning field goal in the late going, a Kilmer pass bounced off of Mul-Key and into the arms of Dale Farley. The linebacker returned the pick 42 yards to the Washington three and, with less than a minute left, Jim Braxton bulled over from the four to win it for the Bills.

NFC Divisional Playoff
Sunday, December 24, 1972
RFK Stadium
Washington, D.C.

12/24/72	**REDSKINS 16, Packers 3**			53,140	
GB	0	3	0	0	3
Was	0	10	0	6	16
GB	FG Marcol 17				
Was	Jefferson 32 pass from Kilmer (Knight kick)				
Was	FG Knight 42				
Was	FG Knight 35				
Was	FG Knight 46				

A perfect strike from Billy Kilmer to Roy Jefferson that went for 32 yards and a second-quarter touchdown would be all the scoring the Redskins would need to move to the NFC Championship game.

The drive began after the Packers took a 3-0 lead on a Chester Marcol field goal. Herb Mul-Key took the ensuing kickoff

three yards deep in the end zone and returned it to the Washington 40. Five plays later, Jefferson got a half step ahead of cornerback Willie Buchanon and caught Kilmer's pass at the goal line for the game's only touchdown 2:06 before halftime. Curt Knight would add three field goals—one with 33 seconds left in the first half and two more in the fourth quarter—to salt the game away.

The Packers had won the Central division with a 10-4 record, a mark built largely on the strength of a powerful rushing game led by John Brockington, who ran for 1,042 yards on the season, and MacArthur Lane. So, this game was tailor-made for George Allen's Washington Redskins. The task was to shut down a one-dimensional offense and not lose the game on offense. This game was won during planning sessions the week before the game.

Manny Sistrunk, a 6-5, 285 pound backup defensive tackle, was the key to the strategy. On obvious running downs, which was most plays for the Packers, Sistrunk lined up at nose guard in a five-man defensive line. The Packers were confused enough by this tactic, but there was another subtle twist that added to the uncertainty. Green Bay, like many teams at the time, was moving away from having the quarterback call the offensive plays. Instead, the Packers used a shuttle system, with a pair of players alternating snaps, each bringing in the play from Coach Dan Devine to the quarterback Hunter. When Allen was going to make a defensive substitution, he would wait until Green Bay's messenger had headed towards the huddle, then would send his defensive personnel into the game.

Sistrunk and the rest of the defensive line of Diron Talbert, Bill Brundidge, Ron McDole and Verlon Biggs wrecked the Packers' blocking schemes. The diminutive cornerback Pat Fischer even got into the act, dropping Brockington for a five-yard loss late in the game. The chess game of situational substitution resulted in a checkmate of Brockington, who managed just nine yards on 13 carries, and Lane, who gained 56 on 14 carries.

The offense played it close to the vest, with Kilmer throwing just 14 passes all day, completing seven for an even 100 yards. He took no chances. Larry Brown, the league MVP who sat out the previous two regular season games with a variety of injuries, carried 25 times for 100 yards. The Redskins were able to win the field position battle with some outstanding punting by Mike Bragg, who booted 6 punts for a 47-yard average. In contrast, Green Bay's punter averaged a full ten yards less per punt.

The favorable field position allowed Washington to move into position for two Knight field goals in the fourth quarter and expand the lead to an insurmountable 16-3. Green Bay got into Washington territory just twice in the second half. They got just as far as the Redskins' 49 the second time before Chris Hanburger intercepted a Hunter pass.

NFC Championship
Sunday, December 31, 1972
RFK Stadium
Washington, D.C.

12/31/72	**REDSKINS 26, Cowboys 3**			53,129	
Dal	0	3	0	0	3
Was	0	10	0	16	26
Was	FG Knight 18				
Was	Taylor 15 pass from Kilmer (Knight kick)				
Dal	FG Fritsch 35				
Was	Taylor 45 pass from Kilmer (Knight kick)				
Was	FG Knight 39				
Was	FG Knight 46				
Was	FG Knight 45				

George Allen said, "It was pretty close to perfect."

How close to perfect?

Allen revealed that he would skip his favored celebratory milk and celebrate the New Year—and the Redskins' 26-3 NFC Championship smashing of the hated Dallas Cowboys—with some "very old" champagne.

Allen certainly will be lifting a glass of the bubbly to the Washington defense. His pride and joy dominated the Cowboys, holding them to 96 yards rushing and a mere eight first downs. Roger Staubach couldn't get untracked and the Dallas quarterback completed just nine of 20 passes for a mere 98 yards. The Redskins sacked him six times.

And it's likely that Allen will toast Billy Kilmer and Charley Taylor. The quarterback completed 14 of 18 passes for 198 yards and two touchdowns. Taylor caught both of those scoring tosses and had a total of seven catches for 146 yards.

While the final score reflected the Redskins' dominance, the game still was a contest entering the fourth quarter. Curt Knight opened the scoring with an 18-yard field goal. Later in the second period, the Redskins scored on a 15-yard Kilmer-to-Taylor touchdown pass. The drive got started on third and ten from the Washington 28 when Taylor shook cornerback Charlie Waters and hauled in Kilmer's pass for a 51-yard game. Two plays later it was 10-0 as Taylor ran a slant and Kilmer hit him perfectly.

Dallas mustered a field goal before halftime and it remained 10-3 going into the final period. Although the scoreboard indicated a competitive game, it seemed to be just a matter of time before the Redskins put it away.

And they did just that early in the fourth quarter. With Waters out of the game with a broken arm, Kilmer picked on his replacement, Mark Washington. On third and ten at the Dallas 45, Taylor blew past Washington and Kilmer hit him in stride for the touchdown.

That sent the sellout crowd into a frenzy. The excitement grew after each of Knight's three fourth-quarter field goals put the Cowboys further and further behind. When it was over, the fans poured onto the field, congratulating their heroes and dancing with joy.

In his postgame prayer, team chaplain James Skinner said, "Lord, help us to be humble." That was a very tall order.

Dec 31

Redskins Favored Over 'Fins by Two
Miami's 16-0 record doesn't impress oddsmakers

Allen Driven to Distraction

Jan 12—George Allen has had it.

"The only thing I have to say is that this is the first meeting I'm going to miss with a team in 23 years," Allen said at the week's final press conference. "I hope the questions we get will be of some value. I've been answering the same questions since Monday."

He noted that 31 players were in interviews for an hour and a half yesterday and "we had our worst practice of the week."

Allen's negative tone prompted one reporter to ask, "Aren't you sounding like a loser?"

"I'm not thinking like one," Allen shot back, although his tirades indicated otherwise.

Meanwhile, Allen's opposite number wasn't fazed by the whole circus. Miami's Don Shula, coaching his third Super Bowl, proclaimed, "My attitude is damned good."

SUPER BOWL VII

Sunday, January 14, 1973
Los Angeles Memorial Coliseum
Los Angeles, California

1/14/73	Dolphins 14, Redskins 7				90,182
Was	0	0	0	7	**7**
Mia	7	7	0	0	**14**
Mia	Twilley 28 pass from Griese (Yepremian kick)				
Mia	Kiick 1 run (Yepremian kick)				
Was	Bass 49 fumble return (Knight kick)				

George Allen's Over the Hill Gang was flying so high going into Super Bowl VII that they were actually installed as three-point favorites over an unbeaten Miami Dolphins team. Sure, Miami had rushed for nearly 3,000 yards that year, but Washington had shut down Green Bay's high-powered rushing game in the first round of the playoffs to gain a 16-3 win. And, yes, star quarterback Bob Griese would be back after missing much of the year with injury, but the return of Roger Staubach—who also was destined for Canton—didn't help the Cowboys much as Washington thrashed the defending champs 26-3 in the NFC Championship game.

It quickly became apparent that the Redskins' status as favorites was unwarranted. The Miami defense—nicknamed the No-Name Defense due to its lack of well-known stars—stuffed the running of Larry Brown by taking away his cutback lanes. Tackle Manny Fernandez was particularly effective; whenever Brown tried to find a hole up the middle, Fernandez was there to give him an inhospitable greeting. During the entire first half the Redskins took one snap in Miami territory, that at the 48. On that play, Billy Kilmer was rushed and his pass intercepted by linebacker Nick Buoniconti and returned 32 yards to set up Miami's second TD just before halftime. They had scored earlier on an 18-yard Griese pass to receiver Howard Twilley near the end of the first quarter.

Trailing 14-0, the Redskins tightened up defensively and made several unsuccessful efforts to get back into the game offensively. Taking possession after the second-half kickoff, Kilmer finally got a hot hand, hitting Charlie Taylor, Roy Jefferson and Jerry Smith to move smartly down the field to the Miami 17. A sack killed the drive, Curt Knight's 32-yard field goal attempt flew wide right and a five-minute drive went for naught. Miami appeared to seize the momentum again when Larry Csonka created a highlight film clip demonstrating the futility of the Redskins defense as tackler after would-be tackler bounced off of the powerful Dolphins running back during a 49-yard run. Washington held on, though, as Brig Owens intercepted a pass in the end zone before embarking on another drive deep into Miami territory.

If it wasn't already clear that it just wasn't the Redskins' day, it became painfully obvious on a second-down play from the Miami 10. Smith broke wide open in the end zone. Kilmer spotted him and threw a pass that seemed destined to hit the tight end in the numbers. It struck the crossbar of the goal posts and fell harmlessly to the ground. On third down, game MVP Jake Scott intercepted Kilmer's pass in the end zone and returned it to the Washington 48. The Redskins appeared to be dead until, in the words of Miami guard Bob Kuchenberg, "Garo did his little thing."

"Garo" was Dolphin kicker Garo Yepremian and the "little thing" was that an attempted pass after his 42-yard field goal attempt with just over two minutes left was blocked by tackle Bill Brundige. Nobody is quite sure to whom the diminutive kicker was trying to pass after he scooped up the ball, which slipped out of his hands as he started into his passing motion. It was so bad that when Mike Bass picked it out of the air and ran it in 49 yards for the TD, he was credited with a fumble recovery, not an interception. Instead of holding a 17-0 lead to build the team's season record to a perfect 17-0, the Dolphins were suddenly sweating it out with 2:07 to play.

Allen eschewed the onside kick and kicked off deep. The defense held and Washington got the ball back with a chance to

tie with 1:14 left. But the Miami defense swarmed all over Kilmer, the drive went nowhere, and Miami took over on downs.

1973
Head Coach: George Allen
Record: 10-4, Second in NFC East
Playoffs: 0-1, lost in Divisional playoff

Honors: Chris Hanburger, Pro Bowl, All-NFC; Ken Houston, Pro Bowl, All-NFC; Herb Mul-Key, Pro Bowl, All-NFC; Charley Taylor, Pro Bowl, All-NFC

Jan 17

Allen Loses Top Assistant
Line coach Mike McCormack takes head job with Eagles

Jan 25

Marv Levy Heads North
Special teams coach takes top job with CFL Montreal Alouettes

---

Feb 3

Pardee Takes on Dual Role
Linebacker will become player-coach for Allen

July 19

Skins Get Duane Thomas in 1-2 Deal
Controversial RB obtained from Chargers for '75 first-round pick and '76 second

---

9/16/73	REDSKINS (1-0) 38, Chargers (0-1) 0			53,589	
SD	0	0	0	0	0
Was	21	0	7	10	38
Was	Biggs 2 fumble recovery (Knight kick)				
Was	Brown 1 run (Knight kick)				
Was	Owens 36 fumble recovery (Knight kick)				
Was	Taylor 32 pass from Kilmer (Knight kick)				
Was	FG Knight 19				
Was	Grant 12 pass from Kilmer (Knight kick)				

RFK Stadium—The Redskins turned three first-quarter fumbles by Chargers running back Mike Garrett into three touchdowns to jump-start an easy 38-0 win over San Diego.

Two of the scores were by defensive players. Early on, Garrett fumbled deep in his own territory and Verlon Biggs picked it up and stepped two yards for a score. Brig Owens had to go a little further to get his six points—36 yards, to be exact—late in the first quarter after Garrett's third fumble. In between, it was Ken Houston with the strip and recovery at the San Diego 28 and Larry Brown with the touchdown from one yard out two plays later.

You know that a team has enjoyed some considerable success when it is up 21-0 and the home team fans are booing. The displeasure stemmed from a lack of offensive production. The home team had netted just 55 yards of offense by the time the halftime gun sounded. The statistics improved, the margin widened and the boobirds quieted in the second half as Billy Kilmer directed touchdown drives of 80 and 52 yards.

The Washington defense held the Chargers in check, sacking quarterback Johnny Unitas five times, and picking off three of the ex-Colts legend's passes.

Sep 17

Some Fans Want Sonny; Allen Not Listening
Coach will stick with Kilmer at QB despite lackluster offense in opener

---

9/23/73	CARDINALS (2-0) 27, Redskins (1-1) 14			50,316	
Was	0	7	3	17	27
StL	7	0	10	17	34
StL	Anderson 1 run (Bakken kick)				
Was	Taylor 23 pass from Kilmer (Knight kick)				
Was	FG Knight 28				
StL	Anderson 1 run (Bakken kick)				
StL	FG Bakken 23				
StL	Anderson 12 pass from Hart (Bakken kick)				
Was	Harraway 10 pass from Jurgensen (Knight kick)				
StL	Shy 97 kickoff return (Bakken kick)				
Was	Mul-Key 97 kickoff return (Knight kick)				
StL	FG Bakken 28				
Was	FG Knight 37				

Busch Stadium—Jim Hart scorched the Redskins' secondary for 286 yards passing in the second half to lead the Cardinals to a 34-27 win over Washington.

After a Curt Knight field goal broke a 7-7 halftime tie, St. Louis ran off 17 unanswered points in the third and early fourth quarters with running back Donny Anderson scoring two touchdowns. Sandwiched in between was a 23-yard field goal by Jim Bakken.

With the Cardinals leading 24-10, Sonny Jurgensen—who had replaced an ineffective Billy Kilmer at quarterback—led the Redskins on a 73-yard, seven-play drive that culminated in Jurgensen's 10-yard touchdown pass to Charley Harraway. Less than a minute later the margin was the same, but only after some considerable excitement. Don Shy took the ensuing kickoff and raced 97 yards for a touchdown. With the crowd still buzzing, Herb Mul-Key fielded the Cardinals' kickoff and matched Shy's return yard for yard, going 97 as well to pull the Redskins back within seven at 31-24.

The 28 points in the first seven minutes of the fourth quarter was the end of the scoring explosion. After Mul-Key's score, St. Louis drove to another Bakken field goal to expand their lead to 10. A Curt Knight three-pointer with just under five minutes left got Washington back within a touchdown, but St. Louis burned off all but a minute and a half of the remaining time and the Redskins' desperation bid at the end failed.

Sep 24

Allen: 'Kilmer is the Quarterback'
Says that benching versus Cards was temporary

10/14/73	**Redskins (4-1) 21, GIANTS (1-3-1) 3**				70,168
Was	7	0	7	7	21
NYG	3	0	0	0	3
NYG	FG Gogolak 24				
Was	Brown 1 run (Knight kick)				
Was	Brown 3 run (Knight kick)				
Was	Robinson 28 interception return (Knight kick)				

Sep 29

Allen: 'I Favor Starting Sonny'
'Tough to bench anyone,' says coach, but Kilmer will take a seat versus Eagles

9/30/73	**Redskins (2-1) 28, EAGLES (1-1-1) 7**				64,147
Was	7	0	7	14	28
Phi	0	7	0	0	7
Was	Taylor 23 pass from Jurgensen (Knight kick)				
Phi	Bulaich 80 pass from Gabriel (Dempsey kick)				
Was	Taylor 10 pass from Jurgensen (Knight kick)				
Was	Brown 1 run (Knight kick)				
Was	Vactor 34 interception return (Knight kick)				

Veterans Stadium—Sonny Jurgensen started his first game in 11 months and shook off some rust to lead the Redskins to a 28-7 win over the Eagles. A torn Achilles' tendon had sidelined him since a 1972 game at Yankee Stadium.

Jurgensen threw the first of his two touchdown passes to Charley Taylor in the first quarter, this one from 23 yards. The Eagles responded with an explosive play. Quarterback Roman Gabriel found running back Norm Bulaich with an 80-yard touchdown bomb to tie the game in the second quarter.

While the offense was struggling, the Washington defense was keeping the Eagles at bay, save for that one bomb. They sacked Gabriel seven times and allowed Philadelphia just 53 yards rushing. In addition, with the Redskins leading just 14-7 in the fourth quarter, the defense made two plays to put it away.

First, Chris Hanburger intercepted a Gabriel pass and returned it 45 yards to the Eagles' 19. Larry Brown carried six straight times from there and his one-yard TD run gave the Redskins some breathing room at 21-7. Then Ted Vactor stepped in front of a Gabriel pass and took it back all the way, 34 yards for the icing on the cake.

10/8/73	**REDSKINS (3-1) 14, Cowboys (3-1) 7**				54,314
Dal	0	7	0	0	7
Was	0	0	0	14	14
Dal	Stowe 15 pass from Staubach (Fritsch kick)				
Was	Taylor 1 pass from Jurgensen (Knight kick)				
Was	Owens 26 interception return (Knight kick)				

RFK Stadium—This game will be remembered for the final play, but the events leading up to Ken Houston's goal line stand were electrifying in their own right.

The Skins fell behind 7-0 late in the second quarter, when Craig Morton found receiver Otto Stowe for 45 yards and a Dallas touchdown. The Washington offense finally got it going late in the fourth quarter, driving 57 yards to tie the game on a one-yard Sonny Jurgensen to Charley Taylor touchdown pass with 3:37 left. Just 63 seconds later, Morton overthrew tight end Billy Joe DuPree and free safety Brig Owens intercepted the pass, dashing 26 yards down the left sideline for the go-ahead touchdown.

Had it not been for an odd hop of the ball, Houston would never have had his moment frozen in time. Dallas went a quick three and out and punted, but the ball bounced off of a Redskin and the Cowboys were back in business at the Washington 31 with two minutes left. Seven plays later, Pat Fischer broke up Morton's pass intended for Stowe, and it was fourth and goal at the four with 24 seconds left.

Morton hit Walt Garrison over the middle at the one. A fraction of a second later, Houston hit Garrison at the one. Just as Garrison's right foot touched the goal line, Houston wrapped his arms around the Dallas fullback in textbook style and drove Garrison backwards. Garrison feebly attempted to lateral the ball, but the whistle had blown. Possession—and the win—belonged to Washington.

Yale Bowl—Once again, the Redskins used a heavy dose of defense and just enough offense to get past the Giants 21-3.

After the Giants opened the scoring with a field goal, the Redskins cranked out their only sustained scoring drive of the day. They moved 80 yards in 12 plays, with Larry Brown scoring from the one. After that, the offense served mostly to kill the clock while the defense was responsible for the two other TD's.

Actually, it appeared that Washington had settled for three points following one turnover: Pat Fischer's interception returned 67 yards to the New York 14. They were unable to move the ball, and Curt Knight was called in to kick a 19-yard field goal. It was successful, but the Giants were flagged for roughing the kicker and George Allen elected to take the three points off the board and go for seven. Six plays later, the gamble paid off as Brown scored from three yards out.

Linebacker Dave Robinson closed out the scoring in the fourth quarter by returning an interception 28 yards for a touchdown. Safety Ken Houston kept the Giants out of the end zone with his second interception late in the game.

Oct 19

Sonny Ailing, Billy Preps
With Jurgensen's knee hurting, Kilmer may start versus Cards

10/21/73	**REDSKINS (5-1) 31, Cardinal (2-4) 13**				54,381
StL	0	6	7	0	13
Was	7	14	0	10	31
Was	Harraway 1 run (Knight kick)				
StL	FG Bakken 32				
Was	Taylor 22 pass from Kilmer (Knight kick)				
Was	Hancock 1 pass from Kilmer (Knight kick)				
StL	FG Bakken 31				
StL	Gray 69 pass from Hart (Bakken kick)				
Was	FG Knight 18				
Was	Bass 56 interception return				

RFK Stadium—Billy Kilmer, starting in place of an injured Sonny Jurgensen, completed 20 of 33 passes for 296 yards and two touchdowns to pace the win over the Cardinals. The point production could have been higher but for seven turnovers by the Redskins, who lost four fumbles and three interceptions.

Kilmer had 245 of his yards through the air in the first half as his team was building a 21-6 lead. The Redskins didn't need Kilmer's arm for their first score, though, as linebacker Dave Robinson returned an interception 39 yards to within six inches of the goal line. Charley Harraway got credit for a one-yard TD run by taking it the rest of the way on the next play.

The home team drove to its two other first-half scores. Charley Taylor made an impressive catch of a 22-yard touchdown pass from Kilmer, and Kilmer's second TD pass went to tight end Mike Hancock.

The Cardinals showed some of their offensive explosiveness in the third quarter when Jim Hart threw a 69-yard touchdown pass to receiver Mel Gray to pull St. Louis to within 21-13. But that was it for the Cardinals; the Redskins added an 18-yard field goal by Curt Knight and a 38-yard touchdown interception return by Mike Bass in the final period.

10/28/73	SAINTS (3-4) 19, Redskins (5-2) 3				66,315
Was	0	0	0	3	3
NO	10	6	0	3	19

NO	FG McLard 35
NO	Butler 9 pass from Manning (McLard kick)
NO	FG McLard 43
NO	FG McLard 30
Was	FG Knight 35
NO	FG McLard 37

Tulane Stadium—The Saints' Bill McLard, just acquired off of waivers earlier in the week, kicked four field goals to pace New Orleans' 19-3 home win over the Redskins.

None of McLard's kicks were chip shots—all of them came from 30 yards or longer.

New Orleans kept getting key plays from quarterback Archie Manning, whose rushing yardage (60) nearly matched his passing total (62). He threw a nine-yard touchdown pass to Bill Butler in the first period to give New Orleans a 10-0 lead.

Given the way the Washington offense was performing, that would have been plenty. They generated just 14 yards rushing in the first half and 24 for the game.

The passing game wasn't much better. Billy Kilmer engineered just 64 yards through the air in the first half. When he came out in the second half and threw an interception on his first attempt, George Allen had seen enough. Sonny Jurgensen came to relieve Kilmer the next series. The results were better, but not nearly good enough. Jurgensen did engineer a drive to the Saints 21 but cornerback Ernie Jackson intercepted his pass from there and that was that. Sonny finished 13 for 25 for 110 yards.

Curt Knight kicked a 35-yard field goal in the fourth quarter to avert a shutout.

11/5/73	STEELERS (7-1) 21, Redskins (5-3) 16				49,230
Was	3	3	3	7	16
Pit	7	7	0	7	21

Was	FG Knight 30
Pit	P. Pearson 7 pass from Hanratty (Gerela kick)
Was	FG Knight 12
Pit	Shanklin 24 pass from Hanratty (Gerela kick)
Was	FG Knight 16
Pit	B. Pearson 46 pass from Gilliam (Gerela kick)
Was	Brown 17 pass from Kilmer (Knight kick)

Three Rivers Stadium—Pittsburgh got three touchdown passes from two different quarterbacks and that, combined with some clutch defense, was enough to get the Steelers past the Redskins 21-16.

Some good Washington defense—an interception by Mike Bass—set up Washington's first score. He returned it to the Washington 23, leading to a 30-yard field goal by Curt Knight.

The home team responded immediately, driving 65 yards to take the lead. The payoff came on Terry Hanratty's seven-yard scoring pass to Preston Pearson.

In the second quarter, a shanked punt gave the Redskins a short field for Knight's second three-pointer. Thirty seconds before halftime, the Steelers extended their lead to 14-6 when Hanratty threw his second TD, this one to Ron Shanklin from 24 yards out.

Unfortunately for the Redskins, the pattern of Pittsburgh answering Washington field goals with touchdowns continued. A 16-yard Knight field goal was followed by Pittsburgh's third touchdown pass. Joe Gilliam, subbing for an injured Hanratty, threw this one 46 yards to Barry Pearson.

The Redskins finally scored a touchdown after Brig Owens' third interception of the game. They had to move just 28 yards, the final play coming on Billy Kilmer's 17-yard pass to Larry Brown. A late threat to steal the game, though, ended when Glen Edwards intercepted a Kilmer pass at the goal line in the closing minute.

11/11/73	REDSKINS (6-3) 33, 49ers (3-6) 9				54,381
SF	0	9	0	0	9
Was	7	3	13	10	33

Was	Brown 18 pass from Jurgensen (Knight kick)
SF	FG Gossett 9
SF	FG Gossett 27
Was	FG Knight 47
SF	FG Gossett 38
Was	Harraway 25 pass from Kilmer (Knight kick)
Was	FG Knight 32
Was	FG Knight 24
Was	FG Knight 41
Was	Hancock 2 pass from Kilmer (Knight kick)

RFK Stadium—The Redskins located their missing wide receivers and, along with them, their offense to thump the 49ers 33-9.

Billy Kilmer completed 22 of 33 passes for 267 yards. The receiver tandem of Charley Taylor and Roy Jefferson, who had combined for just three catches in the team's previous two games—both losses—tallied eleven receptions for 133 yards.

As usual, a big play by the Washington defense considerably boosted the team. With the Redskins up 7-0, the 49ers drove to a first and goal at the Washington one. On first down, Chris Hanburger chased down quarterback Joe Reed, who was attempting to roll into the end zone, and nailed him for a three-yard loss. San Francisco had to settle for a Bruce Gossett field goal.

Gossett kicked two more three-pointers before halftime and Washington's lead was just 10-9 at the break. They got going early in the second half, taking five plays to move 48 yards to a touchdown. Kilmer threw 25 yards to Charley Harraway for that score, making it 17-9.

After that, play got very sloppy for the 49ers and they gave away any chance they had to get back into it. Five turnovers (three fumbles and two interceptions) set up four Washington scores: three Curt Knight field goals and a two-yard TD pass from Kilmer to tight end Mike Hancock.

Sonny Jurgensen participated in one play but made it count, throwing an 18-yard touchdown pass to Larry Brown to give the Redskins their 7-0 first-quarter lead.

11/18/73	REDSKINS (7-3) 22, Colts (2-8) 14				52,675
Bal	0	0	7	7	14
Was	7	6	3	3	22

Was	Brown 1 run (Knight kick)
Was	FG Knight 35
Was	FG Knight 18
Bal	McCauley 1 run (Hunt kick)
Was	FG Knight 37
Was	FG Knight 42
Bal	Speyrer 4 pass from Domres (Hunt kick)
Was	FG Knight 29

RFK Stadium—Curt Knight, who was in danger of losing his job earlier in the season when he hit just three of his first 13 field goal attempts, kicked five field goals to lift the Redskins to a 22-14 win over the Colts. Knight has 12 field goals in the team's last three games.

In the first half, it appeared this might be a laugher for the home team. Larry Brown scored on a one-yard run in the first quarter and Knight got his first two field goals in the second to give Washington a 13-0 halftime lead.

But the Colts were not going quietly. They took the second-half kickoff and chewed up the first 9:17 of the period while in the process of driving 67 yards in 17 plays. The drive culminated with Don McCauley's one-yard touchdown run and the anticipated laugher took on a more serious tone.

It got considerably more serious when Herb Mul-Key fumbled the ensuing kickoff after a 48-yard return and the initial signal from the officials awarded possession to the Colts. When the pile was untangled, though, Washington's Danny Ryczek had the ball at the Baltimore 47. The Redskins drove 17 yards, setting up Knight's third field goal. He kicked another early in the fourth quarter.

That enabled Washington to survive a desperate Baltimore touchdown drive that featured two fourth down conversions and ended up with Marty Domres throwing a four-yard pass to Cotton Speyrer to make it 19-14. That was it for the Colts, as the Redskins drove to Knight's final field goal after the ensuing kickoff and then killed the rest of the clock with the ground game.

11/22/73	Redskins (8-3) 20, LIONS (4-6-1) 0			54,418	
Was	10	3	7	0	20
Det	0	0	0	0	0
Was	Harraway 4 pass from Kilmer (Knight kick)				
Was	FG Knight 25				
Was	FG Knight 23				
Was	Taylor 3 pass from Kilmer (Knight kick)				

Tiger Stadium—Billy Kilmer completed two short touchdown passes, Charley Harraway rushed for 105 yards and the defense held the Lions at bay as Washington got its second shutout win of the season, spoiling Detroit's annual Thanksgiving Day get together with a 20-0 win.

The Redskins had chances to break this one wide open early. On their first possession, they drove 74 yards in 13 plays. Harraway got 28 on the ground during the march, Larry Brown picked up 20 and Kilmer was four of six passing. Kilmer threw four yards to Harraway for the touchdown.

Detroit immediately gave Washington another opportunity when Steve Owens fumbled on the first play after the ensuing kickoff. Ken Houston recovered for the Redskins at the Detroit 23. Soon after that, Curt Knight booted a 25-yard field goal and it was 10-0.

Altie Taylor fumbled the ensuing kickoff and Ken Stone recovered for Washington, but Knight missed a 39-yard field goal.

It remained 10-0 at the half, but the Redskins took control in the third quarter by driving for a TD after taking the second-half kickoff. They moved 75 yards in 12 plays, the capper and game clincher coming on Kilmer's three-yard scoring pass to Charley Taylor.

12/2/73	REDSKINS (9-3) 27, Giants (2-9-1) 24			53,590	
NYG	7	14	0	3	24
Was	3	10	0	14	27
Was	FG Knight 12				
NYG	Ron Johnson 3 run (Gogolak kick)				
NYG	Tucker 12 pass from Ra. Johnson (Gogolak kick)				
NYG	Ron Johnson 25 pass from Ra. Johnson (Gogolak kick)				
Was	Brown 3 run (Knight kick)				
Was	FG Knight 17				
NYG	FG Gogolak 22				
Was	Brown 6 run (Knight kick)				
Was	Brown 16 pass from Jurgensen (Knight kick)				

RFK Stadium—Sonny Jurgensen, bum knee and all, came off the bench to lead the Redskins to two fourth-quarter touchdowns and a 27-24 come-from-behind win over the Giants.

The Giants bolted to a 21-3 lead in the second quarter. First, running back Ron Johnson scored on a three-yard run. Then quarterback Randy Johnson threw a 12-yard scoring pass to tight end Bob Tucker. To complete the Johnson-and-Johnson trifecta, Randy threw a 25-yard TD pass to Ron.

The Redskins responded with a three-yard touchdown run by Larry Brown and Curt Knight's second field goal to cut it to 21-13 at the half.

After a scoreless third quarter, Pete Gogolak kicked a 22-yard field goal early in the fourth and gave the Giants an 11-point margin. Starting quarterback Billy Kilmer reinjured his left ankle,

and in limped Jurgensen, whose nagging injury to his knee had limited him to one practice session per week.

Maybe the rest of the team should practice as infrequently. After missing three of his first four passes, Jurgensen completed 11 straight to spark two long TD drives.

The first one started at the Washington 23. It was nearly dead on arrival three plays later when Jurgensen's pass on third and three at the 30 fell to the turf. A borderline holding call on New York cornerback Pete Athas, however, gave the Redskins new life. Jurgensen took full advantage, hitting four straight passes, including a screen pass on which Brown made a gutsy effort to pick up 20 yards. Two plays after that one, Brown burst up the middle for six yards to cap the drive. Knight's extra point made it 24-20.

Sacking quarterback Johnson helped get the ball back for the offense at its own 34 with 6:43 showing on the game clock. They drove to the Giants 40, but a holding penalty pushed them back into their own territory. It took a 21-yard completion from Jurgensen to Charley Harraway and a tough one-yard run by Brown to get the first down by the length of the ball. Three plays later from the 16, Brown circled out of the backfield, caught Jurgensen's swing pass and lunged over the goal line for the winning score.

Dec 3

Maybe 'No Next Year' for Jurgy
QB 'tired of being inured,' may not come back

Dec 6

Kilmer in Hospital, Jurgensen Will Start
Billy will assume backup role in
Dallas showdown

12/9/73	COWBOYS (9-4) 27, Redskins (9-4) 7			62,195	
Was	0	0	0	7	7
Dal	0	3	14	10	27
Dal	FG Fritsch 9				
Dal	Staubach 5 run (Fritsch kick)				
Dal	Hill 1 run (Fritsch kick)				
Dal	Hill 2 run (Fritsch kick)				
Dal	FG Fritsch 27				
Was	Stone 12 blocked punt return (Knight kick)				

Texas Stadium—The contrast between the pre-game bravado and post-game despair was telling.

Before the game, on the subject of Dallas' mobile quarterback Roger Staubach, George Allen said, "He will scramble at his own risk."

After the game, on the same subject, Allen said, "Staubach hurt us rolling out." You need see no more than those two quotes to figure out who won this one.

Dallas held a 3-0 lead at halftime on the strength of a Tony Fritsch field goal with 29 seconds left in the second quarter. The Redskins had some opportunities to score, but Curt Knight missed field goal attempts of 23, 28 and 37 yards, all of them hooked to the left.

Dallas recovered a Washington fumble at the Redskins 30 early in the third quarter and the visitors would pay for their inability to take advantage of their earlier opportunities. Soon after the recovery, Staubach scored—on a rollout, of course—and it was 10-0.

By the time the third quarter ended, it was 17-0 as Staubach engineered a 70-yard TD drive with Calvin Hill scoring from the one. The Redskins got their only points late in the game when Rusty Tillman blocked a Dallas punt and Ken Stone scooped it up and went in from the 12.

Landry Complains About Skins' Tactics

Dec 11—Dallas coach Tom Landry seems to take wins over the Redskins as poorly as he takes defeats at the hands of Washington.

Earlier this season, after a thrilling 14-7 Redskins win, Landry said that the Redskins weren't as good as his Cowboys, despite the evidence on the scoreboard.

Today, following his team's rout of the Redskins in the return matchup, Landry complained to the league about some of the defensive tactics that Washington employed.

He filed a protest about some of the signals Redskin defenders were calling at the line of scrimmage. According to Landry, they were trying to "jam" quarterback Roger Staubach's signals at the line by imitating his snap count.

Such tactics are illegal, but officials on the field during the game saw no reason to penalize the Redskins at the time.

12/16/73	REDSKINS (10-4) 38, Eagles (5-8-1) 20			49,464	
Phi	10	3	7	0	20
Was	0	24	7	7	38
Phi	FG Dempsey 44				
Phi	Young 34 pass from Gabriel (Dempsey kick)				
Was	Brown 14 pass from Kilmer (Knight kick)				
Was	FG Knight 15				
Was	Jefferson 32 pass from Kilmer (Knight kick)				
Was	Brown 27 pass from Kilmer (Knight kick)				
Phi	FG Dempsey 15				
Was	Brown 64 pass from Kilmer (Knight kick)				
Phi	Sullivan 1 run (Dempsey kick)				
Was	Brown 8 run (Knight kick)				

RFK Stadium—After spotting the Eagles a 10-0 lead in the first quarter, the Redskins ran off 24 unanswered points in the second period to spur the 38-20 win.

Billy Kilmer threw for all three touchdowns during the run, and added a fourth scoring pass in the third quarter.

The win gave the Redskins a Wild Card playoff berth. Although they finished the season tied with Dallas at 10-4, the Cowboys claimed the division title based on tiebreakers.

After the Eagles had taken their 10-0 lead on the strength of a Tom Dempsey field goal and Roman Gabriel's 34-yard touchdown pass to tight end Charley Young, the Redskins got down to business. Taking possession on their own 30 with less than two minutes left in the first quarter, Washington moved 80 yards in eight plays, with 44 of those yards coming on three Kilmer passes to Roy Jefferson. The capper was a seven-yard connection from Kilmer to Larry Brown.

A Philly fumble led to a short Curt Knight field goal that tied the game at 10. After that, the home team rolled to two more touchdowns to take a 24-10 lead. Kilmer found Jefferson for 32 yards for the first TD and Brown caught his second scoring pass—a 27-yarder on a swing pattern. A Dempsey field goal cut the lead to 24-13 at the half.

In the third quarter, Jerry Smith executed a textbook block on a screen pass, springing Brown for 64 yards and another touchdown.

The Eagles responded with a touchdown drive of their own. Gabriel's 73-yard bomb to receiver Harold Carmichael led to a

one-yard run by Tom Sullivan. Soon after that, though, the Redskins wrapped it up when Brown scored his fourth touchdown of the day on a seven-yard run. On the day, Brown carried 26 times for 150 yards.

NFC Divisional Playoff Game
Saturday, December 22, 1973
Metropolitan Stadium
Minneapolis, Minnesota

12/22/73	VIKINGS 27, Redskins 20			45,475	
Was	0	7	3	10	20
Min	0	3	7	17	27
Min	FG Cox 19				
Was	Brown 3 run (Knight kick)				
Min	Brown 2 run (Cox kick)				
Was	FG Knight 52				
Was	FG Knight 42				
Min	Gilliam 28 pass from Tarkenton (Cox kick)				
Min	Gilliam 6 pass from Tarkenton (Cox kick)				
Was	Jefferson 28 pass from Kilmer (Knight kick)				
Min	FG Cox 30				

Fran Tarkenton, appearing in his first playoff game, threw two touchdown passes to receiver John Gilliam in a 65-second span in the fourth quarter to rally the Vikings past the Redskins 27-20.

Washington dominated the first half, but had little to show for its efforts. Curt Knight missed a short field goal attempt in the first quarter to render one drive fruitless. Meanwhile, the Vikings took advantage of their one productive offensive play—a 50-yard hookup from Tarkenton to Oscar Reed—by getting a 19-yard field goal from Fred Cox.

The Redskins got on the board late in the half after the Vikings fumbled a punt and Bob Brunet recovered for Washington at the Minnesota 21. Three plays later, Larry Brown rolled around left end for three yards and a 7-3 lead at the half.

Reed made another big play for the Vikings on their initial second-half possession, weaving through a half dozen would-be tacklers for a 46-yard run down to the two. Bob Brown took it over from there and the Vikings were back in the lead at 10-7.

The visitors responded quickly by moving into Minnesota territory to set up a 52-yard field goal attempt by Knight. The kick was good, tying both an NFL playoff record for distance and the game at 10.

Knight booted another three-pointer, this one from the 42, on the first play of the fourth quarter to push Washington into the lead at 13-10. Tarkenton's first touchdown pass to Gilliam put the Vikings back on top—and then Billy Kilmer made a killer mistake. He threw behind Roy Jefferson on a curl pattern and cornerback Nate Wright intercepted, returning the ball 26 yards to the Washington eight. Two plays later, it was Tarkenton to Gilliam again and the score stood at 24-13.

The defending NFC champions weren't dead yet. They scored on a 28-yard pass from Kilmer to Jefferson and had a chance at a last-minute rally when they held Minnesota to a field goal with a minute and a half left. Trailing by seven, Kilmer completed three straight passes to move near midfield, but his next four attempts missed, and the season ended for the Redskins.

1974
Head Coach: George Allen
Record: 10-4, Second in NFC East
Playoffs: 0-1, Lost in Divisional Playoff

Honors: Chris Hanburger, Pro Bowl, All-NFC; Len Hauss, All-NFC; Ken Houston, Pro Bowl, All-NFC; Diron Talbert, Pro Bowl; Charley Taylor, Pro Bowl, All-NFC

Skins Send Draft Pick for Theismann

March 2—The Redskins have acquired something that they have been lacking in recent seasons: a young, healthy and talented quarterback. Joe Theismann signed a three-year deal with the Redskins today.

Theismann, 24, comes to the Redskins from the Miami Dolphins via the Toronto Argonauts. Miami drafted the former Notre Dame star in the fourth round in 1971 but he opted to sign with the CFL Argonauts. He was a two-time all-star in Canada and the Redskins thought enough of his performance there to send their 1976 first-round pick to the Dolphins to obtain the NFL rights to Theismann.

April 25

Harraway Jumps to WFL
Five-year, $1 million deal lures fullback to Birmingham

Aug 27

Duane Thomas Cut
Redskins gave up 1st- and 2nd-round picks for running back just a year ago

---

Thomas Back On Team—For Now

Aug 31—Controversial running back Duane Thomas is a member of the Redskins again—for the time being, at least.

The team recalled waivers on Thomas after the Kansas City Chiefs put in a claim for him.

But that doesn't necessarily mean he's around for the long haul. Coach George Allen said today that he was still undecided about Thomas' future with the team.

Perhaps Allen wants to try to get something for the first- and second-round draft picks they sent to San Diego in exchange for Thomas last year. Thomas played in 13 games in 1973, but gained up just 95 yards rushing on 13 carries and another 40 yards on five pass receptions.

9/15/74	Redskins (1-0) 13, GIANTS (0-1) 10			51,764	
Was	7	6	0	0	13
NYG	3	0	7	0	10
Was	Bass 28 interception return (Moseley kick)				
NYG	FG Gogolak 33				
Was	Brown 5 run (kick failed)				
NYG	Kotar 6 run (Gogolak kick)				

Yale Bowl—Mike Bass returned an interception for one touchdown and set up the other by recovering a New York fumble, giving the Redskins all the points they needed to beat the Giants.

Bass' interception came in the first quarter and gave Washington a 7-0 lead. New York responded with a 33-yard field goal by Pete Gogolak and the Giants were in possession again when they fumbled at their own 37. After Bass recovered, it took

the Redskins seven plays to drive to a five-yard touchdown run by Larry Brown and Washington led 13-3 at the half.

A Redskins fumble led to a nine-yard touchdown drive by the Giants, but the Washington defense shut the door after that. New York mustered just 70 yards of offense in the second half. Brown converted a critical third and seven in the closing minute with a 15-yard run to convert a third and seven that allowed Washington to kill the clock.

9/22/74	Cardinals (2-0) 17, REDSKINS (1-1) 10			53,888	
StL	7	7	3	0	17
Was	3	7	0	0	10
Was	FG Moseley 28				
StL	Yankowski 71 fumble return (Bakken kick)				
StL	Metcalf 75 run (Bakken kick)				
Was	Reed 11 pass from Kilmer (Moseley kick)				

RFK Stadium—The Cardinals scored two touchdowns in a period of less than two minutes spanning the first and second quarters. Both of the TD plays were more than 70 yards, and they provided enough scoring to beat the Redskins.

The home team had a 3-0 lead and was looking for more when Billy Kilmer dropped back on a third and two play at the St. Louis 14. Linebacker Pete Barnes blindsided the quarterback and the ball popped loose. End Ron Yankowski scooped it up at the 29 and legged the 71 yards into the end zone for a 7-3 Cardinal lead.

That edge was expanded early in the second quarter when Terry Metcalf took a pitchout, dashed around the left end and outran his pursuers to the end zone to complete a 75-yard touchdown run.

Washington managed to narrow the lead to 14-10 before halftime with Kilmer's 11-yard scoring pass to Alvin Reed, but that was all the scoring they would muster. Trailing 17-10 with three minutes left to play, the Skins drove to a first down at the Cardinal 10. It ended there, though, as three incompletions preceded an end zone interception by the Cards' Jim Tolbert to kill the rally.

9/30/74	REDSKINS (2-1) 30, Broncos (1-1-1) 3			54,305	
Den	0	0	3	0	3
Was	7	6	0	17	30
Was	Taylor 3 pass from Kilmer (Moseley kick)				
Was	FG Moseley 37				
Was	FG Moseley 22				
Den	FG Turner 34				
Was	FG Moseley 18				
Was	Taylor 11 pass from Kilmer (Moseley kick)				
Was	Thomas 1 run (Moseley kick)				

RFK Stadium—The Redskins offense finally found itself, rolling up 345 yards in beating the Broncos 30-3. Washington's defense limited Denver to a mere 159 yards of total offense.

Washington got on the board first, driving to a three-yard touchdown pass from Billy Kilmer to Charley Taylor. They continued to move the ball but had to settle for field goals. Mark Moseley hit them from 37 and 22 yards and the Redskins led 13-0 at halftime.

The Redskins' inability to punch the ball into the end zone created a tense moment in the third quarter. The Broncos had mounted a drive that ended with Jim Turner's 34-yard field goal late in the third quarter and it was 13-3. The Redskins fumbled the ensuing kickoff and the Broncos were in possession at the Washington 21. The threat ended, though, when Harold McLinton stuffed Floyd Little on fourth and one at the 12.

The Redskins put the game away after that. Kilmer went to Taylor for 43 yards to set up an 18-yard Moseley field goal and the two hooked up again for 11 yards and a touchdown.

With Washington up 23-3 George Allen game rookie quarterback Joe Theismann his first NFL action. Brig Owens set him up nicely with an interception and return to the Denver 29. Theismann led the Skins to a one-yard Duane Thomas sweep for a touchdown to cap the scoring.

10/6/74	BENGALS (3-1) 28, Redskins (2-2) 17				56,176	
Was	0	3	0	14		17
Cin	7	7	7	7		28
Cin	Parrish 90 punt return (Muhlmann kick)					
Cin	Curtis 24 pass from Anderson (Muhlmann kick)					
Was	FG Moseley 31					
Cin	Parrish 47 fumble return (Muhlmann kick)					
Cin	Clark 3 run (Muhlmann kick)					
Was	Denson 4 pass from Jurgensen (Moseley kick)					
Was	J. Smith 22 pass from Jurgensen (Moseley kick)					

Riverfront Stadium—Lamar Parrish scored on two long returns to spur the Bengals to a 28-3 lead before coasting to an easy 28-17 win over Washington.

Parrish got things going for his team when he returned the Redskins' first punt of the game 90 yards for a quick 7-0 lead. Cincinnati stretched the lead to 14-0 with about 10 minutes left in the second quarter when Ken Anderson threw a 24-yard touchdown pass to receiver Isaac Curtis.

Washington threatened late in the first half by driving to the Cincy 14, but had to settle for a 31-yard Mark Moseley field goal.

In the third quarter, Parrish struck again. He scooped up a Jerry Smith fumble and scooted 47 yards for a 21-3 Bengals lead. After Boobie Clark scored on a three-yard run to make it a full-fledged blowout at 28-3, Sonny Jurgensen replaced Billy Kilmer at quarterback. Jurgy saved some face with a pair of touchdown passes—one to Moses Denson, the other to Smith—but the outcome had already been decided.

Jurgensen went 12 for 20 for 104 yards. The Washington ground game sputtered, totaling just 99 yards. Larry Brown, who has been struggling with a knee injury, got 63 yards on 26 carries.

Oct 7

Jurgy Likely to Start vs. Dolphins
Allen says it makes sense to go with 'best passer'

10/13/74	REDSKINS (3-2) 20, Dolphins (3-2) 17				54,395	
Mia	7	0	3	7		17
Was	0	0	3	17		20
Mia	Ginn 6 run (Yepremian kick)					
Mia	FG Yepremian 32					
Was	FG Moseley 40					
Was	Jefferson 33 pass from Jurgensen (Moseley kick)					
Was	FG Moseley 41					
Mia	Twilley 13 pass from Griese (Yepremian kick)					
Was	L. Smith 6 pass from Jurgensen					

RFK Stadium—It was a Sonny day.

The 40-year-old quarterback led a fourth quarter rally that was the stuff Hall of Famers are made of. This was the first meeting between Washington and Miami since the Fins defeated the Skins in Super Bowl VII. There are many—both Redskins rooters and others—who believe the outcome in that game at the L.A. Coliseum would have been different had No. 9 been taking the snaps that day. The reality is, though, that Jurgensen was out with

---

an Achilles tendon injury and Miami completed its perfect 17-0 season with a 14-7 win.

The stakes weren't nearly as high for this early-season game, with both teams just jockeying for playoff position rather than gunning for the Lombardi Trophy. Still, it was a chance to see how Jurgensen could do against the Dolphins, the two-time defending NFL champs at the time.

In the first half, the answer was "not very well." The Dolphins took the opening kickoff and drove in for a touchdown and a 7-0 lead. After that, Jurgensen threw three interceptions with the final one killing a promising drive near halftime.

Miami got a field goal in the middle of the third quarter to extend its lead to 10-0. Larry Jones returned the ensuing kickoff 57yards to set up a Mark Moseley field goal. Special teams pitched in again when Dennis Johnson forced a fumble on the ensuing kickoff and Brad Dusek recovered it on the Miami 33. Jurgensen converted immediately, throwing a perfect pass to Roy Jefferson on the next play to knot the score at 10 early in the fourth quarter.

On the next drive, the Redskins took the lead after a 19-yard connection from Jurgensen to Jefferson set up a 41-yard Moseley field goal. Washington had a chance to extend its lead with five minutes left, but Moseley missed from 45 yards and opened the door for Miami. Bob Griese converted a third and 10 with a 48-yard completion to Nat Moore that put the Dolphins in business at the Washington 24. Soon after that, Miami faced third and 11 at the 13. Cornerback Mike Bass blitzed, Griese just got his pass off into the area vacated by Bass and Howard Twilley caught it for the touchdown to make it 17-13.

To call the ensuing drive great just doesn't do it justice; nor do other adjectives like heroic or clutch. Here's what happened, and you can come up with your own superlative.

Starting with 1:54 left from the Washington 40 following Herb Mul-Key's 32-yard kickoff return:
• Jurgensen to Moses Denson for six yards;
• Jurgensen to Jerry Smith for 10;
• Jurgensen to Charley Taylor for four;
• Jurgensen to Taylor for 18;
• Jurgensen to Jefferson for 16;
• From the Miami six, Jurgensen pass intended for Larry Smith incomplete;
• Jurgensen to L. Smith for six yards and a touchdown with 16 seconds left on the clock.
Wow.

Larry Smith was tackled by linebacker Doug Swift, a clear infraction that went unflagged, on the incompletion prior to the touchdown. Jurgensen called for the same pattern—a slant—and this time Smith caught the ball over the middle and battled his way through linebackers Swift and Nick Buoniconti to inch the ball over the goal line.

10/20/74	REDSKINS (4-2) 24, Giants (1-5) 3				53,879	
NYG	0	3	0	0		3
Was	0	7	14	3		24
NYG	FG Gogolak 30					
Was	Jefferson 2 pass from Jurgensen (Moseley kick)					
Was	Brown 10 pass from Jurgensen (Moseley kick)					
Was	Denson 15 pass from Jurgensen (Moseley kick)					
Was	FG Moseley 37					

RFK Stadium—Mike Hull sparked the Redskins' 24-3 win over the Giants by blocking a punt late in the first half, a play that set up the go-ahead touchdown.

That TD came on a Sonny Jurgensen pass to Roy Jefferson, one of three touchdown passes by Jurgensen.

The Giants had a 3-0 lead when Mark Moseley missed a 27-yard field goal attempt with 1:56 left in the second quarter.

Washington burned all three of its timeouts to save time for the improbable.

The long shot came through when Hull busted through the line and smothered Dave Jennings' punt. "I got there awfully quick," said the part-time fullback and full-time special teamer. Hull recovered at the Giants' 10.

Following the block, the Skins got into the end zone—but not too easily. It took an uncharacteristic gamble on the part of George Allen, who eschewed a short, tying field goal try and went for the touchdown on fourth and goal at the two. Jurgensen made it pay off by going to Jefferson for a 7-3 lead.

The Redskins held the momentum in the third quarter. Brig Owens picked off a Norm Snead pass at the New York 32 and, although it took 12 plays, Washington moved in to Jurgensen's second scoring pass, 10 yards to Larry Brown. Jurgensen's 15-yard toss to Moses Denson later in the quarter put it out of reach.

10/27/74	**CARDINALS (7-0) 23, Redskins (4-3) 20**		49,410
Was	0	10	3	7	20
StL	9	7	7	0	23

StL	Wehrli 53 interception return (kick failed)
StL	FG Bakken 47
StL	Thomas 52 pass from Hart (Bakken kick)
Was	FG Moseley 48
Was	Brown 2 pass from Jurgensen (Moseley kick)
Was	FG Moseley 48
StL	Anderson 17 pass from Hart (Bakken kick)
Was	Brown 13 pass from Jurgensen (Moseley kick)

Busch Stadium—The Cardinals took advantage of an errant Sonny Jurgensen pass and one of many accurate tosses by Jim Hart to build a 16-0 lead in the game's first 17 minutes and coast to the win over the Redskins.

Early in the game, Roger Wehrli stepped in front of Jurgensen's pass intended for Charley Taylor and was gone, 53 yards for a quick 6-0 lead. Later in the first quarter, Jim Bakken booted a 47-yard field goal to boost the home team's lead to 9-0.

Following a weak Mike Bragg punt, Earl Thomas got behind the Washington secondary and Hart found him with a perfect strike to complete a 52-yard touchdown play. Bakken's extra point was good and it was 16-0 with just two minutes elapsed in the second quarter.

The Redskins rallied to cut it to 16-10 by halftime. After a Mark Moseley field goal, they drove 95 yards in 10 plays, the march culminating in Jurgensen's two-yard touchdown pass to Larry Brown.

Moseley's second field goal in the third quarter ended a nine-minute drive and narrowed the St. Louis lead further at 16-13. Hart struck again, though, finding Donny Anderson for a 17-yard touchdown pass to cap a five-play, 57-yard march.

With 8:47 remaining in the game, Jurgensen again connected with Brown for six, but the Redskins' comeback train ran out of steam after that.

11/3/74	**Redskins (5-3) 17, PACKERS (3-5) 6**		56,287
Was	0	3	7	7	17
GB	3	3	0	0	6

GB	FG Marcol 29
Was	FG Moseley 40
GB	FG Marcol 46
Was	Grant 22 pass from Kilmer (Moseley kick)
Was	McLinton 14 interception return (Moseley kick)

Lambeau Field—Billy Kilmer and the Washington offense suddenly came to life in the third quarter, scoring on Kilmer's 22-yard touchdown pass to Frank Grant to provide the go-ahead points. Harold McLinton provided the clincher in the Redskins' 17-6 win with an interception return for a touchdown in the fourth quarter.

The only scoring in the first half came from each team's placekicker. Chester Marcol booted field goals of 29 and 46 yards for Green Bay while Mark Moseley connected from 40 for the Redskins.

Midway through the third quarter, Washington faced a third and sixteen at its own 44. Kilmer got the first down on a 17-yard strike to Charley Taylor. That worked so well that Kilmer went to Taylor once more, again for 17 yards. Right after that, Kilmer found Frank Grant for 22 yards and a touchdown. Moseley's point after made it 10-6 Washington.

The Redskins' next score came via George Allen's favored formula, favorable field position plus a turnover. Mike Bragg's punt pinned the Pack back at its own three. After two running plays, McLinton picked off Jack Concannon's pass at the 17 and rambled in for the insurance touchdown.

In all, the Redskins intercepted three passes with Pat Fischer and Dave Robinson getting the other two.

11/10/74	**Redskins (6-3) 27, EAGLES (4-5) 20**		65,947
Was	7	0	10	10	27
Phi	7	7	6	0	20

Phi	Carmichael 6 pass from Gabriel (Dempsey kick)
Was	Thomas 1 run (Moseley kick)
Phi	Carmichael 13 pass from Gabriel (Dempsey kick)
Phi	Sullivan 1 pass from Gabriel (kicked failed)
Was	Hanburger fumble recovery in end zone (Moseley kick)
Was	FG Moseley 40
Was	FG Moseley 35
Was	Taylor 30 pass from Jurgensen

Veterans Stadium—A hobbled Sonny Jurgensen came off the bench in the third quarter to rally the Redskins from a 13-point deficit, throwing the winning touchdown pass to Charley Taylor with just over two minutes to play. Washington then held off a late Eagle bid to come out with a 27-20 win.

As usual, defense and special teams played key roles in the scoring for Washington as well. After the Eagles took a 7-0 lead in the first quarter, the Redskins blocked a punt to set up a six-yard touchdown drive, capped by Duane Thomas' one-yard run on fourth down.

After the Eagles got Roman Gabriel's second and third touchdown passes to go up 20-7 in the third quarter (a bad snap caused a missed extra point after last TD), the Washington defense struck. Gabriel fumbled in the end zone and Chris Hanburger pounced on the ball for a quick six points. Mark Moseley's conversion cut the Philly lead to six at 20-14.

Jurgensen led two drives that came up short of the end zone but did set up two Moseley field goals to knot the score at 20. Their last drive went all the way. Jurgensen completed six passes to move the team 75 yards. The sixth completion was to Charley Taylor, who was wide open over the middle and easily completed the 30-yard touchdown play with just over two minutes to go.

After taking the kickoff, the Eagles moved to the Washington nine, but an interception by Ken Stone killed their bid to tie the score.

11/17/74	**REDSKINS (7-3) 28, Cowboys (5-5) 21**		54,395
Dal	0	0	7	14	21
Was	7	21	0	0	28

Was	Theismann 3 run (Moseley kick)
Was	Evans 6 run (Moseley kick)
Was	Houston 58 punt return (Moseley kick)
Was	Jefferson 31 pass from Kilmer (Moseley kick)
Dal	DuPree 40 pass from Staubach
Dal	Newhouse 3 run
Dal	DuPree 4 pass from Staubach

RFK Stadium—The Redskins built up a 28-0 first half lead before having to stave off a furious Dallas rally in the final 30 minutes to claim 28-21 the win.

The home team got out to a 7-0 lead late in the first quarter when Joe Theismann scored a touchdown on a three-yard run. He had come in as, essentially, a pinch runner for the less-mobile Billy Kilmer on third and one at the three. This was just a warm up for a second quarter explosion.

It got started when Washington took 12 plays to drive 77 yards to make it 14-0. The payoff came when fullback Charles Evans went untouched the final six yards for the touchdown. On the next series, the Cowboys were forced to punt and Ken Houston fielded the ball at the Washington 42, hurdled one potential tackle, broke another, reversed his field and outran his other pursuers to the end zone.

The burst of 21 points in 4:05 of play was completed soon after a Deacon Jones sack of Roger Staubach forced Dallas to punt from its own end zone. From the Dallas 31, Roy Jefferson whipped cornerback Mark Washington on a post pattern and Kilmer hit his receiver for the touchdown. By the time the first half was over, the Redskins had outgained their opponents 202 yards to 37.

The atmosphere at RFK Stadium slowly moved from jubilation to concern as Staubach led a second-half rally. He hit tight end Billy Joe Dupree twice for touchdowns, and sandwiched in between those scores was a three-yard scoring run by Robert Newhouse.

The concern grew deeper after Dallas got the ball at its own 39 with 4:15 to go, trailing by seven. Overtime was on everyone's mind when they moved to a first down at the Redskins' seven.

The Redskins held, although it reminded no one of the classic goal-line stand of a year earlier with Ken Houston's classic stop of Walt Garrison at the goal line.

After two running plays gained one yard, Staubach threw to Drew Pearson at the two. Mike Bass broke it up, nearly intercepting the pass. On fourth down, Staubach went for Pearson again. The receiver was open on a quick post, but Staubach misfired and the pass was a little short. The ball bounced harmlessly off of Pearson's arm.

11/24/74	**REDSKINS (8-3) 26, Eagles (4-7) 7**	54,395			
Phi	0	0	7	0	7
Was	3	10	7	6	26
Was	FG Moseley 37				
Was	FG Moseley 38				
Was	J. Smith 2 pass from Kilmer				
Phi	Carmichael 3 pass from Gabriel (Dempsey kick)				
Was	L. Jones 102 kickoff return				
Was	Thomas 3 run (kick failed)				

RFK Stadium—Rookie Larry Jones returned a third-quarter kickoff 102 yards to pull the Redskins out of danger and propel them to a 26-7 win over the Eagles.

The Redskins cruised to a 13-0 lead in the first half on the strength of a pair of Mark Moseley field goals and a two-yard touchdown pass from Billy Kilmer to Jerry Smith. However, Philadelphia was able to hang in the game and move 59 yards in nine plays, eventually scoring on a three-yard connection between Roman Gabriel and Harold Carmichael. It was 13-7 with 13 seconds left in the third quarter. It looked like the Redskins had a game on their hands.

Not for long. Jones took Tom Dempsey's kickoff two yards deep in the end zone and headed up the right hashmark. A block by Brad Dusek cleared a path to the right sideline. One would-be tackler got a hold of Jones' facemask, but the speedy returner shook the illegal grab and went the rest of the way to the end zone. The flag generated by the personal foul caused some consternation on the part of Jones, who was thinking that it might be against the Redskins. His fears were quickly allayed when the foul against the Eagles was signaled and the return—the longest

in team history—went into the books. The Skins cruised home from there.

11/28/74	**COWBOYS (7-5) 24, Redskins (8-4) 23**	63,243			
Was	3	6	7	7	23
Dal	3	0	14	7	24
Dal	FG Hererra 24				
Was	FG Moseley 45				
Was	FG Moseley 34				
Was	FG Moseley 39				
Was	Thomas 9 pass from Kilmer (Moseley kick)				
Dal	DuPree 35 pass from Longley (Hererra kick)				
Dal	Garrison 1 run (Hererra kick)				
Was	Thomas 19 run (Moseley kick)				
Dal	Pearson 50 pass from Longley (Hererra kick)				

Texas Stadium—Be careful what you wish for; you just might get it.

The Redskins couldn't have written the script any better. They held a 16-3 lead in the third quarter. Dave Robinson's vicious hit had knocked starting quarterback Roger Staubach out of the game. The Dallas backup was a rookie from Abilene Christian who, by his own admission, was "a little scared" when he entered the game, his first regular season NFL appearance. A happy ending, a Thanksgiving Day win in Texas Stadium and the playoff berth that would be clinched with a victory appeared to be a certainty.

That rookie quarterback, however, had other ideas. He threw for more than 200 yards and two touchdowns in less than a half of work. His second touchdown pass was the killer—a 50-yard bomb in the game's last minute that lifted the Cowboys over the Redskins.

(Editor's note: Since that quarterback's name makes many Redskins fans physically ill, with memories of a ruined turkey dinner, his name will not be mentioned until the end of this account.)

The Redskins held a 9-3 halftime lead thanks to three Mark Moseley field goals. The visitors stretched the lead after Walt Garrison fumbled early in the third quarter and Robinson recovered for the Redskins at the Dallas 39. Seven plays later, Billy Kilmer threw a nine-yard touchdown pass to Duane Thomas to make it 16-3.

After the ensuing kickoff, Staubach picked up a first down by scrambling for nine yards on second and seven from the Dallas 44. Roger the Dodger couldn't quite elude Robinson, though, and suffered a concussion on the linebacker's clean, hard hit. In came the backup quarterback, nicknamed the Mad Bomber.

"I thought the game was over when we knocked Staubach out," said backup safety Ken Stone. So did almost everyone, except for the rookie quarterback.

He continued the drive that Staubach had kept alive, throwing 35 yards to Billy Joe DuPree for Dallas' first touchdown of the game. The Mad Bomber then led another touchdown drive that ended with Garrison's one-yard touchdown plunge that put Dallas on top 17-16 with just over a minute left in the third.

The Redskins roared back and retook the lead after Kilmer connected with Roy Jefferson for 38 yards. Thomas followed that up with a 19-yard touchdown run to make it 23-17.

Despite holding Dallas at bay for much of the fourth quarter and recovering a fumble with 2:23 left, the Redskins put the ball back into the rookie's hands one more time. After getting just barely six yards to convert a fourth and six at the Dallas 44, the quarterback watched as nickel back Stone did the one thing he wasn't supposed to do: let a receiver get behind him. That receiver was Drew Pearson and Clint Longley threw a perfect bomb to complete the 50-yard touchdown pass with 28 seconds left to play.

12/9/74	**Redskins (9-4) 23, RAMS (9-4) 17**		84,327	
Was	0	20	3	0	23
LA	10	0	7	0	17
LA	FG Ray 37			
LA	Jackson 27 pass from Harris (Ray kick)			
Was	Jefferson 27 pass from Kilmer (kick failed)			
Was	Brown 2 pass from Kilmer (Bragg kick)			
Was	J. Smith 3 pass from Kilmer (Bragg kick)			
LA	McCutcheon 9 run (Ray kick)			
Was	FG Bragg 25			

LA Coliseum—Billy Kilmer threw three touchdown passes in the second quarter to lead the Redskins past the Rams and into the playoffs.

Los Angeles raced to a 10-0 lead in the first quarter with a field goal and a 20-yard touchdown pass from James Harris to Harold Jackson. Washington drove 66 yards in five plays and scored seven seconds into the second quarter on a 27-yard pass from Kilmer to Roy Jefferson. The extra point was missed and it was 10-6.

A failed gamble by Rams coach Chuck Knox gave the Redskins a short field to work with to score the go-ahead touchdown. Punter Mike Burke attempted a pass on fourth and 12 at the LA 23. The pass was incomplete and four plays later Kilmer threw his second TD pass, a two-yard toss to Larry Brown.

Maybe Knox called the ill-fated pass from punt formation because he knew something about his punt team's coverage. Later in the second quarter, Joe Theismann took Burke's punt and returned it 44 yards to the Rams 26. It took five plays to move to Kilmer's third TD pass of the quarter—a three-yarder to Jerry Smith—and the Skins had a 20-10 halftime lead.

Ron Jaworski replaced an injured Harris in the second half and led the Rams to a touchdown on a nine-yard run by Lawrence McCutcheon to cut the margin to 20-17. The Redskins responded with a 25-yard field goal by Mike Bragg and held off the home team for the rest of the way, claiming the win.

12/15/74	**REDSKINS (10-4) 42, Bears (4-10) 0**		52,085	
Chi	0	0	0	0	0
Was	0	21	7	14	42
Was	Brown 1 run (Bragg kick)			
Was	Brown 4 run (Bragg kick)			
Was	Taylor 11 pass from Jurgensen (Bragg kick)			
Was	Taylor 13 pass from Theismann (Bragg kick)			
Was	Thomas 14 run (Bragg kick)			
Was	Evans 1 run (Jones kick)			

RFK Stadium—The Redskins scored 21 points in the second quarter and continued to dominate in the second half as the Redskins routed the Bears.

The win was a hollow one, though, as the St. Louis Cardinals won their game and claimed the NFC East title. The Skins and Cards both finished 10-4 but St. Louis earned the division crown due to their two wins over Washington. The Redskins did earn the NFC Wild Card playoff spot.

After a scoreless first quarter, this one reverted to garbage time very quickly. A 27-yard pass from Sonny Jurgensen to Moses Denson provided nearly half of the distance in a 56-yard drive that culminated in Larry Brown's one-yard plunge for a touchdown.

Jurgensen had found his rhythm. Big throws to Frank Grant and to Charlie Evans were key in two more TD drives in the second quarter. Brown had another touchdown run—this one from four yards—to finish the first march. The second ended with Jurgensen throwing an 11-yard touchdown pass in the second half.

Joe Theismann got his first extended work at quarterback in the second half, throwing one touchdown pass to Taylor and connecting with Frank Grant for 69 yards to set up another TD.

When Evans scored the sixth touchdown, it truly was garbage time. George Allen send veteran defensive end Deacon Jones into the game to kick the extra point. The former member of the LA Rams' Fearsome Foursome put his kick through the uprights, but only after he bounced his kick off of one of them.

NFC Divisional Playoff
Sunday, December 22, 1974
Los Angeles Coliseum
Los Angeles, California

12/22/74	**RAMS 19, Redskins 10**		80,118	
Was	3	7	0	0	10
LA	7	0	3	9	19
LA	Klein 10 pass from Harris (Ray kick)			
Was	FG Bragg 35			
Was	Denson 1 run (Bragg kick)			
LA	FG Ray 37			
LA	FG Ray 26			
LA	Robertson 59 interception return (pass failed)			

The Rams practiced what their former coach preached.

"George Allen always said that if you can get six turnovers in a game, you'll win it," said Merlin Olson, one of Allen's former charges in LA. In this case, the former Rams and current Redskins coach was absolutely right; his team lost three fumbles and threw three interceptions and the other team won the game.

Despite their inability to hold on to the ball, the Redskins were in this game until the late going. After the Rams drove 72 yards to a touchdown, the Redskins responded with a 35-yard Mike Bragg field goal and Moses Denson's one-yard touchdown run to take a 10-7 lead into the locker room at halftime.

In the second half, the self-destruction of the Redskins began in earnest. Olson slammed into Larry Brown, causing a fumble that led to the tying score—a 37-yard field goal by David Ray. On the ensuing kickoff, Doug Cunningham fumbled, leading to another Ray field goal and a 13-10 LA lead early in the fourth quarter.

It took one more turnover for the Rams to put it away. Linebacker Isiah Robertson stepped in front of a Sonny Jurgensen pass and ran it back all the way, 59 yards for the clinching score.

Two Stars Wonder What's Next

Dec 24—Larry Brown and Sonny Jurgensen, two of the Redskins' most popular and productive players, are wondering about their futures.

Although coach George Allen said that he would "like to have Sonny Jurgensen back," Jurgensen is not sure if he wants to take Allen up on that offer.

"I'd like to play as long as I feel I can make a contribution," said Jurgensen, who will turn 41 before the start of the 1975 season. But he said that he wasn't sure if he'd be able to help the team.

Jurgensen was effective when he could play—he completed 64 percent of his passes and the team was 3-1 in games he started—but injuries, particularly one to his knee, severely limited his playing time.

Injuries also limited Brown, the team's all-time leading rusher. He posted career lows in games (11), carries (163) and rushing yards gained (430).

Although Brown is relatively young at 27, his heavy workload carrying the ball (more than 200 regular-season carries in the past five years) and his pounding style of running delivers punishment to his body as well as to opposing defenders.

1975
Head Coach: George Allen
Record: 8-6, Third in NFC East

Honors: Pat Fischer All-NFC; Chris Hanburger Pro Bowl, All-NFC; Len Hauss, All-NFC; Ken Houston Pro Bowl, All-NFL; Charley Taylor Pro Bowl, All-NFC

Jurgensen 'Retirement' All Allen's Decision

May 1—Sonny Jurgensen didn't want it to happen. George Allen called it "the toughest decision I've ever had to make as a coach."

But the decision was made and Jurgensen, one of the best and most popular players in team history, is no longer a Washington Redskin.

His contract expired today and Allen has decided against offering him another one. Money, age and injury all were factors, according to Allen.

Jurgensen was told that he was not in the team's plans last week in a meeting at Redskins Park.

While Jurgensen says he still can play, he did not argue. "I'm not here to criticize the decision," he said. "It's unfortunate at 41 that I'm still not in the picture."

Still in the Redskins' picture are Billy Kilmer, who will become the starter after years of sharing the spot with Jurgensen due to performance and injury issues; Joe Theismann, the No. 2 QB; and newly acquired Randy Johnson.

Tight end Jerry Smith said that Jurgensen will be sorely missed.

"Every pass that man threw fit the situation. Fast, slow, curve, knuckleball, 70 yards, two inches. They were always accurate. If it wasn't complete, it wasn't No. 9's fault."

June 2
Mul-Key Dealt to Colts
Baltimore send 4th-round pick for running back

June 7
Price for No. 9 is a No. 2 and a No. 3
Redskins set two picks as compensation should Jurgensen sign elsewhere

---

July 18
Duane Thomas' Agent: 'Ridiculous Contract'
Contends that club is 'not willing to negotiate'

Aug 5
Skins Sign Cards' Butz
Teams must work out compensation for DT

Aug 23
Aloha: Thomas Signs With WFL Hawaiians
Although Philadelphia franchise claims rights, back appears done with Redskins

Big Price for a Big Man

Sep 4—Dave Butz stands 6-7 and weighs 297 pounds. The Redskins hope he plays up to his size because they have paid a massive price for his services.

The big contract they gave the defensive tackle last month after he played out his option with St. Louis was just the beginning. The matter of compensation to the Cardinals was settled today and the Redskins will be giving up quite a bit.

Washington will send its first-round picks in 1977 and 1978 along with its 1979 second-rounder to St. Louis.

9/21/75	REDSKINS (1-0) 41, Saints (0-1) 3			54,414	
NO	3	0	0	0	3
Was	10	10	0	21	41
Was	FG Moseley 31				
NO	FG McClard 43				
Was	Taylor 11 pass from Kilmer (Moseley kick)				
Was	Taylor 5 pass from Kilmer (Moseley kick)				
Was	FG Moseley 35				
Was	Nelson 27 pass from Kilmer (Moseley kick)				
Was	Smith 14 pass from Kilmer (Moseley kick)				
Was	Dusek 16 fumble recovery return (Moseley kick)				

RFK Stadium—In the first game of the post-Sonny Jurgensen era, the Redskins rallied around Billy Kilmer to dispose of the Saints early. Washington took a 20-3 halftime lead and rolled to a 41-3 victory over New Orleans.

Kilmer completed 14 of 26 passes for 199 yards and four touchdowns. Charley Taylor caught six of Kilmer's throws for 58 yards.

After exchanging field goals with the Saints in the early going, Kilmer and the Redskins got down to business. Kilmer threw for all 65 yards in a three-play TD drive, going to Roy Jefferson for 26, Larry Brown for 28, and Taylor for the final 11 yards. Then Ken Stone blocked a New Orleans punt and the Redskins took over at the Saints' 10. Three plays later, Taylor ran a slant-in pattern and Kilmer hit him with a perfect strike for another touchdown to make it 17-3. The rout was on.

In the third quarter Kilmer threw for two more scores, one of 27 yards to Ralph Nelson and the other 14 yards to Jerry Smith. Brad Dusek picked up a garbage time fumble and ran 16 yards for the game's final score. Dusek and Chris Hanburger led the defensive effort with seven tackles each.

9/28/75	REDSKINS (2-0) 49, Giants (1-1) 13			54,953	
NYG	7	0	6	0	13
Was	0	28	0	21	49
NYG	Johnson 1 run (Hunt kick)				
Was	Brown 4 run (Moseley kick)				
Was	Jefferson 31 pass from Kilmer (Moseley kick)				
Was	McDole fumble recovery in end zone (Moseley kick)				
Was	Jones 52 punt return (Moseley kick)				
NYG	Obradovich 2 pass from Morton (kick failed)				
Was	Jefferson 9 pass from Kilmer (Moseley kick)				
Was	Taylor 13 pass from Johnson (Moseley kick)				
Was	Reed 4 pass from Johnson (Moseley kick)				

RFK Stadium—After spotting New York a 7-0 first quarter lead, the Redskins exploded in the second quarter, scoring four touchdowns four different ways to put away the Giants.

Larry Brown got a four-yard touchdown run around right end on the first play of the second quarter to get things rolling. After the ensuing kickoff, Ken Houston recovered a fumble by Joe Dawkins at the New York 48. It took just three plays for the Redskins to take advantage with Billy Kilmer hitting Roy Jefferson with a 31-yard pass for the score.

After Kilmer threw his only interception of the game, Giants quarterback Craig Morton dropped back into his own end zone to pass. Tackle Bill Brundige sacked Morton, jarring the ball loose. End Ron McDole fell on it for a touchdown.

The final score of the half came on a punt return by Larry Jones that started out looking like a disaster. Jones bobbled the ball as he fielded it at his own 48, and then circled back to his own 35 before picking up blockers down the left sideline and taking it all the way.

As the points soared the defense roared, sacking Giants quarterbacks seven times for 68 yards in losses. Diron Talbert was the ringleader, getting three solo sacks and being credited with assists on two others. New York netted just 65 yards passing and lost three fumbles.

Kilmer threw for another touchdown pass in the fourth quarter before yielding to Randy Johnson, who mopped up nicely going six for six with two scoring tosses of his own.

10/5/75	**EAGLES (1-2) 26, Redskins (2-1) 10**				64,397
Was	3	7	0	0	10
Phi	6	3	7	10	26
Was	FG Moseley 45				
Phi	Carmichael 62 pass from Gabriel (kick failed)				
Phi	FG Muhlmann 20				
Was	Reed 1 pass from Kilmer (Moseley kick)				
Phi	Smith 27 pass from Gabriel (Muhlmann kick)				
Phi	FG Muhlmann 45				
Phi	Gabriel 1 run (Muhlmann kick)				

Veterans Stadium—A second-half charge by the previously winless Eagles put the Redskins away in Philadelphia.

Washington was up 10-9 at halftime on the strength of a Mark Moseley field goal and a one-yard scoring pass from Billy Kilmer to tight end Alvin Reed. The field goal was set up by Ralph Nelson's 50-yard return of the opening kickoff. The Redskins held the lead thanks to a missed extra point following Roman Gabriel's 62-yard touchdown pass to Harold Carmichael.

The Eagles took the lead and control in the third quarter on Gabriel's 27-yard touchdown pass to Charley Smith and finished it off in the fourth with a 45-yard field goal by Horst Muhlmann and a one-yard sneak by Gabriel for another touchdown. The Philly defense shut down a Redskins attack that had scored 90 points in the first two games of the season. Washington aided the Eagles' effort considerably, giving up three fumbles and throwing three interceptions.

10/13/75	**REDSKINS (3-1) 27, Cardinals (2-2) 17**				54,693
StL	0	3	14	0	17
Was	3	7	7	10	27
Was	FG Moseley 47				
StL	FG Bakken 47				
Was	M. Thomas 2 run (Moseley kick)				
StL	Metcalf 93 kickoff return (Bakken kick)				
Was	Pergine 30 pass from Theismann (Moseley kick)				
StL	Gray 48 pass from Hart (Bakken kick)				
Was	M. Thomas 1 run (Moseley kick)				
Was	FG Moseley 34				

RFK Stadium—Mike Thomas, who had been inserted at tailback in place of Larry Brown in the second quarter, rushed for 100 yards and two touchdowns. His second score gave the Redskins a seven-point lead four minutes into the fourth quarter and Washington went on to a 27-17 win over the Cardinals.

Ken Houston smashed into Terry Metcalf in the first quarter, separating the running back from the ball. Brad Dusek recovered, setting up a 47-yard Mark Moseley field goal for the game's first score. Then it was the Cardinals' turn to take advantage of a turnover, getting a 47-yard field goal from Jim Bakken after Larry Jones fumbled away a punt.

The pattern continued, although this time Washington cashed in for a touchdown. Safety Bryant Salter batted a Jim Hart pass into the air and Mike Bass picked it off and returned it to the Cardinal 38. Thomas scored from two yards out to make it 10-3 at the half.

In the third quarter, each team scored a touchdown on special teams. Metcalf returned the second-half kickoff 93 yards for a touchdown to bring the Cardinals back into a tie at 10. The Redskins answered with a bit of trickery. Washington lined up for a field goal attempt from the 30 and holder Joe Theismann took the snap, stood and hit John Pergine with a pass around the 10. The backup linebacker crashed through an attempted tackle at the goal line and gave the lead back to the Redskins at 17-10. St. Louis got it back to even almost immediately as receiver Mel Gray split double coverage and Hart hit him with a perfect pass for a 48-yard touchdown.

Washington started its game-winning drive on its own 24. Kilmer completed five passes on the drive and Thomas' second touchdown run capped it with 4:02 gone in the final quarter. An interception by Chris Hanburger set up a 34-yard Moseley field goal for the final margin. Another pick by Houston snuffed the Cardinals final, desperate bid.

Weekly Intrigue Now Surrounds Tailback

Oct 18—With the near-weekly quarterback controversy now history after the retirement of Sonny Jurgensen, nobody was quite sure where the regular dose of suspense would come from.

Never fear—it's always something when George Allen is around.

Now the weekly debate is about the tailback position. Rookie Mike Thomas has been impressive in his action and he gained 100 yards last week against the Cardinals. Larry Brown is the team's all-time leading rusher, and he still has something left in the tank.

Not wanting to give the Oilers—the Skins' upcoming opponent—a hint as to whether they should repair for the speedy Thomas or the bruising Brown, Allen is keeping his choice of the starter a closely-guarded secret.

Not that it is likely to matter much. Both backs should see plenty of action.

10/13/75	**OILERS (4-1) 13, Redskins (3-2) 10**				51,911
Was	0	7	3	0	10
Hou	0	0	6	7	13
Was	Grant 13 pass from Kilmer (Moseley kick)				
Hou	Hardeman 1 run (kick failed)				
Was	FG Moseley 32				
Hou	Hardeman 1 run (Butler kick)				

Astrodome—What seems to be a good break can sometimes come back to bite you, and that's what happened to the Redskins during the third quarter of their 13-10 loss to Houston.

Washington was leading 7-6 and driving for more when Billy Kilmer was hit out of bounds by linebacker Robert Brazile. The officials not only flagged the Oilers for a personal foul but also tossed Brazile, one of Houston's best defenders, out of the game for giving Kilmer a forearm to the neck. The Redskins had a first and goal at the Houston eight. Both the Oilers and their fans were angered by the ejection and the Redskins were unable to move the ball in, settling for a 32-yard Mark Moseley field goal and a 10-6 lead.

Apparently the Houston offense also was inspired by the ejection. They took the ensuing kickoff and drove 62 yards to the winning score. Don Hardeman plunged one yard for his second touchdown of the half and Skip Butler's extra point gave Houston a 13-10 edge.

The Redskins had taken a 7-0 lead into halftime on the strength of a second-quarter touchdown drive. A 64-yard connection from Kilmer to Charley Taylor set up a 13-yard Kilmer TD pass to Frank Grant.

After Houston took the lead in the fourth, the Redskins' best chance to answer came late in the game when Mike Bass picked off a Dan Pastorini pass at midfield and returned it to the Houston 30. Grant went for 13 yards on an end around, but Curly Culp promptly sacked Kilmer for an 11-yard loss. Mark Moseley was wide right on a 47-yard field goal attempt with 3:13 left and Houston held on the rest of the way.

10/26/75	**Redskins (4-2) 23, BROWNS (0-6) 7** 56,702				
Was	0	6	3	14	23
Cle	0	0	7	0	7
Was	Thomas 3 pass from Kilmer (kick failed)				
Was	FG Moseley 37				
Cle	Roan 15 pass from Sipe (Cockroft kick)				
Was	L. Brown 12 pass from Kilmer (Moseley kick)				
Was	Thomas 1 run (Moseley kick)				

Cleveland Stadium—Mike Thomas led the attack as the Redskins overcame a sluggish start to roll over the winless Browns. The rookie running back gained 124 yards on 27 carries and scored two touchdowns.

Thomas' first touchdown was the only score of the first half and capped an 88-yard drive. The key play came on a spectacular grab by Charley Taylor who tipped an overthrown ball into the air, grabbed it and ran to the Cleveland two for a 34-yard gain. Shortly after that, Billy Kilmer threw a more accurate toss to Thomas from three yards out to make it 6-0. Mark Moseley missed the PAT and the lead remained at six.

The Redskins took the second-half kickoff and drove a 37-yard Mark Moseley field goal to expand the lead to 9-0. Cleveland answered, scoring its first touchdown in nine quarters when Brian Sipe hit tight end Oscar Roan for a 15-yard touchdown pass, making it 9-7. The Redskins began to sweat when Cleveland forced a punt, but the Browns' Pete Athas fumbled and Washington recovered at its own 47. That led to a 12-yard scoring pass from Kilmer to Larry Brown on the second play of the fourth quarter. The Redskins got some breathing room at 16-7.

On its next possession, Washington slowly choked any remaining life out of the Browns with an 85-yard drive that went 16 plays and consumed almost nine minutes. The drive appeared to be ending with a field goal as Moseley connected from 22 yards, but Cleveland was flagged for a personal foul and George Allen decided to take the points off the board and go for the TD. His gamble paid off moments later as Thomas scored from a yard out with 4:38 left in the game.

11/2/75	**REDSKINS (5-2) 30, Cowboys (5-2) 24 OT** 55,004					
Dal	0	17	0	7	0	24
Was	3	7	7	7	6	30
Was	FG Moseley 43					
Dal	P. Pearson 12 pass from Staubach (Fritsch kick)					
Dal	D. Person 10 pass from Staubach (Fritsch kick)					
Was	Grant 46 pass from Kilmer (Moseley kick)					
Dal	FG Fritsch 33					
Was	Taylor 2 pass from Kilmer (Moseley kick)					
Dal	Harris 27 interception return (Fritsch kick)					
Was	Smith 7 pass from Kilmer (Moseley kick)					
Was	Kilmer 1 run					

RFK Stadium—Billy Kilmer hit Jerry Smith with a seven-yard touchdown pass to tie the game with 1:52 left in the fourth quarter

and then snuck over from six inches out in overtime to give the Redskins the win.

The overtime score was set up by an interception by Ken Houston and subsequent personal foul on Dallas quarterback Roger Staubach.

Washington drew first blood with a 43-yard field goal by Mark Moseley, but Dallas got touchdown passes from Staubach to running back Preston Pearson and receiver Drew Pearson in the second quarter to take a 14-3 lead. A 46-yard TD pass from Kilmer to Frank Grant pulled it to 14-10, but the Cowboys scored before halftime on a Tony Fritsch field goal to boost their margin to 17-10.

The Redskins tied the game in the third quarter on Kilmer's two-yard scoring pass to Charley Taylor. After that, the game settled down to a defensive struggle. In fact, a defensive player would score next.

With 5:03 left in regulation, Dallas safety Cliff Harris stepped in front of a Kilmer pass and took it back 27 yards for a touchdown, giving Dallas the lead at 24-17. Kilmer described the ugly toss as "the worst throw I've made all year."

On the drive following the ensuing kickoff, Kilmer made some of his best throws of the year in driving the Redskins 60 yards in nine plays. Rookie running back Mike Thomas atoned for a couple of fumbles earlier in the game by converting a fourth and two by scooting for six yards from the Dallas 13. On the next play, Kilmer hit Smith and Moseley's point after tied the game at 24. Dallas had a chance to win in regulation, but Fritsch's 38-yard field goal try missed badly and the game went into overtime.

With the line of scrimmage at midfield early in overtime, linebacker Chris Hanburger hit Staubach as he was throwing the ball and it fluttered towards Houston, who remarked, "It just seemed to stay up there forever." The safety gathered it in at the 36 and returned it back to the 50. Staubach was flagged for throwing a punch at Pat Fischer and Washington was in business at the Dallas 35. It took 10 plays and a pair of third-down conversions for Kilmer to get in the end zone to end it.

11/9/75	**Redskins (6-2) 21, GIANTS (3-5) 13** 57,242				
Was	7	0	0	14	21
NYG	0	10	3	0	13
Was	Grant 96 pass from Kilmer (Moseley kick)				
NYG	FG Hunt 22				
NYG	Johnson 35 pass from Morton (Hunt kick)				
NYG	FG Hunt 22				
Was	Brown 1 run (Moseley kick)				
Was	Brown 2 run (Moseley kick)				

Shea Stadium—A pair of fourth quarter touchdown runs rallied the Redskins to a win over the Giants. Larry Brown went over from one yard out to put Washington up 14-13 with less than twelve minutes left in the fourth quarter and Bob Brunet added an insurance score from the two with 1:13 remaining.

The Redskins were in a hole late in the first quarter when a Giants punt had them pinned back at their own four yard line. They got out of it immediately as Billy Kilmer hit Frank Grant with a 96-yard TD pass to put Washington up 7-0.

New York scored the next 13 points, with a pair of field goals serving as bookends for a 35-yard TD pass from Craig Morton to running back Ron Johnson. The first FG and the touchdown were set up by New York interceptions of Kilmer passes. Kilmer was replaced by backup Randy Johnson late in the first half. The change was not due to ineffectiveness but because of a shoulder injury that Kilmer sustained.

Following New York's second field goal—this one coming in the third quarter—the Redskins' Johnson went three of four for 39 yards to lead a 10-play, 87-yard drive that spanned the late third and early fourth quarters and culminated in Brown's one-yard run.

Washington ate up five minutes of clock to go 62 yards and notch Brunet's clinching score.

Rookie Mike Thomas gained 123 yards rushing on 25 carries, including three for 37 in the go-ahead TD drive.

11/16/75	CARDINALS (7-2) 20, Redskins (6-3) 17 OT				49,919	
Was	0	7	7	3	0	17
StL	0	3	0	14	3	20
StL	FG Bakken 20					
Was	Taylor 36 pass from Johnson (Moseley kick)					
Was	Thomas 9 pass from Johnson (Moseley kick)					
StL	Cain 8 pass from Hart (Bakken kick)					
Was	FG Moseley 43					
StL	Gray 6 pass from Hart (Bakken kick)					
StL	FG Bakken 37					

Busch Stadium—It was all there for the Redskins: a key win to take sole possession of first place in the division; a chance to steal a win with their backup quarterback. The Skins led most of the way and appeared to have come up with a key goal line stand to save the game. But then the pass went to . . . Mel Gray.

Billy Kilmer had been injured the week before, and with Sonny Jurgensen having retired the previous May and Joe Theismann not yet ready to play, the starting quarterback was journeyman Randy Johnson. The ex-Giant filled in more than adequately, completing 14 of 27 for 252 yards and two touchdowns. The first of those two TD strikes came midway through the second quarter as Johnson found Charley Taylor from 36 yards to erase a 3-0 Cardinal lead. For the next 18 minutes, the Cardinals continually drove down the field only to shoot themselves in the foot with turnovers and penalties. St. Louis racked up 427 yards of offense for the game, including 230 with an effective thunder and lightning ground attack. Terry Metcalf provided the quickness, gaining 79 yards, while Jim Otis was the power back, grinding for 109 on 23 carries.

The Redskins were having their problems with turnovers as well, giving it away five times on the day. But midway through the third quarter, Johnson threw his second touchdown pass—this one to rookie running back Mike Thomas, giving the Redskins a 14-3 lead—but St. Louis responded. A 47-yard pass interference call aided a drive that ended with Jim Hart throwing an eight-yard touchdown pass to tight end J. V. Cain with 13:35 left in the fourth.

Mark Moseley kicked a 42-yard field goal with 6:18 left to put the Redskins up by seven. The Cardinals had to punt back to the Redskins. St. Louis burned all of its time-outs, and one more first down would have allowed Johnson to kneel down on the ball and seal the win. But Washington came up short and punted. Metcalf returned it 19 yards to the Redskins 39 with 1:43 left. Hart quickly completed two passes to move the Cardinals down to the six. After three incompletions, it was fourth and goal with less than thirty seconds left. Hart dropped back and fired over the middle to receiver Mel Gray a couple of yards deep into the end zone. The ball went into Gray's arms and, almost immediately, was knocked out by Pat Fisher. Was it a catch?

It wasn't—at least, that's not what officials said right after the play. Gray did not appear to have possession of the ball in the end zone, as required by the rules. In fact, he didn't appear to have possession at all. The Redskins' defense began to celebrate and the offense headed onto the field.

But wait—the referees were huddling. They conferred and debated and discussed. And then they talked some more.

And eventually, some of them persuaded referee Fred Silva that Gray did have possession with two feet down. So, after what seemed like an eternity but was in reality only about three minutes, the huddle broke and Silva signed a touchdown.

"I've never seen them take so long to make a decision," said George Allen after the game. "That's like having a World Series

and three minutes after the game, ruling that the runner is safe at the plate."

Jim Bakken's extra point tied the game at 17 and the contest went into overtime. The dispirited Redskins lost the toss and offered little resistance as Otis powered a drive to set up a 37-yard field goal attempt by Bakken seven minutes into the extra period. It split the uprights, and the Cards won 20-17.

Nov 17
Allen: 'No Doubt' That Pass Was Incomplete
Independent reviews of replay back his claim that Gray did not have control of tying TD pass

---

11/23/75	Raiders (8-2) 26, REDSKINS (6-4) 23 OT				53,582	
Oak	6	14	0	3	3	26
Was	0	3	7	7	0	23
Oak	Banaszak 1 run (kick failed)					
Was	Taylor 8 pass from Kilmer (kick failed)					
Was	FG Moseley 36					
Oak	Banaszak 27 run (Blanda kick)					
Oak	Banaszak 7 run (Blanda kick)					
Was	Thomas 2 run (Moseley kick)					
Oak	FG Blanda 22					
Was	Grant 33 pass from Kilmer (Moseley kick)					
Oak	FG Blanda 27					

RFK Stadium—The Redskins became another dragon slain in George Blanda's fairy tale season as the 48-year-old kicker booted a 27-yard field goal in overtime to beat the Redskins 26-23.

Oakland's Pete Banaszak ran for three first-half touchdowns and the Raiders held a 20-9 halftime lead. A good turn of fortune helped Washington climb back into the contest in the third quarter. Billy Kilmer's pass was intercepted by Jack Tatum, who returned the ball 28 yards to the Oakland 43. But Tatum fumbled when he was tackled and Washington receiver Frank Grant recovered. Five plays later, the Redskins pulled to 20-16 on Mike Thomas' two-yard touchdown run.

A Blanda field goal in the fourth quarter upped the Oakland lead to seven. Washington knotted it up with 2:37 remaining in regulation when Kilmer found Grant for a 33-yard TD. The Raiders had a shot to win in regulation, but Blanda's 33-yard field goal try with eight seconds left was very wide to the left.

Washington won the overtime toss and its drive stalled at the Oakland 44. Mike Bragg's punt from there covered just 10 yards and the Raiders were in business. Quarterback Ken Stabler moved them 48 yards in eight plays and Blanda's 27-yard attempt was true.

11/30/75	REDSKINS (7-4) 31, Vikings (10-1) 30				55,004	
Min	0	7	7	16		30
Was	7	14	3	7		31
Was	Brown 2 run (Moseley kick)					
Was	Thomas 28 pass from Kilmer (Moseley kick)					
Was	Grant 27 pass from Kilmer (Moseley kick)					
Min	Foreman 8 pass from Tarkenton (Cox kick)					
Min	Foreman 3 run (Cox kick)					
Was	FG Moseley 32					
Min	FG Cox 33					
Min	Tarkenton 21 run (kick failed)					
Min	Foreman 31 run (Cox kick)					
Was	Grant 15 pass from Kilmer (Moseley kick)					

RFK Stadium—"It was the kind of game you have to pinch yourself to make sure you won," said George Allen after the contest, and the 55,004 in attendance and anyone else who watched the Redskins topple the previously unbeaten Vikings would have to agree.

The Redskins lost a 21-0 second-quarter lead but, when normally reliable Minnesota kicker Fred Cox missed a pair of fourth-quarter attempts, the Redskins had an opportunity to top the Vikings' comeback. They did just that when Billy Kilmer hit Frank Grant with a 15-yard touchdown pass in the game's last minute and Mark Moseley made the extra point. Ron McDole blocked Cox's attempt at redemption from 45 yards as time ran out.

The home team started out as though no late heroics would be necessary. Two Kilmer touchdown passes—one to Grant, the other to Mike Thomas—and a Larry Brown touchdown run had the Redskins sitting on a 21-0 lead in the second quarter. The Vikings got their offense going when running back Chuck Foreman scored the first of his three touchdowns, this one on an eight-yard pass from Fran Tarkenton, to pull his team to a 21-7 deficit.

In the third quarter, Foreman scored again, but the Redskins responded with a 32-yard Mark Moseley field goal. Washington led 24-14 going into the wild fourth quarter.

Cox started a 16-0 scoring run by the visitors by hitting a 33-yard field goal. His next kick was not as successful. After Tarkenton scrambled 21 yards for a touchdown to pull his team within one, Cox shanked the point after. "I just plain out missed it," said Cox of the attempt.

The Minnesota offense wasn't done. They took their first lead on Foreman's 31-yard run. Cox's point after attempt was good and the Vikings led 30-24. They then had a chance to put the game away with less than two minutes left, but a 40-yard field goal attempt by Cox went wide left and the Redskins had a shot with 1:51 left.

Kilmer went to work, hitting Grant for 21 yards and then Charley Taylor for another 21 to move to the Minnesota 35. A screen pass to Thomas got them to the 15. On the next play, Grant beat Vikings cornerback Nate Wright on a post pattern and Kilmer hit him with a perfect strike for the touchdown and the crowd went wild. The celebration began in earnest when Moseley hit the extra point and McDole swatted away Cox's final attempt.

12/7/75	**Redskins (8-4) 30, FALCONS (3-9) 27**				52,809
Was	3	7	7	13	30
Atl	0	14	3	10	27
Was	FG Moseley 42				
Was	Brown 3 pass from Kilmer (Moseley kick)				
Atl	Burrow 9 pass from Bartkowski (Mike-Mayer kick)				
Atl	Francis 67 pass from Bartkowski (Mike-Mayer kick)				
Atl	FG Mike-Mayer 23				
Was	Grant 69 pass from Kilmer (Moseley kick)				
Was	FG Moseley 34				
Was	Smith 12 pass from Kilmer (Moseley kick)				
Atl	Hampton 3 pass from Bartkowski (Mike-Mayer kick)				
Atl	FG Mike-Mayer 44				
Was	FG Moseley 39				

Atlanta Fulton County Stadium—"I do what I have to do," Billy Kilmer said after this one. He was referring to the pain-killing shot he took prior to the game, allowing him to play with a broken bone in his foot. But he could have been talking about completing five passes for 56 yards in the game's final minute to get his team in position for Mark Moseley's 39-yard field goal with two seconds left. The score gave Washington a 30-27 win over Atlanta.

As has been the story for most of the Skins' season, this was a seesaw battle all the way. The Redskins took a 10-0 lead early in the second quarter when Kilmer threw a three-yard scoring pass to Larry Brown. Atlanta came roaring back, getting a pair of touchdown passes from Steve Bartkowski to go up 14-10 at halftime. The home team stretched the lead to 17-10 in the third quarter on Nick Mike-Mayer's 23-yard field goal.

Then it was the Redskins' turn again. Kilmer found Frank Grant behind the Atlanta defense and completed a 69-yard scoring pass to the streaking receiver. After a 34-yard Moseley field goal, Kilmer struck again—this time on a 12-yard touchdown

pass to Jerry Smith—and Washington was back up by 10 in the fourth quarter.

But Atlanta wasn't done yet. Bartkowski threw a three-yard touchdown pass to Dave Hampton before leading a game-tying drive that ended with 44-yard field goal by Mike-Mayer as 61 seconds remained. Then Kilmer, with the effects of the pain-killing shot wearing off, led the drive to Moseley's game-winning field goal.

12/13/75	**COWBOYS (9-4) 31, Redskins (8-5) 10**				61,091
Was	10	0	0	0	10
Dal	0	14	0	17	31
Was	FG Moseley 49				
Was	Grant 14 pass from Kilmer (Moseley kick)				
Dal	Richards 57 pass from Staubach (Fritsch kick)				
Dal	Staubach 4 run (Fritsch kick)				
Dal	FG Fritsch 20				
Dal	P. Pearson 5 pass from Staubach (Fritsch kick)				
Dal	Water 20 interception return (Fritsch kick)				

Texas Stadium—Dallas scored two second-quarter touchdowns to erase a 10-0 Washington lead and then turned two fourth-quarter turnovers into touchdowns to secure the 31-10 win. The loss eliminated the Redskins from the NFC playoffs.

Washington had taken its first quarter lead on a 49-yard field goal by Mark Moseley and Billy Kilmer's 14-yard touchdown pass to Frank Grant. Things were going the Skins' way, but it took just one play to turn all that around.

Roger Staubach threw a 17-yarder out to the speedy Golden Richards. Cornerback Mike Bass had the quick receiver in his sights, but Richards spun away from the attempted tackle and cruised down the sideline for 57 yards and a touchdown.

The downhill slide continued for the Redskins when Larry Jones fumbled a Dallas punt and the Cowboys recovered at the Washington 16. With just under two minutes left in the half, Staubach crashed past linebacker Harold McLinton on a quarterback draw from the four and Dallas led 14-10.

The final blow for the Redskins came when Kilmer was knocked out of the game early in the fourth quarter. A rusty Randy Johnson replaced him and threw a lateral pass that missed its target. The Cowboys plucked the free ball off the Texas Stadium carpet. That led to a Preston Pearson touchdown run, putting the game out of Washington's reach at 24-10. Charley Waters provided the final margin when he intercepted another errant Johnson pass and took it back 20 yards for a touchdown.

12/21/75	**Eagles (4-10) 26, REDSKINS (8-6) 3**				49,385
Phi	7	3	10	6	26
Was	3	0	0	0	3
Phi	Smith 28 pass from Boryla (Muhlmann kick)				
Was	FG Moseley 25				
Phi	FG Muhlmann 25				
Phi	FG Muhlmann 23				
Phi	Lavender 35 interception return (Muhlmann kick)				
Phi	LeMaster 89 interception return (kick failed)				

RFK Stadium—The Redskins came into the game with one goal: to get Charley Taylor the NFL career receptions record. It happened eventually, but the Eagles were on the receiving end of seven throws by Washington quarterbacks and easily won the game 26-3.

The other kind of turnover—a fumble—got the Eagles off to an early lead. Randy Logan recovered a Mike Thomas fumble at the Philly 17 and quarterback Mike Boryla led an 83-yard drive that ended with a 28-yard touchdown pass to the wide-open Charles Smith. How wide open was the tight end? He caught the ball on the ten with his back to the goal line and simply backpedaled into the end zone.

It turned from a farce into a rout during the third quarter when Joe Lavender picked off Randy Johnson's pass and returned it 35 yards for a touchdown.

That got Johnson a seat on the bench—and Joe Theismann finally got Taylor the record. It wasn't in the classic fashion that one would have hoped for, perhaps a slant pattern with C. Taylor making a great grab in traffic. No, it was a wide receiver screen, with Taylor catching the forward pass behind the line of scrimmage and dashing 11 yards for a first down. Heroic or not, it was career catch No. 634, moving him past Don Maynard into first place on the all-time receptions list. Taylor got No. 635 later in the game.

1976

Head Coach: George Allen
Record: 10-4, Second in NFC East
Playoffs: 0-1, lost in Divisional Playoffs

Honors: Eddie Brown Pro Bowl; Chris Hanburger All-NFL, Pro Bowl; Ken Houston All-NFL, Pro Bowl; Mike Thomas Pro Bowl

Hall of Fame: Ray Flaherty, Head Coach 1937-1942

June 11
Skins Win Bidding for Riggins
Jets fullback agrees to free agent deal; backfield now boasts trio of 1,000-yard runners

Aug 4
Skins Deal for Joe Lavender
Eagles get Sistrunk, three draft picks for CB

Brown on Bench, Says Riggins is 'Average'

Sep 10—Larry Brown understands why he won't be the Redskins' starting tailback when they open the season on Sunday. He understands that age and the punishment defenders have inflicted on his body over the years have taken their toll on his effectiveness.

But that doesn't mean he is happy John Riggins is starting in his place.

"From what I've seen, John Riggins is an average football player," said Brown, who is the team's all-time leading rusher.

Brown believes that Riggins' contract, not his talent, dictated that the former Jet be inserted into the starting lineup.

Riggins left New York as a free agent and signed a four-year, $1.5 million deal with the Redskins.

9/12/76	**REDSKINS (1-0) 19, Giants (0-1) 17**			55,004	
NYG	3	7	0	7	17
Was	0	3	9	7	19
NYG	FG Danelo 20				
Was	FG Moseley 22				
NYG	Rhodes 63 pass from Morton (Danelo kick)				
Was	Safety Morton tackled in end zone				
Was	Grant 53 pass from Kilmer (Moseley kick)				
NYG	Gillette 62 pass from Morton (Danelo kick)				
Was	M. Thomas 5 pass from Kilmer (Moseley kick)				

RFK Stadium—Billy Kilmer, bloodied but not bowed, led a last-minute touchdown drive to push the Redskins past the Giants.

It was a tough battle all the way. The Giants led 10-3 at halftime on a Joe Danelo field goal and a 63-yard touchdown pass from Craig Morton to Ray Rhodes.

Two plays in a 20-second span in the third quarter put the Redskins into the lead. Ron McDole sacked Morton in the end zone for a safety that made it 10-5. On the first play after the free kick from the Washington 47, Kilmer made a play action fake and found Frank Grant alone over the middle about 10 yards downfield. Grant built up some steam, broke a couple of tackles and cruised 53 yards for the go-ahead touchdown.

Trailing 12-10, the Giants suddenly went ahead in the fourth quarter when Walker Gillette beat Joe Lavender on a post pattern and hauled in Morton's pass to put his team up 17-12.

It wasn't looking good for the home team when, with less than four minutes left, Kilmer was smashed in between two defenders and wound up with blood streaming from his nose. As he went to the sidelines, the drive died and the Redskins had to punt.

The Giants were unable to muster a first down, but burned off all but 1:38 of the clock before punting back to Washington. Eddie Brown's 45-yard punt return gave the Redskins great field position at the New York 42.

Kilmer and assistant trainer Bubba Tyer had managed to stop the bleeding and the player trotted back onto the field, albeit with a wound to the nose that would require five stitches after the game.

Before getting the winning score, the Redskins first had to convert a fourth and ten from the Giant 23. Kilmer did this with a nice 18-yard pass to Roy Jefferson. On the next play, Kilmer found Mike Thomas for five yards and the go-ahead touchdown with 45 seconds left to play. Ken Houston's interception in the waning moments killed the Giants' last hopes.

9/19/76	**REDSKINS (2-0) 31, Seahawks (0-2) 7**			55,004	
Sea	0	0	0	7	7
Was	7	10	7	7	31
Was	Thomas 5 run (Moseley kick)				
Was	FG Moseley 37				
Was	Fugett 12 pass from Kilmer (Moseley kick)				
Was	Thomas 10 pass from Kilmer (Moseley kick)				
Sea	Testerman 1 run (Bitterlich kick)				
Was	Grant 5 pass from Kilmer (Moseley kick)				

RFK Stadium—The Washington defense kept Seattle bottled up in its own territory for the first two and a half quarters of play and the Redskins easily defeated the expansion Seahawks.

As if they needed it, the Redskins got a jump-start to their first scoring drive when Jake Scott recovered a Seahawk fumble at the Washington 48. It took nine plays for the Redskins to score on a five-yard Mike Thomas run.

Following a Mark Moseley field goal in the second quarter, Billy Kilmer threw the first of his three touchdown passes—a 12-yard connection with Jean Fugett. The lead expanded to 24-0 when Kilmer went 10 yards to Mike Thomas for a third-quarter TD.

Seattle scratched the scoring column on a one-yard run by Don Testerman on the first play of the fourth quarter. The

Redskins ground out most of the remaining time, taking almost 10 minutes to drive 93 yards to a touchdown, a five-yard Kilmer to Frank Grant connection with 1:18 left.

Sep 19
Zorn, Patera Say Skins Took Cheap Shots
Seattle QB, Coach talk of dirty hits on Zorn

9/27/76	**Redskins (3-0) 20, EAGLES (1-2) 17, OT**				60,131	
Was	0	10	7	0	3	20
Phi	3	7	0	7	0	17

Phi	FG Muhlmann 22
Phi	Malone 16 run (Muhlmann kick)
Was	FG Moseley 27
Was	Dusek 32 fumble return (Moseley kick)
Was	Thomas 27 run (Moseley kick)
Phi	Smith 41 pass from Boryla (Muhlmann kick)
Was	FG Moseley 29

Veterans Stadium—Mark Moseley booted a 29-yard field goal with 12:49 elapsed in overtime to give the Redskins the win in Philadelphia. Eddie Brown set up the winning kick when he intercepted a pass and returned it to the Eagles 22.

Trailing 10-0 with just over a minute left until halftime, the Redskins struck quickly to tie the game before the break. Moseley connected on a 27-yard field goal to make it 10-3. After the ensuing kickoff, Dave Butz laid a hard hit on rookie running back Herb Lusk, forcing a fumble. Brad Dusek snared the ball and sped 27 yards for the tying touchdown.

The Redskins took advantage of their newfound momentum and took the lead on a 27-yard Mike Thomas run to cap a six-play, 57-yard drive. It was 17-10 Redskins with four minutes gone in the third quarter.

The Eagles fought back, twice driving to the Washington 10-yard line but suffering interceptions on both occasions. With 2:19 left, they got their last chance to tie it up when taking possession at their own 29. After a couple of runs got the drive started, the Eagles faced a fourth and twelve at their own 41 with 1:31 left. Quarterback Mike Boryla calmly found receiver Charley Smith for 14 yards and a first down at the Washington 45. The game-tying, 41-yard TD pass to Smith came on fourth and six with 1:07 to play.

Neither team mounted much of a threat during most of overtime and a tie seemed a distinct possibility—until Brown picked off Boryla's pass at the Philadelphia 30, returning it eight yards. Calvin Hill ran twice to the four, but a holding penalty pushed them back to the 14. After a two-yard run, Moseley was called in and his kick split the uprights.

10/3/76	**BEARS (2-2) 33, Redskins (3-1) 7**				52,105	
Was	0	0	0	7	7	
Chi	10	10	7	6	33	

Chi	Avellini 4 run (Thomas kick)
Chi	FG Thomas 47
Chi	Scott 6 pass from Avellini (Thomas kick)
Chi	FG Thomas 34
Chi	Payton 10 run (Thomas kick)
Chi	FG Thomas 39
Chi	FG Thomas 35
Was	Smith 1 pass from Theismann (Moseley kick)

Soldier Field—Usually when you hear that the turning point of a game was the opening kickoff, it's said as a joke. After Chicago's 33-7 drubbing of the Redskins, however, Bears coach Jack Pardee said it in all seriousness. And he was right.

"The turning point of the game was Brian Baschnagel's opening kickoff return because it established our hitting and field position."

Rookie Baschnagel returned the opening kickoff for 48 yards, setting his team up at the Washington 37. Soon after that, quarterback Bob Avellini scooted four yards to a touchdown on a broken play and the rout was on.

It was 20-0 at halftime. James Scott scored a touchdown on a six-yard pass from Avellini and Bob Thomas booted a pair of field goals. The situation only became worse for Washington in the second half after Walter Payton scored on a 10-yard run in the third quarter. Joe Theismann replaced an ailing and ineffective Billy Kilmer in the second half, but it was too little and way too late.

Even the Redskins' lone score was tainted. Chicago committed pass interference in the end zone on a desperation pass as time was running out in the game, awarding Washington the ball at the Bears one. With one second left, Theismann's pass to Jerry Smith averted the shutout.

The Bears outgained the Redskins on the day 392 yards to 119.

10/10/76	**Chiefs (1-4) 33, REDSKINS (3-2) 30**				55,004	
KC	6	10	7	10	33	
Was	3	7	0	20	30	

Was	FG Moseley 30
KC	FG Stenerud 27
KC	FG Stenerud 52
KC	FG Stenerud 38
Was	Theismann 1 run (Moseley kick)
KC	White 33 pass from Livingston (Stenerud kick)
Was	Smith 5 pass from Theismann (Moseley kick)
Was	Grant 37 pass from Theismann (Moseley kick)
KC	FG Stenerud 45
Was	Riggins 6 run (kick failed)
KC	Brunson 36 pass from Livingston (Stenerud kick)

RFK Stadium—Call it what you will: a trick play, garbage, a gimmick, razzle-dazzle, sandlot stuff. The Chiefs called it the game winner. A 36-yard pass off of a flea flicker gave Kansas City the winning touchdown with 1:03 left in the game.

It took a nice comeback by the Redskins to set up the Chiefs' rally. Trailing 23-10 early in the fourth quarter, the Redskins rallied behind quarterback Joe Theismann, making his first NFL start. Touchdown passes of five yards to Jerry Smith and 37 yards to Frank Grant pushed the Redskins to a 24-23 lead.

The Chiefs responded as Jan Stenerud kicked his fourth field goal of the day to retake the lead a 26-24. A 70-yard drive catapulted the advantage back to the home team after John Riggins scored on a six-yard sweep with 2:50 to play. The Chiefs, though, had time for one last drive.

Starting from the KC 18, quarterback Mike Livingston completed passes of 28 and 14 yards, helping the Chiefs move to the Washington 36. On third and six from there, Livingston handed the ball to running back Woody Green, who in turn gave it to receiver Henry Marshall and the defense pursued the double reverse. Then Marshall flipped the ball back to Livingston, who found receiver Larry Brunson open near the goal line. The receiver caught the pass at the three and dragged a would-be tackler into the end zone. Stenerud's extra point gave the Chiefs a 33-30 lead and Washington couldn't muster a threat after the kickoff.

10/17/76	**REDSKINS (4-2) 20, Lions (2-4) 7**				45,908	
Det	0	0	0	7	7	
Was	0	0	10	10	20	

Was	FG Moseley 42
Was	Grant 8 pass from Theismann (Moseley kick)
Was	Thomas 3 run (Moseley kick)
Was	FG Moseley 45
Det	Jarvis 56 pass from Reed (Mann kick)

RFK Stadium—After having given up 33 points in each of the last two games, the Redskins defense showed up today in Washington's 20-7 win over Detroit. They held the Lions scoreless until the game had less than a minute remaining—and the issue of who would win had already been settled.

The defense allowed the Washington offense to work through a sluggish, scoreless first half. In addition, the D presented the offense with a golden scoring opportunity early in the third quarter when Pat Fischer intercepted Greg Landry's pass at the Detroit 33. The Redskins cashed in with a 42-yard Mark Moseley field goal.

After Detroit missed a field goal, the Skins mounted a drive, going 76 yards in eight plays. The key play in the drive was a 48-yard pass from Joe Theismann to Frank Grant and the same pair connected on an eight-yard pass for the touchdown to cap the drive and make it 10-0.

Another interception—this one by Joe Lavender—gave the Redskins another short field to work with and this time they took full advantage, moving 22 yards to Mike Thomas' three-yard touchdown run on the first play of the fourth quarter. Moseley's 45-yard field goal four minutes later made it 20-0.

Oct 22
Allen: Theismann Just Fill-In Starter
Coach expects Kilmer to start when healthy

10/25/76	REDSKINS (5-2) 20, Cardinals (5-2) 10			48,325	
StL	0	7	0	3	10
Was	6	0	0	14	20
Was	FG Moseley 34				
Was	FG Moseley 33				
StL	Cain 8 pass from Hart (Bakken kick)				
StL	FG Bakken 32				
Was	Thomas 7 run (Moseley kick)				
Was	E. Brown 71 punt return (Moseley kick)				

RFK Stadium—The Redskins' 20-10 win over St. Louis was a sloppy game, both literally and figuratively. It was played on a muddy field in a driving rainstorm. Moreover, the Cardinals fumbled nine times, losing an NFL-record eight of them. Add in two interceptions thrown by Jim Hart and St. Louis suffered 10 giveaways. Add in the two fumbles the Redskins lost (out of four total) and the interception thrown by Billy Kilmer and you have a total of 13 turnovers or more than one every five minutes of play.

Despite their inability to hold on to the ball, the Cardinals built a 10-6 lead early in the fourth quarter. Following a Mike Bragg punt that pinned the Cardinals deep in their own territory, Washington finally cashed in on a takeaway. Terry Metcalf fumbled and Dennis Johnson emerged from the pile with the ball at the seven. On the next play, Mike Thomas swept into the end zone and it was 13-10.

After the ensuing kickoff, St. Louis was unable to garner a first down and punted to Eddie Brown at this own 29. A game with plenty of goats finally found a hero. Brown took advantage of a hole created by Doug Winslow's block, broke three tackles and splashed down the end zone to complete the 71-yard return.

A last-gasp drive by the Cardinals to get back into it ended in—what else?—a fumble; the Redskins slogged off the field with the win.

10/31/76	Cowboys (7-1) 20, REDSKINS (5-3) 7			55,004	
Dal	7	0	10	3	20
Was	0	0	0	7	7
Dal	Dennison 3 run (Herrera kick)				
Dal	Staubach 1 run (Herrera kick)				
Dal	FG Herrera 37				
Dal	FG Herrera 21				
Was	Jefferson 7 pass from Theismann (Moseley kick)				

RFK Stadium—Roger Staubach's one-yard touchdown plunge in the third quarter gave Dallas a 14-0 lead, all they would need to defeat the punchless Redskins 20-7.

All of Dallas' scores except the Staubach run completed drives that started deep in Redskins territory. Butch Johnson's punt return in the first quarter covered 18 yards to the Washington 20. Five plays later Doug Dennison scored on a three-yard run and Dallas led 7-0.

The Washington defense held Dallas at bay for the remainder of the first half, but their offense couldn't take advantage. The Redskins posed just 146 yards of offense on the day, including just 58 through the air. They also damaged their cause by committing three turnovers.

That 7-0 score held until the third quarter when Staubach's run capped a 13-play, 68-yard drive. Efren Herrera kicked field goals after the Cowboys recovered a Mike Thomas fumble at the Washington 20 and after Mel Renfro's interception set Dallas up at the Washington 13.

The home team got on the board with 46 seconds left to play when Joe Theismann threw a seven-yard scoring pass to Roy Jefferson. Eddie Brown's 59-yard punt return to the Dallas 20 set up that score.

11/7/76	Redskins (6-3) 24, 49ERS (6-3) 21			56,134	
Was	0	14	7	3	24
SF	0	14	0	7	21
SF	Williams 80 run (Mike-Mayer kick)				
Was	Fugett 18 pass from Theismann (Moseley kick)				
Was	Fugett 33 pass from Theismann (Moseley kick)				
SF	Williams 85 pass from Plunkett (Mike-Mayer kick)				
Was	Fugett 3 pass from Theismann (Moseley kick)				
SF	Williams 22 run (Mike-Mayer kick)				
Was	FG Moseley 39				

Candlestick Park—Joe Theismann threw three touchdown passes to Jean Fugett and set up Mark Moseley's game-winning field goal with a scrambling first down run from field goal formation as the Redskins beat the 49ers.

Theismann passed for 302 yards on the day, but his best professional effort to date was nearly offset by a spectacular performance by 49ers' running back Delvin Williams. In the second quarter alone, Williams had scoring plays of 80 and 85 yards. For the game, he totaled 269 rushing and receiving.

Williams started off the scoring by reversing his field and picking his way through the Redskins defense in the course of an 80-yard touchdown run to put his team up 7-0. Theismann's first two scoring connections to Fugett put the Redskins in the lead 14-7 but San Francisco had tied it by halftime on Williams' 85-yard touchdown reception on a pass from Jim Plunkett.

The Redskins came out in the third quarter and recaptured the lead on Theismann's third TD pass to Fugett, this one covering three yards. Early in the fourth quarter, Williams, who had 180 yards rushing on the day, tied it again with a 22-yard run.

The Niners were threatening to take the lead later in the fourth, but Joe Lavender picked off a Plunkett pass at the goal line to preserve the deadlock. After that, the Redskins began their drive towards Moseley's game winner. Thinking that a 53-yard try was too long, George Allen called for a fake when the Redskins faced a fourth and six at the San Francisco 36. The holder Theismann took the snap and sprinted out with the option to either run or pass. Seeing he had an angle to the first down stick, Theismann took off towards it. With two yards to spare, he made it. Soon after that, Moseley lined up from a more manageable 39 yards away and booted the game winner with 1:57 left to play

11/14/76	GIANTS (1-9) 12, Redskins (6-4) 9			72,975	
Was	3	3	3	0	9
NYG	3	3	3	3	12
NYG	FG Danelo 30				
Was	FG Moseley 41				
Was	FG Moseley 31				

NYG	FG Danelo 26
NYG	FG Danelo 39
Was	FG Moseley 52
NYG	FG Danelo 50

Giants Stadium—In a battle of three-pointers, the Giants' Joe Danelo bested Washington's Mark Moseley by kicking four field goals to lift New York over the Redskins. Washington lost a chance to tie or take the lead late in the game when Joe Theismann's pass from deep in Giants territory was intercepted.

Danelo and Mosley each kicked a field goal in each of the first three quarters. It was clear, however, that New York's soccer-style kicker was having a better day than Moseley, a straight-ahead kicker who got more height on his kicks. Often the height is a positive thing, but on this day the swirling winds made Moseley's kicks more problematic than Danelo's low line drives. Moseley finished the day three for six, missing twice from 46 and once from 49 yards. Danelo was four for five, his lone miss coming from 53.

With the game tied at nine, the Giants burned almost eight minutes of the fourth quarter to move 40 yards and set up Danelo's go-ahead kick, a 50-yarder.

The Redskins were not done yet. A desperation drive brought them to the New York seven with 41 seconds left. Overtime seemed a certainty and a Washington win a possibility until Theismann's pass—intended for Mike Thomas in the end zone—was a little too soft. Jim Stienke turned around just in time to intercept it and kill the Redskins' chances.

11/21/76	**Redskins (7-4) 16, CARDINALS (8-3) 10**	49,833

Was	3	3	7	3	16
StL	7	0	0	3	10

StL	Metcalf 48 pass from Hart (Bakken kick)
Was	FG Moseley 26
Was	FG Moseley 40
Was	Thomas 22 run (Moseley kick)
Was	FG Moseley 44
StL	FG Bakken 40

Busch Stadium—Mike Thomas rushed for a team-record 195 yards and scored Washington's only touchdown in their win over the Cardinals.

The Cardinals broke on top in the first quarter, scoring on a 48-yard pass from Jim Hart to running back Terry Metcalf. Other than that play, the Redskins defense held Hart largely in check. On the day, the Cardinal QB was nine of 31 passing for 181 yards.

By halftime, the Redskins had pulled to within one at 7-6 on the first two of Mark Moseley's three field goals. They took the lead for good on Thomas' 19-yard touchdown dash with more than six minutes left in the third quarter. Moseley's field goal in the fourth quarter gave his team a nine-point lead.

The Cardinals, as was typical when playing the Redskins, were not done yet. They drove to a Jim Bakken field goal and were threatening to pull the game out when they moved to a first down at the Washington 20 with less than a minute left. From there, though, Hart threw four incompletions and the game was over.

Thomas had some help in the rushing department as John Riggins picked up 49 yards on 18 carries. While the Cardinals didn't match the record nine fumbles they coughed up when the teams met in October, they did hurt their cause with five fumbles, losing three.

11/29/76	**REDSKINS (8-4) 24, Eagles (3-9) 0**	54,292

Phi	0	0	0	0	0
Was	7	7	10	0	24

Was	Grant 41 pass from Kilmer (Moseley kick)
Was	Thomas 17 pass from Kilmer (Moseley kick)
Was	FG Moseley 44
Was	Thomas 14 pass from Kilmer (Moseley kick)

RFK Stadium—The Redskins took control of both the Philadelphia Eagles and their playoff destiny in the course of their shutout win.

Eddie Brown set the offense up with good field position for its second possession of the game with a 43-yard punt return to the Eagles 45. Two plays later from the 41, Billy Kilmer threw a pass to Frank Grant over the middle. The receiver caught the ball at around the 25 and shed a couple of attempted tackles on his way to completing the touchdown play.

Mike Thomas scored on the first of his two touchdown receptions in the second quarter to give the Redskins a 14-0 lead. Later in the game, Thomas pushed past the 1,000-yard rushing mark for the season, becoming the second Redskin to accomplish that (Larry Brown did it in 1970 and 1972). Thomas' second TD catch came in the third period following Mark Moseley's 44-yard field goal and made it 24-0.

Meanwhile, the Redskins defense was harassing Philadelphia quarterbacks Roman Gabriel and Mike Boryla into early and inaccurate throws. The closest the Eagles came to scoring all day was when Horst Muhlmann's 45-yard field goal attempt hit the left upright.

The win put Washington's playoff destiny squarely on its own shoulders. Wins in the last two games of the season would ensure a spot in the postseason.

12/5/76	**Redskins (9-4) 37, Jets (3-10) 16**	46,638

Was	17	7	10	3	37
NYJ	0	3	6	7	16

Was	Fugett 16 pass from Kilmer (Moseley kick)
Was	Jefferson 14 pass from Kilmer (Moseley kick)
Was	FG Moseley 18
NYJ	FG Leahy 47
Was	Riggins 1 run (Moseley kick)
Was	Riggins 2 pass from Kilmer (Moseley kick)
NYJ	Gaines 6 run (kick failed)
Was	FG Moseley 23
NYJ	Giammona 1 run (Moseley kick)
Was	FG Moseley 32

Shea Stadium—Billy Kilmer threw three touchdown passes—including two in the first quarter—to put the team on its way to routing the Jets.

Kilmer's first scoring pass, a 16-yard strike to tight end Jean Fugett, came shortly after Jake Scott recovered a New York fumble. Mark Moseley kicked the extra point and the Redskins led 7-0.

The Redskins drove for their next play, the advance covering 51 yards. Kilmer capped that drive with a 14-yard touchdown pass to Roy Jefferson.

Later in the first quarter the Redskins got close, driving 72 yards, but they couldn't finish off because Fugett dropped Kilmer's pass in the end zone. They settled instead for Mark Moseley's 18-yard field goal to make it 17-0.

Former Jet John Riggins caught Kilmer's third touchdown pass, scored another TD on the ground and rushed for 104 yards on 19 carries in his return to Shea Stadium.

Riggins' scoring run pushed the lead to 24-3 at halftime and allowed the Washington defense to unload on Jets quarterback Richard Todd. They sacked him six times and held him to 61 yards on four of 14 passing.

Dec 9

Cooke Buys 50 More Shares of Stock
Majority owner controls 300 of 350 shares

12/12/76	**Redskins (10-4) 27, COWBOYS (11-3) 14**			59,916	
Was	0	10	3	14	27
Dal	0	7	7	0	14
Was	FG Moseley 25				
Dal	Dennison 12 run (Herrera kick)				
Was	Fugett 6 pass from Kilmer (Moseley kick)				
Dal	B. Johnson 43 pass from Staubach (Hererra kick)				
Was	FG Moseley 27				
Was	Hill 15 run (Moseley kick)				
Was	Riggins 3 run (Moseley kick)				

Texas Stadium—The Redskins moved past the Cowboys and into the NFL playoffs by scoring 14 points in a 50-second span in the fourth quarter.

Washington held a 10-7 halftime lead, but that evaporated less than three minutes into the second half. Roger Staubach hit Butch Johnson with a 43-yard touchdown pass to put Dallas up 14-10. That was largely the extent of Staubach's contributions to his team's effort; thanks to constant pressure by the Redskins defense, he completed just five of 22 passes on the day for 91 yards.

The visitors edged closer on Mark Moseley's 27-yard field goal about five minutes later. Still clinging to their 14-13 lead, the Cowboys punted to Washington with 7:24 left in the game. Starting from midfield, a nine-yard reception by Mike Thomas and John Riggins' three-yard run earned a first down at the 38. After two straight incompletions, the Redskins faced third and ten. Then came what Billy Kilmer called "the play of the game."

Dallas came with an all-out blitz and safety Cliff Harris joined those rushing towards Kilmer. The quarterback barely got off a wobbly pass, but it found Thomas—who snuck into the area over the middle that Harris had vacated—at the 10 yard line. He was tackled at the four.

A couple of penalties pushed the Redskins back to the 15 where they faced second and goal. Ex-Cowboy Calvin Hill followed Riggins around left end and swept in for the go-ahead score with 4:34 left.

Certainly it was not yet time to celebrate, but that would come soon enough. On first down from the 21, Ron McDole sacked Staubach for a loss of twelve. On the next play, Diron Talbert swatted Staubach's pass into the air. It bounced off of Dallas center John Fitzgerald and possibly one other player before it fell into the arms of defensive end Dennis Johnson at the three. The game and playoff spot were secured when Riggins took advantage of some brutal blocking that allowed him to score the clincher untouched.

12/18/76	**VIKINGS 35, Redskins 20**			47,221	
Was	3	0	3	14	20
Min	14	7	14	0	35
Min	Voight 18 pass from Tarkenton (Cox kick)				
Was	FG Moseley 47				
Min	S. White 27 pass from Tarkenton (Cox kick)				
Min	Foreman 2 run (Cox kick)				
Min	Foreman 30 run (Cox kick)				
Was	FG Moseley 35				
Min	S. White 9 pass from Tarkenton				
Was	Grant 12 pass from Kilmer (Moseley kick)				
Was	Jefferson 3 pass from Kilmer (Moseley kick)				

"It was one of those things," said safety Ken Houston after this one. He was specifically talking about a play where he tipped a pass that Minnesota receiver Sammy White caught for a 27-yard touchdown, but he could have been talking about the entire game. The Vikings ran and passed at will and allowed the Redskins very little until it was apparent the Skins would be headed home for the holidays.

The Vikings got out of the gate in a hurry. On their first play from scrimmage, Brent McClanahan turned a simple off tackle play into a 41-yard gain to the Washington 25. Three plays after that, Fran Tarkenton threw an 18-yard touchdown pass to tight end Stu Voight to put the Vikings on top 7-0.

After a Mark Moseley field goal, the Vikings went on a 21-0 scoring run to end the competitive phase of the game, brief as it was. After the pass that Houston tipped and White caught, Chuck Foreman scored on a two-yard run to cap a 66-yard drive that made the halftime score 21-3.

It was more of the same in the third quarter, with Foreman covering the last 30 yards of a 51-yard drive with his second touchdown run that ended any remote possibility of a Redskins comeback. Foreman rushed for 105 yards on the day and McClanahan added 101 on the ground.

After Tarkenton threw another TD to White late in the third quarter to put his team up 35-6, the QB took a seat on the bench to rest up for the NFC Championship game. A pair of Billy Kilmer touchdown passes in the fourth quarter made the final score a bit more respectable, but there was no doubt about who had dominated this game.

"They (the Vikings) had something left and we didn't," said Allen.

1977
Head Coach: George Allen
Record: 9-5, Second in NFC East

Honors: Eddie Brown Pro Bowl; Jean Fugett All-NCF, Pro Bowl;
Ken Houston All-NFL, Pro Bowl

Allen's Return Uncertain

Dec 19—George Allen isn't generally known for being straightforward with the media, but in today's season-ending press conference he revealed a few interesting nuggets.

Foremost among them was that he wasn't sure if he would return as coach of the Redskins for the 1977 season. He said that he would talk to the players before everyone left for the holidays "and then I will make a decision" about next year.

At the end of his previous five seasons at the team's helm, Allen has clearly stated he would be back the following season.

Allen also admitted he didn't think that his team was emotionally ready to play prior to Saturday's playoff loss in Minnesota. They had spent a lot of emotion in their playoff-clinching win in Dallas the week before.

Feb 3

Allen Wants Contract Extension
One year left on original deal,
says 'I would think I'll be here'

July 13

Allen Gets New Contract, Pay Doubles
Extension is for four years at $250K annually

Brown Practices Then Retires

July 26—Larry Brown gave it a go.

He went out onto the practice field at Dickenson College one more time to see if his battered knees would allow him to play another season of football.

They did not.

The Redskins' all-time leading rusher limped off of the field; an hour and a half later, he announced his retirement.

He hangs it up with 5,875 rushing yards. Brown went to four Pro Bowls, was twice an All-Pro selection and was the league MVP in 1972.

'77 Will Be Smith's Last Year

Aug 22—Jerry Smith, who has caught more touchdown passes than any other tight end in NFL history, says that the 1977 season will be his last.

Smith, 34, has been with the Redskins since they drafted him out of Arizona State in the ninth round of the 1965 draft. He has caught 920 passes for 5,490 yards and 60 touchdowns.

Sep 12

Smith, Owens Cut
Tight end, defensive back have
combined 23 years with team

9/18/77	GIANTS (1-0) 20, Redskins (0-1) 17			76,086	
Was	0	0	0	17	17
NYG	7	0	3	10	20
NYG	Martin 30 interception return (Danelo kick)				
NYG	FG Danelo 22				
Was	Thomas 3 run (Moseley kick)				
Was	Riggins 3 pass from Kilmer (Moseley kick)				
Was	FG Moseley 51				
NYG	Shirk 8 pass from Golsteyn (Danelo kick)				
NYG	FG Danelo 30				

Giants Stadium—Joe Danelo kicked a 30-yard field goal with three seconds left to send the Giants past the Redskins by a score of 20-17. This was George Allen's first opening-day loss as a head coach (5-0 with the Rams, 6-0 with Washington).

It appeared that the Skins had pulled this one out of the fire. They trailed 10-0 entering the fourth quarter, but soon got on the board with a three-yard touchdown run by Mike Thomas a minute and a half into it. A little more than five minutes later, they took their first lead when Billy Kilmer pitched a three-yard touchdown pass to John Riggins to make it 14-10.

After Jake Scott's interception set up the "insurance" score—a 51-yard Mark Moseley field goal with 3:36 left—the Giants and their quarterback Jerry Golsteyn rallied. It took a couple of good breaks for them to rally successfully.

After Moseley's score, New York rolled 74 yards to tie the score. Golsteyn completed three of four passes on the drive, including one that represented the first of the Giants' fortunate bounces. Safety Ken Houston tipped a floating Golsteyn pass, but it continued floating right into the hands of receiver Ed Marshall. The play was good for 47 yards and a first down at the Washington eight. From there, Golsteyn found Gary Shirk with nobody anywhere near position to tip the ball. With 1:56 left, it was tied 17-17.

The Giants got their second break when Thomas coughed up the ball and they recovered at the Redskins' 19. After three running plays, they let the clock run down the seven seconds and Danelo's winning boot was good from 30 yards.

Sep 19

Jerry Smith to Return to Redskins
Allen: Move is to 'find a catalyst that
will help the club get going'

9/25/77	REDSKINS (1-1) 10, Falcons (1-1) 6			55,031	
Atl	0	0	3	3	6
Was	0	3	7	0	10
Was	FG Moseley 26				
Atl	FG Mike-Mayer 23				
Was	Thomas 2 pass from Kilmer (Moseley kick)				
Atl	FG Mike-Mayer 27				

RFK Stadium—The Redskins got a touchdown on a two-yard toss from Billy Kilmer to Mike Thomas in the third period to slip past the Falcons 10-6.

Both teams missed numerous scoring opportunities during this sloppy affair.

Washington was clinging to a 3-0 lead in the third quarter when Billy Kilmer was sacked and fumbled and Atlanta recovered at the Redskins 28. Scott Hunter completed a pass to Alfred Jenkins that carried to the ten, but the Washington defense stiffened and Atlanta tied the game with Nick Mike-Mayer's 23-yard field goal.

A pass interference call considerably aided the Redskins' touchdown drive. After the call on linebacker Greg Brezina, the home team had a first and ten at the Atlanta 28. A pass from Kilmer to Charley Taylor carried to the nine and Kilmer flipped the ball to Thomas for the score three plays later, making it 10-3.

The Falcons had two serious threats in the fourth quarter, but came away with just three points. A 36-yard pass from Hunter to running back Haskell Stanback got the Falcons to the Washington 18, but the drive stalled and Mike-Mayer came on and kicked his second field goal.

With a last-gasp drive the Falcons moved from their two to a first down at the Washington 17 with just under two minutes left. Linebacker Mike Curtis delivered a serious setback to Atlanta with a sack of Hunter that lost 13 yards back to the 30, and the defense held from there.

Sep 26

Theismann Says He Doesn't Play for Allen
QB frustrated at backup role but says he wants to stay in Washington

---

Sep 27

Allen, Theismann Meet
QB apologizes for remarks at dinner

Sep 29

Larry Jones Unhappy With Role
Speedy receiver wants more returns, receptions, wants to block less

---

10/2/77	REDSKINS (2-1) 24, Cardinals (1-2) 14			55,031	
StL	0	0	0	14	14
Was	7	0	7	10	24
Was	Grant 12 pass from Kilmer (Moseley kick)				
Was	Fugett 27 pass from Kilmer (Moseley kick)				
StL	Cain 7 pass from Hart (Bakken kick)				
Was	Riggins 53 pass from Kilmer (Moseley kick)				
Was	FG Moseley 41				
StL	Morris 1 run (Bakken kick)				

RFK Stadium—Billy Kilmer threw for 206 yards and three touchdowns to spur the Redskins' win over the Cardinals. Cornerback Joe Lavender made a key interception in the fourth quarter to help preserve the victory.

The home team got off to an early lead with its first possession. From the Cardinals 48, the Redskins drove to Kilmer's first scoring pass, a 12-yarder to Frank Grant. The offense stayed in neutral for much of the rest of the first half, but Mike Bragg kept the Cards at bay by pinning them at their own five, 10, and two yard lines with well-positioned punts.

Kilmer threw a 27-yard TD to Jean Fugett in the third quarter and the lead was 14-0 entering the last period. The Cardinal offense came to life, scoring one touchdown and moving into position to score another with a second and one at the Washington 32. Lavender stepped in front of Jim Hart's pass and picked it off at the 14.

That was just half of the clincher. The other part came when Kilmer led the team 86 yards to a touchdown in three plays. The score came after Kilmer dumped a pass off to John Riggins over the middle. Riggins built up a head of steam, broke a couple of attempted tackles and rolled in to complete the 53-yard touchdown

pass. That and Mark Moseley's 41-yard field goal later in the period allowed the Redskins to survive a last-minute touchdown by the Cardinals.

10/9/77	Redskins (3-1) 10, BUCS (0-4) 0			58,571	
Was	10	0	0	0	10
TB	0	0	0	0	0
Was	FG Moseley 44				
Was	Thomas 6 run (Moseley kick)				

Tampa Stadium—"We had too many mistakes," was one comment heard after this one—and it was from Billy Kilmer, the winning quarterback. The contest, which Kilmer aptly described as "dull," featured nine fumbles, a total of eight turnovers and 14 penalties.

All of the game's scoring came in the first quarter. Washington drove to a 44-yard Mark Moseley field goal early in the game and later embarked on a 57-yard touchdown drive. Kilmer passes to Frank Grant and Jean Fugett got the Redskins close and then Mike Thomas took it over from the six to get it to 10-0.

Washington blew a couple of scoring chances by fumbling the ball away in Tampa Bay territory in the second quarter. Eventually the Redskins decided to keep it close to the vest and see if the Bucs would be able to mount a threat. It turned out to be a sound strategy. The Bucs punted 11 times, didn't convert a third down until the waning moments of the game and lost their one true scoring opportunity when they missed a 38-yard field goal attempt in the third quarter.

Brundige, McKay Trade Barbs

Oct 12—Bill Brundige, who graduated from Colorado with a major in math, doesn't take kindly to being called a "dumb ass idiot."

So, when Buccaneers coach John McKay called Brundige that for questioning his offensive schemes during their game last Sunday, the Redskins defensive tackle fired back.

"I probably know more about offense than he does," Brundige said of McKay. "He's the worst coach in the NFL."

The evidence would seem to back up Brundige. The Redskins shut out Tampa Bay 10-0, sending McKay's Bucs to 0-20 since them came into the NFL last season.

10/16/77	COWBOYS (5-0) 34, Redskins (3-2) 16			62,115	
Was	6	7	3	0	16
Dal	0	14	6	14	34
Was	FG Moseley 25				
Was	FG Moseley 40				
Dal	Richards 50 pass from Staubach (Herrera kick)				
Dal	Newhouse 7 run (Herrera kick)				
Was	Harmon 1 pass from Theismann (Moseley kick)				
Was	FG Moseley 53				
Dal	FG Herrera 44				
Dal	FG Herrera 53				
Dal	Pearson 59 pass from Staubach (Herrera kick)				
Dal	Newhouse 6 run (Herrera kick)				

Texas Stadium—The Redskins held the lead going into the second quarter and again in the third quarter, but don't let that fact fool you into thinking they were ever in this one. Dallas dominated the game from start to finish and dealt the Redskins' hopes for a division title multiple and severe blows.

Fullbacks John Riggins and Bob Brunet both suffered season-ending injuries and several other Redskins were sidelined. The Redskins mustered just one net yard passing, with their 55 yards in gains being offset by 54 yards lost on eight Cowboy sacks. The Cowboys, meanwhile, racked up 435 yards of total offense.

Mark Moseley kicked two field goals in the first quarter to give the Redskins a 6-0 lead. Dallas responded with a pair of second-quarter touchdowns, but Washington pulled back to within one by halftime when Joe Theismann lofted a one-yard scoring pass to running back Clarence Harmon.

The Redskins retook the lead briefly in the second half on Moseley's 53-yard field goal, the longest in team history. Two field goals by Efren Herrera in a four-minute span of the third quarter to push Dallas into a 20-16 lead, though, were the beginning of the end for the Redskins.

The end of the end arrived a couple minutes into the fourth quarter. Dallas faced a third and 13 at its own 41. The Redskins defense went into an all-out blitz, leaving cornerback Gerald Williams one on one with receiver Drew Pearson. From shotgun formation, Roger Staubach saw this and motioned for Pearson to go deep. The Cowboys picked up the blitz, Pearson smoked Williams and gathered in Staubach's perfect pass at the Washington 25 and cruised in for a 27-16 Dallas lead.

Oct 17
Double Whammy: Two FB's Out For Season
Riggins, Brunet out after being injured versus Dallas

10/23/77	Giants (3-3) 17, REDSKINS (3-3) 6			53,903	
NYG	0	0	7	10	17
Was	3	3	0	0	6
Was	FG Moseley 35				
Was	FG Moseley 45				
NYG	Kotar 17 run (Danelo kick)				
NYG	Robinson 23 pass from Pisarcik (Danelo kick)				
NYG	FG Danelo 30				

RFK Stadium—"I can't ever remember a loss this devastating," said George Allen after the Giants' 17-6 defeat of the Redskins.

While the coach is given to hyperbole, it was hard to find much exaggeration in his summation of this one, their third straight loss to the Giants, their former doormats.

While the visitors did plenty to beat Washington, a mistake of the Redskins' own doing was the pivotal moment in this game. Leading 6-0 at halftime on two Mark Moseley field goals, Washington came out in the second half looking to expand its lead. It appeared that they had, but an apparent touchdown was nullified when receiver Frank Grant was flagged for illegal motion on the play. They didn't dent the scoreboard the rest of the game.

Meanwhile, the Giants were busy working their way back into the game. Doug Kotar scored on a 17-yard run later in the third quarter to put them into the lead a 7-6. In the fourth quarter, defensive end John Medenhall—a thorn in the Redskins' side all day—sacked and stripped Billy Kilmer, giving the Giants possession at the Washington 23. Two plays later, Joe Pisarcik threw a 23-yard scoring strike to receiver Jimmy Robinson to stretch the New York margin to 14-6. A Joe Danelo field goal put it out of reach later in the fourth.

Oct 25
QB Shuffle? Theismann May Start
Allen wants offensive spark but downplays importance of change at signal caller

10/30/77	REDSKINS (4-3) 23, Eagles (2-5) 17			55,031	
Phi	7	3	0	7	17
Was	14	6	3	0	23
Was	Fugett 15 pass from Theismann (Moseley kick)				
Was	Fugett 15 pass from Theismann (Moseley kick)				
Phi	Betterson 16 run (Muhlmann kick)				
Phi	FG Muhlmann 44				
Was	FG Moseley 46				
Was	FG Moseley 30				
Was	FG Moseley 51				
Phi	Carmichael 48 pass from Jaworski (Muhlmann kick)				

RFK Stadium—Joe Theismann threw two touchdown passes to tight end Jean Fugett in the first quarter and then watched as his team's defense repelled two late Eagle threats to secure the win.

Both of Theismann's scoring connections with Fugett were from 15 yards and were the ends of drives that started in Eagles territory. The first TD was preceded by Ken Houston's recovery of an Eagle fumble at the Philly 44; the second followed a shanked punt that set the Redskins up at the 29.

Washington's 14-0 lead was cut to 14-10 by the midway point of the second quarter. James Betterson scored on a 16-yard run late in the first quarter and then Horst Muhlmann booted a 44-yard field goal.

Before halftime, the home team had reestablished control with two Mark Moseley field goals and took a 20-10 lead into the locker room. Moseley's third field goal, a 51-yarder, accounted for the Redskins' final points. It would be up to the defense to hang on.

Early in the final period, the defense slipped up, allowing Harold Carmichael to get free to catch a 48-yard touchdown pass from Ron Jaworski to make the score 23-17. Things got tense when the Eagles drove into Washington territory again, but Gerald Williams allowed for a momentary sigh of relief when he intercepted Jaworski's pass at the two yard line.

With the clock winding down, the Eagles made one last push towards the goal line. On fourth down from the Washington 30 with 41 seconds left, tackle Bill Brundige pressured Jaworski, forcing a desperation pass that linebacker Rich Milot batted harmlessly to the ground.

Allen Extension Unsigned?
Oct 31—Redskins team president Edward Bennett Williams had no comment today on a published report that the contract extension he and George Allen agreed to in July has not yet been signed.

According to the report, Allen is not happy with some of the financial details of the four-year, $1 million deal and some other language in the contract.

This is the last year of Allen's original seven-year contract with the Redskins. Absent a new, signed agreement, he could elect to leave Washington and coach another team at the end of this season.

11/7/77	COLTS (7-1) 10, Redskins (4-4) 3			57,740	
Was	0	3	0	0	3
Bal	3	0	0	7	10
Bal	FG Linhart 26				
Was	FG Moseley 40				
Bal	Scott 12 pass from Jones (Linhart kick)				

Memorial Stadium—The Colts scored on a Bert Jones pass early in the fourth quarter and then held on for the win as the clock ran out on Washington's desperation final drive.

The home team dominated the first half, but emerged from the first two quarters with the game tied at three. An interception of Joe Theismann by Stan White set up a Toni Linhart field goal in the first quarter and a 44-yard pass from Theismann to Danny Buggs led to a 40-yarder by Mark Moseley late in the half.

Neither team was able to scratch the scoreboard in the third quarter, but a 23-yard Mike Bragg punt put the Colts in business at their own 39. From there, Baltimore embarked on a 61-yard drive to the go-ahead touchdown. A 24-yard pass from Jones to Glenn Doughty was the big play and Jones' 12-yarder to Freddie Scott gave them a 10-3 lead. They had a shot to stretch it to a 10-point margin with a more than five minutes left, but Linhart missed a 29-yard field goal, leaving the door open for the Redskins—but they couldn't quite get through it.

Starting a final possession at their own 26 with no time-outs left, the Redskins got completions to Frank Grant and Jean Fugett to get to the Colts 34. Theismann then went to Grant again to get to the 13. The offense hustled to the line, and Theismann took the snap, rolled and fired to Calvin Hill in the end zone. It was clear, however, that the clock had ticked to 0:00 before the snap and the Colts had already taken a couple of steps towards the sideline to begin to celebrate their win.

11/13/77	**Redskins (5-4) 17, EAGLES (3-6) 14**		60,702	
Was	0	0	7	10	17
Phi	0	7	0	7	14
Phi	Sullivan 21 pass from Jaworski (Muhlmann kick)			
Was	Grant 14 pass from Theismann (Moseley kick)			
Phi	Jaworski 1 run (Muhlmann kick)			
Was	Buggs 5 pass from Theismann (Moseley kick)			
Was	FG Moseley 54			

Veterans Stadium—Mark Moseley kicked a 54-yard field goal, the longest in team history, to give the Redskins the lead with 3:41 left to play. Moseley and his teammates held their collective breaths and watch while Philly's Horst Muhlmann missed a potential game-tying three pointer from 41 yards in the closing seconds.

A Mike Thomas fumble led to a second-quarter touchdown that gave Philadelphia a 7-0 halftime lead. It might have been worse had Windlan Hall not blocked a Muhlmann field goal attempt in the first quarter.

It took the Redskins just six plays into the second half to tie the score. The rapid 65-yard advance was capped by Joe Theismann's 34-yard touchdown pass to Frank Grant.

Eagles quarterback Ron Jaworski manufactured the game's next score almost single-handedly, rolling for 44 yards on a bootleg to set up his own score on a one-yard sneak early in the fourth quarter to make it 14-7.

Following that, Moseley pushed a 40-yard field goal attempt to the left. The Eagles were unable to get a first down and lined up to punt. Dallas Hickman, a backup defensive lineman, broke through the wall and blocked Spike Jones' kick, then recovered the ball at the Philadelphia 19. Soon after that, Theismann scrambled to the right and tied the game with nine and a half minutes left with a nice pass to Danny Buggs, who tucked the ball away just inside the end line.

Again, the Eagles couldn't move—but this time Jones got his punt off and it rolled dead at the Washington 36. Theismann passed his team to the Philly 37. On fourth and 11 from there, Moseley's boot was true and all that remained was the Eagles' last drive and Muhlmann's failed attempt to send it into overtime.

11/21/77	**REDSKINS (6-4) 10, Packers (2-8) 9**		51,498	
GB	0	3	3	3	9
Was	0	3	0	7	10
Was	FG Moseley 35			
GB	FG Marcol 40			
GB	FG Marcol 42			
Was	Thomas 7 pass from Theismann (Moseley kick)			
GB	FG Marcol 44			

RFK Stadium—Joe Theismann's seven-yard touchdown pass to Mike Thomas gave the Redskins a fourth-quarter lead and they were able to hang on for an uninspiring 10-9 triumph over Green Bay.

Until the Thomas touchdown, which came midway through the fourth quarter, this was a battle of the field goal kickers. Mark Moseley connected in the second quarter and Chester Marcol answered for the Packers with a 40-yarder just before the break and a 42-yard boot 20 seconds before the third quarter ended.

Faced with the 6-3 deficit, Theismann guided the Redskins to the game's lone touchdown. Of the 79 yards on the drive, Theismann accounted for 64 of them by passing for 52 and

scrambling for another 12. The TD toss to Thomas came on the play after his scramble.

The Packers battled back, twice driving into Washington territory. The first foray netted Marcol's third field goal, a 44-yarder with 4:16 to go. Washington managed to burn off some clock on its ensuing possession, but ultimately had to punt back to Green Bay with 39 seconds left. Quarterback Davis Whitehurst quickly passed the Pack downfield from their 16 to the Washington 48 with 23 seconds left. The Pack was one intermediate-length completion away from Marcol's range, but the drive died there, with Joe Lavender intercepting Whitehurst's last desperate heave.

Nov 23
Kilmer Able but Theismann Will Start
Allen says 'nothing to' reports that Billy will start

11/27/77	**Cowboys (9-2) 14, REDSKINS (6-5) 7**		55,031	
Dal	0	0	7	7	14
Was	0	7	0	0	7
Was	Theismann 1 run (Moseley kick)			
Dal	Richards 4 pass from Staubach (Herrera kick)			
Dal	Dorsett 1 run (Herrera kick)			

RFK Stadium—A couple of key special teams mistakes on the part of the Redskins greatly aided Dallas' two touchdown drives as the Cowboys won 14-7 in Washington.

Things did not start well for the Redskins as Roger Staubach completed a 67-yard bomb to Drew Pearson on the third play of the game. The threat ended on the next play when, from the one yard line, Dallas fumbled and Diron Talbert recovered for the Redskins.

Washington had a couple of chances to score in the first period, but Mark Moseley missed two field goals and the game was still scoreless when Washington took possession at its own six with about eight and a half minutes left in the first half. The Redskins consumed just over six minutes of clock in taking 12 plays to move 94 yards to a touchdown. Theismann snuck it in over left guard and Moseley's conversion made it 7-0 2:36 before intermission.

It was still 7-0 when a Mike Bragg punt pinned Dallas back on its own 13 early in the third quarter. However, Pete Wysocki was flagged as an ineligible man downfield and Bragg's rekick carried just 10 yards to the Dallas 41. Buoyed by its good fortune, the Cowboys offense came to life, covering the 59 yards in eight plays with a four-yard scoring pass from Staubach to Golden Richards capping the drive to tie the score at seven.

The Cowboys regained possession late in the third quarter at their own 40 but soon stalled, facing fourth and four at the Washington 49. As the Cowboys lined up in punt formation, Wysocki again donned the goat's horns, jumping offside to give Dallas five yards and a first down. The Redskins argued that the Dallas center had drawn them off, but the discussion, of course, was to no avail.

Dallas converted another fourth down when Staubach slithered for the necessary foot to the one yard line. Right after that, Tony Dorsett got the final yard and Dallas had a 14-7 lead.

Twice the Redskins drove into Dallas territory after that, but all they had to show for it was a missed field goal and a Theismann interception in the dying minutes.

12/4/77	**Redskins (7-5) 10, BILLS (2-10) 0**		22,975	
Was	0	7	0	3	**10**
Buf	0	0	0	0	**0**
Was	Fugett 12 pass from Theismann (Moseley kick)			
Was	FG Moseley 19			

Rich Stadium—The Redskins kept their slim playoff hopes alive as they got a 12-yard touchdown pass from Joe Theismann to

Jean Fugett, giving them all the points they needed to beat the Bills.

The drive that ended with the touchdown pass got a head start when the stiff winds caught the punt of Buffalo's Marv Bateman and the boot netted just 20 yards to the Washington 47. Theismann converted a third down by going to Mike Thomas for a 15-yard completion and then hit Thomas again—this time for 13— and then to Fugett for seven. The eleventh play of the march was the scoring pass from Theismann to Fugett.

Buffalo had but two scoring threats on the day. One of them ended when Joe Harris blocked a 45-yard field goal attempt by Carson Long three seconds before halftime and the other wound up in a missed field goal from 37 yards.

The Redskins pushed deep into Bills territory in the fourth quarter but had to settle for Mark Moseley's 19-yard field goal and a 10-0 lead. Moseley later missed a 45-yard attempt, but it didn't matter; the Bills never threatened.

12/10/77	Redskins (8-5) 26, CARDINALS (7-6) 20				36,067
Was	10	3	3	10	26
StL	0	10	3	7	20
Was	Hill 14 pass from Kilmer (Moseley kick)				
Was	FG Moseley 40				
StL	FG Bakken 32				
StL	Jones 1 run (Bakken kick)				
Was	FG Moseley 23				
StL	FG Bakken 27				
Was	FG Moseley 37				
Was	FG Moseley 42				
Was	Thomas 4 run (Moseley kick)				
StL	Metcalf 68 pass from Hart (Bakken kick)				

Busch Stadium—On a playing surface more suited to a puck and nets rather than a ball and goalposts, Mark Moseley kicked four field goals to help push the Redskins past the Cardinals. Eddie Brown made a diving interception in the end zone with a minute left to preserve the win.

Temperatures of 14 degrees and a slight drizzle created a thin sheet of ice on top of the Busch Stadium artificial turf. Ironically, the conditions turned the home field advantage to the visiting Redskins, the slower of the two teams, rather than the Cards, who relied heavily on speed and quickness.

The Redskins jumped to a 10-0 lead in the first quarter. Billy Kilmer, back in the lineup after missing six weeks, threw a 14-yard touchdown pass to Calvin Hill and Mark Moseley booted a 40-yard field goal.

After Jim Bakken kicked a 32-yard field goal, St. Louis recovered a Hill fumble and turned it into the tying score—a one-yard dive by Steve Jones. Kilmer led a well-executed drive that led to Moseley's 23-yard field goal and a 13-10 lead at the half.

Moseley and Bakken exchanged field goals in the third quarter. The game turned on the kickoff following Moseley's boot. Terry Metcalf fumbled on the return and Windlan Hall recovered for the Redskins at the St. Louis 41. Kilmer converted a third and 11 by scrambling for 12 yards, and another 15 yards were tacked on when St. Louis linebacker Tim Kearney was flagged for roughing Kilmer on the tackle. Four plays after that, Mike Thomas took it into the end zone from four yards out and the Redskins appeared to be in command at 26-13.

That command was a brief one. On the next play from scrimmage, Jim Hart threw to Metcalf over the middle and the speedy running back found his footing on the icy carpet and zoomed into the end zone to complete a 68-yard touchdown play

with 10:52 left in the game—plenty of time for the Cardinals to complete one of their patented killer comebacks.

Twice the Cards drove into Washington territory after that, but the comeback didn't materialize. The first march died when Joe Lavender knocked down Hart's pass on fourth and seven at the Washington 34 with 3:17 left. Brown killed St. Louis' last hope with his spectacular interception with 1:08 left, a theft that George Allen called "one of the best I've ever seen."

12/17/77	REDSKINS (9-5) 17, Rams (10-4) 14				54,308
LA	0	0	0	14	14
Was	14	0	3	0	17
Was	Grant 59 pass from Kilmer (Moseley kick)				
Was	Fugett 3 pass from Kilmer (Moseley kick)				
Was	FG Moseley 45				
LA	Nelson 17 pass from Ferragamo (Septien kick)				
LA	Jodat 2 pass from Ferragamo (Septien kick)				

RFK Stadium—The Redskins carried a 17-0 lead into the fourth quarter but had to withstand two missed field goal attempts by the Rams in the final seconds to claim the win.

By winning this Saturday game, Washington did what it had to do in order to gain a spot in the playoffs on the season's final weekend.

A fluke play gave the Redskins a 7-0 lead in the first quarter. Billy Kilmer threw a long pass intended for tight end Jean Fugett at around the LA 30. Cornerback Monte Jackson tipped the ball. Receiver Frank Grant snared the ball out of the air and, thinking that Fugett had tipped the ball and the play would thus be called an incomplete pass, jogged into the end zone at half speed. Grant was shocked when he saw the officials' raised arms indicating a touchdown.

Another tipped pass led to Washington's second score. Tackle Dave Butz got a paw on a Pat Haden pass and the ball wound up in the arms of safety Jake Scott and the Redskins took over at the Los Angeles 33. Four plays later Fugett was wide open in the end zone and Washington was up 14-0.

Mark Moseley booted a 45-yard field goal to put the home team up 17-0 in the third quarter. Apparently, at that point, the Redskins' collective mind started to wander to the results of upcoming games that would determine their playoff fate. Meanwhile, LA coach Chuck Knox inserted backup quarterback Vince Ferragamo into the game. The sub led a 72-yard drive to one touchdown and then Dave Elmendorf intercepted a Kilmer pass and returned it to his own 38. Rod Phillips ripped off runs of 23 and 25 yards, breaking numerous attempted tackled in the process, setting up Ferragamo's two-yard touchdown pass to Jim Jodat that made it 17-14 with just over five minutes left.

The Redskins managed two first downs, but still had to punt the ball back to the Rams, who took possession at their own 20 with 1:51 left. From there, the Rams moved to the Washington 27 with six seconds left. Rafael Septein was short on a 45-yard field goal attempt, but a borderline roughing the kicker call gave him another shot from five yards closer. The 40-yard try was long enough but well wide to the left, and the Redskins were still alive in the playoff picture.

Dec 18

OT Kick Puts Bears In, Redskins Out
Ex-Redskin Pardee's Team Wins and Gets In

1978
Head Coach: Jack Pardee
Record: 8-8, Third in NFC East

Honors: Tony Green Pro Bowl; Ken Houston Pro Bowl

Jan 4

Allen, Redskins Try To Make a Deal
As openings get filled, coach looks to stay in D.C.

Redskins Lose Patience, Fire Allen

Jan 18—George Allen is no longer the coach of the Redskins.

Team president Edward Bennett Williams announced that the team was withdrawing its contract offer to Allen. The coach and team had announced an agreement on the extension six months ago, but Allen never signed it due to some details over personnel and financial control.

"I just reached the point where I couldn't wait any longer for George to make up his mind," said Williams. "Our negotiations with George Allen are concluded.

"We gave him a deadline to sign and the deadline passed."

He said the team could not afford to wait for Allen to make up his mind while potential replacements landed jobs elsewhere.

"I gave George Allen unlimited patience and he exhausted it," Williams said. "I have him an unlimited budget and he exceeded it."

Among the items straining that big budget were a large coaching staff, a lavish training complex in Virginia, and some big contracts to attract free agents such as Dave Butz and John Riggins.

Allen was informed of the decision last night by his son, who had learned of it in the media. "I thought he was kidding," said Allen.

Jan 19

Pardee Resigns From Bears, Will Talk Here
Ex-Skins linebacker and assistant to Allen appears to be leading candidate

Pardee in the Fold for Three Years

Jan 24—The Redskins have their man—and he won't need a road map to find Redskins Park.

Jack Pardee, who spent three years with the Redskins as a player and as an assistant coach, was given a three-year contract to replace the man he played and coached under here: George Allen.

Pardee was 20-22 in three seasons as head coach of the Bears. Chicago improved every year he was there and even made the playoffs this past season.

Pardee, 42, had a 15-year career as a player with the Rams and Redskins.

Feb 1

Great Circle Route: Allen Back to Rams
Says it's 'a dream' to coach team that fired him in '71

Feb 1

Fischer Won't Return
Team won't offer contract to 38-year-old cornerback

Feb 24

Bobby Beathard Hired as General Manager
Comes from Miami, will share power with Pardee

June 1

Charley Taylor Hangs It Up After 14 Years
End retires as NFL's all-time leading receiver

Skins Deal No. 1 for Parrish, Bacon

June 26—Meet the new boss, same as the old boss.

Bobby Beathard did what George Allen loved to do in trading away a high draft pick for veteran players. He sent the Redskins' No. 1 pick in 1979 to the Bengals in exchange for cornerback Lemar Parrish and defensive end Coy Bacon.

Parrish, 30, will fill the hole created when Pat Fischer was released and Bacon, 35, will add depth on the line.

July 16

Kilmer, Theismann QB Battle Camp Highlight
Pardee has declared open competition for position

Aug 14

Rams Fire Allen
Coached dismissed after two preseason games

9/3/78	Redskins (1-0) 16, PATRIOTS (0-1) 14				55,037
Was	3	0	6	7	16
NE	0	0	7	7	14
Was	FG Moseley 36				
NE	Morgan 33 pass from Grogan (Smith kick)				
Was	Thomas 15 pass from Theismann (kick failed)				
NE	Jackson 45 pass from Grogan (Smith kick)				
Was	Dusek 31 fumble return (Moseley kick)				

Schaefer Stadium—Dave Butz forced the Patriots' Horace Ivory to fumble with less than three minutes left in the game, and Brad Dusek scooped it up and scooted down the left sideline for an improbable 16-14 win.

The only scoring in the first half came courtesy of a 36-yard Mark Moseley field goal in the first quarter. That score was set up on the first play of the game when Joe Theismann unleashed a 51-yard bomb to receiver Danny Buggs.

The Pats erased that deficit in the third period on a 33-yard TD pass from Steve Grogan to Stanley Morgan.

A Ron McDole interception set up the Redskins' first touchdown—a 15-yard pass from Joe Theismann to Mike Thomas. The point after was no good and the Redskins led 9-7.

Grogan connected for his second touchdown pass early in the fourth quarter, this one a 45-yard bomb to Harold Jackson. That gave them a 14-9 lead.

The Redskins were unable to respond and New England was trying to run out the clock when Butz stripped Ivory of the ball.

"When I saw the ball hit the ground, I hesitated," said Dusek. "I wanted to make sure I could pick it up on the run."

9-10-78	REDSKINS (2-0) 35, Eagles (0-2) 30				54,380
Phi	7	3	6	14	30
Was	7	14	7	7	35
Phi	Montgomery 34 run (Mike-Mayer kick)				
Was	Theismann 4 run (Moseley kick)				
Phi	FG Mike-Mayer				
Was	Fugett 49 pass from Theismann (Moseley kick)				
Was	Fugett 19 pass from Theismann (Moseley kick)				
Was	Green 80 punt return (Moseley kick)				
Phi	Montgomery 10 pass from Jaworski (kick failed)				
Was	Buggs 37 pass from Theismann (Moseley kick)				
Phi	Montgomery 8 run (Mike-Mayer kick)				
Phi	Montgomery 5 run (Mike-Mayer kick)				

RFK Stadium—Washington outscored the Eagles 35-7 from late in the first quarter to early in the fourth to hand the Eagles the loss.

In the second quarter, Jean Fugett caught two Joe Theismann touchdown passes—one from 49 yards, and the other from 19—to put the Redskins up 21-10 at the half. Early in the third, Rookie Tony Green contributed an 80-yard punt return to give Washington a 28-10 lead.

The Eagles cut into their deficit with a 10-yard TD pass from Ron Jaworski to running back Wilbert Montgomery. Late in the third, Philly punted to Washington and the Redskins took possession at the Eagles' 48. Theismann threw to receiver Danny Buggs for 11 to the 37.

Then came what turned out to be the game's key play. Theismann handed off to John Riggins, who turned and flipped the ball back to the quarterback. Buggs was wide open and his 37-yard TD catch seemed to be simple—a nice highlight piece and icing on the cake. However, Montgomery scored his third and fourth touchdowns of the game and Philadelphia got two final shots from the Washington 35—the second because the Redskins jumped offside—but both of Jaworski's passes fell incomplete.

9/17/78	Redskins (3-0) 28, CARDINALS (0-3) 20				49,282
Was	7	14	7	0	28
StL	3	0	0	7	10
StL	FG Bakken 30				
Was	Green 99 kickoff return (Moseley kick)				
Was	Fugett 14 pass from Theismann (Moseley kick)				
Was	Thomas 3 run (Moseley kick)				
Was	Harmon 3 pass from Theismann (Moseley kick)				
StL	Gray 22 run (Bakken kick)				

Busch Stadium—For the second week in a row, rookie Tony Green returned a kick for the touchdown as the Redskins won their third straight to open the season.

A Jim Bakken field goal gave St. Louis a 3-0 lead over a lethargic Washington team. Green provided the needed spark by returning the ensuing kickoff 99 yards for the touchdown that put his team ahead to stay. An 11-yard pass from Joe Theismann to Jean Fugett and a three-yard run by Mike Thomas gave Washington a 21-3 halftime bulge.

The Redskins controlled the ball and the clock, rushing for 255 yards, with John Riggins getting 108 of those and Thomas contributing 78. Theismann had to throw just 12 times, completing five for 56 yards. In the third quarter, two of his passes went for scores—the one to Fugett, and another to Clarence—giving Washington a 28-3 lead. St. Louis scored a fourth-quarter touchdown, but was unable to pull off one of the Cardiac Cards'

comebacks of the recent past. They failed to recover an onside kick and then lost the ball on downs on their next possession.

9/24/78	REDSKINS (4-0) 23, Jets (2-2) 3				55,031
NYJ	3	0	0	0	3
Was	0	13	7	3	23
NYJ	FG Leahy 31				
Was	McDaniel 33 pass from Theismann (Moseley kick)				
Was	FG Moseley 39				
Was	FG Moseley 34				
Was	Fugett 20 pass from Theismann (Moseley kick)				
Was	FG Moseley 44				

RFK Stadium—The Jets scratched first, scoring on a Pat Leahy field goal on their first possession, but then Joe Theismann, John Riggins, Mark Moseley and the Washington defense took over. After that score, the Jets would enter Redskins territory just once the rest of the game.

The Washington defense swarmed over Jets' quarterbacks Richard Todd and Matt Robinson, sacking them a combined six times and helping to force two interceptions by Jake Scott. Robinson replaced Todd after the starter suffered a fractured clavicle while being sacked by Karl Lorch and Dave Butz.

Theismann got the Redskins on the board by leading a five play, 71-yard drive in the second quarter, a march considerably aided by a 21-yard pass interference call against New York's Ed Taylor. The call must have spooked Taylor because he let Washington receiver John McDaniel get wide open in the end zone and Theismann's soft toss from 33 yards out put the Redskins ahead to stay at 7-3. On the day, Theismann went 21 for 30 for 209 yards and two TD's

Two subsequent Redskins drives in the second quarter stalled in Jets territory and Moseley kicked field goals of 39 and 34 yards to expand the Redskins' halftime margin to 13-3.

It was all Redskins in the second half as Riggins took over. On the day, he gained 115 yards on 21 carries.

10/2/78	REDSKINS (5-0) 9, Cowboys (3-2) 5				55,031
Dal	0	0	3	2	5
Was	3	3	3	0	9
Was	FG Moseley 52				
Was	FG Moseley 42				
Dal	FG Septien 19				
Was	FG Moseley 27				
Dal	Safety Theismann tackled in end zone				

RFK Stadium—A capacity crowd and a national Monday night TV audience wanted to see if the 4-0 Redskins were legitimate, and if Dallas could continue scoring at the 27 points per game pace they had set so far that season. The second question was answered with an emphatic no, courtesy of the Redskins defense. The answer to the other was a qualified "maybe."

After a rather dull first half with two Mark Moseley field goals providing the only scoring, the pace of the action picked up considerably in the third quarter. Midway through that period, Dallas drove to a first and goal at the Redskins' two. The defense stiffened and the Cowboys had to settle for a 19-yard Rafael Septien field goal. The Redskins moved down the field but stalled in Dallas' red zone and had to settle for a third Moseley FG.

In the fourth quarter, the Cowboys threatened twice but did not score. After a Dallas interception in the end zone stopped a clinching score, Dallas drove to the Washington 14, but Staubach got too much air under a pass intended for Drew Pearson in the end zone and Ken Houston picked it off to snuff out the threat. After forcing the Redskins to punt, the Cowboys mounted one more drive, but they were stopped on downs at the Washington 15. On the game's final snap, Joe Theismann took the ball, raced back into his own end zone with the ball held triumphantly—albeit in a rather risky manner—over his head and, when the clock moved to 0:00, gave himself up for the meaningless safety.

10/8/78	Redskins (6-0) 21, LIONS (1-5) 19			60,555	
Was	0	7	0	14	21
Det	3	6	3	7	19
Det	FG Ricardo 19				
Det	FG Ricardo 23				
Det	FG Ricardo 31				
Was	Williams recovered blocked punt in end zone (Moseley kick)				
Det	FG Ricardo 22				
Was	Fugett 21 pass from Theismann (Moseley kick)				
Det	Kane 6 run (Ricardo kick)				
Was	McDaniel 25 pass from Theismann (Moseley kick)				

Pontiac Silverdome—Washington had to overcome fourth-quarter deficits twice to beat the Lions.

Detroit had led the entire game, taking a 9-0 lead on the strength of three Benny Ricardo field goals. The Redskins' only score came when Gerard Williams fell on a blocked Detroit punt in the end zone.

With the Redskins' offense struggling—the Lions out-rushed them on the day 231 yards to 76—Ricardo's fourth field goal, coming in the third quarter, gave the Lions what seemed to be a safe 12-7 lead.

The home crowd was roaring entering the fourth quarter. Washington quieted them momentarily when Jean Fugett caught a 21-yard touchdown pass from Joe Theismann. Suddenly, the Redskins were on top 14-12. The Lions grabbed the lead back with 5:52 left on a six-yard by Rick Kane, a score earned mostly on second and third efforts.

After an exchange of punts, Washington had the ball at its own 26. A 13-yard Joe Theismann to Mike Thomas pass converted a third and four and then it was Theismann to Thomas again for 30 to the Detroit 25. The next play, receiver John McDaniel beat corner Tony Sumler and Theismann delivered the ball for the winning score.

Pardee Looks Ahead

Oct 10—With his Redskins riding high at 6-0, Jack Pardee took the luxury of looking into the future.

"Three playoff teams could very well come right from our division," Pardee said. "I really think it shapes up that way."

Of course, Pardee has the Redskins penciled in as one of those teams. And he doesn't want to settle for one of the two wild card spots, either.

"Right now, we've got to hold what we've got and we've also got to shoot for home field advantage, divisional titles, those kinds of things."

The road to "those kinds of things" continues on Sunday when the Redskins travel to Philadelphia.

"If we get ready this week, we'll beat the Eagles," Pardee said.

10/15/78	EAGLES (4-3) 17, Redskins (6-1) 10			65,722	
Was	0	3	7	0	10
Phi	7	3	0	7	17
Phi	Sanders 19 interception return (Mike-Mayer kick)				
Was	FG Moseley 49				
Phi	FG Mike-Mayer 29				
Was	Riggins 3 run (Moseley kick)				
Phi	Montgomery 12 run (Mike-Mayer kick)				

Veterans Stadium—Six turnovers and penalties that took a touchdown and a field goal off the board killed the Redskins' chances of staying unbeaten.

The initial turnover cost the Redskins seven points. Eagle safety John Saunders stepped in front of a Joe Theismann pass and scampered 19 yards for a touchdown six and a half minutes into the game. Mark Moseley missed two field goal tries of 41 and 49 yards before finally connecting on a 49-yarder to pull the Redskins within 7-3 in the second quarter. Philly's Nick Mike-

Mayer answered with a 29-yard three-pointer as time expired in the first half to restore the Eagles' lead to seven.

John Riggins tied the game with a three-yard TD run in the third quarter, but Philadelphia regained their margin on a 12-yard TD run by Wilbert Montgomery.

Tony Green committed the final two turnovers that did the Redskins in. With 5:05 left in the game, Green gained the necessary yardage to convert a third and two at the Eagles' 11, but he coughed the ball up and Reggie Wilkes recovered it at the three. The Eagles were forced to punt from there. There was a punt block on and Mike Michel barely got the kick away. Green had an Eagle defender bearing down on him but didn't call for a fair catch and had the ball knocked loose just after he caught it near midfield. Philly recovered and ran out the clock.

10/22/78	GIANTS (5-3), 17 Redskins (6-2) 6			76,192	
Was	0	6	0	0	6
NYG	10	7	0	0	17
NYG	Robinson 43 pass from Pisarcik (Danelo kick)				
NYG	FG Danelo 31				
Was	FG Moseley 41				
Was	FG Moseley 34				
NYG	Pisarcik 3 run (Danelo kick)				

Giants Stadium—New York QB Joe Pisarcik completed just three passes all day, and two of them were killers as the Giants beat the Redskins.

A 46-yard touchdown heave to WR Jimmy Robinson for a first-quarter score did the major damage early. Robinson got just a step on cornerback Gerard Williams, but it was enough for him to snare Pisarcik's pass at the 19 and dive into the end zone.

The other key completion was a second-quarter pass off a flea flicker to James Thompson that covered 46 yards to the Washington four. Before that, the Redskins had climbed back into the game on two Mark Moseley field goals to cut the margin to 7-6. From midfield, Pisarcik handed off to running back Billy Taylor, who handed off to Robinson on an apparent reverse. But Robinson pitched back to Pisarcik, who found Thompson wide open. Two plays later, the quarterback rolled right and into the end zone from three yards out.

Either completion would have beaten an ineffective Redskins offense. Joe Theismann completed as many passes to Giants as Pisarcik did going 15 for 38 for 169 yards and three interceptions.

Oct 25
Kilmer Takes Most First-Team QB Work
Start seems likely but situation still is 'fluid'

10/29/78	REDSKINS (7-2) 38, 49ers (1-8) 20			53,706	
SF	7	6	0	7	20
Was	0	14	14	10	38
SF	Hofer 2 run (Wersching kick)				
SF	FG Wersching 29				
Was	Riggins 1 run (Moseley kick)				
Was	Buggs 50 pass from Kilmer (Moseley kick)				
SF	FG Wersching 35				
Was	McDaniel 17 pass from Kilmer (Moseley kick)				
Was	Riggins 1 run (Moseley kick)				
Was	Green 5 run (Moseley kick)				
SF	Boykin 2 run (Wersching kick)				
Was	FG Moseley 26				

RFK Stadium—Joe Theismann was benched in favor of 39-year-old Billy Kilmer after a 6-0 streak to start the season had come to a screeching halt with a two-game losing streak. After the lowly Niners took a 10-0 lead in the second quarter, chants of "We want Joe" began to arise from the crowd.

As has been the case for years, the Washington defense got the crowd roaring with approval. A John Riggins touchdown following a Ken Houston interception of Steve DeBerg pass soothed the masses and started a 35-3 Redskins run.

After Riggins' run, Washington took the lead on a 50-yard bomb from Kilmer to Danny Buggs. A Ray Wersching field goal before halftime made it 14-13 at intermission.

The Redskins quickly ended any doubt in the third quarter. First Kilmer threw a 17-yard touchdown pass to John McDaniel and then a drive ended in another one-yard touchdown blast for Riggins.

Kilmer's numbers weren't great—he finished 12 for 23 for 185 yards—but he was good enough.

Five 49er turnovers greatly aided the Redskins' cause. In addition to Houston's interception, Jake Scott got two picks and Washington recovered two San Francisco fumbles.

11/6/78	**COLTS (4-6) 21, Redskins (7-3) 17**			57,631
Was	3	7	7	0	17
Bal	0	7	7	7	21

Was	FG Moseley 44
Was	Thompson 31 pass from Kilmer (Moseley kick)
Bal	McCall 19 pass from Jones (Linhart kick)
Bal	Carr 78 pass from Jones (Linhart kick)
Was	Riggins 1 run (Moseley kick)
Bal	Carr 27 pass from Jones (Linhart kick)

Memorial Stadium—Baltimore quarterback Bert Jones shook off the effects of an injured throwing shoulder to connect for three TD passes, including the game winner to Roger Carr with 3:08 left in the game.

Washington held a 10-0 lead in the second quarter on the strength of a 44-yard field goal by Mark Moseley in the first period and Ricky Thompson's 31-yard touchdown pass from Billy Kilmer. The Colts unleashed their firepower, moving to within three at the half and then taking the lead in the third quarter on Jones' 78-yard bomb to Carr. Cornerback Joe Lavender took a futile swipe at the ball as Carr gathered it in near midfield and the receiver raced unchallenged into the end zone.

Joe Theismann replaced the ineffective Kilmer at quarterback and took the team 73 yards in six plays to John Riggins' one-yard touchdown plunge, giving Washington a 17-14 lead with 1:27 left in the third quarter. They survived two Colts field goal attempts in the final period—a 48-yarder blocked by Ron McDole and a 30-yard try that sailed wide right—before Jones and Carr got the game winner.

A final drive into Baltimore territory ended when Theismann threw three straight incompletions from the Colt 39 and then fumbled on the fourth down play.

Nov 8

Theismann Back in the Saddle
QB will start, Kilmer to bench

11/12/78	**REDSKINS (8-3) 16, Giants (5-6) 13 (OT)**				53,271
NYG	0	3	3	7	0	13
Was	0	3	3	7	3	16

NYG	FG Danelo 32
Was	FG Moseley 47
Was	FG Moseley 33
NYG	FG Danelo 29
NYG	Archer 20 fumble return (Danelo kick)
Was	Thomas 1 run (Moseley kick)
Was	FG Moseley 45

RFK Stadium—After missing a 35-yard attempt that would have won the game earlier in overtime, Mark Moseley made good on his second chance, hitting a 45-yard field goal to end the game.

Moseley and his New York counterpart Joe Danelo provided all of the scoring through the first three quarters of play, exchanging field goals in the second and third periods. The Giants

got the game's first touchdown on defense in the fourth quarter when George Martin sacked and stripped Joe Theismann. Tackle Troy Archer was the beneficiary of Martin's heroics as he scooped the ball up and rumbled 20 yards for the go-ahead touchdown.

With time winding down later in the fourth quarter, the home team moved 53 yards in seven plays to Mike Thomas' one-yard scoring run to knot the score at 13 with 1:05 left. Early in the overtime period, a 20-yard run by Theismann set Moseley up for his potential game-winner, but it was wide right.

Pass completions to Thomas and John McDaniel helped the Skins move back into Moseley's range and this time the kick split the uprights to end the game.

The Redskins won, though they got just 99 yards on the ground. John Riggins found particularly tough going against the New York defense, gaining 29 yards on 12 carries.

11/19/78	**Cardinals (4-8) 27, REDSKINS (8-4) 17**				52,460
StL	14	10	3	0	27
Was	0	10	7	0	17

StL	Harrell 70 punt return (Bakken kick)
StL	Stief 21 pass from Hart (Bakken kick)
StL	Chandler 4 pass from Hart (Bakken kick)
StL	FG Bakken 32
Was	Thomas 13 pass from Theismann (Moseley kick)
Was	FG Moseley 50
Was	McDaniel 43 pass from Theismann (Moseley kick)
StL	FG Bakken 27

RFK Stadium—The Cardinals ran up a 24-0 lead in the first 20 minutes of the game and coasted to the win.

Willard Harrell got the Cardinals started with a 70-yard punt return up the middle for their first touchdown. Later in the first quarter, St. Louis caught a break when Jim Hart's pass bounced off the hands of Mel Gray and into those of the Cards' Dave Stief for a 14-0 Cardinal lead.

The Cardinals expanded their lead in the second quarter when they drove 58 yards to another Hart touchdown pass, this one four yards to Al Chandler. Joe Theismann then threw an interception that the Cards turned into a 32-yard Jim Bakken field goal and their 24-0 margin.

Theismann touchdown passes to Mike Thomas and John McDaniel with a Mark Moseley field goal sandwiched in between actually got the Redskins back into it, as they trailed by just seven with more than 25 minutes left to play.

The Washington offense, though, couldn't generate anything more. On the day, St. Louis sacked Theismann nine times and the team rushed for a mere 18 yards. Jim Bakken's 27-yard field goal late in the third quarter wrapped it up for St. Louis.

11/23/78	**COWBOYS (9-4) 37, Redskins (8-5) 10**				64,905
Was	0	0	3	7	10
Dal	13	7	10	7	37

Dal	FG Septien 33
Dal	FG Septien 21
Dal	Laidlaw 1 run (Septien kick)
Dal	D. Pearson 57 pass from Staubach (Septien kick)
Was	FG Moseley 48
Dal	FG Septien 44
Dal	Laidlaw 2 run (Septien kick)
Dal	Brinson 39 run (Septien kick)
Was	Fugett 16 pass from Theismann (Moseley kick)

Texas Stadium—It was supposed to be a Thanksgiving showdown, but the Redskins played the role of the turkey with its neck on the chopping block.

Dallas was ahead 20-0 before the Redskins got their initial first down of the game. For the game, Dallas outgained Washington 507-201.

As noted, it got ugly early. Dallas' first two possessions were smooth marches to Rafael Septien field goals. Then, on

Washington's fourth play from scrimmage, John Riggins fumbled. Benny Barnes recovered for Dallas and raced from the Washington 15 to the six. Scott Laidlaw plunged over from a yard out soon after that and it was 13-0.

The Cowboys failed to score on a possession for the first time when Septien missed a 38-yard field goal early in the second quarter, but they soon made up for that. Roger Staubach opened his team's next offensive series with a 53-yard touchdown strike to Drew Pearson to make it 20-0.

All that was left after that was to finish the turkey and get it on the table. The Redskins were already cooked.

Washington did tally a couple of cosmetic scores in the second half. Mark Moseley booted a 48-yard field goal to get the Redskins on the board in the third quarter. In the fourth, after Dallas had piled the score up to 37-3, Joe Theismann threw a 16-yard touchdown pass to Jean Fugett.

12/3/78	Dolphins (9-5) 16, REDSKINS (8-6) 0				52,860
Mia	0	6	10	0	16
Was	0	0	0	0	0
Mia	FG Yepremian 34				
Mia	FG Yepremian 35				
Mia	Cefalo 40 pass from Griese (Yepremian kick)				
Mia	FG Yepremian 40				

RFK Stadium—"It's the same old story," said John Riggins after this one. Nobody chimed in to disagree as turnovers, penalties and various other misfortunes again combined to do in the Redskins. The Redskins generated 300 yards of offense but failed to score.

A Joe Theismann pass bounced out of Riggins' arms midway through the second quarter and into the grasp of linebacker Rusty Chambers, who returned his interception 29 yards. That set up Miami's first score, a 34-yard field goal by Garo Yepremian. Another three-pointer by Yepremian in the first half's final minute gave the visitors a 6-0 margin.

The lead was looking precarious as the Dolphins started their initial second-half possession at their own four. They were soon out of the hole, however, and into the end zone as six plays into the drive Bob Griese threw a 40-yard scoring pass to receiver Jimmy Cefalo, who had beaten ex-Dolphin Jake Scott. Yepremian's 40-yard field goal near the end of the third quarter accounted for the final score.

The Redskins did threaten late in the game, but on a play from the Dolphins' seven Theismann's pass was again tipped in the air by his intended receiver—this time, Benny Malone—and was again picked off by a Dolphin, now safety Charlie Dabb.

12/10/78	FALCONS (9-6) 20, Redskins (8-7) 17				54,178
Was	0	10	0	7	17
Atl	7	3	7	3	20
Atl	Stanback 1 run (Mazzetti kick)				
Was	Riggins 1 run (Moseley kick)				
Was	FG Moseley 21				
Atl	FG Mazzetti 21				
Atl	Bean 1 run (Mazzetti kick)				
Was	Thomas 1 run (Moseley kick)				
Atl	FG Mazzetti 32				

Atlanta Fulton County Stadium—The Redskins apparently had blocked Tim Mazzetti's attempt at a 37-yard game-winning field goal with two seconds left to avert their fourth straight defeat and take the game into overtime. As befitted the way things had been going, however, Washington was offside on the play and Mazzetti got another chance. The former Philadelphia bartender didn't miss this one, nailing it from 32 yards to win the game for Atlanta.

Mark Moseley's 21-yard field goal gave the Redskins a 10-7 lead in the second quarter, but Mazzetti kicked one from the same distance to tie it up just before halftime. A blocked punt late in the third quarter gave the Falcons possession at the Washington one and Bubba Bean scored from there to push Atlanta into the lead.

The visitors drove to tie it in the fourth. Joe Theismann scrambled for 19 yards to convert a third and nine and Benny Malone ripped off a 31-yard run to help set up Mike Thomas' one-yard touchdown plunge with 6:58 left in the game. On the final Atlanta drive, quarterback Steve Bartkowski completed three passes for 25 yards to get his team in position for Mazzetti's heroics.

12/16/78	Bears (7-9) 14, REDSKINS 10 (8-8)				49,774
Chi	7	0	7	0	14
Was	0	3	0	7	10
Chi	Payton 44 run (Thomas kick)				
Was	FG Moseley 33				
Chi	Schubert 73 punt return (Thomas kick)				
Was	Fugett 17 pass from Kilmer (Moseley kick)				

RFK Stadium—The train wreck that was the conclusion of the Redskins' 1978 season ended with this fifth straight loss. After a 6-0 start and eight wins following 11 games, the Redskins fell to .500 and out of the playoff picture with the loss.

The Bears took a 7-0 lead in the first quarter on Walter Payton's 44-yard touchdown run. On the final play of the half, Mark Moseley pulled the Redskins within 7-3 at the break.

The Bears stretched their lead to 14-3 when Steve Schubert took Mike Bragg's punt at his own 27 and ran it back all the way— 73 yards for a touchdown. After that, Chicago was content to sit on its lead and see if the Redskins could mount a threat. The Bears threw just 10 passes all game.

Billy Kilmer came in and threw that many passes in less than a quarter of work as he relieved Joe Theismann. He completed eight of those 10—one to Jean Fugett that got his team to within 14-10—but that was it for the Redskins.

1979

Head Coach: Jack Pardee
Record: 10-6, Third in NFC East

Honors: Ken Houston All NFC, Pro Bowl;
Mark Moseley All NFC, Pro Bowl: Lamar Parrish All Pro, Pro Bowl

---

Jan 31

McDole Dances Into Retirement
Team did not make DE qualifying offer

May 3

Don Warren Redskins' Top Pick
Tight end taken in fourth round

Hanburger Cut

May 9—Chris Hanburger has made his last tackle for the Redskins.

Washington put the linebacker on waivers today, ending a 14-year career with the team. The move has been long expected as the team did not offer him a new contract last January.

Hanburger played in nine Pro Bowls and was a first-team All-Pro selection four times. He wasn't blessed with great size or speed but made his mark with great preparation and by playing with a high level of intensity.

Kilmer Wobbles Into the Sunset

May 15—The Redskins put Billy Kilmer on waivers today, ending an eight-year career in Washington highlighted by the team's first Super Bowl appearance.

Kilmer spent most of his career in a battle for the starting position—first with Sonny Jurgensen, and recently with Joe Theismann. Noted for his wobbling passes that weren't as pretty as the classic spirals that most NFL quarterback throw, Kilmer's were effective enough earn him two All-Pro selections.

Before George Allen traded for him, Kilmer played with the Saints and 49ers.

May 18

Mike Thomas Dealt to Charger
Ongoing contract disputes led to trade of RB for mid-round draft pick

---

Aug 2

Williams Buys Baltimore Orioles
Team president faces battle; NFL rules prohibit dual role

Aug 29

Riggins Goes AWOL
Wants remaining years of contract guaranteed

Aug 30

Riggins Says 'Fish Weren't Biting,' Returns
Team gives him no contract concession

9/2/79	Oilers (1-0) 29, REDSKINS (0-1) 27				54,262
Hou	6	0	7	16	29
Was	0	17	7	3	27
Hou	FG Fritsch 41				
Hou	FG Fritsch 46				
Was	FG Moseley 27				
Was	Fugett 8 pass from Theismann (Moseley kick)				
Was	Malone 1 run (Moseley kick)				
Hou	Campbell 13 run (Fritsch kick)				
Was	Fugett 30 pass from Theismann (Moseley kick)				
Was	FG Moseley 39				
Hou	Johnson 14 pass from Pastorini (kick failed)				
Hou	FG Fritsch 26				
Hou	Campbell 3 run (Fritsch kick)				

RFK Stadium—Earl Campbell scored on a three-yard run with just over two minutes to go, completing a 16-point Houston rally to push the Oilers past the Redskins.

The Redskins appeared to have taken firm control of this game in the second and third quarters. After Houston took a 6-0 lead on two Tony Fritsch field goals, Washington's defense and special teams sparked a 17-point second period. First, Buddy Hardeman's 52-yard punt returned and led to a 27-yard Mark Moseley field goal. On the next series, Ray Waddy picked off Dan Pastorini's pass and Joe Theismann threw a precise pass to Jean Fugett in the middle of the end zone to put the Redskins in the lead. Then Benny Malone scored on a one-yard run set up when Lamar Parish intercepted a tipped pass at the Houston 36.

After intermission, the teams traded third-quarter touchdowns. Moseley kicked a 39-yard field goal early in the fourth period to push his team's lead to 27-13. That's when Houston began its comeback. Pastorini found his stride, hitting Billy "White Shoes" Johnson, alone in the end zone, with a 14-yard pass. Fritsch missed the extra point, but atoned later when he kicked a 26-yard field goal to pull the Oilers within five points.

The Redskins then made the big blunder as John Riggins fumbled and Bill Currier recovered for the Oilers at the Washington 29. One play after converting a fourth and one with a stumbling five-yard burst, Campbell busted up the middle for nine yards and the go-ahead touchdown. Moseley attempted a 70-yard field goal on the game's final play, but the effort was well short.

9/9/79	Redskins (1-1) 27, LIONS (0-2) 24				54,991
Was	0	17	7	3	27
Det	3	0	0	21	24
Det	FG Ricardo 27				
Was	Thompson 8 pass from Theismann (Moseley kick)				
Was	FG Moseley 35				
Was	Malone 5 run (Moseley kick)				
Was	Fugett 4 pass from Theismann (Moseley kick)				
Det	Robinson 3 run (Ricardo kick)				
Det	Kane 12 run (Ricardo kick)				
Det	Scott 24 pass from Komlo (Ricardo kick)				
Was	FG Moseley 41				

Pontiac Silverdome—The Redskins were cruising with a 24-3 lead in the fourth quarter and a rookie was making his first start at quarterback for the Lions. But that rookie, Jeff Komlo, led the Lions all the way back—and Washington needed a second-chance field goal with eight seconds left to pull this one out.

Washington spotted the home team a 3-0 lead in the first quarter and then scored 24 unanswered points. Theismann's eight-yard TD pass to Ricky Thompson, Benny Malone's five-yard scoring run and, in between, a 35-yard Mark Moseley field goal gave the Redskins a 17-3 halftime lead. In the third quarter, Theismann gave his team a 21-point lead with a four-yard touchdown pass to Jean Fugett.

In the fourth quarter, Komlo got things started by driving his team 54 yards in 10 plays for one touchdown. Then the Silverdome crowd started stirring when John Riggins fumbled at the Detroit 13 and linebacker Charlie Weaver recovered for the Lions. Shortly after that, Rick Kane scooted around end for 12 yards and the touchdown that got the house rocking. With 2:13 left, Komlo hit Freddy Scott at the one and the receiver fell into the end zone to tie the score.

Despite the din in the domed stadium, Theismann patiently moved Washington into position for a field goal attempt. In ten plays, the Redskins moved 53 yards to the Detroit 29. Moseley missed a 46-yard attempt, but the Lions were flagged for having too many men on the field. His 41-yarder was true, and the Redskins escaped with the win.

9/17/79	**REDSKINS (2-1) 27, Giants (0-3) 0**			54,672	
NYG	0	0	0	0	0
Was	3	14	7	3	27
Was	FG Moseley 46				
Was	Lorch 31 interception return (Moseley kick)				
Was	Harmon 4 pass from Theismann (Moseley kick)				
Was	Theismann 7 run (Moseley kick)				
Was	FG Moseley 40				

RFK Stadium—The Redskins methodically built a 17-0 halftime lead and then kept the ball away from New York in the second half to beat the Giants easily.

The Giants' deepest penetration of the game was to the Washington 21. The Redskins defense harassed New York quarterback Joe Pisarcik all night, sacking him three times and intercepting him twice. Defensive tackle Karl Lorch had one of those picks, and he rumbled 31 yards for the game's first touchdown.

Holding a 17-0 halftime lead, the Redskins held the ball for nearly the entire third quarter. They took 16 plays to move 78 yards, scoring a touchdown on a seven-yard Joe Theismann scramble after an eight-minute drive. Starting early in the fourth quarter, Washington ground up much of the rest of the game clock with a drive that lasted 7:55. The result was Mark Moseley's 40-yard field goal to wrap up the scoring.

9/23/79	**Redskins (3-1) 17, CARDINALS (1-3) 7**			50,680	
Was	14	0	0	3	17
StL	0	0	7	0	7
Was	Hover rumble recovery in end zone (Moseley kick)				
Was	Hardeman 41 pass from Theismann (Moseley kick)				
StL	Brown 1 run (Little kick)				
Was	FG Moseley 47				

Busch Stadium—The Redskins scored two quick touchdowns in the first period and held off the Cardinals to take the win.

On the game's second play, Redskins linebacker Rich Milot knocked the ball loose from St. Louis running back Otis Anderson at the St. Louis 18. A mad scramble ensued, knocking the ball back into the end zone where Washington's Don Hover fell on it for a quick 7-0 lead.

Later in the first quarter, Buddy Hardeman caught Joe Theismann's pass at the Cardinal 30 and dashed the rest of the way to complete a 41-yard touchdown play that extended the Washington lead to 14-0.

After losing two first-quarter fumbles in addition to the one that resulted in Hover's touchdown, St. Louis settled down and got back into the game when Theotis Brown scored on a one-yard run in the third quarter. Mark Moseley's 47-yard field goal with 13:01 left in the game provided the final margin.

St. Louis did threaten by driving to the Washington two, but Lamar Parrish intercepted Jim Hart's pass to end the threat.

The turnovers handed Washington the win despite the fact that they were outgained by the Cards 376 yards to 191.

9/30/79	**Redskins (4-1) 16, FALCONS (2-3) 7**			56,810	
Was	3	10	3	0	16
Atl	7	0	0	0	7
Was	FG Moseley 45				
Atl	Andrews 1 run (Mazzetti kick)				
Was	FG Moseley 53				
Was	Riggins 1 run (Moseley kick)				
Was	FG Moseley 37				

Atlanta Fulton County Stadium—Mark Moseley kicked three field goals and the Washington defense stymied Atlanta quarterback Steve Bartkowski to pace the win over the Falcons.

Bartkowski entered the game as the NFC's leading passer, but the Redskins held him to 105 yards in the air on six of 26 passing, sacking him three times and intercepting three of his passes. The Falcons took a 7-3 lead on an 85-yard second quarter drive, but were shut down after that.

The Redskins dominated the rest of the way, with the final score being as close as it was due to some squandered scoring opportunities. In the second quarter, after the Redskins had taken a 13-7 lead, Ray Easterling tipped Joe Theismann's pass from the Atlanta five and Frank Reed intercepted in the end zone.

In the second half, they squandered a great chance to put the Falcons away. Joe Lavender intercepted Bartkowski and returned the ball 16 yards to the Atlanta 30. Aided by penalties, the Redskins gained a first down at the four. From there, however, three tries by Benny Malone and one by John Riggins failed to advance the ball and the Falcons took over on downs.

It didn't matter—the Atlanta offense was completely inept in the second half, gaining a total of just 29 yards.

10/7/79	**EAGLES (5-1) 28, Redskins (4-2) 17**			69,142	
Was	0	7	0	10	17
Phi	7	7	14	0	28
Phi	Montgomery 8 run (Franklin kick)				
Phi	Montgomery 11 pass from Jaworski (Franklin kick)				
Was	Riggins 4 pass from Theismann (Moseley kick)				
Phi	Montgomery 5 run (Franklin kick)				
Phi	Montgomery 4 run (Franklin kick)				
Was	FG Moseley 37				
Was	Riggins 1 run (Moseley kick)				

Veterans Stadium—For the second time in two seasons, Wilbert Montgomery scored four touchdowns against the Redskins. The first two gave the Eagles a 14-0 lead early in the second quarter and the second two put the game away in the third period.

The Eagles took to the air to set up Montgomery's first TD as Ron Jaworski flipped a short pass to tight end Keith Krepele, who got up a head of steam, dispatched safety Mark Murphy with a stiff arm and rumbled down to the Washington eight for a gain of 45 yards. Montgomery ran it over from there for a 7-0 Eagle lead. In the second quarter, Philly took a 14-0 lead with a nine-play, 82-yard drive that ended with Jaworski throwing an 11-yard touchdown pass to Montgomery.

The visitors battled back before halftime, slicing their deficit in half with a ball-control drive that featured short, quick passes by Joe Theismann. The march covered 74 yards in 14 plays and the final short pass was to John Riggins for four yards and a touchdown.

After intermission, the Redskins went back to work and were driving towards Eagle territory when Theismann's pass bounced off of tight end Jean Fugett and into the arms of safety Brenard Wilson. From the Washington 40, Jaworski hit Harold Carmichael on a post pattern down to the five, and Montgomery took it over the goal line on the next play.

Later in the third, the Eagles' game-long domination of the line of scrimmage was in full view as Montgomery and fullback Leroy Harris found huge holes and covered most of the 77 yards to the clinching touchdown. It was Montgomery, of course, who capped the drive with a four-yard run.

10/14/79	Redskins (5-2) 13, BROWNS (4-3) 9			63,323	
Was	0	3	3	7	13
Cle	0	6	3	0	9
Was	FG Moseley 35				
Cle	Hill 1 run (kick blocked)				
Was	FG Moseley 17				
Cle	FG Cockroft 37				
Was	Harmon 15 pass from Theismann (Moseley kick)				

Cleveland Stadium—Joe Theismann threw a 15-yard touchdown pass to Clarence Harmon in the last minute of the game to rally the Redskins past the Browns.

Cleveland took a 6-3 lead in the second quarter on Calvin Hill's one-yard touchdown. The extra point was blocked, so the Redskins were able to tie it up on Mark Moseley's second field goal of the game—a 17-yarder in the third quarter.

The Browns reclaimed the lead just seconds from the end of the third with Don Cockroft's 37-yard field goal. Cleveland regained possession with about ten and a half minutes left and moved in for the kill in classic fashion. They chewed up nearly eight and a half minutes of clock in moving from their 20 to the Washington 15. Cockroft got plenty of leg into a 33-yard field goal attempt, but it missed and the Redskins still trailed by just three.

From the Washington 20 on the next play, Joe Theismann combined with Danny Buggs for a 34-yard pass play to spark the game-winning drive. That drive ended with Theismann throwing to running back Clarence Harmon for the winning touchdown with 27 seconds left.

10/21/79	REDSKINS (6-2) 17, Eagles (6-2) 7			54,432	
Phi	0	0	0	7	7
Was	0	7	7	3	17
Was	Malone 6 run (Moseley kick)				
Was	Theismann 1 run (Moseley kick)				
Was	FG Moseley 46				
Phi	Kreple 40 pass from Jaworski (Franklin kick)				

RFK Stadium—"If you stop number 31, you stop the Eagles," said Diron Talbert, referring to Philadelphia running back Wilbert Montgomery. The Redskins accomplished that goal and beat the Eagles.

Two weeks earlier, Montgomery had scored four touchdowns and gained 127 yards against the Redskins, and coach Jack Pardee and staff wanted to ensure there would be no repeat performance. Pardee used nearly his entire defensive roster, shuttling in players for situational matchups.

The chess game paid off. Not only was Montgomery held to 33 yards and kept out of the end zone, but the Redskins also sacked Eagles QB Ron Jaworski seven times.

Benny Malone got the first score of the game as he capped a drive with a six-yard touchdown run. The Redskins extended their lead in the third quarter with Joe Theismann's one-yard TD run and, finally, got a 46-yard Mark Moseley field goal to give the home team a 17-0 lead. Philly did manage a face-saving score on Jaworski's 40-yard touchdown pass to Keith Kreple with just over four minutes left.

Washington's John Riggins ran for 120 yards on 19 carries, including a 33-yard dash in the fourth quarter that iced the game.

10/28/79	Saints (5-4) 14, REDSKINS (6-3) 10			52,133	
NO	7	7	0	0	14
Was	3	7	0	0	10
NO	Chandler 45 pass from Manning (Yepremian kick)				
Was	FG Moseley 18				
NO	Galbreath 2 run (Yepremian kick)				
Was	Theismann 1 run (Moseley kick)				

RFK Stadium—The last of the Saints' seven sacks of Joe Theismann on the day slammed the door on the Redskins' chances at victory as New Orleans held on to win.

All of the scoring came in the first half. In the opening quarter, Wes Chandler ran a simple down-and-out pattern, beating Ray Waddy, and Archie Manning's pass was on the money for a 45-yard touchdown and a 7-0 Saints lead.

Rich Mauti fumbled a punt, giving the Redskins a first and goal at the nine. As would become the pattern on the day, the Redskins were unable to take full advantage, being forced to settle for an 18-yard Mark Moseley field goal. The teams traded second-quarter touchdowns and the Saints had a 14-10 halftime lead.

In the second half, the Redskins' failure to seize chances to score became more acute and, ultimately, fatal. Scott Galbreath fumbled and Perry Brooks recovered at the Washington 45. In eight plays, they moved to a first and goal at the six, but couldn't score. On the day, the Redskins took 15 snaps in goal to go situations and got only the Moseley field goal.

The last such situation came in the fourth quarter after the Redskins blocked Garo Yepremian's 45-yard field goal attempt. Theismann moved the team from its own 35 to the New Orleans two. From there, the Redskins moved backwards on a horrific series of penalties and other miscues. On fourth down, with less than a minute on the clock, Saints defensive end Elois Grooms slammed Joe Theismann to the turf to put a merciful end to the Redskins chances.

11/4/79	STEELERS (8-2) 38, Redskins (6-4) 7			49,452	
Was	0	7	0	0	7
Pit	7	17	7	7	38
Pit	Stallworth 11 pass from Bradshaw (Bahr kick)				
Was	Riggins 4 run (Moseley kick)				
Pit	Bahr FG 21				
Pit	Cunningham 16 pass from Bradshaw (Bahr kick)				
Pit	Grossman 4 pass from Bradshaw (Bahr kick)				
Pit	Stallworth 65 pass from Bradshaw (Bahr kick)				
Pit	Moser 2 run (Bahr kick)				

Three Rivers Stadium—The Steelers stormed to a 24-7 halftime lead and never looked back in pounding the Redskins.

Washington did manage to tie the game at seven on John Riggins' four-yard touchdown run in the second quarter, but it was all Steelers after that. After a Matt Bahr field goal, Terry Bradshaw threw a 16-yard touchdown pass to tight end Bennie Cunningham. Then cornerback Mel Blount recovered a fumble to set up another Bradshaw scoring toss to a tight end, this one to Randy Grossman.

In a little over a half of work, Terry Bradshaw threw for 311 yards and four touchdowns. He left the game after his 65-yard TD bomb to John Stallworth with just over a minute elapsed in the third quarter to put Pittsburgh up 31-7. Steeler coach Chuck Noll mercifully emptied the bench after that.

The stats did not lie today. The Steelers piled up 545 yards of offense. They more than doubled the Redskins' output in both passing (372 yards to 149) and rushing (173-88)

11/11/79	REDSKINS (7-4) 30, Cardinals (3-8) 28			50,868	
StL	7	0	0	21	28
Was	7	10	3	10	30
Was	Riggins 7 run (Moseley kick)				
StL	Brown 1 run (Little kick)				
Was	FG Moseley 46				

Was	Thompson 8 pass from Theismann (Moseley kick)
Was	FG Moseley 29
Was	Riggins 4 pass from Theismann (Moseley kick)
StL	Morris 2 run (Little kick)
StL	Brown 1 run (Little kick)
StL	Anderson 21 pass from Hart (Little kick)
Was	FG Moseley 39

RFK Stadium—The Redskins were cruising with a 27-7 fourth quarter lead over the Cardinals, but needed a last-minute field goal by Mark Moseley to claim the win.

St. Louis quarterback Jim Hart had been ineffective for the first three quarters of play, throwing three interceptions. Washington built its lead on the strength of two John Riggins touchdown runs, an eight-yard touchdown pass from Joe Theismann to Ricky Thompson, and a pair of Moseley field goals.

In the fourth, Hart started beating the Redskins, leading touchdown drives of 71, 55 and 56 yards. The last culminated in a 21-yard TD pass from Hart to running back Ottis Anderson, giving the Cards a 28-27 lead with 1:55 left in the game.

Theismann calmly got the dormant Washington offense back to life. A 35-yard completion to running back Clarence Harmon got the bulk of the yardage in the drive to get Moseley into position to win the game. He did just that, nailing his 39-yarder with 36 seconds left for a 30-28 win.

Nov 12

Pardee Promises Win
Declares that Redskins 'are going to beat' Dallas

11/18/79	REDSKINS (8-4) 34, Cowboys (8-4) 20				55,031
Dal	0	3	3	14	20
Was	7	7	10	10	34

Was	McDaniel 4 pass from Theismann (Moseley kick)
Dal	FG Septien 34
Was	Riggins 3 run (Moseley kick)
Dal	FG Septien 37
Was	Harmon 10 pass from Theismann (Moseley kick)
Was	FG Moseley 46
Dal	D. Pearson 19 pass from Staubach (Septien kick)
Was	Thompson 11 pass from Theismann (Moseley kick)
Dal	D. Pearson 9 pass from White (Septien kick)
Was	FG Moseley 45

RFK Stadium—Joe Theismann threw three touchdown passes and the Redskins took advantage of numerous Dallas mistakes to beat the Cowboys 34-20.

Late in the second quarter, the Cowboys were threatening to cut into the Redskins' 14-3 lead with possession at the Redskin three. On third and goal, however, blitzing safety Ken Houston sacked Roger Staubach, forcing a fumble that Coy Bacon recovered to end the drive.

Washington extended its lead to 24-6 in the third quarter, but Dallas kept coming, scoring on a 19-yard pass from Staubach to Drew Pearson just over two minutes into the final quarter. The Redskins punted the ball back to Dallas, but linebacker Brad Dusek intercepted a Staubach pass at the Washington 39. That Washington possession ended with Joe Theismann throwing an 11-yard TD pass to Ricky Thompson to clinch the win.

And the scoring was not over. The Redskins felt that the Cowboys had run up the score in defeating them in Dallas the year before so, with nine seconds left, Mark Moseley was called in to kick a 45-yard field goal. "They gave us no excuses last year after what they did to us," Moseley said, "and I'm not going to make any excuses for kicking that field goal."

Nov 18

Williams to Hand Control to Cooke
Dual-ownership prohibition forces Williams, Orioles owner, to cede to majority owner Cooke

11/25/79	GIANTS (6-7) 14, Redskins (8-5) 6				72,641
Was	0	3	3	0	6
NYG	7	0	0	7	14

NYG	Kotar 1 run (Danelo kick)
Was	FG Moseley 21
Was	FG Moseley 41
NYG	Taylor 1 run (Danelo kick)

Giants Stadium—For the fourth straight year, the Redskins laid an egg in the Meadowlands. The Giants rushed for 193 yards, including 126 by Billy Taylor, to grind up the Redskins and get the win.

"I thought today was the day" to finally get a win in Giants Stadium, said center Bob Kuziel. "No such luck."

Actually, luck had little to do with it. New York scored a touchdown on a one-yard run by Doug Kotar and then proceeded to stuff the Washington offense for much of the game. The visitors did manage second- and third-quarter field goals by Mark Moseley to pull within a point, but the Giants had the answer in Taylor.

In New York's game-clinching drive in the fourth quarter, Taylor carried 13 times, gaining 75 of the 79 yards the march covered. He capped it with a one-yard TD run with 8:19 to play. The Redskins did mount one scoring threat after that, but Moseley's 46-yard field goal attempt smacked off the right upright.

The loss was not only costly to the Redskins in the standings—they fell out of a three-way tie for first place—but on the field as well as Ken Houston was sidelined for the rest of the season with a broken right arm.

Nov 26

Houston Wants to Come Back
Out for year with broken arm, safety says he will play in '80 'if they want me'

12/2/79	REDSKINS (9-5) 38, Packers (4-10) 21				51,682
GB	0	21	0	0	21
Was	7	0	7	24	38

Was	Thompson 20 pass from Theismann (Moseley kick)
GB	Tullis 52 pass from Dickey (Birney kick)
GB	Simpson 2 run (Birney kick)
GB	A. Thompson 43 pass from Dickey (Birney kick)
Was	Buggs 8 pass from Theismann (Moseley kick)
Was	McDaniel 39 pass from Theismann (Moseley kick)
Was	Riggins 12 pass from Theismann (Moseley kick)
Was	FG Moseley 33
Was	Forte 20 run (Moseley kick)

RFK Stadium—The Redskins scored 31 unanswered second-half points to erase a 21-7 halftime deficit and beat the Packers 38-21.

Green Bay quarterback Lynn Dickey showed no sign of rust after returning to the lineup for the first time after spending two years on the shelf with a broken leg. After Washington took a 7-0 lead, Dickey led his team to three straight touchdowns. He passed for two of them from long range, going 52 yards to Walter Tullis and 43 to Aundra Thompson. In between, Nate Simpson scored on a one-yard run.

Joe Theismann found his stride after halftime as Dickey began to lose his. The Washington quarterback threw for three TD's during the second half, giving him four for the game. The comeback started with Theismann going to Danny Buggs for an eight-yard touchdown to cut the Green Bay lead to 21-14. On the first play of the fourth quarter, Theismann threw to receiver John McDaniel, who made a leaping catch along the sideline, cut back and bulled between two Green Bay defenders at the goal line to tie the game at 21.

On the Packers' subsequent possession, Monte Coleman intercepted a Lynn Dickey pass and returned it to the Packer 35. Three plays later, Theismann hit John Riggins at the seven. Riggo broke one tackle and outran two Packers into the end zone for the go-ahead score.

12/9/79	**REDSKINS (10-5) 28, Bengals (3-12) 14**				52,882
Cin	14	0	0	0	14
Was	7	14	0	7	28
Cin	A. Griffin 52 pass from Anderson (Bahr kick)				
Was	Riggins 7 run (Moseley kick)				
Cin	Johnson 1 run (Bahr kick)				
Was	Harmon 7 pass from Theismann (Moseley kick)				
Was	Harmon 23 pass from Theismann (Moseley kick)				
Was	Riggins 2 run (Moseley kick)				

RFK Stadium—Former Bengal Coy Bacon sacked Cincinnati quarterback Ken Anderson four times as the Redskins pulled away and beat the Bengals 28-14.

Cincinnati broke on top on their first possession with a 52-yard touchdown pass from Anderson to Archie Griffin. Washington responded with a seven-yard John Riggins run. The visitors had an immediate answer: a 71-yard drive to a one-yard touchdown plunge by fullback Pete Johnson.

After that, though, the Redskins took control thanks to the combination of quarterback Joe Theismann and running back Clarence Harmon. In the second quarter, the pair connected for a seven-yard touchdown to tie the game at 14. Then, as halftime approached, Theismann escaped a heavy rush and got a pass off to Harmon. The back caught it, fought off four would-be tacklers and made his way into the end zone to give his team the lead for good at 21-14 with 42 seconds left in the half.

The defense, led by Bacon, shut the Bengals down for the final three quarters of play. Cincinnati's best shot at a score came midway through the fourth quarter when they drove to the Washington 10. But neither a third and one nor a fourth and one play gained as much as an inch, and the Redskins took over on downs.

12/16/79	**COWBOYS (11-5) 35, Redskins (10-6) 34**				62,867
Was	10	7	0	17	34
Dal	0	14	7	14	38
Was	FG Moseley 24				
Was	Theismann 1 run (Moseley kick)				
Was	Malone 55 pass from Theismann (Moseley kick)				
Dal	Springs 1 run (Septien kick)				
Dal	P. Pearson 26 pass from Staubach (Septien kick)				
Dal	Newhouse 2 run (Septien kick)				
Was	FG Moseley 24				
Was	Riggins 1 run (Moseley kick)				
Was	Riggins 66 run (Moseley kick)				
Dal	Springs 26 pass from Staubach (Septien kick)				
Dal	Hill 7 pass from Staubach (Septien kick)				

Texas Stadium—In their history, the Redskins and their fans have never seen a day quite like Sunday, December 16, 1979. It was a roller coaster ride that will never be forgotten.

Up—The Redskins woke up that morning with a very sunny playoff picture. They were in a three-way tie for the division lead with Dallas and Philadelphia. A win would give them the division title. The Cowboys would play without stars Tony Dorsett and Jethro Pugh, both out with injuries.

Even a loss was unlikely to keep the Redskins out of the postseason. The Bears would have to beat the St. Louis Cardinals by more than 33 points to make up the point differential between the two teams. That was the tiebreaker that would come into play if they both finished 10-6. The Bears hadn't scored more than 28

points in a game all season, so making up 34 points seemed unlikely.

Down—It was unlikely, but the Bears did it, beating the Cardinals 42-6. Their safety net was gone as the Redskins came into Texas Stadium.

Up—The Redskins were opportunistic, recovering three Dallas fumbles to help them take a 17-0 lead early in the second quarter. Two of the fumbles set up a Mark Moseley field goal and a one-yard Joe Theismann touchdown run. Add in a 55-yard pass from Theismann to Benny Malone and the Redskins were flying.

Down—The Redskins led 17-7 with time winding down in the first half, but the Cowboys were driving. Following a holding call, Dallas faced third and 20 at the Washington 26 with 15 seconds left in the half. Roger Staubach found Preston Pearson in the end zone and it was 17-14 at the half. Dallas took the lead early in the third quarter on a one-yard Robert Newhouse run. That finished the 21-0 Dallas run and it was the Redskins' turn.

Up—Early in the fourth quarter, gambling on third and inches at the Cowboys seven, Theismann faked into the line and Clarence Harmon was wide open, but the pass was just beyond Harmon's reach and the Redskins had to settle for a Moseley field goal. Despite the missed opportunity, momentum had clearly swung back to the Redskins. Mark Murphy intercepted a Staubach pass, returning it to the Dallas 25. Two plays later, John Riggins scored from the one and the Redskins were back in the lead, 27-21.

Following a Dallas punt, Washington appeared to put the game away. On second down from the Washington 34, Riggins started up the middle on a draw, but the defense had the middle clogged. He found blocks by George Starke and Ron Saul to the right and took off that way. The running back, building up a full head of steam, brushed off an attempted arm tackle by Cliff Harris and broke into the clear. Safety Dennis Thurman dove for Riggins' ankles at the seven, but he just stumbled a bit as he completed the 66-yard run. Moseley's extra point put Washington up 34-21 with 6:34 to play. Joe Jones sacked Staubach on Dallas' next possession, forcing a punt, and the Redskins had the ball with 5:21 left at the Dallas 40. One first down was all they needed.

Down—The final plunge downward began when Harmon fumbled on third down at the Dallas 42 and Randy White recovered. That set up a 26-yard TD pass to Ron Springs with 2:20 left. Still clinging to the six-point margin, the Redskins again attempted to get that one first down that would give them the division title. But Dallas defensive tackle Larry Cole anticipated the third and two play at the two-minute warning and knifed through the middle of the line to drop Riggins for a two-yard loss.

After the punt, Staubach completed a pass to Drew Hill for 20 yards. Two plays later, for a fleeting second, it seemed that Dallas would be facing fourth as long as tackle Perry Brooks had a bead on Staubach in the backfield. They didn't call him Roger the Dodger for nothing, though, and he ducked under Brooks, righted himself and fired to Pearson for 22 yards to the Washington 33.

The play clearly deflated the defense. On the next one, it was Pearson on the receiving end again for 25. Two plays later, with 42 seconds left, Staubach delivered the killing blow—he took a short drop and lofted the ball to Hill, who had beaten Lamar Parish. The receiver tucked the ball in and Rafael Septien's extra point gave Dallas the 35-34 lead.

The Redskins tried to top Dallas' miracle, but couldn't get the officials' attention to call time-out following a completion to the Dallas 42 and the clock ran out on their season. It would have been a 59-yard field goal attempt but, the way the day had gone, anything seemed possible.

1980
Head Coach: Jack Pardee
Record: 6-10, Third in NFC East

Honors: Mike Nelms Pro Bowl; Lamar Parrish, All-NFL, Pro Bowl

---

Apr 29
Redskins Invest in Art
Take Syracuse receiver Monk in first round

July 19
Is Jack Kent Cooke Now In Charge?
New press guide indicates that Williams must step aside due to baseball conflict

---

July 30
Riggins Wants New Contract
RB may sit out season, team calls demands unacceptable

Aug 21
Redskins Trade for Wilbur Jackson
Deal for 49ers RB signals that team expects to be without Riggins

---

Aug 31
Riggins Put on 'Retired' List
Holdout RB is in Kansas, taking an economics class

9/8/80	Cowboys (1-0) 17, REDSKINS (0-1) 3				55,045
Dal	7	3	0	7	**17**
Was	0	0	0	3	**3**
Dal	Dorsett 6 run (Septien kick)				
Dal	FG Septien 19				
Was	FG Moseley 45				
Dal	Springs 4 run (Septien kick)				

RFK Stadium—This was a Monday night season-opening special, a rematch of the two teams that had staged one of the most compelling battles of the 1979 season, Dallas' miracle 35-34 win the last day of the season. That game had elevated Dallas to the division title and pushed the Redskins out of the playoffs.

In reality, it wasn't a rematch. Roger Staubach, the Dallas quarterback who engineered the rally in Texas Stadium, had retired during the offseason and Danny White had taken his spot as the Cowboys' starting quarterback. Also missing from the lineup was John Riggins, whose 66-yard run had given the Redskins a seemingly insurmountable 13-point fourth-quarter lead. Riggins was in a contract dispute and his return was uncertain. *(Note: Riggins ended up holding out the entire season)*

Of the two, it's apparent that Riggins was missed by his team more than Staubach was by his. Washington mustered just 58 yards on the ground without their leading rusher from 1979 (1,153 yards). Dallas rushed for 177 yards, 66 by Tony Dorsett.

Despite a dismal first half, the Redskins got some life when Ike Forte returned the second-half kickoff 53 yards to the Dallas 45. However, the drive stalled at the Dallas 12, Mark Moseley missed a 29-yard field goal, and the Redskins never seriously threatened after that.

9/13/80	Redskins (1-1) 23, GIANTS (1-1) 21				73,343
Was	6	14	0	3	**23**
NYG	0	14	0	7	**21**
Was	Harmon 20 pass from Theismann (kick failed)				
NYG	Hogan 1 run (Danelo kick)				
Was	Theismann 37 run (Moseley kick)				
NYG	Garrett 32 pass from Simms (Danelo kick)				
Was	Jackson 2 run (Moseley kick)				
NYG	Mullady 20 pass from Simms (Danelo kick)				
Was	FG Moseley 45				

Giants Stadium—Mark Moseley kicked a 45-yard field goal to give the Redskins the lead with 1:55 left in the game, and Lamar Parrish intercepted a Phil Simms pass to seal the win.

Early in the fourth quarter, it didn't appear the Redskins were going to need any last-minute heroics to win this one. They had a six-point lead with the ball deep in Giants territory. Running back Rickey Claitt, however, fumbled at the New York three when Harry Carson hit him hard. Terry Jackson picked it up and returned it to the New York 14. The Giants moved down the field quickly and scored on a 20-yard pass from Simms to tight end Tom Mullady. Joe Danelo's extra point gave New York a 21-20 lead with 5:40 left.

From their own 20, the Redskins answered. After runs by Claitt and Clarence Harmon, Joe Theismann found receivers John McDaniel and Art Monk for a total of 33 yards. Faced with a fourth and inches situation at the Giants 28 at the two-minute warning, coach Jack Pardee didn't hesitate in bringing Moseley despite the fact that the kicker had already had an extra point blocked and was just one of four on field goal attempts for the year. There was never a doubt about the kick once it left Moseley's toe, and the last-gasp Giants rally was shut off by Parrish's interception.

9/21/80	RAIDERS (2-1) 24, Redskins (1-2) 21				45,163
Was	0	7	7	7	**21**
Oak	3	7	7	7	**24**
Oak	FG Bahr 21				
Oak	Casper 20 pass from Pastorini (Bahr kick)				
Was	Walker 15 pass from Theismann (Moseley kick)				
Oak	Whittingham 42 run (Bahr kick)				
Was	Theismann 4 run (Moseley kick)				
Oak	Chandler 5 pass from Pastorini (Bahr kick)				
Was	Thompson 3 pass from Theismann (Moseley kick)				

Oakland-Alameda County Coliseum—The Redskins intercepted three Dan Pastorini passes to stay in the game, but they played catch-up all day and never could overcome an early 10-0 deficit.

The early Raider lead was built on a 21-yard field goal by Matt Bahr and a 20-yard touchdown pass from Pastorini to tight end Dave Casper.

Washington's offense came to life late in the first half. Joe Theismann scrambled 13 yards for a first down, keeping alive a drive that culminated in Theismann's 15-yard touchdown pass to tight end Rick Walker to make it 10-7 at the half.

After halftime, the Raiders responded as Arthur Whittingham swept around the right side and scooted all the way for a 42-yard touchdown to regain a 10-point lead for Oakland. Before the quarter was out, Tony Peters intercepted a Pastorini pass. That led to a four-yard touchdown run by Theismann and it was a three-point game going into the fourth quarter.

Oakland coach Tom Flores was thinking of yanking Pastorini, but decided to give him one more shot. He responded well by directing a 90-yard, 14-play touchdown drive to clinch it for Oakland. Kenny King got the biggest chunk of it with a 30-yard run before Pastorini finished it off with a five-yard touchdown pass to Bob Chandler with 9:45 to go. Washington responded with a four-yard touchdown pass from Theismann to Ricky Thompson, but the home team was able to hang on for the win.

9/28/80	Seahawks (2-2) 14, REDSKINS (1-3) 0				53,263
Sea	0	7	0	7	14
Was	0	0	0	0	0
Sea	Zorn 21 run (Hererra kick)				
Sea	Doornick 8 run (Hererra kick)				

RFK Stadium—The Seahawks took to the ground to control the game against Washington. Seattle outrushed the Redskins 235-78 to take this snoozer.

Not only were the Skins unable to run, their passing game was hampered by four Seattle interceptions, two of them by cornerback Dave Brown. Quarterback Jim Zorn compiled all the points that the Seahawks scored with a 21-yard scramble for a second-quarter touchdown.

It did not help that the normally reliable Mark Moseley was having an off day. The Pro Bowl kicker from 1979 missed all three of his field goal attempts, from 33, 50, and 52 yards.

Despite the Seahawks' dominance, the Redskins still had a chance to tie the game in the fourth quarter. Trailing 7-0, they marched to a first and goal at the Seattle four, but Brown cut in front of Art Monk and intercepted Joe Theismann's pass to end the threat. Seattle then drove to its other TD, an eight-yard run by Dan Doornick.

Zorn did not have much of a game passing the ball, going just 7 for 19 for 86 yards. But his team's dominance on the ground, plus their 4-2 edge in takeaways, rendered that and Joe Theismann's 200 yard of passing, virtually irrelevant.

10/5/80	EAGLES (4-1) 24, Redskins (1-4) 14				69,044
Was	7	0	0	7	14
Phil	7	14	3	0	24
Was	Thompson 54 pass from Theismann (Moseley kick)				
Phil	Harris 51 pass from Jaworski (Franklin kick)				
Phil	Montgomery 3 run (Franklin kick)				
Phil	Carmichael 6 pass from Jaworski (Franklin kick)				
Phil	FG Franklin 39				
Was	Claitt 10 run (Moseley kick)				

Veterans Stadium—The Eagles ran off 24 unanswered points to bury an early Washington lead and take the win.

A 54-yard touchdown pass from Joe Theismann to Ricky Thompson got things going for the Redskins, but the Eagles answered before the first quarter was done with a long TD pass of their own. Ron Jaworski went deep to fullback Leroy Harris for 51 yards to tie the game at seven.

In the second quarter, Philly pulled ahead on a three-yard touchdown run by Wilbert Montgomery and another Jaworski touchdown pass, this one to Harold Carmichael. The Redskins continued to try to advance downfield with the run, fearing taking to the air against the Eagles' 3-4 defensive scheme. This tactic was ineffective as Ricky Claitt and Wilbur Jackson combined for 83 yards on 29 carries.

In addition, little things hurt. Returner Mike Nelms chose not to field two punts inside his ten, thinking they would wind up in the end zone. They both took Eagle bounces and were downed deep in Washington territory, making it a very difficult proposition to drive the length of the field on the ground.

All the Eagles got offensively in the second half was one field goal, but they didn't even need that as the Redskins were able to pile up some yardage, but just one touchdown.

10/13/80	BRONCOS (3-3) 20, Redskins (1-5) 17				74,657
Was	3	0	7	7	17
Den	7	3	3	7	20
Den	Armstrong 8 run (Steinfort kick)				
Was	FG Moseley 23				
Den	FG Steinfort 57				
Was	Jackson 55 run (Moseley kick)				
Den	FG Steinfort 23				
Was	Monk 1 pass from Theismann (Moseley kick)				
Den	Upchurch 32 pass from Morton (Steinfort kick)				

Mile High Stadium—In a wild fourth quarter, the Broncos took a 20-17 lead on Craig Morton's 32-yard touchdown pass to Rick Upchurch with 3:08 left and then survived a furious late drive by the Redskins that ended with a 53-yard field goal attempt going wide right by a narrow margin.

Had the attempt been successful, it would have been only the second-longest field goal of the game. Denver's Fred Steinfort took advantage of the mile-high atmosphere to drill a 57-yarder late in the first half, expanding the Broncos' lead to 10-3. Running back Wilbur Jackson tied the game with a 55-yard touchdown run in the third quarter, but Denver promptly drove to set up another Steinfort field goal, this one a 23-yard chip shot, and took the lead back at 13-10.

In the fourth quarter, the Redskins drove deep into Denver territory and were threatening to take the lead when Clarence Harmon fumbled and the Broncos' Bill Thompson recovered at the Denver seven. But soon after that, Denver running back Lawrence McCutcheon returned the favor by promptly fumbling the ball back at the five and three plays later Joe Theismann found Art Monk in the corner of the end zone for a 17-13 Redskins lead. After that, though, Morton, who had come off the bench in relief of starter Matt Robinson, rallied the Broncos.

10/19/80	REDSKINS (2-5) 23, Cardinals (2-5) 0				51,060
StL	0	0	0	0	0
Was	10	13	0	0	23
Was	Harmon 4 pass from Theismann (Moseley kick)				
Was	FG Moseley 30				
Was	Thompson 36 pass from Theismann (kick failed)				
Was	Harmon 20 run (Moseley kick)				

RFK Stadium—The Redskins defense sacked Cardinal quarterback Jim Hart six times and intercepted him twice to pace the Redskins past the Cardinals.

All of the scoring came in the first half. Washington jumped to a 10-0 lead in the first quarter after driving to Joe Theismann's four-yard touchdown pass to back Clarence Harmon and to a 30-yard field goal by Mark Moseley.

A pair of second-quarter TD's iced it for the home team. Theismann found Ricky Thompson for 36 yards and a touchdown. Then Jeris White, who had both of the interceptions off of Hart, picked off a pass to set up Clarence Harmon's 20-yard scoring run.

Theismann passed for 307 yards and the two touchdowns and the Redskins outgained the Cards by nearly a two to one margin, 453 yards to 227.

10/26/80	REDSKINS (3-5) 22, Saints (0-8) 14				51,375
NO	0	7	0	7	14
Was	3	6	10	3	22
Was	FG Moseley 50				
Was	FG Moseley 28				
Was	FG Moseley 35				
NO	Rogers 10 run (Ricardo kick)				
Was	FG Moseley 52				
Was	Thompson 26 pass from Theismann (Moseley kick)				
Was	FG Moseley 38				
NO	Childs 2 pass from Manning (Ricardo kick)				

RFK Stadium—Mark Moseley was five for six on field goals and the Washington defense intercepted Archie Manning three times and sacked him five times to lead the Redskins over the Saints.

Still, the Redskins had to survive a third-quarter scare against the winless Saints. Trailing just 9-7, Manning ran a quarterback draw that carried inside the Washington 10 early in the third. Fortunately for the Redskins, offsetting penalties negated the play and New Orleans had to punt. Washington drove into position for Moseley to make a 52-yard field goal to expand the lead to 12-7.

Then, two plays after the ensuing kickoff, Rich Milot picked off his second pass of the game, setting the Redskins up at the Saints' 31. It took three plays for Joe Theismann to find receiver Ricky Thompson wide open at the 10 and the receiver zipped past a defender and into the end zone to raise the lead to 19-7. Another Moseley field goal in the fourth quarter sealed the victory.

Wilbur Marshall helped the effort with 86 yards rushing on 16 carries. On the day, Theismann was 15 of 29 for 185 yards.

Oct 31
Ken Houston to Retire
Season will be last for strong safety many call the best ever

---

11/2/80	Vikings (4-5) 39, REDSKINS (3-6) 14			52,060	
Min	7	16	7	9	39
Was	0	7	7	0	14
Min	Young 5 pass from Dils (Danmier kick)				
Min	Senser 2 pass from Dils (Danmier kick)				
Min	Safety Theismann tackled in end zone				
Min	Nord 70 kickoff return (Danmier kick)				
Was	Harmon 1 pass from Theismann (Moseley kick)				
Was	Harmon 1 run (Moseley kick)				
Min	Young 3 run (Danmier kick)				
Min	FG Danmier 31				
Min	FG Danmier 27				
Min	FG Danmier 35				

RFK Stadium—"It wasn't a game to be proud of," said Joe Theismann when it was over, and nobody argued. In their worst home loss since 1966, the Redskins fell behind early and then tried to catch up only to see their comeback collapse under the weight of their own mistakes.

Steve Dils, a last-minute fill-in for regular starting quarterback Tommy Kramer, threw for two touchdowns to forge a 14-0 lead. After Joe Theismann was tackled in his own end zone for a safety, Minnesota's Keith Nord returned the free kick that followed for a touchdown. The lead was 23-0 with the home crowd venting its displeasure with loud and persistent booing.

Theismann threw to Clarence Harmon for a touchdown before halftime before Washington embarked on a 65-yard, 14-play drive after taking the second half kickoff. Harmon again got the six on a one-yard run with 8:01 left in the third. With their team behind by just nine, the boos from the fans turned to cheers. That fired up the defense and the Vikings were forced to punt.

The wheels then came off the comeback bus. John McDaniel just missed blocking the punt—but didn't miss punter Greg Coleman. He was flagged for roughing the kicker. Then a missed tackle by end Joe Jones turned a big loss into an 11-yard gain, followed by two personal foul penalties that placed the Vikings in business at the Washington 3. Rickey Young took it over on the next play, and the rest of the contest was academic.

11/9/80	BEARS (4-6) 35, Redskins (3-7) 21			57,159	
Was	0	0	14	7	21
Chi	21	14	0	0	35
Chi	Payton 50 run (Thomas kick)				
Chi	Scott 40 pass from Evans (Thomas kick)				
Chi	Harper 2 run (Thomas kick)				
Chi	Payton 54 pass from Evans (Thomas kick)				
Chi	Scott 12 pass from Evans (Thomas kick)				
Was	Claitt 3 pass from Theismann (Moseley kick)				
Was	Theismann 7 run (Moseley kick)				
Was	Thompson 16 pass from Theismann (Moseley kick)				

Soldier Field—This one was over shortly after it started. In the first 15 minutes and 10 seconds of the game, the Bears offense had three scoring plays of 40 yards or more and went on to rout the Redskins.

On Chicago's opening drive, Walter Payton busted up the middle for 50 yards and a touchdown. A fumble recovery set up the next Bears TD—a 40-yard pass from Vince Evans to James Scott. The following score was Roland Harper's run from a mere two yards out, but they only had to drive three yards after Gary Campbell intercepted Joe Theismann's pass and returned it 15 yards. Then, on the first play of the second quarter, Evans threw a 54-yard touchdown pass to Payton to make it 28-0.

The Bears added one more touchdown before shutting it down for the day. Theismann did lead the Skins to three second-half touchdowns. He threw touchdown pass of three yards to Ricky Claitt and of 16 yards to Ricky Thompson. In between those, he ran for another score from three yards out.

Theismann was 24 for 34 on the day and he passed for 305 yards but much of his passing came long after the Bears had lost interest in the proceedings.

Redskins Playing for Jobs, Says Pardee

Nov 3—With a record of 3-6, the Redskins' playoff chances are slim and growing slimmer. The team now needs some other goals to play for. Jack Pardee suggested one today: continued employment.

"You better use professionalism every day and you have a chance to succeed," said Pardee.

"I don't like the position we are in either," the coach said. "But we all have to face up to it. We're in it. Whether you are fighting to win each week or whether you are fighting for a job on the team, you better play with aggressiveness and determination."

Pardee indicated that the team's woes against the Vikings (a 39-14 loss) weren't all the fault of the players. He said that he needs to rethink the team's defensive situational substitution schemes.

They need to stick with the concept because, Pardee said, "We aren't good enough just to line up and beat teams." But there likely will be fewer substitutions.

"We have to be aware that other teams are trying to combat what we're doing," Pardee said.

The Vikings, for example, were holding off on making their substitutions until the last possible second, making it difficult for the Redskins to counter.

"We have to be careful that we don't get to the point where we're outsmarting ourselves," said Pardee.

11/16/80	Eagles (10-1) 24, REDSKINS (3-8) 0			51,897	
Phil	14	3	7	0	24
Was	0	0	0	0	0
Phil	Krepfle 7 pass from Jaworski (Franklin kick)				
Phil	Spagnola 14 pass from Jaworski (Franklin kick)				
Phil	FG Franklin 38				
Phil	Robinson 59 fumble return (Franklin kick)				

RFK Stadium—"I'm so embarrassed by the way we played I don't even want to talk to anyone," said Joe Theismann after the Eagles blanked the Redskins 24-0. Wow, now that's pretty bad.

The game started out as though the Eagles would be able to choose what the final score would be. They did it on offense as they took the opening kickoff and drove a methodical 81 yards on

12 plays, scoring on a seven-yard touchdown pass from Ron Jaworski to tight end Keith Krepfle. Right after that, Richard Blackmore intercepted Theismann's pass and Jaworski went to his other tight end, John Spagnola, for 14 yards and a touchdown to make it 14-0 in the first quarter. At that point, the Eagles had outgained the Redskins 122 yards to four.

The final stats weren't that lopsided as the Redskins did manage to venture into Philadelphia territory six times, but they came away empty each trip. The frustration is best illustrated on a two-play sequence in the third quarter with the Redskins trailing 17-0. On third and one from the Eagle 36, Buddy Hardeman lofted a halfback option pass to a wide-open Art Monk, but the ball just eluded the rookie receiver's grasp. On fourth down, not only was Wilbur Jackson thrown for a decisive loss, but he fumbled. Linebacker Jerry Robinson fell on it and hesitated for a second, thinking the play had been blown dead. Teammate Bill Bergy told him to get up and he did. With most of the Redskins playing the role of spectators, Robinson sprinted 59 yards for the game's last score.

Nov 16

Cooke: Pardee Safe—For Now
Owner says he will not fire coach before end of season but won't commit beyond that

---

11/23/80	COWBOYS (9-3) 14, Redskins (3-9) 10			58,809	
Was	0	3	0	7	10
Dal	7	0	0	7	14
Dal	Dorsett 3 run (Septien kick)				
Was	FG Moseley 34				
Dal	Cole 43 interception return (Septien kick)				
Was	Jackson 8 run (Moseley kick)				

Texas Stadium—The Cowboys tried to hand their guests the game, turning the ball over six times, but the Redskins were having no part of it, as they lost to Dallas.

Joe Theismann came into the game hobbled with a hamstring injury. He played gamely for most of the first half, but then aggravated the injury and yielded to Mike Kruczek. The starter was not very effective while he was in and Kruczek was even less successful. Until a drive late in the game, the Redskins had a net of minus nine yards passing.

One sequence effectively told the story of Washington's offensive woes. From a first and ten inside the Dallas 20, a penalty and pair of sacks led to a fourth and 46 to go situation from the Redskin 48.

Still, due to a good rushing effort, the Redskins were in this game until the final quarter. Trailing 7-3 in the third period, a fumble and two interceptions got them the ball near midfield, but they came up empty each time.

Dallas recovered one fumble and made the most out of it. Early in the third quarter, Randy White sacked Kruczek. The ball popped into the air and then off of tackle Larry Cole's helmet. From there, it plopped right into Cole's arms and he took off 43 yards with the gift for the touchdown.

When Washington finally got around to taking advantage of a turnover, it was too late. Monte Coleman's interception set the Redskins up at the Dallas eight with 1:27 left. Wilbur Jackson, who rushed for 128 yards on the day, ran it in from there.

11/30/80	FALCONS (10-3) 10, Redskins (3-10) 6			55,665	
Was	0	3	0	3	6
Atl	0	0	7	3	10
Was	FG Moseley 51				
Atl	Jenkins 14 pass from Bartkowski (Mazzetti kick)				
Atl	FG Mazzetti 23				
Was	FG Moseley 46				

Atlanta-Fulton County Stadium—"A new way to lose a game," said Jack Pardee, as if the Redskins needed to find any more during this lost season. Some others expressed another way.

"It was bull," said Terry Hermeling.

The coach and offensive tackle were referring to an ill-timed and highly controversial penalty that nullified the Redskins tying touchdown in the last five minutes of their 10-6 loss to the Falcons.

With Mike Kruczek starting at quarterback in place of the injured Joe Theismann, Pardee's game plan was extremely conservative, hoping that his defense and Mark Moseley could win the game. It might have worked had it not been for some ill-timed turnovers. In the first quarter Kruczek threw an interception from the Atlanta 21 and later in the same period Wilbur Jackson fumbled at the Falcon 12.

Still, the defense held up its end of the deal and Moseley kicked a 51-yard field goal to stake the Redskins to a 3-0 halftime lead. The Falcons, who had been averaging nearly 30 points a game, broke out on top in the third quarter when Steve Bartkowski threw a 14-yard touchdown pass to James Jenkins. Their other sustained drive of the game resulted in Tim Mazzetti's 23-yard field goal in the fourth quarter that gave Atlanta a 10-3 lead.

Kruczek and the Redskins fought back. The quarterback then threw a 24-yard touchdown pass to Ricky Thompson with 4:27 to play, but the field was littered with laundry. One flag was on Atlanta for roughing the passer. Two more were near the line and, after a conference, the referee announced that Hermeling and Atlanta linebacker Al Richardson had exchanged head slaps. The offsetting personal fouls were during the play, so the down had to be replayed.

The Redskins argued, to no avail, that Hermeling wasn't anywhere near Richardson on the play and, besides, he had put a low block on the end lined up over him. There was no slapping or shoving going on. The drive ended up with Moseley kicking a 46-yard field goal and Washington never got another chance.

12/7/80	REDSKINS (4-10) 40, Chargers (9-5) 17			55,045	
SD	7	3	0	7	17
Was	14	6	6	14	40
Was	Lavender 51 interception return (Moseley kick)				
Was	Jackson 18 pass from Theismann (Moseley kick)				
SD	McCrary 28 pass from Fouts (Benirschke kick)				
Was	FG Moseley 28				
SD	FG Benirschke 26				
Was	FG Moseley 45				
Was	FG Moseley 46				
Was	FG Moseley 46				
SD	Bauer 2 run (Benirschke kick)				
Was	Forte 4 pass from Theismann (Moseley kick)				
Was	Forte 3 run (Moseley kick)				

RFK Stadium—The Redskins broke out of their five-game losing streak in grand style, smashing the playoff-bound Chargers with good performances on both sides of the ball.

Joe Lavender set the tone on San Diego's first possession when he picked off Dan Fouts' pass and returned it 51 yards for a touchdown. It was the first of three interceptions for Lavender on the day and one of seven takeaways for the Redskins on the day (5 interceptions, two fumble recoveries).

It had been six weeks since the Redskins had last enjoyed as much as a seven-point lead and it apparently inspired the offense. So did the return of Joe Theismann at quarterback after he had missed all of one game and parts of two others with a hamstring pull. Washington drove 63 yards for another touchdown as two Theismann passes to Wilbur Jackson covered most of the yardage. A 27-yard connection between the quarterback and running back got the march going and it was finished when

Theismann scrambled and threw to Jackson, who broke a tackle and rolled in from 18 yards out.

A Fouts pass to tight end Greg McCrary sliced the lead to 14-7 and the Chargers were still in it at halftime, trailing just 20-10. They threatened to close the gap even further with their initial drive on the second half, moving to the Washington four. But Monte Coleman, who was the victim on McCrary's TD, intercepted Fouts in the end zone and ran it out to the Washington 39. Two Mark Moseley field goals in the third stretched the lead to 26-10 and Ike Forte scored two touchdowns in the fourth quarter to cap the rout.

12/13/80	REDSKINS (5-10) 16, Giants (4-11) 13			44,443	
NYG	0	10	0	3	13
Was	0	0	7	9	16
NYG	FG Danelo 40				
NYG	Taylor 1 run (Danelo kick)				
Was	Harmon 11 run (Moseley kick)				
Was	FG Moseley 40				
NYG	FG Danelo 40				
Was	Hammond 7 pass from Theismann (kick failed)				

RFK Stadium—Bobby Hammond's seven-yard touchdown catch with 39 seconds left to play gave the Redskins a lackluster 13-10 win over the Giants.

Washington trailed 10-0 at the half and endangered and enraged coach Jack Pardee sarcastically told the team, "You might as well go out and play 30 minutes, because you haven't played any football yet this afternoon."

The Redskins responded, with some help from the equally hapless Giants. New York fumbled the second-half kickoff and Dallas Hickman recovered for the Redskins at the Giant 24. Hammond picked up 13 yards on two carries before Clarence Harmon scored on an 11-yard draw play, cutting the lead to 10-7.

The teams exchanged field goals in the fourth quarter and Washington's final drive started at the Giant 48 with 3:48 to play. A Harmon run converted one third down and Joe Theismann's third and seven pass to Art Monk gained 14 yards to the Giant 19. Again Harmon ran for a first on third and seven and then Hammond, running in an area cleared out by two other receivers, grabbed Theismann's pass in the end zone. The point after was

blocked, opening the door for New York to tie it with a field goal. However, three incompletions preceded Mark Murphy's game-ending interception.

12/21/80	Redskins (6-10) 31, CARDINALS (5-11) 7			35,942	
Was	0	21	3	7	31
StL	0	0	0	7	7
Was	Harmon 1 run (Moseley kick)				
Was	Monk 54 pass from Theismann (Moseley kick)				
Was	Harmon 15 pass from Theismann (Moseley kick)				
Was	FG Moseley 34				
Was	Monk 2 pass from Theismann (Moseley kick)				
StL	Brown 4 run (O'Donoghue kick)				

Busch Stadium—The Redskins limited the Cardinal passing game to a net of minus 12 yards and their offense exploded for 21 second-quarter points to win in St. Louis.

Washington got things going in the second quarter with an 80-yard touchdown drive. Bobby Hammond, who started at running back in place of Wilbur Jackson, rushed for 41 of those yards and Clarence Harmon got the score and a one-yard run.

Hammond's running softened up the Cardinal coverage and Joe Theismann took full advantage with a beautiful 54-yard scoring pass to Art Monk. A 15-yard TD pass from Theismann to Harmon capped the second-quarter scoring outburst, a touchdown set up when fullback Buddy Hardeman turned a short toss into a 46-yard gain.

In the second half, the Washington lead grew to 31-0 on a 34-yard Mark Moseley field goal and Monk's second touchdown catch of the day, this from a more pedestrian distance of two yards. The Cardinals' lone touchdown came against a group of defensive players who normally occupy the bench.

Hammond, who was with the New York Giants to start the season, had a great day, rushing for 135 yards on 17 carries. The Redskins wound up with exactly as many yards rushing, 174, as the Cardinals compiled in total offense.

Dec. 23

Cooke Meets With Beathard, Pardee
'Preliminary' talks on fate of both coach and GM

1981
Head Coach: Joe Gibbs
Record: 8-8, Fourth in NFC East

Honors: Mike Nelms Pro Bowl, All-NFL

Jan. 5

Pardee, 1979 Coach of the Year, Fired
GM Beathard wins power struggle, Pardee is out after three seasons

---

Gibbs Hired as Redskins Coach

Jan. 12—A press conference will be held tomorrow to announce the hiring of Joe Gibbs as head coach of the Washington Redskins. General Manager Bobby Beathard and team owner Jack Kent Cooke decided last night that Gibbs, the San Diego Chargers' offensive coordinator, was the man to replace the fired Jack Pardee.

"Joe appeals to me because of his obvious dedication to the game," Cooke said. "I have confidence that Joe will provide the

Redskins fans with a team that will stir the imagination, win or lose."

Gibbs said that he wanted Cooke to be glad he made the decision to hire him. "I want him to look back on this and say it was the best decision he ever made. I have a sense of urgency. I am ready and fired up."

He won't waste any time starting to earn his salary, reported to be $100,000 annually. After this morning's press conference, he and Beathard will fly to Mobile, Alabama to scout draft prospects at the Senior Bowl. After that, Gibbs will get to work assembling his coaching staff. Cooke has given him an assistant coaches' salary budget that is "top dollar," according to some.

The Redskins also announced that Richie Petitbon will be promoted to defensive coordinator.

Skins Get Draft Day Bonanza

Apr. 29—"This is the best draft I've ever been associated with," said Bobby Beathard following the 1981 NFL Annual Selection Meeting.

The day started off with a deal reminiscent of the ones that Beathard's predecessor as Redskins General Manager, George Allen, loved to make—a draft pick for a disgruntled veteran. The pick was their second-rounder; the player was running back Joe Washington of the Baltimore Colts.

Then the draft got underway and the Redskins moved back in the first round, going from ninth overall to twentieth in a deal with the LA Rams that yielded some later-round selections. There, they picked offensive tackle Mark May.

After that, Beathard made a move on the line between bold and crazy, dealing away his first round pick next year for a third-round pick (plus a few lower selections) to be able to take Pittsburgh center Russ Grimm.

Later on in the draft, using mostly its own selections, the team drafted defensive end Dexter Manley, receiver Charlie Brown, and offensive lineman Darryl Grant.

'Bored, Broke' Riggins is Back

June 11—Declaring, "I'm bored, broke and I'm back," John Riggins took the field for the Washington Redskins today for the first time since the 1979 season finale.

As he prepared to participate in drills at minicamp, Riggins, 31, indicated that this might be his final minicamp. "This might be my last year. I don't know," he said. "I'm taking one year at a time."

Joe Gibbs had gone to Kansas to meet with Riggins in March in an effort to convince the iconoclastic back to return to the Redskins. The coach was obviously pleased that his work paid off, but warned that Riggins had a lot of catching up to do.

"This being his first camp, he has a lot to digest," Gibbs said. "I'm just glad he's here to get started."

Change at Redskins Park—22 new players

Sep 1—The 1981 Redskins may be better than last year's edition and they may be worse, but one thing is certain: they will be different.

Following today's final roster cutdown there were 22 players on the roster who were not there in 1980. Among those, 12 have no NFL playing experience anywhere.

A microcosm of this change is found on the offensive line. Among the eight linemen, four are rookies (Joe Jacoby, Russ Grimm, Mark May, and Darryl Grant), one is a first-year player with no playing experience (Melvin Jones), one has played a very limited number of snaps (Jerry Scanlon), and another has been almost exclusively a long snapper (Jeff Bostic). Only tackle George Starke has any significant playing experience.

Gibbs was shuffling more than just backups. There will be 10 new starters, eight of them on offense. Of the starters who were replaced, five were 30 or older. Their replacements average 23 years of age.

9/6/81	Cowboys (1-0) 26, REDSKINS (0-1) 10			55,045
Dal	0	14	6	6	**26**
Was	0	7	3	0	**10**
Dal	DuPree 33 pass from White (Septien kick)
Was	Washington 15 pass from Theismann (Moseley kick)
Dal	Pearson 42 pass from White (Septien kick)
Dal	FG Septien 29
Was	FG Moseley 42
Dal	FG Septien 42
Dal	FG Septien 23
Dal	FG Septien 18

RFK Stadium—In Joe Gibbs' first game as head coach, the Redskins turned the ball over six times in losing to the Cowboys 26-10.

On the day, the Redskins passed 49 times and ran just 18. "Our basic idea coming in was that we didn't think we could run the ball on them, so we decided to go after them with the pass," Gibbs said. "As it worked out, we weren't very balanced."

Or, for that matter, very effective.

The pattern of the game quickly emerged. The Redskins would move the ball downfield and, as a scoring threat began to develop, Joe Theismann would throw an interception. Of Theismann's four interceptions, three occurred in Dallas territory, one at the 36, another at the 26, and one at the four.

It was that last one that killed any faint hopes the Redskins had of coming back. Trailing 23-10 with more than eight minutes left, they drove to a first down at the Dallas nine. Three plays later on third down from the four, Dennis Thurman stepped in front of Art Monk, picked off Theismann's pass at the goal line and raced 96 yards to the four. Rafael Septien's fourth field goal of the day put it out of reach.

In addition to the four interceptions thrown by Joe Theismann and two lost fumbles, the Redskins' inability to muster a ground game doomed them in this one. John Riggins had returned to the team after a one-year holdout and was supposed to get Washington's ground game going again, but he had eight carries for just 25 yards. As a team, the Skins ran for just 44 yards compared to 206 for Dallas.

9/13/81	Giants (1-1) 17, REDSKINS (0-2) 7			53,343
NYG	0	0	7	10	**17**
Was	0	0	7	0	**7**
Was	Thompson 6 pass from Theismann (Moseley kick)
NYG	Taylor 5 run (Danelo kick)
NYG	FG Danelo 25
NYG	Martin 8 fumble return (Danelo kick)

RFK Stadium—Rookie New York linebacker Lawrence Taylor sacked Joe Theismann twice, but it was turnovers that killed the Redskins in this 17-7 loss to the Giants.

The normally sure-handed Mike Nelms fumbled a Giants punt at the New York 13, leading to a tying touchdown run by Billy Taylor. Then, with less than three minutes left in the game, the Redskins were trying to mount a drive to tie or take the lead when Theismann fumbled after being sacked deep in New York territory. Giants' lineman George Martin got a perfect bounce into his arms, and he rumbled eight yards for the clinching score.

This event was difficult to watch even for the most avid fans. In the scoreless first half, the teams combined for 15 punts and were 0 for 16 on third down conversions. New York quarterback Phil Simms didn't complete a pass until the second quarter and was two for his first 12 attempts.

Despite losing John Riggins, Joe Washington and Russ Grimm to injuries in the first half, the Redskins managed an 82-yard touchdown drive in the third quarter, the payoff coming on a Theismann pass to Ricky Thompson, who carried a Giant safety into the end zone on his back. After the Giants punted on the subsequent possession, though, Nelms fumbled and things came unglued.

9/20/81	CARDINALS (1-2) 40, Redskins (0-3) 30			47,592
Was	10	7	0	13	**30**
StL	9	17	0	14	**40**
StL	FG O'Donoghue 24
Was	FG Moseley 21
Was	Thompson 34 pass from Theismann (Moseley kick)
StL	Green 58 pass from Hart (kick failed)
StL	FG O'Donoghue 47
StL	Mitchell 52 punt return (O'Donoghue kick)
Was	Monk 79 pass from Theismann (Moseley kick)
StL	LaFleur 27 pass from Hart (O'Donoghue kick)

StL	Stief 6 pass from Hart (O'Donoghue kick)
StL	Anderson 7 run (O'Donoghue kick)
Was	Walker 20 pass from Theismann (kick failed)
Was	Thompson 10 pass from Theismann (Moseley kick)

Busch Stadium—The Redskins opened a 10-3 lead in the first quarter when Joe Theismann hit Ricky Thompson with a 34-yard TD pass off of a flea flicker, but Cardinals quarterback Jim Hart took over after that and led St. Louis to a 40-30 win.

The 37-year-old ignited a 37-7 Cardinal scoring run that left the Redskins gasping for breath. Hart, who was a doubtful starter due to a knee injury, completed just 12 passes, but they were good for 226 yards and three touchdowns.

Joe Theismann threw for 388 yards and was intercepted just once, but that one was costly. He rallied the Redskins from a 40-17 fourth-quarter deficit with two touchdown passes. The first one covered 20 yards to Rick Walker and the second went 10 yards to Ricky Thompson.

The interception came with less than a minute left deep in St. Louis territory and ended any hopes the Redskins had for a miracle comeback.

The loss wasted a 521-total yardage effort by the Washington offense. In addition to Theismann's 288 yards through the air, the Redskins rushed for 133 yards, including 104 by Wilbur Jackson.

9/27/81	**EAGLES (4-0) 36, Redskins (0-4) 13**			70,664	
Was	0	6	0	7	**13**
Phil	0	7	7	22	**36**
Phil	Giamonna 13 pass from Jaworski (Franklin kick)				
Was	FG Moseley 19				
Was	FG Moseley 22				
Phil	Giamonna 1 run (Franklin kick)				
Was	Riggins 3 run (Moseley kick)				
Phil	Smith 29 pass from Jaworski (Franklin kick)				
Phil	FG Franklin 28				
Phil	Safety Theismann tackled in end zone				
Phil	FG Franklin 36				
Phil	Brown 7 fumble return (Franklin kick)				

Veterans Stadium—The Eagles broke open a one-point game in the fourth quarter with 22 unanswered points to send Joe Gibbs to his fourth straight loss to start his tenure as Redskins coach by a score of 36-13.

Washington outgained the Eagles 337 yards to 221, but couldn't overcome two lost fumbles, an interception, and 98 yards in penalties.

The Redskins moved up and down the Veterans Stadium carpet in the first half. The problem was that four drives—one to the Eagle 20, the other three to inside the 10—netted just two field goals. Washington trailed 7-6.

That wouldn't cut it against the powerful Eagles. They took the second half kickoff and ground out a 15-play, 72-yard march that resulted in a one-yard touchdown burst by Louie Giamonna. Early in the fourth quarter, though, the Redskins fought back and finally finished off a drive in the preferred fashion, with a three-yard TD run by John Riggins to cut the Philly lead to 14-13.

That was it for the Redskins, however. They were forced to punt on their next possession and the Eagles returned it to their own 49. Soon after that, receiver Charles Smith dusted off Lamar Parrish and caught a 29-yard touchdown pass from Ron Jaworski. Then after the kickoff, Riggins bobbled a swing pass and linebacker Reggie Wilkes intercepted, returning the ball to the Washington 12. That led to a Tony Franklin field goal, making it 24-13. Washington's hopes were fading fast.

Theismann was tackled for a safety and then a Terry Metcalf fumble led to another Franklin field goal. Coach Jack Pardee decided to give quarterback Tom Flick a taste of action and, certainly, the rookie got more than he bargained for. He was sandwiched in between a pair of blitzing Eagles and fumbled. End Greg Brown scooped it up and finished off the scoring with a 22-yard jaunt into the end zone.

10/4/81	**49ers (3-2) 30, Redskins (0-5) 17**			51,843	
SF	14	10	6	0	**30**
Was	0	3	0	14	**17**
SF	Patton 16 run (Bahr kick)				
SF	Hicks 80 fumble return (Bahr kick)				
SF	FG Bahr 43				
Was	FG Moseley 34				
SF	Davis 1 run (Bahr kick)				
SF	Hicks 32 interception return (kick failed)				
Was	Nelms 58 punt return (Moseley kick)				
Was	Washington 5 run (Moseley kick)				

RFK Stadium—"It's the same story," said Joe Gibbs, 0-5 in his head coaching career after this loss and, indeed, it was. Impressive offensive numbers more than offset by ill-timed turnovers was the story of the early 1981 Redskins. This one was no different as the Redskins fell to San Francisco 30-17 in a game that was not as close as the final score would indicate.

After the 49ers had driven to a touchdown after taking the opening kickoff and a 7-0 lead, Washington had a nice drive of its own going. On first down from the San Francisco 22, Terry Metcalf headed to the right on a misdirection play. Niners' safety Ronnie Lott flipped Metcalf into the air as the runner tried to turn the corner and the ball popped out. Safety Dwight Hicks snatched the ball with one hand and raced 80 yards for a touchdown.

The Redskins would not recover from the 14-point turnaround. Hicks later scored another touchdown after intercepting a Theismann pass in the third quarter. It was one of four San Francisco picks. Hicks' return made the score 30-3 and two fourth-quarter touchdowns by the Redskins were mere window dressing.

Gibbs: Cooke is 'Supportive'

Oct 5—Despite an 0-5 record, Redskins owner Jack Kent Cooke is firmly in Joe Gibbs' corner, says the new coach.

"We sit down almost every week and talk, face to face, and he's been nothing but supportive. He's been good to me. He and Bobby Beathard are intelligent men. They are aware of the problems we've been having.

"I'm confident that I'll be here when it all gets straightened out."

Cooke declined to comment, other than saying, "Patience is the key."

Beathard, who hired Gibbs, confirmed that the team intended to stay the course. "Gibbs is the coach who is going to rebuild this team. He shouldn't feel the least bit pressured."

"This is where I should be," Gibbs said. "You don't squirm out of hard times, you 'fess up to them."

10/11/81	**Redskins (1-5) 27, BEARS (1-5) 7**			57,683	
Was	10	7	0	7	**24**
Chi	0	0	0	7	**7**
Was	FG Moseley 38				
Was	Olkewicz 10 interception return (Moseley kick)				
Was	Riggins 1 run (Moseley kick)				
Was	Riggins 2 run (Moseley kick)				
Chi	Anderson 43 pass from Phipps (Roveto kick)				

Soldier Field—Finally, after an 0-5, mistake-filled start to Joe Gibbs' head coaching tenure, the Redskins found an opponent that would hand a game to them. Having been killed by turnovers during the first five games, the Redskins gladly accepted three Bears gifts to build a 17-0 halftime lead and rolled to a 27-7 win.

Joe Lavender's interception of a Vince Evans pass led to a Mark Moseley field goal late in the first quarter. Twenty four seconds later, Evans was intercepted again, this time by Neil Olkewicz, who ran it into the end zone from 10 yards out and it was 10-0.

Late in the first half, it was Dave Butz's turn to pick off Evans, and he rumbled to the Bears' one. John Riggins scored from there, and the lead grew to 17-0.

The Redskins expanded it to 24-0 with 4:45 left in the fourth quarter by putting together their only scoring drive of the game unaided by a Chicago turnover. Riggins capped it off with another short TD run. The Bears averted the shutout when Mike Phipps hit Marcus Anderson for a 43-yard touchdown with 1:43 left.

Gibbs in a Giving Mood After First Win

Oct 12—"Things are a lot more relaxed today. We can laugh and have some fun."

Almost any member of the Redskins could have said that in the glow of their first win of the year. It happened that Joe Gibbs said it and, evidently, his idea of having fun is giving away some swag to his players.

A lot of merchandise has been piling up in the attic at Redskins Park waiting to be awarded to outstanding players after a win. Portable TV's, sport coats, dinners, watches, and shirts were all dished out to deserving gladiators. In return, the players gave Gibbs a game ball.

Gibbs, who came to the Redskins touted as a master of the passing game, attributed the team's success on Sunday to old-fashioned ball control and solid, opportunistic defense.

"We did prove that we can run the ball, that we can move it out from the goal line in tough situations and that we can control it for a long drive," he said. "And our defense also found out that it really is a great unit."

10/18/81	DOLPHINS (5-1-1) 13, Redskins 10			47,367	
Was	0	3	0	7	**10**
Mia	0	3	7	3	**13**
Was	FG Moseley 20				
Mia	FG 37 von Schamann				
Mia	Franklin 1 run (von Schamann kick)				
Was	Riggins 2 run (Moseley kick)				
Mia	FG von Schamann 25				

Orange Bowl—Just two minutes after John Riggins tied the game in the fourth quarter, Uve von Schamann's 25-yard field goal with 9:39 left in the game pushed the Dolphins past the Redskins 13-10.

"We played a very good team very evenly and we still didn't win," said Mark May. "That really hurts."

Part of the Redskins' early season problems seemed to be fading into the distance as they committed just two turnovers and were penalized only three times. The other major source of the team's woes, the inability to finish off drives and take advantage of opportunities, however, remained.

In the second quarter, Joe Theismann completed passes of 25 yards to Don Warren and 12 to Rich Caster to gain a first down at the Miami eight. They had to settle for a field goal after Theismann's third down pass to Joe Washington was incomplete.

Miami tied it up before halftime on von Schamann's 37-yard field goal. In the third quarter, David Woodley tossed a 39-yard completion to Jimmy Cefalo to set up a one-yard scoring run by Aundra Franklin.

The Redskins responded with their only touchdown of the day, driving to a Riggins' one-yard plunge early in the fourth quarter. After that, Woodley went deep again and a 50-yard connection with tight end Joe Rose set up the go-ahead field goal by von Schamann.

Washington had an opportunity to tie or take the lead when they drove to a first down at the Miami 39, but it broke down there and left them to punt with 4:17 left. On third and 13 at the Miami 29, Woodley clinched it with a 54-yard completion to Cefalo and the Dolphins burned off the last minute and a half.

10/25/81	REDSKINS (2-6) 24, Patriots (2-6) 22			50,394	
NE	6	9	0	7	**22**
Was	7	7	10	0	**24**
NE	FG Smith 25				
NE	FG Smith 22				
Was	Washington 13 pass from Theismann (Moseley kick)				
NE	Collins 6 run (kick failed)				
NE	FG Smith 46				
Was	Nelms 75 punt return (Moseley kick)				
Was	FG Moseley 34				
Was	Theismann 1 run (Moseley kick)				
NE	Cunningham 4 run (Smith kick)				

RFK Stadium—A sigh of relief after a penalty flag in a pivotal situation went Washington's way was followed by a cheer of joy as the Patriots' John Smith missed a 51-yard field goal with 51 seconds left, sealing a 24-22 win for the Redskins.

On a third and 20 from the Washington 36, New England's Steve Grogan threw a pass intended for Stanley Morgan at the 10. The receiver got tangled up with CB Lamar Parrish and a flag was thrown. The call was pass interference on Morgan, the Redskins declined the penalty, and Smith's try to give the Patriots the lead fell well short of the crossbar.

The Redskins had erased a 15-7 New England lead with 17 points in the second and third quarters, all of those points either scored or set up by Washington defense and special teams. Mike Nelms returned a punt 75 yards for a TD to pull the Redskins within one. In the third quarter, Mark Murphy intercepted a Grogan pass to set up a Mark Moseley field goal. Later in that period, Nelms stripped the ball from New England's Tony Collins and end Matt Mendenhall recovered at the Patriots' 44. Joe Theismann scored on a fourth and goal run from the one to give the Redskins the cushion they needed.

11/1/81	REDSKINS (3-6) 42, Cardinals (3-6) 21			50,643	
StL	0	0	0	21	**21**
Was	14	7	7	14	**42**
Was	Monk 38 pass from Theismann (Moseley kick)				
Was	Seay 51 pass from Theismann (Moseley kick)				
Was	Riggins 1 run (Moseley kick)				
Was	Riggins 1 run (Moseley kick)				
StL	Green 11 pass from Hart (O'Donoghue kick)				
Was	Monk 10 pass from Theismann (Moseley kick)				
StL	Tilley 14 pass from Hart (O'Donoghue kick)				
StL	Tilley 14 pass from Hart (O'Donoghue kick)				
Was	Riggins 4 run (Moseley kick)				

RFK Stadium—The home crowd had its choice of heroes after this 42-21 romp over the Cardinals. Three stood out, each representing one phase of the game. Rookie free agent linebacker Mel Kaufman was the defensive star, intercepting two Jim Hart passes; Mike Nelms stepped up for the special teams with three big kick returns; and Joe Theismann threw three touchdown passes to spark the Redskins' offense.

Nelms' first big runback came on the game's opening kickoff and was good for 46 yards. Four plays later, Art Monk shook defender Carl Allen and Joe Theismann hit his wide receiver in stride with a 38-yard touchdown pass.

The Redskins again got a short field and again took advantage of it. After Mark Murphy's interception of Jim Hart, Theismann picked on Allen again. That time the cornerback was trying to cover Virgil Seay. Allen made a try for a diving deflection but missed and could just watch from the ground as Seay completed a 51-yard touchdown play. Later in the half, Allen committed pass interference in the end zone, leading to John Riggins' one-yard touchdown run.

Riggins' second rushing TD came in the third quarter and extended the lead to 28-0. Hart and the Cardinals did manage to make the score more respectable with three fourth-quarter touchdowns. The home team kept St. Louis at bay with another Theismann to Monk touchdown connection and Riggins' third rushing score of the day.

Gibbs Sees Progress, But Warns of Tough Battles Ahead

Nov 2—Joe Gibbs said today that while there is reason for real optimism in the wake of his team's 3-1 record following its 0-5 start, he warned that the tough tests are yet to come.

"We are good enough to play four good back-to-back games," he said. "But the teams we have beaten so far have had lesser records. We're going to begin a stretch now against teams that have winning records and are challenging for playoff berths. This will tell us something more."

Of their next five games, four are against teams with winning records and the fifth, 4-5 Detroit, is in the hunt for the Central Division title.

When asked what has caused the turnaround, Gibbs listed five factors: he and the coaches knowing the players' capabilities better; a reduction in turnovers and other errors; the switch to the one-back offense; fewer players being out with injuries and improved confidence.

As to the last factor, Gibbs said, "The first part of the year you say, 'Goodness gracious, when are we going to win?' You have nothing but repeated failure. Now we think we can make the right plays, we think we're a good team."

11/8/81	REDSKINS (4-6) 33, Lions (4-6) 31				52,090	
Det	7	14	0	10		**31**
Was	10	10	3	10		**33**
Was	Washington 7 run (Moseley kick)					
Was	FG Moseley 21					
Det	Scott 36 pass from Hipple (Murray kick)					
Det	Hipple 2 run (Murray kick)					
Was	FG Moseley 33					
Det	Sims 1 run (Murray kick)					
Was	Monk 8 pass from Theismann (Moseley kick)					
Was	FG Moseley 28					
Det	Sims 13 run (Murray kick)					
Was	Washington 12 run (Moseley kick)					
Det	FG Murray 50					
Was	FG Moseley 44					

RFK Stadium—Nearly 1,000 yards of total offense, six lead changes and nine turnovers highlighted this wild affair in Washington. The outcome wasn't settled until a completed Hail Mary pass by the Lions ended as Detroit's Mark Nichols was tackled by Joe Lavender at the Washington two as time ran out.

The Redskins took advantage of two of Detroit's six turnovers to take a 10-0 lead. The Lions' Alvin Hall fumbled the opening kickoff and Jeris White recovered for Washington. Three plays later, Joe Washington, who rushed for 144 yards on the day, scored on a seven-yard run. Soon after the touchdown, the Lions fumbled again, and defensive end Matt Mendenhall recovered at the Detroit 10. Washington settled for a 21-yard Mark Moseley field goal.

Lions' quarterback Eric Hipple then went to work, throwing for one touchdown and scoring another himself on a two-yard run for a 14-10 lead. For the game, Hipple was 14 of 22 for 282 yards. After a Moseley field goal cut it to a one-point lead, it was time for Detroit's star runner Bill Sims to shine. Sims dove over from the one to widen the Lion lead to eight. The former Oklahoma Heisman Trophy winner would score another TD on a 13-yard run in the third quarter, and gained 159 yards on 21 carries on the day.

The Detroit defense was a porous as its offense was productive. After Sims' first TD put the Lions up 21-13 with 2:58 left in the first half, it took the Redskins just two minutes to answer with a six-yard Joe Theismann to Art Monk scoring connection. It was 21-20 Detroit at the half.

The only third quarter score was a 28-yard Moseley field goal that gave the Redskins a two-point lead and set the stage for a wild ride in the fourth. The Lions took advantage of a 43-yard pass interference call against Lamar Parrish that set up Sims' second score to take a 28-23 lead a minute and a half into the final period. Detroit was driving for more when safety Tony Peters intercepted Hipple in the end zone. Given life, the Redskins offense drove 80 yards for a 12-yard run by Washington to seize back the lead at 30-28 with 6:39 left.

The Redskins appeared to have their momentum back when Detroit had to punt, but Joe Washington fumbled the ball back to the Lions. Eddie Murray hit a 50-yard field goal to give Detroit a 31-30 lead with 2:58 to play.

No problem for the Skins. Theismann scrambled for 20 yards to the Detroit 49 on the first play after the ensuing kickoff and the Skins were in business. Joe Washington carried five straight times to move the ball to the 27 and it was up to Moseley to hit a 44-yard field goal to give the Redskins the lead.

Moseley had been bothered by a groin pull since the second game of the season. He had made just one of seven from over 44 yards all year, but Moseley said, "My leg felt good today." It felt good enough to make the points to put the Redskins up 33-31 with 43 seconds left. Washington survived the last-second scare on the Hail Mary and walked off with a well-earned win.

11/15/81	Redskins (5-6) 30, GIANTS (5-6) 27 (OT)					63,133	
Was	7	3	7	10	3		**30**
NYG	7	6	7	7	0		**27**
NYG	Perkins 6 pass from Simms (Danelo kick)						
Was	Thompson 6 pass from Theismann (Moseley kick)						
NYG	Jackson 4 run (kick failed)						
Was	FG Moseley 25						
NYG	Bright 1 run (Danelo kick)						
Was	Riggins 1 run (Moseley kick)						
Was	Warren 3 pass from Theismann (Moseley kick)						
NYG	Mistler 27 pass from Brunner (Danelo kick)						
Was	FG Moseley 49						
Was	FG Moseley 48						

Giants Stadium—In a driving rain, Mark Moseley saved the game for the Redskins with a 49-yard field goal at the end of regulation. He then gave Washington a 30-27 win with another field goal in overtime.

Reserve Giants QB Scott Brunner had given the Giants a 27-24 lead with 45 seconds left in regulation by throwing a 27-yard touchdown pass to John Mistler. Brunner was inserted at signal caller in place of Phil Simms, who had injured his shoulder after being sacked by Dave Butz just a minute before the backup's big play.

On the ensuing kickoff, the Giants tried to keep the ball away from returner Mike Nelms. They were a little too clever as their squib kick was returned to the Washington 46. All it took was 22 yards on six plays for the Redskins to set up Moseley's game-tying attempt from 49 yards out. It was good as time ran out in regulation.

New York's fear of Nelms was well founded. He returned Dave Jennings' punt 26 yards to the Giants' 47 following New York's initial overtime possession. From there, it was Joe Washington for 12, John Riggins for two, and Washington again for another yard. Moseley's 48-yarder ended it 3:44 into the extra period.

11/22/81	COWBOYS (9-3) 24, Redskins (5-7) 10		64,583		
Was	0	7	3	0	**10**
Dal	7	3	7	7	**24**
Dal	Johnson 28 pass from White (Septien kick)				
Dal	FG Septien 25				
Was	Giaquinto 7 pass from Theismann (Moseley kick)				
Was	FG Moseley 26				
Dal	Cosbie 10 pass from White (Septien kick)				
Dal	Springs 1 run (Septien kick)				

Texas Stadium—Even though cornerback Jeris White had dropped a sure interception with open fields in front of him, the Redskins defense still had the Cowboys offense on the ropes. The Redskins had just scored on a 26-yard Mark Moseley field goal to tie the contest at 10. Dallas faced a third and 18 at its own 46.

Dave Butz chased quarterback Danny White out of the pocket and towards the sideline. White then committed what he later called a "cardinal sin" by throwing back across his body towards the middle of the field. Receiver Drew Pearson had broken open and he caught and held onto the ball at the Redskins 20 despite a viscous hit by safety Mark Murphy.

Five plays later, Dallas scored on a 10-yard pass from White to tight end Doug Cosbie and the Cowboys had the lead for good.

It may have been a different story had Joe Washington not torn a rib cartilage late in the first half. The running back was on his way to a career day with 84 yards rushing and another 47 receiving when he felt something pop in his rib cage.

Dallas coach Tom Landry described the Redskins' inability to move the ball without Joe in the lineup best: "Washington isn't Washington without Washington."

11/29/81	BILLS (8-5) 21, Redskins (5-8) 14		59,624		
Was	0	14	0	0	**14**
Buf	7	7	7	0	**21**
Buf	Butler 21 pass from Ferguson (Mike-Mayer kick)				
Buf	Hooks 4 run (Mike-Mayer kick)				
Was	Riggins 2 run (Moseley kick)				
Was	Monk 25 pass from Theismann (Moseley kick)				
Buf	Hooks 18 run (Mike-Mayer kick)				

Rich Stadium—The Redskins were game, rallying from a 14-0 second-quarter deficit to tie the contest with 11 seconds left in the half, but they couldn't overcome five turnovers in losing to the Bills 21-14.

"We just had too many turnovers, too many mistakes," said Joe Gibbs. "And we just had too much other stuff to overcome."

The "other stuff" that Gibbs was referring to was the officiating. Three calls in particular rankled Gibbs and his players.

After finishing off the first half with two touchdowns in just over two minutes to tie the game, they forced a punt on Buffalo's first second-half possession. As Mike Nelms moved in to field the ball, the Bills' Roland Hooks got in his way. The ball hit the ground, bounced off of Nelms' leg and Buffalo pounced on the ball at the Washington 26. That led to Hooks' 18-yard touchdown run for a 21-14 Buffalo lead.

Using one of his strongest curse words, Gibbs said, "Cripes, you are supposed to give him a chance to field the ball. We have the best punt return man in the league and they have to get out of his way."

The non-call was followed by a pair of penalties that thwarted Washington's comeback efforts. First, an illegal procedure wiped out a third and 27 conversion. Joe Theismann was forced to leave the game after being shaken up and Tom Flick went under center. After a false start penalty, Theismann trotted back on the field. A defender tipped Theismann's pass into the arms of Virgil Seay, who had the yardage for the first down.

It turned out to be for naught. Bills defensive coach Tom Catlin complained that Theismann had not sat out the one play required after an injury timeout and the officials agreed, wiping out the play.

Later on, in the fourth quarter, a nice screen play to John Riggins that carried to the Bill 32 was negated by a holding call that was far away from the action. The Redskins were unable to mount a threat after that.

12/6/81	REDSKINS (6-8) 15, Eagles (9-5) 13		52,206		
Phil	0	13	0	0	**13**
Was	6	0	0	9	**15**
Was	Washington 6 run (kick failed)				
Phil	Campbell 25 pass from Jaworski (Franklin kick)				
Phil	Campbell 5 pass from Jaworski (kick blocked))				
Was	FG Moseley 45				
Was	Coleman 52 interception return (kick failed)				

RFK Stadium—With 54 seconds left, nobody was hoping more than Mark Moseley that something would go awry with the Eagles' 24-yard field goal try. The Redskins veteran kicker had flat-out missed two extra point attempts earlier in the game and the Eagles would take the lead on a chip shot for their kicker Tony Franklin.

The first PAT shank came after Joe Washington's six-yard touchdown run to open the scoring. After that, the Eagles dominated the game for the next two quarters, but were only able to put 13 points on the board, failing on an extra point themselves when Dave Butz and Dallas Hickman blocked Franklin's attempt after Philly's second touchdown. "It bounced off my head," Butz said, "and Dallas put it away."

For the game, the Eagles outgained the Redskins 416-176 with Ron Jaworski throwing for 266 yards and Wilbert Montgomery rushing for 116.

But Jaworski threw three interceptions to help the Redskins stay close. The third pick, in fact, gave the Redskins the lead. Monte Coleman grabbed a tipped ball on a screen pass intended for Booker Russell and raced into the end zone untouched. The play was an indication of how the team's fortunes had turned from earlier in the season. "Either Russell or a lineman had tipped it and it fell right into my hands," said Coleman. "If I had stayed on the sideline, he (Jaworski) might have had a chance, but when I cut against the grain, there was no way."

No way, unless a penalty nullified the play and a yellow flag rested on the field. "I dropped my head at first," Coleman said, "and said 'Oh, no!'"

The call, though, was against the Eagles and the Redskins held an improbable 15-13 lead with 6:39 left in the game. The lead stayed right there as Moseley again shanked the extra point. "There's no reason to miss an extra point," said Moseley. "I don't know why I missed them."

No matter what the reason, the misses opened the door for the Eagles to take the lead after Jaworski drove them into field goal position in the last minute. The attempt would be from 24 yards, virtually automatic for the Franklin's powerful leg.

The snap looked good, but Franklin never got the kick off as holder John Sciarra couldn't hold on to the ball. He picked it up off the ground and scrambled to try to find a receiver, but the Redskins buried him at the 23. Washington killed the final seconds.

"The snap was perfect," said Sciarra. "I think I was trying to place the ball down a little too soon. It all happened so fast. My teammates were counting on me. I let them down and I feel really bad." From the Redskins' perspective, better him than Moseley.

12/13/81	REDSKINS (7-8) 38, Colts (1-14) 14		49,706		
Bal	7	0	7	0	**14**
Was	7	21	10	0	**38**
Was	Seay 38 pass from Theismann (Moseley kick)				
Bal	Butler 10 pass from Jones (Wood kick)				
Was	Riggins 8 run (Moseley kick)				
Was	Riggins 14 run (Moseley kick)				

Was	Theismann 8 run (Moseley kick)
Was	Monk 13 pass from Theismann (Moseley kick)
Bal	McCall 6 pass from Jones (Wood kick)
Was	FG Moseley 32

RFK Stadium—The Redskins piled up a 28-7 halftime lead and cruised to an easy 38-14 win over the Colts.

It started well for the Redskins. On their opening possession, they drove in for a touchdown on a 38-yard pass from Joe Theismann to a wide-open Virgil Seay. The Colts fought back to tie it late in the first quarter on a 10-yard pass from Bert Jones to Raymond Butler.

The Redskins took control in the second period. First, they drove to two John Riggins touchdown runs, one of eight yards, the other 14. Then, as time was winding down, Mark Murphy tipped and snared a Jones pass. After that, with less than 30 seconds left in the half, Theismann scored on an eight-yard quarterback draw to stretch the lead to three touchdowns.

Art Monk, who caught seven passes on the day, made a nice, leaping grab of a Theismann pass to score a TD from 13 yards out to make it 35-7 in the third quarter.

Despite the margin that most would think to be comfortable, Joe Gibbs kept on calling aggressive plays, sending Monk deep downfield and running Joe Washington around end. "I just didn't think that we had it put away," said Gibbs. Perhaps, after their 0-5 start, it was difficult for finding fault with the Redskins for wanting to make sure.

Joe Theismann scored on an eight-yard quarterback draw with 17 seconds left in the first half to give the Redskins a 28-7 halftime lead. For the game, the Redskins piled up 486 yards of total offense to 337 for the hapless Colts.

12/20/81	**Redskins (8-8) 30, RAMS (6-10) 7**				52,224	
Was	6	10	14	0		30
LA	0	7	0	0		7
Was	Washington 4 pass from Theismann (kick blocked)
LA	Guman 1 run (Corral kick)
Was	Riggins 1 run (Moseley kick)
Was	FG Moseley 35
Was	Riggins 1 run (Moseley kick)
Was	Seay 37 pass from Theismann (Moseley kick)

Anaheim Stadium—The Redskins rolled for 502 yards of total offense in routing the Rams, who could have mailed in this season finale.

In the first quarter, Washington took the lead when Joe Theismann threw a four-yard touchdown pass to Joe Washington. The conversion attempt was blocked and the Redskins took a 6-0 lead into the second quarter.

After LA took a 7-6 lead on Mike Guman's one-yard touchdown run, Washington took control with two scoring drives. One march ended with John Riggins' one-yard touchdown plunge, another with Mark Moseley's 35-yard field goal and the visitors led 16-7 at the half.

Following intermission, the Redskins put it away with the defense leading the way. First Money Coleman picked off Dan Pastorini's pass, setting up a one-yard Riggins touchdown blast. The Joe Lavender drew a bead on rookie Jeff Kemp's first NFL pass and picked it off. Soon after that Theismann threw a 37-yard touchdown pass to Virgil Seay to make it 30-7.

Joe Theismann was 14 of 22 passing with two TD throws and Joe Washington scampered for 96 yards on 14 carries. Washington's defense allowed just 165 yards to the Rams.

1982
Head Coach: Joe Gibbs
Record: 8-1, First Seed in NFC Super Bowl Tournament
Playoffs: 4-0, Super Bowl XVII Champions

Honors: Joe Gibbs NFL Coach of the Year; Charlie Brown Pro Bowl; Mark Moseley NFL Most Valuable Player, Pro Bowl, All Pro; Mike Nelms Pro Bowl; Tony Peters, Pro Bowl; Joe Theismann Pro Bowl

Hall of Fame: Sam Huff, Linebacker 1964-1967, 1968

Apr 13
Theismann in the Fold
Four-year, $1.5 million deal makes him highest-paid Redskin ever

---

Apr 28
Corner Market: Redskins Trade Lamar Parrish, Draft Vernon Dean
Parrish goes to Buffalo; Skins draft kicker Miller to challenge Moseley

---

Moseley Dangled as Trade Bait

Sep 1—The Redskins will most likely offer their longtime kicker Mark Moseley to several teams as they seek help at defensive end.

It's not clear what value Moseley might have on the trade market, considering that he might soon be released and could be obtained with no compensation.

Sep 3
Oh-fer: Redskins Lose to Bengals to Complete 0-4 Preseason

Moseley Survives Challenge, Kicks Rookie Dan Miller to Bench

Sep 4—Figuring that two legs are better than one, the Redskins have decided to keep both of their kickers.

Mark Moseley, the veteran incumbent, will be on the active roster. The team also decided to keep Dan Miller, a rookie who was drafted in the 11th round to challenge Moseley, on the four-man taxi squad. Reports are that they are still not convinced that Moseley is reliable enough to last the entire season.

Miller's two field goal misses in the final preseason game against Cincinnati probably saved Moseley's job. It also had been rumored that Moseley would be traded.

Moseley offered both praise for Miller and a defense of his capabilities.

About Miller, he said, "He's a good kicker and he's going to do well for some team in this league, I'm sure of that."

He also understands the need to show the coaching staff, in its second season, that he still can get the job done. "Last year I had injury problems, so they did not see me perform like I'm capable of performing.

"I want to show them I am the best, so they know they made the right decision."

9/12/82	**Redskins (1-0) 37, EAGLES (0-1) 34 (OT)**				68,885	
Was	0	14	0	20	3	**37**
Phil	10	3	14	7	0	**34**

Phil	Harrington 4 run (Franklin kick)
Phil	FG Franklin 44
Was	Monk 5 pass from Theismann (Moseley kick)
Was	C. Brown 8 pass from Theismann (Moseley kick)
Phil	FG Franklin 44
Phil	Montgomery 2 run (Franklin kick)
Phil	Montgomery 42 pass from Jaworski (Franklin kick)
Was	C. Brown 78 pass from Theismann (Moseley kick)
Was	Riggins 2 run (Moseley kick)
Was	FG Moseley 30
Phil	Carmichael 4 pass from Jaworski (Franklin kick)
Was	FG Moseley 48
Was	FG Moseley 26

Veterans Stadium—It appeared that the expected Eagle rout was underway. Philadelphia's Tony Franklin had just kicked a 44-yard field goal to give the Eagles a 10-0 lead and Mike Nelms fumbled the ensuing kickoff. Philly recovered at the Washington 18 and visions of the 0-5 start the previous year began to creep into the minds of some Redskins.

"I had visions of early last year happening again," Joe Theismann said. "All too many mistakes too soon. I didn't want us to fall apart."

The Redskins did not fall apart. Wilbert Montgomery lost the handle on an end sweep and Washington pounced on the ball at the 15. It was the Redskins' turn to grab momentum.

Joe Theismann fired two touchdown passes—one to Art Monk, the other to Charlie Brown—to give the Redskins the lead. Monk's catch was a beauty, a leaping grab in the end zone.

Brown's touchdown came with 35 seconds left in the half. After that score, Joe Gibbs made a strategic error that swung the game the Eagles' way. Although the Eagles appeared content to run the clock out, go back into the locker room and regroup, Gibbs called a time out, hoping the Eagles would punt.

Fine, said Eagles quarterback Ron Jaworski, who promptly went to receiver Harold Carmichael for 46 yards to set up a 44-yard Franklin field goal at the gun to pull the Eagles within one.

Buoyed by the events before halftime, the Eagles dominated the third quarter, with Montgomery making up for his earlier miscue to score two touchdowns. It was 27-14 entering the fourth quarter, and time for the game to take yet another turn.

From the Washington 22, Brown zipped past cornerback Roynell Young down the left sideline. Theismann found him and, suddenly, it was 27-21. Nelms took his turn at redemption, returning an Eagle punt 28 yards to the Philadelphia 48. It took just four plays for the Redskins to take the lead on a four-yard John Riggins run and Mark Moseley's extra point.

It was then Eagles coach Dick Vermiel's turn to have strategy backfire on him. Philadelphia was in punt formation at its own 23 on fourth and one. Despite the fact that Redskins were yelling "Fake, fake, watch the fake!" to each other, they snapped the ball to short man Frank LeMaster anyway. He was smothered for a one-yard loss.

Moseley kicked a 30-yard field goal and the Redskins were up 31-27 with 2:48 left. After the kickoff, the Eagles had possession at their own 10. It was the Eagles' turn.

In what Gibbs called "a masterful drive," Jaworski took the Eagles down the field 90 yards for the go-ahead score. Using the sidelines, the Eagles got off 14 plays in just 1:44. Although they took the lead 34-31 on Carmichael's circus catch in the end zone—he batted the ball in the air, fell and made the catch flat on his back—there were still 58 seconds left on the clock. Time for one last momentum change.

Nelms returned Franklin's short kickoff to the Washington 37. A 10-yard completion to Monk got the Skins into Eagles territory. With six seconds left, Theismann scrambled down to the 31. Moseley's kick as time expired would have been good from 60 yards.

In overtime, Monk caught one pass for 27 yards to set the Redskins up at the Philly 42. Three plays later, it was Theismann to Monk again, and Herman Edwards failed in a desperate attempt to knock it down. Monk spun around and rolled down to the nine. Gibbs immediately called for Moseley and his 26-yarder ended it with 4:47 gone in the extra period.

9/19/82	**REDSKINS (2-0) 21, BUCS (0-2) 13**				66,187	
Was	9	9	0	3	**21**	
TB	0	6	0	7	**13**	

Was	Brown 8 pass from Theismann (kick failed)
Was	FG Moseley 35
TB	House 62 pass from Williams (kick failed)
Was	FG Moseley 21
Was	Jordan recovered blocked punt in end zone (kick failed)
TB	Wilder 7 run (Capece kick)
Was	FG Moseley 19

Tampa Stadium—In a Florida downpour, the Redskins pulled out their newest secret weapon—the Riggo Drill.

In fact, the term was coined to describe a segment of practice where John Riggins would run the ball five straight times. On this day where rain made the passing game difficult and the kicking game an adventure, Riggins carried the ball a team record-tying 34 times for 136 yards. Joe Gibbs mentioned the Riggo Drill in his post game comments and the term caught on.

Riggins' running, along with some Tampa miscues, set up three Mark Moseley field goals, a touchdown pass from Joe Theismann to Charlie Brown and kept Doug Williams and the Tampa Bay offense off the field. That, and a blocked punt recovered by Curtis Jordan in the end zone for a touchdown, was enough to beat the Bucs.

After taking a 9-0 lead in the first quarter, the Redskins watched Williams strike back quickly. On the first play of the second quarter, the Bucs quarterback unloaded a 62-yard touchdown bomb to Kevin House and suddenly Tampa Bay was back in it, although they missed the extra point to make it 9-6.

After another Moseley field goal, it was Jordan's turn. He slogged through the line, blocked the Bucs' punt, and splashed down in the end zone with the ball for six. Although the extra point again was missed, the Redskins had a little breathing room at 18-6.

The score remained there until James Wilder ran in for a Buccaneer touchdown from seven yards out early in the fourth quarter. The Skins responded with a nine and a half minute drive to another Moseley field goal and appeared to be in control with 4:16 left to play.

It looked as though they had lost that control two plays later. Williams connected with House on another bomb for 71 yards and an apparent TD. The officials, however, ruled that House had gone out of bounds and then back in to catch the ball, a violation of the rules. Tampa Bay had to punt, and Washington ran out the last 3:37 of the clock with Riggins carrying the ball on the last seven plays.

They're Out: Redskins Join NFL Players in Strike

Sep 20— "I'm really depressed, really down."

The words were spoken at Redskins Park today by Joe Gibbs, but they were spoken all over the country by Joe Fan. The announcement came from NFL Players Association President Gene Upshaw.

"All NFL training facilities will be struck. There will be no practices, no games, until the National Football League bargains in good faith to reach an agreement."

It is the first strike in the history of professional sports.

"How do you act when this happens?" first-year receiver Charlie Brown asked. "I just have a strange feeling in my stomach right now. It's really happened."

Some veterans weren't all that worried about missing a few paychecks. "I'll be okay without a check for a while. I'm not worried about it," said Dexter Manley.

Gibbs Has 'Gut Feeling' That Season is Over as Strike Drags On

Nov 9—As the 1982 NFL players' strike dragged on, it started to appear that there would be no resolution. The players seemed to feel obligated to stay on strike because, well, they'd already been out for so long. The owners seemed to be in no hurry to settle. Meanwhile, around town, fans moped as the grim reality that no settlement was imminent and the financial impact of the strike began to grow to staggering figures.

It was getting to the point for several players where they might have to find jobs, a prospect that they all dreaded. "I hate to work," said running back Nick Giaquinto. "That's why I'm playing football."

Happy Days! Strike Ends, Games to Resume

Nov 16—Then, suddenly, it was over.

A marathon negotiating session ended today with the principal negotiators for the owners and players reaching a tentative agreement to end the strike. The agreement guaranteed that the teams would pay out more than $1.25 billion in player costs over the next four years, plus a severance pay package that would help ease a player's transition into life after his playing career was over.

It was back to work for Gibbs, his coaches, and the Redskins. The players report on Wednesday to prepare for their Sunday game against the Giants. The coach hopes that the team could regain the momentum generated by the Redskins' 2-0 start before the strike.

"The key now is can we get back to where we were before the strike," said Gibbs.

Gibbs isn't going to go easy on the team, but there were no plans to make up for lost time with extra sessions.

"We are going to throw an awful lot at them right away," he said. "It will be a matter of how much they can recall. But we won't have any extra drills or anything like that. We will have a normal work week, which starts on Wednesday anyway."

11/21/82	**Redskins (3-0) 27, GIANTS (0-3) 17**			70,766	
Was	7	14	3	3	**27**
NYG	0	3	7	7	**17**
Was	Wonsley 1 pass from Theismann (Moseley kick)				
Was	Brown 39 pass from Theismann (Moseley kick)				
Was	Riggins 2 run (Moseley kick)				
NYG	FG Danelo 20				
NYG	Perkins 26 pass from Brunner (Danelo kick)				

Was	FG Moseley 37
NYG	Chatman 1 run (Danelo kick)
Was	FG Moseley 29

Giants Stadium—The Redskins ran up a 21-0 lead in the second quarter and managed to hold the Giants at arm's length during the second half to take a 27-17 win.

Washington took the opening kickoff and demonstrated no ill effects of the nine-week layoff that had just concluded with the settling of the player's strike. They drove 73 yards to a touchdown after getting the opening kickoff, the score coming on a one-yard flip from Joe Theismann to fullback Otis Wonsley.

In the second quarter, the Redskins struck quickly to pull away. Charlie Brown caught a Theismann pass, broke away from an attempted tackle, and completed a 39-yard touchdown play. Moments later, Dexter Manley gathered in a tipped ball and Washington was back in business at the Giants' 18. Four plays later, it was John Riggins taking it in from four yards out and it was 21-0.

Trailing 21-3 midway through the third quarter, New York made its bid to get back into it. The Giants' Frank Marion came through the middle untouched and blocked a Jeff Hayes punt. Shortly after that Scott Brunner threw to Johnny Perkins for 26 yards and a touchdown that made it 21-10.

Mark Moseley kicked a field goal to bring the score to 24-10, but the Giants would not go away. A 77-yard drive that culminated in a one-yard scoring run by Cliff Chatman got the Giants back within a touchdown. Finally, one more Moseley field goal—a 29-yarder with 1:23 left—sealed the deal for Washington.

11/28/82	**REDSKINS (4-0) 13, Eagles (1-3) 9**			48,313	
Phil	0	0	9	0	**9**
Was	3	7	3	0	**13**
Was	FG Moseley 45				
Was	Brown 65 pass from Theismann (Moseley kick)				
Phil	FG Franklin 41				
Phil	Carmichael 56 pass from Jaworski (kick failed)				
Was	FG Moseley 43				

RFK Stadium—Three days after Thanksgiving is a bit late to be having an NFL home opener but thanks to a pair of scheduled road games to start the season and the players' strike, that's what the Redskins had this day in a rain-soaked RFK Stadium.

Early on, it appeared that the Skins would dominate. After a 45-yard Mark Moseley field goal in the first quarter, the Redskins were at their own 35 early in the second. Eagle cornerback Roynell Young bit on a pump fake and Charlie Brown burst past him. Theismann hit Brown at the 25 and Brown raced into the end zone for a 65-yard touchdown and a 10-0 lead.

But the rain—and the Eagles defense—started to equalize things. The Eagles had some scoring opportunities but a missed field goal, fumble recovery by Tony Peters and Jeris White interception kept them off the board.

It was a different story in the third quarter. Even though they gambled and failed on a fourth and one at the Washington 18, the Eagles scored on a 41-yard Tony Franklin field goal and a 56-yard strike from Ron Jaworski to Harold Carmichael. The Eagles failed to tie the game, though, when Franklin's point after attempt hit off the left upright and bounced to the turf. That left Washington with a precarious 10-9 lead.

Mike Nelms gave the Redskins a big boost with a 58-yard return on the ensuing kickoff and soon after that Moseley kicked a 43-yard field goal, forcing Philly to score a touchdown to win.

Philadelphia threatened to do that in the fourth quarter but an interception by Mark Murphy shut off one rally. Tony Peters got another pick, the game's eighth turnover, with 1:43 left to close out the Eagles.

12/5/82	**Cowboys (4-1) 24, REDSKINS (4-1) 10**		54,633	
Dal	0	7	10	7	**24**
Was	0	0	0	10	**10**
Dal	Springs 8 pass from White (Septien kick)			
Dal	FG Septien 31			
Dal	Newsome 14 run (Septien kick)			
Was	FG Moseley 38			
Was	Brown 17 pass from Theismann (Moseley kick)			
Dal	Springs 46 run (Septien kick)			

RFK Stadium—The crowd was rocking. The Redskins had fought back from a 17-0 fourth-quarter deficit to within 17-10. Dallas was in punt formation on fourth and three at its own 21.

For the longest time during this game, it appeared certain that the hated Cowboys would spoil the Redskins' perfect 4-0 record. Dallas had taken a 7-0 lead in the second quarter on the strength of an eight-yard touchdown pass from Danny White to Ron Springs. They had made it stand up by blitzing Joe Theismann, sending cornerbacks, safeties, and linebackers. It seemed that every Cowboy except Tom Landry spent time in the Redskins' backfield. Theismann was sacked seven times and Washington was unable to get inside the Dallas 30 during the first half.

It didn't get any better in the third quarter. After a 31-yard field goal by Rafael Septien, receiver Tony Hill gained 22 on a reverse to set up Timmy Newsome's 14-yard touchdown run. Going into the fourth quarter, it was 17-0.

A Washington field goal to cut it to 17-3 didn't inspire much confidence as Theismann was sacked twice during the drive. The next drive was better as Theismann had some time to throw. Virgil Seay caught a pass for 24 yards and Theismann went to Joe Washington for seven. From the Dallas 17, Theismann pump faked to Charlie Brown then threw to him. Brown got by three Dallas defenders on his way to the end zone. Moseley's point after made it 17-10 with 9:45 left and RFK was getting very, very loud.

It got louder after Dallas went nowhere and lined up to punt. The Redskins had a return set up and put no pressure on White, who pulled double duty as the team's punter. Seeing nothing but the backs of Redskin jerseys, White took off running. Rarely has a crowd become so quiet so quickly. After a 20-yard gain, White was tackled but the damage had been done. While Dallas punted and the Redskins regained possession with five and a half minutes to go, it was apparent that White's run had deflated the Redskins. Theismann was sacked again, and Ron Springs' 46-yard touchdown run shortly after the Redskins punted the ball back ended it.

12/12/82	**Redskins (5-1) 12, CARDINAL (3-3) 7**		35,308	
Was	3	3	3	3	**12**
StL	0	0	0	7	**7**
Was	FG Moseley 32			
Was	FG Moseley 30			
Was	FG Moseley 20			
Was	FG Moseley 24			
StL	LaFleur 5 pass from Hart (O'Donoghue kick)			

Busch Stadium—It took a bit of good fortune, but Mark Moseley kept his string of consecutive successful field goal attempts alive. The Redskins needed all four of them to escape with a 12-7 win.

Late in the first quarter, Moseley missed a 37-yard field goal and it seemed that his streak of 14 straight field goals had ended. But the Cardinals were flagged for being offside, wiping the attempt off the records. Moseley's retry from 32 yards was good. Moseley would finish the game with a string of 18 successful field goal attempts, two short of the NFL record.

His next attempt was just as adventurous. This 30-yard attempt was low and wobbling, but it just snuck through near the intersection of the crossbar and the left upright. Style points, zero; points on the board, three.

On the other hand, the Cardinals were suffering from some ill fortune. The first time they touched the ball, Stump Mitchell took a punt back 80 yards into the end zone, but a penalty nullified the runback. Undeterred, running back Ottis Anderson ran for 64 on the next play, but Neil O'Donoghue missed a 26-yard field goal attempt.

The pattern continued for the first three quarters; Washington would drive and settle for a field goal, St. Louis would drive and settle for nothing. Finally, after Moseley's fourth field goal with 10:05 left in the game, St. Louis coach Jim Hanifan replaced quarterback Neil Lomax with Cardinal veteran Jim Hart.

You can take your pick: Hanifan was either a genius for making the move as Hart immediately led St. Louis on a 63-yard touchdown drive, or a fool for waiting so long to make the change. The score came on a five-yard pass to Greg LaFleur with 3:08 left.

The Redskins turned to John Riggins to run out the clock. He carried six straight times, but was unable to complete a classic Riggo drill. On third and two, with just over a minute left and the Cardinals out of time outs, Riggins fumbled as he fought for the first down. It was his first fumble in his last 318 carries.

Hart tried to make some magic, but Mark Murphy batted down a final desperation pass in the end zone.

Gibbs Wants More Points

Dec. 13—Although his team is sitting pretty at 5-1, atop the heap in the combined NFC standings, Joe Gibbs knows that things can fall apart in a hurry if the Redskins can't put the ball in the end zone more often.

"We aren't scoring enough points to consistently win right now," Gibbs said. "We've been very fortunate the last three games.

"It's a concern. We have to score more," he continued. "We've had field goals . . . but we need more touchdowns."

Gibbs would like to be able to breathe easy at the end of a game now and then. "It would be nice to be able to play in the fourth quarter and not worry about hanging on," he said. But I guess we are never going to blow anyone out.

12/19/82	**REDSKINS (6-1) 15, Giants (3-4) 14**		50,030	
NYG	7	7	0	0	**14**
Was	0	3	6	6	**15**
NYG	Perkins 28 pass from Brunner (Danelo kick)			
Was	FG Moseley 20			
NYG	Woolfolk 1 run (Danelo kick)			
Was	Washington 22 run (kick failed)			
Was	FG Moseley 31			
Was	FG Moseley 42			

RFK Stadium—"It was like a Hollywood script," the Redskins' Mark Murphy said. "[You] couldn't have written it any better." Except that even fiction couldn't have been as compelling or exciting as the truth about this one.

A win would give Washington a playoff spot; a loss would put them in the muddled middle of the playoff picture. Before Mark Moseley—who was this close (thumb and index finger an eighth of an inch apart) to losing his job during training camp—had a chance to attempt a game-winning, playoff-clinching record-setting field goal, the Redskins had to scrap and come off the mat and give him a chance to try it.

Washington turned the ball over five times in the first half, four of those being interceptions thrown by Joe Theismann. The first and third picks by the Giants led to touchdowns. The Redskins could only hold on to the ball long enough to tally a Moseley field goal and trailed at halftime 14-3.

After intermission, Washington began to get some control. Their 10-play, 80-yard touchdown drive to open the second half was exactly what Joe Gibbs had asked for at halftime, even though the scoring play wasn't exactly as he had drawn it up in the playbook.

After passes to Don Warren and Charlie Brown led to a first down at the New York 22, Gibbs called for a halfback option. Joe Washington was to sweep right, pull up and throw to Art Monk. New York, though, sniffed it out and Monk was covered. Washington reversed his field and took off around left end. The Giants were caught flat-footed and the only obstacle between Washington and the end zone was cornerback Terry Jackson. Theismann dispatched Jackson with a textbook cross-body block and Washington scooted into the end zone.

It had been snowing off and on the entire day, leaving the field wet and muddy. The point after attempt slipped off Moseley's wet toe, and the Redskins trailed 14-9.

As the fourth quarter began, the snow began to fall harder. It was time for a Riggo Drill, Gibbs decided, calling John Riggins' number eight times in 10 plays. It was good enough to get in position for Moseley to kick a 31-yard field goal with 6:23 left in the game to bring Washington to within 14-12. It was Moseley's 20th straight successful attempt, tying Garo Yepremian's NFL record for consecutive field goals made. He was hoping for an opportunity to break the mark.

Deprived of Washington turnovers, the New York offense did nothing in the second half. They were given a golden opportunity to salt away the game after their defense stopped Riggins short on a fourth and one at the Washington 40, but Scott Brunner was sacked twice and they had to punt. The Redskins took possession at their own 29 with 3:38 left.

On second down, Theismann found tight end Rick Walker over the middle for 20 yards to get the drive started. A facemask call pushed it forward to the Giants 44. Gibbs wanted to get inside the 30 for a field goal attempt.

On third and five from the 39, Theismann squeezed the ball to Brown between two defenders for 14 yards to the 25. Riggins ran for six to the 19 and then six more. Walker, though, was holding on the second run and the ball went back to the 29. After two more Riggins runs, the ball was at the 25 and the Redskins let the clock run down to nine seconds before calling time out. It was snowing as hard as it had been all day.

With the record, playoff spot, and game all riding on the kick, Jeff Bostic's snap and Theismann's hold were perfect. Moseley tried to get a little extra foot into it, giving the Giant's Byron Hunt a chance to get a finger on the ball. The kick wobbled, but it could not have been more beautiful for the Redskins and their fans. It cleared the crossbar with plenty to spare.

12/26/82	Redskins (7-1) 27, SAINTS (3-5) 10			48,667	
Was	7	10	0	10	27
NO	0	7	3	0	10
Was	Brown 57 pass from Theismann (Moseley kick)				
NO	J Rogers 4 run (Anderson kick)				
Was	Brown 58 pass from Theismann (Moseley kick)				
Was	FG Moseley 38				
NO	FG Anderson 36				
Was	FG Moseley 45				
Was	Riggins 1 run (Moseley kick)				

Superdome—It didn't seem like a fair fight, with New Orleans coming into the contest without Kenny Stabler, their starting quarter, and George Rogers, the NFL's leading rusher the year before. But it took a controversial call on a Charlie Brown pass reception and a big run by Joe Washington to put away the spirited Saints, taking a 27-10 win.

Brown had already caught one touchdown pass, a 57-yarder over the middle from Joe Theismann. The Saints had tied it up after Washington fumbled at the New Orleans 40 and Jimmy Rogers took it in from the four. The Redskins wasted a chance to

take the lead when Theismann fumbled at the New Orleans three. Soon, however, the Theismann-to-Brown combination struck again.

New Orleans came with a safety blitz that both quarterback and receiver recognized quickly. Brown ran a go pattern down the sideline with cornerback Johnnie Poe in single coverage. Poe bumped into Brown, knocking the receiver out of bounds for a couple of steps. This drew a flag for pass interference. As the ball arrived, it appeared that Poe tipped it. What's certain is that Brown grabbed it and rolled into the end zone.

Although Brown was an ineligible receiver since he stepped out of bounds, the fact that a defender tipped the ball made all players on the field eligible to catch the ball. Although Poe and New Orleans coach Bum Phillips argued strongly that the defender had not touched the ball, an officials huddle reaffirmed the touchdown call. The Redskins had a 14-7 lead.

In the fourth quarter, after the Saints had pulled within 17-10, a Mark Moseley field goal and John Riggins' one-yard touchdown run wrapped it up for Washington.

1/2/83	REDSKINS (8-1) 28, Cardinals (5-4) 0			52,544	
StL	0	0	0	0	0
Was	7	7	7	7	28
Was	Walker 25 pass from Theismann (Moseley kick)				
Was	Didier 2 pass from Theismann (Moseley kick)				
Was	Harmon 1 run (Moseley kick)				
Was	Washington 8 pass from Theismann (Moseley kick)				

RFK Stadium—"I'm afraid we've got a lot of guys hurt," was Joe Gibbs' most notable post game comment. While the Redskins were happy to have gained home field advantage throughout the NFC playoffs, they weren't in much of a mood to celebrate. The team suffered a rash of injuries in this game, the most serious being Art Monk's broken foot. Some bumps and strains to other players would heal, but Monk was gone for the playoffs.

In Monk's absence, Joe Theismann found that he had some tight ends that could catch the football. After Dexter Manley recovered a shotgun snap that went over the head of Cardinals quarterback Neil Lomax, Theismann hit Rick Walker with a touchdown pass from 25 yards out. It was the first scoring catch for the Redskins' tight end all season. Clint Didier got the second such reception to cap a 52-yard, nine play drive in the second quarter.

The only notable moment in the rest of the first half came when Mark Moseley was wide right on a 40-yard field goal try with six seconds left. It was his first miss of the season and his first after an NFL-record 23 consecutive successful attempts.

Before the Cardinals got their second first down of the game, it was 21-0. Jeris White's interception set up a one-yard run by Clarence Harmon. It looked like St. Louis would dent the scoreboard late in the third, but Lomax fumbled the snap at the Washington one and Dave Butz recovered at the two. It took 12 plays for the Redskins to remove any doubt about the outcome by driving 98 yards to Joe Washington's eight-yard TD pass that closed out the scoring.

Best in Class: Gibbs, Moseley Win NFL Honors

Jan 4—The Redskins got another laurel heaped on them today as the Associated Press named Joe Gibbs the NFL Coach of the Year. This comes on top of kicker Mark Moseley being honored by the same organization by winning the NFL Most Valuable Player award.

Moseley was surprised by the award. "I never thought in my wildest dreams that I'd even be in a position to be nominated," he said. "It's a real shock and a great honor."

The award came because of Moseley's clutch kicking. Of the Redskins eight victories, Moseley field goals provided the margin of victory in five of them. This includes two game-winners in the final seconds of a game.

One of those clutch kicks gave the Redskins a 15-14 win over the Giants and clinched a playoff berth. That boot also enabled Moseley to break the NFL record for the most consecutive successful field goal attempts.

For his part, Gibbs fretted about playoff scheduling and injuries. The Redskins are slated to meet the Detroit Lions in the first round of the playoffs on Saturday. The coach's complaint was that, as the number one seed, the Redskins should get the advantage of playing on Sunday. That would give them an extra day to rest injured players such as Mike Nelms, Joe Washington, and Clarence Harmon.

"I voiced my opinion on that (to league officials)," Gibbs said. "I told them that the number one and number two seeds should play on Sunday."

Gibbs, as usual, expressed concern about the upcoming opponent even though the Lions qualified for the playoffs with a losing record at 4-5.

"They sure have some talented people," he said.

NFC First Round Playoff Game
Saturday, January 8, 1983
RFK Stadium
Washington, D.C.

1/8/83	REDSKINS 31, Lions 7				55,.45
Det	0	0	7	0	7
Was	10	14	7	0	31
Was	White 77 interception return (Moseley kick)				
Was	FG Moseley 26				
Was	Garrett 21 pass from Theismann (Moseley kick)				
Was	Garrett 21 pass from Theismann (Moseley kick)				
Was	Garrett 27 pass from Theismann (Moseley kick)				
Det	Hill 15 pass from Hipple (Murray kick)				

Alvin Garrett came out of nowhere to catch three touchdown passes, John Riggins came out of hiding to rush for 119 yards, and the defense came at the Lions from all directions, forcing five turnovers to lead a 31-7 romp over Detroit.

Detroit had never won in Washington—and their fortunes weren't going to change on this day. The Lions had a nice drive going in the first quarter when Eric Hipple attempted to throw to running back Billy Sims in the flat. Jeris White stepped in front of the pass at the Washington 23 and had nothing in front of him but green grass and white lines. Seventy-seven yards later, the Redskins had a 7-0 lead.

Turnovers continued to plague the Lions. Cornerback Vernon Dean blindsided Hipple on a blitz, causing a fumble that Darryl Grant covered at the Detroit 19, and setting up a 25-yard Mark Moseley field goal. Then it was Garrett's turn to shine.

The 5-7 receiver out of Angelo State had caught just one pass for six yards during the regular season. He was thrust into the starting lineup when Art Monk suffered a broken foot against the Cardinals in the last game of the regular season. Charlie Brown, headed for the Pro Bowl, drew double coverage from the Lions secondary, so it was up to Garrett to help make the passing game productive.

Garrett's first contribution came early in the second quarter when Theismann was under heavy pressure from a Lions blitz. The receiver slipped past cornerback Bruce McNorton and Theismann managed to loft the ball over the defender's head and into Garrett's arms for a 21-yard touchdown to make it 17-0. Six plays after Mike Nelms returned a Detroit punt 39 yards to the

Lions 48, it was again Garrett beating McNorton and Theismann lofting a 21-yard TD pass.

Riggins broke off a 25-yard run to spur a 74-yard touchdown drive to open the second half. That drive ended in, of course, another Theismann to Garrett TD connection, this one from 27 yards out.

Riggins was the team's leading rusher during the abbreviated regular season, gaining 553 yards in nine games, but he hadn't been a focal point of the offense. Sensing that this team had a chance to do something special, Riggins went to Gibbs before the playoffs and told the coach, "Give me the ball." Gibbs told Theismann to give him the ball 25 times and his 119 yards ground up the Lions, killing the clock and setting up Theismann's strikes to Garrett. It was the first game of the best playoff run a running back has ever had.

Gibbs: Skins Will Be Tough
Out 'If We Play Our Game'

Jan. 9—As far as Joe Gibbs is concerned, the Redskins' fate in the playoffs is in their own hands.

"The key now is ourselves," he said, saying that as long as the Redskins play error-free football, they should win no matter what the opposition comes up with.

"If we play our game, we will be hard to beat."

The numbers bear out Gibbs' confidence (come to think of it, for the normally anxious Gibbs, such statements qualify as braggadocio). They have outscored their last three opponents by a combined score of 86-17. In the process they've outgained the opposition by more than 300 yards and are plus nine in turnover ratio (11 forced, two committed).

In addition, two key players on offense—Joe Theismann and John Riggins—are starting to get on a roll. Theismann has thrown 82 passes in a row without an interception and completed over 73 percent of his passes against Detroit. Riggins gained 119 yards and was running with power and authority.

Riggins will have to carry the load. Joe Washington's right knee is bothered by bone chips and he will be limited to spot duty at best. Backing up Riggins is Wilbur Jackson, who has had plenty of knee problems of his own.

Lest anyone think that Gibbs has lost his mind, he did make sure to heap praise on the upcoming opponent: "I saw enough of them . . . to know they are very good and very dangerous."

NFC Divisional Playoff
Saturday, January 15, 1983
RFK Stadium
Washington, D.C.

1/15/83	REDSKINS 21, Vikings 7				54,593
Min	0	7	0	0	7
Was	14	7	0	0	21
Was	Warren 3 pass from Theismann (Moseley kick)				
Was	Riggins 2 run (Moseley kick)				
Min	T. Brown 18 run (Danmeier kick)				
Was	Garrett 14 pass from Theismann (Moseley kick)				

It was a daylong Riggo drill at RFK, with Riggins carrying 37 times for 185 yards as Washington ground the Vikings into submission to move to the NFC Championship game. The Redskins did all of their scoring early, putting up 21 points in just over 20 minutes before letting the defense stuff the Vikings and Riggins chew up the clock.

Riggins carried seven times for 34 yards in the Redskins' first possession as the Redskins drove 66 yards for a touchdown. The payoff came on a three-yard, third down pass from Joe Theismann to Don Warren six minutes into the game.

Having already established Riggins as a threat, the Redskins were able to use the flea flicker two series later. Theismann handed to Riggins, who faked into the middle of the line, stopped, and tossed back to the quarterback, who found Alvin Garrett for 44 yards to the Minnesota 11. The Skins went for it on fourth and inches at the two, and Riggins ploughed over the goal line for the TD to make it 14-0.

A chant that had started mildly a week before began to pick up steam among the 54,593 Redskins faithful in attendance. Rumbles of "We want Dallas, we want Dallas!" started to roll through the stands, expressing a desire for the Redskins to be given an opportunity to avenge their only loss of the season, a home 24-10 loss to the Cowboys in game number five. As the game wore on and it became apparent the Skins would win, the chant grew in volume and intensity.

Minnesota temporarily halted the momentum in the second quarter, scoring on Ted Brown's 18-yard run two minutes into the second quarter, capping a seven-play, 77-yard drive. But the Redskins came right back, moving 70 yards in eight plays and scoring on a 14-yard pass from Theismann to Garrett. The score came with just under 10 minutes left in the half, and it would prove to be the last one of the game for either side.

Both teams would threaten in the second half. Mark Moseley missed two field goal attempts and the Vikings drove into Redskins territory three times. Midway through the third quarter, cornerback Joe Lavender knocked down a fourth-down pass in the end zone to kill one threat and in the fourth period, end Tony McGee sacked Tommy Kramer on fourth and seven at the Washington 15. In between those plays, the Vikings stopped themselves when receiver Sammy White was wide open in the end zone and flat dropped Tommy Kramer's pass.

Enough of this, the Redskins said. In between rousing chants of "We want Dallas," Riggins carried 11 more times to wear down the Vikings and roll down the clock. When he left the game with about a minute left, he acknowledged the emotional cheers of the crowd by stopping around the hash marks, removing his helmet and taking a couple of deep bows, giving the adoring fans a wave. The Redskins and the crowd got Dallas the next day when the Cowboys defeated Green Bay to advance to the NFC title game.

NFC Championship Game
Saturday, January 22, 1983
RFK Stadium
Washington, D.C.

1/22/83	**REDSKINS 31, Cowboys 17**			55,045	
Dal	3	0	14	0	**17**
Was	7	7	7	10	**31**
Dal	FG Septien 27				
Was	Brown 19 pass from Theismann (Moseley kick)				
Was	Riggins 1 run (Moseley kick)				
Dal	Pearson 6 pass from Hogeboom (Septien kick)				
Was	Riggins 4 run (Moseley kick)				
Dal	Johnson 23 pass from Hogeboom (Septien kick)				
Was	FG Moseley 29				
Was	Grant 10 interception return (Moseley kick)				

I t was a wild scene. The ambient crowd noise was much louder than the usual buzz; it was more like a jet airliner on the runway warming up for takeoff. Signs referring to an American Express TV commercial that Dallas coach Tom Landry had done, a spot where he talked about being "surrounded by Redskins," were being waved everywhere. Occasionally, just about every five minutes or so, a chant of "We want Dallas" reached a deafening crescendo. Fans were jumping up and down and giving each other high fives. The stands themselves were rocking and rumbling. Offensive line coach Joe Bugel was giving the one-finger salute to a Dallas defensive coach.

And all of this was just in the two hours before kickoff. After the game started, it really got rowdy.

Dallas took the opening kickoff and promptly drove 75 yards to the Redskins 10. The defense stiffened from there and the Cowboys had to settle for a 27-yard Rafael Septien field goal. The Redskins responded immediately, driving 86 yards to a Joe Theismann-to-Charlie Brown TD pass.

Washington came up empty on its next drive as Mark Moseley missed a 27-yard field goal attempt, but another golden opportunity came shortly after that. Rod Hill muffed a punt at the Dallas 11. It bounced into the end zone where Monte Coleman fell on it, but under NFL rules, the ball was spotted at the point of the muff. It didn't matter, as Riggins went over from a yard out four plays later to make it 14-3.

With 32 seconds left in the first half, Dexter Manley ran over Dallas quarterback Danny White, rendering the signal caller dazed. White left the field under his own power, but he was done for the day with a concussion. Unknown backup Gary Hogeboom would be at the controls of the Dallas offense for the second half.

A short Redskins punt gave Hogeboom a chance to get some confidence and he did just that, leading a six-play, 38-yard drive that ended with a touchdown toss to Drew Pearson. It was 14-10 early in the third quarter and the Redskins' first-half dominance was becoming a distant memory.

Not for long. Mike Nelms made what Joe Gibbs later said was "maybe the key play of the game" when he took the ensuing kickoff 76 yards down the right sideline. Wilbur Jackson threw the key block after Nelms got through the initial wave of defenders, taking out Septien and clearing the way for Nelms to roll all the way down to the Dallas 21. A 22-yard pass from Theismann to Brown preceded Riggins' four-yard TD run to give the Redskins back their breathing room.

They would need it. Hogeboom, not realizing that he was supposed to wilt under the pressure and shrink in fear of the noisy, hostile crowd, calmly led Dallas on an 84-yard, 14-play drive capped by his 23-yard scoring pass to Butch Johnson. The margin was back to just four with 3:25 left in the third quarter. While the crowd noise continued at high volume, a bit of doubt was beginning to creep in: Did we *really* want Dallas?

Dallas threatened to cut the lead further by driving to the Washington 23 early in the fourth quarter, but Septien missed a 42-yard field goal. Following a Washington punt, Dallas started out at the Washington 32. On first down, Hogeboom threw to receiver Tony Hill on the right sideline, but he never saw Mel Kaufman. The linebacker's leaping, over-the-shoulder interception set up a 29-yard Moseley field goal that gave the Redskins a seven-point cushion. Better, but still not safe. That would come on the Cowboys' next play from scrimmage.

From the Dallas 20, the call was a delayed screen pass to running back Tony Dorsett, a play that had gone for 25 yards earlier in the game. Tackle Darryl Grant sensed that this was the call again and stopped his rush, drifting out to the ten yard line. Manley rushed at Hogeboom at full speed, hoping for his second quarterback KO. Instead, he delivered a blow that knocked out the whole Dallas team.

Leaping in the quarterback's face, Manley tipped the ball high into the air. Grant caught it and high stepped the 10 yards to pay dirt. As the crowd exploded with delight, Grant slam-spiked the ball into the end zone turf.

The spike had been driven into the heart of the Cowboys and all that was left was to bury them. The Redskins did that by running Riggins nine straight times on the 50-Gut play. In technical terms, that play is slamming a big guy up the middle behind a bunch of Hogs clearing the way. Riggins had 140 yards rushing in the game, his third straight 100-plus yard effort of the playoffs.

Redskins Are Underdogs, Says Gibbs

Jan. 23—Joe Gibbs tried to get the jump on the Vegas oddsmakers today by declaring that his Redskins would be underdogs against the Miami Dolphins in Super Bowl XVII.

"I'm sure we'll go in as the underdogs," Gibbs said. "I just get the feeling that everybody has more respect for a Miami than for a Washington right now."

Apparently, the respect that was supposed to come as a result of beating the Cowboys hasn't materialized.

"We'll let others evaluate whether we should have respect now or not," said Gibbs. "We just play."

Gibbs wants to make sure that his young team takes nothing for granted. "A chance to be world champions doesn't happen that often," he said. "A lot of people work for years and never get this shot. You can't let it slide by."

Sunday, January 30, 1983
Rose Bowl
Pasadena, California

1/30/83	Redskins 27, Dolphins 17			103,667	
Mia	7	10	0	0	17
Was	0	10	3	14	27
Mia	Cefalo 76 pass from Woodley (von Schamann kick)				
Was	FG Moseley 31				
Mia	FG von Schamann 20				
Was	Garrett 4 pass from Theismann (Moseley kick)				
Mia	Walker 98 kickoff return (von Schamann kick)				
Was	FG Moseley 20				
Was	Riggins 43 run (Moseley kick)				
Was	Brown 6 pass from Theismann (Moseley kick)				

It was a classic matchup of size versus speed. The Miami defense was nicknamed "The Killer Bees," a reference to both their quick, swarming style and the fact that the last names of six starters started with the letter B. Washington countered with the Hogs, who cleared the way for the Diesel. In the end, size would defeat quickness, but it took three quarters for the Redskins to seize the advantage.

The Dolphins struck quickly. Receiver Jimmy Cefalo took advantage of a coverage mixup and turned a little sideline pattern into a 76-yard touchdown on Miami's second offensive series. Two possessions later, Miami was driving in Redskins territory at the 37 when Dexter Manley sacked David Woodley, forcing a fumble that Dave Butz chased down at the Miami 46. The Redskins started the process of wearing down the Bees with Rigging carrying five straight times to set up a 31-yard Mark Moseley field goal to make the score 7-3.

Whatever momentum the Redskins had gained in scratching the scoreboard Miami quickly seized back. In a foreshadowing of a coming event, Fulton Walker returned the kickoff 42 yards to the Miami 47. Using a combination of short passes and quick-hitting runs, the Dolphins moved to the Washington three. From there, Woodley missed Cefalo in the end zone, and the 13-play drive ended in an Uve von Schamann field goal to make it 10-3.

After the ensuing kickoff resulted in a touchback, Joe Gibbs put aside the power game and pulled out his back of tricks. Theismann threw to tight end Rick Walker for 27 yards and then it was Walker again carrying on a reverse for six. After Riggins converted a third and one, it was Theismann to Charlie Brown on a screen and then, after faking a screen left and spinning 360 degrees, the quarterback found Riggins all alone on the right side and the Diesel rumbled for 15. After a Theismann scramble and a couple of Riggins runs, Washington faced third and one on the Miami four.

Earlier in the week, in the wee hours of the morning, Gibbs and his offensive staff came up with the Explode package, a set that had all five eligible receivers in motion before the snap. The idea was to create a moment of confusion in the defense. The Explode worked on the Rose Bowl turf just as well as it had on Gibbs' chalkboard. On that third down play, the shifting left the Miami defenders unsure who was covering whom, helping receiver Alvin Garrett slip past cornerback Gerald Small to catch Theismann's high, arching pass in the right corner of the end zone. Moseley's PAT tied the game at 10 with 1:51 left in the half.

Walker promptly untied it with a 98-yard kickoff return. He started left, found a block, cut up the middle and left the Redskins coverage team in futile pursuit. A Theismann scramble and pass interference call gave the Redskins a shot at some points before halftime, but Garrett couldn't get out of bounds after catching a pass inside the Miami 10. The half ended with Miami leading 17-10.

In the third quarter, a 44-yard reverse to Garrett set up a 20-yard Moseley field goal to pull the Redskins within four midway through the third. The teams then exchanged punts, interceptions and near interceptions for the next twelve minutes of play. One near INT was a big turning point in the game or, rather, a turning point averted by the Redskins.

Late in the third quarter, on first down from the Miami 18, Theismann threw into the right flat. Defensive end Kim Bokamper tipped the ball high into the air and was about to catch it at the four and stroll into the end zone to give Miami an 11-point lead that would have taken Riggins out of the game plan. But Theismann reacted quickly, recovering to bat the ball out of Bokamper's waiting arms.

Disaster averted, the Redskins drove into Miami territory, but they got a little too fancy. On first and ten from the 43, Theismann handed to Riggins who turned and lateraled back to the quarterback. Theismann's pass intended for Brown was picked off by safety Lyle Blackwood at the one. The next time they were at the Miami 43, the Redskins would use a more basic play.

As was the case most of the second half, the Redskins defense put the clamps on Woodley and the Miami offense. Woodley threw incomplete on third and seven from the four, forcing Miami to punt. Woodley was 0 for eight passing in the second half and the Dolphins mustered just two first downs in the final two quarters.

After an illegal block penalty, the Redskins had possession at their own 48 and three plays later faced a fourth and one at the Miami 43. Gibbs didn't hesitate in his call to go for the first down. The call was Seventy Chip, run from goal line formation. As he had been doing all game, Gibbs added motion to the play to try to create just a moment of confusion in the Miami defense.

On this play, the motion caused more than confusion. From the tight, jumbo formation, tight end Don Warren went in motion from the left side of the line to the right. Dolphins' cornerback Don McNeal shadowed Warren. When Warren got to the right end of the line, he reversed his direction. McNeal slipped slightly and was a step or two behind Warren as the ball was snapped.

The Hogs exploded off the line, blocking back Otis Wonsley sealed off the end, and Riggins easily had the first down after taking Joe Theismann's handoff and going off left tackle. McNeal was left unblocked and his attempted arm tackle was useful only to provide a snapshot that adorned the dens of thousands of Redskins fans. After brushing aside McNeal, Riggins easily rolled into the end zone for the TD. The extra point made the score 20-17.

After the defense forced another three and out, the Redskins drove for the kill. From the Miami 41, Riggins carried five straight times to the 23. Five plays later, the Diesel gained the last of his 166 rushing yards to get the Redskins down to the six. Two plays later, right after the two-minute warning, Theismann rolled right and fired it to Brown, who managed to keep both feet in bounds in the right side of the end zone, and the celebration could begin.

1983
Head Coach: Joe Gibbs
Record: 14-2, NFC East Champs
Playoffs 2-1, lost in Super Bowl XVIII

Honors: Jeff Bostic Pro Bowl, All-NFC; Charlie Brown Pro Bowl; Dave Butz Pro Bowl, All-NFL; Russ Grimm Pro Bowl, All-NFL; Joe Jacoby Pro Bowl; Mark Murphy Pro Bowl, All-NFL; Mike Nelms All-NFL; John Riggins All-NFL; Joe Theismann Pro Bowl, All-NFL, NFL Most Valuable Player; Joe Gibbs Coach of the Year

Hall of Fame: Sonny Jurgensen, Quarterback, 1964-74, Bobby Mitchell, Receiver 1962-1968

Feb. 1
Flying the Coop: Falcons Name Dan Henning New Head Coach
Offensive coordinator to mold Falcons in 'Skins' image

Feb. 2
Half a Million Rain-Soaked Fans Join in Championship Celebration

Mar 31
Busted: Harmon Arrested on Drug Charges
Running back charged with cocaine possession

Speed Thrills: Redskins Take Corner Darrell Green in First Round

Apr 27—While Bobby Beathard insists that "he's a football player first," it's hard not to first be impressed by cornerback Darrell Green's speed. That's speed as in a 4.3 time in the 40 and a 9.9 100 meter dash.

Green, selected by the Redskins with the last pick in the first round of today's draft, is a small (5-9, 170) cornerback out of tiny Texas A&I. He's expected to produce big things on the football field. He not only intercepted 16 passes in college, but also averaged more than 20 yards per punt return as a senior.

"He was the player we wanted in the first round," said Beathard. "We kept our fingers crossed that he would last until our pick." He said that they would have traded down, out of the first round, had Green not been available.

There may have been more than sheer talent that drove the Redskins to draft Green. Kick returner Mike Nelms and cornerback Jeris White are expected to be involved in protracted contract holdouts. Green's selection serves as a not-so-gentle nudge for both of them to reconsider their demands.

In the third round Washington tabbed Charles Mann, a defensive end out of Nevada-Reno. "He's a terrific athlete," said Beathard. "He was a late bloomer in college."

Head Hog Bugel Staying In the Pen

July 25—Offensive line coach Joe Bugel, who named and coached the offensive line called "The Hogs" to fame and Super Bowl glory, has declined an offer to become the head coach of the Pittsburgh franchise in the U.S. football league.

Drug Bug Bites Again: Peters Arrested on Narcotics Charges

Aug 3—Tony Peters, the Redskins' Pro Bowl safety, was arrested today on federal charges of conspiracy to sell cocaine. He is free on $50,000 bond while he awaits trial.

He was arrested in Adams hall at Dickinson College in Carlisle, Pennsylvania, the site of the Redskins' training camp. The arrest took place without incident—Mark Murphy, who has a room right next to Peters, wasn't aware that anything had happened—and he was arraigned in Harrisburg.

Joe Gibbs hoped that it was all a mistake. "It would be a tremendous blow to us," said Gibbs on the suspension that Peters faces.

DE Matt Medenhall Walks Out of Camp
Aug 17—Defensive end Matt Mendenhall, who started every game for the champion Redskins last year, walked out of training camp in Carlisle, Pennsylvania yesterday. Team officials did not know why he left or where he was.

Sep 2
Monk on Shelf for Four Weeks
Sprained knee lands WR on IR

9/5/83	Cowboys (1-0) 31, REDSKINS (0-1) 30			55,045
Dal	0	3	14	14	31
Was	10	13	0	7	30
Was	FG Moseley 23			
Was	Riggins 1 run (Moseley kick)			
Dal	FG Septien 28			
Was	FG Moseley 30			
Was	FG Moseley 39			

Was	Brown 41 pass from Theismann (Moseley kick)
Dal	Hill 75 pass from White (Septien kick)
Dal	Hill 51 pass from White (Septien kick)
Dal	White 1 run (Septien kick)
Dal	Cosbie 1 pass from White (Septien kick)
Was	Warren 1 pass from Theismann (Moseley kick)

RFK Stadium—As the two teams walked off of the field at halftime, 55,045 fans chanting "We want Dallas, we want Dallas" in unison taunted the visitors, who were trailing 23-3. Despite the fury in the stands, the Cowboys came out of the locker room for the second half and ran off 28 unanswered points to pull out an improbable 31-30 win.

There were many reasons for the giddy optimism of the Redskins faithful at halftime. The Cowboys had garnered just three first downs and had been outgained 261 yards to 85. Washington held the ball for 22 ½ of the 30 minutes.

Even when Dallas seemed to be doing things right, the Redskins had an answer. After the Redskins took a 10-0 lead on a Mark Moseley field goal and a one-yard touchdown run by John Riggins, Dallas running back Tony Dorsett broke into the clear on a run from his own 17. Before he could score, however, rookie cornerback Darrell Green, coming from the far side of the field, got an angle on the running back. With a jaw-dropping burst of speed, Green caught Dorsett and hauled him down at the six. Dallas had to settle for a field goal to make it 10-3.

After two more Moseley field goals stretched the lead to 16-3, the Redskins got possession at their own 43 with just over two minutes left until halftime. Soon after that, Joe Theismann hit receiver Charlie Brown with a perfect strike at the Dallas 15. Safety Michael Downs fell down and Brown strolled in to make it 23-3 and send the crowd into a frenzy.

Dallas went to work quickly in the second half, taking just five plays to move 90 yards to its first touchdown. The final 75 of those yards came on a bomb from Danny White to receiver Tony Hill. Dallas scored on another long White-to-Hill connection, this one 51 yards, making it a ball game at 23-17 with 6:35 left in the third quarter.

The Redskins had a chance to get some breathing room, but an offensive pass interference call stalled a promising drive and Moseley was wide right on a 31-yard field goal attempt with 9:34 left in the game. Dallas took advantage of the opening, marching 80 yards in 12 plays to take a 24-23 lead on White's one-yard touchdown run with 2:20 left.

Any hope for a comeback died quickly when Brown ran the wrong pattern and cornerback Ron Fellows intercepted Theismann's pass at the Washington 37, returning it to the four. Three plays later, White flipped a one-yard touchdown pass to tight end Doug Cosbie, making Theismann's scoring pass to his tight end Don Warren with 10 seconds left meaningless.

Cosell Under Fire For 'Monkey' Reference to Garrett

Sep 6—If nothing else, Howard Cosell knows how to stir up a controversy.

During Monday night's telecast of the Dallas-Washington game, the ABC commentator said of the Redskins' receiver Alvin Garrett, "That little monkey sure can play."

Although it seemed that Cosell's remark was in a tone that was more complimentary than derisive, the reference to a black man as a "monkey," of course, raised many eyebrows, to say the least. Some have called for Cosell to resign; other, perhaps more reasonable types have asked him to apologize.

So far, Cosell has done neither.

9/11/83	**Redskins (1-1) 23, EAGLES (1-1) 13**			69,542
Was	7	0	3	13	**23**
Phil	0	3	7	3	**13**

Was	Brown 12 pass from Theismann (Moseley kick)
Phil	FG Franklin 29
Phil	Quick 27 pass from Jaworski (Franklin kick)
Was	FG Moseley 36
Was	Riggins 14 run (Moseley kick)
Was	FG Moseley 24
Phil	FG Franklin 33
Was	FG Moseley 23

Veterans Stadium—John Riggins ran 14 yards up the middle for the go-ahead touchdown two minutes into the fourth quarter and the Redskins held on to beat the Eagles 23-13.

Washington jumped to a 7-0 lead in the first quarter when Joe Theismann threw a 12-yard touchdown pass to Charlie Brown. The Eagles responded with a 29-yard Tony Franklin field goal with just over a minute left in the first half. Midway through the third quarter, a 27-yard scoring pass from Ron Jaworski to receiver Mike Quick pushed Philly into a 10-7 lead. The visitors soon responded with a 36-yard Mark Moseley field goal to knot the score at 10 with about three and a half minutes left in the third.

Mike Nelms shed several attempted tackles on his way to an 18-yard punt return that set up Riggins' game-winner. From the Eagles 43, two runs gained eight yards and then, on third and two, Theismann hit third-down back Nick Giaquinto for 21 yards at a first down at the 14. Riggins powered through the middle on the next play, making it 17-10. Two more Moseley field goals held the Eagles at bay for the remainder of the game.

9/18/83	**REDSKINS (2-1) 27, Chiefs (1-2) 12**			52,610
KC	3	9	0	0	**12**
Was	0	0	17	10	**27**

KC	FG Lowery 58
KC	FG Lowery 21
KC	FG Lowery 32
KC	FG Lowery 22
Was	FG Moseley 35
Was	Riggins 2 run (Moseley kick)
Was	Warren 12 pass from Theismann (Moseley kick)
Was	Didier 39 pass from Theismann (Moseley kick)
Was	FG Moseley 34

RFK Stadium—It could have gotten ugly early. In the first half, the Chiefs piled up nearly 300 yards of total offense and held the Redskins in their own territory for all but one drive. Washington had failed to convert a third down in six tries.

The home team was attempting to self-destruct with costly penalties. But the Chiefs took only limited advantage of their host's largesse and held just a 12-0 lead on four Nick Lowery field goals. Washington regrouped in the second half and rallied to a 27-12 win.

A couple of takeaways by the Redskins defense spurred the revival. Early in the second half, cornerback Vernon Dean stripped the ball from KC receiver Anthony Hancock, giving the Redskins the ball at the Chiefs 22, setting up a Mark Moseley field goal. Soon after that, cornerback Darrell Green got his first interception as a pro, returning it seven yards to the Kansas City 28. Washington took full advantage of this turnover, taking six plays to score, the last five being John Riggins runs. His two-yard touchdown run cut the lead to 12-10 with 5:27 left in the third quarter.

The Redskins' go-ahead touchdown symbolized how the fortunes of the game had turned in Washington's favor. On second and ten from the Kansas City 12, Theismann tried to hit back Nick Giaquinto at around the five. The pass was high and Giaquinto leaped and tipped the ball. That's usually bad news when the defense is compacted at the end of the field, but the ball fluttered into the arms of tight end Don Warren at the goal line. He grabbed it and fell into the end zone.

The clincher came with 9:20 to go when Theismann found tight end Clint Didier all alone at the Chiefs 15—no defender was within 20 yards of him—and Didier strolled in for the score.

9/25/83	Redskins (3-1) 27, SEAHAWKS (2-2) 17			60,718
Was	7	13	0	7	27
Sea	3	7	0	7	17

Was	Riggins 1 run (Moseley kick)
Seas	FG N. Johnson 27
Was	Brown 64 pass from Theismann (Moseley kick)
Sea	Largent 13 pass from Zorn (N. Johnson kick)
Was	Garrett 47 pass from Theismann (kick failed)
Was	Walker 4 pass from Theismann (Moseley kick)
Sea	Largent 7 pass from Zorn (N. Johnson kick)

Kingdome—Joe Theismann completed just nine passes, but they were good for 162 yards and three touchdowns as the Redskins downed the Seahawks.

Theismann's efficient passing was augmented by two takeaways by the Redskins defense that led to a pair of short touchdown drives. The first happened early in the game when the Seahawks' running back Curt Warner fumbled and Tony McGee recovered for Washington at the Seattle 19. Soon after that, John Riggins went over from a yard out and the Redskins led 7-0.

The Redskins stretched their lead in the second quarter with a pair of long Theismann touchdown passes, one of 64 yards to Charlie Brown and the other 47 yards to Alvin Garrett. The extra point after the second score was missed, and Washington held a 20-10 halftime lead.

That lead held through the third quarter before Vernon Dean broke it open in the fourth. He intercepted a pass at the Seattle 48 and returned it to the 22. That set up a four-yard touchdown pass from Theismann to tight end Rick Walker that clinched the win with 5:07 left in the game.

10/2/83	REDSKINS (4-1) 37, Raiders (4-1) 35			54,016
LA	0	7	14	14	35
Was	7	10	3	17	37

Was	Riggins 2 run (Moseley kick)
Was	FG Moseley 28
LA	Branch 99 pass from Plunkett (Bahr kick)
Was	J. Washington 5 pass from Theismann (Moseley kick)
Was	FG Moseley 29
LA	Muhammad 35 pass from Plunkett (Bahr kick)
LA	Muhammad 22 pass from Plunkett (Bahr kick)
LA	Christensen 2 pass from Plunkett (Bahr kick)
LA	Pruitt 97 punt return (Bahr kick)
Was	FG Moseley 34 (Bahr kick)
Was	J. Washington 5 pass from Theismann (Moseley kick)

RFK Stadium—This game had more ups and downs, twists and turns than the newest theme park roller coasters.

The Redskins dominated the early going. Interceptions by Curtis Jordan and Mel Kaufman set up scores to give Washington a 10-0 lead. The Raiders responded with the ultimate display of the vertical offense as Jim Plunkett and Cliff Branch hooked up on a 99-yard bomb.

After that quick lapse, the Redskins moved to reassert their control. A Mark Moseley field goal and five-yard touchdown pass from Joe Theismann to Joe Washington made it 20-7 in the third quarter. It appeared that the home team had some breathing room.

The breathing turned to gasping when Plunkett found Calvin Muhammad for touchdown passes of 25 and 22 yards, giving the Raiders the lead. When Greg Pruitt took a punt back 97 yards for a touchdown that gave the Raiders a 35-20 lead with just over seven and a half minutes left in the game, it was positively suffocating.

In fact, although most of them will probably deny it, nearly half of the crowd of 54,016 headed for the exits after that punt return. What ensued was one for the history books, as Theismann would say afterwards. Or, one for the storybooks.

It all got started on the first play after the kickoff when Washington took a screen pass and rocketed 67 yards down the right sideline. Three plays later, Theismann hit Charlie Brown with an 11-yard touchdown pass to draw the Skins within eight. Then Jeff Hayes kicked off and lined a low, hard one off the foot of a Raider. Greg Williams recovered, and the Skins drew within five after a Mark Moseley field goal with 4:28 remaining.

The Raiders managed to kill some clock, but could not get a first down as Plunkett threw to Todd Christensen for nine yards on third and eleven. Washington started at its own 31 with a minute and fifty seconds left. Plenty of time. Theismann completed three straight passes to Brown for nine, 26 and 28 yards, to the Raiders' six with 43 seconds left. On second down from there, Joe Washington snuck through the line, slid to the right and snared Theismann's pass for the winning touchdown. The Redskins won 37-35. The fans in the half full stands exploded in cheers, making more than enough noise to make up for those of little faith who had already departed.

10/2/83	Redskins (5-1) 38, CARDINALS (1-5) 14			42,698
Was	7	17	14	0	38
StL	0	7	7	0	14

Was	Riggins 17 run (Moseley kick)
StL	Green 35 pass from Lomax (O'Donoghue kick)
Was	Monk 20 pass from Theismann (Moseley kick)
Was	Riggins 1 run (Moseley kick)
Was	FG Moseley 22
Was	Walker 10 pass from Theismann (Moseley kick)
StL	Marsh 1 pass from Lisch (O'Donoghue kick)
Was	Riggins 15 run (Moseley kick)

Busch Stadium—The tone of this game was set early on, during the Cardinals' first offensive series. Doug Marsh fumbled, and Curtis Jordan recovered at the St. Louis 29. Four plays later, John Riggins ripped off 17 yards for a touchdown and a 7-0 lead; the Redskins rolled to a 38-14 win.

On the home team's fourth possession with Washington holding a 14-7 lead, quarterback Neil Lomax fumbled deep in Cardinal territory and Todd Liebenstein recovered on the five. Two plays after that, Riggins bulled over from the one to stretch the lead to 21-7.

A Mark Moseley field goal made it 24-7 at halftime and the Redskins removed all doubt about the outcome soon after halftime with, of course, an assist from the Cards. Stump Mitchell took the opening kickoff and put the ball on the Busch Stadium carpet when Alvin Garret hit him. Greg Williams recovered at the St. Louis 23. After four Riggins runs moved it to the ten, Joe Theismann threw to tight end Rick Walker, who bounced off an attempted tackle and scored to make it 31-7.

Riggins scored the final touchdown on a 15-yard run in the fourth quarter. In about three quarters of work, the big back ran for 115 yards on 22 carries, and the three TD's.

10/17/83	PACKERS (4-3) 48, Redskins (5-2) 47			55,255
Was	10	10	13	14	47
GB	10	14	7	17	48

GB	Douglass 22 fumble return (Stenerud kick)
Was	Didier fumble recovery in end zone (Moseley kick)
GB	FG Stenerud 47
Was	FG Moseley 42
GB	Coffman 36 pass from Dickey (Stenerud kick)
Was	Riggins 1 run (Moseley kick)
GB	Coffman 9 pass from Dickey (Stenerud kick)
Was	FG Moseley 26

GB	Ellis 24 run (Stenerud kick)
Was	FG Moseley 31
Was	J. Washington 6 pass from Theismann (Moseley kick)
Was	FG Moseley 26
GB	G. Lewis 2 run (Stenerud kick)
Was	Riggins 1 run (Moseley kick)
GB	Meade 31 pass from Dickey (Stenerud kick)
Was	J. Washington 5 pass from Theismann (Moseley kick)
GB	FG Stenerud 20

Lambeau Field—"We could have done a better job," said cornerback Vernon Dean after the game. And then he walked away.

Presumably, Dean was referring to the Redskins' secondary, which was lit up by Lynn Dickey. The Green Bay quarterback completed 22 of 30 passes for 387 yards and three touchdowns. But Dean could have been speaking on behalf of the entire defenses of both teams. The game featured 1,025 yards of total offense, 56 first downs, and 17 scores.

Perhaps defensive coordinator Richie Petitbon's remark is more apt: "We really stunk."

Actually, one of the defenses did accomplish something early on. Green Bay linebacker Mike Douglass slammed into Joe Washington after the running back caught a short screen pass. The result was the Redskins' first fumble of the season, and Douglass picked it up and returned it 22 yards for a touchdown.

The team's second fumble of the season also resulted in a touchdown. Fighting for yardage on a run from the Packers three, John Riggins fumbled into the end zone. Fortunately for the Redskins, Clint Didier emerged from the bottom of the pile with the ball and the game was tied at seven.

A pair of Dickey touchdown passes to tight end Paul Coffman propelled the Packers to a 24-20 halftime lead. They went to work quickly in the second half to extend the margin, using 43 seconds to move 82 yards in just five plays. "Dickey was throwing the ball so fast it was hard to get a pass rush," said tackle Darryl Grant. Gerry Ellis scored on a 24-yard run and the Packers led 31-20.

The Redskins would retake the lead before the end of the quarter on a pair of Mark Moseley field goals and a six-yard pass from Joe Theismann to Washington.

The 33-31 lead didn't last long. After Moseley's second field goal, Harlan Huckleby returned the kickoff 57 yards and it took just 15 seconds for the Packers to score on a two-yard reverse by tight end Greg Lewis.

The visitors responded, with a hobbled Riggins coming off the bench to carry the ball in a few key short-yardage situations, the last a one-yard touchdown with under ten minutes left and the Skins led by two.

Not for long. On third and 13 from the Washington 31, Dickey flipped a short pass to fullback Mike Meade. Dean gambled and dove for the knockdown and "missed the ball by inches," said Petitbon. "If he goes for the tackle instead, it's fourth and three and they probably have to go for a field goal instead." The few inches turned into 31 yards and a touchdown to push the Pack back ahead.

The Redskins moved smartly down the field and recaptured the lead at 47-45 on Theismann's five-yard TD pass to Washington. There was 2:50 left—plenty of time for more scoring.

Ellis caught a short pass from Dickey, eluded a couple defenders near midfield and ran all the way to the eight. Jan Stenerud accounted for the game's fifth lead change with a 20-yard field goal while 55 seconds remained.

There was still enough time for another score, but Washington didn't get it. The Redskins drove to the Green Bay 22 but Moseley missed a 39-yard field goal attempt with three seconds left. "I hit the ball good," said Moseley. "I just didn't hit it in the right direction. There is no explanation."

Theories Abound on Skins' Pass Defense Woes

Oct 20—Everywhere you turn, you can find instant analysis on what's wrong with the Redskins' pass defense.

"The Pearl Harbor Crew," so named because of their propensity to get bombed with frequency, had one of its worst outings on Monday night against Green Bay. The Pack's bomber was quarterback Lynn Dickey, who completed 22 of 30 passes for 387 yards in Washington's 48-47 loss.

The yardage pushed the Redskins to the bottom on the NFL pack in pass yardage allowed at 278 per game. This stands in stark contrast to their league-best average of just under 84 yards a game allowed on the ground.

Looking at the rush defense gives some insight as to why the pass defense stats are so poor. If opposing teams want to move the ball, the run isn't a very attractive option.

"It's so obvious," said former Eagles coach Dick Vermeil. "Running like them is like throwing popcorn at a battleship."

Another obvious answer is that the Redskins are scoring points at a pace that may threaten the NFL record for scoring in a season. Offenses are constantly playing from behind and, naturally, that means passing.

Going in a little deeper, consider the personnel in the defensive backfield. They lost veteran cornerbacks Joe Lavender (retirement) and Jeris White (contract dispute). In their places are rookie Darrell Green and second-year man Vernon Dean. In addition, nickel linebacker Monte Coleman has missed considerable time with injuries, and 1982 Pro Bowl safety Tony Peters is out on a drug-related suspension.

"If the Redskins' pass defense didn't slip this year, it would be a miracle," said former Dolphins quarterback Bob Griese.

10/23/83	**REDSKINS (6-2) 38, Lions (3-5) 17**			53,189	
Det	0	3	7	7	**17**
Was	14	14	3	7	**38**
Was	Monk 13 pass from Theismann (Moseley kick)				
Was	Evans 2 run (Moseley kick)				
Det	FG Murray 37				
Was	J. Washington 8 pass from Theismann (Moseley kick)				
Was	Evans 2 run (Moseley kick)				
Det	Sims 13 run (Murray kick)				
Was	FG Moseley 22				
Was	Evans 1 run (Moseley kick)				
Det	Norris 2 pass from Danielson (Murray kick)				

RFK Stadium—Due to injuries, the Redskins were without their leading rusher (John Riggins), leading pass catcher (Charlie Brown) and kick returner (Mike Nelms). In their absence, the Washington offense managed to eke out 441 yards of total offense and 38 points in routing the Lions.

The defense responded as well, holding two Detroit quarterbacks to 13 of 34 passing, sacking them five times (2.5 by Dexter Manley), intercepting two passes and recovering one fumble.

Washington jumped out to a 14-0 lead in the first quarter. First Art Monk caught a 14-yard touchdown pass from Joe Theismann and then Reggie Evans powered into the end zone form two yards out.

Evans was part of tag team that the Redskins used to replace Riggins. For most of the game, Joe Washington filled in for Riggins and he rushed for a career high 147 yards on 22 carries and caught three passes, one for a touchdown.

When the Redskins got near the goal line, though, Evans played the Riggo role, scoring three touchdowns on the ground.

After Detroit got on the board with an Eddie Murray field goal the Redskins broke it open. First Washington caught an eight-yard touchdown pass from Joe Theismann and then Evans got his second TD on a two-yard run. That made it 28-3 at halftime and the Redskins never looked back.

10/31/83	Redskins (7-2) 27, CHARGERS (3-6) 24				46,114
Was	7	3	7	10	**27**
SD	7	0	0	17	**24**
Was	Seay 39 pass from Theismann (Moseley kick)				
SD	Muncie 5 run (Benirschke kick)				
Was	FG Moseley 45				
Was	Riggins 2 run (Moseley kick)				
Was	Riggins 1 run (Moseley kick)				
SD	Holohan 23 pass from Luther (Benirschke kick)				
SD	Chandler 27 pass from Luther (Benirschke kick)				
SD	FG Benirschke 43				
Was	FG Moseley 37				

Jack Murphy Stadium—Despite taking the ball away eight times, including six interceptions of San Diego backup quarterback Ed Luther, and piling up 482 yards of total offense, the Redskins needed a Mark Moseley field goal with four seconds left to pull out a 27-24 Halloween night win.

Mike Nelms returned the opening kickoff 40 yards to set up a 39-yard touchdown pass from Joe Theismann to Virgil Seay just 1:46 into the game. Later in the first, Moseley missed a 43-yard field goal attempt—the first of four misses on the day—and the Chargers drove to the tying score. The rest of the half, Redskins threatened often but Moseley was one of two on field goal attempts, missing from 52 and hitting from 45 to give Washington a 10-7 lead at the half.

Special teams, specifically punter Jeff Hayes, helped the Redskins boost their lead in the third quarter. From punt formation on fourth and four at midfield, Hayes took off to the left, easily made the first down, and then cut back to the middle of the field. He rolled all the way to the two yard line before being tackled. On the next play, John Riggins scored to make it 17-7. A Mark Murphy interception led to a second Riggins TD, this one coming from one yard out on the third play of the final period. At 24-7, it seemed that two more Moseley field goal misses which squandered opportunities created by takeaways by Neal Olkewicz and Todd Liebenstein wouldn't make any difference.

After Moseley's second miss, the Chargers offense held on to the ball and came to life. A 78-yard drive ended with Luther going to tight end Pete Holohan and it was 24-17 with less than nine minutes remaining. An onside kick attempt was recovered by the Redskins and, although they couldn't move the ball, a Hayes punt pinned the Chargers back on their own one.

It took just over a minute for San Diego to go the length of the field to pull within three on a Luther touchdown pass to Wes Chandler. This time the Chargers went with a squib kick, a maneuver that pinned the Redskins back at their own six. Washington went three and out and James Brooks returned the punt 30 yards to the Redskins 30. Three plays later, Rolf Benirschke kicked a 43-yard field goal to tie the game with 1:52 left.

After the ensuing kickoff Theismann calmly directed the team 72 yards with a 15-yard pass to Charlie Brown and a five-yard run by Joe Washington getting the final yards to the San Diego 19. Moseley, who had missed at the end of a Monday night game in Green Bay to cost the Redskins a win two weeks before, drilled his 37-yarder with four seconds left to push the Redskins in front, 27-24. Luther suffered his sixth interception on a desperation pass that Mark Murphy gathered in on the game's final play.

11/6/83	REDSKINS (8-2) 45, Cardinals 3-6-1) 7				51,380
StL	0	0	7	0	**7**
Was	7	10	21	7	**45**
Was	Dean recovered fumble in end zone (Moseley kick)				
Was	Riggins 2 run (Moseley kick)				
Was	FG Moseley 42				
Was	Kaufman 70 interception return (Moseley kick)				
StL	R. Green 23 pass from Lomax (O'Donoghue kick)				
Was	Riggins 2 run (Moseley kick)				
Was	Evans 1 run (Moseley kick)				
Was	Giaquinto 1 run (Moseley kick)				

RFK Stadium—Neil Olkewicz forced a first-quarter fumble that was turned into a Redskins touchdown to jump-start the Redskins to a rout of St. Louis.

After Jeff Hayes placed a pooch punt that was downed at the one, Olkewicz slammed into fullback Wayne Morris, who coughed up the ball. The fumble rolled into the end zone where cornerback Vernon Dean pounced on it for a touchdown.

An 87-yard drive ended in a John Riggins touchdown run with less than six minutes left in the half. After that the Redskins' Tony McGee blocked a field goal attempt, setting up a drive to a Mark Moseley field goal that made it 17-0 at halftime.

Any doubt about the outcome ended early in the third quarter when Curtis Jordan tipped a Neil Lomax pass and Mel Kaufman snared it just before it hit the ground. The linebacker raced 70 yards for a touchdown to make it 24-0.

The Cardinals did cut it to 24-7 when they converted a rare Riggins fumble into a 23-yard touchdown pass from Lomax to Roy Green, but that was it for St. Louis. Riggins went over for another score from two yards out and it was garbage time. Backup runner Reggie Evans and third-down specialist Nick Giaquinto each saw action and scored touchdowns to complete the blowout.

11/13/83	Redskins (9-2) 33, GIANTS (2-8-1) 17				71,482
Was	13	3	10	7	**33**
NYG	3	0	0	14	**17**
Was	Riggins 2 run (Moseley kick)				
Was	FG Moseley 47				
NYG	FG Haji-Sheikh 45				
Was	FG Moseley 33				
Was	FG Moseley 38				
Was	FG Moseley 32				
Was	Brown 18 pass from Theismann (Moseley kick)				
Was	Riggins 2 run (Moseley kick)				
NYG	Gray 6 pass from Brunner (Haji-Sheikh kick)				
NYG	Gray 22 pass from Brunner (Haji-Sheikh kick				

Giants Stadium—The Redskins, taking advantage of turnovers and poor special teams play by the Giants, started six scoring drives in New York territory to build a 30-point lead early in the fourth quarter and gaining an easy 33-17 win in the Meadowlands.

The pattern was set on the game's first play when Dave Butz tipped a Scott Brunner pass and Dexter Manley picked it out of the air at the Giants' 22. Four plays later, John Riggins scored from the two. A fumbled punt and a 50-yard kickoff return following a New York field goal set up two Mark Moseley field goals to put Washington up 13-3.

Late in the second quarter, the Giants were threatening, but Brunner and running back Butch Woolfolk botched a handoff. Darryl Grant recovered the loose ball at the Washington 22. From there, the Redskins drove to another Moseley field goal to make it 16-3 at the half.

Another punt mishandled by the Giants led to Moseley's fourth three-pointer early in the third quarter. A short Giants punt gave the Redskins the ball on the New York 40 and the Redskins took advantage with an 18-yard touchdown pass from Joe Theismann to Charlie Brown.

One more punting team gaffe—this one an incomplete pass on a fake punt—gave Washington possession again in Giants territory and a 47-yard drive culminated in a two-yard scoring run by Riggins. Two long New York drives that ended in Brunner touchdown passes to Earnest Gray only slightly placated the boo-birds at Giants Stadium.

Nov 18
Peters Suspended For Two Years
Drug bust will sideline Pro Bowl safety until after '84 season

11/20/83	Redskins (10-2) 42, RAMS (7-5) 20				63,031
Was	10	19	10	3	**42**
LARm	6	0	0	14	**20**
Was	FG Moseley 42				
LARm	D. Hill 12 pass from Ferragamo (kick failed)				
Was	Riggins 1 run (Moseley kick)				
Was	Brown 26 pass from Theismann (Moseley kick)				
Was	Safety Ferragamo tackled in end zone				
Was	Riggins 1 run (Moseley kick)				
Was	FG Moseley 33				
Was	Riggins 1 run (Moseley kick)				
Was	FG Moseley 32				
Was	FG Moseley 19				
LARm	Redden 1 run (Nelson kick)				
LARm	Guman 3 pass from Kemp (Nelson kick)				

Anaheim Stadium—The Redskins scored 16 points in less than five minutes in the second quarter to pull away from the Rams.

With Washington leading 10-6, Rams quarterback Vince Ferragamo overthrew his intended receiver and nickel back Brian Carpenter intercepted the pass at the Los Angeles 26. The Redskins immediately took advantage as Charlie Brown caught a Joe Theismann pass at the 10, broke a tackle, and went into the end zone. Ferragamo was facing a third and 27 on the ensuing possession and, under pressure from rookie defensive end Charles Mann, was flagged for intentional grounding in the end zone. Under the rules, that's a safety and Washington led 19-6.

Washington took possession at its own 39 following the free kick by the Rams. It took nine plays to cover the 61 yards with another Theismann-to-Brown connection getting the ball to the one, setting up John Riggins' run to finish off the drive. A Mark Moseley field goal late in the half made the score 29-6 at intermission.

Linebacker Rich Milot picked off a pair of passes in the third quarter, one setting up another one-yard Riggins TD run and the other a Moseley field goal. The Rams drove for two meaningless touchdowns to make the final a bit more respectable.

11/27/83	REDSKINS (11-2) 28, Eagles (4-9) 24				54,234
Phil	0	21	3	0	**24**
Was	7	21	0	0	**28**
Was	Monk 17 pass from Theismann (Moseley kick)				
Phil	Oliver 2 pass from Jaworski (Franklin kick)				
Was	Riggins 2 run (Moseley kick)				
Phil	Quick 17 pass from Jaworski (Franklin kick)				
Was	Riggins 2 run (Moseley kick)				
Was	Brown 75 pass from Theismann (Moseley kick)				
Phil	Quick 3 pass from Jaworski (Franklin kick)				
Phil	FG Franklin 52				

RFK Stadium—The 15-point underdog Eagles ran and passed almost at will in the second quarter to put a scare into the Redskins. Washington's defense stiffened in the second half, allowing the Skins to escape with a four-point win.

Midway through the first quarter, rookie linebacker Larry Kubin nailed Eagles punt returner John Sciarra as soon as he fielded the ball and Jeff Bostic recovered at the Philly 17. On the next play, cornerback Roynell Young managed to get a hand on Joe Theismann's pass to Art Monk, but Monk gathered in the tipped ball for the reception and touchdown.

Philadelphia tied the score after Jeff Hayes shanked a punt and the Eagles took possession at the Redskin 37 early in the second quarter. The touchdown came on a two-yard play action pass from Ron Jaworski to fullback Hubie Oliver. The teams then exchanged long touchdown drives, with Washington going 67 yards in 11 plays and scoring on a two-yard run by John Riggins. Philly took just three plays to cover 70 yards, the payoff coming on a 17-yard Jaworski pass to receiver Mike Quick that tied the score at 14.

Washington took advantage of two Eagle turnovers to jump out to a two-touchdown lead. Greg Williams recovered a muffed punt at the Eagles three and Riggins scored two plays later. Later, Ken Coffey picked off a Jaworski pass at the Washington six, returning it 19 yards to the 25. The Redskins covered the 75 yards in one play, with Theismann throwing a bomb to Charlie Brown, who shed a tackler around the Philadelphia 35 and rolled into the end zone with a minute and a half left before intermission. Before the Redskins could get too comfortable, though, the Eagles responded with a three-yard Jaworski-to-Quick TD pass with 44 seconds left in the half, closing it at 28-21.

While the Redskins had trouble moving the ball in the second half, all the Eagles could muster was a 42-yard Tony Franklin field goal. Franklin missed from 35 in the fourth quarter to end Philly's last threat.

12/4/83	REDSKINS (12-2) 37, Falcons (6-8) 21				52,074
Atl	0	0	0	21	**21**
Was	7	13	14	3	**37**
Was	Didier 18 pass from Theismann (Moseley kick)				
Was	FG Moseley 25				
Was	J. Washington 11 pass from Theismann (Moseley kick)				
Was	FG Moseley 51				
Was	Kaufman 30 fumble return (Moseley kick)				
Was	Monk 10 pass from Theismann (Moseley kick)				
Atl	Riggs 7 run (Luckhurst kick)				
Was	FG Moseley 43				
Atl	Riggs 4 run (Luckhurst kick)				
Atl	Cain 2 run (Luckhurst kick)				

RFK Stadium—The Redskins built a 34-0 third-quarter lead and coasted to an easy win over the Falcons.

Washington established its offense on the first drive after taking the opening kickoff. They drove 80 yards in nine plays with Clint Didier getting the last 18 gathering in a touchdown pass from Joe Theismann.

After Mark Moseley put the Skins up 10-0 with a second-quarter field goal, the Falcons pulled a couple of plays out of their bag of tricks and cost themselves 10 points. Falcon receiver Floyd Hodge threw a pass on a reverse flea-flicker and cornerback Anthony Washington intercepted it at the Redskins 21. Nine plays later, Theismann threw 11 yards to Joe Washington for a touchdown that made it 17-0 with 58 seconds left before halftime. On its ensuing possession, Atlanta tried again, calling for a hook and lateral play. Receiver Stacey Bailey caught the hook pass, but his lateral was behind the trailing Billy "White Shoes" Johnson. Safety Ken Coffey recovered the loose ball, setting up a 51-yard Moseley field goal at the gun to make it 20-0.

The Washington defense got back into the act in the third quarter. A Mark Murphy interception killed one promising Atlanta drive. Following a rare turnover by the Redskins offense, Dave Butz nailed quarterback Mike Moroski, jarring the ball loose. Mel Kaufmann scooped it up and ran 70 yards for a touchdown. Another interception by Anthony Washington led to the Redskins' final TD, this one coming on a 10-yard pass from Theismann to Art Monk to make it 34-0. The Falcons scored three fourth-quarter touchdowns, two of them by Gerald Riggs, to make the final slightly more respectable.

Redskins Invade Dallas Ready for War

Dec. 10—The Redskins arrived in Dallas today ready to do battle with the Cowboys—and it showed.

About two dozen Redskins wore battle fatigues and combat boots for the flight to the site of tomorrow's game, which will almost certainly decide the NFC East title and home field advantage throughout the conference playoffs.

The participants in the costume party didn't ask Joe Gibbs for permission beforehand. "If they had told me, I probably would have tried to talk them out of it."

Probably? As Russ Grimm said it, "I imagine Joe was about ready to throw up" as he saw the way they were dressed while boarding the team bus.

Earlier in the week at Redskins Park, the players were characteristically cautious in their comments. "It's a game between two great teams," said running back Nick Giaquinto, summarizing most of what the team said.

"Dallas is very good in all respects. I think if you took a poll, most people would pick Dallas as the best team," said Gibbs.

The only remotely hostile comment was by safety Mark Murphy, and that was in response to something the opposition was reported to have said.

It came out in the papers that Dallas coach Tom Landry said he could beat Murphy in a foot race. "I am officially challenging Tom Landry to a race before Sunday's game. Winner takes all, for home field advantage."

Oddsmakers have installed Dallas as a 2 ½ point favorite. No odds have been set on the Murphy versus Landry competition.

12/11/83	Redskins (13-2) 31, COWBOYS (12-3) 10			65,074
Was	14	0	7	10	**31**
Dal	7	3	0	0	**10**
Was	Riggins 3 run (Moseley kick)
Was	Didier 40 pass from Theismann (Moseley kick)
Dal	Cosibe 29 pass from White (Septien kick)
Dal	FG Septien 35
Was	Monk 43 pass from Theismann (Moseley kick)
Was	Riggins 1 run (Moseley kick)
Was	FG Moseley 38

Texas Stadium—This contest was hyped as much as any regular season game in the history of the league. CBS Sports was promoting the meeting between the two 12-2 teams as simply "The Game."

A Dallas win would give the Cowboys the division title and home field advantage throughout the NFC playoffs. Washington would have to beat both Dallas and the New York Giants the following week to claim those prizes. The Redskins, normally a team that shuns hype, added to it by boarding the plane for Dallas dressed in combat fatigues, ready to go to war.

The game started out as though it would be a Redskins blitzkrieg. Washington scored touchdowns on its first two possessions. The first score came on a three-yard run by John Riggins. The threat of Riggins set up the next score as a play fake to the running back left safety Dexter Clinkscale confused and on the ground. Clint Didier was wide open to catch a 40-yard Joe Theismann pass for the touchdown. Then came the first of two momentum swinging fourth down plays. Riggins was stuffed on a fourth and inches play at the Washington 48, and Dallas capitalized two plays later with a touchdown pass from Danny White to tight end Doug Cosbie. The Cowboys added a field goal just before the half ended and it was 14-10.

The second critical fourth down play occurred on Dallas' first possession after halftime. With a yard to go near midfield, Dallas coach Tom Landry apparently told quarterback Danny White to try and draw the Redskins offside with a long snap count, taking the delay of game and punt if the ploy didn't work. White had other

ideas. The TV cameras caught the look of disbelief on the normally stone-faced Landry as White called an audible to a handoff to running back Ron Springs. You didn't have to be a lip reader to make out Landry screaming, "No, Danny, no, no, no!" as the ball was being snapped and then swear as Springs was stuffed for a two-yard loss by a swarm of defenders including Greg Williams and Charles Mann.

While the Redskins would not immediately capitalize on the change of possession, the momentum had clearly swung back their way. After punting and throwing an interception, the Redskins moved in for the kill after rookie cornerback Darrell Green intercepted a deflected pass. From the Dallas 43, Theismann went for it all, hitting Art Monk for the touchdown and a 21-10 lead. An interception by backup safety Greg Williams was followed by a four-yard touchdown run by Riggins and a Mark Moseley field goal with about two minutes in the game left ended the scoring.

The Redskins defense carried the day, taking the ball away on three interceptions and a fumble recovery. Dallas was held to an all-time franchise low of 33 yards rushing and gained just 95 yards of total offense in the second half. Offensively, Theismann was a very efficient 11 for 17 for 201 yards while Monk caught six of those passes for 119.

12/17/83	REDSKINS (14-2) 31, Giants (3-12-1) 22			53,874
NYG	3	9	7	3	**22**
Was	0	7	7	17	**31**
NYG	FG Haji-Sheikh 20
Was	Brown 17 pass from Theismann (Moseley kick)
NYG	FG Haji-Sheikh 39
NYG	FG Haji-Sheikh 19
NYG	FG Haji-Sheikh 45
NYG	Morris 6 pass from Rutledge (Haji-Sheikh kick)
Was	Theismann 3 run (Moseley kick)
Was	FG Moseley 46
NYG	FG Haji-Sheikh 28
Was	Didier 7 pass from Theismann (Moseley kick)
Was	Riggins 2 run (Moseley kick)

RFK Stadium—In a game they had to win to make their victory in Dallas the previous week meaningful, the Redskins came out looking like they were just playing out the string. Quarterback Joe Theismann, who had thrown just nine interceptions in 15 games prior to this one, had three passes picked off in the first period. Not normally given to understatement, Theismann said after the game, "I didn't play well in the first quarter."

Fortunately, the Giants' offense was equally inept early on and Washington got out of the first quarter trailing just 3-0. A roughing call on New York's Lawrence Taylor kept a second-quarter drive alive and the Redskins went in to score on Theismann's 17-yard pass to Charlie Brown. The Redskins had the lead at 7-3.

New York fought back, getting three field goals from Ali Haji-Sheikh to take the lead at halftime. The Redskins were fortunate it wasn't worse as they received a favorable call on a borderline play just prior to Haji-Sheikh's second field goal of the quarter. Giants receiver Byron Williams appeared to have possession in the end zone of a short pass from Jeff Rutledge before dropping it, but the officials ruled that the pass was incomplete; the Giants had to settle for three.

If coach Joe Gibbs had any magic to dispense at halftime, it took a while to take hold. The visitors ground out a 76-yard touchdown drive to open the second half, scoring on a six-yard pass from Rutledge to running back Joe Morris to extend their margin to 19-7. "It was a scared feeling," said guard Russ Grimm.

It must have been a case of getting scared straight, because the Redskins outscored their opponents 24-3 for the rest of the game. A 28-yard return of the second-half kickoff by Reggie Branch and a 44-yard rumble by John Riggins led to Theismann's three-yard bootleg run around left end into the end zone, cutting the deficit to 19-14 with just under three minutes left in the third quarter. Darryl Grant recovered a botched center snap to set up a Mark Moseley field goal to make it a two-point game.

The Giants extended their lead back to five with Haji-Sheikh's fifth field goal of the day, this one coming with 9:13 left in the game. But the Redskins drove 78 yards with the ensuing kickoff and scored on Theismann's seven-yard pass to tight end Clint Didier. The key play on the drive was a 34-yard Theismann to Art Monk connection on a slant pattern.

The game New Yorkers were still alive and down by just five, but the Redskins erased any hopes for a comeback when linebacker Monte Coleman blitzed and separated Rutledge from the ball with a vicious hit. Riggins soon scored his 24th TD of the year, breaking the NFL record held by O. J. Simpson.

NFC Divisional Playoff Game
Sunday, January 1, 1984
RFK Stadium
Washington, D.C.

1/1/84	REDSKINS 51, Rams 7				55,363
LA	0	7	0	0	7
Was	17	21	6	7	51
Was	Riggins 3 run (Moseley kick)				
Was	Monk 40 pass from Theismann (Moseley kick)				
Was	FG Moseley 42				
Was	Riggins 1 run (Moseley kick)				
LA	Dennard 32 pass from Ferragamo (Lansford kick)				
Was	Monk 21 pass from Theismann (Moseley kick)				
Was	Riggins 1 run (Moseley kick)				
Was	FG Moseley 36				
Was	FG Moseley 41				
Was	Green 72 interception return (Moseley kick)				

The table was set for a New Year's Day party. The defending Super Bowl champion Redskins were facing the wild card LA Rams in a divisional playoff game. The Redskins were coming off a bye week; the Rams had to travel to Texas Stadium to eliminate the Cowboys the previous week. The Redskins had gone 14-2 in the regular season; the Rams had snuck into the playoffs with a 9-7 mark. They had met previously, with Washington taking it to the Rams in California 42-20.

Sure, there were some factors in the Rams' favor. There were questions about whether or not the Redskins were hungry for a second title. Los Angeles featured future Hall of Fame running back Eric Dickerson on offense and had the league's leading punt returner in Henry Ellard. And, as they say, anything can happen—that's why they play the games.

Well, they did need to play this game—but only about the first 16 minutes of it. On their opening possession, the Redskins drove 65 yards in eight plays; John Riggins carried six times for 23 yards and capped the drive with a three-yard touchdown run. Five minutes later, Joe Theismann threw 40 yards to Art Monk for a touchdown to make it 14-0. An interception by Anthony Washington set up a 42-yard Mark Moseley field goal with less than a minute left in the first quarter. Then, early in the second, Nick Giaquinto returned a punt 48 yards to set up a one-yard touchdown plunge by Riggins. It was 24-0 with nearly 14 minutes left until halftime.

If it were a Little League game, it would have ended on the massacre rule. If it were a prizefight, the referee would have stopped it. However, NFL rules dictate that they play for 60 minutes, so on it went. The Rams did manage to score a touchdown to close within 24-7, but it took the Redskins just five plays to go 76 yards to answer, with Monk breaking wide open

over the middle and gathering in Theismann's perfect pass for a 21-yard touchdown pass. The score stood at 31-7.

That tally tied the team record for most points scored in a playoff game—an entire game, not just a half. The Redskins broke the mark 43 seconds before halftime on Riggins' third touchdown run of the day, a score set up by a spectacular catch by Charlie Brown that covered 48 yards.

Meanwhile, the defense was doing its part to ensure that the game would not become competitive. They sacked LA quarterback Vince Ferragamo three times. Dickerson gained just 16 yards on 10 carries. Rookie Darrell Green was flying all over the field, batting down passes. And, after two Moseley field goals were the only scoring in the third quarter, Green finished off the scoring and pushed the Redskins over the 50-point mark early in the fourth. A Ferragamo pass bounced off Dickerson's hands and into Green's. In a flash, Green was in the open and on his way to a 72-yard touchdown return.

That score let the Redskins break another team record: the largest margin of victory in any game in team history. It was 51-7 and the rest of the game was garbage time.

NFC Championship Game
Sunday, January 8, 1984
RFK Stadium
Washington, D.C.

1/8/84	REDSKINS 24, 49ers 21				55,363
SF	0	0	0	21	21
Was	0	7	14	3	24
Was	Riggins 4 run (Moseley kick)				
Was	Riggins 1 run (Moseley kick)				
Was	Brown 70 pass from Theismann (Moseley kick)				
SF	Wilson 5 pass from Montana (Wersching kick)				
SF	Solomon 76 pass from Montana (Wersching kick)				
SF	Wilson 12 pass from Montana (Wersching kick)				
Was	FG Moseley 25				

The Redskins came into the 1983 NFC title game flying about as high as a team can. They had scored an NFL-record 541 points during the regular season, had earned home field advantage throughout the playoffs with a 14-2 record and had thrashed the Rams 51-7 in the first round of the playoffs. The Niners were simply another obstacle to be brushed aside on the way to a second straight Super Bowl championship. The 10-6 49ers had barely survived Detroit the week before as Eddie Murray missed a 43-yard field goal attempt with five seconds left, giving the home standing San Francisco team a 24-23 win.

The Redskins dominated the first three quarters, but it didn't show on the scoreboard. Nick Giaquinto fielded a punt and lateraled to rookie Darrell Green, who ran it in for an apparent touchdown. Although replays seemed to show that the pass was legal, the officials said it went forward and the touchdown was nullified. Mark Moseley missed three first-half field goal attempts and Washington had just a 7-0 halftime lead. They got some breathing room in the third on a John Riggins run for one touchdown and a 70-yard Joe Theismann to Charlie Brown pass for another, and it was 21-0 at the end of the third. In seven quarters of playoff football, Washington had outscored the opposition 72-7. The march to the Super Bowl in Tampa could continue.

But then Joe Montana said "not so fast," and proceeded to rain heavily on the celebratory parade. In the span of seven minutes and 29 seconds, Montana threw three touchdown passes, two to Mike Wilson and one to Freddie Solomon. The crowd of 55,363 at RFK sat stunned as a penalty on the kickoff following the last score pushed the Redskins back to their own 14-yard line.

There were just under seven minutes left in regulation. The Redskins needed to score, but not too quickly.

Riggins got things started with a 17-yard run out to the 31. Art Monk kept the drive alive a few plays later with a third-down grab that moved the ball to the San Francisco 45. Two plays later, Eric Wright was called for pass interference on Monk to give Washington a first down at the 18. After the game, Bill Walsh, the coach of the 49ers, said that a "10-foot Boston Celtic" couldn't have caught that ball. Apparently daunted by the legendary "genius" of Walsh, none of the assembled media asked the coach why Wright was mugging Monk if the ball was so far off target.

Later on in the drive, Ronnie Lott made a dumb play by grabbing Brown as he came off the line. Lott complained loudly during and after the game that the official did his job and threw a flag. As the Redskins faced fourth down at the San Francisco eight, the 0-for-4 Moseley came onto the field once more. "I felt like offering him a blindfold and a cigarette," Riggins joked after the game.

Riggo was able to joke because Moseley's 25-yard attempt was right through the uprights, giving the Redskins a 24-21 lead with 44 seconds left. A desperation Montana heave was intercepted on the final play of the game. The Redskins were headed to Tampa.

Gibbs: Redskins Will Need Big Plays to Win

Jan. 20—Joe Gibbs will be thinking big when his Redskins take on the Raiders on Sunday in Super Bowl XVIII.

"I'm sure we are going to throw a lot of balls," said Gibbs. "It's a matter of making the big plays."

While the Redskins certainly will work on establishing a ground game, Gibbs is reluctant to rely on that, citing the fact that the Raiders gave up just 3.7 yards per carry this season.

Raiders coach Tom Flores agreed. "This game has all of the makings of a big-play game," he said.

"I'm more concerned about stopping Theismann, Monk, and Charlie Brown so they don't congregate in the end zone and do whatever they do there," Flores continued, referring to the Redskins' "Fun Bunch" touchdown celebration.

Flores is willing to concede some yards to John Riggins, who has at least 100 rushing yards in six straight playoff games.

"Everything you read in the papers is 'Stop Riggins, stop Riggins,'" Flores said. Citing Riggins' talent and the strength of the Washington offensive line, he said that Riggins will "get his share of yards."

Sunday, January 22, 1984
Tampa Stadium
Tampa, Florida

1/22/84	Raiders 38, Redskins 9				72,920
Was	0	3	6	0	**9**
LA	7	14	14	3	**38**

LA	Jensen recovered blocked punt in end zone (Bahr kick)
LA	Branch 12 pass from Plunkett (Bahr kick)
Was	FG Moseley 24
LA	Squirek 5 interception return (Bahr kick)
Was	Riggins 1 run (kick blocked)
LA	Allen 5 run (Bahr kick)
LA	Allen 74 run (Bahr kick)
LA	FG Bahr 21

The Redskins came to Tampa looking for a second straight crown. Instead, they had their hats handed to them by the Los Angeles Raiders.

The Washington Redskins entered Super Bowl XVIII having lost just two games by a total of two points. The defending Super Bowl Champions had scored an NFL record 541 points and the defense had racked up 61 takeaways.

Looking for a place in history, the Redskins found it—although not in the way they had hoped. They set Super Bowl records by giving up 38 points and losing by 29.

It was apparent early that this was not going to be the Redskins' day. When Washington was forced to punt after its first possession, the Raiders' Derrick Jensen broke through the middle of the line and easily blocked Jeff Hayes' punt at about the 20. The ball rebounded all the way into the end zone, where Jensen fell on it for a quick 7-0 Raider lead.

After Mark Moseley missed a 44-yard field goal attempt, Raiders receiver Cliff Branch beat Anthony Washington for a 50-yard catch to the Washington 15 and two plays later, Jim Plunkett found Branch again for a 12-yard score and a 14-0 Raiders lead.

A promising drive stalled at the Raider six when linebacker Rod Martin broke up a pass intended for Joe Washington. The Redskins had to settle for a 24-yard Moseley field goal to cut it to 14-3. The defense held and the Raiders downed a punt at the 12 with 12 seconds left. The Redskins would receive the second-half kickoff and it appeared to be time to have Joe Theismann take a knee and regroup in the locker room.

Joe Gibbs had different ideas, though. During the regular season, the two teams met in a classic game that the Redskins rallied to win 37-35. The fourth-quarter comeback was sparked by 67-yard pass to Joe Washington on a play called Rocket Screen. Wanting to get field position for perhaps one more scoring attempt before the half, Gibbs sent in Rocket Screen. Problem was, the Raiders remembered that October 2 game, too.

The Raiders' defensive coordinator had a hunch the Redskins might try that play again. He opted to insert linebacker Jack Squirek into the lineup to shadow Washington on that play while the rest of the team played a deep zone to prevent a big play. Theismann read the zone and never expected to see Squirek playing man-to-man on his intended receiver as he tossed the ball towards Washington. The linebacker easily cut in front of Washington at the five, plunging a dagger in the hearts of the Redskins as he dashed into the end zone. The halftime score was Raiders 21, Redskins 3.

The Redskins did manage to drive for a touchdown after the second-half kickoff, finishing off a 70-yard drive with a one-yard touchdown plunge by John Riggins. Some air was let out of the comeback balloon, however, when the extra point was blocked. The balloon was flattened when LA answered with a 70-yard touchdown drive of its own with Marcus Allen scoring on a five-yard run. And even a miracle-type rally was rendered impossible on the last two plays of the third quarter. After Martin stuffed Riggins on fourth and one at the Raiders 26, Allen took a handoff, headed left, cut back to the middle and embarked on a 74-yard scoring run.

Jan. 26
100,000 Hail Runner-Up Redskins
Players vow return to Super Bowl

1984
Head Coach: Joe Gibbs
Record: 11-5, NFC East Champions
Playoffs: 0-1, lost in Divisional Playoff

Honors: Darrell Green Pro Bowl; Russ Grimm All-NFL, Pro Bowl;
Joe Jacoby All-NFL, Pro Bowl; Art Monk All-NFL, Pro Bowl

Aug 1

Mendenhall Goes Home
DE's Career With Redskins Likely Done

Yesterday Gibbs Walks, Today He Talks

Aug 15—The morning after walking out of practice with some 45 minutes left to go and bypassing his daily press conference, Joe Gibbs spoke.

"I spent some time and drove off for a while," he said. "I needed to be by myself."

Obviously, he was displeased with the effort being displayed during the practice session. But, certainly, that's happened before. Why walk out yesterday?

"I guess I just didn't feel like there was anything else I could say to help practice out," Gibbs said.

Although no player was willing to talk about it for the record, there was talk of Gibbs getting agitated at last night's meeting, too. They said that, in a raised voice, Gibbs lectured them on the importance of concentration at practice.

9/2/84	Dolphins (1-0) 35, REDSKINS (0-1) 17			52,683	
Mia	7	7	21	0	**35**
Was	0	10	0	7	**17**
Mia	Duper 26 pass from Marino (von Schamann kick)				
Was	Riggins 1 run (Moseley kick)				
Was	FG Moseley 32				
Mia	Duper 74 pass from Marino (von Schamann kick)				
Mia	Jensen 6 pass from Marino (von Schamann kick)				
Mia	Clayton 9 pass from Marino (von Schamann kick)				
Mia	Jensen 4 pass from Marino (von Schamann kick)				
Was	J. Washington 4 run (Moseley kick)				

RFK Stadium—Dan Marino torched the Redskins with five touchdown passes as the Dolphins pulled away in the second half and claimed a 35-17 win. The second-year quarterback completed 21 of 28 passes for 311 yards with Mark Duper catching six of those tosses for 178 yards.

During most of the first half, this was a competitive game. Miami struck first on a 26-yard Marino-to-Duper TD pass, but the Redskins took the lead in the second quarter. John Riggins, who gained 98 yards on the day, went over from one yard out to tie the game and a 32-yard Mark Moseley field goal gave Washington a 10-7 lead. Just before the two minute warning, Miami took possession at its own 18. It took three plays for them to score, the last a 74-yard bomb to Duper and the Dolphins had a 14-10 halftime lead. The rout was on.

Marino took the Dolphins 68 yards to a touchdown following the second-half kickoff with the key play coming on a 46-yard pass to Duper. Although it was apparent that Marino and the Dolphins needed no help, the Redskins gave them a hand in wrapping up the game. A Joe Washington fumble and an interception of Joe Theismann set up the Dolphins' final two scores which came, of course, on Marino passes.

9/10/84	49ERS (2-0) 37, Redskins (0-2) 31			59,707	
Was	0	3	14	14	**31**
SF	14	13	0	10	**37**
SF	Tyler 1 run (Wersching kick)				
SF	Tyler 5 pass from Montana (Wersching kick)				
SF	FG Wesching 19				
SF	FG Wersching 45				
SF	Clark 15 pass from Montana (Wersching kick)				
Was	FG Moseley 38				
Was	Brown 14 pass from Theismann (Moseley kick)				
Was	Riggins 1 run (Moseley kick)				
SF	Montana 7 run (Wersching kick)				
Was	Riggins 1 run (Moseley kick)				
SF	FG Wersching 38				
Was	Seay 12 pass from Theismann (Moseley kick)				

Candlestick Park—The 49ers built a 27-0 first half lead and then survived a furious second-half comeback attempt. Joe Theismann threw for 235 yards in the second half to help make a game of it, but he was trumped by Joe Montana's 381-yard game. The 37-31 loss dropped the Redskins to 0-2.

The Redskins spent the first half trying to establish the run, but were unable to do so. Joe Washington and John Riggins combined for 13 carries for 17 yards. Meanwhile, Montana enjoyed considerable success, completing his first eight passes for 98 yards and leading touchdown drives on his team's first two possessions. Running back Wendell Tyler scored both of them, one on a one-yard run and the other on a five-yard pass from Montana.

The home team's offensive charge continued barely abated in the second quarter. The Washington defense, such as it was, did manage to hold them to field goals on two occasions to make the score 20-0. But the Niners broke through again, this time on a 15-yard touchdown pass from Montana to Dwight Clark and it was 27-0. At that point, with 1:11 left in the first half, they had outgained the Redskins 322-49.

To their credit, the Redskins did not fold their tents. They battled back with a 38-yard Mark Moseley field goal just before halftime and a pair of third-quarter touchdowns to pull within 27-17. Montana let some of the air out of the comeback balloon by finding receiver Mike Wilson for a 44-yard gain to the Washington six before taking it in himself from seven yards out nine seconds into the fourth quarter, stretching the lead out to 34-17.

But the Redskins still refused to be blown out. Joe Theismann, who passed for 331 yards on the day, led one touchdown drive that ended with a one-yard Riggins run and, after a San Francisco field goal, threw 12 yards to Virgin Seay to pull Washington within six at 37-31 with 3:44 to go.

But Montana, as expected, didn't cooperate with the comeback effort. His 11-yard pass to Clark on third and four allowed the Niners to run out the clock.

9/16/84	**REDSKINS (1-2) 30, Giants (2-1) 14**			52,997
NYG	7	0	7	0	**14**
Was	7	6	0	17	**30**

Was	Riggins 1 run (Moseley kick)
NYG	Carpenter 1 run (Haji-Sheikh kick)
Was	Riggins 1 run (kick missed)
NYG	B. Johnson 27 pass from Simms (Haji-Sheikh kick)
Was	FG Moseley 21
Was	Dean 36 interception return (Moseley kick)
Was	Jordan 29 fumble return (Moseley kick)

RFK Stadium—The Redskins' defense, burned for 72 points in the first two games, showed up with a vengeance today, sacking Giants quarterback Phil Simms five times and intercepting three of his passes. Vernon Dean got all three of the picks, returning one for a touchdown that gave the Redskins some breathing room in their first win of the year, a 30-14 triumph over New York.

Washington entered the fourth quarter trailing as Simms had thrown 27 yards to Bobby Johnson in the third quarter for a 14-13 lead. A Mark Moseley field goal in the final period's first minute put the home team up 16-14. On the Giants' first play after that, Simms tried to go to Johnson again, but Dean had the play sniffed out. Dean cut in front of Johnson to intercept the pass in the left flat and rolled 36 yards for a touchdown with little interference, making it 23-14.

A promising Giants drive came up empty when Ali Haji-Sheikh missed a 38-yard field goal attempt, but the New Yorkers forced a punt and got the ball back with 8:03 left. The call by New York coach Bill Parcells was a double reverse and the result meant disaster for the Giants. Simms handed off to halfback Rob Carpenter, who in turn gave it to receiver Lionel Manuel. Dave Butz and Monte Coleman were not fooled and simultaneously smashed into Manuel, separating him from the ball. Curtis Jordan scooped the ball up and breezed 29 yards to clinch the game.

9/23/84	**Redskins (2-2) 26, PATRIOTS (2-2) 10**			60,503
Was	7	3	13	3	**26**
NE	0	0	7	3	**10**

Was	Riggins 13 run (Moseley kick)
Was	FG Moseley 19
Was	FG Moseley 42
Was	Brown 15 pass from Theismann (Moseley kick)
NE	Starring 38 pass from Eason (Franklin kick)
Was	FG Moseley 22
NE	FG Franklin 22
Was	FG Moseley 27

Sullivan Stadium—The Redskins went into Foxboro and committed assault with a blunt instrument upon their hosts. The weapon was John Riggins, who carried 33 times for 140 yards to help Washington grind out the win. Thanks largely to Riggins' repeated battering, the Redskins held the ball for more than 43 minutes.

The tone was set on the Redskins' second possession when they started at their own seven. Fourteen plays and 7:57 later, Riggins went over from 13 yards out to give Washington a 7-0 lead. Another long drive, this one of eight minutes, resulted in a Mark Moseley field goal and it was 10-0 at halftime.

After another Moseley field goal in the third quarter made it 13-0, Monte Coleman sacked New England quarterback Tony Eason, stripped him of the ball and recovered the fumble at the Patriots 15. The offense immediately took advantage of Coleman's hat trick with Joe Theismann throwing to Charlie Brown for the touchdown on the next play for a 20-0 lead.

New England cut it to 23-10 with 12:06 to play and had a chance to rally, but the Redskins delivered a hard dose of reality by pounding more than 10 minutes off the clock. After 16 plays, Moseley's 27-yard field goal with 1:57 left completed the scoring.

9/30/84	**REDSKINS (3-2) 20, Eagles (1-4) 0**			53,064
Phil	0	0	0	0	**0**
Was	0	10	7	3	**20**

Was	Monk 51 pass from Theismann (Moseley kick)
Was	FG Moseley 35
Was	Riggins 8 run (Moseley kick)
Was	FG Moseley 29

RFK Stadium—A 51-yard touchdown pass on a flea flicker got the Redskins' offense going and Washington cruised to a 20-0 win over Philadelphia.

After having pounded New England for 140 yards on 33 carries the previous week, John Riggins was both a weapon (104 on 28 carries) and a decoy. Early in the second quarter, with the game scoreless, quarterback Joe Theismann handed off to Riggins, who was headed to his favorite spot—right up the middle. But Riggins stopped, turned around and pitched back to Theismann.

"We came up for the run and blew it," said Eagles linebacker Jerry Robinson in a classic understatement. Art Monk was several yards behind the nearest defenders as he caught Theismann's pass in stride at the goal line for a 7-0 lead.

That one play accounted for nearly half of Theismann's 119 passing yards, but Theismann did pitch in with 57 yards rushing, including some clutch gains on the Redskins' second touchdown drive. With the Redskins leading 10-0 in the third quarter, Theismann scrambled for a first down early in what would become a 77-yard drive. Later, he found open ground from the Eagles 35 and wasn't stopped until he reached the eight. From there, he let Riggins do the rest of the work. The big back followed a crunching block by Russ Grimm and easily got into the end zone for a 17-0 lead. Mark Moseley's second field goal topped off the scoring in the fourth quarter.

Meanwhile, the Eagles' offense could to little against the Washington defense. Their biggest scoring threat came in the third quarter when they drove inside the Washington 20 only to lose the ball when Dexter Manley sacked Ron Jaworski, forcing a fumble that Darryl Grant recovered.

Oct 3

Skins Get Raiders' Calvin Muhammad
Draft pick goes to LA for speedy wideout to shore up ailing receiver corps

---

10/7/84	**Redskins (4-2) 35, COLTS (2-4) 7**			60,012
Was	7	21	7	0	**35**
Ind	7	0	0	0	**7**

Was	Monk 10 pass from Theismann (Moseley kick)
Ind	A Moore 2 run (Allegre kick)
Was	Monk 40 pass from Theismann (Moseley kick)
Was	Riggins 1 run (Moseley kick)
Was	Monk 16 pass from Theismann (Moseley kick)
Was	McGrath 11 pass from Theismann (Moseley kick)

Hoosier Dome—Joe Theismann said, "It was a great day." He was speaking of his own performance, but it would be hard to label him as immodest, at least in this particular case. He completed 17 of 20 passes for 267 yards and compensated for his one interception by throwing for four touchdowns as the Redskins routed the Colts 35-7.

This one was over in about 35 minutes. The Colts had tied the game after recovering an Art Monk fumble and driving 19 yards to a touchdown, answering Monk's score earlier in the first quarter. Theismann found that a rookie cornerback was covering Monk and took advantage, throwing 48 yards to the receiver to give the Redskins the lead for good five and a half minutes into the second quarter.

After John Riggins dove in from a yard out, cornerback Vernon Dean made the first of his two interceptions, setting up the third

Theismann-to-Monk scoring connection of the half. From the Colts' 16, Monk ran a fade pattern into the end zone and Theismann dropped the ball over cornerback Tate Randle and into Monk's waiting hands. On the day, Monk caught eight passes for 141 yards and the three TD's.

The Washington defense kept the Colts at bay, holding them to 186 yards of total offense.

10/14/84	**REDSKINS (5-2) 34, Cowboys (4-3) 14**			55,431	
Dal	7	0	0	7	**14**
Was	7	10	10	7	**34**
Dal	Dorsett 29 run (Septien kick)				
Was	Coleman 49 interception return (Moseley kick)				
Was	Didier 8 pass from Theismann (Moseley kick)				
Was	FG Moseley 20				
Was	Muhammad 80 pass from Theismann (Moseley kick)				
Was	FG Moseley 22				
Was	Didier 3 pass from Theismann (Moseley kick)				
Dal	Dorsett 6 run (Septien kick)				

RFK Stadium—A pair of big plays, one by the offense and one by the defense, combined with John Riggins' 165 yards rushing to help the Redskins hammer the Cowboys 34-14.

The first big play came from linebacker Monte Coleman. With Dallas holding a 7-0 lead in the first quarter and looking for more, Coleman stepped in front of a pass intended for running back Ron Springs. "He threw it right to me," Coleman said, referring to Dallas quarterback Gary Hogeboom. The linebacker easily returned the interception 49 yards for a touchdown and Mark Moseley's point after tied the score. The Redskins took a 17-7 lead into the locker room at halftime following an eight-yard touchdown pass from Joe Theismann to tight end Clint Didier and a 20-yard Moseley field goal.

On the first play from scrimmage of the second half, the Redskins moved in for the kill. Theismann rolled out, cranked up and unleashed the longest touchdown pass of his career: 80 yards to Calvin Muhammad. The ball traveled about 55 yards in the air, and Muhammad was well ahead of cornerback Ron Fellows and safety Dextor Clinkscale when he caught it at the 25 to score with no problem. That made it 27-7 and from there a heavy dose of Riggins was all that was needed to wrap this one up.

10/21/84	**CARDINALS (5-3) 26, Redskins (5-3) 24**			50,262	
Was	7	0	14	3	**24**
StL	7	3	7	9	**26**
StL	Green 38 pass from Lomax (O'Donoghue kick)				
Was	Didier 3 pass from Theismann (Moseley kick)				
StL	FG O'Donoghue 29				
Was	Riggins 2 run (Moseley kick)				
Was	R. Walker 7 pass from Theismann (Moseley kick)				
StL	Marsh 19 pass from Lomax (O'Donoghue kick)				
Was	FG Moseley 39				
StL	R. Green 83 pass from Lomax (kick missed)				
StL	FG O'Donoghue 21				

Busch Stadium—The Redskins appeared to be cruising to their sixth straight victory, but the Cardinals struck back on a long bomb and last-second field goal to steal the win. Neil O'Donoghue shook off the effects of having missed his previous three kicks to put the game winner through with three seconds left and give the Cardinals a 26-24 victory.

Washington trailed 10-7 at halftime, but took care of that after taking the second half kickoff. They moved 75 yards to a 14-10 lead, the payoff coming on a two-yard run by John Riggins. Two plays after the ensuing kickoff, end Tony McGee sacked quarterback Neil Lomax, forcing a fumble. Dave Butz recovered and the visitors had possession at the St. Louis 26. Six plays later, Joe Theismann threw to Rick Walker in the end zone and Washington had a 21-10 advantage.

St. Louis responded with a touchdown of its own, and then the Redskins got a Mark Moseley field goal to push their margin back up to seven at 24-17 with just under 12 minutes left to play. Stump Mitchell bobbled the ensuing kickoff and the Cards were in a hole at their own 17.

But not for long. On the first play, Lomax took advantage of tight coverage on the corners to spring Roy Green free on a deep post. Green beat safety Tony Peters gathered in the QB's throw and easily completed the 83-yard touchdown play. Although O'Donoghue's point after attempt bounced off the upright and the Cardinals still trailed 24-23, momentum had clearly swung their way.

O'Donoghue shanked a 40-yard try to put his team ahead with just under three minutes left. Washington gave the ball right back to the Cards, burning off less than a minute before punting back to Lomax and company. Lomax twice converted third and long situations to move from his own 33 to the Washington four. The kicker wasn't about to miss this one, and the home team had a 26-24 win.

10/28/84	**GIANTS (5-4) 37, Redskins (5-4) 13**			76,192	
Was	0	6	0	7	**13**
NYG	14	9	7	7	**37**
NYG	Gray 23 pass from Simms (Haji-Sheikh kick)				
NYG	Morris 2 run (Haji-Sheikh kick)				
NYG	Morris 1 run (kick failed)				
NYG	FG Haji-Sheikh 19				
Was	FG Moseley 23				
Was	FG Moseley 33				
NYG	Morris 5 run (Haji-Sheikh kick)				
NYG	B. Johnson 8 pass from Simms (Haji-Sheikh kick)				
Was	Moore 4 pass from Theismann (Moseley kick)				

Giants Stadium—The Redskins appeared to be off to a good start in their effort for their seventh straight win over the Giants. Early in the game, New York's Phil McConkey fumbled a punt and the Skins had a first down at the Giants 17.

Washington returned the favor, however, fumbling it back a few plays later. The Giants marched in for a touchdown and never looked back. Or, perhaps they did look back to take a peek at Redskins fading further and further behind them. In the end the Giants walked off with a 37-13 win.

That touchdown drive ended with Phil Simms throwing a 23-yard touchdown pass to receiver Earnest Gray. Simms must have sensed that Gray could have his way against the Washington secondary. The next time the Giants got the ball, Gray beat Darrell Green on a streak pattern for 29 yards and then shook Vernon Dean on the same route for 31 yards to the Washington two. Joe Morris took it over on the next play. Three plays, 62 yards, 14-0.

The home team completed a run of 23 unanswered points with another Morris touchdown run (the point after was missed) and a 19-yard field goal by Ali Haji-Sheikh. Before halftime, the Redskins managed two drives inside the New York ten yard line, but came away with just six points on two Mark Moseley field goals. The Giants scored two more touchdowns in the second half before the Redskins finally dented the end zone on a four-yard pass from Joe Theismann to Jeff Moore.

11/5/84	**REDSKINS (6-4) 27, Falcons (3-7) 14**			51,301	
Atl	0	7	7	0	**14**
Was	0	14	6	7	**27**
Was	Riggins 1 run (Moseley kick)				
Was	Theismann 1 run (Moseley kick)				
Atl	Riggs 1 run (Luckhurst kick)				
Atl	Riggs 10 run (Luckhurst kick)				
Was	Riggins 1 run (kick failed)				
Was	Muhammad 7 pass from Theismann				

RFK Stadium—"I had a feeling it wouldn't be pretty," said Joe Gibbs after this game. As usual, he was right. Washington needed an unforced error by the Falcons' backup quarterback to retake the lead after an Atlanta rally had tied the game and then held on for the 27-14 win.

The Redskins appeared to be on their way to an easy win over the lowly Falcons after two second-quarter touchdown drives earned them a 14-0 lead. The first ended when John Riggins bulled over from a yard out; the second came when Joe Theismann faked to Riggins and easily bootlegged around the left side on fourth and goal inside the one. When the Atlanta offense retook the field after the second score, starting quarterback Steve Bartkowski wasn't with them. He was on the bench with a strained knee.

With Mike Moroski filling in, the Falcons put their offense in Gerald Riggs' hands. Riggs keyed an 80-yard touchdown march with eight carries for 49 yards, going in from a yard out for a touchdown that took his team off of the ropes. In the third quarter, he topped off a 79-yard drive by dragging safety Ken Coffey into the end zone to complete a 10-yard scoring run to tie the score at 14.

Atlanta regained possession and was on the move when Moroski made the error that turned the game around. On second and five, without a hand being laid on him, he dropped the ball while trying to elude the rush. Neil Olkewicz fell on it at the Atlanta 32. Theismann threw to Calvin Muhammad for a first down at the 19 and then it was Riggins five straight times, the last a one-yard scoring run. Although Theismann mishandled the snap on the point after attempt, the Redskins still breathed a sigh of relief at being back in the lead. The Washington defense tightened up on Riggs and the Falcons, and Theismann's fourth-quarter TD pass to Muhammad wrapped it up for the home team.

11/11/84	REDSKINS (7-4) 28, Lions (3-7-1) 14			50,212	
Det	0	0	14	0	14
Was	14	7	7	0	28
Was	Moore 2 pass from Theismann (Moseley kick)				
Was	Wonsley 1 run (Moseley kick)				
Was	Wonsley 1 run (Moseley kick)				
Was	Wonsley 3 run (Moseley kick)				
Det	J. Jones 1 run (Murray kick)				
Det	Rubick 19 pass from Danielson (Murray kick)				

RFK Stadium—If the Detroit Lions were ever going to win a game in Washington—something they have never done—today seemed to be the day it could happen. John Riggins was sidelined with a bad back. They blocked three punts, had seven possessions inside the Washington 25, and averaged over seven and a half yards on 22 running plays. The bottom line, however, was the same old story as the Redskins ran up a 28-0 lead and coasted to a 28-14 win.

Two players filled in for Riggins and did so quite ably. In regular situations, it was rookie Keith Griffin, who gained 114 yards on 32 carries. In short yardage, it was Otis Wonsley, normally the blocking back in such circumstances. He scored three touchdowns, the first on a one-yard run that gave the home team a 14-0 lead late in the first quarter.

In the second, Curtis Jordan intercepted a pass, setting up a short touchdown drive that also culminated in another one-yard Wonsley plunge. After halftime, the Lions fumbled a punt, leading to another short TD drive. Wonsley scored it again, this time from three yards out. The score was 28-0.

Detroit had its opportunities to make a game of it by getting their hands on three Jeff Hayes punts. One of those possessions ended when Mel Kaufman tipped Gary Danielson's fourth-down pass and another when Darrell Green picked off Danielson pass in the end zone. Those plays helped push the Lions' record in Washington to 0-12.

11/18/84	EAGLES (5-6-1) 16, Redskins (7-5) 10			63,117	
Was	0	7	3	0	10
Phil	3	3	10	0	16
Phil	FG McFadden 43				
Was	Didier 3 pass from Theismann (Moseley kick)				
Phil	FG McFadden 34				
Phil	FG McFadden 41				
Was	FG Moseley 33				
Phil	Waters 89 kickoff return (McFadden kick)				

Veterans Stadium—Andre Waters returned a kickoff 89 yards in the third quarter to provide the winning points in the Eagles' 16-10 win over Washington. Truth be told, the Redskins had lost the game long before that.

"We lost it in the first half," said Joe Theismann, and it would be difficult to argue with that assessment.

Three times in the first half, Washington had prime scoring opportunities but came up empty. Theismann threw an interception after a shanked Eagle punt netted just three yards, lost a fumble on a first down play inside the Eagles one, and had a Mark Moseley field goal attempt bounce off the right upright.

Even the scoring the Redskins did manage was somewhat tainted. Moseley missed a 23-yard field goal, but the Eagles were flagged for roughing the kicker. Theismann threw three yards to Clint Didier to give Washington a 7-3 lead.

Barefoot kicker Paul McFadden gave the home team the lead with a pair of field goals, one from 34 yards with one second left in the first half and the other from 41 yards early in the third quarter. A 33-yarder by Moseley with five and a half minutes left in the third got the lead back for Washington—but not for long.

Jeff Hayes' kickoff got caught in the wind and floated to Waters at the 11. He burst through an initial wave of tacklers and easily beat Hayes to the end zone. McFadden's point after gave Philly a 16-10 lead.

After having blown so many scoring opportunities, Washington could manufacture no more. They got no closer than the Eagles 34 the rest of the way.

11/25/84	REDSKINS (8-5) 41, Bills (1-12) 14			51,513	
Buf	0	7	7	0	14
Was	17	10	7	7	41
Was	Monk 11 pass from Theismann (Moseley kick)				
Was	FG Moseley 38				
Was	Riggins 1 run (Moseley kick)				
Was	Brown 18 pass from Theismann (Moseley kick)				
Buf	Franklin 8 pass from Ferguson (Nelson kick)				
Was	FG Moseley 51				
Buf	Dennard 36 pass from Ferguson (Nelson kick)				
Was	Dean 11 interception return (Moseley kick)				
Was	Wonsley 3 run (Moseley kick)				

RFK Stadium—Joe Theismann passed for 311 yards and two touchdowns to lead the Redskins to a 41-14 win over Buffalo.

Against the Washington defense, the Bills' offense was balanced, but that's about the only good thing you can say about it. They rushed for 85 yards and passed for 86.

The home team took a 7-0 lead just three and a half minutes into the contest on an 11-yard pass from Theismann to Art Monk. On the day, Monk had 11 catches, boosting his season total to a Redskins record 82. Theismann also broke a team record during the course of the game, surpassing Sonny Jurgensen to become the team's all-time passing yardage leader.

By the end of the first quarter, the Skins had a 17-0 lead. Less than a minute into the second, receiver Charlie Brown celebrated his return from the injured reserve list by catching a pass in the flat, eluding a pair of would-be tacklers and jogging in to complete an 18-yard touchdown play to make it 24-0. The Redskins coasted to the win from there.

11/29/84	Redskins (9-5) 31, VIKINGS (3-11) 17			55,017	
Was	17	14	0	0	**31**
Min	0	0	10	7	**17**

Was	Muhammad 68 pass from Theismann (Moseley kick)
Was	FG Moseley 30
Was	Didier 4 pass from Theismann (Moseley kick)
Was	Jacoby fumble recovery in end zone (Moseley kick)
Was	Grant 22 fumble return (Moseley kick)
Min	FG Stenerud 31
Min	Lewis 14 pass from Manning (Stenerud kick)
Min	Lewis 8 pass from Manning (Stenerud kick)

Metrodome—The Redskins bolted into the lead 18 seconds into the game on the way to a 31-0 halftime margin. Minnesota managed to make it respectable in the second half behind backup quarterback Archie Manning, but they had too much ground to make up as Washington won 31-17.

Washington's early lead came on a 68-yard touchdown bomb from Joe Theismann to Calvin Muhammad. Before the first quarter was over, the Redskins had scored twice more on a Mark Moseley field goal and a four-yard pass from Theismann to Clint Didier. Didier's touchdown was set up when Rich Milot intercepted Wade Wilson's pass and returned it to the Minnesota 12.

In the second quarter, the linemen got into the scoring act. Running back Keith Griffin coughed the ball up after a 12-yard run to the Minnesota seven. As the ball rolled into the end zone, no Minnesota player seemed to be particularly anxious to get in the way of 300-pound tackle Joe Jacoby as he charged towards the ball. The result was Jake's first career touchdown and a 24-0 lead.

Midway through the period, Neil Olkewicz sacked Wilson inside the Minnesota 30. The ball came loose and Darryl Grant scooped it up at the 22. He outran some futile pursuit to make it 31-0.

At the time, those last two scores seemed to be window dressing, albeit with some degree of historical significance—no NFL has ever scored more than two TD's on fumble recoveries in a game. However, they turned out to be decisive.

Coach Les Steckel replaced Wilson with veteran quarterback Manning in the second half. Manning led his team to a field goal and threw a pair of TD passes to Leo Lewis to make the final more respectable.

12/9/85	Redskins (10-5) 30, COWBOYS (9-6) 28			64,286	
Was	0	6	17	7	**30**
Dal	7	14	0	7	**28**

Dal	Donley 6 pass from White (Septien kick)
Was	FG Moseley 31
Dal	Cosbie 2 pass from White (Septien kick)
Was	FG Moseley 34
Dal	Renfro 60 pass from White (Septien kick)
Was	Green 32 interception return (Moseley kick)
Was	Muhammad 22 pass from Theismann (Moseley kick)
Was	FG Moseley 21
Dal	Hill 43 pass from White (Septien kick)
Was	Riggins 1 run (Moseley kick)

Texas Stadium—With the Redskins staring at the short end of a 21-6 halftime score, Darrell Green made the key play, returning an interception 32 yards for a touchdown to start a second-half rally to a 30-28 win. The victory pushed Washington into sole possession of first place in the NFC East.

As the first half unfolded, it appeared that Green would be wearing goat's horns rather than a hero's laurel wreath. He was burned for two of Danny White's three touchdown passes in the half. Green turned the momentum around, though, on Dallas' first series of the second half. He stepped in front of a White pass intended for receiver Doug Donley and ran it back for the score. At 20-13, the comeback was underway.

If Green's return provided the spark, the ensuing kickoff got the fire started in earnest. Otis Wonsley popped Dallas returner

Chuck McSwain, jarring the ball loose and Anthony Washington recovered at the Dallas 31. Soon after that, receiver Calvin Muhammad beat cornerback Ron Fellows on a third and 17 play and Joe Theismann hit him for a 22-yard touchdown pass. The two touchdowns in a span of 1:38 cut the Dallas lead to 21-20.

Later in the third quarter, yet another Dallas turnover helped the Redskins take the lead. Mel Kaufman recovered a Dallas fumble at the Dallas 40. Washington drove down to the four, but John Riggins was stuffed on third and three and Mark Moseley's field goal made it 23-21 late in the third quarter.

The Cowboys recovered for long enough to retake the lead one more time on a 43-yard pass from White to Tony Hill on the first play of the fourth quarter. After that the teams exchanged punts and Washington embarked on its game-winning drive at its own 45 with 9:41 remaining.

Riggins scored the winning points on a one-yard run, but the drive belonged to Art Monk. Taking advantage of a nice block by Theismann, the receiver gained 18 yards on a reverse, and then caught a pass for 14 yards to the one. Following a block by guard Mark May, Riggins found enough daylight to squeeze into the end zone. Moseley's point after made it 30-28.

Dallas had two more possessions, but a sack by tackle Perry Brooks ended one of them and White threw incomplete on fourth down in the last two minutes. The Redskins' playoff fate was firmly in their own hands. A win against the Cardinals next week would give them the division title.

12/16/84	REDSKINS (11-5) 29, Cardinals (9-7) 27			54,299	
StL	0	7	10	10	**27**
Was	6	17	3	3	**29**

Was	Monk 23 pass from Theismann (kick failed)
Was	Monk 12 pass from Theismann (Moseley kick)
StL	Lomax 1 run (O'Donoghue kick)
Was	Riggins 5 run (Moseley kick)
Was	FG Moseley 21
StL	FG O'Donoghue 30
StL	Green 75 pass from Lomax (O'Donoghue kick)
Was	FG Moseley 37
StL	FG O'Donoghue 34
StL	Green 18 pass from Lomax (O'Donoghue kick)
Was	FG Moseley 37

RFK Stadium—Mark Moseley's 37-yard field goal with 1:42 to play lifted the Redskins to a 29-27 win over St. Louis and the NFC East division title. The Cardinals, who would have claimed the division crown, had a shot to steal it back at the end, but Neil O'Donoghue missed a 50-yard field goal attempt on the game's last play. The loss eliminated the Cards from the playoffs.

In an historic sidelight to the contest, Art Monk needed seven catches to break Charley Hennigan's 20-year old record of 101 in a season, set in the AFL with the Houston Oilers. As one would expect from a player of Monk's caliber, he broke the record in style and extended it with clutch plays down the stretch—more on that later.

Monk caught a pair of touchdown passes from Joe Theismann to get the Redskins off to a fast start. Then late in the half, the Redskins blocked a punt to set up a 21-yard Moseley field goal and enjoyed a seemingly comfortable 23-7 lead going into the locker room at halftime. It wasn't long before Neil Lomax and the Cards would begin to make them sweat.

Lomax directed a drive at the outset of the second half that got the Cards a field goal. About three and a half minutes later, Lomax had his team on the board again, this time in more spectacular fashion with a 75-yard touchdown bomb to Roy Green. At 23-17 the Redskins' cruise to the division title had run into some choppy waters.

Monk helped to wake up the offense with a 36-yard catch to set up a 37-yard Moseley field goal, making it 26-17. That was catch number 102 on the season, breaking the record. The mark was noted on the RFK Stadium scoreboard and on the PA system, but there was no on-field celebration as there was still work to be done.

Lomax helped see to that. In the fourth quarter, he led one drive to a field goal, another to his second TD toss to Green. That lifted St. Louis into a one-point lead at 27-26 and the 54,299 in attendance stunned, along with the Redskins. Lomax racked up 468 yards passing on the day, with 314 of them coming in the second half.

The Washington offense responded, but the drive was in trouble after end Elois Grooms sacked Theismann to create a third and 19 at the St. Louis 47. With 2:40 remaining, everyone in the stadium knew the ball was going to Monk.

Therefore, Joe Gibbs had to try to find a way to hide Monk, inasmuch as that was possible. He sent in a play and formation that he had just installed that week called Two Divide. It called for Monk to line up at tight end on the right side. He fought his way off the line, found a hole on the right sideline and, Monk said, "The ball was perfect." It worked for a 20 yards and the first down at the 27. On the day, Monk caught 11 passes for 138 yards.

Three plays later, Moseley came in. "I felt comfortable and positive," Moseley said after the game. His feelings were justified as his 37-yard kick was perfect with room to spare and Washington was ahead 29-27 with 1:42 left to play.

Lomax and the Cards weren't done just yet. The quarterback completed four passes in five plays to move his team to the Washington 39 with 32 seconds left. On third and nine from there Lomax flipped the ball to back Danny Pittman, who had just one obstacle to getting a first down and getting out of bounds to stop the clock, linebacker Rich Milot. The defender made a solid open-field tackle at the 33 and Cardinals rushed their field goal team in to attempt a 50-yard game winner.

"I was so worn out by then that I had a hard time working up the energy to be nervous," said Riggins after the game. He could have been speaking on behalf of most members of both teams.

The snap and hold were good, but Neil O'Donoghue's 50-yard attempt was a couple of yards short and a little wide to the left. As division champs the Redskins had a week off to prepare for a home playoff game. The Cardinals, out of the playoffs due to wild card tiebreakers, had six months to prepare for next year.

12/30/84	Bears 23, REDSKINS 19				55,431
Chi	0	10	13	0	**23**
Was	3	0	14	2	**19**

Was	FG Moseley 25
Chi	FG B. Thomas 34
Chi	Dunsmore 19 pass from Payton (B. Thomas kick)
Chi	Gault 75 pass from Fuller (kick failed)
Was	Riggins 1 run (Moseley kick)
Chi	McKinnon 16 pass from Fuller (B. Thomas kick)
Was	Riggins 1 run (Moseley kick)
Was	Safety Finzer stepped out of end zone

The upstart Bears came into RFK Stadium with the audacity to think that they could compete with the two-time NFC champion Redskins. Not only did they compete, but with a stout defense and some clutch plays, they handed Washington its first-ever playoff defeat at RFK Stadium 23-19.

Chicago coach Mike Ditka was not afraid to try the unconventional. With the score tied at three late in the second period, the Bears had the ball at the Washington 19. Walter Payton took a handoff and started off on a sweep. With the entire defense bearing down on him, Payton pulled up and threw a pass to Pat Dunsmore. The tight end was wide open and he gathered in Payton's pass for an easy touchdown and a 10-3 halftime lead.

It took just two plays in the second half for the upstarts to extend their lead. Receiver Willie Gault caught a simple out pattern from quarterback Steve Fuller, but was able to turn upfield when Darrell Green was too aggressive in trying to make an interception. After getting by Green, Gault was gone on a 75-yard TD play and the Bears had a 16-3 lead. The point after was missed.

The Redskins were beginning to wilt under the pressure of the fierce Chicago pass rush—Joe Theismann was sacked seven times—but they still had something left. They drove 74 yards to a touchdown—a one-yard John Riggins plunge. Theismann passes to Calvin Muhammad for 23 yards and Clint Didier for 29 keyed the march.

Chicago responded with a 77-yard TD drive of its own. The drive was kept alive by a questionable roughing the kicker call against Ken Coffey. Coffey protested the call on the field and was perhaps still distracted when he was beaten for a 16-yard touchdown pass from Fuller to receiver Dennis McKinnon, pushing the Bears' lead back to 13 at 23-10.

Late in the third quarter Rich Milot gave the Redskins some life by recovering a Fuller fumble at the Chicago 36. Washington took full advantage by driving to a touchdown scored on a one-yard John Riggins run and the home team trailed by just six.

After a pair of sacks, the Bears were punting from deep in their own territory. Ditka made a bold strategic call. Although more than eight minutes remained in the game, Ditka ordered punter Dave Finzer to step out of the end zone and give the Redskins a safety to make it 23-19.

Ditka showed great faith in his defense, and it was justified. The Redskins did manage to get a first down at the Bears 24, but Theismann threw three straight incompletions and Mark Moseley missed a 41-yard field goal attempt. Two other Washington possessions went nowhere and Chicago moved on to the NFC championship game. The Redskins headed home.

1985
Head Coach: Joe Gibbs
Record: 10-6, Third in NFC East

Honors: Russ Grimm All Pro, Pro Bowl; Joe Jacoby Pro Bowl; Art Monk All-NFC, Pro Bowl

---

Apr 24
Redskins Trade No. 1 Pick for Saints' RB George Rogers
Heisman Trophy winner has had four 1,000-yard seasons

Aug 26
Let's Make a Deal: WR Brown Dealt to Falcons for G R.C. Thielemann
Skins also get WR Malcolm Barnwell for #2 pick

Aug 27
Moseley Hangs on to Job as Competitor Zendejas is Traded
OT George Starke, KR Mike Nelms waived in second cutdown

Roles of Riggins, Rogers Still Up in the Air

Sep 7—The Redskins traded their first-round pick in the 1985 draft to pry George Rogers away from the New Orleans Saints with the expectation that the former Heisman Trophy winner would, at some point in time, take over for aging legend John Riggins as the team's primary running back. In the days before their season opener, the question is if that time is now.

Joe Gibbs has announced that Riggins would be the starter, but who would be getting the important carries in the fourth quarter remains to be seen. Rogers is built for the task at a powerful 6-2, 230. His main bugaboo has been something that Gibbs absolutely hates—fumbles. Rogers coughed the ball up three times in four exhibition games while Riggins' ability to hold on to the ball is legendary. Said Rogers of fumbles, "They're almost all avoidable and I'd better start avoiding them."

During camp, Gibbs tinkered with a two-back offensive set, perhaps wanting to give Rogers a chance to run from a formation he's more familiar with. The back professes not to care, saying, "Formations don't make a runner. The Redskins understand the running game. I don't foresee any problems."

9/9/85	COWBOYS (1-0) 44, Redskins (0-1) 14				62,292
Was	0	7	0	7	**14**
Dal	3	14	13	14	**44**
Dal	FG Septien 53				
Dal	Newsome 1 run (Septien kick)				
Was	Riggins 1 run (Moseley kick)				
Dal	Renfro 55 pass from White (Septien kick)				
Dal	FG Septien 39				
Dal	FG Septien 43				
Dal	Dorsett 9 run (Septien kick)				
Dal	Scott 26 interception return (Septien kick)				
Was	Didier 19 pass from Theismann (Moseley kick)				
Dal	Thurman 21 interception return (Septien kick)				

Texas Stadium—It was Joe Theismann's 36th birthday, but it was the Washington quarterback who was giving out the gifts. He threw a career-high five interceptions as the Redskins suffered their worst loss of the Joe Gibbs era as they fell to the Cowboys 44-14.

A controversial call helped Dallas get out to a 10-0 lead midway through the second quarter. With the home team up 3-0, Danny White threw to fullback Timmy Newsome for 16 yards to the Washington one. As Newsome was going down, cornerback Barry Wilburn came in and knocked the ball out the back's grasp. It rolled into the end zone where Darrell Green picked it up and started a return. The play, however, had been blown dead as the officials ruled that Newsome was down before coughing it up. Newsome scored on the next play.

The Redskins responded with a 10-play, 77-yard drive to pull within 10-7. John Riggins bulled over from a yard out to cap the march with just less than four minutes left in the half. But that was the high water mark for the Redskins on this Monday night. The beginning of the end came with six seconds left in the half.

White decided he would take advantage of the rookie Wilburn and did so in textbook style. The quarterback threw a six-yard out to Mike Renfro, who stepped out of bounds. From the Dallas 45, Renfro faked another out and Wilburn bit hard, forgetting to keep the receiver in front of him. Wilburn was able only to watch as Renfro blew by him down the sideline, catching White's pass for a 55-yard touchdown and a 17-7 lead.

The misery continued in the third quarter. Theismann threw three interceptions in this period alone, and George Rogers gave up a fumble. The miscues led to a pair of Rafael Septien field goals and a nine-yard touchdown run by Tony Dorsett. It was 30-7 entering the final quarter and the Cowboys piled on with two interception returns for touchdowns. One of the picks was Theismann's fifth; the second came on backup Jay Schroeder's first NFL pass.

9/15/85	REDSKINS (1-1) 16, Oilers (1-1) 13				53,553
Hou	0	10	3	0	**13**
Was	13	3	0	0	**16**
Was	Muhammad 17 pass from Theismann (Moseley kick)				
Was	Rogers 31 run (kick blocked)				
Was	FG Moseley 34				
Hou	FG Zendejas 44				
Hou	Hill 2 pass from Moon (Zendejas kick)				
Hou	FG Zendejas 35				

RFK Stadium—The Redskins built a 16-0 lead in the second quarter and it appeared they were on their way to an expected easy victory. The Oilers, though, had other ideas and, as Joe Gibbs said, "It turned into a real guts job," before Washington pulled out a 16-13 win.

Joe Theismann went to Calvin Muhammad for 17 yards and a touchdown five minutes into the game. Later in the first quarter, George Rogers carried into a pile for what appeared to be a short gain, but he broke loose and, while the Houston defense was looking for him at the bottom of a pile, cruised 31 yards to a touchdown. The extra point was blocked and it was 13-0.

After a Mark Moseley field goal extended the Washington lead to 16-0, Houston began its climb back into the game. Tony Zendejas, who the Redskins had traded to the Oilers during training camp after the kicker had failed to beat out Moseley, kicked a 34-yard field goal.

As halftime neared, the Oilers came after Theismann with an all-out blitz, knocking the ball out of his hands. Houston's Robert Abraham recovered at the Washington 32. Six plays later, quarterback Warren Moon threw a two-yard touchdown pass to receiver Drew Hill with five seconds left in the half and it was 16-10.

After Zendejas' second field goal made it 16-13 in the third quarter, the Oilers got into the end zone three times, but did not score. Cornerback Steve Brown intercepted a Theismann pass and returned it all the way, but a clipping call negated the score. A holding call wiped out a 50-yard touchdown pass from Moon to Hill and a motion penalty killed another apparent Moon touchdown pass, this one to Tim Smith from 11 yards.

Two plays after the last one, Zendejas tried a 33-yard field goal attempt that would have tied the game with 4:18 remaining. It smacked off of the right upright and the Redskins survived.

9/22/85	Eagles (1-2) 19, REDSKINS (1-2) 6			53,748	
Phil	3	3	3	10	19
Was	0	6	0	0	6
Phil	FG McFadden 41				
Phil	FG McFadden 36				
Was	FG Moseley 41				
Was	FG Moseley 26				
Phil	FG McFadden 37				
Phil	E. Jackson 17 pass from Cunningham (McFadden kick)				
Phil	FG McFadden 34				

RFK Stadium—The Redskins failed to score a touchdown for the first time since 1982, made plenty of mistakes and blew a bundle of opportunities in the process of losing 19-6 to the Eagles, who were two-touchdown underdogs.

Attempting to respond to a pair of Paul McFadden field goals, the Redskins twice drove deep into Eagles territory. Both drives stalled and the home team settled for Mark Moseley field goals to tie the game at six.

That score held until midway through the third quarter. On second and long from the Eagles three, Philly receiver Mike Quick turned a short flat pattern into a 69-yard gain when Darrell Green gambled and lost going for an interception. That led to another McFadden field goal and it was 9-6.

In the fourth quarter, the Redskins had two golden opportunities to tie or take the lead. They drove to the Eagles 16, but a dropped pass helped stall the drive and Moseley missed a 32-yard field goal attempt that would have tied the game.

Philadelphia went three and out and another Washington foray into Eagles territory ended in calamity. With the ball at the 35, running back George Rogers fumbled, safety Wes Hopkins gathered in the ball as it bounced right into his arms and then returned the fumble to the Washington 25. Soon after that, rookie quarterback Randall Cunningham scrambled and found a wide-open Earnest Jackson for 17 yards and the clinching touchdown.

Dexter Loads Bears Up With Board Material

Sep 23—With Dexter Manley, you take the bad with the good. The good is an excellent pass rush and an enthusiastic, all-out performance on nearly every play. The bad is an occasional flag for unsportsmanlike conduct and a propensity to talk when he shouldn't.

The 1-2 Redskins are going into Chicago to face the 3-0 Bears. In a session with reporters, Manley took some shots at some of Chicago's stars:

"To win, we have to knock Walter Payton out of the game," he said. And, of quarterback Jim McMahon, Manley opined, "He's a little fragile; he can be hurt."

He saved his biggest shot, though, for his own teammates. "And if you think our offense is having problems now, if they don't

get their act together this week, the Chicago Bears will kill us," he said.

About 700 miles away in Chicago, Bears coach Mike Ditka had the best perspective on Manley's potshots.

"I'm convinced some of those things are said out of frustration and some out of stupidity," he said.

9/29/85	BEARS (4-0) 45, Redskins (1-3) 10			63,708	
Was	7	3	0	0	10
Chi	0	31	7	7	45
Was	Rogers 7 run (Moseley kick)				
Was	FG Moseley 32				
Chi	Gault 99 kickoff return (Butler kick)				
Chi	McKinnon 14 pass from McMahon (Butler kick)				
Chi	McMahon 13 pass from Payton (Butler kick)				
Chi	Moorehead 10 pass from McMahon (Butler kick)				
Chi	FG Butler 28				
Chi	Payton 33 pass from McMahon (Butler kick)				
Chi	Gentry 1 run (Butler kick)				

Soldier Field—A 10-0 Washington lead was buried under an avalanche of 31 unanswered Chicago points in the second quarter as Chicago handed the Redskins a humiliating 45-10 loss.

The Redskins had three scoring chances before Chicago had a first down and took advantage of two of them. George Rogers scored on a seven-yard run and Mark Moseley kicked a 32-yard field goal to give Washington a 10-0 lead on the first play of the second quarter. Things started to go to hell in a hand basket for Washington starting on the next play.

Jeff Hayes, who was also the team's punter, tore a leg muscle in the process of floating the kickoff to Willie Gault, a record-holding sprinter. Gault flashed through the first wave of would-be tacklers and easily beat the hobbled Hayes to finish the 99-yard touchdown return.

Hayes' injury proved to be costly to the Redskins on the very next series. Washington went three and out and Joe Gibbs chose Joe Theismann to serve as the emergency punter. They should have dialed 911 instead as the kick went out of bounds one yard past the line of scrimmage. On the very next play, quarterback Jim McMahon threw to receiver Dennis McKinnon for 14 yards and a touchdown. The Bears still didn't have a first down, but the held a 14-10 lead.

The Redskins didn't have to worry about punting on their next possession. End Richard Dent hit Theismann from the blind side, forcing a fumble that was recovered on the Washington 22. McMahon got into the TD scoring act, handing the ball to Walter Payton, sneaking through the secondary and laying out to catch Payton's 13-yard pass in the end zone.

McMahon returned to his customary role of touchdown thrower before halftime, going to tight end Emory Moorehead for 10 yards with four and a half minutes left until halftime. That and a 28-yard field goal by Kevin Butler made it 31-10. The second half was nothing but extended garbage time.

10/7/85	REDSKINS (2-3) 27, Cardinal (3-2) 10			53,134	
Was	10	7	3	7	27
StL	0	3	0	7	10
Was	Theismann 14 run (Moseley kick)				
Was	FG Moseley 33				
StL	FG O'Donoghue 22				
Was	Clark 10 pass from Theismann (Moseley kick)				
Was	FG Moseley 29				
StL	Anderson 10 run (O'Donoghue kick)				
Was	Didier 12 pass from Theismann (Moseley kick)				

RFK Stadium—The hallmarks of the Redskins' success in recent times—a power running, ball control offense and a solid, opportunistic defense—have been missing all season. With the team teetering on the brink of falling out of the playoff picture, the Skins got their game back in beating the Cardinals. George

Rogers and John Riggins both gained more than 100 yards on the ground and the defense forced six St. Louis turnovers, including five interceptions of Cardinal QB's.

A bit of trickery capped a 45-yard drive for the Redskins' first touchdown. On fourth and short from the 14, Joe Theismann faked to Riggins into the line, sucking in the entire Cardinal defense. The quarterback rolled around the right end for the easy score.

After the teams traded field goals, the Redskins were on the move again. After taking possession at their own 44, they gained 46 yards on eight runs by Riggins and Rogers. Following the old successful formula, Theismann went up top after the defense had been properly softened, throwing ten yards to rookie receiver Gary Clark for the touchdown and a 17-3 lead.

The Redskins' defense kept the Cardinals at bay, stopping them on the ground, allowing just 95 yards rushing, and in the air with the five picks.

Mann: 2-3 Redskins 'Sick of Losing'

Oct 8—After his three-sack performance against the Cardinals, Charles Mann was asked about the state of the team. "There's been some speculation that maybe the Redskins weren't hungry anymore," Mann said. "People said we've been to two Super Bowls, we've done this and done that and maybe we just weren't hungry to win. I think there might have been some truth to that."

But now, "we're psyched up. We were sick of losing and I think everyone's hungry to win again."

10/13/85	REDSKINS (3-3) 24, Lions (3-3) 3				55,692
Det	3	0	0	0	3
Was	3	14	7	0	24
Det	FG Murray 33				
Was	FG Moseley 24				
Was	Riggins 1 run (Moseley kick)				
Was	Riggins 21 run (Moseley kick)				
Was	Riggins 5 run (Moseley kick)				

RFK Stadium—By any definition, it's not news any more. It's like dog bites man or the sun rises in the East. Lions lose in Washington. Detroit is now 0 for 13 in the Nation's Capital. Their latest futile trip to D.C. ended up with a 24-3 loss to the Redskins.

Some of the losses have been taut, exciting affairs; some, like this one, have been routs. The Redskins outrushed their guests 168 yards to 28, accounting in large part for a greater than two-to-one edge in possession time for Washington (40:54 to 19:06).

With the score tied at three in the second quarter, the Redskins used a pair of turnovers to jump to a 14-point lead. Neal Olkewicz forced tight end Dave Lewis to fumble at the Detroit 31. An 18-yard pass from Joe Theismann to Gary Clark got them into John Riggins' range, and he bulled it over from the one.

Riggo showed more range after sucking down some oxygen on the bench. Vernon Dean flattened a Detroit receiver as the ball arrived, sending it into the arms of safety Tony Peters, who returned it to the Lions 25. On second down from the 21, Riggins followed Route 66, big Joe Jacoby, off the left side, and then gained momentum as he got inside the ten. After dragging a couple of defensive backs into the end zone midway through the second period, Washington led at the half 17-3.

The Redskins put the cap on this one by opening the second half with a 66-yard touchdown drive capped, of course, by Riggins. From the five, he ran into a crowd of defenders and kept on going, pushing the pile into the end zone.

10/20/85	GIANTS (4-3) 17, Redskins (3-4) 3				74,389
Was	0	0	0	3	3
NYG	0	7	7	3	17
NYG	Bavaro 29 pass from Simms (Atkinson kick)				
NYG	Adams 2 run (Atkinson kick)				

NYG	FG Atkinson 47
Was	FG Moseley 47

Giants Stadium—"Good defense, good running game," said New York linebacker Lawrence Taylor after the game. "That's how they *used to* beat us." The emphasis is added to underscore the shift of power that appeared to be taking place in the NFC East after the Giants' 17-3 win, which was more dominant than the final score indicated.

Playing without receiver Art Monk and tackle Joe Jacoby, the Redskins still had some chances early in the game. They got into New York territory five times in the first half, but none of the possessions resulted in scores. They came up empty on their deepest penetration when Joe Theismann's pass from the six bounced off of Gary Clark's shoulder pad and into the arms of New York's Herb Welch.

Early in the second quarter the Giants' Phil Simms picked on backup linebacker Chris Keating, who was in the game after Mel Kaufman had his bell rung, for a 29-yard touchdown pass to tight end Mark Bavaro. That would be all the scoring the home team would need.

They widened the gap by driving 80 yards in 5:48 to open the second half, with George Adams carrying over from the two. With Adams and Joe Morris playing the role of John Riggins, the Giants executed the Riggo Drill for much of the rest of the half to grind out the clock.

10/27/85	Redskins (4-4) 14, BROWNS (4-4) 7				78,540
Was	14	0	0	0	14
Cle	0	0	7	0	7
Was	Riggins 1 run (Moseley kick)				
Was	Clark 19 pass from Theismann (Moseley kick)				
Cle	Newsome 14 pass from Danielson (Bahr kick)				

Cleveland Stadium—"Sometimes, we don't look so good," said Joe Gibbs after this game, but at least he was able to say it with a smile on his face for a change. The Redskins took full advantage of a pair of first-quarter turnovers by rookie quarterback Bernie Kosar and held on for a 14-7 win.

On Cleveland's first possession, Kosar underthrew his intended receiver and the ball wound up in the arms of safety Curtis Jordan, who returned it to the Browns 22. After six plays, Washington faced fourth and one at the two. John Riggins picked up the first down on that play and the touchdown on the next with two powerful runs.

Shortly after that, Kosar handed the ball to the Skins again— this time when he botched a handoff attempt to Kevin Mack. Neal Olkewicz recovered and the Redskins were back in business at the Cleveland 37. Four plays later, Joe Theismann threw to Gary Clark in the end zone. The receiver made a nice move on the safety to get free for the 19-yard touchdown reception.

That was all the scoring Washington would need, but the Browns managed to create some tense moments. Coach Marty Schottenheimer pulled Kosar and inserted veteran Gary Danielson at quarterback. Danielson got Cleveland on the board in the third period when he threw a 14-yard touchdown pass to tight end Ozzie Newsome. But two forays into Washington territory in the fourth quarter came up empty.

On the first, cornerback Barry Wilburn raked the ball out of Harry Holt's arms after the tight end had gathered a pass on a short crossing pattern. Curtis Jordan recovered the fumble at the Washington 24. Then the Browns turned it over on downs after moving to a first down at the Washington 20 and the Skins escaped with the win.

11/3/85	Redskins (5-4) 44, FALCONS (1-8) 10		42,209	
Was	3	28	3	10	44
Atl	3	0	0	7	10

Atl	FG Luckhurst 28
Was	FG Moseley 39
Was	Griffin 5 run (Moseley kick)
Was	Theismann 11 run (Moseley kick)
Was	Rogers 1 run (Moseley kick)
Was	Monk 34 pass from Theismann (Moseley kick)
Was	FG Moseley 40
Was	FG Moseley 48
Was	Griffin 66 run (Moseley kick)
Atl	Cox 14 pass from Holly (Luckhurst kick)

Atlanta-Fulton County Stadium—Redskins rookie Reggie Branch acted like a veteran, reading the lips and intentions of the Atlanta punter to sniff out a fake punt. That move created the key play in a 28-0 second quarter that spurred Washington's 44-10 rout of the Falcons.

The Redskins had taken a 10-3 lead early in the period on the strength of a five-yard touchdown run by Keith Griffin. After the ensuing kickoff Atlanta coach Dan Henning, a former Joe Gibbs assistant, gambled and lost on a fake punt. It wasn't just bad luck.

It was fourth and a foot at the Atlanta 29. Branch, a running back with heavy special teams responsibilities, noticed that the huddle took longer than usual and thought he saw punter Rick Donnelly's lips say something about "taking it to the right."

"Sure enough," said Branch, "he faked the kick and headed right." Branch was there waiting for him and the rookie's hunch turned into a five-yard loss for the Falcons.

Three plays later, Joe Theismann ran a naked bootleg and took it in from 11 yards out. Before the half was over, the Redskins scored twice more, on a one-yard run by George Rogers and a 34-yard pass from Theismann to Art Monk. The halftime score was 31-3.

All that was left in the second half was for the Redskins to rack up more rushing yardage. Rogers (16 carries, 124 yards) and Griffin (15 for 164) both went over the 100-yard mark. A good chunk of Griffin's yardage came when he busted a third and inches play off left tackle for 66 yards and his team's final touchdown.

11/10/85	Cowboys (7-3) 13, REDSKINS (5-5) 7		55,750	
Dal	0	3	10	0	13
Was	0	0	0	7	7

Dal	FG Septien 40
Dal	FG Septien 36
Dal	Dorsett 48 pass from White (Septien kick)
Was	Clark 11 pass from Theismann (Moseley kick)

RFK Stadium—"It was a bad day," said Redskins offensive tackle Dan McQuaid, who filled in for the injured Joe Jacoby. He was referring to his own performance—his man, end Jim Jeffcoat, sacked Joe Theismann five times—but his statement rang true for the entire team. Washington lost to Dallas 13-7 to fall two games out of the NFC East lead with precious little time remaining to make up the ground.

While the score was certainly more respectable than the 44-14 blowout the Cowboys recorded in the season opener, the outcome was nearly as decisive. Things started going badly for the home team on their initial possession after they drove 48 yards to the Dallas 23. Theismann, in the face of blitzing safety Michael Downs, badly underthrew Art Monk and cornerback Ron Fellows intercepted to kill the threat.

Then Dallas drove into scoring position at the Washington five. Quarterback Danny White was sacked by tackle Dean Hamel and fumbled. Dexter Manley overran the ball, apparently seeing six points down the open field in front of him, and Dallas recovered. Rafael Septien booted a 40-yard field goal and the Cowboys were ahead 3-0.

Another field goal had Dallas up 6-0 in the third quarter. They got the killer play on third and nine at the Washington 48. The Cowboys had the perfect play against the defense—one that put running back Tony Dorsett on a deep pattern with one-on-one coverage from linebacker Monte Coleman. Still slightly hobbled by a leg injury that had kept him on the shelf for the previous six weeks, Coleman had no chance and Dorsett was wide open at the 15 when he took White's pass to score easily, putting his team up 13-0 with 5:12 left in the third quarter.

The Redskins managed a touchdown drive, scoring a minute and a half into the fourth on an 11-yard pass from Theismann to Gary Clark. In theory Washington had plenty of time to score again to take the lead but in reality, they didn't. Jeffcoat saw to that by sacking Theismann three times in the Redskins' next two offensive series, killing any hopes for a rally.

Theismann Rips Mystery Cowboy Critics

November 14—Although nobody was sure who on the Dallas Cowboys had disparaged him or his team, Joe Theismann ripped into the opposing team.

"I've played a lot of games against the Cowboys," said Theismann, "and nothing they say would ever surprise me.

"We've been fortunate to take some things they want. I'm wearing a world championship ring. They're not. That would be an annoying factor, wouldn't you think? I have an NFC title ring. They don't. Like I say . . . tough."

He went on, saying, "I do think I know more about what's going on than most other people, whether they're in this organization and think they're God's gift to man and live in Texas."

11/18/85	WASHINGTON (6-5) 23, Giants (7-4) 21		53,371	
NYG	7	0	14	0	21
Was	7	0	7	9	23

Was	Warren 10 pass from Theismann (Moseley kick)
NYG	Morris 56 run (Schubert kick)
Was	Riggins 1 run (Moseley kick)
NYG	Morris 41 run (Schubert kick)
NYG	Morris 8 run (Schubert kick)
Was	FG Moseley 28
Was	Didier 14 pass from Schroeder (kick failed)

RFK Stadium—Everyone watching on Monday night football will remember the broken leg, the grotesque angle that Joe Theismann's shin took when Lawrence Taylor took him down from behind, Taylor's frantic gesture towards to Redskins sideline to get help for the quarterback, and the removal of Theismann in the stretcher. Redskins fans will remember all that, too, but will also recall how an untested quarterback came off the bench to save the season for Washington.

Theismann, in the midst of one of his worst seasons, started slowly, able to complete just a couple of short passes on the Redskins' opening drive. On fourth and two at the Washington 43, punter Steve Cox threw to Raphel Cherry for 11 yards and a first down in New York territory. After misfiring on a long pass to Monk, Theismann settled in and completed three passes for 36 yards to finish the drive, including a 10-yard TD pass to tight end Don Warren to give his team a 7-0 lead.

It didn't take long for the Giants to come back. Two series later, running back Joe Morris got loose on a run off left tackle and couldn't be caught, going 56 yards for the tying touchdown.

On first down at the Washington 46, the play call was "50 Gut Pitchback," which asked John Riggins to take a handoff up the middle, stop and pitch back to Theismann. The maneuver was designed to delay the Giants' pass rush long enough for Theismann to find an open receiver downfield.

The Giants weren't fooled. Linebacker Harry Carson and tackle Jim Burt pushed Theismann to his left, where Taylor was waiting. Taylor dragged the quarterback down from behind, falling on Theismann's right leg in the process. The television replays caught the moment where the leg suddenly gave out, bending in mid-shin in a manner that made even the strongest viewers cringe. Those fainter of heart had a much stronger reaction.

A stretcher took Theismann off the field to a thunderous ovation, and the game resumed. It took just two plays for Jay Schroeder to evoke an ovation of his own. The second-year quarterback, who had thrown just eight NFL passes, zipped a 44-yard completion to Art Monk for a first down at the New York 13. Riggins fumbled the ball away three plays later to kill the scoring threat, but things did not seem quite as bleak as they had when Theismann was lying on the turf. The score remained tied at seven at the half.

Apparently, Joe Gibbs was anxious to see what Schroeder could do after halftime, so he called for an onside kick to start the half. Cox executed it to perfection and recovered the ball himself. Schroeder went back to Monk, this time for 50 yards to the New York four. Riggins scored from a yard out three plays later and the Redskins had a 14-7 lead.

Another long Morris touchdown run—this one of 41 yards—soon had the game tied again. Then George Rogers fumbled the ball back to the Giants at the Washington 23. With a shorter field to work with, Morris only had to run eight yards for his third touchdown and a 21-14 New York lead.

With the game getting away from them, the Redskins responded. They drove 65 yards to a 28-yard Mark Moseley field goal with 11:25 left to play. Gibbs called for another onside kick and it worked as well, with Greg Williams making the recovery at the New York 46. Five plays later, cornerback Elvis Patterson tipped Schroeder's pass, but Clint Didier snared it for a 14-yard touchdown. Although Moseley missed the point after, the Redskins held a 23-21 lead with 8:52 left to play.

The Giants were unable to cross midfield after that and Washington had an improbable win. On the day, against the NFC top-ranked defense, Schroeder was 13 for 20 for 221 yards.

Theismann Has Surgery, Laufenberg Added

November 20—Joe Theismann rested with his leg in a cast that went from well up his thigh to his toes following surgery to start the repairs on his severely broken leg. Meanwhile, Babe Laufenberg had his R&R interrupted—and he couldn't be happier about it.

With Jay Schroeder taking over as the starting quarterback, the Redskins needed a new backup. They put out an all-points bulletin to locate Laufenberg, who has spent a couple of years on the team's injured reserve list before being cut in training camp. It turns out he was on a fishing trip in Mexico and watched Theismann get injured on TV at a bar called the Giggling Marlin.

Laufenberg got on the phone to his brother, thinking that the Redskins might call. They hadn't yet, but they did the next morning and he was on a flight to Washington almost immediately.

Schroeder took all of the snaps with the first-team offense and Joe Gibbs said that he "looked good."

"He handles everything real well, he seems to be polished about it all."

11/24/85	**Redskins (7-5) 30, STEELERS (6-6) 23**			59,293	
Was	14	6	7	3	**30**
Pitt	3	14	0	6	**23**
Was	Rogers 1 run (Moseley kick)				
Pit	FG Anderson 22				
Was	Didier 18 pass from Schroeder (Moseley kick)				
Was	FG Moseley 20				
Pitt	Lipps 5 pass from Campbell (Anderson kick)				
Pitt	Erenberg 9 pass from Campbell (Anderson kick)				
Was	FG Moseley 39				
Was	Riggins 1 run (Moseley kick)				
Pitt	FG Anderson 37				
Was	FG Moseley 42				
Pitt	FG Anderson 27				

Three Rivers Stadium—Jay Schroeder completed 15 of 28 passes, including six straight to start the second half, to lead the Redskins to the road win over Pittsburgh. Making his first pro start after coming in for the injured Joe Theismann during the first half the previous week, Schroeder didn't throw an interception and wasn't sacked.

The special teams made the early going easy for Schroeder and the Washington offense. Ken Jenkins returned the opening kickoff 95 yards, leading to George Rogers' one-yard touchdown run for a 7-0 lead. After a Gary Anderson field goal, Otis Wonsley blocked a Steeler punt, setting up an 18-yard touchdown pass from Schroeder to Clint Didier.

The momentum turned towards the home team after a Mark Moseley field goal upped the Washington lead to 17-3. The Steelers scored on a touchdown pass from Scott Campbell to Louis Lipps. On the next possession, Art Monk held onto a pass just long enough to be ruled to have had possession; Pittsburgh recovered the fumble at the Washington 30. Four plays after that Campbell, also making his first NFL start, completed a five-yard TD pass to Rich Erenberg to tie the score at 17 with just over three minutes left in the half.

Washington responded by driving to a 39-yard field goal with three seconds left, and then expanded their lead to ten when Schroeder's precise passing led to a one-yard scoring run by John Riggins to make it 27-14.

The Steelers were game, but two forays inside the Washington 20 generated just two Anderson field goals and they trailed by 27-20 with 11:08 to go. Schroeder took the Redskins to the clinching field goal, burning off six minutes of the clock.

It did get interesting when Pittsburgh recovered an onside kick after scoring a field goal with 2:55 left to go, but Campbell couldn't complete a pass and the win went to Washington.

12/1/85	**49ers (8-5) 35, REDSKINS (7-6) 8**			51,321	
SF	7	14	7	7	**35**
Was	3	5	0	0	**8**
SF	Monroe 95 kickoff return (Wersching kick)				
Was	FG Moseley 25				
Was	Safety Montana intentional grounding in end zone				
SF	Tyler 1 run (Wersching kick)				
SF	Turner 65 fumble return (Wersching kick)				
Was	FG Moseley 21				
SF	Tyler 4 run (Wersching kick)				
SF	Francis 8 pass from Montana (Wersching kick)				

RFK Stadium—Things started going downhill at the outset for the Redskins when Carl Monroe returned the opening kickoff 95 yards for a touchdown. Washington came in needing a win to remain in control of its own playoff destiny. The 49ers, in desperate straits themselves, used the return as a springboard to an easy 35-8 win.

The Redskins did muster five scoring chances in the first half, but wound up further behind than when they started. Mark Moseley kicked a 25-yard field goal but missed a 24-yarder that would have given the Redskins an 8-7 lead. San Francisco took advantage of an interception by Dwight Hicks to take a 14-8 lead.

Washington responded immediately, driving to the San Francisco 25. On second and nine, safety Jeff Fuller blindsided Jay Schroeder, forcing a fumble that linebacker Keena Turner scooped up and took 65 yards for the touchdown to make it 21-5. A final drive into 49er territory late in the half ended up in another short Moseley field goal attempt, this one good from 21 yards.

The home team continued its pattern of futile offensive movement in the second half, the only difference being they couldn't score at all. They were undone by a total of five turnovers on the day with Schroeder committing four of them with two interceptions and two fumbles. Making his second NFL start, Schroeder did post 358 yards passing but needed a team-record 58 attempts to get them (30 completions).

"Just like (the Redskins), we've had a rough season," said San Francisco running back Roger Craig after the game. "Today, I started getting the feeling that things might work out all right after all."

The Washington players had just the opposite feeling—they knew even three wins in their last three games probably wouldn't be enough to gain a playoff spot.

12/8/85	Redskins (8-6) 17, EAGLES (6-8) 12				60,737
Was	0	3	7	7	17
Phil	0	5	7	0	12
Phil	Safety Schroeder intentional grounding in end zone				
Phil	FG McFadden 44				
Was	FG Moseley 32				
Phil	E. Jackson 1 run (McFadden kick)				
Was	Rogers 28 run (Moseley kick)				
Was	Clark 5 pass from Schroeder (Moseley kick)				

Veterans Stadium—George Rogers carried a team record 36 times for 150 yards as the Redskins rallied to beat the Eagles and stay alive in the playoff hunt.

Although Rogers had 76 of his rushing yards at halftime, the Redskins were still staring at the short end of a 5-3 score, a deficit widened to 12-3 late in the third quarter when Ernest Jackson scored on a one-yard run.

The Redskins responded with a 75-yard touchdown drive in just less than two minutes. Jay Schroeder went to Art Monk for 39 yards to start it and Rogers finished it off with a 28-yard TD burst up the middle on third and two. Mark Moseley's extra point made it 12-10 with just over a minute left in the third.

End Charles Mann sacked Eagles quarterback Ron Jaworski on third down, helping the Redskins get good field position after the Eagles punt. From the Philly 49, Rogers carried seven times gaining 32 yards before Schroeder threw five yards to Gary Clark for the go-ahead touchdown.

Jaworski and the Eagles battled back, gaining a first and goal at the Washington five. Mel Kaufman dropped a sure interception in the end zone, but Rich Milot saved the day by making a tackle for a one-yard loss and tipping away Jaworski's fourth-down pass attempt.

12/15/85	REDSKINS (9-6) 27, Bengals (7-8) 24				50,544
Cin	21	3	0	0	24
Was	7	10	3	7	27
Was	Rogers 1 run (Moseley kick)				
Cin	Brown 8 pass from Brooks (Breech kick)				
Cin	Holman 26 pass from Esiason (Breech kick)				
Cin	Holman 51 pass from Esiason (Breech kick)				
Cin	FG Breech 38				
Was	Monk 4 pass from Schroeder (Moseley kick)				
Was	FG Moseley 42				
Was	FG Moseley 39				
Was	Rogers 34 run (Moseley kick)				

RFK Stadium—On the brink of playoff extinction, the Redskins rallied from a 24-7 deficit early in the second quarter to steal a 27-24 win from the Bengals. After rallying, they had to watch with bated breath as Cincinnati's Jim Breech missed a 51-yard field goal attempt with seven seconds left.

Art Monk did much of the work for his team, catching 13 passes for 230 yards. His four-yard touchdown catch started the comeback after three Bengal touchdown passes—two by quarterback Boomer Esiason and one by running back James Brooks—and a 38-yard field goal by Breech had propelled the visitors to the 24-7 lead. It was very close to being worse, but

Curtis Jordan cut in front of receiver Eddie Brown to turn what looked like a six-yard TD pass and 31-7 lead into a saving interception.

Darrell Green's 77-yard punt return for an apparent touchdown was called back for unnecessary roughness, but the Redskins did manage to get a 42-yard field goal to pull within a touchdown at halftime, 24-17.

Although Cincinnati had difficulty moving the ball after taking the lead, particularly on the ground, the Redskins remained reluctant to move in front in this game. Another touchdown was called back due to a penalty and Mark Moseley missed a pair of field goals. George Rogers regained the bad case of the dropsies he suffered from earlier in the year, coughing the ball up three times. Moseley did hit a 39-yard field goal early in the third quarter, but there was no continuity to the offense. It remained 24-20 entering the fourth quarter.

Rogers, temporarily benched, took advantage of his chance at redemption when he was put back into the game. On third and three at the Bengals 38, he followed the interference of rookie guard Raleigh McKenzie, who wiped out two defenders at the point of attack, and raced untouched 38 yards for the go-ahead touchdown midway through the final quarter.

It appeared that Breech might get a chance at tying the game from a much shorter distance when Esiason drove his team to the Washington 21 with 16 seconds left. But Esiason committed a cardinal sin by allowing himself to be sacked by Rich Milot for a 12-yard loss. The difference was critical as the 51-yarder was short.

12/21/85	Redskins (10-6) 27, CARDINALS (5-11) 16				28,09
Was	0	13	7	7	27
StL	9	0	0	7	16
StL	FG Bojovic 42				
StL	R. Green 8 pass from Lomax (kick blocked)				
Was	FG Moseley 21				
Was	Clark 27 pass from Schroeder (Moseley kick)				
Was	FG Moseley 30				
Was	Rogers 1 run (Moseley kick)				
Was	Griffin 1 run (Moseley kick)				
StL	Duncan 2 pass from Lomax (Bojovic kick)				

Busch Stadium—After the previous week's win, Dexter Manley said, "We've just got to beat the hell out of St. Louis and hope the dominos fall the right way next week." The former came to pass as Washington beat the Cardinals 27-16 and the Redskins will see about the other dominos on Sunday.

George Rogers carried the team to the win by becoming the first Washington runner to gain over 200 yards in a game as he racked up 206 on 34 carries.

He was close to watching much of the game on the bench, though, as he fumbled on the game's first play from scrimmage, setting up a quick Cardinal field goal. A 26-yard burst on his next carry apparently settled him down, though, as he went on to his record-setting performance.

The Cardinals went up 9-0 and were looking for more by calling for an onside kick after Roy Green's eight-yard touchdown catch. Washington recovered the attempt and drove to a Mark Moseley field goal. After Novo Bojovic bounced a 39-yard field goal attempt off of the upright, things finally seemed to be moving Washington's way.

The turnaround of momentum was completed when Monte Coleman sacked Neil Lomax, stripping the ball and giving the Redskins possession at the St. Louis 38. Three plays later, Jay Schroeder threw 27 yards to Gary Clark for the go-ahead points. A late Mark Moseley field goal pushed the score to 13-9 at halftime.

Behind Rogers running, the Redskins moved in for the kill in the third quarter. During a 77-yard touchdown march, Rogers carried 13 times for 53 yards, including toting the rock on six straight plays to cover the last 18 yards. The extra point following his one-yard touchdown run put Washington up 20-9.

Consecutive gains of 24 and 17 yards in the fourth quarter helped push Rogers over the 200-yard mark for the game and more than 1,000 for the season (he finished the year with 1,092). He gave way to backup Keith Griffin with just over four minutes left. Griffin tallied the Skins' final score on a one-yard run.

December 22
Go Figure: Cowboys Lose, Redskins Out
Dallas loss gives San Francisco Wild Card spot on tiebreaker

1986
Head Coach: Joe Gibbs
Record: 12-4, Second in NFC East, Wild Card
Playoffs: 2-1, lost in NFC Championship Game

Honors: Gary Clark Pro Bowl; Darrell Green All-NFL, Pro Bowl; Russ Grimm All-NFL, Pro Bowl; Joe Jacoby Pro Bowl; Dexter Manley All-NFL, Pro Bowl; Art Monk Pro Bowl; Jay Schroeder Pro Bowl

Hall of Fame: Ken Houston, Safety 1973-1980

Mar 19
Diesel Runs Out of Gas: Riggins Released

July 24
Broken Down: Theismann Fails Physical
Broken leg vs. Giants ends career

Jackpot: Redskins Reap USFL Talent

August 11—The misfortune of the collapsing USFL turned into the Redskins' good luck as they gained depth at receiver and quarterback. In addition, the team was close to an agreement with a potential starter in running back Kelvin Bryant.

The quarterback added was Doug Williams, who led the Tampa Bay Bucs to the NFL playoffs in 1979 before falling out of favor with both management and the fans and jumping to the new league. His presence puts current backup QB Babe Laufenberg in imminent danger of being cut yet again.

The team's second-round draft pick, Hawaii receiver Walter Murray, also felt the heat turned up several degrees. Washington signed one receiver, Derek Holloway, and were close to agreements with receivers Ricky Sanders, who caught 101 passes in one USFL season, and Clarence Verdin.

Murray has been holding out for first-round money, claiming this was his proper value since the Redskins had traded a first-rounder to get him. These actions showed that team management is in no mood for such negotiating ploys.

August 26
Rally Can't Save the Babe: Skins Cut Laufenberg
QB waived despite stirring preseason comeback vs. Pats

9/7/86	REDSKINS (1-0) 41, Eagles (0-1) 14				53,982
Phil	7	7	0	0	**14**
Was	3	17	14	7	**41**
Was	FG Moseley 19				
Phil	Johnson 17 pass from Jaworski (McFadden kick)				
Was	Bryant 36 pass from Schroeder (Moseley kick)				
Was	Schroeder 1 run (Moseley kick)				
Phil	Tautalatasi 3 pass from Jaworski (McFadden kick)				

Was	FG Cox 55
Was	Didier 36 pass from Schroeder (Moseley kick)
Was	Bryant 16 run (Moseley kick)
Was	Rogers 5 run (Moseley kick)

RFK Stadium—Washington scored two third quarter touchdowns to pull away from the Eagles and roll to an easy 41-14 win. Steve Cox kicked a team-record 55-yard field goal on the last play of the first half to get the Redskins momentum going into the locker room.

Two short TD drives helped the home team stay with the Eagles in the first half. One was set up by a Football Follies type of play. Philly reserve quarterback Randall Cunningham attempted a quick kick on second and 40 inside his 10. He nailed an offensive lineman in the back with the kick, which wobbled and rolled out to the 28. A holding penalty set the Redskins back, but Jay Schroeder hit Kelvin Bryant on a post pattern for 36 yards and a touchdown. Darrell Green intercepted a pass to set up the other touchdown, a one-yard bootleg by Schroeder.

After Cox's boomer at the first-half gun put them up 20-14, the Redskins took the second half kickoff and drove 90 yards to extend the lead. A good mix of short passes and inside runs led to a 36-yard Schroeder TD pass to tight end Clint Didier. Two additional long drives in the third and fourth quarters put it away.

The defense did its part, getting six sacks of Ron Jaworski and two turnovers.

9/14/86	REDSKINS (2-0) 10, Raiders (0-2) 3				55,235
LA	3	0	3	0	**6**
Was	1	0	0	7	**10**
LA	FG Bahr 28				
Was	FG Moseley 45				
LA	FG Bahr 23				
Was	Rogers 3 run (Moseley kick)				

RFK Stadium—Jay Schroeder threw a 59-yard bomb to Clint Didier to set up George Rogers' go-ahead touchdown midway through the fourth quarter, and the Washington defense survived two late drives into its territory to preserve the 10-3 win for the Redskins.

Didier himself suggested the play that resulted in the long gain to Joe Gibbs. Nothing much was working offensively at the time so, when Washington took possession at its own 32 with 9:23 to go in the game, Gibbs took Didier's advice and called the tight end's number on a deep fade. The tight end took a perfect pass from Schroeder and wasn't tackled until he got to the Raiders' nine. Two plays later, George Rogers went outside of a Mark May block and scored from three yards out to give Washington its first lead at 10-6 with 7:27 left to play.

Any relief felt on the part of the Redskins faithful was quickly gone when Napoleon McCallum returned the ensuing kickoff 59 yards to the Redskins' 38. That threat ended on Mel Kaufman's third down sack of Marc Wilson.

A final LA foray into Washington territory ended with a third-down sack by end Charles Mann and cornerback Vernon Dean and Darrell Green's fourth-down interception of Wilson's desperation heave.

9/21/86	Redskins (3-0) 30, CHARGERS (1-2) 27			57,583	
Was	3	7	13	7	30
SD	14	7	3	3	27
Was	FG Moseley 29				
SD	Anderson 13 pass from Fouts (Benirschke kick)				
SD	McGee 1 run (Benirschke kick)				
SD	McGee 1 run (Benirschke kick)				
Was	Rogers 2 run (Moseley kick)				
Was	FG Moseley 24				
Was	FG Moseley 26				
SD	FG Benirschke 50				
Was	Rogers 10 run (Moseley kick)				
SD	FG Benirschke 31				
Was	Clark 14 pass from Schroeder (Moseley kick)				

San Diego-Jack Murphy Stadium—Jay Schroeder teamed up with Gary Clark for two completions in the waning moments of the game to complete a Washington comeback from a 21-3 deficit. First, Clark hauled down a 56-yard bomb before making a sliding catch at the goal line for a 14-yard gain and a 30-27 win.

To get there, the Redskins first had to withstand an assault by Air Coryell, the nickname for coach Don Coryell's high-powered passing attack. Quarterback Dan Fouts completed a swing pass to running back Gary Anderson, who deftly eluded two would-be tacklers on his way to a 14-yard scoring play. Later in the first quarter, tight end Kellen Winslow made a spectacular, left-handed grab of a Fouts pass that set up another Charger touchdown. It got to be 21-3 before the Redskins responded with a two-yard touchdown run by George Rogers with a little over four minutes left before halftime.

Fouts, though, still had the Redskins back on their heels until a goal-line interception by Vernon Dean prevented an answering score and had the visitors happy to be running off the field for the break down by just 11.

San Diego would pay for its inability to put away the Redskins. Washington twice drove for Mark Moseley field goals in the third quarter. After the Chargers responded with a 50-yard three pointer by Rolf Benirschke, Rogers got his second TD run of the day—this one from 10 yards—to pull his team within a point at 24-23 at the end of the third quarter.

The pace slowed considerably in the fourth quarter with the Chargers' offense reduced to short passes and running plays. They did manage another Benirschke field goal to push their lead to four.

Washington took possession at its own 30 at the two minute warning needing a touchdown to win. On first down, Schroeder went deep for Art Monk down the right side, and cornerback Wayne Davis made the play on the ball. The next play, Joe Gibbs lined Clark up on that side, and, as Monk had, Clark drew single coverage from Davis. The corner's coverage was excellent but Schroeder's pass was perfect, dropping into Clark's arms for a 56-yard gain to Chargers 14. With the clock running, the Redskins hurriedly lined up and Clark didn't quite know how to read the coverage so he just ran to the goal line and snared Schroeder's pass.

On the day, Schroeder was only 16 for 36 passing, but he rolled up 341 yards in the air. Clark caught six passes for 144 yards, Monk 7 for 174.

Fouts still had 1:16 and all of the team's timeouts to work with, but a third-down sack by Charles Mann and a fourth-down interception by Curtis Jordan sealed the win for Washington.

9/28/86	REDSKINS (4-0) 19, Seahawks (3-1) 14			54,157	
Sea	7	0	0	7	14
Was	6	3	7	3	19
Sea	Warner 2 run (Johnson kick)				
Was	Rogers 24 run (kick blocked)				
Was	FG Cox 57				
Was	Rogers 7 run (Moseley kick)				
Was	FG Moseley 36				
Sea	Largent 11 pass from Krieg (Johnson kick)				

RFK Stadium—Steve Cox broke a team record that he had set just three weeks earlier when he snuck a 57-yard field goal over the crossbar as time ran out in the first half, putting the Redskins ahead to stay as they slugged out a win over Seattle. The punter, kickoff man and long-distance field goal specialist nailed a 55-yarder in the season opener against Philadelphia.

The teams exchanged first-quarter touchdowns, with Seattle holding a 7-6 lead as the extra point attempt was blocked following Washington's TD, a nice 24-yard run by George Rogers. Seattle was threatening to lengthen its lead with 27 seconds in the first half, poised on the Redskins' 30. Quarterback Dave Krieg, though, made a mistake, trying to squeeze the ball past Rich Milot. The linebacker was having no part of it, intercepting the pass and returning it to the Seattle 48. Following an eight-yard scramble by Jay Schroeder, Joe Gibbs waived in Cox, who gave the Redskins a 9-7 lead.

The Redskins widened their lead on a seven-yard run by Rogers late in the third quarter. Mark Moseley, the regular placekicker, booted a 38-yard field goal to put Washington up 19-7 midway through the fourth. Seattle got back within five points on an 11-yard pass from Krieg to Steve Largent with 1:52 left to play, but a final possession ended with a Hail Mary pass being intercepted by rookie safety Todd Bowles.

10/5/86	Redskins (5-0) 14, SAINTS (1-4) 6			57.378	
Was	7	7	0	0	14
NO	3	3	0	0	6
Was	Rogers 4 run (Moseley kick)				
NO	FG Andersen 34				
NO	FG Andersen 45				
Was	Monk 2 pass from Schroeder (Moseley kick)				

Superdome—Playing without five starters for the entire second half, the Redskins defense held New Orleans without a touchdown to come out with a 14-6 win. The play of the patchwork defense allowed two first-half touchdowns to stand up for Washington.

The Redskins got on the board first. In the first quarter, the Redskins capped a drive when George Rogers dragged a safety the last three yards of a four-yard touchdown run. The former Saint had collected much of the yardage on the scoring drive, with seven carries for 35 yards.

Following two Morten Andersen field goals, Rogers keyed the second touchdown drive, carrying eight times to get the Redskins down to the Saints' two. From there, Jay Schroeder threw to Art Monk, who just got his feet inbounds, and the Redskins had a 14-6 lead.

With five rookies in the lineup at times, the Washington defense preserved the lead by allowing the Saints into their territory just once.

Rogers chewed up yardage and the clock all day long. He had 31 carries for 110 yards and the touchdown. Monk caught 7 passes for 80 yards while Gary Clark chipped in with five receptions for 77.

10/12/86	COWBOYS (4-2) 30, Redskins (5-1) 6			63,264	
Was	0	0	6	0	6
Dal	7	9	0	14	30

Dal	Walker 1 run (Septien kick)
Dal	FG Septien 21
Dal	FG Septien 36
Dal	FG Septien 36
Was	Rogers 2 run (kick failed)
Dal	Sherrard 27 pass from Pelluer (Septien kick)
Dal	Walker 1 run (Septien kick)

Texas Stadium—"Not a bad day. Not a bad day at all." That depends on your perspective. This opinion came from Dallas coach Tom Landry, who had watched his quarterback Steve Pelluer torch the Washington defense for 323 yards passing to help deal the Redskins their first loss of the year.

"It just wasn't our day," was the summary judgment of Joe Gibbs. That was evident early on after penalties and solid defense had forced Dallas into a third and fifteen on its own one-inch line on its opening series. Pelluer apparently threw the ball away, with the pass going way out of bounds, but cornerback Barry Wilburn was flagged for pass interference, giving the Cowboys life at their 19.

Three plays later, Pelluer scrambled and found Herschel Walker deep down the middle. Walker had to adjust to the underthrown pass, but that only gave him more opportunities to elude Redskin defenders. Darrell Green finally chased him down at the one after a 69-yard gain, but Walker pushed it over two plays later. Dallas was up 7-0.

Three Rafael Septien field goals stretched the Dallas lead to 16-0 at halftime. Washington made a bid to climb back into it by driving for a touchdown on its initial second-half possession. After George Rogers' two-yard scoring run, though, much of the air was let out of the comeback balloon when Mark Moseley missed the extra point. In the midst of a severe slump, the 15-year veteran speculated that this might have been his last game with the Redskins saying, "When the snake bites you, he bites hard." (Moseley's feelings turned out to be correct; the Redskins released him days after the game.)

A controversial touchdown pass on the first play of the fourth quarter put it out of reach. From the Washington 27, Pelluer looped a pass into the end zone of which both receiver Mike Sherrard and Darrell Green had possession. Although replays seemed to indicate that Green had possession first and Sherrard wrestled his share of the ball away only after they were both on the ground, the officials awarded the touchdown to Dallas. A fumble on the ensuing kickoff set up Dallas' final score.

After 14 Years, Goodbye: Moseley Cut

Oct 13—The Redskins have waived struggling kicker Mark Moseley.

While nobody was surprised given the fact that Moseley had hit fewer than 50 percent of his last 27 kicks with the Redskins, it still wasn't easy—especially for Joe Gibbs.

In front of the players' locker room at Redskins Park, Gibbs made the announcement. He went on to say, "I wish it never had to come to this with any of our players."

He then brought Moseley out of the locker room and publicly paid tribute to him.

"I just wanted to say in front of everybody how much we appreciate what you've done for us," Gibbs said before turning the session over to Moseley.

"What I'm feeling now is a combination of anxiety and relief," Moseley said. "It's not easy to walk away after 14 years. But, I've

been under an awful lot of pressure the last three or four years here."

Moseley indicated that he'd like to continue playing. Given the option of release or retirement, Moseley chose the former, which delayed a sizeable severance payment but made him a free agent, able to sign with any NFL team.

The kicker summed up his feelings, as well as those of most Redskins fans, saying, "I can't believe what's happening."

10/19/86	REDSKINS (6-1) 28, Cardinals (1-6) 21			53,494	
StL	0	7	7	7	21
Was	7	14	7	0	28

Was	Rogers 2 run (Zendejas kick)
Was	Monk 18 pass from Schroeder (Zendejas kick)
Was	Didier 1 pass from Schroeder (Zendejas kick)
StL	Ferrell 8 pass from Lomax (Lee kick)
Was	Clark 16 pass from Schroeder (Zendejas kick)
StL	J. Smith 7 pass from Lomax (Lee kick)
StL	Ferrell 15 pass from Lomax (Lee kick)

RFK Stadium—The Redskins scored touchdowns on four straight possessions, but had to survive a late Cardinal drive to hang on for the win. Jay Schroeder threw three touchdown passes to pace the Skins.

The Redskins' first score came on a gift from their opponents. A Washington punt bounced off the leg of Cardinal Carl Carter; Anthony Jones covered the ball at the St. Louis two. On the next play, George Rogers took it over for a 7-0 lead.

In the second quarter, Schroeder threw two of his TD passes: one of 16 yards to Art Monk, and the other 21 yards to Clint Didier. St. Louis scratched the board just before halftime when Neal Lomax threw an eight-yard scoring pass to running back Earl Ferrell that cut the Washington lead to 21-7 at the break.

It didn't seem like it would matter as the Redskins responded on their first second-half possession by moving to another score, this one Schroeder's 16-yard touchdown pass to Gary Clark. The home team appeared to be in command with a 28-7 lead.

Nobody told the Cardinals that the game was over. Lomax threw two touchdown passes, the second to Ferrell with 9:28 left in the game to pull his team within seven at 28-21.

A little more than two minutes later, the Cardinals had the ball back on their own 31. Their desperation drive wasn't a thing of beauty, but it did get them to the Washington 14 with 24 seconds left. St. Louis had burned all of its time outs, so it was difficult to explain what followed. Lomax dumped one short over the middle, killing all but six seconds of the remaining time. When Lomax had to go out due to an injury, backup Cliff Stoudt, under heavy pressure, threw a safety valve to Chas Fox who went to his knees to make the catch. Linebacker Calvin Daniels touched Fox down as time ran out.

10/27/86	GIANTS (6-2) 27, Redskins (6-2) 20			75,923	
Was	0	3	14	3	20
NYG	3	10	7	7	27

NYG	FG Allegre 37
NYG	Morris 11 run (Allegre kick)
Was	FG Zendejas 23
NYG	FG Allegre 44
NYG	Johnson 30 pass from Simms (Allegre kick)
Was	Rogers 1 run (Zendejas kick)
Was	Clark 42 pass from Schroeder (Zendejas kick)
Was	FG Zendejas 29
NYG	Morris 13 run (Allegre kick)

Giants Stadium—Joe Morris scored the go-ahead touchdown with 1:38 left to go as the Giants survived a second-half Redskin rally to claim the win. A fourth-down pass from Jay Schroeder to Gary Clark fell incomplete in Giants territory in the final seconds to snuff out the Redskins chances for a second rally.

For much of the first half, the teams tried to out-muscle each other—and Washington was playing the role of the 98-pound weakling. New York ended Washington's first possession by stopping George Rogers on a fourth and one at their 33. The Giants' offensive line continually opened holes for the 5-7 Morris, who gained 92 yards in the game's first 18 minutes (181 on the day). After a Raul Allegre field goal, Morris scored on an 11-yard run to put the Giants up 10-0 two and a half minutes into the second quarter. The teams exchanged field goals and it was 13-3 at the half.

Right after an interception of Schroeder, quarterback Phil Simms found receiver Bobby Johnson for a 30-yard touchdown pass and all of a sudden, it was 20-3 with a little more than nine minutes left in the third quarter. For the Redskins, it was time to abandon the power game and take to the air.

After completing a 71-yard pass to Ricky Sanders to set up a one-yard touchdown run by Rogers, Schroeder found considerable success exploiting the single coverage the Giants were using on Clark. Actually, they had zero coverage on Clark for Schroeder's 42-yard touchdown pass to the receiver, who was completely alone in the end zone. That pulled the Redskins within three at 20-17. On the day, Schroeder passed for 420 yards, with Clark catching 11 for a team-record 241.

After Allegre missed a field goal in the fourth quarter, the Redskins were poised to take the lead, but a sack by Lawrence Taylor forced a tying field goal by Max Zendejas, who had been signed to replace the waived Mark Moseley.

After the ensuing kickoff, Simms completed a 14-yard pass to Johnson to convert a third and ten, but the winning drive was a Morris production. On first and 20 at the New York 44, he scooted up the middle for 34 yards on a draw play and on third and one at the 11, he eluded Darrell Green's attempted tackle in the backfield to scoot 11 yards to the game-winning score.

Schroeder went to Clark three times to get the Redskins down to the Giants' 30, but Clark slipped on a fourth and eight pass and it fell harmlessly to the turf.

11/2/86	REDSKINS (7-2) 44, Vikings (5-4) 38 OT					51,928
Min	14	3	14	7	0	38
Was	10	6	10	12	6	44

Was	Rogers 2 run (Zendejas kick)
Was	FG Zendejas 25
Min	Brown 1 run (C. Nelson kick)
Min	Lewis 67 pass from Kramer (C. Nelson kick)
Was	Manley 26 fumble return (kick blocked)
Min	FG C. Nelson 39
Min	Jordan 68 pass from Kramer (C. Nelson kick)
Was	FG Zendejas 42
Was	Rogers 40 run (Zendejas kick)
Min	Lewis 76 pass from Kramer (C. Nelson kick)
Min	D. Nelson 1 pass from Kramer (C. Nelson kick)
Was	Monk 34 pass from Schroeder (kick failed)
Was	Rogers 2 run (kick blocked)
Was	Clark 38 pass from Schroeder (no attempt)

RFK Stadium—"It feels like we've been playing for about five hours," said Joe Gibbs after this one and the members of the Redskins secondary would have to agree. Tommy Kramer torched them for 490 yards and four touchdowns. Three of the touchdown passes were on plays of more than 65 yards.

Washington did not score the extra point following four of its six touchdowns. The last of those TD's, though, was the game-winner in overtime, so Max Zendejas didn't get an opportunity to blow this one after the Redskins won this wild affair 44-38.

Jay Schroeder managed "only" 378 yards in the air, but he led his team to the game's final three touchdowns, including the 38-yarder to Gary Clark to win it . . . but that's getting way ahead of things.

Washington bolted to a quick 10-0 lead, but the Vikings responded as Kramer heated up. A 67-yard touchdown pass to receiver Leo Lewis gave the Vikings a 14-10 lead by the time the first quarter ended.

They gave the lead right back to Washington when a shotgun snap went over Kramer's head and end Dexter Manley snared it in stride, racing unchallenged 26 yards for a touchdown. The shape of things to come was seen, however, when Zendejas' point after was low and got blocked, allowing the Vikings to claim the halftime lead at 17-16 as Chuck Nelson kicked a 39-yard field goal with about a minute left in the quarter.

The visitors quickly extended their lead in the third quarter with a 68-yard bomb from Kramer to tight end Steve Jordan. After a Zendejas field goal, George Rogers converted a fourth and one at the Minnesota 40 in grand fashion. He broke through the line, cut back and went all the way and the Redskins were up by two at 26-24 following the extra point. They enjoyed the lead for about a minute and a half as Kramer went to Lewis for 76 yards and a touchdown with six seconds left in the third quarter.

A much shorter Kramer TD toss—one yard to Darrin Nelson—followed a pass interference call in the end zone against cornerback Barry Wilburn. Minnesota was up by 12 with less than seven minutes left to play.

The home team responded swiftly, moving 65 yards in three plays, with a 30-yard catch by Clint Didier setting up a 34-yard scoring pass from Schroeder to Art Monk. It didn't seem to matter that Zendejas missed the point after as another touchdown would tie the game and surely, a professional kicker couldn't miss two PAT's in a row. Or could he?

We found out after Schroeder completed a bomb to Didier at the two, who was credited with the catch after replay reviews on the question of if he trapped it were inconclusive. After Rogers ran over from there with 1:03 left, Zendejas did the unthinkable: he missed his second extra point in a row. The roar from the RFK crowd quickly turned to grumbles of disgust as the game headed to overtime tied at 38.

The crowd did go home happy, though. The Redskins won the overtime coin toss. Four plays into the extra period, from the Minnesota 38, Schroeder threw a 15-yard pattern to Clark, who broke away from the Minnesota cornerback and raced down the left sideline for the winning score.

11/9/86	Redskins (8-2) 16, PACKERS (1-9) 7				47,728
Was	6	0	7	3	16
GB	7	0	0	0	7

GB	Epps 3 pass from Wright (Del Greco kick)
Was	Sanders 26 pass from Schroeder (kick failed)
Was	Bryant 6 pass from Schroeder (Zendejas kick)
Was	FG Zendejas 30

Lambeau Field—Playing in 30-mile per hour winds and wind chills near zero, the Redskins scored the go-ahead touchdown late in the third quarter and were able to hang on for the 16-7 win in Green Bay.

The Packers held a 7-6 lead at the half, thanks to Washington kicker Max Zendejas' third consecutive extra point miss, going back to the previous week when he'd missed his last two. Washington had pulled to within 7-6 when, from the Packers 26, Jay Schroeder looped one to Ricky Sanders in the end zone. The receiver was open when cornerback Mossy Cade overran the play, perhaps helped along by a slight shove from Sanders.

The home team was looking to extend its lead in the third quarter when running back Kenneth Davis, who was having a fine game (16 carries for 93 yards), fumbled, and Neal Olkewicz recovered at the Washington 22. That led to a six-yard touchdown pass from Schroeder to Kelvin Bryant and Washington had the lead for good at 13-7. The Packers never threatened after that and a Zendejas field goal with five and a half minutes left clinched it for Washington.

Manley: Wants to 'Ring' Montana

November 13—Frustrated by the perceived lack of respect the 8-2 Redskins are getting around the league, Dexter Manley had something to say.

"Check this," he said. "We're 8-2 and catching a lot of heat. I've NEVER known an 8-2 team to be criticized."

Perhaps the defensive end hadn't checked out the fact that the Redskins, who have made their living pounding out yards on the ground and stuffing the opposing teams' runs, ranked 18th in the league in both rushing yardage allowed and gained.

Asked about the return of Joe Montana, who will make his first start of the season for the 49ers against the Redskins on Monday night, Manley said he wanted to "ring his clock."

Montana is returning following offseason back surgery that was supposed to sideline him for the entire year.

Joe Gibbs, always scared of giving the opposition additional motivation, quickly said that Manley used "a bad choice of words" in his comments on Montana.

11/17/86	**REDSKINS (9-2) 14, 49ers (6-4-1) 6**			54,774
SF	0	3	3	0	**6**
Was	7	0	7	0	**14**
Was	Rogers 1 run (Zendejas kick)			
SF	FG Wersching 34			
Was	Clark 27 pass from Schroeder (Zendejas kick)			
SF	FG Wersching 38			

RFK Stadium—Rarely has so little action been spread out over such a long time frame. In a Monday night game that lasted just under four hours, the Redskins had just enough to defeat Joe Montana and the 49ers 14-6.

Washington took a 7-3 lead into the locker room at halftime on the strength of George Rogers' one-yard touchdown run. It was set up when Dexter Manley forced Montana to fumble. In the days before the game, Manley had promised to "ring (Montana's) clock." He made good on his widely-quoted mixed metaphor by nailing Montana from behind, giving the Redskins possession at their own 47.

The home team extended the lead to 14-3 early in the third quarter after Ken Jenkins returned a punt to the San Francisco 37. It took just three plays for Jay Schroeder to find Gary Clark in the end zone.

Montana has made his reputation on rallying his team, but he was unable to do so this night. Playing in his first game of the season due to back surgery, Montana attempted 60 passes but couldn't get his team into the end zone.

Nov 17
Art Patrons: Monk Tops Fan Voting for Skins' 50th Anniversary Team
Riggins, Jurgensen in next two spots

11/23/86	**REDSKINS (10-2) 41, Cowboys (7-5) 14**			55,642
Dal	0	0	7	7	**14**
Was	14	20	7	0	**41**
Was	Rogers 14 run (Zendejas kick)			
Was	Didier 71 pass from Schroeder (Zendejas kick)			
Was	FG Zendejas 25			
Was	FG Zendejas 41			
Was	Bryant 22 run (Zendejas kick)			
Was	Clark 11 pass from Schroeder (Zendejas kick)			
Dal	Walker 1 run (Septien kick)			
Was	Bryant 1 run (Zendejas kick)			
Dal	Lavette 8 pass from Collier (Septien kick)			

RFK Stadium—"There are about three great things in life," Mark May said. "Winning the lottery, having a baby and beating the Cowboys this badly."

How badly? Badly enough to have the biggest halftime lead ever in the series, 34-0. Badly enough to sack Dallas quarterback Steve Pelluer, who torched the Skins in Texas Stadium earlier this year, five times—and hold the celebrated running back tandem of Tony Dorsett and Herschel Walker to a combined total of 18 yards. Badly enough to rack up 483 yards of offense, just less than twice the Cowboys' total offense of 251 yards. In short, very badly.

Things started in the Redskins' favor right off the bat when Dallas fumbled the opening kickoff. Less than two minutes into the game George Rogers was in the end zone after a 14-yard run off the right side.

Before the first quarter was out, the Redskins had scored again on a 71-yard pass from Jay Schroeder to Clint Didier. The tight end bowled through cornerback Everson Walls at about the Dallas 20 to complete the scoring jaunt. It was 14-0 at the end of the first quarter and things were about to get worse for Dallas.

The Redskins had to settle for field goals after driving into Dallas territory twice in the second quarter, but in the last five minutes of the half, the Redskins maximized their two opportunities. Following a short Dallas punt, Schroeder threw 35 yards to Art Monk for a first down at the Dallas 22 before Kelvin Bryant made a spectacular TD run, spinning away from and running through would-be tacklers in the process. It became 34-0 with 17 seconds left in the half as Gary Clark ran a fade pattern from the Dallas 11 and Schroeder dropped in a perfect pass.

The second half was 30 minutes of garbage time as both teams used their benches liberally to save front-line players for another day. Veteran quarterback Doug Williams made his first appearance as a Redskin, with his only pass attempt going incomplete.

11/30/86	**Redskins (11-2) 20, CARDINALS (3-10) 17**			35,637
Was	7	10	0	3	**20**
StL	3	7	0	7	**17**
StL	FG Schubert 46			
Was	Clark 2 pass from Schroeder			
StL	J. T. Smith 4 pass from Lomax			
Was	Orr 22 pass from Schroeder (Zendejas kick)			
Was	FG Zendejas 30			
StL	Green 35 pass from Lomax (Schubert kick)			
Was	FG Zendejas 27			

Busch Stadium—Despite a solid statistical edge, the Redskins had quite a struggle in beating the lowly Cardinals. Max Zendejas hit a 27-yard field goal with four seconds left in the game to lift the Redskins past the Cardinals, clinching a playoff spot.

Washington turned a 10-7 deficit into a 10-point halftime lead with two scores in the last 3:25 of the first half. Tight end Terry Orr's first NFL catch was a 22-yard touchdown from Jay Schroeder that put his team into the lead. With four seconds left in the half, Zendejas lengthened the margin with a 30-yard field goal and it was 17-7 at the break.

The visitors were unable to put the Cardinals away in the second half. With George Rogers on the bench with an injury, the Redskins offense couldn't generate a consistent rushing attack and St. Louis often employed five defensive backs, even on first down, frustrating the passing game. With 5:23 left to play, Neal Lomax found Roy Green for 35 yards and the tying touchdown.

After the ensuing kickoff Washington started at its own 33. Schroeder went to little-used receiver Ricky Sanders for 19 yards for one key play and carried himself to pick up eight critical yards on a quarterback draw on a third and seven play. That run got the Redskins down to the 16, well within Zendejas' range. His kick from 27 yards out was true.

Zendejas Back From the Brink

December 3—Max Zendejas is safe—for now.

Kicking a game-winning, playoff-clinching field goal is no guarantee of lifetime job security, but it will help your bosses forget about some earlier mistakes, like missing four of your first seven extra point attempts of the season.

One thing that helped get Zendejas out of his slump—he's hit his last 10 extra point attempts and nine of 12 field goals—is an asset every successful kicker must possess: a short memory.

"It wasn't always that way," Zendejas said. "When I was younger, I'd really burn and get mad over a miss. I had to get over that. If I'd missed at St. Louis, I would have just tried to make the next one."

Well, had he missed, his next attempt might well have been for another team.

12/7/86	Giants (12-2) 24, REDSKINS (11-3) 14				55,642
NYG	0	14	10	0	**24**
Was	0	7	0	7	**14**
NYG	Bavaro 9 pass from Simms (Allegre kick)				
Was	Bryant 4 run (Zendejas kick)				
NYG	B. Johnson 7 pass from Simms (Allegre kick)				
NYG	FG Allegre 21				
NYG	McConkey 16 pass from Simms (Allegre kick)				
Was	Bryant 22 pass from Schroeder (Zendejas kick)				

RFK Stadium—Lawrence Taylor sacked Jay Schroeder three times, leading a defense that smothered the Redskins' hopes of claiming the NFC East title. New York's win, much more dominating than the 24-14 final indicated, gave them a one-game lead and the tiebreaker advantage (a head-to-head sweep) with two games to play.

While the New York defense got the accolades, it was the Giants' offense that turned the tide. On the first play following the two-minute warning for the first half, Kelvin Bryan scored on a four-yard for Washington, tying the game at seven and getting the RFK Stadium crowd into the game. The faithful were silenced quickly, however, as the visiting team embarked on an 81-yard touchdown drive. They converted a third and long with Phil Simms going to receiver Bobby Johnson for 34 yards and, with 23 second left in the half, Simms found Johnson again—this time for seven yards and a touchdown.

The lead allowed the Giants to keep the pressure on Schroeder and it paid off. Following a time-consuming drive, a Raul Allegre field goal upped the New York lead to 17-7. The next Redskins series ended quickly as Schroeder finally found an open man. Unfortunately, it was New York linebacker Harry Carson, who intercepted the pass and returned it to the Washington 14. Three plays later, Simms threw a 16-yard touchdown pass to receiver Phil McConkey and it was 24-7.

The prevent defense the Giants employed in the fourth quarter allowed the Redskins to pad their stats and get a touchdown, but the outcome had long since been decided.

12/13/86	BRONCOS (11-4) 31, Redskins (11-4) 30					75,905
Was	6	7	0	17		**30**
Den	0	7	14	10	31	**31**
Was	Sanders 10 pass from Schroeder (kick failed)					
Was	Rogers 15 run (Zendejas kick)					
Den	Elway 11 run (Karlis kick)					
Den	Winder 6 run (Karlis kick)					
Den	Watson 19 pass from Elway (Karlis kick)					
Was	FG Cox 48					
Den	Winder 1 run (Karlis kick)					
Was	Monk 55 pass from Schroeder (Zendejas kick)					
Den	FG Karlis 32					
Was	Rogers 1 run (Zendejas kick)					

Mile High Stadium—All year long, the Redskins had been able to escape serious damage from their shaky kicking game, having enough effectiveness on offense and defense to overcome the weakness at that spot. It was bound to catch up with them, and it did on this day in Denver. A shanked extra point and missed field goal were keys in Washington's 31-30 loss to the Broncos.

The missed PAT came in the opening quarter after Jay Schroeder hit Ricky Sanders with a 10-yard touchdown pass for the game's first score. The attempt was shanked badly and Washington had a 6-0 lead. They stretched it to 13-0 on George Rogers' 15-yard touchdown run in the second quarter and were moving in for more as halftime neared. Zendejas missed a 53-yard field goal attempt, though, and the Broncos walked through the open door.

John Elway completed a 22-yard pass on third and 17 and capped the drive by scoring on a quarterback draw from 11 yards out. Maintaining the momentum after halftime, Denver scored twice more in the third quarter to go up 21-13. The Redskins responded by twice driving into position for field goal tries, but hit on just one of them with Zendejas missing from 41 and Steve Cox coming in to boot one from 48. The kick made it 21-16—and it was a wild start to the fourth quarter.

The home team answered Cox's score by rolling 80 yards to Sammy Winder's one-yard touchdown run. It took just two plays for Washington to respond as Jay Schroeder threw 22 yards to Clint Didier and 55 yards to Art Monk to pull his team back within five.

Washington got the ball back with less than five minutes left, but the comeback attempt was seriously deflated when cornerback Mike Hardin intercepted a Schroeder pass at the Washington 14. Rich Karlis kicked a 32-yard field goal with 3:10 left to go. That rendered George Rogers' one-yard touchdown run a minute and a half later meaningless as the Broncos recovered the onside kick, enabling them to kill the clock.

Zendejas Out, Ex-Terp Atkinson In

December 16—Just two weeks after putting the Redskins in the playoffs with a late field goal, Max Zendejas found out that he'll be watching those playoffs on TV. A shanked extra point in a one-point loss to Denver was the last straw for the Redskins, who put Zendejas on injured reserve, ending his season.

Replacing him will be former Maryland standout Jess Atkinson. After being cut during training camp, Atkinson had gone to work as a mortgage banker in Annapolis, Md. before the Redskins called. He kicked for both the Giants, for whom he scored a touchdown on a fake field goal, and the Cardinals during the 1985 season.

12/21/86	Redskins (12-4) 21, EAGLES (5-10-1) 14				61,816
Was	0	0	0	21	**21**
Phil	14	0	0	0	**14**
Phil	Cunningham 1 run (McFadden kick)				
Phil	Toney 1 run (McFadden kick)				
Was	Didier 26 pass from Schroeder (Atkinson kick)				
Was	Warren 2 pass from Schroeder (Atkinson kick)				
Was	Rogers 5 run (Atkinson kick)				

Veterans Stadium—"We were dead. No, worse than dead," said Dexter Manley.

"It seemed to be one of those days when everything I did and every choice I made was wrong," said Jay Schroeder.

"I've never seen anything like it," said Don Warren of Joe Gibbs' halftime tirade.

These were words from the winning locker room. The Redskins scored 21 unanswered points in the fourth quarter to take a 21-14 win over the Eagles.

Philadelphia had taken a 14-0 lead in the first quarter on a pair on one-yard touchdown runs by quarterback Randall Cunningham and running back Andrew Toney. For the next thirty minutes of play the Redskins continually tried to give the visitors the opportunity to put the game away with turnovers and stalled drives, but Philly refused to accept the offer and it was still 14-0 as the fourth quarter neared.

On the final play of the third period, a promising Redskins drive was kept alive when an Eagles fumble recovery at their 20 was negated by a roughing call and Washington maintained possession. Shortly after that, Schroeder drilled a pass to Clint Didier for 13 yards and the Redskins' first touchdown. Newly-signed kicker Jess Atkinson's extra point was good, and it was 14-7.

Nine plays after a pair of sacks by Manley and Rich Milot had forced an Eagles punt and given the Redskins possession at their own 36, the score was tied. Gibbs crossed the Eagles up by calling for a pass on second and goal at the two and the result was a two-yard TD pass from Schroeder to Warren.

After another Philly three and out, the Redskins were facing third and ten at their own 43. Ricky Sanders, the only eligible receiver who was on a pattern and not double covered, ran a streak down the right sideline. He had a step on cornerback Roynell Young and laid out parallel to the ground to snag Schroeder's pass at the 16. After that spectacular play, the more mundane was utilized as George Rogers carried four straight times, the last for the winning TD with 2:19 remaining.

Gibbs' Halftime Tirade Still Big Topic

December 22—Chairs were flipped. The coach's arms were waving. His voice went several octaves higher than his normal, calm tone.

"Screechy," was the way linebacker Neal Olkewicz described Joe Gibbs' voice. "Definitely screechy."

"I thought maybe Coach Gibbs had been fired, and Mike Ditka (coach of the Chicago Bears) had been hired at halftime," free safety Curtis Jordan said.

But, no, it was Gibbs, riled by his team's lack of intensity in the first half of the game against the Eagles.

"There were veins sticking out of his neck," said linebacker Rich Milot.

There was evidence that this was a very controlled rage. "He never used any four-letter words," said Milot.

Planned or not, controlled or not, the tirade apparently worked. The Redskins rallied from a 14-0 halftime deficit to beat Philadelphia 21-14.

Gibbs was more reflective later on. "Turning it around like that is the toughest challenge there is," he said. "I'll remember that long after I've forgotten what's on the scoreboard."

NFC Wild Card Playoff
Sunday, December 28, 1986
RFK Stadium
Washington, D.C.

12/28/86	WASHINGTON 19, Rams 7				54,180
LA	0	0	0	7	7
Was	10	3	3	3	10
Was	FG Atkinson 25				
Was	Bryant 14 pass from Schroeder (Atkinson kick)				
Was	FG Atkinson 20				
Was	FG Atkinson 38				
LA	House 12 pass from Everett (Lansford kick)				
Was	FG Atkinson 25				

Jess Atkinson remained flawless as the team's place kicker, booting four field goals to provide the winning margin as Washington advanced to the divisional playoff round with a 19-7 win over the Rams.

Four field goals, the longest from 38 yards, and a point after may not seem like a big deal for an NFL kicker, but as Joe Gibbs said, "After what we've been through this year, I'm thrilled about just making an extra point, let alone a field goal."

Late in the first quarter following Atkinson's first field goal, a 25-yarder, the home team drove 60 yards for its first touchdown. The drive was aided greatly when cornerback Leroy Irvin picked up a 13-yard pass interference penalty and then had another 15 tacked on when he protested the call with a "gesture" the officials didn't like. From the LA 14, Jay Schroeder looked off safety Nolan Cromwell and threw to Kelvin Bryant for the score.

The next two Rams' possessions finished with fumbles in Washington territory and the Redskins stretched their lead to 16-0 on two more Atkinson field goals, the second coming with just under three minutes to go in the third quarter.

Early in the fourth, the Rams tried to make a game of it when Jim Everett threw a 12-yard touchdown pass to Kevin House and then drove into Washington territory again at the 39. But linebackers Rich Milot and Calvin Daniels stuffed Dickerson on fourth and one, and the Redskins were headed to Chicago for the second round.

NFC Divisional Playoff
Saturday, January 3, 1987
Soldier Field
Chicago, Illinois

1/3/87	Redskins 27, BEARS 13				65,141
Was	7	0	7	13	27
Chi	0	13	0	0	13
Was	Monk 28 pass from Schroeder (Atkinson kick)				
Chi	Gault 50 pass from Flutie (Butler kick)				
Chi	FG Butler 23				
Chi	FG Butler 41				
Was	Monk 23 pass from Schroeder (Atkinson kick)				
Was	Rogers 1 run (Atkinson kick)				
Was	FG Atkinson 35				
Was	FG Atkinson 25				

The headline in the Chicago paper read: "**Bears Ready—If Redskins Show Up.**"

As the game unfolded, it became clear that the first part of that statement was problematic—and there was not any question about the second part. The Redskins clearly came to play and they knocked off the defending champions in the Bears' own house by a score of 27-13.

The Bears had been on a 32-3 run over the previous two seasons thanks in large part to their ability to snuff the opposing passing game with blitzes. Late in the first quarter, Jay Schroeder made them pay for that strategy when the offensive line gave him enough time to toss a 28-yard scoring pass to Art Monk to put the Redskins up 7-0.

The second quarter belonged to the Bears. Receiver Willie Gault beat Darrell Green badly on a 50-yard touchdown catch from first-year quarterback Doug Flutie, who was starting in place of the injured Jim McMahon. That and two Kevin Butler field goals had the home team up 13-7 at halftime.

It would make for great dramatic reading to say that Green made a super, clutch play by getting revenge on Flutie by intercepting a pass that set up the Redskins' go-ahead score. The truth is, though, that Green merely accepted a gift, intercepting a lollipop that Flutie tossed up somewhere in between Gault and tight end Tim Wrightman. Green's 17-yard return to the Bears' 26 woke up the Redskins' offense.

Three plays later, on third and seven, Schroeder pumped left, Monk broke right, and the quarterback found the receiver for 23 yards and a touchdown. The Redskins were ahead for good at 14-13.

It wasn't over yet, though. Gary Gentry returned the ensuing kickoff 48 yards and shortly after that the Bears were in possession at the Washington 18. From there, though, Darryl Grant got his helmet on the ball, knocking it out of the arms of Walter Payton. Safety Alvin Walton recovered at the 17. Soon, it *was* over.

The Redskins drove 83 yards to the clinching TD. Monk should have had his third touchdown of the day, but cornerback Michael Richardson grabbed him in the end zone, so the score had to come via a one-yard George Rogers run.

The margin widened and the celebration on the sidelines grew more jubilant as Jess Atkinson kicked two fourth-quarter field goals.

Madden: Gibbs a 'Burnout' Candidate

January 9—It's one thing to hear some TV guy spouting off about what they think this coach or that coach will do; most talking heads' only contact with a coach is generally when they are firing questions at him during a press conference. It's another when it comes from John Madden and he's talking about Joe Gibbs.

And Madden thinks that Gibbs is a candidate for coaching burnout.

Not only is Madden a former coach who burned out when it seemed like he had a lot of good coaching years ahead of him, he has worked with Gibbs as a coach. Madden was Gibbs' immediate supervisor when they were both assistant coaches at San Diego State.

Madden think that Gibbs shows the signs of eventual burnout. "I think it will happen to Joe, same as it happened to (Dick) Vermeil, same as it happened to me," he said. "He's not one to do this a hell of a long time."

He said that Gibbs' shelf life was about 10 years due to how intensely he focused on football. As evidence that his focus on the game is all-consuming, he cited a plant that used to be in the Redskins coach's office.

Someone had given Gibbs a large plant for his space. One day he was talking to Madden there and noticed that the plant was gone.

Telling the story, Gibbs goes on, "I say: 'What happened to my plant? Has it melted?'

"The sucker was dead. I hadn't watered it."

"Those things creep up, because you're so intense," Madden said. "You get tunnel vision. And the tunnel's mighty small."

NFC Championship Game
Sunday, January 11, 1987
Giants Stadium
East Rutherford, New Jersey

1/11/87	GIANTS 17, Redskins 0				76,633
Was	0	0	0	0	0
NYG	10	7	0	0	17
NYG	FG Allegre 47				
NYG	Manuel 11 pass from Simms (Allegre kick)				
NYG	Morris 1 run (Allegre kick)				

There are two reasons why the home team generally prevails in playoff games and both were on display in this game.

First, the home team plays in weather conditions that its opponent is not usually accustomed to playing in. This certainly was the case as the Giants seemed unaffected by the cold, swirling winds in the Meadowlands while the visitors, as evidenced by 20 of 50 passing by Jay Schroeder, were ill-equipped to deal with the onslaught.

The second reason is the better team gets the home field advantage—and the Giants were clearly the better team. Even when the ball wasn't in the air, the Giants hit harder, ran faster and were always a step ahead on strategy. New York would have won this game in Washington, at a neutral site, or in any street or cow pasture where the game is played.

The first strategic advantage came on the opening coin toss. The Giants won and elected to have the wind at their backs. This directly led to the Giants' first 10 points as Steve Cox was able to only manage 25 yards on his first two punts. The first led to a Raul Allegre field goal, the second to a touchdown that put the Giants up 10-0.

On that drive, which covered 38 yards, Joe Gibbs gambled and lost when he accepted a holding penalty rather than taking the play, which would have resulted in a fourth and ten at the 26. But Phil Simms hit Lionel Manuel for 25 yards to blow up that bit of strategy. Three plays later, on another third and ten, Simms found Manuel again, this time for 11 yards and the touchdown.

After the Redskins got the wind advantage in the second quarter, they squandered it when a botched snap on a field goal play gave the Giants possession in Washington territory. Seven plays later, Joe Morris scored on a one-yard run to make the score 17-0.

It may as well have been 170-0. The Redskins never challenged, their deepest penetration going to the New York 23. They were a combined zero for 18 on third and fourth down conversions. Schroeder summed it up with simple eloquence: "We were controlled."

1987
Head Coach: Joe Gibbs
Record: 11-5, First in NFC East
Playoffs: 3-0, Super Bowl XXII Champions

Honors: Gary Clark All-NFL, Pro Bowl; Darrell Green All-NFL Pro Bowl;
Charles Mann Pro Bowl; Barry Wilburn All-NFL; Joe Jacoby All-NFL

Mar 13

Manley Enters Rehab Center
Checks into facility for drug, alcohol treatment

Bostic Odd Man Out in O-Line Shuffle

Aug 3—On most offensive lines, a season during which you play every snap and are often recognized by coaches for outstanding performances would earn you a raise. On the Redskins, though, such a performance earned Jeff Bostic a seat on the bench.

Bostic found out during positional meetings to open up camp that Russ Grimm would move over from his left guard spot to Bostic's center position and second-year player Raleigh McKenzie would be the starting left guard. While the official line was this was not a demotion for Bostic since he and Grimm would "compete" for the starting job in the middle of the line, offensive line coach Joe Bugel acknowledged that Grimm would get 99 percent of the snaps with the first team in camp.

"It's time to make some moves, to shift people around and see how they respond," Bugel said.

The reason for the move was threefold. The team wanted to motivate Grimm to prepare and play harder. The thinking was that the competition with Bostic would accomplish just that. In addition, the team is hoping that playing center will cut down on the number of nagging injuries that have plagued Grimm over the past couple of seasons. Finally, the additional size that Grimm would bring to the position (he has three inches and about 15 pounds on Bostic) would help in neutralizing the monster nose tackles that many teams are lining up, especially the Giants' Jim Burt.

"I thought I had as good a year last year as the year I made the Pro Bowl (1983)," Bostic said.

Although perhaps somewhat mystified by the move, he said all the right things. "What I am is a player," Bostic said. "A player who is going to try to help this team win, whatever my role is."

Linebacker Corps Getting Thin

August 16—Coming into training camp, it looked like the only problem the Redskins would have a linebacker would be sorting through the vast, talented corps to see who would start and who would go. Now, following Saturday's preseason win over the Steelers, they might have a tough time fielding a starting three due to injuries.

The worst-hit spot was in the middle. Starter Neal Olkewicz suffered a knee injury that required arthroscopic surgery and will keep him out for four weeks. Kurt Gouveia, his replacement, broke two bones in his fingers. He'll be in a cast for a while, making tackling a difficult proposition at best. On top of that, promising rookie Raven Caldwell received a concussion—but at least he looked great doing it. He lost his helmet during a play on special teams, but went in and made the tackle on the returner anyway.

The good news was that Mel Kaufman was not among the ailing. The seventh-year player is recovering nicely from a ruptured Achilles that sidelined him for most of last season.

9/13/87	**REDSKINS (1-0) 34, Eagles (0-1) 24**				52,188	
Phi	0	10	14	0	-	24
Was	10	7	7	10	-	34
Was	FG Atkinson 27					
Was	Monk 6 pass from Williams (Atkinson kick)					
Phi	Quick 30 pass from Cunningham (McFadden kick)					
Phi	FG McFadden 33					
Was	Rogers 1 run (Cox kick)					
Was	Branch 1 run (Cox kick)					
Phi	Cunningham 2 run (McFadden kick)					
Phi	White 70 fumble recovery return (McFadden kick)					
Was	Monk 39 pass from Williams (Cox kick)					
Was	FG Cox 40					

RFK Stadium—With starting quarterback Jay Schroeder sidelined with a shoulder injury, backup Doug Williams passed for 272 yards and hit Art Monk for two touchdowns as the Redskins beat the Eagles for the fourth straight time.

The Redskins turned a 10-10 tie score in the second quarter into what seemed to be a comfortable 24-10 lead with pair of one-yard touchdown runs, one by George Rogers and the other by Reggie Branch.

That lead held until less than five minutes remained in the third quarter when Eagle quarterback Randall Cunningham scampered into the end zone from two yards out, cutting the lead in half. It seemed Williams and the Redskins had the answer, though, as they drove smartly into Eagle territory. The drive ended abruptly when end Reggie White got to Williams, stripped him of the ball and dashed 70 yards for the tying touchdown.

Keith Griffith helped right the ship for the Redskins by returning the ensuing kickoff 54 yards to the Eagle 39. On the next play, Williams caught the Eagles covering Monk with a linebacker and immediately hit him with the go-ahead touchdown pass. A 46-yard connection between Williams and Gary Clark set up the final score, a 40-yard field goal by Steve Cox. Normally the punter, Cox handled the placements after Jess Atkinson suffered a dislocated knee on an extra point attempt.

9/20/87	**FALCONS (1-1) 21, Redskins (1-1) 20**				63,567	
Was	7	0	6	7	-	20
Atl	7	0	7	7	-	21
Was	Bryant 17 pass from Williams (Haji-Sheikh kick)					
Atl	Dixon 22 pass from Campbell (Luckhurst kick)					
Was	Clark 18 pass from Williams (kick failed)					
Atl	Bailey 23 pass from Campbell (Luckhurst kick)					
Was	Monk 6 pass from Williams (Haji-Sheikh kick)					
Atl	Riggs 4 run (Luckhurst kick)					

Atlanta-Fulton County Stadium—Doug Williams' three touchdown passes in his first start for the Redskins went for naught as bad snaps by center Jeff Bostic on place kicks opened the door for Atlanta to take away the win.

The first two misfires by Bostic occurred late in the second half with the score tied at seven. Twice, newly acquired kicker Ali Haji-Sheikh had a shot at a mid-range field goal—he was roughed on the first attempt—and twice he couldn't get the boot away cleanly because of poor snaps.

The third time wasn't a charm, it was an omen. After Williams put the Redskins ahead 13-7 with an 18-yard touchdown pass to Gary Clark, Bostic's snap bounced behind holder Eric Yarber and the point after attempt was aborted.

"No excuses," said Bostic after the game. "It was just a bad operation all around today."

The Falcons drove in for the tying touchdown, a march that was kept alive when end Marcus Koch was flagged for roughing quarterback Scott Campbell after a third down sack. Mick Luckhurst got the extra point and Atlanta took a 14-13 lead.

Washington drove to take its final lead on Williams' scrambling, six-yard touchdown pass to Art Monk. This time the point after was good, but it would prove useless. The home team embarked on an 80-yard march, retaking the lead on Gerald Riggs' TD run on third and goal at the four and Luckhurst's point after. A final Washington drive went nowhere and Atlanta burned the final 4:43 off the clock.

Sep21

They're Out! NFL Players Go On Strike
Games will go on with replacement players, says league

ScabSkins: Beathard Signs 55 to Contracts

Sep 23—As it became apparent that the NFL players would go on strike following the second game of the season, Redskins General Manager Bobby Beathard got to work identifying players he would like to sign as replacements for the striking regulars. It wasn't a task he particularly relished, but one that he wanted to make sure he did well.

"Since the games will count, it's trying to qualify for the playoffs," said Beathard. "It's the same as always. It's a challenge to put a team on the field that can win."

As the players arrived for their first practice via a bus, they were greeted by the regular Redskins picketing in front of Redskins Park. Evidently, that really affected three of the replacements—they informed the team that they had changed their minds and weren't comfortable replacing the regular players. The Redskins thanked them for coming out and bought them plane tickets back home.

Regular lineman Dean Hamel recognized his former roommate Lionel Vitale out on the field practicing with the strike breakers. Hamel heckled the running back from afar. "Hey Lionel, remember me . . . your roommate?"

"We were roommates for a year and a half," Hamel said. "I bought the house, and he rented from me. We kept in touch. . . Now, he does this."

10-4-87	REDSKINS (2-1) 28, Cardinals (1-2) 21			27,728
StL	0	7	7	7	21
Was	7	7	14	0	28
Was	Allen 34 pass from Rubbert (Tobon kick)			
StL	Ferrell 1 run (Staurovsky kick)			
Was	Allen 88 pass from Rubbert (Tobin Kick			
StL	Ferrell 1 run (Staurovsky kick)			
Was	Vital 8 run (Tobin kick)			
Was	Allen 48 pass from Rubbert (Tobin kick)			
StL	P. Noga 60 interception return (Staurovsky kick)			

RFK Stadium—Nobody quite knew what to expect when the strike-replacement Redskins took the field for the first time. What everyone got was the Anthony Allen show. The wide receiver caught seven passes and set a club record with 255 yards receiving as the ScabSkins outlasted the Cardinals. St. Louis had 14 veteran players who had ignored the strike and crossed the picket line to play in this game.

Quarterback Ed Rubbert quickly established his favorite target, throwing a 34-yard touchdown pass to Allen late in the first quarter. That was the first of two first-half TD connections between those two. The second was an 88-yard bomb in the second

quarter against a Cardinal secondary that had no answer for Allen. The Cards did, however, have a response for the Rubbert-to-Allen quick strikes in the form of a solid running game that gained 167 yards on the day. Earl Ferrell's second one-yard touchdown push of the game even the score at 14 midway through the third quarter.

But Washington scored twice in the third to put it away. First it was Rubbert to Allen for 43 yards, this one not quite making it to the end zone. Lionel Vital took care of that, running it in from eight yards out. Then, from the St. Louis 48 after a short Cardinal punt, Rubbert threw his third touchdown pass of the day to—who else—Allen, giving the Redskins a 28-14 advantage.

In the fourth quarter, Cardinal linebacker Pete Noga made it a bit more interesting when he intercepted Rubbert's pass and scored on a 60-yard return to pull the visitors back within a touchdown. Three ensuing passes for St. Louis, however, came up empty, although the last one did reach the Washington five at the final gun.

10/11/87	Redskins (3-1) 38, GIANTS (0-4) 12			9,123
Was	3	21	7	7	38
NYG	3	0	9	0	12
NYG	FG Benyola 45			
Was	FG Ariri 22			
Was	W. Wilson 1 run (Ariri kick)			
Was	Vital 22 run (Ariri kick)			
Was	W. Wilson 3 run (Ariri kick)			
NYG	Lovelady 23 pass from Busch (kick failed)			
Was	T. Wilson 64 pass from Rubbert (Ariri kick)			
NYG	FG Benyola 20			
Was	Jessie 14 run (Ariri kick)			

Giants Stadium—Lionel Vital ran for 128 yards on 27 carries, including a 22-yard touchdown run, to spur the substitute Redskins to a win at the Meadowlands.

Both teams were playing without any strike-breaking veterans and the Giants sure could have used some. The home team, cheered on by some 67,000 empty seats in a dreary rainstorm, took a 3-0 lead in the first quarter. By halftime, however, the Redskins established their dominance. Wayne Wilson, picked up in the middle of the week, scored two touchdowns, both on short runs. In between, Vital cut back from the Giant 22, got behind guard Derrick Brilz—who took out two Giants with one block—and scampered into the end zone.

New York did pull to within 21-9 with a third-quarter touchdown, but the Redskins responded just over a minute later with a 64-yard touchdown strike from Ed Rubbert to Ted Wilson.

Not So Fast: Strike Ends, But Third Weekend With Replacements Will Go On

Oct 15—They struck as a team and today, they came back to work as a team—or they tried to, anyway.

Two and a half hours after reporting to practice, it was determined that they had missed the deadline for being able to play the next game, so they left. They were not happy, to say the least.

"The team made the decision to leave," said offensive guard R.C. Thielemann. "We didn't want to disrupt Coach Gibbs' practice. We came in because we wanted to challenge the deadline. We didn't think they had the right to tell us when we could play, but apparently they do."

The NFL management council had set 1 P.M. the previous day as the deadline for reporting for players to be eligible to participate this coming weekend. The Redskin players, seeing the futility of the strike, decided yesterday morning to report. The union asked them to wait another day, hoping to be able to settle the strike. The players complied, a decision that got them no settlement and cost them another week of pay.

It also cost the Redskins the opportunity to go into Dallas to play the Cowboys at full strength. Nine Cowboys who have crossed the picket lines, including quarterback Danny White, running back Tony Dorsett and defensive end Ed "Too Tall" Jones, will take the field against a Redskins team manned with 100 percent replacements.

10/19/87	Redskins (4-1) 13, COWBOYS (3-2) 7				60,415
Was	3	0	7	3	**13**
Dal	0	0	7	0	**7**
Was	FG Arari 19				
Was	Wilson 16 run (Arari kick)				
Dal	Edwards 38 pass from D. White (Brady kick)				
Was	FG Arari 39				

Texas Stadium—It's said that courage is when you are afraid, but you go into the fray anyway.

Facing a Dallas team with 11 strikebreaking veterans, including stars such as Randy White and Tony Dorsett as well as other key players like quarterback Danny White and defensive end Too Tall Jones, the replacement Redskins were certainly nervous going into this Monday night contest, but they went in anyway. Not one Redskins veteran had crossed the picket line.

During the week leading up to this game, as it became apparent that the strike would be settled, the Redskins veterans decided to report to play. The NFL, however, ruled that they had come in too late to be able to play that week. The replacements would take the field knowing that it would be for the last time.

Gibbs played that angle to motivate the team. "This is your final audition," the coach said of the Monday night stage that might provide them with an opportunity to show their abilities to scouts and general managers around the league.

Things went the Redskins' way early. Dorsett was stripped of the ball and the Redskins recovered at the Dallas 46, leading to an Obed Arari field goal. The Redskins were frustrated for a while after as quarterback Ed Rubbert left the game with a bruised shoulder, running back Lionel Vital lost a fumble at the Dallas five, and a field goal attempt by Arari from 43 yards hit the upright.

To the delight of Redskins fans, Dallas was doubly frustrated, unable to generate offense despite the presence of Dorsett and Danny White. The quarterback was sacked six times in the first half, Dorsett fumbled again and nothing was working. The first half ended with the Redskins up 3-0. Dallas had not run a play in Washington territory.

"We were disappointed we weren't up by more because we had really been outplaying them," said guard Dan Brilz.

After halftime, the Redskins found their stride. Tony Robinson, subbing for Rubbert, hit tight end Craig McEwen for 42 yards, Vital ran for 17 and receiver Ted Wilson went around left end 16 yards for the touchdown.

The drive allayed fears that Washington's chances were doomed without Rubbert. "When Ed got hurt, I thought we were in big trouble," said tight end Craig McEwen, "but Tony came in all calm, cool and collected. It was just like practice."

Dallas immediately responded with an 80-yard touchdown drive. But the Redskins took control of the clock and ground off over seven minutes before scoring on Arari's 38-yard FG with just over six minutes left to stretch the lead to 13-6. With slightly over two minutes left, the Cowboys started a drive from their own three. With just a few ticks left on the clock, they had made it down to the Washington 13. It was fourth and four.

In the huddle, over the din of 60,000 hostile fans, safety and defensive leader Skip Lane said, "This is our game to win or lose. We've got to win it right now. Play deep, tackle them in front of the goal line, and we win the game." For every player on the field, it would be their last NFL play and they knew it.

As White's pass hit receiver Kelvin Edwards' hands at the six, safety Joe Cofer hit Edwards and the ball bouncing on the Texas Stadium carpet touched off a wild celebration.

"It was kind of a miracle," Gibbs said.

And one courageous performance.

---

13 Replacement Players Will Stay

Oct 20—The Redskins announced that 13 strike-replacement players will stay on the team as the NFL resumes play on Sunday with expanded rosters due to the just-ended strike.

Notable on the list of players who will remain are record-setting receiver Anthony Allen and leading rusher Lionel Vitale. Ed Rubbert, who quarterbacked the replacement team to the first two wins in its 3-0 run, was placed on injured reserve.

Among those waived was quarterback Tony Robinson, who subbed for an injured Rubbert and led the Redskins to their improbable win over the veteran-laden Cowboys. "I didn't feel like this was a good place for him because of our quarterback situation," Washington Coach Joe Gibbs said of Robinson. "We're pretty solid at quarterback."

There are certain to be some hard feelings towards the replacements by the regulars. General Manager Bobby Beathard was not concerned. "It's something they'll have to accept," he said. "The coach runs the team."

10/25/87	REDSKINS (5-1) 17, Jets (3-3) 16				53,497
NYJ	0	3	10	3	**16**
Was	0	7	0	10	**17**
Was	Clark 20 pass from Schroeder (Haji-Sheikh kick)				
NYJ	FG Leahy 33				
NYJ	FG Leahy 23				
NYJ	Shuler 15 pass from O'Brien (Leahy kick)				
NYJ	FG Leahy 21				
Was	Bryant 2 pass from Schroeder (Haji-Sheikh kick)				
Was	FG Haji-Sheikh 28				

RFK Stadium—Returning after a four-week strike, the Redskins stumbled through this one, needing Ali Haji-Sheikh's game-winning field goal with 54 seconds to go to edge the Jets 17-16.

The Redskins took a 7-0 lead early in the second quarter on Jay Schroeder's 20-yard touchdown pass to Gary Clark. The offense went into hibernation for most of the next two quarters, entering Jet territory just twice for the balance of the second and all of the third.

Offering up a double dose of clichés, Schroeder said, "We were a little rusty. We didn't have everybody on the same page."

Fortunately, the Jets were not quite in synch either, but they did build a 16-7 lead on the strength of three Pat Leahy field goals and a 15-yard touchdown pass from Ken O'Brien to Mickey Shuler. A big factor in the Jets' inability to finish off drives was the Washington pass rush, led by Charles Mann. The Redskins sacked O'Brien seven times, with three of those being credited to Mann.

Leahy's third three-pointer came with 4:22 gone in the fourth quarter and woke up the Washington offense. So did the insertion of Kelvin Bryant at running back. He caught passes of 15, 39 and two yards to spur a 61-yard touchdown drive. The last one was good for a touchdown and the Redskins pulled within 16-14 after Haji-Sheikh's extra point.

Dave Butz's sack of O'Brien killed the Jets' ensuing drive and Washington got the ball back at its own 21 with 3:32 to play. On third and 10 from the Washington 32, Schroeder scrambled and found Ricky Sanders streaking down the left sideline. "I just looked up and saw the ball," said Sanders. "I was surprised to see it coming." Sanders recovered from the shock to snare the pass for a 39-yard gain to the New York 29.

Bryant ran for 14 yards to the 15 and, three plays later, Haji-Sheikh's kick was good with 54 seconds to go.

11/1/87	**Redskins (6-1) 27, BILLS (3-4) 7**			71, 640	
Was	3	14	10	0	**27**
Buf	0	0	0	7	**7**
Was	FG Haji-Sheikh 30				
Was	Bryant 12 pass from Schroeder (Haji-Sheikh kick)				
Was	Schroeder 13 run (Haji-Sheikh kick)				
Was	Bryant 7 pass from Schroeder (Haji-Sheikh kick)				
Was	FG Haji-Sheikh 33				
Buf	Reed 17 pass from Kelly (Norwood kick)				

Rich Stadium—The best way to keep an offense from scoring is to keep it off the field. The Redskins did just that to the vaunted Buffalo attack, led by quarterback Jim Kelly, by holding the ball for more than 40 minutes in an easy 27-7 win over the Bills.

George Rogers was the primary ball hog, lugging it 30 times for 125 time-consuming yards. The pattern emerged in the second quarter: Rogers would move the chains until the team got near the goal line before yielding to Kelvin Bryant, who would tally the points.

Early in the second from the Buffalo 12, the Bills apparently forgot about Bryant, who slipped out of the backfield to catch Jay Schroeder's pass for a touchdown and a 10-0 lead. Bryant got another six in the third quarter as he faked two Buffalo defenders onto the ground and twisted in to complete a seven-yard touchdown play. In between those scores, Schroeder got a TD on a 13-yard bootleg.

The Redskins outgained the Bills on the ground 299 yards to 21. Buffalo capitalized on its only threat, scoring on a 17-yard pass from Kelly to Andre Reed, but it was 27-0 by that time.

11/8/87	**EAGLES (4-4) 31, Redskins (6-2) 27**				66,398	
Was	7	14	0	6	-	**27**
Phi	7	10	0	14	-	**31**
Phi	Toney 5 run (McFadden kick)					
Was	Rogers 3 run (Haji-Sheikh kick)					
Was	Monk 19 pass from Schroeder (Haji-Sheikh kick)					
Was	Green 26 fumble recovery return (Haji-Sheikh kick)					
Phi	FG McFadden 37					
Phi	Quick 6 pass from Cunningham (McFadden kick)					
Phi	Quick 32 pass from Cunningham (McFadden kick)					
Was	Clark 47 pass from Schroeder (kick failed)					
Phi	Garrity 40 pass from Cunningham (McFadden kick)					

Veterans Stadium—Randall Cunningham's third touchdown pass of the day, a 40-yarder to Greg Garrity with 1:06 left in the game, lifted the Eagles to a come-from-behind win over the Redskins.

After the Eagles grabbed a 7-0 lead, Washington ran off 21 unanswered points. First George Rogers scored on a three yard run, culminating an 80-yard drive. Then Jay Schroeder led another drive of the same distance, using eight plays (all passes) with the last covering 19 yards to Art Monk for a touchdown and a 14-7 lead. Twenty seconds later, the Redskins were up 21-7 after Andrew Toney fumbled and Darrell Green scooped it up, dashing 26 yards into the end zone.

Philly battled back in the last three minutes of the half. First Roynell Young's interception of a Schroeder pass set up a 37-yard field goal by Paul McFadden. Then receiver Kenny Jackson won a battle with Barry Wilburn and hauled down a Randall Cunningham pass for a 53-yard gain, leading to Cunningham's six-yard TD pass to Mike Quick with just 14 seconds left to cut the lead to 21-17 at the half.

The scoring pace slowed considerably in the third quarter as the quality of Schroeder's play deteriorated significantly. He didn't complete a pass in the period and was on his way to a dismal 16 of 46 performance with two interceptions. The quarterback berated

his contributions afterwards. "There was nothing you could call most of it but stupid, stupid throws. I'll take the heat."

Despite his difficulties, Schroeder did manage to answer Cunningham's second touchdown toss to Quick, this one from 32 yards midway through the fourth quarter. With two and a half minutes left, Schroeder almost couldn't help but complete the 47-yard touchdown to Gary Clark, given that Clark was several yards behind the Eagle defense. The point after was missed and Washington's lead was 27-24 with 2:29 to play.

But the Eagles pulled it out. From the Redskin 40, Garrity got past nickel back Tim Morrison. The defensive back compounded the problem when he made a weak try for an interception on a ball well over his head rather than focusing on tackling Garrity. The receiver made the catch and coasted in for the game winner with 1:06 to play.

Grimm Reality: Center Out Four Weeks

Nov 9—There was bad news for two old Hogs today.

Center Russ Grimm found out the knee injury he suffered in the fourth quarter of Sunday's loss to Philadelphia will require arthroscopic surgery. He will be sidelined for at least four weeks.

Then Jeff Bostic found out that he wouldn't be taking Grimm's spot. Left guard Raleigh McKenzie will slide over into the center spot and Ed Simmons will start at guard. Offensive line coach Joe Bugel said that Bostic would back up both McKenzie and Simmons.

11/15/87	**REDSKINS (7-2) 20, Lions (2-7) 13**				53,593	
Det	3	0	10	0		**13**
Was	0	17	3	0		**20**
Det	FG Murray 40					
Was	FG Haji-Sheikh 33					
Was	Bryant 16 pass from Williams (Haji-Sheikh kick)					
Was	Clark 42 pass from Williams (Haji-Sheikh kick)					
Det	FG Murray 41					
Was	FG Haji-Sheikh 41					
Det	Bernard 2 run (Murray kick)					

RFK Stadium—A simmering quarterback controversy boiled over as Doug Williams replaced an ineffective Jay Schroeder midway through the second quarter and threw two touchdown passes to lead the Redskins to the win.

The game was tied 3-3 with exactly seven minutes left in the first half when Joe Gibbs, going with his "gut feeling," made the switch. Gibbs' gut is generally accurate and this was no exception. On his first possession, Williams led an 80-yard touchdown drive that he capped with a 16-yard touchdown pass to Kelvin Bryant. Then, with time running out in the half, he moved them 61 yards for another touchdown. The bulk of the yardage on the drive came on the payoff, a 42-yard TD from Williams to Gary Clark to put Washington up 17-3 with 27 seconds left.

Williams and the Washington offense cooled down considerably after intermission and Detroit had some opportunities to tie the game after Karl Bernard scored on a two-yard run late in the third quarter. In fact, most of the fourth period was played in Washington territory, but a pair of interceptions stopped Lion incursions inside the 20. Barry Wilburn got the first and Darrell Green made a diving, game saving steal with 1:04 to play. It was Green's third interception of the game.

Nov 16

QB Controversy Becomes Full Blown as Gibbs Announces Williams as Starter
Maybe for one game, maybe for rest of season, says coach

11/23/87	**Rams (3-7) 30, REDSKINS (7-3) 26**				53,614
LARm	14	9	7	0	**30**
Was	9	7	3	7	**26**
LARm	Wilcher 35 fumble recovery return (Lansford kick)				
Was	Monk 17 pass from Williams (kick failed)				
Was	FG Haji-Sheikh 22				
LARm	Brown 95 kickoff return (Lansford kick)				
LARm	FG Lansford 37				
LARm	White 1 run (kick failed)				
Was	FG Haji-Sheikh 29				
LARm	Brown 26 pass from Everett (Lansford kick)				
Was	Monk 5 pass from Williams				

RFK Stadium—The Rams feasted on Redskin mistakes, many of them coming on special teams, to pull off an upset 30-26 win.

The first Redskin blunder was on offense and came on their first series. Doug Williams was sacked and stripped by LA's Gary Jeter and the ball bounced straight to linebacker Mike Wilcher. He accepted the gift and ran 35 yards for a 7-0 lead.

The Redskins recovered, driving to Williams' 17-yard touchdown pass to Art Monk and a 22-yard field Ali Haji-Sheikh field goal. The point after attempt following the touchdown was missed and the Redskins led 9-7. After the three-pointer, though, Ron Brown took the kickoff and showed off his Olympic gold medal winning speed as he flashed through the coverage for 95 yards and a touchdown. With no first downs on their ledger and just six yards of offense, the Rams led 14-9.

Jim Everett then got some offense going for LA, moving them 51 yards to a Mike Lansford field goal. Then another special teams breakdown cost the Redskins six. Nolan Cromwell broke through and blocked a Steve Cox punt and the Rams had possession at the Washington two. They scored on Charles White's one-yard plunge but returned the favor by missing the extra point and led 23-9 with just over four minutes left in the half.

Williams pulled his team back within a touchdown before intermission with a 62-yard pass to Monk that set up the QB's one-yard scoring run. In the third quarter, though, Los Angeles answered a field goal by Haji-Sheikh with a 26-yard touchdown pass from Everett to Brown, pushing their margin up to 11 points.

On the first play of the fourth quarter, Williams threw a five-yard touchdown pass to Monk to pull the home team within four. Alvin Walton intercepted an Everett pass in the end zone to keep it within reach, but the Redskins couldn't quite pull it out. They moved to the Ram 14 with 29 seconds left. Two Williams passes found Monk's hands in the end zone, but the first was poked out at the last instant and the second bounced out of the receiver's hands and into those of cornerback LeRoy Irvin.

With Williams Hurt, Gibbs Turns to Jay

November 28—With quarterback Doug Williams ailing with a back injury, Joe Gibbs has decided to turn back to Jay Schroeder to face the Giants on Sunday.

Williams said he could play if he had to but that his back was "not 100 percent." He will not be on the active roster for the Giants game.

11/29/87	**REDSKINS (8-3) 23, Giants (3-8) 19**				45,815
NYG	10	6	3	0	**19**
Was	0	0	9	14	**23**
NYG	FG Allegre 24				
NYG	Bavaro 30 pass from Simms (Allegre kick)				
NYG	FG Allegre 42				
NYG	FG Allegre 30				
Was	FG Haji-Sheikh 45				
NYG	FG Allegre 45				
Was	Clark 34 pass from Schroeder (kick failed)				
Was	Griffin 6 pass from Schroeder (Haji-Sheikh kick)				
Was	Sanders 28 pass from Schroeder (Haji-Sheikh kick)				

RFK Stadium—"We were better after halftime," said guard R. C. Thielemann. He was referring to his unit, the offensive line, but the statement pertained to the entire team as the Redskins rallied from a 16-0 halftime deficit to beat the Giants 23-19. Jay Schroeder completed just 12 passes but they were good for 331 yards and three touchdowns.

New York marched up and down the field during the first 30 minutes, but had to settle for field goals three times, broaching the end zone just once on Phil Simms' 30-yard touchdown pass to Mark Bavaro. They would pay for their inability to get six instead of three. It would take a while, though.

In the third quarter, the teams exchanged field goals before Schroeder completed four of four passes for 72 yards in a lightning-quick TD drive. The last throw was a 34-yard TD pass to Gary Clark and, although the point after was missed, the Redskins were back in it at 19-9 going into the final quarter.

Solid defense helped the Redskins survive two turnovers early in the fourth quarter before Schroeder took control. From the New York 49, he went five for five to push the home team to another TD, this one on a six-yard toss to a wide-open Keith Griffith.

The go-ahead score was to another receiver that was virtually uncovered: Ricky Sanders. From the Giant 28, Schroeder got it off just as he was being smashed to the ground by defense end Leonard Marshall. "I got awfully nervous waiting for that pass to drop," said Sanders. "It hung up there forever."

Eventually, it came down into Sanders' arms and the Redskins led 23-19. New York wasn't done yet as they drove to the Washington 18 with two seconds left. Simms couldn't find anyone open in the end zone, so he dumped off to running back Tony Galbreath at the nine. He made it to the two, but cornerback Dennis Woodberry met him there and slowed him until the rest of the defense arrived.

12/6/87	**REDSKINS (9-3) 34, Cardinals (5-7) 17**				31,324
Was	10	0	21	3	**34**
StL	0	14	3	0	**17**
Was	Clark 84 pass from Schroeder (Haji-Sheikh kick)				
Was	FG Haji-Sheikh 22				
StL	Mitchell 3 pass from Lomax (Gallery kick)				
StL	Smith 4 pass from Lomax (Gallery kick)				
StL	FG Gallery 48				
Was	Schroeder 7 run (Haji-Sheikh kick)				
Was	Rogers 6 run (Haji-Sheikh kick)				
Was	Didier 19 pass from Schroeder (Haji-Sheikh kick)				
Was	FG Haji-Sheikh 40				

Busch Stadium—In a contest of scoring runs, the Redskins had the final one, scoring the game's last 24 points to clinch the NFC East title with a 34-17 win over the Cardinals.

The Redskins did only a couple of things right in the first half, but they were enough to keep them in the game. Late in the first quarter Jay Schroeder let fly with an 84-yard touchdown bomb to Gary Clark. Shortly after that, they forced a fumble from the Cards' J. T. Smith and got a 22-yard field goal from Ali Haji-Sheikh out of it.

Quarterback Neil Lomax and the St. Louis offense came alive in the second period. Lomax had been sacked three times in the first quarter, but kept his feet under him this period and threw two short TD passes to push his team into a 14-10 halftime lead.

"We were mad in the locker room at halftime," Clark said. "Coach Gibbs didn't throw any chairs, but I know I threw a few."

The airborne seats didn't do much good initially. A field goal early in the second half, set up by Clark's fumble, gave the Cardinals a seven-point lead. After that, though, the Redskins got it going.

It took a bit of good fortune to jump start the dormant offense. It appeared the drive following that field goal was over before it began when Art Monk dropped Schroeder's third-down pass.

However, tackle Mark May goaded linebacker Freddie Joe Nunn into a personal foul penalty and Schroeder completed his next four passes to get to the St. Louis seven. From there, he scored on a quarterback draw to tie it up at 17.

On the ensuing kickoff, Vernon Dean separated returner Ronnie McAdoo from the ball and Brian Davis recovered for the Skins, returning the ball to the Cardinal 16. Three straight handoffs to George Rogers followed, the last resulting in a six-yard touchdown to put the Washington in the lead for good. The Redskins forced a three and out and proceeded to put it away with a 75-yard touchdown drive. The payoff came on Schroeder's 19-yard touchdown pass to Clint Didier.

Dexter Being Dexter

December 9—Holding court with a group of reporters, Dexter Manley spoke about a wide variety of people from heads of state to team owners. His remarks were playfully disparaging to most of them, with the notable exception of the coach of the team he loves to hate.

When asked about Ronald Reagan and Michael Gorbachev and their ongoing summit meeting, Manley said that the whole town in an uproar because Gorbachev is here. "It's slowing things down. I wish he'd get the hell out of town. The Redskins-Cowboys game is bigger than what happens at the summit."

Dallas owner Bum Bright came under Dexter's fire for recently ripping Cowboy coach Tom Landry. Manley, a Houston native, said he'd like "to get a pair of cowboy boots and kick [Bright] in the butt for that one. That would show him what real Texans are like."

The only kind words Manley had to dole out were for Landry. He's "a man I respect," said Manley. As to the Cowboys' recent struggles (they have lost three straight games), he said, "Landry don't go out and play. He's just doing the best he can with what he has."

Not that his respect for Landry made him any less desirous of beating the coach's team, mind you.

"I'd like for us to kick them while they're down," he said

12/13/87	REDSKINS (10-3) 24, Cowboys (5-8) 20				54,882
Dal	3	0	10	7	**20**
Was	7	10	7	0	**24**
Was	Rogers 1 run (Haji-Sheikh kick)				
Dal	FG Ruzek 22				
Was	FG Haji-Sheikh 31				
Was	Clark 56 pass from Schroeder (Haji-Sheikh kick)				
Was	Rogers 1 run (Haji-Sheikh kick)				
Dal	FG Ruzek 37				
Dal	Renfro 25 pass from D. White (Ruzek kick)				
Dal	Barksdale 5 pass from D. White (Ruzek kick)				

RFK Stadium—The Redskins built a 24-3 lead and then disappeared for the final 25 minutes. It took a questionable decision by Tom Landry to go for it on fourth down at the Washington 20 early in the fourth quarter, a four-minute debate over the replay to uphold a Barry Wilburn interception for Washington, a full-scale donnybrook, and a personal foul on Dallas' Bill Bates that kept the Skins' final possession going for the Redskins to get out of this one alive.

"It's one of those wins you're not sure what to say, but you're sure happy you won the game," said Joe Gibbs.

The Redskins went up 7-0 after Herschel Walker fumbled the ball away at his own 25. Jay Schroeder threw to Gary Clark, down to the one. It took George Rogers two tries to bull it over from there.

After Dallas responded with a field goal, Washington proceeded to pad its lead. After Ali Haji-Sheikh kicked a 31-yard field goal, Schroeder again connected with Clark, this time with a 56-yard bomb for a touchdown and a 17-3 lead. Short after

halftime, the Redskins drove to another short Rogers TD and they were cruising at 24-3.

Or at least that appeared to be the case. But, after a Dallas field goal, Clark fumbled after making a reception and, working from the Washington 28, Danny White soon threw a 25-yard touchdown pass to Mike Renfro. It was 24-13 going into what proved to be a wild fourth quarter.

First, with 13:14 to play, Landry decided to go for it on fourth and four from the Washington 20. White's pass to tight end Doug Cosbie was incomplete.

Then, midway through the period, it took the officials nearly four minutes to determine whether or not Barry Wilburn had intercepted a deep White pass. They finally awarded possession to the Redskins.

Dallas regained possession and drove for a touchdown. The play was mundane—a simple five-yard pass from White to Rod Barksdale. But the aftermath was not, resulting in a full-scale brawl. The catalyst was a tussle between Dallas tackle Daryle Smith and Dexter Manley, but the epicenter turned out to be a clash between White and Neal Olkewicz.

"It was all Olkewicz's fault," White said. "There's no place for that on the football field. It was a cheap shot."

Said Olkewicz: "I just went in to knock him off and all hell broke loose."

The touchdown came with 2:42 left, but there was still time for one more controversy. As the Redskins were killing the clock, Rogers gained several inches on third and a few inches. Landry was incensed that the officials did not call for a measurement. He was asked why he didn't request one.

"It's just amazing that you don't measure it," Landry said. "Whether I asked for it or not. That's just foolishness."

No, foolishness was what Bates did after the Cowboys had stopped the Redskins on the next third down. He jumped onto the pile, giving the Redskins a fist down and they killed the clock.

12/20/87	DOLPHINS (8-6) 23, Redskins (10-4) 21				65,715
Was	0	7	7	7	**21**
Mia	0	9	0	14	**23**
Mia	FG Reveiz 48				
Was	Bryant 6 run (Haji-Sheikh kick)				
Mia	Duper 26 pass from Marino (kick failed)				
Was	Schroeder 6 run (Haji-Sheikh kick)				
Mia	Duper 59 pass from Marino (Reveiz kick)				
Was	Rogers 2 run (Haji-Sheikh kick)				
Mia	Duper 6 pass from Marino (Reveiz kick)				

Joe Robbie Stadium—The last six of Dan Marino's 393 passing yards were good for the game-winning touchdown on a throw to Mark Duper with 1:07. That score accounted for the game's fifth lead change, the third of the fourth quarter.

After Miami went on top 3-0 in the second quarter, it took the Redskins just two minutes to respond. Jay Schroeder launched a 55-yard completion to Clarence Verdin, leading to a six-yard touchdown run by Kelvin Bryant. Before the half was out, the Dolphins put together a quick drive with the final 55 of the 70 yards covered with two Marino passes, the second to Duper for 26 yards and the touchdown. The extra point was missed and the Dolphins led 9-7 at intermission.

It stayed that way until 5:46 remained in the third quarter when Schroeder capped a 78-yard drive with a six-yard touchdown run on a bootleg. Leading 14-9, the Redskins mounted another impressive march, but Paul Lankford intercepted Schroeder's pass in the end zone to end the threat.

Soon after that, Miami reclaimed the lead as Duper caught Marino's pass in stride at the Washington 40, broke through two attempted tackles and was gone for 56 yards and the touchdown. This time, the point after was good and it was 16-14 a minute and a half into the fourth quarter.

The Redskins responded quickly, maybe a bit too quickly. They might have burned off more time, but they were handed 30 yards after Schroeder scrambled for 16 yards. Miami's Bud Brown was penalized for 15 yards for spearing the Washington quarterback at the end of the play and then got hit with another 15 when he pushed the official while protesting the call. That set up a first down at the Miami 15 and George Rogers scored four plays later.

Miami's game winner came at the end of an 80-yard drive. The Redskins almost had the drive ended when, on second down at the Washington 17, Todd Bowles had a Marino pass in his hands. However, Barry Wilburn was nearby and ran into Bowles, knocking the ball to the ground. Two plays later, Marino went to Duper to give Miami the lead. A desperation 67-yard field goal attempt on the game's final play was well short.

12/26/87	Redskins (11-4) 27, VIKINGS (8-7) 24 (OT)				59,160	
Was	0	7	7	10	3	27
Min	7	0	17	0		24
Min	Anderson 9 run (C. Nelson kick)					
Was	Wilburn 100 interception return (Haji-Sheikh kick)					
Was	Sanders 46 pass from Williams (Haji-Sheikh kick)					
Min	Anderson 1 run (C. Nelson kick)					
Min	Wilson 1 run (C. Nelson kick)					
Min	FG C. Nelson 20					
Was	FG Haji-Sheikh 37					
Was	Sanders 51 pass from Williams (Haji-Sheikh kick)					
Was	FG Haji-Sheikh 26					

The Metrodome—Doug Williams replaced an ineffective Jay Schroeder at quarterback and, along with Barry Wilburn and Ricky Sanders, sparked a 27-24 overtime win over the Vikings.

Williams entered the game midway through the third quarter with the contest tied at seven. Washington's only score had come courtesy of Wilburn. The Vikings, already leading 7-0, were driving, perched at the Redskin seven. Quarterback Wade Wilson tried to sneak a pass through double coverage, but he found the belly of Wilburn at the goal line. Wilburn headed upfield, broke through the pack and got into the clear. The final obstacle to his team-record 100-yard interception return was removed when Todd Bowles dispatched receiver Anthony Carter with a block around the Minnesota 40.

Williams had an instant impact, throwing a 46-yard touchdown pass to Sanders on his fourth play to put his team up 14-7. After that things cooled for the Redskins and heated up considerably for Minnesota. Starting with the first play of the fourth quarter, the Vikings ran off 17 points in five and a half minutes of play and the Metrodome was rocking as the home team led 24-14.

The Redskins responded quickly, driving to a field goal by Ali Haji-Sheikh to cut the lead to seven. Then, with 2:21 to play, they regained possession at their own 40. On third and one at the 49, Sanders ran a hitch-and-go and was wide open to catch Williams' pass for 51 yards, tying the game at 24. Haji-Sheikh missed a potential game-winning 33-yard field goal attempt in the final minute and the game went into overtime.

The Vikings never saw the ball in the OT. Washington won the toss and Sanders returned the kickoff 36 yards. Sanders then caught two passes for 32 yards to key a foray down inside the Minnesota 10. Joe Gibbs immediately called for Haji-Sheikh, who displayed the kicker's best friend—a short memory—as he ended it by drilling it through from 26 yards.

Dec 30

Gibbs Makes 5th QB Change
Williams gets the nod for playoffs

Bostic Happy to be Back in Lineup

Jan 6—Just weeks ago, it appeared the writing was on the wall for center Jeff Bostic. He was starting games on the bench and finishing many of them there, too. Even an injury to Russ Grimm couldn't elevate Bostic into the first team as the Redskins shuffled other players around to fill the gap. After some long-snapping woes, the team brought in someone off the street to replace Bostic in that capacity. There were whispers, rather loud at times, that Bostic was being pushed out the door by the organization.

As the coaches started to get the team ready for a playoff run, however, they decided to give Bostic, a man with one Super Bowl and one NFC Championship ring, a shot due to his experience. He hasn't disappointed and while Grimm is ready to play, it's Bostic who will be snapping the ball while Grimm is a reserve.

"Seven or eight weeks ago, you've got to think you're trade material, or this is it," Bostic said. "I just tried to keep a positive attitude through it all. I kept telling myself that I was always only one play away from playing."

"I hope I've proved something to them," Bostic said. "I've never felt you have to weigh 280 or 290 to play on the offensive line."

The coaches are in agreement, at least for now.

Manley, Ditka Exchange Barbs

January 7—It all started earlier in the week when somebody told Bears coach Mike Ditka that Redskins defensive end Dexter Manley thought he was a bum. Ditka replied, "Dexter Manley has the IQ of a grapefruit."

Manley denied calling Ditka a bum, but he had no kind words for him, either. "A guy like Mike Ditka, with that ugly face of his, he's one of those guys you have to be able to put up with," Manley said.

"I've got something for him; I've got a case of grapefruit for him. Mike Ditka is a broad, man, he's a broad."

Manley then set his sights on bigger targets. "When we put our minds together, we can beat anybody, even the Russians. Mikhail Gorbachev, we can beat him."

NFC Divisional Playoff
Sunday, January 10, 1988
Soldier Field
Chicago, Illinois

1/10/88	Redskins 21, BEARS 17				65,268
Was	0	14	7	0	21
Chi	7	7	3	0	17
Chi	Thomas 2 run (Butler kick)				
Chi	Morris 14 pass from McMahon (Butler kick)				
Was	Rogers 3 run (Haji-Sheikh kick)				
Was	Didier 18 pass from Williams (Haji-Sheikh kick)				
Was	Green 53 punt return (Haji-Sheikh kick)				
Chi	FG Butler 25				

The Redskins and Bears faced off in a rematch of the previous season's divisional playoff. In that matchup, also played in Soldier Field, Washington had stunned the defending champs to earn a ticket to the NFC title game in New York.

This time, the stakes were a bit higher. The wild card Minnesota Vikings had upset the 49ers the previous day, and the winner of this game between the Central and Eastern division champions would host the NFC title game. It was perfect Midwest football weather: a cold, sunny day where every breath was visible.

The Bears jumped to a 14-0 lead and appeared headed to revenge. But Doug Williams, who had just nailed down the starting quarterback job, had other ideas.

A 32-yard pass from Williams to Ricky Sanders set up a three-yard George Rogers scoring run, and the Redskins tied it before halftime with an 18-yard Williams to Clint Didier touchdown pass.

Bears quarterback Jim McMahon started to find the going a bit tougher when Charles Mann started taking up residence in the Chicago backfield. Mann had three of the Redskins five sacks of McMahon and the Redskins were in control. Then Cap Boso became part of Redskins history.

In the third quarter of a tie game, Darrell Green fielded a punt at his own 48. It appeared that Boso would either tackle Green or knock him out of bounds at around the Bears' 30. That was until Green hurdled the would-be defender and, while in the air, changed direction back to the middle of the field.

The jaw-dropping move cost Green a torn rib cartridge that would keep him out the rest of the game, but it gained the Redskins the go-ahead touchdown as he glided into the end zone, clutching both the ball and his rib cage. Washington had a 21-14 lead. All Chicago could muster was a field goal later in the third period. Washington was headed home to host the NFC title game.

January 11
Monk Out, Green Probable for NFC Title Game
Monk's knee not responding;
Green's ribs still painful

NFC Championship Game
Sunday, January 17, 1988
RFK Stadium
Washington, D.C.

1/17/88	REDSKINS 17, Vikings 10				55,212
Min	0	7	0	3	10
Was	7	0	3	7	17
Was	Bryant 43 pass from Williams (Haji-Sheikh kick)				
Min	Lewis 23 pass from Wilson (C. Nelson kick)				
Was	FG Haji-Sheikh 28				
Min	FG C. Nelson 18				
Was	Clark 7 pass from Williams (Haji-Sheikh kick)				

Joe Gibbs is a humble, religious man and it's doubtful he would trouble God by asking Him for anything as insignificant as a victory in a football game. But there is the vivid mental picture of Joe Gibbs kneeling on the sidelines as the Vikings faced a fourth down at the Washington six. Fifty six seconds remained and the Redskins were clinging to a 17-10 lead. Whether or not divine intervention was involved, Wade Wilson's pass bounced out of Darrin Nelson's hands at the goal line, and the win was preserved.

It probably shouldn't have been that close. When Doug Williams (9-26, 119 yards) wasn't being victimized by drops, he was overthrowing open receivers. Ali Haji-Sheikh missed two field goals. The Redskins were able to get a running game going with rookie Timmy Smith gaining 72 yards on 13 carries.

The Washington defense deserves the credit for this one. They held Minnesota to 76 yards on the ground and the linebacking corps came up with critical plays in the second half. Mel Kaufman intercepted a pass deflected by Dave Butz, setting up Haji-Sheikh's go-ahead field goal in the third quarter. Neal Olkewicz dove in to pile drive running back DJ Dozier backwards just inches short of the goal line on third and goal with 11 minutes left in the game. The Vikings went for the field goal to tie it up at 10.

The Redskins took the lead as Williams found Gary Clark twice, once for 43 yards and moments later, on a broken pattern,

---

for seven yards and the winning touchdown with just over five minutes left. All that was left was to pray the defense could hold on.

Williams Handles Media Circus With Class
January 26—The words "chaos," "mob scene" and "zoo" are often used to describe media day at the Super Bowl. When it came to the group surrounding the Redskins' Doug Williams, though, those terms did not do the scene justice. It was just plain crazy.

Williams did a great job of turning the ridiculous—one reporter tried to start a question by saying, "Doug, you've obviously been a black quarterback all your life," before laughter drowned out the rest of his query—into the sublime.

"All this talk about it bothers me," said Williams. "But what's a guy to do? I know a lot of people want me to elaborate on it."

"But I don't think it is something that should be hit on as much as it has been. The bottom line is: Who is the quarterback and what did he do? Not what color he is."

He tried to turn the topic from being a black quarterback into quarterbacking in general. Answering criticism that he didn't play well in the NFC title game against Minnesota, where he went 9 for 26 passing, he said, "I feel if you're 9 for 26 and throw no interceptions and don't get sacked, that's a good day if you win."

Jan 27
Youth Movement? Coaches Mull Starting Rookie Timmy Smith at RB

Jan 28
Monk Ready to Go For Super Bowl

Sunday, January 31, 1988
Jack Murphy Stadium
San Diego, California

1/31/88	Redskins 42, Broncos 10				73,302
Was	0	35	0	7	42
Den	10	0	0	0	10
Den	Nattiel 56 pass from Elway (Karlis kick)				
Den	FG Karlis 24				
Was	Sanders 80 pass from Williams (Haji-Sheikh kick)				
Was	Clark 27 pass from Williams (Haji-Sheikh kick)				
Was	Smith 58 run (Haji-Sheikh kick)				
Was	Sanders 50 pass from Williams (Haji-Sheikh kick)				
Was	Didier 8 pass from Williams (Haji-Sheikh kick)				
Was	Smith 4 run (Haji-Sheikh kick)				

At the end of the first quarter of Super Bowl XXII, the game was playing out exactly as the pundits hyping John Elway as a one-man team had thought.

On Elway's very first play from scrimmage, he went deep to receiver Ricky Nattiel for a 56-yard touchdown. On Elway's second possession, it was Elway again—this time catching a pass from RB Steve Sewell to set up a field goal for Elway's team to make it 10-0.

While the Elways, actually the Denver Broncos, stalled offensively their next two possessions, the Redskins' offense sputtered too. It seemed to be only a matter of time before The Great Elway would put the Redskins away.

Then Washington took possession at its own 20 with a minute gone in the second quarter or, as it came to be called, The Quarter.

"It was the finest quarter of football I've ever been associated with," said Joe Gibbs. Coaches sometimes exaggerate, but not here.

Williams had gone out with a twisted knee the previous series, but he returned here. After a week of hype about being the first black man ever to start at quarterback in a Super Bowl—and enduring questions like "Have you been a black quarterback all your life?"—it was time for Williams, the other signal caller in this game, to shine.

The play that got The Quarter started wasn't supposed to be a bomb; it was a seven-yard pattern called Charley Hitch. "It wasn't a deep call," said Williams. "Ricky just felt the pressure (from cornerback Mark Haynes) and adjusted. He blew by him." Williams hit the receiver in stride at midfield and Sanders ran untouched for the score. Score 10-7 Denver, drive 80 yards, one play, 10 seconds.

Denver went three and out and Washington took over at its own 36. After Timmy Smith, a surprise starter at running back, gained 19 yards on a second down run, Williams hit receiver Gary Clark on an out pattern at the goal line. Score 14-10 Washington, drive 64 yards, five plays, 2:44.

"Doug was hitting everything," said Clark. "That helped open Timmy up."

Denver missed a field goal before Smith took a handoff and burst off the right side. Tackle Joe Jacoby sealed off the inside and Smith was off to the races. Fortunately, he was racing Denver's Tony Lilly, a slow-footed safety. Smith easily won the duel and got down the sideline for the 58-yard touchdown run. Score 21-10, drive 74 yards, two plays, 51 seconds.

Denver went three and out again and the Redskins went sixty yards on three passes, all of them intended for Sanders. The first was overthrown, but the next two found their targets. After gathering in one for a 10-yard gain to midfield, Sander fielded Williams' perfect strike in stride at the ten and coasted in for the score. The scoreboard read 28-10, drive 60 yards, three plays, 52 seconds.

After the Broncos punted, Smith tore off 43 yards into Denver territory. Williams took it from there, going to Sanders twice for 21 then seven yards. From the seven he hit tight end Clint Didier in the back of the end zone for the TD. Score 35-10, drive 79 yards, seven plays, 1:10.

The Redskins intercepted Elway with seven seconds left in the half, but Williams took a knee to end The Quarter. In just 5:47 of possession time and 18 plays, the Redskins gained 357 yards and ran up the most points ever scored in one quarter of a postseason game. Smith gained 122 yards on the ground and Williams passed for 228 yards, 168 of them to Sanders.

The Redskins rooters who had gathered in San Diego found themselves hoarse from singing "Hail to the Redskins" so many times in such a short period of time. The Elway fans, vocal in the game's opening minutes, had no such problems.

If it was a prizefight, they would have called it here, but NFL rules required that the teams take the field for the second half. After all, there were all of those expensive commercials that had to be run.

All that remained was for Smith to run up his rushing yardage total to 204, a Super Bowl record; for Sanders to gain the rest of his Super Bowl record 193 receiving yards; and for Williams to be announced as the game's MVP.

The Redskin defense made sure the Broncos didn't mount a miracle of their own, pounding Elway often and shutting down his team.

"I was blessed," said Williams afterward. "The rest of the team and its fans felt the same way.

Jan 31

Packers Want to Talk to Gibbs
Redskins coach has one year left on contract

Feb 3

600,000 Hail Redskins in Parade
Reagan greets team at White House, tosses pass to Sanders

1988
Head Coach: Joe Gibbs
Record: 7-9, Third in NFC East

Honors: Charles Mann Pro Bowl, Mark May Pro Bowl

Bear Trap: Redskins Land Bears LB Marshall

Mar 13—The newest—and richest—Redskin met the media today and tried hard to emphasize that he would fit in with a team known for having a blue-collar reputation.

Linebacker Wilber Marshall, formerly of the Bears, said, "If I can help them get (back to the Super Bowl) by playing as hard as I can, I will."

Chicago declined to match an offer sheet that the free agent linebacker signed with Washington. As compensation, the Bears will receive Washington's first-round picks in each of the next two drafts.

"I just want to be the best player I can be. I know I have to earn (my teammates') respect and I hope I can help them win. I think I can help out here. I'll play in any set they want me to. I want to learn the system as quickly as possible."

Marshall, who will earn $6 million over the next five years, tried to downplay the money issue as much as possible.

"I try not to worry about other people's salaries, and I don't think the players care about that," Marshall said. "They care about winning."

Smith Wants to Show Super Bowl Was No Fluke

July 21—Timmy Smith came out of nowhere in Super Bowl XXII to rush for a record 204 yards and two touchdowns to help the Redskins smash the Denver Broncos and take the NFL championship. He now wants to make sure that he doesn't return from whence he came.

According to running backs coach Don Breaux, Smith has a good shot at the starting position. "I'd say right now Timmy has the edge," Washington running backs coach Don Breaux said.

Mindful of the competition—Kelvin Bryant, Keith Griffin and three drafted running backs—Smith decided to nix a notion advanced by his agent that he hold out for a raise over his $90,000 salary.

"I never thought about holding out," Smith said. "I felt like I had to come in and get some work done. I don't want to dwell on the Super Bowl, I want to come in and start working early, just to get a jump."

Offensive Line Shuffle: Thielemann Odd Man Out?

July 29—Four players. Three jobs. Someone is going to get left without a seat when the music stops.

For most of camp, the interior of the offensive line has lined up with Raleigh McKenzie, Jeff Bostic, and R.C. Thielemann from left to right as the starters and Russ Grimm as the primary backup. But that is about to change. It's good news for Grimm and bad news for Thielemann.

"I'm going to start working Grimm at right guard with R.C.," said Redskins' offensive line coach Joe Bugel. "I want to give R.C. as much of a blow as possible since he's in his twelfth season."

That's not something a player like Thielemann likes to hear. "A blow" can quickly turn into a permanent seat on the bench, especially when the guy giving you the rest is a three-time Pro Bowl performer.

"As the season rolls along, inevitably one guy gets hurt, and the other guy is going to get playing time," Thielemann said. "I don't think there will ever be a season where the five guys who started on the line go the whole time without getting hurt."

Wish Granted: Unhappy QB Schroeder Dealt to Raiders for OT Jim Lachey

Sep 4—The long-rumored trade of Jay Schroeder to the Raiders has finally become a reality with the disgruntled second-string quarterback going to Los Angeles in exchange for offensive tackle Jim Lachey and multiple conditional draft picks.

The Redskins wanted a first-round pick in exchange for Schroeder, who made the Pro Bowl following the 1986 season, but the Raiders had traded it away. Washington was happy to settle for Lachey.

"In Jim Lachey, we have a Pro Bowl offensive lineman, who is capable of playing either guard or tackle," said general manager Bobby Beathard. "He should be a dominant force in the NFL for many years."

9/5/88	GIANTS (1-0) 27, Redskins (0-1) 20				76,417
Was	6	7	0	7	20
NYG	0	3	10	14	27
Was	FG Lohmiller 28				
Was	FG Lohmiller 25				
Was	Sanders 29 pass from Williams (Lohmiller kick)				
NYG	FG Allegre 23				
NYG	Morris 9 run (Allegre kick)				
NYG	FG Allegre 32				
NYG	Flynn 27 blocked punt return (Allegre kick)				
NYG	Burt 39 fumble return (Allegre kick)				
Was	Bryant 19 pass from Williams (Lohmiller kick)				

Giants Stadium—The Redskins held a 13-0 lead until the end of the first half, but New York rallied with two return touchdowns, one on special teams and one on defense, to take the game away in the fourth quarter.

After two Chip Lohmiller field goals gave the visitors a 6-0 lead, Doug Williams and Ricky Sanders teamed up to expand the margin early in the second quarter. On third and four from the New York 29, Sanders found a large seam in the zone defense and was in the left corner of the end zone, a good 10 yards from the

nearest defender, when Williams delivered the ball for a touchdown and a 13-0 lead.

The Giants started to climb back into it. Raul Allegre kicked a 23-yard field goal on the last play of the first half and, in the third quarter, another field goal and nine-yard touchdown run by Joe Morris had the game tied at 13 going into the fourth quarter. A classic finish seemed inevitable.

It turned from a classic to a clunker in a hurry. Gary Reasons blocked a Steve Cox punt and safety Tom Flynn scooped the ball up at the Washington 27 and easily went in for the touchdown. A little more than two minutes later, linebacker Pepper Johnson crashed through on a blitz and knocked the ball loose from Williams. Nose tackle Jim Burt plucked the ball off the ground and rumbled 39 yards for a touchdown to make it 27-13. A Williams touchdown pass to Kelvin Bryant came in the dying seconds.

9/11/88	REDSKINS (1-1) 30, Steelers (1-1) 29				55,671
Pitt	3	10	6	10	29
Was	7	3	7	13	30
Pitt	FG Anderson 33				
Was	Sanders 55 pass from Williams (Lohmiller kick)				
Pitt	FG Anderson 24				
Was	FG Lohmiller 37				
Pitt	Lipps 80 pass from Brister (Anderson kick)				
Pitt	Brister 6 run (kick failed)				
Was	Morris 1 run (Lohmiller kick)				
Was	FG Lohmiller 46				
Pitt	Stone 72 pass from Brister (Anderson kick)				
Pitt	FG Anderson 43				
Was	Bryant 7 pass from Williams (Lohmiller kick)				
Was	FG Lohmiller 19				

RFK Stadium—Rookie Chip Lohmiller's 19-yard field goal with 12 seconds left pulled the Redskins past the Steelers 30-29.

After cranking up 52 passes the previous week against the Giants, Doug Williams limbered up his arm again, completing 30 of 52 passes for 430 yards to provide the bulk of his team's offense. Midway through the first quarter, he lofted a 55-yard touchdown pass to Ricky Sanders to give the Redskins a 7-3 lead.

While Steeler quarterback Bubby Brister didn't quite match Williams throw for throw, he was quite effective on some plays. One came from the Washington 20 about seven minutes into the second quarter. Receiver Louis Lipps completely lost Darrell Green and was able to walk into the end zone to complete the 80-yard scoring play after taking Brister's pass.

"I thought the play was over," said Green. "(Lipps) had stopped running. I'd turned around and looked back upfield for someone to tackle. Maybe I gave up too soon, but there's no way they called that in the huddle."

No matter what the play call was, Pittsburgh led 13-10 at the half. Pittsburgh extended the lead in the third quarter when Brister scrambled for six yards and a touchdown. In what would prove to be a costly error, center Mike Webster botched the snap on the extra point try and the Steeler lead was nine.

A one-yard TD run by Jamie Morris and Lohmiller's 46-yard field goal at the outset of the fourth period pulled the Redskins into the lead at 20-19, but it didn't last long. On the Steelers' first play following the kickoff, halfback Dwight Stones outraced linebacker Wilbur Marshall on a crossing pattern and caught Brister's pass in stride, going 72 yards for a touchdown. About five minutes later, Gary Anderson's 43-yard field goal extended the Pittsburgh lead to 29-20.

Williams got his team in striking distance, leading a drive that ended with a seven-yard scoring toss to Kelvin Bryant to make it 29-27 with 4:48 left. When Pittsburgh got the ball back, Marshall stuffed an off-tackle play for a two-yard loss and blitzing linebacker Mel Kaufman batted down Brister's third-down pass attempt.

On the sidelines, Joe Gibbs was exhorting his offense to complete the rally. "Hey, listen, we've been here before and we're there right now," he said.

The offense was aided considerably by some excellent field position, thanks in part to Green and in part to another big special teams mistake by the Steelers. Harry Newsome's first punt rolled out of bounds at the Washington 33, but Pittsburgh was flagged for having an ineligible man downfield. Green returned the re-kick to the Pittsburgh 44.

Williams completed two passes to Art Monk to move to the 19. "I was hoping we'd get in for six," said Lohmiller, perhaps betraying a bit of nerves. He had no reason to worry as a few running plays moved the line of scrimmage closer to the goal posts.

Lohmiller had to make the kick twice. Pittsburgh was offside on the first attempt and the whistle blew before the boot split the uprights. No matter—the second attempt was perfect as well and the Redskins escaped with the win.

9/18/88	REDSKINS (2-1) 17, Eagles (2-1) 10				53,920
Was	14	0	3	0	17
Phil	0	3	0	7	10
Was	Smith 19 run (Lohmiller kick)				
Was	Morris 27 run (Lohmiller kick)				
Phil	FG Dorsey 23				
Was	FG Lohmiller 34				
Phil	Quick 55 pass from Cunningham (Dorsey kick)				

RFK Stadium—The Redskins build a 14-0 lead in the game's first 10 minutes and then got through some anxious moments in the fourth quarter to beat the Eagles 17-10.

Washington drove to touchdowns on its first two possessions as a revamped offensive line blasted away at the Philly front. On the two drives, the Redskins rushed for 94 yards and both touchdowns. The first came on Timmy Smith's 19-yard run; the second was from 27 yards by Jamie Morris.

After that, though, the Eagles clamped down on the Redskins, holding them to just three points and 56 yards rushing in the last 50 minutes of the game. Philadelphia could not quite take advantage. Randall Cunningham threw a 55-yard touchdown pass to Mike Quick early in the fourth quarter to give the Eagles a chance at 17-10.

Their last good opportunity came with 1:31 to play as the Redskins lined up to punt deep in their own territory. However, Junior Tautalatasi was flagged for being offside and the Redskins retained possession. They killed most of the rest of the clock and escaped with the win.

QB Williams has Appendectomy; Untested Rypien will get start

September 21—When the Redskins dealt quarterback Jay Schroeder away to the Raiders, they were gambling that Doug Williams would stay healthy or, failing that, his untested backup Mark Rypien would be able to play well if needed.

The team lost the first part of the bet last night when Williams underwent an emergency appendectomy that will sideline him for up to seven weeks. They will start to find out the result of the second high-stakes proposition on Sunday when Rypien starts against the Cardinals in Arizona.

The Redskins' initial offensive play will represent Rypien's first NFL snap. Rypien has expressed confidence that he's ready to start. Now, he said, it's time "to put up or shut up."

Asked if he thought the team now regretted trading Schroeder, Rypien replied, "I hope I can make it that they don't."

9/25/88	CARDINALS (2-2) 30, Redskins (2-2) 21				61,973
Was	7	7	0	7	21
Pho	2	7	7	14	30
Was	Monk 23 pass from Rypien (Lohmiller kick)				
Pho	Safety Harvey tackled Rypien in end zone				
Pho	Jordan 1 run (Del Greco kick)				
Was	Sanders 18 pass from Rypien (Lohmiller kick)				
Pho	Jordan 1 run (Del Greco kick)				
Pho	Green 27 pass from Lomax (Del Greco kick)				
Was	Allen 2 pass from Rypien (Lohmiller kick)				
Pho	Mack 45 fumble return (Del Greco kick)				

Sun Devil Stadium—Mark Rypien was the emergency starter at quarterback in place of Doug Williams, who had an appendectomy earlier in the week. In his first NFL start, Rypien showed a lot of good things, but also made enough mistakes to help send the Redskins down to a 30-21 defeat at the hands of the Cardinals.

Rypien led his team smartly downfield after taking the opening kickoff. During the 81-yard drive, he completed three passes, each for a gain of more than 20 yards. The last was a 23-yard touchdown strike to Art Monk and the Redskins were up 7-0.

Later in the opening quarter, Rypien failed to get rid of the ball in the end zone and linebacker Ken Harvey nailed him for a safety. That enabled the Cardinals to take the lead a short time later on Tony Jordan's one-yard touchdown run.

It appeared the 9-7 Phoenix lead would hold up until halftime, but Rypien led a masterful two-minute drill that culminated in his 18-yard TD pass to Ricky Sanders with 12 seconds left to give the Redskins a 14-9 lead at intermission.

The Cards recaptured the lead with 4:34 left in the third quarter on another one-yard blast by Jordan. Then, the Redskins made what Joe Gibbs called "a good play . . . that blew up in our face."

Phoenix was punting from its own 23 and an all-out rush by the Redskins left punter Greg Horne with zero chance of getting the punt off. There was, though, a lane that Horne could go through that gave him a very good chance of running for a first down. He did just that, and the drive ended with Neal Lomax throwing a 27-yard touchdown pass to Roy Green to put Phoenix up 23-14.

Washington closed within two on Rypien's third touchdown pass of the day, a two-yard flip to Anthony Allen with 2:30 remaining. The Redskins had a chance to win it, taking over at their own 43 with just over a minute left. The opportunity went fatally awry when linebacker Freddie Joe Nunn nailed Rypien from behind, forcing a fumble. Cornerback Cedric Mack scooped up the ball and scored the clincher on a 45-yard dash.

10/2/88	Giants (3-2) 24, REDSKINS (2-3) 23				54,601
NYG	10	7	7	0	24
Was	6	3	7	7	23
NYG	FG McFadden 32				
Was	Smith 1 run (kick failed)				
NYG	Anderson 1 run (McFadden kick)				
Was	FG Lohmiller 30				
NYG	Carthon 5 run (McFadden kick)				
NYG	Turner 28 pass from Simms (McFadden kick)				
Was	Sanders 49 pass from Rypien (Lohmiller kick)				
Was	Sanders 21 pass from Rypien (Lohmiller kick)				

RFK Stadium—Rookie Chip Lohmiller missed two key place kicks, one in the early going and the other late in the game, and the Redskins couldn't quite finish off a rally. They were defeated at the hands of the Giants by a score of 24-23.

The first errant boot came in the first quarter after Timmy Smith scored on a one-yard touchdown burst. Lohmiller's point after attempt went to the left and the Redskins led 6-3.

New York then took control, leading 17-9 at halftime. They appeared to be running away with it after Phil Simms threw a 28-

yard touchdown pass to receiver Odessa Turner to put New York up by 15 with less than five minutes gone in the third quarter.

That play evidently roused the Redskins, who suddenly turned it around on both sides of the ball and got back into it. Mark Rypien hit Ricky Sanders on a post route for 49 yards and a touchdown to pull the Skins within eight with 4:12 to go in the third. Led by Dexter Manley, the defense came to life. The defensive end got two of his four second half sacks as the Giants went three and out and punted it away. A 63-yard march wound up with Rypien's second touchdown pass to Sanders with less than a minute elapsed in the fourth quarter.

After Darrell Green's 32-yard punt return, the home team got the ball back at the New York 42 still trailing 24-23 with just under six minutes left. Five plays later, the Redskins faced fourth and two at the 19. In came Lohmiller, but his 36-yard attempt went wide left with 2:58 left. The Giants got a key 34-yard completion to receiver Stephen Baker to enable them to kill the clock.

10/9/88	Redskins (3-3) 35, COWBOYS (2-4) 17				63,235
Was	7	21	0	7	35
Dal	7	3	0	7	17
Dal	Newsome 1 run (Ruzak kick)				
Was	Clark 13 pass from Rypien (Lohmiller kick)				
Was	Bryant 10 pass from Rypien (Lohmiller kick)				
Dal	FG Ruzak 45				
Was	Bryant 9 run (Lohmiller kick)				
Was	Rypien 19 run (Lohmiller kick)				
Dal	Martin 35 pass from Pelluer (Ruzak kick)				
Was	Bryant 24 pass from Rypien (Lohmiller kick)				

Texas Stadium—The Redskins maximized their opportunities in the second quarter, turning three takeaways into 21 points to blow away the Cowboys 35-17.

The game was tied at seven entering the second quarter. Monte Coleman got things going for Washington when he intercepted Steve Pelluer's pass at the Dallas 36. Four plays later, Kelvin Bryant took a jarring hit from safety Bill Bates, but held on to Mark Rypien's 10-yard touchdown pass anyway. "Oh, it hurt," Bryant said of the hit, "but it doesn't hurt quite as much when you're in the end zone." Bryant had enough of his wits about him to give the ball a celebratory spike.

After Dallas held on to the ball long enough to get a field goal, Alvin Walton took his turn at picking off Pelluer, returning his interception 29 yards to the Dallas 26. A pair of nice runs by Bryant got it in from there. The second was a real beauty with Bryant twisting and spinning off of left tackle for nine yards and the score, making it 21-10.

It didn't take long for the Redskins to turn it into a rout after that. On the ensuing kickoff, Dean Hamel separated returner Kelvin Martin from the ball and Terry Orr pounced on it at the Dallas 23. On second down from the 19, Rypien went back to pass. He found no open receivers but did find wide open spaces—enough for him to rumble untouched into the end zone.

The 28-10 lead held until early in the fourth quarter when Pelluer threw a 35-yard touchdown pass to Martin. Rypien responded immediately with a 24-yard toss to Bryant for an answering score. Both benches were emptied after that.

10/16/88	REDSKINS (4-3) 33, Cardinals (4-3) 17				54,402
Pho	7	3	0	7	17
Was	9	14	7	3	33
Pho	R. Green 23 pass from Lomax (Del Greco kick)				
Was	Safety Caldwell tackled Lomax in end zone				
Was	Monk 19 pass from Rypien (Lohmiller kick)				
Pho	FG Del Greco 38				
Was	Clark 19 pass from Rypien (Lohmiller kick)				
Was	Monk 45 pass from Rypien (Lohmiller kick)				
Was	Clark 60 pass from Rypien (Lohmiller kick)				
Was	FG Lohmiller 20				

Pho   Novacek 41 pass from Lomax (Del Greco kick)

RFK Stadium—Mark Rypien threw four touchdown passes, two each to Art Monk and Gary Clark, to lead the Redskins over the Cardinals 33-17.

The aerial barrage was sparked by a big defensive play. With Washington trailing 7-0, linebacker Ravin Caldwell busted through on a delayed blitz and, while falling down after a cut block, sacked quarterback Neal Lomax in the end zone for a safety. "This was my first start, my first safety, and my first sack of the year," said Caldwell. "I just got to his legs and pulled up and out."

A little over four minutes later, Monk dove for Rypien's pass and dragged his feet in the end zone to complete a 19-yard scoring pass. After a Phoenix field goal gave the visitors a 10-9 lead, the Redskins poured it on. It took a little luck as Rypien's first TD to Clark went right through the hands of safety Travis Curtis and into those of Clark in the end zone.

No such luck was needed on TD's three and four. The receiver was wide open each time and Rypien delivered the ball on target. The first one was to Monk and covered 45 yards in the final minute of the first half to give the Redskins a 23-10 lead. Then, early in the third quarter, Rypien went to Clark for 60 to put it away for Washington.

Oct 20

Williams Will Replace Ailing Rypien
Bruised ribs sideline NFC's second-rated passer

10/23/88	Redskins (5-3) 20, PACKERS (2-6) 17				51,767
Was	10	0	7	3	20
GB	7	3	7	0	17
Was	FG Lohmiller 33				
Was	Monk 21 pass from Williams (Lohmiller kick)				
GB	Woodside 49 pass from Majkowski (Zendejas kick)				
GB	FG Zendejas 34				
GB	Woodside 8 pass from Majkowski (Zendejas kick)				
Was	Bryant 13 pass from Williams (Lohmiller kick)				
Was	FG Lohmiller 20				

Lambeau Field—Former Redskin kicker Max Zendejas earned the gratitude of his ex-teammates when he missed a 24-yard field goal attempt with 11 seconds left to play, preserving a three-point Washington win. It was Zendejas' second field goal miss of the fourth quarter.

From the Redskins' perspective, it should not have come down to hoping that a kicker would miss a chip shot. The Redskins outgained the Packers 385 yards to 172 and held the ball for just over 40 minutes, but three turnovers kept the Packers in it until the very end.

Washington jumped to a 10-0 lead in the first quarter, but the Packers scored 17 straight points, 10 of them the result of Redskin turnovers. The Redskins tied it up midway through the fourth quarter when Kelvin Bryant made a nice catch of a 13-yard pass from Doug Williams. On the day, Bryant personally outgained the Packers, picking up 140 yards rushing and 70 more on receptions.

After regaining possession, the Redskins embarked on what proved to be the game-winning drive. Bryant carried the load early on, picked up 22 yards on two runs and two receptions. Then Williams hit Gary Clark for 22 on a crossing pattern to move to the Green Bay 19 as the third quarter ended. Timmy Smith squeezed out a fourth and one at the ten, but the drive died at the three. Chip Lohmiller, who was drafted to avoid the kind of anxiety that Zendejas had created the previous season, calmly booted a 20-yarder to put his team ahead 20-17 with 10:59 left.

The Packers had two chances to win it, but Zendejas missed twice. To be fair, the first was a tough chance, from 46 yards in a driving rainstorm with 7:47 left to play. The second one, though, caused great celebration and gratitude on the part of the

Redskins. "I'll send (Zendejas) a Christmas present," said Dexter Manley.

Growing Pains: Gibbs Worries About Building Next to Redskins Park

Oct 27—When George Allen selected the site for Redskins Park, Herndon, Va., was exactly where you wanted such a facility to be—in the middle of nowhere. Not only was there plenty of privacy for practices, but the land was cheap as well.

Now, some 17 years later, Northern Virginia is in the middle of a growth boom and the property around Redskins Park has become quite valuable—too valuable to sit vacant. Buildings have gone up in the vicinity of the facility over the years and, as was inevitable, construction has begun on a building right smack next to Redskins Park.

Joe Gibbs is a worrier, even among the notoriously-paranoid NFL coaching fraternity. A multi-story building next door would be a nightmare, a potential lair for spies from opposing teams who want to peek in on his latest offensive innovations being installed.

He has managed to get his hands on the plans for the building, but he hasn't yet determined the height of it. "The guy sent me the blueprints, but I haven't had time to look at them," Gibbs said. "Not that I could read them if I tried."

Reporters assured Gibbs that it was to be a one-story edifice, but the coach said he would believe it when he saw it.

10/30/88	OILERS (6-3) 41, Redskins (5-4) 17			48,781
Was	0	3	7	7	**17**
Hou	7	17	7	10	**41**
Hou	Hill 22 pass from Moon (Zendejas kick)
Was	FG Lohmiller 46
Hou	Hill 33 pass from Moon (Zendejas kick)
Hou	Moon 3 run (Zendejas kick)
Hou	FG Zendejas 41
Was	T. Smith 1 run (Lohmiller kick)
Hou	Hill 11 pass from Moon (Zendejas kick)
Hou	FG Zendejas
Hou	Pinkett 16 run (Zendejas kick)
Was	Griffin 4 pass from Rypien (Lohmiller kick)

Astrodome—"This won't happen no more," said cornerback Barry Wilburn after this game.

He could have been talking about losing by 24 points to a near-equal opponent. Maybe he was referring to the six turnovers the Redskins made, five of which set Houston up with great field position inside the Washington 30.

Actually, he was referring to his coverage of Houston receiver Drew Hill. It could be said that Hill, who caught nine Warren Moon passes for 148 yards and three touchdowns, had a field day against Wilburn but given that this one was played inside on Astroturf, that was not possible. Let's just say that Wilburn had a very difficult time with Hill.

In the early going, Hill beat Wilburn on a post pattern and dropped a sure TD pass from Warren Moon. It didn't matter as, two plays later, Hill beat Wilburn again on the same pattern, Moon threw the same pass and this time, Hill caught it for a 7-0 Houston lead.

After a Washington field goal, Moon and Hill connected for 70 of the 78 yards that the Oilers traveled for their second TD. The score came after Hill put some visible distance between himself and Wilburn, caught Moon's pass and eluded an attempted tackle by safety Todd Bowles to complete the 33-yard touchdown pass and give Houston a 14-3 lead. The Oilers expanded that advantage to 24-3 at halftime.

To be sure, there were plenty of problems beyond Wilburn's coverage challenges. In order for a receiver to get so free, the quarterback must have time to throw, and the Redskins didn't

pressure Moon consistently. In addition, the aforementioned six turnovers destroyed any chance the Redskins might have had of a miracle comeback.

The real killer occurred after the Redskins had scored a touchdown on Timmy Smith's one-yard run early in the third quarter and forced Houston to punt. With good field position near midfield, Doug Williams' pass was tipped at the line and intercepted by tackle Doug Smith, who returned it to the Washington 28. Two plays later, well, you can figure out what Houston receiver beat what Washington corner for an 11-yard touchdown to turn the fourth quarter into garbage time.

11/6/88	REDSKINS (6-4) 27, Saints (7-3) 24			54,183
NO	7	7	10	0	**24**
Was	0	14	3	10	**27**
NO	Martin 2 pass from Hebert (Anderson kick)
Was	Clark 1 pass from Williams (Lohmiller kick)
NO	Clark 18 pass from Hebert (Anderson kick)
Was	Williams 1 run (Lohmiller kick)
Was	FG Lohmiller 32
NO	Jordan 7 run with fumble return (Anderson kick)
NO	FG Anderson 19
Was	Sanders 8 pass from Williams (Lohmiller kick)
Was	FG Lohmiller 23

RFK Stadium—Chip Lohmiller's 23-yard field goal with 47 seconds left gave the Redskins the lead, but they couldn't rest easily until the Saints' Morten Anderson missed a 49-yard attempt with four seconds on the clock as they hung on to beat New Orleans.

The key and most memorable moment of this contest, however, was not a placekick, nor even a pass or a run. It was provided by Dexter Manley and, well, here's the story:

The Saints had broken on top 24-17 after having been tied at halftime. Early in the fourth quarter, they were in position to make it an uphill struggle for the Redskins to pull this one out with possession at the Washington 20. After a third down incompletion, it appeared Anderson would come in to attempt a near-automatic 37-yard field goal. But New Orleans tackle Jim Dombrowski changed all of that when he took a swing at Manley. Dexter did not retaliate and the dead ball foul made Anderson's attempt a 52-yarder, which was partially blocked.

As it turns out, Dombrowski was the one retaliating as, after the play, Manley spit in the offensive player's face. "He suckered me and I bought into it," said Dombrowski.

"I think I might have sneezed on him," said a coy Manley.

Even after the expectoration situation, the Redskins still trailed by a touchdown and were backed up at their own six. The combination of Doug Williams to Ricky Sanders took care of that little problem. Sanders turned a little hitch pass into a 42-yard gain and later found a seam between a pair of defenders to catch Williams' eight-yard touchdown pass, tying the game with 6:35 to play.

Washington got the ball back less than a minute later on its own 31 and embarked on the winning drive. A pass to tight end Don Warren picked up 32 yards. Then Timmy Smith was called upon to pick up some yardage and burn off some clock as he handled the ball on the next seven plays, six of them runs. Art Monk scooted to the five on a reverse before Lohmiller was called in. Anderson's attempt at the end was wide and short. The Redskins got away with the win.

11/13/88	Bears (9-2) 34, REDSKINS (6-5) 14			52,418
Chi	7	13	0	14	**34**
Was	0	0	7	7	**14**
Chi	Tomczak 1 run (Butler kick)
Chi	Suhey 3 run (Butler kick)
Chi	FG Butler 32

Chi	FG Butler 24
Was	Sanders 4 pass from Rypien (Lohmiller kick)
Chi	Gentry 22 pass from Tomczak (Butler kick)
Was	Clark 3 pass from Rypien (Lohmiller kick)
Chi	Anderson 50 run (Butler kick)

RFK Stadium—Bears coach Mike Ditka had suffered a heart attack 11 days before the game, but it was the Redskins who were in ill health after it. Ditka was calmly roaming the RFK Stadium sidelines during the game as his team dismantled Washington 34-14. The home team's playoff hopes, already on the critical list, were on life support.

The Bears jumped to a 20-0 halftime lead. Quarterback Mike Tomczak went a combined seven for seven on two touchdown drives, one of which ended on one-yard run by Tomczak, the other on a three-yard blast by fullback Matt Suhey. Two Kevin Butler field goals provided Chicago with the 20-point cushion.

Mark Rypien replaced an ineffective Doug Williams at quarterback in the third quarter and led the Redskins to a quick touchdown on a four-yard pass to Ricky Sanders. Washington's defense rose up and forced a three and out, Rypien moved the Skins to a second and one at midfield.

The short-lived comeback attempt died there. Richard Dent sacked Rypien, forcing a fumble. Although Jim Lachey recovered it for Washington, Rypien threw an interception on the third and 13 play to end the threat and the Redskins' chances.

11/21/88	**49ERS (7-5) 37, Redskins (6-6) 21**			59,266	
Was	7	0	7	7	**21**
SF	7	16	0	14	**37**
SF	Jones 18 pass from Montana (Cofer kick)				
Was	Sanders 15 pass from Williams (Lohmiller kick)				
SF	FG Cofer 52				
SF	Taylor 95 punt return (Cofer kick)				
SF	Rathman 1 run (kick blocked)				
Was	Sanders 4 pass from Williams (Lohmiller kick)				
SF	Montana 4 run (Cofer kick)				
SF	Rice 80 pass from Montana (Cofer kick)				
Was	Monk 16 pass from Williams (Lohmiller kick)				

Candlestick Park—Television reruns aren't supposed to appear on Monday night before Thanksgiving, but this loss by the Redskins contained many plot lines common in their five previous losses during the season: turnovers, special teams breakdowns, and a low-powered running game.

Most of it was recycled material, but there were also some new twists to the way things unfolded. For example, Washington had not allowed a punt return for a touchdown to this point in the season, but that changed late in the first half.

Washington had been competitive through the first 25 minutes of the game trailing just 10-7 and punted from around midfield, hoping to pin the Niners back deep in their own territory. As it turns out, it would have been better for the Redskins if Tim McKyer had blocked it, which he nearly did. John Taylor ignored the conventional wisdom about not fielding a punt inside the 10, realizing that this line drive punt by Greg Coleman was a big play opportunity.

And that it was. He was nearly trapped a few times, but he broke those potential tackles and was off to the races—95 yards—to make the score 17-7.

It got worse before halftime as Doug Williams tried to beat double coverage by sneaking a pass to tight end Craig McEwen, but Williams was the one burned as Jeff Fuller made a diving interception. San Francisco took full advantage as Tom Rathman scored on a one-yard run and it was getting ugly at 23-7 at the half.

San Francisco chipped in on the Redskins' next score late in the third quarter as Joe Montana threw an interception to Barry Wilburn. A pair of drive-extending penalties on the 49ers enabled Williams to throw a four-yard TD pass to Ricky Sanders.

The momentum from the touchdown and subsequent defensive stop was killed when Gary Clark fumbled a punt and Bill Romanowski recovered for San Francisco. Montana himself ran it in from the four to terminate any doubts about the eventual outcome.

Nov 25

Gibbs: Williams "Worn Down", Rypien Back in Starting Role
Team needs "a lift" Gibbs says

11/27/88	**Browns (8-5) 17, REDSKINS (6-7) 13**			51,604	
Cle	0	3	0	14	17
Was	0	0	10	3	13
Cle	FG Bahr 37				
Was	Clark 7 pass from Rypien (Lohmiller kick)				
Was	FG Lohmiller 21				
Cle	Mack 1 run (Bahr kick)				
Was	FG Lohmiller 40				
Cle	Byner 27 run (Bahr kick)				

RFK Stadium—Ernest Byner scored on a 27-yard touchdown run with less than two minutes left to give Cleveland a 17-13 win over Washington.

If it's a mark of a good team to play poorly and still win, maybe it's the mark of a mediocre one to play poorly and almost win. The Redskins didn't cross midfield in the first half, possessed the ball for less than 22 minutes to 38 for the Browns and mustered just 11 first downs as Cleveland piled up 25.

After the lackluster first half that ended with Cleveland holding a 3-0 lead, Washington suddenly found its offense, albeit temporarily as things turned out. After receiving the second-half kickoff, the Redskins moved 72 yards to a touchdown. Mark Rypien completed five of seven passes during the drive, including a seven-yard toss to Gary Clark for the score.

A blocked punt about a minute later gave the Redskins a golden opportunity, but they could only convert a first down at the Cleveland nine into a Chip Lohmiller field goal to make it 10-3.

A Cleveland drive that covered 72 yards and consumed nearly 11 minutes of the late third and early fourth quarters resulted in the game being tied on Kevin Mack's one-yard touchdown run. Washington retook the lead by moving 44 yards in six plays and getting another Lohmiller three-pointer with 6:27 to go.

The Browns responded with their game-winning drive. They steadily moved to a third and five at the Washington 27. The play call, a draw to Byner, did not surprise the Redskins. "It was a good defense against a draw play," Joe Gibbs said. "We should have stopped it."

They would have stopped it if Byner hadn't broken a couple of attempted tackles near the line. After that, it was clear sailing into the end zone.

Washington got the ball back with 1:49 remaining and Rypien momentarily raised hopes with a pass to Art Monk to convert a fourth and 22 situation. That was all, though, as Rypien's next pass bounced out of Sanders' hands and into those of Cleveland's Mark Harper.

12/4/88	**Redskins (7-7) 20, EAGLES (8-6) 19**			65,947	
Was	7	0	3	10	**20**
Phil	3	13	3	0	**19**
Phil	FG Zendejas 40				
Was	Sanders 16 pass from Rypien (Lohmiller kick)				
Phil	Byars 2 run (Zendejas kick)				

Phil	Byars 12 pass from Cunningham (kick failed)
Phil	FG Zendejas 19
Was	FG Lohmiller 37
Was	Orr 2 pass from Williams (Lohmiller kick)
Was	FG Lohmiller 44

Veterans Stadium—Chip Lohmiller kicked a 44-yard field goal into a strong breeze with one-second left to cap a late rally and give the Redskins a 20-19 win.

Washington led 7-3 going into the second quarter, but the Eagles took control at that point. Keith Byars scored two touchdowns: one on a short run, and the other on a 12-yard pass from Randall Cunningham. Luis Zendejas missed the extra point after the passing TD, a misfire that would prove fatal to the Eagles.

Still, Philly expanded its lead to 19-7 early in the third quarter on a Zendejas field goal after Gary Clark committed one of the Redskins' four turnovers by fumbling a punt inside his own ten.

A Lohmiller field goal pulled the Redskins within nine going into the fourth, but Washington still couldn't mount much of a threat. Doug Williams had replaced an interception-prone Mark Rypien at quarterback but failed to deliver a touchdown. But they got the jump start they needed when Dave Butz tipped a pass at the line; Alvin Walton picked it off, and set them up in Eagle territory at the 40. Seven plays later the Eagles bit hard on a play action fake and Williams tossed a two-yard touchdown to tight end Terry Orr, making it 19-17 with 8:43 left.

Washington got the ball back at its own 10 with 3:57 to play and Williams was eight of ten passing, converting two third downs and a fourth down on the way to Lohmiller's game winner.

Dec 4

Change is a Constant: Skins Switch QB's, Williams Back as Starter
Rypien didn't play well enough to keep job, says Gibbs

12/11/88	**Cowboys (3-12) 24, REDSKINS (7-8) 17**				51,526
Dal	3	7	7	7	**24**
Was	3	0	14	0	**17**
Dal	FG Ruzek 22
Was	FG Lohmiller 41
Dal	Irvin 24 pass from Pelluer (Ruzek kick)
Dal	Irvin 61 pass from Pelluer (Ruzek kick)
Was	Sanders 40 pass from Williams (Lohmiller kick)
Was	Orr 50 pass from Rypien (Lohmiller kick)
Dal	Irvin 12 pass from Pelluer (Ruzek kick)

RFK Stadium—As Doug Williams' fourth-down pass floated towards a wide-open Don Warren in the end zone, it appeared that the Redskins and Cowboys were headed into overtime. The ball stayed in the air just long enough, however, for safety Michael Downs to get his fingers on it and knock it harmlessly to the turf in the waning seconds to preserve Dallas' win.

That play wasted a good comeback by the Redskins, who found themselves trailing 17-3 early in the third quarter. It was, though, a sloppy effort by the Redskins, who turned the ball over five times to drive their turnover ratio for the season down to a miserable minus 22.

The Cowboys had built their third-quarter margin on the strength of two touchdown passes from Steve Pelluer to receiver Michael Irvin. Darrell Green had exited the game with an injury and, as Irvin said, "When a guy like Darrell Green goes out, it makes your eyes light up." Also lit up was Green's replacement, Dennis Woodberry, who was victimized on Irvin touchdown catches of 24 and 61 yards.

After the second Irving TD, the Redskins started their rally. Ricky Sanders made a nice adjustment on wind-altered Williams pass, looking for the ball over his left shoulder and turning to catch

it to his right to for a 40-yard gain and a touchdown with 8:35 to go in the third. Williams was forced to leave the game with an injured shoulder, but Mark Rypien kept things going with a 50-yard scoring toss to tight end Terry Orr to tie the game at 17.

As it turned out, that was the high point for the Redskins. A dropped pass killed one drive and then Rypien underthrew a wide-open Gary Clark and Dallas intercepted. Soon after that, Woodberry was in the vicinity of Irvin in the end zone, but it didn't matter as the receiver jumped over the defender to grab a 12-yard touchdown pass to push Dallas up by seven with 4:50 to play.

Williams reentered the game at quarterback and the Redskins had two excellent chances to tie the game after that. The first one died on the Dallas 13 with four incompletions, one a drop by a wide-open Clark. The second began at the Dallas 42 with 1:28 left. A minute later, they were at the 20, lining up for a third and one play. Joe Gibbs told Williams to spike the ball to kill the clock with 28 seconds left, a move that Gibbs later said was a mistake as the team still had one timeout left. For a moment, however, it looked like Gibbs would be redeemed as Warren appeared to be free in the end zone, but Downs made a nice recovery and ended Washington's chances.

12/17/88	**BENGALS (12-4) 20, Redskins (7-9) 17 OT**					52,157
Was	3	7	7	0	0	**17**
Cin	0	10	0	7	3	**20**
Was	FG Lohmiller 43
Was	Clark 20 pass from Williams (Lohmiller kick)
Cin	FG Johnson 50
Cin	McGee 17 pass from Esiason (Breech kick)
Was	Sanders 44 pass from Williams (Lohmiller kick)
Cin	Brown 66 pass from Esiason (Breech kick)
Cin	FG Breech 20

Riverfront Stadium—Chip Lohmiller missed a 29-yard field goal attempt with 11 seconds remaining, opening the door for the Bengals to steal the win with a 20-yard Jim Breech field goal 7:01 into overtime.

It never should have been that close. The Redskins controlled the game with running back Jamie Morris grinding out 152 yards rushing on an NFL-record 45 carries. Morris' runs helped give Washington a time of possession edge of nearly 43 minutes to just over 24 for the Bengals. Despite this, they couldn't hold leads of 10-0 in the second quarter or 17-10 midway through the final period. They finished with a losing record for the first time under Joe Gibbs.

Washington patiently built its 10-0 margin by scoring on its first two possessions as Lohmiller kicked a 43-yard field goal and Doug Williams hooked up with Gary Clark for a 20-yard touchdown. Cincinnati tied it up before halftime, however, on a long field goal and a seven-yard pass from Boomer Esiason to Tim McGee.

After retaking the lead on Williams' 44-yard scoring pass to Ricky Sanders, the Redskins twice drove inside the Bengal 20, but came up empty both times. The first time, Gibbs gambled and lost on fourth and one at the 15 as Morris' attempt around right end was stuffed for a one-yard loss. The Redskins soon paid, as Esiason's play action fake sucked in the safeties allowing Eddie Brown to get loose for a 66-yard touchdown to tie the game with 8:31 remaining.

In classic Redskins fashion, they marched down the field running the ball, mostly with Morris. With time winding down, Lohmiller lined up on the right hashmark and attempted a 29-yard field goal. The ball didn't veer an inch from straight forward and smacked off of the right upright to send the game into overtime. On Washington's first possession of overtime, Williams was sacked and fumbled, with David Grant making the recovery for Cincinnati at the Washington 17. Three plays later, Breech chipped it in from 20 yards to win it for the Bengals.

1989
Head Coach: Joe Gibbs
Record: 10-6, third in NFC East

Honors: Jim Lachey All-NFL; Charles Mann Pro Bowl; Mark Rypien Pro Bowl

---

Feb 9

Dan Henning Leaves Again; Hired as Chargers' Head Coach
Redskins get back special teams coach Wayne Sevier

Feb 3

Flash In the Pan: Super Bowl Hero RB Smith, Skins Part Ways
Lack of Preparation for '88 season cited

Darrell Green a Bronco? Trade Talks Get Serious

Apr 4—For how much longer will Darrell Green be a Washington Redskin?

Trade talks with the Denver Broncos have gone from discussion to real negotiation in the past days. The Redskins would take Denver's first-round pick (13th overall) and a player for the rights to Green. Just who that player would be is the sticking point.

The Redskins are willing to part with their 1983 first-round pick for a couple of reasons. One is the nagging injuries that have slowed the 5-9, 185-lb. cornerback to the extent that the team is concerned he may be on the downside of his career.

The other reason is money. Green made $450,000 last year and is looking for a raise to $1 million a year. The Redskins are willing to up his salary, but not to seven figures. The Broncos are willing to pay Green his asking price.

The team has braced for Green's possible departure by signing cornerback Martin Mayhew as a free agent.

Land War: Skins Trade for Riggs, Byner

Apr 23—Looking at the Redskins rushing game, ranked 25th in yardage gained last year, Joe Gibbs asked Bobby Beathard to get him a running back. Beathard thought it was such a good idea that he went out and got him two.

The big trade on draft day was for Atlanta's Gerald Riggs, a classic big back at 6-1, 240 lbs. Not owning a first round draft pick, the Redskins had to give up their 1990 top pick to land Riggs and add their second-rounder this year and their 1990 fifth as well.

Riggs had his best years in Atlanta from 1984-86, gaining more than 1,300 yards each year, most of them from the same one-back set the Redskins employ. The head coach for the Falcons was Dan Henning, who had two stints as one of Gibbs' top assistants.

"It's my favorite offense," said Riggs. "It gives me a chance to run inside, which is what I like to do. Forty Gut, Sixty Gut, Twenty Gut—I have a familiarity with those plays. It'll be like sleepwalking."

While to many the price for Riggs seemed high for a 29-year-old back with a lot of mileage, there was unanimous consent that Beathard virtually stole Ernest Byner from the Browns. He came from the Browns in a straight-up exchange for running back Mike Oliphant. The deal could have come sooner, but Cleveland had

wanted a draft pick in addition to Oliphant. They backed off that demand yesterday and the trade went through.

Who will start? "We'll settle all those things on the field," Byner said. "There's no point in starting a duel in the newspapers now. I can run and catch and block. I'm really a jack-of-all-trades player and, although I don't know what my role will be, I think I can fill one."

With their initial draft pick, in the third round, the Redskins took Auburn defensive tackle Tracy Rocker.

Bobby Beathard Steps Down as GM

May 5—The long-rumored departure of Bobby Beathard from his post as general manager of the Washington Redskins is no longer a rumor. Beathard announced today that he is retiring from the Redskins when his contract is up at the end of this month.

Why is the 52-year-old maverick leaving? "Maybe there has to be a definite reason, but there isn't," Beathard said.

This, of course, led to speculation about why he's stepping down. First, there have been persistent reports of friction with Gibbs and team vice president John Kent Cooke.

"The rumors of the alleged problems with Joe or John Cooke are untrue," Beathard said. "I'm not leaving with any problems between personalities."

Also it has been reported that he has a standing offer from San Diego Chargers owner Alex Spanos to come and be the GM of his team at any time. Beathard has an oceanfront home in the San Diego area and although he has been living in the D.C. area for 10 years, he still considers California to be his home.

Dave Butz Retires

May 18—Dave Butz voluntarily retired from the Redskins today—well, sort of.

"Truthfully, anyone who does it for 14 seasons, anyone who's been at it 26 years is never really ready (to hang it up)," Butz said. "Who in his right mind would turn down several thousand dollars for playing a game to wear a suit and tie? The only problem is I'll have to grow up."

The Redskins were still willing to give Butz a shot at making that several hundred thousand dollars, but they wanted him to move from his Illinois home to the Washington area during the offseason in order to monitor his conditioning. Butz refused to do so and the two sides mutually decided to part ways. Unlike other Redskins stars Joe Theismann and John Riggins, Butz chose to retire immediately rather than wait and see if any other NFL teams would call to give him another shot.

Certainly, there were no hard feelings on either side. Gibbs remembered Butz's toughness. "I think of him coming out of the hospital two years ago to play against the New York Jets. He made one of the biggest plays in the game, and then he checked back into the hospital afterward."

Green Signs New Contract

July 28—Darrell Green, who was nearly traded to the Denver Broncos this spring, agreed to terms with the Redskins and will report to training camp on time.

The cornerback, who has 18 interceptions and three Pro Bowl appearances in six seasons with the team, wanted a salary in the $1 million range. It appears he settled for a salary of about $700,000 with some incentives that could boost the total higher.

Williams in Traction, Rypien Gets Promotion

July 26—Doug Williams is in traction in an Arlington, Va., hospital as training camp is set to open in Carlisle, Pa.

Williams, slated to be the Redskins' starting quarterback this coming season, first injured his back six weeks ago while running on a treadmill at his home in Louisiana. The pain hasn't responded to other treatment options and trainer Bubba Tyer recommended the hospitalization.

The situation with Williams hands the keys to the offense to Mark Rypien, who shared the starting duties with Williams last year. The team's 1986 sixth-round draft pick has been brought along slowly and has had the advantage of working without the pressure of being the full-time starter. That may well change, depending on how quickly Williams' injury gets healed.

Williams Will Undergo Surgery

Aug 23—Quarterback Doug Williams will undergo back surgery tomorrow to repair a herniated disc. The injury hasn't responded to other treatment and tests have indicated that surgery is the best course of action.

Williams will be hospitalized for up to a week and sidelined eight to ten weeks. That would put his potential return to the lineup at midseason or later.

Aug 31

Kelvin Bryant Out for Season
Neck injury shelves RB

Aug 28

Redskins, Williams at Odds Over Sidelined QB's Injury
Origin of back ailment in dispute as team, QB, union try to reach settlement

9/11/89	Giants (1-0) 27, REDSKINS (0-1) 24			54,160	
NYG	7	7	0	13	**27**
Was	0	3	7	14	**24**
NYG	Turner 30 pass from Simms (Allegre kick)				
NYG	Meggett 62 pass from Simms (Allegre kick)				
Was	FG Lohmiller 24				
Was	Sanders 48 pass from Rypien (Lohmiller kick)				
NYG	Anderson 14 run (Allegre kick)				
Was	Coleman 24 interception return (Lohmiller kick)				
NYG	FG Allegre 32				
NYG	FG Allegre 52				

RFK Stadium—It was the usual frustrating day for the Redskins against the Giants. Washington rallied from a 14-0 halftime deficit to take a fourth quarter lead, but two Raul Allegre field goals—the second a 52-yarder with no time left—stole a 27-24 win back for the Giants.

It started off well for the Redskins as Alvin Walton intercepted a Phil Simms pass. The hope turned out to be false, however, as Gerald Riggs, who had gone over 500 carries between fumbles as a member of the Atlanta Falcons, put the ball on the ground and the Giants recovered.

Later in the first quarter, a missed turnover opportunity directly led to New York's first touchdown. From the Washington 30, Simms unleashed a pass for Odessa Turner, who was waiting near the goal line. Darrell Green cut in front of the receiver and had a bead on the ball, but it went right between the defender's hands and into Turner's for a touchdown and a 7-0 lead.

In the second quarter, Dave Meggett took a short pass from Simms, eluded an attempted tackle by Walton and scampered 62 yards for a 14-0 New York lead. A Chip Lohmiller field goal got the Redskins on the board before halftime.

The score remained 14-3 until late in the third quarter when Mark Rypien faked a handoff and found Ricky Sanders all alone on a deep post for a 48-yard touchdown. The Giants responded immediately with a seven-play, 73-yard drive that culminated in Ottis Anderson's 14-yard quick hitter off guard for a touchdown and a 21-10 Giants lead a minute and a half into the final period.

It didn't take long for the Redskins to respond. Rypien was five for five as he moved his team 66 yards in eight plays to pull Washington back within four. The payoff came on Rypien's six-yard touchdown pass to Art Monk.

Then Monte Coleman snagged Simms' pass off of his shoe tops, found a block from Wilbur Marshall and raced 24 yards for the go-ahead touchdown with 9:21 left to play. In most contests, the play would have been a gamebreaker, but not in a Redskins-Giants game.

Simms calmly directed his team downfield, taking his time as he used nearly seven minutes to get in position for Allegre's 32-yard field goal that tied the game with 2:17 to play. A curious play call—a bomb to Art Monk on third and two—led to a Washington punt with 44 seconds left.

Overtime still seemed likely after a couple of completions and a pass interference penalty left New York with a 52-yard field goal attempt by Allegre. Apparently Allegre didn't realize the kick was considered to be out of his range; it just cleared the crossbar.

9/17/89	Eagles (2-0) 42, REDSKINS (0-2) 37			53,493	
Phil	7	7	7	21	**42**
Was	20	10	0	7	**37**
Was	Clark 80 pass from Rypien (Lohmiller kick)				
Was	Riggs 41 run (Lohmiller kick)				
Was	Byner 11 pass from Rypien (Lohmiller kick)				
Phil	Jackson 17 pass from Cunningham (Zendejas kick)				
Was	Clark 5 pass from Rypien (Lohmiller kick)				
Phil	Toney 3 run (Zendejas kick)				
Was	FG Lohmiller 25				
Phil	Jackson 5 pass from Cunningham (Zendejas kick)				
Phil	Carter 5 pass from Cunningham (Zendejas kick)				
Was	Monk 43 pass from Rypien (Lohmiller kick)				
Phil	Quick 2 pass from Cunningham (Zendejas kick)				
Phil	Jackson 4 pass from Cunningham (Zendejas kick)				

RFK Stadium—Bizarre. Shocking. Humiliating. Controversial. Not believed even by those who saw it with their own eyes. But it's in the books—you can look it up.

The Redskins blew a 20-0 first-quarter lead and lost to the Eagles 42-37 on Randall Cunningham's four-yard touchdown pass to tight end Keith Jackson with 52 seconds left to play.

The 20-0 lead took less than 10 minutes to build. In fact, the first 13 points came on Washington's first two snaps from scrimmage. On the first play after the opening kickoff, Mark Rypien found Gary Clark open deep and hit him with an 80-yard touchdown pass. Then Gerald Riggs blasted off of right tackle for 41 yards for a score on the next play. By the time the Redskins had turned Brian Davis' interception into an 11-yard touchdown pass from Rypien to Ernest Byner, the delirious home crowd was taunting Eagles coach Buddy Ryan with chants of "Buuudeee, Buuudeee!"

Bit by bit the visitors crept back into it. They cut the lead to 30-14 by halftime and then scored one touchdown late in the third quarter and another early in the fourth to pull within two at 30-28. Nervous silence replaced the derisive chants.

The Redskins, it seemed, got the wake-up call in time as Rypien threw his fourth touchdown pass of the day, this one 43 yards to Art Monk with 3:06 to play, giving Washington a nine-point lead. Cunningham drove the Eagles to the Washington two and fired a pass to Mike Quick in a crowd at the back of the end zone. Quick went up and caught the ball and a tangle of feet landed, some in and some out of the end zone. After some disagreement, the officials ruled that two of the feet that had landed inbounds belonged to Quick, a judgment the replay officials would not overturn. It was a two-point game with 1:48 to play.

It didn't seem like the controversial TD would matter after Riggs broke off a 58-yard run deep into Philly territory. But a funny thing happened on the way to killing the clock. On third down, Riggs carried up the middle, gaining the last of his team-record 221 yards on the day, trying to set up a field goal attempt. The ball came loose, not due to a solid tackle and strip but because center Raleigh McKenzie's knee knocked it out of Riggs' grasp from behind. That was surprising, but what followed was stunning.

Eagle linebacker Al Harris scooped up the ball and was immediately engulfed by tackle Jim Lachey. Somehow—and exactly how was the crux of much debate—Harris got the ball to safety Wes Hopkins. For a moment, the Redskins hesitated, thinking the play was dead. Hopkins took advantage of the pause, racing down the sideline in front of the Redskins bench until Ricky Sanders tackled him at the four.

The Redskins insisted that Harris had tossed the ball forward to Hopkins. In that case, it still would have been Philadelphia's ball, but back inside their own 20. Again, the replay officials refused to overturn the call on the field. Apparently, the 290-pound Lachey was invisible to both the side judge and the replay official who stated that Harris was free to lateral to Harris because "he had never been touched" by a Washington player.

Cunningham threw to Jackson for the touchdown on the next play and any hopes for a responding miracle died when Rypien fumbled on the next play. The Eagles killed the clock.

9/24/89	Redskins (1-2) 30, COWBOYS (0-3) 7			53,200	
Was	14	3	3	10	**30**
Dal	7	0	0	0	**7**
Was	Walton 29 interception return (Lohmiller kick)				
Dal	Jeffcoat 77 fumble return (Ruzek kick)				
Was	Byner 12 run (Lohmiller kick)				
Was	FG Lohmiller 26				
Was	FG Lohmiller 37				
Was	Morris 12 run (Lohmiller kick)				
Was	FG Lohmiller 33				

Texas Stadium—"Any win beats a loss, period," said Jeff Bostic, commenting on the relative lack of excitement in this easy win over the Cowboys.

A pair of defensive touchdowns opened the scoring. Six minutes into the contest, Alvin Walton picked off Troy Aikman's pass and scooted 29 yards for a touchdown. A couple of minutes later, Washington was threatening to score again when Mark Rypien got blindsided and fumbled. End Jim Jeffcoat scooped the ball up and rambled 77 yards to tie the score.

After that, the Redskins methodically pulled away. In addition to his fumble, Rypien was also having trouble with his accuracy, completing 15 of 37 for 216 yards, so ball control was the order of the day for the Washington offense. Washington held the ball for nearly 40 minutes.

Ernest Byner scored on his first rushing attempt as a Redskin with a 12-yard run to put the Redskins back in the lead for good. Chip Lohmiller kicked two field goals, one each in the second and third quarters, before Washington got back into the end zone. This time it was Jamie Morris, who gained 100 yards on 26 carries,

scoring from 12 yards out early in the fourth. Another Lohmiller field goal finished up the scoring late in the game.

Sep 27

Gibbs Skips Practice to be With Ailing Father
Senior Gibbs suffered massive stroke

10/1/89	Redskins (2-2) 16, SAINTS (1-3) 14			46,358	
Was	3	0	10	3	**16**
NO	7	7	0	0	**14**
Was	FG Lohmiller 48				
NO	Hill 11 pass from Hebert (Andersen kick)				
NO	Hilliard 3 run (Andersen kick)				
Was	FG Lohmiller 19				
Was	Riggs 9 run (Lohmiller kick)				
Was	FG Lohmiller 18				

Louisiana Superdome—The Redskins found themselves trailing 14-3 just 18 minutes into this game. In the first half, they netted just two field goals on three third and goal at the one situations, and rushed for just 11 yards. They managed to bounce back, however, and grind out a 16-14 win over the Saints.

"The boat was sinking," said Russ Grimm, "but we grabbed some buckets instead of running for the life rafts."

Washington's ship began taking on water soon after a New Orleans fumble led to a 48-yard Chip Lohmiller field goal. Just over two minutes later, the Saints completed an impressive drive when Bobby Hebert threw an 11-yard scoring pass to receiver Lonzell Hill. The vessel was surely beginning to list after Dalton Hilliard capped another solid Saints drive with a three-yard touchdown run to push his team's lead up to 14-3.

The buckets got working after that and the Redskins started to get back into it. They blew their first great chance late in the first half after a 55-yard completion from Mark Rypien to Art Monk to the seven. Gerald Riggs was unable to gain an inch on third- and fourth-down carries from the one, and the ball went over on downs.

On their opening drive of the second half, the Redskins faced third down at the New Orleans one again. They didn't come up completely empty, although they did have to settle for a 19-yard Lohmiller field goal after Rypien overthrew tight end Don Warren in the end zone after a play-action fake.

Apparently not convinced that the Redskins would try the run fake on short yardage again, the Saints massed at the line to try to stop a third and one on the Redskins' next drive. New Orleans paid this time, with Rypien's pass to Terry Orr gaining 55 yards. Soon after that, Riggs scored from the nine to pull Washington within a point at 14-13.

A fumbled punt set up Washington's winning score. Derrick Shepard mishandled the ball and snapper Dave Harbour fought the ball away from the returner for a first down at the New Orleans 18. Again, the Redskins were stuffed for no gain on third and goal, this time from well inside the one, and settled for Lohmiller's field goal and a 14-13 lead with just over 10 minutes left in the game.

With 2:43 left, it appeared that the Redskins would live to regret not taking full advantage of their opportunities as New Orleans' Morton Andersen, who had hit more than 85 percent of his attempts inside of 40 yards in his career, launched a field goal try from 36 yards that appeared to be good, but it was a few inches wide. Washington got two first downs to kill the clock after that.

Joe Gibbs' Father Dies
Former law enforcement officer
J. C. Gibbs was 72

10/8/89	REDSKINS (3-2) 30, Cardinals (2-3) 28				53,335
Pho	0	14	7	7	28
Was	10	3	0	17	30
Was	FG Lohmiller 22				
Was	Byner 2 pass from Rypien (Lohmiller kick)				
Was	FG Lohmiller 32				
Pho	J. T. Smith 7 pass from Hogeboom (Del Greco kick)				
Pho	J. T. Smith 20 pass from Hogeboom (Del Greco kick)				
Pho	Farrell 44 run (Del Greco kick)				
Was	FG Lohmiller 37				
Was	Monk 12 pass from Rypien (Lohmiller kick)				
Was	Clark 23 pass from Rypien (Lohmiller kick)				
Pho	J. T. Smith 17 pass from Hogeboom (Del Greco kick)				

RFK Stadium—In a game of scoring runs, the Cardinals' final charge ran out of time and the Redskins held on for the win.

The Redskins jumped out on top first. Darrell Green intercepted two passes to set up the first two scores, a 22-yard field goal by Chip Lohmiller and a two-yard touchdown flip from Mark Rypien to Ernest Byner. Lohmiller booted another three-pointer a minute into the second quarter to boost Washington's lead to 13-0. It appeared the usual rout of the Cardinals was going to be the order of the day.

The Cards weren't about to cooperate. By halftime, two touchdown passes from Gary Hogeboom to J. T. Smith had the visitors up 14-13. When Earl Ferrell took off for 44 yards and a touchdown late in the third period, it was the Cardinals leaving the Redskins in their dust.

Then it was Washington's turn. The Cardinals were poised to respond to a 37-yard Lohmiller field goal with possession at the Washington 47. However, Hogeboom overthrew his intended receiver and Alvin Walton intercepted the pass at the eight. Ninety-two yards later, Rypien eluded a blitzing linebacker and zipped a 12-yard TD to Art Monk to put the Redskins back in the lead at 23-21. They pushed through an insurance score with just under two minutes left on Rypien's third-down, 23-yard touchdown pass to Gary Clark for a 30-21 lead.

As it turned out, the Redskins needed that extra cushion. It took Phoenix just 1:40 to score on Hogeboom's fourth touchdown pass of the day and then they recovered an onside kick to bring flashbacks of improbable, last second losses at RFK earlier in the season. Asked if he was having such unpleasant visions at the time, Joe Gibbs said, "I think that everyone in the stadium was."

After one completion, Phoenix eschewed a 57-yard field goal attempt in favor of a Hail Mary from the Washington 40. Hogeboom never got it off as Charles Mann applied enough pressure to force the play to be aborted. A weak lateral attempt to a back was all the Cardinals could get off before time ran out. Gibbs, the remaining crowd (some of whom had left thinking the Redskins had lost, others thinking that they had won easily), and the team woke up from the recurring nightmare and all was well.

Williams Throws at Practice
QB says he could return in as soon as two weeks

10/15/89	GIANTS (5-1) 20, Redskins (3-3) 17				76,245
Was	0	3	7	7	17
NYG	3	0	3	14	20
NYG	FG Allegre 33				
Was	FG Lohmiller 37				
NYG	FG Allegre 48				

Was	Sanders 29 pass from Rypien (Lohmiller kick)
NYG	Bavaro 12 pass from Simms (Allegre kick)
NYG	Turner 25 pass from Simms (Allegre kick)
Was	Monk 5 pass from Rypien

Giants Stadium—Stop me if you've heard this one before. The Giants rallied in the fourth quarter to edge the Redsk—oh, you *have* heard it before. Well, here goes anyway as this one had its own unique set of frustrations for Washington.

Throughout the first half and much of the third quarter, neither team's offense was able to generate much of anything. New York's Raul Allegre had two field goals, Washington Chip Lohmiller had one and it was 6-3 when Washington took over at its own 18 late in the third.

Suddenly, an offense came to life and it was the Redskins'. In driving the team 82 yards for a touchdown, Mark Rypien never faced a third down and beat a first-down blitz to throw the go-ahead touchdown pass with just over a minute left in the third.

Actually, most of the credit for the TD has to go to receiver Ricky Sanders. It appeared that Rypien had overthrown the pass but Sanders was having none of that, laying out to make a beautiful, diving catch. Lohmiller's extra point had the Redskins up 10-6 entering the final period.

Of course, the Giants offense also was revived. Naturally, they drove 77 yards to a touchdown, converting a fourth and one along the way. Then, as one would suspect, after Gary Clark had converted a third down with a reception over the middle, linebacker Carl Banks' helmet found the football, Clark fumbled and the Giants recovered. New York—no surprise here—converted another fourth down by mere inches before a fumble went right past Washington linebacker Ravin Caldwell and into the hands of one of their offensive linemen. And, you guessed it, Phil Simms threw a 25-yard, third-down touchdown pass to Odessa Turner to put New York up 20-10 with 5:16 left.

The Redskins did respond quickly, taking just two minutes to score on Rypien's five-yard pass to Monk. Needless to say, they never got their hands on the ball again because, as usual, the Giants ground out the final 3:10 of the clock.

10/22/89	REDSKINS (4-3) 32, Bucs (3-4) 28				52,862
TB	7	0	0	21	28
Was	0	12	17	3	32
TB	Reynolds 33 blocked punt return (Igwebuike kick)				
Was	FG Lohmiller 33				
Was	Safety Manley tackled Testaverde in end zone				
Was	Clark 7 pass from Rypien (Lohmiller kick)				
Was	Clark 10 pass from Rypien (Lohmiller kick)				
Was	FG Lohmiller 42				
Was	Riggs 6 run (Lohmiller kick)				
TB	Tate 10 pass from Testaverde (Igwebuike kick)				
TB	Hill 20 pass from Testaverde (Igwebuike kick)				
Was	FG Lohmiller 29				
TB	Carrier 4 pass from Testaverde (Igwebuike kick)				

RFK Stadium—The Redskins scored 29 unanswered points in the second and third quarters and then had to hold off a furious Tampa Bay rally at the end to hold on for the win.

Things did not start well for the home team as the Bucs' Ricky Reynolds blocked a punt and returned it 33 yards for a 7-0 lead with a little over five minutes left in the first quarter.

In the second period, the Redskins started to roll. First, Chip Lohmiller hit a 33-yard field goal. Then Wilbur Marshall flushed Tampa Bay quarterback Vinny Testaverde out of the pocket and into the waiting arms of Dexter Manley, who got the sack in the end zone for a safety. With 13 seconds left in the half, the Redskins took the lead for the first time when Mark Rypien escaped a blitz and tossed a seven-yard touchdown pass to Gary Clark. The receiver made a nice play on the low pass, pinning it against his thigh before taking possession.

The roll continued through the third quarter. At the time that Gerald Riggs rolled six yards for a touchdown to make the score 29-7, Tampa Bay had two first downs and one net yard rushing.

The Bucs abandoned the run—they finished the game with just that one yard—but Testaverde got blazing hot. Less than two minutes after Riggs' TD, Testaverde threw a 10-yard touchdown pass to Lars Tate. Tampa Bay followed that up by recovering an onside kick. Three plays later, Testaverde threw another scoring pass, this one 20 yards to Bruce Hill to make it 29-21. Any premature celebrations taking place in the stands or on the sidelines promptly ceased.

The only way to cool down Testaverde (245 yards passing in the final 16 minutes) was to keep him on the sidelines for a while, and the Washington offense did just that, grinding out a time-consuming drive to a Lohmiller field goal to push the lead up to 32-21 with 3:04 left. Testaverde did get one more touchdown pass with 1:11 left, but Art Monk covered the subsequent onside kick to deprive Vinny of one more shot.

Wrist Injury Lands Green on IR; Wilburn Back to Old CB Spot

Oct 23—The Redskins usually thrive on takeaways from their opponents, but they'd just as soon wish that Todd Bowles' diving interception last Sunday had never taken place.

That's because cornerback Darrell Green collided with Bowles during the play, suffering multiple injuries in the process. The most serious of those were to his left wrist, which required surgery and the placement of some pins to repair.

Green will be placed on the injured reserve list, which means he'll be sidelined for at least six games. Barry Wilburn will be moved back to corner from safety and start in Green's place.

10/24/89	RAIDERS (4-4) 37, Redskins (4-4) 24		52,781	
Was	7	3	7	7	24
LA	14	3	20	0	37
LA	Fernandez 18 pass from Beuerlein (Jaeger kick)			
LA	Fernandez 8 pass from Beuerlein (Jaeger kick)			
Was	Howard 99 kickoff return (Lohmiller kick)			
LA	FG Jaeger 26			
Was	FG Lohmiller 43			
LA	Jackson 73 run (Jaeger kick)			
LA	FG Jaeger 28			
LA	FG Jaeger 37			
LA	Anderson 45 interception return (Jaeger kick)			
Was	Clark 27 pass from Rypien (Lohmiller kick)			
Was	Sanders 14 pass from Humphries (Lohmiller kick)			

Los Angeles Coliseum—The Redskins turned the ball over a nightmarish eight times, five times in the third quarter alone, allowing the Raiders to win easily 37-24.

The worst culprit was quarterback Mark Rypien, who put the ball on the ground four times. "It's a problem, a big problem," said Joe Gibbs. So were the three interceptions Rypien threw.

Although the giveaways were the focus of the post game talk, it's likely that the Raiders would have won easily with any of them. They moved smartly with touchdowns on each of their first two possessions and never were seriously threatened.

The Redskins did manage to pull within seven twice. After LA's second touchdown, Joe Howard fielded the ensuing kickoff, found wide open spaces and rolled untouched for a touchdown. Jeff Jaeger answered with a 26-yard field goal early in the second quarter to push the Oakland lead back up to ten.

Chip Lohmiller's 43-yard field goal as the first half ended again pulled the Skins within seven, but this time the home team had an even better answer. On the second play after the second-half kickoff, Bo Jackson took a pitchout to the left, broke a couple of

attempted tackles and took off down the sideline 73 yards for a touchdown to break it open.

It was only then that the dreadful turnover display commenced. Rypien and Howard each lost a fumble and Rypien threw three interceptions. Gibbs yanked Rypien in favor of Stan Humphries and the replacement quarterback promptly threw an interception to Eddie Anderson, who returned it 45 yards for a touchdown.

Luckily for the Redskins, Beuerlein had been injured and replaced by Jay Schroeder. The ex-Redskin was not sharp, completing just one of eight for a net of one yard. If not for Los Angeles' offensive ineffectiveness in the second half, the Raiders probably could have named their own score. As it was Anderson's touchdown made it 37-10 and two Washington touchdowns over that were scant window dressing.

"This one couldn't have turned out any better," said Schroeder. That's your opinion, Jay.

Nov 1

Williams Back, Named Starter vs. Cowboys
Back injury better, will get first start of the year

11/5/89	Cowboys (1-8) 13, REDSKINS (4-5) 3		53,187	
Dal	0	3	7	3	13
Was	0	0	3	0	3
Dal	FG Ruzek 20			
Was	FG Lohmiller 35			
Dal	Palmer 2 run (Ruzek kick)			
Dal	FG Ruzek 43			

RFK Stadium—The winless Dallas Cowboys came into RFK Stadium and left with a nationally televised win over their rivals. The Redskins left with considerable egg on their faces, a losing record, and playoff hopes that were extremely dim.

"It's a real low point for us," Coach Joe Gibbs said. "We're not getting better, and we're not playing winning football. We're just not getting the job done, starting with me."

Most of the damage was done by running back Paul Palmer who rushed for 110 yards on 18 carries. He also got the game's only touchdown, a score that he set up himself. In the third quarter, Washington had just tied the game at three on Chip Lohmiller's 35-yard field goal. On third and three at the Dallas 47, Palmer took the handoff and eluded Clarence Vaughn, making the safety look foolish in the process. Palmer galloped 47 yards to the six and scored two plays later on a two-yard run.

Washington never seriously threatened after that.

Nov 7

CB Wilburn Test Positive for Cocaine, Gets 4-Game Suspension
Team evidently knew of test result during preseason

11/12/85	Redskins (5-5) 10, EAGLES (6-4) 3		65,443	
Was	3	7	0	0	10
Phil	0	3	0	0	3
Was	FG Lohmiller 34			
Was	Byner 1 run (Lohmiller kick)			
Phil	FG DeLine 49			

Veterans Stadium—A fourth down gamble that paid off set up the game's only touchdown as the Redskins held off the Eagles.

Playing with an offensive line already depleted by injuries, the loss of tackle Joe Jacoby forced Joe Gibbs to change his offensive game plan from conservative to downright Reaganesque. Ball control was the name of the game, and that means clock control. Washington held the ball for more than 37 minutes, keeping it out of the hands of nemesis Randall Cunningham, the Eagle quarterback.

Still, Gibbs figured that he'd have to take a chance somewhere during the course of the game and found the right spot early in the second quarter while holding a 3-0 lead. On fourth and one from the Eagle 33, Gibbs bypassed a field goal try and sent in his goal line offense. It looked as if about fourteen Eagles were piling into the middle of the line, trying to tackle a back who didn't have the ball. Quarterback Doug Williams' play fake took care of the first part of the job; now he had to get the ball to tight end Jimmy Johnson, who was all alone in the secondary. The wind played some tricks with the pass and Johnson had to come back for it. The Eagles tackled him at the nine. Three plays later, Ernest Byner blasted over from the one to give Washington a 10-0 lead.

"I've never run that play in a game before," said Johnson, "but I'll bet it breaks wide open nine times out of ten in practice."

The Eagles scored on a field goal with a second left in the first half, but that would be all. Their best chance came in the third quarter when they drove to the Washington 19, but Monte Coleman blitzed Cunningham and, rather than eat the ball, the quarterback made an ill-advised throw that Kurt Gouveia intercepted to kill the threat. A couple of "Big Ben" rainbows into the end zone in the closing seconds also came up empty.

End of the Road: Positive Drug Test Gets Manley Expelled from NFL

Nov 16—Dexter Manley's controversial career with the Washington Redskins is apparently at an end.

The charismatic but troubled defensive end tested positive for narcotics for the third time last week, resulting in a mandatory expulsion from the NFL.

Although he could apply for reinstatement after a year, it's nearly certain that the Redskins would not be interested in bringing him back.

Nov 16

Rypien Returns as Starter as Williams' Back Problems Resurface

11/20/89	Broncos (9-2) 14, REDSKINS (5-6) 10				52,975
Den	7	7	0	0	**14**
Was	7	0	3	0	**10**
Was	Morris 8 run (Lohmiller kick)				
Den	Bratton 1 pass from Kubiak (Treadwell kick)				
Den	Nattiel 5 pass from Kubiak (Treadwell kick)				
Was	FG Lohmiller 32				

RFK Stadium—Denver quarterback John Elway called in sick for this one, but his backup Gary Kubiak was more than up to the task, throwing two touchdown passes to lead the Broncos past the Redskins.

An unusually strong, swirling wind was present throughout the game. Washington broke on top early. On Denver's third play from scrimmage, Fred Stokes got the defensive lineman's hat trick when he sacked Kubiak, stripped the ball away and recovered the fumble. Stokes returned it to the eight and Jamie Morris ran it in on the next play. Just over a minute into the game, the Redskins held a 7-0 lead.

It didn't take long for Washington to give that touchdown right back. About five minutes later, Morris coughed the ball up deep in his own territory and Denver recovered at the five. On second down, Kubiak, in the game because Elway came down with a severe case of stomach flu a couple of hours before kickoff, flipped a one-yard touchdown pass to Melvin Bratton to tie the game.

In the second quarter, Denver put on the game's only sustained touchdown drive. The Broncos converted five third downs and Kubiak defied the tricky wind to put the perfect touch on his touchdown pass to Ricky Nattiel, getting the ball just over the fingertips of two leaping defenders to make the Denver lead 14-7.

Washington had the wind at its back in the third quarter and manufactured a couple of good chances, but only three points. One foray inside the Denver 20 ended when Morris fumbled the ball away again and they came away with a field goal after reaching the Denver 15.

Later in the third, the Skins attempted to convert a fourth and one at their own 39 with a fake punt. The play was stuffed for a loss—and so were the Redskins' chances. Against the wind in the fourth quarter, Washington couldn't get past its own 33.

11/26/89	REDSKINS (6-6) 38, Bears (6-6) 14				50,044
Chi	0	14	0	0	**14**
Was	0	14	10	14	**38**
Was	Warren 3 pass from Rypien (Lohmiller kick)				
Was	Clark 5 pass from Rypien (Lohmiller kick)				
Chi	T. Sanders 96 kickoff return (Butler kick)				
Chi	McKinnon 12 pass from Tomczak (Butler kick)				
Was	FG Lohmiller 28				
Was	Monk 16 pass from Rypien (Lohmiller kick)				
Was	Monk 9 pass from Rypien (Lohmiller kick)				
Was	Byner 4 run (Lohmiller kick)				

RFK Stadium—The Redskins outscored the Bears 24-0 in the second half to turn a tight game into a rout that brought out the worst in Chicago coach Mike Ditka.

"I refuse to stand back and credit the other team for playing well. We just stink," said Ditka. "We were completely outclassed." He was right about the last part, in more ways than one.

The primary source of the coach's irritation came from the effectiveness of Washington's pass game. Mark Rypien lit them up for 401 yards and four touchdowns. Art Monk and Gary Clark had nine and eight catches, respectively, with each gaining well over 100 yards receiving.

Cornerback Donnell Woolford was the victim on many of those catches. His coach offered these words to console the rookie afterwards: "Evidently, he can't cover his own shadow."

The game turned midway through the third quarter. After Rypien's first two touchdown passes had given Washington a 14-0 lead, the Bears battled back to tie it up at halftime. It appeared that it would be a tight contest to the finish.

The Redskins drove 80 yards and took the lead on Chip Lohmiller's 28-yard field goal with 4:35 left in the third. "We were feeling pretty good about it on the sideline," said Jim Lachey, "then the word came down to stay loose. We were going to try the onside kick."

Lohmiller's bunt was perfectly executed and the only suspense was whether Terry Orr or Joe Howard would recover it. There was no Bear in the area. Ditka, of course, took this in stride: "When our guy (Lorenzo Lynch) was going on the field, the last thing we told him was to watch the onside kick. Does someone like that even belong in the NFL? Or am I just being cruel? It's a joke."

Four plays later, Rypien went to Monk for 18 yards and a touchdown and the rout was on. Early in the fourth quarter, Rypien again threw a TD pass to Monk, and it was all over but the crying. And we know who was crying the loudest.

12/3/89	Redskins (7-6) 29, CARDINALS (5-8) 10				38,870
Was	3	7	14	5	**29**
Pho	0	10	0	0	**10**
Was	FG Lohmiller 29				
Was	Byner 1 run (Lohmiller kick)				
Pho	FG Del Greco 27				

Pho	Ferrell 1 run (Del Greco kick)	
Was	Riggs 1 run (Lohmiller kick)	
Was	Johnson 59 interception return (Lohmiller kick)	
Was	FG Lohmiller 24	
Was	Safety Tupa intentional grounding in end zone	

Sun Devil Stadium—Rookie cornerback A. J. Johnson intercepted two passes, returning one of them for a game-breaking touchdown, as the Redskins beat the Cardinals.

In between his heroics, Johnson learned some lessons the hard way. His first pick set up Chip Lohmiller's 29-yard field goal for a 3-0 Washington lead. It became 10-0 after a 67-yard drive culminated in Ernest Byner's one-yard touchdown run early in the second quarter.

Johnson spent most of the day matched up with Roy Green, a 10-year veteran and notorious Redskin tormentor. First, Green fooled Johnson into mistiming his leap, turning a dangerous, floating pass by Tom Tupa into a 50-yard gain to set up a field goal. Then, late in the second period, Green gave the rookie a little shove as another Tupa floater descended, but it was Johnson who was flagged for interference. That set up the tying touchdown, Earl Ferrell's one-yard run.

Johnson took it in stride. "A 10-year veteran used a trick and stuck me good," he said.

The rally was over for the home team. Joe Howard returned the second-half kickoff 36 yards to the Washington 39 and the Redskins took 11 plays to take it in from there. A 25-yard connection between Mark Rypien got them down to the five. On fourth down from the one, Gerald Riggs followed a path cleared by Jim Lachey, Mark Schlereth and Jimmie Johnson into the end zone.

Phoenix responded by moving smartly to the Washington 45, but Tupa went to Green once too often. Johnson anticipated the out pattern that Green ran, stepped in front of the pass and caught it with nothing but green grass in front of him. Fifty-nine yards later, the Redskins had a two-touchdown lead. The Cards' last real threat expired late in the third quarter when Wayne Davis intercepted Tupa's pass in the end zone.

December 4

No Coach Joe? Oh, No!
Coach says he will consider retirement after season

12/10/89	**REDSKINS (8-6) 26, Chargers (4-10) 21**			47,693	
SD	14	0	0	7	**21**
Was	0	7	9	10	**26**

SD	A. Miller 25 pass from Tolliver (Bahr kick)	
SD	Walker 5 pass from Tolliver (Bahr kick)	
Was	Sanders 45 pass from Rypien (Lohmiller kick)	
Was	FG Lohmiller 38	
Was	FG Lohmiller 31	
Was	FG Lohmiller 32	
SD	Butts 10 run 9Bahr kick)	
Was	Clark 33 pass from Rypien (Lohmiller kick)	
Was	FG Lohmiller 28	

RFK Stadium—Chip Lohmiller kicked four field goals to help the Redskins pull past the Chargers. Washington had to come from behind twice and then survive a late scare before the 26-21 win was ensured.

The win was Joe Gibbs' 100th as head coach of the Redskins.

Billy Joe Tolliver, San Diego's rookie quarterback, looked like an old pro in guiding the Chargers to touchdowns on their first two possessions. He capped each of the drives with scoring passes and the 14-0 lead held until late in the second quarter.

In the final minute of the half, the Washington offense finally got untracked and drove 93 yards for a touchdown. The score came when Ricky Sanders somehow got wide open and made a

nice catch of Mark Rypien's bomb, completing a 45-yard scoring play with just 15 seconds left until halftime.

After intermission, the Redskins began to dominate on the field but couldn't take control on the scoreboard. Three forays inside the Charger 20 resulted in just three Lohmiller field goals. With the Redskin defense having brought Tolliver under control with a heavy dose of blitzes, it appeared that the 16-14 lead might suffice.

That was until back Darrin Nelson made a beautiful, one-handed catch of a screen pass and blew past much of the defense for a 32-yard gain deep into Washington territory. Two plays later, with just over eight minutes left in the game, fullback Marion Butts gave the Chargers a 21-16 lead with a 10-yard touchdown smash.

Joe Howard returned the ensuing kickoff 51 yards to the San Diego 39 and three plays later, the Redskins faced fourth and four at the 33.

Joe Gibbs hadn't won 99 games prior to this one by playing it safe, so he decided to forego a 50-yard Lohmiller field goal attempt and go for it all. The Chargers also rolled the dice, sending eight men on the pass rush. The defensive ploy nearly worked as the defenders buried Rypien just as he released his pass to Gary Clark, who was open on a deep post. The receiver had to slow down a bit to get a bead on the ball, but gathered it in at the goal line just before the defender arrived.

A Tolliver fumble set up Lohmiller's fourth field goal to give Washington a 26-21 lead with 3:24 left. Nobody could breathe easily, however, as the Chargers moved down to the Washington six, where they faced fourth and two with 1:20 remaining. Tolliver got his pass into Wayne Walker's bread basket, but cornerback Martin Mayhew arrived at the receiver the same time the ball did, executed a classic strip, and the ball fell harmlessly to the ground.

12/17/89	**Redskins (9-6) 31, FALCONS (3-12) 30**			37,501	
Was	3	7	21	0	**31**
Atl	3	24	3	0	**30**

Atl	FG Davis 33	
Was	FG Lohmiller 37	
Was	Monk 34 pass from Williams (Lohmiller kick)	
Atl	Haynes 72 pass from Miller (Davis kick)	
Atl	Haynes 17 pass from Miller (Davis kick)	
Atl	FG Davis 24	
Atl	Settle 3 run (Davis kick)	
Was	Monk 60 pass from Rypien (Lohmiller kick)	
Was	Byner 1 run (Lohmiller kick)	
Was	Rypien 9 run (Lohmiller kick)	
Atl	FG Davis 32	

Atlanta-Fulton County Stadium—Nobody would have blamed the Redskins if they had mailed in the second half of this one. Not only were they trailing 27-10, but they also saw that their only shot at keeping playoff possibilities alive—a Rams loss—was very unlikely; Los Angeles held a 21-point halftime lead.

But, as Mark Rypien said afterward, the attitude of the team was, "Heck with it, let's come back and win." And that they did, scoring 21 points in a span of less than five minutes of the third quarter to come away with a 31-30 victory.

That burst answered a similar binge the Falcons had in the second quarter, when they erased a 10-3 Washington lead with 24 points in a little under nine minutes. Atlanta was poised to extend its lead just after halftime with a drive into Washington territory, but Charles Mann sacked Chris Miller to push the Falcons out of field goal range and force a punt.

After intermission the Redskins started at their own 20, and took just three plays to move in for the touchdown. The last play was a 60-yard bomb from Rypien to Art Monk, who was a good 15 yards away from the nearest defender.

Washington got the ball back quickly when A. J. Johnson intercepted Miller's pass at the Washington 31. That led to another quick drive that Ernest Byner capped with a one-yard scoring run. Then Miller threw another interception, this one to defensive tackle Darryl Grant, and the Redskins were in business at the Atlanta 34. They took to the ground this time, running on five of the six plays required to get into the end zone. The TD came on a daring naked bootleg run by Rypien on fourth and one from the nine and the Redskins led 31-27.

Atlanta mustered a field goal to pull within a point with more than 17 minutes left to play, but couldn't move the ball after Miller was knocked out of the game when he was sacked by blitzing linebackers Monte Coleman and Ravin Caldwell.

12/23/89	Redskins (10-6) 29, SEAHAWKS (7-9) 0				60,294
Was	10	3	16	0	29
Sea	0	0	0	0	0
Was	FG Lohmiller 29				
Was	Byner 2 run (Lohmiller kick)				
Was	FG Lohmiller 27				
Was	Clark 44 pass from Rypien				
Was	Safety Krieg tackled in end zone				
Was	Byner 8 run (Lohmiller kick)				

Kingdome—The Redskins used a combination of stout defense and ball-control offense to shut out the Seahawks 29-0.

Seattle held slim playoff hopes prior to the Saturday afternoon contest, but those ended before kickoff when Buffalo beat the Jets. Still, the national media would take note of this game, as it was to be the last for Steve Largent, the Seattle receiver who was retiring with the career Triple Crown: most lifetime receptions, receiving yards and touchdown catches.

Another a pending retirement that was of considerably less note except to the Redskins faithful was that of longtime middle linebacker Neal Olkewicz. While certainly Olkie's teammates understood why the spotlight was on Largent, they still used the relative lack of attention for motivation.

"All we hear about all week was Largent retiring," said defensive end Fred Stokes, "but we had a guy retiring, too. We wanted to give him a shutout and a game ball and send him home happy."

If getting a shutout was indeed his criteria, then Olkewicz certainly went home delighted. Largent caught just two passes, Seattle gained just 26 yards rushing, Stokes sacked quarterback Dave Krieg in the end zone for a safety, and the Redskins forced four turnovers on the way to blanking the Seahawks. "It's hard to see how (my last game) could be more satisfying," said Olkewicz.

The Washington offense received a good deal of satisfaction as well. They took more than seven minutes off the clock in the first period as they marched to Chip Lohmiller's 29-yard field goal. Then, on the ensuing kickoff, Terry Orr sent Seattle's Elroy Harris flying and the ball did not accompany the returner on his airborne journey. Reggie Branch pounced on the ball at the Seahawk 20 and, three plays later, Byner gave his team a 10-0 lead with a two-yard run.

Lohmiller kicked a 27-yard field goal midway through the second quarter to provide his team with a comfortable 13-0 lead. After halftime, it took about five and a half minutes to make the margin downright cushy.

First, Rypien launched a 44-yard touchdown pass to Clark. Then, Stokes sacked harried Seattle quarterback Dave Krieg in the end zone for a safety. Finally, the Redskins drove to Byner's second rushing touchdown—this one from eight yards—to make it 29-0. Washington spent the rest of the game burning minutes off of the clock, building their time of possession edge to more than 20 minutes on the day (41:17 to 18:43).

1990
Head Coach: Joe Gibbs
Record: 10-6, Third in NFC East
Playoffs: Wild Card, lost in Divisional Round

Honors: Ernest Byner Pro Bowl; Gary Clark Pro Bowl; Darrell Green Pro Bowl, All-NFC; Jim Lachey Pro Bowl, All-NFL

Gibbs: 'They'll Have To Usher Me Out'

Jan 17—Even though Joe Gibbs felt that he really didn't have to, he announced today that he will be staying on as coach of the Washington Redskins.

"I said this before in a statement: I had no intention of leaving, and that probably won't ever change," Gibbs said.

"It's all go," said Gibbs. "I think it's the way everything wound up (the team's 5-0 finish)."

In early December, Gibbs didn't seem to be quite so "go" about returning.

"There's been a chance (that I'd leave) for two years," he said then. "I'm just being honest about it. For me, it's every year. I think how we finish this year will have a lot to say about how I feel."

After the season he took a ski trip with his family and during that vacation, he decided to stay.

"They'll have to usher me out," Gibbs said. "I don't think I will ever change on that. I mean it would take something happening to change me, and probably that will never happen. I still feel good about what I'm doing."

Feb. 6
Hog Gone: Bugel Names Cards Head Coach
Skins bring in Hanifan to coach O-Line

Mar 30:
Redskins Release Doug Williams
'Disappointed' former Super Bowl MVP still wants to play

Skins Cut Wilburn, Keep Bryant

May 9—In a surprising move, the Redskins moved talented but fragile running back Kelvin Bryan back onto their active roster. The team is flush with power backs like Gerald Riggs and Ernest Byner, but Bryant brings an element of explosiveness the others lack.

When he's on the *field*, that is. He missed the last six games of 1988 with a knee injury and all of last year with a neck problem.

To make room, Washington dropped defensive back Barry Wilburn.

He was a starter for much of his Redskins career, which started when he was drafted in the eighth round of the 1985 draft.

Wilburn was the victim of both a crowded defensive backfield situation and his off-field problems.

In November Wilburn was suspended for four games due to a positive drug test and was arrested for DWI after the season.

Aug 22
Skins Trade for Steelers DL Johnson
Price is conditional 4th or 5th-round pick

9/9/90	REDSKINS (1-0) 31, Cardinals (0-1) 0			52,649	
Pho	0	0	0	0	0
Was	7	7	14	3	31
Was	Sanders 37 pass from Rypien (Lohmiller kick)				
Was	Byner 4 pass from Rypien (Lohmiller kick)				
Was	Clark 43 pass from Rypien (Lohmiller kick)				
Was	Walton 57 interception return (Lohmiller kick)				
Was	FG Lohmiller 29				

RFK Stadium—Mark Rypien threw three touchdown passes and the Washington defense forced five turnovers as the Redskins easily defeated the Cardinals 31-0.

Two of the takeaways set up Rypien's first two scoring passes. Darrell Green intercepted a pass at the Cardinal 37 and Rypien passed to Ricky Sanders for the score from there. Martin Mayhew got an interception in his own territory at the 20. An eight yard drive culminated in Ernest Byner's four-yard TD catch and the Redskins led 14-0 at halftime.

After yet another turnover set up a 43-yard touchdown pass from Rypien to Gary Clark, the defense took matters into its own hands. Alvin Walton picked off a pass and returned it 57 yards for the touchdown. Chip Lohmiller booted a 29-yard field goal in the fourth quarter to wrap up the scoring.

The turnovers helped make a rout of what was a tight statistical edge for the Redskins. They outgained the Cardinals 347 yards to 294. Byner (17 carries for 63 yards) and Gerald Riggs (13 for 51) shared the load in the rushing game.

Sanders caught six passes for 90 yards while Clark had just three receptions and gained 75.

Gibbs Denies Retirement Report

Sep 10—Joe Gibbs has once again been called upon to comment on a report that his retirement from coaching is drawing near. On NBC's NFL pregame show, Will McDonough said that Gibbs would be one of three successful NFC coaches to quit after the 1990 season. The others were Mike Ditka and Bill Parcells.

Gibbs flatly denied the report, wondering why anyone would listen to McDonough when it comes to the details of his relationship with the Redskins.

"I plan to be here forever," Gibbs said. "He wasn't right last year about me or my contract. He made a statement this year that my contract is up, and that's not true either."

Skins Trade for DT Williams

Sep 11—In an effort to bolster their pass rush, the Redskins traded for Detroit defensive lineman Eric Williams. In exchange for the 6-4, 286-lb Williams the Lions got running back James Wilder and a late-round draft choice.

9/16/90	49ERS (2-0) 26, Redskins (1-1) 13			64,287	
Was	0	10	3	0	13
SF	3	17	3	3	26
SF	FG Cofer 31				
SF	Rice 12 pass from Montana (Cofer kick)				
Was	FG Lohmiller 37				
SF	Taylor 49 pass from Montana				

Was	Monk 35 pass from Rypien (Lohmiller kick)
SF	FG Cofer 29
Was	FG Lohmiller 20
SF	FG Cofer 26
SF	FG Cofer 34

Candlestick Park—San Francisco jumped on top of the Redskins 17-3 and the 49ers were able to keep Washington at arm's length for the remainder of the contest to take a 26-13 win.

Joe Montana's passing prowess was on display early as he cranked out touchdown aerials of 12 yards to Jerry Rice and 49 yards to John Taylor. Matt Cofer and Chip Lohmiller each booted a field goal and San Francisco led 17-3 late in the second quarter.

Joe Gibbs decided the situation was getting desperate enough to go for it on fourth and five at the 49er 35. Art Monk was the secondary receiver on the play and Mark Rypien was forced to go to him. It wasn't a bad choice; the result was a 35-yard touchdown to make it 17-10 with 1:48 left until intermission.

That was a little too much time for Montana and company, who efficiently moved inside the Washington 15. Cofer booted a 29-yard field goal just before the half ended.

In the third quarter, the Redskins had two great chances to dent the 49er lead, but couldn't quite capitalize. After a nice 73-yard drive to open the half, Washington came up empty when Lohmiller's 33-yard field goal attempt was blocked. Then a 40-yard connection from Rypien to Gary Clark gained a first and goal at the one. Two runs, however, were stuffed and safety Ronnie Lott sniffed out the bootleg on third down and dropped Rypien for a two-yard loss. Lohmiller's 20-yard field goal was scant consolation for the blown opportunities.

In fact, the score only served to awaken the Niner offense; they drove to another Cofer field goal with 50 seconds left in the third, keeping Washington two scores behind. The Redskins never threatened in the final stanza and Cofer kicked another field goal to finish up the scoring.

9/23/90	REDSKINS (2-1) 19, Cowboys (1-2) 15			53,804	
Dal	0	3	3	9	15
Was	3	3	6	7	19
Was	FG Lohmiller 37				
Dal	FG Willis 33				
Was	FG Lohmiller 23				
Dal	FG Willis 41				
Was	FG Lohmiller 24				
Was	FG Lohmiller 55				
Was	Green 18 interception return (Lohmiller kick)				
Dal	Smith 2 run (Willis kick)				
Dal	Safety Mojsiejenko stepped out of end zone				

RFK Stadium—Darrell Green scored his team's only touchdown on an interception return and Chip Lohmiller kicked four field goals to pace the Redskins past the Cowboys 19-15.

The pattern for the game was set early on when the Redskins executed a textbook 14-play march into Dallas territory only to see it stall. They settled for a 37-yard Lohmiller field goal.

Starting quarterback Mark Rypien suffered a knee injury in the second quarter and untested (10 NFL pass attempts), Stan Humphries replaced him. Humphries showed that he could hang up 3's on the scoreboard as well as Rypien and Lohmiller kicked field goals of 23, 24, and 55 yards. Ken Willis of Dallas managed a pair of three-pointers and it was 12-6 entering the fourth quarter.

Green's touchdown came on Dallas' first series of the fourth quarter. He stepped in front of a Troy Aikman pass intended for Kelvin Martin at the Dallas 18 and ran a serpentine route into the end zone.

"I must have run 200 yards," Green said. "It just happened so quick, I don't know what happened."

What happened was that the Redskins had some breathing room. Emmitt Smith scored a touchdown on a two-yard run with

3:03 left in the game. Backed up to their own one on the ensuing possession, the Redskins took an intentional safety rather than punting out of their own end zone. After the free kick, Todd Bowles' interception of Aikman sealed it for the Redskins.

Sep 24

Humphries in for Injured Rypien
Starter out 6-8 weeks with injured knee

9/30/90	Redskins (3-1) 38, CARDINALS (1-3) 10				49,303	
Was	0	7	10	21	-	**38**
Pho	0	10	0	0	-	**10**
Pho	FG Del Greco 32					
Was	Riggs 1 run (Lohmiller kick)					
Pho	Green 12 pass from Rosenbach (Del Greco kick)					
Was	FG Lohmiller 26					
Was	Clark 42 pass from Humphries (Lohmiller kick)					
Was	Humphries 1 run (Lohmiller kick)					
Was	Clark 42 pass from Humphries (Lohmiller kick)					
Was	Byner 1 run (Lohmiller kick)					

Sun Devil Stadium—Stan Humphries, filling in for an injured Mark Rypien, was 20 of 25 passing for 257 yards as the Redskins broke the game open in the second half and won 38-10.

After a scoreless first half he Cardinals got on the board first with a 32-yard Al Del Greco field goal. The Redskins countered with a drive that was capped by a one-yard touchdown blast by Gerald Riggs.

Phoenix grabbed a 10-7 lead at halftime, thanks to a 12-yard touchdown pass from Timm Rosenbach to Roy Green just prior to intermission. In the third quarter, Humphries moved the Redskins to the Cardinal nine with some key completions to Gary Clark, but they had to settle for a game-tying field goal by Chip Lohmiller.

Humphries had determined who his favorite target was. On Washington's next possession, Clark drew man coverage. A perfect pump fake sucked in Cedric Mack, the hapless defender, and Clark broke free to catch a 42-yard touchdown pass to put the Redskins in the lead for good.

After Humphries scored himself on a one-yard run, the quarterback and Clark (eight catches, 152 yards) victimized Mack again for another 42-yard TD and the rout was on. Earnest Byner capped the scoring with a one-yard touchdown run.

10/14/90	Giants (5-0) 24, REDSKINS (3-2) 20				54,737	
NYG	0	7	14	3		**24**
Was	3	0	10	7		**20**
Was	FG Lohmiller 42					
NYG	Baker 80 pass from Simms (Bahr kick)					
Was	FG Lohmiller 35					
NYG	Anderson 5 run (Bahr kick)					
Was	Sanders 31 pass from Byner (Lohmiller kick)					
NYG	Bavaro 2 pass from Simms (Bahr kick)					
Was	Riggs 1 run (Lohmiller kick)					
NYG	FG Bahr 19					

RFK Stadium—"I don't know if this was the toughest loss," said Joe Gibbs, "but it's the toughest right now because it happened right now."

With so many difficult losses to the Giants to choose from, the coach could be forgiven if he couldn't choose a least-favorite one. The script for this one was typical with the Giants taking the lead and then allowing the Redskins to rally back into it only to foil the comeback in the end.

New York gained a 7-3 lead in the second quarter. A simple crossing pattern designed to convert a third and 10 at the Giant 20 turned into an 80-yard touchdown from Phil Simms to receiver

Stephen Baker when containment broke down. Said Simms, "I wasn't exactly shocked that we made a few big plays."

Especially against Washington.

In the third quarter, Chip Lohmiller's 35-yard field goal made it a one-point game, but New York responded with a 5-yard touchdown run by Otis Anderson. A halfback option pass from Ernest Byner to Ricky Sanders was good for 31 yards and a touchdown, but the Giants immediately responded as a short dump off to fullback Maurice Carthon turned into a 63-yard gain. That set up a two-yard scoring pass from Simms to tight end Mark Bavaro and the Giants maintained their eight-point lead going into the fourth quarter.

To those who didn't know better, it started looking up for the Redskins after Gerald Riggs scored on a one-yard run with six minutes to play and Washington forced the Giants to punt from near midfield. The better informed knew that something bad would happen to the Redskins, and it did—some unseen hand guided the bouncing ball off of the leg of Washington's Johnny Thomas. Reyna Thompson pounced on the ball at the Washington one. Although the defense held New York to a field goal, the damage was done. A last-gasp drive ended when Greg Jackson picked off Stan Humphries' pass.

10/21/90	REDSKINS (4-2) 13, Eagles (2-4) 7				53,567	
Phil	0	0	0	7		**7**
Was	0	7	0	6		**13**
Was	Riggs 1 run (Lohmiller kick)					
Was	FG Lohmiller 33					
Was	FG Lohmiller 33					
Phil	Barnett 9 pass from Cunningham (Ruzek kick)					

RFK Stadium—The Redskins sacked Eagle quarterback Randall Cunningham five times en route to an ugly but welcome 13-7 win over Philadelphia.

"This one probably wasn't as fancy as the fans would like it," said Joe Gibbs, "but we're really happy to get out of it with a win."

This could have been a classic blowout, but Washington continually had to settle for field goal attempts instead of touchdowns when entering Philly territory. Worse, Chip Lohmiller wasn't converting on the opportunities, pushing four consecutive attempts to the left before finally connecting on two in the final quarter.

Tim Johnson, Fred Stokes, and Eric Williams combined for four sacks and their pressure helped the Redskins hold their nemesis Randall Cunningham to a mediocre outing. He did pass for 220 yards but needed 42 attempts to get there—not exactly an efficient performance.

The Eagles didn't scratch the scoreboard until just 43 seconds were left and Cunningham threw a nine-yard touchdown pass to Fred Barnett.

Gerald Riggs scored the Redskins' only touchdown on a one-yard blast in the second quarter. As has been the case often this year, Riggs (14 carries for 52 yards) and Earnest Byner (16 for 46), split the work on the ground.

10/28/90	GIANTS (7-0) 21, Redskins (4-3) 10				75,321	
Was	0	3	7	0		**10**
NYG	0	14	0	7		**21**
NYG	Baker 4 pass from Simms (Bahr kick)					
NYG	Bavaro 16 pass from Simms (Bahr kick)					
Was	FG Lohmiller 45					
Was	Humphries 5 run (Lohmiller kick)					
NYG	Walls 28 interception return (Bahr kick)					

Giants Stadium—The Redskins rallied from a 14-0 deficit and were knocking at the door, seemingly about to take the lead. But, as usual, nobody answered and Washington was left out in the cold against the Giants once again, losing 21-10.

New York took advantage of excellent field position, driving 41 and 47 yards to two Phil Simms touchdown passes in the second quarter. Then they got a bit greedy and went in for the kill, throwing a long pass to linebacker Lawrence Taylor from field goal formation.

The Redskins, though, always die a slow, painful, torturous death in New York, so rookie defensive back Alvoid Mays didn't bite on the fake and was covering Taylor. The Redskins got the ball on downs. Three passes from Stan Humphries to Don Warren moved Washington into position for a 45-yard Chip Lohmiller field goal and it was 14-3 at the half.

A five-yard TD run by Humphries in the third quarter made it 14-10. Early in the fourth, Washington was at the New York three. Humphries' pass found the hands of Ernest Byner in the end zone, but Byner's hands couldn't find the ball. Instead, it bounced into the arms of safety Terry Jackson, who did manage to gain possession for the interception.

The Redskins had another possession with a chance to take the lead, but Humphries was crushed as he released a pass and Everson Walls clinched the game with an interception and 28-yard touchdown return.

11/4/90	**Redskins (5-3) 41, LIONS (3-5) 38 OT**				69,326	
Was	7	7	7	17	3	**41**
Det	7	21	10	0	0	**38**
Det	Clark 33 pass from Peete (Karlis kick)					
Was	Riggs 8 run (Lohmiller kick)					
Det	Peete 10 run (Karlis kick)					
Det	White 34 interception return (Karlis kick)					
Was	Johnson 4 pass from Humphries (Lohmiller kick)					
Det	Matthews 24 pass from Peete (Karlis kick)					
Det	Sanders 45 run (Karlis kick)					
Was	Riggs 3 run (Lohmiller kick)					
Det	FG Karlis 26					
Was	Clark 34 pass from Rutledge (Lohmiller kick)					
Was	Rutledge 12 run (Lohmiller kick)					
Was	FG Lohmiller 34					

Pontiac Silverdome—The Redskins had beaten the Lions 12 straight times, but with about 10 minutes left in the third quarter, that streak appeared to be in great jeopardy.

Barry Sanders had just broken up the middle for a 45-yard touchdown and the Lions had a 35-14 lead. Redskin quarterback Stan Humphries had set up the touchdown run by throwing his third interception of the day. Humphries had started in place of an injured Mark Rypien so when Joe Gibbs looked down the bench, he saw third stringer Jeff Rutledge. He told Rutledge to start warming up.

Rutledge quickly led the Redskins on a 63-yard TD drive that pulled the Redskins within 14, but the Lions got three back on a field goal on the last play of the third quarter. It was 38-21.

Then Washington got two strokes of good fortune. First, Eric Williams sidelined Lions quarterback Rodney Peete after a hit. Second, Detroit coach Wayne Fontes got brain lock. During the entire fourth quarter, when just a couple of first downs strung together would have clinched the game for the Lions, when he had Bob Gagliano at quarterback, Fontes did not once call the number of his emerging superstar running back, Barry Sanders. Through three quarters, Sanders had 10 carries for 100 yards. When the game ended, Sanders had 10 carries for 100 yards.

After a Chip Lohmiller field goal that made it 38-24, the comeback began in earnest.

With 8:41 to go, Washington took over at its own 20 and moved smartly down the field, taking seven plays to score—a drive finished off with a 34-yard TD pass to Gary Clark.

With Sanders no more than a decoy and spectator, Detroit could only manage to burn two minutes off the clock and punted with 3:24 left. Washington got the ball at its own 15. Rutledge

converted three third downs in moving the ball downfield, completing 8 of 12 passes, the last to Clark moving the ball to the Lions 12. Washington called its final time out with 24 seconds left. The Posse of Clark, Art Monk, and Ricky Sanders was having one of its best days ever, on the way to combining for 32 catches for 432 yards. So it was going to be four shots to the end zone to tie the game, right?

But Gibbs had seen something in the films that somehow made him think that the slow and not-so-nimble Rutledge could score on a quarterback draw. Rutledge seemed to take forever to make his way to pay dirt, but he did and the score was tied.

Each team had a possession in overtime before the Redskins started their game winning drive. The big play was a 40-yard Rutledge to Monk connection on third and fifteen at the Redskin five. Nine plays later, Lohmiller was perfect from 34 yards out, 9:10 into overtime and Washington had a 41-38 win.

Nov 5

Rally Earns Rutledge Starting Job
33-year-old QB rewarded for record comeback vs. Loins

Eagles' White: Bostic Plays Dirty

Nov 8—When the Redskins come in to Veteran's Stadium on Monday night, they'd better watch out, says their star defensive end Reggie White.

Specifically, White said he would be targeting center Jeff Bostic because, according to White, Bostic used illegal chop blocks on him in the two teams' first meeting of the season. White wasn't specific about what he would do to Bostic. "I've got it set in my mind what I want to do," said White. "I know, but I don't want the whole nation to know." White added, "It will be legal."

Bostic and offensive line coach Jim Hanifan profess to have no idea what White was talking about. "I've been through two knee operations myself," said Bostic, "and I wouldn't want to put anybody through the rehab process. We don't teach or use illegal techniques."

The cut block, taking out from down low when he's running free, is perfectly legal. It's when the opponent is engaged with another blocker that taking him out at the knees that the cut becomes a chop block. Hanifan said that Bostic didn't chop White at all in their first meeting and in his only attempt to cut White he whiffed completely.

White's accusations may have had something to do with the four roughness and unsportsmanlike conduct major penalties the Eagles drew earlier at RFK. Afterwards the Eagles complained loudly that such flags were not doled out equally. It's possible that White's words were intended to get the officials to take a closer look at what the Redskins were doing.

11/12/90	**EAGLES (5-4) 28, Redskins (5-4) 14**				65,857
Was	0	7	0	7	**14**
Phil	7	0	21	0	**28**
Phil	Frizzell 30 interception return (Ruzek kick)				
Was	Warren 8 pass from Rutledge (Lohmiller kick)				
Phil	Sherman 9 pass from Byars (Ruzek kick)				
Phil	Simmons 18 fumble return (Ruzek kick)				
Phil	Sherman 3 pass from Cunningham (Ruzek kick)				
Was	Mitchell 1 run (Lohmiller kick)				

Veterans Stadium—The Eagles took control of the game in the second half, knocking both of Washington's active quarterbacks out of the game in the course of racking up three third-quarter touchdowns in less than four minutes.

In all, nine Redskins had to be assisted off of the field, prompting one Eagle to yell tauntingly, "Do you guys need any more body bags out there?"

While still at full strength, Washington did manage to stay in the game, although their offense was unable to mount a scoring drive. With Philadelphia holding a 7-0 lead, Sidney Johnson crashed through on a punt block and Jeff Feagles aborted his kick. The punter got off a pass but was flagged for intentional grounding and Washington gained possession at the Eagle 12. Two plays later, Philly went for a play fake and Don Warren was wide open to catch Jeff Rutledge's eight-yard touchdown pass, tying the game at seven on the first play of the second quarter.

The Philadelphia touchdown barrage started midway through the third quarter. Randall Cunningham flipped a six-yard pass to running back Heath Sherman to convert a fourth and four at the Washington 27. Soon after that, Keith Byars threw to Sherman for nine yards and a touchdown on a halfback option.

Then blitzing safety Wes Hopkins got the first quarterback KO, slamming into Rutledge and knocking the ball loose in the process. End Clyde Simmons picked it up and rumbled 18 yards to make it 21-7. Reggie White's interception of Stan Humphries led to a touchdown pass from Cunningham to Sherman just after that. The Eagles scored their three touchdowns in 3:51.

A crunching hit by White forced Humphries from the game in the fourth quarter and rookie running back Brian Mitchell, a college quarterback, led a touchdown drive in the fourth quarter. He completed three of six passes for 40 yards and scored the TD himself on a one-yard run.

Body Bagged: Humphries, 2 Others on IR

Nov 15—Quarterback Stan Humphries was one of three Redskins placed on the injured reserve list today. Along with Humphries, running back Gerald Riggs and kick returner Walter Stanley will miss a minimum of four games.

Humphries suffered a knee injury after being buried by defensive end Reggie White. It doesn't look like he'll need surgery, so his absence isn't likely to extend beyond the required four weeks. Mark Rypien, who was the starter for the first three games before injuring his knee, is likely to regain his starting job if he's healthy enough to go on Sunday. If he can't go, former Cowboy Gary Hogeboom, signed after Rypien was injured, is likely to get the start since Jeff Rutledge is probably out due to a badly bruised thumb on his throwing hand.

Riggs' injury wasn't due so much to Philly's fierce defense as it was to a set of wheels that may be turning bad. The 30-year-old's left foot, specifically his arch, flared up again during the second quarter. The word "again" is present there because it's the same injury that forced him out of four games and relegated him to part-time duty in four others last year.

"It's a tough time to get injured," said Riggs. "It does feel very similar to what happened last year, but I hope it's something we can work out."

Of the others helped off the field on Monday night, all are expected to play Sunday except kick returner Joe Howard, who is being watched due to a concussion. Tackle Ed Simmons and linebacker Greg Manusky, both of whom suffered knee injuries, are expected to play.

11/18/90	**REDSKINS (6-4) 31, Saints (4-6) 17**				52,573
NO	7	3	0	7	**17**
Was	3	14	7	7	**31**
NO	Perriman 16 pass from Walsh (Andersen kick)				
Was	FG Lohmiller 39				
Was	Clark 8 pass from Rypien (Lohmiller kick)				
NO	FG Andersen 38				
Was	Monk 7 pass from Rypien (Lohmiller kick)				
Was	Clark 19 pass from Rypien (Lohmiller kick)				
Was	Bryant 3 pass from Rypien (Lohmiller kick)				
NO	Turner 8 pass from Walsh (Andersen kick)				

RFK Stadium—Mark Rypien returned to the lineup after missing six games with a knee injury and threw for 311 yards and four touchdowns to lead the Redskins past the Saints.

New Orleans broke on top first after getting a short field to work with. They drove 33 yards to a touchdown on a 16-yard pass from Steve Walsh to Brett Perriman. The Redskins answered with Rypien's first touchdown pass, this one to Gary Clark, early in the second quarter. Each team also got a field goal, making it 10-10 with 4:04 left in the half when Washington took possession at its own 13.

Converting three third downs along the way, Rypien moved his team 87 yards and finished the drive with a seven-yard scoring pass to Art Monk with seven seconds left before intermission.

New Orleans' first two possessions after the break ended in turnovers and Rypien fired touchdown passes after each of those takeaways to push Washington's lead to 31-10.

Nov 19

Manley Reinstated by NFL
Redskins immediately waive former star

11/22/90	**DALLAS (5-7) 27, Redskins (6-5) 17**				60,355
Was	0	7	10	0	**17**
Dal	10	0	7	10	**27**
Dal	FG Willis 49				
Dal	Irvin 12 pass from Aikman (Willis kick)				
Was	Byner 5 run (Lohmiller kick)				
Was	FG Lohmiller 25				
Was	Sanders 6 pass from Rypien (Lohmiller kick)				
Dal	Smith 1 run (Willis kick)				
Dal	FG Willis 41				
Dal	Smith 48 run (Willis kick)				

Texas Stadium—The Redskins rallied from a 10-0 deficit to take a 17-10 lead, but Dallas was stronger in the end and blew past Washington for a 27-17 win.

"This is a real disappointment," Joe Gibbs said. "We just couldn't get it going." Actually, they did get something going, but not for long enough.

Washington rushed for just six yards in the first half, but five of them came on Ernest Byner's second-quarter touchdown run that cut the Cowboys' lead to 10-7 at the break.

Midway through the third quarter, it took the Redskins less than two minutes to take the lead. After Chip Lohmiller kicked a 25-yard field goal, Wilbur Marshall's interception of a Troy Aikman pass led to six-yard touchdown pass from Mark Rypien to Ricky Sanders. The visitors held a 17-10 lead.

But not for long. A 45-yard return of the ensuing kickoff meant that Dallas had to drive just 55 yards to tie the score on Emmitt Smith's one-yard touchdown run. Washington drove into Dallas territory but James Washington's interception killed that threat at the five. From there, Aikman took his team 67 yards in 12 plays, completing three third-down passes for first downs. Keith Willis' 41-yard field goal pushed Dallas into a 20-17 lead and Smith's 48-yard touchdown run later in the fourth quarter sealed it for the Cowboys.

12/2/90	**REDSKINS (7-5) 42, Dolphins (9-3) 20**				53,599
Mia	0	3	3	14	**20**
Was	7	14	14	7	**42**
Was	Byner 2 run (Lohmiller kick)				
Was	Monk 6 pass from Rypien (Lohmiller kick)				
Was	Byner 7 run (Lohmiller kick)				
Mia	FG Stoyanovich 21				
Mia	FG Stoyanovich 44				
Was	Johnson 3 pass from Rypien (Lohmiller kick)				
Was	Byner 13 run (Lohmiller kick)				

Mia	Pruitt 24 pass from Marino (Stoyanovich kick)
Mia	Williams 42 interception return (Stoyanovich kick)
Was	Monk 7 pass from Rypien (Lohmiller kick)

RFK Stadium—Dolphins may travel by water, but the Redskins moved by land and air to trounce Miami 42-20.

Ernest Byner rushed for three touchdowns, two of them in the first half as his team was building a 21-0 lead. In between those runs, Mark Rypien threw a six-yard touchdown pass to Art Monk, the first of three scoring tosses on the day for Rypien. All Miami could muster was a Pete Stoyanovich field goal and it was 21-3 at halftime.

After another Miami field goal, the Redskins put the game away if they hadn't already. Rypien threw a three-yard TD pass to tight end Jimmie Johnson and Byner's final six point run made it 35-6. The rest of the game was garbage time.

The two key stats for the Redskins were zero and 34. The first was the number of sacks the Miami defense, averaging nearly four a game, got of Rypien. Thirty four represented the Dolphins' rushing yardage total—not a good number for a team that came into the game wanting to control the ball on the ground.

Dec 3
Pirating? Bucs Can Coach, Set Sights on Gibbs
Owner Cooke says coach is going nowhere

Dec 4
Changing Feet: Skins Cut Punter Mojsiejenko
Kelly Goodburn signed as replacement

12/9/90	**REDSKINS (8-5) 10, Bears (10-3) 9**				53,990
Chi	3	6	0	0	**9**
Was	0	0	7	3	**10**
Chi	FG Butler 29				
Chi	FG Butler 23				
Chi	FG Butler 26				
Was	Clark 8 pass from Rypien (Lohmiller kick)				
Was	FG Lohmiller 35				

RFK Stadium—Darryl Grant's long arm saved the Redskins from Mark Rypien's errant one, allowing Washington to squeak past the Bears 10-9.

The bad news was that Rypien threw five interceptions; the good news in all of that was that most of them were on the Chicago end of the field, and the Bears could just cash in to the tune of three Kevin Butler field goals.

In the third quarter, Rypien did manage to find a receiver wearing the same colored jersey when he hit Gary Clark with an eight-yard touchdown pass, making it 9-7. Butler smacked a 43-yard field goal attempt off of the right upright and then Chip Lohmiller was just short on a 54-yard attempt. Lohmiller's miss came with 4:16 to play and the Bears had good field position. A few first downs would clinch it.

That's when Grant's long arm got into the act. On first down at the Chicago 38, it appeared that the Bears' Brad Muster had some running room up the middle. Grant reached out to try to slow him down and the ball popped out.

"Honestly, I was just reaching for anything I could grab on the guy," said Grant. "You can try raking the ball out that that all year and not have it work once. My hand, though, kind of stuck to the ball."

Freeing the ball was one thing; recovering the fumble was another. A wild scramble ensued, but Todd Bowles drew a bead on the ball and pounced on it at the Bear 25. Three plays later,

Lohmiller kicked a 35-yard field goal to put the Redskins ahead 10-9 with 2:05 left to play. Interceptions ended each of Chicago's last two possessions.

Injuries Force Another O-Line Shuffle

Dec 12—Needing a win that would all but assure the team of a wild card playoff spot, the Redskins found themselves shuttling players along their offensive line once again.

The catalyst for the moves was right tackle Ed Simmons' knee injury, which requires surgery. Joe Jacoby, benched earlier this year due to both injuries and ineffective play, moves into Simmons' spot.

Mark Schlereth, also sidelined due to injuries earlier in the year, will go back into the lineup at right guard.

12/15/90	**Redskins (9-5) 25, PATRIOTS (1-13) 10**				22,286
Was	9	10	0	6	**25**
NE	0	0	7	3	**10**
Was	Gouveia 39 fumble return (Lohmiller kick)				
Was	Safety snap over punter's head in end zone				
Was	Byner 5 run (Lohmiller kick)				
Was	FG Lohmiller 19				
NE	Stephens 4 run (Staurovsky kick)				
NE	FG Staurovsky 42				
Was	FG Lohmiller 38				
Was	FG Lohmiller 26				

Sullivan Stadium—In a cold rain, Ernest Byner rushed for 149 yards and a touchdown as the Redskins beat the Patriots 25-10 to clinch a wild card spot in the NFL playoffs.

The Redskins scored on offense, defense, and special teams in building a 19-0 halftime lead. The first nine points were virtual gifts. New England's rookie quarterback Tommy Hodson mishandled a snap and linebacker Kurt Gouveia recovered the loose ball, going in from 39 yards out for a 7-0 lead. A minute and a half later a long snap intended for the Patriots' punter came closer to the beer vendor working the front end zone section than to its intended target. The resulting safety expanded the Redskin lead to 9-0.

In the second period Byner scored his touchdown on a five-yard run and Chip Lohmiller booted a 19-yard field goal, giving the Redskins their 19-point halftime margin. The Patriots made some noise in the third and fourth quarters and pulled within 19-10, but two Lohmiller field goals in the fourth put it away.

12/22/90	**COLTS (7-8) 35, Redskins (9-6) 28**				58,173
Was	7	6	5	10	**28**
Ind	0	14	0	21	**35**
Was	Monk 12 pass from Rypien (Lohmiller kick)				
Ind	Dickerson 4 run (Biasucci kick)				
Ind	Morgan 42 pass from George (Biasucci kick)				
Was	FG Lohmiller 53				
Was	FG Lohmiller 56				
Was	Safety George penalized for grounding in end zone				
Was	FG Lohmiller 29				
Was	Clark 53 pass from Rypien (Lohmiller kick)				
Ind	Morgan 8 pass from George (Biasucci kick)				
Was	FG Lohmiller 27				
Ind	Brooks 12 pass from George (Biasucci kick)				
Ind	Grant 25 interception return (Biasucci kick)				

Hoosier Dome—The Redskins played just the kind of game they like to, rushing for 223 yards and holding the ball for nearly 40 minutes, but penalties and an interception that the Colts returned for a touchdown did Washington in as they fell to Indianapolis 35-28.

Washington worked its way back from a 14-7 deficit in the second quarter to a 25-14 lead in the fourth. Two long-distance Chip Lohmiller field goals, from 53 and 56 yards, cut Indy's lead to one at the half. In the third quarter, Jeff George gave the Skins two points when he was caught intentionally grounding a pass in the end zone and then Lohmiller connected on another field goal, this one from the same area code, 29 yards.

Early in the fourth quarter, Mark Rypien hit Gary Clark with a 53-yard touchdown bomb and it appeared that the Redskins had finally grasped control of the contest at 25-14. Even after the Colts scored a touchdown on George's pass to Stanley Morgan, Washington responded with a field goal to maintain a one-touchdown lead.

But the Colts weren't done. George threw another touchdown pass, this one to Robert Brooks. Then, with a minute left and overtime on the horizon, rookie cornerback Alan Grant intercepted Rypien's pass and went untouched 28 yards to complete the shocking comeback.

12/30/90	REDSKINS (10-6) 29, Bills (13-3) 14				52,397
Buf	0	0	7	7	**14**
Was	3	6	3	17	**29**
Was	FG Lohmiller 37				
Was	FG Lohmiller 24				
Was	FG Lohmiller 19				
Buf	Davis 13 pass from Gilbert (Norwood kick)				
Was	FG Lohmiller				
Was	FG Lohmiller				
Was	Riggs 3 run (Lohmiller kick)				
Was	Hobbs 18 pass from Rypien (Lohmiller kick)				
Buf	Tasker 20 pass from Gilbert (Norwood kick)				

RFK Stadium—Both teams were locked into their playoff positions before the game—Washington as a road wild card, Buffalo as AFC East champs with home field advantage throughout the AFC playoffs. Because of that, reserves got considerable action as the Redskins beat the Bills 29-14.

Among the Redskins getting the most action was Chip Lohmiller, who booted five field goals and two extra points, and kicked off eight times. He had the only Washington points through three quarters as the Redskins led 15-7 going into the fourth quarter.

Alvin Walton intercepted a pass from third-string quarterback Gale Gilbert and returned it 61 yards to the Buffalo six to set up the Skins' first trip into the end zone. Gerald Riggs made it on the second of two three-yard runs. Soon after that, another pick set up another TD with Martin Mayhew getting the turnover and Stephen Hobbs getting the score.

NFC Wild Card Game
Saturday, January 5, 1991
Veterans Stadium
Philadelphia, Pennsylvania

1/5/91	Redskins 20, EAGLES 6				65,287
Was	0	10	10	0	**20**
Phil	3	3	0	0	**6**
Phil	FG Ruzek 37				
Phil	FG Ruzek 28				
Was	Monk 16 pass from Rypien (Lohmiller kick)				
Was	FG Lohmiller 20				
Was	FG Lohmiller 19				
Was	Clark 3 pass from Rypien (Lohmiller kick)				

In their Monday night game eight weeks earlier, the Redskins got physically crushed by the Philadelphia Eagles in the "Body Bag" game. That was bad enough, but the Eagles chose to rub it in their faces, taunting and trash talking until the final gun on the field and in the locker room afterwards.

Sometimes, things just fall into place. Washington qualified for the playoffs as a wild card entry, and the seedings called for the Redskins to return to the scene of the crime, Veterans Stadium, for a first-round playoff contest. They would have their shot at revenge.

When facing the press in the days prior to a game, Gibbs was usually overly gracious in his comments about the opposition, making a 2-10 outfit sound like the '60's Packers and their coach the second coming of St. Vincent. Not this week, though. When asked about Ryan, Gibbs stood stone-faced and talked about the challenges ahead.

One reporter caught Gibbs in an unguarded moment. It was January 3, the day before the game. Snow had fallen on New Year's Eve and the journalist noted that the snow still covered Gibbs' car in the parking lot at Redskins Park. In the hallway, the more Gibbs talked about Buddy, the madder he got. "I live to play a game like this one. I live to play this guy," Gibbs said, turning red-faced with rage. While this was hardly headline material or Eagle bulletin board fodder, it was very telling of the mood of the coach and team. They were clearly on a mission as they entered the Vet for the game.

It took them a quarter to get untracked as Philadelphia got two FG's for a 6-0 lead, but the defense stiffened after that, sacking Eagles QB Randall Cunningham five times and forcing three turnovers. Mark Rypien threw two scoring passes and Ernest Byner and Gerald Riggs shared the rushing duties and combined for 94 yards on the ground.

A turnover reversed by replay was the game's turning point. The Redskins had taken a 7-6 lead and were driving for more when the ball popped loose from Byner's grasp when he was tackled at the Philadelphia six. Cornerback Ben Smith scooped the ball up and ran 94 yards for an apparent touchdown. Fortunately for the Redskins, instant replay showed that the ground caused the fumble and the call was reversed, with the Redskins retaining possession. The reversal became a 10-point turnaround as Chip Lohmiller connected on a short field goal and instead of a six-point deficit, the Redskins had a four-point lead. The Eagles' offense never could get untracked and the Redskins won 20-6.

During a players-only meeting in the week before the game, the team had made a pact that they would not sink to the level of Philly and deliver "I told you so's" to the classless Eagles after the game. But the message was delivered to Buddy and his losing team after the game with a certain degree of subtlety.

Clark said, "You'd better not question someone's character unless you're sure of the character you're talking about. This team has character, and hopefully this is just one step."

"People threw dirt on this team all year but they didn't know we had shovels and would keep digging our way out," Coleman added.

NFC Divisional Playoff Game
Saturday, January 12, 1991
Candlestick Park
San Francisco, California

1/12/91	49ERS 28, Redskins 10				65,292
Was	10	0	0	0	**10**
SF	7	14	0	7	**28**
Was	Monk 31 pass from Rypien (Lohmiller kick)				
SF	Rathman 1 run (Cofer kick)				
Was	FG Lohmiller 42				
SF	Rice 10 pass from Montana (Cofer kick)				
SF	Sherrard 8 pass from Montana (Cofer kick)				
SF	M. Carter 62 interception return (Cofer kick)				

Joe Montana passed for 274 yards and two touchdowns to lead the 49ers past the Redskins, eliminating Washington from the playoffs.

Washington twice took the lead in the first quarter. They drove to the San Francisco 31 where Art Monk shed his defender with a stop and go move and caught Mark Rypien's pass for a touchdown. After the Niners tied it up on Tom Rathman's one-yard burst, Chip Lohmiller booted a 44-yard field goal to put Washington on top 10-7.

But the second quarter belonged to Montana and the 49ers. They drove 80 and then 89 yards to Montana touchdown passes. The first went 10 yards to Jerry Rice and the other to Mike Sherrard for eight. Both drives were vintage Montana with the quarterback throwing with just the right touch at just the right time. The TD to Rice is a perfect example as the receiver was well covered in the end zone with Todd Bowles behind him and Darrell

Green in front of him. Montana threw it high and hard. Green got a few fingers on it, but the only one who could catch it was Rice.

You could say that the third quarter belonged to the Redskins, but it didn't really do them any good. Three times they drove into San Francisco territory and totaled zero points. Twice Rypien threw interceptions and once Washington lost the ball on downs. With a minute to play in the game, Rypien was hit while throwing and the ball fluttered into the arms of nose tackle Michael Carter, who lumbered 61 yards for the final touchdown.

1991
Head Coach: Joe Gibbs
Record: 14-2, NFC East Champs
Playoffs: 3-0, Super Bowl XXVI Champions

Honors: Joe Gibbs NFL Coach of the Year; Ernest Byner Pro Bowl; Gary Clark Pro Bowl; Darrell Green All-NFL, Pro Bowl; Jim Lachey All-NFL, Pro Bowl; Chip Lohmiller Pro Bowl; Mark Rypien NFC Player of the Year, Pro Bowl; Mark Schlereth Pro Bowl

Jan 31
Grimm to Retire
Says '91 season will be his last

Mar 1
Hog Gone: Mark May Heading West
Original Hog signs with Chargers

Skins Go To Plan B

Apr 1—The Redskins' Plan B free agency revolving door has spun wildly recently. Coming in are safety Danny Copeland and linebacker Matt Millen.

On the "out" side of the Redskins Park door is safety Todd Bowles.

Millen, a 33-year old veteran who has been on Super Bowl winners with the Raiders and 49ers, is expected to help fill the hole left when incumbent middle linebacker Greg Manusky departed for Minnesota via free agency.

Copeland, who came from Kansas City, will compete with recently-signed Terry Hoage and with holdover Brad Edwards for Bowles' free safety spot.

Apr 18
Bye-Bye Bryant
Skins part company with talented but fragile RB

Redskins Deal with Friends and Foes

Apr 21—The Redskins swung deals with old friends and longtime foes during the first day of the NFL draft.

The friend was former general manager Bobby Beathard, who now holds the same title for the San Diego Chargers. When Beathard saw that guard Eric Moten was available when Washington's second-round pick came up, he just had to have him. He offered up San Diego's 1992 first-round selection for the

rights to take Moten; his replacement Charley Casserly took him up on it. Washington also threw in its 1992 fifth-round pick.

Another deal, this one with the Dallas Cowboys, enabled the Redskins to move up and draft defensive tackle Bobby Wilson out of Michigan State.

Afraid that Wilson wouldn't be there when they picked at number 20 in the first round, Casserly sent that pick and their fifth rounder in this draft to Dallas to move up three spots and nab Wilson.

In the third round, the Redskins took Southern Cal running back Ricky Ervins.

May 23
Williams Wins Million-Dollar Judgment
Judge rules that career-ending back injury happened on the job

Let's Go Racing: Gibbs Forms NASCAR Team

July 4—Joe Gibbs has long been a fan of auto racing. So, as if the NFL wasn't enough competition for him to engage in, Gibbs has decided to enter the growing world of NASCAR.

Gibbs will field a team that will run in stock car racing's Winston Cup series. Dale Jarrett, like Gibbs a North Carolina native, will be the driver for Gibbs' team. Jarrett will drive Chevrolets.

Conklin Moving Up, Humphries Moving Out?

Aug 23—A shuffle in the Redskins' crowded quarterback depth chart is likely to lead to the departure of one of them.

Cary Conklin has been elevated to Mark Rypien's backup at quarterback, moving ahead of Stan Humphries. Jeff Rutledge is a solid number 3, leaving Humphries as the odd man out.

Conklin's elevation wasn't due to anything spectacular, just overall solid play. "Cary's just really moved his game up a step or two," said Joe Gibbs. "He's making the right decisions."

The good thing for the Redskins is that Humphries has some solid trade value, perhaps as high as a first round draft selection. Two potential destinations for Humphries are Phoenix and San Diego. The Cardinals just found out that their starter Timm

Rosenbach will miss at least six weeks of the season with a knee injury.

As for the Chargers, general manager Bobby Beathard liked Humphries enough to draft him in 1988 when Beathard held the same post with the Redskins.

Conklin to IR, Humphries is Top Backup QB

Aug 27—In a surprising twist, Cary Conklin, who appeared to have locked up the job as Mark Rypien's main backup just a week ago, was placed on injured reserve. The reported ailment was a mysterious "click" in his knee.

Joe Gibbs professed that the injury was legitimate. He also said that the league was likely to scrutinize the situation as the Redskins have a reputation for using the IR list to stash young players, particularly quarterbacks, as they develop.

The move was a part of a massive shuffle as the team finalized its 47-man roster.

Conklin was one of six players put on injured reserve, joining offensive linemen Ray Brown and Mo Elewonibi, running back John Settle, cornerback A.J. Johnson and tight end Don Warren.

Since they were placed on the injured list after the final cutdown, they all are eligible to be activated after missing four games. Had they been put on the list prior to the last roster trimming, they would have missed the entire season.

Due to those roster rules, the team had to cut some players that it hoped to get back. The only loss was tight end Ken Whisenhunt, claimed by the New York Jets. To take his spot the Redskins got Terry Orr, who was cut by the Chargers. Back in the fold after 24 hours of unemployment were receivers Stephen Hobbs and Joe Johnson, running back Gerald Riggs, offensive lineman Mark Adickes and cornerback Sidney Johnson.

9/1/91	REDSKINS (1-0) 45, Lions (0-1) 0					52958
Det	0	0	0	0	-	0
Was	21	14	7	3	-	45
Was	Riggs 1 run (Lohmiller kick)					
Was	Johnson 4 pass from Rypien (Lohmiller kick)					
Was	Mitchell 69 punt return (Lohmiller kick)					
Was	Sanders 18 pass from Byner (Lohmiller kick)					
Was	Byner 6 run (Lohmiller kick)					
Was	Clark 38 pass from Rypien (Lohmiller kick)					
Was	FG Lohmiller 26					

RFK Stadium—Normally prime time, nationally televised statements coming out of Washington are from the President of the United States. This one, however, came from the Washington Redskins, who served notice on the rest of the league that they were up to their pre-season billing as Super Bowl favorites. The Redskins scored almost at will in thumping the Lions 45-0. It was Washington's largest shutout victory margin ever.

The first time the Redskins had the ball they crunched out a 62-yard drive that ended in Gerald Riggs' one-yard touchdown run. Darrell Green gave them a short field to work with the next time with his interception at the Detroit 20 and Jimmy Johnson caught a four-yard touchdown pass from Mark Rypien. Hold on a second, the first quarter's not over yet—Brian Mitchell ran through a tackle and bolted 69 yards into the end zone with a punt return.

Ernest Byner had a touchdown pass, coming on a halfback option to Ricky Sanders, before starting Lion quarterback Rodney Peete had a completion. Without star rusher Barry Sanders and Peete thoroughly confused by Richie Petitbon's defensive schemes, the Lions' vaunted Run and Shoot offense could neither run nor shoot. Actually, take that back—the Lions were able to shoot themselves in the foot quite well as they gave up three interceptions.

The pace slowed in the second half as the statement had been completed. If Joe Gibbs were Barry Switzer at Oklahoma, he

could have named his own score. The offense remained very efficient, converting on 10 of 11 third down situations on the day. After the lone failed conversion, Chip Lohmiller booted a 26-yard field goal to close out the scoring.

9/9/91	Redskins (2-0) 33, COWBOYS (1-1) 31					63,025
Was	7	13	3	10	-	33
Dal	14	7	3	7	-	31
Dal	Novacek 3 pass from Aikman (Willis kick)					
Was	Johnson 3 pass from Rypien (Lohmiller kick)					
Dal	E. Smith 75 run (Willis kick)					
Was	FG Lohmiller 53					
Dal	E. Smith 5 pass from Aikman (Willis kick)					
Was	Monk 37 pass from Rypien (Lohmiller kick)					
Was	FG Lohmiller 52					
Was	FG Lohmiller 45					
Dal	Willis FG 51					
Was	Riggs 1 run (Lohmiller kick)					
Was	FG Lohmiller 46					
Dal	Irvin 6 pass from Aikman (Willis kick)					

Texas Stadium—Rarely is a kicker credited with sparking the rally from a big deficit, but the accolades for this game went to NFC Offensive Player of the Week Chip Lohmiller. He kicked four field goals, all of them from 45 yards or longer, to help push the Redskins past Dallas 33-31.

In the first half, Dallas ticked off touchdown drives of 80, 80, and 84 yards. Tight end Jay Novacek scored the first touchdown on a three-yard pass from Troy Aikman. On their next possession, the Cowboys fumbled and Washington had to drive just 28 yards for their first score, a three-yard TD pass from Mark Rypien to tight end Jimmie Johnson.

Then it was Emmitt Smith's turn. He scored on a 15-yard jaunt and a five-yard pass from Aikman. In between, Lohmiller booted a 53-yard field goal to help keep his team within striking distance.

Something else that helped keep the Redskins in the game was Smith's upset stomach. Dallas' star back didn't play much and contributed little after his long scoring run, having been stricken by a stomach ailment.

Trailing 21-10, the Redskins began to pull it together. "We were too ready to play," said Fred Stokes. "We were overhusting, leaving holes open. In the huddle, we started reminding everyone else to do their own job and don't do anyone else's."

Art Monk did his job by catching a 37-yard touchdown pass from Rypien to make it 21-17. Then, eight seconds before halftime, Lohmiller boomed a 53-yard field goal through the uprights to make it a one-point game at intermission.

Early in the third quarter, a fumble recovery provided Lohmiller with another opportunity and he booted a 45-yarder to give his team the lead. Dallas retook the lead on a 51-yard field goal.

Then the Redskins embarked on a 14-play, 85-yard drive to take control of the game. The pivotal moment came near midfield when, from punt formation, up back Brian Mitchell took the snap from center and gained three yards on fourth and one. The drive spanned the third and fourth quarters, consuming 8:20 of the clock. Gerald Riggs scored the touchdown on a one-yard run with 12:48 left in the game.

One more Lohmiller field goal, this one a 46-yarder with just under six minutes left, gave the Redskins a 33-24 lead. That score rendered a late score on an Aikman pass to Michael Irvin meaningless.

Sep 11

Two Starters Shelved
Safety Walton, tackle Simmons go on season-ending IR

9/15/91	**REDSKINS (3-0) 34, Cardinals (1-2) 0**				54,662	
Pho	0	0	0	0	-	**0**
Was	7	7	14	6	-	**34**

Was	Byner 2 run (Lohmiller kick)
Was	Sanders 10 run (Lohmiller kick)
Was	Clark 28 pass from Rypien (Lohmiller kick)
Was	Marshall 54 interception return (Lohmiller kick)
Was	FG Lohmiller 29
Was	FG Lohmiller 48

RFK Stadium—The Redskins pitched their second shutout in two home games, easily beating the Cardinals 34-0.

Ernest Byner proved to be the primary weapon on offense. He opened the scoring in the first quarter with a two-yard run. On the day, Byner gained 109 yards on 23 carries and picked up another 51 on four receptions.

That was all the Redskins really needed as their defense dominated the Cardinals all day long. Particularly bothersome to Phoenix were Wilbur Marshall and Charles Mann. Marshall first deprived the Cards of a TD when he intercepted a pass at the goal line. Then, in the third quarter, he scored six points himself when he picked off a pass and dashed 54 yards.

Mann spent the day in the Phoenix backfield, getting credited with two sacks, three hurries, five tackles, a forced fumble and a fumble recovery.

This was a steady effort by the Redskins. They held a 14-0 lead on Byner's scoring blast and on a 10-yard touchdown run by Ricky Sanders on an end around.

The home team put it away in the second quarter. First Gary Clary hauled in a 28-yard touchdown pass from Mark Rypien and then Marshal made his grab and dash to the goal line later in the third.

The defense did the rest, holding the Cardinals to just 165 total yards.

Sep 16
Gibbs Warns About Overconfidence
3-0 record no guarantee of anything, says coach

9/22/91	**Redskins (4-0) 34, BENGALS (0-4) 27**				52,038	
Was	3	21	3	7	-	**34**
Cin	7	3	14	3	-	**27**

Was	FG Lohmiller 40
Cin	Brooks 1 run (Breech kick)
Was	Riggs 1 run (Lohmiller kick)
Cin	Breech FG 46
Was	Riggs 1 run (Lohmiller kick)
Was	Mitchell 66 punt return (Lohmiller kick)
Was	FG Lohmiller 26
Cin	Taylor 1 run (Breech kick)
Cin	Taylor 34 run (Breech kick)
Cin	Breech FG 25
Was	Riggs 7 run (Lohmiller kick)

Riverfront Stadium—Gerald Riggs' third TD run came with just over two minutes remaining to keep the winless Bengals from taking the unbeaten Redskins into overtime. After a last-second defensive stand, Washington had a 34-27 win.

A 21-point second quarter took the Redskins from a 7-3 deficit to a 24-10 halftime lead. Riggs scored two touchdowns, both on one-yard runs. The third score came when Brian Mitchell took a punt at his own 34, found some wide-open spaces down the middle of the field and went all the way—66 yards for the TD.

Chip Lohmiller booted a 26-yard field goal in the third quarter and the Redskins seemed to be cruising at 27-10. The Bengals, though, had plenty of fight left in them. Before the third period was out, they had scored twice on runs of one and 34 yards by fullback

Craig Taylor. Jim Breech's 25-yard field goal tied it up in the fourth quarter.

Riggs was usually called upon only in short-yardage situations, but with Ernest Byner hurting, Riggs went into the game on first and 10 with 5:17 left to play. On second and three at the Bengal 29, Riggs broke to the outside for 20 yards. Three carries later, he toted the rock into the end zone for a seven-yard touchdown. The Bengals last-gasp effort ended when Boomer Esiason's fourth-down pass fell incomplete thanks largely to linebacker Andre Collins' crunching hit on the intended receiver.

9/30/91	**REDSKINS (5-0) 23, Eagles (3-2) 0**				55,198	
Phi	0	0	0	0	-	**0**
Was	0	10	3	10	-	**23**

Was	Monk 19 pass from Rypien (Lohmiller kick)
Was	FG Lohmiller 37
Was	FG Lohmiller 35
Was	Byner 7 run (Lohmiller kick)
Was	Lohmiller FG 27

RFK Stadium—Using ball control and timely passing, the Redskins battled past a wounded Eagle team 23-0.

The worst Philly injury came at the end of the first quarter when Jim McMahon, who was subbing for injured starter Randall Cunningham, suffered a strained right knee as Wilbur Marshall chased him out of bounds. That meant that third-string quarterback Pat Ryan would have to go the rest of the way at signal caller. He was ill equipped to handle the Redskins' pressure and coverage.

The game was scoreless when the change at quarterback came, but the Skins altered that midway through the second quarter. Mark Rypien finished off a 54-yard drive with a 19-yard touchdown pass to Art Monk. The march was primarily a ground assault with Ernest Byner carrying the ball on seven of the nine plays.

Chip Lohmiller kicked a 37-yard field goal later in the second to make it 10-0 at the half.

The Eagles blew a gift-wrapped scoring chance after a Rypien fumble at the Washington 10 when Darrell Green intercepted Ryan's pass in the end zone.

The way the Eagle offense was playing—on the evening they managed just 89 yards of offense and four first downs—it seemed that 10 points would be more than enough to secure the win, but after another Lohmiller field goal Philly helped the Redskins to another touchdown just to make sure.

Andre Collins intercepted Ryan's pass from the Eagle 14 and returned it to the seven. Three plays and a couple of plays later, Byner took it up the middle seven yards for the score.

10/6/91	**Redskins (6-0) 20, BEARS (4-2) 7**				64,941	
Was	0	10	0	10	-	**20**
Chi	0	0	7	0	-	**7**

Was	FG Lohmiller 47
Was	Monk 26 pass from Rypien (Lohmiller kick)
Chi	Anderson 1 run (Butler kick)
Was	Monk 5 pass from Rypien (Lohmiller kick)
Was	Lohmiller FG 23

Soldier Field—Art Monk caught six passes, two of them for touchdowns, as Washington put away the Bears in the fourth quarter and walked out of Chicago with a 20-7 win.

Monk's first touchdown pass of the day came just after the two-minute warning for the first half when he torched Chicago cornerback Donnell Woolford to get open for Mark Rypien's 26-yard scoring pass. As was typical, Monk deflected credit for the play. "It's a very well-designed play," he said. "Against a two-deep zone, both of the safeties have to commit to Ricky (Sanders). That leaves the man in my position one on one with against a corner who's got a tough angle to come in and make the play."

That gave the Redskins a 10-0 lead that held until less than two minutes remained in the third quarter when Neil Anderson scored on a one-yard run. Suddenly, it was a contest at 10-7.

It remained that way until midway through the fourth quarter. Then Eric Williams got a hand on one of Jim Harbaugh's passes; it settled into the arms of end Fred Stokes at the Chicago 36.

The Redskins converted, but not without a struggle. Facing fourth and four at the 30, Joe Gibbs eschewed a field goal attempt into the wind and Monk went high to snare Rypien's pass for 12 yards to move the chains. Later, on third and goal at the five, Monk got free and caught Rypien's pass in the end zone for a 17-7 lead. Chip Lohmiller's second field goal of the game gave Washington a bit more breathing room.

10/13/91	**REDSKINS (7-0) 42, Cleveland (2-4) 17**					54,715
Cle	7	0	10	0	-	**17**
Was	7	14	7	14	-	**42**

Was	Monk 14 pass from Rypien (Lohmiller kick)
Cle	Slaughter 11 pass from Hansen (Stover kick)
Was	Riggs 1 run (Lohmiller kick)
Was	Byner 21 run (Lohmiller kick)
Cle	FG Stover 26
Cle	Newsome 37 fumble recovery return (Stover kick)
Was	Ervins 12 run (Lohmiller kick)
Was	Riggs 1 run (Lohmiller kick)
Was	Ervins 65 run (Lohmiller kick)

RFK Stadium—Ricky Ervins came off the bench to rush for 133 yards and two touchdowns, including a 65-yard burst to finish off the scoring. The game was closer than the score indicated as the Browns battled and stayed in the game for more than three quarters.

Cleveland became the first team to score at RFK Stadium in 1991 as Webster Slaughter caught an 11-yard touchdown pass off of a fake field goal. That score tied the game at seven in the first quarter. The Redskins answered quickly with second-quarter TD runs by Gerald Riggs and Ernest Byner to take a 21-7 halftime lead.

A Matt Stover field goal made it 21-10 in the third quarter and then linebacker Clay Matthews stripped the ball from Gerald Riggs. Safety Vince Newsome recovered and scooted 37 yards for a touchdown and suddenly, it was a four-point game.

Riggs was in the game because Ernest Byner was injured, so Joe Gibbs turned to Ervins, an untested third-round draft pick. Ervins' first carry was good for 15 yards to start Washington's touchdown drive. The rookie finished it off himself with a 12-yard burst, following a nice block behind Don Warren.

Another TD drive gave the Redskins some real breathing room at 35-17. The march ended with Riggs taking it into the end zone from a yard out, but Ervins was the key, gaining 73 yards on five carries during the drive. The rookie provided an exclamation point when, after the two-minute warning, he bounced outside and broke free for 65 yards and a touchdown.

10/27/91	**Redskins (8-0) 17, GIANTS (4-4) 13**					76,627
Was	0	0	7	10	-	**17**
NYG	10	3	0	0	-	**13**

NYG	FG Allegre 23
NYG	Hampton 1 run (Allegre kick)
NYG	FG Allegre 36
Was	Clark 7 pass from Rypien (Lohmiller kick)
Was	Clark 54 pass from Rypien (Lohmiller kick)
Was	Lohmiller FG 35

Giants Stadium—The Redskins battled back from a 13-0 halftime deficit and stormed past the Giants for a 17-13 win. The victory came thanks largely to two touchdown passes from Mark Rypien to Gary Clark.

It's not often that a 7-0 team with a two-game lead in its division goes into a game with a chip on its collective shoulder, but that was exactly the mood of the Redskins going into this Sunday night contest in Giants Stadium.

The mindset stemmed from the fact that the Giants had beaten the Redskins six straight times. Worse, with the exception of a 1987 game played by strike replacement players, Washington had not won in the Meadowlands since 1983. This led to talk that the 7-0 start was not so impressive since they hadn't faced their nemesis yet.

"I was getting pretty upset about hearing that 7-0 didn't mean a thing," said defensive tackle Eric Williams. "I wasn't going to apologize for our record because the New York Giants hadn't been on the schedule."

The way the game started out, it appeared that the Redskins were going to have to apologize for their performance. The Giants controlled the line of scrimmage and outgained Washington 207 yards to 35. The frustration for the Washington offense was summed up on one play when Gary Clark got open deep, Mark Rypien delivered the pass on target, but Clark dropped the ball.

On the positive side, as badly as they had been outplayed the Redskins weren't out of the game on the scoreboard. Rodney Hampton scored a touchdown on a one-yard run, but two other New York forays deep into Washington territory were stopped short of the end zone. The Giants had to settle for two Raul Allegre field goals and a 13-0 halftime lead.

"The way it started, you have a tendency to say 'Goodness, gracious, here we go again,'" said Gibbs. Most of the players chose stronger language. The mood of the team in the locker room at halftime was one of loud, self-directed anger. Clark, desperate for a chance at redemption for dropping the sure TD pass, was among the most vocal, screaming, "Give me the damn ball!"

Rypien did just that with a seven-yard touchdown pass to Clark to pull the Redskins to within six at 13-7. That capped an 87-yard drive during which the Redskins converted seven straight third downs. The defense stopped the Giants when rookie defensive tackle Bobby Wilson knifed in to nail Hampton for a six-yard loss, forcing a punt.

The Redskins moved to their own 46 yard line where they faced third and 12. Looking for a gamebreaker, Joe Gibbs called a play that assistant Rod Dowhower had suggested in meetings the week before. The Giants were playing their standard defense; a soft, two-deep zone that was designed to prevent the deep pass. The key to beating it long was to get someone out of position.

Rypien took the snap and rolled to his left. Every time that season he had done that previously, he threw to the left. Free safety Greg Jackson knew this and dropped off of Clark, who was running a fly outside the right hashmark. "When he rolls that way," said Jackson, "we have to roll with him."

That left Clark with single coverage from corner Everson Walls. Clark got a step and Rypien got him the ball at the three. The receiver bobbled the ball for just a moment, but this time secured it for a 14-13 lead.

"It was exactly the same play as in the first half," Clark said. "Rip laid it right in my hands."

After getting the ball back, the Redskins did exactly what they needed to do; they ground out a time-consuming drive. Rookie running back Ricky Ervins was the workhouse, carrying the ball on 10 of the 14 plays that chewed nearly eight minutes off the clock. Chip Lohmiller's field goal to make it 17-13 came with 47 seconds left. Wilbur Marshall's interception shut off New York's last-gasp effort.

Gibbs: Byner, Not Ervins, is the Starter

Oct. 28—Joe Gibbs moved yesterday to quash any conversation as to who the team's top running back would be. Despite a stellar performance by rookie Ricky Ervins against the Giants on Sunday night, Ernest Byner would still be the starter.

Going on one of his famously-accurate gut feelings, Gibbs benched Byner in favor of the quicker Ervins at halftime with the Redskins trailing New York 13-0.

Ervins went on to gain 82 yards on 20 carries, allowing the Redskins to control the clock and set up two Mark Rypien to Gary Clark touchdown passes, getting the crucial win for Washington.

Both of the backs said all of the right things. "I like to give credit where it's due," said Byner, "and Ricky deserves it. The kid makes good things happen. He's the future."

For his part, Ervins was properly respectful of the veteran Byner. "I want it (the starting lineup) after Earnest is ready to leave it," said Ervins.

11/3/91	REDSKINS (9-0) 16, Oilers (7-2) 13 (OT)					55,096
Hou	0	6	0	7	0	13
Was	0	3	3	7	3	16

Was	FG Lohmiller 21
Hou	FG Howfield 24
Hou	FG Howfield 23
Was	FG Lohmiller 20
Was	Byner 23 run (Lohmiller kick)
Hou	White 1 run (Howfield kick)
Was	FG Lohmiller 41

RFK Stadium—To win nine straight NFL games to start out a season, you need solid blocking, hard-hitting tackling, inspired play calling, crisp execution and, as was the case today, a little bit of luck. Chip Lohmiller kicked a 41-yard field goal for Washington to give the Redskins a 16-13 overtime victory over Houston.

Darrell Green's interception at the Houston 33 set up the kick.

All of that, however, would not have happened if not for Oiler place kicker Ian Howfield's missed chip shot field goal.

After Houston tied the game on a one-yard run by Lorenzo White with 1:42 left in the game, Brian Mitchell fumbled the ensuing kickoff, giving the Oilers prime field position. Howfield came in for a 33-yard field goal attempt with one second left. It appeared that the winning streak would end at eight. "You don't exactly give up, but you're not far from it," said Andre Collins.

The snap and hold were both perfect, but Howfield's kick was wide right.

On Houston's second offensive play of overtime, Oiler quarterback Warren Moon got bumped as he threw an out pass and Green picked it off. Three Ernest Byner runs preceded Lohmiller's game-ending kick.

11/10/91	REDSKINS (9-0) 56, Falcons (5-5) 17					52,461
Atl	3	0	14	0	-	17
Was	7	21	7	21	-	56

Atl	FG Johnson 31
Was	Orr 9 pass from Rypien (Lohmiller kick)
Was	Clark 61 pass from Rypien (Lohmiller kick)
Was	Rypien 4 run (Lohmiller kick)
Was	Clark 19 pass from Rypien (Lohmiller kick)
Atl	Haynes 75 pass from Tolliver (Johnson kick)
Atl	Rison 15 pass from Tolliver (Johnson kick)
Was	Monk 19 pass from Rypien (Lohmiller kick)
Was	Clark 82 pass from Rypien (Lohmiller kick)
Was	Monk 64 pass from Rypien (Lohmiller kick)
Was	Collins 15 INT return (Lohmiller kick)

RFK Stadium—Mark Rypien threw for 442 yards and a team record-tying six touchdowns to lead the Redskins to a 56-17 pasting of the Falcons.

"We didn't do much of anything right on pass defense," said Atlanta coach Jerry Glanville. Wow, what insight; you just can't get one past ol' Jerry, can you?

Rypien spread the goodies mostly between Art Monk and Gary Clark. Monk caught seven passes for 164 yards and two touchdowns. On both of his scoring catches, his hapless defender was flagged for pass interference, but Monk made the grabs anyway.

Clark wasn't a target quite as often as Monk was, but he made the most of his chances. His four catches gained 203 yards and included touchdown plays of 61, 19, and 82 yards.

The weather, cold with a steady rain, didn't seem to be conducive to a big passing day, but Rypien and his receivers ignored it and focused instead on Atlanta's blitzing schemes, which left Monk and Clark in single coverage much of the day. The extra pass rushers didn't help as Rypien was rarely pressured and never sacked.

The Falcons did throw a minor scare into the Redskins when they scored two quick touchdowns to open up the second half and cut the Washington lead to 28-17. But the Washington defense tightened up, the offense opened back up, and the rout was on.

Andre Collins pushed the Skins over the 50-point mark when he picked off rookie Brett Favre's pass at the 15 and cruised into the end zone.

11/17/91	Redskins (11-0) 41, STEELERS (4-7) 14					56,813
Was	7	10	10	14	-	41
Pit	0	0	0	14	-	14

Was	Riggs 1 run (Lohmiller kick)
Was	FG Lohmiller 36
Was	Monk 11 pass from Rypien (Lohmiller kick)
Was	FG Lohmiller 41
Was	Riggs 1 run (Lohmiller kick)
Pit	Cooper 5 pass from O'Donnell (Anderson kick)
Pit	Stone 40 pass from O'Donnell (Anderson kick)
Was	Clark 49 pass from Rypien (Lohmiller kick)
Was	Sanders 40 pass from Rypien (Lohmiller kick)

Three Rivers Stadium—The Redskins clinched the first berth in the 1991 NFL playoffs as Mark Rypien passed for 225 yards and two touchdowns. The 41-14 win over the Steelers also made Washington one of nine NFL teams ever to start a season with 11 straight wins.

The Redskins jumped to a 17-0 halftime lead, getting it done on both sides of the ball. On their first offensive possession, Mark Rypien completed a 63-yard pass to Art Monk, who was brought down at the Pittsburgh one. Gerald Riggs pounded it over on the next play. After Chip Lohmiller kicked a 36-yard field goal, some fancy footwork by Monk helped the receiver stay inbounds on an 11-yard TD pass from Rypien.

Meanwhile, the defense was giving nothing to the Steeler offense. During the first half, Pittsburgh was permitted to run just one play in Washington territory and that resulted in a sack and fumble. It was one of five sacks on the day for the Washington defense.

Another field goal and another one-yard Riggs run stretched the Washington lead to 27-0 before the Steelers got some offensive life, scoring twice to cut the lead to 27-14 midway through the final period. "I don't know about anyone else," said Joe Gibbs, "but I was worried."

Gibbs' fears were allayed less than three minutes later when Rypien and Gary Clark hooked up on a 49-yard touchdown bomb to put it away for good.

11/24/91	Cowboys (7-5) 24, REDSKINS (11-1) 21					55,561
Dal	0	14	0	10	-	24
Was	7	0	0	14	-	21

Was	Mayhew 31 interception return (Lohmiller kick)
Dal	Smith 32 run (Willis kick)
Dal	Harper 34 pass from Aikman (Willis kick)
Dal	Irvin 24 pass from Beuerlein (Willis kick)
Was	Riggs 1 run (Lohmiller kick)
Dal	FG Willis 42
Was	Sanders 29 pass from Rypien (Lohmiller kick)

RFK Stadium—Dallas rambled into town and gambled early and often. They drew to inside straights several times and cashed in, ending the Redskins' perfect season with a 24-21 win.

The Redskins jumped to a 7-0 lead when Martin Mayhew intercepted a Troy Aikman pass and rolled 31 yards for a touchdown. Dallas tied it with a 75-yard drive in the second period. On third and 15 from the Washington 32, the Redskins were as stunned as anyone else when the play call was a draw to Emmitt Smith. They were so surprised that Smith made it all the way into the end zone.

On the ensuing kickoff, Dallas coach Jimmy Johnson called for an onside kick. Again, the Redskins were caught off guard, but Andre Collins still got his hands on the ball. Dallas' Darrick Brownlow, however, wound up with possession. Although it didn't turn into points, it did get the Redskins further off kilter.

When Aikman's Hail Mary pass from 34 yards out on the last play of the half was descending to earth, it seemed as though the crowd of defenders surrounding receiver Alvin Harper was lost. Harper leaped high to grab the pass and a 14-7 halftime lead.

The home team seemed to have improved its chances on the sixth play of the second half when end Charles Mann and tackle Jumpy Geathers met at the quarterback, sandwiching Aikman and sending him to the bench. But Steve Beuerlein proved to be more than an adequate backup, completing seven of 12 passes for 109 yards and a touchdown.

The scoring pass was to Michael Irvin, who caught nine passes on the day. It capped an 81-yard drive that took six plays. From the Washington 23, Beurlein's pass was behind his receiver, but Irving made an eye-popping play. As he reached back to tip the ball to himself, he turned and caught it for a 21-7 Dallas lead.

Washington went to a no-huddle offense and drove 92 yards to pull within 21-14. On their next possession, though, Dallas chewed seven minutes off of the clock and got a Gary Willis field goal with just 1:14 to play. Mark Rypien threw a 29-yard touchdown pass to Ricky Sanders in the waning seconds, but Dallas recovered the expected onside kick. The Redskins were undefeated no longer.

Was	Orr 47 pass from Rypien (Lohmiller kick)
LARm	FG Zendejas 34
Was	Sanders 30 pass from Rypien (Lohmiller kick)
Was	Ervins 24 pass from Rypien (Lohmiller kick)
Was	FG Lohmiller 35
Was	FG Lohmiller 35

Anaheim Stadium—The Redskins clinched their first NFC East title since 1987 when they broke open a close game with a pair of third-quarter touchdown passes by Mark Rypien, beating the Rams 27-6.

Washington took advantage of a lapse in the Ram defense to take a 7-3 lead in the first quarter. From the LA 47, Rypien rolled to his right and the secondary rolled right along with him. This allowed tight end Terry Orr to sneak out into wide-open spaces down the left hashmark. It seemed as though Rypien's pass took forever to get there. "When you're that wide open," said Orr, "the ball never gets there fast enough."

It got there in plenty of time for Orr to catch it still well in the clear. Safety Michael Stewart was in pursuit but never was a credible threat to Orr's trip to the end zone.

Despite the big play, Washington was unable to shake the Rams in the first half and led by just a point at halftime. As was his usual practice, Joe Gibbs had spent the week prior to the game talking about what a good team the 3-9 Rams were—and members of the media got a good laugh out of it. "You have to admit," said Gibbs, "when we were up only 7-6 at halftime, I didn't look so bad."

Two touchdown drives in the third quarter, however, gave the Redskins some breathing room. The first TD came on a 30-yard touchdown pass from Rypien to Ricky Sanders.

On the second drive, the Redskins unveiled a new twist—a no-huddle offense. They had used it in desperation late in the game against Dallas the previous week and decided to give it a try in different circumstances. It worked to the tune of a seven-play, 62-yard touchdown drive to make it 21-7. Five of the plays were passes, the last a screen to Ricky Ervins for the final 24 yards.

Rams Not Lambs to Gibbs

Nov 29—When oddsmakers came out with the betting line on Sunday's Redskins game in Los Angeles, Washington opened as nine and a half point favorites. To most observers, this seemed logical for an 11-1 team on the road vs. a 3-9 opponent that is in disarray.

To most observers, but not all.

"In my mind, the Rams are the favorite," Gibbs said. "I'm leery of the Rams."

"Every team can beat us," Gibbs said. "The press and everybody else kids me about that."

He even offered some evidence to back up his feelings of apprehension. Said Gibbs, "When you look at the film, you see that the Rams have good football players. Everybody has good players. The Rams have a good quarterback and good receivers." Evidently the coach is referring to Jim Everett, who has thrown 13 interceptions so far this season, and Henry Ellard, a good receiver who generally doesn't give opposing defenders nightmares.

Of course, there are good reasons for Gibbs to publicly state his fear of each and every opponent. He doesn't want to give anyone any bulletin board material—and wants to make sure that his players take nothing for granted.

12/1/91	Redskins (12-1) 27, RAMS (3-10) 6					55,027
Was	7	0	14	6	-	**27**
LARm	3	3	0	0	-	**6**
LARm	FG Zendejas 41					

12/8/91	Redskins (13-1) 20, CARDINALS (4-10) 14					48,373
Was	0	0	14	6	-	**20**
Pho	0	14	0	0	-	**14**
Pho	J. Johnson 1 run (Davis kick)					
Pho	J. Johnson 3 run (Davis kick)					
Was	Orr 4 pass from Rypien (Lohmiller kick)					
Was	Sanders 17 pass from Rypien (Lohmiller kick)					
Was	FG Lohmiller 42					
Was	FG Lohmiller 27					

Sun Devil Stadium—After spotting the Cards a 14-0 halftime lead, the Redskins held the ball for 20 minutes in the second half and rallied for the win.

Just prior to kickoff, Washington was handed home field advantage throughout the playoffs when Dallas' win over New Orleans became final, but word of that did not filter through until the second quarter. By then, it was evident that the Redskins had their hands full. They handed Phoenix one touchdown when Brian Mitchell fumbled a punt deep in Washington territory. The Cards earned their second tally of the half in classic fashion, bottling the Redskins deep in their own territory and then using the resulting field position (their own 48) to launch a short scoring drive. Johnny Johnson scored both of the TD's on short runs and the Redskins were down by 14 at the break.

In the locker room, linebacker Matt Millen was livid. Using language that was almost certainly cleaned up for public consumption after the game, Millen said he told the team, "We were terrible. I told the guys I was glad we were behind. It was an opportunity to see what we were about."

If that's the case, the Redskins were about a potent offense and dominating defense. In the course of scoring 20 unanswered points, Washington outgained the Cardinals 263 yards to 40. Two Mark Rypien touchdown passes tied the game after three quarters and a pair of Chip Lohmiller field goals provided the winning margin in the final period.

12/15/91	REDSKINS (14-1) 34, Giants (7-8) 17					54,722
NYG	3	7	7	0	-	17
Was	7	17	3	7	-	34
NYG	FG Bahr 36					
Was	Clark 65 pass from Rypien (Lohmiller kick)					
NYG	Simms 1 run (Bahr kick)					
Was	Riggs 1 run (Lohmiller kick)					
Was	Orr 22 pass from Rypien (Lohmiller kick)					
Was	FG Lohmiller 36					
Was	FG Lohmiller 36					
NYG	Ingram 18 pass from Simms (Bahr kick)					
Was	Clark 50 pass from Rypien (Lohmiller kick)					

RFK Stadium—Gary Clark opened the Redskins' scoring when he turned a short pass into a 65-yard touchdown and then clinched the 34-17 win over the Giants with a 50-yard TD bomb from Mark Rypien in the fourth quarter.

While Clark provided the bookends, it was a pass reception by tight end Terry Orr that was much of the story. Orr, more accustomed to blocking than receiving, got free for a 22-yard touchdown pass from Rypien with six and a half minutes left in the second quarter. The score gave Washington a 21-10 lead, and the Redskins never looked back.

Safety Danny Copeland led the defense with an interception and a fumble recovery deep in Giants' territory that set up the go-ahead TD in the second quarter, Gerald Riggs' one-yard run.

The Giants' Phil Simms threw for 288 yards and one TD, and added another TD rushing.

12/22/91	EAGLES (10-6) 24, Redskins (14-2) 22					58,988
Was	3	10	3	6	-	22
Phi	7	0	0	17	-	24
Phi	O. Smith 74 INT return (Ruzek kick)					
Was	FG Lohmiller 21					
Was	Ervins 1 run (Lohmiller kick)					
Was	FG Lohmiller 47					
Was	FG Lohmiller 47					
Was	FG Lohmiller 38					
Phi	Keith Jackson 2 pass from Kemp (Ruzek kick)					
Phi	M. Johnson 6 pass from Kemp (Ruzek kick)					
Was	FG Lohmiller 35					
Phi	FG Ruzek 38					

Veterans Stadium—Washington was ahead 19-7 and appeared to be cruising towards a win, but Philadelphia rallied for 17 fourth-quarter points behind quarterback Jeff Kemp. Roger Ruzek kicked the game-winning field goal with 13 seconds remaining to give the Eagles a 24-22 win.

The only thing the Redskins could accomplish here was an NFL-record tying 15th win during the regular season. As the game on the hard artificial surface wore on, that goal became secondary to keeping the front-line players healthy for the playoffs. Joe Gibbs began to pull his starters, including Mark Rypien and Charles Mann.

After spotting the Eagles a 7-0 lead, Washington ran off 19 unanswered points on a one-yard touchdown run by Ricky Ervins and four Chip Lohmiller field goals. After Gibbs began to empty the bench, Kemp rallied the home team, throwing touchdown passes to tight ends Keith Jackson and Mo Johnson to forge a 21-19 Eagle lead with just under 10 minutes to play.

The Redskins fought back behind backup quarterback Jeff Rutledge. His 36-yard completion to Gary Clark set up Lohmiller's go-ahead field goal with just over two minutes remaining.

Kemp and the Eagles had just one time-out to work with, but they used the middle of the field anyway, crossing up the defense. It took eight plays for them to move to the Washington 21, and Ruzek kicked the game winner from there.

Jim Lachey summed up the general feeling; "We all hate to lose, but the object is to win in January."

Lohmiller Outscores Colts for Season

Dec 23—Chip Lohmiller hit five field goals and an extra point against the Eagles on Sunday, enabling him to surpass the point total scored by the entire Indianapolis Colts team this season. Sunday's performance pushed his tally for the season to 149 points while the Colts mustered just 143.

This was the first time an individual player has outscored another NFL team since 1945.

Lohmiller joked that he should have been smart enough to figure out a way to profit from the obscure—but still impressive—accomplishment. "It's not the kind of record you think about, but I wish I had," he said. "I'd have had my agent put something in my contract about it."

NFC Divisional Playoff
Saturday, January 4, 1992
RFK Stadium
Washington, D. C.

1/4/92	REDSKINS 24, Falcons 7					55,181
Atl	0	7	0	0	-	7
Was	0	14	3	7	-	24
Was	Ervins 17 run (Lohmiller kick)					
Was	Riggs 2 run (Lohmiller kick)					
Atl	T. Johnson 1 run (Johnson kick)					
Was	FG Lohmiller 24					
Was	Riggs 1 run (Lohmiller kick)					

In a steady rain and swirling wind, the Redskins got six turnovers and rushed for 162 yards in slopping out a win over the Falcons to advance to the NFC championship game.

Atlanta coach Jerry Glanville tried everything he could to motivate his team and taunt the Redskins. In the days before the game, he accused Washington of running up the score in their earlier meeting, a 56-17 affair during which Joe Gibbs pulled Mark Rypien and many of his starters after three quarters. As he huddled his team prior to kickoff, Glanville held a Redskins helmet up in the air, as though it was a trophy already won. Taking a cue from his coach, cornerback Deion Sanders performed a showy little dance as he was introduced over the PA system.

"Glanville's arrogance had us kind of fired up," said Charles Mann. "You don't do the kind of talking he does and never set foot on the field."

Glanville could control his team's psyche, but he couldn't control the weather. It rained constantly beginning the night before the game, and churning winds kicked up in the morning. The Falcons were a pass-oriented team. The quagmire that was the RFK Stadium field negated Atlanta's speed, its only real advantage. "A (passing) offense in weather like this is like a gun with one bullet," said Sanders.

On the other hand, the Redskins were, according to Jeff Bostic, "A running team that can pass." They smiled when they saw what Mother Nature was dishing out on that day.

"Bad weather. Cold weather. Rainy weather. What kind of weather is it? Redskins weather," said Art Monk.

After a scoreless first quarter, the Redskins embarked on an 11-play, 81-yard touchdown drive. Rypien converted a third down from the Atlanta 31 with a 19-yard pass to Gary Clark. From the

17, Rypien called a draw play that wasn't in the game plan for that week. A huge hole opened up behind blocks by Jim Lachey and Monk. Ricky Ervins busted through, shed a couple of tackles, showed no evidence of any problems with footing as he cut to the outside and high-stepped in for the touchdown.

On Atlanta's next series, Mann forced a fumble and Jumpy Geathers recovered, setting up Gerald Riggs' one-yard TD run. The two scores in 3:11 had the Redskins up 14-0.

The Redskins had opportunities to be up by an even greater margin, but Chip Lohmiller missed three field goal attempts. Atlanta got back into it with an 80-yard drive that made it 14-7 at the half.

In the second half, the home team gradually pulled away. Lohmiller finally found the footing to hit on a field goal, this one from 24 yards. Early in the fourth quarter, Wilbur Marshall recovered a fumble at the Falcon 48. The Redskins used nearly seven minutes to drive in for the clinching touchdown. It came with 6:32 left on another one-yard burst by Riggs.

The soaked fans that attended the game were given souvenir seat cushions on their way through the gates. When Riggs scored, one fan tossed his souvenir up in the air in celebration. A few others followed suit and, within seconds, the stadium air was filled with flying seat cushions.

"I had a big old smile on my face sitting on my butt on the goal line and Gerald is behind me (in the end zone)," said Joe Jacoby. "And all of a sudden I look up and see those yellow things flying down. It was a great feeling. The fans rubbed it back in Glanville's face."

Glanville snubbed Gibbs on the traditional post game handshake, but he did show a modicum of class by not making any excuses.

"We didn't get beat by the rain, we got beat by the Redskins," said Glanville.

NFC Championship Game
Sunday, January 12, 1992
RFK Stadium
Washington, D. C.

1/12/92	**REDSKINS 41, Lions 10**					55,585
Det	0	10	0	0	-	**10**
Was	10	7	10	14	-	**41**
Was	Riggs 2 run (Lohmiller kick)					
Was	FG Lohmiller 20					
Det	W. Green 18 pass from Kramer (Murray kick)					
Was	Riggs 3 run (Lohmiller kick)					
Det	Murray FG 30					
Was	FG Lohmiller 28					
Was	Clark 45 pass from Rypien (Lohmiller kick)					
Was	Monk 21 pass from Rypien (Lohmiller kick)					
Was	D. Green 32 interception return (Lohmiller kick)					

Football seasons are long and often things can change drastically between the beginning of the season and the end. But that was not the case here.

It was apparent that nothing had happened in the eighteen weeks that had elapsed since the Redskins' opening game rout of Detroit to narrow the difference between the two teams. Relying on an opportunistic defense in the first half and efficient offense in the second, Washington beat the Lions 41-10 to advance to Super Bowl XXVI.

There was little doubt which was the better team; in two games, the Redskins outscored Detroit 86-10.

On Detroit's first play from scrimmage Charles Mann got the first of his team's five sacks, forcing a fumble that Fred Stokes recovered at the Detroit 11. Three plays later, Gerald Riggs took it

over from two yards out just 1:06 into the game. A Kurt Gouveia interception just minutes later let up a Chip Lohmiller field goal for a 10-0 lead.

Detroit settled down and embarked on long drives that led to a field goal and a touchdown in the second quarter. Riggs scored on a three-yard run and it was a ballgame at the half with the Redskins up 17-10.

The offense got it rolling in the second half. As a warm-up, Rypien threw to Terry Orr for 45 yards to set up another Lohmiller field goal. On the next possession, from his 27, Rypien went to Art Monk for 31 yards and then threw to Gary Clark, who had gotten behind his defender. The pass couldn't have been prettier as it nestled into Clark's hands in the end zone, making it 27-10—and the celebration started. A 31-yard touchdown pass from Rypien to Monk and Darrell Green's 32-yard interception return for another six points added the exclamation points.

Rypien Tweaks Ankle in Practice

Jan 23—Quarterbacks are always under a magnifying glass. During Super Bowl week, they're under an electron microscope.

It is only because of this that Mark Rypien's ankle injury became news. Such things happen routinely during NFL practices, but when it happens to the starting quarterback days before the Super Bowl, it's treated like man bites dog stuff.

Just minutes before practice ended, some players fell on Rypien during a passing drill. He limped off the field and didn't finish the session.

"He turned his ankle," said Joe Gibbs to anxious media members. "The trainer says it's a mild sprain, and we expect him to practice tomorrow."

Jan 24
Gibbs Retirement Rumors Spring Up (Again)
Coach denies them (again); 'I love what I do,' he says

Sunday, January 26, 1992
The Metrodome
Minneapolis, Minnesota

1/26/92	**Redskins 37, Bills 24**					63,160
Was	0	17	14	6	-	**37**
Buf	0	0	10	14	-	**24**
Was	FG Lohmiller 34					
Was	Byner 10 pass from Rypien (Lohmiller kick)					
Was	Riggs 1 run (Lohmiller kick)					
Was	Riggs 2 run (Lohmiller kick)					
Buf	FG Norwood 21					
Buf	Thomas 1 run (Norwood kick)					
Was	Clark 30 pass from Rypien (Lohmiller kick)					
Was	Lohmiller FG 25					
Was	Lohmiller FG 39					
Buf	Metzelaars 2 pass from Kelly (Norwood kick)					
Buf	Bebe 4 pass from Kelly (Norwood kick)					

Mark Rypien passed for 292 yards and two touchdowns and was named the game's Most Valuable Player as the

Redskins scored the game's first 24 points, gaining their third Super Bowl win in ten seasons.

The Skins looked to have taken the lead on their second possession, but an apparent TD pass to Art Monk was overruled by the replay officials and the subsequent field goal try was botched by a fumbled snap. Later, they blew another opportunity after Brad Edwards returned an interception to the Buffalo 12. Rypien's pass went off of guard Mark Schlereth's helmet and into the arms of Buffalo cornerback Kirby Jackson.

There was concern about the missed opportunities, but there were plenty to come in the second quarter. Chip Lohmiller broke the ice with a 34-yard field goal and a 51-yard drive was topped off by a 10-yard touchdown reception by Earnest Byner.

Buffalo quarterback Jim Kelly, perhaps sensing that things were beginning to get away from the Bills, gambled by throwing into double coverage. Darrell Green intercepted and Washington had possession again at its own 45. It took five plays to move the 55 yards to make it 17-0. The biggest play was a 34-yard completion from Rypien to Gary Clark and the last play was a one-yard burst over the goal line by Gerald Riggs. Buffalo had a couple of threats before halftime, but dropped passes—some of them unforced, some of them provoked by fierce hits by the Washington secondary—and penalties helped keep the Bills off of the scoreboard.

Any realistic hopes Buffalo had for a second half comeback win were quickly erased by Kurt Gouveia's interception on the Bills' first play of the second half. Kelly got pressure up the middle and didn't see Gouveia as he tried to throw to the middle of the field. The linebacker picked the ball off at the 23 and returned it to the two. Riggs scored on a cutback from there.

"It wasn't me," Gouveia said. "Our line got such great pressure that he threw the ball before he wanted to. I was ready, but the tight end wasn't."

Buffalo rallied gamely, getting a touchdown and a field goal to make it 24-10. Rypien answered the challenge and added an exclamation point, throwing a perfect 30-yard strike to Clark in the end zone. Two more Lohmiller field goals made it 37-10 before the Bills pushed across two fourth-quarter touchdowns to make the final a bit more respectable, but no less emphatic.

Joe Gibbs became just the third NFL coach with as many as three Super Bowl titles and, naturally, he deflected the credit. "I've never felt more humble than right now," Gibbs said. "The Lord has blessed me. We've got a great owner [Jack Kent Cooke] and a great team. I've said this was one of my easiest years. Our older players took the leadership upon themselves and the coaches were kind of along for the ride."

It was a ride that Redskins fans will remember for a long, long time.

1992
Head Coach: Joe Gibbs
Record: 9-7, Third in NFC East
Playoffs: 1-1, lost in Divisional Playoff

Honors: Brad Edwards All-NFC; Wilbur Marshall All-NFL, Pro Bowl

Hall of Fame: John Riggins, Running Back, 1976-1979, 1981-1985

July 27
Gibbs Gets 3-Year Contract Extension
Deal worth reported $1.4 million per season

Grimm Retires But Isn't Going Anywhere
Apr 23—Offensive lineman Russ Grimm announced that he is retiring after 11 years with the Redskins.

One of the original members of the Hogs, Grimm made four straight Pro Bowl appearances from 1983 through 1986.

Grimm will still be going to Redskins Park to work, although he will be going to a coach's office rather than to the locker room. He will be the team's tight ends coach.

Strike the Pose: Skins Draft Heisman Winner Howard
Apr 26—The Redskins got their man.

After spending weeks trying to figure out if Michigan wide receiver Desmond Howard would be available when the Redskins picked at number six in the draft, Charley Casserly decided it was better to be safe than to be kicking yourself later on.

He sent the Redskins two first-round picks, numbers 6 and 28 overall, to Cincinnati for the right to move up to number 4 and nab the Heisman Trophy winner.

9/7/92	COWBOYS (1-0) 23, Redskins (0-1) 10				63,538
Was	0	7	0	3	**10**
Dal	9	7	7	0	**23**
Dal	Safety Holt blocked punt out of end zone				

Dal	E. Smith 5 run (Elliott kick)
Was	Clark 30 pass from Rypien (Lohmiller kick)
Dal	Harper 26 pass from Aikman (Elliott kick)
Dal	Martin 79 punt return (Elliott kick)
Was	FG Lohmiller 49

Texas Stadium—The Cowboys rolled up 390 yards of offense and got big plays from their special teams, routing the Redskins 23-10.

The Dallas special teams set the tone when cornerback Isaac Holt eluded his blocker and blocked Kelly Goodburn's punt out of the end zone for two points. After taking the free kick, Dallas grinded out an 84-yard drive that took 13 plays and ate up more than seven and a half minutes of the clock. The drive culminated in a five-yard touchdown run by Emmitt Smith. By the end of the first quarter, the Cowboys had gained 112 yards, the Redskins offense had netted minus two yards.

A Martin Mayhew interception set up the Redskins offense in the second quarter and they responded with Mark Rypien throwing a 30-yard touchdown pass to Gary Clark. Chip Lohmiller's extra point made it 9-7 and, after having been badly outplayed, the Redskins seemed to have climbed back into contention.

But not for long. Troy Aikman engineered a two-minute drill that resulted in a touchdown pass to Alvin Harper. Dallas went into the locker room up 16-7.

The killing blow came in the third quarter. In punt formation, Goodburn took the long snap on a bounce, getting the punt away to Kelvin Martin at the Dallas 21. Martin cut to his left, eluded a tackler, found a wall of blockers and went all the way 79 yards for the clinching score.

9/13/92	REDSKINS (1-1) 24, Falcons (1-1) 17			54,343	
Atl	0	14	0	3	17
Was	0	21	3	0	24
Was	Byner 5 pass from Rypien (Lohmiller kick)				
Was	Howard 55 punt return (Lohmiller kick)				
Atl	Sanders 99 kickoff return (Johnson kick)				
Was	Clark 16 pass from Rypien (Lohmiller kick)				
Atl	Haynes 89 pass from Miller (Johnson kick)				
Was	FG Lohmiller 41				
Atl	FG Johnson 24				

RFK Stadium—The Redskins and Falcons combined for five touchdowns in an explosive second quarter. Washington emerged from that exchange with a 7-point lead and held on for a 24-17 win.

After Ernest Byner opened the scoring by catching a five-yard scoring pass from Mark Rypien, the special teams came up with a trick play. After an Atlanta punt, Desmond Howard took Brian Mitchell's lateral 55 yards for a TD to make it 14-0.

But Atlanta answered with two big plays of its own. After Howard's return, Deion Sanders took the ensuing kickoff all the way, covering 99 yards to make it 14-7. Following a 16-yard touchdown pass from Rypien to Gary Clark, the Falcons got back within seven points again on an 89-yard bomb from Chris Miller to Michael Haynes.

Things settled down to a pace the Redskins preferred in the second half as the two teams exchanged field goals. The Falcons were threatening to tie the game in the late going until Kurt Gouveia sealed the win with a diving interception in the end zone with just less than four minutes left.

9/20/92	REDSKINS (2-1) 13, Lions (1-2) 10			55,818	
Det	0	3	0	7	10
Was	7	3	0	3	13
Was	Byner 6 run (Lohmiller kick)				
Det	FG Hanson 52				
Was	FG Lohmiller 53				
Was	FG Lohmiller 27				
Det	Green 67 pass from Peete (Hanson kick)				

RFK Stadium—The Redskins controlled the ball for nearly 38 minutes, aided greatly by Ernest Byner who gained 120 yards on 30 carries to pace a 13-10 win over the Lions.

The Redskins ground out an 80-yard, 13-play touchdown drive on their first possession, with Byner going over from six yards out. After Jason Hanson connected on a 52-yard field goal, Chip Lohmiller did him one better by connecting from 53 yards to put the Redskins up 10-3 at the half.

Lohmiller provided what would prove to be the winning points with a 27-yard field goal in the third quarter. The Redskins' defense held the Lions to just eight first downs and limited Barry Sanders to 34 yards on 14 carries. Still, the Lions had a chance to tie the game with 1:42 left—but Jason Hanson was short a 49-yard field goal attempt.

While Byner was pounding out yardage on the ground, the Detroit offense could only watch from the sideline. Barry Sanders was held to just 34 yards rushing. The Lions ran 45 offensive plays compared to 66 for Washington.

10-4-92	CARDINALS (1-3) 27, Redskins (2-2) 24			34,488	
Was	14	3	7	0	-	24
Pho	0	0	6	21	-	27
Was	Sanders 19 pass from Rypien (Lohmiller kick)				
Was	Byner 9 run (Lohmiller kick)				
Was	FG Lohmiller 33				
Pho	Brown 1 run (kick failed)				
Was	Byner 3 run (Lohmiller kick)				
Pho	Massey 31 interception return (Davis kick)				
Pho	Massey 41 INT return (Davis kick)				
Pho	Centers 9 pass from Chandler (Davis kick)				

Sun Devil Stadium—The Redskins held leads of 17-0 at halftime and 24-6 entering the fourth quarter, but the wheels came off thanks to a pair of interceptions that the Cardinals' Robert Massey returned for touchdowns. Larry Centers scored the winning touchdown in a 27-24 Phoenix win.

Washington built its first half lead with a 19-yard touchdown pass from Mark Rypien to Ricky Sanders, a 9-yard Ernest Byner run, and Chip Lohmiller's 33-yard field goal. After Ivory Lee Brown brought the Cardinals within 17-6 with a one-yard run, the Redskins answered with Byner's second touchdown run, this one from three yards out. Leading by 18 going into the third quarter, Washington was firmly in control—or so it seemed.

Even after Massey's two scoring returns, the Redskins were still clinging to a four-point lead. The Cardinals took possession at their own 15 with three minutes left. All the defense had to do was keep the home team out of the end zone to sneak out with a win, but they couldn't do it. Phoenix took nine plays to move the 85 yards, scoring with 41 seconds left on a nine-yard pass from Chris Chandler to Larry Centers.

The Redskins got into position for Lohmiller to attempt a 40-yard field goal to force overtime on the game's last play, but the effort to tie the game went wide right.

Oct 8

Bostic Goes on IR, Season Likely Over
Rotator cuff injury sidelines center

10/12/92	REDSKINS (3-2) 34, Broncos (4-2) 3			56,371	
Den	3	0	0	0	3
Was	17	7	7	3	34
Was	Rypien 1 run (Lohmiller kick)				
Den	FG Treadwell 38				
Was	FG Lohmiller 43				
Was	Marshall 20 interception return (Lohmiller kick)				
Was	Clark 44 pass from Rypien (Lohmiller kick)				
Was	Rypien 1 run (Lohmiller kick)				
Was	FG Lohmiller 36				

RFK Stadium—The competitive phase of the game ended early, when Mark Rypien threw a 44-yard touchdown pass to Gary Clark in the third quarter to make the score 24-3. However, suspense remained in the game. Art Monk entered the contest needing seven receptions to break Steve Largent's career catches record.

Monk had four catches as the Redskins took possession late in the fourth quarter. Joe Gibbs decided to call Monk's number on three straight plays to put the receiver over the top. The first two were Monk's trademark dodge routes for six and 18 yards; the third was a sideline pattern for ten yards and the record. In keeping with Monk's low-key style, the celebration was brief and restrained, but number 81 clearly enjoyed the moment, pumping his fist in the air as he was mobbed by his teammates.

While the spotlight rightfully was on Monk, linebacker Wilbur Marshall certainly deserved some recognition as well. In addition to five tackles and a sack, Marshall intercepted a John Elway pass in the second quarter and returned it 20 yards for a touchdown.

Knee Knocks Lachey Out For Four Weeks

Oct. 13—While further testing will be done, preliminary indications are that the knee injury that All-Pro tackle Jim Lachey suffered while blocking on a field goal attempt during last night's game will keep him out of the lineup for three to four weeks, maybe longer.

After it is determined how long Lachey will be out, the team will decide whether or not to place him on the injured reserve—a move which would sideline him for at least four weeks—or to bring in someone to provide some depth on the line.

"We're very worried about the offensive line," Joe Gibbs said. "We thought it was one position we had enough depth. It shows what can happen out there. We're running out of bodies."

No matter what the team does in that regard, Mo Elewonibi will be starting in place of Lachey, considered by many to be the best left tackle in the league. In contrast, Elewonibi's start next Sunday will be his first in the NFL.

In fact, he saw his first extended NFL action when he stepped in for Lachey last night.

10/18/92	**REDSKINS (4-2) 16, Eagles (4-2) 12**			55,198
Phi	0	3	0	9	**12**
Was	7	3	3	3	**16**
Was	Clark 10 pass from Rypien (Lohmiller kick)
Phi	FG Ruzek 39
Was	FG Lohmiller 18
Was	FG Lohmiller 21
Was	FG Lohmiller 28
Phi	Safety Goodburn stepped out of end zone
Phi	C. Williams 6 pass from Cunningham (Ruzek kick)

RFK Stadium—The Redskins drove to a first-quarter lead on the league's top-ranked defense and were able to hold the Eagles off the rest of the game, claiming a 16-12 win.

On the game's opening drive, Ernest Byner carried eight straight times to help move the Redskins down to the Eagle 10. From there, they finished the 11-play, 61-yard, seven and a half minute march with a 10-yard touchdown pass from Mark Rypien to Gary Clark.

Washington found the going considerably tougher after that, driving time after time into Eagle territory only to suffer turnovers or be forced to settle for field goal attempts. Chip Lohmiller connected on three fairly short field goals (18, 21, and 28 yards), giving the home team a 16-3 lead in the fourth quarter.

The Washington defense was up to the task, holding the Eagles to 78 first-half yards and sacking Randall Cunningham five times. Philly's lone touchdown came on a six-yard pass from Cunningham to Calvin Williams with just 25 seconds left to play.

Rypien passed for 240 yards and the one touchdown. Byner and Ricky Ervins tag teamed the rushing game and the two-headed back gained 100 yards on the ground. Each back carried 18 times with Ervins picking up 55 yards and Byner 44.

10/25/92	**Redskins (5-2) 15, VIKINGS (5-2) 13**			59,098
Was	3	9	0	3	**15**
Min	0	0	3	10	**13**
Was	FG Lohmiller 22
Was	FG Lohmiller 52
Was	FG Lohmiller 25
Was	FG Lohmiller 45
Min	FG Reveiz 26
Min	Allen 1 run (Reveiz kick)
Min	FG Reveiz 41
Was	FG Lohmiller 49

Metrodome—Chip Lohmiller, returning to the stadium where he starred for the Minnesota Golden Gophers in college, kicked five field goals and earned NFC Offensive Player of the Week honors as the Redskins beat the Vikings 15-13.

Lohmiller booted four of his three-pointers in the first half, including one from 52 yards and another from 45 as time expired in the first half. That one gave Washington a 12-0 lead at intermission.

The Vikings came back, scoring on a 26-yard field goal by Fuad Reveiz and Terry Allen's one-yard touchdown run.

Then, late in the game, Reveiz went from hero to goat in a matter of seconds. His 41-yard field goal gave the Vikings a 13-12

lead with 2:28 left in the game, but he immediately gave the Redskins great field position when he squibbed the ensuing kickoff out of bounds.

The Redskins needed just over 20 yards to give Lohmiller a shot. That was accomplished on an 11-yard Mark Rypien scramble and a 20-yard pass to Art Monk. Lohmiller's game winner from 49 yards made it through with plenty of distance to spare with just over a minute left.

11/1/92	**Giants (4-4) 24, REDSKINS (5-3) 7**			53,647
NYG	7	14	0	3	**24**
Was	7	0	0	0	**7**
Was	Mitchell 84 punt return (Lohmiller kick)
NYG	Bunch 8 run (Bahr kick)
NYG	McCaffrey 17 pass from Hostetler (Bahr kick)
NYG	Meggett 4 pass from Hostetler (Bahr kick)
NYG	FG Bahr 19

RFK Stadium—New York's Rodney Hampton gained 138 yards rushing, helping the Giants control the ball for nearly 40 minutes in the course of grinding out a 24-7 win over the Redskins.

Things started off well for Washington as Brian Mitchell returned a first-quarter punt 84 yards for a touchdown and a 7-0 lead. However, the Giants responded immediately, driving 65 yards and scoring on an 8-yard run by Jarrod Bunch.

New York took the lead for good in the second quarter on a 17-yard pass from Jeff Hostetler to Ed McCaffrey. The margin stretched to 14 when Hostetler threw a four-yard scoring pass to Dave Meggett with just eight seconds left in the half.

The lead proved to be insurmountable as the Giants continued to dominate on both sides of the ball in the second half. On the day, New York gained 241 rushing yards to the Redskins' 61 and ran 73 offensive plays compared to 49 by Washington.

11/8/92	**Redskins (6-3) 16, SEAHAWKS (1-8) 3**			53,616
Was	0	3	6	7	**16**
Sea	0	3	0	0	**3**
Sea	FG Kasay 22
Was	FG Lohmiller 48
Was	FG Lohmiller 33
Was	FG Lohmiller 37
Was	Orr 26 pass from Rypien (Lohmiller kick)

Kingdome—By the time the fourth quarter rolled around, the Redskins had gone 15 quarters without an offensive touchdown. That string was broken as Mark Rypien found Terry Orr for a 26-yard score to clinch a 16-3 win for Washington.

Until that point, Washington had relied on the leg of Chip Lohmiller to build a 9-3 lead. Lohmiller kicked a 48-yarder to tie the game in the second quarter and booted two more in the third period. The second one, from 37 yards, came after Orr rumbled 46 yards with a Mark Rypien pass to convert a third and one.

The Washington defense held the Seattle passing game in check with two sacks and two interceptions. Seahawks quarterback Stan Gelbaugh was nine for 24 for just 75 yards.

11/15/92	**CHIEFS 35 (6-4), Redskins (6-4) 16**			75,238
Was	0	0	13	3	**16**
KC	7	21	0	7	**35**
KC	Okoye 2 run (Lowery kick)
KC	Barnett 44 pass from Krieg (Lowery kick)
KC	Okoye 3 run (Lowery kick)
KC	Williams 5 run (Lowery kick)
Was	Ervins 5 run (Lohmiller kick)
Was	FG Lohmiller 40
Was	FG Lohmiller 26
Was	FG Lohmiller 38
KC	Barnett 35 pass from Krieg (Lowery kick)

Arrowhead Stadium—The Chiefs scored touchdowns on each of their first four possessions and never looked back in routing Washington.

The home team struck early and often, on the ground and through the air. Kansas City's Dave Krieg passed for 232 yards in the first half alone. Christian Okoye opened the scoring for the Chiefs on a two-yard touchdown run, the first of two rushing TD's for him. Tim Barnett caught a 44-yard touchdown pass from Krieg in the second quarter, followed by Okoye's second touchdown. Then, with 37 seconds left in the first half, Harvey Williams ran in from five yards out to make it 28-0.

The Redskins had some chances to get back into it in the second half, but were unable to take full advantage. After Ricky Ervins' five-yard touchdown run in the third quarter, the Redskins' next three scoring drives all resulted in three points, not seven. It probably wouldn't have mattered. As soon as the Chiefs felt some heat when it became 28-16, they quickly responded with another Krieg touchdown pass to Barnett to extend the lead to 35-16.

11/23/92	SAINTS (8-3) 20, Redskins (6-5) 3				68,591
Was	3	0	0	0	3
NO	0	14	3	3	20
Was	FG Lohmiller 34				
NO	Hilliard 18 run (Anderson kick)				
NO	Early 5 pass from Hebert (Andersen kick)				
NO	FG Andersen 43				
NO	FG Andersen 45				

Superdome—The statistics of the competing quarterbacks don't always tell the story of a game, but they did in this one. The Saints' signal caller Bobby Hebert was the model of efficiency, completing 14 of 18 passes for 142 yards.

Meanwhile, Mark Rypien had to throw 38 passes for his team to net 162 yards in the air. Rypien was sacked four times and threw an interception.

It added up to a 20-3 win for New Orleans.

The Redskins had a nice drive in the first quarter and scored on a 34-yard field goal by Chip Lohmiller.

It was all downhill after that, however, as the Saints scored two touchdowns in the second quarter to take a 14-3 halftime lead. The first came on an 18-yard run by Dalton Hilliard and then Hebert threw a five-yard touchdown pass to Quinn Early. Two field goals by Morten Andersen completed the scoring.

The Redskins rushed for just 58 yards on the day and did not help their cause with five penalties for 92 yards.

11-29-92	REDSKINS (7-5) 41, Cardinals (3-9) 3					53,541
Pho	3	0	0	0	-	3
Was	14	6	7	14	-	41
Pho	FG Davis 42					
Was	Sanders 13 pass from Rypien (Lohmiller kick)					
Was	Edwards 53 INT return (Lohmiller kick)					
Was	FG Lohmiller 32					
Was	FG Lohmiller 22					
Was	Byner 3 run (Lohmiller kick)					
Was	Clark 31 pass from Rypien (Lohmiller kick)					
Was	Monk 10 pass from Conklin (Lohmiller kick)					

RFK Stadium—After having scored just two offensive touchdowns in the previous 23 quarters of play, the Washington attack broke out of that slump in a big way. Mark Rypien threw for 175 yards and two touchdowns while Ernest Byner led a balanced rushing attack with 62 yards as the Redskins thumped the Cardinals 41-3.

While the offensive unit had plenty to be happy about, safety Brad Edwards had reason to smile as well. He picked off three passes and returned one for a touchdown. The scoring return followed a 13-yard touchdown pass from Rypien to Ricky Sanders and gave the home team a 14-3 lead in the first quarter. Two Chip Lohmiller field goals in the second quarter pushed the halftime lead to 20-3.

The fun continued into the second half. Byner scored on a three-yard run in the third quarter and Gary Clark caught a 31-yard

touchdown pass early in the fourth. Backup QB Cary Conklin wrapped up the scoring when he tallied his first NFL touchdown pass, a 10-yarder to Art Monk.

Gibbs Apologizes For Late Passes

Nov 30—Sometimes you just can't win.

Earlier this year, when the Redskins did the kneel-down play near the Denver goal line with a 34-3 lead, the move drew the ire of Broncos coach Dan Reeves. Evidently, he didn't want any mercy and wanted his team to have to stop the Redskins.

Move up to yesterday, when Gibbs put backup quarterback Cary Conklin into the game with five and a half minutes remaining and the Redskins leading the Cardinals 34-3. He called some pass plays, including one on third down at the Arizona 10 that wound up being Conklin's first NFL touchdown pass.

While Conklin celebrated, Cardinal coach Joe Bugel was visibly steamed on the sideline, screaming in the direction of Gibbs on the other side of the field.

Today, Gibbs apologized for calling the pass. "I called that pass without thinking," Gibbs said. "It's 34-3. What are you trying to prove? . . . It's a bad sportsmanship thing."

In Arizona, Bugel, who coached the Redskins offensive line for nine years and to two Super Bowl titles, hadn't yet calmed down. He was particularly disturbed by the fact that he used to work for the organization. "I was a trusty lieutenant for him for nine years, a very loyal lieutenant," Bugel said at a news conference. "Hey, you've got to do what you have to do. I'll just put it that way."

Hey, Buges, how about just stopping the other team?

12/6/92	Redskins (8-5) 28, GIANTS (5-8) 10				62,998
Was	7	7	7	7	28
NYG	0	3	7	0	10
Was	Byner 1 run (Lohmiller kick)				
Was	Byner 11 run (Lohmiller kick)				
NYG	FG Willis 43				
NYG	Hampton 1 run (Willis kick)				
Was	Orr 20 pass from Rypien (Lohmiller kick)				
Was	Monk 42 pass from Rypien (Lohmiller kick)				

Giants Stadium—The Redskins jumped to a 14-0 lead in the second quarter and retook control late in the game to stave off a New York rally and take a 28-10 victory.

Washington gained its two-touchdown margin on the strength of two TD runs by Ernest Byner, who rushed for an even 100 yards on the game. But the Giants battled back to pull within 14-10 on a 43-yard field goal by Ken Willis and a one-yard run by Rodney Hampton.

The Washington offense responded to the wake-up call. Mark Rypien completed four straight passes to lead the Redskins on an 80-yard touchdown march capped by a 20-yard scoring pass to Terry Orr, giving Washington some breathing room. A Rypien touchdown pass to Art Monk in the fourth quarter covered 42 yards and completed the scoring.

12/13/92	REDSKINS (9-5) 20, Cowboys (11-3) 17				56,437
Dal	3	14	0	0	17
Was	0	7	3	10	20
Dal	FG Elliott 23				
Dal	Novacek 5 pass from Aikman (Elliott kick)				
Was	Orr 41 pass from Byner (Lohmiller kick)				
Dal	Novacek 5 pass from Aikman (Elliott kick)				
Was	FG Lohmiller 32				
Was	FG Lohmiller 22				
Was	Copeland fumble recovery in end zone (Lohmiller kick)				

RFK Stadium—Danny Copeland recovered a Troy Aikman fumble in the end zone to complete one of the wildest plays ever witnessed at RFK Stadium to push the Redskins past Dallas 20-17.

The Cowboys seemed to be cruising to a third straight win over Washington, leading 17-10 early in the fourth quarter with the ball at the Washington two. But Aikman gave the Redskins new life when he tried to force the ball into a crowd of defenders and Andre Collins picked it off a yard deep in the end zone and returned it 59 yards to the Dallas 42. Mark Rypien threw to Gary Clark for 16 and to Ricky Sanders for 13, but the drive stalled at the five and Chip Lohmiller's 22-yard field goal cut the lead to 17-13 with 7:02 left.

Dallas started from its own 10 following the kickoff and on third and eight at the 12, Aikman and Michael Irvin made a big play, with the quarterback hitting a streaking Irvin for 20 yards across the middle. Then Darrell Green made a bigger play, stripping the ball from Irvin. Copeland picked the ball up at the 39 and returned it 15 yards. From the Dallas 24, Rypien completed one pass to Clark, but on fourth and one at the two, Rypien barely overthrew Clark. The ball went back to Dallas with three and a half minutes left.

Aikman went back to pass on second and seven from the five. Defensive tackle Jason Buck overpowered center Mark Stepnoski, bull rushing the center back into Aikman. Just before the quarterback started into his passing motion—or just after, depending on your rooting interests—Buck got a hand on the ball, knocking it loose. It rolled free in the end zone and Emmitt Smith picked it up. Rather than falling on it and taking a safety, he tried to flip the ball forward to nobody in particular. It didn't make it far and Copeland pulled it out of a stack of players for the TD.

In celebration, Copeland ran out to midfield, displaying the ball to the cheering but disoriented crowd. The confusion came from the fact that the referees were still trying to find the ball in a pile of players in the end zone and hadn't signaled a touchdown. Monte Coleman directed Copeland back to the goal line, where he showed the ball to the zebras and got the call.

Dallas wasn't done yet. Needing a field goal to tie with more than two minutes left, Aikman completed three straight passes to the Washington 38. But sacks by Shane Collins and Coleman forced Dallas into desperation, and Green knocked away Aikman's last-gasp pass.

12/20/92	**EAGLES (10-5) 17, Redskins (9-6) 13**			65,841	
Was	0	13	0	0	**13**
Phil	0	7	7	3	**17**
Was	FG Lohmiller 29				
Phil	Sherman 21 run (Ruzek kick)				
Was	Sanders 62 pass from Rypien (Lohmiller kick)				
Was	FG Lohmiller 41				
Phi	Williams 28 pass from Cunningham (Ruzek kick)				
Phi	FG Ruzek 23				

Veterans Stadium—The winner of this game would clinch a playoff berth; the loser would have to wait until the next week, the final game of the season. It turned out that the Redskins would be the ones waiting.

Washington led 13-7 at the half on the strength of two Chip Lohmiller field goals and a 62-yard touchdown pass from Mark Rypien to Ricky Sanders. After that, though, the offense went dormant for much of the second half, giving the hosts the opportunity to retake the lead on a 28-yard Randall Cunningham to Calvin Williams TD pass early in the third.

Roger Ruzek's 23-yard field goal with 3:35 left in the game put Philly up by four. Starting at its own 10, the Redskins' offense made a valiant effort, converting three third downs and two fourth downs to get into scoring range. On the 17th play of the drive, Eric Allen knocked away a pass intended for Gary Clark as time ran out, and the Eagles were in the playoffs.

Rypien passed for 272 yards but the offense was hurt by three fumbles, two of them lost, and two Rypien interceptions.

12/26/92	**Raiders (7-9) 21, REDSKINS (9-7) 20**			53,032	
LARd	0	0	7	14	**21**
Was	0	3	7	10	**20**
Was	FG Lohmiller 39				
LARd	Wright 41 pass from Evans (Jager kick)				
Was	Monk 49 pass from Rypien (Lohmiller kick)				
Was	FG Lohmiller 22				
LARd	N. Bell 5 run (Jager kick)				
Was	Ervins 1 run (Lohmiller kick)				
LARd	T. Brown 3 pass from Evans (Jager kick)				

RFK Stadium—The Redskins could wrap up a playoff spot in this season finale, and the 6-9 Raiders were not supposed to provide much of a hindrance. They appeared to be even less of a threat when their starting quarterback, ex-Redskin Pro Bowler Jay Schroeder, went down with an injury in the second quarter and was replaced by 37-year-old Vince Evans. But Evans and the Raiders proved to be quite competitive, taking the lead at 14-13 when Nick Bell scored on a five-yard run with just over four minutes left.

The Redskins answered quickly—too quickly, as it turned out. It took them just four plays to move 55 yards to reclaim the lead on a one-yard Ricky Ervins run. There were just under two minutes left when Washington scored—just enough for Evans. He quieted the 53,032 in attendance by completing a 50-yard bomb to Willie Gault, then silenced the crowd with 13 seconds left by hitting Tim Brown with a 3-yard TD pass on fourth and goal.

The loss did not eliminate the Redskins from the playoff picture, but they would need help.

Dec 27

Skins Take the Back Door In
Minnesota win over Packers; Gives playoff spot to Redskins

NFC Wild Card Playoff Game
Saturday, January 2, 1993
Metrodome
Minneapolis, Minnesota

1/2/93	**Redskins 24, VIKINGS 7**			57,353	
Was	3	14	7	0	**24**
Min	7	0	0	0	**7**
Min	Allen 1 run (Reveiz kick)				
Was	FG Lohmiller 44				
Was	Byner 3 run (Lohmiller kick)				
Was	Mitchell 8 run (Lohmiller kick)				
Was	Clark 24 pass from Rypien (Lohmiller kick)				

Kick returner Brian Mitchell had only six carries from scrimmage all year long but with Ricky Ervins out, Mitchell helped carry the load on offense. He had 16 carries for 109 yards to spur the win over the Vikings.

Mitchell's biggest play came with the Redskins leading 10-7 in the second quarter. From punt formation, he took the snap from center and ran 36 yards to the Minnesota eight. Mitchell ran it in from there to put Washington up 17-7.

In all, the Redskins held the ball for more than 42 minutes in upsetting the Central Division champs. Vikings QB Sean Salisbury completed two passes during Minnesota's opening drive and just four more the rest of the way, finishing 6 for 20 with two interceptions.

On that opening drive it looked as though the Vikings would fulfill their expectations as favorites. The advance covered 79 yards and Terry Allen capped it by powering a yard for a touchdown.

But the Redskins battled back with the defense leading the way. Martin Mayhew picked off a Salisbury pass and returned it to the Vikings 33. That set up a 44-yard Chip Lohmiller field goal to make it 7-3.

Another takeaway, this one a Brad Edwards interception, helped put the Redskins in the lead. That set up a short touchdown drive with Earnest Byner tallying the TD on a three-yard run.

The Mitchell's heroics gave the Redskins a 10-point halftime lead. Washington chewed up a good chunk of the third quarter with a 71-yard touchdown drive. The competitive phase of the game ended shortly before the end of the third period when Mary Rypien hit Gary Clark for 24 yards and a touchdown.

NFC Divisional Playoff Game
Saturday, January 9, 1993
Candlestick Park
San Francisco, California

1/9/93	49ERS 20, Redskins 13				64,991
Was	3	0	3	7	**13**
SF	7	10	0	3	**20**
SF	Taylor 5 pass from Young (Cofer kick)				
Was	FG Lohmiller 19				
SF	FG Cofer 23				
SF	Jones 16 pass from Young				
Was	FG Lohmiller 32				
Was	Rypien 1 run (Lohmiller kick)				
SF	FG Cofer 33				

The Redskins appeared to be dead in the water, trailing the 49ers 17-3 at halftime. Even after Washington got three points back to make it an 11-point game, it appeared that San Francisco was still too much for the defending champs.

Suddenly, though, the Skins were given an opportunity to get back into the contest with a San Francisco turnover. Late in the third quarter, Steve Young fumbled and Washington recovered at the San Francisco 15. Moments later, Mark Rypien snuck over from the one and the Redskins had life at 17-13.

After a 49er punt, the Redskins were driving to take the lead, moving to a first down at the San Francisco 23. The comeback attempt ended right there, however, when Rypien and Brian Mitchell botched a handoff and the 49ers recovered the loose ball. San Francisco took seven minutes off the clock during the subsequent drive, resulting in a field goal that dethroned the reigning Super Bowl champs.

The Niners got on the board first when Steve Young threw a five-yard touchdown pass to John Taylor. The Redskins got close to tying it but they had to settle for a 19-yard Chip Lohmiller field goal.

A Mitchell fumble set up a San Francisco touchdown to help give them that 17-3 halftime lead. The Redskins put up a spirited comeback but it fizzled on the botched handoff.

On a muddy field in San Francisco, the Redskins posted just 73 yards rushing. Rypien threw two interceptions and was sacked five times.

Jan 10
Bear Trap? Petitbon a Candidate in Chicago
Defensive coordinator interviews with Bears, Denver also interested

1993
Head Coach: Richie Petitbon
Record: 4-12, Fifth in NFC East

Feb 14
Big Win: Gibbs' Driver Wins Daytona 500
Dale Jarrett takes NASCAR's premiere event

Say it Ain't So! Citing Family Concerns, Gibbs Resigns

Mar 5—It was a bolt out of the blue.

Millions of Redskins fans who woke up this Friday morning with a chipper disposition were suddenly given a hard jolt of reality when they turned on their TVs or got in their cars to drive to work, tuning to their favorite radio stations.

Joe Gibbs resigns. Press conference at noon.

Before it could sink in—before anyone could really have a chance to reach a state of denial—there the coach was on TV, as promised, confirming the news. He said it was a family decision.

"Every year, we get away and talk about it," he said. "We always reach the same conclusion. This year, it was different. The boys didn't encourage me one way or another, but they understood when I told them what I was thinking. I think Pat's happier than anyone. This isn't an easy lifestyle for a coach's wife. The coach is the guy who stands up and hears everyone tell him how great he is. The wife is the one waiting at home alone while the coach is spending every night at the office.

"I wanted more time with my family. I wanted more time with my sons. I look at this as a window of opportunity with them and I couldn't let it pass."

Although he has been diagnosed with a condition that has caused some pain and some difficulty in sleeping, Gibbs said that health was not a factor in his decision.

Richie Petitbon, the team's longtime defensive coordinator, will be the team's new head coach. It had to be one of the shortest job interviews ever.

"I get a call from Mr. Cooke who tells me Joe has retired and that he wants me to coach the Redskins," Petitbon said. "After I picked myself up off the floor, I said yes."

After hearing the news, most Redskins fans had to pick themselves up as well.

Free Agent Visits Heating Up

Mar 11—The free agent derby is up and running.

San Francisco Linebacker Bill Romanowski spent a full day at Redskins Park, eating breakfast with new coach Richie Petitbon, meeting with Charley Casserly, touring Redskins Park and taking a physical. Romanowski is of interest to the Redskins because all three of their starters at linebacker—Andre Collins, Kurt Gouveia and Wilbur Marshall—are unsigned for 1993.

Romanowski liked what he saw. "I had a pretty good idea what I would find, and what I saw was a very impressive organization," he said.

Meanwhile, the Denver Broncos had their eye on a few free agent Redskins. Defensive end Fred Stokes and defensive tackle Tim Johnson toured their facility today and defensive tackle Jumpy

Geathers got an offer from the Broncos. Geathers did not accept the offer but negotiations could continue.

The Redskins have a total of 20 unrestricted free agents on their roster.

Mar 13

Wilbur Marshall on Trading Block?
*Team puts out feelers for Pro Bowl LB,
unhappy with franchise tag*

Clark Heading West

Mar 22—Gary Clark, a key member of two Super Bowl champion teams in Washington, is heading west.

The team's leading receiver last year signed a three-year, $6 million contract with the Phoenix Cardinals today.

While the contract makes Clark the second-highest paid receiver in the league behind Jerry Rice, he said that it was as much about respect as money.

"It came to a point where it was kind of a respect factor," he said. "I've been in the league eight years. Every year I led the Washington Redskins in receiving or was the go-to guy, we were in the playoffs. When we tried to do different things, we didn't make the playoffs. It's nice to see an organization actually want you. You treat me with respect, I'll treat you with respect."

Apr 8

Monk Offered Backup Role, No Raise
*Petitbon delivers news, receiver
both "relieved" and "disappointed"*

Apr 28

Contract in Way of Marshall Trade to Oilers
*Teams agree on 1st and 5th round picks as
compensation, Marshall must agree to contract*

May 7

Monk Boycotts Minicamp
Money, playing status are issues

June 14

Bank on it—Skins Sign Giants LB
*Carl Banks gets deal from Redskins,
Marshall status still uncertain*

What The #@*%?
Skins Get 3rd and 5th for Marshall

July 2—Wilbur Marshall got his money.

The Houston Oilers got their man.

The Washington Redskins got the shaft.

NFL Commissioner Paul Tagliabue ruled today that the Redskins would get third-and fifth-round draft picks as compensation for Marshall, their Pro Bowl linebacker and franchise player, moving to the Oilers.

This ruling came despite the fact that the Oilers had agreed to send first- and fifth-round picks to Washington for Marshall's services two months ago.

The deal was contingent on Marshall agreeing to a new contract with Houston. After extended negotiations, Marshall

accepted the Oilers' last offer, but the team then withdrew the contract offer.

Tagliabue was called in to arbitrate the three-sided dispute. Apparently he lowered the draft pick from a first to a third because the Redskins had not faxed the paperwork for the trade into the league office.

Of course, they didn't do so because the deal was contingent on Marshall and the Oilers agreeing on the contract.

The commissioner also didn't like the fact that Casserly offered to pay $150,000 of Marshall's salary in order to get the deal done. This was improperly interfering with a two-party negotiation, Tagliabue said.

Washington still will have to pay the $150,000.

The Redskins weren't happy but they have no options.

"So be it," Redskins owner Jack Kent Cooke said tersely. "The commissioner has spoken."

"We'll abide by the decision," Charley Casserly said.

July 15

Monk in the Fold
Signs one-year deal for $1.1 million

July 16

Don Warren Hangs It Up
TE says 14 years of battering "took its toll"

Ouch! Lachey Out For Season With Torn ACL

Aug 16—What was thought to be a sprain turned out to be something much, much worse for Jim Lachey and the Redskins.

Lachey, the team's top offensive lineman and one of the best in the NFL, will undergo season-ending knee surgery for a torn anterior cruciate ligament in his right knee.

After he sustained the injury in a preseason game against the Browns a week ago, Lachey stayed in the game for another eight or 10 plays. Trainer Bubba Tyer thought that the knee was swollen but still structurally sound. After the swelling went down, though, an MRI exam revealed the torn ACL.

Mo Elewonibi, who has been with the team for three years but only has been healthy for five games, will man Lachey's position.

9/6/93	REDSKINS (1-0) 34, Cowboys (0-1) 16				58,345
Dal	6	0	7	3	16
Was	0	14	7	14	35
Dal	Harper 80 pass from Aikman (kick failed)				
Was	Sanders 15 pass from Rypien (Lohmiller kick)				
Was	Mitchell 1 run (Lohmiller kick)				
Was	Middleton 1 pass from Rypien (Lohmiller kick)				
Dal	Harper 33 pass from Aikman (Elliott kick)				
Was	Monk 15 pass from Rypien (Lohmiller kick)				
Dal	FG Elliott 22				
Was	Mitchell 29 run (Lohmiller kick)				

RFK Stadium—Richie Petitbon's head coaching debut was a smashing success as the Redskins pulled away from the defending Super Bowl champion Cowboys to claim an easy 35-16 win.

A blown assignment in the secondary that allowed Alvin Harper to break free for an 80-yard touchdown reception in the first quarter was one of the few things that didn't go right for the Redskins. They responded with a grind-it-out drive that featured rookie Reggie Brooks, who carried on eight of the 13 plays, gaining 48 of the 80 yards. The payoff came when Mark Rypien lofted a pass into the corner of the end zone that Ricky Sanders gathered in for a 15-yard touchdown.

Even when things went poorly for the Redskins, things turned out OK. With a little more than two minutes left before halftime, Kelly Goodburn shanked a punt but the ball bounced off of the leg of Dallas' James Washington. Pat Eilers recovered the free ball at the Dallas 17. Four plays later, Brian Mitchell swept around end from a yard out to give the Redskins a 14-6 lead at intermission.

The home team took command on its initial possession of the second half. Washington moved 78 yards in nine plays, scoring on Rypien's one-TD pass to tight end Ron Middleton. Dallas made some noise with a lightning-quick 80-yard touchdown drive, getting into the end zone with another Aikman-to-Harper hookup, this one of 33 yards.

Mitchell added to Dallas' momentum when, thinking he was in the end zone, he downed the ensuing kickoff on his own one-yard line. "I felt two inches tall," said Mitchell.

But the Washington offense was up to the task. A textbook 13-play, 99-yard drive to the other end zone ensued. Art Monk finished off the seven-minute excursion with a 15-yard touchdown reception. Mitchell's 29-yard burst up the middle topped off the scoring for the Redskins.

Petitbon summed up Monday night's events: "It was very, very nice."

Sep 8

Skins Boot Goodburn, Sign Roby
Former Dolphin a two-time Pro Bowl punter

9/12/93	Cardinals (1-1) 17, REDSKINS (1-1) 10			53,522
Pho	10	7	0	0	17
Was	0	0	7	3	10
Pho	Bailey 58 punt return (Davis kick)
Pho	FG Davis 53
Pho	Moore 18 run (Davis kick)
Was	Sanders 9 pass from Conklin (Lohmiller kick)
Was	FG Lohmiller 23

RFK Stadium—After 14 straight losses in Washington, the Cardinals built a 17-0 first-half lead and held off the Redskins to take a 17-10 win.

Phoenix's cause was greatly aided by the fact that quarterback Mark Rypien was sidelined with a knee injury early in the second quarter, but they already led 10-0 and appeared to be on their way.

Before Rypien went down, they had scored on a 58-yard punt return by Johnny Bailey and on the longest field goal in franchise history, a 53-yarder by Greg Davis.

After Cary Conklin came in at quarterback for Rypien, the Cards padded their lead. They moved 75 yards in short order, with a pass from Steve Beuerlein to ex-Redskin Gary Clark covering 36 yards. Ron Moore then broke a tackle, speeding 18 yards over the goal line to make it 17-0.

It took a trick play on special teams to get the Washington offense jump-started in the third period. On a punt return, Brian Mitchell handed off to Darrell Green, who returned the ball 23 yards to the Redskin 47. It took five plays to score on a nine-yard pass from Conklin to Ricky Sanders.

In the fourth quarter, a first and goal at the Phoenix eight led to just a 23-yard Chip Lohmiller field goal. Still, the Redskins had a chance to tie, getting possession at their own 11 with 4:22 left, but the drive went nowhere. The Cardinals took over on downs.

Sep 14

Rypien Out 3-6 Weeks
Partially-torn knee ligament sidelines QB

9/14/93	EAGLES (3-0) 34, Redskins (1-2) 31			66,421
Was	0	14	7	10	31
Phil	3	7	7	17	34
Phil	FG Bahr 27
Was	McGee 11 pass from Conklin (Lohmiller kick)
Was	Sanders 34 pass from Conklin (Lohmiller kick)
Phil	Williams 80 pass from Cunningham (Bahr kick)
Was	Middleton 1 pass from Conklin (Lohmiller kick)
Phil	Allen 29 interception return (Bahr kick)
Was	FG Lohmiller 38
Phil	Williams 9 pass from Cunningham (Bahr kick)
Was	Brooks 85 run (Lohmiller kick)
Phil	FG Bahr 42
Phil	Williams 10 pass from Cunningham (Bahr kick)

Veterans Stadium—"He did a number on us," said Richie Petitbon. The coach was nearly right. Actually, Randall Cunningham did a few numbers on the Redskins as the Eagles rallied to beat Washington 34-31.

He did numbers like 25 (completions in 39 attempts), 390 (yards), and three (touchdowns, including the game winner with four seconds left).

Cary Conklin, making his first NFL start, helped stake the Redskins to a 14-3 lead in the second quarter with a pair of touchdown passes. The first, 11 yards to Tim McGee, capped an 86-yard drive. Then Philly running back Heath Sherman fumbled and Shane Collins recovered for Washington at the Eagle 34. On the next play, Conklin tossed a 34-yard scoring pass to Ricky Sanders.

It took the Eagles just 19 seconds to respond. On the first play after the kickoff, Calvin Williams beat cornerback A.J. Johnson on a slant. Cunningham hit him in stride, and Williams was gone—80 yards, making it 14-10 at the half.

Another Eagle turnover gave Washington a short field to work with as Jeff Snyder fumbled the second-half kickoff and Pat Eilers recovered at the Eagle 18. On fourth and goal inside the one, Conklin faked to Brian Mitchell and found Ron Middleton all alone for the touchdown.

That got the Washington lead back up until 11 and the margin held until late in the third quarter. Under pressure from end Clyde Simmons, Conklin threw a pass that was, to say the least, ill advised. Cornerback Eric Allen picked it off and easily rolled 29 yards for a touchdown.

"I shouldn't have thrown it," said Conklin. "I should have held it and taken the sack. Or I should have thrown it in the dirt." But he did throw it and the Washington lead was cut to four going into the fourth quarter.

Chip Lohmiller pushed the lead back up to seven with a 38-yard field goal early in the period, but the Eagles came storming back with Cunningham throwing a nine-yard touchdown pass to Williams. Nearly as quickly as the Eagles tied it, Reggie Brooks untied it with an 85-yard burst up the middle, the second-longest run from scrimmage in team history.

That would be all for the Redskins, however. Matt Bahr kicked a 42-yard field goal with 3:57 to go to pull the Eagles within four at 31-27. Despite a fourth-down conversion on a fake punt play, the Redskins were unable to eat up enough clock. The Eagles took possession at their own 17 with 1:54 to play.

Nine plays later, the Eagles were at the Washington ten with ten seconds left. Cunningham had excellent protection and surveyed the field patiently. Williams broke free and Cunningham drilled it in to him for the winning TD.

10/4/93	DOLPHINS (3-1) 17, Redskins (1-3) 10				68,568
Was	0	3	7	0	**10**
Mia	14	0	0	3	**17**
Mia	Martin 80 pass from Marino (Stoyanovich kick)				
Mia	Higgs 1 run (Stoyanovich kick)				
Was	FG Lohmiller 28				
Was	Sanders 12 pass from Gannon (Lohmiller kick)				
Mia	FG Stoyanovich 37				

Joe Robbie Stadium—The Dolphins scored the first two times they had the ball and that was enough to beat the Redskins 17-10.

It took Dan Marino a couple of plays to get warmed up but, after two incompletions, he found Tony Martin slanting across the middle. Martin had a step on rookie cornerback Tom Carter. Marino hit his receiver in stride and, 30 seconds into the contest, Miami held a 7-0 lead.

On their next possession the Dolphins were not as swift but just as sure. Working from the Washington 28, running back Terry Kirby carried for 18 yards and a few plays later caught a Marino pass for 34 to the Washington 20. Mark Higgs scored on a one-yard burst six plays later.

Rich Gannon replaced an ineffective Cary Conklin at quarterback late in the third quarter and led the team to its only touchdown on a 12-yard pass to Ricky Sanders. But with time running out and the Redskins attempting to mount a game-tying drive, Troy Vincent picked off Gannon's pass and Miami killed the clock.

Oct. 7

Rypien Works With First Team
QB set to return after three-game absence

10/10/93	Giants (4-1) 41, REDSKINS (1-4) 7				53,715
NYG	7	20	0	14	**41**
Was	0	7	0	0	**7**
NYG	Tillman 3 run (Treadwell kick)				
NYG	Cross 7 pass from Simms (kick failed)				
NYG	Sherrard 42 pass from Meggett (Treadwell kick)				
NYG	Cross 17 pass from Simms (Treadwell kick)				
Was	McGee 12 pass from Rypien (Lohmiller kick)				
NYG	Sherrard 55 pass from Simms (Treadwell kick)				
NYG	Rasheed 23 run (Treadwell kick)				

RFK Stadium—The Giants ran when they wanted to, passed when they needed to and shut down the Redskins, handing them their worst home loss in 45 years by a score of 41-7.

"It was the most disappointing and embarrassing game I can remember since I've been a Redskin," said 11-year team veteran Darrell Green.

Giants quarterback Phil Simms, naturally, took the opposite point of view. "In the first half, everything went our way," he said. "It was one of the best first halves I've ever been involved in."

The source of Green's woe and Simms' glee was the 27-0 lead the Giants built in the game's first 28 minutes. After Lewis Tillman ran three yards for a touchdown and Simms hit tight end Howard Cross with a seven-yard touchdown pass, New York coach Dan Reeves reached into his own past for a play.

As a member of the Dallas Cowboys in the '60's, he was often called upon to throw the halfback option pass. Here, he called Dave Meggett's number on the play. Meggett, who had beaten the Redskins in the past with his legs, used his arm this time. He lofted a pass to Mike Sherrard, who was wide open thanks to the fact that the Skins were blitzing on the play. Sherrard had to wait a moment for the ball to come down but still had ample time to stroll into the end zone, completing the 42-yard touchdown play.

That broke the Redskins' back, if things hadn't happened already. Simms threw another TD pass to Cross before the Redskins scored on a 12-yard pass from Mark Rypien to Tim

McGee. Brian Mitchell set up that score with a 68-yard kickoff return.

Up 27-7, New York spent most of the second half in cruise control with Tillman's runs (29 carries, 104 yards) eating up yards and time. They did get two more scores when Simms caught the Redskins in an all-out blitz and threw a 55-yard touchdown pass to Sherrard and when David Tate's interception set up a 23-yard scoring run by Kenyon Rasheed.

10/17/93	CARDINALS (2-4) 36, Redskins (1-5) 6				48,143
Was	3	0	3	0	**6**
Pho	0	13	7	16	**36**
Was	FG Lohmiller 43				
Pho	FG Davis 23				
Pho	FG Davis 45				
Pho	Hearst 1 run (Davis kick)				
Pho	Proehl 42 pass from Beuerlein (Davis kick)				
Was	FG Lohmiller 38				
Pho	Safety Brooks tackled in end zone				
Pho	Bailey 14 run (Davis kick)				
Pho	Moore 1 run (Davis kick)				

Sun Devil Stadium—"Right now, we have to be honest. We're not a very good football team. We're not a very well-coached football team," said Richie Petitbon. After this pitiful 36-6 loss to the Cardinals, not a peep of disagreement was heard.

The Redskins' offensive ineptitude was widespread. They fumbled four times, losing three of them. They passed for just 109 yards, needing 29 attempts to get that meager total. Part of the problem with the passing game was the extreme pressure that Phoenix put on Mark Rypien. They got five sacks on the day. Linebacker Freddie Joe Nunn, who forced two of the fumbles and had two of the sacks, had such an awareness of where the ball was that it seemed he was in Washington's offensive huddle.

Still, this game was reasonably close until late in the first half. The Redskins had taken the opening kickoff and put together a nice drive, taking a 3-0 lead on Chip Lohmiller's 43-yard field goal. Greg Davis responded with a pair of field goals of his own and Arizona led 6-3.

Then, facing third and three at his own 43, Cardinal quarterback Steve Beuerlein threw to Anthony Edwards on a crossing pattern. The receiver caught the pass in stride, turned upfield and strode to the Washington eight. Two plays later, Garrison Hearst went around end and just made it into the end zone to make it 13-3 at the half.

A 42-yard touchdown pass from Beuerlein to Ricky Proehl early in the third quarter fairly well wrapped it up for Phoenix. Washington did muster a field goal to make it 20-6, but the Cardinals poured it on in the fourth quarter. They trapped Reggie Brooks for a safety and then had fun in driving for two more touchdowns.

Injuries Taking a Big Toll on 1-5 Redskins

Oct. 23—The injury bug started biting the Redskins in the preseason and hasn't stopped.

Star left tackle Jim Lachey was the first to fall, going down for the season with a torn knee ligament. His replacement, Mo Elewonibi, has been in and out of the lineup, as have fellow linemen Mark Schlereth and Jeff Bostic.

The defensive line hasn't fared much better. Each of the four who started the season opener—Charles Mann, Tim Johnson, Eric Williams and Shane Collins—has missed at least one game. Richie Petitbon has been forced to run a 3-4 defense at times.

On top of that, quarterback Mark Rypien missed three games with a sprained knee and linebacker Andre Collins also was out for three games with a knee problem.

Only 11 players have started all six games this year.

11/1/93	**BILLS (6-1) 24, Redskins (1-6) 10**			79,106	
Was	7	3	0	0	**10**
Buf	14	0	7	3	**24**
Buf	Reed 65 pass from Kelly (Christie kick)				
Was	Brooks 7 run (Lohmiller kick)				
Buf	Brooks 11 pass from Kelly (Christie kick)				
Was	FG Lohmiller 19				
Buf	Thomas 1 run (Christie kick)				
Buf	FG Christie 45				

Rich Stadium—There could be no clearer indication of the sad state of the Redskins than the fact that a two-touchdown loss was considered to be a step in the right direction. But after consecutive losses by a combined score of 77-13, that's how this 24-10 loss to Buffalo was viewed.

"We had a good effort and fought our hearts out," said Jeff Bostic. Apparently, in Bostic's view, those qualities were lacking in the previous two games.

For the first time all year, the Redskins scored a touchdown in the first quarter. It came on a seven-yard run by Reggie Brooks and was the end result of a 71-yard drive during which the Redskins converted three third downs. Chip Lohmiller's extra point tied the game at seven.

After Jim Kelly's second touchdown pass, the Redskins had a great opportunity to tie it up before halftime. Lohmiller kicked a 36-yard field goal, but the Bills were penalized for roughing the kicker. Richie Petitbon took the points off the board and accepted a first down at the nine. The Redskins could get no closer than the two, however, and Lohmiller was called in again and he again converted, making it 14-10 at halftime.

The Bills converted two takeaways, both interceptions by Nate Odomes, into 10 second-half points to put it away.

11/7/93	**REDSKINS (2-6) 30, Colts (3-5) 24**			50,523	
Ind	0	10	0	14	**24**
Was	0	14	6	10	**30**
Was	Green 79 fumble return (Lohmiller kick)				
Was	Rypien 1 run (Lohmiller kick)				
Ind	Langhorne 72 pass from George (Biasucci kick)				
Ind	FG Biasucci 22				
Was	Rypien 1 run (kick failed)				
Was	FG Lohmiller 24				
Was	Mitchell 2 run (Lohmiller kick)				
Ind	Cash 9 pass from George (Biasucci kick)				
Ind	Verdin 1 pass from George (Biasucci kick)				

RFK Stadium—The Redskins took advantage of two second-quarter turnovers to build a 14-0 lead and hang on to beat the Colts 30-24.

After a scoreless first quarter, it looked like Indianapolis was going to break out on top after driving to the Washington 19. That was until running back Roosevelt Potts fumbled after taking a swing pass and was hit by Kurt Gouveia. Darrell Green picked it up at the 21 and disappeared in a flash. No Colt was within 30 yards of Green as he crossed the goal line.

A few minutes later, the Redskins were just hoping to get the Colts pinned back deep, but it turned out much better than that. Reggie Roby's punt soared inside the 20 and Indy return man Clarence Verdin was just trying to get out of the way when the ball bounced off of his shoulder. Rick Hamilton pounced on it and the Redskins were in business at the five. Two plays later, Mark Rypien scored from the one on a quarterback sneak and the Redskins had a 14-0 lead.

The Colts responded, pulling to within 14-10 by halftime on a 72-yard touchdown pass from Jeff George to Reggie Langhorne and a 22-yard Dean Biasucci field goal just before the half ended.

Washington padded its lead with a 79-yard touchdown drive in the third quarter. A 19-yard run by Reggie Brooks got things started and then Rypien connected with Tim McGee for 42 yards

to inside the Colt one. On the next play, Rypien finished the job, scoring a second touchdown on a sneak.

In the fourth quarter, the Redskins put it away by driving to a Chip Lohmiller field goal and two-yard touchdown run by Brian Mitchell. George passed for two more scores, the second coming with just 19 seconds left against the prevent defense to make the final score more respectable.

Nov 8

End of the Line for Jake?
Jacoby goes on IR, back surgery may end 14-year career

11/14/93	**GIANTS (6-3) 20, Redskins (2-7) 6**			76,606	
Was	0	0	3	3	**6**
NYG	7	7	3	3	**20**
NYG	Hampton 1 run (Treadwell kick)				
NYG	Calloway 21 pass from Meggett (Treadwell kick)				
NYG	FG Treadwell 43				
Was	FG Lohmiller 27				
NYG	FG Treadwell 39				
Was	FG Lohmiller 33				

Giants Stadium—Five weeks ago, running back Dave Meggett threw the first touchdown pass of his career. In this game, he threw his second, giving New York a 14-0 lead on the way to an easy 20-6 win over the Redskins. Fool me twice, shame on me.

"We're beyond frustration now," said Richie Petitbon.

They reached frustration in the first quarter when a holding call negated a third-down stop on defense, allowing New York to continue towards a touchdown and a 7-0 lead. They blew past being frustrated in the second quarter when Meggett's pass found a well-covered Chris Calloway for 21 yards and a touchdown, putting New York up 14-0.

Twice in the second half the Redskins drove into New York territory, but settled for field goals both times. Prior to each Chip Lohmiller three-pointer, though, David Treadwell had kicked one for the Giants, so all the Redskins could to is tread water . . . somewhere out there past frustration.

New York prevailed despite being outgained by the Redskins 325 yards to 262. The Giants netted just 110 yards passing and those numbers emphasize how much three turnovers and the Redskins' inability to cash in on touchdown opportunities hurt Washington's chances.

Gannon May Start Over Rypien

Nov 15—Less than two years after being named the Super Bowl MVP, Mark Rypien is about to be named something else—a backup.

Redskins coach Richie Petitbon has instructed the offensive coaches to prepare Rich Gannon to start and if the reserve is healthy—he has been recovering from a broken foot—he will start against the Rams on Sunday.

Rypien wasn't happy about losing the job he has held since midway through the 1989 season, but he understands why it is happening.

"If I'm playing like this and we're winning, it would be a hard move to swallow," Rypien said. "I want to play and I want to compete. But if that's the decision, I'm going to pat Rich on the butt and tell him to get out there and play hard and get this thing going."

11/21/93	**RAMS (3-7) 10, Redskins (2-8) 6**			45,546	
Was	3	0	3	0	**6**
LA	0	0	0	10	**10**
Was	FG Lohmiller 19				
Was	FG Lohmiller 34				

| LA | Drayton 25 pass from Rubley (Zendejas kick) |
| LA | FG Zendejas 23 |

Anaheim Stadium—Backup quarterback T.J. Rubley threw a 25-yard touchdown pass early in the third quarter to push the Rams past the Redskins 10-6.

The Redskins controlled field position and the game for much of the first half, but came away with three points to show for it. They came at the end of a drive after Ernest Byner was shoved out of bounds at the two after taking Rich Gannon's pass on third down from the five. Chip Lohmiller booted the short field goal.

In the third quarter, the Redskins doubled their lead. There was a Desmond Howard sighting as the little-used former Heisman Trophy winner caught a 20-yard pass to help set up Lohmiller's 34-yard effort with three and a half minutes left, giving Washington a 6-0 lead.

Jim Everett had been unable to move the ball so the Rams inserted Rubley into the game. He quickly found himself in the hole, facing a third and 18 at his own 37. Rubley scrambled near the line of scrimmage—over it, the Redskins contended—and launched a pass to tight end Pat Carter for a 38-yard gain to the Washington 25. On the next play, Rubley found his other tight end, Troy Drayton, for the go-ahead touchdown.

Later in the fourth, running back Jerome Bettis spearheaded a drive to a 23-yard field goal by Tony Zendejas. That turned out to be critical as the Redskins were forced to go for the end zone when they drove to the LA 27 with less than a minute to play. Gannon's pass intended for Art Monk was deflected by safety Anthony Newman and corralled in by Michael Stewart to seal it for the Rams.

11/28/93	**Eagles (5-6) 17, REDSKINS (2-9) 14**				46,663
Phil	3	7	0	7	**17**
Was	0	0	0	14	**14**
Phil	FG Bahr 22				
Phil	Hebron 1 run (Bahr kick)				
Was	McGee 17 pass from Gannon (Lohmiller kick)				
Was	Monk 6 pass from Gannon (Lohmiller kick)				
Phil	Joseph 2 pass from Brister (Bahr kick)				

RFK Stadium—Just as they had earlier in the year, the Eagles mounted a long drive to score a game-winning touchdown with less than a minute left. This time, though, it was backup quarterback Bubby Brister leading the charge, not star Randall Cunningham.

Even with Brister in, it's possible that the Eagles didn't need any help to win this game, though they had no wins in their last six games. Nevertheless, the Redskins provided them with a wealth of assistance.

The first big boost for the Eagles came in the second quarter when Richie Petitbon, prodded by special team coach Wayne Sevier, called for a take punt on fourth and seven at the Washington 22. The snap went to up back Brian Mitchell, who exhibited terrible form in launching a pass intended for safety Todd Bowles. Well, the form doesn't really matter; it's the result that counts. That was even worse as Otis Smith intercepted the fling and the Eagles were in business at the Washington 27. Four plays later, Vaughn Hebron covered the final yard to the end zone untouched over right tackle. The Eagles carried their 10-0 lead into intermission.

The Washington offense continued its game-long slumber in the third quarter and it appeared that the Eagles were lulled to sleep as well. It was still 10-0 when the Redskins finally put a drive together, moving 64 yards with the greatest of ease. Rich Gannon completed three passes for 40 yards and didn't face a third down on any of the seven plays in the march. Tim McGee caught Gannon's first-down pass for 17 yards and a touchdown, pulling the Redskins within three.

After not having scored a touchdown in more than 11 quarters, the Skins decided it was so much fun that they'd do it again. The foray was seven plays again, this time covering 77 yards. The big play was a Gannon-to-McGee connection good for 54 yards. Art Monk capped it off with a six-yard TD reception and the Redskins led 14-10 with 5:44 left to play.

So all the Redskins had to do was hold the Eagles out of the end zone—hold a team that hadn't had a sustained touchdown drive all day, an offense that had just one first down to its credit in the second half. That's all they had to do.

Twelve agonizing plays, 75 yards. Two penalties, an offside and a pass interference, helped keep it going. A 16-yard run by Hebron got the Eagles to the Washington three. On third down from the two, Brister faked to Hebron and lofted a pass just beyond the fingertips of a diving Darrell Green and into the arms of tight end Curtis Joseph.

Nov 30

Cooke Gives Praise But No Promises
Although owner likes effort under adversity, fate of Petitbon may be determined in last five games

12/5/93	**Redskins (3-9) 23, BUCCANEERS (3-9) 17**				49,035
Was	7	3	13	0	**23**
TB	0	0	10	7	**17**
Was	Gannon 1 run (Lohmiller kick)				
Was	FG Lohmiller 51				
Was	Brooks 78 run (Lohmiller kick)				
TB	FG Husted 31				
TB	Seals interception in end zone (Husted kick)				
Was	Gouveia 59 interception return (kick failed),				
TB	Hawkins 4 pass from Erickson (Husted kick)				

Tampa Stadium—Reggie Brooks ran for 128 yards, including a 78-yard touchdown run, as the Redskins beat the Buccaneers 23-17.

Brooks' touchdown came on the first play from scrimmage after halftime with the Redskins leading 10-0. From his own 22, he took a handoff, picked his way behind blocks by Reggie McKenzie, Jeff Bostic and Ray Brown and rolled into the end zone.

The Bucs responded with a field goal. They then had Washington backed up to its own eight. Rich Gannon faded back to the goal line and threw, but his pass was deflected. Tampa tackle Ray Seals got a bead on it, juggled it for a moment and, as he fell on his back in the end zone, nestled the ball into his stomach for an easy touchdown.

Trailing now just 17-10, Tampa Bay got the ball back and was beginning to mount a drive when Kurt Gouveia picked off Scott Erickson's pass at the Washington 41. He had open spaces in front of him, but with two bad ankles and not the swiftest afoot even when fully healthy, he seemed a long shot to reach the end zone.

"I felt like I needed to run as fast as I could," Gouveia said.

It turned out to be fast enough; he made it 59 yards for the clinching score.

12/11/93	**Jets (8-5) 3, REDSKINS (3-10) 0**				47,970
NYJ	3	0	0	0	**3**
Was	0	0	0	0	**0**
NYJ	FG Blanchard 45				

RFK Stadium—"I don't know what's going on," said Brian Mitchell.

Rich Gannon said, "I wish I had more answers."

They were talking about this embarrassing game, but they pretty well summed up the entire season for the Redskins. The Jets got a first-quarter field goal from Cary Blanchard and, despite numerous opportunities for the Redskins, it held up for the 3-0 win.

Washington couldn't complain about field position. They partially blocked two Jet punts and, perhaps spooked by the pressure, the Jet punter sent another kick just 12 yards.

But field position means nothing if you can't move the ball, and the Redskins managed just 150 yards of offense with 39 on the ground. In fact, Jet running back Johnny Johnson rushed for more yards (155) than the entire Washington offense gained.

The comic lowlight of the game came late in the first half as the Jets were attempting a field goal. Holder Louie Agular was looking at the ground where he was going to spot the ball and, suddenly, the ball was snapped. It bounced off the side of the holder's helmet and Johnny Thomas picked it up for the Redskins. Blanchard was the only one on the kicking team who knew what was going on; the kicker moved quickly to take down Thomas.

12/19/93	REDSKINS (4-10) 30, Falcons (6-8) 17			50,192
Atl	7	0	7	3	17
Was	0	16	0	14	30
Atl	Pritchard 29 pass from Hebert (Johnson kick)			
Was	Safety Alexander tackled in end zone			
Was	Rypien 1 run (Lohmiller kick)			
Was	Johnson 69 interception return (Lohmiller kick)			
Atl	Broussard 2 run (Johnson kick)			
Atl	FG Johnson 42			
Was	Byner 8 run (Lohmiller kick)			
Was	Coleman 29 fumble return (Lohmiller kick)			

RFK Stadium—The Washington defense got six takeaways and scored touchdowns on two of them as the Redskins rallied past the Falcons for a 30-17 victory.

Monte Coleman, starting at linebacker due to an injury to Carl Banks, was quite busy. He intercepted a pass, forced a fumble, recovered a fumble and returned it for a touchdown in addition to getting credited with two of the team's seven sacks of Atlanta quarterback Bobby Hebert.

The Redskins needed every bit of the defensive effort as they managed just 38 yards rushing, surrendered 182 on the ground and did not convert a single third down on ten attempts. Atlanta's time of possession edge was two to one.

The Falcons jumped on top 7-0 in the first quarter after Brian Mitchell fumbled a punt, setting up Atlanta at the Washington 31. Hebert threw a 29-yard touchdown pass to Mike Pritchard two plays later.

The comedy of errors started for the Falcons in the second quarter. A center snap sailed several feet over the head of punter Harold Alexander. He chased it down in the end zone and decided to take the safety.

After that, Atlanta appeared to have stopped the Redskins on fourth down from the one, but a facemask call gave the offense a fresh set of downs. Mark Rypien rolled to his right and over the goal line for a 9-7 lead.

The gifts kept on rolling in as Hebert didn't see cornerback A.J. Johnson on a pass late in the half. Johnson picked it off and rolled unchallenged 69 yards for a touchdown.

When the Falcons held on to the ball they were fairly effective, driving for a touchdown and a field goal to reclaim the lead at 17-16 with less than five minutes left to play. But the Redskins responded—Desmond Howard returned a kickoff 33 yards to set his team up at its own 48. Rypien completed three of four passes to move the Redskins down to the eight. From there, Ernest Byner went up the middle and dragged Atlanta safety Roger Harper into the end zone to put the Redskins back in front 23-17.

Atlanta had a chance to rally, but it expired when Hebert was hit by Sterling Palmer and coughed the ball up. Coleman scooped it up and easily scored the clincher.

12/26/93	COWBOYS (11-4) 38, Redskins (4-11) 3			64,497
Was	3	0	0	0	3
Dal	7	14	14	3	38
Was	FG Lohmiller 32			
Dal	E. Smith 1 run (Murray kick)			
Dal	Irvin 8 pass from Aikman (Murray kick)			
Dal	Harper 15 pass from Aikman (Murray kick)			
Dal	Coleman 1 run (Murray kick)			
Dal	K. Williams 62 punt return (Murray kick)			
Dal	FG Murray 38			

Texas Stadium—The Redskins have been beaten badly during this season of woe, but rarely have they been completely outclassed and manhandled as they were by the Cowboys. Not just this year, but ever.

The final score, if you must know, was Dallas 38, Washington 3.

There really isn't much of a point in recounting the particulars here. The Redskins took a 3-0 lead after converting a Troy Aikman fumble into a 32-yard Chip Lohmiller field goal, but Dallas took the lead for good four and a half minutes later on Emmitt Smith's one-yard touchdown run.

Trailing 14-3 with less than two minutes to play in the first half, the Redskins were trying to pull closer but a Mark Rypien pass bounced off of Ricky Sanders' hands and James Washington intercepted. Aikman threw a 15-yard TD pass to Alvin Harper with 13 seconds left in the half and the rout was on.

After the game, Rypien, less than two years removed from a Super Bowl MVP performance, said he thought that this might be the end of the line for him in Washington. "As much as I'd like to stay ... finally you get an understanding that it's time to move on," said Rypien. "Not because you want to. But you can just sense from a feeling around you that this might be the time."

Meanwhile, Richie Petitbon was saying, "I wish I could say what I want to say, but I can't."

There was no need, really. The final score said it all.

Dec 26

Rypien: "Time to Move On"
QB says team "leaning in a different direction"

12/31/93	Vikings (9-7) 14, REDSKINS (4-12) 9			42,836
Min	0	7	7	0	14
Was	0	3	3	3	9
Min	Graham 1 run (Revez kick)			
Was	FG Lohmiller 37			
Was	FG Lohmiller 35			
Min	A. Carter 11 pass from McMahon (Revez kick)			
Was	FG Lohmiller 36			

RFK Stadium—A forgettable season ended with a forgettable loss to the Vikings.

Behind backup quarterback Jim McMahon, Minnesota didn't have *much* offensive punch, but they did have just enough. McMahon was three for four passing in leading the Vikings to their first score, a one-yard run by fullback Scottie Graham. In the third quarter, McMahon threw an 11-yard touchdown pass to receiver Anthony Carter.

In between, the Redskins had some good scoring chances but continually shot themselves in the foot. Near the end of the first half, Monte Coleman intercepted McMahon and returned it 14 yards to the Viking 24. A sack followed immediately after that, and they had to settle for a Chip Lohmiller field goal.

Then, in the third quarter, Reggie Brooks busted off a 45-yard run to the Viking 23, but a delay of game penalty followed. Lohmiller was summoned again and it was 7-6.

There were more examples, but you get the idea—especially if you've read about the other 11 losses this season.

1994
Head Coach: Norv Turner
Record: 3-13, Fifth in NFC East

Honors: Reggie Roby All-NFL, Pro Bowl; Ken Harvey Pro Bowl

Jan 4

Cooke Fires Petitbon 'With Regret'
Coach gone after one season; Cowboys' Turner eyed as potential replacement

---

Turner Signs Five-Year Deal to Coach Skins

Feb 2—In a move that has been anticipated for a month, the Redskins introduced Norv Turner as their head coach. The former Cowboys offensive coordinator signed a five-year contract worth $600,000 per year.

When Richie Petitbon was fired on Jan 4, Turner immediately became the leading candidate for his job—but the Redskins had to wait until Dallas' playoff run was over to even interview Turner. The end came Sunday with the Cowboys' second straight Super Bowl triumph.

Team owner Jack Kent Cooke called it "a rebirth for our franchise" and declared it was a "new day."

The day almost didn't happen. The Phoenix Cardinals came in at the last minute with an offer for more money and more authority but Turner cancelled plans to go to Arizona to interview for that job, accepting the Redskins offer instead.

"I have every confidence we will be successful," said Turner. He did not set a timetable, a wise move for a coach taking over a 4-12 team that is suffering from both a declining talent base and a need to trim salaries.

Feb 28

Charley Taylor Fired as Coach
Move by Turner ends 30 years with Redskins for Hall of Fame receiver

---

Mar 10

Center Cut: Bostic Retires
Original Hog hangs it up after release

Mar 14

Mann Waived, Still Wants to Play
DE will seek to play for other team despite three knee operations in 14 months

---

Redskins Say Goodbye to Monk

Apr 6—The fact that it has been over a year in the making didn't make it any less stunning. And the fact that the timing wasn't a surprise didn't make it any less shocking.

After 14 years with the team, Art Monk no longer is a Redskin.

The team announced that contract negotiations with the NFL's all-time leading receiver were over and that they were unable to come to an agreement with Monk.

Monk has been an unrestricted free agent for about two months but there had been faint hopes that he and the team could bridge the $500,000 gap between their contract proposals.

Even if the Redskins had been willing to spend the money to pay him the $1.15 million a year he sought, the new NFL salary cap, which limits how much each team can pay in salaries, makes it very difficult to pay a part-time player that much money.

The beginning of the end came last year when then-coach Richie Petitbon informed Monk that he would become a reserve. Monk—along with many fans—believed that he deserved the right to at least fight for the starting job.

Monk was not available for comment.

"We thank Art for everything he's done for the Redskins over the years," general manager Charley Casserly said. "He's certainly one of the greatest Redskins in the history of the franchise."

Apr 13

Rypien Refuses Pay Cut, Gets Release
Former Super Bowl MVP won't accept pay decrease from $3 million to $1 million

---

Apr 23

Shuler Drafted With Third Pick
'It's a big day,' says Casserly on selection of Tennessee quarterback

---

June 3

Monk Jets to Big Apple
All-time leading receiver signs with New York for $100,000 less than Redskins' offer

---

Aug 2

Shuler in Camp, Signs $19.25 Million Deal
QB ends holdout after agreeing to richest rookie contract in NFL history

---

9/4/94	Seahawks (1-0) 28, REDSKINS (0-1) 7				52,930
Sea	7	14	7	0	**28**
Was	7	0	0	0	**7**
Was	Howard 27 pass from Friesz (Lohmiller kick)				
Sea	Warren 12 run (Kasay kick)				
Sea	Wooden 69 interception return (Kasay kick)				
Sea	Blades 5 pass from Mirer (Kasay kick)				
Sea	Warren 4 run (Kasay kick)				

RFK Stadium—The Redskins scored on their opening drive, but Seattle established control thereafter to spoil the debut of Washington coach Norv Turner, taking a 28-7 win.

Washington drove 82 yards and scored on a touchdown pass from John Friesz to Desmond Howard. They forced the Seahawks to punt, but Brian Mitchell fumbled it and Seattle recovered at the Washington 12. It took just one play to make the Skins pay for their error as Chris Warren ambled around right end 12 yards for the touchdown to tie the game at seven.

The Seahawks pulled away in the second quarter. Terry Wooden intercepted a Friesz pass and went 69 yards for a touchdown. Brian Blades caught a five-yard touchdown pass from Rick Mirer to make it 21-7 at halftime.

Washington's offense was in the middle of an extreme case of the doldrums. After Mitchell's fumble, their next ten possessions resulted in seven punts, two interceptions and one missed field goal attempt. They were unable to get any kind of running game going, gaining just 34 yards rushing on 21 carries.

Warren scored another touchdown in the third quarter to provide the final margin.

9/11/94	Redskins (1-1) 38, SAINTS (0-2) 24			58,049	
Was	14	0	14	10	38
NO	3	0	6	15	24
NO	FG Andersen 29				
Was	Ellard 14 pass from Friesz (Lohmiller kick)				
Was	Mitchell 74 punt return (Lohmiller kick)				
Was	Smith 1 pass from Friesz (Lohmiller kick)				
NO	Haynes 17 pass from Everett (pass failed)				
Was	Ellard 41 pass from Friesz (Lohmiller kick)				
Was	FG Lohmiller 31				
Was	Howard 31 pass from Friesz (Lohmiller kick)				
NO	Small 4 pass from Everett (Small pass from Everett)				
NO	Muster 3 run (Andersen kick)				

Louisiana Superdome—John Friesz threw for four touchdowns and Brian Mitchell got a 74-yard punt return for a touchdown as the Redskins routed the Saints 38-24.

The Redskins got on the board first. Friesz capped a drive with his first scoring toss, a 14-yarder to Henry Ellard. Later on in the first quarter Mitchell fielded a punt and rolled for 74 yards into the end zone. All the Saints could muster was a 49-yard Morten Andersen field goal and the Redskins led 14-0 at intermission.

Washington started to pull away shortly after intermission. Mitchell got another great kick return as he brought the second-half kickoff 86 yards. That set up a one-yard touchdown toss from Friesz to fullback Cedric Smith. and it was 21-3.

The Saints made a brief bid, driving 74 yards to Jim Everett's 17-yard touchdown pass to Michael Haynes. The conversion failed and it was 21-9.

Friesz had the answer as he connected with Ellard for 41 yards and one TD, and with Desmond Howard for 31 yards and a 38-9 lead. Two fourth-quarter touchdowns by the Saints served only to make the final score look a bit more respectable in the next day's papers.

9/18/94	GIANTS (3-0) 31, Redskins (1-2) 23			77,298	
Was	3	17	0	3	23
NYG	10	7	7	7	31
NYG	Meggett 2 run (Treadwell kick)				
Was	FG Lohmiller 25				
NYG	FG Treadwell 34				
Was	Ellard 3 pass from Friesz (Lohmiller kick)				
Was	FG Lohmiller 41				
NYG	Sherrard 30 pass from Brown (Treadwell kick)				
Was	Horton 4 pass from Friesz (Lohmiller kick)				
NYG	Pierce 16 pass from Meggett (Treadwell kick)				
Was	FG Lohmiller 35				
NYG	Meggett 1 run (Treadwell kick)				

Giants Stadium—The Redskins led 20-17 at halftime but were unable to stave off the Giants, who rallied past Washington for a 31-23 win.

Washington scored on four of its first five possessions. Henry Ellard, who caught 10 passes for 197 yards on the day, caught a 3-yard pass from John Friesz to tie the game at 10 in the second period. A Chip Lohmiller field goal and Friesz's second touchdown pass—this one to tight end Ethan Horton—gave the Redskins their three-point halftime lead.

New York resorted to some trickery to reclaim the lead with running back Dave Meggett throwing a halfback option pass to Aaron Pierce for 16 yards and a touchdown. In the fourth quarter, the Redskins threatened to go back on top as they drove to the Giant ten, but a holding call pushed them back. They had to settle for Lohmiller's 35-yard field goal and trailed by just one at 24-23.

The Giants countered with a game-clinching drive that covered 81 yards in 10 plays, ending with a one-yard touchdown plunge by Meggett. A last-gasp effort to tie ended with an interception at the Giant three.

9/25/94	Falcons (2-2) 27, REDSKINS (1-3) 20			53,238	
Atl	7	0	17	3	27
Was	0	13	0	7	20
Atl	Mathis 4 pass from George (Johnson kick)				
Was	Brooks 2 run (Lohmiller kick)				
Was	Ellard 73 pass from Friesz (kick failed)				
Atl	Emmanuel 31 pass from George (Johnson kick)				
Atl	FG Johnson 20				
Atl	Heyward 1 run (Johnson kick)				
Atl	FG Johnson 22				
Was	Ervins 3 run (Lohmiller kick)				

RFK Stadium—Atlanta scored 20 straight points in the second half to erase a 13-7 halftime deficit and then held on to beat the Redskins 27-20.

After spotting the Falcons a 7-0 lead, Washington came roaring back in the second quarter. Reggie Brooks scored on a two-yard run to tie it up before Henry Ellard got deep and John Friesz hit him with a 73-yard touchdown pass.

The Redskins contributed to their own demise in the second half. After Atlanta regained the lead on a touchdown pass from Jeff George to Bert Emmanuel and a 20-yard field goal by Norm Johnson, Friesz fumbled the ball away at his own 27. That led to Craig Heyward's one-yard touchdown run. In the fourth quarter, Friesz threw an interception to set up another Johnson field goal to put Atlanta up 27-14.

Heath Shuler replaced Friesz at quarterback and narrowed the Falcon lead by leading a touchdown drive that culminated in Ricky Ervins' three-yard run. That was all for the Redskins, though, as their last chance died when Shuler was intercepted at the Atlanta 10 with 11 seconds remaining.

Sep 27

Shuler to Get First Start vs. Cowboys
'It's really good timing' to give rookie first start, says Turner

---

10/2/94	Cowboys (3-1) 34, REDSKINS (1-4) 7			55,394	
Dal	7	24	3	0	34
Was	0	0	7	0	7
Dal	E. Smith 4 run (Boniol kick)				
Dal	E. Smith 6 run (Boniol kick)				
Dal	FG Boniol 28				
Dal	Novacek 3 pass from Aikman (Boniol kick)				
Dal	Coleman 7 run (Boniol kick)				
Dal	FG Boniol 47				
Was	Wycheck 8 pass from Shuler (Lohmiller kick)				

RFK Stadium—The Cowboys piled up a 31-0 halftime lead and coasted to a 34-7 win over the Redskins.

Emmitt Smith scored touchdowns in the first and second quarters to put Dallas up 14-0. Rookie quarterback Heath Shuler's first NFL start was a big mountain for the Redskins to climb, but Dallas wasn't nearly done. Chris Boniol booted a 28-yard field goal before they racked up two more TD's before intermission. In all, Dallas scored on five of six first half possessions.

As the defense was getting lit up, the Redskin offense was utterly ineffective. If Shuler wasn't getting pressured by Dallas end Charles Haley, he was misfiring to open receivers. "It wasn't one of our better efforts as an offensive line," said tackle Jim Lachey, beaten by Haley on several occasions.

Reggie Brooks didn't help matters by fumbling twice and contributing to a third turnover when he was involved in a botched handoff with Shuler.

Dallas called the dogs off in the second half, but it didn't help the Redskins much. Through three quarters of play, Washington had a grand total of 41 net yards of offense. They did manage to get to triple digits with 110 before the final gun. It was their worst offensive output in more than 30 years.

10/9/94	EAGLES (4-1) 21, Redskins (1-5) 17				63,947
Was	0	6	11	0	**17**
Phil	7	0	7	7	**21**
Phil	Cunningham 20 run (Murray kick)				
Was	Winans 27 pass from Shuler (kick failed)				
Was	Winans 41 pass from Shuler (Howard pass from Shuler)				
Phil	Barnett 49 pass from Cunningham (Murray kick)				
Was	FG Lohmiller 47				
Phil	Walker 2 run (Murray kick)				

Veterans Stadium—The Redskins took a 17-14 lead into the fourth quarter, but the Eagles played keep-away for most of the final period and took the win from Washington.

Washington's lead came courtesy of two touchdown passes from Heath Shuler to rookie receiver Tydus Winans. The first one covered 27 yards in the second quarter with the Eagles leading 7-0. The point after was missed, however, and the Redskins still trailed 7-6 at the half. The second Shuler to Winans connection came in the third quarter and a two-point conversion gave the Redskins a seven-point lead. Philly tied it back up, and then Chip Lohmiller booted a 47-yard field goal to give his team a three-point lead going into the final period.

Philadelphia then took control. The Eagles drove 80 yards in 11 plays to score on Herschel Walker's two-yard run. After getting the ball back on a punt, they proceeded to grind another seven minutes off the clock with their next possession. They didn't score, but the drive achieved its purpose. After the punt, the Redskins were pinned back at their own eight with 1:48 left. Shuler did manage to get his team to the Eagle 38, but he was intercepted on the three with 40 seconds left.

10-16-94	Cardinals (2-4) 19, REDSKINS (1-6) 16 (OT)					50,019
Ari	0	3	0	13	3	**19**
Was	0	14	0	2	0	**16**
Was	Mitchell 46 pass from Shuler (Lohmiller kick)					
Was	Green 27 interception return (Lohmiller kick)					
Ari	FG Peterson 35					
Ari	Moore 10 run (2-pt. Failed)					
Was	Safety Feagles stepped out of end zone					
Ari	Proehl 5 pass from Beuerlein (Peterson kick)					
Ari	FG Peterson 29					

RFK Stadium—For the fourth time in their last five games, the Redskins led in the second half only to wind up on the short end of the score. This time they were up 14-0 in the fourth quarter but made just enough turnovers and mistakes to lose to the Cardinals 19-16 on Todd Peterson's 29-yard field goal with 4:56 left in overtime.

Washington was cruising on the strength of a 46-yard touchdown pass from Heath Shuler to Brian Mitchell and Darrell Green's 27-yard scoring return with an interception. All the Cardinals had as a rejoinder was a 35-yard field goal by Todd Peterson. That is, that was all until the fourth quarter.

It started when Aneas Williams intercepted a Heath Shuler pass to set up a touchdown on a 10-yard run by Ronald Moore. The two-point conversion failed, though, and Washington held a 5-point lead. That lead was expanded to 16-9 when, in a strategic maneuver that seemed odd at the time, Arizona punter Jeff Feagles intentionally stepped out of the end zone with 4:47 to play.

The ploy worked. The Redskins could only burn a minute and a half off of the clock and punted back to Arizona. The Cardinals tied the game by driving 72 yards and scoring with 19 seconds left on Steve Beuerlein's 5-yard pass to receiver Ricky Proehl.

Chip Lohmiller and Peterson both missed field goals in overtime before Shuler threw his fifth interception of the game to Terry Hoage. The safety returned the ball 12 yards to the Washington 23 and Peterson's game-winner followed soon after that.

Oct. 17

Drive the Bus, Gus: Frerotte to Start at QB
Shuler ailing, rookie 7th-round pick gets nod at Indy

10/23/94	Redskins (2-6) 41, COLTS (3-5) 27				57,879
Was	0	13	14	14	**41**
Ind	3	14	0	10	**27**
Ind	FG Biasucci 50				
Ind	Dawkins 24 pass from Harbaugh (Biasucci kick)				
Was	FG Lohmiller 21				
Ind	Faulk 85 pass from Harbaugh (Biasucci kick)				
Was	FG Lohmiller 27				
Was	Jenkins 1 pass from Frerotte (Lohmiller kick)				
Was	Ervins 1 run (Lohmiller kick)				
Was	Jenkins 5 pass from Frerotte (Lohmiller kick				
Ind	FG Biasucci 28				
Was	Collins 21 interception return (Lohmiller kick)				
Was	Ervins 3 run (Lohmiller kick)				
Ind	Jackson 13 pass from Majkowski (Biasucci kick)				

RCA Dome—On the road with a 17-3 second-quarter deficit and with a rookie seventh-round draft pick at quarterback, it looked like the Redskins' sixth straight defeat was well on its way to becoming a stark reality. But Gus Frerotte, that seventh-round selection, had other ideas; he sparked an improbable rally as the Redskins moved past the Colts for a 41-27 win.

Indianapolis had gained that 17-3 margin on Marshall Faulk's 85-yard touchdown reception from Jim Harbaugh in the second quarter. The Redskins responded with a drive to Chip Lohmiller's second field goal of the day, a 27-yarder.

The Redskins then took possession on their own 21 with 4:32 left in the half. Frerotte played like a seasoned veteran, completing passes to five different receivers and converting three third downs in the process of driving to the Colt one. After throwing the ball away against the blitz, Frerotte guided the ball just past the arms of a defender and into those of tight end James Jenkins with seven seconds left in the half, capping the 14-play drive. Lohmiller's conversion made it 17-13 at the break.

A pass interference call in the end zone led to Washington's go-ahead touchdown midway through the third period. On third and nine from the Colt 23, the Redskins' Tydus Winans got tangled up with Leonard Humphries as Frerotte's pass fell incomplete. When the flag was thrown, it appeared that it could go on either player as there was considerable pushing going on, but it went against the defense. Ricky Ervins took it over from the one on the next play.

Martin Bayless picked off a Harbaugh pass and returned it to the Colt ten, setting up another TD pass from Frerotte to Jenkins, this one from five yards out. Dean Biasucci ended Washington's string of 24 unanswered points with a 28-yard field goal, but the Redskins finished it off with two fourth-quarter touchdowns. One came when Andre Collins stepped in front of a Harbaugh pass and scooted down the sideline 21 yards; the other came on a three-yard run by Ervins.

Frerotte finished the game 17 of 32 passing for 226 yards.

10/30/94	Eagles (6-2) 31, REDSKINS (2-7) 29				53,530
Phil	0	7	7	17	**31**
Was	7	10	3	9	**29**

Was	Howard 13 pass from Frerotte (Lohmiller kick)
Was	Horton 15 pass from Frerotte (Lohmiller kick)
Phil	Walker 11 pass from Cunningham (Lohmiller kick)
Was	FG Lohmiller 54
Phil	Jackson 55 interception return (Murray kick)
Was	FG Lohmiller 23
Phil	Walker 1 run (Murray kick)
Phil	Hebron 6 run (Murray kick)
Was	Jenkins 1 pass from Frerotte (run failed)
Was	FG Lohmiller 40
Phil	FG Miller 30

RFK Stadium—The Redskins led early and led late, but they didn't lead when it counts-- at the end of the game. Eddie Murray kicked a 30-yard field goal with 19 seconds left to give the Eagles a 31-29 win.

The home team jumped to a 14-0 lead on Gus Frerotte touchdown passes of 13 yards to Desmond Howard and 15 to tight end Ethan Horton. Philly answered with a touchdown on a pass from Randall Cunningham to Herschel Walker, but Washington got a booming 54-yard field goal from Chip Lohmiller to push the lead back to 10 points at the half.

The momentum shifted back to the Eagles early in the third quarter. On the third play of the period, Greg Jackson picked off Frerotte's pass and was gone, sprinting 55 yards for a touchdown to cut the lead to three.

Washington came back with another Lohmiller field goal, but Philadelphia drove to two more touchdowns and the Eagles held a 28-20 lead in the fourth quarter. But the Redskins were not done.

They drove 60 yards to a one-yard touchdown pass from Frerotte to James Jenkins and pulled within two as the two-point conversion failed. After getting the ball back, they moved 36 yards and took the lead on Lohmiller's 40-yard field goal for a 29-28 lead.

Cunningham brought the Eagles back, however, driving them 63 yards in 12 time-consuming plays to set up Murray's game winning kick.

11/6/94	49ers (7-2) 37, REDSKINS (2-8) 22				54,335
SF	10	7	13	7	**37**
Was	0	3	3	16	**22**

SF	FG Brien 32
SF	Jones 69 pass from Young (Brien kick)
Was	FG Lohmiller 22
SF	Young 1 run (Brien kick)
SF	McDonald 73 interception return (Brien kick)
Was	FG Lohmiller 23
SF	Carter 96 kickoff return (kick failed)
SF	Rice 28 run (Brien kick)
Was	Horton 4 pass from Friesz (Mitchell run)
Was	Morrison 32 fumble return (Winans pass from Friesz)

RFK Stadium—San Francisco toyed with the Redskins for much of the first half before pulling out to a 37-6 lead and coasting to a 37-22 win.

The 49ers led 10-3 late in the second quarter when they busted out with their big weapons. Steve Young zipped a throw past cornerback Tom Carter to Jerry Rice and the receiver gained 55 yards to the Washington 23. From there, Ricky Watters carried down to the one and Young snuck it over from there.

It didn't take long for the Niners to end any modicum of remaining doubt. In the third quarter, Tim McDonald returned an interception of Gus Frerotte 73 yards for a touchdown.

The Redskins' meek reply—a 23-yard by Chip Lohmiller—was immediately trumped by Dexter Carter's 96-yard kickoff return for a touchdown and a 30-6 lead.

Jerry Rice made it ugly with a 28-yard touchdown run on an end run.

Washington did manage a couple of cosmetic scores in the fourth quarter. Ethan Horton caught a four-yard touchdown pass from John Friesz and then Darrel Morrison scooped up and fumble and ran it 32 yards into the end zone.

Frerotte-Shuler Duel Will Continue in 1995

Nov 7—The battle for the Redskins' starting quarterback position will not be settled until sometime next year, according to Norv Turner.

Heath Shuler, the team's top pick in the draft and holder of a rookie-record contract worth just over $19 million, and Gus Frerotte, the team's seventh-round draft pick and drawing the NFL's minimum wage, will compete for the job in training camp next year, Turner said.

Frerotte will start after this week's bye but "Heath is going to play" at some point, said Turner.

"Sometimes, it doesn't go the way you plan it, but the thing has taken that turn and Gus is a factor in our quarterback situation. One of those guys will be our quarterback for a long time, and it's important that we make sure that they are able to compete for the position."

11/20/94	COWBOYS (9-2) 31, Redskins (2-9) 7				64,644
Was	0	7	0	0	**7**
Dal	17	7	7	0	**31**

Dal	Smith 8 run (Boniol kick)
Dal	Smith 3 run (Boniol kick)
Dal	FG Boniol 32
Was	Howard 19 pass from Friesz (Lohmiller kick)
Dal	Harper 15 pass from Peete (Boniol kick)
Dal	Williams 83 punt return (Boniol kick)

Texas Stadium—Dallas took the suspense out of this one early, scoring 17 first-quarter points on the way to routing the Redskins 31-7.

Emmitt Smith scored both of Dallas' first-quarter touchdowns on runs of eight and three yards and Chris Boniol kicked a 32-yard field goal for a 17-0 Cowboy lead.

The Redskins got on the board before halftime on John Friesz's 19-yard touchdown pass to Desmond Howard.

According to the numbers, Washington didn't play badly from then on, allowing just 95 yards of offense and five first downs to the Cowboys after the first quarter. The Redskins, in fact, outgained the Cowboys 313 yards to 241. It was clear, however, that Dallas was just on cruise control after building that big early cushion. It seemed apparent that the Cowboys could have cranked things back up had they been threatened.

Three different Redskins passers threw interceptions. John Friesz threw two, Gus Frerotte threw one and a Brian Mitchell halfback option pass was picked off as well.

Nov 23

Shuler Will Get Start vs. Giants
Rookie back at QB after six-week absence

11/27/94	Giants (5-7) 21, REDSKINS (2-10) 19				43,384
NYG	7	7	7	0	**21**
Was	3	6	3	7	**19**

Was	FG Lohmiller 43
NYG	Brown 1 run (Treadwell kick)
Was	FG Lohmiller 29
NYG	Calloway 34 pass from Brown (Treadwell kick)
Was	FG Lohmiller 29
NYG	Sherrard 6 pass from Brown (Treadwell kick)
Was	FG Lohmiller 46
Was	Bayless 60 fumble return (Lohmiller kick)

RFK Stadium—Martin Bayless' fumble return for a touchdown gave the Redskins a shot at a win in the late going but the Giants were able to hang on to the ball and, as a result, a 21-19 win.

Before Bayless' run, the Giants had spent the entire game answering Chip Lohmiller field goals with touchdowns. Lohmiller's first three kicks covered 43, 29 and 29 yards, but the bad news was that Washington had been unable to muster a touchdown. The Giants had three of them, and two on Dave Brown passes.

A funny thing happened when the Giants were on their way to yet another touchdown following Lohmiller's fourth field goal, a 46-yarder. They fumbled, Bayless picked it up and ran 60 yards for a touchdown to pull the Redskins within two with 4:44 left in the game.

Washington never got a shot at Lohmiller's fifth field goal as the Giants embarked on a ball control drive that didn't go much of anyplace but ate all but 10 seconds off of the game clock.

12/4/94	BUCCANEERS (4-9) 26, Redskins (2-11) 21			45,121	
Was	7	14	0	0	21
TB	3	14	0	9	26
Was	Collins 92 interception return (Lohmiller kick)				
TB	FG Husted 53				
TB	Rhett 2 run (Husted kick)				
Was	Howard 81 pass from Shuler (Lohmiller kick)				
TB	McDowell 13 pass from Erickson (Husted kick)				
Was	Truitt 77 pass from Shuler (Lohmiller kick)				
TB	FG Husted 22				
TB	Erickson 1 run (pass failed)				

Tampa Stadium—Tampa Bay quarterback Craig Erickson scored on a one-yard sneak with 32 seconds left to play as the Redskins once again snatched defeat from the jaws of victory.

Washington scored three first-half touchdowns, all of them from long distance, to take a 21-17 lead into the locker room. In the first quarter, linebacker Andre Collins intercepted Erickson's pass and bolted 92 yards for a touchdown to give the Redskins a 7-0 lead. The Bucs pulled into the lead with a touchdown run by Errict Rhett and a Michael Husted field goal.

Then Heath Shuler got his arm loosened up. First, he launched an 81-yard scoring strike to Desmond Howard. Following another Tampa Bay touchdown, Shuler found Olanda Truitt for 77 yards and a touchdown for the four-point halftime lead.

The Redskins' lack of a running game—they mustered a team-record low of 10 rushing yards—caught up with them in the second half. In contrast, the Bucs were able to run almost at will with Rhett racking up 192 yards on 40 carries. It was still a 21-17 game going into the fourth quarter, but the home team pulled to within one on Husted's 22-yard field goal. They then ground out an 80-yard, 11-play drive to Erickson's winning TD.

12/11/94	CARDINALS (7-7) 16, Redskins (2-12) 15			53,790	
Was	3	3	0	9	15
Ari	7	0	0	10	17
Ari	Proehl 48 pass from Schroeder (Davis kick)				
Was	FG Lohmiller 34				
Was	FG Lohmiller 31				
Ari	Moore 1 run (Davis kick)				
Was	Ellard 52 pass from Shuler (run failed)				
Was	FG Lohmiller 21				
Ari	FG Davis 27				

Sun Devil Stadium—Chip Lohmiller's 21-yard field goal with 2:54 to play gave the Redskins the lead, but the Cardinals answered as Greg Davis booted a 27-yarder while time ran out, emerging with the 16-15 win.

The Redskins had their chances to score throughout the game. They had four ventures inside of the Cardinal 20, including two first and goal situations, but came away with just three field goals. Prior to Lohmiller's go-ahead three-pointer, the Redskins

got their only touchdown from long distance, on a 52-yard pass from Heath Shuler to Henry Ellard.

Led by ex-Redskin quarterback Jay Schroeder, the Cardinals responded to Lohmiller's boot with a textbook drive that ate up all of the remaining time before Davis' game winner.

The Redskins wasted a good offensive effort with their inability to punch the ball into the end zone. They piled up 406 yards of offense. Shuler was 16 for 27 for 286 yards and Ellard hauled in eight of his passes for 191 yards. There was enough running to keep the Cards honest as Brian Mitchell picked up 60 yards on 17 carries and Shuler scrambled three times for 38 yards.

12/18/94	Buccaneers (6-9) 17, REDSKINS (2-13) 14			47,315	
TB	0	10	0	7	17
Was	0	14	0	0	14
Was	Ervins 15 pass from Shuler (Lohmiller kick)				
TB	FG Husted 42				
TB	Rhett 1 run (Husted kick)				
Was	Ellard 8 pass from Shuler (Lohmiller kick)				
TB	Rhett 3 run (Husted kick)				

RFK Stadium—The Redskins held a lead in the fourth quarter, but wound up on the losing end of things.

Yes, the recurring lead that just won't go away—like Groundhog Day for Bill Murray—popped up for the sixth time during this season as Errict Rhett scored a fourth-quarter touchdown to push the Bucs past Washington 17-14.

The Redskins scored all of their points in the second quarter on two touchdown passes by Heath Shuler. The first went to Ricky Ervins and covered 15 yards, giving Washington a 7-0 lead. After Tampa Bay responded with a Michael Husted field goal and Rhett's one-yard TD run, Shuler hit Henry Ellard for eight yards and a 14-10 lead.

The lead held into the fourth quarter. Unable to sustain a drive, the Redskins punted and Vernon Turner returned the kick 37 yards to the Washington 28. It took five plays for Tampa Bay to move in to Rhett's go-ahead touchdown on a three-yard run.

On two subsequent possessions, Washington couldn't move the ball and the Bucs held on for the win.

12/24/94	Redskins (3-13) 24, RAMS (4-12) 21			25,705	
Was	0	17	7	0	24
LA	7	14	0	0	21
LA	Newman 22 interception return (Zendejas kick)				
Was	Brooks 2 run (Lohmiller kick)				
LA	Kinchen 34 pass from Miller (Zendejas kick)				
Was	Mitchell 78 punt return (Lohmiller kick)				
Was	FG Lohmiller 37				
LA	Ross 36 pass from Miller (Zendejas kick)				
Was	Jenkins 1 pass from Shuler (Lohmiller kick)				

Anaheim Stadium—Heath Shuler threw a one-yard touchdown pass to James Jenkins in the third quarter to push the Redskins past the Rams.

Things got off to a poor start as Anthony Newman intercepted Shuler's pass and scooted 22 yards for a touchdown and the Rams took a 7-0 lead into what would prove to be an action-packed second quarter.

Washington evened it up with a drive to a two-yard Reggie Brooks touchdown run early in the period. After another Los Angeles touchdown, the Rams punted to Brian Mitchell. He found a lane and he was off to the races, returning it 78 yards to tie the game at 14.

A Chip Lohmiller field goal gave the Redskins the lead, but Los Angeles went back on top before the half on a 36-yard touchdown pass from Chris Miller to Jermaine Ross.

The only sustained drive of the second half was produced by Shuler and the Redskins. The 80-yard, 12-play march consumed about five and a half minutes before Shuler flipped a one-yard pass to Jenkins, who was all alone in the end zone.

1995
Head Coach: Norv Turner
Record: 6-10, Third in NFC East

Honors: Brian Mitchell Pro Bowl; Ken Harvey Pro Bowl, All-NFC

Feb 15
Jaguars Take Howard in Expansion Draft
Former Heisman winner a major bust for Redskins

June 14
Redskins Sign RB Terry Allen
Former Viking recovered from knee surgery and gained 1,013 yards last year

---

Aug 8
Lohmiller Gets the Boot
Turner: "I had as much patience as I could" with inconsistent performance; vet Eddie Murray signed

---

Aug 14
First Pick Ends 26-Day Holdout
Receiver Westbrook inks 7-year, $18 million deal

9/3/95	REDSKINS (1-0) 27, Cardinals (0-1) 7				52,731
Ari	0	7	0	0	7
Was	10	0	10	7	27
Was	FG Murray 36				
Was	Westbrook 58 run (Murray kick)				
Ari	McBride 3 pass from Krieg (Davis kick)				
Was	FG Murray 22				
Was	Shepherd 73 pass from Frerotte (Murray kick)				
Was	Galbraith 2 pass from Frerotte (Murray kick)				

RFK Stadium—The Redskins broke open a close game in the second half and easily beat the Cardinals 27-7.

After an Eddie Murray field goal, rookie receiver Michael Westbrook touched the ball in an NFL game for the first time with spectacular results. He took the ball on an end around and raced 58 yards for a touchdown and 10-0 Washington lead.

Arizona responded with a three-yard touchdown pass from Dave Krieg to Oscar McBride and pulled within 10-7 at halftime. The second half, however, belonged to the Redskins.

Gus Frerotte replaced an injured Heath Shuler just before halftime and threw two touchdown passes, one a 73-yard bomb to Leslie Shepherd and the other a two-yard flip to tight end Scott Galbraith.

On the day, the Redskins outgained the Cards by better than a two to one margin, 479 yards to 197.

9/10/95	Raiders (2-0) 20, REDSKINS (1-1) 8				54,584
Oak	0	3	10	7	20
Was	0	3	3	2	8
Oak	FG Ford 19				
Was	FG Murray 21				
Was	FG Murray 43				
Oak	FG Ford 34				
Oak	Glover 1 pass from Hostetler (Ford kick)				
Oak	Fenner 8 pass from Hostetler (Ford kick)				
Was	Safety Brownlow blocked punt out of end zone				

RFK Stadium—The Raiders left their trademark vertical passing game back in Oakland and used the short passes of Jeff Hostetler to beat the Redskins 20-8.

The tone for the day was set during a Raider drive that consumed more than 11 minutes of the first quarter. Hostetler and the Raiders used 18 plays, a mix of short passes and runs, to move 89 yards and capped the drive with a Cole Ford field goal of 19 yards on the first play of the second period.

Washington responded with a pair of Eddie Murray field goals. One came in the second quarter after a 33-yard connection between Gus Frerotte and Michael Westbrook. The second came two minutes after halftime following a Raider fumble.

But that would be all for the Redskins, save for a safety scored on a blocked punt with less than two minutes left to be played. After tying it up on Ford's second field goal, the Raiders recovered a fumble by Terry Allen and drove in for the game's first touchdown which was scored on a one-yard flip from Hostetler to tight end Andrew Glover.

They put it out of reach with a 10-play, 80-yard drive that culminated in Hostetler's eight-yard touchdown pass to running back Derrick Fenner.

9/17/95	BRONCOS (2-1) 38, Redskins (1-2) 31				71,930
Was	0	14	10	7	31
Den	0	24	0	14	38
Den	FG Elam 20				
Was	Mitchell 36 run (Murray kick)				
Den	Bernstine 1 run (Elam kick)				
Den	Davis 8 pass from Elway (Elam kick)				
Den	Davis 6 run (Elam kick)				
Was	Logan 5 pass from Frerotte (Murray kick)				
Was	Shepherd 7 pass from Frerotte (Murray kick)				
Was	FG Murray 21				
Den	Davis 1 run (Elam kick)				
Was	Galbraith 1 pass from Frerotte (Murray kick)				
Den	Smith 43 pass from Elway (Elam kick)				

Mile High Stadium—John Elway has accomplished a lot on the football field, so when he says that he has done something for the first time, you know it has to be very much out of the ordinary.

"I think it's the first time since I started playing football that I've thrown a TD pass on the last play to win a game," Elway said, "so this was extra special. It was awesome.

"It took me a second to realize what had just happened. I was stunned."

So were the Redskins. They watched Rod Smith jump in the air over Darrell Green on the game's final play and catch Elway's 43-yard touchdown pass to snap a 31-all tie with 0:00 showing on the clock.

This was a tough one for the Redskins to take as they had battled back from a 24-7 deficit to tie the game. The game was scoreless going into the second quarter, but the two teams took care of that by combining for 38 points. Washington took a 7-3 lead when Brian Mitchell created a touchdown with a 37-yard kickoff return and then, a few plays later, a 36-yard scoring run from scrimmage.

The Broncos subsequently reeled off 21 unanswered points with three touchdowns. The last one was highly controversial. Actually, there was no dispute that Terrell Davis lost the ball well before crossing the goal line on a run from the six and that Tom Carter fell on the ball in the end zone for Washington; TV replays clearly showed that. The officials, though, huddled and ruled a phantom touchdown to make it 24-7.

The Redskins didn't get mad—they got even. Mitchell returned the ensuing kickoff 38 yards to the Washington 39 and three plays later, the Redskins had negated the TD with which Davis was credited. Gus Frerotte launched a 45-yard completion to Michael Westbrook and got the score with a five-yard pass to fullback Marc Logan. In the third quarter, another Frerotte TD pass—this one of eight yards to Leslie Shepherd—and an Eddie Murray field goal tied the game at 24.

Denver cranked out an 80-yard drive that took 13 plays and pulled ahead with just under five minutes left to play on a one-yard Davis run. Again, Mitchell made a key play, returning the ensuing kickoff 56 yards to the Bronco 40. Eight plays later Frerotte tied the game with an eight-yard pass to Scott Galbraith. There was 1:07 left on the clock.

Too much time, about six seconds too much to be exact. That's how much time was showing when Elway dropped back on fourth down from the Washington 43. Smith, who had never caught an NFL pass, went deep down the left side the Green in pursuit. Elway stepped up to avoid the rush, put it on the money and Smith leapt in the end zone, bringing the ball in for the score.

Smith said, "I saw it coming and I said, 'I've got to get it, no matter what.' I jumped up and made the play. It was just great. I can't describe it."

The Redskins surely had words to describe it, but none of them can be printed here.

Sep 18
Shoulder Injury Shelves Lachey
Torn rotator cuff ends season, threatens career

9/24/95	BUCANEERS (2-2) 14, Redskins (1-3) 6				49,243
Was	3	3	0	0	6
TB	0	0	7	7	14
Was	FG Murray 37				
Was	FG Murray 28				
TB	Rhett 10 run (Husted kick)				
TB	Harper 7 pass from Dilfer (Husted kick)				

Tampa Stadium—A drop and an interception at the goal line ruined a chance for the Redskins to tie this game in the late going. They fell to Tampa Bay 14-6 in Florida heat that could only be described as suffocating.

The Redskins held the Bucs in check during the first half, but failed to take full advantage as two promising drives ended in field goals, not touchdowns. Tampa Bay gained just 52 yards in the first two quarters, using a very conservative game plan consisting mostly of Errict Rhett, who gained 41 of his team's yards.

The fact that the score was still close enabled the Bucs to stick with their design and it began to pay off. Rhett's runs kept the Washington defense on the field and the home team drove to a 10-yard touchdown run by Rhett in the third quarter. Another drive, this one featuring some nice passing by Trent Dilfer, had the Bucs on the Washington seven as the third quarter expired.

On the next snap, Dilfer threw to receiver Alvin Harper near the sideline in the end zone. Harper and Darrell Green went up for the ball and the offensive player came down with it out of bounds. One official called an incompletion and Harper was ejected for arguing the call too strenuously. His protests, however, bore fruit—it was determined that Harper was forced out of bounds and was awarded a touchdown to give the Bucs a 14-6 lead.

Green was blunt, but didn't complain afterwards. "Whether I touched him or not, he wouldn't have gotten two feet down," he said. "This isn't college football. It definitely was no touchdown, and it was very disappointing to see that call."

The Redskins were unable to get anything going offensively until late in the game. A pass interference call helped move them to the Buccaneer one with less than a minute left. Fullback Cedric Smith was wide open in the end zone and just flat dropped Gus Frerotte's pass. Then Frerotte didn't see his tight end Scott Galbraith all alone and instead went to Coleman Bell in the back of the end zone. Tampa corner Martin Mayhew was there, too, and he killed his former team's last gasp with two seconds left when he intercepted the pass.

After 216 Games, Coleman Retires

Sep 26—The Redskins' longest-tenured player is no longer a member of the team.

Linebacker Monte Coleman, who has been out of football since the Redskins declined to offer him a contract last summer, announced his retirement in a press conference at Redskins Park today.

Coleman played in 216 games for Washington, the most of any player in franchise history.

"He's the last of the Mohicans," said Darrell Green. Coleman was the last Redskin to play in all three of the team's Super Bowl champions under Joe Gibbs.

The press conference drew a group of Coleman's former teammates, some reminiscing about the glory days. Art Monk wondered if the camaraderie from those days could ever be rekindled.

"There was just a sense of closeness during that five-, six-, seven-year period," Monk said. "I don't even know how we got that way. It just sort of happened. It's not something you can make happen. It just happens. We didn't have a lot of talent, but we all knew what we had to do to win—play well together."

10/1/95	REDSKINS (2-3) 27, Cowboys (4-1) 23				55,489
Dal	10	0	3	10	23
Was	3	17	7	0	27
Dal	FG Boniol 32				
Was	FG Murray 38				
Dal	Woodson 37 interception return (Boniol kick)				
Was	Logan 9 pass from Frerotte (Murray kick)				
Was	FG Murray 46				
Was	Allen 4 pass from Frerotte (Murray kick)				
Was	Allen 1 run (Murray kick)				
Dal	FG Boniol 34				
Dal	Irvin 28 pass from Wilson (Boniol kick)				
Dal	FG Boniol 23				

RFK Stadium—The Redskins ran off 24 unanswered points in the second and third periods and stunned the unbeaten Cowboys 27-23.

"We knew what we had to do to beat them," Terry Allen said, "and in the huddle there, we realized we were doing it."

Allen was one of the main forces in getting it done. He gained 121 yards rushing on 30 bruising carries and scored two touchdowns: one on the ground, and one on a pass reception.

The Cowboys took a 10-3 lead into the second quarter, having scored when Darren Woodson stepped in front of a Gus Frerotte's pass and dashed 37 yards into the end zone.

Frerotte calmed down after that and started moving his team. On the possession following the interception return, he led a nice drive and capped it off with a nine-yard touchdown pass to Marc Logan to tie it at 10. Before halftime, Eddie Murray kicked a 46-yard field goal and Allen caught a four-yard swing pass from Frerotte. The Redskins held a 20-10 lead.

Allen's catch gave confirmation that this would be the Redskins' day. He juggled the ball and it bounced into the arms of Dixon Edwards. The linebacker couldn't get a handle on it either and it bounced back to Allen, who got possession and dove over the goal line.

More evidence of the Redskins good fortune had come earlier when Dallas' star quarterback Troy Aikman was forced to leave the game after Dallas' first possession without having a hand laid on him. He got his cleats caught in the turf and pulled a calf muscle. Wade Wilson replaced him and the Dallas offense didn't get going until it was too late.

The Redskins took a 27-10 lead in the third when Allen scored on a one-yard burst. Dallas scored a touchdown and a field goal to pull within 74-20 with 7:44 left.

Frerotte, Allen and the Redskins' patched up offense line managed to hold on to the ball for the next 6:59 and Tom Carter intercepted Wilson's last desperate pass.

10/8/95	EAGLES (3-3) 37, Redskins (2-4) 34				65,498	
Was	10	7	7	10	0	34
Phil	10	14	7	3	3	37
Phil	Garner 55 run (Anderson kick)					
Was	FG Murray 36					
Was	Mitchell 59 punt return (Murray kick)					
Phil	FG Anderson 40					
Was	Ellard 40 pass from Frerotte (Murray kick)					
Phil	Garner 1 run (Anderson kick)					
Phil	Barnett 2 pass from Peete (Anderson kick)					
Was	Frerotte 1 run (Murray kick)					
Phil	Garner 17 run (Anderson kick)					
Phil	FG Anderson 43					
Was	Ellard 12 pass from Frerotte (Murray kick)					
Was	FG Murray 46					
Phil	FG Anderson 35					

Veterans Stadium—Gary Anderson kicked a 35-yard field goal in overtime to give the Eagles a 37-34 win in this back-and-forth affair.

There were a lot of big plays in the early going. Charlie Garner bolted 55 yards for a rushing touchdown for the Eagles. Brian Mitchell's 59-yard punt return and Henry Ellard's 40-yard touchdown catch provided plenty of action for the highlight reels. Each team kicked a field goal as well and the Ellard catch of a Gus Frerotte pass gave Washington a 17-10 lead with less than two minutes gone in the second period.

The Eagles scored two more touchdowns before halftime to take a 24-17 lead into the locker room. Coleman Bell returned the second-half kickoff 34 yards to the Eagle 47 and the Redskins were in business. Frerotte converted a third and nine with a 13-yard completion to Mitchell, and Terry Allen tore off 13 yards on a run as they moved to a fourth and goal at the one. After a fake into the line, Frerotte rolled around end on the bootleg and scored untouched to tie the game at 24.

Later on in the third, Frerotte handed the momentum back to the Eagles when he threw an interception to Greg Jackson, setting Philly up in Redskin territory at the 47. Four plays later, they reclaimed the lead on Garner's second TD run of the day, this one of 17 yards. Gary Anderson booted a 43-yard field goal early in the fourth to boost the Eagle lead to 34-24.

Back came the Redskins. They drove 80 yards in 10 plays and pulled within three on Frerotte's 12-yard touchdown pass to Ellard. Later, they took 14 plays to cover 57 yards inching themselves into Eddie Murray's field goal range. Murray's 46-yard boot came with 52 seconds left and sent the game into overtime.

Washington got the kickoff and put together a drive that expired just shy of field goal range; they punted away to the Eagles. Starting from their own 10, Philly steadily moved downfield, relying heavily on the legs of Ricky Watters. Both Watters (139 yards) and Garner (120) surpassed 100 yards on the ground.

"It's no secret that at times we've struggled stopping the run," Norv Turner said.

Facing a third and eight at the Washington 47, Rodney Peete went to Fred Barnett for 16 yards. Watters carried to the 20 and Anderson's kick came a couple of plays later.

10/15/95	CARDINALS (2-5) 24, Redskins (2-5) 20				43,370
Was	7	6	7	0	20
Ari	3	7	7	7	24
Was	Ellard 46 pass from Frerotte (Murray kick)				
Ari	FG Davis 24				
Ari	Williams 28 interception return (Davis kick)				
Was	FG Murray 38				
Was	FG Murray 25				
Ari	Centers 9 run (Davis kick)				
Was	Bell 29 pass from Frerotte (Murray kick)				
Ari	Hearst 1 pass from Krieg (Davis kick)				

Sun Devil Stadium—Dave Krieg flipped a one-yard touchdown pass to Garrison Hearst with just over a minute to play to push the Cardinals past the Redskins 24-20.

The Redskins jumped to a 7-0 lead less than two minutes into the game on Gus Frerotte's 46-yard touchdown pass to Henry Ellard. Following a Greg Davis field goal and Aeneas Williams' 28-yard interception return for a score, Eddie Murray kicked a pair of second-quarter field goals to give Washington a 13-10 lead at the half.

The second half was one of lost opportunities for the Redskins. They appeared to have made a big play on the Cards' opening drive of the third quarter when they recovered a fumble, but a facemask penalty on Ken Harvey gave Arizona a first down instead. That drive culminated in a nine-yard Larry Centers touchdown run to give the home team a 17-13 lead.

The Redskins recaptured the lead when Coleman Bell caught a 29-yard touchdown pass from Frerotte. With the score still 20-17 midway through the fourth quarter, Frerotte overthrew a wide-open Ellard. Instead of getting the clinching touchdown, the Redskins had to punt.

"I looked out to Henry, and he was wide open," Frerotte said. "I thought I put enough air under the ball—it was even fluttering out there—but it was just out of his reach."

The Cards took advantage of the opening. Krieg drove them down the field from their own 42, getting the biggest chunk of yardage on a 20-yard completion to Frank Sanders. His winning toss to Hearst came with 1:16 left on the clock.

Frerotte got the Redskins down to the Arizona 39 with 21 seconds left but they could move no further.

10/22/95	REDSKINS (3-5) 36, Lions (2-5) 30					52,332
Det	3	10	7	10	0	30
Was	6	7	7	10	6	36
Was	FG Murray 26					
Det	FG Hanson 42					
Was	FG Murray 36					
Was	Allen 1 run (Murray kick)					
Det	FG Hanson 20					
Det	Moore 17 pass from Mitchell (Hanson kick)					
Det	Morton 7 pass from Mitchell (Hanson kick)					
Was	Allen 2 run (Murray kick)					
Det	FG Hanson 39					
Was	Ellard 13 pass from Frerotte (Murray kick)					
Det	Perriman 51 pass from Mitchell (Hanson kick)					
Was	FG Murray39					
Was	Green 7 interception return (no try)					

RFK Stadium—After losing four last-minute decisions in the previous five weeks, the Redskins finally won a close one. Darrell Green returned an interception of Scott Mitchell's pass seven yards for a touchdown to give Washington a 36-30 overtime win.

"I was able to jump in there and make what most people think is the greatest play in the world," said Green.

Truth be told, Green and the rest of the members of the Washington secondary needed something to serve as redemption for one of their poorest performances of the year. Mitchell had picked them apart for 350 yards on 30 of 50 passing prior to throwing that final, fatal interception.

This was a back and forth battle from the get-go. Washington earned a 13-3 second quarter lead on the strength of two Eddie Murray field goals and a one-yard Terry Allen touchdown run. Allen's run came five plays after Tony Woods recovered Mitchell's fumble at the Lion 45.

By halftime, the Lions had tied it up on Jason Hanson's second field goal and a 17-yard touchdown pass from Mitchell to Herman Moore. On the TD drive, Mitchell went to Moore three times for a total of 39 yards, including the score.

With the score tied at 13, Mitchell came out firing in the second half. He led an 89-yard, 14-play drive to pay dirt. Two passes to Brett Perriman covered 15 and 19 yards and the payoff came on a seven-yard pop to Johnny Morton.

Apparently wanting to earn MVP honors from both teams, Mitchell again fumbled to set up a Washington touchdown. This time, the Redskins had to travel just 21 yards over the goal line after Tim Johnson fell on the loose ball. Five plays after that Allen tied it up on a two-yard buck through the line.

Each team lost a lead in the final six minutes of regulation. Following Hanson's third field goal, the Redskins took advantage of a 19-yard pass interference flag and a 20-yard Allen run to move to the Lion 13. From there, Gus Frerotte threw to Henry Ellard for 13 yards and a 27-23 lead with 5:26 left.

Just over two minutes later the Lions completed a quick-strike drive to jump back ahead. Working from his own 23, Mitchell completed a pair of 11-yard passes—one each to Perriman and Moore. Then he went deep, finding Perriman streaking over the middle. The receiver outran the secondary into the end zone with 3:21 showing on the clock.

Brian Mitchell's 20-yard run sparked a march that resulted in Murray's 39-yard, game-tying field goal with four seconds remaining.

In the extra period, the Redskins punted the Lions back deep in their own territory. Mitchell was aiming for Morton on a slant and apparently didn't see Green, who snared the pass at the seven and, escorted by linebacker Rod Stephens, easily raced in to end the game.

10/29/95	Giants (3-5) 24, REDSKINS (3-6) 15				53,310
NYG	7	17	0	0	24
Was	3	3	6	3	15
NYG	Glenn 75 interception return (Daluiso kick)				
Was	FG Murray 47				
NYG	Wheatley 1 run (Daluiso kick)				
NYG	Sherrard 57 pass from Brown (Daluiso kick)				
NYG	FG Daluiso 31				
Was	FG Murray 52				
Was	Logan 3 run (run failed)				
Was	FG Murray 27				

RFK Stadium—The Redskins were buried under an avalanche of turnovers in losing to New York 24-15.

Gus Frerotte threw four interceptions and Washington lost two fumbles. Nearly every turnover either led to a Giant score and/or derailed a promising Redskins scoring opportunity.

An example of the "and" situation came on the Redskins' opening drive. They were advancing toward the goal at a steady clip, having moved 48 yards into Giant territory. A simple swing pass turned into a disaster as Marc Logan bobbled Frerotte's toss right into the hands of Vencie Glenn. The safety gladly accepted the gift and blasted off, going 75 unchallenged yards down the sideline for a 7-0 New York lead.

Eddie Murray's 47-yard field goal made it 7-3, but the Redskins were going out of the frying pan and into the fire. Again they drove into Giant territory and again made a play that led to a New York touchdown. Frerotte's pass was batted into the air by end Jamal Duff and Michael Strahan, showing lightning-quick reflexes, picked it out of the air at the 36. He wasn't hauled down until he reached the Washington two. Two plays later, Tyrone Wheatley smashed across from the one to make it 14-3.

Less than two minutes later, New York expanded its lead, scoring without help this time. On first down from his own 43, Dave Brown hit Chris Calloway, who was wide open deep down the middle, but the receiver dropped the ball. No problem—Brown dropped back the next play and found Mike Sherrard equally wide open. Brown again delivered on target and this time his receiver caught it for a 21-3 New York lead.

"We self-destructed both offensively and defensively," Darrell Green said. "We didn't play Redskin football at all. This loss sets us back from where we wanted to go with this season."

The Redskins never made a serious bid to get back into it after that, despite controlling the ball for most of the second half and shutting the Giants out over the final 30 minutes. Logan capped a 52-yard drive with a three-yard scoring run, but the two-point conversion attempt failed and it remained 24-12. Murray kicked a 27-yard field goal in the fourth quarter, but other late scoring bids by Washington ended in a fourth-down sack and, of course, an interception.

11/5/95	CHIEFS (8-1) 24, Redskins (3-6) 3				77,821
Was	0	3	0	0	3
KC	7	10	0	7	24
KC	Allen 1 run (Elliott kick)				
KC	Davis 19 pass from Bono (Elliott kick)				
Was	FG Murray 29				
KC	FG Elliott 38				
KC	Anders 40 run (Elliott kick)				

Arrowhead Stadium—After Kansas City's easy 24-3 win over the Redskins in this one, the following words were heard:

"Our timing just wasn't what it had been. I hate bye weeks," said Chiefs guard Dave Szott.

"Obviously, there were too many misses," said KC quarterback Steve Bono.

"When you sit out a week, the edge falls off a little bit," said center Tim Grunhard.

These, the words from the locker room of the team that won by 21 points. If the Redskins needed any evidence that they were regarded as one of the NFL's "have-nots," there it was.

Washington moved the ball on its opening drive but was forced to punt. Matt Turk dropped a very nice kick that rolled dead at the Chief five. However, an ineligible man downfield cost them a net of 45 yards of field position as Tamrick Vanover returned Turk's rekick 35 yards to midfield. From there the Chiefs embarked on an efficient 10-play touchdown drive. Marcus Allen dove over the pile to take it across on fourth down at the one.

The Chiefs slowly and methodically drained the life out of the Redskins in the second quarter. It was death by a thousand paper cuts as KC ground out scoring drives of 10 and nine plays. The first resulted in a 19-yard touchdown pass from Bono to Willie Davis, the second in a 38-yard Lin Elliott field goal.

While the Redskins managed an Eddie Murray field goal in between those two drives, they never seriously threatened the Chiefs. On the scoreboard, it was still a ball game until Kimble Anders sprinted 40 yards for a TD with 2:26 to go, but those who watched knew it was over long before that.

11/19/95	Seahawks (5-6) 27, REDSKINS (3-8) 20				51,298
Sea	3	7	7	10	**27**
Was	3	7	0	10	**20**

Sea	FG Peterson 39
Was	FG Murray 18
Sea	Galloway 59 pass from Mirer (Peterson kick)
Was	Truitt 18 pass from Frerotte (Murray kick)
Sea	Crumpler 10 pass from Mirer (Peterson kick)
Was	FG Murray 48
Sea	Warren 5 run (Peterson kick)
Sea	FG Peterson 47
Was	Westbrook 5 pass from Shuler (Murray kick)

RFK Stadium—The Redskins turned the ball over five times leading to 13 Seattle points and lost to the Seahawks 27-20.

It didn't take long for the turnover bug to bite. Seattle got a field goal with the game just over four minutes old as the result of an interception and a 15-yard facemask penalty. The Redskins evened the score by driving 66 yards in 13 plays, with Terry Allen converting a fourth and one with a five-yard smash through the line. The drive stalled at the Seahawk one and Washington settled for an 18-yard field goal by Eddie Murray.

The teams exchanged second-quarter touchdown passes. Seattle's came first, on a 59-yard pass from Rick Mirer to speedy wideout Joey Galloway. The Redskins' response was a six-play, 58-yard drive that culminated in Frerotte's 18-yard scoring toss to Olanda Truitt to send the teams into the locker room deadlocked at 10.

The only score of the third quarter came on Mirer's second TD toss of the day and the Redskins responded with a Murray field goal early in the fourth. Midway through the final period, the Redskins took possession deep in their own territory. Heath Shuler had replaced Frerotte at quarterback. He went to a medium-deep pattern, but didn't see safety Robert Blackmon just standing there at the 27.

"I didn't even move," Blackmon said. "I may have back-pedaled probably two yards. The ball was coming."

He returned it 12 yards to the 15. Chris Warren carried for 10 yards to the five, then looked like a man among boys as he carried three Redskin defenders into the end zone with him for a 24-13 lead.

Shuler threw another pick shortly after that, setting up a 47-yard field goal. The second-year QB did manage to get the Skins on the board again with a five-yard pass to Michael Westbrook, but the damage had been done.

Nov 21
Shuler to Start
Poor play by Frerotte prompts benching

11/26/95	Eagles (8-4) 14, REDSKINS (3-9) 7				50,539
Phil	6	0	0	8	**14**
Was	0	0	0	7	**7**

Phil	Watters 9 run (kick failed)
Was	Allen 9 run (Murray kick)
Phil	Watters 1 run (Williams pass from Peete)

RFK Stadium—Eagle quarterback Rodney Peete returned from a third-quarter benching hot, in more ways than one. He was mad about having been benched. And he completed three of three passes to pace a fourth quarter drive that pushed his team past the Redskins 14-7 in a game that was dull to the point of agony.

Philly jumped on top in the first quarter after Ricky Watters scored on a nine-yard run. A holding call forced the conversion to be kicked from the 20, and Gary Anderson hit the upright so it remained 6-0.

Peete then receded into the passing slump that eventually got him benched and the Washington offense continued in its game-long doldrums. In fairness to Heath Shuler, it must be noted that

Michael Westbrook was sidelined with an injury and Henry Ellard saw only very limited playing time; his targets at wide receiver for most of the game were Quinn Early and Olanda Truitt. It didn't help that Eddie Murray missed field goal attempts of 42 and 50 yards in the first half.

While there wasn't much offense, there was some good football being played by Ken Harvey. The linebacker sacked Eagle QB's three times and was, in general, a menace to anything in a green jersey that moved.

Randall Cunningham, who replaced Peete, engineered two consecutive three-and-outs in his stint at signal caller. The Redskins finally pieced together a drive starting late in the third quarter. Shuler completed passes to Jamie Asher for 20 yards and Terry Allen for 13. Less than a minute into the fourth quarter, Terry Allen scored on a seven-yard run, Murray kicked the extra point, and the Redskins found themselves in the lead at 7-6.

Evidently Philly coach Ray Rhodes figured that whatever point he was trying to make to Peete had been made and the starter reentered the game after the kickoff. Peete passed for 53 yards in the ensuing drive, including a throw to Fred Barnett for 31 yards to the Redskin 20. Five plays later the Eagles had worked their way down to the one and Watters pushed over from there. Peete went to Calvin Williams for the two-point conversion, making it 14-7.

Shuler responded by throwing an interception, but was saved when Anderson missed a field goal. The Redskins' last good chance to even it up went by the boards when Shuler underthrew a wide-open Truitt. The receiver still had a shot at it at around the ten, but with safety Greg Jackson closing in, Truitt dropped it.

Landover Stadium Deal (Almost) Done

Dec 3—It appears that Jack Kent Cooke's seven-year quest to find a spot to build a new stadium for the Redskins is finally over.

The stadium will be built on a tract of land adjacent to the Beltway in Landover in Prince George's County, Md.

County executive Wayne Curry removed the final major obstacle by giving his approval to the site, now known as Wilson's Farm. Although some other legal and legislative hurdles remain, it seems likely that the Redskins will be able to begin playing in their 78,600 stadium in 1997.

Cooke announced in 1998 that he wanted to pay for a new stadium with his own money. Political and neighborhood opposition spiked attempts to build it in the District, Alexandria, Va., and Laurel, Md.

12/3/95	Redskins (4-9) 24, COWBOYS (10-3) 17				64,866
Was	0	7	7	10	**24**
Dal	0	10	0	7	**17**

Dal	Smith 7 run (Boniol kick)
Was	Allen 2 run (Murray kick)
Dal	FG Boniol 37
Was	Ellard 10 pass from Shuler (Murray kick)
Was	Allen 1 run (Murray kick)
Was	FG Murray 47
Dal	Irvin 3 pass from Aikman (Boniol kick)

Texas Stadium—You could get better odds on lightning striking twice in a frozen-over hell during a blue moon than you could of this happening. As far as news, this was real man-bites-dog stuff.

Timely defense, clutch offense, and a dash of good fortune worked together to help the Redskins beat the Cowboys for the second time this year. "This is my Super Bowl," said James Washington, a former Cowboy.

There was hardly a big game atmosphere present in Texas Stadium when the game started, with most writing off Washington's 27-23 shocker over the Cowboys on Oct. 1 as a fluke. After all, Troy Aikman had missed all but a few plays of that one after going out with an injury and Heath Shuler, who had been erratic all year, was calling the signals for the visitors. In addition, the change of venue would favor Dallas; the Redskins were 0-6 on the road coming in.

The game was scoreless until midway through the second quarter. A questionable pass interference call on Darrell Green greatly aided Dallas' 69-yard drive for a touchdown. Emmitt Smith carried it over from seven yards out to give his team a 7-0 lead.

The Redskins responded with a drive paced by Terry Allen, who gained 41 of the 73 yards, including runs of 16 and 13 yards, as well as an eight-yard jaunt to convert a fourth and one. It was Allen who took it over the goal line from two yards out on the 13th play of the march.

Allen's score came with just 1:22 left in the first half, but that left enough time for Aikman to pass Dallas downfield into position for Chris Boniol's 37-yard field goal as time expired.

Anyone thinking that score would give Dallas a lift was mistaken. Dallas punted on its initial possession of the second half and the Redskins embarked on an 83-yard thrust ending with Shuler throwing a 10-yard TD pass to Henry Ellard. The Redskins took a 14-10 lead.

Still, it was assumed that one of the Cowboy stalwarts such as Smith or Aikman would stand up, make some big plays, and Dallas would prevail. As it turned out, though, the player stepping up in the fourth quarter wore burgundy: safety Stanley Richard.

First, he stepped in front of an Aikman pass near midfield and returned it to the Dallas 27 to set up a one-yard touchdown blast by Allen to make it 21-10. Dallas drove downfield and, on fourth and one at the three, Smith went wide to the left and aimed for the flag. Richard came up and stripped the ball from the runner's grasp. Although Smith wound up with the ball back in his hands, the officials eventually ruled that he had gained possession in the end zone while his feet were out of bounds. That made it a touchback and the Redskins took over at the 20.

It took one more big play for Washington to wrap it up. Shuler had taken off on planned rollout runs to the right several times. On this play, he took off right, stopped and fired deep to the left to Leslie Shepherd for 44 yards. That set up the clinching score—Murray's 47-yard field goal.

The Cowboys handled their defeat with the grace that one has come to expect from this bunch. "This team had no business beating us," Deion Sanders said. "I wouldn't say the best team won today."

12/10/95	GIANTS (5-9) 20, Redskins (4-10) 13			48,247
Was	0	3	0	10	**13**
NYG	3	10	0	7	**20**
NYG	FG Daluiso 36
Was	FG Murray 34
NYG	Lewis 90 kickoff return (Daluiso kick)
NYG	FG Daluiso 42
Was	FG Murray 30
Was	Allen 1 run (Murray kick)
NYG	Calloway 40 pass from Brown (Daluiso kick)

Giants Stadium—Despite holding edges of around two to one in first downs, total yardage and time of possession, the Redskins managed to find a way to lose to the Giants. A successful gamble by coach Dan Reeves on a fourth-down play proved to be decisive.

Early in the second quarter, Eddie Murray kicked a field goal, matching an earlier successful boot by New York's Brad Daluiso. On the ensuing kickoff, Thomas Lewis made the first of two big plays for New York as he sped 90 yards for a touchdown and a 10-3 Giant lead. Before halftime, a Tito Wooten interception led to another Daluiso field goal and New York led 13-3 at halftime.

The Redskin defense continued to hold the Giants at bay and the game was tied going into the fourth quarter. At the outset of

the fourth, Washington was in the process of completing a 13-play drive that ended with a 30-yard field goal by Murray, making it 13-6 with just over a minute gone in the fourth.

On their next possession, the Redskins finally punched it into the end zone, going 80 yards in 16 plays. Terry Allen pushed his way in on fourth down from the one with 3:35 to play.

That decision to go for it on fourth down was fairly easy, given the fact that the Redskins were deep in Giant territory and trailing by 12. After the kickoff, however, Reeves faced a quite different set of circumstances. It was fourth and inches at the Giant 41. Faced with this state of affairs, most NFL coaches will punt at least 99 percent of the time. But not Reeves—not this time. He sent Rodney Hampton into the line and the running back bulled through for two yards and the first down. A few plays later, Chris Calloway got open deep down the middle and quarterback Dave Brown hit him with a perfect strike with 1:12 to play to give the Giants the win.

When it works, you're a genius. "In that situation, you're just trying to win the game," Reeves said. "We thought we had the play to do it."

Actually, it wasn't quite over. Brian Mitchell returned the ensuing kickoff 53 yards and with a facemask penalty tacked on, the Skins had a shot from the Giant 23. But Heath Shuler threw four straight incompletions to kill the comeback chance.

12/17/95	**Redskins (5-8) 35, RAMS (7-8) 23**			63,760
Was	7	7	14	7	**35**
StL	10	0	0	13	**23**
StL	FG Biasucci 25
StL	Bettis 1 run (Biasucci kick)
Was	Mitchell 22 pass from Shuler (Murray kick)
Was	Carter 51 interception return (Murray kick)
Was	Allen 1 run (Murray kick)
Was	Shepherd 8 run (Murray kick)
StL	Bailey 5 run (Biasucci kick)
StL	Wright 21 pass from Rypien (pass failed)
Was	Woods 3 fumble return (Murray kick)

Trans World Dome—The Redskins built an 18-point lead by running off 28 unanswered points and were able to hang on at the end to beat the Rams 35-23.

St. Louis jumped off to a 10-0 lead in the first quarter. Former Redskin quarterback Mark Rypien completed a 50-yard pass to Alexander Wright on a flea flicker on the game's first play from scrimmage, setting up a 25-yard field goal by Dean Biasucci. Then Sean Gilbert recovered Terry Allen's fumble at the Redskin 28 and, six plays later, Jerome Bettis pounded in from the one.

The Redskins were in the lead to stay before halftime. On the last play of the first quarter, Brian Mitchell darted through the middle 22 yards with a shovel pass from Heath Shuler, capping a 62-yard drive. In the second period, Tom Carter stepped in front of Isaac Bruce, picked off Rypien's pass and was gone—51 yards for the touchdown.

Two touchdowns in a bit more than two minutes gave the Redskins a large lead in the third quarter. A couple of big penalties against the Rams aided a 54-yard, 13-play foray that ended with Allen bashing his way to pay dirt from the one. The Rams then fumbled the ensuing kickoff, with Matt Vanderbeek recovering for the Redskins at the St. Louis 27. It took four plays to cash in, with Leslie Shepherd covering the last eight yards on a reverse to make it 28-10.

A hurry-up, no-huddle offense led to a pair of fourth-quarter TD's for the Rams and, suddenly, it was 28-23 with more than 10 minutes left to play. Washington had to punt and although the kick backed the Rams up inside the 10, it was still tense. After all, St. Louis had driven 92 yards for their first TD of the quarter.

The tension ended when Tony Woods scored the easiest touchdown that a defensive lineman will ever get. Rypien threw to tight end Todd Kinchen at around the 10. Marvcus Patton came in like a missile and made contact. Kinchen went down; the ball went flying. Observing all of this at around the three was Woods, who was as surprised as anyone when the ball bounced to him. "The ball hopped right into my arms," Woods said. "I made a U-turn and ran right into the end zone. I'm keeping the ball, it's right here in my locker."

He should give at least partial custody of it to Patton.

12/24/95	REDSKINS (6-10) 20, Carolina (7-9) 17			42,903
Car	3	7	0	7	17
Was	7	3	7	3	20
Car	FG Kasay 42			
Was	Allen 1 run (Murray kick)			
Was	FG Murray 29			
Car	Moore 1 run (Kasay kick)			
Was	Allen 1 run (Murray kick)			
Was	FG Murray 32			
Car	Green 2 pass from Collins (Kasay kick)			

RFK Stadium—The Redskins broke a 10-10 tie with a third-quarter offensive explosion that propelled them past the Panthers.

Each team scored on a field goal and short touchdown run in the first half. After a John Kasay field goal got Carolina on the board first, Brian Mitchell returned the ensuing kickoff to the Washington 42. The offense took advantage of the short field, moving the 58 yards to the end zone in seven plays. The biggest chunks of yardage were eaten up when Gus Frerotte threw to Michael Westbrook for 21 yards and Leslie Shepherd weaved his way for 17 yards on a reverse. Terry Allen got the last chunk, one yard over the goal line to make it 7-3.

James Washington's interception set up Eddie Murray's 29-yard field goal, putting the score at 10-3, but the Panthers put together a drive just before halftime that culminated in Derrick Moore's one-yard TD run 22 seconds before intermission.

It wasn't until late in the third quarter that the Redskins offense came back to life. At the end of the lightning quick blitzkrieg was another one-yard Allen run, but the previous two plays of the 93-yard, three-play advance were considerably less pedestrian. First, Frerotte found a favorable matchup as rookie corner Tyrone Poole was covering Henry Ellard. The veteran receiver blew by Poole's coverage attempt and hauled in Frerotte's pass for a 59-yard gain. Before the defense could catch its breath, it was trying to chase Westbrook down on a reverse. Carolina eventually succeeded, but not before Westbrook had ripped off 33 yards down to the one, where Allen got the TD.

A drive not as eye-catching but just as important came right after that as the Skins moved 43 yards in seven plays to set up a 32-yard Murray field goal, stretching their lead to 20-10. That enabled them to withstand a Panther touchdown with 35 seconds left to play. The Redskins covered the onside kick and ran out the remaining seconds.

1996

Head Coach: Norv Turner
Record: 9-7, Third in NFC East

Honors: Terry Allen Pro Bowl, AP All Pro; Gus Frerotte Pro Bowl; Darrell Green Pro Bowl; Matt Turk Pro Bowl, AP All Pro

Hall of Fame: Joe Gibbs, Head Coach 1981-1992

Jan 27

Gibbs Elected to Hall of Fame
Three-time Super Bowl winning coach gets in on first vote

Apr 8

Skins Get Gilbert From Rams
Send 1st-round pick, #6 overall, for DT, 26

Aug 19

Turner Names Frerotte Starter
Shuler, relegated to bench, pledges "full support"

9/1/96	Eagles (1-0) 17, REDSKINS (0-1) 14				53,415
Phi	7	10	0	0	-	17
Was	7	0	7	0	-	14
Phi	Fryar 18 pass from Peete (Anderson kick)				
Was	Allen 2 run (Blanton kick)				
Phi	C. Jones 9 pass from Peete (Anderson kick)				
Phi	FG Anderson 26				
Was	Allen 49 run (Blanton kick)				

RFK Stadium—Philadelphia gave the Redskins every opportunity to stay in the game, but Washington was unable to take advantage. They fell to the Eagles 17-14.

The Eagles outgained the hosts 310 yards to 77 in the first half, but were unable to put to game away. In the second quarter, Eagles running back Ricky Watters fumbled the ball away inside the Redskins five and later in the same period receiver Mark Ingram dropped a sure touchdown pass at the goal line, so the Eagles held just a 17-7 halftime lead.

The Redskins pulled within three on the second play of the third quarter on Terry Allen's 49-yard TD burst, but could not muster a serious threat after that. Philly's Mike Mamula kept constant pressure on quarterback Gus Frerotte, harassing him into a 12 for 25, 119-yard passing performance. After Allen's run, the closest the Redskins got to the Eagles goal line was the 31. That series concluded when Eddie Murray was well short on a potential game-tying field goal from 53 yards out with six minutes left in the game. Washington did not threaten further and the final was 17-14.

9/8/96	REDSKINS (1-1) 10, Bears (1-1) 3				52,711
Chi	3	0	0	0	-	3
Was	0	3	7	0	-	10
Chi	FG Huerta 37				
Was	FG Blanton 50				
Was	Allen 28 run (Blanton kick)				

RFK Stadium—The Redskins held an opponent without a touchdown for the first time since 1993 in beating the Bears 10-3. Norv Turner awarded every member of the defense a game ball in honor of the effort.

The first half was a punting duel between Washington's Matt Turk and the Bears' Todd Sauerbraun. Each team scratched the scoreboard with a field goal and it was 3-3 at the half.

The game's key moment came in the third quarter. The Bears were driving in Redskins territory in the third quarter when receiver Michael Timpson caught a third down pass at the 25. Stanley Richard forced the ball out with a jarring hit and Darrell Green recovered, advancing the ball to the Washington 49. It took just three plays for the Redskins to convert the turnover into points. After two Gus Frerotte to Henry Ellard passes moved the ball to the Bears 28, Chicago gambled and lost on a blitz, letting Terry Allen go virtually untouched 28 yards for a touchdown.

Chicago got inside the Washington 20 twice in the fourth quarter, but the Washington defense kept them out of the end zone. One drive ended when Ken Harvey sacked Bears QB Eric Kramer on third and nine, the second when Kramer's fourth-down pass fell incomplete in the waning moments of the game.

9/15/96	Redskins (2-1) 31, GIANTS (0-3) 10				71,693
Was	3	14	0	14	-	31
NYG	0	7	3	0	-	10

Was	FG Blanton 36
Was	Logan 3 run (Blanton kick)
Was	Galbraith 30 pass from Frerotte (Blanton kick)
NYG	Pierce 7 pass from Brown (Daluiso kick)
NYG	FG Daluiso 19
Was	Allen 7 run (Blanton kick)
Was	Davis 39 run (Blanton kick)

Giants Stadium—The Redskins built a 17-0 lead first half then responded to a Giants rally with a pair of fourth-quarter touchdown runs that salted away a 31-10 win.

Leading 10-0 in the second quarter, the Redskins lined up for a 47-yard field goal attempt. Holder Gus Frerotte took the snap and assumed his normal role, that of quarterback. He rolled to the right and found tight end Scott Galbraith wide open at the 19. The Giants were totally fooled; Galbraith strolled in for a 17-0 lead.

The Giants cut the lead to 17-7 before halftime and threatened again in the third quarter, driving to the Washington two. On fourth down, Giants coach Dan Reeves elected to kick a field goal to make it 17-10.

The decision was unpopular with the Giants Stadium crowd and their opinion was justified after the ensuing kickoff. Washington drove 76 yards to a touchdown, the score coming on a seven-yard run by Terry Allen. Allen gained 38 yards on that drive and 146 on the day. Stephen Davis closed out the scoring by breaking through the line on fourth and one and rolling 39 yards for the TD.

9/22/96	Redskins (3-1) 17, RAMS (1-2) 10				62,303
Was	7	3	7	0	-	17
StL	0	0	3	7	-	10

Was	Galbraith 2 pass from Frerotte (Blanton kick)
Was	FG Blanton 38
StL	FG Lohmiller 19
Was	Allen 9 run (Blanton kick)
StL	Ross 3 run (Lohmiller kick)

Trans World Dome—Tom Carter's interception at the Washington 13 with 2:40 left was the Redskins' third of the game and it preserved the win.

Washington took a 10-0 lead in the first half on the strength of a two-yard touchdown pass from Gus Frerotte to tight end Scott Galbraith and a 38-yard Scott Blanton field goal. The Redskins took advantage of a short field to get both of the scores. The touchdown was the result of a 49-yard drive after a St. Louis punt and Marvcus Patton picked off a pass at the Rams 34 to set up the field goal.

In the third quarter, Rams nickel back Torin Dorn intercepted a tipped pass and returned it to the Washington five, but St. Louis had to settle for a 19-yard Chip Lohmiller field goal to cut the lead

to 10-3. Later in the third, the Redskins went up 17-3 when Terry Allen scored on a 9-yard run.

The home team made a run at it, but the Redskins held on. After the Rams got a touchdown run early in the fourth quarter, they were driving to tie the game with less than three minutes left. Quarterback Steve Walsh tried to throw the ball away, but instead it went to the flat to Carter, who gathered it in at the Washington 13 with 2:40 left in the game.

9/29/96	REDSKINS (4-1) 31, Jets (0-5) 16				52,068
NYJ	0	13	3	0	-	16
Was	0	10	7	14	-	31

Was	FG Blanton 28
NYJ	Murrell 9 run (Lowery kick)
NYJ	FG Lowery 26
Was	Shepherd 12 run (Blanton kick)
NYJ	FG Lowery 35
Was	Allen 8 run (Blanton kick)
NYJ	FG Lowery 33
Was	Shepherd 52 pass from Frerotte (Blanton kick)
Was	Allen 28 run (Blanton kick)

RFK Stadium—The Redskins scored on a flea-flicker and a reverse, also using some solid running in beating the Jets 31-16.

The Jets took a 13-10 lead into intermission. The Redskins scored first on Scott Blanton's 28-yard field goal but the Jets responded with an Adrian Murrell touchdown run and a pair of field goals. Washington got a 12-yard touchdown run on an end around by receiver Leslie Shepherd.

It was apparent that the winless Jets were not going down easily. After a Terry Allen touchdown run and another New York field goal Washington was clinging to a 17-16 lead going into the fourth quarter.

The Redskins expanded their lead to 24-16 on Leslie Shepherd's 52-yard touchdown catch off of the flea flicker in the early in the fourth.

The Jets fought back, driving deep in Redskins territory. On first and goal at the three, Neil O'Donnell threw the ball and the Jets' Keyshawn Johnson and Redskins' Tom Carter wrestled for the pass in the end zone.

After a long delay, the officials came out of their huddle and declared the result of the play to be the one that replays indicated was the least likely: an interception by Carter. An argument ensured, but it was to no avail.

The Redskins gladly accepted the gift and put the game away on Terry Allen's 28-yard burst on fourth and one.

10/13/96	Redskins (5-1) 27, PATRIOTS (3-3) 22				59,638
Was	3	7	14	3	-	27
NE	6	10	0	6	-	22

NE	FG Vinatieri 24
Was	FG Blanton 21
NE	FG Vinatieri 35
Was	Shepherd 32 run (Blanton kick)
NE	Martin 3 run (Vinatieri kick)
NE	FG Vinatieri 29
Was	Asher 13 pass from Frerotte (Blanton kick)
Was	Ellard 14 pass from Frerotte (Blanton kick)
NE	Martin 2 run (run failed)
Was	FG Blanton 24

Foxboro Stadium—Henry Ellard caught eight passes for 152 yards, including some clutch grabs in the second half, to pace the Redskins win.

Gus Frerotte threw touchdown passes on the Redskins' first two second-half possessions to move Washington from a 16-10 halftime deficit to a 24-16 lead. The first covered 13 yards and went to tight end Jamie Asher. The second scoring pass was to Ellard, who was just getting warmed up.

After a two-yard touchdown run by the Patriots' Curtis Martin, it took a stop on a two-point conversion attempt with 5:33 left to hold the lead.

Then Ellard, taking advantage of a safety blitz, caught a 40-yard pass from Frerotte to convert a third and nine. After that, on second and 19, Frerotte knew just where to go, finding Ellard for 10 yards to the 20 and 15 more to the five. Ellard masterfully dragged his feet just inbounds on the second catch.

That allowed Washington to burn most of the rest of the time off the clock before Scott Blanton's field goal provided the final margin with 56 seconds left.

10/20/96	REDSKINS (6-1) 31, Giants (2-5) 21					52,684
NYG	0	0	14	7	-	21
Was	7	21	0	3	-	31
Was	Allen 2 run (Blanton kick)					
Was	Allen 1 run (Blanton kick)					
Was	Allen 2 run (Blanton kick)					
Was	Green 68 INT return (Blanton kick)					
NYG	Lewis 31 pass from Brown (Daluiso kick)					
NYG	Calloway 13 pass from Brown (Daluiso kick)					
NYG	Wheatley 1 run (Daluiso kick)					
Was	FG Blanton 45					

RFK Stadium—After a pass bounced out of the hands of the Giants' Thomas Lewis and into Darrell Green's arms, it seemed as though Green's 68-yard TD run giving the Redskins a 28-0 lead was icing on the cake. But New York refused to go away easily—the Redskins had to survive some anxious moments in the late going to beat the Giants 31-21.

The Redskins had pushed the Giants around all half, building a 21-0 lead on three short Terry Allen touchdown runs. But their attempt to mail in the second half of the game almost cost them dearly. The Redskins allowed the Giants 292 second-half yards, and a one-yard TD blast by Tyrone Wheatley with 6:35 left pulled the Giants within seven. "I think everybody was just going out, just trying to get the game over in the second half instead of putting it to 'em," Redskins lineman Joe Patton said.

Up until Wheatley's run, the Washington offense had gained just 35 yards and one first down in the second half. They finally woke up and put together a drive that ended with Scott Blanton's field goal with 2:33 left preserved the win.

10/27/96	REDSKINS (7-1) 31, Colts (5-3) 16					54,254
Ind	0	13	3	0	-	16
Was	10	7	7	7	-	31
Was	FG Blanton 20					
Was	Allen 4 run (Blanton kick)					
Ind	FG Blanchard 21					
Was	Shepherd 7 pass from Frerotte (Blanton kick)					
Ind	Faulk 1 run (Blanchard kick)					
Ind	FG Blanchard 29					
Was	Allen 1 run (Blanton kick)					
Ind	FG Blanchard 51					
Was	Allen 32 run (Blanton kick)					

RFK Stadium—Terry Allen gained 79 of his 124 yards in the second half as the Redskins pulled away to beat the Colts 31-16. The Redskins running back scored three touchdowns, the second of which was set up by a clutch punt return by Brian Mitchell.

For a while, it appeared that no second-half heroics would be needed. Washington took a 17-3 lead with less than five minutes left until halftime when Gus Frerotte capped a 73-yard drive with a seven-yard scoring pass to Leslie Shepherd. But the Colts responded with a touchdown and field goal before the break, making it a four-point game.

The score held until late in the third quarter. Mitchell took a punt at the Washington 28 and didn't stop until he was collared at the Indianapolis one. Allen went over on the next play, and the

Redskins had some breathing room at 24-13 with 2:41 left in the third.

In the fourth quarter, Ken Harvey stripped quarterback Jim Harbaugh of the ball and Darryl Morrison recovered for Washington. Three plays later, Allen got loose down the right sideline for a 32-yard TD to put it away.

11/3/96	BILLS (9-3) 38, Redskins (7-2) 13					78,002
Was	7	0	0	6	-	13
Buf	0	17	14	7	-	38
Was	Allen 1 run (Blanton kick)					
Buf	Thomas 10 run (Christie kick)					
Buf	FG Christie 33					
Buf	Holmes 3 run (Christie kick)					
Buf	Holmes 5 run (Christie kick)					
Buf	Kelly 4 run (Christie kick)					
Was	Allen 1 run (pass failed)					
Buf	Holmes 13 run (Christie kick)					

Rich Stadium—Washington scored first, but the Bills ran off 31 unanswered points over the second and third quarters, bringing an emphatic end to a seven-game Redskins winning streak with a 38-13 win.

The Redskins drove 80 yards to a first-quarter touchdown, with Terry Allen finishing it on a one-yard run. The Bills weren't warmed up yet. They were in the second quarter as they drove 80 and 58 yards to touchdowns. Darick Holmes got sizeable chunks of yardage on both drives and got one of the TD's; Thurman Thomas claimed the other. Sandwiched in between was a 33-yard Steve Christie field goal set up when Marc Logan fumbled and the Bills recovered at the Washington 35. Thomas and Holmes both gained more than 100 yards rushing on the day, and Holmes scored three touchdowns.

The Redskins made a bid to get back into it with the score still 17-7 in the third quarter. They were driving in Buffalo territory when Bryce Paup sacked Gus Frerotte, who fumbled. Buffalo recovered at midfield and drove for a touchdown to make it 24-7. All that was left was for Buffalo to grind out the rest of the clock.

11/10/96	Cardinals 37, REDSKINS 34 (OT)					51,929
Ari	3	10	0	21	3	37
Was	3	10	14	7	0	34
Ari	FG Butler 26					
Was	FG Blanton 53					
Was	Logan 36 run (Blanton kick)					
Ari	FG Butler 39					
Ari	Dowdell 64 pass from Esiason					
Was	FG Blanton 24					
Was	Westbrook 17 pass from Frerotte (Blanton kick)					
Was	Allen 1 run (Blanton kick)					
Ari	McWilliams 13 pass from Esiason (Butler kick)					
Ari	Edwards 12 pass from Esiason (Butler kick)					
Ari	FG Butler 32					

RFK Stadium—In one of the most bizarre games in the history of RFK Stadium, Kevin Butler's 32-yard field goal with seconds left in overtime gave Arizona a 37-34 win over Washington.

The Redskins seemed to have put away the pesky Cards with a pair of third-quarter TD's. Arizona rallied, but the Redskins again appeared to seal the win when Darryl Pounds picked off Boomer Esiason at the Washington 6 with less than two minutes left. The Redskins were desperately clinging to a seven-point lead.

On third and five, the Cardinals were flagged for pass interference and all the Redskins would have to do was fall on the ball a couple of times to preserve the win.

But one official saw a tip of the ball that nobody else in the stadium or on TV did, and the flag was picked up. After the ensuing punt, Esiason easily drove the Cardinals to the tying score. Esiason was in the midst of a career day, passing for 531 yards, the third-highest single-game total in NFL history.

The Redskins appeared to have the game won again when Scott Blanton connected on a 38-yard field goal attempt in overtime. But the Redskins were flagged for holding, Blanton missed the second try, and Arizona had new life. Kevin Butler, who had blown a 32-yard FG attempt early in OT, missed his second overtime chip shot in the final minute of the extra period, but the Redskins were offside. After 74 minutes and 27 seconds of play, this one was over when the third time was a charm for Butler—his 32-yarder was good.

11/17/96	**Redskins (8-3) 26, EAGLES (7-4) 21**			66,834	
Was	3	10	10	3	-	**26**
Phi	0	7	7	7	-	**21**
Was	FG Blanton 37				
Was	Asher 12 pass from Frerotte (Blanton kick)				
Phi	Watters 1 run (Anderson kick)				
Was	FG Blanton 22				
Was	Asher 7 pass from Frerotte (Blanton kick)				
Phi	Jones 13 pass from Detmer (Anderson kick)				
Was	FG Blanton 30				
Phi	Watters 1 run (Anderson kick)				
Was	FG Blanton 33				

Veterans Stadium—The Redskins recovered from the previous week's devastating loss in style, going on the road to beat the Eagles 26-21 and take over first place in the NFC East.

A pair of TD passes from Gus Frerotte to tight end Jamie Asher staked the Redskins to a 20-7 lead early in the third quarter. The Eagles came right back, taking the kickoff after the second score and drove 78 yards, finishing it with a 13-yard scoring pass from Ty Detmer to Chris T. Jones. Late in the same period, Scott Blanton made a 30-yard field goal to stretch the lead to 23-14, setting up a tense fourth quarter.

After Ricky Watters scored on a one-yard run to cut the lead to two, the Redskins were unable to move and punted back to the Eagles, who took possession at their own 17 with 4:40 left. The march was a retreat. Rich Owens nailed Watters for an eight-yard loss on first down, and then Ken Harvey sacked Detmer for a loss of seven. On fourth and 25 from the two, the Eagles punted.

The Redskins executed a short drive to Blanton's fourth field goal of the game, coming with 1:20 left to provide the final margin. The Eagles made the Skins sweat before they could chalk up the W, driving to the Washington 21 before four straight incompletions ended the threat with five seconds to go.

11/24/96	**49ers (9-3) 19, REDSKINS (8-4) 16**				54,235	
SF	3	3	0	10	3	**19**
Was	0	6	3	7	0	**16**
SF	FG Wilkins 19					
Was	FG Blanton 19					
Was	FG Blanton 22					
SF	FG Wilkins 48					
Was	FG Blanton 31					
SF	FG Wilkins 44					
Was	Asher 20 pass from Frerotte (Blanton kick)					
SF	Floyd 1 run (Wilkins kick)					
SF	FG Wilkins 38					

RFK Stadium—There the ball sat, rocking on the RFK Stadium turf. The Redskins had just scored to take a 16-9 lead midway through the fourth quarter. A solid tackle had knocked the ball loose from the Niners' returner Dexter Carter. It appeared that the Redskins' Scott Turner was about to recover the fumble, giving his team the chance to wrap up the critical victory.

The touchdown—a 20-yard pass from Gus Frerotte to tight end Jamie Asher—was the first of the game. It capped an eight-play, 78-yard drive. The stadium was alive as Scott Blanton kicked off to San Francisco.

The ball popped loose as Carter was hit and Turner had a bead on it at the 27. But San Francisco's Junior Bryant pulled the

ball away in the bottom of the pile and the Niners were still alive. Steve Young was nine for nine on the subsequent drive, his last pass covering 21 yards to the Washington five. William Floyd carried over from the one soon after that and the extra point tied the game at 16 with 1:58 left in the game. Washington could not threaten in the last two minutes, and the contest went to overtime.

The 49ers took the overtime kickoff and moved to the Redskins 20 in seven plays, the biggest chunk coming on a 25-yard run by Terry Kirby. Jeff Wilkins' 38-yard field goal ended it 3:24 into overtime.

11/28/96	**COWBOYS (8-5) 21, Redskins (8-5) 10**				64,955	
Was	0	3	7	0	-	**10**
Dal	0	7	7	7	-	**21**
Dal	E. Smith 4 run (Boniol kick)					
Was	FG Blanton 21					
Was	Shepherd 26 pass from Frerotte (Blanton kick)					
Dal	E. Smith 4 run (Boniol kick)					
Dal	E. Smith 3 run (Boniol kick)					

Texas Stadium—The Redskins took a 10-7 lead early in the third quarter, but Dallas ground down Washington, piling up a 201-46 advantage in rushing yards. Emmitt Smith was the chief culprit, gaining 155 yards and three touchdowns on the ground. Dallas pulled away for a 21-10 win.

Smith, who had been benched in the fourth quarter of a loss to the Giants the week before, broke a scoreless tie with just over two minutes left in the first half by going over from four yards out. That score was set up when quarterback Gus Frerotte and center Jeff Uhlenhake missed connections on the snap, and Dallas' Fred Strickland recovered at the Washington 33. The Redskins responded with a 21-yard Scott Blanton field goal just before the gun to make it 7-3 at the half.

Leslie Shepherd gave Washington the lead with a 26-yard touchdown catch to cap the opening drive of the second half, but it was a costly score. Shepherd suffered a strained Achilles' tendon that put him on the sidelines alongside the Redskins' other starting receiver Michael Westbrook, out with a bruised knee.

It probably wouldn't have mattered anyway. Smith was just too much for the Redskins' defense. Following Shepherd's score, Smith busted loose for a 42-yard run that was the key play in a drive that ended when Smith scored from the four, giving Dallas lead at 14-10. In the fourth quarter, Dallas took eight minutes off of the clock in driving to the clinching touchdown scored, of course, by Smith.

12/8/96	**BUCS (5-9) 24, Redskins (8-6) 10**			44,733	
Was	0	3	0	7	-	**10**
TB	10	3	11	0	-	**24**
TB	Harris 22 pass from Dilfer (Husted kick)				
TB	FG Husted 42				
Was	FG Blanton 29				
TB	FG Husted 35				
TB	FG Husted 19				
TB	Alstott 13 run (Harris pass from Dilfer)				
Was	Ellard 3 pass from Frerotte (Blanton kick)				

Houlihan's Stadium—It was one thing to be chewed up on the ground by Emmitt Smith and the Cowboys the week before, but this was quite another matter. The Buccaneers rushed for 209 yards, more than twice their per-game average for the season, and handily beat the Redskins.

The Bucs led 13-3 at halftime on the strength of a touchdown pass from Trent Dilfer to Jackie Harris and a pair of Michael Husted field goals. Between the strength of their ground game and Washington's offensive ineptitude, Tampa Bay found it necessary to throw just four times in the second half, and only once in the fourth quarter.

Washington did manage a lone touchdown with three minutes left to make the final 24-10 as they scored on a three-yard touchdow toss from Gus Frerotte to Henry Ellard but the damage had been done. The Redskins slipped out of a first-place tie with Dallas and were a loss away from possible playoff elimination after a 7-1 start.

The Redskins mustered just 41 yards in 16 rushing attempts. Frerotte did manage 219 yards passing but he needed 39 attempts to get there.

12/15/96	CARDINALS (7-8) 27, Redskins (8-7) 26					34,260
Was	3	13	7	3	-	26
Ari	7	7	3	10	-	27
Ari	Centers 6 pass from Graham (Butler kick)					
Was	FG Blanton 20					
Ari	Miller 26 lateral from Swann (Butler kick)					
Was	Turner fumble recovery in end zone (Blanton kick)					
Was	FG Blanton 22					
Was	FG Blanton 23					
Was	Allen 14 run (Blanton kick)					
Ari	FG Butler 22					
Ari	Sanders 21 pass from Graham (Butler kick)					
Was	FG Blanton 35					
Ari	FG Butler 28					

Sun Devil Stadium—Kevin Butler's overtime field goal at RFK Stadium in early November was the beginning of the end of the Redskins' playoff aspirations. His field goal on the last play of this game was the end of the end.

Twice in the first half, the Redskins drove to the Cardinals' two yard line, but had to settle for field goals both times as defensive tackle Eric Swann made key plays to stall the Skins. Washington did manage a touchdown in between those drives, but it came on special teams as Scott Turner recovered a fumbled punt in the end zone. The Redskins led 16-14 at halftime.

Terry Allen gave the Redskins a 23-14 cushion with a 14-yard scoring run in the third quarter. Butler kicked a field goal to cut the lead to six going into the fourth quarter.

Things began to unravel for the Redskins when Arizona blocked a Matt Turk punt. It appeared that Washington's James Jenkins had made a clutch play by scooping the ball up and advancing past the first-down marker. But the officials ruled that Jenkins couldn't advance the ball, and Arizona had possession at the Washington 37. Three plays later they had a 24-23 lead on a 21-yard touchdown pass from Kent Graham to Frank Sanders.

After the Redskins drove to a 35-yard Scott Blanton field goal to retake the lead at 26-24, the Cardinals commenced their game-winning drive that, to the Redskins, was like death by a thousand paper cuts. With 7:02 left, Arizona started at its own 20. Kent Graham went four for six as the Cardinals took 15 plays to move 69 yards. Leeland McElroy inflicted the final wound when he scooted 21 yards to the 14. Shortly after that, Butler booted the Redskins out of the playoffs with a 28-yard field goal as time expired.

12/22/96	REDSKINS (9-7) 37, Cowboys (10-6) 10					56,454
Dal	0	3	0	7	-	10
Was	3	13	7	14	-	37
Was	FG Blanton 45					
Was	FG Blanton 29					
Dal	FG Boniol 34					
Was	Allen 1 run (Blanton kick)					
Was	FG Blanton 18					
Was	Allen 2 run (Blanton kick)					
Was	Allen 6 run (Blanton kick)					
Was	S. Davis 4 run (Blanton kick)					
Dal	Walker 39 run (Boniol kick)					

RFK Stadium—The game was the backdrop and the venue took center stage—this was the final Redskins game at venerable RFK Stadium. Dallas had clinched its playoff position and Washington had been eliminated, so the contest was an exhibition. The Redskins didn't disappoint the 56,464 fans as they thumped the Cowboys.

Scott Blanton booted field goals of 45 and 29 yards to get the Redskins on the board first. After Dallas responded with a three-pointer of its own, the Redskins drove to the first of three Terry Allen touchdown runs. During the game Allen moved his rushing yardage total for the season to 1,353, a team record for a single season. John Riggins formerly held the record and was there along with dozens of other ex-Skins including Sonny Jurgensen, Dexter Manley, Monte Coleman and other luminaries from the RFK era. They marched onto the field at halftime to give the stadium a final hurrah.

By then the Redskins were up 16-3 and gave the crowd plenty more to enjoy in the second half. Allen scored two more touchdowns on runs on two and six yards before yielding to rookie Stephen Davis, who bulled over from four yards out for Washington's final TD. That put Washington up 37-3 and was the last touchdown scored by a Redskin at RFK.

"A lot of memories will be lost," said Billy Kilmer, "but they'll never die.

1997
Head Coach: Norv Turner
Record: 8-7-1, Second in NFC East

Honors: Cris Dishman Pro Bowl; Darrell Green Pro Bowl, All-NFL;
Ken Harvey Pro Bowl; Matt Turk Pro Bowl, All-NFL

Jan 24
Officially a Bust—Skins Set Shuler Free
*Team declines to pay $4 million option; former
3rd overall pick becomes a restricted free agent*

Feb. 6
Tagged—Gilbert Named Franchise Player
*Agent Sunferi says salary 'substantially lower'
than value, hints at holdout*

Cooke Gives Turner 3-Year Extension

Mar 4—Norv Turner may not have a playoff appearance on his list of accomplishments, but he does have some pretty solid job security. Jack Kent Cooke, in announcing that he had given Turner a three-year, $3 million contract extension, professed his loyalty to Turner.

"I want Norv to be our coach as long as I own the club," Cooke said.

The fact that Turner has an 18-30 record in three season in Washington did not stop Cooke from declaring that he believed him to be "one of the best coaches in the NFL."

Apr 6
Jack Kent Cooke Dies at 84
*Owner succumbs to heart attack;
son John expected to take over as team
president*

Apr 10
Stadium to Bear Owner's Name, Son Says
Jack Kent Cooke Stadium slated to open this fall

Apr 17
Shuler Shipped to Saints
Skins get 3rd and 5th round picks for QB

Apr 25
Darrell Green Inks 5-year Deal
Cornerback, 37, will finish career in Washington

July 17
Out Pattern: Monk Signs With Skins, Retires
Receiver 'very happy' with retirement

John Cooke May Not Be Able to Keep Team

July 26—Due to a complex will that donates the bulk of the estate of Jack Kent Cooke to a charitable foundation, the late owner's son may not be able to keep the Redskins in the family.

The will sets up a foundation to pay for college scholarships and requires that the bulk of the elder Cooke's assets be liquidated with the proceeds given to the foundation. This means

that the team must be sold to the highest bidder, with no favoritism granted to anyone, John Cooke included.

While John certainly is a man of great means, purchasing the team may be beyond those means. The open market is likely to set the value of the team and Jack Kent Cooke Stadium well over $500 million. It is unlikely that John Cooke will be able to muster enough capital to be a serious contender without substantial help from outside investors.

Aug 19
Westbrook Faces Fine For Attack on Davis
*Turner calls incident 'unfortunate';
attack apparently unprovoked*

Aug 20
Stadium Will Seat More Than 80,000
*Room found for 2,000 additional seats makes
it NFL's biggest; will open on schedule*

Aug 24
'96 Top Pick Andre Johnson Cut
Offensive tackle never played a single snap

Aug 26
Gilbert Packs Up, Leaves Town
*DT empties Ashburn house, remains $900k/year
apart from Skins*

8/31/97	Redskins (1-0) 24, PANTHERS (0-1) 10				72,633
Was	0	10	0	14	**24**
Car	3	0	0	7	**10**
Car	FG Kasay 52				
Was	FG Blanton 38				
Was	Allen 1 run (Blanton kick)				
Car	Walls 24 pass from Beuerlein (Kasay kick),				
Was	Allen 1 run (Blanton kick)				
Was	Shepherd 5 pass from Frerotte (Blanton kick)				

Ericsson Stadium—Terry Allen ran for 141 yards and two touchdowns to pace the Redskins to an upset 24-10 win on the road against Carolina.

The Panthers, surprise participants in the NFC title game the previous season, contributed greatly to their own demise by turning the ball over four times and racking up 10 penalties for 101 yards. The first Carolina turnover occurred deep in Washington territory with the game tied at three when running back Fred Lane fumbled and safety Jesse Campbell recovered at the nine. From there, the Redskins embarked on a 91-yard drive, taking 11 plays to score on Allen's one-yard burst to take a 10-3 lead with 28 seconds left in the half.

The home team tied it up early in the fourth quarter when Steve Beuerlein hit tight end Wesley Walls with a 24-yard touchdown pass. Washington came right back, going 67 yards with Gus Frerotte hitting tight end Jamie Asher twice for gains of nine and 15 yards. The payoff came on another one-yard run by Allen. Washington led 17-10.

The lead soon doubled. Michael Bates fumbled the ensuing kickoff and four plays later, Frerotte threw the clinching TD pass to Leslie Shepherd with six and a half minutes left.

9/7/97	STEELERS (1-1) 14, Redskins (1-1) 13				58,059
Was	0	3	10	0	13
Pit	7	0	0	7	14
Pit	Stewart 1 run (N. Johnson kick)				
Was	FG Blanton 37				
Was	Mitchell 97 kickoff return (Blanton kick),				
Was	FG Blanton 28				
Pit	Bettis 1 run (N. Johnson kick)				

Three Rivers Stadium—A pair of red-zone interceptions made Gus Frerotte's homecoming to Pittsburgh an unhappy one. The Redskins fell to the Steelers 14-13.

Twice, the Redskins executed long drives deep into Pittsburgh territory only to come up empty. Frerotte threw end-zone interceptions on second and goal from the seven and on second and ten at the 20.

The visitors got across the goal line just once, on Brian Mitchell's 97-yard return of the second-half kickoff. That score and a pair of Scott Blanton field goals staked Washington to a 13-7 lead in the third quarter. But the Redskins' inability to stop the Pittsburgh running game, particularly Jerome Bettis, caught up with them.

The Steelers ground out a nine-play, 72-yard drive spanning the third and fourth quarters. Bettis gained 46 of those yards, including the final one that gave the Steelers a one-point lead with 13:23 left in the game after Norm Johnson's extra point.

Bettis rushed for 134 yards and the Steelers racked up 222 on the ground as a team.

The Redskins had opportunities after that, but couldn't covert. The final nail was Frerotte's third interception, coming from the Washington 41 with 23 seconds left and the Redskins desperately trying to get into position for a potential game-winning field goal.

9/14/97	REDSKINS (2-1) 19, Cardinals (1-2) 13					78,270
Ari	7	0	3	3	0	13
Was	3	7	0	3	6	19
Was	FG Blanton 20					
Ari	Bennett recovered blocked punt in end zone (Butler kick)					
Was	Westbrook 5 pass from Frerotte (Blanton kick)					
Ari	FG Butler 32					
Was	FG Blanton 19					
Ari	FG Butler 47					
Was	Westbrook 40 pass from Frerotte					

Jack Kent Cooke Stadium—Michael Westbrook, under fire for a lack of productivity in the season's first two games, caught two touchdown passes, the second a spectacular, diving game-winner in overtime. The catch made for a successful christening of the Redskins' new 78,000-seat stadium in suburban Landover, Md., as the Redskins beat Arizona 13-10.

Westbrook's first scoring catch, from five yards out, boosted the Redskins to a 10-7 halftime lead. The second half was a battle of field goals, with Arizona's Kevin Butler twice tying the score. Butler's second field goal came with two seconds left and the score was 13-13.

Prior to that, the Redskins had missed a chance to put the game away when they couldn't punch it over on first and goal at the one. Scott Blanton's 19-yard field goal had put the Redskins up 13-10 with 1:13 left.

The Cardinals' first overtime possession ended at their own 35 when Redskins' defensive end Kennard Lang forced a fumble and linebacker Derek Smith recovered.

Two plays later, Gus Frerotte sidestepped a heavy rush and threw to Westbrook. The receiver dove, his feet leaving the ground just inside the five, gathered the pass in and landed just over the goal line.

9/28/97	REDSKINS (3-1) 24, Jaguars (3-1) 12				74,421
Jax	6	3	3	0	12
Was	0	14	0	10	24
Jax	FG Hollis 30				
Jax	FG Hollis 42				
Jax	FG Hollis 25				
Was	Shepherd 10 pass from Frerotte (Blanton kick)				
Was	Asher 8 pass from Frerotte (Blanton kick)				
Jax	FG Hollis 47				
Was	FG Blanton 41				
Was	Shepherd 13 pass from Frerotte (Blanton kick)				

Jack Kent Cooke Stadium—The Redskins overcame a shaky start and ran their record at their new stadium to 2-0 with a 24-12 win over the Jaguars.

Jacksonville had the league's highest-scoring offense coming into the game and had opportunities to put the Redskins in the hole early. Twice in the first half, the Jaguars got turnovers deep in Redskins territory, but had to settle for a pair of Mike Hollis field goals. A third Hollis field goal was the result of a 52-yard drive by the Jags and the visitors had a 9-0 lead.

In the last six minutes of the half, it was the Redskins' turn to get a favorable field position—and they took full advantage. Jacksonville was flagged for unnecessary roughness following a 24-yard punt return by Brian Mitchell, setting up the offense at the Jaguars' 28-yard line. Six plays later, Gus Frerotte threw a 10-yard touchdown pass to Leslie Shepherd to pull Washington to within 9-7. Darrell Green batted a Mark Brunell pass into the air and Stanley Richard intercepted it, setting up a 37-yard TD drive that ended with another Frerotte scoring pass, this one to Jamie Asher. That put the Redskins up 14-9 at halftime.

Hollis' fourth field goal was the only scoring in the third quarter and the home team closed it out in the fourth. They drove 55 yards to a Scott Blanton field goal early in the period. Jacksonville had possession for a potential game-tying drive, but another batted ball fell into Washington hands. This time it was cornerback Cris Dishman tipping and tackle Marc Boutte catching, returning it 10 yards to the Jags' 17. A second Frerotte-to-Shepherd scoring pass iced the contest.

The Redskins held their opponent to 204 total yards of offense while Terry Allen, playing with a cast on his broken thumb, rushed for 122 yards on 36 carries.

10/5/97	EAGLES (2-3) 24, Redskins (3-2) 10				67,008
Was	0	3	7	0	10
Phil	7	10	0	7	24
Phil	Detmer 3 run (Boniol kick),				
Phil	Watters 1 run (Boniol kick),				
Was	FG Blanton 37				
Phil	FG Boniol 34				
Was	Allen 5 pass from Frerotte (Blanton kick)				
Phil	Watters 1 run (Boniol kick)				

Veterans Stadium—The Eagles rushed for 203 yards and controlled the ball for nearly 40 minutes, grinding up the Redskins in a dominating 24-10 win.

Eagles quarterback Ty Detmer, who also made a hefty contribution to the offense by going 17 for 27 for 246 yards, scored first on a three-yard run in the opening period. Early in the second, Ricky Watters plunged over from the one to put the Eagles up 14-0.

Marc Boutte recovered a Philly fumble to set up a Scott Blanton field goal and cut the lead to 14-3, but the Eagles responded before halftime with a 34-yard field goal by Chris Boniol to stretch the lead back to two touchdowns.

Unable to move the ball on the ground, the Redskins took to the air to score a third-quarter touchdown. All of the six plays and 70 yards of the drive were passes, the last a five-yarder to Terry Allen for a touchdown to bring the score to 17-10.

But the Eagles came right back, executing a 10-play, 75-yard drive that consumed five and a half minutes and ended in Watters' second one-yard scoring run.

10/13/97	REDSKINS (4-2) 21, Cowboys (3-3) 16				76,159
Dal	3	0	6	7	16
Was	7	7	7	0	21
Dal	FG Cunningham 19				
Was	S. Davis 2 run (Blanton kick)				
Was	Jenkins 13 pass from Frerotte (Blanton kick)				
Was	Davis 4 run (Blanton kick)				
Dal	Coakley 16 fumble return (pass failed)				
Dal	Irvin 14 pass from Aikman (Cunningham kick)				

Jack Kent Cooke Stadium—Stephen Davis, filling in for an injured Terry Allen, scored a pair of touchdowns to pace the Redskins to a 21-16 win. For the game, Davis gained 94 yards on 22 carries.

After Dallas scored first on a 19-yard field goal by Richie Cunningham, Washington steadily built a 21-3 lead. An 80-yard drive, paced by throws from Gus Frerotte to Michael Westbrook and Leslie Shepherd, ended with Davis' first scoring run, a two-yard burst late in the first quarter. Another 80-yard drive, this one in the second quarter, culminated with a 13-yard touchdown pass from Frerotte to tight end James Jenkins.

The home team didn't have to go as far for their third-quarter touchdown, scored on a 4-yard Davis run. The Redskins gained possession at the Dallas 25 when Rich Owens recovered a Troy Aikman fumble.

The Cowboys rallied, scoring touchdowns on a 16-yard fumble return by Dexter Coakley and a 14-yard touchdown pass from Aikman to Michael Irvin, but the Redskins held on for the win.

Frerotte scattered his 12 completions among eight different receivers with Shepherd catching two for 60 yards.

10/19/97	OILERS (3-4) 28, Redskins (4-3) 14				31,042
Was	0	0	14	0	14
Ten	0	14	7	7	28
Ten	McNair 2 run (Del Greco kick)				
Ten	George 3 run (Del Greco kick)				
Ten	R. Thomas 5 run (Del Greco kick)				
Was	Ellard 13 pass from Frerotte (Blanton kick)				
Was	Ellard 10 pass from Frerotte (Blanton kick)				
Ten	George 6 run (Del Greco kick)				

Liberty Bowl—Early in the fourth quarter, the Redskins were threatening to come all the way back from a 21-point deficit. Gus Frerotte had hit Henry Ellard with a pair of third-quarter touchdown passes to make a 21-0 Oilers lead a more manageable 21-14.

The Redskins regained possession and were driving for the tying score when Frerotte was hit as he passed, sending the ball into the arms of the Oilers' Denard Wilson. Following an Eddie George touchdown run, another interception later in the fourth quarter sealed the Redskins' fate in a 28-14 loss.

Tennessee had built its lead on the strength of George's running and the timely scrambling of quarterback Steve McNair. A 21-yard dash by McNair on third and five led to McNair's two-yard scoring run and George scored the Oilers' second touchdown on a three-yard run. On the day, George carried 31 times for 125 yards and McNair kicked in 53 yards on 10 carries.

Ellard caught six passes for 84 yards. The Redskins had a tough time controlling the ball on the ground. It's not a good sign when one scramble by your quarterback accounts for a fourth of your rushing yards. That was the case here, however, as Frerotte's 26-yard scramble was a good chunk of the Redskins' 94 yards on the ground.

10/26/97	Ravens (4-4) 20, REDSKINS (4-4) 17				75,067
Bal	7	7	3	3	20
Was	7	0	7	3	17
Bal	Alexander 13 pass from Testaverde (Stover kick)				
Was	Shepherd 15 pass from Frerotte (Blanton kick)				
Bal	Morris 4 run (Stover kick)				
Bal	FG Stover 34				
Was	Mitchell 6 pass from Frerotte (Blanton kick)				
Bal	FG Stover 28				
Was	FG Blanton 26				

Jack Kent Cooke Stadium—In a driving rainstorm, Baltimore's Bam Morris ran through the Redskins' feeble run defense for 179 yards as the Ravens dealt the Redskins a 20-17 loss, their first defeat at their new stadium.

Morris racked up 101 yards in the first half alone, grinding through the middle time after time for large gains.

Baltimore took a 7-0 lead in the first quarter, but the Redskins came right back when Brian Mitchell returned the ensuing kickoff 61 yards to set up a 15-yard touchdown pass from Gus Frerotte to Leslie Shepherd.

The Ravens responded by grinding out a 20-play, 78-yard drive that chewed more than 11 minutes off the clock. They converted two fourth downs in the process and scored on Morris' four-yard run. Baltimore led 14-7 at halftime.

The Ravens expanded the lead to 17-7 on a 34-yard Matt Stover field goal. The Redskins then got back into it by defying the conventional wisdom and taking points off of the board. Scott Blanton nailed a 49-yard field goal attempt and the Ravens were offside on the play. The Redskins took the penalty, the yardage being sufficient to give them a first down. Soon after that, Frerotte threw six yards to Brian Mitchell to make it 17-14.

Stover kicked another field goal in the fourth quarter to stretch the Ravens' lead to six. Washington recovered a fumble at the Baltimore 25, but could muster only a field goal.

11/2/97	Redskins (5-4) 31, BEARS (1-8) 8				53,032
Was	14	10	7	0	31
Chi	0	0	0	8	8
Was	Jenkins 9 pass from Frerotte (Blanton kick)				
Was	Bowie 5 run (Blanton kick)				
Was	Frerotte 1 run (Blanton kick)				
Was	FG Blanton 38				
Was	Shepherd 39 pass from Frerotte (Blanton kick)				
Chi	Proehl 2 pass from Kramer (Proehl pass from Kramer)				

Soldier Field—Terry Allen, returning from a two-week absence due to injuries, rushed for 125 yards as the Redskins built a 24-0 halftime lead en route to an easy win. The visitors took advantage of numerous Bears penalties and turnovers in the process of racking up a 31-8 triumph.

Washington rushed for 98 yards in the first quarter in the course executing a pair of touchdown drives. The first score followed a 76-yard drive highlighted by a 30-yard Allen run. The payoff came when Gus Frerotte threw a nine-yard scoring pass to James Jenkins. A pass interference call greatly aided the next drive, setting the Redskins up at the Chicago five. Fullback Larry Bowie took it in from there.

Another pass interference call led to the Redskins' third touchdown, and a fumbled punt set the Redskins up for a field goal before halftime. Washington ran the lead to 31-0 in the third quarter before the Bears got a face-saving touchdown with just over five minutes left in the game.

Nov 4

Deadline Comes and Goes, Gilbert Out for '97
Franchise player continues holdout, won't be able to play this year; two sides $500K/year apart

11/9/97	**REDSKINS (6-4) 30, Lions (4-6) 7**				75,261
Det	0	0	7	0	**7**
Was	3	10	7	10	**30**
Was	FG Blanton 22				
Was	Jenkins 1 pass from Frerotte (Blanton kick)				
Was	FG Blanton 50				
Was	Allen 1 run (Blanton kick)				
Det	B. Sanders 51 run (Hanson kick)				
Was	FG Blanton 45				
Was	Pounds 22 interception return (Blanton kick)				

Jack Kent Cooke Stadium—The Lions had never beaten the Redskins in 18 tries in the District of Columbia, and they were unsuccessful in their attempt to break the road jinx in the state of Maryland. Two pass interference penalties were keys in two touchdown drives that boosted the Redskins to a 20-0 third-quarter lead and Washington went on to win 30-7.

Following a Scott Blanton field goal, Jesse Campbell intercepted a Scott Mitchell pass and returned it seven yards to the Detroit 30. Shortly after that, Detroit's Corey Raymond was flagged for pass interference in the end zone, moving the ball to the one. With everyone expecting a Terry Allen dive, Gus Frerotte threw to James Jenkins to make it 10-0.

With the score 13-0 in the third quarter, another interference call—this one on the Lions' Bryant Westbrook—helped get Washington into scoring position at the three. And this time, it was Allen who pushed it over from the one, making the score 20-0.

Lions star running back Barry Sanders did get a Sports Center moment when he reversed his field and broke into the clear for a 51-yard touchdown run, but Blanton's third field goal and a 22-yard interception return ran the final to 30-7.

11/16/97	**COWBOYS (6-5) 17, Redskins (6-5) 14**				64,559
Was	0	0	7	7	**14**
Dal	0	6	0	11	**17**
Dal	FG Cunningham 34				
Dal	FG Cunningham 40				
Was	Allen 4 run (Blanton kick)				
Was	Ellard 24 pass from Frerotte (Blanton kick)				
Dal	Irvin 6 pass from Aikman (E. Smith pass from Aikman)				
Dal	FG Cunningham 42				

Texas Stadium—It seemed that the Redskins had the Cowboys just where they wanted them. It turned out that Dallas' Troy Aikman, Michael Irvin and Emmitt Smith were the ones who truly had the upper hand.

The Redskins, needing a win to stay in first place tie in the division, had built a 14-6 lead on the strength of a pair of second-half touchdowns. With about six minutes left in the game, Dallas took possession at its own three.

Aikman got the drive started by getting the Cowboys out of the hole with a 21-yard pass to tight end Eric Bjornson. One pass to Irvin went for 18 yards and then came a real killer: a 31-yard Aikman-to-Irvin connection to convert a fourth and two at midfield. Soon after that, the same combination teamed up for a six-yard touchdown connection. Aikman then completed the comeback by throwing to Smith for the two-point conversion.

Actually, the comeback wasn't complete—it was a tie game with just under two minutes left—but in reality, it was all over but the crying.

Washington could not move the ball and punted back to Dallas. Matt Turk shanked the kick and it traveled just 28 yards to the Dallas 47. Aikman engineered an eight-play, 28-yard drive that had burned all but four seconds off of the clock when Richie Cunningham kicked a 42-yard field goal to give the Cowboys the 17-14 win.

11/23/97	**REDSKINS (6-5-1) 7, Giants (7-4-1) 7 OT**					75,703
NYG	0	0	7	0	0	**7**
Was	0	7	0	0	0	**7**
Was	Frerotte 1 run (Blanton kick)					
NYG	Calloway 4 pass from Kanell (Daluiso kick)					

Jack Kent Cooke Stadium—"This game was a very pitiful kind of game," said Redskins cornerback Darrell Green after the Redskins and Giants stumbled to a 7-7 tie. "It was sort of embarrassing. Maybe the fans enjoyed it."

Green was absolutely correct until his last sentence. Not even the most masochistic of those in attendance at Jack Kent Cooke Stadium or in the national TV audience watching the Sunday night game on ESPN could possibly have derived much pleasure from a game featuring 22 punts, six turnovers, 10 sacks, and 14 accepted penalties. One starting quarterback left the game with a self-inflicted injury; the other managed just 105 net yards passing through five quarters of play.

The injured QB was Washington's Gus Frerotte. Five plays after the Redskins' Kennard Lang recovered a fumble at the New York 26, Frerotte rolled in for a touchdown from one yard out. Frerotte celebrated the score by head butting some padding on the stadium wall near the end zone. Unfortunately, there was thick concrete behind the thin padding and Frerotte would up going to the hospital with a jammed neck. He would certainly recover from the neck injury, but not from the jokes about his ill-conceived celebration.

Jeff Hostetler came in for Frerotte and promptly threw an interception to set up New York's touchdown. The interception came when Sam Garnes tipped the pass and cornerback Phillipi Sparks picked it off at the Washington 46. Seven plays later, shortly after a 20-yard pass interference call on Green, Danny Kanell threw four yards to Chris Calloway for the tying score.

The rest of the game was an exercise in futility. The Redskins had a drive of nine plays that netted one yard. The Giants had a field goal blocked. When it turned out that Washington had called time out negating the play, they said the heck with it and punted. Washington committed three turnovers in overtime, but the Giants couldn't take advantage of any of them.

The biggest mistake was saved for near the end. With time running out in the extra period, Hostetler threw to Michael Westbrook, who gathered in the pass at the Giants' 30 while going out of bounds. The officials ruled that he was out of bounds. Westbrook yanked his helmet off in anger, perhaps wishing to make his protests more clear. He was flagged for unsportsmanlike conduct, moving the Redskins back 15 yards into their own territory with 43 seconds left. Scott Blanton's 54-yard field goal attempt fell short with two seconds left.

"That might be an all-timer," Green said. "I don't think you can ever do anything worse on the football field." He was referring to Westbrook's outburst, but he could have been talking about any number of other moments in this one.

11/30/97	**Rams (3-10) 23, REDSKINS (6-6-1) 20**				74,772
StL	0	10	7	6	**23**
Was	7	3	0	10	**20**
Was	Bowie 39 pass from Frerotte (Blanton kick),				
StL	FG Wilkins 30				
Was	FG Blanton 43				
StL	Lee 36 pass from Banks (Wilkins kick)				
StL	Moore 5 run (Wilkins kick)				

Was	FG Blanton 19				
StL	FG Wilkins 23				
Was	Mitchell 2 run (Blanton kick)				
StL	FG Wilkins 25				

Jack Kent Cooke Stadium—The Redskins' playoff chances took a severe hit in this stunning 23-20 loss to the lowly Rams. A gutsy drive to tie the game in the fourth quarter was negated when the Rams' Amp Lee scooted 45 yards with a pass to set up Jeff Wilkins' game-winning field goal with four seconds left.

Washington took the opening kickoff and smartly drove 76 yards in nine plays, scoring on a 39-yard pass from Frerotte to fullback Larry Bowie. After an exchange of field goals, the Rams had tied the game with just over a minute left in the half when Tony Banks threw a 36-yard touchdown pass to Lee.

In the third quarter, Jerald Moore scored on a five-yard run to put the Rams up by seven. The home team drove to a first and goal at the Rams two, but had to settle for a field goal after a false start penalty and a sack pushed them back. Wilkins' second field goal of the game pushed the lead back to seven with just under five minutes left.

Washington took possession at their own 22 following the kickoff and embarked on a 15-play drive to tie the game. The offense converted a third and ten when Frerotte went to Michael Westbrook for 15 yards, then kept the desperate drive alive with a pair of fourth and long conversions. Brian Mitchell scored the tying touchdown with 1:50 left.

The heroics were erased when Banks threw to Lee, who was wide open on the hash mark, and Wilkins converted the game winner.

Frerotte Out For Season With Broken Hip

Dec 1—Redskins quarterback Gus Frerotte led a heroic drive to tie Sunday's game against the Rams late in the fourth quarter. It was learned today that he led that drive with a broken hip.

He suffered the injury when he was thrown to the ground on the first play of the fourth quarter. His right knee was jammed into the ground, causing a fracture of the acetabulum, a hip socket bone.

Despite the injury he led the Redskins on a 15-play, 78-yard drive to tie the game with 1:50 left to play. The Rams won 23-20 with a field goal at the end of regulation time.

Frerotte didn't seek medical attention during or after the game, but he awoke with severe pain this morning. He was driven to Arlington Hospital, where tests revealed the injury.

Jeff Hostetler will replace Frerotte as the team's starting quarterback.

12-7-97	**Redskins (7-6-1) 38, CARDINALS (3-11) 28**				41,537
Was	7	10	7	14	**38**
Ari	0	14	7	7	**28**
Was	Mitchell 63 punt return (Blanton kick)				
Was	Bowie 3 pass from Hostetler (Blanton kick),				
Was	FG Blanton 40				
Ari	Rb. Moore 4 pass from Plummer (Nedney kick)				
Ari	Rb. Moore 29 pass from Plummer (Nedney kick)				
Was	Dishman 29 interception return (Blanton kick)				
Ari	Gedney 37 pass from Plummer (Nedney kick)				
Was	Ellard 23 pass from Hostetler (Blanton kick),				
Ari	Rb.Moore 47 pass from Plummer (Nedney kick),				
Was	Connell 7 pass from Hostetler (Blanton kick),				

Sun Devil Stadium—Brian Mitchell made a pair of big plays to stake the Redskins to a 17-0 lead and the Redskins held off the Cardinals 38-28 in Jeff Hostetler's debut as the Redskins starting quarterback.

In the first quarter, Mitchell fielded a 57-yard punt by Jeff Feagles at the Washington 37, started to his right and then cut

back to the middle. He faked out a would-be tackler at about the 30, completing a 67-yard touchdown run untouched with just less than five minutes left in the period. Then, in the second quarter, Mitchell made the key play in a 91-yard touchdown drive. He took a short pass from Hostetler and turned it into a 69-yard gain to the Arizona 29. Soon after that, Hostetler threw to Larry Bowie for three yards and a touchdown to make the score 14-0. Later, a 40-yard Scott Blanton field goal boosted the lead to 17-0 with 9:26 remaining in the half.

But the Cards would not fall easily. Quarterback Jake Plummer threw two touchdown passes to receiver Rob Moore, the second a 29-yarder with just seven seconds left in the half, cutting the Washington halftime lead to 17-14.

Washington got some breathing room when Cris Dishman returned an interception 29 yards for a touchdown early in the third period, but it was still no time to breathe easy. Plummer responded by throwing a 37-yard TD pass to Chris Gendey. Again, the Skins pulled back out to a 10-point lead on a 23-yard pass from Hostetler to Henry Ellard. Again, Plummer responded, going to Moore again for 47 yards to make it 31-28 with just over 10 minutes left.

Arizona got the ball back, but Plummer was out of magic. Marvcus Patton sacked him, forced a fumble, and Kennard Lang recovered at the Cardinals 22. Three plays later, Hostetler threw seven yards to Albert Connell with 4:17 left to seal the win.

12/13/97	**GIANTS (9-5-1) 30, Redskins (7-7-1) 10**				77,571
Was	0	3	7	0	**10**
NYG	17	3	0	10	**30**
NYG	FG Daluiso 41				
NYG	Way 15 run (Daluiso kick				
NYG	Calloway 7 pass from Kanell (Daluiso kick),				
Was	FG Blanton 33				
NYG	FG Daluiso 28				
Was	Connell 43 pass from Hostetler (Blanton kick)				
NYG	FG Daluiso 28				
NYG	Sehorn 35 interception return (Daluiso kick)				

Giants Stadium—In what was the worst big game performance in memory, the Redskins laid an egg on the Meadowlands carpet. The best way to go through this one is by the numbers:

419—The official number of no-shows for the game. It's unclear if that count includes the Redskins and their coaches.

297—The number of seconds it took for the Giants to build a 10-0 lead. First Jessie Armstead recovered a Jeff Hostetler fumble to set up a Brad Daluiso field goal. Then punter Matt Turk then fumbled the snap from center to give the Giants a short field again. This time they took full advantage, with Charles Way running 15 yards for a touchdown with 4:57 elapsed.

110—The Giants net yards passing behind rookie quarterback Danny Kanell. Thirty-nine of them came on the only extended drive that was necessary. It came in the first quarter, a 13-play, 76-yard march that culminated in Chris Calloway's 7-yard touchdown catch from Kanell.

45—The Redskins' net rushing yardage total. Stephen Davis mustered 41 of those on 10 carries, but the running game was not a factor after those initial 297 seconds.

35—The yardage on Jason Sehorn's fourth-quarter interception return for a touchdown. Despite everything that went wrong, there was still some slim hope for a miracle Redskins win until Sehorn's runback.

22—The Redskins third down conversion percentage (2-9). They were 0-3 on fourth down.

6—The number of turnovers the Redskins committed; four interceptions and two fumbles. That tally doesn't count what was possibly the game's most damaging play: the fumbled snap by Turk. Since Turk recovered his fumble and was tackled, that went down in the books as a failed fourth down conversion.

0—Washington's chances of winning the NFC East after this game was over. Also, their chances of making the playoffs at all without help.

12/21/97	REDSKINS (8-7-1) 35, Eagles (6-9-1) 32				75,939
Phil	7	7	3	15	32
Was	14	14	0	7	35
Was	Pounds 18 fumble return (Jacke kick)				
Was	Green 83 interception return (Jacke kick)				
Phil	Dunn 31 pass from Hoying (Boniol kick)				
Was	Davis 1 run (Jacke kick)				
Phil	Garner 9 run (Boniol kick)				
Was	Bowie 3 run (Jacke kick)				
Phil	FG Boniol 33				
Phil	Garner 1 run (Solomon pass from Hoying)				
Was	Westbrook 7 pass from Hostetler (Jacke kick)				
Phil	Solomon 14 pass from Hoying (Boniol kick)				

Jack Kent Cooke Stadium—The Redskins had in interest in the outcome of three games on this last Sunday of the season. After they won the contest over which they had control by taking a 35-32 win over the Eagles, all they could do was hope that one of the other two turned out in their favor.

Neither one did, though. Both the Vikings and Lions won their games to claim the final two playoff berths and leave the Redskins out of the postseason for the fifth consecutive year.

The Washington defense got things jump started. Less than two minutes into the game, Darryl Pounds got the football defender's equivalent of a grand slam when he sacked quarterback Bobby Hoying, stripped him of the ball, recovered the fumble and returned it 18 yards for a touchdown and a 7-0 lead.

Two possessions later, the Eagles were driving in Redskins territory when a poor pass by Hoying was intercepted by a diving Darrell Green. The cornerback jumped up untouched and, before most of the Eagles realized that he was not down, was off on an 83-yard touchdown jaunt.

The teams traded scores for most of the rest of the game, with the Redskins able to keep the visitors at arm's length due to their early cushion. The Eagles took advantage of an interception to score a touchdown and a two-point conversion to pull within 28-25 with 6:41 remaining.

The air came out of the Eagles' comeback balloon, however, when Brian Mitchell returned the ensuing kickoff 74 yards to the 14. Three plays later, Jeff Hostetler threw a seven-yard touchdown pass to Michael Westbrook.

1998
Head Coach: Norv Turner
Record: 6-10, Fourth in NFC East

Honors: Matt Turk All-NFL, Pro Bowl

Feb. 11
Franchise Tag Remains Fixed to Gilbert
Team will try to trade unhappy defender

Feb. 23
49ers DT Stubblefield Signed as Free Agent
Defensive Player of the Year gets six years, $36 million

Feb. 26
Skins Pull Sign and Trade for DT Wilkinson
Bengals get 1st and 3rd round picks for 'Big Daddy'

Gilbert Saga Over, Skins to Get Two Firsts

Apr 16—The rocky relationship between the Redskins and defensive tackle Sean Gilbert will soon come to an end.

The Carolina Panthers will sign Gilbert to an offer sheet soon after this weekend's draft. As soon as the Redskins decline to match it, which they are likely to do before the ink on the contract is dry, Washington will get Carolina's first-round draft picks in 1999 and 2000 as compensation.

Gilbert sat out the entire 1997 season after the Redskins made him their franchise player. Although both sides tried to hammer out a long-term agreement, they never could.

The Panthers struck a deal with Gilbert last month and tried to work out lesser compensation with the Redskins. Carolina, however, was unwilling to give up its first pick in this year's draft and the Redskins wouldn't budge. Because of that the Panthers will execute the offer sheet right after the draft so the price will not have to be paid until the two following drafts.

The Panthers will make Gilbert the highest-paid defensive player in NFL history, giving him a seven-year, $46.5 million contract with a $10 million signing bonus.

9/7/98	GIANTS (1-0) 31, Redskins (0-1) 24					76,269
Was	7	3	7	7	-	24
NYG	0	10	21	0	-	31
Was	Shepherd 17 pass from Frerotte (Blanton kick).					
NYG	FG Daluiso 35					
Was	FG Blanton 46					
NYG	Calloway 5 pass from Kanell (Daluiso kick).					
NYG	Way 2 run (Daluiso kick)					
NYG	Strahan 24 INT return (Daluiso kick)					
Was	Bowie 4 pass from T. Green (Blanton kick).					
NYG	Toomer 22 pass from Kanell (Daluiso kick).					
Was	Alexander 1 pass from T. Green (Blanton kick)					

Giants Stadium—Giant interceptions of consecutive Gus Frerotte passes helped New York to 21 third-quarter points in less than four minutes. Trent Green came in to relieve Frerotte, who suffered a bruised shoulder, but a late rally fell short. The Redskins lost 31-24.

Frerotte got the Redskins off to a good start, leading the offense 46 yards in four plays following a 37-yard punt return by Brian Mitchell. The payoff came on a 17-yard pass from Frerotte to Shepherd. The game's pivotal moments came after the Giants scored on Brad Daluiso's 35-yard field goal.

Frerotte dropped back and hit Michael Westbrook with a beautiful pass for a 31-yard touchdown and apparent 14-3 lead, but tackle Shar Pourdanesh was flagged for holding and the drive came up empty. Soon after that, Stephen Davis was dropped for a loss on third and one in Giants territory and Washington had to settle for a field goal.

With the door left ajar by Washington's inability to convert opportunities, the Giants crashed through. They got a five-yard TD pass From Danny Kanell to Chris Calloway with just seconds left before halftime. Then disaster struck in the third quarter as

Frerotte threw one interception to Conrad Hamilton and a second to Michael Strahan. The first was returned to the two to set up a short scoring run and defensive end Strahan took his back all the way—24 yards for a touchdown.

Green, getting his first extended NFL action, led one touchdown drive and the Redskins had possession late in the third quarter to try to tie the game. But Green was sacked and stripped of the ball. New York covered at the Washington 22 and scored a touchdown on the next play.

Sep 8

Skins Going Green—Trent Gets Starting Nod
Turner says 'He gave us a chance to win'

Sep 9

Cooke Estate Hangs 'For Sale' Sign on Skins
Bidding for team and stadium will start at $530 million; final price of over $600 million expected

---

9/14/98	49ers (2-0) 45, REDSKINS (0-2) 10				76,798
SF	7	14	7	17	-	45
Was	7	3	0	0	-	10
Was	Shepherd 9 pass from T. Green (Blanton kick).
SF	Owens 20 pass from S. Young (Richey kick)
SF	S. Young 3 run (Richey kick)
Was	FG Blanton 37
SF	Smith 16 pass from S. Young (Richey kick)
SF	Edwards 2 pass from S. Young (Richey kick)
SF	Hearst 5 run (Richey kick).
SF	FG Richey 22
SF	Levy 21 run (Richey kick).

Jack Kent Cooke Stadium—San Francisco toyed with the Redskins for most of the first half before turning it up on both sides of the ball to finish off the Redskins and roll to a 45-10 win.

Trent Green, making his first NFL start, completed four of four on the Redskins first possession—an eight-play, 86-yard drive that culminated in Green's 9-yard touchdown pass to Leslie Shepherd. For the game, Green was 14 of 25 for 201 yards, with the one touchdown and one interception.

The 49ers soon responded with a long drive of their own, moving 83 yards and getting a 20-yard touchdown pass from Steve Young to Terrell Owens. Early in the second quarter, Terry Allen fumbled, the Niners recovered and quickly moved to a three-yard touchdown run by Young.

The Redskins had a chance to tie it, but an unusual facemask penalty on Michael Westbrook negated what would have been a second Green-to-Shepherd touchdown pass, and the Redskins had to settle for a field goal.

They would regret missing the opportunity. San Francisco scored another touchdown before halftime to go up 21-10. The visitors dominated the second half, on their way to rolling up 503 yards of offense on the night.

9/20/98	SEAHAWKS (3-0) 24, Redskins (0-3) 14				63,336
Was	7	0	0	7	-	14
Sea	7	3	14	0	-	24
Sea	Broussard 90 kickoff return (Peterson kick).
Was	Westbrook 36 pass from T. Green (Akers kick).
Sea	FG Peterson 32
Sea	Watters 13 run (Peterson kick).
Sea	Pritchard 21 pass from Moon (Peterson kick).
Was	Westbrook 26 pass from T. Green (Akers kick).

Kingdome—Seattle returned the opening kickoff for a touchdown, and then watched the Redskins make enough mistakes to lose 24-14.

One Trent Green interception stopped a promising drive; another set up an easy six points for the Seahawks. On top of that fumbles and penalties killed whatever chance Washington may have had to recover.

The game got off to an ominous start for the visitors when newly signed kicker David Akers kicked off to Steve Broussard at the 10. Broussard was untouched in the process of taking the kick back all the way.

The Redskins answered with a 68-yard drive that ended with a 36-yard touchdown pass from Green to Michael Westbrook. But missed field goals, interceptions and a Terry Allen fumble helped Seattle run off 17 unanswered points in the second and third quarters to put the Redskins away.

Westbrook caught another Green touchdown pass in the fourth quarter, this one from 26 yards. But it was way too little and far too late.

Washington lost despite out gaining the home team 465 yards to 299. Green piled up 383 yards passing, many of them after the running game had been abandoned in an effort to play catch up.

9/27/98	Broncos (4-0) 38, REDSKINS (0-4) 16				71,880
Den	7	10	14	7	-	38
Was	0	7	3	6	-	16
Den	McCaffrey 19 pass from Brister (Elam kick).
Den	FG Elam 37
Den	Gordon 55 interception return (Elam kick).
Was	Allen 5 run (Blanchard kick)
Den	Davis 42 run (Elam kick)
Den	Griffith 14 pass from Brister (Elam kick).
Was	FG Blanchard 37
Den	Loville 1 run (Elam kick).
Was	Westbrook 75 pass from T. Green (pass failed).

Jack Kent Cooke Stadium—"It's rock bottom," Redskins wide receiver Leslie Shepherd said. "It's 0-and-4. You always say, 'Don't panic. Don't worry.' Well, panic. Worry. We've got to get out of it."

It wasn't quite rock bottom yet, but this one was bad. Bubby Brister was in for an injured John Elway as Denver scored the game's first 17 points on the way to the win.

As in the season's previous three losses, the Redskins played a big role in their own demise. Trent Green's first interception was returned by cornerback Darrien Gordon 55 yards for a touchdown that would give Denver all the points it would need to win. The Redskins were flagged for eight penalties, one of which wiped out a successful field goal attempt. The Redskins fumbled four times, losing one.

The Broncos also helped themselves a great deal. Terrell Davis rushed for 119 yards including a 42-yard TD run early in the third quarter that gave his team a 24-10 lead. Denver never looked back from there.

Sep 30

Cooke Gives Turner Full Support
Says fans 'have every right to be upset' but winning 'is only a matter of time'

Turner Calls SI Criticism 'Very Predictable'

Oct 1—Norv Turner dismissed critical comments about him in a Sports Illustrated article, saying that such statements were par for the course for an 0-5 team.

Some of the shots at Turner were attributed to anonymous players, who ripped the coach for releasing kickers Scott Blanton and David Akers when there were much bigger problems.

"Norv tries to scare guys and act like he'll get rid of them if they don't perform, but nobody believes him," SI quotes one source. "Who did he cut? The kicker? Wow, guys are shaking."

"I'd like people to be accountable for their statements," said Turner.

During a recent game Dana Stubblefield reportedly challenged Turner's leadership on the sideline, an incident that Turner says he barely noticed.

10/5/98	Cowboys (3-2) 31, REDSKINS (0-5) 10				72,284
Dal	3	14	7	7	-	31
Was	7	3	0	0	-	10
Was	Shepherd 40 pass from T. Green (Blanchard kick)
Dal	FG Cunningham 42
Dal	E. Smith 3 run (Cunningham kick)
Dal	Mills 43 pass from Garrett (Cunningham kick)
Was	FG Blanchard 31
Dal	Warren 6 run (Cunningham kick).
Dal	Warren 6 run (Cunningham kick)

RFK Stadium—Washington took a quick 7-0 lead, but the Cowboys ground down the Redskins the rest of the game to take a 31-10 win.

Dallas running backs Emmitt Smith and Chris Warren both topped 100 yards rushing.

The Redskins' touchdown came after Ken Harvey recovered a fumble by quarterback Jason Garrett at midfield. Four plays later, Trent Green threw 40 yards to Leslie Shepherd for a touchdown and a 7-0 Washington lead.

But Green made a key error after Dallas had cut the lead to 7-3 with a 42-yard field goal. The quarterback threw way over the head of tight end Jamie Asher and into the arms of Dallas corner Deion Sanders, who returned the pick 21 yards to the Redskins' 22. Four plays later, Smith went over from three yards out and Dallas had the lead for good.

Dallas expanded their margin to ten points on a 43-yard touchdown pass from Garrett to receiver Ernie Mills. Warren closed it out in the second half with a pair of six-yard touchdown runs.

Green struggled passing all day, completing 13 of 29 attempts for 129 yards. He was sacked four times for 29 yards in losses.

10/11/98	EAGLES (1-5) 17, Redskins (0-6) 12				66,123
Was	0	3	3	6	-	12
Phi	7	3	0	7	-	17
Phi	Peete 19 run (Boniol kick)
Was	FG Blanchard 46
Phi	FG Boniol 44
Was	FG Blanchard 44
Phi	Sinceno 3 pass from Peete (Boniol kick)
Was	Mitchell 1 run (run failed)

Veterans Stadium—This game between 0-5 teams lived down to its billing. It was the Redskins who remained winless as the Eagles dumped them 17-12.

A fumble by Trent Green set up the Eagles' first score, a 19-yard scramble by quarterback Rodney Peete. It was the first of three Washington turnovers.

The second giveaway also cost the Redskins seven points. Struggling for extra yardage near the goal line, Terry Allen coughed the ball up and the Eagles recovered. The Redskins argued in vain that Allen's forward progress had been stopped.

Trailing 10-3 at halftime, Gus Frerotte replaced Trent Green at quarterback and led a comeback attempt. Washington scored on a 44-yard field goal by Kerry Blanchard to pull within 10-6, but Philadelphia answered with a Peete touchdown pass early in the fourth quarter.

Washington got to within striking distance by driving to a one-yard touchdown run by Brian Mitchell. A two-point conversion failed, however, at 17-12 the Redskins needed a touchdown.

A desperation drive that began at the Washington 40 with just over a minute to go ended when a fourth-down pass from Frerotte to Jamie Asher came up a yard short of a first down.

Oct 10

Gus' Turn—Frerotte to Start
Green, 0-5 as starter, heads to bench

10/18/98	VIKINGS (6-0) 41, Redskins (0-7) 7				64,004
Was	7	0	0	0	-	7
Min	14	7	3	17	-	41
Was	Allen 2 run (Blanchard kick)
Min	Glover 11 pass from Cunningham (Anderson kick)
Min	Hoard 1 run (Anderson kick)
Min	Carter 1 pass from Cunningham (Anderson kick)
Min	FG Anderson 49
Min	Smith 19 run (Anderson kick)
Min	FG Anderson 46
Min	Hoard 1 run (Anderson kick)

Metrodome—The Redskins hit "rock bottom" according to Darrell Green, falling to 0-7 in an all-around miserable performance.

"That's as poor a performance as I can say I've ever been involved with," said Norv Turner, who called the Redskins' offense "totally inept."

There isn't much more to say about this one. As they had done three other times prior to this game, the Redskins jumped to a 7-0 lead. A drive culminated in a two-yard touchdown run by Terry Allen. But, as had been the case every other time, the lead soon vaporized in a barrage of mistakes, penalties and other assorted errors.

Oct. 27

Musical QB Chairs Continues, Green to Start
Frerotte unhappy over losing starting job for second time this year

---

Oct. 29

Stubby Slips, Will Miss 3-5 Weeks
$42-million DT Stubblefield injures knee on stairs at home, has surgery

11/1/98	REDSKINS (1-7) 21, Giants (3-5) 14				67,976
NYG	7	0	7	0	-	14
Was	7	7	7	0	-	21
Was	T. Green 1 run (Blanchard kick)
NYG	Patten 90 KO ret (Daluiso kick)
Was	Davis 12 pass from T. Green (Blanchard kick)
Was	Hicks 4 run (Blanchard kick)
NYG	Hilliard 11 pass from Kanell (Daluiso kick)

Jack Kent Cooke Stadium—No turnovers and solid defense ended the seven-game, season opening losing streak, gaining the team its first win in 44 weeks, a 21-14 triumph over the Giants.

Trent Green was reinserted into the starting lineup at quarterback in place of the ineffective Gus Frerotte and Green immediately made Norv Turner's decision look like a good one. Green was four of four passing during a game-opening drive that ended when Green himself ran over from a yard out to put the Redskins ahead 7-0.

But the Redskins had blown early leads in several of their previous losses and it seemed to be "oh, no, here we go again" when David Patten ran the kickoff back 90 yards to tie the score.

This time, it was different. For the first time all year, the Redskins took a lead into halftime on the strength of Green's 12-yard touchdown pass to Stephen Davis. The scoring pass was Green's fifth completion in five attempts during the 11-play, 69-yard drive.

In the unfamiliar position of not having to play catch up in the second half, the Redskins were able to give rookie running back Skip Hicks some work in the third quarter. During a 10-play, 79-yard drive, Hicks gained 50 yards on five carries, including the capper: a four-yard touchdown run.

The score allowed the Redskins to withstand a fourth-quarter score by the Giants and celebrate victory for the first time since Dec 21, 1997.

11/8/98	CARDINALS (5-4) 29, Redskins (1-8) 27		45,950	
Was	3	14	0	10	-	**27**
Ari	0	7	7	15	-	**29**

Was	FG Blanchard 34
Was	Hicks 2 run (Blanchard kick)
Ari	Bates 1 run (Nedney kick)
Was	Mitchell 6 run (Blanchard kick)
Ari	Centers 4 pass from Plummer (Nedney kick)
Ari	Bates 1 run (Nedney kick)
Ari	Safety M. Turk fumbled out of end zone
Ari	FG Nedney 26
Wash	Shepherd 35 pass from Green (Blanchard kick)
Wash	FG Blanchard 54
Ari	FG Nedney 47

Sun Devil Stadium—Opposing kickers made field goals to give their teams the lead in the last 35 seconds for the first time in nearly 30 years. Unfortunately, it was the Cardinals' Joe Nedney that got the last of the two, a 47 yard shot with two seconds left, trumping Carey Blanchard's 54-yarder just 33 seconds earlier.

The game was frustrating for the Redskins for more than just the ending. Brian Mitchell was coasting to a 100-yard touchdown return of the opening kickoff when Patrise Alexander threw an illegal block, negating the return. The Redskins gained a 10-0 lead early in the second quarter on a two-yard run by Skip Hicks. They got the lead back to 10 after the Cardinals scored a touchdown when Mitchell ran in from six yards out in the last minute of the first half.

But they blew all of that lead—and more. Cardinal quarterback Jake Plummer, in the course of completing 15 of 16 second-half passes, led two touchdown drives in the second half. On top of that, punter Matt Turk fumbled a snap in the end zone, giving Arizona two points that would prove decisive. Nedney's field goal with 3:09 left in the game gave the home team a 26-17 lead.

But the Redskins weren't done. They quickly drove to a touchdown on a 35-yard pass from Trent Green to Leslie Shepherd, pulling within two. Stephen Davis recovered an onside kick and suddenly the Redskins had a chance. Green converted a fourth and five with an eight-yard pass to Mitchell and, soon after that, Blanchard's field goal was good with plenty of distance to spare.

Problem was, there was also plenty of time to spare for Plummer. In the remaining 35 seconds, he managed to get off five plays, moving the Cardinals to the Washington 30. From there, Nedney's boot was the killing blow.

11/15/98	REDSKINS (2-8) 28, Eagles (2-8) 3		67,704	
Phi	0	3	0	0	-	**3**
Was	7	7	7	7	-	**28**

Was	Hicks 1 run (Blanchard kick),
Phi	FG Boniol 19
Was	Hicks 1 run (Blanchard kick)
Was	Connell 56 pass from Green (Blanchard kick0
Was	Hicks 5 run (Blanchard kick)

Jack Kent Cooke Stadium—Cris Dishman intercepted two passes and the Redskins sacked Eagle quarterbacks five times to lead the way in a 28-3 Washington win.

From the Philly 20, Eagles quarterback Bobby Hoying tried to throw a screen pass, but defensive end Kelvin Kinney tipped it and tackle Dan Wilkinson picked it off for the Redskins. From the ten, it took three plays for the Redskins to score on Skip Hicks' one-yard run.

The home team dodged a bullet when quarterback Trent Green was sacked and fumbled, with the Eagles recovering on the Washington eight. The Washington defense stiffened, and Philadelphia had to settle for a field goal to make it 7-3.

Runs of 13 and 16 yards by Brian Mitchell were the key plays in a 66-yard drive that ended when Hicks lunged over from the one to give the Redskins a 14-3 lead.

Washington clinched it in the third quarter when Green dodged a blitz to find receiver Albert Connell wide open at the Eagles' 26. Connell took advantage of a Michael Westbrook block to complete the 56-yard touchdown play. Dishman returned one of his interceptions to the Eagles' one and Hicks scored his third touchdown in the fourth quarter to close out the scoring.

11/22/98	Cardinals (6-5) 45, REDSKINS (2-9) 42		63,435	
Ari	17	14	7	7	-	**45**
Was	0	6	21	15	-	**42**

Ari	FG Nedney 26
Ari	McWilliams 6 pass from Plummer (Nedney kick)
Ari	Plummer 1 run (Nedney kick)
Ari	Murrell 13 run (Nedney kick)
Ari	Plummer 10 run (Nedney kick)
Was	Westbrook 15 pass from Green (kick failed)
Was	Westbrook 12 pass from Green (Blanchard kick)
Ari	Centers 9 pass from Plummer (Nedney kick)
Was	Westbrook 11 pass from Green (Blanchard kick)
Was	Shepherd 16 pass from Green
Was	Hicks 5 run (Shepherd pass from Green)
Ari	Plummer 1 run (Nedney kick)
Was	Green 2 run

Jack Kent Cooke Stadium—The Redskins scored six touchdowns in the game's final 31 minutes, but it wasn't enough to overcome a 31-0 deficit as the Cardinals were able to hang on for a 45-42 win.

As had been the pattern for most of the season, things got off to a bad start for the Redskins when, after Arizona went three and out on its first possession, Brian Mitchell muffed a punt. The Cardinals recovered, setting up a 26-yard field goal by Joe Nedney.

That opened the floodgates for Arizona. Before halftime, Jake Plummer threw for one touchdown and ran for two more. Adrian Murrell scored on a 13-yard run in the midst of all that and it was 31-0 Cardinals.

The Redskins began to show a pulse just before halftime. On a third and 15 play, quarterback Trent Green threw to Michael Westbrook on a hitch pattern and the receiver spun, completing the 15-yard touchdown play. A bad snap sent the extra point attempt awry, so it was 31-6 at intermission.

Green and Westbrook connected for another TD early in the third quarter, but Arizona responded when Plummer eluded a near-sack by Kennard Lang and threw a nine-yard touchdown pass to Larry Centers.

Training 38-13, the comeback attempt cranked up in earnest. First, it was another Green to Westbrook scoring hookup. Then Leomont Evans made two big plays. First, he recovered the onside kick following the third Westbrook TD. That set up a 16-yard Green touchdown pass to Leslie Shepherd five plays later.

On the subsequent Arizona possession, Evans intercepted Plummer's pass in the end zone and ran it out 54 yards to the

Cardinal 48. Later, on fourth and one at the Cardinal five, Skip Hicks carried the ball in for the touchdown to pull within five at 38-33. Shepherd caught the two-point conversion on a pass from Green, but he committed what proved to be a fatal error. He spiked the ball in the face of the Cardinals, drawing an unsportsmanlike conduct penalty that was enforced on the ensuing kickoff.

Brett Conway had to kick off from his 15 and the Cardinals started their drive from their own 45. A key third-down completion from Plummer to Frank Sanders kept the drive alive and Plummer finished the drive off with a one-yard sneak on fourth down. Green threw his fourth touchdown pass of the game to make it a three-point game again, but time was running out. Arizona recovered the onside kick. Although they gave up possession on downs to give Washington one last shot, Green threw his only interception of the day with 1:16 left, killing the last chance at a miracle.

The Redskins' 36 second-half points represented the highest-scoring half of football ever for a team that wound up losing.

11/29/98	Redskins (3-9) 29, RAIDERS (7-5) 19					41,409
Was	7	10	2	10	-	29
Oak	7	0	0	12	-	19
Was	Davis 19 pass from T. Green (Blanchard kick)					
Oak	Kaufman 23 run (Davis kick)					
Was	Shepherd 43 pass from T. Green (Blanchard kick)					
Was	FG Blanchard 28					
Was	Safety Boutte tackled Hollas in end zone					
Was	Alexander 2 pass from T. Green (Blanchard kick)					
Oak	Mickens 12 pass from Hollas (2-point try failed)					
Was	FG Blanchard 47					
Oak	Brown 2 pass from Hollas (2-point try failed)					

Oakland/Alameda County Coliseum—The Redskins ran off 19 unanswered points from the first through third quarters and held off the Raiders to win in Oakland by a score of 29-19.

Washington got off to a great start as Brian Mitchell returned the opening kickoff 57 yards to the Oakland 40. That led to a 19-yard touchdown pass from Trent Green to fullback Stephen Davis. After the Raiders went three and out on their ensuing possession, Mitchell got another nice return, this one of 19 yards with a punt. The Redskins couldn't take advantage of the field position as, on first and goal at the three, tight end Stephen Alexander fumbled after catching Green's pass and the Raiders recovered in the end zone.

Oakland then drove 80 yards to a touchdown, scoring on Napoleon Kaufman's 23-yard run. Soon after that, it looked as though the speedy Kaufman would give his team the lead as he broke into the clear on a run from his own 24. Darrell Green chased him down after a gain of 55, however, and the Raiders fumbled the ball away a few plays later.

With the score still tied at seven, Washington had possession at the Oakland 43 following a Sean Barber interception. Green lofted a pass in the general direction of receiver Leslie Shepherd that appeared certain to either be picked off or out of bounds. Cornerback Marquis Walker jumped to make the interception near the goal line, but the ball bounced off the defender and Shepherd drew a bead on it. He managed to come down with it and get both feet inbounds for a 14-7 Washington lead with about six minutes left in the half. Before halftime, Washington drove for a Kerry Blanchard field goal and a 10-point lead.

The Raiders made a change at quarterback, but the change from Jeff George to Bob Hollas did little good. Following a Matt Turk punt that pinned Oakland back to its two yard line, tackle Marc Boutte sacked Hollas in the end zone, forcing a fumble. Hollas recovered his own miscue, but the resulting safety gave Washington a 12-point lead and possession after the ensuing free kick. Davis took a swing pass for 30 yards and then Skip Hicks ran twice for 29 down to the one. On second down from there, a play

fake paralyzed the defense and Alexander was wide open for the touchdown.

The home team did manage two fourth-quarter touchdowns, but never seriously threatened the Redskins' lead.

12/6/98	REDSKINS (4-9) 24, Chargers (5-8) 20					65,713
SD	3	11	3	3	-	20
Was	7	10	0	7	-	24
SD	FG Carney 32					
Was	Thrash 25 pass from T. Green (Blanchard kick)					
SD	FG Carney 27					
Was	Mitchell 101 kickoff return (Blanchard kick)					
SD	Jones 23 pass from Fletcher (Jones pass from Whelihan)					
Was	FG Blanchard 35					
SD	FG Carney 40					
SD	FG Carney 25					
Was	Shepherd 20 pass from T. Green (Blanchard kick)					

Jack Kent Cooke Stadium—Trent Green's 20-yard touchdown pass to Leslie Shepherd with just less than two minutes to play rallied the Redskins past San Diego 24-20.

In the first quarter, Washington drove to a 25-yard scoring pass from Green to receiver James Thrash to take a 7-3 lead. In the second quarter, after a second James Carney field goal had pulled the Chargers within a point, Brian Mitchell took the ensuing kickoff a yard deep in the end zone. What followed was one of the most hard-fought returns you'll ever see.

Mitchell followed James Thrash to get past the initial wall, but he wasn't fast enough to break completely free. For the last 20 yards, he battled off multiple would-be tacklers with a stiff arm and managed to stay in bounds to complete the 101-yard touchdown return.

The Chargers responded with a touchdown and two-point conversion to tie it up. A sack by Jamal Duff forced a fumble that Dan Wilkinson recovered, setting up a 35-yard Kerry Blanchard field goal to push Washington back ahead 17-14 at halftime.

In the third quarter, San Diego controlled the ball for all but about four minutes, but came out of the period with just a tying field goal. The Redskins were unable to move the ball and Carney put his team ahead with his fourth three-pointer of the day, this one from 25 yards out with about four and a half minutes left to play.

The Redskins couldn't move and San Diego regained possession, but had to punt with two and a half minutes left. Mitchell again made a key play, returning the punt 19 yards to the San Diego 44. On the play after the two minute warning, Green pump faked and three players in the secondary bit. That left Shepherd wide open to catch Green's 20-yard touchdown pass for a 24-20 lead. Leomont Evans' interception snuffed out San Diego's final chance at the Washington 36.

Dec 6

Westbrook Out For Season With Neck Injury
Herniated disk threatens career

12/13/98	Redskins (5-9) 28, PANTHERS (2-12) 25					46,940.
Was	14	7	7	0	-	28
Car	3	14	0	8	-	25
Was	Connell 16 pass from Green (Blanchard kick),					
Was	Hicks 4 run (Blanchard kick),					
Car	FG Kasay 26					
Was	Hicks 5 run (Blanchard kick),					
Car	Biakabutuka 29 pass from Beuerlein (Kasay kick),					
Car	Stone recovered blocked punt in end zone (Kasay kick),					
Was	Alexander 17 pass from Green (Blanchard kick)					
Car	Biakabutuka 2 run (Muhammad pass from Beuerlein)					

Ericsson Stadium—The Redskins mounted long scoring touchdown drives on their first three possessions to take a 21-3 lead in the third quarter, but they needed the late interception by Stanley Richard and Darrell Green to hang on for a 28-25 win.

The three drives were textbook material, covering 82, 80 and 79 yards, mixing the run and pass with great effectiveness. The first one culminated in Trent Green's 16-yard pass to Albert Connell. Terry Allen's 45-yard run was the key in that drive.

Carolina threatened to retaliate almost immediately as receiver Muhsin Muhammad took a Steve Beuerlein pass and appeared to be headed for a 65-yard touchdown reception. Cris Dishman was the defender who had been beaten, but he recovered to catch Muhammad from behind and strip the ball away at the Washington two. The ball rolled out of the end zone for a touchback.

The following Washington drive ended when Skip Hicks scampered four yards for a touchdown and a 14-0 lead. On the ensuing kickoff, a Carolina player again appeared headed to a long touchdown play. In fact, Michael Bates did cross the goal line with the ball, but a holding penalty nullified the runback and the Panthers had to settle for a field goal. Washington drove to Hicks' second TD run of the day to take a 21-3 lead with just under four minutes elapsed in the second quarter.

Much of the lead had vanished by halftime. Running back Tshimanga Biakabutuka scored a touchdown on a screen pass from Beuerlein with 2:43 left in the half. Bates then blocked a punt, Dwight Stone recovered in the end zone, and suddenly it was a four-point game at intermission.

In the third quarter, the Redskins regained some measure of control with a 17-yard touchdown from Green that tight end Stephen Alexander made a nice diving catch on. But the Panthers had the answer as Biakabutuka scored on a two-yard run and a two-point conversion pulled Carolina within 28-25 with more than 12 minutes left to play.

With three possessions to either tie or take the lead, Carolina couldn't do it. They punted on the first. Their second opportunity was their best as Biakabutuka turned a short dump-off reception into a 46-yard gain to the Washington 26. On third down at the 19, Beuerlein went for Mark Carrier at the five, but Stanley Richard stepped in front and made the interception to end the threat.

On Carolina's final possession, a couple of sacks led to a fourth and long play and Darrell Green intercepted Beuerlein's desperation heave to secure the win for Washington.

12/20/98	REDSKINS (6-9) 20, Bucs (7-8) 16				66,309	
TB	7	6	3	0	-	16
Was	7	0	0	13	-	20
TB	Moore 8 pass from Dilfer (Husted kick).					
Was	Shepherd 16 run (Blanchard kick).					
TB	FG Husted 20					
TB	FG Husted 42					
TB	FG Husted 24					
Was	FG Blanchard 26					
Was	FG Blanchard 35					
Was	Alexander 15 pass from T. Green (Blanchard kick)					

Jack Kent Cooke Stadium—Stephen Alexander's 15-yard touchdown reception capped a 13-point fourth-quarter rally as the Redskins got past the Bucs by a score of 20-16.

Tampa scored on its first possession, getting an eight-yard touchdown pass from Trent Dilfer to tight end Dave Moore. The

Redskins responded soon after that, with Brian Mitchell getting things started with a 32-yard punt return. Trent Green converted a third and nine with a 12-yard pass to Chris Thomas to keep the drive alive. Then, from the Tampa Bay 16, Green handed off to receiver Albert Connell, who in turn handed it to other receiver Leslie Shepherd. The play used the aggressiveness of the Bucs' defense against itself and Shepherd cut to his left, zipping into the end zone to tie the game at seven.

After that, a fumble by Green set up one Bucs' field goal before Green threw an interception that led to another three-pointer and 13-7 halftime lead for the visitors.

The Redskins were fortunate to come out of the third quarter down by just an additional three points. They mustered just one first down against the stout Buccaneer defense. Tampa Bay's offense controlled the ball, but managed just one more Michael Husted field goal to take what seemed to be a safe 16-7 lead into the fourth quarter.

Connell hauled in a Green pass for 61 yards that set up a Kerry Blanchard field goal to start the Washington comeback. The Redskins got the ball back and mounted another drive to the Tampa 15 where Blanchard again was called on. He delivered again, pulling the Redskins within three with about ten minutes left.

And with just under six minutes left, the Redskins got the break they needed. Tampa Bay's Jacquez Green fumbled a punt and Mike Sellers recovered for Washington at the Bucs' 15. On the next play, Green fired a touchdown pass to Sellers to give the Skins their first lead at 20-16. Interceptions by linebacker Greg Jones and Darrell Green killed Tampa's late bids.

Dec 23
Frerotte: 'I Want to Go Where I Can Start'
Twice-benched '96 Pro Bowl QB has two years left on contract

12/27/98	Cowboys (10-6) 23, Redskins (6-10) 7				63,565	
Was	7	0	0	0	-	7
Dal	3	17	0	3	-	23
Dal	FG Cunningham 27					
Was	Shepherd 6 pass from T. Green (Blanchard kick)					
Dal	Smith 1 run (Cunningham kick)					
Dal	Smith 26 run (Cunningham kick)					
Dal	FG Cunningham 23					
Dal	FG Cunningham 26					

Texas Stadium—The Redskins reverted back to early season form, losing an early lead by committing turnovers and ill-timed penalties in losing to the Cowboys 23-7.

Washington took a 7-3 lead in the first quarter on Trent Green's six-yard touchdown pass to Leslie Shepherd. A 39-yard connection between those same two set up the score.

That was Washington's last score. Dallas took control in the second quarter with two drives that took just eight plays and covered a combined 153 yards. Both drives ended with Emmitt Smith touchdown runs: one from a yard out, the other from 26. Richie Cunningham kicked a 23-yard field goal before halftime and it was 20-7. A listless second half ensured with Cunningham's third field goal of the day providing the only scoring.

1999

Head Coach: Norv Turner
Record: 10-6, NFC East Champions
Playoffs: 1-1, lost in Divisional Playoff

Honors: Stephen Davis Pro Bowl; Brad Johnson Pro Bowl; Tre Johnson Pro Bowl

Cooke Out—Skins Sold For $800 Million

Jan 10—The trustees of the estate of Jack Kent Cooke has signed an agreement to sell the Washington Redskins for a cool $800 million.

Cooke's son, John, was unable to top the bid by New York banker Howard Milstein and Daniel M. Snyder of Bethesda, Md.

The price is over $250 million more than the previous record paid for an NFL franchise. The sale must be approved by three-fourths of the NFL owners.

Jan 20

Free Agent Green On Hold
QB awaits ownership situations, says team is 'strapped' by NFL

QB Shuffle—Green Gone, Vikes' Johnson In

Feb. 15—Redskins fans have been used to quarterbacks shuffling in and out of the lineup, but they've never seen a week quite like this.

After Gus Frerotte, the on-and-off starter since 1994, was waived earlier this week, the other two shoes dropped tonight.

As Trent Green, the starter for most of last season and the man the Redskins wanted to make their quarterback of the future, was signing a free agent contract with the St. Louis Rams, the Redskins were acquiring his replacement.

In a trade with the Minnesota Vikings, the Redskins got Brad Johnson.

They were going to pay a hefty price in either case. Green signed for four years and $16.5 million. Washington had offered him $16 million over four years but had trouble negotiating further due to the team's unsettled ownership situation.

To get Johnson, 30, Washington gave up first- and third-round picks in this year's draft, plus their second-round pick in 2000.

Mar 17

Milstein Group Asks For Delay
Tagliabue grants request, says 'votes are not there';
some owners not happy with financing

Apr 8

Dead Deal: Committee Rejects Sale
Finance group votes down Milstein-Snyder proposal; bidding to restart immediately

Dealing Like Champs-Skins Get Bailey, Picks

Apr 17—The Redskins went into the draft hoping to get Georgia cornerback Champ Bailey with the fifth overall pick. They wound up getting Bailey and a whole lot more.

The key was the New Orleans Saints' strong desire to acquire Texas running back Ricky Williams. When the Heisman Trophy winner was on the board as the fifth pick rolled around, Redskins general manager Charley Casserly pulled the trigger on a deal he had already set up with the Saints.

In exchange for that selection, Washington got the Saints' top pick, 12th overall, plus their third through seventh-round picks this year and their first- and third-rounders in 2000.

Casserly had more dealing to do to get in position to land Bailey, who wouldn't last until the 12th pick. In another deal he already had set up, he sent the Bears that pick plus the third, fourth, and fifth picks he'd just obtained from New Orleans. That netted Chicago's pick, the seventh, and the Redskins snared Bailey with that selection.

Apr 18

Leading Rusher Allen Cut
$3.1 million saved; Davis, Hicks will battle for RB job

Apr 22

New Deal: Snyder is in Line to Buy Team
Cooke withdraws after Snyder constructs new $800 million bid

May 25

Done Deal: NFL Approves Snyder Deal
$800 million sale gets unanimous endorsement

May 26

Snyder Promises 'Active Control'
"Redskin at heart" will have office at Redskins Park

July 23

Casserly Out as Redskins GM
Will stay in consultant role; former 49er executive Vinny Cerrato is Director of Player Personnel

Aug 13

Hurtin' Harvey Hangs It Up
Knee injury hobbled Pro Bowl LB, says 'It was time to go'

Aug 17

What's in a Name? Not Cooke!
Home field now Redskins Stadium until naming rights can be sold; Raljon address also dropped

Sep 1

Davis Wins Running Back Job
Beats out favored Hicks; Peete will be No. 2 QB

9-12-99	Cowboys (1-0) 41, REDSKINS (0-1) 35 (OT)				79,237	
Dal	7	7	0	21	6	**41**
Was	3	10	22	0	0	**35**
Dal	LaFleur 15 pass from Aikman (Cunningham kick)					
Was	FG Conway 25					
Dal	LaFleur 14 pass from Aikman (Cunningham kick)					
Was	Westbrook 41 pass from Johnson (Conway kick)					
Was	FG Conway 24					
Was	Davis 3 run (Davis run)					
Was	Davis 7 run (Blanchard kick)					
Was	Connell 50 pass from Johnson (Conway kick)					
Dal	Smith 1 run (Cunningham kick)					
Dal	Irvin 37 pass from Aikman (Cunningham kick)					
Dal	Irvin 12 pass from Aikman (Cunningham kick)					
Dal	Ismail 76 pass from Aikman					

Redskins Stadium—In a contest that evoked nightmares of Texas Stadium in '79 and of Clint Longley, the Cowboys, behind five TD passes by Troy Aikman, rallied from a 21-point fourth-quarter deficit to a 41-35 overtime win.

The game was three separate contests. The first, in which Dallas outscored the Redskins 14-3, spanned the first quarter and first play of the second. Then it was Washington's turn, scoring 32 unanswered points in the second and third quarters. Brad Johnson made his Redskins debut in grand fashion, continually finding WR's Albert Connell and Michael Westbrook wide open, throwing a scoring pass to each of them. In between those scores, RB Stephen Davis got two touchdowns and added a two-point conversion. The Johnson-to-Connell scoring aerial, from 50 yards out with just over a minute left in the third quarter, seemingly wrapped up the game.

But then phase three of the game began. Dallas crossed up the Redskins by keeping the ball on the ground to score once, and then Aikman went to Michael Irvin twice to tie the score.

The Redskins drove into field goal range and had a chance to win in regulation, but the snap was fumbled and the 41-yard attempt had to be aborted.

On Dallas' first series in OT, Aikman faked into the line, sucking in the entire Redskins secondary. Rocket Ismail was all alone as he gathered in the pass and ran unobstructed into the end zone, finishing the game.

9/19/99	Redskins (1-1) 50, GIANTS (1-1) 21				78,717	
Was	21	12	10	7	-	**50**
NYG	0	14	0	7	-	**21**
Was	Davis 1 run (Conway kick)					
Was	Davis 1 run (Conway kick)					
Was	Davis 19 run (Conway kick)					
NYG	Way 7 run (Daluiso kick)					
Was	Barber 70 INT return (kick blocked)					
NYG	Johnson 11 run (Daluiso kick)					
Was	Alexander 1 pass from Johnson (2 pt. conversion failed)					
Was	FG Conway 48					
Was	Westbrook 15 pass from Johnson (Conway kick)					
Was	Alexander 27 pass from Johnson (Conway kick)					
NYG	Hilliard 7 pass from Graham (Daluiso kick)					

Giants Stadium—The Redskins scored early and often on their way to a 50-21 rout of the Giants.

Stephen Davis scored three first-quarter TD's as the Redskins amassed 165 yards of offense and 12 first downs in the opening frame alone. The third touchdown was made on second effort as Davis found nothing up the middle, bounced back and scooted around left end. Receiver Michael Westbrook was there to serve as an escort, but he didn't have to block anyone; the Giants seemed to think the whistle had blown. The two strolled the 19 yards into the end zone.

The Giants seemed poised to mount a comeback in the second quarter. They had scored one touchdown and were driving for another until linebacker Shawn Barber picked off a pass and went 70 yards the other way to make it 27-7.

The competitive phase of the game was over, but the Redskins weren't done as Brad Johnson, who went 20 of 28 for 231 yards, threw two touchdown passes to tight end Stephen Alexander and one to Westbrook.

The second scoring pass to Alexander pushed the Redskins point total to 50, their best single-game scoring total ever in a road game and their fifth-best in any game.

9/26/99	Redskins (2-1) 27, JETS (0-3) 20				78,161	
Was	0	10	3	14	-	**27**
NYJ	7	0	7	6	-	**20**
NYJ	Ward 35 pass from Mirer (Hall kick)					
Was	FG Conway 26					
Was	Davis 1 run (Conway kick)					
Was	FG Conway 50					
NYJ	Martin 3 run (Hall kick)					
NYJ	FG Hall 37					
Was	Davis 4 run (Conway kick)					
Was	Davis 7 run (Conway kick)					
NYJ	FG Hall 34					

Giants Stadium—Stephen Davis scored three touchdowns, the last two moving the Redskins from a 17-13 deficit with eight minutes left to a 27-20 win.

New York scored first on a touchdown pass from Rick Mirer to Dedric Ward. The Redskins then seemingly took control, with Davis' first touchdown being sandwiched by a pair of Brett Conway field goals.

But Washington couldn't put the Jets away and New York decided to get back into it. Curtis Martin scored on a three-yard run late in the third quarter and John Hall kicked a field goal with 8:10 left in the game. Suddenly, the Redskins were down 17-13.

The Redskins' offense responded by going 80 yards to a four-yard Davis touchdown run, retaking the lead at 20-17 with 4:11 remaining. On the Jets' next series, defensive end Kennard Lang stripped Mirer of the ball and tackle Dan Wilkinson recovered at the Jets' 21. Four plays later, Davis ran in for the clinching score.

On the day, Davis rushed for 93 yards on 24 attempts. Martin picked up 85 on 20 carries while Bernie Parmalee provided effective relief with 51 yards in 10 tries.

10/3/99	REDSKINS (3-1) 38, Panthers (1-3) 36				76,831	
Car	21	3	3	9	-	**36**
Was	0	28	7	3	-	**38**
Car	Biakabutuka 60 run (Kasay kick)					
Car	Biakabutuka 1 run (Kasay kick)					
Car	Biakabutuka 45 run (Kasay kick)					
Was	S. Davis 1 run (Conway kick)					
Car	FG Kasay 43					
Was	Westbrook 17 pass from B. Johnson (Conway kick)					
Was	Westbrook 11 pass from B. Johnson (Conway kick)					
Was	Connell 62 pass from B. Johnson (Conway kick)					
Was	Connell 32 pass from B. Johnson (Conway kick)					
Car	FG Kasay 43					
Car	FG Kasay 42					
Car	Walls 6 pass from Beuerlein (pass failed),					
Was	FG Conway 31					

Redskins Stadium—Washington matched the biggest comeback win in the team's history with a 38-36 win over Carolina.

The Redskins spent the first quarter trying and failing to catch Carolina's Tim Biakabutuka. The RB scored on runs of 60, one and 45 yards as Carolina built a 21-0 lead in the first nine minutes of the game.

The Redskins recovered nicely, taking a 28-24 lead before halftime on Brad Johnson's third TD pass of the second quarter, a 62-yard bomb to a wide-open Albert Connell. After another Johnson-to-Connell scoring connection built the lead to 35-24, Carolina clawed back into the lead. A pair of field goals and a touchdown pass gave the Panthers a one-point lead halfway through the fourth quarter.

All seemed lost when Brian Mitchell fumbled after fielding a punt and Carolina recovered. However, the Redskins retained possession when replays revealed the Mitchell's knee had hit the ground prior to the fumble. The Redskins took full advantage of their second life. Soon after Stephen Davis converted a fourth and one near midfield at the two-minute warning, Johnson found Michael Westbrook for 19 yards to the Carolina 12. Brett Conway's game-winning 31-yard FG came with six seconds left.

10/17/99	**Redskins (4-1) 24, CARDINALS (2-4) 10**				55,893	
Was	0	10	7	7	-	**24**
Ari	3	0	0	7	-	**10**
Ari	FG Jacke 44					
Was	FG Conway 36					
Was	Bailey 59 INT return (Conway kick)					
Was	Alexander 1 pass from Johnson (Conway kick)					
Ari	Moore 10 pass from Brown (Jacke kick)					
Was	Hicks 14 run (Conway kick)					

Sun Devil Stadium—Champ Bailey returned one of his three interceptions 59 yards for a touchdown that sparked the team to score 17 straight points in the Redskins' win.

Arizona got on the board first with field goal and Washington responded in the second quarter with a 36-yard field goal by Brett Conway.

With the game tied at three in the second quarter, Arizona quarterback Jake Plummer tried to hit David Boston on a third and ten play from the Washington 49. Bailey stepped in front of the receiver, intercepted the ball and was gone down the sidelines to give the Redskins a 10-3 lead.

Plummer left the game early in the third quarter when he broke a finger after getting it caught in blitzing linebacker Sean Barber's helmet. The Redskins expanded their lead in the third quarter on a 14-yard touchdown pass from Brad Johnson to Stephen Alexander. Arizona threatened to make a game of it in the fourth quarter when Dave Brown, Plummer's replacement, threw a 10-yard touchdown pass to Rob Moore. But the Redskins sealed it a short time later a 14-yard run by Skip Hicks.

10/24/99	**COWBOYS (4-2) 38, Redskins (4-2) 20**				64,377	
Was	0	10	10	0	-	**20**
Dal	10	7	7	14	-	**38**
Dal	Ismail 13 pass from Aikman (Cunningham kick)					
Dal	FG Cunningham 32					
Dal	Smith 1 run (Cunningham kick)					
Was	Sellers 33 pass from Johnson					
Was	FG Conway 36					
Was	FG Conway 24					
Dal	Lafleur 4 pass from Aikman (Cunningham kick)					
Was	Connell 44 pass from Johnson (Conway kick)					
Dal	Aikman 1 run (Cunningham kick)					
Dal	Sanders 70 punt return (Cunningham kick)					

Texas Stadium—The Redskins clawed back from a 17-0 deficit to pull within 17-13 and 24-20, but Dallas converted key plays to pull away in the fourth quarter.

It appeared that the rout was on as the Cowboys seemed to have the Redskins intimidated early on. On Dallas' first eight possessions, they got four touchdowns and a field goal. The Redskins did manage to stay in the game on the strength of a pair of Brad Johnson touchdown passes. The first went to Mike Sellers and broke the scoring ice for Washington, putting them within 17-7 in the second quarter. The second was a 44-yard bomb to Albert

Connell and it appeared that the battle was joined as that made it 24-20 late in the third quarter.

Dallas got the ball at its own seven after the kickoff and soon faced a third and 19. But nickel back Darryl Pounds was flagged for a pass interference penalty and the drive was alive. They went the whole 93 yards with quarterback Troy Aikman culminating the march with a one-yard TD run. Deion Sanders added insult to his own injury—he had been knocked out of the game with a concussion earlier—by returning a punt 70 yards to close out the scoring.

Oct. 27

FedEx Deliver Big Bucks to Redskins
$200 million deal for stadium naming rights

10/31/99	**REDSKINS (5-2) 48, Bears (3-5) 22**				77,621	
Chi	0	0	14	8	-	**22**
Was	14	17	14	3	-	**48**
Was	Davis 76 run (Conway kick)					
Was	Wilkinson 88 INT return (Conway kick)					
Was	FG Conway 50					
Was	Johnson 1 run (Conway kick)					
Was	Westbrook 13 pass from Johnson (Conway kick)					
Was	Davis 2 run (Conway kick)					
Was	Centers 22 pass from Johnson (Conway kick)					
Chi	Robinson 30 pass from McNown (Boniol kick)					
Chi	Robinson 52 pass from McNown (Boniol kick)					
Was	FG Conway 51					
Chi	Wetnight 3 pass from McNown (McNown run)					

Redskins Stadium—Stephen Davis' 75-yard touchdown run in the game's first minute and Dan Wilkinson's 88-yard rumble with an interception keyed a 48-22 rout of the Bears.

Davis' score started a 45-0 run for the Redskins and Wilkinson's interception was one of five takeaways for the Washington defense. Davis' run came as the fans were barely settled in their seats. He got a huge hole up the middle and was gone.

The Bears tried to respond by driving to the Washington 10. As quarterback Shane Matthews went back to pass, defensive end Marco Coleman nailed him, causing the ball to flutter into the air. "Big Daddy," listed at a svelte 313 pounds, grabbed it out of the air and began the long journey to pay dirt. Darrell Green pulled up beside him for the last half of the journey and played the role of both escort and cheerleader, urging Wilkinson into the end zone.

"Not in my wildest dreams did I think I could go 88 yards," Wilkinson said. Neither did the Bears or anyone else watching at the stadium.

The play took the fight out of the Bears and the Redskins got two more touchdowns before halftime. The first came on a broken play when quarterback Brad Johnson bobbled the snap, recovered, and went around the end to a one-yard scoring run and the second when Michael Westbrook made a spectacular catch of a Johnson pass for a 13-yard TD. It was 31-0 at the half.

After two more Washington TD's in the third quarter made it 45-0, play began to get sloppy. The Bears drove to a 30-yard scoring pass from Cade McNown to receiver Marcus Robinson and then recovered an onside kick to set up TD connection between the same pair, but it was all window dressing.

Davis wound up with 143 yards on just 12 carries and Johnson was a very efficient 15 of 25 for 204 yards with no interceptions and two touchdowns.

11/7/99	**Bills (6-3) 34, REDSKINS (5-3) 17**			78,721	
Buf	3	14	14	3	-	34
Was	7	3	0	7	-	17
Was	Davis 8 run (Conway kick)
Buf	FG Christie 23
Buf	Collins 6 pass from Flutie (Christie kick)
Was	FG Conway 41
Buf	Smith 1 run (Christie kick)
Buf	Smith 10 run (Christie kick)
Buf	Moulds 14 pass from Flutie (Christie kick)
Was	Connell 16 pass from Johnson (Conway kick)
Buf	FG Christie 21

Redskins Stadium—Thanks to 204 rushing yards and crucial plays by quarterback Doug Flutie, the Bills controlled the ball for 41 minutes and pulled away in the second half for the win over the Redskins.

Washington started out well with a snappy, efficient touchdown drive that covered 66 yards in eight plays. Brad Johnson passed to Michael Westbrook for 23 yards to the Buffalo 40, then Westbrook took a handoff on an end around for 11 more. After that it was Stephen Davis' turn as he caught a screen pass for 21 yards to the 12. He found a solid wall of blockers a couple of plays later and scored from the eight for a 7-0 lead.

But that represented the high water mark for the Redskins as Buffalo outscored them 31-3 through the third quarter. After getting a Steve Christie field goal, the Bills drove for their first touchdown. Flutie made the key play in that drive with a 13-yard scramble on third and three.

After the Redskins tied the game on a 41-yard Brett Conway field goal, Flutie kept his team's go-ahead drive alive with as spectacular an eight-yard run as you'll ever see. He made two Redskins miss as he darted to the Washington 15 to convert a fourth and five. Soon after that, Antowain Smith scored on a one-yard run 21 seconds before halftime and Buffalo had a 17-10 lead.

A 14-yard Flutie scramble preceded Smith's ten-yard TD run in the third quarter and, later in the period, Flutie pitched a 14-yard scoring pass to Eric Moulds to break it open for Buffalo.

11/14/99	**EAGLES (3-7) 35, Redskins (5-4) 28**			66,591	
Was	14	7	0	7	-	28
Phi	10	3	11	11	-	35
Was	Davis 2 run (Conway kick)
Phi	FG Johnson 49
Was	Connell 54 pass from Johnson (Conway kick)
Phi	Rossum 89 kickoff return (Johnson kick)
Was	Davis 1 run (Conway kick)
Phi	FG Johnson 29
Phi	FG Johnson 20
Phi	Staley 20 run (McNabb run)
Phi	FG Johnson 30
Was	Westbrook 43 pass from Johnson (Conway kick)
Phi	Bienemy 11 run (McNabb pass to Weaver)

Veterans Stadium—The Redskins turned the ball over six times and threw in some untimely penalties, special teams breakdowns and mental errors for good measure in losing an ugly game to the Eagles by a score of 35-28.

Washington bolted to a 14-3 lead on Stephen Davis' two-yard touchdown run and a 54-yard touchdown pass from Brad Johnson to Albert Connell. The Eagles served notice, though, that they were not going to be the victims of the anticipated rout as Allen Rossum returned the kickoff after the second score 89 yards for a touchdown.

After Davis scored his second touchdown to put the Redskins up 21-10, the self-destruction commenced. An interception and fumble gave the Eagles great field position in Washington territory, but the defense held them to field goals both times—the lead was down to 21-16. Late in the third quarter Philly drove for a

touchdown and rookie quarterback Donovan McNabb, making his first NFL start, ran in for the two-point conversion. The Eagles led 24-21.

A field goal following another interception pushed the Philadelphia lead to 27-21 before the Redskins offense got it going again. They drove 91 yards in two plays, both of them Brad Johnson bombs to Michael Westbrook. The first covered 48 yards, the second 43 for the score and a 28-27 lead with just over four minutes elapsed in the fourth quarter.

It appeared that the Redskins might hang on as they were driving into Eagle territory midway through the fourth quarter. Cornerback Al Harris, however, stripped the ball from Connell—it went down as an interception as Connell never had control—at the 33 and returned it to midfield with 5:49 left.

On third and eight from the 48, it once again appeared that the Redskins would escape from the Vet alive as Matt Stevens intercepted McNabb's pass and returned it deep into Eagle territory. However, the officials huddled—never a good sign on the road. The ruling was that a facemask penalty away from the ball by cornerback Mark McMillian negated the interception and the Eagles retained possession. Again, the Redskins' hopes were raised as McNabb's third-down pass fell incomplete, but Washington was flagged for holding, giving the Eagles an automatic first down. After that, Philly ran through a dispirited defense to Eric Bienemy's 11-yard touchdown run. They again converted for two points to take a seven-point lead with 3:17 to play.

In attempting to answer, the Redskins converted one fourth down, but Johnson was sacked on fourth and four at the Eagle 28 to end it.

11/21/99	**REDSKINS (6-4) 23, Giants (5-5) 13**			78,641	
NYG	0	6	0	7	-	13
Was	7	3	3	10	-	23
Was	Davis 1 run (Conway kick)
NYG	FG Blanchard 44
Was	FG Conway 44
NYG	FG Blanchard 44
Was	FG Conway 21
Was	Coleman 42 fumble return (Conway kick)
NYG	Way 1 run (Blanchard kick)
Was	FG Conway 37

FedEx Field—Tough defense and the power running of Stephen Davis led the Redskins to a 23-13 win over the Giants.

Davis, who rushed for 183 yards on the day, ran one yard for a touchdown to cap an eight-play, 55-yard drive in the first quarter to give Washington a 7-0 lead. After that, touchdowns became very difficult to come by for the Redskins. Following a New York field goal, a 49-yard run by Davis to the Giants 11 resulted in just a Brett Conway field goal. New York answered with another three points before halftime and it was 10-6.

It was still tight at 13-6 when, on the first play of the fourth quarter, Ndukwe Kalu forced New York quarterback Kerry Collins to fumble. Fellow defensive end Marco Coleman picked it up and ran 42 yards for a touchdown, making it 20-6.

The Giants answered with a one-yard run by Charles Way and seemed to have stopped the Redskins on the subsequent drive, but a personal foul penalty on the Giants kept the drive alive. Conway kicked the clinching field goal in the last minute.

11/28/99	REDSKINS (7-4) 20, Eagles (3-9) 17 (OT)				74,741.	
Phi	0	3	0	14	0	17
Was	3	7	7	0	3	20

Was	FG Conway 43
Was	Sellers 6 pass from Johnson (Conway kick)
Phi	FG Johnson 34
Was	Davis 1 run (Conway kick)
Phi	Broughton 3 pass from McNabb (Johnson kick),
Phi	Broughton 26 pass from McNabb (Johnson kick),
Was	FG Conway 27

FedEx Field—After missing a game-winning field goal at the end of regulation, Brett Conway converted a 27-yard three-pointer in overtime to pull the game out for the Redskins.

For the game's first three quarters, it didn't seem likely that any late heroics would be necessary. Washington built a 10-0 lead on Conway's 43-yard field goal in the first quarter and a six-yard touchdown pass from Brad Johnson to Mike Sellers. The Eagles got a field goal to make it 10-3 at halftime, but the home team responded with a one-yard Stephen Davis run in the third period. The Redskins were cruising at 17-3.

Things began to get a bit less comfortable as the Eagles embarked on an 18-play drive that bridged the third and fourth quarter. The march consumed nearly nine minutes and culminated in Donovan McNabb's three-yard touchdown pass to tight end Luther Brighton.

The Eagles got the ball back and drove in to tie the game with 1:52 left. McNabb scrambled for 26 yards to get into Washington territory, then dumped a short pass to Brighton, who broke some tackles to turn it into a 26-yard touchdown reception to tie the game at 17.

The stunned crowd came back to life as Brian Mitchell returned the ensuing kickoff 45 yards and the Redskins moved into range for a chip-shot opportunity for Conway, but he missed the 28-yard attempt with five seconds left to force overtime.

Again a long kickoff return, this one 48 yards by James Thrash, gave the home team a short field to work with. On third down from the Eagle two, Norv Turner called on Conway. It was a good thing they had a margin for error as holder Johnson fumbled the snap and fell on it at the nine. On fourth down, the hold was good and the kick was true.

12/5/99	LIONS (8-4) 33, Redskins (7-5) 17				77,693	
Was	3	7	7	0	-	17
Det	0	20	0	13	-	33

Was	FG Conway 42
Det	FG Hanson 50
Was	Thrash 95 kickoff return (Conway kick)
Det	Moore 23 pass from Frerotte (Hanson kick)
Det	Howard 68 punt return (Hanson kick
Det	FG Hanson 45
Was	Westbrook 39 pass from Johnson (Conway kick)
Det	FG Hanson 37
Det	FG Hanson 52
Det	Ellis 11 fumble return (Hanson kick)

Pontiac Silverdome—The Redskins had as much to do with ending their 18-game winning streak versus Detroit as the Lions did. Washington came unraveled in the Silverdome, committing 14 penalties, allowing five sacks, throwing two interceptions and fumbling six times.

It's not that Detroit did nothing to earn its win. Two former Redskins, in fact, contributed greatly to their former team's demise. Quarterback Gus Frerotte threw a 23-yard scoring pass to receiver Herman Moore and Desmond Howard took a punt back 68 yards for another touchdown. Those tallies and two Jason Hanson field goals accounted for a 20-point second-quarter

outburst that put the Lions up 20-10 at the half. James Thrash's 95-yard return of the kickoff following Hanson's first field goal was the only play keeping the Redskins in the game.

The Washington offense finally scratched in the third quarter on a 39-yard pass from Brad Johnson to Michael Westbrook to close the score to 20-17. But the Redskins made too many mistakes to complete the comeback. A sack of Johnson and the quarterback's fumble that the Lions returned 11 yards for the final touchdown was the final and fatal error.

12/13/99	REDSKINS (8-5) 28, Cardinals (6-7) 3				75,851	
Ari	3	0	0	0	-	3
Was	7	14	0	7	-	28

Was	Davis 50 run (Conway kick)
Ari	FG Jacke 31
Was	Fryar 7 pass from Johnson (Conway kick)
Was	Westbrook 25 pass from Johnson (Conway kick)
Was	Hicks 11 run (Conway kick)

FedEx Field—Four minutes into the game, Stephen Davis took a handoff, found a hole that was both wide and deep, ran through it and coasted 50 yards for a touchdown.

Arizona was caught in a blitz on the play and the Redskins had a quick 7-0 lead on their way to a 28-3 win.

Davis ran for 189 yards on the day.

The Cardinals responded with a field goal later in the first quarter to pull within 7-3. The Redskins, however, took control of the game before halftime with two Brad Johnson touchdown passes. The first went to Irvin Fryar and covered seven yards. Then Johnson found Michael Westbrook from 25 yards out to the Redskins a 21-3 halftime lead.

The Redskins' defense kept the Cardinals at bay all day. Arizona got just 173 yards of offense, including 53 on the ground, and Washington intercepted quarterback Jake Plummer three times.

That allowed the offense to operate on cruise control most of the second half. Backup running back Skip Hicks capped the scoring with an 11-yard touchdown run in the fourth quarter.

12/19/99	COLTS (12-2) 24, Redskins (8-6) 21				57,013	
Was	3	10	0	8	-	21
Ind	7	3	0	14	-	24

Ind	James 37 pass from Manning (Vanderjagt kick)
Was	FG Conway 23
Was	Connell 48 pass from Johnson (Conway kick)
Ind	FG Vanderjagt 43
Was	FG Conway 32
Ind	Dilger 1 pass from Manning (Vanderjagt kick)
Ind	James 2 run (Vanderjagt kick)
Was	Mitchell 6 run (Westbrook pass from Johnson)

RCA Dome—The Colts scored two fourth quarter touchdowns to erase a 13-10 Washington lead and then held off a late rally by the visitors to claim the win.

Running back Edgerrin James scored Indy's first touchdown on a 37-yard pass from Payton Manning. The Redskins responded quickly, getting a 29-yard kickoff return to start their drive at their own 40. Stephen Davis converted a key third and one play and then a 25-yard aerial from Brad Johnson to Stephen Alexander got them down to the Colt 12. The defense stiffened there and Brett Conway got his team on the board with a 23-yard field goal.

A second-quarter turnover helped get the Redskins into the lead. Manning was pressured by a blitz, was sacked and fumbled, with Sam Shade making the recovery at the Washington 42. Three plays later, Johnson unleashed a bomb that Albert Connell gathered in for a 48-yard touchdown and a 10-7 Washington lead.

The teams exchanged field goals before halftime, but the Redskins came out it for the worse. Davis, the NFL's leading rusher, had 70 first-half yards on the ground, but had to come out with a sprained ankle late in the second period. That put a serious crimp in the Washington offense for the remainder of the game.

Indianapolis was unable to take advantage of the Skins' lack of offense, though, until late in the third period. In the final three minutes of the quarter, they drove from their own 20 to the Washington one. James got the final 20 yards on a nice run as time expired in the third. On the first play of the fourth quarter, the Colts reclaimed the lead on Manning's one-yard pass to tight end Ken Dilger. Then the Colts blocked a Conway field goal attempt, setting up a 51-yard drive to another James touchdown and a 24-13 lead.

Then the Washington offense finally came to life. One drive ended with a failed fourth and four conversion attempt at the Colt 26 when Mitchell came up with three yards. The next got the Redskins what they needed—a touchdown, on a six-yard run by Mitchell, and a two-point conversion, on a pass from Johnson to Michael Westbrook. That made it 24-21 with 1:24 left.

The Redskins got one last chance when James Thrash zeroed in on Conway's bouncing onside kick and recovered for Washington. A first-down sack put them in a hole, however, and Johnson's fourth-down pass sailed over Westbrook's head to end their chances.

Turner Denies Buyout Story

Dec 21—Norv Turner today refused to comment on a published story that he was considering taking a buyout from the remaining two years of his contract.

Turner reportedly was tired of dealing with new team owner Daniel Snyder.

Turner may or may not have an option if the Redskins fail to make the playoffs. Snyder has let it be known that Turner will be gone if the Redskins don't make the playoffs, something they haven't done in Turner's previous five years as head coach.

However, the Redskins are on the verge of clinching a spot in the postseason and if Snyder is true to his word and retains the coach, Turner will have to decide if he wants to stay.

12/26/99	Redskins (9-6) 26, 49ERS (4-11) 20				68,329	
Was	0	7	3	10	6	**26**
SF	7	6	7	0	0	**20**
SF	Garner 4 run (Richey kick)					
Was	Westbrook 65 pass from Johnson (Conway kick)					
SF	FG Richey 29					
SF	FG Richey 25					
Was	FG Conway 47					
SF	Stokes 5 pass from Garcia (Richey kick)					
Was	FG Conway 34					
Was	Johnson 1 run (Conway kick)					
Was	Centers 33 pass from Johnson					

3Com Park—Brad Johnson capped a comeback from a 10-point fourth-quarter deficit with a 33-yard touchdown pass to fullback Larry Centers to beat San Francisco in overtime. The Redskins had clinched a playoff spot before taking the field but had to survive some scary moments before escaping with a 26-20 win.

The Niners scored first, consuming more than seven minutes of the first quarter to drive 80 yards to Charlie Garner's four-yard touchdown run. In the second period, the Redskins managed an 80-yard TD drive of their own, but this one was much quicker, taking just four plays and two minutes. After Johnson converted a third and five with a 10-yard completion to Irvin Fryar, he unloaded a 65-yard touchdown pass to Michael Westbrook. The score was tied at seven.

Garner was the featured player in two San Francisco drives to field goals, giving them a 13-7 halftime lead. On the first one, his

26-yard reception from Jeff Garcia got his team to the Washington 15, setting up a 29-yarder by Wade Richey. On the next drive, he carried the ball 17 yards to the Washington seven and Richey booted a 25-yard field goal with 1:28 left in the half.

In the second half, the Redskins were still unable to mount a sustained drive, but did get a Brett Conway field goal after Johnson's 47-yard completion to Albert Connell about midway through the third quarter. The Niners answered, driving 78 yards to Jeff Garcia's five-yard touchdown pass to receiver J. J. Stokes to stretch the lead to 20-10 entering the fourth quarter.

Matt Steven's interception set up a 34-yard Conway field goal to pull Washington within a touchdown with a little less than three minutes elapsed in the fourth. The Redskins regained possession about midway through the quarter and embarked on a game-tying drive. The march appeared over when Johnson's 20-yard pass to Irving Fryar was ruled to have hit the ground before the receiver gathered it in at the San Francisco 11, but a replay reversal gave them new life. Johnson soon scored on a one-yard sneak with 3:28 remaining.

Garcia scrambled for 25 yards and it appeared that the Skins' efforts would be for naught as San Francisco moved into field goal range. Then Sean Barber made a game-saving play as he stripped the ball away from running back Terry Jackson. Anthony Cook recovered at the Washington 21 to preserve the tie and send it into overtime.

Washington won the toss and it took just four plays to cover 78 yards to end it: a 25-yard pass from Johnson to running back Skip Hicks, an eight-yard connection between the same two, a 12-yard run by Centers and Johnson's easy pass to Centers, who was all alone near the right sideline and jogged in for the 33-yard touchdown.

Dec 28

Turner, Snyder Agree: Norv to Stay On
Owner says he will retain coach; Turner says he won't resign but status of some assistants uncertain

---

1/2/00	REDSKINS (10-6) 21, Dolphins (9-7) 10				78,106	
Mia	0	3	0	7	-	**10**
Was	0	7	7	7	-	**21**
Was	Hicks 8 run (Conway kick)					
Mia	FG Mare 29					
Was	Fryar 30 pass from Peete (Conway kick)					
Was	Centers 4 pass from Peete (Conway kick)					
Mia	Gadsden 4 pass from Huard (Mare kick)					

FedEx Field—Backup quarterback Rodney Peete threw two touchdown passes to lead the Redskins past Miami 21-10. Both teams had locked in their playoff positions before kickoff, so this amounted to an exhibition game.

A pass interference call set up the lone first-half touchdown. The call gave the Redskins 41 yards to the Miami eight and Skip Hicks zipped around the left side for the score from there.

Peete replaced Brad Johnson after intermission and his first big contribution was running interference for James Thrash, throwing a key block to spring the receiver for a 37-yard gain on a reverse. Then Peete capped the drive with a 30-yard touchdown pass to Irving Fryar.

Things got very sloppy after that as both coaches substituted liberally.

Wild Card Playoff Game
Saturday, January 8, 2000
FedEx Field
Landover, Maryland

1/8/00	REDSKINS 27, Lions 13					79,411
Det	0	0	0	13	-	13
Was	14	13	0	0	-	27
Was	Davis 1 run (Conway kick)					
Was	Davis 4 run (Conway kick)					
Was	FG Conway 33					
Was	FG Conway 23					
Was	Connell 30 pass from Johnson (Conway kick)					
Det	Rice 94 blocked FG return (2-point conversion failed)					
Det	Rivers 5 pass from Frerotte (Hanson kick)					

Stephen Davis ran for 119 yards and two TD's before leaving the game before halftime with an injured knee. Washington wrapped this one up in the first half, racking up 275 yards of offense and intercepting two Gus Frerotte passes. The Redskins coasted to a 27-13 win.

It was not a good homecoming to Washington for Frerotte, the Redskins' former quarterback. Besides the two interceptions, linebacker Greg Jones sacked him on the game's very first snap from scrimmage, dislocating the quarterback's left pinky.

As the game wore on and the points piled up for Washington, it got worse and worse for Frerotte. "When you have to throw it on every down, they're going to come flying at you," Frerotte said after the game. "It's like a big buffet for those defensive linemen." The Redskin defense feasted on the Lions for five sacks.

The Redskin got fat on Lion penalties during their first drive. A roughing the punter penalty kept it alive after a three and out start and a pass interference call moved Washington from the Detroit 42 to the one. Davis went over from there and it was 7-0.

On their next possession, Davis cut behind a block from guard Keith Sims on the left side, cut towards the sideline and was off for a 58-yard gain. Soon after that, Davis scored from the four.

Champ Bailey's interception set up a field goal by Brett Conway and on their next drive, Brad Johnson handed to Davis five straight times to set up another Conway three-pointer to make the score 20-0. Shortly before halftime, the competitive phase of the game ended when Johnson connected with Albert Connell for a 30-yard touchdown pass.

With a 27-0 lead, the Redskins got conservative—and a bit sloppy. In the fourth quarter, the Lions blocked a field goal attempt and Ron Rice picked it up and returned it 94 yards for a touchdown. On the very last play of the game, Frerotte got off a five-yard touchdown pass to Ron Rivers to make the final look a bit more respectable.

T. Johnson Won't Miss a Game

Jan 10—The Redskins can exhale. The Banga won't miss a playoff game.

A suspension was thought to be a possibility for Pro Bowl Guard Tre Johnson after he accidently struck an official during a fight in the Redskins' playoff win over Detroit.

This does not mean that Johnson's conduct will not draw some sort of sanction, including a fine and a suspension for a game next season.

"The only thing being ruled out is a suspension from Saturday's game," Greg Aiello, the NFL's vice president of public relations, said from New York.

NFC Divisional Playoff
Sunday, January 16, 2000
Raymond James Stadium
Tampa, Florida

1/16/00	BUCS 14, Redskins 13					65,835
Was	0	3	10	0	-	13
TB	0	0	7	7	-	14
Was	FG Conway 28					
Was	Mitchell 100 KO return (Conway kick)					
Was	FG Conway 48					
TB	Alstott 2 run (Gramatica kick)					
TB	Davis 1 pass from King (Gramatica kick)					

The Redskins were eliminated from the playoffs despite holding a 13-0 lead late in the third quarter. A good bounce kept the Bucs go-ahead drive alive and a bad snap denied Brett Conway a shot at a game-winning field goal.

Both teams struggled offensively in the first half and Washington led 3-0 on Conway's 28-yard field goal late in the half, which was the only score.

Brian Mitchell changed that when he took the second-half kickoff at the goal line, found a seam and sought daylight as he cut to the right. He dismissed kicker Martin Gramatica with a stiff arm and outran a couple more Bucs into the end zone. It was the longest kick return in NFL playoff history and, more importantly, gave the Redskins a 10-0 lead. Darrell Green's interception and Conway's subsequent 48-yard field goal stretched the lead to 13-0 midway through the third quarter.

The Redskins got the ball back and were moving into Tampa Bay territory when Brad Johnson overthrew his intended receiver and John Lynch intercepted at the 27. The Bucs offense suddenly came to life, driving 73 yards in six plays to Mike Alstott's two-yard, second-effort touchdown run.

The game then turned on a pair of fumbles by the opposing quarterbacks. Johnson was sacked, fumbled, and Warren Sapp recovered for the Bucs at the Washington 32. Three plays later on third and three at the 25, Tampa quarterback Shaun King was sacked and stripped by linebacker Sean Barber. The ball managed to find running back Warrick Dunn, who gladly scooped up the gift and ran 13 yards for a first down. Then Alstott converted a fourth and one with a five-yard gain to the three. On third and goal at the one, King was in the process of getting decked by the onrushing Ndukwe Kalu but managed to squeeze the trigger on a one-yard scoring pass to tight end John Davis. Grammatica's extra point made it 14-13 with 7:29 to play.

The Redskins got one last chance after getting possession with just over three minutes remaining. They moved downfield to the Bucs 33 and Conway was called on to kicked a 52-yarder with 1:17 to play. "It's a 50-50 kick with a 50-yard field goal," the holder Johnson said. "But you'd like to have a chance."

Conway didn't get it as Dan Turk's snap rolled back to Johnson and the holder turned back into a quarterback and desperately sought someone to whom to pass the ball. He was sacked and Tampa Bay killed the clock to advance to the NFC title game.

2000

Head Coach: Norv Turner (7-6), Terry Robiskie (1-2)
Record: 8-8, third in NFC East

Honors: Stephen Alexander Pro Bowl; Champ Bailey All-NFC, Pro Bowl;
Marco Coleman Pro Bowl; Stephen Davis Pro Bowl

Jan 18

Davis to get Franchise Tag
Price is conditional 4th or 5th-round pick

Turk Wants to be Cut

Jan 18—Punter Matt Turk, a three-time Pro Bowl performer, has heard rumors that the will be cut from the team—and he is hoping those rumors are correct.

"I haven't been told anything yet, so I'm more or less hoping that what I read [about being released] is true," said Turk.

When asked if he would rather get his walking papers, he said, "Oh, absolutely. Absolutely. It's just the way this organization has treated me and the way things have gone. I'm really looking forward to a fresh start and moving on."

Last season was a tough one for Turk. In the season opener he fumbled a snap and a potential game-winning field goal against Dallas was aborted. Washington lost in overtime. There was some controversy over the origin of a finger injury. And his brother Dan became the goat in the team's playoff loss after he botched a snap on a last-second field goal try.

Feb 12

Bruce Smith Signs With Redskins
36-year-old pass rusher gets $25 million over five years, $4.5 million is guaranteed

---

Skins Make Deal, Will Pick 2-3

Feb 26—The Redskins aren't waiting until draft day to start making deals. They have moved up in the April draft and will have the second and third selections in the first round.

They already had the No. 2 overall pick as a result of the Sean Gilbert trade. They packaged their own selection, the 24th, along with the 12th pick they had acquired from New Orleans for the rights to Ricky Williams, and their fourth- and fifth-rounders to San Francisco in exchange for the third overall.

Apr 11

George Signed as Backup QB
Former first overall pick gets four-year, $18 million deal

Apr 16

Skins Tab Arrington, Samuels
Penn State LB, Alabama OT greet fans at FedEx Field

June 1

Mitchell Cut
Release of all-time return leader paves way for Sanders

Sanders Intro at Prime Time Presser

June 6—The Redskins unveiled their latest acquisition tonight as Deion Sanders was introduced to Washington.

"If your top priority is not to win the Super Bowl, I don't know why you're playing football," Sanders said. The Redskins are paying him in hopes that he will be the last piece of the puzzle to a title.

And they are paying him well. His contract is worth $56 million over seven years with $8 million in guaranteed money. There is no clause in the contract that would keep him from playing baseball. He has been a two-sport player from time to time during his NFL career.

Sep 2

Davis Cashes In Big
Back gets $90 million deal, $7.5 million guaranteed

9/3/00	**REDSKINS (1-0) 20, Panthers (0-1) 17**				80,257
Car	10	0	0	7	17
Was	7	0	3	10	20
Was	Davis 2 run (Conway kick)				
Car	Bates 92 kickoff return (Cunningham kick)				
Car	FG Cunningham 30				
Was	FG Conway 24				
Was	Johnson 1 run (Conway kick)				
Was	FG Conway 21				
Car	Walls 20 pass from Beuerlein (Cunningham kick)				

FedEx Field—The Redskins recorded six sacks and held the Panthers to just 126 passing yards in recording the season-opening 20-17 victory.

Washington took the opening kickoff and executed a classic touchdown march, going 79 yards in 12 plays and burning more than seven minutes off the clock. Stephen Davis went over from two yards out to cap the drive to make it 7-0.

Michael Bates of the Panthers quickly dissipated any thoughts the Redskins may have had of turning this one into a rout. He returned the ensuing kickoff 92 yards for a touchdown and the battle was joined. The Redskins offense could not move effectively after that opening drive, and a Richie Cunningham field goal gave Carolina a 10-7 halftime lead.

The visitors seemed poised to advance their lead in the third quarter, taking the second-half kickoff and driving to the Washington 46. On third and fifteen from the Carolina 49, Bruce Smith sacked Steve Beuerlein, swatting the ball out of his hand. Ndukwe Kalu recovered at the 28, setting up a 24-yard field goal by Brett Conway that tied the game at 10.

Later in the third, the Redskins drove for the go-ahead touchdown. Brad Johnson completed a 22-yard pass to Irving Fryar to convert a third and 11 at the Washington 34, a play that got things moving. Johnson threw for 13 yards to Davis, Davis ran for 11, and then it was Johnson throwing to James Thrash for 11 more to the 21 on the first play of the fourth quarter. From there, three straight Davis runs put it down to the one and Johnson snuck it into the end zone. Conway's extra point made it 17-10.

The Redskins got a scare when Bates returned the ensuing kickoff 90 yards to the five, but they were saved by a holding call that pushed the Panthers back to their own 17. Marco Coleman sacked Beuerlein for a 14-yard loss back to the two, and Washington had possession at the Carolina 40 after the punt. The offense took five and a half minutes off of the clock in driving to the three. Conway's 20-yard field goal with just less than five minutes left proved to be the winning points.

The Panthers were able to score again, on a 20-yard TD pass from Beuerlein to Wesley Walls at the two-minute warning, but Washington recovered the attempted onside kick and killed the clock.

Davis ran for 133 yards on 23 carries and Smith and Coleman each recorded two sacks.

9/10/00	**LIONS (2-0) 15, Redskins (1-1) 10**				74,159
Was	0	7	3	0	10
Det	3	3	3	6	15

Det	FG Hanson 49
Det	FG Hanson 20
Was	Alexander 5 pass from Johnson (Conway kick)
Det	FG Hanson 54
Was	FG Conway 26
Det	FG Hanson 37
Det	FG Hanson 35

Silverdome—The Washington defense held the Lions without a touchdown, but Brad Johnson threw four interceptions, preventing the Redskins from getting much going offensively. Five Jason Hanson field goals were all Detroit needed for the 15-10 win.

Trailing 3-0, the Redskins had a nice drive going with a first and ten at the Lions 21. But Larry Centers juggled Johnson's pass, Detroit lineman Kelvin Pritchett snagged the ball out of the air and raced down the sideline to the Washington one, where Tre Johnson took him down. A gritty goal line stand minimized the damage and held the Lions to Hanson's second field goal to make it 6-0.

Washington responded to the defensive effort, driving 75 yards in 8:43 to take the lead. Brad Johnson completed passes to five different receivers during the drive, with four completions converting third downs. The final third-down pass went five yards to Stephen Alexander for a touchdown. Champ Bailey ended a Lions threat near halftime by picking off a pass at the Washington six and the Redskins led 7-6 at the break.

The teams exchanged field goals in the third quarter. Hanson's 54-yarder put Detroit back into the lead. Faced with a fourth and inches at the Lions nine, Norv Turner decided to take the safe three points and Conway's 26-yarder put Washington back up 10-9.

A 44-yard kickoff return by Desmond Howard gave the Lions good field position and they took advantage, needing to drive just 33 yards to another Hanson field goal—this one from 37 yards—and Detroit led 12-10 early in the final period.

James Thrash returned the kickoff 49 yards to the Lions 49, but at that point, the game quickly started spiraling downward for the Redskins. On the first play from scrimmage, Johnson horribly overthrew Alexander and safety Kurt Shulz intercepted at the Lions' 12, returning it six yards to the 18. A controversial roughing the passer call on Bruce Smith kept the drive alive, and Hanson connected again to put Detroit up 15-10. Two more interceptions—the last coming at the Detroit 32 with just under a minute left—snuffed out any hope for a comeback.

Sep 11

Knee Knocks Out Westbrook
Torn ligament will sideline receiver for the year; Ex-Bill Andre Reed probable replacement

10/18/00	**Cowboys (1-2) 27, REDSKINS (1-2) 21**				84,431
Dal	7	7	3	10	27
Was	7	0	7	7	21

Was	Davis 7 run (Husted kick)
Dal	Warren 76 pass from Cunningham (Seder kick)
Dal	Smith 3 run (Seder kick)
Dal	FG Seder 32

Was	Davis 1 run (Husted kick)
Dal	Harris 16 pass from Cunningham (Seder kick)
Was	Sellers 7 pass from Johnson (Husted kick)
Dal	FG Seder 38

FedEx Field—Dallas ran off 17 unanswered points to take a 17-7 third-quarter lead and the Redskins never recovered, falling to the Cowboys 27-21.

Washington used a bit of special teams trickery to set up its first score. Deion Sanders fielded a punt at his own 13 and lateraled to Champ Bailey, who returned it 54 yards to the Dallas 33. Six plays later, Stephen Davis scored from seven yards, and it was 7-0 Redskins.

After an exchange of punts, Dallas had a first down at its own 24. Quarterback Randall Cunningham fumbled in the pocket, but the ball bounced back into his hands. The miscue distracted the secondary for a moment, allowing running back Chris Warren to get free on the left sideline. Cunningham found him and Warren raced untouched into the end zone to tie the game.

A Brad Johnson fumble gave the Cowboys a short field to work with and Emmitt Smith scored on a three-yard run to give Dallas a 14-7 halftime lead. They expanded it to 17-7 by driving to a field goal after taking the second-half kickoff. A Sam Shade interception at the Dallas 23 set up Davis' second touchdown run, this one from one yard out, and the Dallas lead was cut to 17-14.

Dallas answered with a score of its own, a 16-yard touchdown pass from Cunningham to tight end Jackie Harris, allowing the team to regain its 10-point lead at 24-14 with just over nine minutes left. The Redskins responded, going 69 yards in nine plays, with Johnson passing seven yards to Mike Sellers for the touchdown to pull the Redskins back with three.

The Cowboys went three and out and the Redskins took possession at its own 24 with 4:33 to go. But the comeback hopes ended when Johnson overthrew Irving Fryar on a deep pass attempt, and Dallas' Izell Reece intercepted and returned it 46 yards to the Washington 23. Tim Seder's field goal put Dallas up by six and the Redskins' final desperation drive fizzled near midfield.

Conway Cut, Finds Out Through Agent
Sep 20—The Redskins waived their kicker today, but they neglected to tell him.

Brett Conway wasn't shocked that he was waived. He has been suffering from a strained quadriceps this year and the team couldn't hold a roster spot while he recovered.

He was taken aback, however, that the team did not inform him in person. Redskins' salary cap expert Mark Levin called Conway's agent to tell him the news and the agent got word to the now-former player.

Michael Husted will take over as the Redskins' place kicker.

9/24/00	**Redskins (2-2) 16, GIANTS (3-1) 6**				78,216
Was	0	10	6	0	16
NYG	0	0	0	6	6

Was	Fryar 23 pass from Johnson (Husted kick)
Was	FG Husted 25
Was	Reed 21 pass from Johnson (kick failed)
NYG	Hilliard 7 pass from Collins

Giants Stadium—The Giants came into this Sunday night home game on a high with a 3-0 record. The Redskins, on the other hand, were reeling under heavy pressure created by a disappointing 1-2 start. Quarterback Brad Johnson, in particular, was under fire, having thrown five interceptions in the previous two games, four of them in the fourth quarter. His longest completion had been for 26 yards.

Johnson saved his job, saved the day and, for the moment, saved the season. On consecutive possessions in the second quarter, he completed long passes to set up scores. The first came when James Thrash hauled in Johnson's pass for a 46-yard gain on a third and two play from the Washington 31. On the very next play, Johnson found Irvin Fryar for a 23-yard touchdown and a 7-0 lead. The next bomb was to Albert Connell for 48 yards from the Washington 35 to the New York 17 to set up Michael Husted's 25-yard field goal, giving Washington a 10-point lead at halftime.

It took Johnson—suddenly transformed into the Mad Bomber—just four plays after halftime to give Washington a commanding 16-0 lead. On third and three from the Washington 26, he found Connell open again and hit him for a 53-yard gain to the Giants 21. Again, it took just one play for the Redskins to convert as Johnson found Andre Reed for the touchdown.

The Giants threatened to score early in the fourth quarter but Deion Sanders ended it with an interception in the end zone. New York averted a shutout by scoring a touchdown with two and a half minutes left, but it was just window dressing.

Washington held the Giants to 93 yards rushing and sacked quarterback Kerry Collins four times.

10/1/00	REDSKINS (3-2) 20, Bucs (3-2) 17 OT					83,532
TB	7	0	0	10	0	17
Was	0	7	3	7	3	20
TB	Alstott 2 run (Gramatica kick)					
Was	Davis 50 run (Husted kick)					
Was	FG Husted 28					
Was	Centers 8 pass from Johnson (Husted kick)					
Was	Anthony 46 pass from King (Gramatica kick)					
Was	FG Gramatica 42					
Was	FG Husted 20					

FedEx Field—Deion Sanders' 57-yard punt return set up a short, game-winning field goal by Michael Husted and Washington had salvaged a game it looked like it may have blown. The Redskins lost a 10-point lead with four minutes left to let the game get into overtime.

Tampa Bay got on the board first, scoring on a two-yard Mike Alstott run set up when Brad Johnson was sacked and fumbled, with the Bucs getting the ball at the Redskins' 25. Five plays later, with a minute and a half left in the first quarter, it was 7-0.

The two defenses dominated much of the second quarter, but the Redskins broke through with five minutes left before halftime. Following a third-down conversion on a pass from Brad Johnson to Irving Fryar that moved the ball to midfield, Stephen Davis took a handoff from Johnson. He went off of right end, zigged and zagged through the secondary and went all the way for the tying touchdown.

Relying heavily on Davis' running, Washington drove to take the lead on their first possession of the second half on Husted's 28-yard field goal. Davis gained 141 yards on 28 carries against a Tampa defense that was notably stingy against the run. Washington's David Terrell partially blocked a 40-yard field goal attempt by the Bucs' Martin Gramatica early in the fourth quarter and the lead held.

Washington extended the lead after recovering Keyshawn Johnson's fumble at the Tampa Bay 21. The Redskins burned 3:36 off of the clock in taking six plays to score on an eight-yard pass from Johnson to Larry Centers. The Buccaneers seemed dead in the water at 17-7 with 3:57 to play.

But the Bucs got just what they needed when Bruce Smith sacked quarterback Sean King and stripped him of the ball. Just as in the previous season's playoff game between the teams, the Bucs made chicken salad out of it. King recovered the ball and heaved a 46-yard TD pass to Ridell Anthony to pull the Bucs within three at the two-minute warning. The Redskins failed to kill the clock and Tampa drove into position for a 42-yard field goal by Martin Gramatica that tied the game at 17.

The Redskins punted to Tampa after failing to move with the overtime's first possession. The Bucs went three and out and were forced to punt from their own 15. Deion Sanders fielded it at his own 35, broke an attempted shoestring tackle and ran into the clear down the right side. The punter forced Sanders back to the middle and he was tackled at the eight after a 57-yard return. Davis ran it three times to the three and Husted's 20-yarder ended it.

Oct 2

Banged-up Knee Puts Johnson Out
Knee injury puts Pro Bowl guard out for season

10/8/00	Redskins (4-2) 17, EAGLES (3-3) 14				65,491
Was	7	0	0	10	17
Phil	0	7	0	7	14
Was	Davis 12 run (Husted kick)				
Phil	Johnson 30 pass from McNabb (Akers kick)				
Phil	Brown 8 pass from McNabb (Akers kick)				
Was	Hicks 3 run (Husted kick)				
Was	FG Husted 24				

Veterans Stadium—Some good play combined with a few good breaks let Washington survive this visit to Philly. The Redskins outgained the Eagles 402-275. Quarterback Donovan McNabb was Philadelphia's leading rusher with 43 yards. Washington seemed in control for much of the game, but needed an immaculate fumble, a very questionable play call by the Eagles and a quick whistle to escape with a 17-14 win.

The Redskins engineered a masterful opening drive, starting with a reverse to James Thrash that went for 34 yards to the Eagles' 35. After a nine-yard pass from Brad Johnson to Irving Fryar, Stephen Davis covered the remaining 26 yards on three carries, the last one coming from 12 yards out. Davis followed a block by Larry Centers up the middle and then found daylight to the left side thanks to a solid downfield block by Albert Connell.

For the remainder of the first half, penalties and breakdowns killed some promising Redskins drives. One of those ended on the Philadelphia 15 when Michael Husted missed a 33-yard field goal attempt. And penalties and breakdowns helped the Eagles drive 92 yards on six plays to tie the game with a minute and a half left before intermission. McNabb threw to Charles Johnson 30 yards for the score to make it 7-7.

It was more of the same for the Redskins in the third quarter. A sack and a couple of penalties led to the squandering of their great field position after the second-half kickoff. Husted missed a 43-yard field goal after two false starts pushed the Redskins back from a first down at the Philly 30.

Apparently the Eagles said, Hey, as long as they're letting us hang around in this game, we might as well go ahead and win it. They drove 68 yards in 11 plays to take the lead, the payoff coming on the first play of the fourth quarter when McNabb hit receiver Na Brown on an eight-yard slant.

Washington answered—but not without the help of one of the oddest plays of the year. Starting from their own 20, the Redskins drove down the field mostly on the strength of Johnson's passing. On second and eight from the Philadelphia 25, though, one of Johnson's passes went errant and was intercepted by safety Damon Moore at the seven. Moore took a few steps upfield to return his INT and just flat-out dropped the ball without being touched. Thrash pounced on it at the 15 and the Redskins had a first down. Two plays later, Skip Hicks scored on a three-yard run to tie the game at 14 with 10:15 left.

Neither team could mount another offensive threat. The Redskins dodged a bullet when replay reversed a fumble call on a Deion Sanders punt return that would have given the Eagles the ball deep in Redskins territory. After stalling at the Philadelphia 40 with 40 seconds left, the Redskins punted and the Eagles took over at the Washington 24. Eagles coach Andy Reid chose to try to make something happen rather than run out the clock and play for overtime. Something happened, but it wasn't good for the Eagles.

On second and 13, McNabb rolled right and, under pressure, launched the ball downfield. Darrell Green was there to pick it off at the Washington 48. He returned it 33 yards to the Washington 19. On the next play, Davis rolled 13 yards to the 6, where the ball came loose. Although replays indicated he had fumbled, the officials ruled that he was down by contact and the whistle had blown, so there was no official review. Husted's field goal with two seconds left won it for Washington.

Oct 10
Husted Wins Game Sunday, Cut Tuesday
Rookie Kris Heppner becomes team's 3rd kicker in '00

10/15/00	REDSKINS (5-2) 10, Ravens (5-2) 3				83,252
Bal	0	3	0	0	3
Was	0	3	0	7	10

Was	FG Heppner 37
Bal	FG Stover 51
Was	Davis 33 run (Heppner kick)

FedEx Field—An interception by linebacker Kevin Mitchell just before halftime gave the Redskins a huge boost and propelled them to victory over Baltimore.

The game was tied at three when a pass interference call gave the Ravens a first and goal at the one with 10 seconds left in the half. Banks dropped back and fired the ball towards tight end Shannon Sharpe in the back of the end zone. Both Mitchell and fellow LB Derek Smith were in the vicinity and Mitchell stepped in front of Sharpe to get the interception.

The Redskins returned the favor, although in a less dramatic fashion, when a good drive to open the second half was ended at the Baltimore 25 when Brad Johnson's first-down pass intended for Albert Connell was intercepted. Both defenses kept the opposing offenses at bay until the Redskins took possession at their own 20 with 2:34 left in the third.

Runs by Stephen Davis and Johnson completions to Larry Centers and Stephen Alexander moved Washington down to the Baltimore 33 after the first play of the fourth quarter. On second down from there, Davis followed blocks by Centers and tackle Chris Samuels and broke into the clear down the left side. Safety Rod Woodson had the only shot at stopping Davis, but the running back dismissed him with a classic stiff arm and completed the scoring run.

The Ravens never seriously threatened in their last two possessions and the Redskins held the ball the last five and a half minutes.

Davis gained 91 yards rushing and the Washington defense held Baltimore to 199 yards of offense, 109 of them passing.

10/22/00	Redskins (6-2) 35, JAGUARS (2-6) 16				69,061
Was	7	14	7	7	35
Jack	3	13	0	0	16

Was	Davis 1 run (Heppner kick)
Jack	FG Hollis 23
Jack	Soward 33 pass from Brunell (Hollis kick)
Was	Connell 11 pass from Johnson (Heppner kick)
Was	Connell 49 pass from Johnson (Heppner kick)
Jack	FG Hollis 33
Jack	FG Hollis 51
Was	Connell 77 pass from Johnson (Heppner kick)
Was	Davis 16 run (Heppner kick)

Alltel Stadium—After seven weeks of close losses and tight wins, the Redskins finally got an easy victory. Albert Connell caught

three touchdown passes from Brad Johnson and the Washington defense recorded six sacks of Jaguars QB Mark Brunell.

The Redskins got in front early as Deion Sanders intercepted a pass that bounced off of a Jacksonville receiver's hands. From the Jaguars 38, the Redskins used five plays to get into the end zone on Stephen Davis' one-yard run.

Jacksonville responded by driving 86 yards to a first and goal at the Washington five, but had to settle for a field goal by Mike Hollis. On their next possession, though, the Jags broke through, scoring on a 33-yard pass from Brunell to R. Jay Soward to take a 10-7 lead with 2:32 elapsed in the second quarter.

The Johnson-to-Connell connection then got going in earnest, with Connell gathering in TD passes of 11 and 49 yards on consecutive drives in the second quarter. The first drive was a short one, set up when Soward muffed a punt and David Terrell fell on it at the Jaguars' 12. Two plays after a 25-yard punt return by James Thrash, Connell caught the 49-yard score to make it 21-10 with five and a half minutes left in the half.

Jacksonville did manage a couple of field goals before intermission to pull within five, but that would be all for them. The Redskins held them to just 128 yards of offense in the second half.

The Redskins pulled away with their second possession of the second quarter, taking just one play to do it. From the 23, Connell got behind the Jacksonville defense and hauled in Johnson's bomb just past midfield and racing in untouched to make it 28-16. On the day, Connell caught seven passes for 211 yards.

The final score came on a one-yard run by Davis in the fourth quarter. Davis gained 114 yards on 24 carries.

10/30/00	Titans (7-1) 27, REDSKINS (6-3) 21				83,472
Ten	0	20	0	7	27
Was	7	0	7	7	21

Was	Sellers 5 pass from Johnson (Heppner kick)
Ten	FG Del Greco 46
Ten	Mason 69 punt return (Del Greco kick)
Ten	FG Del Greco 21
Ten	Rolle 81 interception return (Del Greco kick)
Was	Davis 1 run (Heppner kick)
Ten	Wycheck 18 pass from McNair (Del Greco kick)
Was	Centers 3 pass from Johnson (Heppner kick)

FedEx Field—The areas of weakness that cost the Redskins during their slow start to the season—turnovers and poor special team play—caught up to them with a vengeance in the second quarter. Tennessee returned one punt for a touchdown, got great field position to set up a field goal after the Redskins couldn't execute a punt, and finally got a touchdown on an 81-yard interception return as time ran out in the first half. The Redskins made a game second half rally, but the Titans responded to come away with a 27-21 win.

Washington got on the board first with a 15-play, 84-yard touchdown drive that consumed 8:19. The Redskins converted four third downs and Brad Johnson completed passes to five different receivers, the last one to tight end Mike Sellers for five yards and the touchdown. The Titans responded with a grinding drive of their own, moving 45 yards in 11 plays to score on a 46-yard field goal by Al Del Greco.

Then came the beginning of the end for the Redskins. Eddie Mason field Tommy Barnhardt's punt at his own 31 and busted it right up the middle, going 69 yards for the go-ahead score. The Redskins were forced to punt again two possessions later and the results were disastrous once more. A poor snap forced Barnhardt to try to run for a first down. Not only did he fail to make it—it was fourth and 27—but he was flagged for unnecessary roughness for a scuffle after the play. Starting from the Washington 26, the Titans stalled at the four, and Del Greco's 21-yard field goal made it 13-7 with a minute left until halftime.

After the kickoff, the Redskins drove from their own 34 to the Titans' 34 with 10 seconds left. Trying to get into position for a field goal attempt, Johnson forced a pass in to Irving Fryar and defensive back Samari Rolle picked it off at the 19. Rolle did a masterful job of finding openings and reading his blocking, crisscrossing the field on his way to an 81-yard touchdown return. Just like that it was 20-7.

The Redskins tried to make a game out of it in the second half, but the Titans had just enough to beat them. Stephen Davis scored on a one-yard run with a minute left in the third quarter to pull the Redskins within six. Tennessee came back in its next possession with an 11-play, 71-yard drive to a touchdown to pull back out to a 13-point lead at 27-14. A three-yard pass from Johnson to Larry Centers made it 27-21, but interceptions on Washington's final two possessions sealed the deal for Tennessee.

Nov 2

B. Johnson Out With Knee Sprain
Will miss 2-4 weeks; George to start

11/5/00	CARDINALS (3-6) 16, Redskins (6-4) 15			52,244	
Was	3	9	3	0	15
Ari	10	0	6	0	16
Ari	Williams 103 fumble return (Blanchard kick)				
Ari	FG Blanchard 30				
Was	FG Heppner 35				
Was	Davis 1 run (kick failed)				
Was	Heppner FG 28				
Ari	Pittman 7 run (run failed)				
Was	FG Heppner 29				

Sun Devil Stadium—It was one thing having turnovers and bad special teams play beat you against a good team like Tennessee the week before. It was quite another when it happened against the lowly Cardinals. Despite outgaining Arizona 431-178 and getting 16 more first downs (27-11), the Redskins played just poorly enough when it counted and lost 16-15.

The Redskins moved smartly down the field on their first possession, but when Stephen Davis tried to take it over on a second and goal at the one, the ball popped out and defensive back Aneas Williams scooped it up and ripped off the second-longest fumble return in NFL history—103 yards— to give the Cardinals an early 7-0 lead. Two plays later, Williams intercepted a pass by Jeff George, subbing for an injured Brad Johnson, to set up a Cardinal field goal.

The Redskins again moved into the red zone, but had to settle for a 35-yard field goal by Chris Heppner. They dodged a bullet when Arizona quarterback Jake Plummer fumbled deep in Washington territory, with the Redskins recovering at their own nine. On the ensuing drive, the Redskins did find pay dirt after moving downfield with a good mix of runs and passes. Davis went in from a yard out to cap the 91-yard, 10-play march, but a bad snap forced the point after attempt to be aborted and the Redskins still trailed 10-9 with just under nine minutes left in the half.

After Arizona missed a 56-yard field goal attempt, Davis took a George pass and rumbled 39 yards to the Arizona 15. Reverting to form, the offense stalled there and Heppner kicked a 28-yard field goal to put the Redskins in front 12-10 at halftime.

The lead lasted just 1:16 into the third quarter. MarTay Jenkins returned the second-half kickoff 71 yards to the Washington 20 and three plays later Michael Pittman scored on a seven-yard run to make it 16-12. The two-point conversion attempt was no good.

It didn't matter. Three forays deep into Cardinal territory resulted in just three points for the Redskins. The final drive ended when Heppner missed a 33-yard field goal attempt with a little over five minutes left.

Redskins Double Down on Kickers

Nov 8—When it comes to their kicking situation, the Redskins have decided that two feet are better than one.

Eddie Murray and Scott Bentley became the fourth and fifth kickers the team has employed this year. Murray, 44 and a veteran of 18 seasons, including one with Washington in 1995, will kick field goals. Bentley, who has yet to kick in an NFL game, will kick off.

Kris Heppner, who missed a 33-yard field goal in the final minutes of a one-point loss against the Cardinals, was waived.

11/20/00	Redskins (7-4) 33, RAMS (8-3) 20			66,087	
Was	3	10	12	8	33
StL	10	3	7	0	20
StL	FG Hall 30				
StL	Faulk 19 pass from Green (Hall kick)				
Was	FG Murray 37				
StL	FG Hall 43				
Was	Thrash 19 pass from George (Murray kick)				
Was	FG Murray 47				
Was	Centers 3 pass from George (kick failed)				
StL	Proehl 15 pass from Green (Hall kick)				
Was	Fryar 34 pass from George (pass failed)				
Was	FG Murray 41				
Was	FG Murray 39				
Was	Safety Green tackled in end zone by Smith				

Trans World Dome—The Redskins survived an early onslaught by the high-powered Rams offense and rallied to a tough road win by a score of 33-20. Newly signed kicker Eddie Murray kicked four field goals and Jeff George threw three touchdown passes.

At the beginning, this one was all Rams. St. Louis easily converted a first and 21 after a personal foul penalty and scored on a 30-yard Jeff Hall field goal. The Redskins committed a false start on their first offensive play and, on their third snap, George threw to a wide-open Dexter McCleon—who was, unfortunately, a cornerback for the Rams. He returned the pick 23 yards to the Washington 24 and two plays later former Redskins quarterback Trent Green threw to Marshall Faulk 19 yards for a touchdown, making it 10-0 with five and a half minutes gone. The home crowd was rocking and the Skins were reeling.

The Redskins scored on a 37-yard field goal just before the end of the first quarter, but the Rams came right back and matched that with a 60-yard drive to a 43-yard field goal by Hall.

George, who was starting in place of an injured Brad Johnson, kept the Redskins' next drive alive with a 14-yard scramble on third and eight. Just after the two-minute warning, Stephen Davis scampered 16 yards into the end zone, but the score was nullified by a holding penalty that was enforced from the nine. No problem. On the next snap, George fired a frozen rope to James Thrash in the end zone and it was 13-10.

The Rams were bottled up at their own eight after the kickoff, but were not content to run out the clock. Deion Sanders fell down while covering receiver Tory Holt and Green connected with Holt, who was headed for a huge gain down the sideline. Sanders got up, chased Holt down and knocked the ball out of the receiver's hands. Matt Stevens recovered at the Redskins 28. Washington then went on the attack, with two passes from George to Albert Connell putting the Redskins in position for a 47-yard Murray field goal to tie the game at 13 as time expired in the first half.

The Redskins and Rams both drove for touchdowns with their initial possessions of the second half, the difference being that Murray's attempted point after bounced off the upright and St. Louis' Hall made his PAT. The Rams had a 20-19 lead.

After the Rams' score, it was all Redskins. First, they drove 44 yards to a touchdown, the last 34 coming on another George laser-beam thrown, this one to Irving Fryar. The two-point conversion attempt failed and it was 25-20. After that score, the Redskins' Norv Turner completely departed from his character and called for a surprise onside kick. It worked perfectly as kickoff specialist Scott Bentley chased down his own kick and recovered at the Washington 41. That led to a Murray field goal to boost Washington's lead to 28-20. The Rams fumbled the ensuing kickoff, Sam Shade recovered and Washington was back in business at the Rams' 21. Another Murray field goal boosted the Redskins' margin to 31-20.

The Rams were threatening, but Champ Bailey picked off a pass in the end zone and returned it to near midfield. After a Tommy Barnhardt punt pinned the Rams back at their own one, Bruce Smith sacked Green in the end zone for a safety that made the final 33-20.

11/26/00	**Eagles (9-4) 23, REDSKINS (7-5) 20**				83,284
Phil	7	3	7	6	23
Was	7	7	3	3	20
Was	Thrash 36 pass from George (Murray kick)				
Phil	Thomason 3 pass from McNabb (Akers kick)				
Phil	FG Akers 27				
Was	Alexander 19 pass from George (Murray kick)				
Phil	McNabb 21 run (Akers kick)				
Was	Murray FG 26				
Phil	FG Akers 33				
Was	Murray FG 20				
Phil	FG Akers 30				

FedEx Field—The Redskins were unable to punch the ball into the end zone on seven plays from the Eagles' three-yard line, costing Washington a chance to take control of the NFC East. Second-year quarterback Donovan McNabb took control for the Eagles, rushing for 125 yards and passing for 137.

The Eagles' second-best friend behind McNabb was the Redskins. Both Eagles touchdowns were due to Washington fumbles. The Redskins were holding a 7-0 lead on the strength of a 36-yard TD pass from Jeff George to James Thrash when the Eagles punted from near midfield. Thrash muffed the catch, Philadelphia fell on it on the 11 and got into the end zone two plays later.

Then, early in the second half, George mishandled the snap from center and the Eagles pounced on the miscue again. On the next play, McNabb faked a handoff and scrambled around the left end, dodged some would-be tacklers, and got into the end zone for a 17-14 Philly lead with just over nine minutes left in the third quarter.

In a foreshadowing of things to come, the Redskins couldn't get it into the end zone after a 15-yard connection from George to Larry Centers gave them a first and goal at the Eagles' six. They had to settle for a 26-yard Murray field goal to tie it at 17. Another David Akers field goal put the Eagles back up 20-17 with 11:47 left in the game.

A borderline pass interference call set the Redskins up with a first and goal at the Eagles three. With power back Stephen Davis inactive for the game with a broken bone in his arm, things bogged down from there. Even though they got a new life with a defensive holding call on third down, Washington still couldn't get the ball into the end zone and had to settle for a tying 20-yard field goal with just under six minutes left in the game.

With the Eagles facing third and ten at their own 39 following the kickoff, McNabb found daylight around the right side, dodged a couple of potential tacklers and got loose in the open field. He got a block from one of his receivers and wasn't caught until he'd gained 54 yards to the Washington seven. The defense held from there,

but the Eagles got the field goal to take a 23-20 lead with just over three minutes left.

George saved the day temporarily with a 50-yard completion to Thrash to convert a third and 21. But that drive stalled at the Eagles' 26 and Eddie Murray's 44-yard field goal attempt was wide left, allowing McNabb to kneel on the ball to kill the clock.

12/3/00	**Giants (9-4) 9, REDSKINS (7-6) 7**				83,485
NYG	0	6	3	0	9
Was	0	0	0	7	7
NYG	FG Daluiso 46				
NYG	FG Daluiso 27				
NYG	FG Daluiso 28				
Was	Fryar 5 pass from George (Murray kick)				

FedEx Field—The Redskins' hopes of winning the division title ended as Eddie Murray's 49-yard field goal attempt in the game's last minute fell short. After the game, Norv Turner's tenure as head coach of the team ended in a move that was announced the following day.

Neither team was able to get much going offensively for the entire game. The Giants had a 6-0 halftime lead and were moving towards more with a first down at the Washington 47, but Deion Sanders intercepted a Kerry Collins pass and Washington had the ball back at their own 34. The Redskins gave it right back three plays later when Brad Johnson was rushed and threw up a wounded duck that safety Sam Garnes picked off and returned to the Washington 32. Seven plays later, Brad Daluiso kicked his third field goal of the game and it was 9-0 with a little over six minutes left in the third quarter.

As Johnson was ineffective and the Redskins were unable to mount a running game, it became clear that Washington would need some help if it were to stay in the game. They got it when Giants tight end Dan Campbell fumbled early in the fourth quarter and Washington's Sean Barber recovered at the New York 31. Turner had been contemplating pulling Johnson in favor of Jeff George, but decided to give his starter another series. The decision may have cost Turner his job.

On second down from the Giants 21, Johnson threw another ugly interception—this one aimed at nobody in particular—and cornerback Emmanuel McDaniel stepped in to pick it off and end the threat. The Giants burned over four minutes off the clock before punting the ball back to the Redskins, who took over at their own three.

George then came into the game and drove the team 97 yards in 10 plays for a touchdown, with the last five yards coming on a George pass to Irving Fryar for the touchdown to make it 9-7 with just under five minutes to go. The Giants managed one first down after the kickoff, but punted back to Washington. The Redskins had a last chance at their own 14 with 2:39 left.

They nearly pulled it off. George completed three passes to move Washington to the New York 35. It appeared he had completed a fourth, but James Thrash's catch at the 19 was nullified on replay review. Murray's field goal attempt from 49 yards was several yards short.

Turner Fired

Dec 4—Even though the Redskins have a winning record at 7-6 and still have mathematical chance of making the playoffs, Norv Turner was fired as the team's coach after Sunday's 9-7 loss to the Giants.

"This was something out of need," Daniel Snyder said. "There are three games to go. We are in the playoff hunt. We felt it was in the best interest of the organization."

Offensive assistant Terry Robiskie will take over as interim coach.

Turner, three games shy of completing his seventh season, was 49-59-1. "We all know at some point you're going to move on," he said. "It's time for me to move on."

Dec 5

Spurrier: If Skins Call, I'll Listen
Florida coach says he's not looking to leave UF

12/10/00	COWBOYS (5-9) 32, Redskins (7-7) 13			63,467
Was	0	7	0	6	13
Dal	6	6	10	10	32

Dal	FG Seder 33
Dal	FG Seder 19
Was	Davis 1 run (Murray kick)
Dal	McGarity 22 run (pass failed)
Dal	Smith 2 run (Seder kick)
Dal	FG Seder 20
Dal	Tucker 17 run (Seder kick)
Was	Fryar 32 pass from George (pass failed)
Dal	FG Seder 43

Texas Stadium—Meet the new boss, same as the old boss. Well, the results were the same, anyway.

Terry Robiskie was at the helm, replacing the fired Norv Turner, but the former receivers coach couldn't stem the downward slide of the Redskins as they lost miserably to the Cowboys.

A fierce hit by LaVar Arrington knocked Dallas quarterback Troy Aikman out of the game in the early going. In came third stringer Anthony Wright, but it didn't matter who was at QB. Aikman and Wright combined for just eight pass attempts all day, completing five of them. Wright did quite well spending the game handing off to Emmitt Smith, who racked up 150 of the Cowboys' 242 rushing yards.

For a change of pace, Wright handed off to wide receivers running end around plays twice, with very positive results for Dallas. The first time, Wayne McGarity scooted 22 yards to erase a 7-6 Washington lead in the second quarter. While the two-point conversion failed, Dallas took a 12-7 lead at halftime.

The home team expanded its lead soon after intermission. On Washington's first play, Dallas stripped the ball away from Stephen Davis and recovered the ball at the Redskin 22. Smith first carried for 20 and then for two, giving his team a 19-7 lead. It was downhill from there as sacks, fumbles and penalties aborted any attempts for the Redskins to get back into it.

12/16/00	STEELERS (8-7) 24, Redskins (8-7) 3			58,183
Was	3	0	0	0	3
Pitt	0	17	0	7	24

Was	FG Murray 32
Pitt	FG Brown 28
Pitt	Poteat 53 punt return (Brown kick)
Pitt	Huntley 3 run (Brown kick)
Pitt	Huntley 30 run (Brown kick)

Three Rivers Stadium—In a game that was a microcosm of a season gone wrong, the Steelers pounded the Redskins to close down Three Rivers Stadium—the scene of four NFL championship seasons during the 1970's—in style.

The game was lost late in the second quarter, during a four-minute span that showcased the bad play and bad luck that ruined the Redskins' season. Poor special teams play was on display as Pittsburgh's Hank Poteat fielded Tommy Barnhardt's line drive punt at the Steeler 47 and returned it for a touchdown with embarrassing ease.

On the Redskins' ensuing possession, receiver Albert Connell had Jeff George's third-down pass in his grasp, but it slipped and he had it pinned against his hip. Cornerback Chad Scott plucked the ball out, getting credit for an interception and giving his team the ball at the Washington 38. A few plays later, Kordell Stewart mishandled a snap, but it squirted back to Jerome Bettis, who turned the potential disaster into a two-yard gain. Five plays later, Richard Huntley gave Pittsburgh a two-touchdown lead with a three-yard scoring run.

12/24/00	REDSKINS (8-8) 20, Cardinals (3-13) 3			65,711
Ari	0	3	0	0	3
Was	14	6	0	0	20

Was	Bailey 7 run (Murray kick)
Was	Fryar 7 pass from Johnson (Murray kick)
Was	FG Murray 41
Was	FG Bentley 50
Ari	FG Blanchard 37

FedEx Field—The Redskins mopped up the season with an easy win over the Cardinals as Pro Bowl cornerback Champ Bailey played a starring role on offense.

Bailey wasn't the first wrinkle the Redskins introduced offensively. Receiver Irving Fryar lined up at running back, took the handoff and ran for 15 yards off tackle to get a 10-play, 65-yard touchdown drive started. It was capped off when, on third and goal from the seven, Bailey took a pitchout, turned the corner, and put on a burst of speed to just sneak into the end zone at the pylon.

Then the Redskins got a break similar to the ones they had been handing to their opponents all year long. Arizona's Michael Pittman caught a swing pass and was heading for a good gain. As he neared the sideline, though, he lost the handle on the ball without a Redskin anywhere near him. Derek Smith recovered at the Arizona 33. Five runs by Stephen Davis and a quarterback draw by Brad Johnson moved it to the seven. From there, Johnson threw to Fryar in the end zone to make it 14-0.

The Redskins expanded their lead to 20-0 with a pair of field goals in the second quarter, one by regular placekicker Eddie Murray and the other, from 50 yards out, by kickoff specialist Scott Bentley. As the teams played out the rest of the clock, Bailey caught two passes for 54 yards and practiced his usual specialty—intercepting a pass.

2001
Head Coach: Marty Schottenheimer
Record: 8-8, Second in NFC East

Honors: LaVar Arrington Pro Bowl; Chris Samuels Pro Bowl

Schottenheimer Flips, Signs on With Skins

Jan 3—A month ago, Marty Schottenheimer said he didn't think he could work for Daniel Snyder. Today, he signed on the dotted line to do just that.

The former Browns and Chiefs coach also will be the director of football operations. His contract is for four years and $10 million.

Schottenheimer made his remarks about being incompatible with Snyder's hands-on ownership style while working as an analyst for ESPN. They met for the first time last week and Schottenheimer changed his tune.

"At first, I felt our management styles were not similar, but when I met him I felt him to be a very engaging guy," Schottenheimer said. He added that Snyder is "totally committed" to winning.

Jan 23
Marty Dismisses Vinny
Cerrato out as personnel director despite Snyder assurances of job security

Mar 1
Big Buck Bust: Stubblefield Cut
Team will eat $7.75 million cap hit to release prize '98 free agent DT

Apr 13
Past is Present—Skins to Train in Carlisle
Team near deal at Dickinson College, site of camp from 1963-1994

Sanders' Fate Still Unclear

June 5—June 1 has come and gone and Deion Sanders still is a Redskin.

There was speculation that Sanders, who doesn't seem to be in new coach Marty Schottenheimer's plans, would be cut on June 1, the first day that the salary cap impact of the $8 million signing bonus the Redskins paid him last year could be passed off into 2002.

"There's nothing we have to do [immediately]," said Schottenheimer.

Meanwhile Sanders, who is struggling with the Cincinnati Reds, is hoping to be cut—and the sooner, the better. He said that when it happens "I'll jump up in the air and kick my heels twice. They'll be paying me . . . for doing nothing."

Sanders' contract allows him to play baseball, but the Reds may be on the verge of releasing the 33-year-old part-time player who is batting .174. If that happens, he will have to report to training camp in July or be in violation of his contract. That could force him to repay a good chunk of that bonus. It seems unlikely he would be clicking his heels if he should have to write out that check.

July 28

Prime Time Slate Cancelled: Sanders Retires
Will repay some of bonus; still keeps $7.5 million for one year

Aug 16
Redskins Bank Some Insurance
QB Tony Banks signs in case George's shoulder problems persist

Sep 4
Darrell Green's Odyssey Will End After 2001
Cornerback says he will retire after 19th season to run foundation full time

9/9/01	CHARGERS (1-0) 30, Redskins (0-1) 3				60,629
Was	0	0	3	0	3
SD	10	10	0	10	30
SD	Dwight 84 punt return (Richey kick)				
SD	FG Richey 21				
SD	Tomlinson 3 run (Richey kick)				
SD	FG Richey 48				
Was	FG Conway 40				
SD	FG Richey 32				
SD	Tomlinson 1 run (Richey kick)				

Qualcomm Stadium—The Marty Schottenheimer regime in Washington got off to a very rocky start as the Chargers matched their 2000 win total in the season opener by trouncing the Redskins.

Tim Dwight got things started for the Chargers when he fielded a booming, 47-yard punt by Bryan Barker and got a few nice blocks to help him cover the 84 yards to the end zone untouched. Following a three and out by the Redskins, the Chargers drove into position for a 21-yard Wade Richey field goal for a 10-0 lead.

It got twice as bad for Washington in the second quarter. Rookie running back LaDainian Tomlinson capped a seven-play, 45-yard drive with a three-yard run and Richey kicked another field goal to put San Diego up 20-0 at the half. The Washington offense remained mired in neutral, with dropped passes and no running game, at the times when it wasn't in reverse due to penalties and interceptions.

It got so bad that Schottenheimer's pledge to stick with Jeff George as his starter at quarterback lasted less than 45 minutes into the season. Tony Banks replaced George, who had thrown two interceptions and fumbled three snaps.

Things got a little bit better as a Charger fumble set up a Brett Conway field goal to get the Redskins on the board.

The Chargers dismissed the threat, such as it was, by again pairing up a Tomlinson TD run and a Richey field goal to score 10 more points, this time in the fourth quarter, to account for the final score.

Games Postponed After Attacks

Sep 13—In the wake of the terrorist attacks against New York and Washington, D.C., on Tuesday, NFL Commissioner Paul Tagliabue decided to cancel this weekend's slate of games.

Said Tagliabue, "We tried to be sensible, sensitive and right, and certainly not quick or superficial."

A decision about if and when the games will be made up will be made later in the season.

The Redskins were to have their home opener against the Cardinals on Sunday. Given that FedEx Field is about 20 miles from the Pentagon, the site of one of the attacks, the Redskins wholeheartedly supported the commissioner's decision.

"The canceling of a game or two is the least of our concerns," said defensive end Bruce Smith. "Right now, we're more concerned for the state of America."

9/24/01	PACKERS (2-0) 37, Redskins (0-2) 0		59,771	
Was	0	0	0	0	0
GB	7	3	10	17	37
GB	Freeman 12 pass from Favre (Longwell kick)			
GB	FG Longwell 28			
GB	FG Longwell 32			
GB	Schroeder 41 pass from Favre (Longwell kick)			
GB	Franks 4 pass from Favre (Longwell kick)			
GB	FG Longwell 30			
GB	Mealey 33 fumble return (Longwell kick)			

Lambeau Field—The Redskins staggered through their second straight lopsided defeat before a national TV audience, making key mistakes in all three phases of the game in getting pounded by the Packers in a Monday night massacre.

Green Bay had an easy road to its first score, thanks to a shanked Bryan Barker punt that covered all of 12 yards to the Redskins 42. After converting a fourth and two with a 22-yard pass to Corey Bradford, Brett Favre zipped a 12-yard dart to receiver Antonio Freeman for a 7-0 Packer lead.

A play emblematic of the woes of the Washington offense came after that. On third down, Michael Westbrook ran a nice pattern and caught Jeff George's pass for a gain of six yards. Problem was, eight yards were needed for the first down and the Redskins punted back to Green Bay.

Despite the lack of offensive productivity, the Redskins were still in it as the third quarter opened, trailing just 10-0. That changed quickly, however, as George threw an interception to set up Ryan Longwell's second field goal of the game.

Still, it was only 13-0 and the Redskins offense was beginning to show some signs of life. It appeared the Redskins had stopped the Packers on a third and seven play near midfield and would get the ball back. Champ Bailey, though, was called for holding, giving the Pack's drive new momentum. Soon after that the Redskins paid the ultimate price for the mistake—Bailey slipped just a bit as Bill Schroeder caught Favre's pass over the middle. The stumble gave the speedy Packer receiver all the edge he needed as he streaked into the end zone to make it 20-0.

The Redskins managed just 137 yards of offense on the evening and didn't threaten to score the rest of the game. Meanwhile Green Bay, which racked up 386 total yards, scored 17 more points in the fourth quarter to complete the rout.

George Sacked, Banks to Start

Sep 26—After having led the Redskins to no points in their first two games, Jeff George was fired as the team's quarterback.

Not benched. Fired.

Marty Schottenheimer decided to release George after the team's 0-2 start because he didn't think the team could win with

him. It's likely that Schottenheimer was concerned that the notoriously-temperamental would not take a benching well.

Tony Banks, signed during training camp, will become the 11th Redskin to start at quarterback since 1994.

9/30/2001	Chiefs (1-2) 45, REDSKINS (0-3) 13		76,573	
KC	0	28	7	10	45
Was	3	7	3	0	13
Was	FG Conway 30			
KC	Richardson 4 run (Peterson kick)			
KC	Holmes 24 pass from Green (Peterson kick)			
Was	Gardner 24 pass from Banks (Conway kick)			
KC	Holmes 7 run (Peterson kick)			
KC	Holmes 24 run (Peterson kick			
Was	FG Conway 28			
KC	Gonzalez 3 pass from Green (Peterson kick)			
KC	FG Peterson 33			
KC	Thomas 3 pass from Green (Peterson kick)			

FedEx Field—Kansas City scored touchdowns on five consecutive possessions in the second and third quarters to hand the Redskins their third straight humiliating loss.

On Washington's first possession, a nice mix of Stephen Davis runs and Banks passes to a variety of receivers got Washington deep into Chief territory. Brett Conway booted a 30-yard field goal to give the Redskins their first lead of the year.

A subsequent drive reached the KC 30 before an incomplete pass on fourth down killed that effort. The Chiefs took possession with a minute and a half left in the first quarter and embarked on the first of their five straight touchdown drives. Tony Richardson capped the 12-play, 70-yard march with a four-yard touchdown run up the middle.

Kansas City's next foray across the goal line was quicker, as they used just five plays to move 64 yards, scoring on a 24-pass from Trent Green to Holmes. The Redskins responded immediately. After Michael Bates returned the kickoff 37 yards to the Washington 43, a pass interference penalty gave the Skins a first down at the Chief 26. On the very next play, Banks found a crack in between two defenders and delivered to Gardner in the end zone. Conway's point after made it 14-10 with three and a half minutes left in the first half. It looked like a competitive ballgame was brewing.

The Redskins, though, had developed a knack for making the killer mistake at the wrong time. Conway's kickoff went out of bounds, giving the Chiefs possession at their own 40. It took them just six plays to take advantage with Holmes covering the last 18 on two carries, the second one seven yards into the end zone with 1:20 left before intermission.

After a Redskin three and out, the Chiefs appeared to be content to run out the last 37 seconds—but the Washington defense wouldn't let them. From the KC 30, Holmes went off tackle to use up some time but nobody bothered to tackle him, so he took off for 27 yards. After a Green pass to Chris Thomas gained 19, Holmes bolted up the middle for the final 24 yards of the embarrassingly easy 70-yard drive.

That turned the sound of booing at FedEx Field from ambient noise into a roar. Things didn't get any better in the second half as Green threw for two more touchdowns to cap a 21 for 26 day.

Oct 1

Barber Out for Season
Starting LB has torn ACT, will undergo surgery

Snyder Defends Schottenheimer

Oct 2—With the Redskins sitting at 0-3, Marty Schottenheimer has both his critics and defenders.

Put Daniel Snyder—the only person whose opinion really counts in this matter—in the latter category.

In a question-and-answer session at the National Press Club, Snyder showed strong support for the coach.

"Marty Schottenheimer's record is impeccable. I believe in him. We all must have a little more faith than we do," Snyder said. "Joe Gibbs was 0-5 in his first year here. We need to give Coach Schottenheimer a little more time.

"It takes time to put together a winning organization, clearly longer than I anticipated," he continued. "Losing's never fun. This Sunday and every Sunday, I want to be competitive. I want to leave it on the field."

10/7/01	GIANTS (3-1) 23, Redskins (0-4) 9			78,651	
Was	3	3	3	0	9
NYG	3	6	0	14	23
NYG	FG Andersen 50				
Was	FG Conway 35				
NYG	FG Andersen 26				
Was	FG Conway 55				
NYG	FG Andersen 22				
Was	FG Conway 41				
NYG	Campbell 1 pass from Collins (Andersen kick)				
NYG	Sehorn 34 interception return (Andersen kick)				

Giants Stadium—The Redskins played their best game of the season by far, but a moral victory is just another name for a "loss." That was the result after the Giants broke open a tie game with a pair of fourth-quarter touchdowns to take a 26-9 victory.

The kickers accounted for all of the scoring in the first three periods. Each one dialed one up from long distance, with Morton Andersen booting a 50-yarder to give the Giants a 3-0 lead and Brett Conway bettering that with a 55-yard effort in the second quarter that tied the game at six.

After Conway had tied the game for the third time—this time at nine—New York finally grasped control of the game. They moved 71 yards in a drive that spanned the third and fourth quarters. The main force was running back Damon Washington, who tore off runs of 15 and 22 yards. The second one moved the ball down to the Redskin one and Kerry Collins flipped a TD toss to Dan Campbell from there to put the Giants up 16-9.

The Redskins fought back as a 52-yard pass from Tony Banks to rookie receiver Rod Grander got them deep in New York territory. Then came the inevitable foul-up, however, as Kevin Lockett slipped while running to a Banks pass and all Giant cornerback Jason Sehorn had to do was stand in the end zone and catch the ball. He did, killing that threat.

Sehorn snuffed out Washington's last-gasp hope, as he stepped in front of Banks' intended receiver and had an easy 34-yard jaunt to the clinching score with just under three minutes left.

10/15/01	COWBOYS (1-4) 9, Redskins (0-5) 7			63,941	
Was	0	0	0	7	7
Dal	0	3	0	6	13
Dal	FG Seder 28				
Was	Westbrook 31 pass from Banks (Conway kick)				
Dal	FG Seder 39				
Dal	FG Seder 26				

Texas Stadium—In battle of two 0-4 teams, it was the Redskins who left unscathed in the win column. Washington held its initial second-half lead of the season, but a Stephen Davis fumble with 2:40 left led to a 26-yard field goal by Tim Seder as time expired to pull out the win for Dallas.

The game lived down to its expectations. The only scoring for the first three quarters was a 28-yard Seder field goal just before halftime.

Well, the Redskins said, as long as they are going to let us hang around, we might as well take advantage of it. After Seder missed a 52-yard field goal attempt on the first play of the fourth quarter, Washington embarked on a drive that resulted in its second touchdown of the season. Davis pounded for 27 yards on four straight carries, including a 19-yard burst, to set up third and six at the Cowboy 31. Michael Westbrook broke open down the middle of the field and caught Tony Banks' pass at the goal line, stepping into pay dirt for a sudden 7-3 Washington lead.

Dallas chipped into the lead with a 39-yard Seder field goal on its next drive, but when the Redskins retook possession with 6:32 remaining they cranked up what looked like a classic clinching drive—Davis ate up yardage and ground up clock with hard running. Banks converted one third down with a pass in the flat to Ki-Jana Carter that gained 15 yards to the Dallas 49. Davis got six on the next play as the clock ticked down with less than three minutes remaining. One more first down would force Dallas to burn all of its time-outs and put the Cowboys in a desperate position.

Then it happened. Davis got the necessary yardage for the first but, as replays confirmed, he lost possession of the ball a fraction of a second before his knee touched the Texas Stadium carpet. The Cowboys took over at their own 33 with 2:40 left. Dallas got a surge, the Redskins noticeably deflated and another loss for Washington quickly became inevitable. Wright completed two passes and Emmitt Smith ran twice to move the ball to the Redskin 26, putting the winning field goal well within Seder's range. Smith made sure a few plays later with a 13-yard scamper down to the eight. Seder came on to boot his game-winner as the clock turned to 0:00.

10/21/01	REDSKINS (1-5) 17, Panthers (1-5) 14, OT			74,480	
Car	7	0	0	7	0	14
Was	0	0	0	14	3	17
Car	Wells 2 pass from Weinke (Kasay kick)				
Car	Biakabutuka 10 run (Kasay kick)				
Was	Arrington 67 interception return (Conway kick)				
Was	Gardner 85 pass from Banks (Conway kick)				
Was	FG Conway 23				

FedEx Field—After three and a half quarters of football that strongly resembled the first 20 quarters of a dismal season, lightning struck twice for the Redskins in the final period as they tied the game on big plays by LaVar Arrington and Rod Gardner. Brett Conway's 23-yard field goal beat Carolina 17-14 in overtime.

"You hate to say you don't believe it, but I really don't believe we won," Arrington said. "There were a lot of crazy turns and twists in that game."

Perhaps his comprehension was somewhat affected by the concussion he had suffered in the first half. He went back into the locker room, rested until he regained his senses, and then went back into the game.

"I didn't think it would take this long, but it did," Marty Schottenheimer said. "We are growing. I'm more delighted, frankly, for the players than myself because they're the ones that had to endure in the circumstances that unfolded in the ballgame [today] and they wouldn't give up."

As mentioned, the game started out as though it would be no different from the futile experience of the first five games. The Panthers drove to a touchdown on their second possession after an exchange of punts gave them good field position at their own 47. It took them six plays to move the 53 yards and Wesley Walls caught a two-yard scoring pass from Chris Weinke to account for the score.

While the Redskin offense was utterly ineffective, the defense did step up with a pair of second-quarter interceptions by defensive linemen to snuff out Panther drives deep into Redskin territory. First, with the line of scrimmage at the eight, linebacker

Antonio Pierce smashed into Weinke, forcing a fluttering pass that tackle Kenard Lang picked off. Then, with time running out in the half Carolina had the ball at the Redskin one. Out of time-outs, Weinke had to pass. Tackle Dan Wilkinson tipped the ball, however, and rookie defensive end Otis Leverette got the pick with eight seconds left.

No inspiration was drawn from the clutch defensive plays, however, and a sense that another loss was inevitable began to grow. An 83-yard drive that spanned the third and fourth quarters ended with Tim Biakabutuka's one-yard touchdown run to make it 14-0. Washington went three and out and a 27-yard Biakabutuka run had Carolina in Washington territory at the 31. Two plays later, it was third and seven at the 28.

It wasn't a particularly risky play that Carolina called, a little toss in the flat to Chris Hetherington. Arrington was nearby and zeroed in on the fullback as the ball came into his hands. The ball bounced out, though, and in a flash, Arrington went from tackler to pass defender, snatching the ball out of the air and taking off for the goal line. He cruised the 68 yards unchallenged and the game—perhaps the season—took on a new complexion.

Another play was needed, however, for Arrington's to do any good and the Redskins got it in short order. The Panthers failed to get a first down and their punt rolled dead at the Washington 15. On first down, Tony Banks, who had been booed lustily for most of the game, saw that rookie receiver Rod Gardner had worked his way past the Carolina zone. The quarterback delivered the ball on target and the receiver easily coasted into the end zone to tie it up midway through the fourth quarter.

The Panthers were clearly broken and meekly went three and out. The energized Redskins would eventually score the winning field goal, but it would take them two tries to get it. First they drove smartly to the Panther 13, but Conway missed a 32-yard field goal with 36 seconds left in regulation. After winning the toss in overtime, it took the Redskins just four plays to end it.

From the Washington 14, Stephen Davis carried for two yards before Banks threw to fullback Bryan Johnson for 32 yards to the 48. On the next play, Banks connected with Gardner again. The rookie made a diving catch at around the five, bounced up and bolted into the end zone. A wild celebration was cut off, however, when a replay revealed that Gardner had been touched while on the ground. The festivities resumed shortly as Conway came in and kicked the game-winner from 23 yards.

10/28/01	REDSKINS (2-5) 35, Giants (3-4) 21			80,316	
NYG	0	14	0	7	21
Was	14	3	10	8	35
Was	Gardner 12 pass from Banks (Conway kick)				
Was	Metcalf 89 punt return (Conway kick)				
NYG	Toomer 6 pass from Collins (Andersen kick)				
NYG	Hilliard 27 pass from Collins (Andersen kick)				
Was	FG Conway 43				
Was	Thompson 31 pass from Lockett (Conway kick)				
Was	FG Conway 20				
NYG	Comella 1 pass from Collins (Andersen kick)				
Was	Westbrook 76 pass from Banks (Bennett pass from Banks)				

FedEx Field—The resourceful Redskins got an 89-yard punt return from newly signed Eric Metcalf, a touchdown pass by wide receiver Kevin Lockett, and a clinching touchdown bomb to Michael Westbrook to beat the Giants 35-21.

Washington had to drive all of 15 yards for its first touchdown. On New York's second offensive play, an attempted handoff on an end around went awry and Kenard Lang was there to gather in the loose ball. Three plays later Tony Banks threw a 12-yard touchdown pass to Rod Gardner and the Redskins led 7-0 less than two minutes into the game.

They doubled that lead later in the first. Metcalf, who had not played in nearly two years, touched the ball for the first time as a Redskin when he fielded Rodney Williams' line drive punt near the left sideline at his own 11. He bolted straight ahead, encountering heavy traffic. There was daylight—and lots of it—to the right, and Metcalf cut that way. Only one Giant remained as a potential obstacle after the returner crossed midfield and Metcalf outran him to the end zone.

New York drove to two touchdowns to tie it up at 14. A 43-yard Brett Conway field goal as time expired in the first half gave the Redskins the lead for good.

The Redskins opened it up on their first drive of the second half. On second down from the Giant 31, Banks turned and whipped a lateral to Lockett. The receiver turned into a passer and found Derrius Thompson all alone in the end zone and the Redskins led 24-14. They pushed it to a 13-point margin as the revitalized offense consumed nearly seven minutes of clock in driving 63 yards to a 20-yard Conway field goal.

New York put one more scare into the home team with a touchdown early in the fourth quarter to cut it to 27-21. They had possession with a chance to take the lead but the drive fizzled after a couple of first downs and punted back to Washington.

Three plays later it was over. It was third and 19 following a sack and Banks dropped back from his own 24. He found Westbrook just behind the Jason Sehorn and Shaun Williams down the right sideline and delivered the ball to his receiver at around midfield. Westbrook won the footrace as he cut back to the middle and rolled over the goal line for the clincher.

11/4/01	REDSKINS (3-5) 27, Seahawks (3-4) 14			82,352	
Sea	7	0	7	0	14
Was	10	10	7	0	27
Was	Rasby 7 pass from Banks (Conway kick)				
Sea	Alexander 41 run (Lindell kick)				
Was	FG Conway 43				
Was	FG Conway 23				
Was	Davis 1 run (Conway kick)				
Was	Westbrook 13 pass from Banks (Conway kick)				
Sea	Jackson 46 pass from Dilfer (Lindell kick)				

FedEx Field—Stephen Davis ran for 142 yards and a touchdown as the Redskins easily beat Seattle.

Washington jumped on top on its first possession. Davis runs of 12 and 11 yards keyed a nine-play, 71-yard drive that culminated in a seven-yard touchdown pass from Tony Banks to tight end Walter Rasby. The Seahawks drew even midway through the opening period when Shaun Alexander found a hole up the middle and scooted 41 yards over the goal line.

It was the Redskins' game after that as they scored 20 unanswered points. A pair of interceptions—one by Champ Bailey, the other by David Terrell—set up Brett Conway field goals of 43 and 23 yards to give Washington a 13-7 lead.

Later in the second quarter the Redskins moved to the Seattle 44 on a few short Banks passes. From there, Davis carried eight straight times, finally bashing over the goal line from a yard out with five and a half minutes left in the second.

"All week, people were saying, 'You can't run the ball on these guys,' " Davis said. "We proved them wrong."

Conway's conversion pushed the Redskin lead to 20-7 at halftime. They wrapped it up midway through the third with a 69-yard touchdown drive. This one was manufactured on the legs of not Davis, but Banks, who scrambled for gains of 17 and 15 yards to key the drive. Banks finished off the march—and the Seahawks—with a 13-yard touchdown pass to Michael Westbrook.

11/18/01	Redskins (4-5) 17, BRONCOS (5-5) 10			71,045	
Was	0	3	0	14	17
Den	0	10	0	0	10
Den	FG Elam 33				

Den	Smith 1 pass from Griese (Elam kick)
Was	FG Conway 48
Was	Westbrook 5 pass from Graham (Conway kick)
Was	Flemister 3 pass from Graham (Conway kick)

Invesco Field—Kent Graham came off the bench in place of the injured Tony Banks and rallied the Redskins past the Broncos. The game-winning points came on Graham's three-yard touchdown pass to Zeron Flemister with two and a half minutes left to play.

Denver took advantage of two Redskins fumbles to build a 10-0 lead in the second period.

After the ensuing kickoff, Banks completions of five yards to Ki-Jana Carter and seven to Rod Gardner sandwiched around a 10-yard run by Carter got the Redskins into Bronco territory at the 48. On second and three from there, Banks was hit by Leon Lett as he threw an incompletion. That left Banks with a concussion and put him down and out for the rest of the game and Graham trotted in. The veteran backup calmly converted the third down with a 12-yard completion to Gardner, getting the Skins in Brett Conway's field goal range. Into the teeth of a stiff wind, Conway nailed his 48-yard attempt with 17 seconds remaining in the half to get the Skins on the board.

It took a while for the Redskins to get the tying score. The game bogged down in the third quarter as the rain intensified with neither team able to string together more than a couple of first downs on offense. The break that Washington needed came late in the third. Denver tight end Desmond Clark fumbled after a reception and LaVar Arrington recovered for the Redskins at midfield. Graham capitalized with a five-yard touchdown pass to Westbrook.

With eight and a half minutes left the Redskins embarked on their game-winning drive from their own 46. It didn't get off to a promising start as Graham was sacked for a 10-yard loss on the very first play, but a controversial pass interference penalty converted a third down to keep it alive.

Davis ripped off a 13-yard run down to the Bronco 28. Flemister then nabbed a 14-yard pass from Graham to move it down to the three. Davis pounded into the line twice to no avail, but Denver went for the play fake to Davis and Graham found Flemister open in the back of the end zone. The Broncos' ensuing drive died near midfield with four straight incompletions.

11/25/01	**Redskins (5-5) 13, Eagles (6-4) 3**				65,666
Was	0	10	0	3	13
Phil	0	0	3	0	3
Was	Carter 5 run (Conway kick)				
Was	FG Conway 43				
Phil	FG Akers 49				
Was	FG Conway 32				

Veterans Stadium—The Redskins became the first NFL team ever o reach 5-5 after starting 0-5 by earning a hard-fought 13-3 victory over the Eagles.

Washington got all the points it would need early in the second quarter when Ki-Jana Carter slipped an attempted tackle in the backfield and scooted five yards for a touchdown. A 23-yard pass from Tony Banks to Zeron Flemister was the big play in the six-play, 59-yard drive.

The Redskin defense, meanwhile, was making life miserable for the Philly offense. The Eagles went three and out in their first five possessions and held the ball for just nine minutes in the first half. All game long, quarterback Donovan McNabb, whose strength was scrambling and creating plays on the run, was bottled up in the pocket and was clearly confused and frustrated.

Brett Conway pushed the lead to 10-0 with a 43-yard field goal just before intermission. The home team answered with just over four minutes left in the third quarter with a 49-yard three-pointer by

David Akers, setting the stage for two dramatic fourth-down plays in the final period.

The first was on the initial play of the last quarter. Facing fourth and three from the Redskin 33, McNabb rolled out and fired incomplete to Freddie Mitchell. The intended receiver was blanketed by Darrell Green. Philly's next possession carried to the Washington 35, where it was fourth and one. They tried to pick it up on the ground this time but linebackers LaVar Arrington and Kevin Mitchell smothered running back Correll Buckhalter at the line; the Skins offense took over with 9:25 left to play.

"Any time you stop a team on fourth down, that's huge," Arrington said. And when you do it twice, that's colossal.

Marty Schottenheimer's book in this situation called for a sustained drive by the offense to kill the clock and score a field goal—and that's exactly what the coach got. Banks converted one third down with a completion to Rod Gardner and Stephen Davis and Carter found first-down yardage on two other third-down situations. The Eagles burned all of their time-outs and were helpless as the clock ticked down to 33 seconds remaining as Conway kicked the clinching field goal from 32 yards out.

12/2/01	**Cowboys (3-8) 20, REDSKINS (5-6) 14**				85,112
Dal	7	0	0	13	20
Was	0	0	7	7	14
Dal	Smith 5 run (Hilbert kick)				
Was	Banks 1 run (Conway kick)				
Dal	FG Hilbert 38				
Dal	Ismail 62 pass from Carter (Hilbert kick)				
Dal	FG Hilbert 39				
Was	Gardner 15 pass from Banks (Conway kick)				

FedEx Field—In sixty minutes of uninspired football, the Redskins managed to undo much of the good they had done in the previous five games as they fell to the lowly Cowboys.

The embarrassment was a team effort, with the Cowboys rushing for 215 yards to 81 for the Redskins. The offense was unproductive, particularly in the first half. Washington had mustered fewer than 50 yards of offense before a futile drive late in the half boosted the yardage output to a whopping 90. Meanwhile, the Cowboys were controlling the clock, holding the ball for 20 minutes in the half.

Dallas scored on its first possession, driving 68 yards in nine plays. After that, the Cowboys missed a field goal and otherwise stopped themselves with ill-timed penalties and incompletions to allow Washington to stay in the game.

The Redskins took advantage of Dallas' kindness in the third quarter as they finally put together a drive to tie the game. It was largely a Stephen Davis production as he handled the ball on 10 of the 12 plays and gained all but 10 of the 63 yards covered. After six carries for 24 yards, with a nine-yard pass from Tony Banks to Eric Metcalf worked into the mix, Davis took a screen pass from Banks and rambled 29 yards down to the Dallas one. Davis' next three carries netted nothing, but Banks scored on a fourth-down bootleg to tie the game.

The Cowboys retook the lead on a 38-yard Jon Hilbert field goal. They wrapped it up with a 64-yard touchdown pass from Carter to Raghib Ismail.

"It's a setback. We know we should have won that game," said LaVar Arrington. "I hate Dallas. I have to wait all the way till next year to get another shot at Dallas."

12/9/01	**Redskins (6-6) 20, CARDINALS (5-7) 10**				40,056
Was	0	10	0	10	20
Ari	0	3	0	7	10

Was	Flemister 2 pass from Banks (Conway kick)
Ari	FG Gramatica 24
Was	FG Conway 22
Was	FG Conway 42
Was	Davis 1 run (Conway kick)
Ari	Jenkins 10 pass from Plummer

Sun Devil Stadium—In a prototypical display of Marty Ball, the Redskins used a conservative but efficient offense and a stout defense to earn the win over Arizona.

The Redskins came up empty after an impressive opening push as they moved 77 yards in 14 plays, but Brett Conway's 47-yard field goal attempt smacked off of the left upright.

Later in the first quarter, Washington embarked on another drive and this one paid off. Stephen Davis carried much of the load, gaining 29 yards rushing during the thrust. The payoff came on Tony Banks' two-yard touchdown pass to Zeron Flemister on the opening play of the second quarter. Later in the game, Davis would pass the 1,000-yard mark in rushing for the third consecutive season, becoming the first Redskin ever to accomplish that feat.

Arizona responded with a nice drive of its own, winding up with a 24-yard Bill Gramatica field goal. It appeared that the half would end with the score still 7-3 after Conway again hit the left upright with a field goal attempt—this one of 44 yards—with 38 seconds to go in the half.

The Cardinals chose not to run out the clock and LaVar Arrington made them pay for that decision. Jake Plummer completed three straight passes, but his fourth attempt bounced out of David Boston's hands and into those of Arrington. The linebacker roared 43 yards down the sideline to the Cardinal eight. Only nine seconds remained and after one play Marty Schottenheimer called in Conway, who avoided the upright as his kick from 22 yards was good.

The Redskins put it away in the fourth quarter with another Conway field goal and a one-yard touchdown run by Davis. The TD was set up when Banks completed a 40-yard pass to Rod Gardner, who made a leaping catch at the Arizona two.

12/16/01	**Eagles (9-4) 20, REDSKINS (6-7) 6**				84,936
Phil	0	10	7	3	20
Was	3	3	0	0	6
Was	FG Conway 47
Was	FG Conway 25
Phil	Mitchell 4 pass from McNabb (Akers kick)
Phil	FG Akers 40
Phil	Pinkston 62 pass from McNabb (Akers kick)
Phil	FG Akers 49

FedEx Field—The usual suspects—interceptions, dropped passes, ill-times penalties, missed field goals, fumbles—were all culprits as the Redskins slipped out of contention for the NFC East title as they lost to the Eagles.

"Philly played outstanding, but we missed a lot of opportunities," Redskins left tackle Chris Samuels said. "We made a lot of crucial mistakes, and they killed us."

The Redskins built a 6-0 lead as a 30-yard punt return by Eric Metcalf and a 57-yard completion from Tony Banks to Rod Gardner led to a pair of Conway field goals. Before halftime, though, the Eagles had seized both the lead and control of the game.

Immediately after the second three-pointer, they embarked on a 66-yard touchdown march. McNabb kept it alive by converting a fourth and one at the Redskin 42 with a two-yard sneak and finished it off with a four-yard scoring pass to Freddie Mitchell. The rookie receiver worked his way to a tiny opening on Darrell Green and dove for McNabb's low pass in the end zone.

Before halftime, the Redskins handed Philadelphia three points as Metcalf fumbled a punt at his own 44, setting up a 40-yard David Akers field goal.

The door slammed shut on the Redskins on a sequence of plays early in the third quarter. Washington put together a nice drive into Eagle territory, but a couple of dropped passes killed it and Conway was wide and short on a 48-yard field goal attempt. On the next play, McNabb faked a screen and then a reverse. Rookie cornerback Fred Smoot was sucked in by one or both of the fakes and receiver Todd Pinkston broke free, catching McNabb's pass and legging it 62 yards into the end zone for a 17-6 lead.

After Akers' field goal early in the fourth pushed the lead to 20-6, the Redskin defense did provide a couple of opportunities, with Darrell Green's interception and Smith's forced fumble and subsequent recovery giving Washington possession in Philly territory. The threats ended on a fourth-down incompletion and an end-zone interception by safety Brian Dawkins.

Dec 17

Green Will Be Back For 20th

Cornerback recants September retirement announcement, says fans convinced him to play in '02

12/23/01	**Bears (11-3) 20, REDSKINS (6-8) 15**				78,884
Chi	3	7	0	10	20
Was	7	3	3	2	15
Chi	FG Edinger 39
Was	Davis 3 run (Conway kick)
Chi	Johnson 32 run (Edinger kick)
Was	FG Conway 34
Was	FG Conway 26
Chi	Urlacher 27 pass from Maynard (Edinger kick)
Chi	FG Edinger 37
Was	Safety Maynard stepped out of end zone

FedEx Field—Chicago linebacker Brian Urlacher caught a 27-yard touchdown pass on a fake field goal to give his team a fourth-quarter lead and the Bears held on to beat the Redskins.

"Nobody should come to our house and walk away with their heads held high," Bruce Smith said. That, however, is what happened for the third time in three key December contests at FedEx Field. Home losses to Dallas and Philadelphia put the Redskins' playoff hopes in serious jeopardy, and they were eliminated after losing this one.

The teams played to a 10-10 deadlock in the first half. Washington scored its touchdown after a drive that covered 57 yards in 12 plays. Stephen Davis covered the last 39 yards of the march himself with a reception for nine yards and six carries for 30, getting the six points from the three.

The Redskins took a 13-10 third-quarter lead by driving to a 26-yard field goal by Brett Conway. Chicago responded, converting two fourth downs during a TD drive that spanned the third and fourth quarters. The first was relatively mundane: a two-yard sneak by quarterback Jim Miller with one yard to go at the Bear 41. The second, though, was highlight-film stuff and a killer for the Redskins.

On fourth and six at the Redskin 27, the Bears lined up in field goal formation. Urlacher, who isn't normally in the game on such plays, lined up at wingback. He went in motion across the line. Holder Brad Maynard took the snap, stood up and fired to Urlacher who, despite the motion, had failed to draw much attention from the Redskins, at around the 15. He easily ran the rest of the way to put the Bears up 17-13.

Chicago again drove into field goal position on their next possession and this time Paul Edinger kicked it, giving the Bears a one-touchdown lead. A Redskin drive reached the Bear three, but it went back to the Bears on downs right there.

12/30/01	**Redskins (7-8) 40, SAINTS (7-8) 10**				70,020
Was	0	13	17	10	40
NO	10	0	0	0	10

NO	McAllister 22 pass from Brooks (Carney kick)
NO	FG Carney 29
Was	Davis 6 run (Conway kick)
Was	FG Conway 53
Was	FG Conway 22
Was	FG Conway 34
Was	Banks 2 run (Conway kick)
Was	Carter 2 run (Conway kick)
Was	FG Conway 37
Was	Carter 1 run (Conway kick)

Superdome—The Redskins spotted the Saints a 10-0 lead before reeling off 40 unanswered points to defeat New Orleans.

Washington was fortunate that it wasn't in worse shape before embarking on its comeback. After the defense allowed the Saints a fairly easy 66-yard opening drive to a touchdown, the Redskins offense put New Orleans right back in business when Tony Banks threw an interception to Kevin Mathis. The cornerback's return and a 15-yard facemask penalty had the home team knocking on the door at the Washington 11.

For a few minutes, New Orleans had a 13-0 lead. Aaron Brooks had lofted a third-down pass caught by Willie Jackson while going out of bounds in the end zone, and officials signaled a touchdown. The Redskins won a replay reversal when the tape clearly showed that Jackson got only one foot inbounds. John Carney kicked a 29-yard field goal for a 10-0 Saint lead.

The scoring binge started after a 76-yard drive that ended early in the second quarter on Stephen Davis' six-yard touchdown run. A shanked punt led to a 53-yard Brett Conway field goal to tie the game and Champ Bailey set up another three points with an interception deep in New Orleans territory late in the half.

After driving to another field goal on their initial possession of the second half, the Redskins gladly accepted a string of gifts from the Saints to expand their 16-10 lead. Under pressure from a blitzing Darrell Green, Brooks threw an ill-advised pass that Green batted and tackle Dan Wilkinson intercepted at the Saint 18. Six plays later Banks scooted around left end into the end zone. The Saints gave the ball up on downs near midfield and a 25-yard Davis run set up Ki-Jana Carter's two-yard touchdown run for a 30-10 lead. Ricky Williams' fumble led to Conway's fourth field goal and Carter capped the scoring with another short run midway through the final period.

| Jan 4 |
| **Report: Skins Will Pursue Spurrier** |

| Team would fire Schottenheimer |
| to hire ex-Florida coach |

1/6/02	**REDSKINS (8-8) 20, Cardinals (7-9) 17**				61,721
Ari	7	10	0	0	17
Was	0	6	6	8	20
Ari	Wilson 61 interception return (Oglesby kick)				
Was	FG Conway 36				
Ari	Jones 4 run (Oglesby kick)				
Was	FG Conway 33				
Ari	FG Oglesby 26				
Was	Rasby 5 pass from Banks (pass failed)				
Was	Davis 2 run (Davis run)				

FedEx Field—Trailing 17-6 in a game with no playoff implications in a cold, steady rain, one would have difficulty blaming the Redskins if they had mailed in the second half of this one and lost to the Cardinals. The Redskins, however, fought on and earned the win over Arizona.

In the forefront of the fight was Stephen Davis, who carried the ball 38 times for 147 yards. In the process, he broke his own team record for rushing yardage in a season, running his total to 1,432.

"We didn't pack it in for the same reason we didn't pack it in when we were 0-5: This team has a lot of heart," Redskins guard Dave Szott said. "I had a lot of faith we would come back and play a good football game."

Not many present would agree with Szott's assessment of it being a good football game on the part of the Redskins—not in the first half, at least. Arizona took a 7-0 lead in the first quarter when Adrian Wilson stepped in front of a Tony Banks pass and sprinted down the sideline 61 yards for a touchdown. It got worse after Brett Conway kicked a field goal as Jake Plummer went over the middle to receiver David Boston for 48 yards. That play led to a four-yard Thomas Jones touchdown run and it was 14-3.

The teams traded field goals before intermission and the Redskins seized control in the second half. Davis carried on eight of the 12 plays of an 82-yard foray that culminated in a five-yard TD pass from Banks to Walter Rasby. A two-point conversion attempt failed and it remained 17-12 at the end of the third quarter.

Antonio Pierce's interception at the Arizona 23 set up Davis' game-winning TD, which came when he smashed over the goal line from two yards out. Davis then crashed up the middle for the two points that gave the Redskins a 20-17 lead. Arizona thought it had received a break when Boston was bumped on a long Plummer pass attempt, but officials kept their flags in their pockets and the Redskins were able to hold on

2002
Head Coach: Steve Spurrier
Record: 7-9, Third in NFC East

Honors: LaVar Arrington Pro Bowl; Chris Samuels Pro Bowl;
Champ Bailey Pro Bowl

Hall of Fame: George Allen, Head Coach 1971-1977

Jan 13

Marty Fired, Clearing Way for Spurrier
Snyder cites 'irreconcilable difference'

Spurrier is Skins' New Ball Coach

Jan 14—Steve Spurrier was introduced tonight as the new head coach of the Redskins. He comes armed with a confidence bordering on arrogance, cloaked in disarming Southern charm. And, more importantly, a five-year, $25 million contract.

He made some points with his players by speaking of easier practices, saying, "Soldiers don't train with live bullets."

Spurrier also said that, while owner Daniel Snyder will get the final say in any arguments, ". . . [H]e'll listen pretty good, too."

It should be noted, however, that the 56-year-old Spurrier did defer to the 37-year-old team owner, referring to him as "Mister Snyder."

Jan 27

Bobby Won't Be Back, Vinny Will
Talks with Beathard break down,
Cerrato rehired as player personnel director

Aug 29

Matthews Gets Starting QB Nod
Wuerffel, Ramsey will stand in reserve

9/8/02	REDSKINS (1-0) 31, Cardinals (0-1) 23				85,140
Ari	10	3	3	7	23
Was	3	7	14	7	31
Was	FG Conway 35				
Ari	FG Gramatica 36				
Ari	Plummer 7 run (Gramatica kick)				
Was	Lockett 26 pass from Matthews (Conway kick)				
Ari	FG Gramatica 20				
Was	Davis 3 run (Conway kick)				
Ari	FG Gramatica 39				
Was	Gardner 43 pass from Matthews (Conway kick)				
Was	Thompson 17 pass from Matthews (Conway kick)				
Ari	Boston 29 pass from Plummer (Gramatica kick)				

FedEx Field—Shane Matthews gunned for three touchdowns and everyone had a lot of fun as the Redskins made Steve Spurrier's NFL coaching debut a success with a 31-23 win over the Cardinals.

Matthews did suffer an embarrassing gaffe prior to getting warmed up. With the score tied at three in the first quarter, he threw a pass into the back of guard Brenden Stai. The ball bounced into the air, Arizona tackle Barron Tanner made the interception and the Cards were in business at the Washington eight after his 17-yard return. Arizona cashed in when quarterback Jake Plummer scrambled seven yards for a touchdown.

Matthews responded in the second quarter with a nice throw that went over the cornerback and into the arms of Kevin Lockett for 26 yards and a touchdown. Arizona's Bill Gramatica booted a

20-yard field goal and the Cardinals took a 13-10 lead into the locker room.

The Redskins took command with two third-quarter touchdowns. Stephen Davis, who carried 26 times for 104 yards, got the first one. He powered over from three yards out to cap a seven-play, 71-yard drive.

Gramatica kicked another field goal to pull Arizona within a point at 17-16, but that would be as close as they would get. Matthews capped back-to-back drives with touchdown passes. The first one, to Rod Gardner, covered 43 yards. The receiver wasn't wide open, but Matthews put the ball on the money and Gardner outfought the defender for the ball.

Arizona tried to respond with another field goal, but Gramatica's 52-yard attempt was wide right. It took just eight plays for the Redskins to move 58 yards to Matthews' 17-yard TD toss to Derrius Thompson and it was 31-16 with about 12 minutes left to play.

David Boston caught a touchdown pass from Plummer, but the Washington defense held after that. Champ Bailey's interception in the last minute sealed it for the Redskins.

9/16/02	Eagles (1-1) 37, Redskins (1-1) 7				84,982
Phil	14	9	7	7	37
Was	0	7	0	0	7
Phil	McNabb 8 run (Akers kick)				
Phil	Thomason 2 pass from McNabb (Akers kick)				
Was	J. Green 90 punt return (Tuthill kick)				
Phil	FG Akers 22				
Phil	FG Akers 40				
Phil	FG Akers 47				
Phil	Thrash 39 pass from McNabb (Akers kick)				
Phil	Levens 47 run (Akers kick)				

FedEx Field—When a head coach apologizes after a loss, you know that it got ugly. And that's a good description of the Redskins' 37-7 loss to Philadelphia.

"They outplayed us, outcoached us, everything," Spurrier said. "I apologize to the Redskins' fans."

The outplaying starting on the Eagles' first snap from scrimmage as James Thrash pulled in a 33-yard pass from Donovan McNabb. That drive culminated in an eight-yard McNabb touchdown run and it was 7-0.

It looked like the Eagles' next drive had ended with a David Akers field goal, but the Redskins were offside on the play. Philly took the points off the board and accepted a first down at the seven. Their fling against conventional wisdom paid off as McNabb threw a two-yard touchdown pass to Jeff Thomason to give his team a 14-0 lead.

Jacquez Green got the Redskins back into it briefly with the second-longest punt return in team history. He fielded Sean Landeta's punt at the 10, started up the middle and then found a wall giving him a lane up the left sideline. His 90-yard dash is surpassed only by Bill Dudley's 96-yard punt runback in 1950.

But the Eagles started to put it away before halftime. Three drives came up short of the end zone, but Akers nailed a trio of field goals to make it 23-7 at halftime.

The nail in the coffin came early in the third quarter as McNabb fired a 39-yard touchdown pass to Thrash to make it 30-7.

Pepper Spray Subdues Fans--and Eagles

Sep 16—It's not all that unusual for fans of opposing teams to scuffle in the stands, especially on a Monday night when alcohol consumption tends to be high. It *is* unusual for players on the bench to be affected by it, however.

That's what happened near the end of tonight's Redskins-Eagles game at FedEx field, a 37-7 loss for the home team. As authorities used pepper spray to subdue some fighting fans, some of it drifted over to the end of the Philadelphia bench. Several players were exposed to the spray and had to be treated.

An Eagles spokesman said that the team was not looking for an apology from the Redskins.

"It was a freak thing," he said.

9/22/02	49ERS (2-1) 20, Redskins (1-2) 10				67,541
Was	0	10	0	0	10
SF	7	10	3	0	20
SF	Barlow 7 run (Cortez kick)				
Was	FG Tuthill 33				
SF	Owens 38 run (Cortez kick)				
Was	Flemister 19 pass from Matthews (Tuthill kick)				
SF	FG Cortez 33				
SF	FG Cortez 35				

San Francisco Stadium—San Francisco quarterback Jeff Garcia left the game early with stomach pains, but it was the Redskins who were the ones feeling ill after the 49ers' 20-10 victory.

Things started going downhill in a hurry. On Washington's second offensive play, Stephen Davis fumbled and safety Tony Parrish recovered. His 10-yard return to the Skins' 14 set up a seven-yard Kevan Barlow touchdown run and San Francisco was in the lead for good.

The Redskins responded with a 33-yard James Tuthill field goal to make it 7-3 before San Francisco answered with the play of the game. Receiver Terrell Owens took a reverse handoff and looked to launch an option pass. He didn't have a receiver, though, so he started to run. Both LaVar Arrington and Renaldo Wynn had shots at him in the backfield, but Owens shook them loose and bolted 38 yards for a touchdown to make it 14-3.

By halftime the Redskins had narrowed the lead to 17-10, scoring on a 19-yard pass from Shane Matthews to tight end Zeron Flemister. When Garcia went out after his team's initial third-quarter possession, it looked like the Redskins had an opportunity to steal a win.

However, their inability to stop the run—the 49ers racked up 252 yards on the ground—and their problems generating any offense spiked any chance the Redskins had of winning. San Francisco defensive end Andre Carter had two sacks and forced a Matthews fumble.

Danny Wuerffel replaced Matthew at quarterback in the second half, but the change of ex-Gators didn't matter. The Redskins were shut out in the second half and they mustered just 217 yards of offense on the day.

Oct 4
Wuerffel to Get Starting Nod vs. Titans
Spurrier: Ramsey still 'looks like a rookie'

10/6/02	Redskins (2-2) 31, TITANS (1-4) 14				78,651
Was	3	7	14	7	31
Ten	0	14	0	0	14
Was	FG Tuthill 31				
Ten	McNair 11 run (Nedney kick)				
Was	Gardner 20 pass from Ramsey (Tuthill kick)				
Ten	Simon 8 pass from McNair (Nedney kick)				
Was	Davis 1 run (Tuthill kick)				
Was	Lockett 23 pass from Ramsey (Tuthill kick)				
Was	Davis 14 pass from Lockett (Tuthill kick)				

The Coliseum—Rookie quarterback Patrick Ramsey make his NFL debut in grand fashion, passing for 268 yards and two touchdowns to lead the Redskins to a 31-14 win over Tennessee.

Ramsey was one of three Skins to throw passes on the day. Danny Wuerffel started the game and had three attempts before leaving after the first series with an injured shoulder. Wide receiver Kevin Lockett was one-for-one passing with a touchdown on a gimmick play that nearly went awry.

With Washington up 24-14 in the first minute of the fourth quarter, Ramsey threw a lateral to Lockett at the Titans 19. The receiver fumbled the toss but tracked down the ball, continued to roll out and calmly hit Stephen Davis for 14 yards and the clinching score.

Wuerffel did lead the Redskins to a score in his one drive, a 31-yard James Tuthill field goal. Davis keyed the advance with a 23-yard run.

Soon after that, however, things didn't look so good for Washington. Wuerffel was out and the rookie Ramsey was in, taking his initial NFL snaps. A running back like Davis can be a novice QB's best friend, but he found himself sidelined with a sprained knee.

The Titans, led by veteran signal caller Steve McNair, took a 14-10 lead into the locker room. McNair scrambled 11 yards for one touchdown and threw an eight-yard scoring pass to John Simon for another.

In between those scores, Ramsey started to find his stride. He crafted a 90-yard drive and capped it with a 20-yard touchdown pass to Rod Gardner.

Washington took the lead for good on the first possession of the second half. The Redskins drove 74 yards to a one-yard TD blast by Davis, who has returned to action.

A 14-yard touchdown toss from Ramsey to Lockett gave the Redskins some breathing room later in the third before the Lockett touchdown pass clinched it.

The Washington defense did its part, allowing just 59 yards rushing and sacking McNair four times.

10/13/02	Saints (5-1) 43, REDSKINS (2-3) 27				80,768
NO	13	16	7	7	43
Was	0	21	0	6	27
NO	FG Carney 21				
NO	FG Carney 23				
NO	Williams 2 pass from Brooks (Carney kick)				
NO	Horn 17 pass from Brooks (Tuthill kick)				
Was	Davis 1 run (Tuthill kick)				
NO	Lewis 90 kickoff return (run failed)				
Was	Ramsey 1 run (Tuthill kick)				
Was	Ohalete 78 interception return (Tuthill kick)				
NO	FG Carney 36				
NO	Lewis 83 punt return (Carney kick)				
NO	Reed 31 pass from Brooks (Carney kick)				
Was	Watson 62 pass from Ramsey (pass failed)				

FedEx Field—In a starting debut that was the stuff nightmares are made of, Patrick Ramsey threw four interceptions and got sacked seven times as the Saints pummeled Washington 43-27.

Despite all of the issues, Ramsey might have had a chance to make a game of it if not for the heroics of one Michael Lewis. The Saints' kick returner—who had been driving a beer truck for a living two years ago—returned a kickoff 90 yards for a second-quarter touchdown, a score that blunted any momentum the Redskins may have gained from a one-yard Stephen Davis TD blast for Washington's first score.

Then, after two more Washington touchdowns made it a legitimate contest at 29-21 at halftime, Lewis did it again. This time the former Arena League star scampered 83 yards with a punt return, breaking the game open in the third quarter.

Ramsey's woes started on his third snap of the game. He fired a pass down the middle of the field. He didn't see safety Jay Bellamy, who intercepted the pass and set up his team at the Washington five. New Orleans had to settle for a 21-yard John Carney field goal.

Another interception thrown by Ramsey—he was being hit by defensive end Darren Howard as he passed—came early in the next series. Sammy Knight's return and a personal foul had the Saints deep in Washington territory again, this time at the nine. Again, they settled for three to make it 6-0.

The Redskins weren't so fortunate after turning the ball over on their next two possessions. After Bellamy recovered a Davis fumble, tight end Boo Williams eluded the coverage and snared a two-yard TD pass from Aaron Brooks. The Ramsey threw his third interception—this one bounced off of receiver Rod Gardner—leading to Joe Horn's 17-yard scoring reception on a pass from Brooks.

A 40-yard screen pass to Ladell Betts set up Davis' TD run. Lewis, however, got those seven points right back with his 90-yard return and it was 26-7.

The Redskins weren't quite done yet. Ramsey led an 81-yard touchdown drive and capped it with a one-yard sneak. Ifeanyi Ohalete picked off a Brooks pass and rolled 78 yards for a touchdown and all of a sudden, it was 26-21.

That would prove to be the high water mark for the Redskins. Carney booted a 36-yard field goal as time expired in the half. Any further comeback hopes were dashed on Lewis' punt return.

10/20/02	PACKERS (6-1) 30. Redskins (2-4) 9				63,363
Was	3	3	3	0	9
GB	7	10	0	13	30
Was	FG Tuthill 25				
GB	Green 24 run (Longwell kick)				
Was	FG Tuthill 53				
GB	Green 2 run (Longwell kick)				
GB	FG Longwell 36				
Was	FG Tuthill 31				
GB	FG Longwell 41				
GB	Green 8 run (Longwell kick)				
GB	FG Longwell 28				

Lambeau Field—Although they knocked Packer quarterback Brett Favre out of the game with a knee injury, the Redskins couldn't overcome a collective foot injury. They kept on shooting themselves there, allowing the Packers to take an easy 30-9 win.

For the second straight week, Patrick Ramsey committed multiple turnovers. The week before, the rookie threw four interceptions; this week, fumbles were the bugaboo. Ramsey coughed the ball up five times, losing three of them.

Washington took a 3-0 lead by driving to James Tuthill's 25-yard field goal on their first possession of the game. Favre and the Packers responded, taking the ensuing kickoff at their own 31 and driving to a 24-yard Amahn Green touchdown run.

Tuthill's second field goal was a 53-yard boomer midway through the second quarter and it cut the deficit to 7-6. That was as close as the Redskins would get. Green again scored to cap a Packer drive, this time from two yards out. The teams exchanged field goals, but every time it seemed like the Redskins would have a chance to get back into it, a fumble would kill any building momentum. The Packers pulled away in the fourth quarter with

Green tallying his third TD of the day to cap a drive led by Doug Pederson, Favre's replacement at quarterback.

'Banga' Back; Ramsey Benched

Oct 21—The Redskins today sent their future to the bench and welcome back a part of the past.

Steve Spurrier announced that Shane Matthews would replace rookie Patrick Ramsey at quarterback. After a sterling debut in a win against the Titans, Ramsey, the team's top draft pick, has struggled in losses to the Saints and Packers. Against Green Bay, Ramsey fumbled five times.

Meanwhile, the team signed guard Tre Johnson in an attempt to bolster their offensive line. Johnson, known as "The Banga," was a Redskin from 1994 through 2000 and made the Pro Bowl in 1999.

10/27/02	REDSKINS (3-4) 26, Colts (4-3) 21				80,169
Ind	0	7	0	14	21
Was	10	13	0	3	26
Was	FG Tuthill 40				
Was	McCants 9 pass from Matthews (Tuthill kick)				
Was	Doering 33 pass from Matthews (Tuthill kick)				
Was	FG Tuthill 23				
Ind	Manning 1 run (Vanderjagt kick)				
Was	FG Tuthill 41				
Ind	James 2 run (James run)				
Ind	Williams 20 run (pass failed)				
Was	FG Tuthill 22				

FedEx Field—The Redskins jumped out to a 20-0 lead and then had to hang on for dear life to beat the Colts 26-21.

Shane Matthews returned to the lineup as the starting quarterback and was effective in leading the Redskins to scores on each of their first four possessions. Matthews passed for two of those scores, a nine-yard toss to Darnerien McCants and a 33-yard strike to Chris Doering. James Tuthill contributed field goals of 40 and 23 yards and the Redskins were coasting at 20-0 with just over six minutes left in the first half.

The Colts got the break they needed to get back into it when Stephen Davis fumbled at the Colt 10-yard line and defensive tackle James Cannida scooped it up, returning it to the seven. Three plays later Peyton Manning bootlegged it in from the one with just over a minute to go in the first half. Even a 60-yard kickoff return by Ladell Betts that set up a 41-yard Tuthill field goal at the gun didn't shake the feeling that Indy had the momentum going into the second half.

The Redskins had a chance to put the game away for good in the third quarter after Fred Smoot intercepted a Manning pass and returned it to the Colt 14. On fourth and one from the five, however, Steve Spurrier elected to go for the first rather than kick the field goal. Things continued to go the Colts' way as Matthews' pass fell incomplete.

Manning and the Colts faced just one third down in covering the 95 yards to the end zone with relative ease, the quarterback going eight for eight during the drive. The payoff came on a two-yard toss from Manning to Edgerron James on the first play of the fourth.

The Colts pulled to within eight at 23-15 when James swept across the goal line for a two-point conversion.

A pair of Washington three and outs later, Indianapolis got a 34-yard punt return from Troy Edwards and the Colts were in business at the Redskin 41. Again they scored with almost stunning ease with running back Ricky Williams covering all of the ground. After gaining 21 yards on three carries, Williams gathered in a 20-yard TD pass from Manning to make it 23-21.

It was then, however, that the momentum switched back to the home team. Smoot knocked away Manning's attempt to pass for two points to tie the game.

After the ensuing kickoff, Washington took possession at its own 30 with 6:41 to go. Running back Stephen Davis—the man the Redskins would normally rely upon to move the chains and eat up clock—was on the sideline with a knee injury. Kenny Watson filled in quite ably, gaining all but 14 of the 66 yards the Redskins moved to set up Tuthill's clinching field goal, a 22-yarder with 18 seconds left to play.

Oct 31

Goodbye Carlisle, Hello Ashburn
Team will opt out of contract in Pennsylvania, hold training camp at home facility

---

11/3/02	**Redskins (4-4) 14, SEAHAWKS (2-6) 3**				64,325
Was	7	7	0	0	14
Sea	0	3	0	0	3
Was	McCants 11 pass from Matthews (Tuthill kick)				
Sea	FG Lindell 23				
Was	Gardner 19 pass from Matthews (Tuthill kick)				

Seahawks Stadium—"A win is a win," said Shane Matthews, and that's about all the Redskins had to take away from this drab affair in Seattle.

This wasn't a great offensive performance, with Kenny Watson's 110 yards rushing in his first NFL start against the league's worst rushing defense being the lone high point. Matthews did pass for both of the Redskins' scores, going to Darnerien McCants for 11 yards in the first quarter and 19 yards to Rod Gardner in the second. Other than those two throws, Matthews completed eight passes for 84 yards.

And, despite the near shutout posted by the defense, it was hardly a dominant performance on the other side of the ball for the Redskins, either. Seattle racked up 324 yards of offense, with Matt Hasselbeck completing 28 of 44 for 264 yards.

Depending on your point of view, you can say the Seahawks gave the game away or the Redskins were opportunistic. Seattle coach Mike Holmgren made two highly questionable calls to go for it on fourth down in Redskins territory, and both times the Redskins made plays to get the ball back. One was the game's key play as Bruce Smith sacked Hasselbeck for a nine-yard loss in the closing seconds of the first half on a fourth and goal from the two.

Another Smith sack of Hasselbeck resulted in a fumble in the third quarter, quashing a Seahawk drive that had reached the Redskin 21. Seattle never again mounted a serious threat until just over two minutes remained in the game. Another sack of Hasselbeck ended the threat, this one by Daryl Gardener at the Washington 15.

11/10/02	**JAGUARS (4-5) 26, Redskins (4-5) 7**				66,665
Was	7	0	0	0	7
Jax	0	10	13	3	26
Was	Gardner 20 pass from Matthews (Tuthill kick)				
Jax	Mack 2 run (Seder kick)				
Jax	FG Seder 27				
Jax	FG Seder 43				
Jax	FG Seder 27				
Jax	Taylor 12 run (Seder kick)				
Jax	FG Seder 42				

Alltel Stadium—Even though he had called the plays, Steve Spurrier seemed to be dumbfounded. Fifty one passes and just 16 running plays against one of the NFL's worst run defenses added up to just seven points in this embarrassing loss to the Jags.

"I was dumb enough to think we could throw it up and down the field," said Spurrier, who also made a comment that suggested

he threw his run-oriented game plan out the window when he saw how nice the weather in Jacksonville would be.

The Redskins had a chance to build a big early lead. They went up 7-0 when their initial possession of the game ended in a 20-yard touchdown pass from Shane Matthews to Rod Gardner. After forcing a Jaguar punt, Washington drove to a first down at the Jacksonville 35. Matthew threw into the end zone for Jacquez Green, but his receiver was tightly covered by cornerback Jason Craft, who intercepted the pass in the end zone to end the threat.

Even at that, the Jaguars didn't score until they got a huge break on special teams, a 12-yard punt by Bryan Barker that set them up at the Redskin 21. Stacey Mack took it over from the two three plays later and the cheap TD tied the game at seven.

Good field position gained on an exchange of punts lifted Jacksonville to a go-ahead field goal just before half. The Jaguars owned the second half, scoring a touchdown and three field goals on four consecutive possessions in the third and fourth quarter to salt this one away.

Gators 'Cheap & Available' For a Reason?

Nov 13—When Steve Spurrier brought a collection of players who performed for him at the University of Florida to the Redskins, he quipped that they were here because they were "cheap and available."

When the Redskins waived one of those players, receiver Jacquez Green, it became apparent why they could be had for a low price: their ability to perform in the NFL is questionable.

Quarterbacks Shane Matthews and Danny Wuerffel have yet to make a consistent impact. Green and fellow Gator receivers Reidel Anthony and Chris Doering aren't lighting it up, either.

Spurrier's Gators were known for a high-octane passing game; the Redskins currently rank 22nd in the NFL in yards gained through the air.

11/17/02	**GIANTS (6-4) 19, Redskins (4-6) 17**				78,727
Was	0	10	7	0	17
NYG	3	7	6	3	19
NYG	FG Bryant 43				
Was	Jackson 6 pass from Matthews (Tuthill kick)				
Was	FG Tuthill 31				
NYG	Toomer 35 pass from Collins (Bryant kick)				
Was	Gardner 11 pass from Matthews (Tuthill kick)				
NYG	FG Bryant 34				
NYG	FG Bryant 33				
NYG	FG Bryant 19				

Giants Stadium—The Redskins had a shot to steal away a game that they probably didn't deserve to win, but James Tuthill's plant foot slipped on a 42-yard field goal attempt with 3:11 to play and the attempt was blocked. The Giants held on for a 19-17 win.

The Redskin offense was particularly, well, offensive. They mustered just 166 yards of offense. Quarterback Shane Matthews likely earned a ticket back onto the bench with a performance where he averaged just 3.2 yards on 35 pass attempts.

The two teams each tallied a touchdown and a field goal in the first half, with the Redskins' TD coming on a six-yard pass from Matthews to Willie Jackson. Washington jumped on top 17-10 early in the third quarter after safety David Terrell intercept a Kerry Collins pass at the Giant 30 and returned it to the 11. Matthews threw his second touchdown pass of the day on the next play, this one to Rod Gardner.

After that, however, many of the bugaboos that have popped up throughout the season for the Redskins came along again to allow the Giants to chip away at the lead and, ultimately, win the game. First it was poor kick coverage—a 28-yard punt return by Delvin Joyce set up a 34-yard Matt Bryant field goal. Then it was fumbleitis as Ladell Betts coughed it up at the Redskin 37, leading to another Bryant field goal to make it 17-16.

Matthews' interception was thrown to Jason Sehorn, who was pushed out of bounds at the Washington 40. Nine plays later New York called on Bryant again, and his 19-yard field goal gave the Giants a 19-17 lead with just under 11 minutes left to play.

After that the Redskins had three more possessions to try to take the lead. The second one was the most promising as the Redskins moved from their own 31 to the Giant 25. With 3:11 left, Tuthill's kick never had a chance as his plant foot slipped in the muck and the ball slammed into the middle of the line.

Nov 20

Wuerffel's Turn Again
Matthews to bench, Ramsey still waiting

11/24/02	**REDSKINS (5-6) 20, Rams (5-6) 17**				79,823
StL	7	3	0	7	17
Was	0	7	13	0	20
StL	Edwards 4 pass from Warner (Wilkins kick)				
StL	FG Wilkins 30				
Was	Davis 1 run (Tuthill kick)				
Was	Davis 3 run (Tuthill kick)				
Was	Davis 4 run (kick failed)				
StL	Proehl 5 pass from Warner (Wilkins kick)				

FedEx Field—Danny Wuerffel played the best game of his NFL career and LaVar Arrington made a game-saving play as the Redskins held off the Rams.

Arrington slapped the ball out of Rams quarterback Kurt Warner's hand on a first down play from the Washington six. Tackle Daryl Gardener recovered the fumble with 11 seconds left to play, preserving the Redskins' 20-17 lead.

Such heroics are expected out of Arrington; Wuerffel's solid play was much more of a surprise. Steve Spurrier turned to his former Heisman Trophy-winning quarterback almost out of desperation with Shane Matthews struggling and Patrick Ramsey still too green to play. Wuerffel responded by completing 16 of 23 passes for 235 yards and made it through the game without throwing an interception or being sacked.

St. Louis raced to a 10-0 lead and the Redskins responded immediately. They drove 75 yards to a one-yard scoring run by Stephen Davis after the ensuing kickoff. It was 10-7 Rams heading into intermission.

Washington continued to hold the momentum in the second half. Champ Bailey returned a punt 39 yards into St. Louis territory at the 42. With the exception of an 18-yard Wuerffel-to-Gardner pass, it was all Davis again, with Stephen bulling in from the three to give the Redskins the lead at 14-10.

Following a holding penalty, the Rams had to punt from the hole, giving the Redskins great field position once again at the St. Louis 40. On fourth and one from the four, Davis followed an excellent block by fullback Bryan Johnson into the end zone. The hold on the extra point was botched, however, and the Redskins' lead was 20-10.

James Tuthill missed another chance to expand the Washington lead, but he pulled a 34-yard field goal attempt wide left early in the fourth quarter. The Rams responded by driving 75 yards in 12 plays to pull within three at 20-17. Warner passed on 11 of the 12 plays, the last one to Ricky Proehl for five yards and the touchdown with 6:08 left to play.

Washington moved into Ram territory on its next possession but couldn't burn up much clock before punting. Taking over at his own 20 with 3:28 to play, Warner moved the Rams to a third down and ten at the Redskins 28. A draw play to Trung Canidate caught the Redskins by surprise and the speedy back motored 22 yards to the six with 17 seconds left.

With overtime a near certainty and a gut-wrench loss a strong possibility, Arrington saved the day. Lined up a left end, he zipped

---

around offensive tackle John St. Clair, spied the ball in Warner's grasp and slapped it away. Gardner just beat St. Clair to the ball. A replay review confirmed the fumble call on the field and the Redskins had a much-needed win.

11/28/02	**COWBOYS (5-7) 27, Redskins (5-7) 20**				63,606
Was	0	14	6	0	20
Dal	0	10	7	10	27
Dal	Bryant 29 pass from Hutchinson (Cundiff kick)				
Was	Gardner 40 pass from Wuerffel (Tuthill kick)				
Dal	FG Cundiff 21				
Was	Flemister 16 pass from Wuerffel (Tuthill kick)				
Was	Thompson 11 pass from Wuerffel (kick failed)				
Dal	Williams 5 interception return (Cundiff kick)				
Dal	Galloway 41 pass from Hutchinson (Cundiff kick)				
Dal	FG Cundiff 42				

Texas Stadium—"Since I've been here, we always have control of the game against this team," said Fred Smoot, "and then something happens."

"This team" referred to the Dallas Cowboys, to whom the Redskins lost their tenth straight game. The "something" that happened was safety Roy Williams' gift-wrapped five-yard interception return for a touchdown that sparked Dallas' rally from a 20-10 third-quarter deficit en route to their 27-20 win.

Although the Redskins did build that lead, one still got the feeling that this would be another one of those days against the Cowboys. In the first quarter Kevin Mitchell blocked a Cowboy punt, setting the Redskins up at the Dallas 25. Three plays later James Tuthill's field goal attempt was swatted back by the Cowboys' Flozell Adams. In the ensuing chase for the loose ball, holder (and punter) Bryan Barker ended up with a grotesquely broken nose. Dallas recovered the ball at the Redskin 49 and moved quickly to a 29-yard touchdown pass from Chad Hutchison to Antonio Bryant.

The Redskins managed to shake off the adverse events and proceeded to outscore the Cowboys 20-3 over the next 15 minutes of play. Wuerffel threw touchdown passes to Rod Gardner, Zeron Flemister and Derrius Thompson to take a 20-10 lead.

The game turned on Washington's next possession. A well-placed punt had them pinned back at their own three. On third down from the one, Wuerffel threw a little pass to Watson over the middle just past the line of scrimmage. The play was designed to get a little working room for Tuthill, who was filling in as the punter. Instead, it was disastrous. The ball bounced out of Watson's hands and right into those of Williams, who caught the ball in stride at the five and easily rolled into the end zone.

Even though they still led, it seemed the Redskins were done—and they were. The effectiveness of the Dallas rushing game, which gained 231 yards on the day, began to wear down the Redskins. The aging Emmitt Smith racked up 144 of those yards. Although it didn't come until a few series after Williams' touchdown, the go-ahead score was inevitable. It came on a 41-yard pass from Hutchison to Joey Galloway with 11 minutes left to play.

Washington responded with a three and out and Dallas drove to a field goal to extend its lead to 27-20. The Redskins were able to get as close as the Cowboy 34, but Davis was stuffed on a fourth and one play and, for the tenth straight time, that was that.

Dec 2

Slumping Tuthill Cut, Punter Barker to IR
Team signs Joe Cortez to kick, Craig Jennings to punt

12/8/02	**Giants (7-6) 27, REDSKINS (5-8) 21**				78,635
NYG	3	14	7	3	27
Was	0	3	11	7	21

NYG	FG Bryant 42
NYG	Stackhouse 2 pass from Collins (Bryant kick)
NYG	Toomer 29 pass from Collins (Bryant kick)
Was	FG Cortez 24
Was	FG Cortez 44
Was	Gardner 13 pass from Ramsey (Ramsey pass to Doering)
NYG	Barber 1 run (Bryant kick)
NYG	FG Bryant 35
Was	Davis 1 run (Cortez kick)

FedEx Field—If you expect to snap out of a slump and want to win with a rookie quarterback at the helm, you don't want to turn the ball over five times. That's what the Redskins did, though, in going down to their fourth defeat in their last five games.

The rookie quarterback, Patrick Ramsey, came into the game after starter Danny Wuerffel injured his shoulder in the third quarter. The Redskins trailed 17-3 at that point and Ramsey nearly led a comeback win, but a key turnover in the late going—a fumble by receiver Darnerian McCants at the Giant 30—killed the potential rally.

Ramsey entered with the Redskins trailing 17-3 after Wuerffel was sacked and fumbled on the second series of the second half. Stephen Davis recovered the fumble and Ramsey led a drive to another Cortez field goal, cutting the New York lead to 17-6.

The comeback train started steaming in earnest after a Bruce Smith sack of Kerry Collins led to a three and out by the Giants and the punt carried just 33 yards to the Washington 45. Davis chugged for nine then 33 yards and Ramsey completed the drive with a 13-yard scoring pass to Rod Gardner. Ramsey threw to Chris Doering for the two-point conversion and all of a sudden it was 17-14.

But after the Redskins defense forced a punt, Champ Bailey muffed the catch and New York recovered at the Washington 21. It took just two plays for New York to score, a 20-yard pass from Collins to tight end Jeremy Shockey and a one-yard Tiki Barber run.

After the Giants padded their lead with another field goal to go up 27-14, the Redskins took one last shot at it. They moved 62 yards on seven plays—an 18-yard pass from Ramsey to Gardner to convert fourth and nine the big one—to Davis' one-yard TD burst to pull within six with 8:42 left to play.

On their next possession, Ladell Betts' 24-yard jaunt with a screen pass got the Skins into Giant territory at the 44 with just over five minutes left on the clock. Two plays later on second and eight, Ramsey hit Darnerian McCants over the middle for a first down but, just before his knees hit the ground, former Redskin Kato Serwanga stripped the ball away. The Giants recovered and ran out all but the final 55 seconds. A desperation drive expired near midfield as the clock ran out.

12/15/02	**EAGLES (11-3) 34, Redskins (5-9) 21**				65,615
Was	0	7	0	14	21
Phil	7	10	14	3	34

Phil	Staley 38 pass from Feeley (Akers kick)
Phil	FG Akers 28
Phil	Staley 1 run (Akers kick)
Was	Doering 15 pass from Ramsey (Cortez kick)
Phil	Emmons 44 fumble return (Akers kick)
Phil	Freeman 6 pass from Feeley (Akers kick)
Was	Gardner 30 pass from Ramsey (Cortez kick)
Was	Thompson 21 pass from Ramsey (Cortez kick)
Phil	FG Akers 45

Veterans Stadium—"I admire the way their team plays. They play hard, they play smart and they don't give away the ball," said Steve Spurrier after this one, perhaps with a touch of envy in his voice. His Redskins seemed to be in a daze at times, didn't play intelligently and committed three turnovers to help the Eagles rout the team 34-21.

The Redskins set the tone right off the bat when Stephen Davis fumbled on the game's second play. Davis dislocated his shoulder on the play, putting him out for the rest of the game and perhaps the season.

That particular turnover wasn't costly as Fred Smoot intercepted A. J. Feeley's pass a few plays later, but the next two giveaways gave the Eagles 10 points. Late in the first quarter with Philadelphia leading 7-0, Champ Bailey muffed a punt, giving the Eagles possession at the Washington 27. That led to a 28-yard Davis Acres field goal on the first play of the second quarter.

Then in the third quarter, Patrick Ramsey and Ladell Betts—who had come in to replace Davis—botched a handoff. Carlos Emmons of the Eagles fell on the ball at the Redskin 44. Emmons stayed on the turf for a moment and, noting that no Redskin had touched him, sprang up and ran uncontested into the end zone.

"That was a sad play for us," said Spurrier.

It wasn't as though they needed the Redskins' largesse to score. Before the Bailey turnover they drove 65 yards in four plays to their first touchdown. After taking the 10-0 lead, they drove 80 yards to make it 17-0. The Redskins scored on a 15-yard pass from Ramsey to Chris Doering to make it 17-7 at halftime, but after taking their nap during Emmons' touchdown they were down by 17.

A six-yard touchdown reception by Antonio Freeman made it 31-7 and Ramsey touchdown passes to Rod Gardner and Derrius Thompson were mere window dressing.

Jansen Signs Extension

Dec 18—Although they still have two regular season games left, the Redskins got started on their offseason today by signing tackle Jon Jansen to a contract extension.

The contract is worth $25 million over eight years with $8 million guaranteed.

Jansen has been the team's starting right tackle since he stepped onto the field after being drafted in the second round out of Michigan in 1999. He would have been an unrestricted free agent this spring.

12/22/02	**REDSKINS (6-9) 26, Texans (4-11) 10**				70,020
Hou	3	0	0	7	10
Was	7	9	0	10	26

Hou	FG Brown 46
Was	Cartwright 12 pass from Ramsey
Was	Safety Miller holding in end zone
Was	Thompson 13 pass from Ramsey
Was	Betts 3 run (Cortez kick)
Hou	Williams recovered blocked punt in end zone (Brown kick)
Was	FG Cortez 23

FedEx Field—For the first time since 1985, two Redskins running backs rushed for more than 100 yards in a game. Both Ladell Betts (116 yards) and Kenny Watson (100) passed the century mark as the Redskins pulled away from the Houston Texans for a 26-10 victory.

To be sure, rookie quarterback Patrick Ramsey's passing did contribute to the Redskins' success as well. His 12-yard touchdown pass to fullback Rock Cartwright put the Redskins up 7-3 in the first quarters and Ramsey was on his way to his first win as a starter.

Washington's lead was upped to 9-3 when Houston tight end Billy Miller was flagged for holding in the end zone during a punt, a no-no that means an automatic safety. To call the expansion

Texans' play on the day ragged would be charitable, although they did play hard.

Betts, who gained 116 yards rushing this game, got things going on a drive late in the second half with runs of four and 10 yards. Ramsey then took to the air, throwing to Rod Gardner for 13 and then 33 yards. The second pass got them to the Houston 13 with just over a minute left in the half. Wasting no time, Ramsey fired a 13-yard TD pass to Derrius Thompson to make it 16-7 at the half.

The third quarter was scoreless, although the Redskins did embark on a drive with 2:34 remaining in that period that led to a three-yard Betts touchdown run 44 seconds into the final stanza. Houston's Kevin Williams recovered a blocked punt in the end zone to make the score 23-10.

But the Redskins had the answer—make that the *answers*—as Betts and Watson took turns gobbling up yardage and chewing up the clock. A drive that consumed more than six and a half minutes resulted in a 23-yard Jose Cortez field goal to close out the scoring.

12/29/02	**REDSKINS (7-9) 20, Cowboys (5-11) 14**				84,142
Dal	0	7	0	7	14
Was	0	7	10	3	20

Was	Watson 5 run (Cortez kick)
Dal	Williams 85 interception return (Cundiff kick)
Was	Arrington recovered fumble in end zone (Cortez kick)
Was	FG Cortez 22
Was	FG Cortez 38
Dal	Bryant 46 pass from Hutchinson

FedEx Field— This was Darrell Green's last game after 20 seasons with the Redskins, and his emotional remarks before the game and joyous victory lap afterwards rendered anything in between forgettable.

Well, this 20-14 win over Dallas wasn't very pretty. Green, however, provided the memories—and any win over the Cowboys after 10 straight losses to them helped make it bearable.

Green provided one of the game's few highlights (outside of ones that will make "Football Follies") when he ran 35 yards after taking a reverse handoff on a punt return. He even hurdled a would-be tackler, reminding many of his daring play in his younger days.

Other than that, the play mostly was ragged. Watson's touchdown was set up when Renaldo Wynn sacked Dallas quarterback Chad Hutchinson and stripped the ball away. LaVar Arrington recovered at the Cowboy 24 and Watson went off right guard for the score four plays later. In the third quarter, Arrington put the Redskins ahead to stay.

On a third and 22 play from the Dallas 14, end Bruce Smith blew by two blockers and blindsided Hutchinson. The ball went flying back to the end zone where Arrington pounced on it for a 14-7 Washington lead.

A pair of Jose Cortez field goals put the Redskins up 20-7 in the fourth quarter. After the first one, the Redskins appeared to have wrapped the game up. The Cowboys' Woodrow Dantzler fumbled the ensuing kickoff. The ball was lying on the ground and nobody realized it was still alive until the Redskins' Bryan Johnson scooped it up and ran 12 yards into the end zone. In the confusion, however, the Washington defense had started to take the field and the Redskins lost both the score and possession due to the subsequent penalty.

Washington got a scare when Hutchinson converted a fourth and 14 play with a 46-yard touchdown pass to Antonio Bryant to make it 20-14 with 3:10 left to play. The Redskins could breathe easy only after Watson gained seven yards on a third and six carry and Ramsey could kneel down to kill the rest of the clock. The Redskins' first win over Dallas since October of 1997 was in the books, as was Green's amazing career.

Green Hits Right Notes in Swan Song

Dec 29—The Redskins didn't formally proclaim it to be Darrell Green Day, but the retiring cornerback and the 84,142 in attendance at FedEx Field knew that it was.

Nobody has played with one team longer than the 20 years Green spent with the Redskins, and he has built a strong bond with the fans. And Green and those fans held a mutual love fest prior to the game against the Cowboys.

Before the game he delivered an emotional address; his attempts to hold back tears were unsuccessful.

And after the final gun he took a final victory lap around the stadium, greeting fans, accepting a bouquet of flowers and generally reveling in the affection.

"This will not sink in—this day, not playing again—for quite some time," Green said.

2003
Head Coach: Steve Spurrier
Record: 5-11, Third in NFC East

Honors: LaVar Arrington Pro Bowl; Champ Bailey Pro Bowl; Laveranues Coles Pro Bowl

---

Jan 14
Lewis To Be Bengals' Head Man
LB coach George Edwards to head Skins' defense, will retain Lewis' system

---

Davis' Run With Redskins Is Over

Feb 26—In a long-anticipated move, the Redskins said goodbye to running back Stephen Davis.

The two-time Pro Bowl performer is third on the team's all-time rushing list with 5,790 yards.

His release this offseason almost was inevitable from the moment he signed a contract extension in 2000. By the terms of that deal, Davis' salary cap number was scheduled to take up more than $11 million of the $74.8 million limit.

Mar 10
Redskins Raid Jets Again, Sign Coles to Offer
Jets WR will get $35 million over seven years; New York can match or get Skins' 1st-round pick

---

Mar 19
Coles a Redskin; Top Draft Pick to Jets
New York declines to match Washington's offer

July 29
Daddy's Gone: Skins Cut Wilkinson
DT refuses to take pay cut, is released

Snyder Makes Final Roster Moves

Aug 30—When asked why the Redskins waived Danny Wuerffel during the final roster cuts, leaving the team with just two quarterbacks, Steve Spurrier didn't have an answer.

The head coach wasn't holding back. He didn't know the reasoning behind the decision because it wasn't his call. The choice to release Wuerffel—who starred for Spurrier at Florida—and running back Kenny Watson were made by team owner Daniel Snyder.

This raised some eyebrows as Snyder pays Spurrier $5 million a year to make such decisions. The fact that two such critical decisions were taken out of his hands raises questions about who is in charge of football operations at Redskins Park.

9/4/03	**REDSKINS (1-0) 16, Jets (0-1) 13**				85,420
NYJ	7	0	3	3	13
Was	3	10	0	3	16
Was	FG Hall 50				
NYJ	Jordan 1 run (Brien kick)				
Was	McCants 4 pass from Ramsey (Hall kick)				
Was	FG Hall 22				
NYJ	FG Brien 30				
NYJ	FG Brien 41				
Was	FG Hall 33				

FedEx Field—John Hall's 33-yard field goal with five seconds left to play lifted the Redskins past the New York Jets 16-13.

Hall is one of five players on the Washington roster who wore the Jets' green last season. Another ex-Jet, receiver Laveranues Coles, caught a 25-yard pass from Patrick Ramsey to set up the game's first score, a 50-yard Hall field goal.

A 15-yard personal foul penalty on Washington safety Ifeanyi Ohalete jump-started a Jet drive on their ensuing possession. LaMont Jordan capped the drive when he bulled over on fourth and goal at the one and New York led 7-3.

Washington took back the lead on its next possession, grinding out a 14-play, 74-yard drive that consumed more than eight and a half minutes of clock. Running back Trung Canidate kept the drive alive when he fought for a yard to convert a fourth and one at the New York 28. Ramsey culminated the drive with a fluttering pass that Darnerien McCants gathered in with a leaping catch for four yards and the score.

The Redskins extended their lead as a 48-yard Ramsey-to-Coles bomb set up a 22-yard Hall field goal. That made it 13-7 at the half.

In the second half, the Washington offense bogged down and made some key mistakes that got the Jets back into it. Early in the third quarter Donnie Abraham swooped in and picked off a Ramsey pass, returning it 12 yards to the Washington 26. Safety Matt Bowen saved a touchdown when he knocked away a third-down pass intended for Chrebet. New York settled for a 30-yard Doug Brien field goal to pull within 13-10.

Another Brien field goal tied the game at 13-13.

The teams exchanged punts and Washington took over at its 39 with 2:16 left. After Ladell Betts gained six yards, Ramsey—not known for being fleet of foot—took off on a scramble around left end, gaining 24 yards to the Jets 31.

Betts made Hall's task a bit easier with runs of three, 11 and three yards and the Redskins called time-out at the New York 17 with eight seconds left. Hall's kick for the win was true.

9/14/03	**Redskins (2-0) 33, FALCONS (1-1) 31**				70,241
Was	0	17	9	7	33
Atl	3	21	0	7	31
Atl	FG Feely 37				
Atl	Duckett 13 run (Feely kick)				
Atl	Duckett 1 run (Feely kick)				
Was	Betts 13 run (Hall kick)				
Was	Cartwright 1 run (Hall kick)				
Atl	Crumpler 1 pass from Johnson (Feely kick)				
Was	FG Hall 54				
Was	Gardner 21 pass from Ramsey (Hall kick)				
Was	Safety Johnson tackled in end zone by Armstead				
Was	Coles 19 pass from Ramsey				
Atl	Farris 42 pass from Johnson (Feely kick)				

Georgia Dome—The visiting Redskins responded to a 17-point second-quarter deficit by outscoring the Falcons 33-7 over the next 31 minutes of play. There were some scary moments at the end, but Washington held on for a 33-31 win over Atlanta.

There were offense stars aplenty for the winners, especially quarterback Patrick Ramsey and wide receiver Laveranues Coles. Ramsey completed 25 of 39 passes for a career-best 356 yards and two touchdowns while Coles gathered in 11 of Ramsey's throws for 180 yards and a touchdown.

The Redskins would need every bit of their production and more. "We came out a little bit shaky," said Ramsey, showing a penchant for understatement.

After the Falcons drove to a 37-yard Jay Feely field goal and a 13-yard touchdown run by T. J. Duckett, Ramsey was blindsided and fumbled. Atlanta recovered at the one and Duckett bulled his way to pay dirt on the next play to put the Falcons up 17-0 with less than two minutes gone in the second quarter.

A little later in the second period, the Redskins' comeback started in earnest. A five-play, 65-yard drive capped by a 13-yard touchdown run by Ladell Betts got the Redskins on the scoreboard. Soon after that Ifeanyi Ohalete intercepted a Johnson pass and returned it 30 yards to the Atlanta one. Three plays later Rock Cartwright scored from there and it was suddenly a ballgame at 17-14.

A 52-yard return of the ensuing kickoff set up a Falcon touchdown to push their lead up to 24-14. But the Redskins regained the momentum going into the locker room as John Hall nailed a 54-yard field goal seven seconds before intermission.

Washington tied it up with 9:52 left in the third quarter on a 21-yard touchdown pass from Ramsey to Rod Gardner. Then, after Bryan Barker dropped a punt down at the Atlanta five, Jesse Armstead blitzed and sacked Johnson in the end zone for a safety and a 26-24 Redskin lead.

The Skins took maximum advantage of the safety, taking the ensuing free kick and driving 71 yards in five plays to a touchdown. Coles got the score as he broke free and Ramsey hit him for 19 yards and Washington was up 33-24.

A late Atlanta touchdown pass made it 33-31 with 2:21 left to play, but the Falcons' onside kick attempt traveled only nine yards and the Redskins ran out all but 19 seconds of the clock.

9/21/03	**Giants (2-1) 24, REDSKINS (2-1) 21 OT**				84,856	
NYG	7	14	0	0	3	24
Was	3	0	7	11	0	21
Was	FG Hall 42					
NYG	Hilliard 5 pass from Collins (Bryant kick)					
NYG	Toomer 54 pass from Collins (Bryant kick)					
NYG	Hilliard 5 pass from Collins (Bryant kick)					
Was	McCants 4 pass from Ramsey (Hall kick)					
Was	Gardner 6 pass from Ramsey (Hall kick)					
Was	FG Hall 33					
NYG	FG Bryant 29					

FedEx Field—For the second straight week the Redskins battled back from a deep early hole to get back into a game. Unlike a week ago, however, they couldn't finish the deal—they lost to the Giants 24-21 on Matt Bryant's 29-yard field goal 4:15 into overtime.

Washington contributed greatly to its own demise, tying a team record by committing 17 penalties. It seemed as though every one of the flags came at a very inopportune time.

"We were the Redskins killers ourselves," said cornerback Fred Smoot.

It started on the Redskins' very first drive. Wide receiver Darnerien McCants drew a flag for taunting after catching a pass for a first down at the Giants 21, short-circuiting that drive. On their next possession a holding penalty against Chris Samuels negated a touchdown pass and the Skins had to settle for a 42-yard John Hall field goal to take a 3-0 lead.

New York responded with three Kerry Collins touchdown passes before intermission. He never should have had the opportunity to throw the last one, but a personal foul penalty on Washington linebacker Jeremiah Trotter kept alive a late drive. Collins took full advantage of the gaffe a few plays later by throwing a five-yard touchdown pass to Ike Hilliard to give the Giants a 21-3 halftime lead.

Patrick Ramsey got the comeback going as he fired a four-yard TD pass to McCants, making it 21-10 with 3:47 left in the third quarter.

After the teams exchanged punts and field goal misses, the Redskins took possession at their own 27 with 4:10 left to play. A 22-yard Ramsey pass to Laveranues Coles converted one third down and a seven-yard Ramsey to Patrick Johnson pass converted another. On first and goal at the six, Ramsey found Rod Gardner free for the TD. Ramey then displayed some mobility as he bought time to find McCants for the two-point conversion to make it 21-18 with 2:27 left to play.

The Giants did a quick (19 seconds) three and out and the Skins were back in business at their own 28 with 2:01 left to play.

Ramsey passes of 21 yards to Coles and 32 yards to McCants got the Redskins in Hall's range and his boot from 33 yards sent the game into overtime at 21-21.

All of the momentum seemed to be with the home team as a holding penalty on the overtime kickoff game New York possession at its own six. However, Collins engineered a drive to Bryant's game winner. The big play was a 27-yard pass to fullback Jim Finn.

9/28/03	**REDSKINS (3-1) 20, Patriots (2-2) 17**				83,623
NE	3	0	7	7	17
Was	3	3	14	0	20
Was	FG Hall 38				
NE	FG Vinatieri 23				
Was	FG Hall 29				
Was	Betts 1 run (Hall kick)				
Was	Cartwright 3 run (Hall kick)				
NE	Givens 29 pass from Brady (Vinatieri kick)				
NE	Centers 7 pass from Brady (Vinatieri kick)				

FedEx Field—The Redskins ran off 17 unanswered points to take a 20-3 lead over the Patriots, but nothing comes easy for this team. They needed a last-minute defensive stand to pull out a 20-17 win over the Patriots.

Washington got on the board first as running back Chad Morton took a short pass and turned it into a 30-yard gain to set up a 38-yard John Hall field goal.

The Patriots responded immediately with a drive to a 23-yard field goal by Adam Vinatieri to knot the game at 3-3.

In the second quarter, another Hall field goal pushed the Redskins to a 6-3 lead.

The Redskins took full advantage of a break just after intermission. On a play from the New England 26, Bailey nailed running back Kevin Faulk, forcing a fumble that bounced back to the six. Matt Bowen scooped it up there and bolted to the one-yard line. Ladell Betts cut behind a Derrick Dockery block and scored for a 13-3 Redskin lead.

After Vinatieri was wide left on a 46-yard field goal, the Redskins drove 64 yards to up their lead to 17. Actually, a good chunk of that yardage was on a roll. From the Washington 42, Trung Canidate broke loose for a gain of 23, but he fumbled at the end of the run. The ball kept going, bouncing and rolling from the Patriot 35 all the way down to the 12, where receiver Rod Gardner chased it down and made the recovery.

Two plays later Rock Cartwright ran it in from the three and the Redskins were up 20-3 with just over five minutes left in the third quarter.

The Patriots closed the gap almost immediately, taking just 2:55 to move 71 yards to a 29-yard TD pass from Brady to David Givens, making it 20-10 going into the fourth quarter.

Rashad Bauman picked off a Brady pass to kill one Patriot drive. With 2:10 left Brady found Larry Centers for seven yards and a touchdown and it was a three-point game at 20-17.

The Redskins offense hadn't done much on its own in the second half, so Bill Belichick decided to kick away rather than going for the onside kick. The strategy almost worked as the Redskins committed three false start penalties and punted from their own seven with 1:48 left. After a weak boot by Bryan Barker, New England had its last chance from the Washington 45.

The Pats went nowhere and after Ohalete knocked down Brady's fourth-down pass, one Patrick Ramsey kneel down ended it.

10/5/03	**EAGLES (2-2) 27, Redskins (3-2) 25**			67,792	
Was	0	10	3	12	25
Phi	3	10	7	7	27
Phi	FG Akers 52				
Phi	Ritchie 4 pass from McNabb (Kers kick)				
Was	Ramsey 1 run (Hall kick)				
Phi	FG Akers 36				
Was	FG Hall 48				
Was	FG Hall 45				
Phi	Kalu 15 Interception return (Akers kick)				
Was	FG Hall 37				
Phi	Westbrook 19 run (Akers kick)				
Was	FG Hall 53				
Was	McCants 32 pass from Ramsey (pass failed)				

Lincoln Financial Field—The Redskins had a chance to tie the Eagles in the late going but Patrick Ramsey was wild high on a pass for a two-point conversion attempt in the closing minute of the game.

"Laveranues [Coles] was wide open, and I missed the throw," Ramsey said. "It was as simple as that."

The Redskins did plenty to lose the game prior to Ramsey's late misfire. They committed 11 penalties and were generally sloppy in their play.

Despite all of that, the Redskins very nearly rallied back from an 11-point deficit with just over three minutes left to play.

After Brian Westbrook scooted over the goal line to put the Eagles up 27-16 with 3:10 left to play, Ramsey moved Washington into position for a 53-yard John Hall Field goal, his fourth of the day.

Hall followed that up with a well-executed onside kick and Bryan Johnson recovered the bouncing ball. Ramsey then fired to Darnerien McCants for 32 yards and a touchdown that made the score 27-25.

A Philly blitz left Coles open on the attempt to put the game into overtime, but the throw was off target.

Two Ramsey interceptions earlier in the game helped the Eagles build a lead the Redskins couldn't quite overcome. Soon after a Rod Hood interception set up Philadelphia at the Washington 18, Donovan McNabb threw a four-yard touchdown pass to fullback Don Richie.

With the game tied at 13 in the third quarter Ramsey was hit as he attempted a screen pass to Ladell Betts. The ball floated into the air and into the waiting arms of defensive end N. D. Kalu at the Washington 15. He dashed into the end zone to put the Eagles up to stay.

10/12/03	**Buccaneers (3-2) 35, REDSKINS (3-3) 13**			85,490	
TB	0	7	7	21	35
Was	3	7	3	0	13
Was	FG Hall 33				
TB	Yoder 1 pass from B. Johnson (Gramatica kick)				
Was	McCants 2 pass from Ramsey (Hall kick)				
Was	FG Hall 51				
TB	Yoder 11 pass from B. Johnson (Gramatica kick)				
TB	Heller 4 pass from B. Johnson (Gramatica kick)				
TB	K. Johnson 39 pass from B. Johnson (Gramatica kick)				
TB	Brooks 44 interception return (Gramatica kick)				

FedEx Field—A six-point Redskin lead early in the third quarter was buried under an avalanche of 28 unanswered points by the Buccaneers, who cruised to a 35-13 win.

The Redskins got on the board on their second possession, but they wanted more than John Hall's 33-yard field goal out of their 18-play drive.

A one-yard pass from Brad Johnson to Todd Yoder capped an 85-yard drive that gave Tampa Bay a 7-3 lead in the second quarter.

Washington retook the lead before halftime. Patrick Ramsey threw a dart to Rod Gardner for a 22-yard gain to the Bucs two. On the next play Ramsey found Darnerien McCants in the end zone to put the Redskins up 10-7 at intermission.

Things were looking pretty good for the Redskins when they expanded their lead with a drive to a 51-yard Hall field goal. Then a taunting penalty on Tampa Bay receiver Keenan McCardell had the Bucs in a third and 15 at their own 15.

But Johnson beat a blitz with a toss to running back Michael Pittman that gained 18 yards. The Bucs cruised the rest of the way to the end zone, taking the lead for good when Johnson again hit a wide-open Yoder for a touchdown, this time from 11 yards out.

It got ugly in the fourth quarter. Ramsey threw an interception to set up another Johnson touchdown pass. It went again to a tight end on the same misdirection play that had worked twice before, but this time it went to Will Heller to make it 21-13.

Keyshawn Johnson caught Brad Johnson's fourth touchdown pass of the game, a 39-yard toss, and Derrick Brooks capped the scoring with a 44-yard return of an interception.

10/19/03	**BILLS (4-3) 24, Redskins (3-4) 7**			73,149	
Was	0	0	7	0	7
Buf	3	7	7	7	24
Buf	FG Lindell 20				
Buf	Henry 4 run (Lindell kick)				
Was	Gardner 25 pass from Ramsey (Hall kick)				
Buf	Reed 10 pass from Bledsoe (Lindell kick)				
Buf	Henry 14 run (Lindell kick)				

Ralph Wilson Stadium—The Bills came into this game ranked last in the entire NFL in total offense. When it was over they had racked up 432 yards of offense in the course of pounding the Redskins 24-7.

Buffalo's Travis Henry nearly outgained the entire Washington offense himself. The running back pounded for 167 yards while the Patrick Ramsey-led Redskins offense mustered just 169.

There were a lot of reasons why defensive end Renaldo Wynn said that "the whole roof caved in." Ramsey was charged with three fumbles in a two-play span in the second quarter. The first of those three came when rookie guard Derrick Dockery knocked the ball out of his hand on a third and goal play from the one. The Bills' Lawyer Milloy recovered and one of the Redskins' few solid scoring threats went by the wayside.

Washington was down 10-0 before earning a first down. Buffalo drove to a 20-yard Rian Lindell field goal on its first possession.

The Bills got a good break during their second scoring drive. LaVar Arrington executed a perfect strip, punching the ball out of the arms of fullback Sam Gash, who had caught a Drew Bledsoe pass. The ball zipped straight into the arms of receiver Bobby Shaw, who ran for 10 more yards. That drive culminated in a four-yard Henry touchdown run.

The Redskins made the appearance of getting back into the game on their initial possession of the second half. Rock Cartwright powered for five yards on fourth and one to keep alive a drive that ended when Rod Gardner made a nice touchdown catch from 25 yards out. Hall's conversion made it 10-7.

Buffalo responded immediately, however, by marching 80 yards to extend the lead back to 10. Josh Reed got the six points on a 10-yard pass from Bledsoe.

Meanwhile, the Bills defense pounded on Ramsey, hitting him on almost every play. Eventually he came out and ex-Bill Rob

Johnson came in. To the delight of the crowd, he was sacked on his second snap.

Henry finished up the scoring with a 14-yard touchdown jaunt in the fourth quarter.

Spurrier Tempers Harsh Comments

Oct 20—Steve Spurrier today attempted to soften some harsh remarks he made in the wake of Sunday's 24-7 loss to Buffalo.

After the game, Spurrier questioned the effort and commitment of some unspecified members of the team. "We may go out on the street and pick up guys who will play hard," Spurrier said after the game.

"Maybe that was an on-the-moment thought to get our guys' attention," Spurrier said today. He acknowledged the fact that it would be difficult to make any significant personnel changes in late October.

"This is our team," he said.

Quarterback Carousel: Johnson Cut

Oct 22—The Redskins again shuffled their quarterback contingent, waiving Rob Johnson and replacing him with Tim Hasselbeck.

Johnson, who signed a two-year, $2 million contract last March, never was comfortable running Steve Spurrier's offense nor did he mesh with the coach personally.

Hasselbeck has never thrown an NFL pass and will get a crash course in the offense over the coming bye week.

11/2/03	COWBOYS (6-2) 21, Redskins (3-5) 14				64,002
Was	6	0	0	8	14
Dal	0	7	7	7	21
Was	Coles 7 pass from Ramsey (kick failed)				
Dal	Hambrick 2 run (Cundiff kick)				
Dal	Hambrick 1 run (Cundiff kick)				
Dal	Glenn 19 pass from Carter (Cundiff kick)				
Was	Jacobs 19 pass from Ramsey (McCants pass from Ramsey)				

Texas Stadium—The Dallas Cowboys tried very hard to play the role of generous hosts, but the Redskins were not able to take advantage of the hospitality. Despite the fact that the Cowboys turned the ball over four times in the first half, the Redskins scored just one touchdown and eventually fell to Dallas 21-14.

The one break that Washington did turn into points was a first-quarter interception of Quincy Carter. Actually, while Carter was charged with the turnover, the blame should go to his intended receiver, Terry Glenn. Carter's pass was on the mark but Glenn first dropped it and then knocked it into the air with his leg. It was an easy pick for safety Ifeanyi Ohalete and his subsequent 30-yard return had the Redskins in business at the Dallas six.

From the seven two plays later, Laveranues Coles ran a fade and did a nice job of getting both feet down inbounds as he gathered in Patrick Ramsey's pass. Dallas offensive tackle Flozell Adams got a hand on John Hall's conversion attempt and it remained 6-0.

In the second quarter a dropped interception and personal foul penalty helped move Dallas to the Washington four. On fourth down from there, the Cowboys lined up to attempt a field goal. A penalty flag flew and Washington linebacker Antonio Pierce was charged with unsportsmanlike conduct for imitating Dallas' snap count. After the penalty nobody had seen before and hasn't seen since, Troy Hambrick dove in for a touchdown to put Dallas up 7-6.

The Cowboys extended their lead on their first possession of the second half. LaVar Arrington appeared to have ended that possession with an interception, but it was overturned when a replay revealed the ball had hit the ground before Arrington had

control. Hambrick again powered for the touchdown, this time from a yard out.

A 91-yard drive that spanned the third and fourth quarters clinched it for Dallas. Carter dodged a blitzing Arrington and found Glenn for a 19-yard scoring pass with just over 11 minutes left to play.

Ramsey suffered a dislocated pinky during a late drive but returned to throw a 19-yard touchdown pass to rookie receiver Taylor Jacobs. A two-point conversion attempt was successful to put the Redskins in striking distance at 21-14 but Dallas ran out the remaining time.

11/9/03	REDSKINS (4-5) 27, Seahawks (6-3) 20				80,728
Sea	14	3	0	3	20
Was	3	14	3	7	27
Was	FG Hall 20				
Sea	Ingram 5 pass from Hasselbeck (Brown kick)				
Sea	Alexander 1 run (Brown kick)				
Was	Coles 15 pass from Ramsey (Hall kick)				
Sea	FG Brown 27				
Was	Gardner 14 pass from Ramsey				
Was	FG Hall 34				
Sea	FG Brown 48				
Was	Canidate 10 pass from Gardner				

FedEx Field—Rod Gardner caught a touchdown pass and threw for a TD as the Redskins' beat Seattle 27-20.

Gardner's scoring pass culminated the game-winning drive with just under two minutes left to play. The march was kept alive a few minutes earlier when coach Steve Spurrier took the NFL's book of conventional wisdom and tossed it out. In a tie game, he kept his offense on the field on fourth and inches from his team's own 25. Rock Cartwright made him look good by fighting for a yard.

Spurrier's gambling side came out again on the winning play. Facing third and five at the Seattle 10, many NFL coaches would have gone for a safe play to keep a chip-shot field goal try alive.

That's what Spurrier was going to do before the Seahawks called time-out; the coach then changed the play. Quarterback Patrick Ramsey dropped back and fired a lateral over to Gardner, who was wide left. The high-school quarterback backpedaled long enough for running back Trung Canidate to sneak over to the right side. No Seahawk was in shouting distance of Canidate as he gathered in Gardner's pass for the easy touchdown.

Aside from the final drive, most of the game's action came in the first half. Seattle took a 14-3 lead in the first quarter and it looked like it was about to get worse early in the second period. Safety Damien Robinson picked off a Ramsey pass at the Washington 28 and nothing but green grass and white stripes seemed to be between Robinson and the goal line. Receiver Laveranues Coles hustled to the ball, though, and knocked it loose at the two. Guard Randy Thomas didn't quit on the play either, recovering in the end zone for a touchback.

The Redskins resumed the drive at their 20 and moved to a touchdown. They received a break along the way when Ramsey appeared to have thrown an interception to Shawn Springs, but the play was negated by a pass interference call on Marcus Trufant. Ramsey went to Coles to cap the drive with a 15-yard scoring strike to make it 14-10.

A Seattle drive built primarily on Matt Hasselbeck passes set up a Josh Brown field goal just before the two-minute warning but the Redskins stormed back to tie it at halftime. Ramsey finished off a 66-yard foray with a 14-yard pass to Gardner.

The teams exchanged second-half field goals prior to the Redskins' winning drive.

11/16/03	PANTHERS (8-2) 20, Redskins (4-6) 17			73,263	
Was	0	3	0	14	17
Car	0	3	7	10	20
Car	FG Kasay 25				
Was	FG Hall 23				
Car	Delhomme 1 run (Kasay kick)				
Was	McCants 4 pass from Ramsey (Hall kick)				
Car	FG Kasay 26				
Was	Johnson 10 pass from Ramsey (Hall kick)				
Car	Davis 3 run (Kasay kick)				

Ericsson Stadium—Former Redskins star Stephen Davis scored a late touchdown to snatch a 20-17 victory away from his old team. The play was controversial, but counted just the same.

Washington had rallied to score two fourth-quarter touchdowns to take a 17-13 lead. With just over a minute left quarterback Jake Delhomme led his team down to the Washington one.

On second and goal from the three, Davis took a handoff, encountered some traffic and extended the ball towards the goal line. The ball popped loose. One of three things had happened—and two of them were good for the Redskins: Davis had broken the plane of the goal line with the ball and scored a touchdown; his knee hit the ground before the ball got to the end zone; or the Redskins had knocked the ball out of his hands before either the knee hit or he scored.

After the way things have gone for the Redskins this year, it was no surprise the call went against them. The line judge ruled that Davis had scored; the referee didn't see anything on replay to counter that ruling.

Truth be told, the Redskins should not have been in position to have a close call cost them the game. Blunders of their own making cost them 21 first-half points. Patrick Ramsey overthrew two wide-open receivers who almost certainly would have scored, and Rock Cartwright fumbled the ball away at the Carolina goal line.

Trailing 10-3 entering the fourth quarter the Redskins tied it up when Darnerien McCants made a great catch of a Ramsey pass in the back of the end zone. Carolina retook the lead on John Kasay's 26-yard field goal with 5:24 to go but the Redskins moved quickly—perhaps too quickly—to seize the lead.

A 29-yard pass interference penalty greatly aided the drive and Ramsey finished it off with a 10-yard touchdown pass to receiver Patrick Johnson with 4:19 left.

Panthers coach John Fox gambled on fourth and one at the Carolina 38 and it paid off in a big way as Delhomme found Davis for 28 yards to the Washington 37. Steve Smith made a leaping catch to get the Panthers down to the seven and Davis squeaked the ball into the end zone two plays later.

11/23/03	DOLPHINS (7-4) 24, Redskins (4-7) 23			73,578	
Was	6	14	3	0	23
Mia	7	3	0	14	24
Mia	McKnight 80 pass from Griese (Mare kick)				
Was	FG Hall 28				
Was	FG Hall 31				
Was	Coles 37 pass from Hasselbeck (Hall kick)				
Was	Canidate 2 run (Hall kick)				
Mia	FG Mare 51				
Was	FG Hall 22				
Mia	Williams 1 run (Mare kick)				
Mia	Williams 24 run (Mare kick)				

Pro Player Stadium—The Redskins had leads of 20-7 in the first half and 23-10 in the third quarter but Miami rallied with two fourth-quarter touchdowns to take a 24-23 win.

With the beating he has been taking all year it seemed to be only a matter of time before Patrick Ramsey took one too many hits and got knocked out of a game. The time came in the second quarter when he was thrown to the ground on a sack. Ramsey

suffered a slight concussion and Tim Hasselbeck entered the game, getting his first significant NFL entry in the process.

The Redskins were trailing 7-3 when Hasselbeck came in and immediately had a positive impact, leading three straight scoring drives. After a pair of John Hall field goals, Hasselbeck found Laveranues Coles on a pump-and-go for 37 yards and a touchdown to put the Redskins up 13-7 in the second quarter.

The Redskins expanded their lead to 20-7 later in the second. Chad Morton's 27-yard run keyed the drive, an 11-yard Hasselbeck scramble got them down to the Miami five and Trung Canidate scooted untouched around right end for the final two yards.

Miami drove to an Olinda Mare field goal before intermission but the Redskins scored the only points of the third quarter on a 22-yard Hall field goal, taking a 23-10 lead into the fourth quarter.

After Hall's field goal, Miami coach Dave Wannstedt gave the hook to quarterback Brian Griese, who had been struggling since throwing an 80-yard touchdown pass in the first quarter. Jay Fiedler came in as the spark the Dolphins needed. He immediately completed a 31-yard pass to Chris Chambers and the Dolphins were on their way. Ricky Williams capped the drive with a one-yard scoring drive on fourth and goal.

Miami got the ball back and moved in for the kill. Williams dashed through the Washington defense for 24 yards and the go-ahead score with 4:19 left to play.

The Redskins had two shots to get into position for a winning field goal but Hasselbeck threw an interception and Patrick Johnson fumbled a punt to squander those opportunities.

Skins Hoping For Ramsey, Not Playoffs

Nov 24—Steve Spurrier conceded that the Redskins have almost no shot at reaching the playoffs, but he'd like to get injured quarterback Patrick Ramsey back behind center at some point.

With the team at 4-7 and three games behind the last NFC Wild Card spot, Spurrier acknowledged reality in saying, "The playoffs are very, very unrealistic right now."

Ramsey was knocked out of Sunday's game in Miami with a concussion and he also has been struggling with an old foot injury that has flared up lately.

"Patrick is still our starting quarterback as long as he's healthy to play," said Spurrier.

Nov 29

Ramsey Knocked to Sideline
Injuries sideline QB; Hasselbeck will start vs. Saints

11/30/03	Saints (6-6) 24, REDSKINS (4-8) 20			76,821	
NO	0	10	7	7	24
Was	0	14	3	3	20
NO	Brooks 7 run (Carney kick)				
Was	Cartwright 2 run (Hall kick)				
NO	FG Carney 25				
Was	Morton 94 kickoff return (Hall kick)				
Was	FG Hall 45				
NO	Brooks 3 run (Carney kick)				
Was	FG Hall 49				
NO	Williams 15 pass from Brooks				

FedEx Field—For the third straight week the Redskins had a fourth-quarter lead—and for the third straight week, they blew it. This time they fell victim to Aaron Brooks and the New Orleans Saints by a score of 24-20.

Tim Hasselbeck started at quarterback in place of the injured Patrick Ramsey and was respectable in his first NFL start, going 22 of 42 for 231 yards.

After a scoreless first quarter, things heated up. First the teams traded touchdowns, the Saints scoring on a seven-yard

Brooks scramble and Washington answering with a two-yard run by Rock Cartwright.

New Orleans recaptured the lead at 10-7 on a 25-yard John Carney field goal but they didn't hold it for long. Chad Morton fielded the ensuing kickoff at the six and took the shortest route to the goal line, going straight up the middle for 94 yards and a touchdown. He broke an ankle tackle along the way and had the speedy Patrick Johnson serve as an escort on his way to the end zone.

After the Redskins extended their lead to 17-10 on a 45-yard John Hall field goal, the Saints evened things up with another Brooks touchdown scamper, this one from three yards out.

The kickoff went out of bounds, setting the Redskins up at their own 40. A 16-yard Laveranues Coles reception helped move Washington into range for Hall to give the Redskins the lead when he boomed a 49-yard field goal.

Unfortunately, the Redskins special teams returned the favorable field position favor the Saints had just granted. Keyuo Craver returned the kickoff to the Washington 40. From there, four Deuce McAllister runs gained 23 yards and Brooks then capped the drive with a pinpoint pass to Boo Williams, who was stationed between two defenders in the end zone.

The Redskins still had time to respond but, as has been the pattern lately, they couldn't get it done. Hasselbeck overthrew a wide-open Coles on third and two to kill the drive and their last chance was shot down with four straight incompletions.

Ramsey Carted Off Practice Field

Dec 3—Patrick Ramsey's season could be over after all.

His foot, revealed to have a previously-undetected break, gave out as he attempted to plant it today during practice. The second-year quarterback fell and was carted off the field. Ramsey missed his first start of the season due to the injury last week. It was thought that he could be able to play with it until it could be repaired with offseason surgery.

While examination revealed no new injury to his foot, the team may decide to shut him down for the season to prevent further damage.

12/7/03	**Redskins (5-8) 20, GIANTS (4-9) 7**			78,217	
Was	3	7	7	3	20
NYG	7	0	0	0	7
Was	FG Hall 28				
NYG	Levens 5 run (Bryant kick)				
Was	McCants 6 pass from Hasselbeck (Hall kick)				
Was	Gardner 7 pass from Hasselbeck (Hall kick)				
Was	FG Hall 41				

Giants Stadium—In a cold, blustery Giants Stadium, Tim Hasselbeck was a very efficient 13 for 19 for 153 yards and two touchdowns to help the Redskins past the Giants 20-7.

There was an historic highlight to the game as Bruce Smith sacked backup quarterback Jesse Palmer in the fourth quarter to surpass Reggie White and become the career leader in that category. It was one of six sacks the Washington defense collected on the day.

John Hall got the scoring going for the Redskins with a 28-yard field goal, a score set up by a Tiki Barber fumble at the New York 27. The Giants responded, driving to a five-yard Dorsey Levens touchdown run.

That would prove to be the high-water mark for the Giants. Patrick Johnson returned the ensuing kickoff 50 yards. Soon after that the Redskins scored on a six-yard pass from Hasselbeck to Darnerien McCants. It was 10-7 and the Redskins were ahead to stay.

The Giants had a chance to score near the end of the first half but one of Kerry Collins' passes went through the hands of Tim Carter and Camp Bailey got the interception to kill the drive.

Washington extended its lead early in the third quarter. On third and five at the New York seven, Hasselbeck fired a touchdown pass to Rod Gardner. Another Hall field goal—this one from 41 yards with 10:42 left—stretched the Washington lead to 20-7.

The Giants had one more shot. From the New York 25, Barber took a swing pass from Palmer and nothing but green grass and white stripes stood between him and the end zone. However, he had Jeremiah Trotter behind him and the middle linebacker ran down the speedy back after a gain of 36.

The Giants did make it down to the Redskins 12, but a fourth-down incompletion clinched the Washington win.

Dec 10

Snyder: Spurrier Will Be Back in '04
Owner says coach 'absolutely' will be retained despite team's struggles

---

12/14/03	**Cowboys (9-5) 27, REDSKINS (5-9) 0**			70,284	
Dal	7	7	3	10	27
Was	0	0	0	0	0
Dal	Anderson 21 pass from Carter (Cundiff kick)				
Dal	Carter 3 run (Cundiff kick)				
Dal	FG Cundiff 34				
Dal	FG Cundiff 20				
Dal	Bickerstaff 2 run (Cundiff kick)				

FedEx Field—You know it was a bad game when the home fans throw snowballs at you . . . and you think they were being kind.

Some FedEx Field fans—out of the few that remained at the end of this 27-0 spanking at the hands of the Cowboys—pitched snowballs at Redskins players towards the end of the contest made even more miserable by the damp, chilly and snowy weather.

Fred Smoot did not feel that the action was without merit. "They should have thrown a glacier out there," he said. "We stunk. We stunk the place up."

Quarterback Tim Hasselbeck had a historically bad day. He completed six passes to Redskins and four to Cowboys. His six of 26 day for 56 yards added up—or added down, if that's possible—to a quarterback rating of 0.0. In case you're wondering, no, it is not possible to get a negative QB rating.

Hasselbeck was far from the only goat. Chad Morton lost a fumble, as did tight end Zeron Flemister.

And the Redskins defense gave little more than token resistance to a Dallas offense that wasn't exactly a powerhouse. The Cowboys got all of the points they would need on their first drive. They cruised 74 yards in 10 plays with Troy Hambrick chewing up big chunks of the field with runs of 12 and 15 yards. The payoff came on a 21-yard pass from Quincy Carter to Troy Hambrick.

The Redskins' best scoring chance came in the second quarter. Bryan Barker completed a three yard pass on a fake punt play to keep the drive alive. A few plays later Hasselbeck thought he had the perfect matchup with rookie cornerback Terrace Newman covering Laveranues Coles one on one. Good setup; poor execution. The pass was badly underthrown and Newman had an easy interception.

Later in the second Hasselbeck sailed a pass well over Rock Cartwright's head. Newman picked it off and his 25-yard return had the Cowboys in business at the Washington 9. Three plays later Carter took a shotgun snap and bolted into the end zone.

The Cowboys cruised in the second half and the Redskins never mounted much of a threat.

12/21/03	**BEARS (7-8) 27, Redskins (5-10) 24**				61,719
Was	10	7	0	7	24
Chi	10	0	14	3	27

Was	FG Hall 27
Chi	Booker 59 pass from Grossman (Edinger kick)
Chi	FG Edinger 19
Was	Morton 36 pass from Gardner (Hall kick)
Was	Coles 14 pass from Hasselbeck (Hall kick)
Chi	Gage 11 pass from Hasselbeck (Edinger kick)
Chi	Thomas 3 run (Edinger kick)
Was	Coles 19 pass from Hasselbeck (Hall kick)
Chi	FG Edinger 45

Soldier Field—As Chicago's Paul Edinger lined up for a 45-yard field goal against a stiff wind with time running out, virtually everyone thought that the game was headed to overtime. The breeze wasn't just blowing the streamers on top of the goal posts; the uprights themselves were swaying. There seemed to be no way that Edinger could undo the 24-24 tie.

But these are the 2003 Redskins, and it seems as though every break that could go against them *would* go against them. And, against all odds, Edinger's boot slipped through the swirling currents and snuck over the crossbar with less than two feet to spare with five seconds left. The Bears had a 27-24 win.

"It's the story of our season," said Chris Samuels.

Of course, there is more to the story than the field goal. A few plays before that attempt, the Bears faced fourth and inches at the Redskins 38. Tailback Anthony Thomas slammed into the pile and shifted it just enough to move the chains. The drive stayed alive and Chicago won it a few plays later.

Washington got a Fred Smooth interception deep in Chicago territory at the nine, but after three Tim Hasselbeck incompletions they had to settle for a 27-yard John Hall field goal.

The Bears took a 10-3 lead before Hasselbeck—who posted a worse-than-dismal 0.0 quarterback rating a week ago against Dallas—got heated up. He moved the Redskins down to the Chicago 36 and, from there, he lateraled to receiver Rod Gardner. The high-school quarterback had an easy toss to a wide-open Chad Morton for the touchdown.

It looked like Gardner had another TD pass to his credit just before halftime. The target of his pass was Hasselbeck but officials ruled that the ball hit the ground before he gathered it in. The Redskins got the six points anyway as Hasselbeck rifled a 14-yard strike to Laveranues Coles, giving Washington a 17-10 halftime lead.

The offense essentially took the third quarter off as Chicago controlled the ball for 13 minutes while scoring two touchdowns and retaking the lead. A second Hasselbeck-to-Coles scoring strike—this one from 19 yards—evened it up early in the fourth, setting the stage for Edinger's late dramatics.

LaVar's Salary Takes a Leap

Dec 26—Linebacker LaVar Arrington's penchant for making big plays has earned him some big bucks.

He inked a contract extension worth $68 million over eight years. There is approximately $20 million in guaranteed money.

The deal clears considerable cap space for the 2004 season and was designed to have Arrington remain a Redskin for the rest of his career.

12/27/03	**Eagles (12-4) 31, REDSKINS (5-11) 7**				76,766
Phi	7	14	7	3	31
Was	0	7	0	0	7

Phi	Lewis 3 pass from McNabb (Akers kick)
Phi	McNabb 1 run (Akers kick)
Phi	Mitchell 8 pass from McNabb
Was	Cartwright 1 run (Hall kick)
Phi	Buckhalter 11 pass from McNabb
Phi	FG Akers 26

FedEx Field—The Eagles scored touchdowns the first three times they had the ball and cruised to a 31-7 win over the Redskins.

The outcome was fitting of the Redskins' dismal season. After a 3-1 start, they won just two of their final 12 games.

The only time it appeared this game might be competitive was during the Redskins' opening drive. Tim Hasselbeck found receiver Laveranues Coles for gains of 13 and 14 yards to move Washington into Eagle territory. But John Hall's 52-yard field goal attempt faded wide left.

Philadelphia moved quickly after taking possession. Donovan McNabb completed passes of 24 yards to Todd Pinkston and 17 yards to Brian Westbrook to move the Eagles deep into Washington territory. On second and goal at the three, the Redskins simply failed to cover tight end Chad Lewis and he caught a touchdown pass from McNabb.

The Eagles had considerably further to travel the next time they had the ball thanks to Bryan Barker's 69-yard punt that was downed at their four. Fourteen plays later they were in the end zone. McNabb went to Todd Pinkston for 40 yards to get things going and McNabb scrambled in from the one after executing a nice play action fake. A Hasselbeck fumble set up the Eagles' third score of the half.

A 40-yard rumble by Rock Cartwright helped the Redskins get on the board before halftime. He tallied the six points when he powered into the end zone to make it 21-7.

Any thoughts that the late score would create any momentum for the home team quickly were quashed as the Eagles moved smartly downfield for a touchdown.

2004
Head Coach: Joe Gibbs
Record: 6-10, Tied for Second in NFC East

Honors: Marcus Washington Pro Bowl

Fun 'n' Run: Spurrier Resigns

Dec 30—While Steve Spurrier was playing golf in Florida two days after the Redskins' season ended, his agent was speaking with Daniel Snyder. The purpose of the meeting was to negotiate the terms of Spurrier's resignation as coach of the Redskins.

The now-ex coach acknowledged his departure and that he may have made a mistake in coming to the NFL.

"The whole thing wasn't working," Spurrier said. "This is the best thing for everyone concerned."

"I've been a head coach for 20 years," he said. "That's a long time, a long grind. Coming to the NFL, I certainly didn't think it would be to have 5-11 seasons. It's probably time for me to ease on out a little bit."

There was some early confusion as to whether or not Spurrier had resigned earlier in the day. When reached by phone, he originally denied that he was quitting. His agent was actually in with Snyder negotiating the terms of his departure when the phone call was made; Spurrier thought it best not to say anything.

Snyder had indicated that he had every intention of bringing back Spurrier, who had a 12-20 record in two seasons, but he accepted the resignation "with regret."

By resigning, Spurrier walked away from the $15 million remaining on his original five-year contract.

Do You Believe in Miracles? Gibbs is Back!

Jan 7—In a move that stunned and delighted Redskins fans everywhere, Joe Gibbs—architect of the team's glory days in the 1980's and early 1990's—has agreed to return to coach the Redskins.

Gibbs has carved a successful stint as a champion NASCAR team owner in the 11 years since he left Washington. He has been mentioned in connection with numerous coaching openings, but has never seriously considered any of them.

For Washington, the return of Gibbs was the impossible dream. That dream has come true.

Gibbs: 'I Couldn't Coach Anywhere Else'

Jan 8—Yes, it really is true. Coach Joe is back.

There he was at the podium in the packed auditorium at Redskins Park. In front of him were the three Lombardi Trophies that he won. In the audience were dozens of the players that helped him win those Super Bowls.

After being formally introduced by Daniel Snyder, he admitted to being "nervous and excited." And he was talking about the challenges of coming back.

"There is no net, so I'm going to pray a lot!" said Gibbs. "But that may be the biggest thrill—knowing how hard it is."

When talking about being approached for other coaching jobs since he left the Redskins, he said that he turned them down because he enjoyed the freedom that NASCAR team ownership offered him. But, this time, when contacted by Daniel Snyder shortly after Steve Spurrier resigned last week, he said yes.

"I couldn't coach anyplace else," he said.

He admitted that it would take him a while to catch up on the technical aspects of the game. "But more than anything, it's our people, our players, picking the right guys that are Redskins and really care about it."

Gibbs Announces Coaching Staff

Feb 3—Joe Gibbs announced his coaching staff today. It was a lengthy press session and a crowded room because the staff is one of the largest in league history.

Counting Gibbs, there will be 17 men wearing headsets, reviewing film, instructing in fundamentals, and coming up with game plans. And there are a lot of impressive titles.

There are two assistant head coaches. Joe Bugel is AHC/offense while Gregg Williams is AHC/defense. Williams actually will run the defense while Bugel's responsibilities won't range much beyond the offensive line.

And then there are two coordinators, but they are that in title only. Don Breaux is the offensive coordinator but will coach the backs, while defensive coordinator Greg Blache will keep all of his attention on the defensive line.

Feb 18

QB Competition is on: Brunell Agrees to Deal
Jags QB will get $43 million over seven years, $8.6 million signing bonus; will compete with Ramsey for starting job

---

Free Agent Haul Climbs to Six in 24 Hours; Bailey Dealt for Portis, 2nd-Round Pick

Mar 5—The remaking of the Washington Redskins in Joe Gibbs' image began in earnest over the past few days.

In the first 24 hours of free agency the team has signed six players to contracts. In addition, the team executed trades for Clinton Portis and Mark Brunell.

Brunell was obtained for a third-round pick. Portis came from Denver in exchange for the rights to Washington's franchise player, cornerback Champ Bailey, and a second-round pick. The Redskins were unable to sign Bailey to a long-term contract and elected to trade him rather than have him play the year under the franchise tender.

The free agent haul centered on the defense, including end Phillip Daniels, tackle Cornelius Griffin, linebacker Marcus Washington and cornerback Shawn Springs.

Aug 8

The Rock Goes Down: Jansen Out for Season
Achilles' tendon tear sidelines tackle

Aug 30

Youth Not Served: Brunell to Start at QB
Ramsey will start season as backup

9/12/04	REDSKINS (1-0) 16, Buccaneers (0-1) 10			90,098	
TD	0	3	7	0	10
Was	7	3	0	6	16
Was	Portis 64 run (Hall kick)				
Was	FG Hall 20				
TB	FG Gramatica 47				
TB	Barber 9 fumble return (Gramatica kick)				
Was	FG Hall 30				
Was	FG Hall 34				

FedEx Field—A throng more than 90,000 strong greeted Joe Gibbs back to the Redskins, and the legendary coach and his new/old team did not disappoint. Washington exhibited a tough, ball-control offense and a swarming, aggressive defense while beating Tampa Bay 16-10.

"It was huge for me," Gibbs said. "I can tell you that."

It started out as though it was going to be a dominant performance reminiscent of the old glory days under Gibbs. On Clinton Portis' first carry as a Redskin, the line opened up a hole that would have made the old Hogs proud and he scooted 64 yards for a touchdown.

The Washington offense wasn't as dynamic the rest of the way, but it was effective. As a team the Redskins rushed for 166 yards, with Portis picking up 148 on 29 carries.

Much of the credit has to go to the Washington defense led by coordinator Gregg Williams, also making his Redskins debut. His aggressive schemes had Tampa Bay quarterback Brad Johnson confused and running for his life all day long.

The Bucs mustered just 169 yards of total offense, a mere 30 of them on the ground. Johnson was sacked four times, two of them by safety Matt Bowen.

Despite all of this, it was a tie game going into the fourth quarter. The Redskins' early superiority was wiped out in an instant with about five minutes left in the third quarter. Center Cory Raymer stepped on Mark Brunell's foot as the quarterback was handing off to Portis. The ball came loose and bounced into the arms of cornerback Ronde Barber, who stepped nine yards for a touchdown to tie it at 10.

An Antonio Pierce interception caused by defensive lineman Jermaine Haley's good pressure set up the go-ahead score. Haley forced an errant pass by Johnson and Pierce made a leaping interception. His return to the Washington 36 gave the Redskins good field position and Portis keyed the drive to Hall's field goal to make it 13-10.

A Portis conversion of a third and one allowed the Redskins to kill most of the remaining time before Hall's 34-yarder pushed the final score to 16-10.

9/19/04	GIANTS (1-1) 20, Redskins (1-1) 14			78,767	
Was	7	0	0	7	14
NYG	0	20	0	0	20
Was	Cooley 2 pass from Brunell (Hall kick)				
NYG	Carter 38 pass from Warner (Christie kick)				
NYG	Green 16 fumble return (Christie kick)				
NYG	FG Christie 38				
NYG	FG Christie 22				
Was	Portis 13 pass from Ramsey (Hall kick)				

Giants Stadium—The Giants posted 20 unanswered points in the third quarter, giving them all they would need for their 20-14 win over Washington.

The Redskins' sloppy play—four interceptions, three lost fumbles, and various other sins of commission and omission—contributed both to the Giants building that lead and the Redskins being unable to overcome it.

"We made so many mistakes today," Gibbs said. "I think back and I don't know that I have seen that many."

Things started off well for the Redskins as they drove 53 yards to the game's first touchdown. The payoff came from the Giants'

two-yard line when Brunell executed a nifty bootleg fake and tossed to Chris Cooley for the TD.

The mistakes began to snowball in the second quarter. First Brunell was sacked and stripped by defensive tackle Fred Robbins. Michael Strahan recovered and it took Kurt Warner exactly one play to make the Redskins pay for the error. His 38-yard touchdown strike to Tim Carter tied the score at seven.

The turnover bug soon bit the Redskins again. Clinton Portis fumbled and linebacker Barrett Green scooped up the loose ball and rolled 16 yards to put the Giants ahead to stay at 14-7.

Brunell threw an interception to set up a Steve Christie field goal and before halftime, Warner crafted a 72-yard drive to put the Giants up 20-7 late in the second period.

John Hall bounced a 41-yard field goal attempt off the right upright, beginning a parade of blown opportunities for the Redskins. Brunell went out with a pulled hamstring early in the third quarter and Patrick Ramsey came in at quarterback.

Ramsey showed why the Redskins are intrigued by him as he completed a 51-yard pass to Rod Gardner, who made a diving catch at the New York seven. He then showed why he's on the bench by forcing a pass in to Laveranues Coles that was picked off in the end zone by safety Brent Alexander.

Things started looking up for Washington early in the fourth quarter. Ramsey zipped a touchdown pass to Portis and Todd Franz recovered a Giant fumble on the ensuing kickoff. The Redskins were in business at the New York 45 and a touchdown away from taking the lead.

But a few plays later Ramsey threw the ball right to safety Gibril Wilson. One later foray into Giant territory ended in another Alexander interception.

Sep 23

Arrington Out 2-4 Weeks
Pro Bowl LB has surgery on knee

9/27/04	Cowboys (2-1) 21, REDSKINS (1-2) 18			90,367	
Dal	7	0	7	7	21
Was	0	3	7	8	18
Dal	George 1 run (Cundiff kick)				
Was	FG Hall 19				
Dal	Whitten 10 pass from Testaverde (Cundiff kick)				
Was	Gardner 1 pass from Brunell (Hall kick)				
Dal	Glenn 26 pass from Anderson (Cundiff kick)				
Was	Gardner 15 pass from Brunell (Jacobs pass from Brunell)				

FedEx Field—Bill Parcells always had Joe Gibbs' number when the two coached against each other in the 1980's. The Cowboys had won 12 of the last 13 games against Washington. Put Parcells in charge of the Cowboys and you have a double jinx that the Redskins were unable to overcome as they fell to Dallas 21-18.

The Cowboys scored first on a one-yard Eddie George run and held their rivals at arm's length the rest of the way.

Washington had an excellent opportunity to tie it up just before halftime. A steady march that had consumed nearly half of the second quarter had the Redskins knocking on the door with a first and goal at the one. However, Brunell got nowhere on a first-down sneak, Clinton Portis was stuffed on second down and Brunell threw incomplete on third. John Hall kicked a 19-yard field goal and it was 7-3 at the half.

The magnitude of those four points left on the field became apparent when Dallas exploded for a touchdown on its second possession of the third quarter. On second down from the Dallas 19, Testaverde completed consecutive passes to Antonio Bryant for 48 yards, to Keyshawn Johnson for 23, and to Jason Witten for 10 yards and a touchdown. That made it 14-3 and the Redskins were playing catch up.

The Skins did answer with a nice touchdown drive and pulled to within 14-10 on a one-yard flip from Brunell to Rod Gardner. That still left them trailing by four, however.

And that's when Richie Anderson put them away. Early in the fourth quarter he caught a Testaverde pass and scampered 28 yards to the Washington 39. Then, two plays later, Anderson got the call on a halfback option and threw a 26-yard touchdown pass to Terry Glenn. The receiver displayed some fancy footwork to keep both feet in bounds as he gathered in the pass. Gibbs challenged the call but it was upheld.

Thirteen minutes remained to be played—plenty of time, except the Redskins needed two scores. They got one as Brunell threw a 15-yard touchdown pass to Gardner to complete a two-play, 64-yard drive. A two-point conversion got the Redskins within 21-18 with 4:30 to play.

But the Cowboys were able to run all but 21 seconds off of the remaining clock. A desperation pass to Gardner got the Redskins down to the Dallas 21, but time expired before they could run another play.

10/3/04	BROWNS (2-2) 17, Redskins (1-3) 13			73,348	
Was	3	7	0	3	13
Cle	3	0	7	7	17
Was	FG Hall 31				
Cle	FG Dawson 30				
Was	Portis 1 run (Hall kick)				
Cle	Shea 15 pass from Garcia (Dawson kick)				
Was	FG Hall 26				
Cle	Suggs 3 run (Dawson kick)				

Cleveland Browns Stadium—The Cleveland Browns were missing seven starters but the Redskins seemingly played without their entire offense, losing 17-13.

Washington held leads of 3-0, 10-3, and 13-10 but an inability to sustain drives and the failure of the defense to make key stops let the Browns hang around.

Oh, and don't forget the mistakes. After John Hall's 31-yard field goal gave Washington that 3-0 lead, James Thrash committed a face mask penalty on the ensuing kickoff. That allowed Cleveland to start with a short field at its own 46 and Phil Dawson tied the game with a 30-yard field goal.

The Washington offense had one more nice drive before disappearing for the day. Clinton Portis runs and Mark Brunell passes—including a 30-yarder to Laveranues Coles to convert a fourth and six at the Cleveland 37—moved the Redskins into position for a one-yard Portis TD blast. Hall converted and it was 10-3 at the half.

At that point the Redskins had controlled the ball for 18 minutes. They would have it for another 11 minutes the entire second half. The third quarter started ugly when Portis fumbled the ball away at the Washington 32. Four plays later the game was tied as Jeff Garcia threw a 15-yard touchdown pass to Aaron Shea.

The Redskins did muster one more sustained drive, but they couldn't punch it in after getting a first down at the Cleveland 12. They settled for Hall's 26-yard field goal and a 13-10 lead six seconds into the fourth quarter.

Washington held defensively but after the punt, all the offense could muster was a three and out. That opened the door for Cleveland and Garcia led a nine-play, 80-yard touchdown drive. Lee Suggs capped it with a three-yard touchdown run with 6:55 left to play.

Trailing by four, the Redskins had two more possessions to try to retake the lead. The first one went three and out; the second ended on a Coles fumble recovered by defensive back Earl Little.

10/10/04	Ravens (3-2) 17, REDSKINS (1-4) 10			90,287	
Bal	0	0	14	3	17
Was	0	10	0	0	10
Was	FG Hall 26				
Was	Cooley 7 pass from Brunell (Hall kick)				
Bal	Reed 22 fumble return (Stover kick)				
Bal	Sams 78 punt return (Stover kick)				
Bal	FG Stover 33				

FedEx Field—The Ravens rallied from a 10-0 halftime deficit without scoring an offensive touchdown and beat the Redskins 17-10.

The Washington offense was nothing to write home about either. They did have a balanced "attack," gaining 52 yards on the ground and 55 passing. Add two turnovers to that and you have a picture of futility.

Three times in the second quarter the Redskins defense intercepted passes in Ravens territory. They only managed 10 points out of those three chances.

Poor offense? Great defense? Probably a little of both on the part of both teams—and it added up to a whole lot of nothing offensively.

Washington finally got a touchdown following the last of those three picks. Todd Franz returned the pick of Kyle Boller down to the Baltimore eight. Two plays later Mark Brunell found Chris Cooley for seven yards and a touchdown. That made it 10-0 at halftime.

Safety Ed Reed got the Ravens on the board midway through the third quarter by notching a defender's grand slam. He sacked Brunell, stripped away the ball, recovered the fumble and returned it 22 yards for a touchdown. All of a sudden it was 10-7.

The Redskins went three and out and punted away the ball to B. J. Sams. He faked a reverse handoff and flew up the right sideline. Khary Campbell had the last shot at Sams, but the ankle tackle near the goal line was futile.

A Brunell interception near the end of the third quarter set up a Matt Stover field goal early in the fourth. The Redskins had two more possessions after that and went nowhere. Along with the rest of the crowd at FedEx Field they watched Jamal Lewis chew up yardage and the clock. The only truly productive offensive player on the field got most of his 168 yards rushing against a worn-down Washington defense in the second half.

10/17/04	Redskins (2-4) 13, BEARS (1-4) 10			61,945	
Was	3	7	0	3	13
Chi	0	7	0	3	10
Was	FG Kimrin 41				
Was	Gardner 18 pass from Brunell (Kimrin kick)				
Chi	Azumah 70 interception return (Edinger kick)				
Was	FG Kimrin 26				
Chi	FG Edinger 26				

Soldier Field—All year long, the Redskins have been trying and failing to field an offense that would live up to the standards Joe Gibbs' teams set in the 1980's.

Today, against the Bears, they got it half right. The Redskins ran for 218 yards—171 of them by Clinton Portis—and beat Chicago 13-10. Portis had six runs of 10 yards or more, matching his total for the previous five games.

Portis had to have a good day because quarterback Mark Brunell did not. He went eight for 22 for just 95 yards. One of his passes was intercepted and returned 70 yards for a touchdown.

Portis alone outgained the Bears, who mustered just 160 total yards. But the interception and touchdown return by Jerry Azumah in the second quarter allowed the Bears to stay in it until the late going when rookie safety Sean Taylor's interception sealed it.

With John Hall injured, the Redskins went all the way to Scandinavia to find a kicker. Native Swede Ola Kimrin hopped on a plane and overcame jet lag in time to boot a 41-yard field goal to put the Redskins up 3-0.

The Bears went three and out and the Redskins expanded their lead after taking over at their own 21. Brunell converted a third and nine with a 21-yard strike to Laveranues Coles and Portis bolted for 19 yards to key the drive. Rod Gardner capped it by catching an 18-yard touchdown pass from Brunell on the first play of the second quarter. Kimrin's conversion made it 10-0.

That may have been enough for the Redskins to win, but the game took a shocking twist midway through the second quarter. After runs of 19 yards by Portis and of 14 by Ladell Betts, the Redskins were in Chicago territory threatening to score again. But Brunell's second-down pass was deflected, Azumah grabbed it and he was off to the races.

The Redskins defense, aided by the ball-control Washington offense, managed to make the lead stand up. A drive that spanned the third and fourth quarters expanded the lead to 13-7 with another Kimrin field goal.

The Bears drove to a 46-yard Paul Edinger field goal on their ensuing possession but the Washington defense held them at bay the rest of the way. Taylor's interception came at the Washington 40 with 25 seconds left.

Oct 25

Setback for LaVar?
Arrington slips during practice, hurts repaired knee

10/31/04	**Packers (4-4) 28, REDSKINS (2-5) 14**				89,925
GB	3	14	3	8	28
Was	0	7	0	7	14
GB	FG Longwell 37				
GB	Green 1 run (Longwell kick)				
GB	Walker 9 pass from Favre (				
Was	Gardner 12 pass from Brunell (Kimrin kick)				
GB	FG Longwell 39				
Was	Gardner 12 pass from Brunell (Kimrin kick)				
GB	Green 11 run (Ferguson pass from Favre)				

FedEx Field—It appeared to be one of those plays that can turn around a season, a bolt out of the blue that sparks an improbable comeback and recharges the team and, indeed, an entire city.

It *appeared* to be, anyway. But it didn't count.

With just under three minutes to play, the Redskins trailed 20-14 and faced a third and eight at the Green Bay 43. The play sent receiver James Thrash in motion and running back Clinton Portis on a post pattern. Mark Brunell had time and found Portis open. He burst through a crowd of bodies and dove into the end zone. The FedEx Field crowd erupted and Washington was an extra point away from taking the lead after they had trailed 17-0 in the second quarter.

But there was a piece of yellow laundry in the backfield—one of those penalty flags that make conspiracy theorists light up the Internet message boards. The official call was illegal motion on Thrash, but nobody in a striped shirt seemed to know exactly what motion Thrash had made that was illegal. There was not a flag on the ground when Brunell released the pass and, considering that such a call can be made only at the snap of the ball, well, you have to wonder.

All the Redskins could do about it was wonder. And they still had the ball with a couple of chances to convert a third and 13 and keep the drive alive. But Brunell threw an interception on the very next play and an Ahman Green touchdown run soon after that put it out of reach.

The way the game started out, it seemed unlikely there would be any late dramatics. Favre was 14 for 18 for 234 yards in the first half and his nine-yard touchdown pass to Javon Walker gave his team that 17-0 lead.

The defense tightened up in the second half and Washington got back into it. Brunell threw a pair of touchdown passes to Rod Gardner, both of them covering 12 yards. A Shawn Springs interception and subsequent return to the Packer 17 set up the second of those.

That made it 20-14 and Fred Smoot's interception of Favre at the Washington 38 set the stage for the Redskins' ultimately-futile last chance.

11/7/04	**Redskins (3-5) 17, LIONS (4-4) 10**				62,657
Was	0	3	14	0	17
Det	0	3	0	7	10
Was	FG Kimrin 24				
Det	FG Hanson 40				
Was	Coles 15 pass from Portis (Kimrin kick)				
Was	Harris 15 return of blocked punt (Kimrin kick)				
Det	Schlesinger 1 pass from Harrington (Kimrin kick)				

Ford Field—Clinton Portis rushed for 147 yards on 34 carries and threw a 15-yard touchdown pass to pace the Redskins past the Lions 17-10.

There is plenty of credit to spread beyond Portis. What ultimately proved to be the winning points came in the third quarter when Taylor Jacobs blocked Nick Harris' punt at the Lions 27. Walt Harris scooped up the loose ball at the 13 and, with a convoy of teammates, dashed into the end zone.

One other special teams thumbs-up went to James Thrash. Three times he downed punts inside the Lions five. Thanks to the poor field position, the Lions racked up 322 yards of offense but couldn't score a touchdown until the outcome was settled.

Mark Brunell struggled passing—he completed just six of 17 passes for 58 yards on the day—and the Redskins struggled to score. The teams traded field goals in the first half.

The Redskins took the second half kickoff and Portis immediately bolted for 21 yards to midfield. From the 15 soon after that, Portis took a handoff, cocked and fired to Laveranues Coles for the touchdown.

Harris' big play came later in the third, putting the Redskins in the driver's seat at 17-3 with 4:32 left in the quarter.

Joey Harrington threw an interception to Fred Smoot to kill a foray deep into Redskins territory with just over six minutes to play. The Lions scored a touchdown on Cory Schlesinger's one-yard run with 2:11 to play and forced a Washington punt with 1:48 left. But Ladell Betts downed the ball at the two and the Lions ran out of time before they could seriously threaten.

11/14/04	**Bengals (4-5) 17, REDSKINS (3-6) 10**				87,786
Cin	7	10	0	0	17
Was	0	0	0	10	10
Cin	R. Johnson 1 run (Graham kick)				
Cin	Stewart 1 pass from Palmer				
Cin	FG Graham 41				
Was	FG Kimrin 33				
Was	Cooley 9 pass from Ramsey (Kimrin kick)				

FedEx Field—Midway through the second quarter of this game against the Bengals, Joe Gibbs made the move many fans had been urging him to make for several weeks. He inserted Patrick Ramsey at quarterback and benched Mark Brunell.

It was a classic case of too little, too late. It was too late because the score already was 17-0 in favor of Cincinnati. It was too little because Ramsey didn't provide much of a spark, although he was clearly better than Brunell, who was one for eight for six yards with one interception at the time Gibbs showed him the bench. Ramsey threw for 210 yards—but needed 37 attempts to get there. He threw one touchdown and two interceptions.

The only true professional-grade quarterback performance came from the Bengals' Carson Palmer, making just his ninth NFL start. He did toss two first-half interceptions, but in between completed 14 of 17 passes to stake the Bengals to that 17-point advantage.

Ramsey started to settle in during the third quarter but he and the Redskins blew some key opportunities. The Redskins punted on their first possession and the Bengals fumbled. James Thrash recovered at the Cincinnati 33. However, Ladell Betts was flagged for being illegally downfield and the Redskins had to kick it again.

Later in the third, Joe Salave'a forced Rudi Johnson to fumble and Marcus Washington recovered at the Washington 39. Three plays later, though, Tory James picked off Ramsey's pass and that opportunity went by the boards.

Ramsey finally got the Redskins into the end zone just before the two-minute warning. He threw consecutive passes to Darnerien McCants for 27 and 19 yards. Chris Cooley caught a nine-yard touchdown pass a few plays later.

Nov 15
No Controversy—Ramsey for Rest of '04
At 3-6, Gibbs, Redskins look to future

11/21/04	EAGLES (9-1) 28, Redskins (3-7) 6				67,720
Was	3	3	0	0	6
Phil	7	0	7	14	28
Was	FG Kimrin 35				
Phi	Lewis 2 pass from McNabb (Akers kick)				
Was	FG Kimrin 24				
Phi	Owens 10 pass from McNabb (Akers kick)				
Phi	Westbrook 1 pass from McNabb (Akers kick)				
Phi	Westbrook 14 pass from McNabb (Akers kick)				

Lincoln Financial Field—Patrick Ramsey passed the eyeball test in his first start under Joe Gibbs. But even though he looked like a somewhat competent NFL starting quarterback, the results were much the same as they had been under Mark Brunell. In fact, the scoring output was the lowest of the season as the Redskins fell to the Eagles 28-6.

Again the other team had a distinct advantage at the most important position on the field. Donovan McNabb threw four touchdown passes as he went 18 for 26 for 222 yards.

The Redskins did manage to stay in the game during the first half. They got two Ola Kimrin field goals, one each in the first and second quarter. All the Eagles could post was one touchdown, that coming on a two-yard toss from McNabb to Greg Lewis. The Eagles led 7-6 at intermission.

But the Washington offense couldn't stick with Joe Gibbs' game plan to control the ball on the ground with Clinton Portis carrying to load to take the pressure off of Ramsey. But the Eagles figured this out very quickly and stuffed Portis time after time. He gained just 37 yards on 17 carries.

That forced Ramsey to attempt 34 passes, probably a good dozen or so more than what Gibbs wanted.

The Eagles started to pull away in the third quarter as McNabb hit Terrell Owens with a 10-yard touchdown pass. Still, it was a one-score ballgame at 14-6 going into the fourth quarter.

At the start of the fourth the Redskins were in the midst of a drive that had started at their own 20. It reached the Eagle 10 where they had first and goal.

It fell apart at that point. Ray Brown was flagged for a false start, and then Chris Samuels backed it up 15 more by drawing flags for holding and then for a false start. Kimrin missed a 48-yard field goal wide right.

The Eagles put it away with touchdowns on their next two possessions.

11/28/04	STEELERS (10-1) 16, Redskins (3-8) 7				63,707
Was	0	0	7	0	7
Pit	3	10	0	3	16
Pit	FG Reed 33				
Pit	Bettis 4 run (Reed kick)				
Pit	FG Reed 36				
Was	Cooley 2 pass from Ramsey (Hall kick)				
Pit	FG Reed 32				

Heinz Field—Once again, the Redskins paired solid defense with anemic offense. Throw in a couple of turnovers and some penalties and you have the recipe for yet another Redskins defeat—and yet another game where they fail to score as many as 20 points. The Steelers led 13-0 at halftime and survived a mild Washington rally to take a 16-7 win.

This is the team's 11th game this year, and they have yet to hang 20 points on the scoreboard.

The Steelers' first 10 points were set up by Antwaan Randle El. The elusive receiver twice gained his team favorable field position with punt returns. His first of 60 yards set up a Jeff Reed field goal.

He took the next punt down the sideline for 43 yards and punter Tom Tupa knocked him out of bounds at the Washington 39. Six plays later, Jerome Bettis toted the rock into the end zone from six yards out.

The Redskins made it a game by driving for a touchdown late in the third quarter, and advance that covered 79 yards. The last yard was the hardest. It took them four cracks to get it into the end zone after getting a first and goal at the one. Two Ladell Betts lost a yard and then Patrick Ramsey's pass for tight end Brian Kozlowski fell incomplete. Finally, on fourth down, Ramsey fired a two-yard touchdown pass to Chris Cooley and all of sudden it was a ballgame at 13-7 with 3:23 left in the third quarter.

The Washington defense rose up and forced a three and out. But Betts was stuffed for no gain on third and one and Joe Gibbs elected to punt. The Steelers drove for the clinching field goal after that.

12/5/04	REDSKINS (4-8) 31, Giants (5-7) 7				87,872
NYG	0	0	7	0	7
Was	7	14	3	7	31
Was	Portis 1 run (Hall kick)				
Was	Portis 4 pass from Ramsey (Hall kick)				
Was	Royal 9 pass from Ramsey (Hall kick)				
Was	FG Hall 46				
NYG	Ward 92 kickoff return (Christie kick)				
Was	Cooley 6 pass from Ramsey (Hall kick)				

FedEx Field—The Redskins, who had not scored more than 18 points in a game all year, ran up a 21-0 halftime lead and went on to bury the Giants 31-7.

Clinton Portis led the offensive attack with 148 yards on 38 carries. Patrick Ramsey enjoyed what was by far his best game since he took over the starting job three games ago, completing 19 of 22 passes for 174 yards and three touchdowns.

And Ramsey's stat line included a zero in the interceptions column. In the second game of the season, he threw three in less than a half of play.

The Redskins defense has played well all year and this game was no exception. They held Tiki Barber to just 38 yards rushing on 13 carries and made rookie quarterback Eli Manning look like, well, a rookie.

New York did not score an offensive point. The Giants' only points came on Derrick Ward's 92-yard kickoff return for a touchdown.

The Redskins set the tone early. Backed up at their own seven on their first drive, Joe Gibbs' called five straight Portis runs. When the dust settled, they were at their own 42.

The advance continued until Portis smashed through the line and scored from the one. The touchdown drive was the longest of the season, covering 93 yards in 13 plays and 7:15.

They did it again in the second quarter, moving 91 yards in 10 plays. The payoff here came on a shovel pass from Ramsey to Portis good for four yards and a 14-0 lead.

The next time the Redskins got their hands on the ball, they did not have to go nearly as far. Walt Harris blocked a punt and Washington took over at the Giants 31. Five plays later from the nine, Ramsey rolled right and threw a dart to tight end Robert Royal to push the Redskins past that elusive 20-point mark.

While the scoring pace slowed in the second half, the Redskins maintained a firm grip on the football. They ended up with more than 40 minutes of possession time compared to just 19 and change for New York.

12/12/04	**Eagles(12-1) 17, REDSKINS (4-9) 14**				90,089	
Phil	7	0	10	0		17
Was	7	0	0	7		14
Was	Portis 5 run (Hall kick)					
Phi	Smith 2 pass from McNabb (Akers kick)					
Phi	FG Akers 38					
Phi	Levens 1 run (Akers kick)					
Was	Portis 2 run (Hall kick)					

FedEx Field—Patrick Ramsey went to the well once too often.

After going to tight end Chris Cooley every time he needed a big play all day, Ramsey tried it with the game on the line. With 1:47 left, Ramsey had just gone to Cooley for a first down at the Eagles 27 with the Redskins trailing by three at 17-14. But the Eagles were ready for it this time and Ramsey threw to Cooley in double coverage in the end zone.

Brian Dawkins came up with a fairly easy interception. Instead of claiming a huge upset, the Redskins left empty-handed with a 17-14 loss.

In defeat, the Redskins squandered excellent performances on both sides of the ball. Ramsey looked sharp for the second game in a row and Clinton Portis ran for 80 yards on 23 carries. Along with Cooley, who had five catches for 75 yards, Laveranues Coles had a good receiving day, catching 12 passes for 100 yards. The Washington defense held an Eagle offense that had put up 47 points a week ago in check.

Washington jumped to a 7-0 lead in a hurry. Ladell Betts returned the opening kickoff all the way to the Eagles 14 and a face mask penalty moved the ball to the seven. Two plays later Portis scored from the seven.

The Eagles responded immediately with a 66-yard drive that consumed just 1:28. Donovan McNabb hit L. J. Smith with a two-yard strike and it was tied at 7-7.

The Eagles nearly stretched their lead as McNabb connected with a wide-open Todd Pinkston on a long bomb that went for 80 yards. Pinkston, however, tripped over his own feet four yards shy of the goal line. On the next play, Antonio Pierce knocked the ball out of the hands of Terrell Owens and recovered the fumble to end the threat.

It looked like the Eagles were going to pull away when they scored 10 third-quarter points on a David Akers field goal and a one-yard touchdown run by Dorsey Levens.

But the Redskins were not done. Shawn Springs intercepted a McNabb pass to set up a one-yard Portis touchdown run to make it 17-14. Their final, ultimately futile chance started with four minutes left.

12/18/04	**Redskins (5-9) 26, 49ERS (2-12) 16**				65,710	
Was	7	16	3	0		26
SF	7	2	0	7		16
Was	Royal 12 pass from Ramsey (Chandler kick)					
SF	Lloyd 17 pass from Dorsey (Peterson kick)					

Was	FG Chandler 49
Was	FG Chandler 25
Was	FG Chandler 20
SF	Safety blocked punt went out of end zone
Was	Pierce 78 interception return (Chandler kick)
Was	FG Chandler 26
SF	Conway 11 pass from Dorsey (Peterson kick)

Monster Park—The Redskins intercepted four Ken Dorsey passes and Antonio Pierce returned one of those 78 yards for a touchdown as the Redskins knocked off San Francisco 26-16.

Washington drove 78 yards for a touchdown on its very first possession. The drive featured a lot of Clinton Portis runs mixed in with Patrick Ramsey completions to Rod Gardner for 11 and 21 yards. The drive culminated in Ramsey's 12-yard touchdown pass to tight end Robert Royal.

The 49ers came right back on their first possession, driving 71 yards to a 17-yard touchdown pass from Dorsey to Brandon Lloyd.

Late in the first quarter it looked like the Redskins had scored their first defensive touchdown of the year. Safety Sean Taylor jumped high to intercept a pass at the Redskins 16 and after a scrambling 30-yard return, he pitched the ball to teammate Lemar Marshall, who ran the remaining 54 yards into the end zone. San Francisco challenged the play, however, and it was determined that Taylor's pitch went forward. The Redskins drove into scoring position but had to settle for a 49-yard Jeff Chandler field goal.

Two more forays deep into Niner territory—one the result of a sustained drive, the other due to defensive end Ron Warner's interception and 39-yard return—also resulted in Chandler field goals.

Late in the first half, the momentum switched to the home team. Tom Tupa's punt was blocked and the ball rolled out of the end zone for a safety. After the free kick it looked like the 49ers were going to make it a nine-point swing as they drove to the Washington 23 with just over a minute left in the second quarter.

On third and eight from there, Dorsey threw to the left sideline and Pierce was waiting. The linebacker grabbed interception and sprinted down the field. He coasted into the end zone for a 23-9 Redskins lead at halftime.

Another Chandler field goal expanded the lead to 26-9 and essentially salted this one away.

Dec 20
Gibbs: It's Ramsey's Job in '05
Coach says no veteran will come in,
no camp competition with Brunell

12/26/04	**COWBOYS (6-9) 13, Redskins (5-10) 10**				63,705	
Was	3	0	0	7		10
Dal	0	6	0	7		13
Was	FG Chandler 25					
Dal	FG Cundiff 26					
Dal	FG Cundiff 23					
Was	Royal 5 pass from Ramsey (Chandler kick)					
Dal	Crayton 39 pass from Testaverde (Cundiff kick)					

Texas Stadium—In an ending reminiscent of Texas Stadium nightmares of the past, Vinny Testaverde threw a 39-yard touchdown pass to Patrick Crayton with 37 seconds left to play to push the Cowboys past the Redskins 13-10.

Washington had a shot at pulling off a bigger miracle at the end, but Jeff Chandler's 57-yard field goal attempt at the final gun was short.

There were no touchdowns scored in the first three quarters of play. Joe Gibbs' Redskins like to control the ball on the ground but with Clinton Portis and Ladell Betts combining for just 75 yards rushing, that was not happening. Julius Jones of the Cowboys was somewhat more effective, but his 57 yards on 22 rushing attempts worked out to an average of just 2.6 yards per carry.

Patrick Ramsey was hot early and late. His early hot streak ended one pass too soon. After commanding an opening drive that reached the Dallas 11, Lynn Scott picked off his attempt at the five and the drive died.

Dallas was unable to move, going four and out, and Antonio Brown bolted 39 yards on a punt return and the Redskins were back in business at the Dallas 23. They got as far as the seven but Ramsey misfired on consecutive passes and they had to settle for a 25-yard Chandler field goal.

The Cowboys put together a couple of sustained drives in the second quarter. Both of them reached inside the Washington 10 but stalled short of the end zone and Billy Cundiff booted field goals. The second came as time expired in the second half to give Dallas a 6-3 lead.

Ramsey got hot again in the fourth quarter. The Redskins steadily marched 80 yards in 13 plays to reclaim the lead at 10-6. Ramsey threw a nifty pass on the run to Robert Royal for the touchdown with 6:44 left to play.

The Redskins had the ball two more times and one first down probably would have salted the game away, but they couldn't get there. A defense that had been on the field for most of the game came out with 1:25 remaining to try and get one more stop.

But they couldn't get it. On third down from the Washington 39, veteran Testaverde looked rookie safety Sean Taylor off of Crayton. The receiver was wide open on the right sideline to catch the pass and apply the dagger.

12/26/04	**REDSKINS (6-10) 21, Vikings (8-8) 18**				76,876
Min	0	3	7	8	18
Was	7	7	0	7	21

Was	Cooley 6 pass from Ramsey (Chandler kick)
Min	FG Andersen 23
Was	Royal 4 pass from Ramsey (Chandler kick)
Min	Moss 28 pass from Culpepper (Andersen kick)
Was	Betts 1 run (Chandler kick)
Min	Robinson 38 pass from Culpepper (O. Smith pass from Culpepper)

FedEx Field—The Redskins played like they wanted to all year, displaying a swarming, dominant defense and a smash mouth, ball-control offense as they beat the Vikings 21-18.

Washington took the lead on the game's opening possession and never gave it up. Antonio Brown jump-started the drive with a 66-yard return of the opening kickoff. From the Minnesota 32, it was mostly Ladell Betts, who carried five times for 15 yards and a few Patrick Ramsey passes. The last one went to Chris Coley for six yards and a touchdown.

Later in the first the Redskins had another promising drive going, but Kory Williams intercepted a Ramsey pass from the Viking 21. The Vikings turned that takeaway into three points in the form of a 23-yard Morton Andersen field goal.

Washington tallied another TD before halftime. Ramsey passes to James Thrash for 15 yards and to Laveranues Coles for 14 were the key plays and Ramsey finished off the drive with a four-yard touchdown pass to Robert Royal. That came with 1:17 left in the first half and the Redskins took a 14-3 lead into the locker room.

The Washington defense snuffed out a Viking drive at the outset of the third quarter with consecutive sacks of Daunte Culpepper. On second and nine at midfield, Antonio Pierce and Lemar Marshall blitzed and teamed up to nail Culpepper for a loss of eight. On the next play, it was another loss of eight as Cornelius Griffin came in low and brought down the 6-4 quarterback.

Minnesota did score the next time it had the ball on a 28-yard pass from Culpepper to Randy Moss to make it 14-10. The Washington defense stiffened after that.

The Redskins put it away early in the fourth quarter. Taylor Jacobs hauled in a bomb from Ramsey, made a nice move to elude a defender and scampered all the way to the one for a gain of 45. Ladell Betts scored on the next play.

The Vikings did put together a late desperation drive and Culpepper hit Marcus Robinson with a 38-yard touchdown pass with two seconds left. A two-point conversion theoretically left the Vikings in position to pull out a miracle, but Mike Sellers recovered the onside kick and one Ramsey kneel down ended it.

Dec 30

Pierce, Smoot Remain Unsigned for '05
Pierce 'big-time confident it will get done,'
Smoot says return not certain

2005

Head Coach: Joe Gibbs
Record: 10-6, Second in NFC East
Playoffs: 1-1, Lost in Divisional Round

Honors: Santana Moss Pro Bowl; Chris Samuels Pro Bowl

Coles On His Way Out?

Feb 21—Laveranues Coles caught 90 passes in Joe Gibbs' offense in 2004. Apparently, that wasn't enough from him.

According to media reports, Coles has asked to be released or traded and Gibbs is inclined to honor his request. Of course, it's not that simple. The Redskins gave Coles a $13 million signing bonus just two years ago. They would have to absorb a sizeable salary cap hit if they were to cut him loose. And then there's the matter of the first-round pick the team sent to the Jets as compensation. The Redskins don't want that to go into the trash can.

So, if Coles does go, it appears he would have to give back some of that signing bonus to lessen the cap hit and/or a player would have to come to the Redskins via a trade.

Stay tuned.

Mar 2

Pierce Heads to New York
Leading tackler in '04 agrees to terms with Giants

Mar 5

On and Off Coles Deal Finally Done
*Disgruntled receiver goes back to Jets;
Redskins get Santana Moss in return*

Skins, Broncos Make a Deal

Apr 19—In a surprising move, the Redskins dealt for another first-round pick in the upcoming draft. They got Denver's first-round pick, the 25th overall. In exchange, Washington gave up their 2006 No. 1 and No. 6 and their third-round pick in this draft.

Apr 24

A Pair of Tigers by the Tail
*CB Rogers drafted at No. 9, QB Campbell at No. 25;
were teammates at Auburn*

Taylor Faces Felony Charges

June 4—Redskins safety Sean Taylor has turned himself in to Miami-Dad police after being charged with aggravated assault with a firearm and simple assault.

Details of the incident are unclear, but Taylor faces serious jail time if he is convicted on felony charges.

9/11/05	REDSKINS (1-0) 9, Bears (0-1) 7				90,138
Chi	0	0	7	0	7
Was	0	6	3	0	9
Was	FG Hall 40				
Was	FG Hall 43				
Chi	Thomas 1 run (Brien kick_				
Was	FG Hall 19				

FedEx Field—It wasn't pretty and not for the faint of heart, but the Redskins will take their 9-7 opening day win over the Bears and won't apologize for it.

"When it comes down to getting that 'W,' any way you can do it," said Santana Moss. "That's all that matters."

The Redskins won despite losing quarterback Patrick Ramsey to what appeared to be a cheap shot by Lance Briggs on a second-quarter sack. Ramsey fumbled and Tommie Harris recovered for the Bears. Mark Brunell replaced Ramsey on the next series.

The Redskins moved in for their first score in that drive. The big play first appeared to be a disaster. Brunell threw one deep and Nathan Vasher intercepted the pass at the Bears 27. However, Mike Green was flagged for pass interference and the Redskins had a first down at the Bears 29. A few plays later John Hall kicked a 40-yard field goal to give the Redskins a 3-0 lead. Hall booted another three-pointer, this one from 43.

That would have been enough for the Redskins to win had Antonio Brown not fumbled away the second-half kickoff at his own 23. Seven plays later Thomas Jones plunged in from a yard out and, despite having been outplayed, the Bears led 7-6.

The Redskins responded immediately, driving 63 yards. The problem was that the end zone was 64 yards away from their starting point; they had to settle for another field goal. Hall's 19-yarder made it 9-7.

The Bears were not done. Their ensuing drive ended at the Washington 22 when Lemar Marshall picked off Kyle Orton's first-down pass. The Redskins were backed up at their own six after that but Clinton Portis got them out of the hole with a 41-yard run off right tackle.

That drive fizzled out, giving the Bears one more chance. They moved into Washington territory and the folks in the home crowd decided they'd had enough. After Thomas Jones lost three yards on first and 10 at the Washington 34, the noise became deafening. That rattled the Bears and they committed not one, not two, but *three* consecutive false starts.

When the Bears finally got off a snap, Demetric Evans broke free and nailed Orton for a 10-yard loss.

Chicago got the ball back with 1:43 to go but on second down Cornelius Griffin sacked Orton, causing a fumble that Griffin recovered to preserve the win.

Gibbs: Change 'Happens', Brunell to Start

Sep 12—Washington is the home of the quarterback controversy, but they usually take longer to brew than one game into the season.

Joe Gibbs announced today that Patrick Ramsey, who was named the starter for this season 10 months ago, will be benched in favor of Mark Brunell.

Ramsey strained his neck while being sacked in the second quarter. Brunell came in, passed for just 70 yards and the Redskins didn't score a touchdown. Nevertheless, Gibbs saw enough to make the change.

"You don't like doing this. I don't," said Gibbs. "Sometimes you don't chart the circumstances or what happens. It just happens."

> There are reports that Ramsey requested a trade when Gibbs informed him of the decision in a meeting today.

9/19/05	Redskins (2-0) 14, Cowboys (1-1) 13				65,207	
Was	0	0	0	14		14
Dal	0	3	7	3		13
Dal	FG Cortez 33					
Dal	Glenn 70 pass from Bledsoe					
Dal	FG Cortez 41					
Was	Moss 39 pass from Brunell (Novak kick)					
Was	Moss 39 pass from Brunell (Novak kick)					

Texas Stadium—Maybe it didn't make up for Clint Longley on Thanksgiving or Captain Comeback in the 1979 season finale.

But it sure was sweet.

For 54 minutes the Redskins had done nothing offensively and trailed the Cowboys 13-0. It could have been worse, but it didn't seem to matter. With 3:55 to play Mark Brunell lined them up for a fourth and 15 play at the Dallas 39. Redskins fans everywhere reached for their remotes to shut off the TV before heading to bed on this Monday night.

But Brunell launched a perfect strike to Santana Moss between two defenders in the end zone. All of a sudden it was 13-7 and, well, the remote controls went back on the table.

The ensuing Dallas drive burned off less than a minute and they punted for a touchback. On first down Brunell went to Portis for 10. Fans looked at their remotes, believing this would be a typical dink-and-dunk drive that would run out of time before reaching pay dirt. Why bother watching?

But on second down, Brunell launched another bomb towards Moss. Could he do it again?

Yes. As objects were tossed in the air in celebration, Moss again split two defenders, hauled in Brunell's bomb and dashed into the end zone.

There was celebrating—but still work to be done. The Cowboys' Tyson Thompson returned the ensuing kickoff 49 yards to the Washington 48. All it would take would be 20 yards to good field goal position to spoil the pending celebration.

On third and four, Drew Bledsoe had Patrick Crayton for the first down, but Sean Taylor separated the receiver from the ball with a booming hit. And on fourth down Walt Harris tackled Terry Glenn a yard shy of the first-down marker.

Dallas did have one more chance after the Redskins went three and out, but the clock ran out at the Cowboys 41.

Prior to those last six minutes there isn't much to talk about from a Redskins perspective. Washington couldn't pass and couldn't run. Brunell threw a second-quarter pass that Terence Newman picked off to set up a Dallas field goal and it was 3-0 at halftime.

On Dallas' second play of the third quarter, they executed a flea flicker to perfection. Julius Jones took a handoff and both safety Sean Taylor and cornerback Shawn Springs bit hard. Jones turned and flipped to Bledsoe, who found Glenn wide open for 70 yards and a touchdown.

Another Cortez field goal to make it 13-0 almost seemed to be unnecessary. After a blitzing Roy Williams sacked Brunell for a loss of 17, the Redskins faced third and 27.

Brunell couldn't find anyone open so he took off running and wasn't tackled until he had picked up 25 yards. On fourth and two, he hit James Thrash in the flat and picked up the first down and much more, gaining 20 yards to the Dallas 34.

Four plays later, the miracle commenced.

10/2/05	REDSKINS (3-0) 20, Seahawks (2-2) 17 OT					90,215	
Sea	3	0	7	7	0		17
Was	0	7	10	0	3		20
Sea	FG Brown 53						
Was	Royal 1 pass from Brunell (Novak kick)						
Was	Sellers 4 pass from Brunell (Novak kick)						

Sea	Alexander 3 run (Brown kick)
Was	FG Novak 40
Sea	Jackson 6 pass from Hasselbeck (Brown kick)
Was	FG Novak 39

FedEx Field—The Redskins blew leads of 14-3 in the third quarter and of 17-10 in the fourth. They had to watch as 48-yard field goal attempt that would have beaten them smacked off the left upright.

But they survived and Nick Novak's 39-yard field goal five and a half minutes into overtime gave them a 20-17 white-knuckle win over Seattle.

Washington dominated the first quarter but the Seahawks blocked a field goal to end one lone drive and another died at the Seattle 42. In between, Josh Brown kicked a field goal for a 3-0 Seattle lead.

The Redskins chewed up almost eight minutes of the second quarter and the third time was a charm when it came to sustained drives. Mark Brunell tossed a one-yard touchdown pass to Robert Royal to put the Redskins up 7-3.

A pass interference call midway through the second quarter set up another Brunell TD toss, this one going to Mike Sellers from four yards out.

Just on the verge of being out of it, Seattle responded immediately. A 34-yard Shaun Alexander run keyed an 85-yard drive on the Seahawks' ensuing possession. Alexander also capped the drive with a three-yard touchdown run and all of a sudden it was a ballgame at 14-10.

Novak stretched the lead to 17-10 with eight seconds left in the third quarter with a 40-yard field goal, but it wasn't enough. With 1:27 left to play, Matt Hasselbeck threw a six-yard touchdown pass to Darrell Jackson, tying the game at 17-17.

The Redskins turned the ball over only once all day but it came at a bad time. On the second play after the ensuing kickoff, Brunell's pass went off of the fingertips on Clinton Portis and into the hands of cornerback Kelly Herndon at the Washington 33. But it hit the upright to send it into overtime.

Novak's winning field goal was set up on a third and 10 play from the Seattle 45. Brunell hit Santana Moss on a slant and the receiver dashed down to the 15.

109/05	BRONCOS (4-1) 21, Redskins (3-1) 19				75,880	
Was	7	3	0	9		19
Den	7	7	7	0		21
Den	Bell 34 run (Elam kick)					
Was	Sellers 2 pass from Brunell (Novak kick)					
Den	Lelie 5 pass from Plummer (Elam kick)					
Was	FG Novak 34					
Den	Bell 55 run (Elam kick)					
Was	FG Novak 36					
Was	Cooley 11 pass from Brunell (pass failed)					

Invesco Field at Mile High—The Redskins have been walking a tightrope during their first three games of the season, pulling out three wins that were in doubt until the final seconds. Today, however, they lost their balance and fell off of the tightrope as they lost to the Broncos 21-19.

They had a shot at sending the game into overtime with 1:09 left to play after Mark Brunell hit Chris Cooley with an 11-yard touchdown pass to make it a two-point game.

Receiver David Patten was wide open in the back of the end zone on the two-point conversion attempt. Brunell saw him and fired, but linebacker Ian Gold stuck his hand up and knocked away the ball.

"It was straight up luck," Patten said. "He just happened to be Johnny on the spot."

The Redskins were driving on their opening possession but Brunell and Clinton Portis botched a handoff at their 48, allowing linebacker Al Wilson to pounce on the ball. Four plays later on fourth and one, Tatum Bell scampered around left end and broke free for 34 yards and a touchdown.

Washington chased after those easy seven points it had given up all day long.

The Redskins came right back and tied it up with a 78-yard drive that culminated in Brunell flipping a two-yard touchdown pass to Mike Sellers.

Denver reclaimed the lead with a touchdown drive of its own and Nick Novak booted a 34-yard field goal to make it 14-10 at halftime.

After Carlos Rogers downed a punt at the Denver two, Jake Plummer went back to pass in the end zone. The ball slipped out of his hand after a pump fake and fell to the ground. Plummer recovered the ball in the end zone for what was called a safety.

After a replay review, however, the referee invoked the tuck rule and it was an incomplete pass. Two series later, after a 38-yard Novak field goal attempt was blocked, Bell again broke a long touchdown run, this one covering 55 yards.

Trailing 21-10, the Redskins nearly pulled it out in the final period. Novak kicked a 36-yard field goal midway through the fourth before the Redskins saw their last chance get tipped away.

Arrington: I'm in the 'Doghouse'

Oct 11—Linebacker LaVar Arrington had been a Pro Bowl performer the last three seasons he's been healthy. Now, he's healthy—and he can't even get onto the field.

"I've put myself in the doghouse somehow," said Arrington, who participated in just seven plays combined against the Cowboys and Seahawks before riding the bench the entire game in Denver.

When asked about Arrington's lack of playing time earlier, defensive coordinator Gregg Williams said that players "have to do it in practice" to play on Sunday.

Arrington said: "Like Coach Williams says, I've got to show them in practice. Well, in practice, give me some reps so you can see what I can do. If you're not going to play me, then don't play me. Just don't make things up about why I'm not playing."

10/16/05	CHIEFS (3-2) 28, Redskins (3-2) 21			78,083
Was	0	7	14	0	21
KC	3	3	15	7	28

KC	FG Tynes 20
Was	Moss 4 pass from Brunell (Novak kick)
KC	FG Tynes 38
KC	Holmes 6 run (Boerigter pass from Green)
Was	Moss 78 pass from Brunell (Novak kick)
KC	Knight 80 fumble return (Tynes kick)
Was	Cooley 11 pass from Brunell (Novak kick)
KC	Holmes 60 pass from Green (Tynes kick)

Arrowhead Stadium—Priest Holmes took a screen pass 60 yards for a touchdown early in the fourth quarter and the Kansas City defense made it stand up for a 28-21 win over the Redskins.

The Redskins eked out wins in their first three games despite turning the ball over more than their opponents. Usually that's a recipe for disaster, and the last two weeks it has caught up with them.

Today the Redskins gave it up three times with one resulting in what may have been a 14-point turnaround. Midway through the third quarter, Washington was driving with a second and three at the Chiefs 23. They were looking for their second straight touchdown after Santana Moss had bolted 78 yards for a touchdown with a screen pass to tie the game at 14-14 on their previous possession.

Rock Cartwright battled for the three yards to get the first, but the ball popped out and safety Sammy Knight scooped it up. He was off to the races and 80 yards later, it was 21-14 Kansas City.

The Redskins came right back and tied it up with a 67-yard touchdown drive. It looked like the drive had died at the K.C. 33 when a Brunell pass was intercepted in the end zone. But an illegal contact penalty gave the Redskins possession and a first down and five plays later Brunell threw an 11-yard touchdown pass to Chris Cooley and Nick Novak's conversion knotted the game at 21-21.

But Holmes united it a few plays later as he navigated through the Redskins' secondary with awesome precision, breaking a few tackles and making some defenders fall down as he eluded them.

At that point, the two teams had combined to score 36 points in a 13-minute span. But that was the last score of the game. The Redskins' best shot came on their last possession but Brunell threw four straight incompletions from the Kansas City 33 to end the threat.

10/23/05	REDSKINS (4-2) 52, 49ers (1-5) 17			90,224
SF	7	0	0	10	17
Was	14	21	10	7	52

Was	Sellers 2 pass from Brunell (Novak kick)
Was	Portis 5 run (Novak kick)
SF	Barlow 17 run (Nedney kick)
Was	Portis 1 run (Novak kick)
Was	Moss 32 pass from Brunell (Novak kick)
Was	Sellers 19 pass from Brunell (Novak kick)
Was	Portis 1 run (Novak kick)
Was	FG Novak 27
Was	Cartwright 4 run (Novak kick)
SF	FG Nedney 47
SF	Gore 72 run (Nedney kick)

FedEx Field—The Redskins posted 457 yards of offense and ran up their highest point total of the decade as they thumped the 49ers 52-17.

This one was a laugher before halftime. Washington scored touchdowns on five of its six first-half possessions. Only one of the scoring drives lasted longer than 3:06 and took more than six plays.

The first scoring drive was typical. From the Washington 39, Clinton Portis (19 carries, 101 yards) ran for 10 yards and then for two. Mark Brunell (156.2 quarterback rating) launched one to Santana Moss (five receptions for 112 yards) that was good for 43 yards to the six. Portis then picked up four yards in two carries. On third down, Brunell found Mike Sellers for one of the tight end's two touchdowns on the day.

Kickoff. Retake possession. Repeat.

San Francisco was in it for a brief period of time. After Portis scored on a five-yard run to make it 14-0, the 49 scored on a 17-yard Kevan Barlow touchdown run and then the Redskins were forced to punt for the only time in the half.

But the Niners went three and out and the Redskins drove 76 yards to Portis' second touchdown of the day—a one-yard blast—and it was 21-7.

Washington removed any doubt in the final two minutes of the half. On the first play after the warning, Brunell finished off a four-play, 67-yard drive with a 32-yard touchdown pass to Moss. After the ensuing kickoff Marcus Washington sacked Alex Smith and knocked the ball loose. Phillip Daniels recovered at the San Francisco 19. On the next play it was Brunell to Sellers again for the touchdown to make it 35-7 at intermission.

The Redskins surpassed the 50-point mark when Rock Cartwright powered four yards of a touchdown with just over nine minutes left.

10/30/05	**GIANTS (5-2) 36, Redskins (4-3) 0**				78,630
Was	0	0	0	0	0
NYG	6	13	17	0	36
NYG	FG Feely 39				
NYG	FG Feely 50				
NYG	Jacobs 3 run (Feely kick)				
NYG	FG Feely 33				
NYG	FG Feely 39				
NYG	Shockey 10 pass from Manning (Feely kick)				
NYG	FG Feely 44				
NYG	Barber 4 run (Feely kick)				

Giants Stadium—The Redskins came into this game looking to be taken seriously as contenders in the NFC East. Instead they put on a performance worthy of being laughed at.

It got ugly in a hurry. On the first scrimmage play of the game Tiki Barber took a handoff and went left. A huge hole greeted him there and he raced 57 yards to the Washington 16. The defense then stiffened and the Giants had to settle for a Jay Feely field goal.

That was one of four Feely field goals in the first half. The defense bent with great regularity in the first 30 minutes, but it only broke early in the second quarter when Brandon Jacobs powered three yards for a touchdown. Barber set up that score with a 59-yard run down to the one.

Barber had 202 yards rushing in the first half, topping his career best for a game.

Nominally, at least, the game was still competitive as the two-minute warning approached with the Redskins trailing just 13-0. But a pair of Feely field goals, both set up by Washington turnovers, made the mountain even taller at 19-0.

Miracle scenarios faded in the first two minutes of the second half. Ladell Betts fumbled the second-half kickoff and the Giants recovered at the Washington 23. A first-down holding penalty that made it first and 20 was scarcely an obstacle as Barber bolted for 18 yards. Two plays later Eli Manning threw a 10-yard touchdown pass to Jeremy Shockey.

It was obvious the Redskins had brought a knife to a gun fight. Their longest drive covered 60 yards but their best chance at scoring perished on downs at the New York five.

Their second-longest drive traversed all of 14 yards. The Skins lost yardage on six of their 16 possessions.

11/6/05	**REDSKINS (5-3) 17, Eagles (4-4) 10**				90,298
Phi	7	0	3	0	10
Was	0	10	7	0	17
Phi	Brown 56 pass from McNabb (Akers kick)				
Was	FG Hall 24				
Was	Sellers 1 run (Hall kick)				
Phi	FG Akers 34				
Was	Portis 6 run (Hall kick)				

FedEx Field—Ryan Clark intercepted a Donovan McNabb pass near the goal line to snuff out a threat with 90 seconds left to play and clinch a 17-10 Redskins victory.

The Eagles had to deal with distractions created by star wide receiver Terrell Owens, who was suspended for this game. The situation didn't seem to have an effect on the Eagles either mentally or in terms of the talent on the field—at least, not at the outset. Donovan McNabb hit Reggie Brown, Owens' replacement in the starting lineup, for 56 yards and a touchdown with just over three minutes left in the first quarter.

The Redskins responded with a drive to a 24-yard John Hall field goal. They took the lead with 4:17 remaining in the first half with a 79-yard touchdown drive. The big play was a pass interference call on cornerback Lito Sheppard, setting the Redskins up at the one. The 280-pound fullback Mike Sellers got the call and poked the nose of the ball past the goal line before it got knocked loose. Hall's conversion put the Redskins up 10-7.

It looked like the Eagles would at least tie it up before halftime, but McNabb got a bit too clever. After he completed a pass to Billy McMullen for 15 yards to the Washington 24, the clock still was ticking and the Eagles were out of time-outs. With 28 seconds left, McNabb feigned a spike to stop the clock but dropped back to find a receiver. Phillip Daniels was not fooled; he nailed McNabb for a seven-yard loss.

Philly drove to a tying field goal midway through the third quarter but the Redskins responded immediately. Ladell Betts returned the ensuing kickoff 40 yards to the Eagles 48 to get things going. Three plays later Betts converted a third and 11 by going over the middle, finding a soft spot in the coverage and getting open to haul in a 26-yard pass from Mark Brunell.

The other hero on the drive was guard Derrick Dockery. He hustled downfield during Chris Cooley's 13-yard reception to the six and was in position to make the recovery when Cooley fumbled. Clinton Portis scored on the next play and the Redskins led 17-10 with 2:47 left in the third.

The Redskins defense clamped down until the Eagles' final drive that started from the Philadelphia 15 with 2:41 left to play. It reached the seven where, on fourth and four, Clark latched on to McNabb's pass at the three. The Redskins ran out the clock.

11/13/05	**BUCCANEERS (6-3) 36, Redskins (5-4) 35**				65,421
Was	3	10	15	7	35
TB	7	14	7	8	36
TB	Alstott 2 run (Bryant kick)				
Was	FG Hall 33				
TB	Alstott 1 run (Bryant kick)				
Was	Betts 94 kickoff return (Hall kick)				
TB	Galloway 24 pass from Simms (Bryant kick)				
Was	FG Hall 40				
Was	Sellers 7 pass from Brunell (Portis pass from Brunell)				
Was	Betts 17 pass from Brunell (Hall kick)				
TB	Hilliard 4 pass from Simms (Bryant kick)				
Was	Portis 8 run (Hall kick)				
TB	Shepherd 30 pass from Simms (Alstott run)				

Raymond James Stadium—Mike Alstott scored a two-point conversion—at least, the officials *said* that he did—with 58 seconds left to play to push the Buccaneers past the Redskins 36-35.

The play was the final turn of a back-and-forth contest. Chris Simms got the Bucs in a position to take the lead with a late drive as the Redskins were ahead 35-28. A touchdown pass to Edell Shepherd made it 35-34 and the Bucs lined up to kick the extra point.

The first of two dubious calls by the officials came when Walt Harris blocked the conversion and started to celebrate. Washington was penalized for being offside on the play. That did not appear to be the case but, nonetheless, the ball was moved half the distance to the one.

At that point, Bucs coach Jon Gruden decided to roll the dice and go for two points and the win. He called for Alstott to power his way up the middle. At some point the ball crossed the plane of the goal line but it appeared that the runner's elbow had hit the ground first. However, the conversion was called good and the replay was deemed to be inconclusive.

Turnovers damaged the Redskins early. Mark Brunell threw an interception to set up one Alstott touchdown run before he fumbled, leading to another. It was 14-3 midway through the second quarter.

It took the Redskins 16 seconds to get back into after Alstott's second TD. Ladell Betts took the ensuing kickoff back all the way—94 yards for a touchdown. He danced near the left sideline while doing this and that prompted Gruden to throw a challenge flag, saying that Betts had stepped out of bounds. The play stood and it was 14-10.

It was 21-13 early in the third quarter when the Redskins flipped the tables and capitalized on a Tampa Bay turnover. Demetric Evans recovered a fumble at the Bucs seven and Brunell tossed a seven-yard touchdown pass to Mike Sellers three plays later. Brunell threw to Clinton Portis for the two-point conversion to knot the score at 21.

The teams exchanged touchdowns later in the third and it was tied at 28 as the fourth quarter started. At that time the Redskins were in the midst of a 16-play, 76-yard drive to take the lead. It was a steady advance with the longest gain coming on Santana Moss' 10-yard reception. Portis skirted around right end for eight yards and the go-ahead score.

The Redskins got the ball back with 3:37 to play, but they couldn't get a first down to kill the clock.

11/20/05	**Raiders (4-6) 16, REDSKINS (5-5) 13**			90,129	
Oak	3	0	7	6	16
Was	7	6	0	0	13
Was	Marshall 17 interception return (Hall kick)				
Oak	FG Janikowski 30				
Was	FG Hall 24				
Was	FG Hall 45				
Oak	Porter 49 pass from Collins (Janikowski kick)				
Oak	FG Janikowski 25				
Oak	FG Janikowski 19				

FedEx Field—Sebastian Janikowski kicked a 19-yard field goal with 1:08 left to play to push the Raiders past the Redskins 16-13.

Washington is in a 2-5 funk since starting 3-0 and today they found a different way to lose. The offense disappeared in the second half and the defense let up just enough to let Oakland sneak out of town with the win.

Things started off well for Washington. On the Raiders' first possession, Chris Clemons popped Kerry Collins as he was passing and the ball fell into the arms of linebacker Lemar Marshall. He rolled 17 yards into the end zone and, less than five minutes into the game, it was 7-0.

But then the Redskins made life easy for the other side when Clinton Portis fumbled deep in Washington territory at the 18. That set up a Janikowski field goal to make it 7-3.

Washington made two forays into Oakland territory but came out both times with just three points. Still, a 13-3 lead seemed solid against a punchless Oakland defense.

However, the Raiders had other ideas. On their initial second half possession receiver Jerry Porter had a free release into the secondary and blew past Marshall to catch a 49-yard touchdown pass. All of a sudden it was 13-10.

And suddenly, the Washington offense couldn't do anything. Penalties and turnovers bogged things down and the Raiders tied it up with a 25-yard field goal early in the fourth quarter. Washington had two possessions to try to take the lead, but both wound up going three and out.

Oakland moved in for the kill. They got a first and goal at the one with 2:20 to go. It looked like LaMont Jordan had fumbled the ball away to the Redskins but he was called down by contact. Janikowski kicked the winning field goal three plays later.

Brunell got his only two completions of the fourth quarter while moving the Redskins to the Oakland 43. They couldn't finish the deal, though, as Brunell was sacked and fumbled to seal it.

12/27/05	**Chargers (7-4) 23, REDSKINS (5-6) 17 OT**					84,930	
SD	0	7	0	10	6	23	
Was	3	7	7	0	0	17	
Was	FG Hall 38						
SD	Tomlinson 1 run (Kaeding kick)						
Was	Moss 22 pass from Brunell (Hall kick)						
Was	Cartwright 13 run (Hall kick)						

SD	FG Kaeding 48
SD	Tomlinson 32 run (Kaeding kick)
SD	Tomlinson 41 run

FedEx Field—The Redskins continued their catch-and-release program as they let another opponent off the hook in a 23-17 overtime loss to the Chargers.

LaDainian Tomlinson, held in check for much of the game, bolted 41 yards for a touchdown to win it in overtime. Washington had a chance to avert overtime but a holding call in a critical situation pushed back a field goal attempt. John Hall missed from 53 yards with 35 seconds left in regulation.

The Redskins built a 17-7 third-quarter lead. They went ahead 10-7 midway through the second period when Mark Brunell threw to Santana Moss for 22 yards and a touchdown. Brunell hit Chris Cooley and Taylor Jacobs for 17 yards each earlier in the drive.

Washington expanded the lead in the third quarter. Brunell twice went to Moss for good gains and Rock Cartwright scooted through a hole over left guard for 13 yards and a touchdown.

After that, however, the offense went into a shell. Tomlinson started to heat up and after a Nate Kaeding field goal made it 17-10, the Redskins defense got an interception (Carlos Rogers) and forced a three and out. But the Redskins couldn't move the ball and the Chargers got another chance at their 33 with 4:36 left to play. Three plays later, Tomlinson scooted 32 yards to tie it at 17.

The Redskins got the break they needed when Shawn Springs picked off a Drew Brees pass at the Chargers 31 with just over a minute left. After Clinton Portis picked up six yards on first down, disaster struck. Casey Rabach was flagged for holding and Washington was pushed back to the 35. Hall's miss from 53 followed.

San Diego won the overtime coin toss and Tomlinson's winning TD came soon after that.

12/4/05	**Redskins (6-6) 24, RAMS (5-7) 9**				65,701	
Was	7	3	0	14	**24**	
StL	0	7	02	7	**9**	
Was	Portis 47 run (Hall kick)					
StL	Fitzpatrick 7 run (Wilkins kick)					
Was	FG Hall 38					
Was	Portis 1 run (Hall kick)					
StL.	Safety Brunell fumbled out of end zone					
Was	Cooley 4 pass from Brunell					

Edward Jones Dome—Both Rock Cartwright and Clinton Portis rushed for more than 100 yards to pace the Redskins' 24-9 win over the Rams.

Cartwright racked up 118 yards on just nine carries. Portis (27 att., 136) scored the first of his two touchdowns on a 47-yard run to open the scoring with less than five minutes elapsed.

The Rams were resilient behind rookie quarterback Ryan Fitzpatrick, however. He scored on a seven-yard scramble midway through the second quarter to tie the game at 7-7.

Cartwright's 52-yard run set up a 38-yard John Hall field goal with 3:16 remaining in the first half. While the Redskins outplayed the Rams, they still held just that 10-7 lead going into the fourth quarter.

Early in the final period, however, it appeared they had put away the pesky Rams as they capped a 69-yard drive with a one-yard Portis touchdown run.

This Washington team, however, rarely makes things easy. After holding the Rams they took over at their six. On first down from there, Brunell went back into the end zone to pass and fumbled. He managed to knock the ball out of the end zone for a safety before any Ram could pounce on it for six. Still, the Redskins would be kicking away to St. Louis and with the score at 17-9 and almost 12 minutes left to play all the Rams needed was a touchdown and two-point conversion to tie the game.

The Redskins didn't have to sweat the situation for long. Two plays into the ensuing possession, Fitzpatrick fumbled a snap and Renaldo Wynn snagged it at the St. Louis 44. Nine plays later Brunell threw a four-yard touchdown pass to Chris Cooley and Washington had breathing room at 24-9.

Carlos Rogers' interception at the Redskins eight snuffed out the Rams' last chance.

12/11/05	**Redskins (7-6) 17, CARDINALS ((4-9) 13**				46,654
Was	0	3	14	0	17
Ari	0	10	3	0	13
Was	FG Hall 41				
Ari	McCoy 2 pass from Warner (Rackers kick)				
Ari	FG Rackers 44				
Was	Portis 15 run (Hall kick)				
Ari	FG Rackers 20				
Was	A. Brown 91 kickoff return (Hall kick)				

Sun Devil Stadium—Antonio Brown's 91-yard kickoff return for a touchdown pulled the Redskins past the Cardinals 17-13.

The Redskins may want to take the films from the first half and burn them. For that matter, the Cardinals might want to do the same. The first five possessions of the game ended in turnovers. Late in the first half, after Arizona had taken a 10-3 lead, the two teams again had turnovers on back-to-back possessions.

Mark Brunell threw three interceptions in the half, and all three came in the red zone. Kurt Warner, his counterpart with the Cards, threw an interception and lost a fumble in the first quarter.

Frustrated and dismayed, Joe Gibbs and the Redskins retreated to the locker room at halftime to devise a new strategy. They had passed 75 percent of the time in the latter stages of the first half and the coaches decided to go with more of a ground-oriented attack.

They came out and turned things around on their first possession of the second half. Brunell passed just three times during the 13-play, 80-yard drive. Clinton Portis and Ladell Betts carried the load and Portis capped off the drive with a 15-yard dash around right end. H-back Mike Sellers led the way, pancaking the remaining opposition at the five while Portis stuck the ball over the plane of the goal line before going out of bounds.

Arizona came back fast, driving to a 20-yard Neil Rackers field goal. Brown and the Redskins came back faster as a perfect wall opened the way for the speedy returner to break free down the left sideline on the ensuing kickoff.

The Washington defense tightened after that. Arizona's deepest penetration came on their last possession and ended on downs with 2:09 left to play.

Portis clinched it by powering his way for a first down on third and six at midfield.

12/18/05	**REDSKINS (8-6) 35, Cowboys (8-6) 7**				90,588
Dal	0	0	0	7	7
Was	7	21	7	0	35
Was	Cooley 8 pass from Brunell (Hall kick)				
Was	Cooley 2 pass from Brunell (Hall kick)				
Was	Sellers 3 pass from Brunell (Hall kick)				
Was	Cooley 30 pass from Brunell (Hall kick)				
Was	Betts 1 run (Hall kick)				
Dal	Whitten 2 pass from Bledsoe (Cundiff kick)				

FedEx Field—In the most important game between the two teams in over a decade, the Redskins busted out the whippin' stick on the Dallas Cowboys, burying their arch rivals 35-7.

It was Washington's largest margin of victory over Dallas ever. The last time the division rivals played in December with heavy playoff implications on the line for both teams was in 1992.

Things started going well early for the Redskins. On the Cowboys' very first offensive play, defensive end Phillip Daniels

batted Drew Bledsoe's pass into the air and Cornelius Griffin made a nifty over-the-shoulder interception at the Dallas 21.

Daniels spent a lot of time harassing Bledsoe all day long. He racked up four sacks of the Dallas quarterback.

Four plays after the turnover Mark Brunell threw an eight-yard touchdown pass to Chris Cooley (three TD receptions) and the rout was on.

Actually, the blowout didn't start in earnest until late in the second quarter. A 42-yard pass from Brunell to Santana Moss—who made a sensational, diving catch—set up a two-yard scoring toss from Brunell to Cooley. It still was 14-0 and Dallas had the ball with 3:00 left in the first half. At halftime, it looked to still be a somewhat competitive game.

But then Matt McBriar shanked a punt and the Redskins were in business at the Dallas 34. Brunell to Moss picked up 31 yards and Brunell to Cooley picked up the remaining three to make it 21-0.

The Redskins weren't done yet. Marcus Washington, who was all over the field all day long, intercepted Bledsoe and scampered 41 yards to the Dallas 30. Cooley then gave the game its signature play by taking a short pass from Brunell and blasting his way 30 yards, leaving several Cowboys lying on the field in his wake.

Just to disabuse any notion of a comeback on the part of the Cowboys, the Redskins punched them in the mouth one more time early in the third quarter. On Dallas' first possession of the half Washington sacked Bledsoe, forcing a fumble that Daniels recovered at the Cowboys 21. Six plays later Ladell Betts punched it in from the one and it was 35-0.

Joe Gibbs had only two more things about which to be concerned the rest of the way. One was a serious worry as standout guard Randy Thomas had to be taken off the field with a broken fibula, an injury that will end his season.

The other was relatively minor. As the clock wound down, strains of a song about not letting babies grow up to be cowboys came over the speakers at FedEx Field. Ever mindful of giving the slightest incentive in a future game to the opposition, Gibbs was scrambling around trying to find someone to stop the music.

The music had stopped for the Cowboys considerably earlier.

Dec 19

Skins' Playoff Fate In Their Hands
Wins in final two games means playoffs for first time since '99

12/24/05	**REDSKINS (9-6) 35, Giants (10-5) 20**				90,477
NYG	10	7	3	0	20
Was	14	7	7	7	35
Was	Moss 17 pass from Brunell (Hall kick)				
NYG	FG Feely 47				
NYG	Blackburn 31 interception return (Feely kick)				
Was	Moss 59 pass from Brunell (Hall kick)				
Was	Cooley 17 pass from Portis (Hall kick)				
NYG	Toomer 25 pass from Manning (Feely kick)				
Was	Moss 72 pass from Ramsey (Hall kick)				
NYG	FG Feely 38				
Was	Portis 19 run (Hall kick)				

FedEx Field—One week after winning The Game of the Decade, the Redskins had to go out and do it again.

For their smashing victory over rival Dallas to mean anything the Redskins would have to beat the rival New York Giants. A loss this week would undo much of the good that the win over the Cowboys had done.

While the win was not as easy as the one the week before, the Redskins put up 35 points for the second week in a row and dispatched the Giants 35-20, keeping their playoff hopes very much alive.

Patrick Ramsey, who had the starting quarterback job taken from him 19 minutes into the season, came off the bench in the third quarter after starter Mark Brunell went out with a knee injury. With the Redskins leading by just 21-17, it appeared that disaster loomed as Ramsey had to call two time-outs in a seven-second span to get the signals straight.

But it turns out those time-outs were well spent. Ramsey saw that Santana Moss had single coverage and threw a well-placed pass to the speedy receiver. Moss plucked the ball out of the air, executed a jaw-dropping spin move, and easily outran the Giants secondary to the end zone to complete a 72-yard touchdown play.

That gave the Redskins some breathing room at 28-17, but it wasn't over yet. New York drove to a 38-yard Jay Feely field goal to make it a one-possession game going into the fourth quarter.

The Redskins, though, weren't going to blow this final-period lead as they had done with annoying frequency all year long. On third and two at the New York 21, Clinton Portis powered for the first down. On the next play Portis dashed around left end for 19 yards and the clinching score.

The first half went back and forth. The Giants took a 10-7 lead when Chase Blackburn returned an interception of a Brunell pass 31 yards for a touchdown. Brunell got that back and more with touchdown passes to Moss (59 yards) and Chris Cooley (17 yards).

An Eli Manning touchdown pass to Amani Toomer trimmed the lead to 21-17 and on their first possession of the third quarter, the Giants were driving for more, reaching the Redskins 12. But the advance stalled, Renaldo Wynn swatted down Feely's 29-yard field goal attempt and Ramsey went to Moss a few minutes later.

A Few Scenarios Will Put Skins In

Dec 24—On New Year's Day the Redskins could be celebrating a Wild Card playoff berth. They might pop the cork on a bottle of fine champagne and toast themselves as the NFC East division champs.

Or they might pour a beer to cry in after missing out on the playoffs altogether.

The simplest way for the Redskins to avoid the latter scenario is to beat the Eagles in Philadelphia, clinching at least a Wild Card berth. Should they get help in the form of an Oakland upset of the Giants, they would be division champs.

They're not definitely out if they lose to the Eagles, but they would need cooperation from Minnesota and Dallas. Both of those teams would have to lose to allow the Redskins back into a Wild Card berth.

1/1/06	**Redskins (10-6) 31, EAGLES (6-10) 20**			67,700	
Was	7	3	7	14	31
Phi	10	7	3	0	20
Phi	FG Akers 59				
Was	Sellers 4 pass from Brunell (Hall kick)				
Phi	Brown 33 pass from McMahon (Akers kick)				
Phi	Brown 8 pass from McMahon (Akers kick)				
Was	FG Hall 25				
Was	Portis 2 run (Hall kick)				
Phi	FG Akers 35				
Was	Portis 22 run (Hall kick)				
Was	Taylor 39 fumble return (Hall kick)				

Lincoln Financial Field—The Redskins won their fifth straight game and clinched a Wild Card spot in the NFC playoffs with a 31-20 win over the Eagles.

The win was not nearly as easy as the final score might indicate. The Redskins trailed 17-7 in the second quarter and 20-17 early in the fourth period.

But they came up with three plays in the last 13 minutes to propel them to the win. The first one came with the Eagles in possession with a third and 15 at their 20. Middle linebacker Lemar Marshall drew a bead on Mike McMahon's pass to the left flat. He tipped the ball into the air with his left hand, located it in midair, and snared it for the interception. The Redskins were in business at the Philly 22.

One play later they were in the lead. Clinton Portis took a handoff and started up the middle, spun out of a tackle, and took off to the left. He broke into the clear and, with an assist from Santana Moss in the form of a nice block, bolted into the end zone.

That gave the Redskins a 24-20 lead—nice, but far from secure. The Eagles had three possessions to try to drive for a go-ahead touchdown. The first ended in Redskins territory at the 36 when McMahon fumbled a snap and Joe Salave'a recovered at the Washington 36. The Eagles punted on their next possession.

Still, the Redskins couldn't put together a drive to wrap it up so Sean Taylor took care of it for them. Phillip Daniels sacked Koy Detmer, who had come in the replace McMahon, and the ball flew forward. A pile formed at the ball but it squirted away and Taylor scooped it up. He punctuated his game-clinching, playoff-clinching 39-yard touchdown return by diving into the end zone.

The first half made those Redskins fans who had partied a bit too hard the night before feel even worse. McMahon threw two touchdown passes to rookie Reggie Brown. Washington couldn't get going on offense with Brunell, recovering from a sprained knee suffered the previous week, frequently misfiring.

The Redskins' only touchdown of the half came after the Eagles muffed a punt and the Redskins took possession at the Philadelphia 37 after Mike Sellers recovered. After Brunell hit Moss for 16 yards to the four, he flipped one to Sellers just beyond the line and the big H-back rumbled in for the score.

That gave the Redskins something to hang on to until they could rally in the fourth quarter.

Jan 3

Williams Cashes In, Will Stay
Defensive chief signs for 3 years at $2.5 million per

NFC Wild Card Playoff
Raymond James Stadium
Tampa, Florida
Saturday, January 7, 2006

1/7/06	**Redskins 17, BUCCANEERS 10**			65,514	
Was	14	3	0	0	17
TB	0	3	7	0	10
Was	Portis 6 run (Hall kick)				
Was	Taylor 51 fumble return (Hall kick)				
TB	FG Bryant 43				
Was	FG Hall 47				
TB	Simms 2 run (Bryant kick)				

The Redskins turned two takeaways into two first-quarter touchdowns and their defense—and some good fortune—made those scores stand up as Washington beat Tampa Bay 17-10. It was the Redskins' first playoff game since 1999.

It was a good thing that the defense was able to set up a score. Washington struggled offensively, gaining a net of just 120 yards. No team in NFL history has won a postseason game while gaining so few yards.

A LaVar Arrington interception set up the first score. A crucial assist goes to defensive tackle Joe Salave'a, who tipped Chris Simms' first pass of the day into the air. Arrington came down with it and sprinted to the Bucs' six-yard line. Clinton Portis took it in on the next play and John Hall's conversion made it 7-0.

The Redskins doubled their lead on the Buccaneers' next possession. Tampa Bay was on the move with a first down at the Washington 34. Carnell Williams took a handoff and started up the middle. Marcus Washington stripped away the ball and grabbed it while on the ground. As no Buccaneer had touched him, Washington got up and started to run with the ball— until it got knocked out of his hands. Sean Taylor swooped into the picture, gathered up the bouncing ball while barely breaking stride, and had nothing but green grass and white stripes between himself and the end zone. His 51-yard return put the Redskins up 14-0.

It was a defensive struggle throughout. After the Bucs drove to a field goal late in the first quarter, the Redskins responded with their only sustained scoring march of the game. They moved 40 yards in 10 plays to get into position for Hall to kick a 47-yard field goal and reestablish their two-touchdown lead.

After that the Redskins had eight more possessions. They did not net more than nine yards on any one of them. They did muster a couple of first downs, but a fumble and a sack knocked them back below double-digit yardage each time.

Simms heated up a bit and led a 51-yard touchdown drive, running it in himself from two yards out. The going got a bit easier for him after Shawn Springs left with a groin injury and Taylor was ejected after spitting in a player's face. Brian Kelly's interception of a Brunell pass gave Simms a shot at tying it up with 3:43 left to play.

On third down from the Washington 35, Simms launched one for Edell Shepherd in the end zone. The receiver lunged, caught the ball and controlled it momentarily, but when he hit the ground the ball fell loose. Officials correctly ruled the pass incomplete, citing the rule that the receiver must maintain control of the pass if he hits the ground. After a replay review, the referee said the same thing. Simms' fourth-down attempt was incomplete.

Marcus Washington snuffed out Tampa Bay's last chance with an interception in the last minute.

NFC Divisional Playoff
Qwest Field
Seattle, Washington
Saturday, January 14, 2006

1/14/06	**SEAHAWKS 20, Redskins 10**				67,551
Was	0	3	0	7	10
Sea	0	7	7	6	20
Was	FG Hall 26				
Sea	Jackson 29 pass from Hasselbeck (Brown kick)				
Sea	Hasselbeck 6 run (Brown kick)				
Sea	FG Brown 33				
Was	Moss 20 pass from Brunell (Hall kick)				
Sea	FG Brown 31				

The Seattle Seahawks will spend the next week preparing for the NFC Championship Game. The Redskins will spend the week—and probably many more after it—ruing the opportunities they missed in their 20-10 playoff loss to the Seahawks.

Seattle starting out the game playing like the favorites they were. A drive to the Washington 11, however, ended when NFL MVP Sean Alexander fumbled and Lemar Marshall recovered.

The Seattle offense stalled after that, going three and out four straight times. Late in the first quarter they lost Alexander to a concussion. They appeared to be on the ropes.

But the Redskins did not deliver any punches. They one-upped their opponents by reeling off five consecutive three-and-out series. After the fifth, they got the break they needed. The punt was muffed and Pierson Prioleau recovered at the Seattle 41.

The Redskins did string together a couple of first downs but failed to take full advantage of the turnover. The drive died at the seven and John Hall's 26-yard field goal gave Washington a 3-0 lead.

Soon after that from the Seattle 26, Seahawks quarterback Matt Hasselbeck threw a pass right into the hands of Carlos Rogers. The rookie cornerback had nothing but empty field turn between himself and the goal line and, for a moment, it looked like the Redskins would take control of the game.

But the ball bounced off of Rogers' hands. Seattle continued the drive that culminated in a 26-yard touchdown pass from Hasselbeck to Darrell Jackson. That made it 7-3 and the score held until halftime.

The Washington offense remained in the deep freeze and the Seahawks stretched their lead to 17-3 on a six-yard Hasselbeck touchdown run and a Josh Brown field goal. When the Redskins finally cranked out a sustained drive into Seattle territory, it died when Brunell was sacked and fumbled on fourth down from the 33 with 1:55 left in the third quarter.

The Redskins, however, managed to create one last chance. After Brown's field goal with 14:20 left to play, Chris Cooley grabbed a Brunell pass and rumbled 52 yards to the Seattle 24. On third down from the 20, Brunell's pass was knocked away by cornerback Andre Dyson. But the ball hung in the air long enough for Moss to seize it out of the air for a touchdown and suddenly, it was 17-10.

As if that wasn't enough good fortune, Josh Scobey fumbled the ensuing kickoff. The Redskins moved from the Seattle 40 down to the 18 but couldn't seal the deal. Brunell misfired while trying to hit Moss on third down and Hall pushed his 36-yard field goal attempt wide left.

Seattle then burned off all but the last three minutes and Brown's 31-yard field goal put it out of reach at 20-10.

2006
Head Coach: Joe Gibbs
Record: 5-11, Fourth in NFC East

Honors: Chris Samuels Pro Bowl; Sean Taylor Pro Bowl

Arrington Buys His Freedom

Mar 5—Only a couple of years ago it was easy to envision LaVar Arrington making big plays and going to Pro Bowls wearing burgundy and gold well into the next decade.

But now, after two years filled with injuries, unexplained benchings and a very public dispute over the terms of the contract he signed in late 2003—the one that was supposed to keep him in a Redskins uniform for the remainder of his career—Arrington wanted out of town so badly he was willing to pay for his freedom.

And the Redskins, in a salary cap fix and tired of dealing with him, were willing to cut a deal to let the second overall pick in the 2000 NFL draft walk.

Arrington will forego a $4.4 million payment due to him on one of the bonuses from that 2003 deal. The Redskins will have that amount credited to their 2006 salary cap and Arrington will be free to sign with any team.

June 1
Taylor Case Ends In Plea Deal
No jail time for safety; may face NFL suspension

Aug 14
Portis Out With Shoulder Injury
Occurred while making tackle after an interception; duration of absence uncertain

Aug 15
A Bad Gut Feeling: Springs Out With Injury
Surgery to repair abdominal muscle tear will sideline corner 3-6 weeks

9/11/06	Vikings (1-0) 19, REDSKINS (0-1) 16				90,608
Min	6	3	7	3	19
Was	3	10	3	0	16
Min	Taylor 4 run (kick failed)				
Was	FG Hall 27				
Was	Portis 5 run (Hall kick)				
Was	FG Hall 27				
Min	FG Longwell 46				
Min	Robinson 20 pass from Johnson (Longwell kick)				
Was	FG Hall 22				
Min	FG Longwell 31				

FedEx Field—Ryan Longwell kicked a 31-yard field goal with 1:04 left to play to lift the Vikings over the Redskins 19-16.

Washington had a chance to send it into overtime with 17 seconds remaining but John Hall's 48-yard field goal wandered wide left.

Things did not start off well for the Redskins. On the opening kickoff, Pierson Prioleau, a special teams stalwart who also was to start at safety, suffered a knee injury that may end his season.

Former Redskins quarterback Brad Johnson took advantage of the depleted secondary from the get-go. On the opening drive he converted a third and nine and a third and seven with passes to receiver Troy Williamson. The second one covered 46 yards to the six. Three plays later, on third down from the four, the Vikings crossed up the Redskins with a run and Chester Taylor scored

easily. The snap on the conversion was fumbled and it was 6-0 Vikings.

The teams exchanged field goals and then Washington took the lead midway through the second quarter. Clinton Portis capped a 51-yard drive by following a crunching Mike Sellers block around left end for five yards and a touchdown.

With 2:21 left in the first half Washington started a drive at the Minnesota 43 and immediately threatened to put the Vikings away after Brunell found Santana Moss for 37 yards to the six. But Brunell fumbled the first snap and then threw two incompletions. Hall kicked a field goal with 1:03 left. Not only had the Redskins failed to maximize the opportunity, they left the Vikings with plenty of time to strike back.

And that they did. Williamson returned the ensuing kickoff 44 yards and Longwell made it 13-9 with a field goal as time expired.

The momentum had swung back to the Vikings. Another nice return—this one a 20-yard punt runback by Mewelde Moore—jump-started a drive that culminated in Johnson's 20-yard touchdown pass to Marcus Robinson. This time the extra point was good and the Vikings led 16-13.

A drive that got as far as the Minnesota four fizzled and another Hall field goal tied it at 16. Neither offense could do much until the Vikings launched their game-winning drive with 5:30 left.

9/17/06	COWBOYS (1-1) 27, Redskins (0-2) 10				63,152
Was	0	10	0	0	10
Dal	10	7	0	10	27
Dal	FG Vanderjagt 26				
Dal	Crayton 4 pass from Bledsoe (Vanderjagt kick)				
Was	FG Hall 39				
Dal	Barber 1 run (Vanderjagt kick)				
Was	Cartwright 100 kickoff return (Hall kick)				
Dal	Glenn 40 pass from Bledsoe (Vanderjagt kick)				
Dal	FG Vanderjagt 50				

Texas Stadium—The Redskins struggled on offense and let down at some key moments on defense while losing to Dallas 27-10.

Dallas scored on each of its two possessions, driving to a field goal and then moving 56 yards to a touchdown pass from Drew Bledsoe to Patrick Crayton. Both drives were marred with penalty flags against the Redskins, who totaled 11 penalties for 117 yards on the day.

The Redskins got on the board by driving to a John Hall field goal early in the third quarter. The Cowboys went up 17-3 with a touchdown drive spurred by a 41-yard pass interference penalty on defensive back Kenny Wright.

But the game took at turn at that point. Rock Cartwright fielded the ensuing kickoff at the goal line and chugged the length of the field, 100 yards for a touchdown. It was a ballgame at 17-10 at halftime.

The Redskins offense, however, did not participate in the change of momentum. They had six possessions with the score 17-10. On none of the first five did they get out of their own territory. On the sixth they got a gift and started on the Cowboys' side of the field after Sean Taylor forced a fumble and Marcus Washington recovered at the Dallas 39.

But two plays went nowhere and on third down, Brunell floated a pass towards the end zone. Safety Roy Williams got an easy interception before running out of bounds at the one.

After a couple of penalties against Washington got them out of the hole, the Cowboys embarked on a 99-yard touchdown drive. The drive capper and game clincher came when Bledsoe, with plenty of time to throw, hit Terry Glenn in the end zone from 40 yards out.

9/24/06	Redskins (1-2) 31, TEXANS (0-3) 15				70,059
Was	7	14	7	3	31
Hou	7	0	0	8	15
Hou	Bruener 2 pass from Carr (Brown kick)				
Was	Betts 9 run (Hall kick)				
Was	Randle El 23 pass from Brunell (Hall kick)				
Was	Portis 30 run (Hall kick)				
Was	Portis 1 run (Hall kick)				
Was	FG Hall 46				
Hou	Daneils 2 pass from Carr (Dayne run)				

Reliant Stadium—Mark Brunell, under fire for a lack of productivity in the first two games on the season, set an NFL record by completing 22 consecutive passes as the Redskins beat Houston 31-15.

The effective passing game, composed mostly of short throws, opened up things for the runners. As a team, the Redskins rushed for 234 yards with Ladell Betts racking up a career best 124 on 16 carries.

The first five minutes of the game were similar to what had transpired in the first two games. After being penalized on the opening kickoff, the Redskins went three and out. After the punt, the Texans scored easily, with a 53-yard bomb from David Carr to Andre Johnson being the key play. Tight end Mark Bruener got the TD on a two-year pass from Carr.

Yet another penalty backed the Redskins up inside their own ten after the ensuing kickoff. Two plays later it was third and six at the 13. Washington lined up with four wide receivers. That left the middle of the field open for Brunell to flip a shovel pass to Clinton Portis, who was on the move. He didn't stop until he was pushed out of bounds at the Houston 13. Two plays later Betts followed a nice Santana Moss block to score from nine yards out.

That pass started Brunell's streak. Washington took the lead for good on the first play of the second quarter when Brunell threw a 23-yard touchdown pass to Antwaan Randle El. Although the pass traveled just a few yards downfield, it was on the money and allowed Randle El to catch it in stride and roll the rest of the way.

Evidence of the dink-and-dunk nature of the Redskins' passing game came in a series in the second quarter. Brunell completed three straight passes but they covered a total of just eight yards, forcing the team to punt.

With nine seconds left in the half Washington had driven to the Houston 30. On second and six, Portis ran a draw to try and improve John Hall's field goal chances. Hall ended up kicking an extra point as Portis dashed up the middle all the way to the end zone.

It looked like Brunell's consecutive completions streak had ended in the midst of what would turn out to be a 70-yard touchdown drive. On first and 10 at the 13, Brunell threw incomplete for Brandon Lloyd but a roughing the pass flag negated the attempt.

Clinton Portis ran in for the clinching touchdown from a yard out a few plays later.

Brunell's streak ended on the next series when he misfired going to Lloyd. For the game he was 24 of 27 for 261 yards.

10/1/06	REDSKINS (2-2) 36, Jaguars (2-2) 30 OT					89,450
Jax	10	7	0	13	0	30
Was	7	6	7	10	6	36
Jax	FG Scobee 46					
Was	Moss 55 pass from Brunell (Hall kick)					
Jax	Williams 33 pass from Leftwich (Scobee kick)					
Was	FG Hall 44					
Jax	Jones-Drew 51 pass from Leftwich (Scobee kick)					
Was	FG Hall 37					
Was	Portis 1 run (Hall kick)					
Was	Moss 8 pass from Brunell (Hall kick)					
Jax	Williams 21 pass from Leftwich					
Jax	FG Scobee 43					
Was	FG Hall 37					
Jax	FG Scobee 41					
Was	Moss 68 pass from Brunell					

FedEx Field—A taught, exciting game came to an explosive end when Santana Moss snared a pass that Mark Brunell perhaps should not have thrown and streaked to the end zone, giving the Redskins a 36-30 overtime win over Jacksonville.

The reason the throw was risky was that two defenders were near Moss as Brunell fired it to the speedy receiver. Somehow both of them missed it. Moss grabbed it, spun around and bolted the rest of the way to complete the 68-yard game winner.

There were three lead changes and three ties in this one. After a Josh Scobee field goal made it 3-0 Moss pulled off his first breathtaking play of the day. From the Redskins 45 he caught a deep pass from Brunell. It looked like he was going to be tackled short of the goal line, but he dismissed the bewildered defender with a 360-degree spin move and went the rest of the way to make it 7-3.

Then the Jaguars went on a 14-3 run. The second TD came when Byron Leftwich threw a short pass to running back Maurice Jones-Drew, who turned on the afterburners to finish the 51-yard touchdown play.

Trailing 17-10, the Redskins reeled off 17 unanswered points, seeming to take control of the game. Defensive end Phillip Daniels set up the last of those points with an interception of Leftwich at the Jacksonville 29. That set up another Brunell-to-Moss touchdown pass, this one coming from a pedestrian eight yards. John Hall converted to make it 27-17 with 12:24 left to play.

The Jags wasted little time getting back into it. Leftwich went to Reggie Williams for 35 yards, Mercedes Lewis for 31 and then to Williams again for 21 yards and a touchdown. Williams was crunched between two defenders on the scoring play and his helmet flew off, but the receiver held on.

Brandon Lloyd handed the ball right back to Jacksonville with a fumble after catching a second-down pass. That set up a Scobee field goal to tie it at 27-27 with 6:40 left in regulation.

Rock Cartwright's 46-yard return of the ensuing kickoff set up a Hall field goal to put the Skins back on top at 30-27 with 1:55 left to play. Leftwich, however, was able to move the Jags into position to tie it up and Scobee did just that with a 41-yard field goal with 11 seconds left.

The Redskins won the toss and three plays and 1:49 into the extra session, Moss worked his magic.

10/8/06	GIANTS (2-2) 19, Redskins (2-3) 3				78,653
Was	3	0	0	0	3
NYG	0	9	7	3	19
Was	FG Hall 39				
NYG	FG Feely 24				
NYG	FG Feely 34				
NYG	FG Feely 32				
NYG	Burress 2 pass from Manning (Feely kick)				
NYG	FG Feely 40				

Giants Stadium—After two weeks of flying high the Redskins offence came crashing back to Earth in their 19-3 loss to the Giants. After posting nearly 1,000 yards in the last two games combined, Washington mustered just 164 yards against New York.

The Redskins took a 3-0 first-quarter lead by driving to a 39-yard John Hall field goal. In all, they held the ball for about eight minutes in the first quarter. For the last 45 minutes of play the

Giants had a time of possession advantage of roughly two to one (29 minutes to 16 for the Redskins).

Jay Feely missed a field goal on the Giants' first possession. They came away with points after each of their next four possessions. Had they been more efficient in the red zone this game would have resembled the 36-0 pasting that New York delivered to the Redskins in this stadium last year.

As it was, the Redskins still were very much alive, trailing 6-3 when the Giants took possession at their own two-yard line with 4:28 left in the first half. If the defense could hold them to a quick three and out, there was a chance to grab momentum going into the locker room.

Instead, it was the beginning of the end for Washington. New York burned off all but two seconds of the first-half clock while executing a 14-play drive to a 32-yard Feely field goal to make it 9-3.

Then the Giants took the second half kickoff and pulled off another drive that was death by a thousand paper cuts. This one took 15 plays to cover 69 yards to a two-yard touchdown pass from Eli Manning to Plaxico Burress. They converted three first downs including a third and 16 on a Manning to Amani Toomer pass to the sideline. Toomer did not get both feet in, but Reed Doughty was ruled to have pushed him out of bounds.

The Redskins' last shot at making the game competitive came on their ensuing possession. They moved to the New York 24 where they faced third and one. Mark Brunell couldn't make connections to Chris Cooley and the subsequent 42-yard field goal attempt was wide left.

10/15/06	Titans (1-5) 25, REDSKINS (2-4) 22			88,550	
Ten	3	10	9	3	25
Was	7	7	0	8	22
Ten	FG Bironas 32				
Was	Portis 10 run (Novak kick)				
Was	Cooley 24 pass from Brunell (Novak kick)				
Ten	FG Bironas 26				
Ten	Jones 3 pass from Young (Bironas kick)				
Ten	Henry 2 run (Bironas kick)				
Ten	Safety punt blocked out of end zone				
Was	Portis 4 run (Moss pass from Brunell)				
Ten	FG Bironas 30				

FedEx Field—The hype and hope of the preseason gave way to grim reality as the Redskins blew a 14-3 lead and lost to a winless team playing with a rookie quarterback. Rob Bironas kicked a 30-yard field goal with just over five minutes left to play to give Tennessee a 25-22 win over Washington.

After Bironas kicked a field goal on the Titans' opening drive, it looked like the Redskins were going to take care of business. On their ensuing possession the Redskins smartly moved down the field 78 yards and scored on Clinton Portis' 10-yard touchdown run.

The Washington defense stepped up and forced a three and out. Mark Brunell culminated a 70-yard touchdown drive on the first play of the second quarter with a 24-yard scoring toss to Chris Cooley.

At 14-3 it appeared that the rout was on and the Redskins were on their way to righting their season—but that appearance was deceiving.

The Titans fought back with a field goal and a touchdown on their next two possessions. The Redskins were on the move in the last two minutes of the half, but Antwaan Randle El fumbled the ball away after taking a Brunell pass into Titans territory.

The visitors picked up right where they left off after halftime. The FedEx Field crowd began to grow very restless as rookie quarterback Vince Young led the Titans on a 74-yard touchdown drive on their initial second-half possession. They stretched their

lead to eight points when he blocked David Frost's punt out of the end zone.

The Redskins did put on a quick drive early in the fourth quarter to tie it up. Brunell connected with Brandon Lloyd for 52 yards to the Tennessee four. Two plays later Portis powered in from there and the two-point conversion tied the game at 22.

Washington had possessions before and after Bironas' winning field goal and they went three and out on each of them. In the second half the Titans had a time of possession advantage of 19 minutes to 11 for the Redskins.

The Redskins' last chance died when Brunell threw an interception with 54 seconds left.

Oct 16

Not Yet--Brunell to Remain at QB
Despite 2-4 record, inefficient offense, Campbell will remain on bench

---

10/22/06	COLTS (6-0) 36, Redskins (2-5) 22			57,274	
Was	0	14	0	8	22
Ind	7	6	20	3	36
Ind	Clark 1 pass from Manning (Vinatieri kick)				
Was	Cooley 13 pass from Brunell (Novak kick)				
Ind	FG Vinatieri 30				
Was	Randle El 87 punt return (Novak kick)				
Ind	FG Vinatieri 19				
Ind	Harrison 4 pass from Manning (Vinatieri kick)				
Ind	Wayne 51 pass from Manning (Vinatieri kick)				
Ind	Harrison 1 pass from Manning (pass failed)				
Ind	FG Vinatieri 47				
Was	Thrash 5 pass from Brunell (Cooley pass from Brunell)				

RCA Dome—A 14-10 Washington lead was buried under an avalanche of 26 unanswered points as the Redskins fell to the Colts 36-22.

After the Colts took a 7-0 first-quarter lead on Payton Manning's one-yard touchdown pass to Dallas Clark, the Redskins got moving late in the first quarter thanks to Antwaan Randle El. He returned a punt 24 yards to set up Washington in Colts territory at the 45. A 13-yard pass from Mark Brunell to Santana Moss got things going and Brunell capped the drive with a 13-yard touchdown pass to Chris Cooley to tie the game at 7-7.

A few series later Indy punted again and this time Randle El took it all the way back, 87 yards for a touchdown. He bolted straight up the middle of the field, put on a move to elude the punter at around the 20, and rolled in for the score. The extra point put the Redskins up 14-10 with 2:24 left in the half.

But, typical of the way the Redskins' season has gone this year, they handed the momentum right back to the other team. Randle El was flagged for excessive celebration, pushing the kickoff back 15 yards. The Redskins were offside on the kickoff and they lined up to kick from the 10. Then punter David Frost was penalized for removing his helmet and, incredibly, Washington kicked off from its own five.

The Colts drove to the Washington one and settled for an Adam Vinatieri field goal to make it 14-13.

Any hopes the Redskins had for hanging with the Cowboys vanished quickly in the third quarter. Manning led three touchdown drives during that period. To call them brutally efficient would be an understatement.

Four plays, 55 yards, four-yard touchdown pass to Marvin Harrison.

Four plays, 81 yards, 51-yard touchdown pass to Reggie Wayne.

Seven plays, 66 yards, one-yard touchdown pass to Harrison.

While all of this was going on the Washington offense ran all of eight plays.

Game over.

Washington did get a late touchdown on a Brunell pass to James Thrash, but it was far too little and way too late.

11/5/06	REDSKINS (3-5) 22, Cowboys (4-4) 19				90,250
Dal	0	12	7	0	19
Was	5	7	0	10	22
Was	Safety Marshall tackled Jones in end zone				
Was	FG Novak 28				
Dal	Glenn 10 pass from Romo (pass failed)				
Dal	FG Vanderjagt 33				
Was	Portis 38 run (Novak kick)				
Dal	FG Vanderjagt 30				
Dal	Owens 4 pass from Romo (Vanderjagt kick)				
Was	Cooley 18 pass from Brunell (Novak kick)				
Was	FG Novak 47				

FedEx Field—In one of the most bizarre games in the storied history of the Cowboys-Redskins series, Nick Novak kicked a 47-yard field goal at the end of regulation—actually, one play *after* the end of regulation—to give Washington a 22-19 win.

Novak had missed a go-ahead attempt from 49 yards with 35 seconds to go. It looked like the miss would be fatal. Tony Romo completed three of four passes and quickly got the Cowboys down to the Washington 17 with six seconds left. Mike Vanderjagt came on for an easy 35-yard field goal attempt that almost certainly would win the game.

Well, *almost* certainly. Safety Troy Vincent—who never had lined up with a field goal block team prior to this season—found a seam in the protection and broke through to block the kick. Overtime.

Sean Taylor, however, was thinking touchdown. He picked up the ball and scrambled around, looking for running room as the clock ticked down to 0:00. Dallas' Kyle Kosier grabbed Taylor's face mask, turning his head around. A flag flew and Taylor kept on running all the way to the Dallas 44. The call was for a 15-yard face mask penalty.

Not only did the penalty move the ball to the 29 but since a half can't end on a defensive penalty, the game was extended by one untimed down. That gave Novak his opportunity for redemption and he had just enough distance to touch off a celebration.

The Redskins started the game with a nice drive deep into Cowboy territory. After getting a first and goal at the four, however, they could not punch it in, despite getting a total of seven chances thanks to a defensive holding call.

The drive did lead to points. After Clinton Portis got stuffed on fourth down at the one, Lemar Marshall tackled Julius Jones in the end zone for a safety. After the free kick the Redskins moved into position for a 28-yard Novak field goal to take a 5-0 lead.

The game was tied at 12 at halftime and it looked like the Cowboys were on their way in the third quarter. They scored once on a four-yard pass from Romo to Terrell Owens. Leading 19-12, Owens got open deep down the seam but dropped what probably would have been a clinching 74-yard touchdown pass.

The Redskins tied it up early in the fourth quarter on an 18-yard touchdown pass from Mark Brunell to Chris Cooley. Fittingly, that score was set up by a 48-yard pass interference penalty on an option pass by Antwaan Randle El.

11/12/06	EAGLES (5-4) 27, Redskins (3-6) 3				69,143
Was	0	3	0	0	3
Phi	10	7	10	0	27
Phi	FG Akers 37				
Phi	Stallworth 84 pass from McNabb (Akers kick)				
Phi	Buckhalter 55 pass from McNabb (Akers kick)				
Was	FG Novak 32				
Phi	FG Akers 25				
Phi	Brown 70 interception return (Akers kick)				

Lincoln Financial Field—The Redskins' label as one of the NFL's most disappointing teams for the 2006 season was cemented today as they were barely competitive, losing 27-6 to an Eagles team that was not on the top of its game.

The Redskins held the ball for 20 minutes in the first half but couldn't do anything with it. The prototypical possession for the game—perhaps for the 2006 season—was their third. They held the ball for more than five and a half minutes and ran 14 plays, but netted just 37 yards.

They staggered from their 33 to the Eagles 30. Early in the drive Clinton Portis suffered a broken hand and he will be lost for at least a few weeks. His replacement, Ladell Betts, had some positive runs and also lost yardage on two carries and fumbled out of bounds on another. Mark Brunell completed two passes for four and six yards. It ended when Nick Novak went wide right on a 48-yard field goal attempt.

At that point the Redskins already trailed 7-0. It soon got worse after the Eagles took over following the missed field goal. On third and 15 at the Philly 45, Donovan McNabb passed to Reggie Brown for 20 yards. Shawn Springs smacked Brown and the ball popped out, though it went directly into the hands of running back Correll Buckhalter. He snared it out of the air and rumbled the rest of the way for the touchdown to make the score 17-0.

Brunell completed a long pass to Brandon Lloyd—good for 43 yards to the Eagle 17—midway through the second quarter. But all the Redskins could get out of the drive was a 32-yard Novak field goal to make it 17-3.

The Eagles put it away quickly in the third quarter. They drove to a field goal and then Sheldon Brown picked off a Brunell pass and bolted 70 yards for a touchdown.

Nov 12

Broken Hand KO's Portis
Back will miss at least four games

Campbell Takes the Reigns

Nov 13—After 28 games as a spectator, Jason Campbell finally gets his shot.

Joe Gibbs announced today that Mark Brunell will be benched and Campbell will start at quarterback on Sunday against Tampa Bay and for the rest of the season.

"We want to give Jason every opportunity," Gibbs said. "When we drafted him we felt like we had a very talented person there, and certainly when we give him the starting job we're going to do everything we can to support him."

Gibbs reported that Brunell accepted the move "with class."

Campbell said he was "shocked" by the move. Given the performance of Brunell and the offense for most of the season, he is one of the few who is.

11/19/06	BUCCANEERS (3-7) 20, Redskins (3-7) 17				65,699
Was	3	0	7	7	17
TB	3	0	7	10	20
TB	FG Bryant 26				
Was	FG Novak 45				
Was	Cooley 3 pass from Campbell (Novak kick)				
TB	Becht 2 pass from Gradkowski (Bryant kick)				
TB	Galloway 34 pass from Gradkowski (Bryant kick)				
TB	FG Bryant 31				
Was	Yoder 4 pass from Campbell (Novak kick)				

Raymond James Stadium—The Redskins made a change at quarterback, inserting the untested Jason Campbell in place of the struggling Mark Brunell. Unfortunately, they had to field the same defense that has been ineffective all year and Washington fell to Tampa Bay 20-17.

The Bucs piled up 181 rushing yards, more than twice their paltry 81-yard season average.

"It's just unacceptable," defensive end Renaldo Wynn said. "We just let teams run up and down on us. It's just not right."

Campbell's first NFL pass came on the Redskins' first offensive play. The long bomb went off the fingertips of Brandon Lloyd and the Redskins lost an opportunity for a quick score.

The Bucs were the ones who blew opportunities the rest of the half. They came up empty in two long drives into Washington territory. One ended when quarterback Bruce Gradkowski fumbled at the 33 and Marcus Washington recovered. The other started at the Tampa Bay five and ended when Shawn Springs intercepted Gradkowski in the end zone just before halftime.

It was 3-3 at intermission, and for a moment it looked like the Redskins might make the Bucs pay for missing their opportunities. Campbell completed pass of 14 yards to Antwaan Randle El and of 11 yards to Ladell Betts and then he hit James Thrash for 17. T. J. Duckett and Betts picked up some good chunks of yardage rushing. It all added up to a 74-yard touchdown drive that Campbell finished off with a three-yard touchdown pass to Chris Cooley.

The ball then began to bounce the Bucs' way. On a third and goal play at the Washington two, Gradkowski threw a pass for Joey Galloway in the end zone. The ball bounced off of the intended receiver and into the arms of tight end Anthony Becht for the tying touchdown.

Early in the fourth quarter Campbell completed a short pass to Betts, who fumbled when he was tackled. The Bucs recovered and three plays later Galloway got behind the coverage as Gradkowski hit him with a 34-yard touchdown pass.

After the Redskins went three and out, the Bucs padded their lead by driving to a 31-yard Matt Bryant field goal. The drive was composed exclusively of Carnell Williams runs, six of them for 42 yards.

That made it 20-10, rendering Campbell's touchdown pass to Todd Yoder with 37 seconds left meaningless.

11/26/06	**REDSKINS (4-7) 17, Panthers (6-5) 13**				85,450
Car	3	3	0	7	13
Was	0	3	7	7	17
Car	FG Kasay 42				
Was	FG Novak 42				
Car	FG Kasay 51				
Was	Randle El 4 pass from Campbell (Novak kick)				
Car	Smith 8 pass from Delhomme (Kasay kick)				
Was	Cooley 66 pass from Campbell (Novak kick)				

FedEx Field—Playing in just his second NFL game, Jason Campbell threw a 66-yard touchdown pass to Chris Cooley with 4:26 left to play to lead the Redskins past the Panthers 17-13.

After the game, the play was discovered to have been even more dramatic than it first seemed. Campbell's helmet headset—his communication link to the coaches on the sideline—started delivering nothing but static as the play was being called. Not wanting to burn a time-out despite the fact that it was third and eight and the Redskins trailed 13-10, Campbell went ahead and called the play he thought the coaches would call.

That sent Cooley over the middle and Campbell fired a pass to him near midfield. The tight end shook off one tackle attempt and then another, headed to the sideline and rolled into the end zone.

Sean Taylor intercepted Jake Delhomme's desperation pass in the end zone to seal it for the Redskins.

The offenses struggled in the first half. Carolina took a 6-3 lead just before halftime. The score was set up when a partially-blocked Derrick Frost punt netted just two yards to the Washington

44. Two plays gained 10 yards and John Kasay's 51-yard attempt was good at the gun.

The Redskins went three and out five times in the half.

Washington took the lead the same way that Carolina did: on a partially-blocked punt. Rocky McIntosh got a hand on a punt that ended up netting just 11 yards and the Redskins were in business at the Carolina 36. Seven plays later, Campbell went over the middle to Antwaan Randle El for four yards and a touchdown.

Carolina responded immediately with a 74-yard touchdown drive that culminated in Steve Smith making a spectacular catch of a Delhomme pass for eight yards and a touchdown.

Campbell wanted to answer right back, throwing deep for Moss on the first play of the ensuing drive. The pass was intercepted and Campbell had to wait until the next series to find Cooley for the winning TD.

12/3/06	**Falcons (6-6) 24, REDSKINS (4-8) 14**				86,436
Atl	0	10	7	7	24
Was	14	0	0	0	14
Was	Betts 8 run (Suisham kick)				
Was	Moss 42 pass from Campbell (Suisham kick)				
Atl	FG Andersen 34				
Atl	Crumpler 16 pass from Vick (Andersen kick)				
Atl	Jenkins 22 pass from Vick (Andersen kick)				
Atl	Norwood 69 run (Andersen kick)				

FedEx Field—The Redskins bolted to a 14-0 first-quarter lead and then watched it fade away as they lost to the Falcons 24-14.

Ladell Betts got Washington's first drive going by carrying four straight times for 25 yards. Five plays later Betts capped the drive with an eight-yard touchdown run behind a Mike Sellers block to make it 7-0 midway through the first quarter.

Atlanta went three and out and punted to the Washington 30. They fed Betts the rock again and after four carries the Redskins were at the Falcons 42. From there, Jason Campbell arched a pass to Santana Moss at the five. The receiver, surrounded by two defenders, leapt and plucked the ball out of the air. He fell to the ground untouched and literally rolled the final yard or so into the end zone.

The Falcons didn't score until midway through the second quarter when Morten Andersen kicked a 34-yard field goal. The Redskins tried to respond but Shaun Suisham's 50-yard field goal attempt went wide left.

Given the good field position after the miss, Atlanta quickly moved in and Michael Vick fired a 16-yard touchdown pass to tight end Algae Crumpler, making it 14-10 at halftime.

Washington's next drive came to a disastrous conclusion. They were on the move at the Atlanta 21 when Campbell couldn't shake blitzing safety Lawyer Milloy—but he threw the ball anyway. Chauncey Davis accepted the easy interception and bolted 41 yards to the Washington 25. Two plays later the Falcons had the lead as Vick went to receiver Michael Jenkins on a slant for 22 yards and a touchdown.

"I tried to shake him," Campbell said of Milloy. "He grabbed the back of my jersey. I tried to throw it away to set up good field goal position."

The Redskins had two possessions trailing by just 17-14. The second one made it to the Atlanta 36 but fizzled there. Early in the fourth quarter Jerious Norwood bolted 69 yards for a clinching TD.

12/10/06	**Eagles (7-6) 21, REDSKINS (4-9) 19**				84,164
Phil	7	14	0	0	21
Was	3	3	10	3	19
Was	FG Suisham 31				
Phi	Smith 10 pass from Garcia (Akers kick)				
Phi	Lewis 84 interception return (Akers kick)				
Phi	Stallworth 3 pass from McNabb (Akers kick)				

Was	FG Suisham 45
Was	FG Suisham 32
Was	Randle El 34 pass from Campbell (Suisham kick)
Was	FG Suisham 35

FedEx Field—When someone once said that statistics are for losers, they must have had a game like this one in mind. The Redskins outgained the Eagles by 150 yards and had a 15-minute edge in time of possession. But they lost to the Eagles 21-19 in a game that really wasn't as close as the final indicated.

The Redskins started off well, holding the Eagles three and out and then driving to a 31-yard Shaun Suisham field goal. Then, on their next possession it started to come apart. As has happened so often this year, a turnover shifted the momentum.

Omar Gaither picked off Jason Campbell's pass at the Redskins 47 and returned it to the 31. Five plays later Jeff Garcia threw a 10-yard touchdown pass to L. J. Smith.

Early in the second quarter the Redskins moved to the Eagles 23. A Campbell pass intended for Chris Cooley was deflected and then intercepted by safety Michael Lewis. He was off to the races, returning the pick 84 yards for a touchdown.

The Redskins got a break when the Eagles fumbled a punt and Ade Jimoh recovered at the Washington 47. Three plays later, however, they were punting again—and the Eagles drove to their third consecutive touchdown.

Washington was game, posting a field goal a minute before halftime and another one on their first third-quarter possession. Late in the third they finally penetrated the end zone, scoring on a 34-yard touchdown pass from Campbell to Antwaan Randle El. That made it a five-point game at 21-16.

The Redskins' best shot at taking the lead came on a drive that started at their own 15. When Campbell scrambled 15 yards the Redskins had a first and goal at the 15. But a penalty and a sack spiked the drive and facing fourth and goal and the 17, Suisham kicked a 35-yard field goal with 5:02 left.

The Redskins never regained possession as the Eagles ran out the clock.

12/17/06	**Redskins (5-9) 16, SAINTS (9-5) 10**			69,052	
Was	10	3	0	3	16
NO	0	7	0	3	10
Was	FG Suisham 37
Was	Moss 31 pass from Campbell (Suisham kick)
NO	McAllister 1 run (Carney kick)
Was	FG Suisham 37
NO	FG Carney 41
Was	FG Suisham 22

Superdome—All year long the Redskins have been putting up ineffective defensive efforts against mediocre offensive teams. Today they were facing the high-powered offense of New Orleans and there was every reason to suspect the Saints would post Arena-league type numbers.

But that's why they play the games. The Redskins got a lead and protected it, playing their best defensive game of the year in beating New Orleans 16-10.

The Redskins established a 10-0 lead in the first quarter. They drove to a field goal the first time they had the ball. Later in the first Jason Campbell engineered a lightning-quick 80-yard touchdown drive. On third and five at the Redskins 25, Campbell found Chris Cooley, who rumbled 44 yards to the Saints 31. On the very next play Campbell fired a strike to Moss for a touchdown and a 10-0 lead.

New Orleans came back with a touchdown drive, scoring on a one-yard Deuce McAllister run. But Washington managed to keep the Saints at arm's length by responding with a 37-yard Suisham field goal on their next possession to make it 13-7.

The third quarter was scoreless but the Saints pulled to within 13-10 early in the fourth and got the ball back. Drew Brees

launched a deep pass and Carlos Rogers made a juggling interception. The Redskins burned off more than six minutes of clock while driving to a 22-yard Suisham field goal. The score as 16-10 with 4:19 left to play.

New Orleans threatened to steal it away, driving to the Washington 15 in the last two minutes. Brees flipped a screen pass to speedy rookie Reggie Bush. It looked like Bush had a path to the end zone, but Cornelius Griffin and Andre Carter, two linemen, flashed into the picture and nailed Bush for a one-yard loss. Brees' fourth-down pass fell incomplete

12/24/06	**RAMS (7-8) 37, Redskins (5-10) 31 OT**				62,324	
Was	7	14	7	3	0	31
StL	0	14	14	3	6	37
Was	Duckett 5 run (Suisham kick)
StL	Bruce 10 pass from Bulger (Wilkins kick)
StL	Byrd 27 pass from Bulger (Wilkins kick)
Was	Betts 6 run (Suisham kick)
Was	Cooley 9 pass from Campbell (Suisham kick)
Was	Betts 7 run (Suisham kick)
StL	Jackson 64 pass from Bulger (Wilkins kick)
StL	Davis 10 pass from Bulger (Wilkins kick)
StL	FG Wilkins 21
Was	FG Suisham 52
StL	Jackson 21 run

Edward Jones Dome—Tailback Stephen Jackson bolted 21 yards for a touchdown in overtime to give the Rams a 37-31 win over the Redskins.

Both teams had good reason to think they had the game won at various points. The Redskins' best chance to wrap up a victory came with the score tied at 31 just before the two-minute warning. From the Rams 29 Ladell Betts broke a run well into field goal range. However, he fumbled at the 25 and the ball bounced toward the goal line. Corey Chavous recovered at the 13 and the threat was gone.

Betts ran for 129 yards on 29 attempts with two touchdowns. He tied a team record by getting more than 100 yards for a fifth straight game.

After the Rams went up 14-7 in the second quarter, the Redskins put up 21 unanswered points to take a two-touchdown lead. Betts scored the first and third TD's from six and seven yards, respectively. The first once came after Vernon Fox blocked a Rams punt out of bounds at the St. Louis eight.

In between Betts' scores, Chris Cooley hauled in a nine-yard touchdown pass from Jason Campbell with 30 left in the first half.

After Betts' second touchdown early in the third quarter made it 28-14, the Rams got back into it in a hurry. Jackson caught a short pass from Mark Bulger, found a seam and dashed 64 yards to the end zone. Washington went three and out and the Rams put Jackson to work on the ground. He carried four straight times for 37 yards to key a drive that culminated in Bulger throwing a 10-yard touchdown pass to former Redskin Stephen Davis. That tied the game at 28.

The teams traded fourth-quarter field goals to set up the late dramatics.

12/30/06	**Giants (8-8) 34, REDSKINS (5-11) 28**			86,141	
NYG	3	17	7	7	34
Was	7	0	7	14	28
NYG	FG Feely 34
Was	Moss 48 pass from Randle El (Suisham kick)
NYG	Barber 15 run (Feely kick)
NYG	Barber 55 run (Feely kick)
NYG	FG Feely 31
NYG	Carter 6 pass from Manning (Feely kick)
Was	Betts 7 pass from Campbell (Suisham kick)
Was	Duckett 1 run (Suisham kick)
NYG	Barber 50 run
Was	Sellers 1 pass from Campbell (Suisham kick)

FedEx Field—The Redskins' season came to an end with yet another inconsistent performance as they fell to the Giants 34-28.

Washington started off with a nice drive that reached the New York 18. But Ladell Betts fumbled from there and Fred Robbins scooped up the ball and returned it all the way to the Washington 12. Andre Carter sacked Eli Manning and the Giants had to settle for a field goal.

The Redskins came back on their next possession with Antwaan Randle El executing a nice touchdown pass to Santana Moss that put them up 7-3.

After that, the Skins' inability to stop Tiki Barber reared its ugly head. First Barber capped a 58-yard drive with a 15-yard touchdown run. Then, later in the second quarter, the Giants drove 97 yards to a touchdown. Barber scored it, dashing 55 yards off left guard.

A six-yard Eli Manning touchdown pass to Tim Carter capped a 24-0 scoring run for the Giants and had the Redskins looking at the short end of a 27-7 deficit.

While nobody would have remembered if they'd just packed it in after that, the Redskins kept fighting. Jason Campbell threw a seven-yard touchdown pass to Ladell Betts late in the third quarter and T. J. Duckett capped another drive with a one-yard touchdown burst.

The Redskins were within striking distance at 27-21 with 9:30 left to play. It looked like they were going to get the ball back into their hot hands as Manning's third-down pass fell incomplete.

But there was laundry on the field; Kenny Wright was penalized for defensive holding, keeping the drive alive. Two plays later Barber ripped off another long TD run—this one from 55 yards—to make it 34-21.

Still, the Redskins were game. They drove to a Campbell-to-Mike-Sellers touchdown pass and got the ball back with 2:18 to go. But four straight Campbell incompletions ended it.

2007
Head Coach: Joe Gibbs
Record: 9-7, Third in NFC East
Playoffs 0-1, Lost in Wild Card Round

Honors: Chris Cooley Pro Bowl; Chris Samuels Pro Bowl; Sean Taylor Pro Bowl: Ethan Albright Pro Bowl

---

Mar 3
Smoot Back, Fletcher in the Fold
LB comes from Buffalo for five years, $25 million;
Smoot back after disappointing season in Minnesota

9/9/07	REDSKINS (1-0) 16, Dolphins (0-1) 13 OT				90,163
Mia	0	7	3	3	0	13
Was	0	3	7	3	3	16
Was	FG Suisham 31
Mia	Peele 1 pass from Green (Feely kick)
Was	Portis 19 run (Suisham kick)
Mia	FG Feely 20
Was	FG Suisham 44
Mia	FG Feely 36
Was	FG Suisham 39

FedEx Field—Shaun Suisham kicked a 39-yard field goal 5:36 into overtime to give the Redskins a 16-13 win over the Dolphins.

The Redskins were ragged offensively to say the least. Jason Campbell's first pass was intercepted and Clinton Portis had trouble getting going on the ground. Their one score of the half came after they drove from their own 20 to the Miami five. On third down from there, however, Zach Thomas sacked Campbell and Shaun Suisham came on to kick a 31-yard field goal.

On the play where Campbell was sacked, right tackle Jon Jansen suffered a fracture dislocation of his right ankle, an injury that seems likely to end his season. Stephon Heyer, a rookie free agent, stepped in for Jansen. Despite the fact that he never had played right tackle in his life, he filled in admirably.

Miami got on the board with a touchdown on the last play of the first half. Miami coach Cam Cameron, coaching his first NFL game, rolled the dice by eschewing a short field goal attempt running a pass play from the one yard line with four seconds left. The clock ran out during the play but Trent Green made Cameron look good by finding tight end Justin Peele in the end zone. Jay Feely's conversion gave Miami a 7-3 lead.

A nice pass from Campbell to Antwaan Randle El that covered 49 yards was the key play in a 78-yard touchdown drive to open the second half. That play carried to the Dolphins 24 before Portis hid behind the interference of fullback Mike Sellers as he motored 19 yards for a touchdown.

The 10-7 lead lasted until late in the third quarter when Jay Feely tied it up with a 20-yard field goal. The Redskins drove into Miami territory, but on the first play of the fourth quarter a deep Campbell pass intended for Brandon Lloyd was intercepted.

The teams exchanged fourth-quarter field goals to set up overtime. The Redskins won the toss and got rolling on Portis runs of six and 14 yards. After Portis ran for nine yards to the Miami 22, Joe Gibbs called for the field goal on first down.

9/17/07	Redskins (2-0) 20, EAGLES (0-2) 12				67,726
Was	3	7	3	7	20
Phi	0	6	3	3	12
Was	FG Suisham 35
Phi	FG Akers 24
Phi	FG Akers 39
Was	Cooley 16 pass from Campbell (Suisham kick)
Was	FG Suisham 37
Phi	FG Akers 26
Was	Portis 6 run (Suisham kick)
Phi	FG Akers 22

Lincoln Financial Field—Jason Campbell threw a touchdown pass to Chris Cooley just before halftime, providing a key momentum swing that sent the Redskins on to a 20-12 win over the Eagles.

With the Eagles leading 6-3, confusion reigned after Campbell completed a pass to Antwaan Randle El that carried 17 yards to the Eagles one. With Washington out of time-outs, Campbell spiked the ball to stop the clock with 14 seconds left. A delay of game and a false start pushed the line of scrimmage back to the 11. Joe Gibbs, wanting to get some points before anything else could go wrong, sent out the field goal team.

Apparently this move threw off the Eagles; they called time-out. Gibbs then sent his offense back on the field. After another false start, Cooley got a step on safety Brian Dawkins and the Redskins took the lead for good.

"That was a big momentum swing," Gibbs said.

Shaun Suisham's second field goal of the game midway through the third quarter expanded Washington's lead to 13-6.

The Eagles got a David Akers field goal to make it 13-9 but Washington got some breathing room early in the fourth quarter. Campbell dumped a short pass to Ladell Betts, who dashed 28 yards to the Eagle 35. On third and 10 from the 26, Campbell flipped the ball to tight end Todd Yoder, who lumbered for 18 yards and a first down at the six. On the next play Clinton Portis scored from six yards out and it was 20-9.

Donovan McNabb led a drive to a field goal and threatened to send the game into overtime with a late bid. On fourth down and the nine, however, LaRon Landry broke up McNabb's pass to receiver Kevin Curtis with a wicked hit and the Redskins ran out the clock.

9/23/07	Giants (1-2) 24, REDSKINS (2-1) 17			90,803
NYG	3	0	7	14	24
Was	7	10	0	0	17
NYG	FG Tynes 34			
Was	Portis 1 run (Suisham kick)			
Was	Cooley 8 pass from Campbell (Suisham kick)			
Was	FG Suisham 47			
NYG	Droughns 1 run (Tynes kick)			
NYG	Droughns 1 run (Tynes kick)			
NYG	Burress 33 pass from Manning (Tynes kick)			

FedEx Field—The Redskins blew a 17-3 halftime lead—and a chance at redemption—as they fell to the Giants 24-17.

Washington scored 10 of those 17 first-half points thanks largely to New York turnovers. With the Giants up 3-0, Andre Carter made a big play, sacking Eli Manning at the Giants 12 and stripping the ball loose. London Fletcher recovered and returned to the six and two plays later Clinton Portis blasted over from the one to make it 7-3.

The Redskins put together their only sustained scoring drive of the game early in the second quarter. The big play was a 49-yard pass from Jason Campbell to Santana Moss that moved the Redskins down to the New York 10. Three plays later Campbell fired an eight-yard touchdown pass to Chris Cooley to make it 14-3.

Fletcher intercepted a Manning pass with 1:33 left in the half and that led to a 47-yard Shaun Suisham field goal as time expired in the half.

Washington drew no momentum from the events just before halftime. New York came out of the locker room and embarked on a 61-yard touchdown drive. They converted three third downs along the way to Reuben Droughns' one-yard touchdown burst.

Sean Taylor picked off a Manning pass, but the offensive response was to go three and out. The Giants put together a drive that spanned the third and fourth quarters and tied the game on another Droughns one-yard TD burst. That tied the game at 17 and the Redskins were reeling.

And it got worse. Campbell and Portis botched a handoff and Antonio Pierce pounced on the ball at the Redskins 44. It took five plays for the Giants to take the lead. From the 33, Manning got rid of the ball against an all-out blitz and Plaxico Burress broke Carlos Rogers' tackle attempt and easily ran into the end zone.

The Redskins got their last chance with 2:19 left. They had good field position at the New York 35 thanks to Antwaan Randle El's 27-yard punt return. Campbell kept hope alive when he converted a fourth and eight with a 15-yard pass to Moss. A 20-yard pass to Randle El got them down one. Although there was nearly a minute left, Campbell spiked the ball rather than trying to run a play with no huddle. A pass to Mike Sellers was incomplete and then two straight cracks at the left side by Ladell Betts went nowhere.

10/7/07	REDSKINS (3-1) 34, Lions (3-2) 3			88,944
Det	0	0	3	0	3
Was	0	14	2	18	34
Was	Cooley 7 pass from Campbell (Suisham kick)			
Was	Sellers 1 run (Suisham kick)			
Det	FG Hansen 39			
Was	Safety Carter sacked Kitna in end zone			
Was	Sellers 8 pass from Campbell (Cooley pass from Campbell)			
Was	FG Suisham 28			
Was	Rogers 61 interception return (Suisham kick)			

FedEx Field—The Redskins dominated all phases of the game and pounded the Lions 34-3.

Jason Campbell had his best day as a pro, completing 23 of 29 passes for 248 yards and two touchdowns.

Washington's first two drives reached Lions territory, but both stalled outside of scoring range. The third time was a charm as they put together a 14-play, 80-yard touchdown drive. Campbell went to Antwaan Randle El three times for 39 yards during the advance and he capped it with a seven-yard touchdown pass to Chris Cooley.

The next time they got the ball, the Redskins expanded their lead with a drive covering 83 yards. The video highlight came when Campbell threw a short pass to Mike Sellers, his 280-pound fullback. Seller worked up a full head of steam and flattened safety Kenoy Kennedy, picking up 24 yards on the play. Sellers got the TD by powering in from the one at the two-minute warning.

Things became moderately uncomfortable late in the third quarter when Jason Hanson kicked a 39-yard field goal and the Redskins went three and out. Derrick Frost got off a nice punt and the Lions were bottled up at their own eight with a chance to make a game of it.

On second down, however, Andre Carter broke through and sacked John Kitna in the end zone for a safety. Even though the Redskins' ensuing possession ended on a fumble at the Detroit 10, it seemed to be just a matter of time before the Redskins put this one away.

Detroit punted and three players contributed to a huge special teams play. James Thrash returned the punt 62 yards, thanks to an absolutely devastating block by Sean Taylor. The ball was punched away at the end of the return and Rock Cartwright recovered the bouncing ball at the three. After a false start penalty, Campbell went to Sellers for eight yards and the touchdown.

Carlos Rogers capped the scoring by picking off a Kitna pass and cruising 61 yards down the sideline for a touchdown.

10/14/07	PACKERS (5-1) 17, Redskins (3-2) 14			70,761
Was	7	7	0	0	14
GB	7	0	10	0	17
GB	Wynn 3 run			
Was	Campbell 6 run (Suisham kick)			
Was	Cooley 14 pass from Campbell (Suisham kick)			
GB	FG Crosby 37			
GB	Woodson 57 fumble return (Crosby kick)			

Lambeau Field—A chance to upset a quality opponent on the road disappeared under an avalanche of penalties, turnovers and dropped passes as the Redskins fell to the Packers 17-14.

The biggest blunder committed came in the third quarter. Green Bay had just kicked a field goal but Washington still held a 14-10 lead. Rock Cartwright gave the offense excellent field position with a 40-yard kickoff return to the Packers 48.

But two plays later Santana Moss took a handoff from Clinton Portis on a reverse. He didn't have much running room as he cut upfield, and the ball popped loose as he tackled. Charles Woodson picked it up and was gone—47 yards for a touchdown.

The Packers got on the board first after Bret Favre hit Donald Lee with a short pass over the middle. The tight end had gotten lost in coverage and rolled for 60 yards to the Washington three. DeShawn Wynn powered for the touchdown on the next play.

The Redskins responded immediately as Jason Campbell led a 68-yard touchdown drive on Washington's ensuing possession. A 28-yard pass to Chris Cooley got them close and, on second and goal at the six, Campbell couldn't find a receiver. He pulled the ball down, headed up the middle and lunged over the goal line to tie the game at 7-7.

Washington got into Packer territory again midway through the second quarter, but Woodson intercepted Campbell's pass to end that threat.

Towards the end of the half the Redskins did find pay dirt again. This was a 63-yard march that culminated in Campbell throwing a 14-yard to Chris Cooley with just over a minute left in the first half.

The Packers ate up almost seven minutes of the third quarter in driving to a Mason Crosby field goal that cut the Washington lead to 14-10.

The Moss fumble and Woodson return came a few plays later. On Washington's next possession Campbell laid out a perfect deep sideline pass for Moss, who dropped the ball.

The Redskins had more chances—but they couldn't get it done. One possession reached Packer territory at the 33, but Campbell's pass to Ladell Betts on fourth and two was stopped for no gain.

The Redskins were able to stay in the game thanks largely to the efforts of Sean Taylor. The Redskins safety was all over the field, intercepting two Favre passes and having a shot at a few others.

10/21/07	**REDSKINS (4-2) 21, Cardinals (3-4) 19**		85,640
Ari	0	6	0	13	19
Was	7	7	7	0	21
Was	Portis 2 run (Suisham kick)		
Was	Fletcher 27 interception return (Suisham kick)		
Ari	Boldin 2 pass from Warner (kick failed)		
Was	Portis 1 run (Suisham kick)		
Air	Boldin 10 pass from Warner (Rackers kick)		
Ari	Pope 1 pass from Rattay (pass failed)		

FedEx Field—The Redskins had a 21-6 lead going into the fourth quarter but they had to wait until a Neil Rackers field goal attempt drifted wide with seven seconds left to be assured of a win.

Washington built its lead with very little help from its offense. Both the ground game (73 yards for the game) and passing game (87 yards) were ineffective. They were able to post 21 points thanks almost entirely to the Washington defense.

It's not as though the Cardinals were shut down. Kurt Warner passed for 283 yards and was especially hard to stop in the fourth quarter. But he did throw two interceptions, and the Redskins managed to parlay those into 14 points.

Sean Taylor, patrolling the deep part of the field, picked off a Warner pass and dashed down the sideline for 48 yards to the 25. It looked like the Redskins might have to settle for three points off of the opportunity, but a flag flew after Jason Campbell's third and six pass to Mike Sellers came up short of the first down. The call was a personal foul, giving Washington a fresh set of downs. Two plays later Clinton Portis powered into the end zone and it was 7-0.

That score held until midway through the second quarter. Warner threw a pass right to London Fletcher at the Cardinals 27. The linebacker had a trio of blockers in front of him and he followed them to the pylon, diving in for a 14-0 lead.

Arizona responded with a touchdown drive just before halftime. The point after was missed and it was 14-6.

The Redskins extended their lead with their only sustained scoring drive of the day. Going 59 yards, they moved to what

seemed to be a very comfortable 14-6 lead with just under six minutes left in the third quarter on Portis' one-yard touchdown run.

Things got a little less comfortable when the Cardinals drove for a touchdown early in the fourth quarter. It became pins and needles time when Warner mastered a 71-yard drive to a touchdown that pulled his team to within 21-19 with 26 seconds left. The two-point conversion failed—wide receiver Anquan Boldin took the snap and threw a pass that safety LaRon Landry intercepted—but Arizona recovered the onside kick. Rackers' 55-yard attempt was long enough, but it was wide.

10/28/07	**PATRIOTS (8-0) 52, Redskins (4-3) 7**		68,756
Was	0	0	0	7	7
NE	7	17	14	14	52
NE	Brady 3 run (Gostkowski kick)		
NE	Vrabel 2 pass from Brady (Gostkowski kick)		
NE	FG Gostkowski 36		
NE	Moss 6 pass from Brady (Gostkowski kick)		
NE	Brady 2 run (Gostkowski kick)		
NE	Colvin 11 fumble return (Gostkowski kick)		
NE	Welker 2 pass from Brady (Gostkowski kick)		
NE	Cassel 15 run (Gostkowski kick)		
Was	Cooley 15 pass from Campbell (Suisham kick)		

Gillette Stadium—The New England Patriots scored at will and shut down the Redskins, handing Washington a humiliating 52-7 defeat.

"We got utterly embarrassed in every facet of the football game," said linebacker London Fletcher.

New England outgained the Redskins by better than a two-to-one margin, putting up 486 yards to 224 for Washington. Actually, it was worse than that as it was close to a three-to-one ratio before the Redskins drove 63 yards against a soft Patriots defense, averting the shutout. Jason Campbell threw a 15-yard touchdown pass to Chris Cooley with three minutes left for Washington's only points.

There isn't much of a reason to go over the particulars of this one. New England cranked out a 90-yard touchdown drive on their first possession, setting the tone early. The Patriots were up 24-0 at halftime and 38-0 after three quarters.

There was some controversy generated in the fourth quarter. The Patriots twice went for it on fourth down in Washington territory instead of trying a field goal or punting. This prompted some to say that the Patriots were running up the score. Washington defensive coordinator Gregg Williams was having none of such talk.

"It's our job to stop them," he said.

11/4/07	**Redskins (5-3) 23, JETS (1-8) 20 OT**		76,663
Was	3	6	3	8	3	23
NYJ	10	7	0	3	0	20
NYJ	Washington 86 kickoff return (Nugent kick)		
Was	FG Suisham 46		
NYJ	FG Nugent 29		
NYJ	Kowalewski 1 pass from Clemens (Nugent kick)		
Was	FG Suisham 40		
Was	FG Suisham 22		
Was	FG Suisham 40		
Was	Portis 1 run (Randle El pass from Campbell)		
NYG	FG Nugent 30		
Was	FG Suisham 46		

Giants Stadium—The Redskins trailed early, led late and had to go into overtime to beat the lowly Jets 23-20.

Washington, in fact, trailed very early. The Jets' Leon Washington took the opening kickoff near the right sideline, cut back to the left and dashed past the coverage, going 86 yards for a touchdown.

The Redskins responded by driving to a 46-yard Shaun Suisham field goal on their next possession, but things got worse before they got better. The Jets reeled off 10 more points and the Redskins trailed 17-3 with 9:28 left in the first half.

Washington responded with a field goal, the drive paced by Clinton Portis' hard running. Reacting to something he'd seen on film, Joe Gibbs decided to call a surprise onside kick. It worked perfectly as Rock Cartwright jumped on the ball just after it had traveled the required 10 yards.

The Redskins got as far as the Jets four on that possession, but the drive stalled there. Suisham kicked another field goal to make it 17-9 at halftime.

After another Suisham field goal cut the deficit to five points, the Jets threatened to put it away early in the fourth quarter. But on third down from the Washington 25, Jerricho Cotchery caught a short pass in a crowd of Redskins. One member of the crowd knocked the ball free and LaRon Landry scooped up the ball and returned it 15 yards to the Washington 36.

A 32-yard run by Portis (196 yards, 36 carries) was the key play in the Redskins' only touchdown of the day. Portis, of course, scored it on a one-yard blast. A two-point conversion put Washington up 20-17 with just over 11 minutes left to play.

The Jets were not done. They took possession at their own 25 and drove to a 30-yard Mike Nugent field goal to send it into overtime. And then they won the toss, quickly moving into Redskins territory with a 39-yard pass from Kellen Clemens to Cotchery. But the Washington defense tightened and New York punted.

Starting from their 10, the Redskins moved to the game winner. Again, Portis was the linchpin, carrying six times for 37 yards. Suisham's fifth field goal of the day was good from 46 yards to end it.

11/11/07	Eagles (4-5) 33, REDSKING (5-4) 25			90,218
Phi	7	0	6	20	33
Was	0	12	3	10	25
Phi	Westbrook 4 pass from McNabb (Akers kick)			
Was	Thrash 4 pass from Campbell (kick failed)			
Was	Thrash 12 pass from Campbell (pass failed)			
Was	FG Suisham 23			
Phi	Smith 8 pass from McNabb (pass failed)			
Was	McCardell 6 pass from Campbell (Suisham kick)			
Phi	Brown 45 pass from McNabb (Akers kick)			
Was	FG Suisham 21			
Phi	Westbrook 57 pass from McNabb (pass failed)			
Phi	Westbrook 10 run (Akers kick)			

FedEx Field—The Eagles' Brian Westbrook scored on a magnificent, 57-yard scamper with a screen pass to give the Eagles a fourth-quarter lead and Philadelphia held on the beat the Redskins 33-25.

Washington blew a halftime lead and, shortly before Westbrook's dash, a chance to wrap it up in the fourth quarter.

The Redskins ran off 15 unanswered points after the Eagles took a 7-0 lead. Jason Campbell threw two touchdown passes to James Thrash in the second quarter and Shaun Suisham booted a 23-yard field goal in the third quarter.

That was the good news. The bad news was they left some points on the table—and they would pay for that later on. After the first Thrash touchdown, Suisham missed the conversion. Joe Gibbs decided to try and make up for that after the second TD, but Campbell's two-point pass attempt went incomplete. And Suisham kicked that field goal after 280-pound fullback Mike Sellers was stuffed on third and one at the Eagles five.

Donovan McNabb threw a touchdown pass late in the third quarter, but they failed on a two-point conversion. The Redskins responded with a 68-yard touchdown drive with Campbell working out the no huddle. On third and goal at the six, Campbell fired a six-yard touchdown pass to veteran receiver Keenan McCardell.

The conversion was good this time and Washington held a 22-13 lead with 12:36 left to play.

The beginning of the end came when an illegal contact penalty got the Eagles out of a second and 20 jam. On the next play, the Redskins had double coverage deep but misplayed McNabb's rainbow. It came down to Reggie Brown for a 45-yard touchdown to make it 22-20.

Washington punted, but it looked like they got the break they needed on the Eagles' first play when Andre Carter sacked and stripped McNabb and Anthony Montgomery recovered at the Eagles 24.

Two plays later it was first and goal at the seven. The Redskins ran seven plays from there and were unable to get it into the end zone. A defensive holding flag after a third-down incompletion generated a fresh set of downs, but they got no closer than the one. They settled for another Suisham field goal and the Redskins led 25-20.

Two plays later Westbrook took a short screen pass from McNabb and weaved 57 yards to the end zone, finding some nice blocks and making defenders miss on his own along the way.

Washington still was very much alive, especially after the Eagles again failed on a two-point conversion. But Campbell was sacked and stripped on the next series and Philly recovered at the Washington 10. Westbrook scored the clincher on the next play.

The Redskins did have a final shot trailing by eight but the drive died at their own 40.

11/18/07	COWBOYS (9-1) 28, Redskins (5-5) 23			63,706
Was	7	3	3	10	23
Dal	0	7	7	14	28
Was	Cooley 19 pass from Campbell (Suisham kick)			
Dal	Owens 4 pass from Romo (Folk kick)			
Was	FG Suisham 45			
Dal	Owens 31 pass from Romo (Folk kick)			
Was	FG Suisham 39			
Dal	Owens 46 pass from Romo (Folk kick)			
Was	FG Suisham 44			
Dal	Owens 52 pass from Romo (Folk kick)			
Was	Moss 5 pass from Campbell (Suisham kick)			

Texas Stadium—There were plenty of key plays and twists and turns in this game, but the reason the Redskins lost to the Cowboys 28-23 boiled down to one thing: they couldn't cover Terrell Owens.

Every time Tony Romo needed a play, he dialed up the controversial but talented wide receiver. Owens caught eight passes for 173 yards and all four Dallas touchdowns.

The Redskins got on the board first, driving 59 yards to a touchdown. The score came when Jason Campbell found Chris Cooley open at the goal line from 19 yards.

Dallas evened things up with a drive that consumed almost half of the second quarter. After converting a third and 15 with a 20-yard pass to Owens, Romo went back to his favorite target for four yards for the score with 1:16 left in the first half.

That left enough time, however, for Campbell to lead a dink-and-dunk drive to a 45-yard Shaun Suisham field goal, putting Washington up 10-7 at halftime.

That score held until late in the third quarter when Dallas faced another third and long. With 19 yards to go from the Washington 31, Owens somehow got behind the secondary and hauled in Romo's pass to give Dallas a 14-10 lead.

They would not relinquish that advantage, but the Redskins would threaten it numerous times. They drove into Dallas territory on their ensuing possession but settled for a Suisham field goal.

The Cowboys expanded their lead as Owens caught two more touchdown passes and Suisham kicked another field goal. Owens' last score came with 7:50 to go and put Dallas up 28-16.

Campbell, who passed for 348 yards, led a rally that didn't quite get finished. An efficient, no huddle drive led to a five-yard touchdown to Santana Moss. A Phillip Daniels sack of Romo led to a Dallas three and out and great field position at the Cowboys 40 after the punt. Four plays later they were in the red zone at the 19.

But on third and 10 from there, Campbell forced a pass and Terence Newman intercepted at the 12. Washington had one more shot but a Campbell Hail Mary from midfield was incomplete.

11/25/07	BUCCANEERS (4-7) 19, Redskins (5-6) 13			65,596	
Was	0	3	7	3	13
TB	10	9	0	0	19
TB	Graham 1 run (Bryant kick)				
TB	FG Bryant 35				
TB	FG Bryant 27				
TB	FG Bryant 48				
Was	FG Suisham 43				
TB	FG Bryant 39				
Was	Cooley 39 pass from Campbell (Suisham kick)				
Was	FG Suisham 38				

Raymond James Stadium—The Redskins turned the ball over early—and they turned it over late. In between they played OK, but couldn't overcome the giveaways. They lost to the Buccaneers 19-13.

Washington should have been blown out in the first half. They fumbled on four of their first five possessions. On the Redskins' first play Santana Moss fumbled after catching Jason Campbell's pass. The Bucs recovered and returned it to the Redskins 19. Three plays later Earnest Graham plunged in from the one.

Three more fumbles followed with Tampa Bay taking possession at the Washington 19, the 20, and the 30. Each time the Washington defense stepped up and held the Bucs to Matt Bryant field goals. It was "only" 16-0 with less than five minutes gone in the second quarter.

The teams exchanged field goals before halftime and then the Redskins started to climb back into it on their first possession of the second half. Campbell led a sharp 73-yard drive to a touchdown. The capper came when, from the Bucs 39, Campbell stepped up in the pocket and found Chris Cooley open at the 10. The tight end hauled in the pass and easily made it to pay dirt.

The game turned on Washington's next series. They had a nice series underway, converting two third downs and reaching the Tampa Bay four. From there they faced fourth and one. With a nine-point deficit and two minutes remaining in the third quarter the Redskins had to score twice to take the lead. But Joe Gibbs elected to go for the yard and the first down. Clinton Portis went nowhere and it went back to the Buccaneers on downs.

Portis did convert a fourth and one on the Redskins' next series with an eight-yard run, but the drive stalled when Campbell was sacked. Suisham kicked a 38-yard field goal and it was 19-13 with 11:24 left to play.

Twice the Redskins had great shots at taking the lead. They had a second and five at the Tampa Bay 32 but cornerback Ronde Barber baited Campbell into an interception.

The other chance came after Campbell had moved the Redskins all the way from their seven to the Bucs 16 with 25 seconds left. But Campbell was picked again, this time by Brian Kelly in the end zone.

Taylor Shot in Home, In Critical Condition

Nov 26—Redskins safety Sean Taylor was shot in his Miami home this morning, sending him into surgery and Redskins Park into shock.

Taylor suffered one gunshot wound to his leg by an intruder. He underwent seven hours of surgery in an attempt to control bleeding and repair the damage.

Meanwhile, the Redskins players and coaches came in for what was supposed to be a light Monday of discussions breaking down Sunday's loss to Tampa Bay. Instead, they went into a team meeting and Joe Gibbs informed them of the news.

"You never think about entering a team meeting and addressing this kind of issue," said safety Pierson Prioleau.

Gregg Williams is particularly close to Taylor, having been his mentor since they both came to the team in 2004. Choking back tears, he said, "It's been a long, difficult day for all of us. Most people came here today thinking about how to get over a tough loss in Tampa [Sunday]. But things like this put things into perspective in a hurry."

"It's just unbelievable," tight end Chris Cooley said. "You don't ever expect anything like this to happen. It's crazy to have somebody so close to you go through this."

A contingent of members of the organization left for Miami, including Daniel Snyder and Clinton Portis.

Taylor Dies, Team Rocked

Nov 27—After some hopeful signs last night, Sean Taylor died from a gunshot wound early today.

Last night there seemed to be some hope as Taylor responded to a request from a doctor following seven hours of surgery during the day. But the hope turned out to be false and the condition of Taylor, 24, deteriorated overnight. He died at approximately 5 a.m.

At Redskins Park on an off day, Coach Joe Gibbs and other players were stunned. They talked about Taylor as a player and a person.

"For him, the sky was the limit," Gibbs said. "What was cut short here was a career that was going to go to a lot of Pro Bowls and have a lot of fun. That's what we're going to miss."

"Sean was a good friend to all of us," said Jason Campbell. "It's like we lost a family member. Through this tragedy, we all have to pull together, stay strong for each other."

12/2/07	Bills (6-6) 17, REDSKINS (5-7) 16			85,831	
Buf	0	2	6	9	17
Was	3	6	7	0	16
Was	FG Suisham 27				
Was	FG Suisham 28				
Buf	Safety Crowell sacked Campbell in end zone				
Was	FG Suisham 33				
Buf	FG Lindell 38				
Was	Portis 3 run (Suisham kick)				
Buf	FG Lindell 43				
Buf	FG Lindell 24				
Buf	FG Lindell 33				
Buf	FG Lindell 36				

FedEx Field—In a cruel ending to a very cruel week, the Redskins lost to the Bills on Rian Lindell's 36-yard field goal with eight seconds left.

The week was brutal as the Redskins had to deal with the death of star safety Sean Taylor, who was shot in his Miami home. The ending was ugly because of Joe Gibbs, who made Lindell's attempt much easier by making a gaffe that moved the field goal 15 yards closer.

Lindell was lining up for a 51-yard try with the score 16-14. Gibbs called one time-out to try to ice the kicker and then called another one. The second time-out request was a violation of the rules and moved the attempt 15 yards closer.

"To be quite truthful, I made a decision there at the end that very likely cost us the game," Gibbs said. "That's on me."

Truth be told, plenty happened before the strategic blunder that cost the Redskins the contest. In the first half Washington drives reached Bills territory at the five, five and 15 yard lines. Each time the advance stalled and Shaun Suisham had to come in and kick field goals. Buffalo sacked Campbell in the end zone for a safety midway through the second quarter and it was 9-3 at halftime.

The Bills drove to a field goal on their initial second-half possession, but the Redskins responded with the game's only touchdown. Rock Cartwright's 38-yard kickoff return got things going and Clinton Portis capped the drive with a three-yard touchdown run. Suisham's conversion gave the Redskins a 16-5 lead with 5:42 left in the third quarter.

Football is a game of emotion—and the human body has a limited supply of that. The Redskins expended much of theirs during the week and were sky high to start the game. It appeared that after that touchdown drive, the Redskins were emotionally spent. Buffalo inched its way back into it as Lindell kicked three field goals to make it 16-14.

Still, it looked like Washington might hang on and win one for their fallen teammate. They took possession with 3:42 to go, needing two first downs to burn the clock.

They picked up one but couldn't get the other. Buffalo took over at its own 22 with 56 seconds left after the punt. A 30-yard pass from Trent Edwards to Josh Reed set up the final sequence.

Dec 3

Thousands Attend Taylor Funeral
Entire Redskins organization at three-hour service; tribute to man, father, and football player

---

12/6/07	REDSKINS (6-7) 24, Bears (5-8) 16			82,213
Chi	0	0	10	6	16
Was	0	7	7	10	24
Was	Yoder 21 pass from Collins (Suisham kick)
Was	Sellers 1 run (Suisham kick)
Chi	FG Gould 30
Chi	Berrian 17 pass from Griese (Gould kick)
Was	FG Suisham 23
Chi	FG Gould 22
Was	Betts 16 pass from Collins (Suisham kick)
Chi	FG Gould 22

FedEx Field—The thread by which the Redskins' playoff hopes were hanging seemed to have broken as starting quarterback Jason Campbell lay on the turf with a dislocated kneecap. Surely backup Todd Collins, who had seen scant action in a decade, would be unable to lead a Redskins team exhausted from having attended Sean Taylor's funeral three days ago to victory in this game so critical to their playoff chances.

But not so fast. Collins came in and—for one game, at least—got the job done in gritty fashion as the Redskins beat the Bears 24-16. He went 15 for 20 for 224 yards and two touchdowns and generally looked the part of a competent NFL quarterback despite the fact that he has seen only mop-up action since 1997. He gave a lift to a team that was badly in need of one.

The game was scoreless late in the second quarter when Campbell went down under the weight of two Bears linemen falling on his leg at the same time. It looked like Chicago would be the first to dent the scoreboard as they had a first down at the Washington 31 with 36 seconds left in the half. But Shawn Springs picked off a Brian Griese pass and made a nice 53-yard return to the Bears 21. On the next play Collins calmly dropped back and found Todd Yoder a few yards shy of the end zone. The tight end turned and went in to put Washington up 7-0.

The Redskins doubled their lead on the first series on the second half. The big play in the 63-yard drive was a little swing pass to Clinton Portis. He cut back to the left sideline, picked up some blocking and powered his way the last 10 yards down to the one. Mike Sellers went up the gut and blasted it in from there.

The Bears rallied and a Robbie Gould field goal with 6:48 left to play made it a four-point game at 17-13. The Redskins responded with a drive to the Chicago 16, where they faced third and six. Joe Gibbs' *modus operandi* in these situations was to play it safe, call a run and kick the field goal, giving the Bears a chance to tie it with a single score.

But Gibbs threw out his own book this time, calling a pass up the middle to Ladell Betts. He made the catch in stride and bolted into the end zone for the clincher.

12/16/07	Redskins (7-7) 22, GIANTS (9-5) 10			77,899
Was	3	13	6	0	22
NYG	0	3	7	0	10
Was	FG Suisham 49
Was	FG Suisham 31
Was	Betts 14 run (Suisham kick)
NYG	FG Tynes 35
Was	FG Suisham 28
Was	Portis 5 run (pass failed)
NYG	Boss 19 pass from Manning (Tynes kick)

Giants Stadium—Redskins quarterback Todd Collins overcame a slow start in challenging weather conditions to lead the Redskins over the Giants 22-10. The win kept alive the Redskins' faint playoff hopes.

One might have thought that Collins looked like a journeyman quarterback making his first start in 10 years as his first eight passes went incomplete. However, with the wind whipping and swirling around Giants Stadium, Eli Manning—the Giants' quarterback who was the first pick in the draft a few years ago—also struggled mightily.

Washington got into position to take a first-quarter lead when Clinton Portis broke off a couple of nice runs to set up a Shawn Suisham field goal. Early in the second quarter, Collins got his first completion on a 36-yard deep sideline pattern to Santana Moss. Collins then found Todd Yoder on a short pass and the tight end rumbled for 30 yards to the Giants 14. That set up another field goal for a 6-0 lead.

Later in the second Collins went deep to Moss again, this time for 34 yards to the New York 15. On third down from the 14 Collins pump faked and put the ball into the belly of Ladell Betts. He took it straight up the gut to make it 13-0.

The teams exchanged field goals in the last two minutes before the Redskins confirmed control on their first series of the second half. A short kickoff into the wind with a personal foul tacked on to the return had Washington in business at the Giants 46. Five plays later Portis bolted in from the five. The two-point conversion failed, but the Redskins still had a comfortable 22-3 lead.

It got slightly less comfortable when New York scored a touchdown with 4:37 left in the third. But the defense tightened up and two fourth-quarter Giants forays into Washington territory ended on downs.

Dec 17

Gibbs May Stay Beyond Contract
Snyder has offered two-year extension beyond '09

12/23/07	**Redskins (8-7) 32. VIKINGS (8-7) 21**			63,634	
Was	9	13	3	7	32
Min	0	0	7	14	21

Was	Safety Golston tackled Richardson in end zone
Was	Cooley 33 pass from Collins (Suisham kick)
Was	Moss 32 pass from Collins (Suisham kick)
Was	Randle El 15 pass from Portis (pass failed)
Was	FG Suisham 26
Min	Kleinsasser 2 pass from Jackson (Longwell kick)
Min	Jackson 6 run (Longwell kick)
Was	Portis 13 run (Suisham kick)
Min	Jackson 1 run (Longwell kick)

Metrodome—Rarely do you hear quality control coaches and video personnel receive credit for a key play in a big win. But that's exactly what was happening after the Redskins' 32-21 victory over the Vikings.

What once seemed to be an insurmountable 25-point Washington lead had shrunk to an 11-point margin with ten minutes to play. The Metrodome crowd was rocking and the Redskins were trying to quiet them with a clinching drive.

Todd Collins threw a deep sideline pass to Santana Moss. Up in the booth, offensive coordinator Al Saunders didn't think that Moss had been able to get both feet inbounds and he was afraid that the Vikings would challenge the play. So he called for Collins to go hurry-up and get the snap off before the Minnesota coaches could throw the red flag.

It was too hurried, however. The center exchange was botched and the Vikings recovered the fumble. The crowd roared and Redskins fans everywhere were thinking, "Here we go again."

Except for some low-ranking assistant coaches and camera operators stationed high above the field. They yelled, "12 men, 12 men, challenge it, challenge it!" into their headsets. Trusting his coaches, Joe Gibbs threw the flag. And, indeed, the replay revealed that the Vikings weren't quite able to get extra defenders off of the field prior to the snap. The referee dropped a flag for 12 men on the field and the Redskins retained possession. Seven plays later Clinton Portis scooted 13 yards around right end to put the game away.

It looked like it had been put away long before that. The Redskins appeared to have come away empty after Fred Smoot intercepted a Tavaris Jackson pass and returned it to the Vikings eight. Mike Sellers was stopped inches short on fourth and goal (a touchdown was signaled but overturned on replay). But on the Vikings' first snap, defensive tackle Kedric Golston sliced through and nailed Tony Richardson for a safety.

The Redskins than took the ensuing free kick and launched a 67-yard drive that culminated in Collins throwing a 33-yard touchdown pass to Chris Cooley.

The Vikings could go nowhere. Washington defensive coordinator Gregg Williams often went with four linemen and four linebackers in order to stop star running back Adrian Peterson. It worked as drawn up; Peterson gained just 27 yards on nine carries.

The Redskins went up 22-0 at halftime on Portis' 15-yard touchdown pass to Antwaan Randle El. Minnesota rallied but their shot at a miracle came apart thanks to the alert young coaches and Gibbs' willingness to trust them.

Win and They're In

Dec 29—If the Redskins extend their winning streak to four as they close out the season, they will get a chance to win a fifth straight.

A Washington win over Dallas would put the Redskins into the playoffs as a Wild Card team.

They still could get in if they should lose to the Cowboys. If the Broncos beat the Vikings in Denver, the Redskins will be in no matter what.

12/30/07	**REDSKINS (9-7) 27, Cowboys (13-3) 6**			90,910	
Dal	0	3	0	3	6
Was	7	6	7	7	27

Was	Portis 23 run (Suisham kick)
Was	FG Suisham 46
Dal	FG Folk 37
Was	FG Suisham 21
Was	Portis 1 run (Suisham kick)
Was	Moss 42 pass from Collins (Suisham kick)
Dal	FG Folk 30

FedEx Field—Clinton Portis and Santana Moss paid tribute to Sean Taylor, their fallen friend and teammate, in a big way, leading the Redskins' 27-6 win over the Cowboys. The win clinches a Wild Card playoff spot.

Portis rushed for 104 yards on 25 carries and scored both of Washington's touchdowns. Moss caught a pass to account for the other touchdown and caught eight in all for 115 yards.

The Cowboys already had their spot as the No. 1 playoff seed wrapped up and, while they did rest some banged-up front line players, most of their starters were in the lineup as the Redskins built a 13-3 halftime lead. Washington's first drive fizzled at the Dallas 37, but they got a touchdown on their second possession. One play after an apparent interception of Todd Collins was nullified by a 20-yard pass interference penalty, Portis took a handoff up the middle, broke free, blew through a pair of would-be tacklers and scored from 23 yards out.

That would be all the Washington defense would need. They held the Cowboys to a net of one yard rushing, the lowest total ever for a Dallas team. Two Cowboy forays into the red zone—one a result of a Collins fumble at the Washington 18—gained just three points for Dallas.

Portis' second touchdown came at the end of a 63-yard drive that chewed up almost half of the third quarter.

Collins and Moss ended all doubt that the Redskins were going to the playoffs early in the fourth quarter. From the Dallas 42, Collins rolled right. Moss was wide open down the sideline and Collins' pass was on the money for a 27-3 Washington lead.

Players Credit Taylor's Inspiration

Dec 30—On their first play after the death of Sean Taylor, the Redskins defense ran with 10 men on the field as a tribute to their missing man.

For the past four games, the team believes they have been playing with 12 on the field.

"Sean's death brought us closer together," said London Fletcher after the Redskins beat the Cowboys 27-6 to earn a playoff spot. "We're like family right now. We played with our angel out there."

"Sean pulled us together and made us realize you don't get no tomorrow in this game," end Phillip Daniels said. "You gotta play hard as you can today. The funeral was closure for us. You get closure, and you can move on and concentrate on the things you've got to do. That's what we've done."

At the end of last night's team meeting, the defense got an extra jolt of inspiration. On the screen, there appeared a picture of Taylor—one he had autographed for a fan. Over his signature he had written, "We want Dallas." The picture had been posted on Extremeskins.com, the team's official message board.

And they did indeed get the Cowboys, holding them to one net yard of rushing in 16 attempts and controlling the action all day.

NFC Wild Card Playoff
Saturday, January 5, 2008
Qwest Field
Seattle, Washington

1/5/08	SEAHAWKS 35, Redskins 14				68,297
Was	0	0	0	14	14
Sea	7	3	3	22	35
Sea	Weaver 17 run (Brown kick)				
Sea	FG Brown 50				
Sea	FG Brown 33				
Was	Randle El 7 pass from Collins (Suisham kick)				
Was	Moss 30 pass from Collins (Suisham kick)				
Sea	Hackett 20 pass from Hasselbeck (Pollard pass from Hasselbeck)				
Sea	Trufant 78 interception return (Brown kick)				
Sea	Babineaux 57 interception return (Brown kick)				

It was all the Redskins could ask for. After trailing 13-0, they had rallied for two fourth-quarter touchdowns to take a one-point lead. On the kickoff after gaining that lead, the wind had blown the ball around and the Seahawks could not track it down. Anthony Mix recovered the free ball and the Redskins were in business at the Seattle 14. One more touchdown would quiet the Qwest Field throng and continue the Redskins' improbable run one more week.

But they didn't get it. Chris Cooley couldn't handle a Todd Collins pass near the five. Clinton Portis was stopped after picking up two yards and Collins threw incomplete. Well, at least a field goal would force Seattle to score a touchdown.

They didn't get that, either. Shaun Suisham's 30-yard attempt strayed wide right. The Seahawks drove to a touchdown two series later and then clinched it with a pair of interceptions returned for six.

There isn't much to say about the game preceding the late rally except that the Redskins were fortunate to be in a position to get back into the game. The Seattle pass rush was fierce and while they only posted three sacks, Collins was harassed and harried all afternoon. The running game, a reliable force during the four-game winning streak that got the Redskins into the playoffs, didn't get much done, either.

The Seahawks scored a touchdown on their first possession, driving to a 17-yard Leonard Weaver touchdown run. Josh Brown tacked on field goals in the second and third quarters.

After the last field goal, the Redskins finally got some offense going. From their own 16 they went no-huddle with Collins hitting Cooley and Antwaan Randle El for key gains. On third down at the Seattle seven, Collins went over the middle to Randle El for a touchdown to make it 13-7.

The Redskins got the ball back quickly as rookie safety LaRon Landry picked off a pass at the Seattle 42. Three plays later Collins threw a strike to Santana Moss for 30 yards and an improbable 14-13 lead.

That, however, proved to be it.

Family Man Gibbs Retires Again

Jan 8—At his press conference on Monday, Joe Gibbs left open the door to retirement just a bit. He would not commit to being back to coach in 2008.

Today, he opened that door and walked through it.

Citing a need to spend more time with his family, Gibbs retired as Redskins coach. He made the decision at about 2:30 a. m. after a long meeting with owner Daniel Snyder.

"I just did not feel like I could make the kind of commitment that I needed to make going forward this year, knowing what my family situation was," he said at a press conference. "I felt like they needed me."

"I tried very, very hard to convince Joe to not retire," Snyder said.

2008
Head Coach: Jim Zorn
Record: 8-8, Fourth in NFC East

Honors: Clinton Portis Pro Bowl; Mike Sellers Pro Bowl; Chris Cooley Pro Bowl; Chris Samuels Pro Bowl

Hall of Fame: Art Monk, receiver 1980-1993, Darrell Green, cornerback, 1983-2002

Williams, Saunders Fired; Search Continues

Jan 26—Gregg Williams and Al Saunders, two of the most respected and highest-paid assistant coaches in the NFL, were given their walking papers today as the Redskins' search for a new head coach took a turn to the weird.

Williams, who headed up the defense, was thought to be the leading candidate to replace Joe Gibbs and was interviewed for the job four times. Evidently, Daniel Snyder didn't like what he heard.

Despite his previous experience as a head coach, Saunders was never considered for the job.

The two men have already been replaced. Jim Zorn will move from Seattle to be the offensive coordinator, and Greg Blache will move from coaching the defensive line to running the defense.

Everything is all wrapped up except for—oh yeah—the head coaching job. Earlier this week many outlets were reporting that the hiring of former Giants coach Jim Fassel was imminent. That possibility appears to have fallen by the wayside.

So, Snyder must continue to search for a head coaching candidate willing to accept the fact that he will not be able to choose his own coordinators.

Feb 2

Double Dip of Fame: Monk, Green to be Enshrined

At end of Gibbs II era, two stars from glory days elected to Hall of Fame

Shocker: Zorn is Named Head Coach

Feb 9—Jim Zorn got a quick promotion.

After a search lasting just over a month, the Redskins have hired Zorn, brought in just last month to be their offensive coordinator, as their new head coach.

The 54-year-old Zorn played quarterback in the NFL for Seattle and was the quarterbacks coach there last year. He has never been a head coach at any level.

"I know about the history of this franchise as well as the passion of its fans," Zorn said in a statement. "I won't let you down."

July 20

With Daniels Out, Skins Move Fast
After knee fells Daniels in morning, Redskins trade 2009 2nd, 2010 5th for Miami's Taylor

9/4/08	GIANTS (1-0) 16, Redskins (0-1) 7				79,742
Was	0	7	0	0	7
NYG	10	6	0	0	16
NYG	Manning 1 run (Carney kick)				
NYG	FG Carney 24				
NYG	FG Carney 25				
NYG	FG Carney 47				
Was	Moss 12 pass from Campbell (Suisham kick)				

Giants Stadium—The Jim Zorn era in Washington got off to a shaky start as the Redskins were uncompetitive, losing to the Giants 16-7.

New York scored on its first four possessions. Eli Manning had a hot hand while leading an 84-yard touchdown drive the first time they had the ball. The Super Bowl MVP converted a couple of third and long situations, rolling out and running it in himself from the one.

The tone for the Washington offense was set on the first series. Jason Campbell dropped back to pass and barely had time to set before Justin Tuck was in his face. After the eight-yard loss on the sack, Clinton Portis ran a draw for three yards, then a false start penalty backed them up five. Another Portis draw and a punt then followed.

After carving up the Washington defense on the first drive, the Giants chose the blunt instrument on their next one. Brandon Jacobs had runs of 7, 17 and nine yards to help set up a John Carney field goal.

Up until they took possession with two minutes left in the first half, the Redskins' only first down had come via penalty and they had yet to take a snap in New York territory. Rock Cartwright took care of the latter by returning a kickoff 50 yards to the Giants 45. Their initial first down came two plays later on Campbell's 13-yard completion to Antwaan Randle El. And Washington dented the scoreboard with 20 seconds left in the half on Campbell's 12-yard touchdown pass to Santana Moss.

The Redskins maintained no momentum from that late score. They had three third-quarter possessions and went three and out in each of them. Meanwhile, the Giants were doing little offensively—but they really had no need to.

Still, it was a two-score margin going into the fourth quarter and Washington did start to piece together some drives. But there was no urgency to the offense, and no hurry-up tactics. Precious seconds ticked away as plays were sent in and signals were called.

The Redskins' second and third drives into New York territory were their final two possessions. The first one ended on downs at the 43; the other died when the clock ran out.

9/14/08	REDSKINS (1-1) 29, Saints (1-1) 24				88,246
NO	0	10	14	0	24
Was	3	6	6	14	29
Was	FG Suisham 22				
Was	FG Suisham 36				
NO	Thomas 1 run (Gramatica kick)				
Was	FG Suisham 35				
NO	FG Gramatica 49				
NO	Meachem 19 pass from Brees (Gramatica kick)				
Was	Portis 9 run (pass failed)				
NO	Bush 55 punt return (Gramatica kick)				
Was	Portis 8 run (Suisham kick)				
Was	Moss 67 pass from Campbell (Suisham kick)				

FedEx Field—Jason Campbell remembered what Jim Zorn had drilled into him: avert, reset, throw.

With the game on the line, Campbell averted a Saints defender by stepping up in the pocket, resetting his feet and throwing a perfect strike to the streaking Santana Moss. The receiver gathered in the pass and bolted the rest of the way to the end zone to complete the 67-yard touchdown.

That play completed a fourth-quarter comeback and gave the Redskins a lead with 3:29 left to play. Washington held on and beat the Saints 29-24.

The Redskins could have averted a tense ending had they been able to punch the ball into the end zone in the first half. They got close enough to have Shaun Suisham attempt five field goals during the first two quarters. He made three of them and Washington trailed 10-9 at halftime.

One of the field goals was set up by a Chris Horton interception. Due to Reed Doughty falling ill, the rookie safety was informed just that morning that he would be starting. He made the most of it, getting a second interception and recovering a fumble.

The teams each scored a touchdown on their initial second-half possessions. Washington's came on a nine-yard Clinton Portis dash around left end. Jim Zorn went for two in an effort to tie the score but the try failed and it was 17-15.

Late in the third quarter the Redskins' task grew significantly more difficult as Reggie Bush fielded a punt, picked up some great blocking and rolled 55 yards for a touchdown, giving the Saints a 24-15 lead going into the fourth quarter.

They were in a bigger hole a few series later after a first-down sack set up second and 22. Campbell calmly stepped back and fired a pass to Chris Cooley that gained 23 yards and a first. The quarterback got on a roll and passed the team downfield until letting Portis cover the last eight yards into the end zone to make it 24-22.

The defense forced a three and out, and it took Campbell just one play to put the Redskins in the lead. In all, he completed his last eight passes. The last one—a dart to Moss to convert a fourth and two—allowed the Redskins to assume the victory formation.

9/21/08	REDSKINS (2-1) 24, Cardinals (2-1) 17				90,060
Ari	0	7	10	0	17
Was	7	3	7	7	24
Was	Portis 3 run (Suisham kick)				
Was	FG Suisham 48				
Ari	Boldin 4 pass from Warner (Rackers kick)				
Ari	FG Rackers 26				
Was	Yoder 2 pass from Campbell (Suisham kick)				
Ari	Fitzgerald 62 pass from Warner (Rackers kick)				
Was	Moss 17 pass from Campbell (Suisham kick)				

FedEx Field—Santana Moss scored on a 17-yard wide receiver screen pass with 12:10 left to play to lead the Redskins past the Cardinals 24-17.

The play followed an interception by Carlos Rogers with an assist by Leigh Torrence. The two cornerbacks were covering receiver Steve Breaston, who was running after a Kurt Warner pass deep down the middle. Torrence caught up with the receiver and tipped the ball in the air. Rogers was a step behind and lunged to make the interception. He got up, picked up some blocks and rolled 42 yards down to the 15.

Two plays later Jason Campbell dropped back and fired to Moss a couple of yards behind the line of scrimmage. He had a phalanx of blockers—including Randy Thomas and Todd Yoder—to serve as escorts while he darted into the end zone.

The Redskins took a 7-0 lead on their first possession of the game. Campbell led a 60-yard touchdown drive that culminated in Clinton Portis' three-yard touchdown burst up the middle.

Early in the second period Washington parlayed a turnover into three points. Edgerrin James fumbled after catching a Warner pass and Rogers recovered at the Arizona 34. Shaun Suisham booted a 48-yard field goal a few plays later and the Redskins led 10-0.

The Washington offense went dormant and the Cardinals got back into the game. They scored late in the first half on a touchdown pass from Warner to Anquan Boldin and drove to a Neil Rackers field goal on their initial possession of the second half.

Washington responded immediately, driving 80 yards after taking the ensuing kickoff. Campbell heated up again, spreading the ball around as the team moved downfield. His favorite target was Chris Cooley and his 16-yard reception set up the Redskins at the Arizona two. On the next play, Campbell flipped a two-yard touchdown pass to Todd Yoder and the Redskins led 17-10.

But not for long. About a minute and a half later Warner went deep for Larry Fitzgerald and the 62-yard touchdown play tied the game at 17-17.

After Moss' touchdown, the Redskins defense shut down the Cardinals and the Washington offense played keep away. Arizona was limited to just two possessions and they went three and out on both.

9/28/08	**Redskins (3-1) 26, COWBOYS (3-1) 24**				63,462
Was	0	17	3	6	26
Dal	7	3	7	7	24
Dal	Witten 21 pass from Romo (Folk kick)				
Was	Thrash 3 pass from Campbell (Suisham kick)				
Was	Randle El 2 pass from Campbell (Suisham kick)				
Was	FG Suisham 20				
Dal	FG Folk 36				
Dal	Owens 10 pass from Romo (Folk kick)				
Was	FG Suisham 33				
Was	FG Suisham 33				
Was	FG Suisham 29				
Dal	Austin 11 pass from Romo (Faulk kick)				

Texas Stadium—Clinton Portis rushed for 121 yards and Jason Campbell was very efficient in passing for two touchdowns as the Redskins won in Dallas 26-24.

Washington trailed 7-0 going into the second quarter and then exploded, scoring 17 unanswered points. First Campbell capped an 80-yard drive with a three-yard touchdown pass to James Thrash. Then a 28-yard pass from Campbell to Santana Moss keyed a drive that culminated in another short TD toss, this one two yards to Antwaan Randle El.

The Redskins had a chance to break the game wide open when Moss got free on a fly pattern and Campbell hit him for 53 yards to the Dallas eight. However, the drive stalled at the two and they settled for a 20-yard Shaun Suisham field goal.

Dallas battled back and tied the game at 17-17 with a Nick Folk field goal late in the first half and a 10-yard touchdown pass

from Tony Romo to Terrell Owens to cap their opening drive of the second half.

A 31-yard Portis run jump-started a drive that led to a 33-yard Suisham field goal on Washington's next possession. Twice the Redskins entered the end zone, but both touchdowns were called back on penalties on center Casey Rabach. The first was a highly questionable holding call; the other was for Rabach being downfield.

A few series later the Cowboys were on the move when safety Chris Horton came out of nowhere to pick off a Romo pass at the Dallas 44. Again, the Redskins couldn't punch it in, but Suisham's 33-yard field goal gave them a 23-17 lead.

After the ensuing kickoff, Romo targeted Owens on three straight passes—and all three went incomplete. After the punt, the Redskins executed a textbook clock-killing drive, grinding up almost seven minutes in moving to another Suisham field goal to make it a two-score game at 26-17 with 3:26 left.

The Cowboys scored a touchdown on a desperation drive, but the attempted onside kick flew out of bounds.

10/5/08	**Redskins (4-1) 23, EAGLES (2-3) 17**				69,144
Was	0	9	7	7	23
Phi	14	0	0	3	17
Phi	Westbrook 9 run (Akers kick)				
Phi	Jackson 68 punt return (Akers kick)				
Was	FG Suisham 41				
Was	FG Suisham 48				
Was	FG Suisham 50				
Was	Cooley 18 pass from Randle El (Suisham kick)				
Was	Portis 4 run (Suisham kick)				
Phi	FG Akers 23				

Lincoln Financial Field—The Redskins found themselves in a 14-0 hole early, but they fought back and ran off 23 unanswered points to beat the Eagles 23-17.

Philadelphia came out roaring after the opening kickoff, moving smartly down the field for 80 yards and a touchdown. Brian Westbrook powered his way up the middle from nine yards out for the score.

That was an ugly start for the Redskins—and it got uglier very quickly. After the Redskins went three and out, rookie DeSean Jackson fielded the punt, eluded the first wave of would-be tacklers and outran everyone else to the end zone for a 68-yard touchdown return.

Washington's comeback did not start right away. After the Eagles missed a field goal late in the first quarter they drove to a 41-yard Shaun Suisham field goal. A long drive to another field goal followed. Starting from their three, the Redskins steadily advanced downfield, consuming over eight minutes. They only got as far as the Philly 30 and Suisham was good from 48 at the two-minute warning.

They weren't done yet. After the Eagles went three and out, Jason Campbell again navigated through the Eagles defense for another field goal as time expired in the half.

As the Washington defense continued to hold Donovan McNabb and the Eagles at bay, the Redskins offense went back to work in the second half. A 21-yard Clinton Portis run up the middle keyed a drive that put the Redskins in the lead. The score came when Campbell handed off to Antwaan Randle El, who stopped a yard shy of the line and fired an 18-yard pass to Chris Cooley. The tight end caught the pass at the five, turned and rolled in for the score.

After a pair of Philadelphia three and outs, the Redskins moved in for the kill. A 21-yard punt return by Randle El and a 15-yard personal foul set up the Redskins at the Eagles 43. Portis ran for nine and then 27 yards to move them to the seven. Three plays later from the four, the line opened up a huge hole for Portis and he dashed into the end zone to make it 23-14.

The Eagles did pull to within six with a field goal with 7:21 left, but they never got the ball back. With 2:48 left Jim Zorn decided to go for it on fourth and one at the Eagle 38. Portis made his coach look good by suggesting the play and then executing it, moving the pile for three yards. Three Campbell knee-downs ensued.

10/12/08	**Rams (1-4) 19, REDSKINS (4-2) 17**			90,376
StL	3	7	6	3	19
Was	7	0	0	10	17

Was	Portis 3 run (Suisham kick)
StL	FG Brown 51 (Brown kick)
StL	Atogwe 75 fumble return (Brown kick)
StL	FG Brown 25
StL	FG Brown 44
Was	FG Suisham 38
Was	Portis 2 run (Suisham kick)
StL	FG Brown 49.

FedEx Field—It's dangerous to let a winless team stay in the game with you, especially when you're at home. It's even more dangerous to hand them a gift touchdown on a bonehead play.

The Redskins tempted fate on both of those counts yesterday and lost to the Rams 19-17 on Josh Brown's 49-yard field goal as time expired.

Things were a little too easy for the Redskins at the beginning. Their opening drive stalled near midfield but the punt pinned the Rams back at their own three. Two plays later running back Stephen Jackson fumbled and LaRon Landry recovered at the three. One the next play Clinton powered into the end zone and it was 7-0.

Nobody seemed to be particularly concerned when the Rams' Josh Brown booted a 51-yard field goal—or when a promising drive went awry when Chris Cooley fumbled and the Rams recovered. Or when a Jason Campbell fumble killed another drive that had reached the St. Louis 34.

In fact, things were looking pretty good as halftime approached. Campbell fired a pass to Cooley good for 28 yards and a first down at the Rams 16.

The next play, though, was the beginning of the end. Campbell passed and the ball was batted up in the air. It started to fall to the ground near Pete Kendall. For reasons he was unable to explain, he chose to catch the ball rather than bat it to the ground. After a couple of steps the Rams pried the ball loose and O. J. Atogwe scooped it up and was off to the races—75 yards for a touchdown. The Rams led 10-7 at halftime.

The play did not seem to serve as much of a wakeup call as St. Louis maneuvered for two third-quarter field goals to up their lead to 16-7.

Washington did come alive in the fourth quarter with a field goal and a two-yard Portis touchdown run to take a 17-16 lead with 3:53 left. But on third and 13, St. Louis Receiver Donnie Avery somehow got open deep and hauled in Marc Bulger's pass for 43 yards to the Washington 16. A personal foul penalty made Brown's attempt longer but his kick was true as the clock hit 0:00.

10/19/08	**REDSKINS (5-2) 14, Browns (2-4) 11**			90,487
Cle	0	0	3	8	11
Was	0	0	7	7	14

Was	Portis 3 run (Suisham kick)
Cle	FG Dawson 37
Was	Moss 18 pass from Campbell (Suisham kick)
Cle	Cribbs 1 pass from Anderson (Edwards pass from Anderson)

FedEx Field—The Redskins couldn't find their offense all day, so they had to rely on solid defense to beat the Browns 14-11.

They saved their best for last. With Washington up 14-3, Cleveland drove to a first and goal at the one with more than eight minutes left in the game. They eventually reached the end zone

but not until nine plays had been run and nearly five minutes had burned off the clock.

The first four plays were stonewall jobs with London Fletcher flying all over the field to make stops. The Redskins took over at the three and on first down, Clinton Portis broke free down the right sideline. Cornerback Eric Wright then poked the ball out and the Browns recovered at the Washington 29.

Two plays later it was second and goal at the one. Twice Washington stuffed Jamal Lewis runs before Derrick Anderson found Josh Cribbs in the end zone for the touchdown with 2:44 left to play.

The Browns did get the ball back and got into position for a field goal try. Phil Dawson had the leg from 54 yards, but his try was wide right with 32 seconds left.

Unless you are a fan of punting, there wasn't much to watch in the first half. Of the game's first 14 possessions, extending into the third quarter, there were 13 punts and a missed field goal. The miss came on the last play of the half when the best chance for a score was squandered as Shaun Suisham's 36-yard field goal attempt hit the upright.

On their second possession of the third quarter, the Redskins finally got the offensive spark they were looking for. Jason Campbell found Santana Moss open on a deep out. Moss spun out of a couple of tackles and scampered to the Cleveland 27. Six plays later from the three, Portis started to the right, cut back towards the middle and just made it over the goal line.

The Browns responded with a Dawson field goal but the Redskins extended their lead with a quick drive early in the fourth quarter. Portis dashed 27 yards to the Cleveland 18. On the next play Campbell threw to Moss in the right flat. The elusive receiver danced down the sideline and into the end zone.

The Browns drove to one on their ensuing possession before the defense erected the wall.

10/26/08	**Redskins (6-2) 25, LIONS (0-7) 17**			54,312
Was	3	3	10	9	25
Det	7	3	0	7	17

Was	FG Suisham 25
Det	R. Johnson 11 run (Hanson kick)
Det	FG Hanson 43
Was	FG Suisham 47
Was	FG Suisham 45
Was	Moss 50 pass from Campbell (Suisham kick)
Was	Moss 80 punt return (pass failed)
Det	C. Johnson 17 pass from Orlovsky (Hanson kick)
Was	FG Suisham 42

Ford Field—Santana Moss scored two long touchdowns in the second half to save the Redskins from what would have been a humiliating defeat to the Lions. The speedy receiver scored on a long pass reception and on an 80-yard punt return to push the Redskins past Detroit 25-17.

Washington was in a dogfight—or, more appropriately, a cat fight—from the beginning. The Redskins drove to a field goal on their first possession but the Lions captured the lead on Rudi Johnson's 11-yard touchdown run late in the first quarter. The teams exchanged field goals in the second quarter and Detroit had a 10-6 lead at halftime.

The Redskins' comeback started with a field goal on their initial second-half possession. An illegal block pushed them back to the five the next time they had the ball. A 17-yard pass from Campbell to Chris Cooley converted a third down and got them out of the hole. From midfield a few plays later, Campbell stepped up in the pocket and fired deep for Moss. The receiver gathered the pass in around the 20, turned and sprinted to the end zone. Shaun Suisham's conversion put the Redskins up 16-10.

The score remained the same until early in the fourth quarter. Moss went back to field a punt for just the second time this year.

He fielded the ball at the 20, survived a collision with teammate Devin Thomas, made a couple of Lions miss and outran everyone else for the touchdown. A two-point conversion failed and the Redskins led 22-10.

The Lions were game. They drove 76 yards for a touchdown—converting two fourth downs along the way—to make it 22-17. They still had hope after holding the Redskins to a field goal on their next drive, but their final drive expired on downs at their own 45.

11/3/08	Steelers (6-2) 23, REDSKINS (6-3) 6			90,512
Pit	0	10	6	7	23
Was	6	0	0	0	6
Was	FG Suisham 44			
Was	FG Suisham 43			
Pit	FG Reed 35			
Pit	Roethlisberger 1 run (Reed kick)			
Pit	Parker 1 run (kick failed)			
Pit	Holmes 5 pass from Leftwich (Reed kick)			

FedEx Field—Washington native Byron Leftwich came in for the injured Ben Roethlisberger and helped the Steelers beat the Redskins 23-6.

Pittsburgh had taken a 10-6 lead late in the first half on Roethlisberger's touchdown on a one-yard quarterback sneak. But he was injured either on that play or shortly before it and Leftwich came in to steer his team to a pair of second-half touchdowns.

The Redskins had a chance to grab a large early lead but instead left points on the table. Steelers coach Mike Tomlin called a surprise onside kick on the game's opening kickoff but Alfred Fincher was not fooled—he recovered at the Pittsburgh 36. But Clinton Portis was stuffed on third and two and the Redskins settled for a 44-yard Shaun Suisham field goal.

They had to settle again after another break. On the next series, Andre Carter tipped a Roethlisberger pass that bounced off of the helmet of a Steeler lineman and into the hands of defensive tackle Cornelius Griffin at the Pittsburgh 30. But three plays netted just five yards and Suisham came on again to make it 6-0.

A 43-yard pass interference penalty early in the second quarter set up the Steelers' first score, a 35-yard Josh Reed field goal.

The next time Pittsburgh had the ball, Roethlisberger threw to the right sideline and Carlos Rogers jumped in and had his hands on the ball with nothing but green grass and white stripes in between himself and the goal line. But he dropped the ball and another scoring chance went by the board.

It seemed likely that the Redskins would hold that 6-3 lead going into the locker room until one member of a Steeler jailbreak blocked Ryan Plackenmeier's punt and Roethlisberger's sneak came four plays later to make it 10-6 at intermission.

Four plays into the second half Leftwich launched a bomb that Nate Washington hauled in for 50 yards to the Redskins 11. Willie Parker capped that drive with a one-yard blast for a touchdown. The conversion missed, but the game was slipping away from the Redskins at 16-6.

The tough Steelers defense held the Redskins at bay until Leftwich threw a five-yard touchdown pass to Santonio Holmes early in the fourth quarter. The Redskins' ensuing drive ended on downs at the Pittsburgh one.

11/16/08	Cowboys (6-4) 14, REDSKINS (6-4) 10			90,830
Dal	0	7	0	7	14
Was	7	3	0	0	10
Was	Sellers 2 pass from Campbell (Suisham kick)			
Dal	Barber 2 run			
Was	FG Suisham 41			
Dal	Bennett 25 pass from Romo (Folk kick)			

FedEx Field—The Redskins offense went dormant in the second half and they lost to the Cowboys 14-10.

Washington started out well, driving to a touchdown on their initial possession. They started off in great field position after a face mask penalty on the Dallas punt moved the ball to the Cowboys 50. Ten plays later Jason Campbell flipped a two-yard touchdown pass to Mike Sellers and the Redskins led 7-0 midway through the first quarter.

The Cowboys were on the move on their ensuing drive, but newly-acquired cornerback DeAngelo Hall ended the advance with an interception at the Redskins 18. In the second quarter the Redskins were moving at the Dallas 36 but a penalty and a sack short-circuited that drive, forcing them to punt.

After taking possession at their own 20 the Cowboys drove to tie the score. The big plays came when Tony Romo threw to Jason Witten for 28 yards and to Terrell Owens for 28. Marion Barber took the handoff and powered in from two yards out, just breaking the plane of the goal line with 1:01 left in the first half.

Rock Cartwright's 58-yard return of the ensuing kickoff put the Redskins in great shape at the Dallas 37. A Campbell pass to Chris Cooley got them in position for Shaun Suisham to boot a 41-yard field goal, giving Washington a 10-7 halftime lead.

After taking the second-half kickoff the Redskins had a nice drive going until Terence Newman picked off Campbell's pass at the Dallas 33. Another opportunity went by the boards the next time the Redskins had the ball. After gaining a first down at the Dallas 17 the Redskins moved backwards and Suisham's attempt from 46 yards was short.

It remained 10-7 going into the fourth quarter. But Dallas embarked on a drive from their 33 and took the lead. From the Washington 25, rookie tight End Martellus Bennett made a nice catch of a Romo pass for the touchdown to make it 14-10 with 10:36 left to play.

Washington moved into Dallas territory, but the drive died on downs at the 37. The Cowboys killed the rest of the clock with running back Marion Barber carrying the load.

11/23/08	Redskins (7-4) 20, SEAHAWKS (2-9) 17			67,771
Was	0	7	10	3	20
Sea	3	7	0	7	17
Sea	FG Mare 45			
Was	Betts 1 run (Suisham kick)			
Sea	Morris 4 pass from Hasselbeck (Mare kick)			
Was	FG Suisham 26			
Was	Randle El 8 pass from Campbell (Suisham kick)			
Sea	Carlson 10 pass from Hasselbeck (Mare kick)			
Was	FG Suisham 22			

Qwest Field—Shaun Suisham kicked a 22-yard field goal with 9:19 left to play to lift the Redskins past the Seahawks 20-17.

Despite the fact that he missed most of practice during the week while suffering from a sprained knee, Clinton Portis carried the load for Washington. He had 143 yards in 29 rushing attempts.

Redskins coach Jim Zorn was triumphant in his return to Seattle where he was a star quarterback and later a longtime assistant coach.

For all of Portis' "heroics," as Zorn called them, the Redskins had to battle every inch of the way to beat the 2-8 home team. Seattle got on the board first as Maurice Morris broke off a 44-yard run to set up a field goal.

The Redskins took the lead with about four and a half minutes remaining in the first half. They embarked on a 12-play, 62-yard drive with Portis getting into Seattle territory with a 20-yard run to the 37. Portis carried five times for 36 yards during the advance. Ladell Betts gave him a breather near the goal line and he got the six points on a one-yard burst to put up the Redskins up 7-3.

Seattle regained the advantage with 35 seconds left in the half as Matt Hasselbeck capped a drive with a four-yard touchdown toss to Morris.

It looked like the Redskins were going to take control of the game in the third quarter. First they drove to a 26-yard Suisham field goal to tie the game at 10-10. On Seattle's next possession, LaRon Landry made a diving interception of a Hasselbeck pass and after a 13-yard return, the Redskins were in business at the Seattle 35.

Jason Campbell went to Chris Cooley for 21 yards and two plays later, Campbell threw over the middle to Antwaan Randle El for a touchdown and a 17-10 lead with three and a half minutes left in the third quarter.

Hasselbeck and the Seahawks battled right back. They moved 62 yards to a touchdown, the score coming on a 10-yard pass from Hasselbeck to John Carlson.

The Redskins then drove to Suisham's tiebreaking field goal. After a Seattle punt, it looked like the Redskins were going to run out the clock. They burned play time down from just over seven minutes to 1:39 as Seattle used its last time-out. But Portis took a breather then and Ladell Betts fumbled the ball back to Seattle at the Seahawks 22.

Their last chance lasted just one play as Shawn Springs intercepted Hasselbeck's pass.

11/30/08	Giants (11-1) 23, REDSKINS (7-5) 7				85,912
NYG	10	3	3	7	23
Was	0	7	0	0	7
NYG	Toomer 40 pass from Manning (Carney kick)				
NYG	FG Carney 31				
NYG	FG Carney 38				
Was	D. Thomas 25 run (Suisham kick)				
NYG	Jacobs 1 run (Carney kick)				
NYG	FG Carney 39				

FedEx Field—The Redskins dared the Giants to pass by stacking defenders at the line of scrimmage. New York took them up on the dare and thumped the Redskins 23-7.

Eli Manning's pass for 63 of the 71 yards to the Giants covered their opening possession. Manning made it look easy as he threw 40 yards to Amani Toomer for the touchdown.

Manning passed for 305 yards on the day, including 223 in the first half.

After the Redskins' second consecutive three and out series, the Giants were on the move again. Anthony Montgomery sacked Manning on a third down play from the Washington seven so New York had to settle for a 31-yard John Carney field goal.

The Redskins started to make some noise early in the second quarter. They moved from their 43 to the New York 29. On first down from there, receiver Devin Thomas took the ball on reverse and, with Jason Campbell leading interference, he dashed towards the end zone. He broke a tackle at the five and lunged over the goal line.

It remained 13-7 at halftime, but the Giants started to put it away soon after that. A face mask penalty set them up at the Washington 48 after a punt and eight plays later Brandon Jacobs battered up the middle for a touchdown.

The Redskins tried to respond but Aaron Ross intercepted Campbell's pass at the Giants five.

After Carney kicked another field goal to put New York up by 17, the Redskins twice drove into Giants territory to try to get back into it. The first one expired on downs at the 34 and the second ended at the eleven when the clock ran out.

12/7/08	RAVENS (9-4) 24, Redskins (7-6) 10				71,438
Was	0	0	0	10	10
Bal	14	0	3	7	24
Bal	McClain 8 run (Stover kick)				
Bal	Reed 32 fumble return (Stover kick)				
Bal	FG Stover 32				
Was	FG Suisham 43				
Was	Randle El 5 pass from Campbell				
Bal	Mason 28 pass from Flacco (Stover kick)				

M&T Bank Stadium—The Ravens jumped out to a 14-0 lead less than six minutes into the game and never looked back in beating the Redskins 24-10.

The Ravens were the aggressors and the tone was set early. On the Redskins' third play, Jason Campbell was hit as he threw and a wounded duck floated downfield. Ed Reed intercepted the pass and returned it to the Baltimore 45. Then Joe Flacco went deep on his first pass and completed it to Derrick Mason for 26 yards. Four plays later Le'Ron McClain scored from four yards out to make it 7-0.

The teams traded punts and the Redskins started from their 11. Clinton Portis popped one up the middle for 11 yards but just before he hit the ground, Reed pried the ball loose. Reed scooped up the ball, found some blocking and scurried into the end zone.

In the second quarter Washington was able to penetrate to the Baltimore 30, but the drive stalled there and Shaun Suisham was wide on a 48-yard field goal attempt. That was as close as the Redskins came to scoring in the first half.

A good chunk of the third quarter was burned up during a Ravens field goal drive. They took six and a half minutes driving from their 21 to the Washington 14. The key play was a 24-yard Flacco completion to tight end Todd Heap on fourth and one. Stover's 32-yard field goal made it 17-0 with just over four minutes left in the third quarter.

A couple of turnovers got Washington back into the game, albeit briefly. LaRon Landry zeroed in on a Flacco pass and picked it off, returning it five yards to the Baltimore 26. The Redskins got down to the 12 but Campbell was sacked; they had to settle for a 43-yard Shaun Suisham field goal.

Washington got the ball right back two plays after the ensuing kickoff. Willis McGahee lost the ball as he was fighting for extra yardage. DeAngelo Hall recovered and returned it to the Ravens 30. Five plays later Antwaan Randle El caught Campbell's pass in a crowd a yard deep in the end zone. All of a sudden it was 17-10 with 11 and a half minutes left to play.

The comeback train stopped there. The Ravens rammed the ball down the throats of the Washington defense with McClain carrying nine times during a drive that covered 83 yards in just over seven and a half minutes. Flacco finished off the drive—and the Redskins—with a 28-yard touchdown pass to Mason.

Portis Rips Zorn on Radio

Dec 9—Clinton Portis is not one to keep his feelings to himself. Combine that propensity with a big megaphone and you have an instant controversy when he feels he's been crossed.

His big megaphone is a weekly radio appearance, and he took that opportunity this week to take shots at Jim Zorn for the running back's paucity of carries over the past two games.

When asked why he thought he has just 22 carries over the past two weeks and was benched for virtually the entire second half against the Ravens last Sunday, Portis replied sarcastically, "We got a genius for a head coach, so I don't know. I'm sure he's got everything figured out. All I can do is when he calls a play is to go out and execute to the best of my ability."

After the game, Zorn pointed out that Portis missed most of practice during the week, an occurrence that has become a pattern as he has struggled with various injuries.

"If I could practice, I'd practice," Portis said. "If my injuries weren't legit, the trainers wouldn't hold me out and they'd have me at practice."

He also said that his lack of practice time did not lead to his making any errors.

"If you go back and watch the film, I guarantee you won't see me make mistakes," he said. "But maybe [Zorn is] watching a different film than me."

12/14/08	**BENGALS (2-11-1) 20, Redskins (7-7) 13**			63,996	
Was	0	10	0	3	13
Cin	14	3	0	3	20
Cin	Fitzpatrick 1 run (Graham kick)				
Cin	Henry 12 pass from Fitzpatrick (Graham kick)				
Cin	FG Graham 32				
Was	Moss 10 pass from Campbell (Suisham kick)				
Was	FG Suisham 23				
Cin	FG Graham 45				
Was	FG Suisham 36				

Paul Brown Stadium—It was one thing when the playoff-contending Ravens ran up a 17-0 lead a week ago. The one-win Bengals doing it today was quite another.

As they did against Baltimore, the Redskins rallied to make a game of it. But, again, the rally fell short and Washington lost, this time by a score of 20-13.

The Redskins started self-destructing early. On their third play from scrimmage, Chris Cooley caught a Jason Campbell pass, rumbled for 19 yards and then fumbled. The Bengals recovered and six plays later, quarterback Ryan Fitzpatrick scored from a yard out on a naked bootleg, making it 7-0.

The Redskins punted a few plays later and had the Bengals pinned back at their own six. But Chris Benson took a screen pass of 79 yards. After another two plays, Fitzpatrick arched a pass to the end zone and Chris Henry ran under it and made the catch for a touchdown. The score was 14-0 with more than three minutes left in the first quarter.

An illegal formation penalty negated a third and three conversion and the Redskins punted. Cincinnati drove to a 32-yard Shayne Graham field goal and they had a 17-0 lead.

The Redskins finally got things going offensively later in the second quarter. A 28-yard Santana Moss punt return put them in business at the Bengals 40. On third down at the 10, Campbell fired to Moss in the back of the end zone to get the Redskins on the board.

The Washington defense forced a three and out and after the punt, the Redskins moved from their 24 to the Cincinnati five. They couldn't punch it in, however, and settled for Shaun Suisham's 23-yard field goal with 15 seconds left in the half.

Down 17-10, the Redskins moved from the 12 to a first and goal at the one. The officials signaled touchdown after Mike Sellers' second-down carry, but the call was challenged and reversed. On third down Sellers was stopped and he reached out to try to poke the ball across the goal line. It was batted out of his hand and the Bengals recovered for a touchback.

That was the Redskins' last good chance. After a Graham field goal made it 20-10, Rock Cartwright's 87-yard kickoff return gave them a shot at a miracle but Washington settled for a 36-yard field goal. The onside kick went out of bounds with 1:43 left.

Zorn Says He's 'The Worst'

Dec 16—The day after the Redskins allowed the Cincinnati Bengals to double their win total from one to two at their expense, Jim Zorn was feeling the heat.

"I just feel like the worst coach in America to have to lose the way we're losing," said Zorn. "I'm deeply concerned, and I want to look internally, and it starts with me."

The Bengals game was the latest of the losses piling up since the middle of the season. At that point, the Redskins were 6-2 and

the only question there seemed to be about the playoffs was what their seeing would be.

But they have gone 1-5 since, and their postseason prospects are very dim.

During the course of the slump, Zorn has continually blamed execution problems—not anything that he might have been doing wrong.

"Even before this juncture but certainly now, I have to look at myself," he said. "To me, it's all about me. I need to check my plan of attack, and all of our staff needs to re-evaluate what we're doing to see if we're going in the right direction."

12/21/08	**REDSKINS (8-7) 10, Eagles (8-6-1) 3**			82,412	
Phi	0	0	3	0	3
Was	0	3	7	0	10
Was	FG Suisham 33				
Was	Portis 1 run (Suisham kick)				
Phi	FG Akers 22				

FedEx Field—LaRon Landry and Fred Smoot teamed up to make a goal-line tackle that will go down in Redskins lore to preserve a 10-3 win over the Eagles.

The play came after the Eagles, trailing by that seven-point margin, drove from their nine down to the Washington 18. Quarterback Donovan McNabb spiked the ball to stop the clock with 12 seconds left. Philadelphia was out of time-outs.

McNabb threw to receiver Reggie Brown just short of the goal line. As soon as he caught the ball, Landry hit him high and Smoot nailed him low. The receiver went backwards and the ball was spotted at the one. The clock ticked down to 0:00 before the Eagles could line up for another play.

Before the Redskins could celebrate, they had to survive a video review of the play. The call on the field was upheld and the Redskins had the win.

The first quarter was a fierce exchange of punts. Washington got something going on offense late in the period but Shaun Suisham missed a 54-yard field goal attempt early in the second quarter.

The next time the Redskins got the ball, they moved far enough to give Suisham a shorter attempt—and this time he nailed it from 33 yards.

Philadelphia had just one foray into Washington territory in the first half, and that ended with a punt from the 36. On their initial possession of the third quarter Jason Taylor blindsided McNabb and the ball popped loose. London Fletcher scooped it up and returned it to the Eagles 18.

Five plays later, on third and goal at the one, the left side of the Redskins line got enough push to get Clinton Portis over the goal line for a 10-0 Washington lead.

The Eagles responded with a field goal to make it 10-3 with 4:22 left in the third quarter. The game then reverted to the earlier pattern of a punting duel. Neither team mounted a serious threat until the Eagles' final, desperate try came up a yard short thanks to Landry and Smoot.

Despite the win, the Redskins were eliminated from the playoffs.

12/28/08	**49ERS (7-9) 27, Redskins (8-8) 24**			67,519	
Was	0	17	0	7	24
SF	7	0	7	13	27
SF	S. Hill 2 run (Nedney kick)				
Was	Portis 4 run (Suisham kick)				
Was	FG Suisham 41				
Was	Randle El 6 pass from Campbell (Suisham kick)				
SF	Foster 1 run (Nedney kick)				
SF	J. Hill 9 pass from S. Hill (Nedney kick)				
SF	FG Nedney 34				
Was	Campbell 2 run (Suisham kick)				
SF	FG Nedney 40				

Candlestick Park—San Francisco's Joe Nedney kicked a 39-yard field goal as time expired to give the 49ers a 27-24 win over the Redskins.

Like so many other games during Washington's 2-6 season-ending skid, the Redskins fell behind early. San Francisco took the opening kickoff and drove 65 yards for a touchdown. Quarterback Shaun Hill capped the drive with a two-yard dash into the end zone.

The Redskins appeared to have seized control of the game when they ran off 17 unanswered points in the second quarter. First Clinton Portis capped a drive that spanned the first and second periods with a four-yard touchdown run. Then, after Carlos Rogers picked off a Hill pass and returned it 31 yards, Shaun Suisham kicked a 41-yard field goal.

With 9:38 left in the half, the Redskins embarked on a 78-yard scoring drive. Along the way they converted three third downs and one fourth down. From the San Francisco six with 26 seconds remaining, Jason Campbell found Antwaan Randle El who squeezed into the end zone. The score withstood a replay challenge and Washington led 17-7 at halftime.

As the second half started the Redskins quickly lost the momentum they had built. Portis fumbled on the fourth play of the period and San Francisco recovered at the Washington 38. It took them six plays to score with DeShaun Foster powering in and it was 17-14.

The score remained the same until the fourth quarter. The Hill got hot and the 49ers ripped off an 80-yard touchdown drive. Then, after the Redskins went three and out, they extended their lead to 24-17 on a 33-yard Nedney field goal with just under five minutes to play.

Rock Cartwright got the desperation drive jump-started with a 43-yard kickoff return to the Washington 45. Two Campbell scrambles were the key plays. A 23-yard run moved the Redskins to the 10. Four plays later on fourth and goal at the two, Campbell couldn't find a receiver, tucked the ball in and lunged into the end zone. After a replay review confirmed the touchdown Suisham kicked the extra point to tie the game at 24-24 with 1:09 left.

They left just enough time for the 49ers to win it. Hill completed passes to Michael Johnson for 19 yards and to Bryant Johnson for 24. That last one got them to the Redskins 21 and Nedney's game winner came three plays later.

CPSIA information can be obtained at www.ICGtesting.com
Printed in the USA
BVOW03s1725050716

454396BV00050B/197/P